Corporate and
White Collar Crime

ASPEN CASEBOOK SERIES

Corporate and White Collar Crime
Cases and Materials

Fifth Edition

Kathleen F. Brickey

James Carr Professor of Criminal Jurisprudence
Washington University

Wolters Kluwer
Law & Business

Published by Wolters Kluwer Law & Business in New York.

Wolters Kluwer Law & Business serves customers worldwide with CCH, Aspen Publishers, and Kluwer Law International products. (www.wolterskluwerlb.com)

To contact Customer Service, e-mail customer.service@wolterskluwer.com, call 1-800-234-1660, fax 1-800-901-9075, or mail correspondence to:

> Wolters Kluwer Law & Business
> Attn: Order Department
> PO Box 990
> Frederick, MD 21705

Printed in the United States of America.

1 2 3 4 5 6 7 8 9 0

ISBN 978-0-7355-9021-2

Library of Congress Cataloging-in-Publication Data

Brickey, Kathleen F.
    Corporate and white collar crime : cases and materials / Kathleen F. Brickey.—5th ed.
        p. cm.
    Includes bibliographical references and index.
    ISBN 978-0-7355-9021-2 (casebound : alk. paper)

1. White collar crimes—United States—Cases. 2. Commercial crimes—United States—Cases. 3. Corporation law—United States—Criminal provisions—Cases. I. Title.

    KF9350.B75 2011
    345.73'0268—dc23

2011015316

About Wolters Kluwer Law & Business

Wolters Kluwer Law & Business is a leading global provider of intelligent information and digital solutions for legal and business professionals in key specialty areas, and respected educational resources for professors and law students. Wolters Kluwer Law & Business connects legal and business professionals as well as those in the education market with timely, specialized authoritative content and information-enabled solutions to support success through productivity, accuracy and mobility.

Serving customers worldwide, Wolters Kluwer Law & Business products include those under the Aspen Publishers, CCH, Kluwer Law International, Loislaw, Best Case, ftwilliam.com and MediRegs family of products.

CCH products have been a trusted resource since 1913, and are highly regarded resources for legal, securities, antitrust and trade regulation, government contracting, banking, pension, payroll, employment and labor, and healthcare reimbursement and compliance professionals.

Aspen Publishers products provide essential information to attorneys, business professionals and law students. Written by preeminent authorities, the product line offers analytical and practical information in a range of specialty practice areas from securities law and intellectual property to mergers and acquisitions and pension/benefits. Aspen's trusted legal education resources provide professors and students with high-quality, up-to-date and effective resources for successful instruction and study in all areas of the law.

Kluwer Law International products provide the global business community with reliable international legal information in English. Legal practitioners, corporate counsel and business executives around the world rely on Kluwer Law journals, looseleafs, books, and electronic products for comprehensive information in many areas of international legal practice.

Loislaw is a comprehensive online legal research product providing legal content to law firm practitioners of various specializations. Loislaw provides attorneys with the ability to quickly and efficiently find the necessary legal information they need, when and where they need it, by facilitating access to primary law as well as state-specific law, records, forms and treatises.

Best Case Solutions is the leading bankruptcy software product to the bankruptcy industry. It provides software and workflow tools to flawlessly streamline petition preparation and the electronic filing process, while timely incorporating ever-changing court requirements.

ftwilliam.com offers employee benefits professionals the highest quality plan documents (retirement, welfare and non-qualified) and government forms (5500/PBGC, 1099 and IRS) software at highly competitive prices.

MediRegs products provide integrated health care compliance content and software solutions for professionals in healthcare, higher education and life sciences, including professionals in accounting, law and consulting.

Wolters Kluwer Law & Business, a division of Wolters Kluwer, is headquartered in New York. Wolters Kluwer is a market-leading global information services company focused on professionals.

To Jim

Summary of Contents

Contents

2

**Personal Liability in an
Organizational Setting**   **39**

5

Securities Fraud	**153**

6

False Statements 199

7

Perjury and False Declarations   **243**

9

Bribery of Public Officials   **339**

10

12

Currency Reporting Crimes
and Money Laundering   519

13

Preface

Despite its familiar ring, the term "white collar crime" is dauntingly difficult to define. Edwin Sutherland, who first coined the term in 1939, developed a construct that relied on the social status of the offender and the circumstances surrounding the crime as the relevant points of reference. As the concept of white collar crime evolved over time, the focus shifted away from the offender to the nature of the offense, the locus of the wrong, or the means used to commit it. Nevertheless, decades of academic debate have neither resolved the threshold definitional issue nor provided a coherent organizing principle. Yet notwithstanding the vagaries of defining the subject, white collar crime has become a growth industry in the wake of Enron and its progeny and is fast becoming an established part of the law school curriculum.

This book endeavors to provide a theoretical and policy framework for considering the respective roles of institutional and individual responsibility and for systematically examining the principal federal statutes that prosecutors regularly invoke in corporate and white collar crime cases. In addition to relying on reported judicial decisions as vehicles for discussion, the book uses problems, case studies, and other similar materials to illustrate the context within which the issues are framed. The fifth edition nonetheless retains a strong focus on substantive criminal law. And because major federal criminal statutes are the organizing principle of the course, the book is designed to be used with the companion statutory supplement.

As has been true in the past, the similarities between this edition and its predecessors are greater than the differences, although recent statutory and case law developments have, of course, required some shifts in emphasis and coverage.

As was true of the earlier editions, for the sake of brevity and clarity I have omitted some footnotes and citations in the edited cases and have eliminated most parallel citations without indication. Footnotes that have been retained are renumbered consecutively throughout each chapter. Explanatory footnotes that I have added to cases and other quoted material are identified by the legend " — ED."

KATHLEEN F. BRICKEY

March 2011

Acknowledgments

I have benefitted greatly from feedback I have received from students and colleagues on earlier editions of the book, and I thank them for their helpful comments.

I owe a special word of thanks to my faculty assistant, Beverly Owens, for her exceptional organizational and technical assistance, as well as to my research assistants, whose contributions to the new edition have been invaluable.

I am also indebted to the following authors, organizations, and copyright holders for permission to reprint excerpts from their works:

3 Kathleen F. Brickey, Corporate Criminal Liability § 13:10.10 (2d ed. 1991-1994 & 2010-2011 Cumulative Supplement), copyright currently held by Thomson Reuters.

Kathleen F. Brickey, Enron's Legacy, 8 Buff. Crim. L. Rev. 221, 232-234, 234-237 (2004). Copyright © 2004 by Kathleen F. Brickey.

Kathleen F. Brickey, Rethinking Corporate Liability Under the Model Penal Code, 19 Rutgers L.J. 593, 597-598, 625-626 (1988). Reprinted with permission of the Rutgers Law Journal. Copyright © 1988 by Rutgers School of Law — Camden.

Francis T. Cullen, Gray Cavender, William J. Maakestad, & Michael L. Benson, Corporate Crime Under Attack, 355-356, 362-363 (2d ed. 2006). Copyright © 1987, 2006, Matthew Bender & Company, Inc. Reprinted with permission.

Sanford H. Kadish, Some Observations on the Use of Criminal Sanctions in Enforcing Economic Regulations, 30 U. Chi. L. Rev. 423, 430-431 (1963). Reprinted with permission.

1

Corporate Criminal Liability

I. INTRODUCTION

For nearly a century, Congress has viewed criminal sanctions as appropriate mechanisms for controlling corporate misconduct. The federal government's early predisposition to incorporate criminal penalties in statutes that regulate corporate behavior is nowhere better illustrated than in its enactment of the Sherman Act in 1890. Even though corporate criminal liability was not yet widely recognized, Congress nonetheless made the Sherman Act's criminal and civil prohibitions expressly applicable to corporations. Because the financial impact of imposing criminal fines on corporations would ultimately be borne by innocent shareholders, it seemed inevitable that the Supreme Court would be called upon to consider the wisdom, fairness, and legality of doing so at a relatively early date.

A. CORPORATE CRIMINAL LIABILITY

NEW YORK CENTRAL & HUDSON RIVER RAILROAD v. UNITED STATES
212 U.S. 481 (1909)

Mr. Justice DAY delivered the opinion of the court.

[New York Central, its general traffic manager, and its assistant traffic manager were indicted for paying rebates to sugar refiners in violation of the Elkins Act. Correspondence between New York Central's traffic managers and the refiners' managers established that New York Central agreed to charge the refiners five cents less than the published rate per hundred pounds to ship the sugar from New York to Detroit. The refiners obtained the rebate by sending claims to New York Central's assistant freight traffic manager, who then forwarded them to the general manager. The claims were satisfied by cashier's drafts that were paid from New York Central's funds. The correspondence made clear that New York Central made this concession to prevent the refiners from shipping their sugar by barge and to give the refiners some competitive relief. New

York Central and the assistant freight traffic manager were convicted and sentenced to pay, respectively, fines of $102,000 and $6,000.]

The principal attack in this court is upon the constitutional validity of certain features of the Elkins Act. That act, among other things, provides:

> (1) That anything done or omitted to be done by a corporation common carrier subject to the act to regulate commerce . . . which, if done or omitted to be done by any director or officer thereof, or any receiver, trustee, lessee, agent or person acting for or employed by such corporation, would constitute a misdemeanor . . . under this act, shall also be held to be a misdemeanor committed by such corporation, and upon conviction thereof it shall be subject to like penalties as are prescribed . . . by this act. . . .

It is contended that these provisions of the law are unconstitutional because Congress has no authority to impute to a corporation the commission of criminal offenses, or to subject a corporation to a criminal prosecution by reason of the things charged. The argument is that to thus punish the corporation is in reality to punish the innocent stockholders, and to deprive them of their property without opportunity to be heard, consequently without due process of law. . . . It is urged that as there is no authority shown by the board of directors or the stockholders for the criminal acts of the agents of the company, in contracting for and giving rebates, they could not be lawfully charged against the corporation. As no action of the board of directors could legally authorize a crime, and as indeed the stockholders could not do so, the arguments come to this: that owing to the nature and character of its organization and the extent of its power and authority, a corporation cannot commit a crime of the nature charged in this case.

Some of the earlier writers on common law held the law to be that a corporation could not commit a crime. It is said to have been held by Lord Chief Justice Holt (Anonymous, 12 Modern 559) that "a corporation is not indictable, although the particular members of it are." In Blackstone's Commentaries, chapter 18, § 12, we find it stated: "A corporation cannot commit treason, or felony, or other crime in its corporate capacity, though its members may in their distinct individual capacities." The modern authority, universally, so far as we know, is the other way. In considering the subject, Bishop's New Criminal Law, § 417, devotes a chapter to the capacity of corporations to commit crime, and states the law to be: "Since a corporation acts by its officers and agents[,] their purposes, motives, and intent are just as much those of the corporation as are the things done. If, for example, the invisible, intangible essence of air, which we term a corporation, can level mountains, fill up valleys, lay down iron tracks, and run railroad cars on them, it can intend to do it, and can act therein as well viciously as virtuously." Without citing the state cases holding the same view, we may note Telegram Newspaper Company v. Commonwealth, 172 Mass. 294, in which it was held that a corporation was subject to punishment for criminal contempt, and the court, speaking by Mr. Chief Justice Field, said: "We think a corporation may be liable criminally for certain offenses of which a specific intent may be a necessary element. There is no more difficulty in imputing to a corporation a specific intent in criminal proceedings than in civil. A corporation cannot be arrested and imprisoned in either civil or criminal proceedings, but its property may be taken either as compensation for a private wrong or as punishment for a public wrong." . . .

It is now well established that, in actions for tort, the corporation may be held responsible for damages for the acts of its agent within the scope of his employment.

And this is the rule when the act is done by the agent in the course of his employment, although done wantonly or recklessly or against the express orders of the principal. In such cases the liability is not imputed because the principal actually participates in the malice or fraud, but because the act is done for the benefit of the principal, while the agent is acting within the scope of his employment in the business of the principal, and justice requires that the latter shall be held responsible for damages to the individual who has suffered by such conduct.

A corporation is held responsible for acts not within the agent's corporate powers strictly construed, but which the agent has assumed to perform for the corporation when employing the corporate powers actually authorized, and in such cases there need be no written authority under seal or vote of the corporation in order to constitute the agency or to authorize the act.

In this case we are to consider the criminal responsibility of a corporation for an act done while an authorized agent of the company is exercising the authority conferred upon him. It was admitted by the defendant at the trial that, at the time mentioned in the indictment, the general freight traffic manager and the assistant freight traffic manager were authorized to establish rates at which freight should be carried over the line of the New York Central & Hudson River Company, and were authorized to unite with other companies in the establishing, filing, and publishing of through rates, including the through rate or rates between New York and Detroit referred to in the indictment. Thus, the subject-matter of making and fixing rates was within the scope of the authority and employment of the agents of the company, whose acts in this connection are sought to be charged upon the company. Thus clothed with authority, the agents were bound to respect the regulation of interstate commerce enacted by Congress, requiring the filing and publication of rates and punishing departures therefrom. Applying the principle governing civil liability, we go only a step farther in holding that the act of the agent, while exercising the authority delegated to him to make rates for transportation, may be controlled, in the interest of public policy, by imputing his act to his employer and imposing penalties upon the corporation for which he is acting in the premises.

It is true that there are some crimes which, in their nature, cannot be committed by corporations. But there is a large class of offenses, of which rebating under the Federal statutes is one, wherein the crime consists in purposely doing the things prohibited by statute. In that class of crimes we see no good reason why corporations may not be held responsible for and charged with the knowledge and purposes of their agents, acting within the authority conferred upon them. If it were not so, many offenses might go unpunished and acts be committed in violation of law where, as in the present case, the statute requires all persons, corporate or private, to refrain from certain practices, forbidden in the interest of public policy. . . .

We see no valid objection in law, and every reason in public policy, why the corporation which profits by the transaction, and can only act through its agents and officers, shall be held punishable by fine because of the knowledge and intent of its agents to whom it has intrusted authority to act in the subject-matter of making and fixing rates of transportation, and whose knowledge and purposes may well be attributed to the corporation for which the agents act. While the law should have regard to the rights of all, and to those of corporations no less than to those of individuals, it cannot shut its eyes to the fact that the great majority of business transactions in modern times are conducted through these bodies, and particularly that interstate commerce is almost entirely in their hands, and to give them immunity from all punishment because of the old and exploded doctrine that a corporation cannot commit a crime would virtually take away the only means of effectually controlling the subject-matter and correcting the abuses aimed at.

There can be no question of the power of Congress to regulate interstate commerce, to prevent favoritism and to secure equal rights to all engaged in interstate trade. It would be a distinct step backward to hold that Congress cannot control those who are conducting this interstate commerce by holding them responsible for the intent and purposes of the agents to whom they have delegated the power to act in the premises. . . .

Affirmed.

Notes and Questions

1. In what sense was the act of giving rebates the act of the corporation? What evidence supports that conclusion?

2. What policy considerations led the Court to conclude that corporations can be held criminally responsible? Is the Court's reasoning persuasive?

3. Some commentators have suggested that *New York Central* has historically been misconstrued as establishing a general rule that corporations are criminally liable under respondeat superior principles. What was the Court's precise holding in *New York Central* and what were the critical steps in the Court's reasoning? How broadly (or narrowly) should the Court's opinion be read?

4. Most corporations are creatures of state law. They operate under charters issued by the state and must comply with state requirements to remain in good standing. Why does the federal government have the power to sanction corporations like N.Y. Central?

FRANCIS T. CULLEN, GRAY CAVENDER,
WILLIAM J. MAAKESTAD & MICHAEL L. BENSON,
CORPORATE CRIME UNDER ATTACK
355-356, 362-363 (2d ed. 2006)

Corporate Criminals or Criminal Corporations?
The Rise of Organizational Liability

On June 16, 2002, a Chicago jury declared the accounting firm of Arthur Andersen guilty of a felony charge of obstructing justice for destroying more than a ton of documents and deleting more than 30,000 e-mails and computer files related to one of its most important clients: Enron. At the time of the conviction, Andersen was one of the five largest accounting firms in the world, with nearly 85,000 employees worldwide. Within a year of the conviction, employees of Andersen numbered less than 300. The Arthur Andersen trial marked the most publicized criminal prosecution of a business organization since the Ford Pinto case. And, though the firm's conviction was later overturned by the U.S. Supreme Court on technical grounds, the Andersen case highlighted a core issue identical to one that had been raised in Ford Pinto more than 20 years before: Can a corporation — or any other form of business enterprise — commit a crime?

While the very idea of holding a business enterprise criminally responsible was attacked on several legal fronts during the pretrial stage of the Ford Pinto prosecution, by the time of the Andersen prosecution, corporate criminal liability presented far fewer legal and conceptual obstacles. As Kathleen Brickey has observed, the Pinto case served as an important catalyst for getting us to think more broadly about the spectrum of liability for business crimes. In short, viewed after a quarter-century, Ford Pinto has left "less a product liability legacy, and more an enterprise liability legacy." . . .

Commentators on corporate social control have long debated whether it is better for individual executives or business organizations to be the target of criminal sanctions. That is, is it best to apply the law to "corporate criminals" or "criminal corporations"? The most common answer — and one that is embedded in prevailing American law — is that the preferred statutory scheme should generally provide for both individual and enterprise liability, with the appropriateness of each to be determined case by case through the exercise of sound prosecutorial discretion. Current legal rules concerning enterprise liability came into being after many years of discussion over such foundational issues as whether an organization could even possess the requisite mental state (*mens rea,* or guilty mind) to commit a crime. . . .

Despite these developments and the relatively small number of corporate prosecutions, the concept of organizational crime remains controversial, and some critics continue to argue against the application of criminal sanctions to corporate and other business enterprises, primarily on three grounds. First, they challenge the deterrent effect of the sanction, essentially because "corporations don't commit crimes, people do." Second, they question the retributive function because corporate criminal sanctions may actually end up punishing innocent shareholders (by reducing the value of their shares) and consumers (by increasing the costs of goods and services). Third, they contest the efficiency of organizational liability, arguing that economic analysis shows that, on the whole, civil liability may deter unlawful corporate conduct at less cost than criminal liability. Although a detailed analysis of each objection is beyond the scope of this chapter, a few comments are in order, particularly because the Pinto prosecution — along with other important cases like the Arthur Andersen prosecution — involved organizational rather than individual defendants. We suggest that, in many instances, sanctioning the organization is the most prudent and equitable policy, and thus prosecutors' options should not be confined to imposing individual criminal liability.

The critics' first objection — that people, not corporations, commit crimes — ignores the reality that the labyrinthian structure of many modern corporations often makes it extremely difficult to pinpoint individual responsibility for specific decisions. Even in cases in which employees who carried out criminal activities can be identified, controversial questions remain. John S. Martin, a former U.S. Attorney who actively prosecuted corporate and white-collar crime cases, comments that when individual offenders can be identified they "often turn out to be lower-level corporate employees who never made a lot of money, who never benefited personally from the transaction, and who acted with either the real or mistaken belief that if they did not commit the acts in question their jobs might be in jeopardy." Further, says Martin, "they may have believed that their superior was aware and approved of the crime, but could not honestly testify to a specific conversation or other act of the superior that would support an indictment of the superior." Thus, a thorough investigation may well lead a prosecutor to conclude that indictments against individuals simply cannot be justified, even though the corporation benefited from a clear violation of a criminal statute. Such a result would disserve the deterrent function.

The existence of corporate criminal liability also provides a powerful incentive for top officers to supervise middle- and lower-level management more closely. Individual liability, in the absence of corporate liability, encourages just the opposite: top executives may take the attitude of "don't tell me, I don't want to know." In the words of Peter Jones, former chief legal counsel at Levi Strauss, "a fundamental law of organizational physics is that bad news does not flow upstream." Only when directives come from the upper echelon of the corporation "will busy executives feel enough pressure to prevent activities that seriously threaten public health and safety." For a similar reason, proponents of the conservative "Chicago School" of law and economic thought advocate corporate rather than individual sanctioning: a firm's control mechanisms will be more efficient than the state's in deterring misconduct by its agents and will bring about adequate compliance with legal standards as long as the costs of punishment outweigh the potential benefits.

risk to shareholders

The second objection — that the cost of corporate criminal fines is actually borne by innocent shareholders and consumers — also seems unfounded. With regard to shareholders, whether individual or institutional, incidents of corporate criminal behavior may give the owners the right to redress the diminution of their interest by filing a derivative suit against individual officers and/or members of the board of directors. Although the cost and the uncertainty of winning such a suit may be high, shareholders must regard this cost as one of the risks incurred when they invest in securities. Just as shareholders may occasionally be enriched unjustly through undetected misbehavior by their company, it is only fair to expect them to bear a part of the burden on those occasions when illegality is discovered and duly sanctioned.

Consumer Cost

Next, it is simplistic, if not untenable, to argue that corporate criminal fines will simply be passed on to the consuming public through higher prices. Stephen Yoder, among others, notes that in such instances our economic system allows consumers to exert a type of indirect, collective control. If we assume that competition exists in the offending corporation's industry, the firm cannot simply decide to raise its prices to absorb the fine or the costs related to the litigation. If it does so, it risks becoming less competitive and suffering such concomitant problems as decreased profits, difficulty in securing debt and equity financing, curtailed expansion, and the loss of investors to more law-abiding corporations.

Civil

The final objection — that civil remedies may be a cheaper and hence more efficient deterrent of unlawful conduct than criminal sanctions — also misses the mark. First, . . . it is common for corporate wrongdoing to be met by both criminal and civil responses, each seeking different moral and instrumental ends. Second, as Lawrence Friedman reminds us, deterrence and efficiency are not the only interests in play. Deterrence has never been regarded as the sole justification for criminal liability, and efficiency is but one basis for social policy. The pursuit of justice and the imposition of just deserts are also traditional and worthwhile considerations. Civil and criminal liabilities have distinct social meanings, and in the real world findings of civil and criminal liability are not transmutable for purposes of moral condemnation.

. . . Dan Kahan concludes his broad investigation for social meaning in the context of corporate wrongdoing with a passage that emphasizes the civil-criminal distinction:

> Just as crimes by natural persons denigrate social values, so do corporate crimes. Members of the public show that they feel this way, for example, when they complain that corporations put profits ahead of the interests of workers, consumers, or the environment. Punishing corporations, just like punishing natural persons, is also understood to be the right way for society to repudiate the false valuations that their crimes express. Criminal liability "sends the message" that people matter more than profits and reaffirm the value of those who were sacrificed to "corporate greed."

Notes and Questions

1. What are the principal arguments for and against criminally prosecuting corporations and other entities? What purposes do such prosecutions serve?

2. To what extent does a corporate prosecution impose the cost of corporate wrongdoing on the corporation's shareholders? Is fining the corporation the equivalent of punishing the shareholders as well? Is it fair to impose the economic burden of a criminal fine on shareholders?

3. If, as the authors posit, corporations are often subject to both civil and criminal sanctions, what is the rationale for having a dual system of parallel remedies? Do criminal and civil actions against a corporation serve the same purposes?

B. CORPORATE PROSECUTION POLICY

Notwithstanding continued controversy over the wisdom of prosecuting corporations and other business entities, the notion of corporate criminal liability is now firmly embedded in American jurisprudence. The recent corporate fraud scandals heightened public consciousness of the need for greater transparency and accountability in corporate governance matters. That, in turn, spawned a number of reforms to promote consistency and coordination among federal prosecutors and other members of the enforcement community, particularly regarding the criteria prosecutors use in deciding whether to charge a corporation or other business entity. One of the most visible and, at times, controversial initiatives has been the Justice Department's ongoing effort to articulate a clear corporate prosecution policy by promulgating formalized — though not formally enforceable — prosecutorial guidelines.

KATHLEEN F. BRICKEY, ENRON'S LEGACY
8 BUFF. CRIM. L. REV. 221, 234-237 (2004)

JUSTICE DEPARTMENT CORPORATE PROSECUTION GUIDANCE

Corporate prosecutions constitute a small minority of federal criminal cases. But as the government's prosecution of Arthur Andersen for obstruction of justice attests, federal prosecutors will charge business entities in cases they believe are truly egregious.

In 1999, the Justice Department issued non-binding guidelines to provide United States Attorneys offices a framework for deciding whether to bring charges against a corporation. Called Federal Prosecution of Corporations, the guidance identified eight factors that would generally be relevant to the charging decision: (1) the nature and seriousness of the crime, including potential harm to the public; (2) the pervasiveness of wrongdoing within the company; (3) the company's prior history of similar misconduct; (4) the company's timely and voluntary disclosure of the wrongdoing and the degree of its cooperation in identifying responsible individuals and providing evidence; (5) the effectiveness of the company's compliance program in preventing and detecting wrongdoing; (6) remedial measures the company took upon discovery of the wrongdoing; (7) potential collateral consequences of a corporate conviction, including adverse effects on third parties; and (8) the adequacy of available non-criminal remedies as an alternative to criminal prosecution.

The guidance recommended that when prosecutors decide to indict a corporation they should bring the most serious sustainable charge, and cautioned that it is generally inappropriate to condition corporate plea agreements on the government's promise to forgo prosecuting culpable individuals.

1. CORPORATE COOPERATION

In January of 2003, the Justice Department issued revised corporate prosecution principles that respond to the corporate fraud scandals. Now called Principles of Federal Prosecution of Business Organizations,[1] the revised guidance retains the same analytical framework but calls for "increased emphasis on and scrutiny of the authenticity of a corporation's cooperation" with the investigation.[2] Like the original guidance on cooperation, the revised principles take into account the company's willingness to disclose the results of its internal investigation, to identify culpable individuals, to make witnesses available and assist in locating evidence, and to waive attorney-client and work product protections. But the revised principles emphasize the importance of scrutinizing whether the corporation is really cooperating or whether it is merely going through the motions while actually impeding the investigation. Examples of conduct that impedes include:

> overly broad assertions of corporate representation of employees or former employees; inappropriate directions to employees or their counsel, such as directions not to cooperate openly and fully with the investigation including, for example, the direction to decline to be interviewed; making presentations or submissions that contain misleading assertions or

---

1. U.S. Dept. of Justice, Principles of Federal Prosecution of Business Organizations, Jan. 20, 2003 [hereinafter Principles of Prosecution].

2. Memorandum on Principles of Federal Prosecution of Business Organizations, from Larry D. Thompson, Deputy Attorney General, to Heads of Department Components, United States Attorneys, Jan. 20, 2003 [hereinafter Thompson Memorandum].

> Too often business organizations, while purporting to cooperate with a Department investigation, in fact take steps to impede the quick and effective exposure of the complete scope of wrongdoing. The revisions make clear that such conduct should weigh in favor of a corporate prosecution.

Id. As Deputy Attorney General, Mr. Thompson also chaired the Corporate Fraud Task Force.

omissions; incomplete or delayed production of records; and failure to promptly disclose illegal conduct known to the corporation.[3]

The clear import is that conduct that impedes prompt and full exposure of wrongdoing should weigh in favor of prosecuting the corporation.

Conversely, exemplary corporate cooperation can reap handsome rewards. Homestore, the largest online provider of real estate listings, is an illustrative case in point. Homestore executives enriched themselves through a series of fraudulent transactions that inflated the company's revenue. As soon as its audit committee learned of the fraud, Homestore promptly reported it to the SEC. Homestore also hired outside counsel to conduct an internal investigation, provided the investigative report to the government, and waived attorney-client and work product protections applicable to materials it supplied to the SEC. Homestore also fired the responsible individuals and implemented remedial measures to prevent the fraud from recurring.

As of the date of this writing, the government's investigation has resulted in the filing of criminal charges against seven Homestore executives and managers, including the COO, the CFO, and the Vice President of Planning.[4] As is often the case, the SEC simultaneously sued the top executives.

In view of the company's extensive cooperation, it is not surprising that Homestore was not criminally charged. But its assistance in the investigation also apparently induced the SEC to forgo filing a civil enforcement action against the corporation as well.

2. CORPORATE COMPLIANCE PROGRAMS

A second substantive change in the guidance relates to evaluating the effectiveness of corporate compliance policies and procedures to ensure that they are not "mere paper programs." The new emphasis here is on scrutinizing the role of the board of directors.[5]

---

3. Principles of Prosecution, supra note 1, at VI, Comment.

4. All of the defendants pled guilty, and most became cooperating witnesses.

5. Corporate boards have received bad report cards in the wake of the corporate scandals. See, e.g., The Role of the Board of Directors in Enron's Collapse, S. Rep. No. 107-70, at 11-59 (2002) (finding that Enron's Board must assume significant responsibility for the company's collapse; the Board abdicated its fiduciary responsibilities by tolerating high-risk accounting practices and transactions with blatant conflicts of interest, by failing to address extensive undisclosed off-books transactions, by awarding excessive executive compensation, by failing to curb abusive use of a personal multi-million dollar credit line by CEO Ken Lay, and by allowing its own independence to be compromised); Richard C. Breeden, Restoring Trust: Report to The Hon. Jed S. Rakoff, The United States District Court For the Southern District of New York, on Corporate Governance for the Future of MCI, Inc., 1-2, 5-6, 45-76 (Aug. 2003) (report by court-appointed corporate monitor criticizing WorldCom Board's lack of independence and cronyism, and providing a blueprint for reform); Dennis R. Beresford, Nicholas deB. Katzenbach & C.B. Rogers, Jr., Report of Investigation by the Special Investigative Committee of the Board of Directors of WorldCom, Inc., 29-35, 264-337 (Mar. 31, 2003) (criticizing WorldCom Board for relinquishing too much power to CEO Bernard Ebbers and exercising too little restraint over him, and detailing an almost complete breakdown of corporate governance mechanisms); First Interim Report of Dick Thornburgh, Bankruptcy Court Examiner, In re: WorldCom, Inc., Case No. 02-15533 (AJG), 6-7, 37-43 (Bankr. S.D.N.Y. Nov. 4, 2002) (making preliminary findings that WorldCom's Board and its audit and compensation committees virtually abdicated their responsibilities to CEO Ebbers); Second Interim Report of Dick Thornburgh, Bankruptcy Court Examiner, In re: WorldCom, Inc., Case No. 02-15533 (AJG), 114-115 (Bankr. S.D.N.Y. June 9, 2003) (finding "significant and troubling questions" about WorldCom Board's due diligence in making hundreds

Did the board independently review management's proposals, or did it serve as a rubber stamp? Did management provide sufficient information to enable the board to exercise independent judgment? Were the company's internal audit controls adequate to ensure independence and accuracy? Did the directors establish an information and reporting system designed to facilitate informed decision making by management and the board on corporate legal matters? These questions probe not only whether the design of the compliance program is adequate, but also whether management has conscientiously enforced it.

The corporate compliance criteria in the guidance also complement corporate governance reforms, imposed by [the Sarbanes-Oxley Act of 2002], that subject corporate boards to increased scrutiny. Thus, for example, Sarbanes-Oxley relieves senior management of the responsibility for hiring, compensating, and monitoring outside auditors and assigns it to the board's audit committee. Sarbanes-Oxley also endeavors to eliminate financial conflicts of interest from the audit oversight function by requiring directors who serve on audit committees to satisfy statutory financial independence criteria. Under the new standards, audit committee members may not receive fees or compensation from the corporation other than their compensation as board members. Nor may they be affiliated with the corporation or its subsidiaries in any capacity other than as members of the board. And to help ensure informed decision making, Sarbanes-Oxley requires that at least one member of the audit committee qualify as a "financial expert." Sarbanes-Oxley also assigns the audit committee the responsibility of establishing procedures for receiving internal and external complaints relating to financial and audit matters.

Thus, prosecutors may look to corporate governance requirements imposed by Sarbanes-Oxley to assist their evaluation of a company's compliance program as they assess the merits of charging the corporation. Indeed, while corporate prosecutions are likely to remain the exception rather than the rule, the revised guidance sends a clear message that the Justice Department believes the threat of criminal prosecution can serve as a catalyst for positive change in a corporation's culture.

Notes and Questions

1. If, as the Justice Department predicts, corporate prosecutions are likely to remain a small minority of federal criminal prosecutions, is it realistic to believe that the threat of criminal prosecution will serve as a catalyst for change?

2. Like the Principles of Federal Prosecution of Business Organizations (hereinafter Principles of Prosecution) codified in the U.S. Attorneys' Manual, the Federal Sentencing Guidelines for organizational offenders emphasize the twin elements of corporate cooperation and corporate compliance programs. While the Principles of Prosecution treat corporate cooperation and effective compliance programs as highly relevant factors in determining whether to prosecute a corporation, the Sentencing Guidelines consider them highly relevant to the decision whether the corporation is

---

of millions of dollars in loans to CEO Bernard Ebbers); Westar Energy, Inc., Report of the Special Committee to the Board of Directors, 81- 82 (Apr. 29, 2003) (faulting Westar Board for failing to curb abusive use of company airplanes for personal use).

entitled to a mitigated sentence. Does this potential "double whammy" increase the likelihood that the threat of corporate prosecution will serve as a catalyst for change?

3. Even though corporate prosecutions are relatively rare, the recent prosecution of Arthur Andersen for shredding Enron documents demonstrates the government's willingness to prosecute business organizations for what they believe is egregious conduct.[6] What role does a case like the Andersen prosecution play in making the threat of prosecution credible to the business community?

4. Why would the Justice Department give priority to a corporation's cooperation and voluntary disclosure? What benefits might flow from corporate — as opposed to individual — cooperation?

5. If a corporation cooperates fully, should that automatically entitle it to immunity from prosecution?

6. What are the hallmarks of an effective compliance program? Should an effective compliance program be expected to prevent all or virtually all criminal wrongdoing within the organization?

7. Are career prosecutors qualified to evaluate the effectiveness of corporate compliance programs? If not, does this diminish the appropriateness of considering corporate governance as a factor in the decision whether to prosecute? Are there reliable (and fair) alternative ways to implement this component of the Principles of Prosecution?

8. While the Principles of Prosecution caution that prosecutors should make sparing use of their ability to charge corporations, they also see potential benefits of corporate prosecutions — particularly when there is pervasive criminal conduct in a particular sector of the business community. What benefits could be derived from prosecuting one or more corporations when there is industry-wide criminal conduct? Can you identify particular industries in which pervasive, nationwide misconduct has occurred?

9. Are there particular types of crimes that are most likely to be committed by businesses? If so, is there a stronger reason to prosecute corporations whose employees engage in that kind of wrongdoing?

The Principles of Prosecution discussed in the preceding excerpt continue to be an evolving work in progress, partly because the factors relating to corporate cooperation and waiver of the corporate attorney-client privilege proved to be highly volatile. Although the basic structure and themes of the Principles of Prosecution remain essentially the same, the Justice Department has since refined them on several more occasions to respond to critics in the business community and the defense bar, and to ward off legislation — including the proposed Attorney-Client Privilege Protection Act — designed to curtail some prosecutorial policies and practices.

---

6. See Kathleen F. Brickey, Andersen's Fall from Grace, 81 Wash. U. L.Q. 917 (2004).

UNITED STATES ATTORNEYS' MANUAL
TITLE 9
PRINCIPLES OF FEDERAL PROSECUTION OF BUSINESS ORGANIZATIONS[7]
(August 2008)

9-28.100 DUTIES OF FEDERAL PROSECUTORS AND DUTIES OF CORPORATE LEADERS

The prosecution of corporate crime is a high priority for the Department of Justice. By investigating allegations of wrongdoing and by bringing charges where appropriate for criminal misconduct, the Department promotes critical public interests. These interests include, to take just a few examples: (1) protecting the integrity of our free economic and capital markets; (2) protecting consumers, investors, and business entities that compete only through lawful means; and (3) protecting the American people from misconduct that would violate criminal laws safeguarding the environment. . . .

9-28.200 GENERAL CONSIDERATIONS OF CORPORATE LIABILITY

A. General Principle: Corporations should not be treated leniently because of their artificial nature nor should they be subject to harsher treatment. Vigorous enforcement of the criminal laws against corporate wrongdoers, where appropriate, results in great benefits for law enforcement and the public, particularly in the area of white collar crime. Indicting corporations for wrongdoing enables the government to be a force for positive change of corporate culture, and a force to prevent, discover, and punish serious crimes. . . .

9-28.300 FACTORS TO BE CONSIDERED

A. General Principle: Generally, prosecutors apply the same factors in determining whether to charge a corporation as they do with respect to individuals. Thus, the prosecutor must weigh all of the factors normally considered in the sound exercise of prosecutorial judgment: the sufficiency of the evidence; the likelihood of success at trial; the probable deterrent, rehabilitative, and other consequences of conviction; and the adequacy of noncriminal approaches. However, due to the nature of the corporate "person," some additional factors are present. In conducting an investigation, determining whether to bring charges, and negotiating plea or other agreements, prosecutors should consider the following factors in reaching a decision as to the proper treatment of a corporate target:

1. the nature and seriousness of the offense, including the risk of harm to the public, and applicable policies and priorities, if any, governing the prosecution of corporations for particular categories of crime;

---

7. While these guidelines specifically refer only to corporations, they also apply to the consideration of prosecuting all types of business organizations, including partnerships, sole proprietorships, government entities, and unincorporated associations.

2. the pervasiveness of wrongdoing within the corporation, including the complicity in, or the condoning of, the wrongdoing by corporate management;

3. the corporation's history of similar misconduct, including prior criminal, civil, and regulatory enforcement actions against it;

4. the corporation's timely and voluntary disclosure of wrongdoing and its willingness to cooperate in the investigation of its agents;

5. the existence and effectiveness of the corporation's pre-existing compliance program;

6. the corporation's remedial actions, including any efforts to implement an effective corporate compliance program or to improve an existing one, to replace responsible management, to discipline or terminate wrongdoers, to pay restitution, and to cooperate with the relevant government agencies;

7. collateral consequences, including whether there is disproportionate harm to shareholders, pension holders, employees, and others not proven personally culpable, as well as impact on the public arising from the prosecution;

8. the adequacy of the prosecution of individuals responsible for the corporation's malfeasance; and

9. the adequacy of remedies such as civil or regulatory enforcement actions.

B. Comment: The factors listed in this section are intended to be illustrative of those that should be evaluated and are not an exhaustive list of potentially relevant considerations. . . .

9-28.500 PERVASIVENESS OF WRONGDOING WITHIN THE CORPORATION

A. General Principles: A corporation can only act through natural persons, and it is therefore held responsible for the acts of such persons fairly attributable to it. Charging a corporation for even minor misconduct may be appropriate where the wrongdoing was pervasive and was undertaken by a large number of employees, or by all the employees in a particular role within the corporation, or was condoned by upper management. On the other hand, it may not be appropriate to impose liability upon a corporation, particularly one with a robust compliance program in place, under a strict respondeat superior theory for the single isolated act of a rogue employee. There is, of course, a wide spectrum between these two extremes, and a prosecutor should exercise sound discretion in evaluating the pervasiveness of wrongdoing within a corporation. . . .

9-28.600 THE CORPORATION'S PAST HISTORY

A. General Principle: Prosecutors may consider a corporation's history of similar conduct, including prior criminal, civil, and regulatory enforcement actions against it, in determining whether to bring criminal charges and how best to resolve cases.

B. Comment: A corporation, like a natural person, is expected to learn from its mistakes. A history of similar misconduct may be probative of a corporate culture that encouraged, or at least condoned, such misdeeds, regardless of any compliance programs. . . .

9-28.700 THE VALUE OF COOPERATION

A. General Principle: In determining whether to charge a corporation and how to resolve corporate criminal cases, the corporation's timely and voluntary disclosure of wrongdoing and its cooperation with the government's investigation may be relevant factors. In gauging the extent of the corporation's cooperation, the prosecutor may consider, among other things, whether the corporation made a voluntary and timely disclosure, and the corporation's willingness to provide relevant information and evidence and identify relevant actors within and outside the corporation, including senior executives. . . .

9-28.800 CORPORATE COMPLIANCE PROGRAMS

A. General Principle: Compliance programs are established by corporate management to prevent and detect misconduct and to ensure that corporate activities are conducted in accordance with applicable criminal and civil laws, regulations, and rules. The Department encourages such corporate self-policing, including voluntary disclosures to the government of any problems that a corporation discovers on its own. However, the existence of a compliance program is not sufficient, in and of itself, to justify not charging a corporation for criminal misconduct undertaken by its officers, directors, employees, or agents. In addition, the nature of some crimes, e.g., antitrust violations, may be such that national law enforcement policies mandate prosecutions of corporations notwithstanding the existence of a compliance program. . . .

9-28.1000 COLLATERAL CONSEQUENCES

A. General Principle: Prosecutors may consider the collateral consequences of a corporate criminal conviction or indictment in determining whether to charge the corporation with a criminal offense and how to resolve corporate criminal cases.

B. Comment: One of the factors in determining whether to charge a natural person or a corporation is whether the likely punishment is appropriate given the nature and seriousness of the crime. In the corporate context, prosecutors may take into account the possibly substantial consequences to a corporation's employees, investors, pensioners, and customers, many of whom may, depending on the size and nature of the corporation and their role in its operations, have played no role in the criminal conduct, have been unaware of it, or have been unable to prevent it. Prosecutors should also be aware of non-penal sanctions that may accompany a criminal charge, such as potential suspension or debarment from eligibility for government contracts or federally funded programs such as health care programs. Determining whether or not such non-penal sanctions are appropriate or required in a particular case is the responsibility of the relevant agency, and is a decision that will be made based on the applicable statutes, regulations, and policies.

Virtually every conviction of a corporation, like virtually every conviction of an individual, will have an impact on innocent third parties, and the mere existence of such an effect is not sufficient to preclude prosecution of the corporation. . . .

9-28.1300 PLEA AGREEMENTS WITH CORPORATIONS

A. General Principle: In negotiating plea agreements with corporations, as with individuals, prosecutors should generally seek a plea to the most serious, readily provable offense charged. In addition, the terms of the plea agreement should contain appropriate provisions to ensure punishment, deterrence, rehabilitation, and compliance with the plea agreement in the corporate context. Although special circumstances may mandate a different conclusion, prosecutors generally should not agree to accept a corporate guilty plea in exchange for non-prosecution or dismissal of charges against individual officers and employees.

B. Comment: . . . A corporation should be made to realize that pleading guilty to criminal charges constitutes an admission of guilt and not merely a resolution of an inconvenient distraction from its business. As with natural persons, pleas should be structured so that the corporation may not later "proclaim lack of culpability or even complete innocence." Thus, for instance, there should be placed upon the record a sufficient factual basis for the plea to prevent later corporate assertions of innocence. . . .

In negotiating a plea agreement, prosecutors should also consider the deterrent value of prosecutions of individuals within the corporation. Therefore, one factor that a prosecutor may consider in determining whether to enter into a plea agreement is whether the corporation is seeking immunity for its employees and officers or whether the corporation is willing to cooperate in the investigation of culpable individuals as outlined herein. Prosecutors should rarely negotiate away individual criminal liability in a corporate plea. . . .

In plea agreements in which the corporation agrees to cooperate, the prosecutor should ensure that the cooperation is entirely truthful. To do so, the prosecutor may request that the corporation make appropriate disclosures of relevant factual information and documents, make employees and agents available for debriefing, file appropriate certified financial statements, agree to governmental or third-party audits, and take whatever other steps are necessary to ensure that the full scope of the corporate wrongdoing is disclosed and that the responsible personnel are identified and, if appropriate, prosecuted. . . .

Notes and Questions

1. What are the most significant changes in the current version of the Justice Department's Principles of Prosecution? Do they signal substantial departures from previous Justice Department policy, or are they more akin to explanations and qualifications of previous versions of published corporate prosecution policies?

2. Which of the factors enumerated in the current Principles of Prosecution seem most important? Which are most likely to be difficult to gauge?

3. In deciding whether to prosecute a corporation, is it fair for prosecutors to attach importance to the organization's willingness (1) to voluntarily turn itself in (and thus initiate a criminal investigation into its own affairs); (2) to cooperate with the investigation; and (3) possibly to waive the attorney-client privilege and work product protection? What kind of cooperation do the Principles of Prosecution anticipate? Might a corporation's voluntary disclosure of wrongdoing ultimately expose it to civil liability as well?

4. The Principles of Prosecution also recommend that prosecutors consider corporate remedial actions such as implementing or revising a compliance program, reshuffling management, and disciplining or firing officers and agents. Why are these factors relevant? Does this give prosecutors power to influence internal corporate management decisions? If so, is that appropriate?

5. The Principles of Prosecution state that, as a general rule, a plea bargain with the corporation should not carry with it an agreement not to prosecute individual officers and employees. What considerations support that approach? Why would a corporation be willing to incur substantial criminal fines in exchange for dismissal of charges against its officers and agents?

II. THE RESPONDEAT SUPERIOR RULE

A. CRIMINAL ACTS

A considerable body of case law, including federal law, allows imposition of corporate liability for criminal acts performed by officers and agents in the course of their employment, without regard to their status in the corporate hierarchy. Under this established line of authority, corporations have been convicted not only for the criminal acts of managers and supervisors, but also for the acts of subordinate, even menial, employees.

The only general limitation on corporate liability under the respondeat superior rule is that the agent who commits the crime must be acting within the scope of his or her authority and on behalf of the corporation.

COMMONWEALTH v. BENEFICIAL FINANCE CO.
360 Mass. 188, 275 N.E.2d 33 (1971)

Spiegel, Justice.

We have before us appeals emanating from 2 separate series of indictments and 2 separate jury trials of various individual and corporate defendants. . . .

These cases have become generally known as the "small loans" cases. In each case the defendants were charged with various offences under numerous indictments returned in 1964 by a special grand jury. The offences charged were offering or paying, or soliciting or receiving bribes or conspiring to do so. . . .

[The] evidence tends to show that during the year 1962, several licensed small loans companies (corporate defendants), together with certain of their officers and employees (some of whom are defendants), conspired to bribe . . . public officials. The purpose of the alleged conspiracy and the payment of the bribe money was to insure the maintenance of a maximum interest rate which companies licensed to do business in the Commonwealth were permitted to charge. Proceedings on this matter were conducted by the Small Loans Regulatory Board (Rate Board) in 1962 and the bribe money allegedly paid to Hanley was intended to "fix" the results of these hearings. . . .

The defendants and the Commonwealth have proposed differing standards upon which the criminal responsibility of a corporation should be predicated. The defendants argue that a corporation should not be held criminally liable for the conduct of its servants or agents unless such conduct was performed, authorized, ratified, adopted or tolerated by the corporations' directors, officers or other "high managerial agents" who are sufficiently high in the corporate hierarchy to warrant the assumption that their acts in some substantial sense reflect corporate policy. This standard is that adopted by the American Law Institute Model Penal Code. . . .

The Commonwealth, on the other hand, argues that the standard applied by the judge in his instructions to the jury was correct. These instructions, which prescribe a somewhat more flexible standard than that delineated in the Model Penal Code, state in part, as follows:

[T]he Commonwealth must prove beyond a reasonable doubt that there existed between the guilty individual or individuals and the corporation which is being charged with the conduct of the individuals, such *a relationship that the acts and the intent of the individuals were the acts and intent of the corporation.* . . .

It does not mean that the Commonwealth must prove that the individual who acted criminally was a member of the corporation's board of directors, or that he was a high officer in the corporation, or that he held any office at all. . . . The Commonwealth must prove that the individual for whose conduct it seeks to charge *the corporation criminally was placed in a position by the corporation where he had enough power, duty, responsibility and authority to act for and in behalf of the corporation to handle the particular business or operation or project of the corporation in which he was engaged at the time that he committed the criminal act, with power of decision as to what he would or would not do while acting for the corporation, and that he was acting for and in behalf of the corporation in the accomplishment of that particular business or operation or project, and that he committed a criminal act while so acting.* . . .

You will note from what I said that it is not necessary that the Commonwealth prove that an individual had any particular office or any office at all or that he had any particular title or any title at all. It isn't the title that counts. *It isn't the name of the office that counts, but it's the position in which the corporation placed that person with relation to its business, with regard to the powers and duties and responsibilities and authority which it gave to him which counts.* If it placed him in a position with such power, duty, authority, and responsibility that it can be found by you that, when he acted in the corporation's business, the corporation was acting, then you may find the corporation equally guilty of the criminal acts which he commits and of the intent which he holds, if you first find that the individual was guilty of the crime.

Now, this test doesn't depend upon the power, duty, the responsibility, or the authority which the individual has with reference to the entire corporation business. The test should be applied to his position with relation to the particular operation or project in which he is serving the corporation.

The difference between the judge's instructions to the jury and the Model Penal Code lies largely in the latter's reference to a "high managerial agent" and in the Code requirement that to impose corporate criminal liability, it at least must appear that its directors or high managerial agent "authorized . . . or recklessly tolerated" the allegedly criminal acts. The judge's instructions focus on the authority of the corporate agent in relation to the *particular* corporate business in which the agent was engaged. . . . The judge correctly charged the jury on the basis of the decided cases, rather than on the basis of a proposed model code.

It may also be observed that the judge's standard is somewhat similar to the traditional common law rule of respondeat superior. However, in applying this rule to a criminal case, the judge added certain requirements not generally associated with that common law doctrine. He further qualified the rule of respondeat superior by requiring that the conduct for which the corporation is being held accountable be performed *on behalf of the corporation.*

[After considering existing Massachusetts precedent the court examined *New York Central* and a number of federal court of appeals decisions that adopted a respondeat superior rule of corporate responsibility.]

Juxtaposition of the traditional criminal law requirement of ascertaining guilt beyond a reasonable doubt (as opposed to the civil law standard of the preponderance of the evidence), with the rule of respondeat superior, fully justifies application of the standard enunciated by the judge to a criminal prosecution against a corporation for a crime requiring specific intent.

The foregoing is especially true in view of the particular circumstances of this case. In order to commit the crimes charged in these indictments, the defendant corporations either had to offer to pay money to a public official or conspire to do so. The disbursal of funds is an act peculiarly within the ambit of corporate activity. These corporations by the very nature of their business are constantly dealing with the expenditure and collection of moneys. It could hardly be expected that any of the individual defendants would conspire to pay, or would pay, the substantial amount of money here involved, namely $25,000, out of his own pocket. The jury would be warranted in finding that the disbursal of such an amount of money would come from the corporate treasury. A reasonable inference could therefore be drawn that the payment of such money by the corporations was done as a matter of corporate policy and as a reflection of corporate intent, thus comporting with the underlying rationale of the Model Penal Code, and probably with its specific requirements.

Moreover, we do not think that the Model Penal Code standard really purports to deal with the evidentiary problems which are inherent in establishing the quantum of proof necessary to show that the directors or officers of a corporation authorize, ratify, tolerate, or participate in the criminal acts of an agent when such acts are apparently performed on behalf of the corporation. Evidence of such authorization or ratification is too easily susceptible of concealment. As is so trenchantly stated by the judge: "Criminal acts are not usually made the subject of votes of authorization or ratification by corporate Boards of Directors; and the lack of such votes does not prevent the act from being the act of the corporation."

It is obvious that criminal conspiratorial acts are not performed within the glare of publicity, nor would we expect a board of directors to meet officially and record on the corporate records a delegation of authority to initiate, conduct or conclude proceedings for the purpose of bribing a public official. Of necessity, the proof of authority to so act must rest on all the circumstances and conduct in a given situation and the reasonable inferences to be drawn therefrom.

Additional factors of importance are the size and complexity of many large modern corporations which necessitate the delegation of more authority to lesser corporate agents and employees. As the judge pointed out: "There are not enough seats on the

Board of Directors, nor enough offices in a corporation, to permit the corporation engaged in widespread operations to give such a title or office to every person in whom it places the power, authority, and responsibility for decision and action." This latter consideration lends credence to the view that the title or position of an individual in a corporation should not be conclusively determinative in ascribing criminal responsibility. In a large corporation, with many numerous and distinct departments, a high ranking corporate officer or agent may have no authority or involvement in a particular sphere of corporate activity, whereas a lower ranking corporate executive might have much broader power in dealing with a matter peculiarly within the scope of his authority. Employees who are in the lower echelon of the corporate hierarchy often exercise more responsibility in the *everyday operations* of the corporation than the directors or officers. Assuredly, the title or office that the person holds may be considered, but it should not be the decisive criterion upon which to predicate corporate responsibility. . . .

To permit corporations to conceal the nefarious acts of their underlings by using the shield of corporate armor to deflect corporate responsibility, and to separate the subordinate from the executive, would be to permit "endocratic" corporations to inflict widespread public harm without hope of redress. It would merely serve to ignore the scramble and realities of the market place.[8] This we decline to do. We believe that stringent standards must be adopted to discourage any attempt by "endocratic" corporations' executives to place the sole responsibility for criminal acts on the shoulders of their subordinates. . . .

Considering everything we have said above, we are of [the] opinion that the quantum of proof necessary to sustain the conviction of a corporation for the acts of its agents is sufficiently met if it is shown that the corporation has placed the agent in a position where he has enough authority and responsibility to act for and in behalf of the corporation in handling the *particular* corporate business, operation or project in which he was engaged at the time he committed the criminal act. The judge properly instructed the jury to this effect and correctly stated that this standard does not depend upon the responsibility or authority which the agent has with respect to the entire corporate business, but only to his position with relation to the particular business in which he was serving the corporation. . . .

All judgments affirmed.

Notes and Questions

1. The requirement that agents must act within the scope of their authority does not mean that express authorization to engage in the wrongful conduct is needed. It means, instead, that the agent must perform the acts "on behalf of" the corporation and that the acts must be "directly related to the performance of the type of duties the employee has general authority to perform."[9] In what sense did the defendants' participation in the conspiracy to bribe public officials satisfy these requirements in *Beneficial Finance*?

---

8. The term "endocratic" was coined by Dean Rostow and means a "large, publicly-held corporation, whose stock is scattered in small fractions among thousands of stockholders." Note, Increasing Community Control Over Corporate Crime — A Problem in the Law of Sanctions, 71 Yale L.J. 280, 281, n.3.

9. United States v. American Radiator & Standard Sanitary Corp., 433 F.2d 174, 204-205 (3d Cir. 1970).

2. The requirement that the agent must be acting "on behalf of" the corporation is sometimes expressed as one of "intent to benefit" the corporation. The gist of this requirement is that the agent must act with the purpose of forwarding corporate business. By stealing *from*, as opposed to *for* the corporation, for example, the agent commits a crime against the entity rather than on its behalf.[10] In what sense were the defendants who conspired to bribe public officials acting on behalf of the corporation in *Beneficial Finance*?

3. The court observed that under the respondeat superior theory, agents who are relatively low-level operatives may commit criminal acts that are imputable to the corporation. What policy considerations support this relaxed standard of corporate liability? Why shouldn't imposition of corporate criminal liability require proof that policy-level managers participated in the criminal conduct?

4. The court in *Beneficial Finance* rejected the Model Penal Code's high managerial agent requirement in favor of a more traditional respondeat superior standard. If the court had applied the Model Penal Code rule, is it likely that the defendants' convictions would have been upheld?

5. The court in *Beneficial Finance* justified recognition of the respondeat superior theory of liability partly because of the impenetrability of the layers of bureaucracy that characterize large, publicly held corporations. That, in turn, influenced the court's conclusion that the Model Penal Code's high managerial agent rule was unworkable. Is a rule of liability that requires proof of high managerial complicity likely to be (in practice, if not in theory) a rule of no liability at all? Consider the following excerpt.

> Without first inquiring into how modern business corporations are structured and how they allocate responsibility among corporate officers, directors, and operatives, we cannot gauge whether a rule of liability premised upon a showing of participation by the Board of Directors or a high managerial agent is workable.
>
> Most large or diversified corporate operations are characterized by a system of delegation through which authority for setting and implementing policy is purposefully diffused. Consider two examples that are roughly contemporaneous with the Model Penal Code.
>
> As early as 1961 General Electric informed its stockholders that it had adopted an extensive system of decentralization and delegation. The corporation decentralized into more than one hundred profit-seeking departments, each under separate managers who had "extensive authority to function without first 'checking back' with headquarters . . . [and] responsible for such operations as establishing production schedules, setting inventory levels, determining the flow of cash, keeping organization structure sound, arriving at acceptable prices with customers, and maintaining favorable relations with employees."[11]
>
> At about the same time Allis-Chalmers, an electrical equipment manufacturer, established an operating policy that sought to decentralize the operation by delegating authority to "the lowest possible management level capable of fulfilling the delegated responsibility."[12] This company employed 31,000 people to work in 24 plants, 145 sales offices, and 5000 dealers and distributors.[13] The Board of Directors met once a month for several hours to consider a pre-set agenda. The Board set general business policy for the corporation,

---

10. Cf. Standard Oil Co. v. United States, 307 F.2d 120 (5th Cir. 1962).

11. Note, Corporate Criminal Liability for Acts in Violation of Company Policy, 50 Geo. L.J. 547, 552 n.27 (1962) (quoting General Electric Share Owners Quarterly, Jan. 25, 1961, at 2).

12. Graham v. Allis-Chalmers Mfg. Co., 41 Del. Ch. 78, 81, 188 A.2d 125, 128 (1963).

13. Id.

but "[b]y reason of the extent and complexity of the company's operations, it [was] not practicable for the Board to consider in detail specific problems of the various divisions."[14]

Do the organizational changes that General Electric and Allis-Chalmers implemented in the early 1960s provide a better context for evaluating the *Beneficial Finance* court's concerns about the Model Penal Code rule?

6. To what extent should the fate of the corporation be tied to the fate of the individual wrongdoer? If for some reason the agent is not (or cannot be) prosecuted — or is tried and acquitted — should that have any bearing on the corporation's liability? Since corporate liability rests on the imputation of an agent's wrongful acts and intent, should acquittal of the agent exonerate the corporation? What reasons might explain a jury's acquitting the presumably culpable agent while convicting the corporation on whose behalf the agent acted? If that scenario should occur, should the court uphold the corporation's conviction?[15]

7. Under the respondeat superior rule, a corporation may incur criminal liability for the conduct of agents who are not, in the usual sense, its employees. Wrongful acts committed by an independent contractor, a subsidiary, or a division may also be imputed to the corporation.[16] Does this rule extend the principle of corporate criminal liability to its illogical extreme? What policy considerations are likely to have shaped the rule?

NOTE ON RESPONDEAT SUPERIOR RULE

Although the respondeat superior rule is well ensconced in federal law and in the law of many states, one hundred years of precedent have not insulated it from criticism by academics, the criminal defense bar, and — more recently — the business community itself. A recent broadside attack on the rule in an amicus brief[17] revived interest in debating whether the rule should be retained in its present form.

In United States v. Ionia Management S.A.,[18] *amici* argued that while the Supreme Court's decision in *New York Central* clearly upheld the constitutional authority of

---

14. Kathleen F. Brickey, Rethinking Corporate Liability Under the Model Penal Code, 19 Rutgers L.J. 593, 625-626 (1988) (quoting id. at 82, 188 A.2d at 128) [hereinafter Brickey, Rethinking Corporate Liability].

15. Cf. United States v. General Motors Corp., 121 F.2d 376, 411 (7th Cir. 1941) ("We can not understand how the jury could have acquitted all of the individual defendants."); United States v. Austin-Bagley Corp., 31 F.2d 229, 233 (2d Cir. 1929) ("How an intelligent jury could have acquitted any of the defendants we cannot conceive.").

16. Cf. United States v. Wilshire Oil Co., 427 F.2d 969 (10th Cir. 1970) (corporate division); United States v. Parfait Powder Puff Co., 163 F.2d 1008 (7th Cir. 1947) (corporation is liable for Food, Drug, and Cosmetic Act violation for acts of independent contractor who, contrary to instructions, substituted unauthorized ingredient in finished product); United States v. Johns-Manville Corp., 231 F. Supp. 690 (E.D. Pa. 1963) (corporate subsidiary).

17. Brief for the Association of Corporate Counsel et al. as Amici Curiae Supporting Appellant, United States v. Ionia Management S.A., 555 F.3d 303 (2d Cir. 2009) (No. 07-5801-CR). The brief-writing effort was spearheaded by Andrew Weissmann, a former Enron prosecutor who served as co-lead counsel in the prosecution of Arthur Andersen. Weissmann, who was Counsel of Record on the *Ionia* brief, led an eclectic coalition of the Association of Corporate Counsel, the Chamber of Commerce, the National Association of Criminal Defense Lawyers, the National Association of Manufacturers, the New York State Association of Criminal Defense Lawyers, and the Washington Legal Foundation in urging reversal of the corporation's conviction.

18. 555 F.3d 303 (2d Cir. 2009).

Congress to impose criminal liability on corporations — as it expressly did in the Elkins Act — *New York Central* has been erroneously construed as a template for applying the least demanding standards for corporate criminal liability, without express guidance from Congress.

Amici urged the Second Circuit to adopt a more stringent rule that would require the government to prove that accused corporations lacked "effective policies and procedures to deter and detect criminal actions by their employees" or, alternatively, to recognize due diligence as an affirmative defense. The brief also noted with approval the Model Penal Code's general requirement that corporate actors be high managerial agents before their misconduct is imputable to the entity.

The Second Circuit summarily dismissed these challenges to settled precedent.

> We find that Ionia's claim that there was not sufficient evidence to convict it on a respondeat superior theory to be meritless. . . . The record reflects that there was ample evidence for a jury to have reasonably found that the [ship's] crew acted within the scope of their employment. The crew members acted within their authority to maintain the engine room, discharge waste, and record relevant information, when they used the [bypass hose to discharge untreated waste into the sea]. They testified that they acted at the direction of their supervisors not just (a) in the discharging of the oil, and (b) in the making and maintaining of [false entries in required records], but also (c) in lying to the Coast Guard. The jury could, moreover, infer from the expert testimony about the maintenance and expense involved in using the Oil Water Separator that the crew used the bypass hose to benefit Ionia and subsequently lied to protect the company.
>
> Ionia's appeal that the jury charge on respondeat superior was erroneous . . . also fails. . . . Ionia contends that the District Court erred because, inter alia, it failed to instruct the jury that corporate criminal liability can only stem from the actions of so-called "managerial" employees. That contention seems at odds with our precedents in United States v. Twentieth Century Fox Film Corp., 882 F.2d 656, 660 (2d Cir. 1989), and United States v. George F. Fish, Inc., 154 F.2d 798, 801 (2d Cir. 1946) (per curiam). But regardless of these, there was overwhelming evidence that the [ship's] Chief Engineers specifically directed crew members to use the "magic hose," and so Ionia's argument is without merit in any event.
>
> Furthermore, we refuse to adopt the suggestion that the prosecution, in order to establish vicarious liability, should have to prove as a separate element in its case-in-chief that the corporation lacked effective policies and procedures to deter and detect criminal actions by its employees. We note that this argument is made only by *amici curiae* and not by Ionia, and so we are not obligated to consider it. But the argument, whoever made it, is unavailing. Adding such an element is contrary to the precedent of our Circuit on this issue. *See* Twentieth Century Fox Film Corp., 882 F.2d at 660 (holding that a compliance program, "however extensive, does not immunize the corporation from liability when its employees, acting within the scope of their authority, fail to comply with the law"). And this remains so regardless of asserted new Supreme Court cases in other areas of the law. As the District Court instructed the jury here, a corporate compliance program may be relevant to whether an employee was acting in the scope of his employment, but it is not a separate element. . . .[19]

---

19. Id. at 309-310.

Notes and Questions

1. Why would the existence of a corporate compliance program be relevant to the determination whether a corporate agent who committed a crime was acting within the scope of his employment?

2. As a matter of policy, would allowing a corporate defendant to assert an effective compliance policy as an affirmative defense be more consistent with the goals of the criminal law? If a corporation has a rigorous compliance policy, what additional deterrent value does the respondeat superior rule provide?

PEOPLE v. LESSOFF & BERGER
608 N.Y.S.2d 54 (N.Y. Sup. Ct. 1994)

MICHAEL R. JUVILER, Justice.

This is a written version of an oral decision on a motion to dismiss the indictment. The defendant Lessoff is a lawyer whose office is in Manhattan. The co-defendant is the law partnership in which the defendant Lessoff is a partner. The issue is whether a law partnership may be indicted for crimes of fraud, and if so, whether a partnership may be indicted if only one partner is involved in the alleged crimes.

The evidence before the Grand Jury showed that the defendant Lessoff referred clients in personal-injury accident cases to a radiologist in Brooklyn for examination and report. The indictment, as clarified by a bill of particulars, alleges that Lessoff instructed the radiologist to change MRI reports to delete references to nontraumatic damage and to abnormalities or injuries predating the accidents.

The crimes alleged are insurance fraud, for soliciting the doctor to change the MRI findings with intent to defraud insurers; falsifying business records, the MRI reports at the radiologist's office; and attempted grand larceny, an attempt by false pretenses to gain money in a lawsuit against the New York City Transit Authority. At the time of the crimes charged in the indictment, the doctor, unknown to the defendant Lessoff, was working undercover with the District Attorney's Office during the Grand Jury investigation and was secretly recording his telephone conversations with Lessoff. The indictment alleges ten separate transactions involving ten separate clients of Lessoff and the partnership. At all times Lessoff was acting in the name of the law firm. There is no evidence implicating anyone else in the firm in the alleged crimes. . . .

The partnership defendant has moved to dismiss the entire indictment on the ground that the evidence before the Grand Jury shows, at most, culpable involvement by only one partner, the defendant Lessoff.

The plain language of Penal Law § 10.00(7) authorizes an indictment of the partnership on such facts. That section provides that a "person" — which includes a person charged with a crime — means, "where appropriate," "a partnership." Similarly, the section defining the crime of insurance fraud, § 176.00, provides that a "person" chargeable with the crime of insurance fraud includes any "*firm, association* or corporation"; under the Partnership Law, a partnership is "an *association* of two or more persons to carry on as co-owners a business for profit." § 10(1). Unmistakably, therefore, the Penal Law applies to a law "firm," whether it be a partnership or a professional corporation, and the law firm may be charged if one partner has committed a crime in the name of the law firm, as alleged in this case. Presumably, if there is a conviction of a partnership, the sentence can be a fine, a conditional discharge, or an unconditional discharge, as for a corporation.

The background of these Penal Law provisions confirms this interpretation. The quoted language was adopted as part of the Penal Law after federal criminal statutes had been construed by the Supreme Court of the United States to apply to partnerships, without reference to individual responsibility. United States v. A & P Trucking Co., 358 U.S. 121, 126-127, had held that "a partnership can violate each of the statutes here in question quite apart from the participation and knowledge of the partners as individuals."

Application of the Penal Law to a partnership when only one partner is alleged to have been culpable may be harsh, but it is rational. It is analogous to the criminal responsibility of a corporation for conduct of a "high managerial agent." See Penal Law § 20.20. And it is consistent with the settled principle in torts that a partnership is responsible for conversion of funds by one partner, even if the other partners are unaware of the misconduct.

Criminal liability for one partner's frauds is particularly appropriate in the case of a law partnership. Not only do law partners, as any partners, benefit financially from the fruits of one partner's fraudulent conduct committed in the name of the firm, but there is a strong public interest in regulating the ethics of the legal profession. Cf. People v. Smithtown General Hospital, 399 N.Y.S.2d 993 (Sup. Ct. Suffolk Co.) (public regulation of hospitals in the public interest supports criminal prosecution of a hospital partnership even without evidence of culpability of individual partners).

The partnership's motion to dismiss the indictment is denied.

Notes and Questions

1. The court stated that imposition of liability on the partnership under these circumstances is "harsh but rational." In what respect is it harsh? In what respect rational?

2. The New York legislature decided to treat partnerships like corporations for purposes of imposing criminal liability. Are partnerships sufficiently like corporations to warrant this treatment? In what respects are corporations different?

3. Assume that the lawyer who committed the fraud had been an associate rather than a partner in the firm. Would the partnership be criminally liable for the associate's misconduct?

4. The court observed that there is a strong public policy favoring the regulation of legal ethics. Is the criminal law an appropriate mechanism for achieving that end?

UNITED STATES v. HILTON HOTELS CORP.
467 F.2d 1000 (9th Cir. 1972)

BROWNING, Circuit Judge.

This is an appeal from a conviction under an indictment charging a violation of section 1 of the Sherman Act, 15 U.S.C. § 1.

Operators of hotels, restaurants, hotel and restaurant supply companies, and other businesses in Portland, Oregon, organized an association to attract conventions to their city. To finance the association, members were asked to make contributions in predetermined amounts. Companies selling supplies to hotels were asked to contribute an amount equal to one per cent of their sales to hotel members. To aid collections, hotel members, including appellant, agreed to give preferential treatment to suppliers who paid their assessments, and to curtail purchases from those who did not.

I

The jury was instructed that such an agreement by the hotel members, if proven, would be a per se violation of the Sherman Act. Appellant argues that this was error.

We need not explore the outer limits of the doctrine that joint refusals to deal constitute per se violations of the Act, for the conduct involved here was of the kind long held to be forbidden without more. "Throughout the history of the Sherman Act, the courts have had little difficulty in finding unreasonable restraints of trade in agreements among competitors, at any level of distribution, designed to coerce those subject to a boycott to accede to the action or inaction desired by the group or to exclude them from competition." Barber, Refusals to Deal under the Federal Antitrust Laws, 103 U. Pa. L. Rev. 847, 872-873 (1955).

Appellant argues that in cases in which the per se rule has been applied to refusals to deal, the defendants intended "to destroy a competitor or a line of competition," while the purpose of the defendants in the present case "was solely to bring convention dollars into Portland." But the necessary and direct consequence of defendants' scheme was to deprive uncooperative suppliers of the opportunity to sell to defendant hotels in free and open competition with other suppliers, and to deprive defendant hotels of the opportunity to buy supplies from such suppliers in accordance with the individual judgment of each hotel, at prices and on terms and conditions of sale determined by free competition. Defendants therefore "intended" to impose these restraints upon competition in the only sense relevant here. . . .

II

Appellant's president testified that it would be contrary to the policy of the corporation for the manager of one of its hotels to condition purchases upon payment of a contribution to a local association by the supplier. The manager of appellant's Portland hotel and his assistant testified that it was the hotel's policy to purchase supplies solely on the basis of price, quality, and service. They also testified that on two occasions they told the hotel's purchasing agent that he was to take no part in the boycott. The purchasing agent confirmed the receipt of these instructions, but admitted that, despite them, he had threatened a supplier with loss of the hotel's business unless the supplier paid the association assessment. He testified that he violated his instructions because of anger and personal pique toward the individual representing the supplier.

Based upon this testimony, appellant requested certain instructions bearing upon the criminal liability of a corporation for the unauthorized acts of its agents. These requests were rejected by the trial court. The court instructed the jury that a corporation is liable for the acts and statements of its agents "within the scope of their employment," defined to mean "in the corporation's behalf in performance of the agent's general line of work," including "not only that which has been authorized by the corporation, but also that which outsiders could reasonably assume the agent would have authority to do." The court added: "A corporation is responsible for acts and statements of its agents, done or made within the scope of their employment, even though their conduct may be contrary to their actual instructions or contrary to the corporation's stated policies."

Appellant objects only to the court's concluding statement. . . .

The breadth and critical character of the public interests protected by the Sherman Act, and the gravity of the threat to those interests that led to the enactment of the statute, support a construction holding business organizations accountable, as a general rule, for violations of the Act by their employees in the course of their businesses. In enacting the Sherman Act, "Congress was passing drastic legislation to remedy a threatening danger to the public welfare. . . ." United Mine Workers v. Coronado Coal Co., 259 U.S. 344, 392 (1922). The statute "was designed to be a comprehensive charter of economic liberty aimed at preserving free and unfettered competition as the rule of trade. It rests on the premise that the unrestrained interaction of competitive forces will yield the best allocation of our economic resources, the lowest prices, the highest quality and the greatest material progress, while at the same time providing an environment conducive to the preservation of our democratic political and social institutions." Northern Pacific Ry. v. United States, supra 356 U.S. at 4.

With such important public interests at stake, it is reasonable to assume that Congress intended to impose liability upon business entities for the acts of those to whom they choose to delegate the conduct of their affairs, thus stimulating a maximum effort by owners and managers to assure adherence by such agents to the requirements of the Act. . . .

Because of the nature of Sherman Act offenses and the context in which they normally occur, the factors that militate against allowing a corporation to disown the criminal acts of its agents apply with special force to Sherman Act violations.

Antitrust violations are usually motivated by a desire to enhance profits. They commonly involve large, complex, and highly decentralized corporate business enterprises, and intricate business processes, practices, and arrangements. More often than not they also involve basic policy decisions, and must be implemented over an extended period of time.

Complex business structures, characterized by decentralization and delegation of authority, commonly adopted by corporations for business purposes, make it difficult to identify the particular corporate agents responsible for Sherman Act violations. At the same time, it is generally true that high management officials, for whose conduct the corporate directors and stockholders are the most clearly responsible, are likely to have participated in the policy decisions underlying Sherman Act violations, or at least to have become aware of them.

Violations of the Sherman Act are a likely consequence of the pressure to maximize profits that is commonly imposed by corporate owners upon managing agents and, in turn, upon lesser employees. In the face of that pressure, generalized directions to obey the Sherman Act, with the probable effect of [forgoing] profits, are the least likely to be taken seriously. And if a violation of the Sherman Act occurs, the corporation, and not the individual agents, will have realized the profits from the illegal activity.

In sum, identification of the particular agents responsible for a Sherman Act violation is especially difficult, and their conviction and punishment is peculiarly ineffective as a deterrent. At the same time, conviction and punishment of the business entity itself is likely to be both appropriate and effective.

For these reasons we conclude that as a general rule a corporation is liable under the Sherman Act for the acts of its agents in the scope of their employment, even though contrary to general corporate policy and express instructions to the agent.

Thus the general policy statements of appellant's president were no defense. Nor was it enough that appellant's manager told the purchasing agent that he was not to participate in the boycott. The purchasing agent was authorized to buy all of appellant's supplies. Purchases were made on the basis of specifications, but the purchasing agent exercised complete authority as to source. He was in a unique position to add the corporation's buying power to the force of the boycott. Appellant could not gain exculpation by issuing general instructions without undertaking to enforce those instructions by means commensurate with the obvious risks. . . .

Affirmed.

Notes and Questions

1. If the object of criminal sanctions is to deter — that is, to cause management to take steps to prevent violations of the law — should a corporation be liable for criminal acts committed contrary to corporate policy or express instructions? Is an employee's intentional misconduct within the corporation's control?[20]

2. Does the reasoning in *Hilton Hotels* apply with equal force to offenses requiring an element of moral culpability — e.g., mail fraud, which requires intent to defraud? Should a jury be permitted to consider a corporation's compliance policy when deliberating the corporation's guilt? If so, why would the compliance policy be relevant to the issue of guilt?[21] If a corporate compliance program is relevant to the jury's deliberations, are there circumstances under which it should provide the corporation a complete defense? If so, what would they be and why? What characteristics should the compliance program have?[22]

3. Corporate compliance programs have now taken on greater significance at the sentencing stage of a criminal prosecution. In 1991, the U.S. Sentencing Commission promulgated guidelines for sentencing organizational offenders, which calculate a corporation's "culpability score" on the basis of aggravating and mitigating factors. If the corporation had an effective program to prevent and detect violations of the law, that

---

20. Cf. United States v. Harry L. Young & Sons, Inc., 464 F.2d 1295 (10th Cir. 1972) (drivers of truck laden with explosives left truck unattended despite dispatcher's warning upon their original departure from California and upon drivers' later report of mechanical breakdown in Utah).

21. Compare United States v. Twentieth Century Fox Film Corp., 882 F.2d 656, 660-661 (2d Cir. 1989) (corporation's efforts to comply with consent decree are irrelevant to criminal contempt charge) with United States v. Basic Constr. Co., 711 F.2d 570 (4th Cir. 1983) (court correctly permitted jury to consider corporation's antitrust compliance policy in determining whether relatively minor officials were working for corporation's benefit).

22. Cf. Charles J. Walsh & Alissa Pyrich, Corporate Compliance Programs as a Defense to Criminal Liability: Can a Corporation Save Its Soul?, 47 Rutgers L. Rev. 605 (1995).

will result in a reduction of sentence unless high-level personnel participated in or condoned the offense.[23]

If a corporation's compliance program is relevant to the degree of culpability for sentencing purposes, should it be equally relevant at trial on the issue of guilt?

4. The Model Penal Code recognizes a limited due diligence defense for regulatory offenses that do not impose strict liability. In prosecutions brought under § 2.07(1)(a), it is a defense that the high managerial agent with supervisory responsibility over the offending transaction exercised due diligence to prevent the commission of the offense.[24]

Although two early federal cases recognized a company's good-faith compliance efforts as a defense,[25] the overwhelming weight of authority is to the contrary today. Even among states that have adopted legislation resembling Model Penal Code § 2.07, only a few recognize any form of due diligence defense.

B. CRIMINAL INTENT

The earliest cases that recognized corporate liability for crime arose in the context of nuisance prosecutions and, to a lesser extent, regulatory crimes, neither of which required proof of culpability. Not surprisingly, when courts were first asked to hold corporations accountable for crimes requiring mens rea, they were reluctant to ascribe moral blame to a juristic person. But by the turn of the century, that barrier to holding corporations criminally accountable also began to erode. After all, if corporations could possess the wrongful state of mind required for the commission of an intentional tort, why should it be conceptually more difficult to impute wrongful intent to commit a crime?

UNITED STATES v. BANK OF NEW ENGLAND, N.A.
821 F.2d 844 (1st Cir. 1987)

BOWNES, Circuit Judge.

The Bank of New England appeals a jury verdict convicting it of thirty-one violations of the Currency Transaction Reporting Act (the Act). Department of Treasury regulations promulgated under the Act require banks to file Currency Transaction Reports (CTRs) within fifteen days of customer currency transactions exceeding $10,000. 31 C.F.R. § 103.22. The Act imposes felony liability when a bank willfully fails to file such reports "as part of a pattern of illegal activity involving transactions of more than $100,000 in a twelve-month period. . . ." 31 U.S.C. § 5322(b).

---

23. See U.S. Sentencing Commission, Guidelines Manual § 8C2.5(f) (2009). Cf. Dan K. Webb & Steven F. Molo, *Some Practical Considerations in Developing Effective Compliance Programs: A Framework for Meeting the Requirements of the Sentencing Guidelines*, 71 Wash. U. L.Q. 375 (1993).

24. Model Penal Code § 2.07(5) (Official Draft and Revised Comments 1980).

25. See Holland Furnace Co. v. United States, 158 F.2d 2 (6th Cir. 1946); John Gund Brewing Co. v. United States, 204 F. 17 (8th Cir.), modified, 206 F. 386 (1913).

I. THE ISSUES

The Bank was found guilty of having failed to file CTRs on cash withdrawals made by James McDonough. It is undisputed that on thirty-one separate occasions between May 1983 and July 1984, McDonough withdrew from the Prudential Branch of the Bank more than $10,000 in cash by using multiple checks — each one individually under $10,000 — presented simultaneously to a single bank teller. The Bank contends that such conduct did not trigger the Act's reporting requirements. . . . The Bank also argues that the trial judge's instructions on willfulness were fatally flawed, and that, in any event, the evidence did not suffice to show that it willfully failed to file CTRs on McDonough's transactions. Finally, the Bank submits that during her charge to the jury, the trial judge erroneously alluded to evidence of the Bank's conduct after the dates specified in the indictment. . . .

IV. WILLFULNESS OF THE BANK'S CONDUCT

A. THE TRIAL COURT'S INSTRUCTION ON WILLFULNESS

Criminal liability under 31 U.S.C. § 5322 only attaches when a financial institution "willfully" violates the CTR filing requirement. A finding of willfulness under the Reporting Act must be supported by "proof of the defendant's knowledge of the reporting requirements and his specific intent to commit the crime." United States v. Hernando Ospina, 798 F.2d 1570, 1580 (11th Cir. 1986). Willfulness can rarely be proven by direct evidence, since it is a state of mind; it is usually established by drawing reasonable inferences from the available facts.

The Bank contends that the trial court's instructions on knowledge and specific intent effectively relieved the government of its responsibility to prove that the Bank acted willfully. The trial judge began her instructions on this element by outlining generally the concepts of knowledge and willfulness:

> Knowingly simply means voluntarily and intentionally. It's designed to exclude a failure that is done by mistake or accident, or for some other innocent reason. Willfully means voluntarily, intentionally, and with a specific intent to disregard, to disobey the law, with a bad purpose to violate the law.

The trial judge properly instructed the jury that it could infer knowledge if a defendant consciously avoided learning about the reporting requirements. The court then focused on the kind of proof that would establish the Bank's knowledge of its filing obligations. The judge instructed that the knowledge of individual employees acting within the scope of their employment is imputed to the Bank. She told the jury that "if any employee knew that multiple checks would require the filing of reports, the bank knew it, provided the employee knew it within the scope of his employment. . . ."

The trial judge then focused on the issue of "collective knowledge":

> In addition, however, you have to look at the bank as an institution. As such, its knowledge is the sum of the knowledge of all of the employees. That is, the bank's knowledge is the totality of what all of the employees know within the scope of their employment.

So, if Employee *A* knows one facet of the currency reporting requirement, *B* knows another facet of it, and *C* a third facet of it, the bank knows them all. So if you find that an employee within the scope of his employment knew that CTRs had to be filed, even if multiple checks are used, the bank is deemed to know it. The bank is also deemed to know it if each of several employees knew a part of that requirement and the sum of what the separate employees knew amounted to knowledge that such a requirement existed.

After discussing the two modes of establishing knowledge — via either knowledge of one of its individual employees or the aggregate knowledge of all its employees — the trial judge turned to the issue of specific intent:

There is a similar double business with respect to the concept of willfulness with respect to the bank. In deciding whether the bank acted willfully, again you have to look first at the conduct of all employees and officers, and, second, at what the bank did or did not do as an institution. The bank is deemed to have acted willfully if one of its employees in the scope of his employment acted willfully. So, if you find that an employee willfully failed to do what was necessary to file these reports, then that is deemed to be the act of the bank, and the bank is deemed to have willfully failed to file. . . .

Alternatively, the bank as an institution has certain responsibilities; as an organization, it has certain responsibilities. And you will have to determine whether the bank as an organization consciously avoided learning about and observing CTR requirements. The Government, to prove the bank guilty on this theory, has to show that its failure to file was the result of some flagrant organizational indifference. In this connection, you should look at the evidence as to the bank's effort, if any, to inform its employees of the law; its effort to check on their compliance; its response to various bits of information that it got in August and September of '84 and February of '85; its policies, and how it carried out its stated policies. . . .

If you find that the Government has proven with respect to any transaction either that an employee within the scope of his employment willfully failed to file a required report or that the bank was flagrantly indifferent to its obligations, then you may find that the bank has willfully failed to file the required reports.

The Bank contends that the trial court's instructions regarding knowledge were defective because they eliminated the requirement that it be proven that the Bank violated a known legal duty. It avers that the knowledge instruction invited the jury to convict the Bank for negligently maintaining a poor communications network that prevented the consolidation of the information held by its various employees. The Bank argues that it is error to find that a corporation possesses a particular item of knowledge if one part of the corporation has half the information making up the item, and another part of the entity has the other half.

A collective knowledge instruction is entirely appropriate in the context of corporate criminal liability. The acts of a corporation are, after all, simply the acts of all of its employees operating within the scope of their employment. The law on corporate criminal liability reflects this. Similarly, the knowledge obtained by corporate employees acting within the scope of their employment is imputed to the corporation. Corporations compartmentalize knowledge, subdividing the elements of specific duties and operations into smaller components. The aggregate of those components constitutes the corporation's knowledge of a particular operation. It is irrelevant whether employees administering one component of an operation know the specific activities of employees administering another aspect of the operation:

> [A] corporation cannot plead innocence by asserting that the information obtained by several employees was not acquired by any one individual who then would have comprehended its full import. Rather the corporation is considered to have acquired the collective knowledge of its employees and is held responsible for their failure to act accordingly.

United States v. T.I.M.E.-D.C., Inc., 381 F. Supp. at 738. Since the Bank had the compartmentalized structure common to all large corporations, the court's collective knowledge instruction was not only proper but necessary.

Nor do we find any defects in the trial court's instructions on specific intent. The court told the jury that the concept of willfulness entails a voluntary, intentional, and bad purpose to disobey the law. Her instructions on this element, when viewed as a whole, directed the jury not to convict for accidental, mistaken or inadvertent acts or omissions. It is urged that the court erroneously charged that willfulness could be found via flagrant indifference by the Bank toward its reporting obligations. With respect to federal regulatory statutes, the Supreme Court has endorsed defining willfulness, in both civil and criminal contexts, as "a disregard for the governing statute and an indifference to its requirements." Trans World Airlines, Inc. v. Thurston, 469 U.S. 111, 127 & n.20 (1985). . . .

B. EVIDENCE OF WILLFULNESS

[An internal bank memorandum and evidence that a bank auditor discussed the reporting requirements with the bank's tellers supported the conclusion that the bank was well aware that McDonough's transactions should have been reported.]

Regarding the Bank's specific intent to violate the reporting obligation, Simona Wong testified that head teller Patricia Murphy knew that McDonough's transactions were reportable, but, on one occasion, deliberately chose not to file a CTR on him because he was "a good customer." In addition, the jury heard testimony that bank employees regarded McDonough's transactions as unusual, speculated that he was a bookie, and suspected that he was structuring his transactions to avoid the Act's reporting requirements. An internal Bank memo, written after an investigation of the McDonough transactions, concluded that a "person managing the branch would have to have known that something strange was going on." Given the suspicions aroused by McDonough's banking practices and the abundance of information indicating that his transactions were reportable, the jury could have concluded that the failure by Bank personnel to, at least, inquire about the reportability of McDonough's transactions constituted flagrant indifference to the obligations imposed by the Act.

We hold that evidence was sufficient for a finding of willfulness. . . .

C. INSTRUCTIONS PERTAINING TO THE BANK'S POST-JULY 1984 CONDUCT

At trial, the government introduced evidence of the Bank's CTR compliance efforts after July 31, 1984, the last date on which the Bank was charged with failing to file a CTR. On August 7, 1984, the Bank learned that McDonough's transactions were being investigated by law-enforcement agencies. In addition, the branch manager and head teller were told specifically that McDonough's transactions were reportable. The government introduced evidence of the Bank's conduct after July 1984, which could be found to show scant effort by the Bank to comply with its legal obligations, even after it had learned that McDonough had come under suspicion. The Bank's failure to file a CTR on McDonough's July 31, 1984, transaction was highlighted specifically. The government argued that when the Bank was told directly by law-enforcement officers on August 7 that McDonough's transactions were reportable, it should have at least completed a CTR on the July 31 withdrawal, while it still had time to meet the statute's fifteen-day filing deadline. The government also pointed to the fact that between August 1984 and May 1985 there occurred a flurry of law-enforcement activity surrounding McDonough's transactions with the Bank. The Bank, however, did not make any effort to report McDonough's 1983 and 1984 transactions until May 1985, after it received a federal grand jury subpoena.

This evidence was admitted originally on the Count One conspiracy charge which the trial court dismissed after all testimony had been taken. The Bank did not move to strike this evidence once the conspiracy charge was dismissed. During closing argument, the government urged that the post-July 1984 evidence manifested the Bank's disregard of its reporting duty, and thus inferentially illuminated its mental state during the time period charged in the indictment. The trial court instructed the jury that it could consider post-July 1984 conduct as probative of the Bank's intent to violate the Act. Specifically, the court told the jury that the evidence might shed light on whether the Bank had been flagrantly indifferent to its reporting obligations. . . .

[W]e uphold the district court's instruction that post-July 1984 conduct was probative of the Bank's mental state. . . .

Affirmed.

Notes and Questions

1. What is the theoretical basis for holding that corporations are capable of forming mens rea? Does the collective knowledge doctrine extend the rationale beyond its logical extreme? What justifies imputing the collective knowledge of corporate agents to the corporate entity?

2. One commentator has stated that "[t]he fiction of collective intent, although perhaps needed, is simply a desperate, but disingenuous application of the respondeat superior or MPC standards."[26] Do you agree?

3. When culpability is premised on the collective knowledge doctrine, does liability reflect true corporate blameworthiness?

4. What facts support a finding of "flagrant" institutional disregard? What kinds of steps can (or should) corporate management take to avoid liability under this theory?

5. What is the difference between the collective knowledge doctrine and negligence?

---

26. Pamela H. Bucy, Corporate Ethos: A Standard for Imposing Corporate Criminal Liability, 75 Minn. L. Rev. 1095, 1157 (1991).

6. Is the collective knowledge doctrine consistent with the text and theoretical underpinnings of Model Penal Code § 2.07?

7. Did the trial court's instructions concerning the bank's post-July conduct invite the jury to convict the bank for acts that were not charged in the indictment? Did those instructions in effect make failure to file a CTR a continuing offense?

III. THE MODEL PENAL CODE RULE

The theory that corporations may be held criminally responsible is rooted in seventeenth-century English law. By the beginning of the twentieth century a coherent rule based upon respondeat superior principles had begun to evolve in federal law, and it had matured into a relatively settled rule by mid-century. Development of a doctrinal basis for holding corporations criminally liable under state law was quite another matter. The states lagged behind in recognizing corporate criminal liability, and the developing rules were by no means uniform or even consistent with the federal rule.

In 1956, the American Law Institute reluctantly included a corporate liability provision in the Model Penal Code. Section 2.07 creates a "trifurcated scheme of corporate liability that draws intersecting lines between acts and omissions, between true crimes and regulatory offenses, and between the operatives who are the 'hands' of the corporation and the policy makers who constitute its 'mind.'"[27]

Among the most expansive of the three rules is section 2.07(1)(a), which adopts a broad respondeat superior theory of liability. Under this rule, a corporation may incur liability for minor infractions[28] and for non-Code penal offenses when a legislative purpose to impose liability on corporations "plainly appears," provided that the conduct constituting the offense is performed by a corporate agent acting within the scope of his employment and on behalf of the corporation.

The potential reach of the (1)(a) liability rule is limited, however, by the availability of a due diligence defense. Proof that "the high managerial agent having supervisory responsibility over the subject matter of the offense employed due diligence to prevent its commission" exonerates the corporation from criminal liability.[29]

The second rule of corporate liability pertains to omissions as opposed to acts. Subsection (1)(b) provides that a corporation is accountable for failure to discharge specific duties imposed on corporations by law. Neither the text of this provision nor the comments address the question of whose omission may lead to liability.

The third rule of liability is by far the most restrictive. Under subsection (1)(c), a corporation will incur liability for true crimes — that is, for an offense defined in the Penal

---

27. Brickey, Rethinking Corporate Liability, supra note 14, at 596.

28. Section 2.07(1)(a) uses the term "violation" to denote these minor infractions, which are ordinarily punishable by nothing more serious than a fine. Violations are not considered crimes, and a conviction for committing a violation does not carry with it any disability that would be associated with being convicted of a crime. Model Penal Code and Commentaries § 1.04(5) (1985) [hereinafter Model Penal Code]. — ED.

29. Id. § 2.07(5). This defense is unavailable if the offense charged imposes strict liability or if the defense is "plainly inconsistent with the legislative purpose in defining the particular offense." Id.

The due diligence defense transforms a legislative directive ("Do this" or "Don't do this") into a request ("Try to do this" or "Do all you reasonably can").

Code — only if the conduct constituting the offense is authorized, commanded, solicited, performed, or recklessly tolerated[30] by the board of directors or a "high managerial agent" whose acquiescence to the wrongdoing — by virtue of his position of authority — may fairly be regarded as reflecting corporate policy.[31]

As the court observed in *Beneficial Finance*, the size and structural complexity of many corporations require increased delegation of responsibility. This fact of modern corporate life influenced the court's decision to adopt the respondeat superior rule of corporate liability, which permits the acts and intent of low-level operatives to be imputed to the corporation. In contrast, the Model Penal Code requires the participation or approval of a high managerial agent as a prerequisite to corporate liability for non-regulatory crimes.

The Model Penal Code defines the term "high managerial agent" as follows:

"high managerial agent" means an officer of a corporation or an unincorporated association, or, in the case of a partnership, a partner, or any other agent of a corporation or association having duties of such responsibility that his conduct may fairly be assumed to represent the policy of the corporation or association.[32]

Although the Code definition of "high managerial agent" adopts as key criteria the agent's degree of responsibility and proximity to corporate policy making, the Comments observe that, "[g]iven the wide variations in corporate structure, these criteria are necessarily very general."[33] By way of example, however, the Comments state that a corporation would incur liability for the acts of its president or general manager but not for the acts of a foreman in a large plant or an insignificant branch manager.[34]

STATE v. CHAPMAN DODGE CENTER, INC.
428 So. 2d 413 (La. 1983)

FRED C. SEXTON, Jr., Justice Ad Hoc.

[Chapman Dodge Center and its owner, John Swindle, were charged with 20 counts of theft in connection with the dealership's failure to pay sales taxes due on the sale of more than one hundred automobiles.]

Chapman Dodge Center, Inc., a Baton Rouge Dodge dealership, closed its doors because of financial difficulty on September 12, 1980. Shortly thereafter the district attorney's office began receiving complaints from Dodge customers that they had not received their permanent license plates for their cars because the dealership had neither registered the cars purchased, nor paid the sales tax due. The usual practice was for the

---

30. Under the Model Penal Code, "recklessness" means conscious disregard of a substantial and unjustifiable risk under circumstances that reflect a gross deviation from the standard of care that a person in the actor's situation would be expected to observe. Model Penal Code § 2.02(2)(c). — ED.

31. Brickey, Rethinking Corporate Liability, supra note 14, at 597-598.

32. Model Penal Code § 2.07(4)(c).

33. Model Penal Code § 2.07, Comment at 339.

34. Id. But see People v. Deitsch, 470 N.Y.S.2d 158 (App. Div. 1983) (characterizing the foreman of a warehouse as a high managerial agent).

customer to pay the amount due for sales tax to the car dealer who, in turn, would register the car with the state and tender the tax. After a car is registered and the tax paid, the state issues a permanent license plate. In the meantime, the dealership is authorized to give the customer a temporary plate that is valid for 35 days. Dodge customers were being stopped for expired temporary license plates since they had not received their permanent tags.

Chapman Dodge had been in financial difficulty for about a year prior to its closing. Aside from the general economic situation, Chapman's difficulties were due in great part to Chapman's financial relationship to the financially troubled Chrysler Corporation. According to the trial record, at the time Chapman closed, Chrysler Corporation owed between $250,000 and $400,000 to Chapman Dodge. In addition, Chrysler Credit Corporation, a subsidiary of Chrysler Motors, had $140,000 of Chapman's money "on reserve" for potential losses on loans Chrysler Credit made to Chapman customers.

After Chapman Dodge closed its doors, Chrysler Credit Corporation took possession of Chapman Dodge. On the premises, employees of Chrysler Credit Corporation found between 180 and 190 registration forms for purchased cars which had not been filed with the state and for which no sales tax had been paid. Since Chrysler Credit Corporation owned the mortgages on 159 of these cars, it paid the sales taxes due on them (approximately $68,000) in order to register the cars and the chattel mortgages with the state.

The defendant, John Swindle, personally paid the sales taxes (about $11,000) on the remaining cars which had not been financed by Chrysler Credit Corporation. The defendant did so after he was notified by the district attorney's office that the taxes were due. The defendant's attorney in Mississippi, however, testified that he advised the defendant that Chrysler Credit Corporation should be responsible for all taxes due since it had possession of all of Chapman Dodge's assets, and was therefore responsible for discharging Chapman's tax liability. . . .

Defendant John Swindle testified that he was the sole owner of Barony Corporation, a holding company for several food service corporations. Barony Corporation owned a subsidiary called Center Management which was formed to hold automobile dealerships when Swindle expanded his operations to include that business. Chapman Dodge was one of four dealerships owned by Center Management. Center Management, after acquiring the necessary funding, then purchased Chapman Dodge. Subsequently Chapman Dodge endorsed the notes Center Management had signed in obtaining financing. Each month a check was sent by Chapman Dodge to Center Management to cover the payment due by Center Management on the notes.

The evidence showed that the defendant, a resident of Jackson, Mississippi, was seldom at the dealership more than twice a month. It was Donald Barrett that was in charge of the daily operations of Chapman Dodge as general manager. All department managers were responsible to Barrett, who in turn answered to Swindle. According to the testimony of James Duvall, Chapman Dodge's accountant, he and Barrett made the decisions as to which bills were to be paid.

Swindle testified that when the dealership was showing continued financial trouble, he discussed this matter with James Duvall. Since the dealership was behind in paying withholding taxes, as well as sales taxes, he ordered Duvall to pay all of the taxes owed, particularly the federal withholdings. When the dealership was closed, Swindle asked Barrett if all the taxes had been paid. The record shows that in the presence of Johnilyn Smith, an administrative assistant to Swindle, and Frank Peel, a business associate of Swindle, Barrett stated that *all* taxes had been paid. Barrett testified that he did not say *all* the taxes had been paid, only that the *federal* taxes had been paid. On cross-examination however Barrett stated that he "may" have said that all the taxes were paid.

The defendant received no indication that the sales taxes were not paid until a week or ten days after closing the dealership when the district attorney contacted Chapman Dodge's lawyer. Duvall testified that he was instructed by Donald Barrett to retain the sales tax money. Donald Barrett however testified that he had told James Duvall in June of 1980 to pay only those obligations necessary to keep the dealership open; but that he never told Duvall to retain the contracts and sales taxes on the purchased vehicles.

Donald Barrett was originally indicted on the theft charges along with John Swindle and Chapman Dodge. Both he and James Duvall were granted "use" immunity in order to compel their testimony against Chapman Dodge and John Swindle. . . .

[Although the jury did not convict Swindle and Chapman Dodge on the theft charges, it convicted them of the lesser included offense of unauthorized use of a movable, an offense that required a finding of fraudulent intent. On appeal, the court found the evidence insufficient to sustain Swindle's conviction because he had so little contact with the dealership and, upon learning of the unpaid taxes, had instructed Duvall to pay all taxes owed.]

The question of the criminal liability of the corporate defendant in this case is a more difficult proposition involving fundamental issues of the nature of criminal responsibility. These issues have not been generally considered with respect to corporations in this jurisdiction. Certainly our law contemplates corporate criminal defendants. Louisiana law delineates a number of acts the commission or omission of which creates corporate criminal responsibility.[35]

The problem of what criminal liability a corporation should bear for the unauthorized acts of its officers and managers is indeed a grave and troubling one. Recent allegations of corporate responsibility for large train derailments and massive pollution of water sources underscore the importance of this troubling topic. Certainly there is civil responsibility under such circumstances. The question is whether a corporation should be criminally responsible in the absence of a specific statute which defines and describes the corporate act, prohibits that act, and establishes a specific punishment therefor. . . .

A corporation by the very nature of its operation is dependent upon people to carry out its business. Some of these people may rightfully be regarded as the "mind" of the corporation. This group, known as the board of directors, is responsible for the direction that the corporation takes in its business activity. Plans for the corporation, developed by the board of directors, are transmitted to the officers of the corporation and through them to the employees. This latter group may be regarded as the "hands" of the corporation. But here our analogy to the human form must end. For unlike ordinary human hands, corporate "hands" have minds of their own and are capable of self direction.

---

35. LSA-R.S. 12:172 (Failure to Keep Records); LSA-R.S. 37:850 (Violation of Embalming Laws); LSA-R.S. 14:106 (Obscenity); LSA-R.S. 47:1953 (Tax Assessment of Corporations); LSA-R.S. 51:125, 126 (Transactions Lessening Competition); LSA-R.S. 30:217 (Unauthorized Prospecting); LSA-R.S. 30:1096 (Pollution).

When a corporation is accused of committing a crime which requires intent, it must be determined who within the corporate structure had the intent to commit the crime. If the crime was the product of a board of directors' resolution authorizing its employees to commit specific criminal acts, then intent on the part of the corporation is manifest. However, a more difficult question arises if the crime is actually committed by an employee of the corporation not authorized to perform such an act. Holding a corporation criminally responsible for the acts of an employee may be inconsistent with basic notions of criminal intent, since such a posture would render a corporate entity responsible for actions which it theoretically had no intent to commit.

Common law jurisdictions hold corporations criminally liable for the acts of low-ranking employees. In such jurisdictions, corporate criminal liability is based on an extension of the tort doctrine of vicarious liability. The theme of vicarious criminal liability, however, is varied. Some jurisdictions impose criminal liability where there has been an act or an authorization to act by a managerial officer, some where there has been an act committed within the scope of the actor's employment, and still others where there has been an act done which benefits the corporation. These varied applications notwithstanding, common law jurisdictions have found corporations liable for forms of homicide, theft, extortion — in short, virtually every crime other than rape and carnal knowledge.

The instant defendant is a closely held holding corporation which is accused of a basic "Ten Commandment Crime" — theft — and convicted of a lesser included offense. Thus the finder of fact in effect determined that the defendant corporation kept the money in question with fraudulent intent, but with the intent to eventually return the funds. The evidence further indicates that "retention" of the funds was not specifically authorized by the board of directors or by the president or any other officer of the corporation. The record does not indicate, moreover, that any of these entities had any real knowledge of that action. Of course the corporation, its board of directors, its parent corporations and its president are for all practical purposes the same entity — the individual defendant Swindle.

Furthermore, as discussed earlier, the evidence preponderates that it was a party other than Swindle who determined to "retain the funds."

Thus, the facts of this case can be narrowed to a fine point. In so doing, however, broad questions of a complex nature are visited upon us. While recognizing the potential disservice to the jurisprudence we are nevertheless unable, within the confines of this appeal, to resolve these extremely complex issues. We simply determine that under the circumstances of this case, criminal intent has not been adequately established. We determine that under the circumstances of this case, there was insufficient intent shown in the trial court . . . , and therefore this corporate defendant may not be found criminally responsible. We hold that since this record reveals no evidence of complicity by the officers or the board of directors, explicit or tacit, that the actions of these managers and/or employees were insufficient to cause this corporate entity to be guilty of the offense of an unauthorized use of a movable.

We thus reverse as to both defendants and order their discharge.

Reversed and discharged as to both defendants.

LEMMON, Justice, dissenting in part.

The evidence supports a conclusion that a high managerial agent, in whom the corporation had vested the authority to manage its day-to-day business operations, knowingly committed a criminal offense on behalf of the corporation and for its benefit while acting in the scope of his employment. The corporation should therefore be held criminally liable.[36]

Notes and Questions

1. Why was the evidence insufficient to sustain Swindle's conviction? Is conviction of the responsible corporate agent a prerequisite to holding the corporation liable for his wrongful acts?

2. How important is it that the corporation was charged with a "Ten Commandment crime"?

3. Is the manager of an automobile dealership a person whose conduct reflects corporate policy? Why is it *not* important that Barrett, who was responsible for the dealership's day-to-day operations, withheld sales tax payments for the dealership's benefit on multiple occasions? Is the lesson of this case that the owner of a corporation can shield the company from liability by keeping himself aloof from its business operations?

---

36. To support this conclusion, the dissent cited Model Penal Code § 2.07(1)(c) and State v. Adjustment Department Credit Bureau, Inc., 483 P.2d 687 (Idaho 1971), both of which require participation by a high managerial agent; the Study Draft for a New Federal Criminal Code § 402 (1970) and C.I.T. Corp. v. United States, 150 F.2d 85 (9th Cir. 1945), neither of which requires participation by a high managerial agent; and Commonwealth v. Beneficial Finance Co., 275 N.E.2d 33 (Mass. 1971), which specifically rejects the high managerial agent requirement. — ED.

2

Personal Liability in an Organizational Setting

I. INTRODUCTION

When we consider the potential liability of individual participants in corporate and white collar crimes, we find ourselves on more familiar ground. It is axiomatic that one who violates a criminal statute is personally responsible in the eyes of the law. But should the rule be different in an organizational setting? Are corporate officers and agents criminally liable for conduct they engage in on behalf of the corporation? They are, after all, acting under the cloak of authority and within the scope of their employment. And if they are criminally liable for acts they personally commit, are they also liable for acts committed by their subordinates? It is to these issues that we now turn.

II. DIRECT PARTICIPANTS

The question whether corporate agents are liable for crimes committed during the course of their employment seemed to be settled in the early eighteenth century. As Chief Justice Holt uttered in a now familiar dictum: "A corporation is not indictable but the particular members of it are."[1] But once it became established that corporations could be held accountable for crimes committed by their agents, it was inevitable that corporate agents would argue they should not be personally liable for official acts they performed on behalf of the corporation. Because their acts were corporate acts, the argument ran, the law should look "to the principal rather than the mere agent" in accordance with established agency law principles.[2]

The Supreme Court definitively resolved this issue in United States v. Wise,[3] a case in which a corporation and one of its officers had been charged with price fixing, in violation of the Sherman Act. The government alleged that the officer had acted

---

1. Anonymous, 88 Eng. Rep. 1518 (K.B. 1701).
2. State v. Morris & Essex R.R., 23 N.J.L. 360, 369 (1852).
3. 370 U.S. 405 (1962).

"solely in his capacity as an officer, director, or agent who authorized, ordered, or did some of the [illegal] acts."

The Court in *Wise* rejected the argument that a corporate officer or agent is not personally liable for acts committed solely in a representative capacity. Even though the acts Wise committed were corporate acts in the sense that they were imputable to the corporation,[4] the Court found no evidence of legislative intent to exempt corporate officers and agents from personal liability for conduct they engage in.

> No intent to exculpate a corporate officer who violates the law is to be imputed to Congress without clear compulsion; else the fines established by the Sherman Act to deter crime become mere license fees for illegitimate corporate business operations. . . . [A] corporate officer is subject to prosecution under § 1 of the Sherman Act whenever he knowingly participates in effecting the illegal contract, combination, or conspiracy — be he one who authorizes, orders, or helps perpetrate the crime — regardless of whether he is acting in a representative capacity.[5]

Thus, it is well settled that absent clear legislative intent to exclude corporate agents from personal responsibility for crimes they commit, they "cannot use the corporate entity as a shield against liability for [their] own misdeeds."[6]

Notes and Questions

1. What are the implications of the argument that corporate agents should not bear personal responsibility for acts they commit on behalf of the corporation?

2. When a corporation is prosecuted for criminal wrongdoing, should corporate agents be prosecuted as well? Is imposition of criminal liability on both the entity and its agent needlessly redundant?[7]

SANFORD H. KADISH, SOME OBSERVATIONS ON THE USE OF CRIMINAL SANCTIONS IN ENFORCING ECONOMIC REGULATIONS
30 U. Chi. L. Rev. 423, 430-431 (1963)

Fixing criminal liability upon the immediate actors within a corporate structure generally poses no special problem. But the immediate actors may be lower echelon officials or employees who are the tools rather than the responsible originators of the violative conduct. Where the corporation is managed by its owners, the task of

---

4. The Sherman Act defines the term "person" to include corporations and associations. The Court in *Wise* thought it was logical for Congress to expressly include organizations in the definition of "persons" subject to liability since the Sherman Act was enacted before the doctrine of corporate criminal liability had become well established. Id. at 408.

5. Id. at 409, 416.

6. Kathleen F. Brickey, Corporate Criminal Liability: A Primer for Corporate Counsel, 40 Bus. Law. 129, 138-139 (1984).

7. Cf. U.S. Dept. of Justice, Principles of Federal Prosecution of Business Organizations 2 (Dec. 2006) (stating that prosecuting a corporation is not a proxy for prosecuting culpable individuals).

identifying the policy formulators is not acute. But where the stock of the corporation is widely held, the organization complex and sprawling, and the responsibility spread over a maze of departments and divisions, then, as has recently been shown, there may be conspicuous difficulties in pinpointing responsibility on the higher echelon policy-making officials. The source of the difficulty is the conventional requirement that to hold one person criminally liable for the acts of another he must have participated in the acts of the other in some meaningful way, as by directing or encouraging them, aiding in their commission or permitting them to be done by subordinates whom he has power to control.

Notes and Questions

1. Should only policy initiators be prosecuted for committing crimes on behalf of the corporation? Or should lower-echelon employees who are the "tools" through which the crimes are committed also be prosecuted? Why would lower-echelon employees engage in misconduct like price fixing?

2. As we saw in Chapter 1, a corporation may be criminally liable for the misdeeds of its agents. Is the converse also true?[8]

NOTE ON ACCOMPLICE LIABILITY

Federal law does not recognize arcane distinctions between principals and accessories. Instead, it holds those who participate in the commission of a crime and those who assist the perpetrators equally responsible for the resulting crime. The federal complicity statute, 18 U.S.C. § 2, provides as follows:

> (a) Whoever commits an offense against the United States or aids, abets, counsels, commands, induces or procures its commission, is punishable as a principal.
>
> (b) Whoever willfully causes an act to be done which if directly performed by him or another would be an offense against the United States, is punishable as a principal.

As the language of this statute makes clear, aiders and abettors who assist in the planning of a crime or who induce or encourage others to commit the crime are punishable as principals. Section 2 thus provides a vehicle for imposing vicarious liability on aiders and abettors, regardless of the respective roles they play. Thus, for example, the chief executive of a corporation who tells the bookkeeper to destroy subpoenaed records, the bank supervisor who instructs subordinates to make false entries in the bank's records, and the business owner who authorizes employees to sign false Medicare and Medicaid claims are all punishable as if they had personally performed the act constituting the crime.[9]

---

8. Cf. Bourgeois v. Commonwealth, 227 S.E.2d 714 (Va. 1976).

9. See, e.g., United States v. Precision Medical Lab., Inc., 593 F.2d 434 (2d Cir. 1978); United States v. Berger, 456 F.2d 1349 (2d Cir. 1972); Meredith v. United States, 238 F.2d 535 (4th Cir. 1956).

$\boxed{\text{PROBLEM 2-1}}$

Carl Cole, a business owner, enlisted the assistance of his employees in making campaign contributions to candidates for federal office. Because he was subject to strict limits on the amount he could personally contribute in any election cycle, he asked his employees to write personal checks to the various candidates' campaign committees. Cole immediately reimbursed the employees with cash or by check, thus circumventing the contribution limits by creating the false appearance that the employees were the source of the contributions.

The treasurers of each of the candidates' campaigns were required to file reports, including contributor lists, with the Federal Election Commission. Unknown to the campaign treasurers, the reports were false because Cole had successfully concealed the source of the contributions. The federal false statements statute, 18 U.S.C. § 1001, makes it a crime to knowingly and willfully falsify, conceal, or cover up a material fact or make a false statement in any matter within the jurisdiction of the executive branch, including the Federal Election Commission.

Has Cole violated § 1001? Have the campaign treasurers violated § 1001? What mental state does 18 U.S.C. § 2 require? How does § 2 interface with § 1001?[10]

III. RESPONSIBLE CORPORATE OFFICERS

The recent convictions of Enron CEOs Jeff Skilling and Ken Lay, WorldCom CEO Bernie Ebbers, and Adelphia CEO John Rigas make it abundantly clear that corporate officers are personally liable for crimes they commit during the course of their employment. But what about crimes of omission? Are corporate officers personally liable for crimes they fail to prevent if they have responsibility for the business process that results in the violation?

This question gained importance with the rise of public welfare offenses. A typical public welfare offense is found in the Food, Drug, and Comestic Act, which makes it a crime to introduce adulterated or misbranded drugs into the stream of commerce. As the Supreme Court observed in United States v. Dotterweich,[11] public welfare statutes are needed to protect the lives and health of innocent consumers who are put at risk by the marketing of adulterated or misbranded products.

In *Dotterweich*, the Court upheld the conviction of the president and general manager of a small drug jobber for shipping misbranded and adulterated drugs in violation of the Food, Drug, and Cosmetic Act. The Court ruled that the manager could be held criminally responsible for the violation even though there was no evidence that he knew the drugs were misbranded and adulterated or that he personally participated in shipping them. The Court was of the view that the Act "puts the burden of acting at hazard upon a person otherwise innocent but standing in responsible relation to a public

---

10. Compare United States v. Curran, 20 F.3d 560 (3d Cir. 1994), with United States v. Hsia, 176 F.3d 517 (D.C. Cir. 1999).
    11. 320 U.S. 277 (1943).

danger."[12] As long as he shared "responsibility in the business process resulting in unlawful distribution," he would be personally liable.[13]

During the three decades following *Dotterweich*, most individuals prosecuted under the Food, Drug, and Comestic Act held relatively high office or had general authority over the business enterprise. That led to the perception that officers of small businesses were exposed to "a particularly high risk since they generally are involved in plant operations, in addition to their overall responsibilities."[14]

In response to a 1972 General Accounting Office report that sanitation problems in the food industry were on the increase, the Food and Drug Administration (FDA) warned industry representatives that enforcement efforts would be stepped up. Dissatisfied with the response to that warning, the FDA wrote letters to the presidents of several food chains, warning:

> We regard you as the person who ultimately has the authority to order correction of such conditions, and thus who ultimately must bear the responsibility for any failure to correct them. Should it become necessary to bring criminal action to prevent a continuation of violative conditions, therefore, we wish you to understand that you and the other high corporate officials in your organization who are specifically responsible for sanitation practices will be held accountable.[15]

The prosecution in United States v. Park occurred shortly thereafter.

UNITED STATES v. PARK
421 U.S. 658 (1975)

Mr. Chief Justice BURGER delivered the opinion of the Court.

We granted certiorari to consider whether the jury instructions in the prosecution of a corporate officer under § 301(k) of the Federal Food, Drug, and Cosmetic Act, 21 U.S.C. § 331(k), were appropriate under United States v. Dotterweich, 320 U.S. 277 (1943).

Acme Markets, Inc., is a national retail food chain with approximately 36,000 employees, 874 retail outlets, 12 general warehouses, and four special warehouses. Its headquarters, including the office of the president, respondent Park, who is chief executive officer of the corporation, are located in Philadelphia, Pa. In a five-count information filed in the United States District Court for the District of Maryland, the Government charged Acme and respondent with violations of the Federal Food, Drug, and Cosmetic Act. Each count of the information alleged that the defendants had received food that had been shipped in interstate commerce and that, while the food was being held for sale in Acme's Baltimore warehouse following shipment in interstate commerce, they caused it to be held in a building accessible to rodents and to be exposed to contamination by rodents. These acts were alleged to have resulted in the

---

12. Id. at 281.

13. Id. at 284.

14. Daniel F. O'Keefe, Jr. & Marc H. Shapiro, Personal Criminal Liability Under the Federal Food, Drug, and Cosmetic Act — The *Dotterweich* Doctrine, 30 Food Drug Cosm. L.J. 5, 20 (1975).

15. Id. at 29.

food's being adulterated within the meaning of 21 U.S.C. §§ 342(a)(3) and (4), in violation of 21 U.S.C. § 331(k).

Acme pleaded guilty to each count of the information. Respondent pleaded not guilty. The evidence at trial demonstrated that in April 1970 the Food and Drug Administration (FDA) advised respondent by letter of insanitary conditions in Acme's Philadelphia warehouse. In 1971 the FDA found that similar conditions existed in the firm's Baltimore warehouse. An FDA consumer safety officer testified concerning evidence of rodent infestation and other insanitary conditions discovered during a 12-day inspection of the Baltimore warehouse in November and December 1971. He also related that a second inspection of the warehouse had been conducted in March 1972. On that occasion the inspectors found that there had been improvement in the sanitary conditions, but that "there was still evidence of rodent activity in the building and in the warehouses and we found some rodent-contaminated lots of food items."

The Government also presented testimony by the Chief of Compliance of the FDA's Baltimore office, who informed respondent by letter of the conditions at the Baltimore warehouse after the first inspection.[16] There was testimony by Acme's Baltimore division vice president, who had responded to the letter on behalf of Acme and respondent and who described the steps taken to remedy the insanitary conditions discovered by both inspections. The Government's final witness, Acme's vice president for legal affairs and assistant secretary, identified respondent as the president and chief executive officer of the company and read a bylaw prescribing the duties of the chief executive officer.[17] He testified that respondent functioned by delegating "normal operating duties," including sanitation, but that he retained "certain things, which are the big, broad, principles of the operation of the company," and had "the responsibility of seeing that they all work together."

At the close of the Government's case in chief, respondent moved for a judgment of acquittal on the ground that "the evidence in chief has shown that Mr. Park is not personally concerned in this Food and Drug violation." The trial judge denied the motion, stating that United States v. Dotterweich, 320 U.S. 277 (1943), was controlling.

Respondent was the only defense witness. He testified that, although all of Acme's employees were in a sense under his general direction, the company had an "organizational structure for responsibilities for certain functions" according to which

---

16. The letter, dated January 27, 1972, included the following:

   We note with much concern that the old and new warehouse areas used for food storage were actively and extensively inhabited by live rodents. Of even more concern was the observation that such reprehensible conditions obviously existed for a prolonged period of time without any detection, or were completely ignored. . . .

   We trust this letter will serve to direct your attention to the seriousness of the problem and formally advise you of the urgent need to initiate whatever measures are necessary to prevent recurrence and ensure compliance with the law.

17. The bylaw provided in pertinent part:

   The Chairman of the board of directors or the president shall be the chief executive officer of the company as the board of directors may from time to time determine. He shall, subject to the board of directors, have general and active supervision of the affairs, business, offices and employees of the company. . . .

   He shall, from time to time, in his discretion or at the order of the board, report the operations and affairs of the company. He shall also perform such other duties and have such other powers as may be assigned to him from time to time by the board of directors.

different phases of its operation were "assigned to individuals who, in turn, have staff and departments under them." He identified those individuals responsible for sanitation, and related that upon receipt of the January 1972 FDA letter, he had conferred with the vice president for legal affairs, who informed him that the Baltimore division vice president "was investigating the situation immediately and would be taking corrective action and would be preparing a summary of the corrective action to reply to the letter." Respondent stated that he did not "believe there was anything [he] could have done more constructively than what [he] found was being done."

On cross-examination, respondent conceded that providing sanitary conditions for food offered for sale to the public was something that he was "responsible for in the entire operation of the company," and he stated that it was one of many phases of the company that he assigned to "dependable subordinates." Respondent was asked about and, over the objections of his counsel, admitted receiving, the April 1970 letter addressed to him from the FDA regarding insanitary conditions at Acme's Philadelphia warehouse.[18] He acknowledged that, with the exception of the division vice president, the same individuals had responsibility for sanitation in both Baltimore and Philadelphia. Finally, in response to questions concerning the Philadelphia and Baltimore incidents, respondent admitted that the Baltimore problem indicated the system for handling sanitation "wasn't working perfectly" and that as Acme's chief executive officer he was responsible for "any result which occurs in our company."

At the close of the evidence, respondent's renewed motion for a judgment of acquittal was denied. The relevant portion of the trial judge's instructions to the jury challenged by respondent is set out in the margin.[19] Respondent's counsel objected to the instructions on the ground that they failed fairly to reflect our decision in United States v. Dotterweich and to define "'responsible relationship.'" The trial judge overruled the objection. The jury found respondent guilty on all counts of the information, and he was subsequently sentenced to pay a fine of $50 on each count.

The Court of Appeals reversed the conviction and remanded for a new trial. That court viewed the Government as arguing "that the conviction may be predicated solely

18. The April 1970 letter informed respondent of the following "objectionable conditions" in Acme's Philadelphia warehouse:

"1. Potential rodent entry ways were noted via ill fitting doors and door in repair at Southwest corner of warehouse; at dock at old salvage room and at receiving and shipping doors which were observed to be open most of the time.

"2. Rodent nesting, rodent excreta pellets, rodent stained bale bagging and rodent gnawed holes were noted among bales of flour stored in warehouse.

"3. Potential rodent harborage was noted in discarded paper, rope, sawdust and other debris piled in corner of shipping and receiving dock near bakery and warehouse doors. Rodent excreta pellets were observed among bags of sawdust (or wood shavings)."

19. [The jury instructions provided in pertinent part:]

In order to find the Defendant guilty on any count of the Information, you must find beyond a reasonable doubt on each count. . . .

Thirdly, that John R. Park held a position of authority in the operation of the business of Acme Markets, Incorporated. . . .

The individual is or could be liable under the statute, even if he did not consciously do wrong. However, the fact that the Defendant is pres[id]ent and is a chief executive officer of the Acme Markets does not require a finding of guilt. Though, he need not have personally participated in the situation, he must have had a responsible relationship to the issue. The issue is, in this case, whether the Defendant, John R. Park, by virtue of his position in the company, had a position of authority and responsibility in the situation out of which these charges arose.

upon a showing that . . . [respondent] was the President of the offending corporation," and it stated that as "a general proposition, some act of commission or omission is an essential element of every crime." 499 F.2d 839, 841 (CA4 1974). It reasoned that, although our decision in United States v. Dotterweich had construed the statutory provisions under which respondent was tried to dispense with the traditional element of "'awareness of some wrongdoing'" the Court had not construed them as dispensing with the element of "wrongful action." The Court of Appeals concluded that the trial judge's instructions "might well have left the jury with the erroneous impression that Park could be found guilty in the absence of 'wrongful action' on his part," 499 F.2d, at 841-842, and that proof of this element was required by due process. It held, with one dissent, that the instructions did not "correctly state the law of the case," id., at 840, and directed that on retrial the jury be instructed as to "wrongful action," which might be "gross negligence and inattention in discharging . . . corporate duties and obligations or any of a host of other acts of commission or omission which would 'cause' the contamination of food." Id., at 842.

The Court of Appeals also held that the admission in evidence of the April 1970 FDA warning to respondent was error warranting reversal, based on its conclusion that, "as this case was submitted to the jury and in light of the sole issue presented," there was no need for the evidence and thus that its prejudicial effect outweighed its relevancy. . . . 499 F.2d, at 843.

We granted certiorari because of an apparent conflict among the Courts of Appeals with respect to the standard of liability of corporate officers under the Federal Food, Drug, and Cosmetic Act as construed in United States v. Dotterweich, and because of the importance of the question to the Government's enforcement program. We reverse. . . .

II

The rule that corporate employees who have "a responsible share in the furtherance of the transaction which the statute outlaws" are subject to the criminal provisions of the Act was not formulated in a vacuum. Cases under the Federal Food and Drugs Act of 1906 reflected the view both that knowledge or intent were not required to be proved in prosecutions under its criminal provisions, and that responsible corporate agents could be subjected to the liability thereby imposed. Moreover, the principle had been recognized that a corporate agent, through whose act, default, or omission the corporation committed a crime, was himself guilty individually of that crime. The principle had been applied whether or not the crime required "consciousness of wrongdoing," and it had been applied not only to those corporate agents who themselves committed the criminal act, but also to those who by virtue of their managerial positions or other similar relation to the actor could be deemed responsible for its commission.

In the latter class of cases, the liability of managerial officers did not depend on their knowledge of, or personal participation in, the act made criminal by the statute. Rather, where the statute under which they were prosecuted dispensed with "consciousness of wrongdoing," an omission or failure to act was deemed a sufficient basis for a responsible corporate agent's liability. It was enough in such cases that, by virtue of the relationship he bore to the corporation, the agent had the power to prevent the act complained of.

The rationale . . . in *Dotterweich* . . . has been confirmed in our subsequent cases. . . .

Thus *Dotterweich* and the cases which have followed reveal that in providing sanctions which reach and touch the individuals who execute the corporate mission — and this is by no means necessarily confined to a single corporate agent or employee — the Act imposes not only a positive duty to seek out and remedy violations when they occur but also, and primarily, a duty to implement measures that will insure that violations will not occur. The requirements of foresight and vigilance imposed on responsible corporate agents are beyond question demanding, and perhaps onerous, but they are no more stringent than the public has a right to expect of those who voluntarily assume positions of authority in business enterprises whose services and products affect the health and well-being of the public that supports them.

The Act does not, as we observed in *Dotterweich*, make criminal liability turn on "awareness of some wrongdoing" or "conscious fraud." The duty imposed by Congress on responsible corporate agents is, we emphasize, one that requires the highest standard of foresight and vigilance, but the Act, in its criminal aspect, does not require that which is objectively impossible. The theory upon which responsible corporate agents are held criminally accountable for "causing" violations of the Act permits a claim that a defendant was "powerless" to prevent or correct the violation to "be raised defensively at a trial on the merits." United States v. Wiesenfeld Warehouse Co., 376 U.S. 86, 91 (1964). If such a claim is made, the defendant has the burden of coming forward with evidence, but this does not alter the Government's ultimate burden of proving beyond a reasonable doubt the defendant's guilt, including his power, in light of the duty imposed by the Act, to prevent or correct the prohibited condition. Congress has seen fit to enforce the accountability of responsible corporate agents dealing with products which may affect the health of consumers by penal sanctions cast in rigorous terms, and the obligation of the courts is to give them effect so long as they do not violate the Constitution.

III

We cannot agree with the Court of Appeals that it was incumbent upon the District Court to instruct the jury that the Government had the burden of establishing "wrongful action" in the sense in which the Court of Appeals used that phrase. The concept of a "responsible relationship" to, or a "responsible share" in, a violation of the Act indeed imports some measure of blameworthiness; but it is equally clear that the Government establishes a prima facie case when it introduces evidence sufficient to warrant a finding by the trier of the facts that the defendant had, by reason of his position in the corporation, responsibility and authority either to prevent in the first instance, or promptly to correct, the violation complained of, and that he failed to do so. The failure thus to fulfill the duty imposed by the interaction of the corporate agent's authority and the statute furnishes a sufficient causal link. The considerations which prompted the imposition of this duty, and the scope of the duty, provide the measure of culpability. . . .

IV

Our conclusion that the Court of Appeals erred in its reading of the jury charge suggests as well our disagreement with that court concerning the admissibility of evidence demonstrating that respondent was advised by the FDA in 1970 of insanitary conditions in Acme's Philadelphia warehouse. We are satisfied that the Act imposes the highest standard of care and permits conviction of responsible corporate officials who, in light of this standard of care, have the power to prevent or correct violations of its provisions. Implicit in the Court's admonition that "the ultimate judgment of juries must be trusted," United States v. Dotterweich, 320 U.S. at 285, however, is the realization that they may demand more than corporate bylaws to find culpability.

Respondent testified in his defense that he had employed a system in which he relied upon his subordinates, and that he was ultimately responsible for this system. He testified further that he had found these subordinates to be "dependable" and had "great confidence" in them. By this and other testimony respondent evidently sought to persuade the jury that, as the president of a large corporation, he had no choice but to delegate duties to those in whom he reposed confidence, that he had no reason to suspect his subordinates were failing to insure compliance with the Act, and that, once violations were unearthed, acting through those subordinates he did everything possible to correct them.

Although we need not decide whether this testimony would have entitled respondent to an instruction as to his lack of power, had he requested it, the testimony clearly created the "need" for rebuttal evidence. That evidence was not offered to show that respondent had a propensity to commit criminal acts or that the crime charged had been committed; its purpose was to demonstrate that respondent was on notice that he could not rely on his system of delegation to subordinates to prevent or correct insanitary conditions at Acme's warehouses, and that he must have been aware of the deficiencies of this system before the Baltimore violations were discovered. The evidence was therefore relevant since it served to rebut respondent's defense that he had justifiably relied upon subordinates to handle sanitation matters. And, particularly in light of the difficult task of juries in prosecutions under the Act, we conclude that its relevance and persuasiveness outweighed any prejudicial effect.

Reversed.

Mr. Justice STEWART, with whom Mr. Justice MARSHALL and Mr. Justice POWELL join, dissenting.

Although agreeing with much of what is said in the Court's opinion, I dissent from the opinion and judgment, because the jury instructions in this case were not consistent with the law as the Court today expounds it.

As I understand the Court's opinion, it holds that in order to sustain a conviction under § 301(k) of the Federal Food, Drug, and Cosmetic Act the prosecution must at least show that by reason of an individual's corporate position and responsibilities, he had a duty to use care to maintain the physical integrity of the corporation's food products. A jury may then draw the inference that when the food is found to be in such condition as to violate the statute's prohibitions, that condition was "caused" by a breach of the standard of care imposed upon the responsible official. This is the language of negligence, and I agree with it.

To affirm this conviction, however, the Court must approve the instructions given to the members of the jury who were entrusted with determining whether the respondent was innocent or guilty. Those instructions did not conform to the standards that the Court itself sets out today.

The trial judge instructed the jury to find Park guilty if it found beyond a reasonable doubt that Park "had a responsible relation to the situation. . . . The issue is, in this case, whether the Defendant, John R. Park, by virtue of his position in the company, had a position of authority and responsibility in the situation out of which these charges arose." Requiring, as it did, a verdict of guilty upon a finding of "responsibility," this instruction standing alone could have been construed as a direction to convict if the jury found Park "responsible" for the condition in the sense that his position as chief executive officer gave him formal responsibility within the structure of the corporation. But the trial judge went on specifically to caution the jury not to attach such a meaning to his instruction, saying that "the fact that the Defendant is pres[id]ent and is a chief executive officer of the Acme Markets does not require a finding of guilt." "Responsibility" as used by the trial judge therefore had whatever meaning the jury in its unguided discretion chose to give it.

The instructions, therefore, expressed nothing more than a tautology. They told the jury: "You must find the defendant guilty if you find that he is to be held accountable for this adulterated food." In other words: "You must find the defendant guilty if you conclude that he is guilty." The trial judge recognized the infirmities in these instructions, but he reluctantly concluded that he was required to give such a charge under United States v. Dotterweich, which, he thought, in declining to define "responsible relation" had declined to specify the minimum standard of liability for criminal guilt. . . .[20]

To be sure, "the day [is] long past when [courts] . . . parsed instructions and engaged in nice semantic distinctions," Cool v. United States, 409 U.S. 100, 107 (Rehnquist, J., dissenting). But this Court has never before abandoned the view that jury instructions must contain a statement of the applicable law sufficiently precise to enable the jury to be guided by something other than its rough notions of social justice. And while it might be argued that the issue before the jury in this case was a "mixed" question of both law and fact, this has never meant that a jury is to be left wholly at sea, without any guidance as to the standard of conduct the law requires. The instructions given by the trial court in this case, it must be emphasized, were a virtual nullity, a mere authorization to convict if the jury thought it appropriate. Such instructions — regardless of the blameworthiness of the defendant's conduct, regardless of the social value of the Food, Drug, and Cosmetic Act, and regardless of the importance of convicting those who violate it — have no place in our jurisprudence. . . .

---

20. In response to a request for further illumination of what he meant by "responsible relationship" the District Judge said:

Let me say this, simply as to the definition of the "responsible relationship." *Dotterweich* and subsequent cases have indicated this really is a jury question. It says it is not even subject to being defined by the Court. As I have indicated to counsel, I am quite candid in stating that I do not agree with the decision; therefore, I am going to stick by [my original instruction].

Notes and Questions

1. The Court in *Park* stated that "[t]he concept of a 'responsible relationship' to, or a 'responsible share' in, a violation of the Act indeed imports some measure of blameworthiness. . . . The considerations which prompted the imposition of [the defendant's] duty, and the scope of the duty, provide the measure of culpability." Did the Court adopt a negligence theory of liability or a strict liability theory? Is the Court's conclusion that the Act requires a finding of minimal culpability consistent with its rejection of a requirement that the government must establish "wrongful action" in the sense that the court of appeals required it?

2. What implications do *Dotterweich* and *Park* have for the privilege of delegating authority and responsibility to subordinate agents? Is it possible that high-ranking corporate officers and managers may be held personally accountable for violations that occur in a sphere of operations in which they have little or no involvement?

3. The Court said that Park would not have been liable if he had been powerless to prevent or correct the violation. At what point during the trial does Park's responsibility for the activity that results in the violation become an issue? Is it relevant only if he raises an objective impossibility defense? Who has the burden of proving his responsibility for the offending activity?

PROBLEM 2-2

Suppose the efforts to clean up the warehouse in *Park* had been successful. Suppose further that a competitor of Acme Markets hires a saboteur to impersonate an FDA inspector and, on the eve of the next FDA inspection, sends the saboteur to "inspect" Acme's warehouse. While in the Acme warehouse complex, the saboteur surreptitiously deposits rat and mouse pellets in strategic locations. The following day, a real FDA inspector arrives on the scene and discovers the contamination. Is Park responsible for the violation?[21]

PROBLEM 2-3

Suppose that Park was at the warehouse when the first inspection occurred and that, in the presence of the inspector, Park reprimanded the warehouse janitor and gave him specific orders to correct the problem. The janitor, who held a grudge against Park and Acme, purposely failed to follow those orders. One month later, a second FDA inspection occurred. To Park's surprise, the inspector discovered the same contamination problem. Is Park liable for the violation? Or does he have an impossibility defense based upon employee sabotage?[22]

---

21. Compare Norman Abrams, Criminal Liability of Corporate Officers for Strict Liability Offenses — A Comment on *Dotterweich* and *Park*, 28 UCLA L. Rev. 463, 468-469 (1981), with Kathleen F. Brickey, Criminal Liability of Corporate Officers for Strict Liability Offenses — Another View, 35 Vand. L. Rev. 1337, 1366-1367 (1982).

22. Cf. United States v. Starr, 535 F.2d 512 (9th Cir. 1976).

PROBLEM 2-4

Suppose that Acme had an unenclosed food storage facility in Hawaii. When the FDA inspection occurred, the inspector saw birds flying in and out of the warehouse, perching on overhead sprinklers, and eating from bags of rice stored there. When charged with the violation, Park raised the following defense. "I have been working on this contamination problem a long time, but my efforts to solve it during the past months have not been effective. I initially tried to scare the birds away with scarecrows. When I saw that scarecrows wouldn't work, I shot starter pistols every morning, thinking the noise would frighten them away. But that didn't solve the problem either. My current plan is to enclose the food storage area in a huge wire cage to keep the birds out. But right now, I can't construct the cage because the materials I need to build it haven't arrived from the mainland United States."

Does the unavailability of the materials give Park a valid impossibility defense?[23]

Dotterweich and *Park* were the genesis of the responsible corporate officer doctrine, which, in both cases, added judicial gloss to the Food, Drug, and Cosmetic Act. Although there are arguably good reasons to confine the doctrine to statutes defining public welfare offenses, in some jurisdictions it has spilled over into other regulatory contexts where the statutory offenses are not — strictly speaking — public welfare crimes.

UNITED STATES v. JORGENSEN
144 F.3d 550 (8th Cir. 1998)

HANSEN, Circuit Judge.

I

In the mid-1980s, Gregory Jorgensen conceived the idea of gathering a group of South Dakota cattle producers together to market and sell the processed beef derived from their own cattle, hoping to increase the net return from their raised cattle while enabling them to better control their own production. Acting on this idea, Gregory and his father, Martin Jorgensen, incorporated Dakota Lean, Inc. in South Dakota and began slaughtering cattle raised by them and their neighbors. Deborah Jorgensen became involved in the company after its initial organization. The company decided to concentrate on marketing and selling "heart healthy" meat products, produced from cattle raised on the Jorgensen ranch or from Jorgensen-bred animals.

When Dakota Lean sold its meat to customers, the product was accompanied by brochures making various claims about the product. Included in these claims were statements that the cattle were "genetically selected," that "strict quality control [was] maintained through individualized tracking and processing of each animal," and that the cattle were "raised on a wholesome diet of native prairie grass and selected feed

---

23. Cf. United States v. Y. Hata & Co., 535 F.2d 508 (9th Cir. 1976).

stuffs without any growth hormones or implants." Other brochures sent to customers stated that the meat had "No Substitutes" and "No Additives" and came from cattle "selectively bred for over 30 years to yield a much lower fat and cholesterol content." Some brochures also claimed Dakota Lean meat was produced from cattle which had been "raised on a carefully controlled diet of mother's milk and prairie grasses" which was "supplemented with corn and milo, a coarse, rough-seeded sorghum, grown and milled on Dakota Lean's 16,000 acre ranch in South Dakota" as the cattle matured. Additionally, according to the brochures, "computerized records keep track of each animal's food, and fat and cholesterol content levels are measured every three months."

In 1989, when demand for their products outstripped their capacity to fill the orders from slaughtering their own cattle and those of their neighbors having the same attributes as their own cattle, the Jorgensens decided to start buying commercial beef trim from outside suppliers. Beef trim is meat purchased from packing plants which is ordinarily used to make hamburger. None of the outside suppliers claimed their beef trim was hormone or antibiotic free, or that the cattle producing the meat had been genetically bred or fed a special diet. The Jorgensens blended this ordinary commercial outside beef trim with their own Dakota Lean meat product. Dakota Lean then sold this blended product to its customers while at the same time making the representations outlined above to its customers in the accompanying brochures. The company did not tell its customers that it was blending outside beef trim with its own meat. All told, it purchased more than a million pounds of outside beef trim to blend with its own meat.

[The jury convicted the Jorgensens and Dakota Lean of conspiracy, fraudulent sale of misbranded meat in violation of the Federal Meat Inspection Act, and — with the exception of Martin Jorgensen — mail and wire fraud.]

II

A. SUFFICIENCY OF THE EVIDENCE

The defendants first argue that there was insufficient evidence to support any of the counts of conviction and, therefore, that the district court erred in denying their motions for judgment of acquittal. . . .

[The Federal Meat Inspection Act makes it a felony to distribute misbranded meat products in interstate commerce with intent to defraud. Meat products are misbranded if the label is "false or misleading in any particular," and the definition of labeling includes "all labels and other written, printed or graphic matter (1) upon any article or any of its containers or wrappers, or (2) accompanying such article."]

The evidence supports the jury's verdicts in this case. First, the brochures that accompanied the Dakota Lean meat products qualify as "labeling," [and the] brochures were "written matter" that was "accompanying" Dakota Lean's meat product when it was distributed in commerce. Contrary to the defendants' assertions, Dakota Lean customers testified at trial that the literature describing the meat arrived with the product. Second, the Dakota Lean meat products sold were "misbranded." Dakota Lean's own meat had been blended with outside beef trim that did not have the qualities specified in the claims contained in the brochures. Thus, the labeling was false and misleading resulting in the misbranding. Third, the defendants caused the misbranded meat to be distributed in commerce when they sold the products to customers in various states.

There was evidence that each defendant had the requisite intent to defraud. When tours were given of the processing plant, boxes of outside beef trim were hidden behind boxes of Dakota Lean marked product to create the illusion that it was all Jorgensen-bred beef. Gregory Jorgensen gave the final order to purchase outside beef trim and to blend it with Dakota Lean's own product. He told employees that the company was mixing the outside beef trim with the company's own product but that this information was not to leave the plant. He also approved the continued use of the false and misleading brochures.

Martin Jorgensen knew of the blending of outside beef trim with the Dakota Lean product. He told the sales manager to represent the blended product as it was described in the misleading brochures. He loaned the corporation $25,000 so it could buy outside beef. Martin himself also promoted the blended product by making these same representations.

Deborah Jorgensen was actively involved in the daily operations of the company. This included selling the product to customers. She also knew that the company was blending its own meat with outside beef trim. She was personally involved in the purchasing of some of the outside beef trim. She represented the product as it was described in the misleading brochures. She was also the contact person within Dakota Lean for an advertising firm that produced many of the false and misleading brochures. While her involvement with the company was interrupted, the jury convicted her on substantive counts that occurred only after she returned to the company in September 1992, and of the conspiracy count. . . .

B. JURY INSTRUCTIONS . . .

The defendants . . . argue that the district court abused its discretion in refusing to give a proposed jury instruction concerning when a corporate officer may be held criminally responsible for the actions of the company. The proposed instruction would have informed the jury that "a person is not responsible for the acts performed by other people on behalf of a corporation, even if those persons are officers, employees or other agents of the corporation." . . .

A corporate officer who is in a "'responsible relationship'" to an activity within a company that violates provisions of the federal food laws, such as meat misbranding, "can be held criminally responsible even though that officer did not personally engage in that activity." *Cattle King*, 793 F.2d at 240 (quoting *Park*, 421 U.S. at 673-74). As previously noted, the misbranding provisions of which the corporate officers were convicted require the officer to act with an "intent to defraud." Thus, the jury could convict a defendant corporate officer if it found a defendant: (1) had an intent to defraud; and (2) either personally participated in the misbranding or was in a "responsible relationship" within the company regarding the misbranding of meat.

We first note that the defendants' proposed jury instruction does not accurately state the law set out above as it applies in this case. Under the proposed instruction the jury could not have convicted a defendant based on the actions of any officers, employees, or other agents of Dakota Lean, Inc. However, a defendant can be held criminally responsible for the acts of other people who are officers, employees or other agents of the company if the defendant is in a "responsible relationship." See *Cattle King*, 793

F.2d at 240. Thus, the district court did not abuse its discretion in refusing to give the proposed instruction.

We also find no error in the instructions that were given. They correctly required the jury to find that each defendant had a specific intent to defraud and that each of them had caused misbranding of meat to occur. Because the jury found the corporation guilty of six counts of misbranding without also finding any of the Jorgensens guilty of these counts, we are convinced that the jury did not find any of the Jorgensens guilty of misbranding merely because they held positions of authority in the company. We cannot say the district court abused its discretion in giving these instructions. We reject the defendants' claims on this issue. . . .

III

We have considered all other arguments raised by the defendants in their appeal and find them to be without merit. We therefore affirm the judgments of the district court.

Notes and Questions

1. What are the differences between the Food and Drug Act provisions at issue in *Park* and the Meat Inspection Act provisions at issue in *Jorgensen*? Are the differences important?

2. Are the defendants in *Jorgensen* liable for the same reasons that Park was liable, or does *Jorgensen* stretch the responsible corporate officer doctrine beyond what the Court in *Park* envisioned? What are the outer boundaries of the responsible corporate officer doctrine?

3. In what sense did the defendants in *Jorgensen* cause the Meat Inspection Act violations? Is the causal relationship between their conduct and the violations the same as the causal relationship between Park's conduct and the FDA violations?

4. Is liability in *Jorgensen* based on acts or omissions? Was it necessary for the trial court to give a responsible corporate officer instruction?

5. To convict the defendants in *Jorgensen*, the jury had to find intent to defraud. What evidence points to fraudulent intent?

Congress has also contributed to the expansion of the responsible corporate officer doctrine. Thus, for example, the criminal provisions in two major environmental statutes — the Clean Water Act and the Clean Air Act — define the term "person"[24] to include "any responsible corporate officer."

---

24. See 33 U.S.C. § 1319(c)(6) (Clean Water Act); 42 U.S.C. § 7413(c)(6) (Clean Air Act).

UNITED STATES v. IVERSON
162 F.3d 1015 (9th Cir. 1998)

GRABER, Circuit Judge. . . .

BACKGROUND . . .

Defendant was a founder of CH2O, Inc., and served as the company's President and Chairman of the Board. CH2O blends chemicals to create numerous products, including acid cleaners and heavy-duty alkaline compounds. The company ships the blended chemicals to its customers in drums.

CH2O asked its customers to return the drums so that it could reuse them. Although customers returned the drums, they often did not clean them sufficiently. Thus, the drums still contained chemical residue. Before CH2O could reuse the drums, it had to remove that residue.

To remove the residue, CH2O instituted a drum-cleaning operation, which in turn generated wastewater. In the early to mid-1980s, defendant approached the manager of the local sewer authority to see whether the sewer authority would accept the company's wastewater. The sewer authority refused, because the wastewater "did not meet the parameters we had set for accepting industrial waste. It had too high of a metal content." Thereafter, defendant and the general manager of CH2O made two other attempts to convince the sewer authority to accept the wastewater. Both times, it refused.

Beginning in about 1985, defendant personally discharged the wastewater and ordered employees of CH2O to discharge the wastewater in three places: (1) on the plant's property, (2) through a sewer drain at an apartment complex that defendant owned, and (3) through a sewer drain at defendant's home. (The plant did not have sewer access.) Those discharges continued until about 1988, when CH2O hired Bill Brady.

Brady initially paid a waste disposal company to dispose of the wastewater. Those efforts cost the company thousands of dollars each month. Beginning in late 1991, CH2O stopped its drum-cleaning operation and, instead, shipped the drums to a professional outside contractor for cleaning.

In April 1992, CH2O fired Brady. Around that same time, defendant bought a warehouse in Olympia. Unlike the CH2O plant, the warehouse had sewer access. After the purchase, CH2O restarted its drum-cleaning operation at the warehouse and disposed of its wastewater through the sewer. CH2O obtained neither a permit nor permission to make these discharges. The drum-cleaning operation continued until the summer of 1995, when CH2O learned that it was under investigation for discharging pollutants into the sewer.

A few months before CH2O restarted its drum-cleaning operation, defendant announced his "official" retirement from CH2O. Thereafter, he continued to receive money from CH2O, to conduct business at the company's facilities, and to give orders to employees. Moreover, the company continued to list him as the president in documents that it filed with the state, and the employee who was responsible for running the day-to-day aspects of the drum-cleaning operation testified that he reported to defendant.

During the four years of the operation at the warehouse, defendant was sometimes present when drums were cleaned. During those occasions, defendant was close enough to see and smell the waste.

In some instances, defendant informed employees that he had obtained a permit for the drum-cleaning operation and that the operation was on the "up and up." At other times, however, defendant told employees that, if they got caught, the company would receive only a slap on the wrist.

[Iverson was charged in a five count indictment with violating the Clean Water Act (CWA) and related water pollution laws, and was convicted on all counts.]

RESPONSIBLE CORPORATE OFFICER

Defendant . . . argues that the district court erred in formulating its "responsible corporate officer" jury instruction. We are not persuaded. . . .

B. "RESPONSIBLE CORPORATE OFFICER" LIABILITY

The district court instructed the jury that it could find defendant liable under the CWA as a "responsible corporate officer" if it found, beyond a reasonable doubt:

1. That the defendant had knowledge of the fact that pollutants were being discharged to the sewer system by employees of CH2O, Inc.;
2. That the defendant had the authority and capacity to prevent the discharge of pollutants to the sewer system; and
3. That the defendant failed to prevent the on-going discharge of pollutants to the sewer system.

Defendant argues that the district court misinterpreted the scope of "responsible corporate officer" liability. Specifically, defendant suggests that a corporate officer is "responsible" only when the officer in fact exercises control over the activity causing the discharge or has an express corporate duty to oversee the activity. We have not previously interpreted the scope of "responsible corporate officer" liability under the CWA. We do so now and reject defendant's narrow interpretation.

. . . The CWA holds criminally liable "any person who . . . knowingly violates" its provisions. The CWA defines the term "person" to include "any responsible corporate officer." However, the CWA does not define the term "responsible corporate officer."

When a statute does not define a term, we generally interpret that term by employing the ordinary, contemporary, and common meaning of the words that Congress used. As pertinent here, the word "responsible" means "answerable" or "involving a degree of accountability." Webster's Third New Int'l Dictionary 1935 (unabridged ed. 1993). Using that meaning, "any corporate officer" who is "answerable" or "accountable" for the unlawful discharge is liable under the CWA.

The history of the "responsible corporate officer" liability supports the foregoing construction. The "responsible corporate officer" doctrine originated in a Supreme Court case interpreting the Federal Food, Drug, and Cosmetic Act (FFDCA), United States v. Dotterweich, 320 U.S. 277 (1943).

In *Dotterweich*, the president and the general manager of a corporation each argued that he was not a "person" as that term is defined in the FFDCA. The Court disagreed, holding that "the offense is committed . . . by all who do have such a responsible share in the furtherance of the transaction which the statute outlaws." Id. at 284. The Court refused to define the boundaries of the doctrine, however, leaving the question for district courts and juries. See id. at 285 ("To attempt a formula embracing the variety of conduct whereby persons may responsibly contribute in furthering a transaction forbidden by an Act of Congress . . . would be mischievous futility. . . . [T]he question of responsibility [is properly left] to the jury.").

Because Congress used a similar definition of the term "person" in the CWA, we can presume that Congress intended that the principles of *Dotterweich* apply under the CWA. Under *Dotterweich*, whether defendant had sufficient "responsibility" over the discharges to be criminally liable would be a question for the jury.

After Congress initially enacted the CWA in 1972, the Supreme Court further defined the scope of the "responsible corporate officer" doctrine under the FFDCA. In United States v. Park, 421 U.S. 658 (1975), a corporate president argued that he could not be "responsible" under *Dotterweich*, because he had delegated decision-making control over the activity in question to a subordinate. The Court rejected that argument, holding that

> the Government establishes a prima facie case when it introduces evidence sufficient to warrant a finding by the trier of the facts that the defendant had, by reason[] of his position in the corporation, responsibility and authority either to prevent in the first instance or promptly to correct, the violation complained of, and that he failed to do so.

Id. at 673-74. Stated another way, the question for the jury is whether the corporate officer had "authority with respect to the conditions that formed the basis of the alleged violations." Id. at 674. The Court did not, however, require the corporate officer actually to exercise any authority over the activity. . . .

Moreover, this court has interpreted similar terms in other statutes consistently with the Court's decision in *Park*. . . .

Taken together, the wording of the CWA, the Supreme Court's interpretations of the "responsible corporate officer" doctrine, and this court's interpretation of similar statutory requirements establish the contours of the "responsible corporate officer" doctrine under the CWA. Under the CWA, a person is a "responsible corporate officer" if the person has authority to exercise control over the corporation's activity that is causing the discharges. There is no requirement that the officer in fact exercise such authority or that the corporation expressly vest a duty in the officer to oversee the activity. . . .

Affirmed.

Notes and Questions

1. Since Iverson had "officially" retired from CH20, what is the basis for holding him liable as a responsible corporate officer? Does it matter whether he continued to have a formal affiliation with the company?[25]

2. How important is it that Iverson was occasionally present when the drums were cleaned?

3. What policy supports imposing criminal liability on an individual who is not personally involved in committing the violation?

NOTE ON FINES AND INDEMNIFICATION

To the extent that courts rely on the threat of personal liability as a deterrent to criminal wrongdoing, modern corporate indemnification statutes seem to undercut its deterrent value. Delaware corporation law provides a good example. Under Delaware law, a corporation may pay any criminal fine imposed on a corporate agent if the board of directors determines that the agent acted in good faith, that his conduct was not contrary to the corporation's best interests, and that he had no reason to believe his conduct was unlawful.[26] The corporation is required to indemnify the agent, if acquitted, for legal costs — including attorneys' fees — incurred in defending the prosecution.[27]

In the federal system, some statutes and regulations clearly disfavor indemnification. The Foreign Corrupt Practices Act (FCPA), for example, flatly prohibits direct or indirect indemnification of fines imposed on corporate officers, directors, and agents convicted of FCPA violations.[28] The Securities and Exchange Commission (SEC) also frowns on indemnification. The Commission requires corporations to disclose in their registration statements the SEC's position that indemnification of those in control of the organization is against public policy and that indemnification agreements are thus unenforceable.[29]

The Sentencing Reform Act of 1984, in contrast, defers to state law. The Act forbids corporations from indemnifying their officers and agents *unless* indemnification is expressly authorized by state law.[30] Delaware corporation law, discussed above, is a prime example of just such a law.

---

25. Cf. United States v. Hong, 242 F.3d 528 (4th Cir. 2001).

26. Del. Code Ann. tit. 8, § 145(a), (c) (2009).

27. Id. § 145(c).

28. 15 U.S.C. §§ 78dd-2(g)(3), 78ff(c)(3). See generally 2 William E. Knepper & Dan A. Bailey, Liability of Corporate Officers and Directors § 22.21 (2002).

29. See Regulation S-K Item 510, 17 C.F.R. § 229.510 (2009). Courts generally uphold the SEC's position. See, e.g., In re U.S. Oil & Gas Litig., 967 F.2d 489, 495 (11th Cir. 1992); Globus, Inc. v. Law Research Serv., 318 F. Supp. 955, 958 (S.D.N.Y. 1970), aff'd, 442 F.2d 1346 (2d Cir. 1971).

30. 18 U.S.C. § 3572(f).

Notes and Questions

1. Is it sound public policy to permit corporations to indemnify criminal fines? Why would the SEC conclude that indemnification agreements are against public policy? Why would the Delaware legislature conclude they are not?

2. Assuming that a corporation is authorized to indemnify its agents, which agents are most likely to benefit?

3. Are corporations likely to be insured against the risk that they may need to indemnify their top officials? Or does the indemnification payment come from the corporate treasury? If, as the SEC posits, indemnification payments made from corporate coffers would "nullify the liability provisions of the Securities Act," why wouldn't indemnifying officers through insurance procured with corporate assets be similarly objectionable?

3

Conspiracy

I. INTRODUCTION

Conspiracy is an inchoate offense. It consists of an agreement between two or more parties to commit an unlawful act. The agreement is punishable whether or not the criminal objective is achieved, because group danger poses a greater threat than individual wrongdoing does. "[T]o unite, back of a criminal purpose, the strength, opportunities and resources of many is obviously more dangerous and more difficult to police than the efforts of a lone wrongdoer."[1] By combining their efforts to engage in criminal activity, conspirators increase their chances of bringing about their unlawful goal, make it easier to pursue complex objectives, and make it more likely that they will expand their horizons to include criminal activities well beyond the original purpose of the group.[2]

Conspiracy has been called the darling of the modern prosecutor's nursery. Because conspiracy law gives prosecutors a number of procedural and evidentiary advantages, it is one of the most frequently charged federal crimes.[3]

Conspiracy doctrine is important partly because of the frequency with which federal prosecutors rely on it and partly because members of a conspiracy may be held vicariously liable for crimes committed by their co-conspirators in furtherance of the conspiratorial objective.[4]

The general federal conspiracy statute, 18 U.S.C. § 371, contains two distinct prohibitions: (1) conspiring to commit an offense against the United States; and (2) conspiring to defraud the United States. In contrast with common law conspiracy doctrine, § 371 requires at least one member of the conspiracy to commit an overt act to show the conspiracy is at work. The overt act need not be unlawful, however. *Any* act performed to further the conspiratorial objective will suffice, even though the conduct would be wholly innocent in another context. Overt acts committed by one member of the conspiracy are chargeable to all.

---

1. Krulewitch v. United States, 336 U.S. 440, 448-449 (1949).
2. Callanan v. United States, 364 U.S. 587, 593-594 (1961).
3. See Paul Marcus, Conspiracy: The Criminal Agreement in Theory and Practice, 65 Geo. L.J. 925, 947 (1977); Shirley A. Selz, Conspiracy Law in Theory and in Practice: Federal Conspiracy Prosecutions in Chicago, 5 Am. J. Crim. L. 35, 48-49 (1977).
4. Pinkerton v. United States, 328 U.S. 640, 647-648 (1946).

Section 371 is only one of many conspiracy statutes in the federal criminal code.[5] The Sarbanes-Oxley Act, enacted in the wake of the Enron and WorldCom financial accounting scandals, provided additional grist for the mill by adding a special conspiracy provision, 18 U.S.C. § 1349, applicable primarily to conspiracies to violate the mail, wire, and bank fraud statutes, in addition to newly enacted securities and corporate financial accountability laws.

The primary differences between the general federal conspiracy statute and the Sarbanes-Oxley conspiracy statute are that: (1) unlike § 371, which explicitly requires proof of an overt act, § 1349 does not require an overt act;[6] (2) unlike § 371, which imposes a fixed maximum fine and imprisonment for most conspiracies, the maximum penalty for a § 1349 conspiracy is the same as the penalty authorized for the object offense; and (3) unlike § 371, which applies generally to offenses throughout Title 18, § 1349 applies to only a limited range of crimes.

II. THE PLURALITY REQUIREMENT

Because conspiracy liability is predicated on a group danger rationale, a plurality of parties is required. Thus, at least two actors must participate in the unlawful scheme. The prosecution need not, however, indict or convict all participants in the scheme to establish the guilt of one. The government may prosecute only one member of the conspiracy, provided that the evidence otherwise establishes a plurality of parties acting in concert.

UNITED STATES v. STEVENS
909 F.2d 431 (11th Cir. 1990)

RONEY, Senior Circuit Judge.

In this criminal conspiracy case, we hold that a sole stockholder who completely controls a corporation and is the sole actor in performance of corporate activities, cannot be guilty of a criminal conspiracy with that corporation in the absence of another human actor. We therefore reverse the conspiracy conviction of defendant Gary S. Stevens. . . . The indictment alleged the following scheme: Stevens formed four separate corporations in the state of Florida for the purpose of performing government contract work. The corporations entered into a government contract with the U.S. Navy to build an automated storage and retrieval system at the Portsmouth Naval Shipyard in Kittery, Maine. The contract provided for periodic progress payments from the Government as designated aspects of the project were completed.

Stevens was the sole shareholder of these corporations and exercised sole control over them. He was also the only agent of the corporations who executed forms relating

---

5. See, e.g., 21 U.S.C. §§ 846, 963 (drug conspiracies); 18 U.S.C. § 1962(d) (racketeering conspiracies); 15 U.S.C. § 1 (antitrust conspiracies).

6. See United States v. Shabani, 513 U.S. 10, 13-17 (1994) (overt act requirement is a departure from common law; proof of an overt act is not required under a conspiracy statute that does not explicitly require one).

to these contracts. Stevens misrepresented that certain work had been performed in several requests for progress payments. Stevens applied for both personal and commercial loans at several federally insured banks, duplicitously listing as security the income derived from this contract.

The jury focused on the issue, presented by this appeal, concerning the alleged conspiracy between Stevens and his corporations. During deliberations, it submitted several written questions to the district court, including the following:

> Can a person conspire with his own corporation, realizing that he is the primary (only) agent of his own corporation?

> Can we have a definition of conspiracy as it applies to a wholly owned corporation?

The district court judge responded in writing that a person was legally able to conspire with his wholly owned corporation, and that the general definition of conspiracy applies to both humans and corporations.

Although a conspiracy under 18 U.S.C. § 371 requires an agreement between two or more persons, we have held that a corporation may be held criminally liable under § 371 when conspiring with its officers or employees. In so holding, we rejected the "single entity" theory that all agents of a corporation engaging in corporate conduct form a single, collective legal person — that is, the corporation — and that the acts of each agent constitute the acts of the corporation. The single entity theory shielded intracorporate associations of individuals from conspiracy liability on the rationale that a corporation cannot conspire with itself any more than a private individual can. *[single entity theory]*

Distinguishing the antitrust context in which the single entity theory first arose, this Court decided that in the context of a criminal conspiracy to defraud the Government, the single entity theory contravened "the underlying purpose that led to the creation of the fiction of corporate personification. It originated to broaden the scope of corporate responsibility; we will not use it to shield individuals or corporations from criminal liability." United States v. Hartley, 678 F.2d 961, 972 (11th Cir. 1982).

Hartley makes two important holdings in the field of intracorporate conspiracy. *First*, it holds that a group of conspirators cannot escape conspiracy responsibility merely because they all act on behalf of a corporation. *Second, Hartley* holds that liability for a conspiracy may be imputed to the corporation itself on a respondeat superior theory. *[Hartley]*

> The [corporate] fiction was never intended to prohibit the imposition of criminal liability by allowing a corporation or its agents to hide behind the identity of the other. We decline to expand the fiction only to limit corporate responsibility in the context of the criminal conspiracy now before us.
>
> . . . In these situations, the action by an incorporated collection of individuals creates the "group danger" at which conspiracy liability is aimed, and the view of the corporation as a single legal actor becomes a fiction without a purpose. *[group danger]*

678 F.2d at 970.

In this case, we confront a different situation: there is only one human actor, acting for himself and for the corporate entity which he controls. In the great majority of reported decisions involving intracorporate conspiracies under § 371, there were multiple human conspirators in addition to the corporate coconspirator. Some cases have expressly indicated that multiple actors must be involved.

The argument that a single human actor can be convicted of conspiracy under § 371 under the circumstances of this case flies in the face of the traditional justification for criminal conspiracies. Conspiracy is a crime separate from the substantive criminal offense which is the purpose of the conspiracy. This separate punishment is targeted not at the substantive offenses themselves, but at the danger posed to society by combinations of individuals acting in concert.

> This settled principle derives from the reason of things in dealing with socially reprehensible conduct: collective criminal agreement — partnership in crime — presents a greater potential threat to the public than individual delicts. Concerted action both increases the likelihood that the criminal object will be successfully attained and decreases the probability that the individuals involved will depart from their path of criminality. Group association for criminal purposes often, if not normally, makes possible the attainment of ends more complex than those which one criminal could accomplish. Nor is the danger of a conspiratorial group limited to the particular end toward which it has embarked. Combination in crime makes more likely the commission of crimes unrelated to the original purpose for which the group was formed. In sum, the danger which a conspiracy generates is not confined to the substantive offense which is the immediate aim of the enterprise.

Callanan v. United States, 364 U.S. 587, 593-94 (1961).

The threat posed to society by these combinations arises from the creative interaction of two autonomous minds. It is for this reason that the essence of a conspiracy is an *agreement*. The societal threat is of a different quality when one human simply uses the corporate mechanism to carry out his crime. The danger from agreement does not arise.

Even if it can be said that Stevens made up his mind as an individual to pursue fraudulent ends and at the same time made up the "minds" of his corporations to pursue these same ends, this case lacks any interaction between multiple autonomous actors. The basis for punishing Stevens for the separate offense of conspiracy, in addition to the substantive offenses he committed, is not present in this case.

Although it takes three incorporators to form a corporation in Florida, the Government does not assert that the incorporators, other than Stevens, were in any way involved in the criminal objective.

We accordingly reverse Stevens's conviction for conspiracy under § 371. . . .

Notes and Questions

1. The court said the group danger rationale for imposing conspiracy liability is not present when there is only one human actor. Is that necessarily true? Suppose that one of Stevens's corporations (Stevens Electronics Co.) supplies electronic components to be used in the automated retrieval system to his other corporation (Stevens Assembly Inc.), which will manufacture the system. He then causes Stevens Electronics to bill Stevens Assembly for components that were never delivered. He next causes Stevens Assembly to pay the bogus bills. And last, he causes Stevens Assembly to file false claims against the government, seeking payment for the cost of

acquiring the nonexistent components. Have the two corporations conspired? Is there an element of group danger here?

2. Is the group danger rationale sufficiently strong to warrant convicting parties to an agreement who never attempt to commit the object offense? What special dangers are posed by concerted activity?

3. The court in *Stevens* made it clear that the essence of a conspiracy is an agreement, but it goes without saying that conspirators rarely reduce their agreement to writing. That being true, what evidence is needed to prove the agreement element of a conspiracy offense?

4. The court observed that the single entity theory (also known as the intra-enterprise conspiracy theory) shields related corporations from antitrust conspiracy liability, but distinguished the case at hand. The distinction is important only in the context of § 1 of the Sherman Act, which prohibits "every contract, combination . . . or conspiracy in restraint of trade."[7]

The reason for the exception is that § 1 prohibits concerted action that would otherwise be lawful if engaged in by a single party. Price fixing provides an illustrative case. Suppose that Acme Airlines and Chip's Commuter Line provide the only airline service into Podunk. To provide this service, Acme's managers must discuss and decide what fares the airline will charge for flights to Podunk from various points of origin. That is a legitimate and necessary business decision for Acme to make. But it is a decision that Chip's management must make for its airline as well. The potential problem arises if managers from Acme and Chip's get together to discuss pricing and agree to charge identical fares — say, fares that would be much higher than either company could get away with if they priced their flights competitively. That constitutes a conspiracy to restrain trade in violation of § 1.

In multicorporate enterprises like those in *Stevens*, the question is whether related corporations should be treated as separate entities for purposes of § 1 violations — e.g., our price fixing example. The leading case in point is Copperweld Corp. v. Independence Tube Corp.,[8] where the Supreme Court held that a parent corporation and its wholly owned subsidiary cannot conspire under § 1. The Court found that § 1 requires a joining of independent economic powers that normally pursue separate interests (e.g., those of Acme and Chip's). Because parent and subsidiary corporations normally have congruent interests and because coordinated conduct between them is consistent with competitive conduct, the Court in *Copperweld* concluded that they should be treated as a single economic entity and thus cannot combine to restrain trade.

Does this rationale apply with equal force to intra-enterprise conspiracies outside the antitrust context? If not, why not?

NOTE ON INCONSISTENT VERDICTS

As the court in *Stevens* made clear, to establish that a conspiracy exists, the government must prove that a plurality of actors acted in concert. But consider the following scenario. Smith and Taylor are partners in a business that manufactures

---

7. 15 U.S.C. § 1.
8. 467 U.S. 752 (1984).

specialized electronic components designed for use in nuclear weapons systems. They successfully bid on a multi-million-dollar contract with the federal government to supply components for a new missile system. The contract requires them to test the components and, in addition, to certify in writing that all components they supply have been tested and that they meet or surpass the performance standards specified in the contract. Smith and Taylor decide to cut corners in order to speed up the production process, so they test only half of the components they supply under the contract. To avoid detection of their ruse, they falsely certify that all of the components have been tested and that each component they delivered has passed all of the tests.

After the deception is discovered, the grand jury indicts Smith and Taylor for conspiring to defraud the government and for making false statements. At trial, the jury convicts Smith but acquits Taylor on the conspiracy charge. Smith then moves to have his conviction set aside on the ground that the government failed to prove an essential element of a conspiracy — viz., a plurality of parties. Simply put, the argument is that Smith cannot have conspired with himself, so no evidentiary basis for a conspiracy conviction exists. Should Smith's motion be granted?

At an earlier point in time, the rule of consistency would have worked in Smith's favor. Notwithstanding that there has never been a rule requiring that all members of the conspiracy must be charged and tried, the rule of consistency provided that the conviction of a lone conspirator could not be sustained if all of the other alleged members of the conspiracy had been acquitted.[9] But in more recent times, the rule of consistency has fallen by the wayside in federal courts, so that most jurisdictions would allow Smith's conspiracy conviction to stand, even though Thomas — the only other alleged member of the conspiracy — has been acquitted.[10]

What might support recognition of a conviction under these circumstances? Does Taylor's acquittal necessarily mean that the jury found there was insufficient evidence to convict? Not necessarily: "[I]n the face of inconsistent verdicts, one cannot 'necessarily assume[] that the acquittal . . . was proper — the one the jury really meant.' It is equally possible that the jury, convinced of guilt, properly reached its conclusion on [one] offense, and then through mistake, compromise, or lenity, arrived at an inconsistent conclusion on the [other] offense."[11] Thus, courts are reluctant to speculate about what motivated a given jury verdict and will allow inconsistent verdicts to stand. As in other contexts, in the event that there may have been a miscarriage of justice, trial and appellate courts routinely review the record to determine whether there was sufficient evidence to support the jury's decision to convict.

NOTE ON SCOPE OF CONSPIRACY

When the government alleges a conspiracy comprised of more than two members, courts must often decide the scope of the conspiratorial agreement. The question usually

---

9. See, e.g., United States v. Sangmeister, 685 F.2d 1124 (9th Cir. 1982).

10. See, e.g., United States v. Bucuvalas, 909 F.2d 593 (1st Cir. 1990) (the rule of consistency is no longer viable).

11. Id. at 595. The move away from the rule of consistency has been prompted in large measure by two Supreme Court decisions that approved upholding logically inconsistent verdicts in other statutory contexts. See United States v. Powell, 469 U.S. 57 (1984); Dunn v. United States, 284 U.S. 390 (1932).

boils down to whether there is a single overarching conspiracy or multiple conspiracies. Consider the following scenario. Adams, an investment banker, is often privy to confidential inside information relating to securities. Adams agrees to give stock tips based on the inside information to Baker, his mistress. Baker routinely passes the same information on to Cooper, Baker's other lover. Are Adams, Baker, and Cooper part of a single insider trading conspiracy?[12]

It depends. Did the agreement between Adams and Baker contemplate the participation of anyone else, or did Baker share the information with Cooper on the sly? Did Adams reasonably foresee that Baker would pass the tips to a third party? Did Adams know of or consent to Baker's sharing the inside information with other parties? If the answer to any of these questions is yes, there is a good chance that Adams, the originating tipper, is in a conspiracy with Cooper, the remote tippee.[13] But if Adams took precautions to maintain the secrecy of his arrangement with Baker, it is less likely that Adams and Cooper are co-conspirators.[14] In that event, a court could find two separate conspiracies: one between Adams and Baker, another between Baker and Cooper.

But what if Adams is unaware of Cooper, but Cooper is aware of Adams's role? A court might then ask whether Adams and Cooper mutually benefited from Cooper's participation in the scheme, or whether Cooper alone benefited from his receipt of the tips from Baker. If Adams did not benefit, there is no mutual dependence among the three participants and likely no single conspiracy.[15] The more remote the tippee is from the originating tipper — i.e., the more parties there are — the more complex the issues become.[16]

These points can have immensely practical implications relating to the venue where the parties can be tried, whether they must be tried jointly in a single trial, and whether the co-conspirator exception to the hearsay rule will allow otherwise inadmissible evidence to be used against other members of the conspiracy.[17]

III. THE OBJECT OFFENSE

Section 371 defines two categories of conspiracies that are distinguished by their criminal objectives: (1) conspiracy *to commit an offense* against the United States (e.g., to violate a federal criminal statute); and (2) conspiracy *to defraud* the United States in any manner or for any purpose (e.g., to cheat or trick a government agency). Although the objective of the conspiracy must be commission of an independent crime, the conspirators need not achieve their criminal objective to be guilty of conspiracy to commit the crime.

---

12. See United States v. McDermott, 245 F.3d 133 (2d Cir. 2001). See also United States v. Carpenter, 791 F.2d 1024 (2d Cir. 1986).

13. United States v. Geibel, 369 F.3d 682, 690-692 (2d Cir. 2004).

14. Id. at 691.

15. Id. at 692.

16. Cf. id. at 686-688 (describing insider trading scheme in which securities-related information was passed on to 15 or 20 individuals).

17. See Wayne R. LaFave, Criminal Law § 12.1(b) (5th ed. 2010).

A. THE "OFFENSE" AND "DEFRAUD" CLAUSES

UNITED STATES v. ARCH TRADING CO.
987 F.2d 1087 (4th Cir. 1993)

NIEMEYER, Circuit Judge.

On August 2, 1990, Iraq invaded Kuwait. On that same day President Bush invoked the emergency powers provided to him by Congress and issued executive orders prohibiting United States persons from, among other things, traveling to Iraq and dealing with the government of Iraq and its agents. In the present appeal, Arch Trading Company, Inc., a Virginia corporation, challenges its convictions for various crimes arising from violations of these prohibitions. The company was convicted of conspiring to commit an offense against the United States, in violation of 18 U.S.C. § 371; of disobeying the emergency executive orders, in violation of the International Emergency Economic Powers Act (IEEPA), 50 U.S.C. §§ 1701 et seq., and of lying to the Department of Treasury's Office of Foreign Assets Control (OFAC) about its conduct, in violation of 18 U.S.C. § 1001. . . .

Arch Trading contends principally that (1) the indictment charging it with conspiracy to *commit an offense* under § 371 was defective because in the circumstances the company could only have been charged with conspiracy *to defraud.* . . .

I

In November 1988 Arch Trading entered into a $1.9 million contract with Agricultural Supplies Company, a "quasi-governmental body owned by the government of Iraq" (Agricultural of Iraq), to ship to Iraq and install there laboratory equipment, including a "virology fermenter" and a "bacteriology machine," purportedly for veterinary use. . . .

From April 1990 through July 1990 Arch Trading acquired the equipment and related chemicals and arranged for their delivery to Iraq. By early August 1990, five of a planned six shipments had arrived in Iraq, but none had been installed. The sixth shipment, which was never actually delivered, was en route. On August 2, 1990, when Iraq invaded Kuwait, President Bush, invoking the powers given him under the IEEPA, issued Executive Order No. 12722 prohibiting United States persons from, among other things, exporting goods, technology, or services to Iraq; performing any contract in support of an industrial, commercial or governmental project in Iraq; and engaging in any transaction related to travel to Iraq by United States persons. At Arch Trading's request, that same day the Treasury Department's OFAC faxed a copy of the Executive Order to Arch Trading's offices. A week later the President issued a slightly more detailed order. Both executive orders were formally implemented through regulations published in the Code of Federal Regulations.

Notwithstanding the prohibitions of the first executive order, two executives of Arch Trading immediately attempted to enter Iraq via Cyprus to install the laboratory equipment that had already been delivered. When that effort failed, Arch Trading retained a Jordanian firm, Biomedical Technologies, Inc., to perform the installation. One of the Arch Trading executives who had earlier attempted to enter Iraq later joined

Biomedical employees in Baghdad to help coordinate the installation, which was accomplished between October 24 and November 2, 1990. The travel expenses of both the Arch Trading executive and the Biomedical Technologies employees were reimbursed by Arch Trading, on authority of its president, Kamal Sadder, and upon completion of the installation, Biomedical Technologies was paid a bonus. . . .

[Arch Trading submitted backdated documents in an effort to recover its $200,000 deposit in the Kuwaiti bank. In furtherance of that effort, it made false statements to the Office of Foreign Assets Control of the Department of the Treasury. Arch Trading's dealings with Iraq were discovered by the Customs Service during an unrelated investigation.]

II

Arch Trading first contends that it was improperly charged under 18 U.S.C. § 371. That section criminalizes conspiracies of two sorts: conspiracies *to commit an offense* against the United States and conspiracies *to defraud* the United States. Arch Trading was charged with, and convicted of, conspiring to commit an "offense" against the United States government. It asserts, however, it could only have been charged, if at all, with having conspired to "defraud" the United States, because violations of executive orders and regulations do not constitute an "offense." Arch Trading argues that the conspiracy count must therefore be dismissed, relying on United States v. Minarik, 875 F.2d 1186, 1193-94 (6th Cir. 1989).

We reject this argument because we do not agree that violation of an executive order cannot constitute an offense as that term is used in 18 U.S.C. § 371. While it may be that executive orders cannot alone establish crimes, when such orders are duly authorized by an act of Congress and Congress specifies a criminal sanction for their violation, the consequence is different. In this case the IEEPA authorized the President to issue executive orders proscribing conduct, and 50 U.S.C. § 1705(b) makes criminal the disobedience of an order issued under the Act. There is no question that violation of a federal criminal statute may properly be charged under the "offense" clause. We therefore hold that when Congress provides criminal sanctions for violations of executive orders that it empowers the President to issue, such violation constitutes an "offense" for the purposes of 18 U.S.C. § 371.

While Arch Trading's conduct could arguably have been charged also as a conspiracy "to defraud," the two prongs of § 371 are not mutually exclusive. Because of the broad interpretation which has been given the "defraud" clause, § 371's two clauses overlap considerably. The wide breadth of the "defraud" clause has long been established:

> To conspire to defraud the United States means to cheat the government out of property or money, but it also means to interfere with or obstruct one of its lawful functions by deceit, craft or trickery, or at least by means that are dishonest. It is not necessary that the government shall be subjected to property or pecuniary loss by the fraud, but only that its legitimate official actions and purpose shall be defeated by misrepresentation, chicane, or the overreaching of those charged with carrying out the governmental intention.

Hammerschmidt v. United States, 265 U.S. 182, 188 (1924).

Because of this overlap, given conduct may be proscribed by both of the section's clauses. In such a situation, the fact that a particular course of conduct is chargeable under one clause does not render it immune from prosecution under the other. When both prongs of § 371 apply to the conduct with which a particular defendant is charged, the government enjoys considerable latitude in deciding how to proceed. Convictions under the "defraud" clause for conspiracies *to commit particular offenses* are commonly upheld. Conversely, convictions under the "offense" clause for conspiracy to engage in conduct which would defraud the United States are also proper. Many courts have even found it permissible to list both prongs of § 371 in a single indictment count rather than specifying whether the alleged conspiracy was one to defraud or one to commit an offense. . . .

In short, the evidence in this case against Arch Trading would have supported conviction under either the "offense" or the "defraud" clause, and absent an improper motive, which is not alleged here, the government's choice of invoking the offense clause was an appropriate exercise of discretion. . . .

Affirmed.

Notes and Questions

1. What differentiates a conspiracy to commit an offense against the United States from a conspiracy to defraud the United States? Are these really two distinct crimes? Or are there times when the two crimes are in actuality one and the same?

2. How can violating an executive order be equated with violating a criminal statute? Under *Arch Trading*, would all violations of executive orders be "offenses" for purposes of § 371?

3. The court said that absent an improper motive, the government may proceed at its discretion under either the offense clause or the defraud clause. What would constitute an improper motive?

4. The government's choice of which clause to proceed under can be a matter of considerable practical significance to the defendant. Section 371 conspiracies are classified as felonies unless the object offense is a misdemeanor.

Consider, for example, two law partners who conspire not to file a partnership tax return that is required by law. The government could charge this as a conspiracy to defraud — i.e., to cheat the government out of tax revenue or to impede the proper administration of the revenue laws. In that case, the indictment would charge a felony. On the other hand, the government could charge this as a conspiracy to commit an offense against the United States — i.e., willful failure to pay a tax or make a return.[18] In that case, the indictment would charge a misdemeanor.

Notwithstanding the overlap between these two theories, most courts hold that the defraud clause provides an independent basis for imposing felony liability.

If the government's reason for charging this as a conspiracy to defraud is to seek the more serious penalty, is that an improper motive?[19]

---

18. See 26 U.S.C. § 7203.
19. Cf. United States v. Batchelder, 442 U.S. 114 (1979).

B. MENS REA

Mere association with members of a conspiracy is insufficient to prove participation in it. Instead, the defendant must know the conspiracy exists, must know its general scope and purpose, and must voluntarily join in the scheme. But knowledge alone is insufficient. The defendant must intend to agree and, in addition, must possess the mental state required to commit the object offense.

UNITED STATES v. LICCIARDI
30 F.3d 1127 (9th Cir. 1994)

NOONAN, Circuit Judge.

Michael Licciardi appeals his conviction under 18 U.S.C. § 371 of conspiracy to defraud the United States by obstructing the functions of the Bureau of Alcohol, Tobacco and Firearms (the BATF); of two convictions under 18 U.S.C. § 1341 of mail fraud; and of his conviction under 18 U.S.C. § 1001 of making a false statement. This case involves an effort of the government to extend substantially the scope of the general conspiracy statute. . . .

THE INDICTMENT

Licciardi was indicted for the following offenses:

Count 1. From January 1987 to April 1989 Licciardi was charged with a conspiracy whose "object" was to "defraud the United States and its agency, the BATF, by obstructing, impairing and defeating the lawful function of the BATF to assure the integrity and varietal designations of wine through examination and analysis of records maintained honestly and accurately and free from deceit, trickery, fraud and dishonesty, in violation of Title 18 U.S.C. § 371."

[The indictment also charged that the object of the conspiracy was to defraud Delicato Vineyards (Delicato) and other wine producers by selling mislabeled grapes.]

FACTS. . .

Licciardi was a partner with his father in a grape brokerage business, Corvette Company (Corvette). Corvette bought grapes from the growers and sold them, almost exclusively, to Delicato; almost 90 percent of Delicato's purchases from brokers were from Corvette. During the crush in the fall of the year, Licciardi had 24-hour access to Delicato, including the areas where the grapes were received, weighed and dumped into the crushers. During this period Licciardi occupied an office at Delicato's from which he scheduled and supervised deliveries of grapes from Corvette. His position gave him the opportunity for the deceitful transactions set out here.

[Licciardi and several wine growers hatched a scheme to misrepresent the variety and origin of grapes they sold so they could charge prices that greatly exceeded the actual value of the grapes.]

MENS REA

On appeal, Licciardi argues that there was no evidence that he had an intention to defraud the United States. It is true that the general conspiracy statute has been given a very broad meaning so that "defraud" extends beyond its common law usage and includes interference or obstruction of a lawful governmental function "by deceit, craft or treachery or at least by means that are dishonest." Hammerschmidt v. United States, 265 U.S. 182, 188 (1923). If all the government had to prove was that Licciardi had used dishonest means and that these means had the effect of impairing a function of the BATF, the government would easily have prevailed. [I]t is unlawful for a winery to sell in interstate commerce wine unless it is packaged in conformity with regulations prescribed by the Treasury with respect to labeling which will provide the consumer "with adequate information as to the identity and quality of the product." . . . Licciardi's dishonest methods would have had the effect of preventing Delicato from complying with the regulations and would have therefore prevented the BATF from enforcing the regulations.

The difficulty for the government is Licciardi's mens rea for commission of the federal crime. Mens rea is, of course, a fundamental requirement of our criminal jurisprudence. In the case of a charge of conspiracy to violate the federal statute the government "must prove at least the degree of criminal intent necessary for the substantive offense itself." United States v. Feola, 420 U.S. 671, 686 (1975). This requirement has been the rule for at least a century.

Much of the reason for insisting on mens rea is to prevent "ostensibly innocuous conduct" from unwittingly becoming criminal. It will be observed that Licciardi was far from innocent morally or in terms of the law of California. But the question is whether he was innocent of any design to commit a federal crime. . . .

[T]he government has failed to prove its case against Licciardi for conspiracy to defraud the United States by impairing the functions of the BATF. That the incidental effects of Licciardi's actions would have been to impair the functions of the BATF does not confer upon him the mens rea of accomplishing that object.

It might have been easy for the government to establish that Licciardi was familiar with the federal regulations on the labelling of wine and that it was a necessary part of his plan of deceit that Delicato provide information to the government that would frustrate these regulations. But we cannot speculate as to what the government might have proved when it did not make the effort to show that Licciardi had "conspired to cause" Delicato to provide false information to the BATF. . . .

The government relies on *Feola*, but does so mistakenly. There the substantive criminal statute was violated when someone assaulted a federal officer, whether or not he knew his victim was a federal officer. By the same token, the conspiracy statute did not require knowledge that the victim was a federal officer, because no greater knowledge and intent were required for the conspiracy than for violation of the substantive statute. . . .

Long ago Learned Hand referred to the general conspiracy statute as the "darling of the modern prosecutor's nursery." Harrison v. United States, 7 F.2d 259, 263 (2d Cir. 1925). It is understandable why that should be so, and it is perhaps understandable but regrettable that prosecutors should recurrently push to expand the limits of the statute in order to have it encompass more and more activities which may be deeply offensive or immoral or contrary to state law but which Congress has not made federal crimes. It is instructive that *Pettibone* in 1893, *Hammerschmidt* in 1924 and Tanner v. United States, 483 U.S. 107 in 1989 are all instances where the Supreme Court rebuffed a prosecutor's imaginative and unjustified expansion of the statute. We have only recently had to do the same.

The Supreme Court has very recently had occasion to observe that where "a severe penalty" is attached to a crime, it is unlikely that *mens rea* need not be proved. In the instant case we note that a regulatory scheme, which does not have criminal penalties attached to it, has been converted by the government's theory into a system whose violation by commercial cheating is subject to the severe felony penalties of the conspiracy law. We do not accept that theory.

The government has a second string to its bow or, to use Hand's metaphor, a second darling in the modern prosecutor's nursery. If there is sufficient evidence of a second object of the charged conspiracy, we cannot set aside the jury verdict. The government says nothing on this appeal about the charged objective of Licciardi conducting financial transactions to conceal unlawful activities. The government does, however, refer to the charged objective of the conspiracy to obtain money from Delicato by fraudulent representations in violation of 18 U.S.C. §§ 1341 & 2. The government points to the mail fraud counts on which Licciardi was convicted.

In 1987, the first year of the conspiracy, Licciardi arranged with Alfieri for the establishment of a post office box in the name of a fictitious company, intending to use the mails to keep his fraud secret. In 1988, a check representing the proceeds of one of the fraudulent transactions was sent through the mails to this post office box and at Licciardi's direction recovered from this box. These facts established that Licciardi had the requisite mens rea to commit mail fraud. His conviction of conspiracy must [therefore] be sustained. . . .

FLETCHER, J., concurring specially.

I concur in Judge Noonan's opinion except as I express my disagreements below. . . .

II

I disagree with the majority's conclusion that "the absence of mens rea" requires reversal of the conspiracy conviction under the first of the government's two conspiracy theories.

To understand my point, it is important to keep in mind that 18 U.S.C. § 371 consists of both an "offense" clause and a "defraud" clause: it criminalizes both conspiracies "to commit any offense against the United States" and conspiracies "to defraud the United States or any agency thereof." The offense clause is premised on a conspiracy to commit a predicate act that violates a statute other than the conspiracy statute; the defraud clause involves a violation of the conspiracy statute itself. Count 1 included a charge under both clauses. Judge Noonan would affirm the conspiracy conviction under the offense clause, on the basis that Licciardi conspired to commit mail fraud; a conviction under the defraud clause, according to the majority, cannot stand. My focus is on the charge under the defraud clause.

United States v. Feola, 420 U.S. 671 (1975), clarified the body of conspiracy law relating to conduct falling under the offense clause: *Feola* held that the level of intent required to meet the jurisdictional element of a conspiracy charged under the offense clause was the same as the level of intent required to meet the jurisdictional element of the underlying offense. In *Feola*, intent to assault was all that was required; knowledge that the victim was a federal officer was *not* required. The majority is certainly correct that the outcome in *Feola* provides only limited assistance to the government in this case, since the underlying offense in *Feola* clearly did *not* require anti-federal intent, while the same cannot be said here. But by the same token, cases like Ingram v. United States, 360 U.S. 672 (1959), in which the underlying statute *did* require knowledge that the United States was being deprived of money which was its due, offer no support for the assertion that knowledge of federal involvement is required in this case. In contrast to both *Feola* and *Ingram*, the charge in this case falls under the defraud clause, and hence involves no underlying offense at all. Without an underlying offense and without *Feola*'s formulation to guide us, the matter of determining what level of intent is required is more difficult than it is in the case of an offense clause conspiracy. The issue should not be confused, however, by reference to cases like *Ingram*.

The Supreme Court case which addresses conspiracy charges brought under the defraud clause is Tanner v. United States, 483 U.S. 107 (1987). I disagree with the majority's reading of that case. The majority emphasizes *Tanner*'s statement that a conspiracy criminalized by § 371 is "most importantly" defined by the "target of the conspiracy." The majority derives from the latter phrase the conclusion that a person whose conspiratorial acts have the effect of defrauding the federal government escapes § 371 liability unless he knew that his acts would have the effect of defrauding the government. In fact, however, the Supreme Court's disposition in *Tanner* indicates just the opposite.

In *Tanner*, the prosecution tried to link the defendants' deceptive acts to an effect on the federal government in two distinct ways. The Court rejected the first way, but accepted the second. The government's first argument, which the Court disposed of in that part of the opinion on which the majority relies, was that a fraud on a private corporation which receives government funding is a fraud on the government. In dismissing that argument, the Court pointed out that such a "sweeping interpretation of § 371 . . . would in effect substitute 'anyone receiving federal assistance and supervision' for the phrase 'the United States or any agency thereof.'"

The prosecution's second argument was encapsulated in the language of the indictment, which the *Tanner* Court quoted:

> "It was further a part of the conspiracy that the defendants would and did cause [a third person] to falsely state and represent to the [government] that a [government]-approved competitive bidding procedure had been followed. . . ."

483 U.S. at 132. The Court *accepted* this method of connecting the conspiracy to the defrauding of the government, and remanded the case to the Eleventh Circuit for a determination of whether the evidence presented at trial was sufficient to establish that petitioners conspired to cause [the third person] to make misrepresentations to [the government]."

The evidence in this case was sufficient to establish just such a conspiracy. There is no question but that Licciardi conspired with Bavaro, Alfieri and others to provide false field tags, and that Delicato passed these on to the BATF in compliance with its reporting obligations. This linkage between the conspiracy and the government — in which the defendant directly manipulated a third person and caused that person to *make a false statement to the government* — appears to be precisely what the *Tanner* Court held *would* be sufficient to uphold a § 371 conviction. And it is entirely distinct from the linkage which was rejected by *Tanner* — where the fraud perpetrated on a private person may have some impact on the government simply because the government has a fiscal relationship with the private person.

This case can also be conceptualized as one in which *defendant himself* made false statements to the government, passing them along through the conduit provided by the third person. In this light, the government's election to charge under the defraud clause is ironic. The government easily instead could have charged Licciardi with conspiring to commit an offense against the United States — making false statements in violation of 18 U.S.C. § 1001. Under United States v. Yermian, 468 U.S. 63 (1984), the lack of anti-federal intent does not bar a conviction for the substantive offense. And under *Feola*, the same would pertain to the offense of conspiracy. In other words, Licciardi's conviction could easily be sustained under the offense clause of § 371 had the government simply drafted the indictment differently.

Irony aside, of course, we must evaluate the charges against Licciardi as they were framed by the government. The government has made precisely the linkage between the conspiracy and its federal "target" that was endorsed as adequate in *Tanner*: it has shown that Licciardi "conspired to cause [a third person] to make misrepresentations to [the government]." The prosecution need not show that Licciardi knew that the federal government was the ultimate recipient of the misrepresentations. Because this case seems to fall precisely within that portion of *Tanner* in which the Supreme Court held that the government had correctly charged a conspiracy under the defraud clause of § 371, I do not agree that a conviction under the defraud clause must be reversed on the grounds that the government failed to show anti-federal intent.

Because the conviction can be affirmed on the basis of a conspiracy under the defraud clause, I would not reach the question of whether a conviction based on conspiracy to violate the mail fraud statute could be affirmed in this case. I am not suggesting that it cannot be affirmed on that basis, but I am uncomfortable relying on a theory eschewed by the government.

Notes and Questions

1. To be guilty of conspiracy, what must the defendant know and what must he intend? What is the difference between knowledge and intent in this context? Are the mens rea requirements under the "offense" and "defraud" clauses of § 371 the same?

2. The majority in *Licciardi* thought *Feola* was inapposite, but the dissent thought it directly applied. Which view seems more sound? Is the gist of the problem in *Licciardi* whether the defendant had anti-federal intent?

3. What constitutes fraud under the "defraud" clause of § 371? Must the fraud be punishable as an independent crime?

C. VICARIOUS LIABILITY

PINKERTON v. UNITED STATES
328 U.S. 640 (1946)

Mr. Justice DOUGLAS delivered the opinion of the Court.

Walter and Daniel Pinkerton are brothers who live a short distance from each other on Daniel's farm. They were indicted for violations of the Internal Revenue Code. The indictment contained ten substantive counts and one conspiracy count. The jury found Walter guilty on nine of the substantive counts and on the conspiracy count. It found Daniel guilty on six of the substantive counts and on the conspiracy count. Walter was fined $500 and sentenced generally on the substantive counts to imprisonment for thirty months. On the conspiracy count he was given a two year sentence to run concurrently with the other sentence. Daniel was fined $1,000 and sentenced generally on the substantive counts to imprisonment for thirty months. On the conspiracy count he was fined $500 and given a two year sentence to run concurrently with the other sentence. The judgments of conviction were affirmed by the Circuit Court of Appeals. . . .

It is contended that there was insufficient evidence to implicate Daniel in the conspiracy. But we think there was enough evidence for submission of the issue to the jury.

There is, however, no evidence to show that Daniel participated directly in the commission of the substantive offenses on which his conviction has been sustained, although there was evidence to show that these substantive offenses were in fact committed by Walter in furtherance of the unlawful agreement or conspiracy existing between the brothers. The question was submitted to the jury on the theory that each petitioner could be found guilty of the substantive offenses, if it was found at the time those offenses were committed petitioners were parties to an unlawful conspiracy and the substantive offenses charged were in fact committed in furtherance of it.[20]

Daniel relies on United States v. Sall, 116 F.2d 745 (3d Cir. 1940). That case held that participation in the conspiracy was not itself enough to sustain a conviction for the substantive offense even though it was committed in furtherance of the conspiracy. The court held that, in addition to evidence that the offense was in fact committed in furtherance of the conspiracy, evidence of direct participation in the commission of the substantive offense or other evidence from which participation might fairly be inferred was necessary.

We take a different view. We have here a continuous conspiracy. There is here no evidence of the affirmative action on the part of Daniel which is necessary to establish his withdrawal from it. Hyde v. United States, 225 U.S. 347, 369. As stated in that case, "having joined in an unlawful scheme, having constituted agents for its performance, scheme and agency to be continuous until full fruition be secured, until he does some act to disavow or defeat the purpose he is in no situation to claim the delay of the law. As the offense has not been terminated or accomplished, he is still offending. And we think, consciously offending, offending as certainly, as we have said, as at the first moment of his confederation, and consciously through every moment of its existence." And so long as the partnership in crime continues, the partners act for each other in

---

20. . . . Daniel was not indicted as an aider or abettor, nor was his case submitted to the jury on that theory.

carrying it forward. It is settled that "an overt act of one partner may be the act of all without any new agreement specifically directed to that act." United States v. Kissel, 218 U.S. 601, 608. Motive or intent may be proved by the acts or declarations of some of the conspirators in furtherance of the common objective. . . . The governing principle is the same when the substantive offense is committed by one of the conspirators in furtherance of the unlawful project. The criminal intent to do the act is established by the formation of the conspiracy. Each conspirator instigated the commission of the crime. The unlawful agreement contemplated precisely what was done. It was formed for the purpose. The act done was in execution of the enterprise. The rule which holds responsible one who counsels, procures, or commands another to commit a crime is founded on the same principle. That principle is recognized in the law of conspiracy when the overt act of one partner in crime is attributable to all. An overt act is an essential ingredient of the crime of conspiracy. If that can be supplied by the act of one conspirator, we fail to see why the same or other acts in furtherance of the conspiracy are likewise not attributable to the others for the purpose of holding them responsible for the substantive offense.

A different case would arise if the substantive offense committed by one of the conspirators was not in fact done in furtherance of the conspiracy, did not fall within the scope of the unlawful project, or was merely a part of the ramifications of the plan which could not be reasonably foreseen as a necessary or natural consequence of the unlawful agreement. But as we read this record, that is not this case.

Affirmed.

Mr. Justice RUTLEDGE, dissenting in part.

The judgment concerning Daniel Pinkerton should be reversed. In my opinion it is without precedent here and is a dangerous precedent to establish.

Daniel and Walter, who were brothers living near each other, were charged in several counts with substantive offenses, and then a conspiracy count was added naming those offenses as overt acts. The proof showed that Walter alone committed the substantive crimes. There was none to establish that Daniel participated in them, aided and abetted Walter in committing them, or knew that he had done so. Daniel in fact was in the penitentiary, under sentence for other crimes, when some of Walter's crimes were done.

There was evidence, however, to show that over several years Daniel and Walter had confederated to commit similar crimes concerned with unlawful possession, transportation, and dealing in whiskey, in fraud of the federal revenues. On this evidence both were convicted of conspiracy. Walter also was convicted on the substantive counts on the proof of his committing the crimes charged. Then, on that evidence without more than the proof of Daniel's criminal agreement with Walter and the latter's overt acts, which were also the substantive offenses charged, the court told the jury they could find Daniel guilty of those substantive offenses. They did so.

I think this ruling violates both the letter and the spirit of what Congress did when it separately defined the three classes of crime, namely, (1) completed substantive offenses; (2) aiding, abetting or counseling another to commit them; and (3) conspiracy to commit them. Not only does this ignore the distinctions Congress has prescribed shall be observed. It either convicts one man for another's crime or punishes the man convicted twice for the same offense.

The three types of offense are not identical. Nor are their differences merely verbal. The gist of conspiracy is the agreement; that of aiding, abetting or counseling is in consciously advising or assisting another to commit particular offenses, and thus becoming a party to them; that of substantive crime, going a step beyond mere aiding, abetting, counseling to completion of the offense.

These general differences are well understood. But when conspiracy has ripened into completed crime, or has advanced to the stage of aiding and abetting, it becomes easy to disregard their differences and loosely to treat one as identical with the other, that is, for every purpose except the most vital one of imposing sentence. And thus the substance, if not the technical effect, of double jeopardy or multiple punishment may be accomplished. Thus also may one be convicted of an offense not charged or proved against him, on evidence showing he committed another. . . .

. . . Daniel has been held guilty of the substantive crimes committed only by Walter on proof that he did no more than conspire with him to commit offenses of the same general character. There was no evidence that he counseled, advised or had knowledge of those particular acts or offenses. There was, therefore, none that he aided, abetted or took part in them. There was only evidence sufficient to show that he had agreed with Walter at some past time to engage in such transactions generally. As to Daniel this was only evidence of conspiracy, not of substantive crime.

The court's theory seems to be that Daniel and Walter became general partners in crime by virtue of their agreement and because of that agreement without more on his part Daniel became criminally responsible as a principal for everything Walter did thereafter in the nature of a criminal offense of the general sort the agreement contemplated, so long as there was not clear evidence that Daniel had withdrawn from or revoked the agreement. Whether or not his commitment to the penitentiary had that effect, the result is a vicarious criminal responsibility as broad as, or broader than, the vicarious civil liability of a partner for acts done by a co-partner in the course of the firm's business.

Such analogies from private commercial law and the law of torts are dangerous, in my judgment, for transfer to the criminal field. Guilt there with us remains personal, not vicarious, for the more serious offenses. It should be kept so. . . .

Notes and Questions

1. What is the rationale supporting liability under the *Pinkerton* rule? Is it strong enough to warrant holding Daniel liable for crimes his brother committed?

2. Does *Pinkerton* establish a broad rule of vicarious liability? What are the limits on liability under *Pinkerton*? Are they adequate to avoid unjustly punishing co-conspirators for crimes they did not commit?

3. The Court notes that Daniel was neither charged nor tried as an aider and abettor. Is aiding and abetting a species of vicarious liability? What is the difference between *Pinkerton* liability and aider and abettor liability? Could Daniel have been convicted as an aider and abettor?

NOTE ON OVERT ACTS

The Court in *Pinkerton* based its reasoning in part on the established principle that the overt act of one conspirator is chargeable to all. Thus, only one member of the conspiracy needs to commit an overt act in furtherance of the conspiracy. But what is the context for the Court's observation?

Although not all federal conspiracy statutes require proof of an overt act,[21] the general federal conspiracy statute, 18 U.S.C. § 371, specifically requires the government to prove that at least one of the conspirators committed an overt act "to effect the object of the conspiracy." But rather than contemplating independently unlawful conduct, the overt act element only requires some evidence that the conspiracy is at work. It need not constitute a substantial step in a course of conduct designed to culminate in the commission of the object offense.

Although the overt act requirement suggests that a member of the conspiracy must have performed an independently unlawful act, nothing could be further from the truth. The overt act need not be unlawful to constitute an element of the substantive crime the conspirators plan to commit. All that is required is objective evidence that the conspiracy is at work. Any act performed with the purposes of furthering the conspiracy will suffice. Thus, for example, something as innocuous as making a telephone call or arranging a meeting may satisfy this element of a § 371 violation.

IV. WITHDRAWAL AND TERMINATION

Conspiracy is ordinarily a continuing offense. Its natural termination point is when the conspiratorial objective is achieved or all of the conspirators have disavowed its purpose. Consider, for example, a conspiracy among three high-level managers of XYZ Corporation to offer a $100,000 bribe to a public official to induce the official to award XYZ a valuable contract. If the public official accepts the bribe and corruptly designates XYZ as the successful bidder, the conspiracy ends when XYZ receives the contract award. Conversely, suppose the three managers have a change of heart before they offer the bribe. In consequence, they close the Swiss bank account from which the $100,000 would have been paid and abandon their plan to make the corrupt payment. Because they have all disavowed the illicit scheme, the conspiracy would come to an end and the statute of limitations would begin to run.

Individual members may terminate their own participation in an ongoing conspiracy by withdrawing from it — i.e., by taking affirmative steps to disassociate themselves from the conspiracy and its criminal objectives. Although withdrawal does not extinguish the withdrawing member's liability for the crime of conspiracy or for crimes already committed in furtherance of the conspiratorial objective, it insulates him

---

21. See, e.g., 15 U.S.C. § 1 (conspiracy to restrain trade); 18 U.S.C. § 1962(d) (conspiracy to violate RICO statute); 21 U.S.C. § 846 (conspiracy to violate controlled substances act). Because conspiracies at common law did not require proof of an overt act as an element of the offense, the Supreme Court has made it abundantly clear that proof of an overt act is not required under statutes that do not explicitly require one. United States v. Shabani, 513 U.S. 10, 13-17 (1994) (construing drug conspiracy statute). See also Salinas v. United States, 522 U.S. 52 (1997) (construing RICO conspiracy provision).

from *Pinkerton* liability for future crimes committed by fellow members of the conspiracy and causes the statute of limitations to begin to run on conspiracy charges that could be brought against him. The question then becomes what constitutes withdrawal and how the burden of proof is allocated between the prosecution and defense.

> Mere cessation of activity in furtherance of an illegal conspiracy does not necessarily constitute withdrawal. The defendant must present evidence of some affirmative act of withdrawal on his part, typically either a full confession to the authorities or communication to his co-conspirators that he has abandoned the enterprise and its goals. See United States v. United States Gypsum Co., 438 U.S. 422, 464-65 (1978). When a defendant has produced sufficient evidence to make a prima facie case of withdrawal, however, the government cannot rest on its proof that he participated at one time in the illegal scheme; it must rebut the prima facie showing either by impeaching the defendant's proof or by going forward with evidence of some conduct in furtherance of the conspiracy subsequent to the act of withdrawal.[22]

PROBLEM 3-1

Smith & Jones is a large metropolitan law firm that specializes in representing plaintiffs in personal injury litigation. Seven of the firm's attorneys and investigators committed massive fraud and bribery in personal injury trials, filing counterfeit claims and using false testimony. They pursued these nefarious goals variously by pressuring accident witnesses to commit perjury; bribing individuals who had not witnessed accidents to testify that they had; bribing witnesses whose testimony would be unfavorable not to testify; and creating false photographs, documents, and other physical evidence. The firm earned millions of dollars in contingency fees from these suits.

Wilson, an in-house investigator for the firm who participated in the fraud, resigned in 1994. Although he worked for the firm on an ad hoc basis after that date, none of the work he performed after he left involved fraud, bribery, or any other form of wrongdoing.

Johnson, a junior partner who participated in the fraud, also left the firm in 1994. Although he did no work for the firm after his departure, he continued to receive a percentage of the recovery in cases he had tried before he resigned from the firm.

Wilson and Johnson were indicted in 2000. Both claim that the prosecution is time-barred because they withdrew from the conspiracy when they left the firm in 1994, and the applicable statute of limitations is five years. Is either of them likely to prevail on the withdrawal defense?[23]

---

22. United States v. Steele, 685 F.2d 793, 803-804 (3d Cir. 1982).
23. Cf. United States v. Eisen, 974 F.2d 246 (2d Cir. 1992); United States v. Misle Bus & Equip. Co., 967 F.2d 1227 (8th Cir. 1992).

UNITED STATES v. JIMENEZ RECIO
537 U.S. 270 (2003)

Justice BREYER delivered the opinion of the Court.

We here consider the validity of a Ninth Circuit rule that a conspiracy ends automatically when the object of the conspiracy becomes impossible to achieve — when, for example, the Government frustrates a drug conspiracy's objective by seizing the drugs that its members have agreed to distribute. In our view, conspiracy law does not contain any such "automatic termination" rule.

I

In United States v. Cruz, 127 F.3d 791, 795 (9th Cir. 1997), the Ninth Circuit, following the language of an earlier case, United States v. Castro, 972 F.2d 1107, 1112 (9th Cir. 1992), wrote that a conspiracy terminates when "'there is affirmative evidence of abandonment, withdrawal, disavowal *or defeat of the object of the conspiracy*.'" It considered the conviction of an individual who, the Government had charged, joined a conspiracy (to distribute drugs) after the Government had seized the drugs in question. The Circuit found that the Government's seizure of the drugs guaranteed the "defeat" of the conspiracy's objective, namely, drug distribution. The Circuit held that the conspiracy had terminated with that "defeat," i.e., when the Government seized the drugs. Hence the individual, who had joined the conspiracy after that point, could not be convicted as a conspiracy member.

In this case the lower courts applied the *Cruz* rule to similar facts: On November 18, 1997, police stopped a truck in Nevada. They found, and seized, a large stash of illegal drugs. With the help of the truck's two drivers, they set up a sting. The Government took the truck to the drivers' destination, a mall in Idaho. The drivers paged a contact and described the truck's location. The contact said that he would call someone to get the truck. And three hours later, the two defendants, Francisco Jimenez Recio and Adrian Lopez-Meza, appeared in a car. Jimenez Recio drove away in the truck; Lopez-Meza drove the car away in a similar direction. Police stopped both vehicles and arrested both men.

A federal grand jury indicted Jimenez Recio, Lopez-Meza, and the two original truck drivers, charging them with having conspired, together and with others, to possess and to distribute unlawful drugs. A jury convicted all four. But the trial judge then decided that the jury instructions had been erroneous in respect to Jimenez Recio and Lopez-Meza. The judge noted that the Ninth Circuit, in *Cruz*, had held that the Government could not prosecute drug conspiracy defendants unless they had joined the conspiracy before the Government seized the drugs. That holding, as applied here, meant that the jury could not convict Jimenez Recio and Lopez-Meza unless the jury believed they had joined the conspiracy before the Nevada police stopped the truck and seized the drugs. The judge ordered a new trial where the jury would be instructed to that effect. The new jury convicted the two men once again. . . .

II

In *Cruz*, the Ninth Circuit held that a conspiracy continues "'until there is affirmative evidence of abandonment, withdrawal, disavowal or defeat of the object of the conspiracy.'" The critical portion of this statement is the last segment, that a conspiracy ends once there has been "defeat of [its] object." The Circuit's holdings make clear that the phrase means that the conspiracy ends through "defeat" when the Government intervenes, making the conspiracy's goals impossible to achieve, even if the conspirators do not know that the Government has intervened and are totally unaware that the conspiracy is bound to fail. In our view, this statement of the law is incorrect. A conspiracy does not automatically terminate simply because the Government, unbeknownst to some of the conspirators, has "defeated" the conspiracy's "object."

Two basic considerations convince us that this is the proper view of the law. First, the Ninth Circuit's rule is inconsistent with our own understanding of basic conspiracy law. The Court has repeatedly said that the essence of a conspiracy is "an agreement to commit an unlawful act." Iannelli v. United States, 420 U.S. 770, 777 (1975). That agreement is "a distinct evil," which "may exist and be punished whether or not the substantive crime ensues." Salinas v. United States, 522 U.S. 52, 65 (1997). The conspiracy poses a "threat to the public" over and above the threat of the commission of the relevant substantive crime — both because the "combination in crime makes more likely the commission of [other] crimes" and because it "decreases the probability that the individuals involved will depart from their path of criminality." Callanan v. United States, 364 U.S. 587, 593-594 (1961); see also United States v. Rabinowich, 238 U.S. 78, 88 (1915) (conspiracy "sometimes quite outweighs, in injury to the public, the mere commission of the contemplated crime"). Where police have frustrated a conspiracy's specific objective but conspirators (unaware of that fact) have neither abandoned the conspiracy nor withdrawn, these special conspiracy-related dangers remain. So too remains the essence of the conspiracy — the agreement to commit the crime. That being so, the Government's defeat of the conspiracy's objective will not necessarily and automatically terminate the conspiracy.

Second, the view we endorse today is the view of almost all courts and commentators but for the Ninth Circuit. No other Federal Court of Appeals has adopted the Ninth Circuit's rule. Three have explicitly rejected it. . . . One treatise, after surveying lower court conspiracy decisions, has concluded that "impossibility of success is not a defense." 2 LaFave & Scott, Substantive Criminal Law § 6.5, at 85. And the American Law Institute's Model Penal Code § 5.03, p. 384 (1985), would find that a conspiracy "terminates when the crime or crimes that are its object are committed" or when the relevant "agreement . . . is abandoned." It would not find "impossibility" a basis for termination. . . .

In tracing the origins of the statement of conspiracy law upon which the *Cruz* panel relied, we have found a 1982 Ninth Circuit case, United States v. Bloch, 696 F.2d 1213, in which the court, referring to an earlier case, United States v. Krasn, 614 F.2d 1229 (9th Cir. 1980), changed the language of the traditional conspiracy termination rule. *Krasn* said that a conspiracy is "'presumed to continue unless there is affirmative evidence that *the defendant* abandoned, withdrew from, or disavowed the conspiracy *or defeated its purpose*.'" Id., at 1236. The *Bloch* panel changed the grammatical structure. It said that "a conspiracy is presumed to continue until *there is* . . . defeat of the purposes of the conspiracy." 696 F.2d at 1215. Later Ninth Circuit cases apparently read the change to mean that a conspiracy terminates, not only when the *defendant* defeats its objective, but also when *someone else* defeats that objective, perhaps the police. In *Castro*, the panel followed *Bloch*. In *Cruz*, the panel quoted *Castro*. This history may help to explain the origin of the *Cruz* rule. But, since the Circuit's earlier cases nowhere give any reason for the critical change of language, they cannot help to justify it.

III

We conclude that the Ninth Circuit's conspiracy-termination law holding set forth in *Cruz* is erroneous. . . .

[Opinion by Justice STEVENS, concurring in part and dissenting in part, omitted.]

Notes and Questions

1. What is the rationale for upholding convictions of would-be conspirators who join an already defeated conspiracy? Does this stretch conspiracy law too far?

2. At what point would the conspiracy in *Jimenez Recio* come to an end?

3. Justice Rutledge's dissent in *Pinkerton* observed that Daniel was in prison when Walter committed some of the crimes. Was Daniel's imprisonment enough to terminate the conspiracy? If not, was the fact of his imprisonment tantamount to an effective withdrawal from the conspiracy?

4

Mail Fraud

I. INTRODUCTION

The mail fraud statute, 18 U.S.C. § 1341, has long provided federal prosecutors with a powerful weapon to combat an infinite variety of frauds. First enacted in 1872, the mail fraud statute enabled the government to prosecute a multitude of frauds — including loan sharking, real estate swindles, securities fraud, and credit card fraud — well before Congress enacted legislation that specifically addressed them.[1] Thus, a scheme to defraud need not contemplate the commission of an independent crime.[2]

The statute's broad proscription against using the mails to execute fraudulent schemes provides virtually open-ended liability, in part because the statute does not define the term "defraud." Nor have courts succeeded in providing useful guidance. "To try to delimit 'fraud' by definition," as one court explained, "would tend to reward subtle and ingenious circumvention and is not done."[3] Thus, the mail fraud statute "condemns conduct which fails to match the reflection of moral uprightness, of fundamental honesty, fair play and right dealing in the general and business life of members of society."[4]

The fraud itself need not be something that Congress can independently punish, moreover. The gist of the offense is the use of the mails to further fraudulent activity. Thus, by virtue of its power to regulate the use of the United States mails, Congress can forbid using the mails to execute a fraudulent scheme "whether it can forbid the scheme or not."[5] Schemes involving the mailing of fraudulent state tax returns are within the reach of the statute, for example, notwithstanding that Congress lacks jurisdiction over

---

1. See United States v. Maze, 414 U.S. 395, 405, 406 (1974) (Burger, C.J., dissenting).
2. United States v. Bush, 522 F.2d 641, 646 (7th Cir. 1975).
3. Foshay v. United States, 68 F.2d 205, 211 (8th Cir. 1933). Cf. Weiss v. United States, 122 F.2d 675, 681 (5th Cir. 1941) (the term "fraud" simply "needs no definition").
4. Blachly v. United States, 380 F.2d 665, 671 (5th Cir. 1967). At an early date the government invoked the mail fraud statute in a case in which the defendant had used the mails to obtain money through threats of murder or lesser bodily harm. The Supreme Court held that although "the obtaining of money by threats to injure or kill is more reprehensible than cheat, trick or false pretenses," extortionate threats are beyond the ambit of the mail fraud statute. Fasulo v. United States, 272 U.S. 620, 628 (1926). "[B]road as are the words 'to defraud,' they do not include threat and coercion through fear or force." Id.
5. Badders v. United States, 240 U.S. 391, 393 (1916).

state tax matters.[6] Not surprisingly, the breadth of the mail fraud statute has prompted criticism that it places too much power in the prosecutor's hands.

The wire fraud statute, 18 U.S.C. § 1343, is patterned after the mail fraud statute. Both laws prohibit use of a specific jurisdictional facility to execute a scheme to defraud. Because the statutes are in pari materia,[7] they are subject to the rule that they should be given parallel construction. Thus, principles developed in the mail fraud cases that appear in this chapter apply with equal force to wire fraud prosecutions, and vice versa.

II. SCHEMES TO DEFRAUD

A. INTENT TO DEFRAUD

UNITED STATES v. HAWKEY
148 F.3d 920 (8th Cir. 1998)

HEANEY, Circuit Judge.

Lester A. Hawkey, a sheriff in Minnehaha County, South Dakota, was charged in a forty-one count indictment for misusing funds belonging to the Minnehaha Sheriff's Department (MSD) and the Minnehaha County Sheriff and Deputies Association (MCSDA). A jury convicted Hawkey on all but two counts. . . .

I. BACKGROUND

In 1988, Hawkey, on behalf of the MSD and the MCSDA, entered into an agreement with Wildwood Productions, a benefit concert promoter,[8] to conduct annual benefit concerts each April. The proceeds of the annual concerts were purportedly intended to aid local youth programs. Prompted by Hawkey's representations, Wildwood's telemarketers solicited money from individuals and businesses in South Dakota and neighboring states for the purchase of tickets, donations, and/or to purchase advertising space in the concert program book. By United States mail, Wildwood sent statements or invoices to individuals and businesses who agreed to purchase tickets, advertise, or make donations. Individuals and businesses also sent their checks to either the MSD or MCSDA via the United States mail.

Wildwood's contracts with the MSD and MCSDA called for the establishment of two bank accounts. One account was to hold proceeds of ticket sales and the other was to hold the proceeds of advertisement sales. Shortly after the 1991 concert, Hawkey began using the concert accounts for a variety of personal and business expenses. While

---

6. See United States v. Mirabile, 503 F.2d 1065 (8th Cir. 1974). Cf. United States v. Sylvanus, 192 F.2d 96 (7th Cir. 1951) (mailing related to state-regulated insurance business).

7. "Statutes are considered to be in pari materia — to pertain to the same subject matter — when they relate to the same person or thing, or the same class of persons or things, or have the same purpose or object." 2 A. Sands, Statutes and Statutory Construction § 51.03, at 298 (4th ed. 1973).

8. Wildwood provides telemarketing operations, promotes ticket sales, solicits donations, and promotes advertisement sales for charitable organizations.

making some contributions to youth programs and charities, Hawkey spent a significant portion of the benefit concert proceeds for personal items. Hawkey also made deposits of business and personal funds to the concert account to replace depleted funds.

II. Sufficiency of the Evidence...

A. MAIL FRAUD

In Hawkey's challenge to the sufficiency of the evidence used to support his twenty-four count conviction for mail fraud, he argues that no one suffered any property loss and that there was no scheme or intent to defraud. Title 18 U.S.C. § 1341 prohibits the use of the mails to execute "any scheme or artifice to defraud, or for obtaining money or property by means of false or fraudulent pretenses, representations, or promises." Accordingly, to obtain a conviction for mail fraud under § 1341, the government must prove "(1) the existence of a scheme to defraud, and (2) the use of the mails . . . for purposes of executing the scheme." United States v. Manzer, 69 F.3d 222, 226 (8th Cir. 1995). The scheme "need not be fraudulent on its face but must involve some sort of fraudulent misrepresentations or omissions reasonably calculated to deceive persons of ordinary prudence and comprehension." United States v. Coyle, 63 F.3d 1239, 1243 (3d Cir. 1995). The term "property" extends to intangible property rights.

Hawkey argues that, because the businesses received their advertisements and ticket purchasers were able to attend the concerts, they were not deprived of money or property because they received what they paid for. We disagree. The record reveals that Hawkey solicited, or caused to be solicited, funds that were intended for charitable organizations; and, while some money was in fact paid to the charitable organizations, Hawkey converted most of the money for his own personal use. The businesses and concert-goers who responded to Hawkey's solicitations did not intend to merely purchase a ticket or advertising; they intended part of their payment as a contribution to a charitable organization.

Hawkey alternatively argues that there is insufficient evidence of a scheme to defraud because he did not control the telemarketers' solicitations, and the telemarketers did not represent to consumers that all of the concert proceeds would go to charity. Likewise, this argument is unavailing. A reasonable jury could have found that Hawkey intentionally engaged in a scheme by which money intended and solicited for charitable purposes was diverted from its designated charitable purpose to his personal benefit through false representations. The record reflects that the concerts were designed to raise money for charitable purposes; Hawkey knowingly diverted these funds for his personal benefit; and Hawkey failed to inform Wildwood, his accountant, the contributors, and the benefactors that he removed the funds for his personal benefit. Consequently, the jury permissibly concluded that there was a scheme in which Hawkey knowingly participated.

Hawkey contends that there was insufficient evidence to prove that he intended to defraud citizens responding to his solicitations. The jury was instructed that "to act with intent to defraud means to act knowingly and with the intent to deceive someone for the purpose of causing some financial loss . . . to another or bringing about some financial gain to oneself or another to the detriment of a third party." The jury found that Hawkey possessed the required intent to obtain personal gain from his misrepresentations and found him guilty of mail fraud. We conclude that this finding is supported by the record. . . .

V

For the foregoing reasons, we affirm the district court as to the sufficiency of the evidence supporting Hawkey's convictions. . . .

Notes and Questions

1. If the concerts were performed as promised and some of the money went to charities, the ticket purchasers received what they paid for. How were they defrauded? Is evidence that the concertgoers were satisfied with the performance relevant?

2. Suppose that a charity solicits contributions to feed malnourished children in an impoverished country overseas. Although 25 percent of the contributions are used for the stated purpose, 75 percent of the money the charity collects is used to pay overhead and administrative expenses. Has the charity committed fraud?[9]

NOTE ON FRAUD AND FALSE PRETENSES

The mail fraud statute proscribes devising "any scheme or artifice to defraud, or for obtaining money or property by means of false or fraudulent pretenses. . . ." In Durland v. United States,[10] the Supreme Court found that the concept of fraud encompasses a broader array of mischief than the crime of false pretenses. What differentiates fraud and false pretenses?

The crime of false pretenses is committed when the actor, intending to defraud, knowingly makes a false representation of a past or present fact to induce another to part with title to property. Promises and representations as to the future do not qualify under most false pretenses statutes. Thus, falsely stating that a gem has been appraised at $1,000 constitutes a false representation for purposes of false pretenses liability, but falsely stating that the gem will appreciate in value over the next year does not. Nor do false promises historically fall within the ambit of false pretenses, even though the promisor may be viewed as misrepresenting a fact (i.e., promisor's state of mind). Thus, the law of false pretenses is fraught with technicalities.

Fraud, in contrast, is a fluid concept, and courts have been unwilling to confine the term to a single, definite meaning. Notwithstanding that reluctance to pin the term down, a good working definition might be as follows: Fraud consists of an effort to gain

---

9. Cf. United States v. Lyons, 453 F.3d 1222 (9th Cir. 2006) (while telemarketers' failure to disclose that they keep 80-90 percent of contributions they receive is not per se fraudulent, undisclosed high fundraising costs may be evidence of fraud if fundraisers make misleading statements about how charitable contributions will be spent).

10. 161 U.S. 306 (1896).

an undue advantage or to bring about some harm through misrepresentation or breach of duty. Because we are dealing with a relatively elastic concept, misrepresentations that have historically been excluded from the realm of false pretenses — e.g., false statements of opinion and false promises relating to future events — may constitute fraudulent representations in contexts such as the mail fraud statute. Thus, a misrepresentation that the promisor will reset the gem free of charge and that the gem will thereby appreciate in value is fraud if it is made with the purpose of harming the promisee or obtaining an undeserved advantage.

PROBLEM 4-1

A-1 Office Supply sells stationery and other office supplies over the telephone. A-1's sales representatives solicit purchases through scripted sales pitches that contain blatant misrepresentations. They include such statements as "I'm a good friend of your office manager and he asked me to call your purchasing agent" (the salesperson does not know the manager), or "Due to a clerical error, we ordered excess inventory that we need to clear out in a hurry, so I can offer you some really good buys on national brand name supplies" (there is no excess inventory). The sales representatives readily admit that they use these kinds of devices to "get by" secretaries who answer the phone and to "get the purchasing agent to listen to our pitch." The merchandise they sell is of good quality, and they always discuss price and quality honestly with the customer. The merchandise is normally delivered by mail.

Do these sales practices constitute fraud under the mail fraud statute? How, if at all, do the misrepresentations differ from those in *Hawkey*? Are intent to deceive and intent to defraud necessarily the same thing?[11]

NOTE ON MATERIALITY

Although the mail and wire fraud statutes contain no express materiality requirements, courts have traditionally assumed that false or fraudulent representations must be material. In Neder v. United States,[12] the Supreme Court held that materiality is required. The Court relied on the common law understanding of what constitutes fraud in reaching this result. "It is a well-established rule of construction that '[w]here Congress uses terms that have accumulated settled meaning under . . . the common law, a court must infer, unless the statute otherwise dictates, that Congress means to incorporate the established meaning of those terms.'"[13] Because "the common law could not have conceived of 'fraud' without proof of materiality"[14] and the statutes do not dictate to the contrary, Congress must have implicitly intended to incorporate the common law meaning of fraud, including the requirement of materiality, into the statutes.

The Court relied on the Restatement (Second) of Torts for a definition of materiality. A statement is material if:

---

11. Cf. United States v. Regent Office Supply, 421 F.2d 1174 (2d Cir. 1970).
12. 527 U.S. 1 (1999).
13. Id. at 21.
14. Id. at 22.

(a) a reasonable man would attach importance to its existence or nonexistence in determining his choice of action in the transaction in question; or

(b) the maker of the representation knows or has reason to know that its recipient regards or is likely to regard the matter as important in determining his choice of action, although a reasonable man would not so regard it.[15]

LUSTIGER v. UNITED STATES
386 F.2d 132 (9th Cir. 1967)

HAMLEY, Circuit Judge.

[Lustiger formed the Lake Mead Land and Water Company, which bought or acquired options to buy approximately 64 sections of land in Mohave County, Arizona. The company subdivided the sections and offered them for sale to the public, calling the unincorporated subdivision "Lake Mead City." Between September 1960 and May 1962 the company advertised the land in newspapers and other publications across the country. Individuals who responded to the advertisements received an "Investor's Kit" that contained, among other things, a 32-page color brochure. The contents of the brochure formed the basis for Lustiger's mail fraud indictment. Following a nonjury trial, the district court convicted him of 17 counts of mail fraud. Lustiger appealed.]

The advertising brochure which Lustiger had the company distribute, entitled "Join Us for Pleasure and Profit at Lake Mead City," contained numerous statements describing the asserted advantages of Lake Mead City. In addition, the brochure contained many photographs purporting to depict scenes in the area. Sales generated by this extensive advertising program continued until May, 1962. At that time the advertising campaign was discontinued as the result of litigation over the company's title to the land. By March 10, 1962, three thousand lots had been sold.

Paragraphs 7 through 11 of Count I of the indictment, made applicable to all counts, charge that Lustiger's advertising materials contained misleading, deceptive, false and fraudulent pretenses, representations and promises concerning the property. These paragraphs further charge that these alleged misleading, deceptive, false and fraudulent pretenses were part of a scheme by Lustiger to defraud land purchasers. . . .

One of the categories of alleged misleading, deceptive and false statements contained in Lustiger's advertising materials relates to the availability of water, both for recreational and domestic uses. The color brochure contains numerous photographs, most of which depict water scenes on or around Lake Mead. The lake is said to be only five miles from Lake Mead City. Other photographs show small lakes and ponds, purportedly located within the boundaries of Lake Mead City. One body of water is colorfully described as the "Favorite swimming hole." Another picture shows a large metal water tank lying horizontally alongside a windmill, with the printed declaration: "IMPORTANT! Plenty of Water." A vicinity map "Depicting Lake Mead City Area," distributed by Lustiger, shows two wells, three springs and a water pipe line.

Lustiger does not deny that these representations were made, nor does he question the materiality of the facts presented. He argues, however, that the court's presumptive

---

15. Restatement (Second) of Torts § 538 (1976).

finding that the representations were misleading, deceptive and false was not supported by the requisite degree of proof.

Our examination of Lustiger's advertising materials reveals that the statements, photographs and maps, unaccompanied by true statements concerning the lack of available water, could reasonably have led a person of average intelligence and experience to believe that all parcels offered for sale had reasonable access to a water supply.[16] While the statements in the advertising materials may not have been literally false, taken as a whole they were fraudulently misleading and deceptive.

It is true that, measured by a straight line, Lake Mead is only five miles from the boundary of Lake Mead City. However, Lustiger did not reveal that by existing roads Lake Mead is fifteen miles from the nearest and forty miles from the farthest Lake Mead City unit. Moreover, most of the units did not have access presently available by ordinary motor vehicles. Thus, a purchaser may in fact have a long, if not impossible, route to travel to enjoy the benefits of Lake Mead.

Likewise, all the water scenes in Lustiger's brochure were taken within the boundaries of Lake Mead City. Undisclosed to the prospective purchaser, however, was the fact that none of the pictured bodies of water were on land owned or optioned by Lustiger's company. These photographs were taken at the Diamond Bar Ranch, which is near the center of the general area where Lake Mead City is located. There was evidence that a few children had used the pictured water pond for swimming. The foreman of this ranch testified, however, that the "Favorite swimming hole" depicted in the brochure was not a swimming hole but was a dirt stock tank for stock water with perhaps two feet of mud on its bottom.

The vicinity map depicting several sources of water for domestic use follows a similar pattern of deception. Lustiger failed to disclose that the only source of water on the property owned by the company and available to purchasers during the period charged in the indictment was the Clearwater Well, located in the far northwestern corner of the Lake Mead City units, a distance of twenty-eight miles from some subdivision units.[17] In order to obtain water for domestic use, practically all lot purchasers would have to haul their water from the Clearwater Well and provide storage on their own lots. Moreover, as noted above, most of the subdivision units were not accessible by ordinary motor vehicles. . . .

The story is the same with regard to other matters of interest to one considering the purchase of property in a rural subdivision. The evidence is overwhelming that Lustiger's advertising materials were in some respects false and, apart from falsity were, when considered as a whole, fraudulently deceptive and misleading, exhibiting an intent and purpose to defraud.

---

16. This is not to say that representations and concealments will necessarily pass muster if they do not deceive a person of average intelligence and experience. In Lemons v. United States, 9 Cir., 278 F.2d 369, 373, this court said:

> It is immaterial whether only the most gullible would have been deceived by this technique. Section 1341 protects the naive as well as the worldly-wise, and the former are more in need of protection than the latter. United States v. Sylvanus, 7 Cir., 192 F.2d 96, 105. As a matter of fact, ". . . the lack of guile on the part of those solicited may itself point with persuasion to the fraudulent character of the artifice." Norman v. United States, 6 Cir., 100 F.2d 905, 907.

17. After the indictment was returned the company acquired another well and built a water tank. It also obtained options on other water resources.

If a scheme is devised with the intent to defraud, and the mails are used in executing the scheme, the fact that there is no misrepresentation of a single existing fact is immaterial. It is only necessary to prove that it is a scheme reasonably calculated to deceive, and that the mail service of the United States was used and intended to be used in the execution of the scheme.

Moreover, deceitful statements of half truths or the concealment of material facts is actual fraud violative of the mail fraud statute. In addition, as the Tenth Circuit said in Gusow v. United States, 10 Cir., 347 F.2d 755, 756, the deception need not be premised upon verbalized words alone. The arrangement of the words, or the circumstances in which they are used may convey the false and deceptive appearance.

Lustiger argues that the above-mentioned advertising statements constitute "seller's puffing" and are not indictable under the mail fraud statute. While it is true that exaggeration within reasonable bounds under the circumstances will not support a finding of a scheme to defraud, a substantial deception, as evidenced here, is sufficient. Moreover, here prospective buyers were expected to rely almost entirely on the advertising materials in making their purchase. Only a few buyers saw the property before signing the purchase contract. Under these circumstances courts cannot be blind to the increased potential for a fraudulent scheme to trap the unwary. . . .

We conclude that the evidence is sufficient to support a finding that Lustiger intentionally engaged in a scheme to defraud. . . .

Affirmed.

Notes and Questions

1. In *Lustiger*, why did the making of literally true statements amount to fraud? When, if ever, will literally false statements not be fraudulent?

2. Would it have made any difference in *Lustiger* if only the credulous would have purchased land in reliance on the material contained in the Investor's Kit? [18]

3. What is the difference between puffing and fraud?

4. Did the investors in *Lustiger* act prudently? Are there steps they could have taken to avoid being defrauded? If so, should fraud laws be used to protect people who are capable of protecting themselves but are careless in their business dealings? If reasonable investors can avoid obvious frauds by using common sense, should the criminal law help those who won't help themselves? [19]

---

18. Compare United States v. Coffman, 94 F.3d 330 (7th Cir. 1996), with United States v. Brown, 79 F.3d 1550 (11th Cir. 1996).

19. Cf. United States v. Svete, 556 F.3d 1157 (11th Cir. 2009)

B. PROTECTED INTERESTS

1. Intangible Rights Theory

UNITED STATES v. GEORGE
477 F.2d 508 (7th Cir. 1973)

CUMMING, Circuit Judge.

[Three defendants were charged with mail fraud in connection with a scheme to defraud Zenith Radio Corporation. The scheme consisted of a plan under which Greensphan, a cabinet supplier, paid Yonan, Zenith's purchasing agent, kickbacks to ensure that Zenith would continue to purchase Greensphan's cabinets. The kickbacks were paid through George, who did business as A & G Woodworking Co. All three were convicted and appealed.]

The evidence brought forward at the trial disclosed a novel scheme. Yonan went to work for Zenith in 1961 and was a buyer in the cabinet division of Zenith's Purchasing Department. He had "primary responsibility" for negotiating with cabinet vendors, and, in the words of his immediate supervisor, that meant "his responsibility was to send out the blueprints and gather in quotations, and where the price was too high, to try to negotiate it down to a proper level." Of course, the quotations Yonan negotiated were reviewed by his superiors and by other departments of Zenith. In 1966, Yonan was given the responsibility for finding and negotiating with a supplier of cabinets for Zenith's newly conceived "Circle of Sound" product. His responsibility also included arranging for delivery and monitoring the quality of the cabinets. His friend since the mid-fifties, defendant Greensphan, the owner of Accurate Box Corporation ("Accurate"), was tapped as the supplier. During the indictment years, Accurate was the sole bidder on and supplier of these cabinets. Yonan's supervisor thought Accurate's prices to be fair and reasonable, but in the absence of other bidders, could not conclude they were competitive. Zenith normally allowed its suppliers a maximum of 10% profit, and Accurate's prices reflected that profit margin. The Circle of Sound product proved to be a tremendous financial success. . . .

Without recounting any actual threat by Yonan, Greensphan testified that he agreed to pay Yonan $1 per cabinet kickback on the model 565 Circle of Sound unit and later per cabinet kickbacks on other models because he was afraid he was otherwise going to lose Zenith's business. Yonan assertedly told him that "everybody and their uncle would like to get into this to manufacture this unit." He stated that Yonan's requests for such payments originated in October 1967. When he asked Yonan how the kickbacks were to be paid, Greensphan was told to pay A & G Woodworking Co.'s commission invoices. Greensphan never related these events to anyone at Zenith. He had known defendant George since 1960. He denied inflating any quotations to cover monies paid to Yonan.

Commencing in December 1967, Accurate received commission invoices from defendant George's A & G Woodworking Co. even though neither George nor A & G Woodworking Co. provided any services to Accurate. Accurate paid these invoices on the basis of a commission per unit on the types of models it shipped to Zenith.[20]

---

20. On two Circle of Sound models, the commission was $1.00 per unit shipped, and on two others it was $.75 and $.20 per unit respectively.

Greensphan also cashed a $3,000 Accurate check payable to himself and gave the proceeds to George because he was fearful of losing Zenith's business. To conceal the set fee per unit commission on the cabinets shipped, Accurate's records showed the payments to George's company as 3.4% on monies Accurate received from Zenith rather than as fixed sums on each cabinet. However, on these records the total prices of the cabinets shipped to Zenith were not correct, but were altered to make the commissions correspond to 3.4% thereof. From December 1967 until December 1970, Accurate paid George's company in excess of $300,000 in commissions. During the period in which Greensphan's company was paying the commission invoices of George's company, the latter paid Yonan kickbacks in excess of $100,000 through checks made out by George.

The Government's theory, credited by the jury, was that the kickbacks to Yonan were accomplished by Greensphan's payments of George's company's fictitious commission invoices, with George then acting as a kickback conduit to Yonan. In this connection, it should be noted that in 1969 or 1970, Yonan asked Greensphan's company's controller for a report of the total commission payments then made by that company to George. Shipping quantities on at least one A & G invoice were confirmed to Yonan by Accurate's plant superintendent.

Zenith had a conflict-of-interest policy providing that no gratuities of any nature were to be bestowed on its Purchasing Department employees by suppliers. Yonan twice signed documents embodying that policy, which was annually brought to the attention of all suppliers of Zenith through letters sent out to them. Greensphan admitted receiving these letters during the period of time he was channeling the payments to Yonan.

A number of Zenith's employees testified that Yonan did not request preferential treatment for Greensphan and his company and that they had no knowledge of Yonan providing such treatment for them. It appears Yonan was insistent on quality and efficiency from Accurate.

EVIDENTIARY SUFFICIENCY OF A SCHEME TO DEFRAUD

[The defendants argued that there was no fraud because "the kickbacks were never shown to come out of Zenith's pockets, as opposed to Greensphan's, because Yonan was never shown to provide or secure any special services for Greensphan and his company, and because Zenith was never shown to be dissatisfied with Accurate's cabinets or prices."]

Since the gravamen of the offense is a "scheme to defraud," it is unnecessary that the Government allege or prove that the victim of the scheme was actually defrauded or suffered a loss. If there was intent on the part of a schemer to deprive Zenith of Yonan's honest and loyal services in the form of his giving Greensphan preferential treatment, it is simply beside the point that Yonan may not have had to (or had occasion to) exert special influence in favor of Greensphan or that Zenith was satisfied with Accurate's product and prices. And it is of no moment whether or not the kickback money actually came from Zenith. Thus the district court correctly charged the jury that it was unnecessary for the Government to prove "that anyone actually be defrauded." Contrary to defendant's contentions, the evidence hardly shows that it was impossible for Yonan to exercise favoritism toward Greensphan. As the Court noted in Shushan v. United States, 117 F.2d 110, 115 (5th Cir. 1941): "The fact that the official who is bribed is only one of several and could not award the contract by himself does not change the character of the scheme where he is expected to have influence enough to secure the end in view." In our view the evidence shows that Yonan did have opportunities to give Greensphan preferential treatment, particularly by avoiding the solicitation of potential competitors. Of course, the actual exercise of any such opportunity by a person in Yonan's position may be practically undetectable.

Furthermore, even if Yonan never intended to give Greensphan preferential treatment, and the Government does not argue that the evidence was sufficient to support a conclusion that he did, the defendants' argument still misses the mark. The evidence shows Yonan actually defrauded Zenith. We need not accept the Government's far-ranging argument that anytime an agent secretly profits from his agency he has committed criminal fraud. Not every breach of every fiduciary duty works a criminal fraud. But here Yonan's duty was to negotiate the best price possible for Zenith or at least to apprise Zenith that Greensphan was willing to sell his cabinets for substantially less money. Not only did Yonan secretly earn a profit from his agency, but also he deprived Zenith of material knowledge that Greensphan would accept less profit. There was a very real and tangible harm to Zenith in losing the discount or losing the opportunity to bargain with a most relevant fact before it. . . . Here the fraud consisted in Yonan's holding himself out to be a loyal employee, acting in Zenith's best interests, but actually not giving his honest and faithful services, to Zenith's real detriment.

No refuge can be taken in Zenith's policy "normally" to allow suppliers a 10% profit and in Accurate's prices being within that margin. Nothing would have prevented Zenith from bargaining with Accurate for a lesser profit margin, and it would be unrealistic to presume that Zenith would consider the fact of better than $100,000 in actual kickbacks to its buyer — over $300,000 in agreed-to-kickbacks — to be immaterial in its dealings with Greensphan. It is preposterous to claim that Zenith would have spurned such a discount if offered.

In this case, whether Zenith was to be deprived of Yonan's honest and faithful performance of his duties to the extent of his secretly profiting from his agency and concealing knowledge of the availability of that material sum from Zenith, or to the further extent of his meriting the payments which he received, a fraud within the reach of the mail fraud statute would be present. The statute requires the existence of a scheme to perpetrate this fraud, and the question of evidentiary sufficiency boils down to whether the Government has proven that the defendants contemplated that Zenith suffer the loss of Yonan's honest and loyal services.

Indubitably the evidence showed a "scheme." The critical element is fraudulent intent. Each of the defendants asserts that there was insufficient evidence as to his intent to defraud Zenith of Yonan's loyalty and honesty, but we conclude to the contrary.

As to Yonan, his undisclosed receipt of the kickbacks by itself warrants a finding that he intended to defraud Zenith of his honest and loyal services. His employment duty was to negotiate the best possible deal for Zenith, or at least to apprise Zenith that Greensphan would be satisfied with a lesser profit margin. He is presumed to know that he could not personally profit by any decrease in price he could negotiate with Greensphan and that any such decrease should be made available to Zenith. In sum, the jury could hardly help but infer that Yonan intended to do exactly what he did. Hence it was not necessary for the jury to conclude that when Yonan received the kickbacks, he intended to defraud Zenith further by giving Greensphan the favored treatment for which Yonan was paid.

The evidence also supports a finding that George contemplated Zenith would be defrauded of Yonan's honest and faithful services. George billed Greensphan for "commissions" on the Circle of Sound cabinets Greensphan sold Zenith though he provided no services to Greensphan. Checks totalling about $100,000, approximately one-third of the commissions, then passed from George to Yonan, with George apparently retaining an unmerited two-thirds. That George's payments to Yonan had their source in Greensphan's commission payments is shown by Yonan's call to Greensphan's accountant asking about the commission sums paid to George by Greensphan and by Yonan's checking the shipping quantities on an A & G invoice with Greensphan's plant superintendent. George can hardly claim to have been an unwitting conduit for the payments from Greensphan to Yonan. He submitted spurious invoices based on the number of cabinets Greensphan shipped to Zenith and made an enormous profit in the process. He, Greensphan, and Yonan were mutual friends at the inception of the scheme, and, at least on one occasion, were observed together in Accurate's plant. He must have known Yonan's position at Zenith and the relationship between Yonan and Greensphan. If the substantial payments from Greensphan to Yonan were not designed to compromise Yonan's fiduciary duties to Zenith, why were they not made directly and openly instead of through George and disguised as commission payments to him? Why would the transaction be so shrouded in secrecy and spuriousness if Yonan could legitimately make and hide from Zenith an enormous profit from his employment position or curry Greensphan's favor? It would take a man of incredible naivete to play George's role in this scheme and not understand that Yonan was giving less than full measure of loyalty and honesty to Zenith. At least George must have known that some actual injury to Zenith was the reasonably probable result of this scheme. . . .

Thus we conclude that there was sufficient evidence for the jury to find that each defendant intended to defraud Zenith. . . .

Judgments affirmed.

Notes and Questions

1. The court in *George* noted that Zenith had a conflict of interest policy and that Yonan was aware of it. How important is that? Does it matter whether Greensphan and George knew about the policy?[21]

2. The facts in *George* indicate that Zenith received what it expected to get. The product supplied was satisfactory, the normal quality control mechanisms were in place, and the price Zenith paid Accurate was within the normal profit margin for Zenith's suppliers. Where is the fraud?

---

21. Cf. Restatement (Second) of Agency § 387 (1958) ("Unless otherwise agreed, an agent is subject to a duty to his principal to act solely for the benefit of the principal in all matters connected with his agency.").

2. Money or Property Requirement

CARPENTER v. UNITED STATES
484 U.S. 19 (1987)

Justice WHITE delivered the opinion of the Court. . . .

I

In 1981, [R. Foster] Winans became a reporter for the Wall Street Journal (the Journal) and in the summer of 1982 became one of the two writers of a daily column, "Heard on the Street." That column discussed selected stocks or groups of stocks, giving positive and negative information about those stocks and taking "a point of view with respect to investment in the stocks that it reviews." Winans regularly interviewed corporate executives to put together interesting perspectives on the stocks that would be highlighted in upcoming columns, but, at least for the columns at issue here, none contained corporate inside information or any "hold for release" information. Because of the "Heard" column's perceived quality and integrity, it had the potential of affecting the price of the stocks which it examined. The District Court concluded on the basis of testimony presented at trial that the "Heard" column "does have an impact on the market, difficult though it may be to quantify in any particular case."

The official policy and practice at the Journal was that prior to publication, the contents of the column were the Journal's confidential information. Despite the rule, with which Winans was familiar, he entered into a scheme in October 1983 with Peter Brant and petitioner Felis, both connected with the Kidder Peabody brokerage firm in New York City, to give them advance information as to the timing and contents of the "Heard" column. This permitted Brant and Felis and another conspirator, David Clark, a client of Brant, to buy or sell based on the probable impact of the column on the market. Profits were to be shared. The conspirators agreed that the scheme would not affect the journalistic purity of the "Heard" column, and the District Court did not find that the contents of any of the articles were altered to further the profit potential of petitioners' stock-trading scheme. Over a four-month period, the brokers made prepublication trades on the basis of information given them by Winans about the contents of some 27 "Heard" columns. The net profits from these trades were about $690,000.

In November 1983, correlations between the "Heard" articles and trading in the Clark and Felis accounts were noted at Kidder Peabody and inquiries began. Brant and Felis denied knowing anyone at the Journal and took steps to conceal the trades. Later, the Securities and Exchange Commission began an investigation. Questions were met by denials both by the brokers at Kidder Peabody and by Winans at the Journal. As the investigation progressed, the conspirators quarreled, and on March 29, 1984, Winans and Carpenter went to the SEC and revealed the entire scheme. This indictment and a bench trial followed. Brant, who had pleaded guilty under a plea agreement, was a witness for the Government.

[Both the district court and the court of appeals found that Winans' misappropriation of prepublication information violated § 10(b) of the Securities Exchange Act. The

Supreme Court was evenly divided on the question whether Winans and his confederates violated the securities laws and for that reason affirmed their convictions on those counts of the indictment.]

II

Petitioners assert that their activities were not a scheme to defraud the Journal within the meaning of the mail and wire fraud statutes; and that in any event, they did not obtain any "money or property" from the Journal, which is a necessary element of the crime under our decision last Term in McNally v. United States, 483 U.S. 350 (1987). We are unpersuaded by either submission and address the latter first.

We held in *McNally* that the mail fraud statute does not reach "schemes to defraud citizens of their intangible rights to honest and impartial government," id., at 355, and that the statute is "limited in scope to the protection of property rights." Id. at 360. Petitioners argue that the Journal's interest in prepublication confidentiality for the "Heard" columns is no more than an intangible consideration outside the reach of § 1341; nor does that law, it is urged, protect against mere injury to reputation. This is not a case like *McNally*, however. The Journal, as Winans' employer, was defrauded of much more than its contractual right to his honest and faithful service, an interest too ethereal in itself to fall within the protection of the mail fraud statute, which "had its origin in the desire to protect individual property rights." *McNally*, supra, at 358, n.8. Here, the object of the scheme was to take the Journal's confidential business information — the publication schedule and contents of the "Heard" column — and its intangible nature does not make it any less "property" protected by the mail and wire fraud statutes. *McNally* did not limit the scope of § 1341 to tangible as distinguished from intangible property rights.

Both courts below expressly referred to the Journal's interest in the confidentiality of the contents and timing of the "Heard" column as a property right, and we agree with that conclusion. Confidential business information has long been recognized as property. "Confidential information acquired or compiled by a corporation in the course and conduct of its business is a species of property to which the corporation has the exclusive right and benefit, and which a court of equity will protect through the injunctive process or other appropriate remedy." 3 W. Fletcher, Cyclopedia of Law of Private Corporations § 857.1, p. 260 (rev. ed. 1986). The Journal had a property right in keeping confidential and making exclusive use, prior to publication, of the schedule and contents of the "Heard" columns. As the Court has observed before:

> [N]ews matter, however little susceptible of ownership or dominion in the absolute sense, is stock in trade, to be gathered at the cost of enterprise, organization, skill, labor, and money, and to be distributed and sold to those who will pay money for it, as for any other merchandise. International News Service v. Associated Press, 248 U.S. 215, 236 (1918).

Petitioners' arguments that they did not interfere with the Journal's use of the information or did not publicize it and deprive the Journal of the first public use of it miss the point. The confidential information was generated from the business and the business had a right to decide how to use it prior to disclosing it to the public. Petitioners cannot successfully contend based on *Associated Press* that a scheme to defraud requires a monetary loss, such as giving the information to a competitor; it is sufficient that the Journal has been deprived of its right to exclusive use of the information, for exclusivity is an important aspect of confidential business information and most private property for that matter.

We cannot accept petitioners' further argument that Winans' conduct in revealing prepublication information was no more than a violation of workplace rules and did not amount to fraudulent activity that is proscribed by the mail fraud statute. Sections 1341 and 1343 reach any scheme to deprive another of money or property by means of false or fraudulent pretenses, representations, or promises. As we observed last Term in *McNally*, the words "to defraud" in the mail fraud statute have the "common understanding" of "'wronging one in his property rights by dishonest methods or schemes,' and 'usually signify the deprivation of something of value by trick, deceit, chicane or overreaching.'" 483 U.S. at 358. The concept of "fraud" includes the act of embezzlement, which is "'the fraudulent appropriation to one's own use of the money or goods entrusted to one's care by another.'" Grin v. Shine, 187 U.S. 181, 189 (1902). The District Court found that Winans' undertaking at the Journal was not to reveal prepublication information about his column, a promise that became a sham when in violation of his duty he passed along to his co-conspirators confidential information belonging to the Journal, pursuant to an ongoing scheme to share profits from trading in anticipation of the "Heard" column's impact on the stock market. . . . As the New York courts have recognized, "It is well established, as a general proposition, that a person who acquires special knowledge or information by virtue of a confidential or fiduciary relationship with another is not free to exploit that knowledge or information for his own personal benefit but must account to his principal for any profits derived therefrom." Diamond v. Oreamuno, 248 N.E.2d 910, 912 (N.Y. 1969); see also Restatement (Second) of Agency §§ 388, Comment c, 396(c) (1958).

We have little trouble in holding that the conspiracy here to trade on the Journal's confidential information is not outside the reach of the mail and wire fraud statutes, provided the other elements of the offenses are satisfied. The Journal's business information that it intended to be kept confidential was its property; the declaration to that effect in the employee manual merely removed any doubts on that score and made the finding of specific intent to defraud that much easier. Winans continued in the employ of the Journal, appropriating its confidential business information for his own use, all the while pretending to perform his duty of safeguarding it. In fact, he told his editors twice about leaks of confidential information not related to the stock-trading scheme, demonstrating both his knowledge that the Journal viewed information concerning the "Heard" column as confidential and his deceit as he played the role of a loyal employee. Furthermore, the District Court's conclusion that each of the petitioners acted with the required specific intent to defraud is strongly supported by the evidence.

Lastly, we reject the submission that using the wires and the mail to print and send the Journal to its customers did not satisfy the requirement that those mediums be used to execute the scheme at issue. The courts below were quite right in observing that circulation of the "Heard" column was not only anticipated but an essential part of the scheme. Had the column not been made available to Journal customers, there would have been no effect on stock prices and no likelihood of profiting from the information leaked by Winans.

The judgment below is affirmed.

Notes and Questions

1. The Court in *McNally* adopted the "money or property" requirement without defining *property.* Is that apt to be problematic? Does *Carpenter* clear up the ambiguity?[22]

2. Could the conviction in *George* be sustained after *McNally* and *Carpenter*? How would *McNally* and *Carpenter* change the focus?

3. To set the stage for the ruling in *Carpenter*, the Court in *McNally* had to give the text of § 1341 a relatively cramped construction. The majority in *McNally* interpreted the statutory language as follows:

> After 1909, . . . the mail fraud statute criminalized schemes or artifices "to defraud" or "for obtaining money or property by means of false or fraudulent pretenses, representation, or promises. . . ." Because the two phrases identifying the proscribed schemes appear in the disjunctive, it is arguable that they are to be construed independently and that the money-or-property requirement of the latter phrase does not limit schemes to defraud to those aimed at causing deprivation of money or property. This is the approach that has been taken by each of the Courts of Appeals that has addressed the issue: schemes to defraud include those designed to deprive individuals, the people or the government of intangible rights, such as the right to have public officials perform their duties honestly.
>
> As the Court long ago stated, however, the words "to defraud" commonly refer "to wronging one in his property rights by dishonest methods or schemes," and "usually signify the deprivation of something of value by trick, deceit, chicane or overreaching." Hammerschmidt v. United States, 265 U.S. 182, 188 (1924).[23] The codification of the holding in *Durland* in 1909 does not indicate that Congress was departing from this common understanding. As we see it, adding the second phrase simply made it unmistakable that the statute reached false promises and misrepresentations as to the future as well as other frauds involving money or property. . . .
>
> . . . Rather than construe the statute in a manner that leaves its outer boundaries ambiguous and involves the Federal Government in setting standards of disclosure and good government for local and state officials, we read 1341 as limited in scope to the protection of property rights. . . .

Justice Stevens, joined in part by Justice O'Connor, registered a stinging rebuke to the majority's methodology as well as its holding.

> The mail fraud statute sets forth three separate prohibitions. It prohibits the use of the United States mails for the purpose of executing
>
> > [1] *any* scheme or artifice to defraud, [2] *or* for obtaining money or property by means of false or fraudulent pretenses, representations, or promises, [3] *or* to sell,

---

22. Cf. John C. Coffee, Jr., Hush!: The Criminal Status of Confidential Information After *McNally* and *Carpenter* and the Enduring Problem of Overcriminalization, 26 Am. Crim. L. Rev. 121 (1988).

23. *Hammerschmidt* concerned the scope of the predecessor of 18 U.S.C. § 371, which makes criminal any conspiracy "to defraud the United States, or any agency thereof in any manner or for any purpose." *Hammerschmidt* indicates, in regard to that statute, that while "[t]o conspire to defraud the United States means primarily to cheat the Government out of property or money, . . . it also means to interfere with or obstruct one of its lawful governmental functions by deceit, craft or trickery, or at least by means that are dishonest." 265 U.S. at 188. Other cases have held that § 371 reaches conspiracies other than those directed at property interests. . . . However, we believe that this broad construction of § 371 is based on a consideration not applicable to the mail fraud statute.

dispose of, loan, exchange, alter, give away, distribute, supply, or furnish or procure for unlawful use any counterfeit, or spurious coin, obligation, security, or other article, or anything represented to be or intimated or held out to be such counterfeit or spurious article. . . . 18 U.S.C. § 1341.

As the language makes clear, each of these restrictions is independent. One can violate the second clause — obtaining money or property by false pretenses — even though one does not violate the third clause — counterfeiting. Similarly, one can violate the first clause — devising a scheme or artifice to defraud — without violating the counterfeiting provision. Until today it was also obvious that one could violate the first clause by devising a scheme or artifice to defraud, even though one did not violate the second clause by seeking to obtain money or property from his victim through false pretenses. Every court to consider the matter had so held. Yet, today, the Court, for all practical purposes, rejects this longstanding construction of the statute by imposing a requirement that a scheme or artifice to defraud does not violate the statute unless its purpose is to defraud someone of money or property. I am at a loss to understand the source or justification for this holding. Certainly no canon of statutory construction requires us to ignore the plain language of the provision.

Which of the two readings of § 1341 seems most persuasive and why?

CLEVELAND v. UNITED STATES
531 U.S. 12 (2000)

Justice GINSBURG delivered the opinion of the Court.
This case presents the question whether the federal mail fraud statute, 18 U.S.C. § 1341, reaches false statements made in an application for a state license. . . .

OPINION OF THE COURT

video poker machines

I

Louisiana law allows certain businesses to operate video poker machines. The State itself, however, does not run such machinery. The law requires prospective owners of video poker machines to apply for a license from the State. The licenses are not transferable and must be renewed annually. To qualify for a license, an applicant must meet suitability requirements designed to ensure that licensees have good character and fiscal integrity.

In 1992, Fred Goodson and his family formed a limited partnership, Truck Stop Gaming, Ltd. (TSG), in order to participate in the video poker business at their truck stop in Slidell, Louisiana. Cleveland, a New Orleans lawyer, assisted Goodson in preparing TSG's application for a video poker license. The application required TSG to identify its partners and to submit personal financial statements for all partners. It also required TSG to affirm that the listed partners were the sole beneficial owners of the business and that no partner held an interest in the partnership merely as an agent or nominee, or intended to transfer the interest in the future.

TSG's application identified Goodson's adult children, Alex and Maria, as the sole beneficial owners of the partnership. It also showed that Goodson and Cleveland's law firm had loaned Alex and Maria all initial capital for the partnership and that Goodson was TSG's general manager. In May 1992, the State approved the application and issued a license. TSG successfully renewed the license in 1993, 1994, and 1995 pursuant to La. Admin. Code, tit. 42, § 2405(B)(3). Each renewal application identified no ownership interests other than those of Alex and Maria.

In 1996, the FBI discovered evidence that Cleveland and Goodson had participated in a scheme to bribe state legislators to vote in a manner favorable to the video poker industry. The Government charged Cleveland and Goodson with multiple counts of money laundering under 18 U.S.C. § 1957, as well as racketeering and conspiracy under § 1962. Among the predicate acts supporting these charges were four counts of mail fraud under § 1341. The indictment alleged that Cleveland and Goodson had violated § 1341 by fraudulently concealing that they were the true owners of TSG in the initial license application and three renewal applications mailed to the State. They concealed their ownership interests, according to the Government, because they had tax and financial problems that could have undermined their suitability to receive a video poker license.

Before trial, Cleveland moved to dismiss the mail fraud counts on the ground that the alleged fraud did not deprive the State of "property" under § 1341. The District Court denied the motion, concluding that "licenses constitute property even before they are issued." 951 F. Supp. 1249, 1261 (ED La. 1997). A jury found Cleveland guilty on two counts of mail fraud (based on the 1994 and 1995 license renewals) and on money laundering, racketeering, and conspiracy counts predicated on the mail fraud. The District Court sentenced Cleveland to 121 months in prison.

On appeal, Cleveland again argued that Louisiana had no property interest in video poker licenses, relying on several Court of Appeals decisions holding that the government does not relinquish "property" for purposes of § 1341 when it issues a permit or license. See United States v. Shotts, 145 F.3d 1289, 1296 (CA11 1998) (license to operate a bail bonds business); United States v. Schwartz, 924 F.2d 410, 418 (CA2 1991) (arms export license); United States v. Granberry, 908 F.2d 278, 280 (CA8 1990) (school bus operator's permit); Toulabi v. United States, 875 F.2d 122, 125 (CA7 1989) (chauffeur's license); United States v. Dadanian, 856 F.2d 1391, 1392 (CA9 1988) (gambling license); United States v. Murphy, 836 F.2d 248, 254 (CA6 1988) (license to conduct charitable bingo games).

The Court of Appeals for the Fifth Circuit nevertheless affirmed Cleveland's conviction and sentence, considering itself bound by its holding in United States v. Salvatore, 110 F.3d 1131, 1138 (1997), that Louisiana video poker licenses constitute "property" in the hands of the State. Two other Circuits have concluded that the issuing authority has a property interest in unissued licenses under § 1341. United States v. Bucuvalas, 970 F.2d 937, 945 (CA1 1992) (entertainment and liquor license); United States v. Martinez, 905 F.2d 709, 715 (CA3 1990) (medical license).

We granted certiorari to resolve the conflict among the Courts of Appeals and now reverse the Fifth Circuit's judgment.

II

In McNally v. United States, 483 U.S. 350, 360 (1987), this Court held that the federal mail fraud statute is "limited in scope to the protection of property rights." . . . At the time *McNally* was decided, federal prosecutors had been using § 1341 to attack various forms of corruption that deprived victims of "intangible rights" unrelated to money or property.[24] Reviewing the history of § 1341, we concluded that "the original impetus behind the mail fraud statute was to protect the people from schemes to deprive them of their money or property." Id., at 356. . . .

Soon after *McNally*, in Carpenter v. United States, 484 U.S. 19, 25 (1987), we again stated that § 1341 protects property rights only. . . .

The following year, Congress amended the law specifically to cover one of the "intangible rights" that lower courts had protected under § 1341 prior to *McNally*: "the intangible right of honest services." Significantly, Congress covered only the intangible right of honest services even though federal courts, relying on *McNally*, had dismissed, for want of monetary loss to any victim, prosecutions under § 1341 for diverse forms of public corruption, including licensing fraud.

III

In this case, there is no assertion that Louisiana's video poker licensing scheme implicates the intangible right of honest services. The question presented is whether, for purposes of the federal mail fraud statute, a government regulator parts with "property" when it issues a license. For the reasons we now set out, we hold that § 1341 does not reach fraud in obtaining a state or municipal license of the kind here involved, for such a license is not "property" in the government regulator's hands. Again, as we said in *McNally*, "if Congress desires to go further, it must speak more clearly than it has." 483 U.S. at 360.

To begin with, we think it beyond genuine dispute that whatever interests Louisiana might be said to have in its video poker licenses, the State's core concern is *regulatory*. Louisiana recognizes the importance of "public confidence and trust that gaming activities . . . are conducted honestly and are free from criminal and corruptive elements." La. Rev. Stat. Ann. § 27:306(A)(1). The video poker licensing statute accordingly asserts the State's "legitimate interest in providing strict regulation of all persons, practices, associations, and activities related to the operation of . . . establishments licensed to offer video draw poker devices." Ibid. The statute assigns the Office of State Police, a part of the Department of Public Safety and Corrections, the responsibility to promulgate rules and regulations concerning the licensing process. It also authorizes the State Police to deny, condition, suspend, or revoke licenses, to levy fines of up to $1,000 per violation of any rule, and to inspect all premises where video poker devices are offered for play. In addition, the statute defines criminal penalties for unauthorized use of video poker devices and prescribes detailed suitability requirements for licensees.

24. E.g., United States v. Clapps, 732 F.2d 1148, 1153 (CA3 1984) (electoral body's right to fair elections); United States v. Bronston, 658 F.2d 920, 927 (CA2 1981) (client's right to attorney's loyalty); United States v. Bohonus, 628 F.2d 1167, 1172 (CA9 1980) (right to honest services of an agent or employee); United States v. Isaacs, 493 F.2d 1124, 1150 (CA7 1974) (right to honest services of public official).

In short, the statute establishes a typical regulatory program. It licenses, subject to certain conditions, engagement in pursuits that private actors may not undertake without official authorization. In this regard, it resembles other licensing schemes long characterized by this Court as exercises of state police powers. E.g., Ziffrin, Inc. v. Reeves, 308 U.S. 132, 138 (1939) (license to transport alcoholic beverages); Hall v. Geiger-Jones Co., 242 U.S. 539, 558 (1917) (license to sell corporate stock); Fanning v. Gregoire, 57 U.S. 524 (1854) (ferry license).

Acknowledging Louisiana's regulatory interests, the Government offers two reasons why the State also has a property interest in its video poker licenses. First, the State receives a substantial sum of money in exchange for each license and continues to receive payments from the licensee as long as the license remains in effect. Second, the State has significant control over the issuance, renewal, suspension, and revocation of licenses. Without doubt, Louisiana has a substantial economic stake in the video poker industry. The State collects an upfront "processing fee" for each new license application ($10,000 for truck stops), a separate "processing fee" for each renewal application ($1,000 for truck stops), an "annual fee" from each device owner ($2,000), an additional "device operation" fee ($1,000 for truck stops), and, most importantly, a fixed percentage of net revenue from each video poker device (32.5% for truck stops). It is hardly evident, however, why these tolls should make video poker licenses "property" in the hands of the State. The State receives the lion's share of its expected revenue not while the licenses remain in its own hands, but only after they have been issued to licensees. Licenses pre-issuance do not generate an ongoing stream of revenue. At most, they entitle the State to collect a processing fee from applicants for new licenses. Were an entitlement of this order sufficient to establish a state property right, one could scarcely avoid the conclusion that States have property rights in any license or permit requiring an upfront fee, including drivers' licenses, medical licenses, and fishing and hunting licenses. Such licenses, as the Government itself concedes, are "purely regulatory."

Tellingly, as to the character of Louisiana's stake in its video poker licenses, the Government nowhere alleges that Cleveland defrauded the State of any money to which the State was entitled by law. Indeed, there is no dispute that TSG paid the State of Louisiana its proper share of revenue, which totaled more than $1.2 million, between 1993 and 1995. If Cleveland defrauded the State of "property," the nature of that property cannot be economic.

Addressing this concern, the Government argues that Cleveland frustrated the State's right to control the issuance, renewal, and revocation of video poker licenses. The Fifth Circuit has characterized the protected interest as "Louisiana's right to choose the persons to whom it issues video poker licenses." Salvatore, 110 F.3d at 1140. But far from composing an interest that "has long been recognized as property," Carpenter, 484 U.S. at 26, these intangible rights of allocation, exclusion, and control amount to no more and no less than Louisiana's sovereign power to regulate. Notably, the Government overlooks the fact that these rights include the distinctively sovereign authority to impose criminal penalties for violations of the licensing scheme, including making false statements in a license application. Even when tied to an expected stream of revenue, the State's right of control does not create a property interest any more than a law licensing liquor sales in a State that levies a sales tax on liquor. Such regulations are paradigmatic exercises of the States' traditional police powers.

The Government compares the State's interest in video poker licenses to a patent holder's interest in a patent that she has not yet licensed. Although it is true that both involve the right to exclude, we think the congruence ends there. A patent not only confers the right to exclude others from using an invention, it also protects the holder's right to use, make, or sell the invention herself. Louisiana does not conduct gaming operations itself, it does not hold video poker licenses to reserve that prerogative, and it does not "sell" video poker licenses in the ordinary commercial sense. Furthermore, while a patent holder may sell her patent, the State may not sell its licensing authority. Instead of a patent holder's interest in an unlicensed patent, the better analogy is to the Federal Government's interest in an unissued patent. That interest, like the State's interest in licensing video poker operations, surely implicates the Government's role as sovereign, not as property holder.

The Government also compares the State's licensing power to a franchisor's right to select its franchisees. On this view, Louisiana's video poker licensing scheme represents the State's venture into the video poker business. Although the State could have chosen to run the business itself, the Government says, it decided to franchise private entities to carry out the operations instead. However, a franchisor's right to select its franchisees typically derives from its ownership of a trademark, brand name, business strategy, or other product that it may trade or sell in the open market. Louisiana's authority to select video poker licensees rests on no similar asset. It rests instead upon the State's sovereign right to exclude applicants deemed unsuitable to run video poker operations. A right to exclude in that governing capacity is not one appropriately labeled "property." Moreover, unlike an entrepreneur or business partner who shares both losses and gains arising from a business venture, Louisiana cannot be said to have put its labor or capital at risk through its fee-laden licensing scheme. In short, the State did not decide to venture into the video poker business; it decided typically to permit, regulate, and tax private operators of the games.

We reject the Government's theories of property rights not simply because they stray from traditional concepts of property. We resist the Government's reading of § 1341 as well because it invites us to approve a sweeping expansion of federal criminal jurisdiction in the absence of a clear statement by Congress. Equating issuance of licenses or permits with deprivation of property would subject to federal mail fraud prosecution a wide range of conduct traditionally regulated by state and local authorities. We note in this regard that Louisiana's video poker statute typically and unambiguously imposes criminal penalties for making false statements on license applications. As we reiterated last Term, "'unless Congress conveys its purpose clearly, it will not be deemed to have significantly changed the federal-state balance' in the prosecution of crimes." Jones v. United States, 529 U.S. 848, 858 (2000).

Moreover, to the extent that the word "property" is ambiguous as placed in § 1341, we have instructed that "ambiguity concerning the ambit of criminal statutes should be resolved in favor of lenity." Rewis v. United States, 401 U.S. 808, 812 (1971). This interpretive guide is especially appropriate in construing § 1341 because, as this case demonstrates, mail fraud is a predicate offense under RICO, 18 U.S.C. § 1961(1), and the money laundering statute, § 1956(c)(7)(A). In deciding what is "property" under § 1341, we think "it is appropriate, before we choose the harsher alternative, to require that Congress should have spoken in language that is clear and definite." United States v. Universal C.I.T. Credit Corp., 344 U.S. 218, 222 (1952).

Finally, in an argument not raised below but urged as an alternate ground for affirmance, the Government contends that § 1341, as amended in 1909, defines two independent offenses: (1) "any scheme or artifice to defraud" and (2) "any scheme or artifice . . . for obtaining money or property by means of false or fraudulent pretenses, representations, or promises." Because a video poker license is property in the hands of the licensee, the Government says, Cleveland "obtained . . . property" and thereby committed the second offense even if the license is not property in the hands of the State. Although we do not here question that video poker licensees may have property interests in their licenses,[25] we nevertheless disagree with the Government's reading of § 1341. In *McNally*, we recognized that "because the two phrases identifying the proscribed schemes appear in the disjunctive, it is arguable that they are to be construed independently." 483 U.S. at 358. But we rejected that construction of the statute, instead concluding that the second phrase simply modifies the first by "making it unmistakable that the statute reached false promises and misrepresentations as to the future as well as other frauds involving money or property." Id. at 359. Indeed, directly contradicting the Government's view, we said that "the mail fraud statute . . . had its origin in the desire to protect individual property rights, and any benefit which the Government derives from the statute must be limited to *the Government's interests as property holder.*" Id. at 359, n.8 (emphasis added). We reaffirm our reading of § 1341 in *McNally*. Were the Government correct that the second phrase of § 1341 defines a separate offense, the statute would appear to arm federal prosecutors with power to police false statements in an enormous range of submissions to state and local authorities. For reasons already stated, we decline to attribute to § 1341 a purpose so encompassing where Congress has not made such a design clear.

IV

We conclude that § 1341 requires the object of the fraud to be "property" in the victim's hands and that a Louisiana video poker license in the State's hands is not "property" under § 1341. Absent clear statement by Congress, we will not read the mail fraud statute to place under federal superintendence a vast array of conduct traditionally policed by the States. Our holding means that Cleveland's § 1341 conviction must be vacated. Accordingly, the judgment of the United States Court of Appeals for the Fifth Circuit is reversed, and the case is remanded for further proceedings consistent with this opinion.

It is so ordered.

---

25. Notwithstanding the State's declaration that "any license issued or renewed . . . is not property or a protected interest under the constitutions of either the United States or the state of Louisiana," La. Rev. Stat. Ann. § 27:301(D) (West Supp. 2000), "the question whether a state-law right constitutes 'property' or 'rights to property' is a matter of federal law," Drye v. United States, 528 U.S. 49, 58 (1999). In some contexts, we have held that individuals have constitutionally protected property interests in state-issued licenses essential to pursuing an occupation or livelihood. See, e.g., Bell v. Burson, 402 U.S. 535, 539 (1971) (driver's license).

Notes and Questions

1. Since the state has an economic interest in the video poker operations that it licenses, why don't its economic expectations constitute a property right?

2. Is it clear why the Wall Street Journal's right to control the timing of the release of confidential business information is property while Louisiana's right to control who receives state-issued video poker licenses is not?

3. Does the decision in *Cleveland* clarify what status a video poker license has in the hands of the licensee? Does the issued license constitute "property"? Is Louisiana's power to revoke the license relevant?

4. In rejecting the government's position, the Court in *Cleveland* sounded a strong federalism theme. Why did the government's interpretation of the statute provoke this concern?

5. The Court also invoked the rule of lenity, a canon of statutory construction often used to narrow the scope of criminal laws. Why did the Court find it particularly appropriate to invoke the rule in this context?

PASQUANTINO v. UNITED STATES
544 U.S. 349 (2005)

Justice THOMAS delivered the opinion of the Court. . . .

I

Petitioners Carl J. Pasquantino, David B. Pasquantino, and Arthur Hilts were indicted for and convicted of federal wire fraud for carrying out a scheme to smuggle large quantities of liquor into Canada from the United States. According to the evidence presented at trial, the Pasquantinos, while in New York, ordered liquor over the telephone from discount package stores in Maryland. They employed Hilts and others to drive the liquor over the Canadian border, without paying the required excise taxes. The drivers avoided paying taxes by hiding the liquor in their vehicles and failing to declare the goods to Canadian customs officials. During the time of petitioners' smuggling operation, between 1996 and 2000, Canada heavily taxed the importation of alcoholic beverages. Uncontested evidence at trial showed that Canadian taxes then due on alcohol purchased in the United States and transported to Canada were approximately double the liquor's purchase price.

Before trial, petitioners moved to dismiss the indictment on the ground that it stated no wire fraud offense. . . . The District Court denied the motion and the case went to trial. The jury convicted petitioners of wire fraud. [Sitting en banc, the Fourth Circuit Court of Appeals affirmed the convictions.]

We granted certiorari to resolve a conflict in the Courts of Appeals over whether a scheme to defraud a foreign government of tax revenue violates the wire fraud statute. . . . We agree with the Court of Appeals that it does and therefore affirm the judgment below.

II

We first consider whether petitioners' conduct falls within the literal terms of the wire fraud statute. The statute prohibits using interstate wires to effect "any scheme or artifice to defraud, or for obtaining money or property by means of false or fraudulent pretenses, representations, or promises." 18 U.S.C. § 1343. Two elements of this crime, and the only two that petitioners dispute here, are that the defendant engage in a "scheme or artifice to defraud," and that the "object of the fraud . . . be '[money or] property' in the victim's hands," Cleveland v. United States, 531 U.S. 12, 26 (2000).[26] Petitioners' smuggling operation satisfies both elements.

Taking the latter element first, Canada's right to uncollected excise taxes on the liquor petitioners imported into Canada is "property" in its hands. This right is an entitlement to collect money from petitioners, the possession of which is "something of value" to the Government of Canada. Valuable entitlements like these are "property" as that term ordinarily is employed. Had petitioners complied with this legal obligation, they would have paid money to Canada. Petitioners' tax evasion deprived Canada of that money, inflicting an economic injury no less than had they embezzled funds from the Canadian treasury. The object of petitioners' scheme was to deprive Canada of money legally due, and their scheme thereby had as its object the deprivation of Canada's "property."

The common law of fraud confirms this characterization of Canada's right to excise taxes. The right to be paid money has long been thought to be a species of property. Consistent with that understanding, fraud at common law included a scheme to deprive a victim of his entitlement to money. For instance, a debtor who concealed his assets when settling debts with his creditors thereby committed common-law fraud. That made sense given the economic equivalence between money in hand and money legally due. The fact that the victim of the fraud happens to be the Government, rather than a private party, does not lessen the injury.

Our conclusion that the right to tax revenue is property in Canada's hands, contrary to petitioners' contentions, is consistent with Cleveland, supra. In that case, the defendant, Cleveland, had obtained a video poker license by making false statements on his license application. We held that a State's interest in an unissued video poker license was not "property," because the interest in choosing particular licensees was "'purely regulatory'" and "[could not] be economic." Id., at 27. We also noted that "the Government nowhere alleged that Cleveland defrauded the State of any money to which the State was entitled by law." Id.

Cleveland is different from this case. Unlike a State's interest in allocating a video poker license to particular applicants, Canada's entitlement to tax revenue is a straightforward "economic" interest. There was no suggestion in Cleveland that the defendant aimed at depriving the State of any money due under the license; quite the opposite, there was "no dispute that [the defendant's partnership] paid the State of Louisiana its proper share of revenue" due. Id., at 22. Here, by contrast, the Government alleged and proved that petitioners' scheme aimed at depriving Canada of money to which it was

---

26. Although Cleveland interpreted the term "property" in the mail fraud statute, 18 U.S.C. § 1341, we have construed identical language in the wire and mail fraud statutes in pari materia. See Neder v. United States, 527 U.S. 1, 20 (1999) ("'scheme or artifice to defraud'"); Carpenter v. United States, 484 U.S. 19, 25 and n. 6 (1987) ("scheme or artifice to defraud"; "money or property").

entitled by law. Canada could hardly have a more "economic" interest than in the receipt of tax revenue. *Cleveland* is therefore consistent with our conclusion that Canada's entitlement is "property" as that word is used in the wire fraud statute.

Turning to the second element at issue here, petitioners' plot was a "scheme or artifice to defraud" Canada of its valuable entitlement to tax revenue. The evidence showed that petitioners routinely concealed imported liquor from Canadian officials and failed to declare those goods on customs forms. By this conduct, they represented to Canadian customs officials that their drivers had no goods to declare. This, then, was a scheme "designed to defraud by representations," Durland v. United States, 161 U.S. 306, 313 (1896), and therefore a "scheme or artifice to defraud" Canada of taxes due on the smuggled goods. . . .

IV

[O]ur interpretation of the wire fraud statute does not give it "extraterritorial effect."[27] 125 S. Ct. 1784 (Ginsburg, J., dissenting). Petitioners used U.S. interstate wires to execute a scheme to defraud a foreign sovereign of tax revenue. Their offense was complete the moment they executed the scheme inside the United States; "the wire fraud statute punishes the scheme, not its success." United States v. Pierce, 224 F.3d 158, 166 (CA2 2000). This domestic element of petitioners' conduct is what the Government is punishing in this prosecution, no less than when it prosecutes a scheme to defraud a foreign individual or corporation, or a foreign government acting as a market participant. In any event, the wire fraud statute punishes frauds executed "in interstate or foreign commerce," 18 U.S.C. § 1343, so this is surely not a statute in which Congress had only "domestic concerns in mind." Small v. United States, 125 S. Ct. 1752, 1755. . . .

It may seem an odd use of the Federal Government's resources to prosecute a U.S. citizen for smuggling cheap liquor into Canada. But the broad language of the wire fraud statute authorizes it to do so and no canon of statutory construction permits us to read the statute more narrowly. The judgment of the Court of Appeals is affirmed.

It is so ordered.　　　　●　　●　　●　　●

Justice GINSBURG, with whom Justice BREYER joins, and Justice SCALIA and Justice SOUTER join as to Parts II and III, dissenting.

This case concerns extension of the "wire fraud" statute to a scenario extraterritorial in significant part: The Government invoked the statute to reach a scheme to smuggle liquor from the United States into Canada and thereby deprive Canada of revenues due under that nation's customs and tax laws. . . .

The scheme at issue involves liquor purchased from discount sellers in Maryland, trucked to New York, then smuggled into Canada to evade Canada's hefty tax on imported alcohol.[28] Defendants below, petitioners here, were indicted under § 1343 for devising a scheme "to defraud the governments of Canada and the Province of Ontario

---

27. As some indication of the novelty of the dissent's "extraterritoriality" argument, we note that this argument was not pressed or passed upon below and was raised only as an afterthought in petitioners' reply brief, depriving the Government of a chance to respond.

28. The Government offered a Canadian customs officer's testimony at trial that if alcohol is purchased for $56 per case in the United States, the Canadian tax would be approximately $100 per case.

of excise duties and tax revenues relating to the importation and sale of liquor." Each of the six counts in question was based on telephone calls between New York and Maryland.

The Court today reads the wire fraud statute to draw into our courts, at the prosecutor's option, charges that another nation's revenue laws have been evaded. . . .

As I see it, and as petitioners urged, the Court has ascribed an exorbitant scope to the wire fraud statute, in disregard of our repeated recognition that "Congress legislates against the backdrop of the presumption against extraterritoriality." See EEOC v. Arabian American Oil Co., 499 U.S. 244, 248 (1991) (*ARAMCO*). . . .

Today's novel decision is all the more troubling for its failure to take account of Canada's primary interest in the matter at stake. United States citizens who have committed criminal violations of Canadian tax law can be extradited to stand trial in Canada.[29] Canadian courts are best positioned to decide "whether, and to what extent, the defendants have defrauded the governments of Canada and Ontario out of tax revenues owed pursuant to their own, sovereign, excise laws." 336 F.3d 321, 343 (CA4 2003) (en banc) (Gregory, J., dissenting).

I

The Government's prosecution of David Pasquantino, Carl Pasquantino, and Arthur Hilts for wire fraud was grounded in Canadian customs and tax laws. The wire fraud statute, 18 U.S.C. § 1343, required the Government to allege and prove that the defendants engaged in a scheme to defraud a victim — here, the Canadian Government — of money or property. To establish the fraudulent nature of the defendants' scheme and the Canadian Government's entitlement to the money withheld by the defendants, the United States offered proof at trial that Canada imposes import duties on liquor, and that the defendants intended to evade those duties. The defendants' convictions for wire fraud therefore resulted from, and could not have been obtained without proof of, their intent to violate Canadian revenue laws.

The United States Government's reliance on Canadian customs and tax laws continued at sentencing. The United States Sentencing Guidelines mandated that the defendants be sentenced on the basis of, among other things, the amount by which the defendants defrauded the Canadian Government. See United States Sentencing Commission, Guidelines Manual § 2F1.1(b)(1) (Nov. 2000). Accordingly, the District Court calculated the number of cases of liquor smuggled into Canada and the aggregate amount of import duties evaded by the defendants. The court concluded that the Pasquantinos avoided over $2.5 million in Canadian duties, and Hilts, over $1.1 million. The resulting offense-level increases yielded significantly longer sentences for the defendants.[30] As Judge Gregory stated in dissent below, the fact that "the bulk of the defendants' sentences were related, not to the American crime of wire fraud, but to

---

29. Indeed, the defendants have all been indicted in Canada for failing to report excise taxes and possession of unlawfully imported spirits, but Canada has not requested their extradition.

30. I note that petitioners' sentences were enhanced on the basis of judicial factfindings, in violation of the Sixth Amendment. See United States v. Booker, 125 S. Ct. 738, 755-756 (2005) (Stevens, J., for the Court); see also Blakely v. Washington, 542 U.S. 296 (2004). Despite the Court's affirmance of their convictions, therefore, the petitioners may be entitled to resentencing. . . .

the Canadian crime of tax evasion," shows that "this case was primarily about enforcing Canadian law." 336 F.3d at 342-343.

Expansively interpreting the text of the wire fraud statute, which prohibits "any scheme or artifice to defraud, or for obtaining money or property by means of . . . fraudulent pretenses," the Court today upholds the Government's deployment of § 1343 essentially to enforce foreign tax law. This Court has several times observed that the wire fraud statute has a long arm, extending to "everything designed to defraud by representations as to the past or present, or suggestions and promises as to the future." Durland v. United States, 161 U.S. 306, 313 (1896). But the Court has also recognized that incautious reading of the statute could dramatically expand the reach of federal criminal law, and we have refused to apply the proscription exorbitantly.

Construing § 1343 to encompass violations of foreign revenue laws, the Court ignores the absence of anything signaling Congress' intent to give the statute such an extraordinary extraterritorial effect. . . .

III

Finally, the rule of lenity counsels against adopting the Court's interpretation of § 1343. It is a "close question" whether the wire fraud statute's prohibition of "any scheme . . . to defraud" includes schemes directed solely at defrauding foreign governments of tax revenues. We have long held that, when confronted with "two rational readings of a criminal statute, one harsher than the other, we are to choose the harsher only when Congress has spoken in clear and definite language." *McNally*, 483 U.S., at 359-360.

This interpretive guide is particularly appropriate here. Wire fraud is a predicate offense under the Racketeer Influenced and Corrupt Organizations Act (RICO), 18 U.S.C. § 1961(1), and the money laundering statute, § 1956(c)(7)(A). A finding that particular conduct constitutes wire fraud therefore exposes certain defendants to the severe criminal penalties and forfeitures provided in both RICO, see § 1963, and the money laundering statute, § 1956(a), (b). . . .

For the reasons stated, I would hold that § 1343 does not extend to schemes to evade foreign tax and customs laws. I would therefore reverse the judgment of the Court of Appeals.

Notes and Questions

1. How is Canada's right to receive taxes on alcoholic beverages different from Louisiana's right to receive video poker license fees and a percentage of revenues generated by video poker machines? What makes *Cleveland* distinguishable from *Pasquantino*?

2. Are the dissenters correct in saying that *Pasquantino* gives the wire fraud statute extraterritorial effect? Why would the issue of extraterritorial jurisdiction trouble them?

3. What if the phone calls had been made between New York and Toronto? Would the wire fraud statute still apply? Would allowing a wire fraud prosecution to proceed on these facts be tantamount to giving the statute extraterritorial effect?

4. What if the defendants had ordered liquor via phone calls to out-of-state discount package stores intending to smuggle it into Canada, but never actually made any bootleg shipments? Would they still have violated the wire fraud statute?

5. Another issue the Court confronted in *Pasquantino* was whether application of the wire fraud statute to a scheme to defraud the Canadian government of excise taxes ran afoul of the common law revenue rule. The revenue rule prohibits courts from enforcing the tax laws of foreign countries. Is the wire fraud prosecution in *Pasquantino* the functional equivalent of U.S. enforcement of Canadian tax laws?

6. The defendants in *Pasquantino* were also indicted in Canada, but the Canadian government had not requested extradition. Should U.S. prosecutors consider the defendants' amenability to prosecution in Canada before bringing a wire fraud prosecution like this?

a. Intent to Deprive

UNITED STATES v. CZUBINSKI
106 F.3d 1069 (1st Cir. 1997)

TORRUELLA, Chief Judge.

Defendant-appellant Richard Czubinski ("Czubinski") appeals his jury conviction on nine counts of wire fraud, 18 U.S.C. §§ 1343, 1346, and four counts of computer fraud, 18 U.S.C. § 1030(a)(4). . . .

BACKGROUND

I. PERTINENT FACTS . . .

For all periods relevant to the acts giving rise to his conviction, the defendant Czubinski was employed as a Contact Representative in the Boston office of the Taxpayer Services Division of the Internal Revenue Service ("IRS"). To perform his official duties, which mainly involved answering questions from taxpayers regarding their returns, Czubinski routinely accessed information from one of the IRS's computer systems known as the Integrated Data Retrieval System ("IDRS"). Using a valid password given to Contact Representatives, certain search codes, and taxpayer social security numbers, Czubinski was able to retrieve, to his terminal screen in Boston, income tax return information regarding virtually any taxpayer — information that is permanently stored in the IDRS "master file" located in Martinsburg, West Virginia. In the period of Czubinski's employ, IRS rules plainly stated that employees with passwords and access codes were not permitted to access files on IDRS outside of the course of their official duties.[31]

---

31. In 1987 Czubinski signed an acknowledgment of receipt of the IRS Rules of Conduct, which contained the following rule:

In 1992, Czubinski carried out numerous unauthorized searches of IDRS files. He knowingly disregarded IRS rules by looking at confidential information obtained by performing computer searches that were outside of the scope of his duties as a Contact Representative, including, but not limited to, the searches listed in the indictment. Audit trails performed by internal IRS auditors establish that Czubinski frequently made unauthorized accesses on IDRS in 1992. For example, Czubinski accessed information regarding: the tax returns of two individuals involved in the David Duke presidential campaign; the joint tax return of an assistant district attorney (who had been prosecuting Czubinski's father on an unrelated felony offense) and his wife; the tax return of Boston City Counselor Jim Kelly's Campaign Committee (Kelly had defeated Czubinski in the previous election for the Counselor seat for District 2); the tax return of one of his brothers' instructors; the joint tax return of a Boston Housing Authority police officer, who was involved in a community organization with one of Czubinski's brothers, and the officer's wife; and the tax return of a woman Czubinski had dated a few times. Czubinski also accessed the files of various other social acquaintances by performing unauthorized searches.

Nothing in the record indicates that Czubinski did anything more than knowingly disregard IRS rules by observing the confidential information he accessed. No evidence suggests, nor does the government contend, that Czubinski disclosed the confidential information he accessed to any third parties. The government's only evidence demonstrating any intent to use the confidential information for nefarious ends was the trial testimony of William A. Murray, an acquaintance of Czubinski who briefly participated in Czubinski's local Invisible Knights of the Ku Klux Klan ("KKK") chapter and worked with him on the David Duke campaign. Murray testified that Czubinski had once stated at a social gathering in "early 1992" that "he intended to use some of that information to build dossiers on people" involved in "the white supremacist movement." There is, however, no evidence that Czubinski created dossiers, took steps toward making dossiers (such as by printing out or recording the information he browsed), or shared any of the information he accessed in the years following the single comment to Murray. No other witness testified to having any knowledge of Czubinski's alleged intent to create "dossiers" on KKK members.

The record shows that Czubinski did not perform any unauthorized searches after 1992. He continued to be employed as a Contact Representative until June 1995, when a grand jury returned an indictment against him on ten counts of federal wire fraud under 18 U.S.C. §§ 1343, 1346, and four counts of federal interest computer fraud under 18 U.S.C. § 1030(a)(4).

The portion of the indictment alleging wire fraud states that Czubinski defrauded the IRS of confidential property and defrauded the IRS and the public of his honest services by using his valid password to acquire confidential taxpayer information as part of a scheme to: 1) build "dossiers" on associates in the KKK; 2) seek information regarding an assistant district attorney who was then prosecuting Czubinski's father on

---

Employees must make every effort to assure security and prevent unauthorized disclosure of protected information data in the use of Government owned or leased computers. In addition, employees may not use any Service computer system for other than official purposes.

In addition, Czubinski received separate rules regarding use of the IDRS, one of which states:

Access only those accounts required to accomplish your official duties.

an unrelated criminal charge; and 3) perform opposition research by inspecting the records of a political opponent in the race for a Boston City Councilor seat. The wire fraud indictment, therefore, articulated particular personal ends to which the unauthorized access to confidential information through interstate wires was allegedly a means.

The portion of the indictment setting forth the computer fraud charges stated that Czubinski obtained something of value, beyond the mere unauthorized use of a federal interest computer, by performing certain searches — searches representing a subset of those making up the mail fraud counts.

II. PROCEEDINGS BELOW

[After the trial court denied his motions to dismiss and for judgment of acquittal, the jury convicted Czubinski on 13 counts of fraud.]

DISCUSSION

I. THE WIRE FRAUD COUNTS

We turn first to Czubinski's conviction on the nine wire fraud counts.[32] To support a conviction for wire fraud, the government must prove two elements beyond a reasonable doubt: (1) the defendant's knowing and willing participation in a scheme or artifice to defraud with the specific intent to defraud, and (2) the use of interstate wire communications in furtherance of the scheme. Although defendant's motion for judgment of acquittal places emphasis on shortcomings in proof with regard to the second element, by arguing that the wire transmissions at issue were not proved to be interstate, we find the first element dispositive and hold that the government failed to prove beyond a reasonable doubt that the defendant willfully participated in a scheme to defraud within the meaning of the wire fraud statute.[33] That is, assuming the counts accurately describe unauthorized searches of taxpayer returns through interstate wire transmissions, there is insufficient record evidence to permit a rational jury to conclude that the wire transmissions were part of a criminal scheme to defraud under sections 1343 and 1346.

---

32. The federal wire fraud statute, 18 U.S.C. § 1343, provides in pertinent part:

Whoever, having devised or intending to devise any scheme or artifice to defraud, or for obtaining money or property by means of false or fraudulent pretenses, representations, or promises, transmits or causes to be transmitted by means of wire . . . communication in interstate or foreign commerce, any writings, signs, signals, pictures, or sounds for the purpose of executing such scheme or artifice, shall be fined under this title or imprisoned not more than five years, or both.

33. We do not find that it was irrational for a trier of fact to conclude beyond a reasonable doubt that Czubinski's searches caused information from the IDRS master file in Martinsburg, West Virginia, to be sent to his terminal in Boston. The interstate element could reasonably be inferred from circumstantial evidence. See, e.g., Testimony of Edward Makaskill, Trial Transcript, Vol. 3 at 82 (explaining that certain command codes used by Czubinski generally access information from out-of-state computers).

The government pursued two theories of wire fraud in this prosecution: first, that Czubinski defrauded the IRS of its property, under section 1343, by acquiring confidential information for certain intended personal uses; second, that he defrauded the IRS and the public of their intangible right to his honest services, under sections 1343 and 1346. We consider the evidence with regard to each theory, in turn.

A. Scheme to Defraud IRS of Property

The government correctly notes that confidential information may constitute intangible "property" and that its unauthorized dissemination or other use may deprive the owner of its property rights. Where such deprivation is effected through dishonest or deceitful means, a "scheme to defraud," within the meaning of the wire fraud statute, is shown. Thus, a necessary step toward satisfying the "scheme to defraud" element in this context is showing that the defendant intended to "deprive" another of their protected right.

The government, however, provides no case in support of its contention here that merely accessing confidential information, without doing, or clearly intending to do, more, is tantamount to a deprivation of IRS property under the wire fraud statute. In *Carpenter*, for example, the confidential information regarding the contents of a newspaper column was converted to the defendants' use to their substantial benefit. We do not think that Czubinski's unauthorized browsing, even if done with the intent to deceive the IRS into thinking he was performing only authorized searches, constitutes a "deprivation" within the meaning of the federal fraud statutes.

Binding precedents, and good sense, support the conclusion that to "deprive" a person of their intangible property interest in confidential information under section 1343, either some articulable harm must befall the holder of the information as a result of the defendant's activities, or some gainful use must be intended by the person accessing the information, whether or not this use is profitable in the economic sense. Here, neither the taking of the IRS' right to "exclusive use" of the confidential information, nor Czubinski's gain from access to the information, can be shown absent evidence of his "use" of the information. Accordingly, without evidence that Czubinski used or intended to use the taxpayer information (beyond mere browsing), an intent to deprive cannot be proven, and, *a fortiori*, a scheme to defraud is not shown.

All of the cases cited by the government in support of their contention that the confidentiality breached by Czubinski's search in itself constitutes a deprivation of property in fact support our holding today, for they all involve, at a minimum, a finding of a further intended use of the confidential information accessed by the defendants. The government's best support comes from United States v. Seidlitz, 589 F.2d 152, 160 (4th Cir. 1978), in which a former employee of a computer systems firm secretly accessed its files, but never was shown to have sold or used the data he accessed, and was nevertheless convicted of wire fraud. The affirming Fourth Circuit held, however, that a jury could have reasonably found that, at the time the defendant raided a competitor's computer system, he intended to retrieve information that would be helpful for his own start-up, competing computer firm. In the instant case, Czubinski did indeed access confidential information through fraudulent pretenses — he appeared to be performing his duties when in fact he used IRS passwords to perform unauthorized searches. Nevertheless, it was not proven that he intended to deprive the IRS of their property interest through either disclosure or use of that information. . . .

The fatal flaw in the government's case is that it has not shown beyond a reasonable doubt that Czubinski intended to carry out a scheme to deprive the IRS of its property interest in confidential information. Had there been sufficient proof that Czubinski intended either to create dossiers for the sake of advancing personal causes or to disseminate confidential information to third parties, then his actions in searching files could arguably be said to be a step in furtherance of a scheme to deprive the IRS of its property interest in confidential information. The government's case regarding Czubinski's intent to make any use of the information he browsed rests on the testimony of one witness at trial who stated that Czubinski once remarked at a social gathering that he intended to build dossiers on potential KKK informants. We must assume, on this appeal, that Czubinski did indeed make such a comment. Nevertheless, the fact that during the months following this remark — that is, during the period in which Czubinski made his unauthorized searches — he did not create dossiers (there was no evidence that he created dossiers either during or after the period of his unauthorized searches); given the fact that he did not even take steps toward creating dossiers, such as recording or printing out the information; given the fact that no other person testifying as to Czubinski's involvement in white supremacist organizations had any knowledge of Czubinski's alleged intent to create dossiers or use confidential information; and given the fact that not a single piece of evidence suggests that Czubinski ever shared taxpayer information with others, no rational jury could have found beyond a reasonable doubt that, when Czubinski was browsing taxpayer files, he was doing so in furtherance of a scheme to use the information he browsed for private purposes, be they nefarious or otherwise. In addition, there was no evidence that Czubinski disclosed, or used to his advantage, any information regarding political opponents or regarding the person prosecuting his father.

Mere browsing of the records of people about whom one might have a particular interest, although reprehensible, is not enough to sustain a wire fraud conviction on a "deprivation of intangible property" theory. Curiosity on the part of an IRS officer may lead to dismissal, but curiosity alone will not sustain a finding of participation in a felonious criminal scheme to deprive the IRS of its property. . . .

The defendant's conviction is thus reversed. . . .

Notes and Questions

1. Czubinski used IRS passwords to perform unauthorized searches of the computer files under the pretext of doing his job. Is it important that he gained access to the files under fraudulent pretenses?

2. What if Czubinski intended to build dossiers on potential KKK informants if he found worthwhile information, but discovered nothing of real interest? Would the court find a violation of the statute under those circumstances? Would an employer (government or private) who learned that Czubinski was improperly accessing confidential information — whether state secrets or trade secrets — be willing to permit the intrusion to continue until Czubinski actually used the information? If not, does the court's reading of the statute effectively confer immunity on the dishonest employee?

3. It is well settled that a scheme to defraud need not be successful to violate the statute. Does *Czubinski* undercut this long-established rule?

4. Czubinski was prosecuted for wire fraud. The wire fraud statute is patterned after the mail fraud statute but differs in that the jurisdictional element is *interstate* transmission of wire, radio, or television communications in furtherance of a scheme to defraud, rather than use of the mails to further the fraud.[34] As is true under the mail fraud statute, the use of wire communications need only be reasonably foreseeable. Because the interstate character of the transmission is jurisdictional only, the defendant need not know or foresee that the communication will travel interstate.[35] As long as it is reasonably foreseeable that a wire communication will be sent in furtherance of the fraud, that is enough.

Does the wire fraud statute provide the government unfair opportunities to "manufacture" federal jurisdiction? Suppose the FBI sets up a sting operation as part of an investigation into allegations that a local judge in Kansas City, Missouri, is taking bribes in exchange for dismissing felony charges against drug dealers and gang members. As part of the sting operation, an undercover FBI agent is "charged" with a drug felony and is scheduled to appear before the corrupt judge. Before his scheduled arraignment, the undercover agent drives a few miles to Kansas City, Kansas, for the express purpose of calling the judge and arranging a payoff. If the strategy is successful and the judge agrees over the phone to accept the bribe, can the U.S. Attorney short-circuit the local corruption investigation by charging the judge with wire fraud?[36]

3. Honest Services Theory

Thus far our consideration of post-*McNally* developments has focused on what constitutes property under the mail and wire fraud statutes. But another significant change in the law — the enactment of 18 U.S.C. § 1346 — was a direct response to *McNally* that was unquestionably meant to "overrule" it. Section 1346, which provides that, for purposes of the mail, wire, and bank fraud statutes,[37] "the term 'scheme or artifice to defraud' includes a scheme or artifice to deprive another of the intangible right of honest services."

As might be expected, Congress did not statutorily define what is encompassed by the term "honest services" or delineate the circumstances under which a right of honest services exists. That, in turn, generated conflicting views about the contours of this newly revived theory of fraud. The conflict was fed in part by the state of pre-*McNally* case law, which did not articulate a unified set of rules. Instead, the contours of the doctrine were amorphous, and some courts' expressions of its meaning were "far broader than their holdings,"[38] leaving a multitude of unresolved issues for courts to consider.

---

34. Cf. United States v. Cowart, 595 F.2d 1023 (5th Cir. 1979) (interstate transmission via telecopier); United States v. King, 590 F.2d 253 (8th Cir. 1978) (telephone communication transmitted by microwave).

35. Cf. United States v. Bryant, 766 F.2d 370 (8th Cir. 1985) (telegrams defendants sent from Kansas City, Missouri, to Bridgeton, Missouri, were — unbeknownst to them — routed electronically through a Western Union installation in Middletown, Virginia).

36. Cf. United States v. Archer, 486 F.2d 670 (2d Cir. 1973).

37. 18 U.S.C. § 1343 (wire fraud); 18 U.S.C. § 1344 (bank fraud).

38. United States v. Brumley, 116 F.3d 728, 733 (5th Cir. 1997).

SKILLING v. UNITED STATES
130 S. Ct. 2896 (2010)

Justice GINSBURG delivered the opinion of the Court. . . .

I

Founded in 1985, Enron Corporation grew from its headquarters in Houston, Texas, into one of the world's leading energy companies. Skilling launched his career there in 1990 when Kenneth Lay, the company's founder, hired him to head an Enron subsidiary. Skilling steadily rose through the corporation's ranks, serving as president and chief operating officer, and then, beginning in February 2001, as chief executive officer. Six months later, on August 14, 2001, Skilling resigned from Enron.

Less than four months after Skilling's departure, Enron spiraled into bankruptcy. The company's stock, which had traded at $90 per share in August 2000, plummeted to pennies per share in late 2001. Attempting to comprehend what caused the corporation's collapse, the U.S. Department of Justice formed an Enron Task Force, comprising prosecutors and FBI agents from around the Nation. The Government's investigation uncovered an elaborate conspiracy to prop up Enron's short-run stock prices by overstating the company's financial well being. In the years following Enron's bankruptcy, the Government prosecuted dozens of Enron employees who participated in the scheme. In time, the Government worked its way up the corporation's chain of command: On July 7, 2004, a grand jury indicted Skilling, Lay, and Richard Causey, Enron's former chief accounting officer.

These three defendants, the indictment alleged,

engaged in a wide-ranging scheme to deceive the investing public, including Enron's shareholders, . . . about the true performance of Enron's businesses by: (a) manipulating Enron's publicly reported financial results; and (b) making public statements and representations about Enron's financial performance and results that were false and misleading.

Skilling and his co-conspirators, the indictment continued, "enriched themselves as a result of the scheme through salary, bonuses, grants of stock and stock options, other profits, and prestige."

Count 1 of the indictment charged Skilling with conspiracy to commit securities and wire fraud; in particular, it alleged that Skilling had sought to "depriv[e] Enron and its shareholders of the intangible right of [his] honest services." The indictment further charged Skilling with more than 25 substantive counts of securities fraud, wire fraud, making false representations to Enron's auditors, and insider trading. . . .

Following a 4-month trial and nearly five days of deliberation, the jury found Skilling guilty of 19 counts, including the honest services fraud conspiracy charge, and not guilty of 9 insider trading counts. The District Court sentenced Skilling to 292 months' imprisonment, 3 years' supervised release, and $45 million in restitution.

[On appeal to the Fifth Circuit, Skilling argued, inter alia, that he was denied a fair trial because of extensive pre-trial publicity and community prejudice, and that he was wrongly convicted of conspiring to commit honest services wire fraud. He argued that the government had applied an incorrect honest services theory to his case and, if not, the government's theory—as applied to his conduct—rendered § 1346 unconstitutionally vague. Affirming his convictions, the court of appeals rejected both arguments, ruling (1) that the government had overcome the presumption of prejudice and Skilling had failed to establish actual prejudice; and (2) that the jury was entitled to convict upon a showing that Skilling had committed a material breach of a fiduciary duty, to Enron's detriment. The court did not address Skilling's constitutional challenge to § 1346.

After upholding the court of appeals' ruling that Skilling could not prevail on his fair trial argument, the Supreme Court took strong exception to the lower court's ruling on the honest services issue.]

III

We next consider whether Skilling's conspiracy conviction was premised on an improper theory of honest services wire fraud. The honest services statute, § 1346, Skilling maintains, is unconstitutionally vague. Alternatively, he contends that his conduct does not fall within the statute's compass.

A

[The Court first traced the evolution of the honest services doctrine. The Court observed that, historically, most honest services prosecutions involved bribery of public officials, but that over time, the lower courts had extended the theory to cases involving bribery and kickbacks among private parties. Although all of the courts of appeals had recognized the honest services theory by 1982, the high Court's 1987 decision in *McNally* had, in the Court's words, "stopped the development of the intangible rights doctrine in its tracks."]

3

Congress responded swiftly. The following year, it enacted a new statute "specifically to cover one of the intangible rights that lower courts had protected . . . prior to *McNally:* 'the intangible right of honest services.'" Cleveland v. United States, 531 U.S. 12, 19-20 (2000). In full, the honest services statute stated:

"For the purposes of th[e] chapter [of the United States Code that prohibits, inter alia, mail fraud, § 1341, and wire fraud, § 1343], the term scheme or artifice to defraud includes a scheme or artifice to deprive another of the intangible right of honest services." § 1346.

B

Congress, Skilling charges, reacted quickly but not clearly: He asserts that § 1346 is unconstitutionally vague. To satisfy due process, "a penal statute [must] define the criminal offense [1] with sufficient definiteness that ordinary people can understand what conduct is prohibited and [2] in a manner that does not encourage arbitrary and discriminatory enforcement." Kolender v. Lawson, 461 U.S. 352, 357 (1983). The void for vagueness doctrine embraces these requirements.

According to Skilling, § 1346 meets neither of the two due process essentials. First, the phrase "the intangible right of honest services," he contends, does not adequately define what behavior it bars. Second, he alleges, § 1346's "standardless sweep allows policemen, prosecutors, and juries to pursue their personal predilections," thereby "facilitat[ing] opportunistic and arbitrary prosecutions."

In urging invalidation of § 1346, Skilling swims against our case law's current, which requires us, if we can, to construe, not condemn, Congress' enactments. Alert to § 1346's potential breadth, the Courts of Appeals have divided on how best to interpret the statute. Uniformly, however, they have declined to throw out the statute as irremediably vague.

We agree that § 1346 should be construed rather than invalidated. First, we look to the doctrine developed in pre-*McNally* cases in an endeavor to ascertain the meaning of the phrase "the intangible right of honest services." Second, to preserve what Congress certainly intended the statute to cover, we pare that body of precedent down to its core: In the main, the pre-*McNally* cases involved fraudulent schemes to deprive another of honest services through bribes or kickbacks supplied by a third party who had not been deceived. Confined to these paramount applications, § 1346 presents no vagueness problem.

1

There is no doubt that Congress intended § 1346 to refer to and incorporate the honest services doctrine recognized in Court of Appeals decisions before *McNally* derailed the intangible rights theory of fraud. Congress enacted § 1346 on the heels of *McNally* and drafted the statute using that decision's terminology. As the Second Circuit observed in its leading analysis of § 1346:

> "The definite article 'the' suggests that intangible right of honest services had a specific meaning to Congress when it enacted the statute — Congress was recriminalizing mail- and wire-fraud schemes to deprive others of *that* 'intangible right of honest services,' which had been protected before *McNally,* not *all* intangible rights of honest services whatever they might be thought to be." United States v. Rybicki, 354 F.3d 124, 137-138 (2003) (en banc).

2

Satisfied that Congress, by enacting § 1346, "meant to reinstate the body of pre-*McNally* honest services law," we have surveyed that case law. In parsing the Courts of Appeals decisions, we acknowledge that Skilling's vagueness challenge has force, for honest services decisions preceding *McNally* were not models of clarity or consistency. While the honest services cases preceding *McNally* dominantly and consistently applied the fraud statute to bribery and kickback schemes — schemes that were the basis of most honest services prosecutions — there was considerable disarray over the statute's application to conduct outside that core category. In light of this disarray, Skilling urges us, as he urged the Fifth Circuit, to invalidate the statute *in toto.*

It has long been our practice, however, before striking a federal statute as impermissibly vague, to consider whether the prescription is amenable to a limiting construction. See, e.g., Hooper v. California, 155 U.S. 648, 657 (1895) ("The elementary rule is that *every reasonable construction* must be resorted to, in order to save a statute from unconstitutionality.""). We have accordingly instructed "the federal courts . . . to avoid constitutional difficulties by [adopting a limiting interpretation] if such a construction is fairly possible."

Arguing against any limiting construction, Skilling contends that it is impossible to identify a salvageable honest services core; "the pre-*McNally* caselaw," he asserts, "is a hodgepodge of oft-conflicting holdings" that are "hopelessly unclear." We have rejected an argument of the same tenor before. In *Civil Service Comm'n v. Letter Carriers,* federal employees challenged a provision of the Hatch Act that incorporated earlier decisions of the United States Civil Service Commission enforcing a similar law. "[T]he several thousand adjudications of the Civil Service Commission," the employees maintained, were "an impenetrable jungle" — "undiscoverable, inconsistent, [and] incapable of yielding any meaningful rules to govern present or future conduct." 413 U.S., at 571. Mindful that "our task [wa]s not to destroy the Act if we c[ould], but to construe it," we held that "the rules that had evolved over the years from repeated adjudications were subject to sufficiently clear and summary statement." Id. at 571-572.

A similar observation may be made here. Although some applications of the pre-*McNally* honest services doctrine occasioned disagreement among the Courts of Appeals, these cases do not cloud the doctrine's solid core: The "vast majority" of the honest services cases involved offenders who, in violation of a fiduciary duty, participated in bribery or kickback schemes. Indeed, the *McNally* case itself, which spurred Congress to enact § 1346, presented a paradigmatic kickback fact pattern. Congress' reversal of *McNally* and reinstatement of the honest services doctrine, we conclude, can and should be salvaged by confining its scope to the core pre-*McNally* applications.

As already noted, the honest services doctrine had its genesis in prosecutions involving bribery allegations.

In view of this history, there is no doubt that Congress intended § 1346 to reach *at least* bribes and kickbacks. Reading the statute to proscribe a wider range of offensive conduct, we acknowledge, would raise the due process concerns underlying the vagueness doctrine. To preserve the statute without transgressing constitutional limitations, we now hold that § 1346 criminalizes *only* the bribe and kickback core of the pre-*McNally* case law.

3

The Government urges us to go further by locating within § 1346's compass another category of proscribed conduct: "undisclosed self-dealing by a public official or private employee — *i.e.,* the taking of official action by the employee that furthers his own undisclosed financial interests while purporting to act in the interests of those to whom he owes a fiduciary duty." "[T]he theory of liability in *McNally* itself was nondisclosure of a conflicting financial interest," the Government observes, and "Congress clearly intended to revive th[at] nondisclosure theory." Moreover, "[a]lthough not as numerous as the bribery and kickback cases," the Government asserts, "the pre-*McNally* cases involving undisclosed self-dealing were abundant."

Neither of these contentions withstands close inspection. *McNally,* as we have already observed, involved a classic kickback scheme: A public official, in exchange for routing Kentucky's insurance business through a middleman company, arranged for that company to share its commissions with entities in which the official held an interest. This was no mere failure to disclose a conflict of interest; rather, the official conspired with a third party so that both would profit from wealth generated by public contracts. Reading § 1346 to proscribe bribes and kickbacks — and nothing more — satisfies Congress' undoubted aim to reverse *McNally* on its facts.

Nor are we persuaded that the pre-*McNally* conflict of interest cases constitute core applications of the honest services doctrine. Although the Courts of Appeals upheld honest services convictions for "some schemes of non-disclosure and concealment of material information," they reached no consensus on which schemes qualified. In light of the relative infrequency of conflict of interest prosecutions in comparison to bribery and kickback charges, and the intercircuit inconsistencies they produced, we conclude that a reasonable limiting construction of § 1346 must exclude this amorphous category of cases.

Further dispelling doubt on this point is the familiar principle that "ambiguity concerning the ambit of criminal statutes should be resolved in favor of lenity." *Cleveland,* 531 U.S., at 25. "This interpretive guide is especially appropriate in construing [§ 1346] because . . . mail [and wire] fraud [are] predicate offense[s] under [the Racketeer Influenced and Corrupt Organizations Act] and the money laundering statute." *Cleveland,* 531 U.S., at 25. Holding that honest services fraud does not encompass conduct more wide-ranging than the paradigmatic cases of bribes and kickbacks, we resist the Government's less constrained construction absent Congress' clear instruction otherwise.

In sum, our construction of § 1346 "establish[es] a uniform national standard, define[s] honest services with clarity, reach[es] only seriously culpable conduct, and accomplish[es] Congress's goal of 'overruling' *McNally.*" "If Congress desires to go further," we reiterate, "it must speak more clearly than it has." *McNally,* 483 U.S., at 360.[39]

4

Interpreted to encompass only bribery and kickback schemes, § 1346 is not unconstitutionally vague. Recall that the void for vagueness doctrine addresses concerns about (1) fair notice and (2) arbitrary and discriminatory prosecutions. A prohibition on fraudulently depriving another of one's honest services by accepting bribes or kickbacks does not present a problem on either score.

As to fair notice, "whatever the school of thought concerning the scope and meaning of § 1346, it has always been 'as plain as a pikestaff that' bribes and kickbacks constitute honest services fraud," Williams v. United States, 341 U.S. 97, 101 (1951), and the statute's *mens rea* requirement further blunts any notice concern.

---

39. If Congress were to take up the enterprise of criminalizing "undisclosed self-dealing by a public official or private employee," it would have to employ standards of sufficient definiteness and specificity to overcome due process concerns. The Government proposes a standard that prohibits the "taking of official action by the employee that furthers his own undisclosed financial interests while purporting to act in the interests of those to whom he owes a fiduciary duty," so long as the employee acts with a specific intent to deceive and the undisclosed conduct could influence the victim to change its behavior. That formulation, however, leaves many questions unanswered. How direct or significant does the conflicting financial interest have to be? To what extent does the official action have to further that interest in order to amount to fraud? To whom should the disclosure be made and what information should it convey? These questions and others call for particular care in attempting to formulate an adequate criminal prohibition in this context.

As to arbitrary prosecutions, we perceive no significant risk that the honest services statute, as we interpret it today, will be stretched out of shape. Its prohibition on bribes and kickbacks draws content not only from the pre-*McNally* case law, but also from federal statutes proscribing — and defining — similar crimes. A criminal defendant who participated in a bribery or kickback scheme, in short, cannot tenably complain about prosecution under § 1346 on vagueness grounds.

C

It remains to determine whether Skilling's conduct violated § 1346. Skilling's honest services prosecution, the Government concedes, was not "prototypical." The Government charged Skilling with conspiring to defraud Enron's shareholders by misrepresenting the company's fiscal health, thereby artificially inflating its stock price. It was the Government's theory at trial that Skilling "profited from the fraudulent scheme . . . through the receipt of salary and bonuses, . . . and through the sale of approximately $200 million in Enron stock, which netted him $89 million."

The Government did not, at any time, allege that Skilling solicited or accepted side payments from a third party in exchange for making these misrepresentations. It is therefore clear that, as we read § 1346, Skilling did not commit honest services fraud.

Because the indictment alleged three objects of the conspiracy — honest services wire fraud, money or property wire fraud, and securities fraud — Skilling's conviction is flawed. See Yates v. United States, 354 U.S. 298 (1957) (constitutional error occurs when a jury is instructed on alternative theories of guilt and returns a general verdict that may rest on a legally invalid theory). This determination, however, does not necessarily require reversal of the conspiracy conviction; we recently confirmed, in Hedgpeth v. Pulido, 129 S. Ct. 530 (2008) (per curiam), that errors of the *Yates* variety are subject to harmless error analysis. The parties vigorously dispute whether the error was harmless. We leave this dispute for resolution on remand.

Whether potential reversal on the conspiracy count touches any of Skilling's other convictions is also an open question. All of his convictions, Skilling contends, hinged on the conspiracy count and, like dominoes, must fall if it falls. The District Court, deciding Skilling's motion for bail pending appeal, found this argument dubious, but the Fifth Circuit had no occasion to rule on it. That court may do so on remand.

For the foregoing reasons, we affirm the Fifth Circuit's ruling on Skilling's fair trial argument, vacate its ruling on his conspiracy conviction, and remand the case for proceedings consistent with this opinion.

It is so ordered.

Justice SCALIA, with whom Justice THOMAS joins, and with whom Justice KENNEDY joins except as to Part III, concurring in part and concurring in the judgment. . . .

The Court strikes a pose of judicial humility in proclaiming that our task is "not to destroy the Act . . . but to construe it." But in transforming the prohibition of "honest services fraud" into a prohibition of "bribery and kick-backs" it is wielding a power we long ago abjured: the power to define new federal crimes.

I

A criminal statute must clearly define the conduct it proscribes. A statute that is unconstitutionally vague cannot be saved by a more precise indictment nor by judicial construction that writes in specific criteria that its text does not contain. Our cases have described vague statutes as failing "to provide a person of ordinary intelligence fair notice of what is prohibited, or [as being] so standardless that [they] authoriz[e] or encourag[e] seriously discriminatory enforcement." Here, Skilling argues that § 1346 fails to provide fair notice and encourages arbitrary enforcement because it provides no definition of the right of honest services whose deprivation it prohibits. In my view Skilling is correct.

The Court maintains that "the intangible right of honest services" means the right not to have one's fiduciaries accept "bribes or kickbacks." Its first step in reaching that conclusion is the assertion that the phrase refers to "the doctrine developed" in cases decided by lower federal courts prior to our decision in McNally v. United States, 483 U.S. 350 (1987). I do not contest that. I agree that Congress used the novel phrase to adopt the lower court case law that had been disapproved by McNally — what the Court calls "the pre-McNally honest services doctrine." The problem is that that doctrine provides no "ascertainable standard of guilt," and certainly is not limited to "bribes or kickbacks." . . .

[P]re-McNally Court of Appeals opinions were not limited to fraud by public officials. Some courts had held that those fiduciaries subject to the "honest services" obligation included private individuals who merely participated in public decisions and even private employees who had no role in public decisions. Moreover, "to say that a man is a fiduciary only begins [the] analysis; it gives direction to further inquiry. . . . What obligations does he owe as a fiduciary?" None of the "honest services" cases, neither those pertaining to public officials nor those pertaining to private employees, defined the nature and content of the fiduciary duty central to the "fraud" offense.

There was not even universal agreement concerning the *source* of the fiduciary obligation — whether it must be positive state or federal law, or merely general principles, such as the "obligations of loyalty and fidelity" that inhere in the "employment relationship." The decision McNally reversed had grounded the duty in general (not jurisdiction specific) trust law, a *corpus juris* festooned with various duties. Another pre-McNally case referred to the general law of agency, which imposes duties quite different from those of a trustee.

This indeterminacy does not disappear if one assumes that the pre-McNally cases developed a federal, common law fiduciary duty; the duty remained hopelessly undefined. Some courts described it in astoundingly broad language. Blachly v. United States, 380 F.2d 665 (5th Cir. 1967), loftily declared that "[l]aw puts its imprimatur on the accepted moral standards and condemns conduct which fails to match the 'reflection of moral uprightness, of fundamental honesty, fair play and right dealing in the general and business life of members of society.'" Other courts unhelpfully added that any scheme "contrary to public policy" was also condemned by the statute. Even opinions that did not indulge in such grandiloquence did not specify the duty at issue beyond loyalty or honesty. Moreover, the demands of the duty were said to be greater for public officials than for private employees, but in what respects (or by how much) was never made clear.

The indefiniteness of the fiduciary duty is not all. Many courts held that some *je-ne-sais-quoi* beyond a mere breach of fiduciary duty was needed to establish honest services fraud. There was, unsurprisingly, some dispute about that, at least in the context of acts by persons owing duties to the public. And even among those courts that did require something additional where a public official was involved, there was disagreement as to what the addition should be. For example, in United States v. Bush, 522 F.2d 641 (1975), the Seventh Circuit held that material misrepresentations and active concealment were enough. But in *Rabbitt,* 583 F.2d 1014, the Eighth Circuit held that actual harm to the State was needed.

Similar disagreements occurred with respect to private employees. Courts disputed whether the defendant must use his fiduciary position for his own gain. . . . The Court's statement today that there was a deprivation of honest services even if "the scheme occasioned a money or property *gain* for the betrayed party," is therefore true, except to the extent it is not.

In short, the first step in the Court's analysis — holding that "the intangible right of honest services" refers to "the honest services doctrine recognized in Court of Appeals' decisions before *McNally,*" — is a step out of the frying pan into the fire. The pre-*McNally* cases provide no clear indication of what constitutes a denial of the right of honest services. The possibilities range from any action that is contrary to public policy or otherwise immoral, to only the disloyalty of a public official or employee to his principal, to only the secret use of a perpetrator's position of trust in order to harm whomever he is beholden to. The duty probably did not have to be rooted in state law, but maybe it did. It might have been more demanding in the case of public officials, but perhaps not. At the time § 1346 was enacted there was no settled criterion for choosing among these options, for conclusively settling what was in and what was out.

II

The Court is aware of all this. It knows that adopting by reference "the pre-*McNally* honest services doctrine" is adopting by reference nothing more precise than the referring term itself ("the intangible right of honest services"). Hence the *deus ex machina*: "[W]e pare that body of precedent down to its core." Since the honest services doctrine "had its genesis" in bribery prosecutions, and since several cases and counsel for Skilling referred to bribery and kickback schemes as "core" or "paradigm" or "typical" examples, or "[t]he most obvious form," of honest services fraud, and since two cases and counsel for the Government say that they formed the "vast majority," or "most" or at least "[t]he bulk" of honest services cases, THEREFORE it must be the case that they are *all* Congress meant by its reference to the honest services doctrine.

Even if that conclusion followed from its premises, it would not suffice to eliminate the vagueness of the statute. It would solve (perhaps) the indeterminacy of what acts constitute a breach of the "honest services" obligation under the pre-*McNally* law. But it would not solve the most fundamental indeterminacy: the character of the "fiduciary capacity" to which the bribery and kickback restriction applies. Does it apply only to public officials? Or in addition to private individuals who contract with the public? Or to everyone, including the corporate officer here? The pre-*McNally* case law does not provide an answer. Thus, even with the bribery and kickback limitation the statute does not answer the question "What is the criterion of guilt?"

But that is perhaps beside the point, because it is obvious that mere prohibition of bribery and kickbacks was not the intent of the statute. To say that bribery and kick-backs represented "the core" of the doctrine, or that most cases applying the doctrine involved those offenses, is not to say that they *are* the doctrine. All it proves is that the multifarious versions of the doctrine *overlap* with regard to those offenses. But the doc-trine itself is much more. Among all the pre-*McNally* smorgasbord offerings of variet-ies of honest services fraud, *not one* is limited to bribery and kickbacks. That is a dish the Court has cooked up all on its own.

Thus, the Court's claim to "respec[t] the legislature" is false. It is entirely clear (as the Court and I agree) that Congress meant to reinstate the body of pre-*McNally* honest services law; and entirely clear that that prohibited much more (though precisely what more is uncertain) than bribery and kickbacks. Perhaps it is true that "Congress intended § 1346 to reach *at least* bribes and kickbacks." That simply does not mean, as the Court now holds, that "§ 1346 criminalizes *only*" bribery and kickbacks.

Arriving at that conclusion requires not interpretation but invention. . . .

[Opinion of Justice SOTOMAYOR, concurring in part and dissenting in part, omitted.]

Notes and Questions

1. Is it fair to say, as the majority does, that because most prosecutions under the pre-*McNally* honest services theory involved bribery or kickbacks, § 1346 therefore applies to only those forms of dishonesty? Or does Justice Scalia hit the mark when he says that although prosecutions involving bribery and kickbacks may be the most com-mon examples of pre-*McNally* honest services theory, the prevalence of this category of prosecutions doesn't necessarily mean that those cases define the contours of the theory itself?

2. In paring the pre-*McNally* body of honest services precedent down to its "core" — i.e., bribery and kickbacks — is the majority interpreting or rewriting § 1346? Does the majority's opinion carry out or thwart what Congress intended when it enacted § 1346?

3. Although the Court ruled that § 1346 applies only to schemes involving bribery and kickbacks, it did not define either term. Does the term "bribery" encompass the crime of "gratuity"?[40] Are the definitions of bribery and kickbacks limited by conduct that is prohibited by federal statutory and/or case law,[41] or do they also include more expansive forms of corruption prohibited under state law? Is there a sufficiently shared understanding of the generic meaning of these terms to provide the average person fair notice of what behavior is punishable?[42] Or has the Court merely substituted one ambiguity for another?

---

40. Cf. 18 U.S.C. § 201 (defining bribery as the giving or receipt of something of value (i.e., a quid pro quo) to influence a public official's performance of his duties but defining the crime of gratuity as the giving or receipt of something of value on account of (i.e., as a reward for) official action that has been taken or will be taken in the future).

41. Cf. United States v. Copeland, 143 F.3d 1439 (11th Cir. 1998) (construing the federal program bribery statute, 18 U.S.C. § 666, as excluding purely commercial transactions with the government).

42. Cf. United States v. Garner, 837 F.2d 1404 (7th Cir. 1987) (construing the RICO definition of state predicate crimes under 18 U.S.C. § 1961(1)(A) as including any act involving bribery to mean

4. Does *Skilling* apply only to bribery and kickbacks involving a public official, or does it apply to cases of private commercial bribery as well? Why should it make any difference whether one of the participants in the scheme is a public official? And just who is a public official? What sources of authority should lower courts look to in resolving these questions?

5. Is breach of a fiduciary duty required under the honest services theory after *Skilling*? If so, how should the lower courts interpret what constitutes a fiduciary duty? What sources of authority should govern the resolution of this question?

6. The Court makes it clear that it is within the province of Congress to overturn *Skilling* by enacting legislation that "speaks more clearly" to what conduct is criminal.[43] If Congress wants to amend § 1346 to include the government's theory that the honest services statute should be applied to conflict of interest cases in which there is undisclosed self dealing, what must the legislation do to pass muster after *Skilling*? Is it clear how such a bill should be drafted? What hurdles does Congress still face?

7. Is it clear whether Skilling's conviction must be thrown out? If not, what decisions remain for the lower courts to resolve?

8. After *Skilling*, could the government prosecute the defendants in *George* under § 1346? Is there more than one mail fraud theory the government could pursue if it prosecuted a case involving facts similar to those in *George*?

III. USE OF THE MAILS

Even though the use of the mails is the heart of § 1341, the mailings need not be central to the scheme to defraud. Use of the mails need only be "incident to an essential part of the scheme."[44]

SCHMUCK v. UNITED STATES
489 U.S. 705 (1989)

Justice BLACKMUN delivered the opinion of the Court.

I

In August 1983, petitioner Wayne T. Schmuck, a used-car distributor, was indicted in the United States District Court for the Western District of Wisconsin on 12 counts of mail fraud, in violation of 18 U.S.C. §§ 1341 and 2.

---

anything encompassed under state law that makes bribery or bribery-like conduct — in its generic sense — a crime).

43. Within three months of the *Skilling* decision, Senator Patrick Leahy (then Chairman of the Senate Judiciary Committee), proposed legislation that would broaden the definition of honest services fraud and attempt once again to reinstate pre-*McNally* case law.

44. Pereira v. United States, 347 U.S. 1, 8 (1954).

The alleged fraud was a common and straightforward one. Schmuck purchased used cars, rolled back their odometers, and then sold the automobiles to Wisconsin retail dealers for prices artificially inflated because of the low-mileage readings. These unwitting car dealers, relying on the altered odometer figures, then resold the cars to customers, who in turn paid prices reflecting Schmuck's fraud. To complete the resale of each automobile, the dealer who purchased it from Schmuck would submit a title-application form to the Wisconsin Department of Transportation on behalf of his retail customers. The receipt of a Wisconsin title was a prerequisite for completing the resale; without it, the dealer could not transfer title to the customer and the customer could not obtain Wisconsin tags. The submission of the title-application form supplied the mailing element of each of the alleged mail frauds.

[The jury returned guilty verdicts on all 12 counts. On appeal, Schmuck argued unsuccessfully that the mailings of the title applications were not in furtherance of the fraudulent scheme.]

II

"The federal mail fraud statute does not purport to reach all frauds, but only those limited instances in which the use of the mails is a part of the execution of the fraud, leaving all other cases to be dealt with by appropriate state law." Kann v. United States, 323 U.S. 88, 95 (1944). To be part of the execution of the fraud, however, the use of the mails need not be an essential element of the scheme. Pereira v. United States, 347 U.S. 1, 8 (1954). It is sufficient for the mailing to be "incident to an essential part of the scheme," ibid., or "a step in [the] plot," Badders v. United States, 240 U.S. 391, 394 (1916).

Schmuck, relying principally on this Court's decisions in *Kann*, supra, Parr v. United States, 363 U.S. 370 (1960), and United States v. Maze, 414 U.S. 395 (1974), argues that mail fraud can be predicated only on a mailing that affirmatively assists the perpetrator in carrying out his fraudulent scheme. The mailing element of the offense, he contends, cannot be satisfied by a mailing, such as those at issue here, that is routine and innocent in and of itself, and that, far from furthering the execution of the fraud, occurs after the fraud has come to fruition, is merely tangentially related to the fraud, and is counterproductive in that it creates a "paper trail" from which the fraud may be discovered. We disagree both with this characterization of the mailings in the present case and with this description of the applicable law.

We begin by considering the scope of Schmuck's fraudulent scheme. Schmuck was charged with devising and executing a scheme to defraud Wisconsin retail automobile customers who based their decisions to purchase certain automobiles at least in part on the low-mileage readings provided by the tampered odometers. This was a fairly large-scale operation. Evidence at trial indicated that Schmuck had employed a man known only as "Fred" to turn back the odometers on about 150 different cars. Schmuck then marketed these cars to a number of dealers, several of whom he dealt with on a consistent basis over a period of about 15 years. Indeed, of the 12 automobiles that are the subject of the counts of the indictment, 5 were sold to "P & A Sales," and 4 to "Southside Auto." Thus, Schmuck's was not a "one-shot" operation in which he sold a single car to an isolated dealer. His was an ongoing fraudulent venture. A rational jury could have concluded that the success of Schmuck's venture depended upon his continued harmonious relations with and good reputation among retail dealers, which in turn required the smooth flow of cars from the dealers to their Wisconsin customers.

Under these circumstances, we believe that a rational jury could have found that the title-registration mailings were part of the execution of the fraudulent scheme, a scheme which did not reach fruition until the retail dealers resold the cars and effected transfers of title. Schmuck's scheme would have come to an abrupt halt if the dealers either had lost faith in Schmuck or had not been able to resell the cars obtained from him. These resales and Schmuck's relationships with the retail dealers naturally depend on the successful passage of title among the various parties. Thus, although the registration-form mailings may not have contributed directly to the duping of either the retail dealers or the customers, they were necessary to the passage of title, which in turn was essential to the perpetuation of Schmuck's scheme. As noted earlier, a mailing that is "incident to an essential part of the scheme," *Pereira*, 347 U.S., at 8, satisfies the mailing element of the mail fraud offense. The mailings here fit this description.

Once the full flavor of Schmuck's scheme is appreciated, the critical distinctions between this case and the three cases in which this Court has delimited the reach of the mail fraud statute — *Kann*, *Parr*, and *Maze* — are readily apparent. The defendants in *Kann* were corporate officers and directors accused of setting up a dummy corporation through which to divert profits into their own pockets. As part of this fraudulent scheme, the defendants caused the corporation to issue two checks payable to them. The defendants cashed these checks at local banks, which then mailed the checks to the drawee banks for collection. This Court held that the mailing of the cashed checks to the drawee banks could not supply the mailing element of the mail fraud charges. The defendants' fraudulent scheme had reached fruition. "It was immaterial to them, or to any consummation of the scheme, how the bank which paid or credited the check would collect from the drawee bank." 323 U.S., at 94.

In *Parr*, several defendants were charged, inter alia, with having fraudulently obtained gasoline and a variety of other products and services through the unauthorized use of a credit card issued to the school district which employed them. The mailing element of the mail fraud charges in *Parr* was purportedly satisfied when the oil company which issued the credit card mailed invoices to the school district for payment, and when the district mailed payment in the form of a check. Relying on *Kann*, this Court held that these mailings were not in execution of the scheme as required by the statute because it was immaterial to the defendants how the oil company went about collecting its payment.[45]

Later, in *Maze*, the defendant allegedly stole his roommate's credit card, headed south on a winter jaunt, and obtained food and lodging at motels along the route by

---

45. *Parr* also involved a second fraudulent scheme through which the defendant school board members misappropriated school district tax revenues. The Government argued that the mailing element of the mail fraud charges was supplied by the mailing of tax statements, checks, and receipts. This Court held, however, that in the absence of any evidence that the tax levy was increased as part of the fraud, the mailing element of the offense could not be supplied by mailings "made or caused to be made under the imperative command of duty imposed by state law." 363 U.S., at 391. No such legal duty is at issue here. Whereas the mailings of the tax documents in *Parr* were the direct product of the school district's state constitutional duty to levy taxes, and would have been made regardless of the defendants' fraudulent scheme, the mailings in the present case, though in compliance with Wisconsin's car-registration procedure, were derivative of Schmuck's scheme to sell "doctored" cars and would not have occurred but for that scheme.

placing the charges on the stolen card. The mailing element of the mail fraud charge was supplied by the fact that the defendant knew that each motel proprietor would mail an invoice to the bank that had issued the credit card, which in turn would mail a bill to the card owner for payment. The Court found that these mailings could not support mail fraud charges because the defendant's scheme had reached fruition when he checked out of each motel. The success of his scheme in no way depended on the mailings; they merely determined which of his victims would ultimately bear the loss.

The title-registration mailings at issue here served a function different from the mailings in *Kann*, *Parr*, and *Maze*. The intrabank mailings in *Kann* and the credit card invoice mailings in *Parr* and *Maze* involved little more than post-fraud accounting among the potential victims of the various schemes, and the long-term success of the fraud did not turn on which of the potential victims bore the ultimate loss. Here, in contrast, a jury rationally could have found that Schmuck by no means was indifferent to the fact of who bore the loss. The mailing of the title-registration forms was an essential step in the successful passage of title to the retail purchasers. Moreover, a failure in this passage of title would have jeopardized Schmuck's relationship of trust and good-will with the retail dealers upon whose unwitting cooperation his scheme depended. Schmuck's reliance on our prior cases limiting the reach of the mail fraud statute is simply misplaced.

To the extent that Schmuck would draw from these previous cases a general rule that routine mailings that are innocent in themselves cannot supply the mailing element of the mail fraud offense, he misapprehends this Court's precedents. In *Parr* the Court specifically acknowledged that "innocent" mailings — ones that contain no false information — may supply the mailing element. In other cases, the Court has found the elements of mail fraud to be satisfied where the mailings have been routine. See, e.g., Carpenter v. United States, 484 U.S. 19, 28 (1987) (mailing newspapers).

We also reject Schmuck's contention that mailings that someday may contribute to the uncovering of a fraudulent scheme cannot supply the mailing element of the mail fraud offense. The relevant question at all times is whether the mailing is part of the execution of the scheme as conceived by the perpetrator at the time, regardless of whether the mailing later, through hindsight, may prove to have been counterproductive and return to haunt the perpetrator of the fraud. The mail fraud statute includes no guarantee that the use of the mails for the purpose of executing a fraudulent scheme will be risk free. Those who use the mails to defraud proceed at their peril.

For these reasons, we agree with the Court of Appeals that the mailings in this case satisfy the mailing element of the mail fraud offenses. . . .

It is so ordered.

Justice SCALIA, with whom Justice BRENNAN, Justice MARSHALL, and Justice O'CONNOR join, dissenting. . . .

The purpose of the mail fraud statute is "to prevent the post office from being used to carry [fraudulent schemes] into effect." Durland v. United States, 161 U.S. 306, 314 (1896); Parr v. United States, 363 U.S. 370, 389 (1960). The law does not establish a general federal remedy against fraudulent conduct, with use of the mails as the jurisdictional hook, but reaches only "those limited instances in which the use of the mails is *a part of the execution of the fraud*, leaving all other cases to be dealt with by appropriate state law." Kann v. United States, 323 U.S. 88, 95 (1944) (emphasis added). In other words, it is mail fraud, not mail and fraud, that incurs liability. This federal statute is not violated by a fraudulent scheme in which, at some point, a mailing happens to occur — nor even by one in which a mailing predictably and necessarily occurs. The mailing must be in furtherance of the fraud.

In Kann v. United States, we concluded that even though defendants who cashed checks obtained as part of a fraudulent scheme knew that the bank cashing the checks would send them by mail to a drawee bank for collection, they did not thereby violate the mail fraud statute, because upon their receipt of the cash "[t]he scheme . . . had reached fruition," and the mailing was "immaterial . . . to any consummation of the scheme." Id. at 94. We held to the same effect in United States v. Maze, declining to find that credit-card fraud was converted into mail fraud by the certainty that, after the wrongdoer had fraudulently received his goods and services from the merchants, they would forward the credit charges by mail for payment. These cases are squarely in point here. For though the Government chose to charge a defrauding of retail customers (to whom the innocent dealers resold the cars), it is obvious that, regardless of who the ultimate victim of the fraud may have been, the fraud was complete with respect to each car when petitioner pocketed the dealer's money. As far as each particular transaction was concerned, it was as inconsequential to him whether the dealer resold the car as it was inconsequential to the defendant in *Maze* whether the defrauded merchant ever forwarded the charges to the credit-card company. . . .

What Justice Frankfurter observed almost three decades ago remains true: "The adequate degree of relationship between a mailing which occurs during the life of a scheme and the scheme is . . . not a matter susceptible of geometric determination." Parr v. United States, supra, at 397 (Frankfurter, J., dissenting). All the more reason to adhere as closely as possible to past cases. I think we have not done that today, and thus create problems for tomorrow.

Notes and Questions

1. All of the mailings were title applications submitted by the retail dealers on behalf of their buyers, but Schmuck knew it was customary for the dealers to mail the applications. In what sense is there a nexus between Schmuck and the dealers' use of the mails? Is this sufficient to elevate Schmuck's scheme to mail fraud? Or, as Justice Scalia complained, does this amount to nothing more than mail and fraud?

2. The Court informs us that Schmuck sold cars with rolled-back odometers to Wisconsin retail dealers. The following additional facts came to light during oral arguments. Schmuck was an Illinois resident operating an Illinois car business. The cars he sold to the Wisconsin dealers came from and were titled in Illinois. At the time the sales occurred, Illinois titling laws did not require a statement of the odometer mileage. Thus, when Schmuck hand delivered the false odometer slips (and presumably the Illinois title documents) to the Wisconsin dealers, the discrepancy between the actual and recorded mileage figures would not have been apparent.

The Wisconsin titles were essential to the dealers' ability to resell the cars. You could not get a license plate or drive a car on Wisconsin roads without a title, and in Wisconsin you could not get a title without an odometer mileage statement. Thus, the first mileage that appeared in Wisconsin title records was the rolled back mileage the

Wisconsin dealers unwittingly put in the title application forms and mailed to the Wisconsin Department of Transportation on behalf of the buyers. Simply put, when the Wisconsin dealers resold the cars, the odometer readings recorded in the Wisconsin title applications would not have revealed evidence of Schmuck's odometer tampering.

Do these facts help explain the government's theory that the Wisconsin dealers' submission of the title applications supplied the mailing element?

3. In *Carpenter*, the Supreme Court said that the mailing of the Wall Street Journal was essential to the insider trading scheme. In what sense was it essential? And what about the timing? Was the fraud on the Journal complete *before* the mails were used? If so, how could the mailings have "furthered" the scheme to defraud?

4. Who mailed the Wall Street Journal and the title applications in *Carpenter* and *Schmuck*? Does it matter who mailed them?

5. Were there any fraudulent misrepresentations in the Wall Street Journal's "Heard on the Street" columns? If not, why would the mailings be within the reach of the mail fraud statute?

UNITED STATES v. SAMPSON
371 U.S. 75 (1962)

Mr. Justice BLACK delivered the opinion of the Court.

[The defendants were officers, directors, and employees of a large corporation that purported to assist business people to obtain loans or sell their businesses. Although the defendants made elaborate representations about the services they would supply, they did not intend and made no effort to perform them.

Their modus operandi was to call upon prospects, encourage them to apply for the defendants' services, and urge them to give the defendants a refundable "advance fee," which the defendants immediately deposited into their own bank account. All applications that were signed and accompanied by a check in the right amount were accepted. After the money was received, the accepted applications were routinely mailed to the victims, together with a form letter that was "'for the purpose of lulling [the] victims by representing that their applications had been accepted and that the defendants would therefore perform for said victims the valuable services which the defendants had falsely and fraudulently represented that they would perform.'"

In reliance on *Kann* and *Parr*, the district court dismissed the indictment on the ground that the mailings were not for the purpose of executing the scheme.]

The use of the mails relied on in the 34 dismissed counts was the mailing by the defendants of their acceptances of the victims' applications for their services. As conceded by the Government, prior to each mailing of an acceptance to a victim the defendants had obtained all the money they expected to get from that victim. The district judge's reason for holding that these counts did not charge a federal offense was that, since the money had already been obtained by the defendants before the acceptances were mailed, these mailings could not have been "for the purpose of executing" the scheme. For this holding the court relied chiefly on Kann v. United States, 323 U.S. 88 (1944), and Parr v. United States, 363 U.S. 370 (1960). . . .

We are unable to find anything in either the *Kann* or the *Parr* case which suggests that the Court was laying down an automatic rule that a deliberate, planned use of the mails after the victims' money had been obtained can never be "for the purpose of executing" the defendants' scheme. Rather the Court found only that under the facts in those cases the schemes had been fully executed before the mails were used. And Court of Appeals decisions rendered both before and after *Kann* have followed the view that subsequent mailings can in some circumstances provide the basis for an indictment under the mail fraud statute[].

Moreover, as pointed out above, the indictment in this case alleged that the defendants' scheme contemplated from the start the commission of fraudulent activities which were to be and actually were carried out both before and after the money was obtained from the victims. The indictment specifically alleged that the signed copies of the accepted applications and the covering letters were mailed by the defendants to the victims for the purpose of lulling them by assurances that the promised services would be performed. We cannot hold that such a deliberate and planned use of the United States mails by defendants engaged in a nationwide, fraudulent scheme in pursuance of a previously formulated plan could not, if established by evidence, be found by a jury under proper instructions to be "for the purpose of executing" a scheme within the meaning of the mail fraud statute. For these reasons, we hold that it was error for the District Court to dismiss these 34 substantive counts. . . .

Reversed.

Mr. Justice DOUGLAS, dissenting.

I think that today the Court materially qualifies Parr v. United States, 363 U.S. 370. . . .

It is possible that in this case indictments could be drawn which charge the use of mails *to lull existing victims* into a feeling of security so that a scheme to obtain money *from other victims* could be successfully consummated. The opinion does not so construe the indictment but concludes, as I read it, that the mere lulling of existing victims into a sense of security is enough. . . .

We should not struggle to uphold poorly drawn counts. To do so only encourages more federal prosecution in fields that are essentially local.

Notes and Questions

1. Why are "lulling letters" deemed to be "in furtherance" of a scheme to defraud? Is it important that the defendants in *Sampson* received all the money they intended to get from the victims *before* the letters were sent?

2. Is *Sampson* consistent with *Kann* and *Parr*? Justice Douglas thought not.

3. Do the mailings in *Sampson* bear the same or a similar relationship to the fraud as those in *Schmuck*, or are they altogether different?

4. The requirement that the mailings be "in furtherance of" the fraudulent scheme precludes the government from relying on mailings that work against the scheme. Thus, a mailing that "serves to put the defrauded person on notice of the fraud, makes the execution of the fraud less likely, opposes the scheme, or discloses the nature of the fraud" generally will not violate the statute.[46]

---

46. United States v. Koen, 982 F.2d 1101, 1107 (7th Cir. 1992).

But whether a mailing is in furtherance of the scheme is determined at the time of the mailing. If the mailing was part of the execution as the defendant perceived it, the mailing violates the statute notwithstanding that it may have fortuitously accelerated discovery of the scheme.[47]

Were the mailings by the victims in *Sampson* in furtherance of the scheme? If so, why didn't the prosecutor rely on them to bring the scheme within the ambit of § 1341?

NOTE ON PROOF OF MAILING

The government may use circumstantial evidence to prove the mails were used to further a scheme to defraud. In effect, this relieves the government of the burden of proving who actually mailed the communications in question and precisely how and when they were mailed. The proof may consist of evidence concerning routine office procedures for processing documents like those in question[48] or evidence of conduct that is consistent with a response to the material that was mailed.[49]

Because the gist of the mail fraud offense is use of the mails in furtherance of a fraudulent scheme rather than commission of the fraud itself, each separate mailing in furtherance of the scheme constitutes a separate offense.

In 1994, Congress broadened the mail fraud statute by expanding the jurisdictional element to allow depositing anything to be delivered by a *private* or *commercial interstate carrier* to serve as a substitute for the mailing requirement. Thus, sending a package via Federal Express or UPS in furtherance of a scheme to defraud can now be prosecuted as mail fraud. Is this expansion of federal jurisdiction warranted?

IV. MAIL AND WIRE FRAUD AFFECTING A FINANCIAL INSTITUTION

In 1989, Congress amended the mail and wire fraud statutes to increase the maximum penalties to 30 years in prison and a fine of up to $1 million and to provide a longer statute of limitations if the fraud affected a financial institution.[50] Neither the text of the amended statutes nor the legislative history provides guidance on when mail or wire fraud will be deemed to "affect" a financial institution, or how the financial institution must be affected by the fraud.

---

47. Id. at 1109.

48. United States v. Joyce, 499 F.2d 9 (7th Cir. 1974) (proof of mailing was established through witness who testified that he dictated the letter in question and that under standard office procedure his secretary mailed all dictated letters except interoffice correspondence).

49. United States v. Hopkins, 357 F.2d 14 (6th Cir. 1966) (mailing was established by proof that advertiser, who solicited prospective purchasers to mail inquiries to a post office box number, called a prospective purchaser in an apparent response to a solicited inquiry).

50. The term "financial institution" is defined in 18 U.S.C. § 20.

UNITED STATES v. BOUYEA
152 F.3d 192 (2d Cir. 1998)

PER CURIAM. . . .

BACKGROUND

On February 22, 1996, a federal grand jury returned a three-count indictment charging Bouyea and one co-defendant with two counts of bank fraud and one count of wire fraud. The first bank fraud count alleged that Bouyea engaged in a scheme to defraud Chester Bank by causing Chester Bank to lend money on the basis of forged, false, and fraudulent documents. The second count charged Bouyea with wire fraud for using an interstate facsimile transmission to fraudulently obtain $150,000 in money and property from the Center Capital Corporation ("Center Capital") in a manner affecting Centerbank, a financial institution of which Center Capital is a wholly-owned subsidiary. The third count of the indictment charged Bouyea with bank fraud for devising a scheme or artifice to defraud Founders Bank, a financial institution.

On November 7, 1996, after a five day trial, a jury returned a verdict of guilty on counts two and three, but acquitted the defendants on the first count. . . . On February 12, 1997, the district court sentenced the defendant, in principal part, to thirty months' imprisonment, and ordered restitution in the amount of $450,000.

Bouyea appealed. . . .

DISCUSSION . . .

First, Bouyea argues that there is insufficient evidence to prove "intent" and "materiality." In order to convict Bouyea of wire fraud, the government was obligated to prove that he devised a scheme "to defraud, or for obtaining money or property by means of false or fraudulent pretenses, or promises . . . ," and that he used interstate wires or communications to execute the scheme. In addition, the government had to prove that Bouyea had a fraudulent intent. The false representation or failure to disclose must relate to material information. The government presented more than sufficient evidence for a rational juror to conclude that Bouyea engaged in a scheme to defraud Center Capital; that Bouyea made misstatements in furtherance of that scheme; that he knew of the misstatements and intentionally made them in order to get a loan from Center Capital; that those misstatements were material; and that Bouyea used the interstate wires (that is, a facsimile machine) in order to effectuate his scheme. Accordingly, we decline to reverse the wire fraud conviction on this ground.

The second question is whether the evidence supported the jury's conclusion that Bouyea's scheme "affected a financial institution." Normally, conviction under the federal wire fraud statute does not require proof of an effect on a financial institution. A five-year statute of limitations generally applies to the filing of a wire fraud indictment. However, "if the offense affects a financial institution," then a ten-year statute of limitations applies. In the present case, the indictment was filed six years after the wire fraud took place. Therefore, the district court charged the jury that in order to convict, the government was required to prove that Bouyea's wire fraud against Center Capital affected a financial institution.

The defrauded institution, Center Capital, is a wholly-owned subsidiary of Centerbank, which is a financial institution. However, Center Capital is not itself a financial institution within the meaning of the statute. Nonetheless, the evidence presented to the jury was sufficient to allow it to conclude that, by defrauding a wholly-owned subsidiary of Centerbank, Bouyea did "affect" Centerbank, a financial institution, for purposes of § 3293(2). John Coates, credit manager and director of remarketing for Center Capital, testified that Center Capital borrowed the money for its transaction with Bouyea from its parent, Centerbank, and that when Center Capital suffered a $150,000 loss as a result of Bouyea's fraudulent scheme, Centerbank was affected by this loss. This testimony was sufficient to support the finding that a financial institution was affected by the wire fraud.

Insofar as Bouyea argues that the defrauding of a financial institution's subsidiary — leading to a reduction of the financial institution's assets — is insufficient as a matter of law to meet the "affecting a financial institution" requirement of § 3293(2), we easily reject his argument. As the Third Circuit Court of Appeals has found:

> We may quickly dispose of the . . . argument [that Congress meant to exclude fraud affecting a bank's service subsidiary from § 3282(2)] for it assumes that a fraud perpetrated against a financial institution's wholly owned subsidiary cannot affect the parent, a clearly untenable assumption. Moreover, whether or not it is possible to perpetrate a fraud against a wholly owned subsidiary without affecting its parent, the statute is clear: it broadly applies to any act of wire fraud "that affects a financial institution." [The defendant's] argument would have more force if the statute provided for an extended limitations period where the financial institution is the object of fraud. Clearly, however, Congress chose to extend the statute of limitations to a broader class of crimes.

United States v. Pelullo, 964 F.2d 193, 215-16 (3d Cir. 1992). On the facts of this case, the effect of the wire fraud on Centerbank was sufficiently direct so as to support the jury's finding. Accordingly, there was sufficient evidence to support the jury's necessary finding that the wire fraud affected a financial institution.

Because we affirm Bouyea's conviction for wire fraud, Bouyea's claim that his bank fraud conviction should be vacated . . . is moot. . . .

The judgment of the district court is affirmed.

Notes and Questions

1. How was the bank in *Bouyea* affected by the wire fraud?
2. Why would Congress provide more severe penalties and a longer statute of limitations for mail and wire fraud violations that affect a financial institution? Why wouldn't Congress require that the bank be the object of the fraud?
3. Bouyea was charged with wire fraud and bank fraud. The practice of tacking mail or wire fraud charges onto allegations that the defendant's conduct also violated another more specific statute is common. Defense lawyers sometimes argue that when Congress enacts a specific statute (e.g., bank fraud), it intends for the specific statute to trump statutes of general applicability (e.g., mail fraud). The argument largely falls on

deaf ears.[51] Thus, the government often gets at least two bites at the apple by charging the defendant under overlapping statutes. Why would courts be unsympathetic to the argument that the statutes should be construed as mutually exclusive?

V. STATUTES PROHIBITING SPECIFIC FRAUDS

A. BANK FRAUD

The bank fraud statute, 18 U.S.C. § 1344, is patterned after the mail and wire fraud statutes. It has two distinct prohibitions: (1) knowingly executing or attempting to execute a scheme or artifice to defraud a financial institution;[52] and (2) knowingly executing or attempting to execute a scheme or artifice to obtain moneys, assets, or other property owned by or under the custody or control of a financial institution through false or fraudulent pretenses, representations, or promises.

UNITED STATES v. DOKE
171 F.3d 240 (5th Cir. 1999)

JONES, Circuit Judge. . . .

I. FACTS

Doke was a real estate developer in Houston. Bass was his attorney and had negotiated several of Doke's real estate transactions. In 1984, one of Doke's entities sold a 200-acre tract of undeveloped land in north Houston to General Homes Corporation, retaining two options to buy back small parcels of it. The first option, pertaining to 6.028 acres, was set to expire on August 1, 1985.

On July 11, 1985, Bass notified General Homes that Doke would exercise his option to buy the land. The purchase price would be nearly $788,000. On July 19, Bass requested a $600,000 loan from Champions Point National Bank ("Champions") to pay for the land. Champions approved the loan on July 30, and the next day, in a simultaneous closing, General Homes sold the land to a Doke entity, which sold it to Bass for the same price. This prosecution arose from that loan. The government argues — and the jury must have believed — that Bass told Champions he was borrowing the money to buy the land from Doke, without revealing Doke's continued involvement with the land or the loan.

---

51. See, e.g., United States v. Dowling, 739 F.2d 1445 (9th Cir. 1984), rev'd in part, 473 U.S. 207 (1985) (rejecting argument that statute punishing copyright infringement and mail fraud statute are mutually exclusive); United States v. Computer Sciences Corp., 689 F.2d 1181 (4th Cir. 1982) (rejecting argument that false claims statute and mail and wire fraud statutes are mutually exclusive); United States v. Weatherspoon, 581 F.2d 595 (7th Cir. 1978) (rejecting argument that false statements statute and mail fraud statute are mutually exclusive); Edwards v. United States, 312 U.S. 473 (1941) (rejecting argument that securities laws preempt mail fraud statute); United States v. Shareef, 634 F.2d 679 (2d Cir. 1980) (Commodity Futures Trading Commission Act of 1974 does not preempt mail fraud statute).

52. For the applicable definition of the term "financial institution," see 18 U.S.C. § 20.

It is undisputed that Doke gave to Bass the $200,000 Bass used for the down payment. Every six months for the next two years, Doke sent to Bass the money Bass used to make each payment on the loan. By late 1987, however, the Houston real estate market and the stock market had crashed. Doke was no longer able to pay Bass for the loan payments. Just before the February 1988 payment was due, Bass asked Champions to restructure his loan by extending more credit and extending the repayment terms. In the letter making this request, Bass made no mention of Doke. Champions denied Bass's request, and Bass did not make the February 1988 loan payment. Later that year, Champions foreclosed on the property. In 1990, Champions failed and was taken over by the FDIC. Shortly thereafter, the property was sold for a loss.

When regulators took over the bank in 1990, they were unable to find Bass's credit file, in which they were especially interested because the loan was made to an insider and had not been repaid. At the time of the loan, Bass had been on the Champions board of directors. Doke had also been an insider because he was a significant shareholder.

The theory of the government's case is that Doke and Bass failed to disclose Doke's involvement in the loan because Champions could not have loaned the $600,000 directly to Doke without violating civil regulations. Under the limits of the loan-to-one-borrower rule, Champions could loan Doke only about $40,000 more than he had already borrowed. It could, however, lend over $300,000 to Bass. Thus, when Bass borrowed the $600,000, Champions participated out $300,000 of the loan to Park 45 National Bank, a "sister bank" that had several directors in common with Champions.

Doke and Bass were indicted in July 1995. A jury trial was held in February and March 1997. They were found guilty on all four counts: one count of conspiracy under 18 U.S.C. § 371, one count of bank fraud under 18 U.S.C. § 1344, and two counts of making false statements to a financial institution under 18 U.S.C. § 1014.

II. SUFFICIENCY OF EVIDENCE . . .

. . . [T]he government argues that Doke and Bass concealed Doke's involvement from Champions, and that the loan exposed Champions to the risk of being in violation of banking regulations. Doke and Bass contend that there was not enough evidence to show that Bass failed to disclose Doke's involvement to the bank. In addition, however, they argue that, even assuming non-disclosure of Doke's involvement, this nominee loan could not have defrauded the bank because the bank received exactly the risk it bargained for: it knew Bass's credit-worthiness, knew what the money would be used for, and knew what collateral would secure the loan.

In order to prove bank fraud under 18 U.S.C. § 1344, the government must show that Doke and Bass

> knowingly executed, or attempted to execute, a scheme to defraud a federally-chartered or -insured financial institution. A scheme to defraud includes any false or fraudulent pretenses or representations intending to deceive others in order to obtain something of value, such as money, from the institution to be deceived. The requisite intent to defraud is established if the defendant acted knowingly and with the specific intent to deceive, ordinarily for the purpose of causing some financial loss to another or bringing about some financial gain to himself.

United States v. Hanson, 161 F.3d 896, 900 (5th Cir. 1998). In this case, the crux is whether Doke and Bass had the intent to deceive and whether the financial gains and losses in the offing demonstrated a scheme to defraud. . . .

Doke and Bass argue that Bass disclosed their partnership to the bank when he applied for the loan. They contend that several pieces of evidence, in addition to Bass's own testimony at the trial, show that Bass made this disclosure. The loan file presented at trial was missing the documents that would prove the disclosure. Other documents in the file showed Doke's continued involvement. The files on Bass at other banks show that Bass was not concealing anything. Doke's payments to Bass were routed through Champions. Two bank officers testified they knew of Doke's involvement. Finally, Doke had sufficient credit available at another bank to eliminate any motive to circumvent the lending limits at Champions.

The government, on the other hand, presented testimony from the president of the bank, Ron Karel, who was also Bass's loan officer. Karel strenuously maintained that Bass did not reveal Doke's continued involvement with the loan. Although he knew that Doke was involved in the original sale of the land (selling it to Bass), Karel maintained he did not know Doke would be paying off Bass's loan. The loan application (not filled out by Bass but purportedly reflective of what he had told the bank) stated that Bass would repay the loan out of his "personal income and sale of property." Furthermore, Karel testified that at the board of directors meeting where Bass's loan was approved, Bass commented: "This has got to be a good deal because, after all, I'm putting in $200,000 of my own money toward the purchase price of this land." Several other directors testified about the approval of the loan. Bobby Newman testified that he had seen no indication that Doke was involved with the loan. Keith Franze testified that he did not know of Doke's involvement and would not have voted to approve the loan if he had known. Robert Russ testified that he "never heard" that Doke would be the one paying off the loan, but he admitted it had happened so long before trial he could not be sure he would remember if he had.

Aside from the documents in Bass's file at Champions, which were ambiguous because of their incomplete state, this was largely a swearing contest between Bass's and Karel's versions of events. Two bank officers testified that Karel knew of Doke's involvement with the loan. But Karel and the other directors who denied knowledge of Doke's involvement were subject to extensive cross-examination by Bass's able trial counsel. This court is not inclined to interfere with the jury's decision about witnesses' credibility when that issue was so squarely set before it. . . .

Separate from the issue of how much they concealed from the bank, Doke and Bass argue that the economic validity of the transaction underlying the loan precluded it from being fraudulent. . . .

We agree that the transaction in this case had economic substance and was not a sham. We also agree that a nominee loan is not illegal where there is no evidence that the transaction is concealed from the bank, and where the loan documents "make the relationship between the various transactions very clear." United States v. Grossman, 117 F.3d 255, 260-61 (5th Cir. 1997). This court has held, however, that fraudulent actions, such as concealing the identity of a silent partner in violation of banking regulations, contravene § 1344. Further, the creditworthiness of the borrower is no defense against a § 1344 bank fraud conviction.

The type of proof of fraud is what distinguishes the cases upholding bank fraud convictions from *Beuttenmuller*, *Baker*, and *Schnitzer*, which overturned such convictions. In the latter cases, the government could not prove that the defendants knew and concealed material information from the banks, so it attempted to draw an inference of fraudulent intent by proving the transactions were economic shams. This court disagreed with the government's characterization of the deals and necessarily found insufficient proof of intent to defraud. In cases like *Henderson*, *Saks*, *Parekh* — and this one — there was proof of intent to defraud irrespective of the economic substance of the transactions. See also United States v. Hanson, 161 F.3d 896, 900-01 (5th Cir. 1998). Because Doke's and Bass's failure to disclose Doke's involvement with the loan put the bank in violation of banking regulations, and a reasonable juror could have concluded beyond a reasonable doubt that they did fail to disclose Doke's involvement, the evidence was sufficient to support their convictions for bank fraud. . . .

[T]he judgment and sentences of the district court are affirmed.

Notes and Questions

1. The court finds it irrelevant that the loan transaction had economic substance and was not a sham. If the transaction was bona fide, the bank knew the extent of Bass's creditworthiness, and the bank knew what collateral secured the loan, where is the fraud?

2. Assume that Bass lacked the ability to repay when the loan was made. Assume further that it was clear that he sincerely believed that he would be able to make the payments if Doke defaulted and that he had good faith intent to repay if called upon to do so. Would his sincere belief and good faith intent constitute a defense?

3. If Bass had had sufficient assets to repay the loan, would he still be guilty if he failed to disclose Doke's continued involvement in the transaction?

UNITED STATES v. REAUME
338 F.3d 577 (6th Cir. 2003)

COLE, Circuit Judge. . . .

I

On August 19, 1999, a federal grand jury returned a one-count indictment charging Reaume with bank fraud. The indictment alleged that Reaume knowingly executed a scheme to defraud Monroe Bank and Trust ("the Bank").

Reaume's jury trial began on August 14, 2001. At trial, testimony was presented that Reaume opened two checking accounts at the Bank using the aliases Steven D. McIlveen and Robert Sandor. Accounts also were opened at the Bank by Adam Rodriguez and Danny K. Drummond in their own names. Drummond opened an additional account under the alias of John S. Woods.

Reaume, Rodriguez, and Drummond used checks drawn from their accounts to purchase merchandise at various branches of national-chain retailers, and subsequently returned most of the merchandise for cash refunds at other branches of the stores. The Bank flagged the five accounts early on and refused to honor the checks for which there were insufficient funds ("NSF checks"). The losses resulting from the passing of these NSF checks, therefore, fell on either the retailers themselves or the check-guarantee companies that insured the retailers.

On August 16, 2001, the jury returned a guilty verdict. . . .

II

A. SUFFICIENCY OF THE EVIDENCE AND INTENT TO DEFRAUD

Reaume argues that there was insufficient evidence to find that he specifically intended to defraud the Bank, as opposed to the merchants or their insurers. He contends that an intent to defraud the payee of an NSF check does not provide a basis for a finding that there was an intent to subject the issuing bank to a loss. . . .

Three elements are required for a conviction of bank fraud pursuant to § 1344: (1) the defendant must have knowingly executed or attempted to execute a scheme to defraud a financial institution; (2) the defendant must have done so with the intent to defraud; and (3) the financial institution must have been insured by the Federal Deposit Insurance Corporation. United States v. Everett, 270 F.3d 986, 989 (6th Cir. 2001).

This Court previously addressed the intent element of the bank fraud statute in United States v. Hoglund, 178 F.3d 410 (6th Cir. 1999), and Everett. While neither of these cases are directly controlling, their explication here is critical because it is from these cases that we distill the principle which we apply to the present case.

In Hoglund, an attorney was convicted under § 1344 after settling his clients' cases without their permission, forging their signatures on the settlement checks he received, and depositing the money into his own account. In Hoglund, we addressed the issue of whether the Government must prove that the defendant exposed a bank to a risk of loss as part of the "scheme to defraud" element. Hoglund resolved this question by holding that "risk of loss" is simply "one way of establishing intent to defraud in bank cases." Thus, this Court found that a defendant need not have exposed a bank to a risk of loss as an element of bank fraud. Instead, proof that the defendant "intended to put a bank at a risk of loss" was sufficient to maintain a bank fraud conviction. Thus, Hoglund held that the bank fraud statute is violated, even when there is no actual risk of loss on the part of the bank, if the defendant's intent is to expose the bank to such a risk. While informative, Hoglund is not controlling in the present case. Here, in contrast to Hoglund, the defendant claims that, regardless of whether there was an actual risk of loss, there was no intent to expose the Bank to a risk of loss.

In Everett, the defendant, a certified public accountant, was found guilty of bank fraud by a jury. On appeal, the defendant argued that the Government failed to prove the specific intent required by § 1344, namely, the intent to defraud a federally insured bank, or at least to put the bank at a risk of loss. The defendant acknowledged that there was evidence that she intended to defraud her client, but argued that the manner in which she defrauded her client did not impose a risk of loss on the bank in question. In affirming the conviction, we held that the specific intent required for bank fraud does not require putting the bank at a risk of a loss or intending to do so "in the usual sense." 78 F.3d at 991. "It is sufficient if the defendant in the course of committing fraud on *someone* causes a federally insured bank to transfer funds under its possession and control." Id. *Everett*, therefore, can be said to stand for the proposition that the bank fraud statute is violated, even if the intended victim of the fraudulent activity is an entity other than a federally insured financial institution, when the fraudulent activity causes the bank to transfer funds. Thus, the holding of *Everett* is also instructive but not squarely on point, as there was no evidence in the present case indicating that the Bank actually did transfer funds in connection with Reaume's fraudulent activities.

Unlike the defendant in *Hoglund*, Reaume contends that he harbored no intent to expose the financial institution to a risk of loss. Moreover, unlike the situation in *Everett*, Reaume contends, and the evidence substantiates, that the Bank never transferred any funds in connection with the fraudulent activity. Thus, it appears that Reaume's particular fact pattern does not fall neatly under the *Hoglund* or *Everett* rubric, which consider both the intended victim and actual loss.

We nevertheless affirm Reaume's conviction. The specific issue that Reaume appeals is the evidence of his intent to defraud the Bank itself. In *Everett*, this Court held that an intent to put the financial institution at a risk of loss is not required, and that the fact that the defendant defrauded someone was sufficient, given that the fraud caused the bank to transfer funds. In the present case, the Bank was clearly at a risk of loss. Evidence was presented at trial to demonstrate that, when the Bank receives an NSF check, it makes a decision to either honor the check anyway or to dishonor the check. If the check is dishonored, the Bank does not lose any money, but if the check is honored, and the account holder fails to pay back that debt to the Bank, the Bank suffers a loss. Therefore, it is clear that Reaume's fraudulent activity, regardless of the intended victim, could have caused the Bank to transfer funds. If in fact the Bank had transferred funds, then this case would clearly be governed by *Everett*, because an intent to defraud someone would have caused the Bank to transfer funds. The issue of Reaume's intent simply cannot logically turn on the course of action chosen by the Bank after receiving the NSF checks. Accordingly, it is a necessary extension of *Everett* to find the intent element of § 1344 satisfied in this case.

Everett contains language to support this outcome. In *Everett*, this Court stated that the Government is probably better advised to proceed under the wire or mail fraud statutes where the bank has "minimal involvement, such as where a swindler deceives someone into voluntarily writing checks to the swindler on a good account." Id. Nevertheless, the Court indicated that even such a minimal involvement of the bank is sufficient to find liability under § 1344 when the specific intent to defraud someone is present. Therefore, we need not address the question of whether the evidence presented at trial was sufficient for a reasonable jury to find that Reaume intended to defraud the Bank specifically. Applying the reasoning of *Hoglund* and *Everett*, we find that intent to defraud the federally insured institution itself is satisfied where: (1) the intent to defraud some entity was present; and (2) that intended fraud placed a federally insured financial institution at a risk of loss. . . .

III

For the foregoing reasons, we affirm the judgment of the district court.

Notes and Questions

1. The court in *Reaume* seems to recognize three sustainable theories of liability under § 1344 based on variables relating to the actor's intent and the consequences of his conduct: (1) intent to put a *bank* at risk of loss, regardless of whether the bank was actually exposed to loss; (2) intent to defraud *some* party and the fraud causes the bank to transfer funds under its possession and control; and (3) intent to defraud *some* party and the fraud puts the bank at risk of loss. Are all three theories supported by the statute's language?

2. Is it logical to impose liability for bank fraud when the actor has no intent to defraud the bank? Does extending the reach of § 1344 to this type of case unnecessarily duplicate the offenses defined in §§ 1341 and 1343 relating to fraud "affecting" a financial institution?

B. COMPUTER FRAUD

Congress enacted the first federal computer fraud statute in 1984. A modest start at best, the statute provided limited protection against unauthorized use of government computers and information stored in government computer systems. Two years later, Congress substantially overhauled the statute, expanded its coverage, and renamed it the Computer Fraud and Abuse Act of 1986. The statute has been an evolving work in progress ever since. Subsequent amendments enacted in 1990, 1994, and 1996 broadened its scope and corrected deficiencies embedded in successive versions of the law. Codified as 18 U.S.C. § 1030, the statute currently defines seven categories of crimes that target harms resulting from accessing protected computers without authorization or in excess of one's authorization. The statute defines the term "protected computer" to mean a computer:

> (A) exclusively for the use of a financial institution or the United States Government, or, in the case of a computer not exclusively for such use, used by or for a financial institution or the United States Government and the conduct constituting the offense affects that use by or for the financial institution or the Government;[53] or
> (B) which is used in interstate or foreign commerce or communication. . . .

Id. § 1030(e)(2)(A), (B).

---

53. The statute designates eight categories of financial institutions whose computers it protects. Most of them can be generically described as federal or federally insured banks or credit unions.

UNITED STATES v. MIDDLETON
231 F.3d 1207 (9th Cir. 2000)

GRABER, Circuit Judge.

Defendant Nicholas Middleton challenges his conviction for intentionally causing damage to a "protected computer" without authorization, in violation of 18 U.S.C. § 1030(a)(5)(A). Defendant asks us to interpret the statute, which prohibits conduct causing damage to "one or more individuals," 18 U.S.C. § 1030(e)(8)(A), to exclude damage to a corporation. Defendant also argues that the trial court incorrectly instructed the jury on the "damage" element of the offense and that the government presented insufficient evidence of the requisite amount of damage. We disagree with each of Defendant's contentions and, therefore, affirm the conviction.

I. FACTUAL AND PROCEDURAL BACKGROUND

Defendant worked as the personal computer administrator for Slip.net, an Internet service provider. His responsibilities included installing software and hardware on the company's computers and providing technical support to its employees. He had extensive knowledge of Slip.net's internal systems, including employee and computer program passwords. Dissatisfied with his job, Defendant quit. He then began to write threatening e-mails to his former employer.

Slip.net had allowed Defendant to retain an e-mail account as a paying customer after he left the company's employ. Defendant used this account to commit his first unauthorized act. After logging in to Slip.net's system, Defendant used a computer program called "Switch User" to switch his account to that of a Slip.net receptionist, Valerie Wilson. This subterfuge allowed Defendant to take advantage of the benefits and privileges associated with that employee's account, such as creating and deleting accounts and adding features to existing accounts.

Ted Glenwright, Slip.net's president, discovered this unauthorized action while looking through a "Switch User log," which records all attempts to use the Switch User program. Glenwright cross-checked the information with the company's "Radius Log," which records an outside user's attempt to dial in to the company's modem banks. The information established that Defendant had connected to Slip.net's computers and had then switched to Wilson's account. Glenwright immediately terminated Defendant's e-mail account.

Nevertheless, Defendant was able to continue his activities. Three days later, he obtained access to Slip.net's computers by logging in to a computer that contained a test account and then using that test account to gain access to the company's main computers. Once in Slip.net's main system, Defendant accessed the account of a sales representative and created two new accounts, which he called "TERPID" and "SANTOS." Defendant used TERPID and SANTOS to obtain access to a different computer that the company had named "Lemming." Slip.net used Lemming to perform internal administrative functions and to host customers' websites. Lemming also contained the software for a new billing system. After gaining access to the Lemming computer, Defendant changed all the administrative passwords, altered the computer's registry, deleted the entire billing system (including programs that ran the billing software), and deleted two internal databases.

Glenwright discovered the damage the next morning. He immediately contacted the company's system administrator, Bruno Connelly. Glenwright and Connelly spent an entire weekend repairing the damage that Defendant had caused to Slip.net's computers, including restoring access to the computer system, assigning new passwords, reloading the billing software, and recreating the deleted databases. They also spent many hours investigating the source and the extent of the damage. Glenwright estimated that he spent 93 hours repairing the damage; Connelly estimated that he spent 28 hours; and other employees estimated that they spent a total of 33 hours. Additionally, Slip.net bought new software to replace software that Defendant had deleted, and the company hired an outside consultant for technical support.

Defendant was arrested and charged with a violation of 18 U.S.C. § 1030(a)(5)(A). He moved to dismiss the indictment, arguing that Slip.net was not an "individual" within the meaning of the statute. The district court denied the motion, holding that "the statute encompasses damage sustained by a business entity as well as by a natural person." United States v. Middleton, 35 F. Supp. 2d 1189, 1192 (N.D. Cal. 1999).

The case was then tried to a jury. Defendant filed motions for acquittal, arguing that the government had failed to prove that Slip.net suffered at least $5,000 in damage. The district court denied the motions. Defendant requested a jury instruction on the meaning of "damage." This request, too, was denied, and the court gave a different instruction.

The jury convicted Defendant. The district court sentenced him to three years' probation, subject to the condition that he serve 180 days in community confinement. The court also ordered Defendant to pay $9,147 in restitution. This timely appeal ensued. . . .

DISCUSSION

A. "ONE OR MORE INDIVIDUALS"

Title 18 U.S.C. § 1030(a)(5)(A) prohibits a person from knowingly transmitting "a program, information, code, or command, and as a result of such conduct, intentionally causing damage without authorization, to a protected computer." A "protected computer" is a computer "which is used in interstate or foreign commerce or communication." 18 U.S.C. § 1030(e)(2)(B). Defendant concedes that Slip.net's computers fit within that definition. The statute defines "damage" to mean "any impairment to the integrity or availability of data, a program, a system, or information, that causes loss aggregating at least $5,000 in value during any 1-year period to one or more individuals." 18 U.S.C. § 1030(e)(8)(A). Defendant argues that Congress intended the phrase "one or more individuals" to exclude corporations. We disagree. . . .

We examine first the ordinary meaning of "individuals." That word does not necessarily exclude corporations. Webster's Third New Int'l Dictionary 1152 (unabridged ed. 1993) provides five definitions of the noun "individual," the first being a single or particular being or *thing or group of* beings or *things*." To the extent that a word's dictionary meaning equates to its "plain meaning," a corporation can be referred to as an "individual."

Neither is "individual" a legal term of art that applies only to natural persons. As Black's Law Dictionary 773 (6th ed. 1990) states:

> Individual. As a noun, this term denotes a single person as distinguished from a group or class, and also, very commonly, a private or natural person as distinguished from a partnership, corporation, or association; *but it is said that this restrictive signification is not necessarily inherent in the word, and that it may, in proper cases, include artificial persons.* . . .

. . . Defendant was convicted of violating § 1030(a)(5)(A), which criminalizes damage to "protected computers." A "protected computer" is a computer that is "used in interstate or foreign commerce or communication." 18 U.S.C. § 1030(e)(2)(B). A large number of the computers that are used in interstate or foreign commerce or communication are owned by corporations. Cf. S. Rep. No. 104-357, pt. II (1996) (noting that "computers continue to proliferate in businesses and homes"). It is highly unlikely, in view of Congress' purpose to stop damage to computers used in interstate and foreign commerce and communication, that Congress intended to criminalize damage to such computers only if the damage is to a natural person. Defendant's interpretation would thwart Congress' intent. . . .

Defendant also relies on the statute's legislative history. We have examined that history, but conclude that the statute's history confirms our reading of the word "individuals." Congress originally enacted the Computer Fraud and Abuse Act in 1984. The 1990 version of § 1030(a)(5)(A) prohibited conduct that damages a "Federal interest computer" and "causes loss to one or more others of a value aggregating $1,000 or more." A "Federal interest computer" was defined as a computer owned or used by the United States Government or a financial institution, or "one of two or more computers used in committing the offense, not all of which are located in the same State." 18 U.S.C. § 1030(e)(2)(A) & (B). In 1994, Congress replaced the term "Federal interest computer" with the phrase "computer used in interstate commerce or communication" and changed the damage provision to read, "causes loss or damage to one or more other persons of value aggregating $1,000 or more." 18 U.S.C. § 1030(a)(5)(A)(ii)(II)(aa) (1995). Before the 1994 amendment, a hacker could escape the statute's prohibitions by containing activities within a single state. Congress' 1994 amendment attempted to "broaden the statute's reach." S. Rep. No. 104-357, pt. IV(E) (discussing 1994 amendment). Congress' 1994 amendments also added a private cause of action for victims of computer crime. 18 U.S.C. § 1030(g).

In 1996, Congress amended § 1030(a)(5) to its current form, using the term "protected computer" and concomitantly expanding the number of computers that the statute "protected." 18 U.S.C. § 1030(a)(5) & (e)(2).[54] The 1996 amendments also

---

54. The 1996 amendments corrected deficiencies in the 1990 version of the statute and the 1994 version. In 1994, when Congress substituted the phrase "computer used in interstate commerce or communication" for "Federal interest computer," it inadvertently removed protection from those computers belonging to or used by the United States Government or a financial institution, but not used in interstate commerce. See S. Rep. No. 104-357. The 1996 amendments included within the definition of "protected computer" those computers used in interstate commerce or communication, as well as computers "exclusively for the use of a financial institution or the United States Government, or . . . used by or

altered the definition of damage to read, "loss aggregating at least $5,000 in value during any 1-year period to one or more individuals." 18 U.S.C. § 1030(e)(8)(A). We have found no explanation for this change. We do not believe, however, that this change evidences an intent to limit the statute's reach.

To the contrary, Congress has consciously broadened the statute consistently since its original enactment. The Senate Report on the 1996 amendments notes:

> As intended when the law was originally enacted, the Computer Fraud and Abuse statute facilitates addressing in a single statute the problem of computer crime. . . . *As computers continue to proliferate in businesses and homes, and new forms of computer crimes emerge, Congress must remain vigilant to ensure that the Computer Fraud and Abuse statute is up-to-date and provides law enforcement with the necessary legal framework to fight computer crime.*

S. Rep. No. 104-357, pt. II. The report instructs that "the definition of 'damage' is amended to be sufficiently broad to encompass the types of harm against which people should be protected." Id. pt. IV(1)(E). The report notes that the interaction between § 1030(a)(5)(A) (the provision that prohibits conduct causing damage) and § 1030(e)(8) (the provision that defines damage) will prohibit a hacker from stealing passwords from an existing log-on program, when this conduct requires "all system users to change their passwords, *and requires the system administrator to devote resources to resecuring the system.* . . . If the loss to the victim meets the required monetary threshold, the conduct should be criminal, and the victim should be entitled to relief." Id. The reference to a "system administrator" suggests that a corporate victim is involved. That is, if Congress intended to limit the definition of the crime to conduct causing financial damage to a natural person only, its report would not use the example of a "system administrator" devoting resources to fix a computer problem as illustrative of the "damage" to be prevented and criminalized. The Senate Report's reference to the proliferation of computers in businesses as well as homes provides additional evidence of the Senate's intent to extend the statute's protections to corporate entities.

On the basis of the statutory text taken in context . . . and the statute's purpose and legislative history, we conclude that 18 U.S.C. § 1030(a)(5) criminalizes computer crime that damages natural persons and corporations alike. The district court did not err in so ruling.

B. JURY INSTRUCTIONS ON "DAMAGE"

Defendant next argues that the district court instructed the jury improperly on the definition of "damage." Defendant requested this instruction: "Damage does not include expenses relating to creating a better or making a more secure system than the one in existence prior to the impairment." The court refused the request and gave a different instruction. The court explained to the jury that "damage" is an impairment to Slip.net's computer system that caused a loss of at least $5,000. The court continued:

---

for a financial institution or the United States Government and the conduct constituting the offense affects the use." 18 U.S.C. § 1030(e)(2)(A).

The term "loss" means any monetary loss that Slip.net sustained as a result of any damage to Slip.net's computer data, program, system or information that you find occurred.

And in considering whether the damage caused a loss less than or greater than $5,000, you may consider any loss that you find was a natural and foreseeable result of any damage that you find occurred.

In determining the amount of losses, you may consider what measures were reasonably necessary to restore the data, program, system, or information that you find was damaged or what measures were reasonably necessary to resecure the data, program, system, or information from further damage.

"In reviewing jury instructions, the relevant inquiry is whether the instructions as a whole are misleading or inadequate to guide the jury's deliberation." United States v. Dixon, 201 F.3d 1223, 1230 (9th Cir. 2000). In this case, the district court's instructions on "damage" and "loss" correctly stated the applicable law. Defendant concedes that "damage" includes any loss that was a foreseeable consequence of his criminal conduct, including those costs necessary to "resecure" Slip.net's computers. He does not argue, therefore, that the court misstated the law.

Defendant contends instead that the court's instruction might have led the jury to believe that it could consider the cost of creating a better or more secure system and that his proposed additional instruction was needed to avoid that possibility. The district court's instruction, when read in its entirety, adequately presented Defendant's theory. The court instructed the jury that it could consider only those costs that were a "natural and foreseeable result" of Defendant's conduct, only those costs that were "reasonably necessary," and only those costs that would "resecure" the computer to avoid "further damage." That instruction logically excludes any costs that the jury believed were excessive, as well as any costs that would merely create an improved computer system unrelated to preventing further damage resulting from Defendant's conduct. In particular, the term "resecure" implies making the system as secure as it was before, not making it more secure than it was before. We presume that the jury followed the court's instructions. . . .

C. SUFFICIENCY OF THE EVIDENCE

Defendant's final argument is that the government presented insufficient evidence of the requisite $5,000 in damage. The government computed the amount of damage that occurred by multiplying the number of hours that each employee spent in fixing the computer problems by their respective hourly rates (calculated using their annual salaries), then adding the cost of the consultant and the new software. The government estimated the total amount of damage to be $10,092. Defendant and the government agree that the cost of Glenwright's time made up the bulk of that total.

Defendant observes that Slip.net paid Glenwright a fixed salary and that Slip.net did not pay Glenwright anything extra to fix the problems caused by Defendant's conduct. There also is no evidence, says Defendant, that Glenwright was diverted from his other responsibilities or that such a diversion caused Slip.net a financial loss. Defendant argues that, unless Slip.net paid its salaried employees an extra $5,000 for the time spent fixing the computer system, or unless the company was prevented from making $5,000 that it otherwise would have made because of the employees' diversion, Slip.net has not suffered "damage" as defined in the statute. We disagree.

In United States v. Sablan, 92 F.3d 865, 869 (9th Cir. 1996), this court held that, under the Sentencing Guidelines for computer fraud, it was permissible for the district court to compute "loss" based on the hourly wage of the victim bank's employees. The court reasoned, in part, that the bank would have had to pay a similar amount had it hired an outside contractor to repair the damage. Analogous reasoning applies here. There is no basis to believe that Congress intended the element of "damage" to depend on a victim's choice whether to use hourly employees, outside contractors, or salaried employees to repair the same level of harm to a protected computer. Rather, whether the amount of time spent by the employees and their imputed hourly rates were reasonable for the repair tasks that they performed are questions to be answered by the trier of fact.

Our review of the record identifies sufficient evidence from which a rational trier of fact could have found that Slip.net suffered $5,000 or more in damage. Glenwright testified that he spent approximately 93 hours investigating and repairing the damage caused by Defendant. That total included 24 hours investigating the break-in, determining how to fix it, and taking temporary measures to prevent future break-ins. Glenwright testified that he spent 21 hours recreating deleted databases and 16 hours reloading and configuring the billing software and its related applications. Glenwright estimated that his time was worth $90 per hour, based on his salary of $180,000 per year. He also testified, among other things, that he did not hire an outside contractor to repair the damage because he believed that he, as a computer expert with a pre-existing knowledge of the customized features of his company's computers, could fix the problems more efficiently. It is worth noting that, because the jury had to find only $5,000 worth of damage, it could have discounted Glenwright's number of hours or his hourly rate considerably and still have found the requisite amount of damage.

Other Slip.net employees testified to the hours that they spent fixing the damage caused by Defendant, and to their respective salaries. The government then presented expert testimony from which a jury could determine that the time spent by the employees was reasonable. Defendant cross-examined the government's witnesses on these issues vigorously, and he presented contrary expert testimony. By the verdict, the jury found the government witnesses' testimony to be more credible, a finding that was within its power to make. We hold, on this record, that the conviction was not based on insufficient evidence.

Affirmed.

Notes and Questions

1. The materials in Chapter 1 explored how courts came to recognize that corporations and other legal entities could be deemed "persons" in the eyes of the law. The court in *Middleton* concluded that corporations can also be deemed "individuals." Is it conceptually more difficult to justify treating corporations as individuals? What is the strongest argument that, in the context of the computer fraud statute, the term "individuals" includes corporations?

2. The court observed that the computer fraud statute originally covered "Federal interest computers" but that Congress subsequently extended its coverage to "protected computers." What difference does this change make? What was the rationale behind it?

3. Middleton deleted Slip.net's billing software. Suppose the deleted software could not be reinstalled and Slip.net had to replace it. Although the deleted version was commercially available, a newer, more powerful version had just come out. If Slip.net purchased the new version, would that have any bearing on the determination of what damage Middleton's hacking had caused? How should aggregate loss be determined? Can aggregate loss be calculated with precision? If so, should precise calculations be required?[55]

4. Why would the statute require a loss of $5,000 or more?

UNITED STATES v. CZUBINSKI
106 F.3d 1069 (1st Cir. 1997)

TORRUELLA, Chief Judge. . . .
[Please review the facts in *Czubinski*, supra.]

II. THE COMPUTER FRAUD COUNTS

Czubinski was convicted on all four of the computer fraud counts on which he was indicted; these counts arise out of unauthorized searches that also formed the basis of four of the ten wire fraud counts in the indictment. Specifically, he was convicted of violating 18 U.S.C. § 1030(a)(4), a provision enacted in the Computer Fraud and Abuse Act of 1986. Section 1030(a)(4) applies to:

> Whoever . . . knowingly and with intent to defraud, accesses a Federal interest computer[56] without authorization, or exceeds authorized access, and by means of such conduct furthers the intended fraud and obtains anything of value, unless the object of the fraud and the thing obtained consists only of the use of the computer.

We have never before addressed section 1030(a)(4). Czubinski unquestionably exceeded authorized access to a Federal interest computer.[57] On appeal he argues that he did not obtain "anything of value." We agree, finding that his searches of taxpayer return information did not satisfy the statutory requirement that he obtain "anything of value." The value of information is relative to one's needs and objectives; here, the government had to show that the information was valuable to Czubinski in light of a fraudulent scheme. The government failed, however, to prove that Czubinski intended anything more than to satisfy idle curiosity.

The plain language of section 1030(a)(4) emphasizes that more than mere unauthorized use is required: the "thing obtained" may not merely be the unauthorized use.

---

55. Cf. United States v. Millot, 433 F.3d 1057 (8th Cir. 2006) (finding that losses incurred by contractor hired to manage secure computer system of defendant's former employer could be taken into account in determining whether defendant caused more than $5,000 in damage to the system).

56. A 1996 amendment deleted the term "Federal interest computer" from the statute and inserted "protected computer" in its stead. — ED.

57. "The term 'exceeds authorized access' means to access a computer with authorization and to use such access to obtain or alter information in the computer that the accesser is not entitled so to obtain or alter." 18 U.S.C. § 1030(e)(6).

It is the showing of some additional end — to which the unauthorized access is a means — that is lacking here. The evidence did not show that Czubinski's end was anything more than to satisfy his curiosity by viewing information about friends, acquaintances, and political rivals. No evidence suggests that he printed out, recorded, or used the information he browsed. No rational jury could conclude beyond a reasonable doubt that Czubinski intended to use or disclose that information, and merely viewing information cannot be deemed the same as obtaining something of value for the purposes of this statute.[58]

The legislative history further supports our reading of the term "anything of value." "In the game of statutory interpretation, statutory language is the ultimate trump card," and the remarks of sponsors of legislation are authoritative only to the extent that they are compatible with the plain language of section 1030(a)(4). Here, a Senate co-sponsor's comments suggest that Congress intended section 1030(a)(4) to punish attempts to steal valuable data, and did not wish to punish mere unauthorized access:

> The acts of fraud we are addressing in proposed section 1030(a)(4) are essentially thefts in which someone uses a federal interest computer to wrongly obtain something of value from another. . . . Proposed section 1030(a)(4) is intended to reflect the distinction between the theft of information, a felony, and mere unauthorized access, a misdemeanor.

132 Cong. Rec. 7128, 7129, 99th Cong., 2d Sess. (1986). The Senate Committee Report further underscores the fact that this section should apply to those who steal information through unauthorized access as part of an illegal scheme:

> The Committee remains convinced that there must be a clear distinction between computer theft, punishable as a felony [under section 1030(a)(4)], and computer trespass, punishable in the first instance as a misdemeanor [under a different provision]. The element in the new paragraph (a)(4), requiring a showing of an intent to defraud, is meant to preserve that distinction, as is the requirement that the property wrongfully obtained via computer furthers the intended fraud.

S. Rep. No. 132, 99th Cong., 2d Sess., reprinted in 1986 U.S.C.C.A.N. 2479. For the same reasons we deemed the trial evidence could not support a finding that Czubinski deprived the IRS of its property . . . under section 1343, we find that Czubinski has not obtained valuable information in furtherance of a fraudulent scheme for the purposes of section 1030(a)(4). . . .

The defendant's conviction is thus reversed. . . .

---

58. The district court, in denying a motion to dismiss the computer fraud counts in the indictment, found that the indictment sufficiently alleged that the confidential taxpayer information was itself a "thing of value" to Czubinski, given his ends. The indictment, of course, alleged specific uses for the information, such as creating dossiers on KKK members, that were not proven at trial. In light of the trial evidence — which, as we have said, indicates that there was no recording, disclosure or further use of the confidential information — we find that Czubinski did not obtain "anything of value" through his unauthorized searches.

Notes and Questions

1. At the time when Czubinski engaged in his unauthorized browsing, the statute provided that his conduct would be a crime if he thereby obtained anything of value, "unless the object of the fraud and the thing obtained consists only of the use of the computer." The statute has since been amended to read "unless the object of the fraud and the thing obtained consists only of the use of the computer *and the value of such use is not more than $5,000 in any 1-year period*." How, if at all, would the amendment affect the analysis in *Czubinski*? What is the amendment's apparent purpose?

2. What distinguishes conduct that "exceeds authorized access" from conduct that is "without authorization"? Which category of conduct did Czubinski's wrongful browsing fall under? Did Middleton's misconduct fit within the same category?

5

Securities Fraud

I. INTRODUCTION

The Securities Act of 1933 and the Securities Exchange Act of 1934 were the federal government's first ventures into the regulation of corporate securities. The 1933 Act is principally a disclosure statute designed to promote truth in the offering and sale of securities. The Act employs two mechanisms — registration requirements and broad antifraud provisions — to achieve that goal. In addition to amplifying those disclosure requirements, the 1934 Act regulates trading and market practices as well.

Both Acts contain a general criminal penalty provision that elevates willful violations of virtually all of the civil provisions to felonies. Thus, the conduct elements of criminal securities violations will ordinarily be defined in the Acts' civil regulatory provisions.[1]

To illustrate, consider a corporate insider who trades on the basis of undisclosed confidential information in violation of Rule 10b-5. The insider trading may well trigger a Securities and Exchange Commission (SEC) investigation, and, if warranted, the SEC may impose administrative sanctions and file an action for injunctive relief. If there is reason to believe the scheme was willful, the SEC may also refer the matter to the Justice Department. If the Department decides to bring criminal charges, the prosecutor must establish all of the elements of the civil 10b-5 violation *plus* the additional element of a willful state of mind.

Even though the SEC does not have criminal enforcement authority, it often works closely with prosecutors and assists them in building a criminal case. Because the two agencies may have common interests in the same matter — e.g., Enron's financial accounting fraud — it is not uncommon for them to conduct parallel civil and criminal investigations of the same conduct and to reach a global settlement of all of the issues in the parallel cases. Table 5-1 illustrates just how closely the Enron civil and criminal cases paralleled one another.

---

1. The criminal penalty provision in the 1934 Act also defines and punishes the independent crime of willfully making false and misleading statements in a registration statement or other document.

TABLE 5-1[2]
ENRON-RELATED PARALLEL CIVIL AND CRIMINAL PROCEEDINGS

DEFENDANT	CIVIL FILING	CIVIL SETTLEMENT	CRIMINAL FILING	GUILTY PLEA
Lay	July 8, 2004		July 8, 2004	
Rieker	May 19, 2004	May 19, 2004	May 19, 2004	May 19, 2004
Skilling	Feb. 19, 2004		Feb. 19, 2004	
Causey	Jan. 22, 2004		Jan. 22, 2004	
CIBC	Dec. 22, 2003	Dec. 22, 2003	Dec. 22, 2003	Dec. 22, 2003
John Doe #1	Dec. 22, 2003		None	
John Doe #2	Dec. 22, 2003		None	
John Doe #3	Dec. 22, 2003		None	
Gordon	Dec. 19, 2003	Dec. 19, 2003	Dec. 19, 2003	Dec. 19, 2003
Delainey	Oct. 30, 2003		Oct. 29, 2003	
Colwell	Oct. 9, 2003		None	
Glisan	Sept. 10, 2003	Sept. 10, 2003	Apr. 30, 2003	Sept. 10, 2003
J. P. Morgan Chase	July 28, 2003	July 28, 2003	None	
Citigroup	July 28, 2003	July 28, 2003	None	
Rice	May 1, 2003		Apr. 29, 2003	
Hirko	May 1, 2003		Apr. 29, 2003	
Hannon	May 1, 2003		Apr. 29, 2003	
Shelby	May 1, 2003		Apr. 29, 2003	
Yeager	May 1, 2003		Apr. 29, 2003	
Howard	May 1, 2003[3]		Apr. 29, 2003	
Krautz	May 1, 2003[4]		Apr. 29, 2003	
Merrill Lynch	Mar. 17, 2003	Mar. 17, 2003	None	
Furst	Mar. 17, 2003		Oct. 14, 2003	
Tilney	Mar. 17, 2003		None	
Bayly	Mar. 17, 2003		Oct. 14, 2003	
Davis	Mar. 17, 2003		None	
Fastow	Oct. 2, 2002	Jan. 14, 2004	Oct. 1, 2002	Jan. 14, 2004
Kopper	Aug. 21, 2002	Aug. 21, 2002	Aug. 21, 2002	Aug. 21, 2002

II. WILLFULNESS

Violations of the Securities Exchange Act constitute crimes only if they are committed "willfully." Although its meaning is context specific, when "willfully" is specified as the mental state for a federal crime, Congress ordinarily designates it as an element of the offense but does not define it. Thus, more often than not Congress leaves it to the courts to sort out on a case by case basis what willfulness means in the context of any given statute. The Securities Exchange Act is no exception.

---

2. Adapted from Kathleen F. Brickey, Enron's Legacy, 8 Buff. Crim. L. Rev. 221, 253-254 (2004). Cases appear in reverse chronological order by date of civil filing.
    3. Amended complaint. Original complaint filed Mar. 12, 2003.
    4. Amended complaint. Original complaint filed Mar. 12, 2003.

UNITED STATES v. TARALLO
380 F.3d 1174 (9th Cir. 2004)

GRABER, Circuit Judge. . . .

FACTUAL AND PROCEDURAL BACKGROUND

[Tarallo and two co-defendants, Colvin and Larson, devised a fraudulent telemarketing scheme through which they solicited investments in three fictitious businesses that the court refers to in this opinion as Medical Advantage, Lamelli, and R.A.C.]

Defendant and his co-defendants falsely represented to potential investors that Medical Advantage operated independent weight loss clinics around the country and had a projected 1997 revenue of $8.2 million, and that C. Everett Koop and Tom Brokaw supported or were affiliated with the company. Defendant and his co-defendants falsely represented to potential investors that Lamelli had developed a detoxification system that could detoxify a person of all alcohol or drugs in 15 minutes, that the system had won FDA approval, and that $187 million in revenue was expected to be generated by this alleged invention in 1998. Defendant and his co-defendants falsely represented to potential investors that R.A.C. had generated $2.3 million in revenue in 1997 from sales of motor oil, car batteries, and tools, and that the company projected for 1998 revenues of approximately $3.5 million.

Defendant and his co-defendants told potential investors that they would be investing by means of promissory notes, which would be held in a "trust" for a fixed term of between 90 and 180 days. In return, the investors would receive 12 percent interest per annum and shares of "restricted stock" in the company. Defendant told investors that the company's Initial Public Offering ("IPO") would occur on or before the date on which the promissory note was to mature, at which point investors could (at their option) either receive back their invested principal or use it to purchase shares offered in the IPO. Instead of holding the invested funds in trust as promised, however, Colvin and others used those funds for the benefit of Colvin, Larson, Defendant, and their associates, and the investors never saw their money again.

After a nine-day trial, a jury convicted Defendant on six counts of securities fraud and four counts of mail fraud. The district court sentenced him to 37 months' imprisonment on each count, with the sentences to run concurrently. Defendant timely appealed.

DISCUSSION

[On appeal, Tarallo argued, inter alia, that the evidence was insufficient to support his fraud convictions.]

A. EVIDENCE SUPPORTING THE FRAUD CONVICTIONS . . .

2. Defendant Knowingly Made False Statements

A defendant may be convicted of committing mail fraud in violation of 18 U.S.C. § 1341 only if the government proves beyond a reasonable doubt that the defendant had the specific intent to defraud. Likewise, a defendant may be convicted of committing securities fraud only if the government proves specific intent to defraud, mislead, or deceive.

Defendant argues that there was insufficient evidence that he knew that the statements he made to potential investors were false. If he did not even know that the statements were false, of course, he could not have had the specific intent to defraud. He points out that Colvin and Larson distributed typewritten scripts for salespeople to use during sales calls, and he asserts that the investment materials they provided to Defendant (and passed along to investors) were sophisticated and were not recognizably false. In essence, Defendant claims that no evidence at trial established that he was anything other than an innocent who was duped right along with the investors.

The record does not support Defendant's claim. A reasonable factfinder could have found beyond a reasonable doubt that Defendant knew of the fraudulent nature of the scheme in which he was participating.

[Summarizing evidence that would support the jury's finding that Tarallo knew he was lying, the court observed that, among other things, he told investors that their money would be invested and safely held in trust, when in fact he and his confederates used the funds for their own personal benefit.]

The jury also heard evidence that Defendant lied to potential investors about where he was located, telling them during telephone conversations that he was in a different office from Colvin, an office that did not exist. Investor-victim John Wiedmer testified that Defendant told him that he was in a Washington, D.C., office, while Colvin was in California. Wiedmer testified that this statement influenced his decision to invest because it made the publishing company Defendant was pitching sound like "a pretty big operation," and that representation added some credence to the legitimacy of the enterprise. Likewise, investor-victim Keith Crew testified that Defendant sometimes claimed to be in Washington, D.C., when they spoke on the telephone and that Defendant provided him with a business card from Al Tarall (Defendant's alias) in Washington, D.C. However, Agent Steven Goldman of the FBI testified that, in the course of his investigation into the telemarketing scheme, he learned that the "Washington office" was only a "virtual office" that consisted simply of a service that answered the telephones and forwarded mail.

The foregoing evidence supported the jury's finding beyond a reasonable doubt that Defendant knew of the fraudulent nature of the telemarketing scheme and that he acted with the intent to defraud.

C. JURY INSTRUCTIONS

Defendant claims several errors in the jury instructions relating to the fraud counts as to which there was sufficient evidence. . . .

2. Instructions Equating "Willfully" and "Knowingly"

Defendant was charged with, and convicted of, securities fraud under 15 U.S.C. § 78ff and under 17 C.F.R. § 240.10b-5, which was promulgated under the authority of 15 U.S.C. § 78j. Section 78ff(a) states:

(a) Willful violations; false and misleading statements

Any person who *willfully* violates any provision of this chapter (other than section 78dd-1 of this title), or any rule or regulation thereunder the violation of which is made unlawful or the observance of which is required under the terms of this chapter, or any person who *willfully and knowingly* makes, or causes to be made, any statement in any application, report, or document required to be filed under this chapter or any rule or regulation thereunder or any undertaking contained in a registration statement. . . . which statement was false or misleading with respect to any material fact, shall upon conviction be fined not more than $5,000,000, or imprisoned not more than 20 years, or both, except that when such person is a person other than a natural person, a fine not exceeding $25,000,000 may be imposed; but no person shall be subject to imprisonment under this section for the violation of any rule or regulation if he proves that he had no knowledge of such rule or regulation.

15 U.S.C. § 78ff(a).

The district court instructed the jury on "knowingly" and "willfully" as follows:

Each of the crimes charged in the indictment requires proof beyond a reasonable doubt that the defendant acted knowingly. An act is done knowingly if the defendant is aware of the act and does not act or fail to act through ignorance, mistake, or accident.

The government is not required to prove that the defendant knew that his acts or omissions were unlawful. Thus, for example, to prove a defendant guilty of securities fraud or mail fraud based on making a false or misleading representation, the government must prove beyond a reasonable doubt that the defendant knew the representation was false or was made with reckless indifference to its truth or falsity, but it need not prove that in making the representation the defendant knew he was committing securities fraud, mail fraud, or any other criminal offense.

In these statutes, willfully has the same meaning as knowingly.

Defendant argues that the court erred by instructing that "willfully" and "knowingly" mean the same thing, and by instructing that the government did not have to prove that defendant knew that his conduct was unlawful. He argues that the "willful" instruction runs afoul of Bryan v. United States, 524 U.S. 184, 191-92 (1998), in which the Supreme Court stated:

As a general matter, when used in the criminal context, a "willful" act is one undertaken with a "bad purpose." In other words, in order to establish a "willful" violation of a statute, "the Government must prove that the defendant acted with knowledge that his conduct was unlawful." Ratzlaf v. United States, 510 U.S. 135, 137 (1994).

Because 15 U.S.C. § 78ff requires a showing of "willfulness," Defendant argues, it was error to instruct the jury that Defendant could be convicted even if the jury found that he did not know that his conduct was unlawful.

As an initial matter, we note that the district court *did* err in this instruction, although not in the way that Defendant claims. As quoted above, the district court instructed that "[e]ach of the crimes charged in the indictment requires proof beyond a reasonable doubt that the defendant acted *knowingly.*" However, § 78ff(a) states that a person who "willfully" violates any provision of the chapter or any rule or regulation promulgated thereunder is subject to criminal penalty. "Knowingly" is not a required element. "Knowingly" *is* an element for the conviction of any individual who "makes, or causes to be made, any statement in any application, report, or document required to be filed under this chapter or any rule or regulation thereunder or any undertaking contained in a registration statement. . . ." As § 78ff makes clear, such a person must be found to have engaged in the proscribed conduct "willfully and knowingly."

The conduct for which Defendant was indicted, tried, and convicted did not involve the filing of an application, report, or document required by the securities laws. Instead, his conduct was covered by 17 C.F.R. § 240.10b-5. That conduct clearly falls under the first provision of § 78ff, which requires only that the act be done "willfully," but does *not* require that the act be done "knowingly." Therefore, the district court's instruction that "[e]ach of the crimes charged in the indictment requires proof beyond a reasonable doubt that the defendant acted knowingly" was erroneous.

However, the district court then went on to equate "willfully" with "knowingly." The district court's error in including "knowingly" in the instructions is therefore harmless so long as the definition the court provided for knowingly *and* willfully satisfies the statutory definition of "willfully." We turn now to that question.

The Supreme Court has taken pains to observe that the word "willful" "is a word of many meanings" and that "its construction is often influenced by its context." *Ratzlaf,* 510 U.S. at 141; see also *Bryan,* 524 U.S. at 191. We must consider, then, the context in which "willfully" is found in the securities fraud statutes. The question is whether the securities fraud statutes' use of the term "willfully" means that a defendant can be convicted of securities fraud only if he or she *knows that the charged conduct is unlawful*, or whether "willfully" simply means what the district court instructed it means: "knowingly" in the sense that the defendant *intends those actions* and that they are not the product of accident or mistake.

Defendant's argument — that willfulness requires that he knew that he was breaking the law at the time he made his false statements — has been previously rejected by this and other courts. In United States v. Charnay, 537 F.2d 341, 351-52 (9th Cir. 1976), we cited with approval the Second Circuit's interpretation of § 78ff in United States v. Peltz, 433 F.2d 48, 54 (2d Cir. 1970). The Second Circuit explained there that "[t]he language makes one point entirely clear. A person can willfully violate an SEC rule even if he does not know of its existence. This conclusion follows from the difference between the standard for violation of the statute or a rule or regulation, to wit, 'willfully,' and that for false or misleading statements, namely 'willfully and knowingly.'" Id. at 54. We quoted a law review article cited in *Peltz,* 433 F.2d at 55, which "concluded it was necessary only that the prosecution establishes a realization on the defendant's part that he was doing a wrongful act." *Charnay,* 537 F.2d at 352. . . .

Even were we not bound by our existing precedent, we would reach the same result. The final clause of § 78ff(a) provides that "no person shall be subject to imprisonment under this section for the violation of any rule or regulation if he proves that he had no knowledge of such rule or regulation." The opening sentence of subsection (a) explains that "[a]ny person who *willfully* violates any provision of this chapter . . . or any rule or regulation thereunder the violation of which is made unlawful or the observance of which is required under the terms of this chapter" commits a crime. If "willfully" meant "with knowledge that one's conduct violates a rule or regulation," the last clause proscribing imprisonment — but not a fine — in cases where a defendant did *not* know of the rule or regulation would be nonsensical: If willfully meant "with knowledge that one is breaking the law," there would be no need to proscribe imprisonment (but permit imposition of a fine) for someone who acted *without* knowing that he or she was violating a rule or regulation. Such a person could not have been convicted in the first place.

Under our jurisprudence, then, "willfully" as it is used in § 78ff(a) means intentionally undertaking an act that one knows to be wrongful; "willfully" in this context does *not* require that the actor know specifically that the conduct was unlawful. The district court's instructions correctly informed the jury that it had to find that defendant intentionally undertook such an act:

> To prove a defendant guilty of securities fraud or mail fraud based on making a false or misleading representation, the government must prove beyond a reasonable doubt that the defendant knew the representation was false or was made with reckless indifference to its truth or falsity, but it need not prove that in making the representation the defendant knew he was committing securities fraud, mail fraud, or any other criminal offense.

The district court's instructions thus required the jury to find that Defendant had made statements that he knew at the time were false, or else made them with a reckless disregard for whether they were false. The district court therefore required the jury to find that Defendant undertook acts that he knew at the time to be wrongful, meeting the standard for defining "willfully" in this circuit. The district court's importation of the term "knowingly" into the jury instructions was harmless beyond a reasonable doubt, because the court equated "knowingly" with "willfully," and the court's definition properly explained "willfully.". . .

Notes and Questions

1. The court rejected the argument that a defendant cannot be shown to have acted willfully without proof that he knew his conduct was unlawful. Instead, the court found that in the context of securities fraud prosecutions, the government need only prove that the defendant knew his conduct was wrongful. What is the difference between "unlawful" and "wrongful" in this context? To establish knowledge of wrongfulness, does the government have to prove that the defendant acted with a bad purpose?

2. What evidence supports the jury's finding that Torallo acted willfully?

3. One important link in the court's chain of reasoning is that under the 1934 Act's general criminal penalty provision, § 78ff(a), violations of other provisions of the Act or rules or regulations promulgated thereunder must be committed willfully, while violations of the false statements prong of § 78ff(a) must be committed willfully *and knowingly* to be punishable. Is there a meaningful distinction between knowledge and willfulness in this context?

4. Although the court found that the jury instructions were erroneous because they equated knowledge with willfulness, the court nonetheless upheld Tarallo's conviction. Is there a rational explanation for upholding a conviction based on instructions that misstated the mens rea requirement, which is the sole distinction between civil and criminal violations?

5. Did the investors in *Tarallo* act prudently? Are there steps they could have taken to avoid being defrauded? If so, should fraud laws be used to protect people who are capable of protecting themselves but are careless in their business dealings? Stated differently, if reasonable investors can avoid obvious frauds by using common sense, should the criminal law help those who won't help themselves?[5]

NOTE ON THE "NO KNOWLEDGE" PROVISO

The penalty provision in the 1934 Act contains an unusual "no knowledge" proviso that may preclude imposition of a sentence of imprisonment for willful violations.

> [N]o person shall be subject to imprisonment under this section for the violation of any rule or regulation if he proves that he had no knowledge of such rule or regulation.[6]

This provision may protect ostensibly innocent business executives from serving a term of imprisonment for violating some obscure rule or unpublicized administrative action, but it does not insulate them from criminal liability for the violation itself. As the court in *Tarallo* observed, implicit in this statutory scheme is the premise that you can willfully violate a prohibition of which you are unaware. But if, as *Tarallo* held, willfulness does not require proof of knowledge of illegality, what does the "no knowledge" proviso mean?

In United States v. Lilley,[7] a prosecution related to the collapse of Westec Corporation, two defendants pled guilty to violating SEC Rule 10b-5 by engaging in stock manipulation. In their plea agreements, they admitted all of the manipulative acts charged in the indictment. Both defendants then invoked the "no knowledge" proviso and moved to exclude the possibility of a sentence of imprisonment. At an evidentiary hearing before sentencing, both defendants testified that they had no knowledge of Rule 10b-5 when the stock manipulation occurred.

In denying their motions, the court was doubtful that the proviso applied to the facts of the case but was quite certain that if it did, Congress only meant to permit defendants "to rebut the presumption that [they] had knowledge of the rule or regulation under which [they were] charged," but did not intend to eliminate the presumption that every person has knowledge of the *standards* contained in the securities laws.[8]

---

5. Cf. United States v. Svete, 556 F.3d 1157 (11th Cir. 2009).
6. 15 U.S.C. § 78ff(a).
7. 291 F. Supp. 989 (S.D. Tex. 1968).
8. Id. at 991.

[I]f the "no knowledge" clause is applicable under the facts of their situation, I find that defendants have failed to satisfy their burden of showing no knowledge of Rule 10b-5. Proof of no knowledge cannot mean proof that defendants did not know, for example, the precise number or common name of the rule, the book and page where it was to be found, or the date upon which it was promulgated. It does not even mean proof of a lack of knowledge that their conduct was proscribed by rule rather than by statute. Proof of "no knowledge" of the rule can only mean proof of an ignorance of the substance of the rule, proof that they did not know that their conduct was contrary to law.

Here, neither defendant has discharged his burden, whether the standard for measuring same be that of "beyond a reasonable doubt" or, "by a preponderance of the evidence." The rule does not attempt to itemize specific kinds of fraud. Therefore, proof that a defendant knew securities fraud to be prohibited by law should prevent him from discharging his burden under the "no knowledge" clause of proving ignorance of Rule 10b-5.

In pleading guilty to the charges . . . , each of these defendants admitted that he knew securities fraud was a violation of law. Each also testified that he did not consider his manipulative conduct as fraudulent, but Rule 10b-5 does not expressly prohibit the fraudulent manipulation of securities prices. It prohibits fraud, and leaves to the courts the task of defining the specific kinds of securities fraud. A lack of knowledge that manipulative activity is fraudulent is thus irrelevant. What is relevant is that each defendant has admitted that he knew his conduct was manipulative and that he knew securities fraud was illegal. These admissions by each defendant preclude him from discharging his burden of showing "no knowledge" of Rule 10b-5. To the contrary, they affirmatively demonstrate that defendants were familiar with the import of the rule. The "no knowledge" requirement of § 78ff(a) is not met by proof that defendants did not know that their specific conduct was within the prohibition of the rule.

By pleading guilty to the charges . . . defendants admitted that they knew securities fraud was prohibited, which is the substance of Rule 10b-5. No more knowledge is required.

Notes and Questions

1. Does the "no knowledge" proviso cut against the maxim that ignorance of the law is no excuse?

2. In what sense did the defendants in *Lilley* possess knowledge of the relevant rule or regulation? Is this a meaningful standard? Or does it virtually assure that few or no defendants will qualify?

3. The "no knowledge" proviso imposes the burden of proof squarely on the defendant. It does not, however, specify what the standard of proof is. Does the statute require the defendant to disprove an element of the offense? If it does, is it constitutional?[9]

---

9. Cf. In re Winship, 397 U.S. 358 (1970); United States v. Mandel, 296 F. Supp. 1038 (S.D.N.Y. 1969); United States v. Guterma, 189 F. Supp. 265 (S.D.N.Y. 1960). See also Lisa Mann Burke, The Tension Between *In re Winship* and the Use of Presumptions in Jury Instructions After *Sandstrom, Allen* and *Clark*, 17 N.M. L. Rev. 55 (1987).

Would it make a difference if the statute provided that "no person shall be *convicted* under this section for the violation of any rule, regulation, or order if he proves that he had no knowledge of such rule, regulation, or order"?[10]

4. Because the defendant raises the "no knowledge" claim at the sentencing phase of the trial, the claim will succeed or fail solely on the basis of judicial fact finding. In the context of a jury trial, does this violate the recently established rule, beginning with Apprendi v. New Jersey[11] and culminating in United States v. Booker,[12] that any fact other than a prior conviction that would increase the maximum penalty for the defendant's crime must be proved — to the satisfaction of the trier of fact — beyond a reasonable doubt?[13]

5. The "no knowledge" proviso has generated so little reported case law that one might reasonably assume that it is largely ignored in practice.[14] While that is generally true, some prosecutors have discovered that when put to creative use, it can play an instrumental role in facilitating plea negotiations. In some instances, for example, the plea agreement provides that the defendant may avoid a prison sentence by proving that he had no knowledge of the rule he admitted violating.[15] More importantly, however, some plea agreements *stipulate* that the defendant lacked knowledge of the relevant rule or regulation[16] and thus effectively narrow the range of sentencing options available to the court.

The court in *Lilley* found that Congress included the "no knowledge" proviso in the statute because of "fears generated by the spectre of a severe penalty ensuing from violation of a rule or regulation . . . of which the person charged had no knowledge." Is it likely that Congress anticipated it would be used to insulate knowledgeable defendants from imprisonment through carefully crafted plea agreements? Is this an appropriate use of the clause?

III. INSIDER TRADING

Insider trading is a controversial subject. Those who oppose insider trading, including the SEC and the Justice Department, believe the practice must be curbed if

---

10. See 15 U.S.C. § 79z-3 (penalty provision in Public Utility Holding Company Act of 1935); 15 U.S.C. § 80a-48 (penalty provision in Investment Company Act of 1940).

11. 350 U.S. 466 (2000).

12. 543 U.S. 220 (2005).

13. Cf. United States v. Tarallo, 380 F.3d 1174, 1192 (9th Cir. 2004).

14. But cf. United States v. O'Hagan, 139 F.3d 641, 646-648 (8th Cir. 1998) (rejecting defendant's argument that in light of the no knowledge proviso, the willfulness element of criminal securities violations should be construed to require proof that he knew his conduct was illegal).

15. *See, e.g.,* United States v. Westgard, Cr. No. 4-94-82, Government's Memorandum of Law Relating to Validity of Plea Agreements ("Pursuant to § 78ff(a), commonly referred to as section 32 of the Securities Exchange Act of 1934, the defendants may avoid any term of imprisonment by demonstrating that they had no knowledge of the regulation referenced in the Information.") (on file with the author).

16. *See, e.g.,* United States v. Adams, Cr. No. 4-94-82, Plea Agreement and Sentencing Stipulations ("The parties stipulate and agree that, pursuant to Title 15, United States Code, Section 78ff(a), the defendant had no knowledge of the substance of the rules and regulations set forth within Title 17, Code of Federal Regulations, Sections 240.17a-3(a)(8) and 240.17a-4(b)(1), and therefore, as provided by statute, the defendant may not be subjected to a term of imprisonment based on a conviction entered in connection with Count I of the Information.") (on file with the author).

investors are to have confidence in the market. In contrast, insider trading proponents argue that it should remain unregulated because it promotes market efficiency.[17]

The controversy was thrust into the limelight during the 1980s due to unprecedented levels of civil and criminal enforcement activity. SEC and Justice Department investigations uncovered widespread and large-scale insider trading schemes within the country's most respected brokerage houses, law firms, and corporations. The prosecution of Dennis Levine in 1986 targeted the biggest scheme ever to be uncovered. Shortly thereafter, the investigation of Ivan Boesky revealed an even bigger one. What we learned from the dozens of related prosecutions is that insider trading is a prevalent practice that, in some quarters at least, is business as usual.

Notwithstanding the volume of high-profile insider trading prosecutions, insider trading is neither defined nor expressly forbidden by statute or regulation. Instead, federal prosecutors reach insider trading activities through a general antifraud provision, § 10b of the Securities Exchange Act of 1934, together with SEC Rule 10b-5.

Section 10b prohibits use of a manipulative or deceptive device in connection with the purchase or sale of securities in violation of SEC rules and regulations. 15 U.S.C. § 78j(b). Rule 10b-5, promulgated by the SEC pursuant to this provision, prohibits three categories of manipulative and deceptive devices. Under Rule 10b-5, it is illegal to

(1) employ a device, scheme, or artifice to defraud;
(2) make any untrue statement of a material fact or omit any such fact necessary to make the statement not misleading; or
(3) engage in a transaction, practice or course of business that would operate as a fraud or deceit.

17 C.F.R. § 240.10b-5. Insider trading is prosecuted under this rule on the theory that it constitutes a scheme to defraud.

A. THE EVOLVING DOCTRINAL RULES

1. Classical Theory

CHIARELLA v. UNITED STATES
445 U.S. 222 (1980)

Mr. Justice POWELL delivered the opinion of the Court.

The question in this case is whether a person who learns from the confidential documents of one corporation that it is planning an attempt to secure control of a second corporation violates § 10(b) of the Securities Exchange Act of 1934 if he fails to disclose the impending takeover before trading in the target company's securities.

---

17. Indeed, a Heritage Foundation task force report recommended that corporations be authorized to amend their charters to permit insider trading. Conservative Group Urges Easing of Restrictions, Narrower Definition, Corporate Counsel Weekly (BNA), Dec. 14, 1988, at 2.

I

Petitioner is a printer by trade. In 1975 and 1976, he worked as a "markup man" in the New York composing room of Pandick Press, a financial printer. Among documents that petitioner handled were five announcements of corporate takeover bids. When these documents were delivered to the printer, the identities of the acquiring and target corporations were concealed by blank spaces or false names. The true names were sent to the printer on the night of the final printing.

The petitioner, however, was able to deduce the names of the target companies before the final printing from other information contained in the documents. Without disclosing his knowledge, petitioner purchased stock in the target companies and sold the shares immediately after the takeover attempts were made public. By this method, petitioner realized a gain of slightly more than $30,000 in the course of 14 months. Subsequently, the Securities and Exchange Commission (Commission or SEC) began an investigation of his trading activities. In May 1977, petitioner entered into a consent decree with the Commission in which he agreed to return his profits to the sellers of the shares. On the same day, he was discharged by Pandick Press.

In January 1978, petitioner was indicted on 17 counts of violating § 10(b) of the Securities Exchange Act of 1934 (1934 Act) and SEC Rule 10b-5. After petitioner unsuccessfully moved to dismiss the indictment, he was brought to trial and convicted on all counts.

The Court of Appeals for the Second Circuit affirmed petitioner's conviction. We granted certiorari, and we now reverse.

II

Section 10(b) of the 1934 Act, 15 U.S.C. § 78j, prohibits the use "in connection with the purchase or sale of any security . . . [of] any manipulative or deceptive device or contrivance in contravention of such rules and regulations as the Commission may prescribe." Pursuant to this section, the SEC promulgated Rule 10b-5 which provides in pertinent part:

> It shall be unlawful for any person, directly or indirectly, by the use of any means or instrumentality of interstate commerce, or of the mails or of any facility of any national securities exchange,
> (a) To employ any device, scheme, or artifice to defraud, [or]. . .
> (c) To engage in any act, practice, or course of business which operates or would operate as a fraud or deceit upon any person, in connection with the purchase or sale of any security. 17 C.F.R. § 240.10b-5.

This case concerns the legal effect of the petitioner's silence. The District Court's charge permitted the jury to convict the petitioner if it found that he willfully failed to inform sellers of target company securities that he knew of a forthcoming takeover bid that would make their shares more valuable. In order to decide whether silence in such circumstances violates § 10(b), it is necessary to review the language and legislative history of that statute as well as its interpretation by the Commission and the federal courts.

Although the starting point of our inquiry is the language of the statute, § 10(b) does not state whether silence may constitute a manipulative or deceptive device. Section 10(b) was designed as a catchall clause to prevent fraudulent practices. But neither the legislative history nor the statute itself affords specific guidance for the resolution of this case. When Rule 10b-5 was promulgated in 1942, the SEC did not discuss the possibility that failure to provide information might run afoul of § 10(b).

The SEC took an important step in the development of § 10(b) when it held that a broker-dealer and his firm violated that section by selling securities on the basis of undisclosed information obtained from a director of the issuer corporation who was also a registered representative of the brokerage firm. In Cady, Roberts & Co., 40 S.E.C. 907 (1961), the Commission decided that a corporate insider must abstain from trading in the shares of his corporation unless he has first disclosed all material inside information known to him. The obligation to disclose or abstain derives from

> [a]n affirmative duty to disclose material information[, which] has been traditionally imposed on corporate "insiders," particularly officers, directors, or controlling stockholders. We, and the courts, have consistently held that insiders must disclose material facts which are known to them by virtue of their position but which are not known to persons with whom they deal and which, if known, would affect their investment judgment. Id., at 911.

The Commission emphasized that the duty arose from (i) the existence of a relationship affording access to inside information intended to be available only for a corporate purpose, and (ii) the unfairness of allowing a corporate insider to take advantage of that information by trading without disclosure.

That the relationship between a corporate insider and the stockholders of his corporation gives rise to a disclosure obligation is not a novel twist of the law. At common law, misrepresentation made for the purpose of inducing reliance upon the false statement is fraudulent. But one who fails to disclose material information prior to the consummation of a transaction commits fraud only when he is under a duty to do so. And the duty to disclose arises when one party has information "that the other [party] is entitled to know because of a fiduciary or other similar relation of trust and confidence between them." In its *Cady, Roberts* decision, the Commission recognized a relationship of trust and confidence between the shareholders of a corporation and those insiders who have obtained confidential information by reason of their position with that corporation. This relationship gives rise to a duty to disclose because of the "necessity of preventing a corporate insider from . . . tak[ing] unfair advantage of the uninformed minority stockholders." Speed v. Transamerica Corp., 99 F. Supp. 808, 829 (Del. 1951).

The federal courts have found violations of § 10(b) where corporate insiders used undisclosed information for their own benefit. E.g., SEC v. Texas Gulf Sulphur Co., 401 F.2d 833 (CA2 1968). The cases also have emphasized, in accordance with the common-law rule, that "[t]he party charged with failing to disclose market information must be under a duty to disclose it." Frigitemp Corp. v. Financial Dynamics Fund, Inc., 524 F.2d 275, 282 (CA2 1975). Accordingly, a purchaser of stock who has no duty to a prospective seller because he is neither an insider nor a fiduciary has been held to have no obligation to reveal material facts. . . .

III

In this case, the petitioner was convicted of violating § 10(b) although he was not a corporate insider and he received no confidential information from the target company. Moreover, the "market information" upon which he relied did not concern the earning power or operations of the target company, but only the plans of the acquiring company. Petitioner's use of that information was not a fraud under § 10(b) unless he was subject to an affirmative duty to disclose it before trading. In this case, the jury instructions failed to specify any such duty. In effect, the trial court instructed the jury that petitioner owed a duty to everyone; to all sellers, indeed, to the market as a whole. The jury simply was told to decide whether petitioner used material, nonpublic information at a time when "he knew other people trading in the securities market did not have access to the same information."

The Court of Appeals affirmed the conviction by holding that "*[a]nyone* — corporate insider or not — who regularly receives material nonpublic information may not use that information to trade in securities without incurring an affirmative duty to disclose." 588 F.2d at 1365 (emphasis in original). Although the court said that its test would include only persons who regularly receive material, nonpublic information, its rationale for that limitation is unrelated to the existence of a duty to disclose.[18] The Court of Appeals, like the trial court, failed to identify a relationship between petitioner and the sellers that could give rise to a duty. Its decision thus rested solely upon its belief that the federal securities laws have "created a system providing equal access to information necessary for reasoned and intelligent investment decisions." Id. at 1362. The use by anyone of material information not generally available gives certain buyers or sellers an unfair advantage over less informed buyers and sellers.

This reasoning suffers from two defects. First, not every instance of financial unfairness constitutes fraudulent activity under § 10(b). See Santa Fe Industries, Inc. v. Green, 430 U.S. 462, 474-477 (1977). Second, the element required to make silence fraudulent — a duty to disclose — is absent in this case. No duty could arise from petitioner's relationship with the sellers of the target company's securities, for petitioner had no prior dealings with them. He was not their agent, he was not a fiduciary, he was not a person in whom the sellers had placed their trust and confidence. He was, in fact, a complete stranger who dealt with the sellers only through impersonal market transactions.

We cannot affirm petitioner's conviction without recognizing a general duty between all participants in market transactions to forgo actions based on material, nonpublic information. . . .

Section 10(b) is aptly described as a catchall provision, but what it catches must be fraud. When an allegation of fraud is based upon nondisclosure, there can be no fraud absent a duty to speak. We hold that a duty to disclose under § 10(b) does not arise from the mere possession of nonpublic market information. The contrary result is

---

18. The Court of Appeals said that its "regular access to market information" test would create a workable rule embracing "those who occupy . . . strategic places in the market mechanism." 588 F.2d at 1365. These considerations are insufficient to support a duty to disclose. A duty arises from the relationship between parties, and not merely from one's ability to acquire information because of his position in the market. . . .

without support in the legislative history of § 10(b) and would be inconsistent with the careful plan that Congress has enacted for regulation of the securities markets.[19]

The judgment of the Court of Appeals is reversed.

Mr. Justice STEVENS, concurring.

Before liability, civil or criminal, may be imposed for a Rule 10b-5 violation, it is necessary to identify the duty that the defendant has breached. Arguably, when petitioner bought securities in the open market, he violated (a) a duty to disclose owed to the sellers from whom he purchased target company stock and (b) a duty of silence owed to the acquiring companies. I agree with the Court's determination that petitioner owed no duty of disclosure to the sellers, that his conviction rested on the erroneous premise that he did owe them such a duty, and that the judgment of the Court of Appeals must therefore be reversed.

The Court correctly does not address the second question: whether the petitioner's breach of his duty of silence — a duty he unquestionably owed to his employer and to his employer's customers — could give rise to criminal liability under Rule 10b-5. Respectable arguments could be made in support of either position. On the one hand, if we assume that petitioner breached a duty to the acquiring companies that had entrusted confidential information to his employers, a legitimate argument could be made that his actions constituted "a fraud or a deceit" upon those companies "in connection with the purchase or sale of any security." On the other hand, inasmuch as those companies would not be able to recover damages from petitioner for violating Rule 10b-5 because they were neither purchasers nor sellers of target company securities, it could also be argued that no actionable violation of Rule 10b-5 had occurred. I think the Court wisely leaves the resolution of this issue for another day.

I write simply to emphasize the fact that we have not necessarily placed any stamp of approval on what this petitioner did, nor have we held that similar actions must be considered lawful in the future. Rather, we have merely held that petitioner's criminal conviction cannot rest on the theory that he breached a duty he did not owe. . . .

Mr. Justice BRENNAN, concurring in the judgment.

The Court holds, correctly in my view, that "a duty to disclose under § 10(b) does not arise from the mere possession of nonpublic market information." Prior to so holding, however, it suggests that no violation of § 10(b) could be made out absent a breach of some duty arising out of a fiduciary relationship between buyer and seller. I cannot subscribe to that suggestion. On the contrary, it seems to me that Part I of The Chief Justice's dissent correctly states the applicable substantive law — a person violates § 10(b) whenever he improperly obtains or converts to his own benefit nonpublic information which he then uses in connection with the purchase or sale of securities.

While I agree with Part I of The Chief Justice's dissent, I am unable to agree with Part II. Rather, I concur in the judgment of the majority because I think it clear that the legal theory sketched by The Chief Justice is not the one presented to the jury. . . .

---

19. The government also argued that Chiarella "breached a duty to the acquiring corporation when he acted upon information that he obtained by virtue of his position as an employee of a printer employed by the corporation," but the Court did not consider this theory because it was not submitted to the jury. — ED.

Mr. Chief Justice BURGER, dissenting.

I believe that the jury instructions in this case properly charged a violation of § 10(b) and Rule 10b-5, and I would affirm the conviction.

I

As a general rule, neither party to an arm's-length business transaction has an obligation to disclose information to the other unless the parties stand in some confidential or fiduciary relation. This rule permits a businessman to capitalize on his experience and skill in securing and evaluating relevant information; it provides incentive for hard work, careful analysis, and astute forecasting. But the policies that underlie the rule also should limit its scope. In particular, the rule should give way when an informational advantage is obtained, not by superior experience, foresight, or industry, but by some unlawful means. . . . I would read § 10(b) and Rule 10b-5 to encompass and build on this principle: to mean that a person who has misappropriated nonpublic information has an absolute duty to disclose that information or to refrain from trading. . . .

Mr. Justice BLACKMUN, with whom Mr. Justice MARSHALL joins, dissenting.

Although I agree with much of what is said in Part I of the dissenting opinion of The Chief Justice, I write separately because, in my view, it is unnecessary to rest petitioner's conviction on a "misappropriation" theory. The fact that petitioner Chiarella purloined, or, to use The Chief Justice's word, "stole," information concerning pending tender offers certainly is the most dramatic evidence that petitioner was guilty of fraud. He has conceded that he knew it was wrong, and he and his co-workers in the printshop were specifically warned by their employer that actions of this kind were improper and forbidden. But I also would find petitioner's conduct fraudulent within the meaning of § 10(b) of the Securities Exchange Act of 1934, and the Securities and Exchange Commission's Rule 10b-5, even if he had obtained the blessing of his employer's principals before embarking on his profiteering scheme. Indeed, I think petitioner's brand of manipulative trading, with or without such approval, lies close to the heart of what the securities laws are intended to prohibit.

The Court continues to pursue a course, charted in certain recent decisions, designed to transform § 10(b) from an intentionally elastic "catchall" provision to one that catches relatively little of the misbehavior that all too often makes investment in securities a needlessly risky business for the uninitiated investor. . . .

I, of course, agree with the Court that a relationship of trust can establish a duty to disclose under § 10(b) and Rule 10b-5. But I do not agree that a failure to disclose violates the Rule only when the responsibilities of a relationship of that kind have been breached. As applied to this case, the Court's approach unduly minimizes the importance of petitioner's *access* to confidential information that the honest investor, no matter how diligently he tried, could not legally obtain. . . .

Notes and Questions

1. Did Chiarella owe a duty to the acquiring corporation that was a customer of his employer?

2. Did Chiarella breach the duty of loyalty and confidentiality that he owed his employer? If so, would his breach of duty have violated § 10b? Could that breach have constituted the violation?

3. What if Chiarella had been an insider in the acquiring corporation and had knowledge of the takeover plans? If he had purchased stock in the target companies, would he have violated § 10b and Rule 10b-5?

2. Misappropriation Theory

UNITED STATES v. O'HAGAN
521 U.S. 642 (1997)

Justice GINSBURG delivered the opinion of the Court. . . .

I

Respondent James Herman O'Hagan was a partner in the law firm of Dorsey & Whitney in Minneapolis, Minnesota. In July 1988, Grand Metropolitan PLC (Grand Met), a company based in London, England, retained Dorsey & Whitney as local counsel to represent Grand Met regarding a potential tender offer for the common stock of the Pillsbury Company, headquartered in Minneapolis. Both Grand Met and Dorsey & Whitney took precautions to protect the confidentiality of Grand Met's tender offer plans. O'Hagan did no work on the Grand Met representation. Dorsey & Whitney withdrew from representing Grand Met on September 9, 1988. Less than a month later, on October 4, 1988, Grand Met publicly announced its tender offer for Pillsbury stock.

On August 18, 1988, while Dorsey & Whitney was still representing Grand Met, O'Hagan began purchasing call options for Pillsbury stock. Each option gave him the right to purchase 100 shares of Pillsbury stock by a specified date in September 1988. Later in August and in September, O'Hagan made additional purchases of Pillsbury call options. By the end of September, he owned 2,500 unexpired Pillsbury options, apparently more than any other individual investor. O'Hagan also purchased, in September 1988, some 5,000 shares of Pillsbury common stock, at a price just under $39 per share. When Grand Met announced its tender offer in October, the price of Pillsbury stock rose to nearly $60 per share. O'Hagan then sold his Pillsbury call options and common stock, making a profit of more than $4.3 million.

The Securities and Exchange Commission (SEC or Commission) initiated an investigation into O'Hagan's transactions, culminating in a 57-count indictment. The indictment alleged that O'Hagan defrauded his law firm and its client, Grand Met, by using for his own trading purposes material, nonpublic information regarding Grand Met's planned tender offer. According to the indictment, O'Hagan used the profits he gained through this trading to conceal his previous embezzlement and conversion of unrelated client trust funds.[20] O'Hagan was charged with 20 counts of mail fraud; 17 counts of securities fraud, in violation of § 10(b) of the Securities Exchange Act of 1934 (Exchange Act) and SEC Rule 10b-5; 17 counts of fraudulent trading in connection with a tender offer, in violation of § 14(e) of the Exchange Act, and SEC Rule 14e-3(a); and 3 counts of violating federal money laundering statutes, 18 U.S.C. §§ 1956(a)(1)(B)(i), 1957. A jury convicted O'Hagan on all 57 counts, and he was sentenced to a 41-month term of imprisonment.

A divided panel of the Court of Appeals for the Eighth Circuit reversed all of O'Hagan's convictions. Liability under § 10(b) and Rule 10b-5, the Eighth Circuit held, may not be grounded on the "misappropriation theory" of securities fraud on which the prosecution relied. . . .

II . . .

A . . .

The statute . . . proscribes (1) using any deceptive device (2) in connection with the purchase or sale of securities, in contravention of rules prescribed by the Commission. The provision, as written, does not confine its coverage to deception of a purchaser or seller of securities; rather, the statute reaches any deceptive device used "in connection with the purchase or sale of any security.". . .

Under the "traditional" or "classical theory" of insider trading liability, § 10(b) and Rule 10b-5 are violated when a corporate insider trades in the securities of his corporation on the basis of material, nonpublic information. Trading on such information qualifies as a "deceptive device" under § 10(b), we have affirmed, because "a relationship of trust and confidence [exists] between the shareholders of a corporation and those insiders who have obtained confidential information by reason of their position with that corporation." Chiarella v. United States, 445 U.S. 222, 228 (1980). That relationship, we recognized, "gives rise to a duty to disclose [or to abstain from trading] because of the 'necessity of preventing a corporate insider from . . . taking unfair advantage of . . . uninformed . . . stockholders.'" Id., at 228-229. The classical theory applies not only to officers, directors, and other permanent insiders of a corporation, but also to attorneys, accountants, consultants, and others who temporarily become fiduciaries of a corporation. See Dirks v. SEC, 463 U.S. 646, 655, n.14 (1983).

The "misappropriation theory" holds that a person commits fraud "in connection with" a securities transaction, and thereby violates § 10(b) and Rule 10b-5, when he misappropriates confidential information for securities trading purposes, in breach of a duty owed to the source of the information. Under this theory, a fiduciary's undisclosed, self-serving use of a principal's information to purchase or sell securities, in breach of a duty of loyalty and confidentiality, defrauds the principal of the exclusive use of that information. See Brief for United States 14. In lieu of premising liability on a fiduciary relationship between company insider and purchaser or seller of the company's stock, the misappropriation theory premises liability on a fiduciary-turned-trader's deception of those who entrusted him with access to confidential information.

---

20. O'Hagan was convicted of theft in state court, sentenced to 30 months' imprisonment, and fined. See State v. O'Hagan, 474 N.W.2d 613, 615, 623 (Minn. App. 1991). The Supreme Court of Minnesota disbarred O'Hagan from the practice of law. See In re O'Hagan, 450 N.W.2d 571 (Minn. 1990).

The two theories are complementary, each addressing efforts to capitalize on nonpublic information through the purchase or sale of securities. The classical theory targets a corporate insider's breach of duty to shareholders with whom the insider transacts; the misappropriation theory outlaws trading on the basis of nonpublic information by a corporate "outsider" in breach of a duty owed not to a trading party, but to the source of the information. The misappropriation theory is thus designed to "protect the integrity of the securities markets against abuses by 'outsiders' to a corporation who have access to confidential information that will affect the corporation's security price when revealed, but who owe no fiduciary or other duty to that corporation's shareholders." Ibid.

In this case, the indictment alleged that O'Hagan, in breach of a duty of trust and confidence he owed to his law firm, Dorsey & Whitney, and to its client, Grand Met, traded on the basis of nonpublic information regarding Grand Met's planned tender offer for Pillsbury common stock. This conduct, the Government charged, constituted a fraudulent device in connection with the purchase and sale of securities.[21]

B

We agree with the Government that misappropriation, as just defined, satisfies § 10(b)'s requirement that chargeable conduct involve a "deceptive device or contrivance" used "in connection with" the purchase or sale of securities. We observe, first, that misappropriators, as the Government describes them, deal in deception. A fiduciary who "[pretends] loyalty to the principal while secretly converting the principal's information for personal gain," Brief for United States 17, "dupes" or defrauds the principal. See Aldave, Misappropriation: A General Theory of Liability for Trading on Nonpublic Information, 13 Hofstra L. Rev. 101, 119 (1984).

We addressed fraud of the same species in Carpenter v. United States, 484 U.S. 19 (1987), which involved the mail fraud statute's proscription of "any scheme or artifice to defraud." Affirming convictions under that statute, we said in *Carpenter* that an employee's undertaking not to reveal his employer's confidential information "became a sham" when the employee provided the information to his co-conspirators in a scheme to obtain trading profits. 484 U.S. at 27. A company's confidential information, we recognized in *Carpenter*, qualifies as property to which the company has a right of exclusive use. The undisclosed misappropriation of such information, in violation of a fiduciary duty, the Court said in *Carpenter*, constitutes fraud akin to embezzlement — "'the fraudulent appropriation to one's own use of the money or goods entrusted to one's care by another.'" Id., at 27. *Carpenter*'s discussion of the fraudulent misuse of confidential information, the Government notes, "is a particularly apt source of guidance here, because [the mail fraud statute] (like Section 10(b)) has long been held to require deception, not merely the breach of a fiduciary duty." Brief for United States 18, n.9.

---

21. The Government could not have prosecuted O'Hagan under the classical theory, for O'Hagan was not an "insider" of Pillsbury, the corporation in whose stock he traded. Although an "outsider" with respect to Pillsbury, O'Hagan had an intimate association with, and was found to have traded on confidential information from, Dorsey & Whitney, counsel to tender offeror Grand Met. Under the misappropriation theory, O'Hagan's securities trading does not escape Exchange Act sanction, as it would under the dissent's reasoning, simply because he was associated with, and gained nonpublic information from, the bidder, rather than the target.

Deception through nondisclosure is central to the theory of liability for which the Government seeks recognition. As counsel for the Government stated in explanation of the theory at oral argument: "To satisfy the common law rule that a trustee may not use the property that [has] been entrusted [to] him, there would have to be consent. To satisfy the requirement of the Securities Act that there be no deception, there would only have to be disclosure." Tr. of Oral Arg. 12; see generally Restatement (Second) of Agency §§ 390, 395 (1958) (agent's disclosure obligation regarding use of confidential information).[22]

The misappropriation theory advanced by the Government is consistent with Santa Fe Industries, Inc. v. Green, 430 U.S. 462 (1977), a decision underscoring that § 10(b) is not an all-purpose breach of fiduciary duty ban; rather, it trains on conduct involving manipulation or deception. In contrast to the Government's allegations in this case, in *Santa Fe Industries*, all pertinent facts were disclosed by the persons charged with violating § 10(b) and Rule 10b-5; therefore, there was no deception through nondisclosure to which liability under those provisions could attach. Similarly, full disclosure forecloses liability under the misappropriation theory: Because the deception essential to the misappropriation theory involves feigning fidelity to the source of information, if the fiduciary discloses to the source that he plans to trade on the nonpublic information, there is no "deceptive device" and thus no § 10(b) violation — although the fiduciary-turned-trader may remain liable under state law for breach of a duty of loyalty.[23]

We turn next to the § 10(b) requirement that the misappropriator's deceptive use of information be "in connection with the purchase or sale of [a] security." This element is satisfied because the fiduciary's fraud is consummated, not when the fiduciary gains the confidential information, but when, without disclosure to his principal, he uses the information to purchase or sell securities. The securities transaction and the breach of duty thus coincide. This is so even though the person or entity defrauded is not the other party to the trade, but is, instead, the source of the nonpublic information. See Aldave, 13 Hofstra L. Rev., at 120 ("a fraud or deceit can be practiced on one person, with resultant harm to another person or group of persons"). A misappropriator who trades on the basis of material, nonpublic information, in short, gains his advantageous market position through deception; he deceives the source of the information and simultaneously harms members of the investing public. . . .

The misappropriation theory comports with § 10(b)'s language, which requires deception "in connection with the purchase or sale of any security," not deception of an identifiable purchaser or seller. The theory is also well-tuned to an animating purpose of the Exchange Act: to insure honest securities markets and thereby promote investor confidence. Although informational disparity is inevitable in the securities markets, investors likely would hesitate to venture their capital in a market where trading based

---

22. Under the misappropriation theory urged in this case, the disclosure obligation runs to the source of the information, here, Dorsey & Whitney and Grand Met. Chief Justice Burger, dissenting in *Chiarella*, advanced a broader reading of § 10(b) and Rule 10b-5; the disclosure obligation, as he envisioned it, ran to those with whom the misappropriator trades. 445 U.S. at 240 ("a person who has misappropriated non-public information has an absolute duty to disclose that information or to refrain from trading"); see also id., at 243, n.4. The Government does not propose that we adopt a misappropriation theory of that breadth.

23. Where, however, a person trading on the basis of material, nonpublic information owes a duty of loyalty and confidentiality to two entities or persons — for example, a law firm and its client — but makes disclosure to only one, the trader may still be liable under the misappropriation theory.

on misappropriated nonpublic information is unchecked by law. An investor's informational disadvantage vis-à-vis a misappropriator with material, nonpublic information stems from contrivance, not luck; it is a disadvantage that cannot be overcome with research or skill. See Brudney, Insiders, Outsiders, and Informational Advantages Under the Federal Securities Law, 93 Harv. L. Rev. 322, 356 (1979); Aldave, 13 Hofstra L. Rev., at 122-123.

In sum, . . . it makes scant sense to hold a lawyer like O'Hagan a § 10(b) violator if he works for a law firm representing the target of a tender offer, but not if he works for a law firm representing the bidder. The text of the statute requires no such result. The misappropriation at issue here was properly made the subject of a § 10(b) charge because it meets the statutory requirement that there be "deceptive" conduct "in connection with" securities transactions. . . .

The judgment of the Court of Appeals for the Eighth Circuit is reversed, and the case is remanded for further proceedings consistent with this opinion. . . .

Justice THOMAS, with whom THE CHIEF JUSTICE joins, concurring in the judgment in part and dissenting in part. . . .

Today the majority upholds respondent's convictions for violating § 10(b) of the Securities Exchange Act of 1934, and Rule 10b-5 promulgated thereunder, based upon the Securities and Exchange Commission's "misappropriation theory." Central to the majority's holding is the need to interpret § 10(b)'s requirement that a deceptive device be "used or employed, in connection with the purchase or sale of any security." 15 U.S.C. § 78j(b). Because the Commission's misappropriation theory fails to provide a coherent and consistent interpretation of this essential requirement for liability under § 10(b), I dissent. . . .

I

I do not take issue with the majority's determination that the undisclosed misappropriation of confidential information by a fiduciary can constitute a "deceptive device" within the meaning of § 10(b). Nondisclosure where there is a pre-existing duty to disclose satisfies our definitions of fraud and deceit for purposes of the securities laws. See Chiarella v. United States, 445 U.S. 222, 230 (1980).

Unlike the majority, however, I cannot accept the Commission's interpretation of when a deceptive device is "used . . . in connection with" a securities transaction. . . .

[T]he Government's . . . misappropriation theory [should not] cover cases, such as this one, involving fraud on the source of information where the source has no connection with the other participant in a securities transaction. . . .

[Opinion of Justice SCALIA, concurring in part and dissenting in part, omitted.]

Notes and Questions

1. When is misappropriated inside information used "in connection with" the purchase or sale of a security after *O'Hagan*? Is the majority's theory incoherent, as Justice Thomas suggests?

2. Is breach of a fiduciary duty an element of liability under the misappropriation theory? If so, to whom does the duty run? Would it matter if, as O'Hagan claimed, he did not know the identity of the company that planned to make a takeover bid for Pillsbury?

3. If the government were confronted with the facts in *Chiarella* today, could it craft a viable theory of insider trading liability? If so, what would it be?

4. What kinds of conduct does the concept of misappropriation encompass? Suppose the security guard in the building where Dorsey & Whitney's offices are located hears a rumor that the firm is working on a big takeover deal. Late one night the guard picks the lock on the firm's door and looks around until he finds the Grand Met file on O'Hagan's desk. If the guard copies the file and then trades on the basis of information the file contains, has he violated Rule 10b-5?

5. What constitutes nonpublic confidential information? In *O'Hagan*, it was important that Grand Met's potential tender offer for Pillsbury stock should remain confidential, but Dorsey & Whitney could not provide the needed legal services unless Grand Met disclosed information about the planned transaction. Thus, lawyers, paralegals, and secretaries at the firm became privy to information about Grand Met's plans during the course of Dorsey & Whitney's representation of Grand Met. It seems clear that Grand Met's limited and confidential disclosure to the law firm did not strip the information of its confidential or nonpublic character.

O'Hagan argued that because the impending takeover bid had been the subject of intense media interest, the information was no longer nonpublic. On remand, the Eighth Circuit summarily rejected this claim.

> Despite O'Hagan's claims to the contrary, contemporaneous media reports speculating that Pillsbury would be taken over by Grand Met do not render the information O'Hagan learned immaterial or nonpublic. Financial analysts testified that these media reports were "not taken seriously," and were dismissed because "newspapers are always having articles of rumors." The market as a whole attributed little to these reports as evidenced by the lack of significant movement in Pillsbury stock price upon dissemination of the stories. The reports themselves concerned only *speculation* about a takeover of Pillsbury, whereas O'Hagan now had firsthand, concrete knowledge that a client and his law firm were preparing a plan to take over Pillsbury. The information that O'Hagan obtained went beyond that which had been publicly disseminated.[24] We believe a reasonable investor would have considered this additional information about what Dorsey & Whitney and its client were doing vis-a-vis Pillsbury to have "significantly altered the 'total mix' of information [then] available."[25]

At what point along the continuum should intense media coverage strip inside information of its nonpublic character?

6. Suppose O'Hagan's best friend was a Special FBI Agent who had access to law enforcement reports about publicly traded companies with potential regulatory problems. As a favor to his friend, the Special Agent misappropriated confidential FBI and SEC reports containing law enforcement data about the companies and passed the

---

24. The Second Circuit reached the same conclusion on facts similar to this case. *See* United States v. Mylett, 97 F.3d 663, 666-67 (2d Cir. 1996) (inside information of a merger that had been the subject of media speculation is nonpublic information).

25. United States v. O'Hagan, 139 F.3d 641, 648 (8th Cir. 1998).

information along to O'Hagan. Although someone who "knows where to look" could have lawfully discovered — "albeit with difficulty" — some of the reported enforcement data, the reports were compiled from a mix of discoverable information and purely private data. Do the contents of the reports qualify as "nonpublic" confidential information?[26]

3. Tipper/Tippee Theory

DIRKS v. SECURITIES AND EXCHANGE COMMISSION
463 U.S. 646 (1983)

Justice POWELL delivered the opinion of the Court.

Petitioner Raymond Dirks received material nonpublic information from "insiders" of a corporation with which he had no connection. He disclosed this information to investors, who relied on it in trading in the shares of the corporation. The question is whether Dirks violated the antifraud provisions of the federal securities laws by this disclosure.

I

In 1973, Dirks was an officer of a New York broker-dealer firm who specialized in providing investment analysis of insurance company securities to institutional investors. On March 6, Dirks received information from Ronald Secrist, a former officer of Equity Funding of America. Secrist alleged that the assets of Equity Funding, a diversified corporation primarily engaged in selling life insurance and mutual funds, were vastly overstated as the result of fraudulent corporate practices. Secrist also stated that various regulatory agencies had failed to act on similar charges made by Equity Funding employees. He urged Dirks to verify the fraud and disclose it publicly.

Dirks decided to investigate the allegations. He visited Equity Funding's headquarters in Los Angeles and interviewed several officers and employees of the corporation. The senior management denied any wrongdoing, but certain corporation employees corroborated the charges of fraud. Neither Dirks nor his firm owned or traded any Equity Funding stock, but throughout his investigation he openly discussed the information he had obtained with a number of clients and investors. Some of these persons sold their holdings of Equity Funding securities, including five investment advisers who liquidated holdings of more than $16 million.

While Dirks was in Los Angeles, he was in touch regularly with William Blundell, the Wall Street Journal's Los Angeles bureau chief. Dirks urged Blundell to write a story on the fraud allegations. Blundell did not believe, however, that such a massive fraud could go undetected and declined to write the story. He feared that publishing such damaging hearsay might be libelous.

During the 2-week period in which Dirks pursued his investigation and spread word of Secrist's charges, the price of Equity Funding stock fell from $26 per share to

---

26. Cf. United States v. Royer, 549 F.3d 886 (2d Cir. 2008).

less than $15 per share. This led the New York Stock Exchange to halt trading on March 27. Shortly thereafter California insurance authorities impounded Equity Funding's records and uncovered evidence of the fraud. Only then did the Securities and Exchange Commission (SEC) file a complaint against Equity Funding[27] and only then, on April 2, did the Wall Street Journal publish a front-page story based largely on information assembled by Dirks. Equity Funding immediately went into receivership.[28]

The SEC began an investigation into Dirks' role in the exposure of the fraud. After a hearing by an Administrative Law Judge, the SEC found that Dirks had aided and abetted violations of § 17(a) of the Securities Act of 1933, § 10(b) of the Securities Exchange Act of 1934, and SEC Rule 10b-5, by repeating the allegations of fraud to members of the investment community who later sold their Equity Funding stock. The SEC concluded: "Where 'tippees' — regardless of their motivation or occupation — come into possession of material 'corporate information that they know is confidential and know or should know came from a corporate insider,' they must either publicly disclose that information or refrain from trading." 21 S.E.C. Docket 1401, 1407 (1981) (quoting Chiarella v. United States, 445 U.S. 222, 230, n.12 (1980)). Recognizing, however, that Dirks "played an important role in bringing [Equity Funding's] massive fraud to light," 21 S.E.C. Docket, at 1412, the SEC only censured him.[29]

Dirks sought review in the Court of Appeals for the District of Columbia Circuit. The court entered judgment against Dirks "for the reasons stated by the Commission in its opinion." . . .

III

We were explicit in *Chiarella* in saying that there can be no duty to disclose where the person who has traded on inside information "was not [the corporation's] agent, . . . was not a fiduciary, [or] was not a person in whom the sellers [of the securities] had placed their trust and confidence." 445 U.S., at 232. Not to require such a fiduciary relationship, we recognized, would "[depart] radically from the established doctrine that duty arises from a specific relationship between two parties" and would amount to "recognizing a general duty between all participants in market transactions to forgo actions based on material, nonpublic information." Id., at 232, 233. This requirement of a specific relationship between the shareholders and the individual trading on inside information has created analytical difficulties for the SEC and courts in policing tippees who trade on inside information. Unlike insiders who have independent fiduciary duties

---

27. As early as 1971, the SEC had received allegations of fraudulent accounting practices at Equity Funding. Moreover, on March 9, 1973, an official of the California Insurance Department informed the SEC's regional office in Los Angeles of Secrist's charges of fraud. Dirks himself voluntarily presented his information at the SEC's regional office beginning on March 27.

28. A federal grand jury in Los Angeles subsequently returned a 105-count indictment against 22 persons, including many of Equity Funding's officers and directors. All defendants were found guilty of one or more counts, either by a plea of guilty or a conviction after trial.

29. Section 15 of the Securities Exchange Act, 15 U.S.C. § 78o(b)(4)(E), provides that the SEC may impose certain sanctions, including censure, on any person associated with a registered broker-dealer who has "willfully aided [or] abetted" any violation of the federal securities laws. See 15 U.S.C. § 78ff(a) (providing criminal penalties).

to both the corporation and its shareholders, the typical tippee has no such relation-ships.[30] In view of this absence, it has been unclear how a tippee acquires the *Cady, Roberts* duty to refrain from trading on inside information.

A

The SEC's position, as stated in its opinion in this case, is that a tippee "inherits" the *Cady, Roberts* obligation to shareholders whenever he receives inside information from an insider:

> In tipping potential traders, Dirks breached a duty which he had assumed as a result of knowingly receiving confidential information from [Equity Funding] insiders. Tippees such as Dirks who receive non-public, material information from insiders become "subject to the same duty as [the] insiders." Such a tippee breaches the fiduciary duty which he assumes from the insider when the tippee knowingly transmits the information to some-one who will probably trade on the basis thereof. . . . Presumably, Dirks' informants were entitled to disclose the [Equity Funding] fraud in order to bring it to light and its per-petrators to justice. However, Dirks — standing in their shoes — committed a breach of the fiduciary duty which he had assumed in dealing with them, when he passed the infor-mation on to traders. 21 S.E.C. Docket, at 1410, n. 42.

This view differs little from the view that we rejected as inconsistent with congressional intent in *Chiarella*. . . .

In effect, the SEC's theory of tippee liability in both cases appears rooted in the idea that the antifraud provisions require equal information among all traders. This conflicts with the principle set forth in *Chiarella* that only some persons, under some circumstances, will be barred from trading while in possession of material nonpublic information. . . .

B

The conclusion that recipients of inside information do not invariably acquire a duty to disclose or abstain does not mean that such tippees always are free to trade on the information. The need for a ban on some tippee trading is clear. Not only are insiders forbidden by their fiduciary relationship from personally using undisclosed corporate information to their advantage, but they also may not give such information

---

30. Under certain circumstances, such as where corporate information is revealed legitimately to an underwriter, accountant, lawyer, or consultant working for the corporation, these outsiders may become fiduciaries of the shareholders. The basis for recognizing this fiduciary duty is not simply that such persons acquired nonpublic corporate information, but rather that they have entered into a special confidential relationship in the conduct of the business of the enterprise and are given access to information solely for corporate purposes. When such a person breaches his fiduciary relationship, he may be treated more prop-erly as a tipper than a tippee. See Shapiro v. Merrill Lynch, Pierce, Fenner & Smith, Inc., 495 F.2d 228, 237 (CA2 1974) (investment banker had access to material information when working on a proposed pub-lic offering for the corporation). For such a duty to be imposed, however, the corporation must expect the outsider to keep the disclosed nonpublic information confidential, and the relationship at least must imply such a duty.

to an outsider for the same improper purpose of exploiting the information for their personal gain. . . .

Thus, some tippees must assume an insider's duty to the shareholders not because they receive inside information, but rather because it has been made available to them *improperly*. And for Rule 10b-5 purposes, the insider's disclosure is improper only where it would violate his *Cady, Roberts* duty. Thus, a tippee assumes a fiduciary duty to the shareholders of a corporation not to trade on material nonpublic information only when the insider has breached his fiduciary duty to the shareholders by disclosing the information to the tippee and the tippee knows or should know that there has been a breach. As Commissioner Smith perceptively observed in In re Investors Management Co., 44 S.E.C. 633 (1971): "[T]ippee responsibility must be related back to insider responsibility by a necessary finding that the tippee knew the information was given to him in breach of a duty by a person having a special relationship to the issuer not to disclose the information. . . ." Id., at 651 (concurring in result). Tipping thus properly is viewed only as a means of indirectly violating the *Cady, Roberts* disclose-or-abstain rule. . . .

IV

Under the inside-trading and tipping rules set forth above, we find that there was no actionable violation by Dirks. It is undisputed that Dirks himself was a stranger to Equity Funding, with no preexisting fiduciary duty to its shareholders. He took no action, directly or indirectly, that induced the shareholders or officers of Equity Funding to repose trust or confidence in him. There was no expectation by Dirk's sources that he would keep their information in confidence. Nor did Dirks misappropriate or illegally obtain the information about Equity Funding. Unless the insiders breached their *Cady, Roberts* duty to shareholders in disclosing the nonpublic information to Dirks, he breached no duty when he passed it on to investors as well as to the Wall Street Journal.

It is clear that neither Secrist nor the other Equity Funding employees violated their *Cady, Roberts* duty to the corporation's shareholders by providing information to Dirks. The tippers received no monetary or personal benefit for revealing Equity Funding's secrets, nor was their purpose to make a gift of valuable information to Dirks. As the facts of this case clearly indicate, the tippers were motivated by a desire to expose the fraud. In the absence of a breach of duty to shareholders by the insiders, there was no derivative breach by Dirks. Dirks therefore could not have been "a participant after the fact in [an] insider's breach of a fiduciary duty." *Chiarella*, 445 U.S. at 320, n.12.

V

We conclude that Dirks, in the circumstances of this case, had no duty to abstain from use of the inside information that he obtained. The judgment of the Court of Appeals therefore is *reversed*.

Justice BLACKMUN, with whom Justice BRENNAN and Justice MARSHALL join, dissenting.

The Court today takes still another step to limit the protections provided investors by § 10(b) of the Securities Exchange Act of 1934. The device employed in this case engrafts a special motivational requirement on the fiduciary duty doctrine. This innovation excuses a knowing and intentional violation of an insider's duty to shareholders if the insider does not act from a motive of personal gain. Even on the extraordinary facts of this case, such an innovation is not justified. . . .

I . . .

C

The fact that the insider himself does not benefit from the breach does not eradicate the shareholder's injury. Cf. Restatement (Second) of Trusts § 205, Comments *c* and *d* (1959) (trustee liable for acts causing diminution of value of trust); 3 A. Scott, Law of Trusts § 205, p. 1665 (3d ed. 1967) (trustee liable for any losses to trust caused by his breach). It makes no difference to the shareholder whether the corporate insider gained or intended to gain personally from the transaction; the shareholder still has lost because of the insider's misuse of nonpublic information. The duty is addressed not to the insider's motives, but to his actions and their consequences on the shareholder. Personal gain is not an element of the breach of this duty. . . .

Notes and Questions

1. Why was the absence of personal gain so important to the majority of the Court?

2. If Chiarella had been prosecuted on the theory that his position was analogous to that of a tippee, how would the case have come out in light of *Dirks*?[31]

3. What is the substance of the duty to disclose or abstain? There is little doubt about the "abstain" part of the equation, but what does its "disclosure" counterpart entail? This question has particular salience in the context of cases like *Dirks*, where Mr. Dirks did his best to spread word of the Equity Funding fraud. He openly discussed Equity Funding's financial problems with various clients and investors, tried in vain to persuade the Wall Street Journal to publish a story about the firm's precarious financial condition, and shared his findings with the SEC. Moreover, the SEC and the California Insurance Department had previously ignored allegations of financial wrongdoing at Equity Funding. If Dirks had had a duty to disclose, would these circumstances add up to disclosure under insider trading rules? What more could Dirks be expected to do? Under what circumstances does limited disclosure strip what would otherwise be confidential material of its status as "nonpublic" information?[32]

---

31. The SEC has specifically addressed this problem in a related context. Rule 14e-3 provides that buying or selling securities on the basis of material nonpublic information relating to a tender offer is a fraudulent, deceptive, or manipulative act or practice. 17 C.F.R. § 240.14e-3.

32. Cf. United States v. Royer, 549 F.3d 886, 898 (2d Cir. 2008) ("[w]hen an investor with [confidential] information chooses to disclose it, the non-public information remains non-public for purposes of the insider trading laws until it has been disseminated in a manner sufficient to insure its availability to the investing public or to insure that the market has had an opportunity to 'absorb' the disclosed information such that the company's stock price has already adjusted to reflect that information").

PROBLEM 5-1

Suppose that Dirks invites Secrist to dinner at a posh restaurant. Over the course of the evening, Dirks plies Secrist with a generous amount of wine. Toward the end of the meal — and after consuming far more wine than he should have — Secrist becomes a bit tipsy and begins to confide in Dirks on a range of personal and professional matters. Then, while Secrist sips an after-dinner brandy, Dirks gently prods him into talking about internal matters at Equity Funding. He also orders Secrist a second brandy. Now highly intoxicated, Secrist talks freely about Equity Funding's financial condition and unwittingly discloses the massive accounting fraud that threatens to bring the firm down. The next morning, Dirks sells all of his Equity Funding stock.

Is Dirks liable under the tipper/tippee theory of liability? Is Secrist liable as a tipper? How, if at all, is this scenario distinguishable from the situation the Court addressed in *Dirks*?[33]

PROBLEM 5-2

The security guard at the building where Dorsey & Whitney's offices are located hears a rumor that the firm is working on a second big takeover deal. Unwilling to risk getting caught breaking into the firm's offices again, he devises another way to find out the details. The guard knows that Dorsey & Whitney employs a courier whose sole responsibility is to deliver documents to Minneapolis clients. The guard introduces himself to the courier and offers him $20 per file to let him look at all files to be delivered that bear O'Hagan's name. Knowing that O'Hagan has recently been the source of many urgent and highly confidential deliveries, the courier eagerly agrees. If the guard learns the terms of the second takeover deal by perusing the yet-to-be delivered files and he trades on the basis of the information before the takeover is announced, has he violated the prohibition against insider trading? Cf. United States v. Libera, 989 F.2d 596 (2d Cir. 1993).

UNITED STATES v. CHESTMAN
947 F.2d 551 (2d Cir. 1991) (en banc)

MESKILL, Circuit Judge, joined by CARDAMONE, PRATT, MINER and ALTIMARI, Circuit Judges. . . .

BACKGROUND

Robert Chestman is a stockbroker. Keith Loeb first sought Chestman's services in 1982, when Loeb decided to consolidate his and his wife's holdings in Waldbaum, Inc. (Waldbaum), a publicly traded company that owned a large supermarket chain. During their initial meeting, Loeb told Chestman that his wife was a granddaughter of Julia

---

33. Cf. United States v. Evans, 486 F.3d 315 (7th Cir. 2007).

Waldbaum, member of the board of directors of Waldbaum and the wife of its founder. Julia Waldbaum also was the mother of Ira Waldbaum, the president and controlling shareholder of Waldbaum. From 1982 to 1986, Chestman executed several transactions involving Waldbaum restricted and common stock for Keith Loeb. To facilitate some of these trades, Loeb sent Chestman a copy of his wife's birth certificate, which indicated that his wife's mother was Shirley Waldbaum Witkin.

On November 21, 1986, Ira Waldbaum agreed to sell Waldbaum to the Great Atlantic and Pacific Tea Company (A&P). The resulting stock purchase agreement required Ira to tender a controlling block of Waldbaum shares to A&P at a price of $50 per share. Ira told three of his children, all employees of Waldbaum, about the pending sale two days later, admonishing them to keep the news quiet until a public announcement. He also told his sister, Shirley Witkin, and nephew, Robert Karin, about the sale, and offered to tender their shares along with his controlling block of shares to enable them to avoid the administrative difficulty of tendering after the public announcement. He cautioned them "that [the sale was] not to be discussed," that it was to remain confidential.

In spite of Ira's counsel, Shirley told her daughter, Susan Loeb, on November 24 that Ira was selling the company. Shirley warned Susan not to tell anyone except her husband, Keith Loeb, because disclosure could ruin the sale. The next day, Susan told her husband about the pending tender offer and cautioned him not to tell anyone because "it could possibly ruin the sale."

The following day, November 26, Keith Loeb telephoned Robert Chestman at 8:59 A.M. Unable to reach Chestman, Loeb left a message asking Chestman to call him "ASAP." According to Loeb, he later spoke with Chestman between 9:00 A.M. and 10:30 A.M. that morning and told Chestman that he had "some definite, some accurate information" that Waldbaum was about to be sold at a "substantially higher" price than its market value. Loeb asked Chestman several times what he thought Loeb should do. Chestman responded that he could not advise Loeb what to do "in a situation like this" and that Loeb would have to make up his own mind.

That morning Chestman executed several purchases of Waldbaum stock. At 9:49 A.M., he bought 3,000 shares for his own account at $24.65 per share. Between 11:31 A.M. and 12:30 P.M., he purchased an additional 8,000 shares for his clients' discretionary accounts at prices ranging from $25.75 to $26.00 per share. One of the discretionary accounts was the Loeb account, for which Chestman bought 1,000 shares.

Before the market closed at 4:00 P.M., Loeb claims that he telephoned Chestman a second time. During their conversation Loeb again pressed Chestman for advice. Chestman repeated that he could not advise Loeb "in a situation like this," but then said that, based on his research, Waldbaum was a "buy." Loeb subsequently ordered 1,000 shares of Waldbaum stock.

Chestman presented a different version of the day's events. Before the SEC and at trial, he claimed that he had purchased Waldbaum stock based on his own research. He stated that his purchases were consistent with previous purchases of Waldbaum stock and other retail food stocks and were supported by reports in trade publications as well as the unusually high trading volume of the stock on November 25. He denied having spoken to Loeb about Waldbaum stock on the day of the trades.

At the close of trading on November 26, the tender offer was publicly announced. Waldbaum stock rose to $49 per share the next business day. In December 1986, Loeb learned that the National Association of Securities Dealers had started an investigation concerning transactions in Waldbaum stock. Loeb contacted Chestman who, according to Loeb, "reassured" him that Chestman had bought the stock for Loeb's account based on his research. Loeb called Chestman again in April 1987 after learning of an SEC investigation into the trading of Waldbaum stock. Chestman again stated that he bought the stock based on research. Similar conversations ensued. After one of these conversations, Chestman asked Loeb what his "position" was, Loeb replied, "I guess it's the same thing." Loeb subsequently agreed, however, to cooperate with the government. The terms of his cooperation agreement required that he disgorge the $25,000 profit from his purchase and sale of Waldbaum stock and pay a $25,000 fine. . . .

DISCUSSION . . .

B. RULE 10B-5

Chestman's Rule 10b-5 convictions were based on the misappropriation theory, which provides that "one who misappropriates nonpublic information in breach of a fiduciary duty and trades on that information to his own advantage violates Section 10(b) and Rule 10b-5." SEC v. Materia, 745 F.2d 197, 203 (2d Cir. 1984). With respect to the shares Chestman purchased on behalf of Keith Loeb, Chestman was convicted of aiding and abetting Loeb's misappropriation of nonpublic information in breach of a duty Loeb owed to the Waldbaum family and to his wife Susan. As to the shares Chestman purchased for himself and his other clients, Chestman was convicted as a "tippee" of that same misappropriated information. Thus, while Chestman is the defendant in this case, the alleged misappropriator was Keith Loeb. The government agrees that Chestman's convictions cannot be sustained unless there was sufficient evidence to show that (1) Keith Loeb breached a duty owed to the Waldbaum family or Susan Loeb based on a fiduciary or similar relationship of trust and confidence, and (2) Chestman knew that Loeb had done so. We have heretofore never applied the misappropriation theory — and its predicate requirement of a fiduciary breach — in the context of family relationships. . . .

3. Fiduciary Duties and Their Functional Equivalent

Against this backdrop, we turn to our central inquiry — what constitutes a fiduciary or similar relationship of trust and confidence in the context of Rule 10b-5 criminal liability? We begin by noting two factors that do not themselves create the necessary relationship.

First, a fiduciary duty cannot be imposed unilaterally by entrusting a person with confidential information. Walton v. Morgan Stanley & Co., 623 F.2d 796, 799 (2d Cir. 1980) (applying Delaware law). . . .

Second, marriage does not, without more, create a fiduciary relationship. "'[M]ere kinship does not of itself establish a confidential relation.' . . . Rather, the existence of a confidential relationship must be determined independently of a preexisting family relationship." *Reed*, 601 F. Supp. at 706 (quoting G.G. Bogert, The Law of Trusts and Trustees § 482, at 300-11 (Rev. 2d ed. 1978)). Although spouses certainly may by their conduct become fiduciaries, the marriage relationship alone does not impose fiduciary status. In sum, more than the gratuitous reposal of a secret to another who happens to be a family member is required to establish a fiduciary or similar relationship of trust and confidence.

We take our cues as to what *is* required to create the requisite relationship from the securities fraud precedents and the common law. See *Chiarella*, 445 U.S. at 227-30. The common law has recognized that some associations are inherently fiduciary. Counted among these hornbook fiduciary relations are those existing between attorney and client, executor and heir, guardian and ward, principal and agent, trustee and trust beneficiary, and senior corporate official and shareholder. While this list is by no means exhaustive, it is clear that the relationships involved in this case — those between Keith and Susan Loeb and between Keith Loeb and the Waldbaum family — were not traditional fiduciary relationships.

That does not end our inquiry, however. The misappropriation theory requires us to consider not only whether there exists a fiduciary relationship but also whether there exists a "similar relationship of trust and confidence." As the term "similar" implies, a "relationship of trust and confidence" must share the essential characteristics of a fiduciary association. Absent reference to the adjective "similar," interpretation of a "relationship of trust and confidence" becomes an exercise in question begging. Consider: when one *entrusts* a secret (read *confidence*) to another, there then exists a relationship of trust and confidence. *Walton*, however, instructs that entrusting confidential information to another does not, without more, create the necessary relationship and its correlative duty to maintain the confidence. A "similar relationship of trust and confidence," therefore, must be the functional equivalent of a fiduciary relationship. To determine whether such a relationship exists, we must ascertain the characteristics of a fiduciary relationship. . . .

A fiduciary relationship involves discretionary authority and dependency: One person depends on another — the fiduciary — to serve his interests. In relying on a fiduciary to act for his benefit, the beneficiary of the relation may entrust the fiduciary with custody over property of one sort or another. Because the fiduciary obtains access to this property to serve the ends of the fiduciary relationship, he becomes duty-bound not to appropriate the property for his own use. What has been said of an agent's duty of confidentiality applies with equal force to other fiduciary relations: "an agent is subject to a duty to the principal not to use or to communicate information confidentially given him by the principal or acquired by him during the course of or on account of his agency." Restatement (Second) of Agency § 395 (1958). These characteristics represent the measure of the paradigmatic fiduciary relationship. A similar relationship of trust and confidence consequently must share these qualities.

In *Reed*, 601 F. Supp. 685, the district court confronted the question whether these principal characteristics of a fiduciary relationship — dependency and influence — were necessary factual prerequisites to a similar relationship of trust and confidence. There a member of the board of directors of Amax, Gordon Reed, disclosed to his son on several occasions confidential information concerning a proposed tender offer for Amax. Allegedly relying on this information, the son purchased Amax stock call options. The son was subsequently indicted for violating, among other things, Rule 10b-5 based on breach of a fiduciary duty arising between the father and son. The son then moved to dismiss the indictment, contending that he did not breach a fiduciary duty to his father. The district court sustained the indictment.

Both the government and Chestman rely on *Reed*. The government draws on *Reed*'s application of the misappropriation theory in the family context and its expansive construction of relationships of trust and confidence. Chestman, without challenging the holding in *Reed*, argues that *Reed* cannot sustain his Rule 10b-5 convictions because, unlike Reed senior and junior, Keith and Susan Loeb did not customarily repose confidential business information in one another. Neither party challenges the holding of *Reed*. And we decline to do so *sua sponte*. To remain consistent with our interpretation of a "similar relationship of trust and confidence,". . . we limit *Reed* to its essential holding: the repeated disclosure of business secrets between family members may substitute for a factual finding of dependence and influence and thereby sustain a finding of the functional equivalent of a fiduciary relationship. We note, in this regard, that *Reed* repeatedly emphasized that the father and son "frequently discussed business affairs." Id. at 690; see also id. at 705, 709, 717-18. . . .

4. Application of the Law of Fiduciary Duties . . .

We have little trouble finding the evidence insufficient to establish a fiduciary relationship or its functional equivalent between Keith Loeb and the Waldbaum family. The government presented only two pieces of evidence on this point. The first was that Keith was an extended member of the Waldbaum family, specifically the family patriarch's (Ira Waldbaum's) "nephew-in-law." The second piece of evidence concerned Ira's discussions of the business with family members. "My children," Ira Waldbaum testified, "have always been involved with me and my family and they know we never speak about business outside of the family." His earlier testimony indicates that the "family" to which he referred were his "three children who were involved in the business."

Lending this evidence the reasonable inferences to which it is entitled, it falls short of establishing the relationship necessary for fiduciary obligations. Kinship alone does not create the necessary relationship. The government proffered nothing more to establish a fiduciary-like association. It did not show that Keith Loeb had been brought into the family's inner circle, whose members, it appears, discussed confidential business information either because they were kin or because they worked together with Ira Waldbaum. Keith was not an employee of Waldbaum and there was no showing that he participated in confidential communications regarding the business. The critical information was gratuitously communicated to him. The disclosure did not serve the interests of Ira Waldbaum, his children or the Waldbaum company. Nor was there any evidence that the alleged relationship was characterized by influence or reliance of any sort. Measured against the principles of fiduciary relations, the evidence does not support a finding that Keith Loeb and the Waldbaum family shared either a fiduciary relation or its functional equivalent.

The government's theory that Keith breached a fiduciary duty of confidentiality to Susan suffers from similar defects. The evidence showed: Keith and Susan were married; Susan admonished Keith not to disclose that Waldbaum was the target of a tender offer; and the two had shared and maintained confidences in the past.

Keith's status as Susan's husband could not itself establish fiduciary status. Nor, absent a pre-existing fiduciary relation or an express agreement of confidentiality, could the coda — "Don't tell." That leaves the unremarkable testimony that Keith and Susan had shared and maintained generic confidences before. The jury was not told the nature of these past disclosures and therefore it could not reasonably find a relationship that inspired fiduciary, rather than normal marital, obligations. . . .

In sum, because Keith owed neither Susan nor the Waldbaum family a fiduciary duty or its functional equivalent, he did not defraud them by disclosing news of the pending tender offer to Chestman. Absent a predicate act of fraud by Keith Loeb, the alleged misappropriator, Chestman could not be derivatively liable as Loeb's tippee or as an aider and abettor. Therefore, Chestman's Rule 10b-5 convictions must be reversed. . . .

WINTER, Circuit Judge (joined by OAKES, Chief Judge, NEWMAN, KEARSE, and McLAUGHLIN, Circuit Judges), concurring in part and dissenting in part:

1) INSIDER TRADING . . .

C) THE INSTANT CASE

When this analysis is applied to a family-controlled corporation such as that involved in the instant case, I believe that family members who have benefitted from the family's control of the corporation are under a duty not to disclose confidential corporate information that comes to them in the ordinary course of family affairs. In the case of family-controlled corporations, family and business affairs are necessarily intertwined, and it is inevitable that from time to time normal familial interactions will lead to the revelation of confidential corporate matters to various family members. Indeed, the very nature of familial relationships may cause the disclosure of corporate matters to avoid misunderstandings among family members or suggestions that a family member is unworthy of trust.

Keith Loeb learned of the pending acquisition of Waldbaum's by A&P through precisely such interactions. His wife Susan was asked one day by her sister to take carpool responsibilities for their children. When Susan inquired as to why this was necessary, the sister was vague and said that she had to take their mother somewhere. After further inquiry, the sister flatly declined to tell Susan what was going on. Susan did not say, "Gee, confidential corporate information must be involved, and I have no right to such information." Instead, concerned about her mother's ongoing health problems, Susan made direct inquiry of her mother, who revealed that Susan's sister took her to get stock certificates to give to Ira Waldbaum for the initial phase of the A&P acquisition. The mother swore Susan to secrecy, telling Susan that the acquisition would be very profitable to the family and premature disclosure could ruin the deal. Susan then asked whether she could tell her husband Keith. Instead of saying, "No, Keith may be your husband but you are to button your lips in his presence," her mother assented but warned against disclosure to anyone else.

Susan and Keith Loeb jointly owned a large number of Waldbaum shares at that time, all of which had been a gift from her mother. The Loebs' children also owned shares received as a gift from their grandmother. Susan told Keith about the A&P acquisition in the course of discussing the financial benefits they and their children would receive as a result of that transaction. She stressed the need for absolute secrecy. Susan testified that she and her husband had shared confidences in the past and that on each such occasion they had indicated to each other that the confidences would be respected. Thereafter, Keith Loeb informed Chestman about the A&P acquisition in the hope of making a profit.

I have little difficulty in concluding that Chestman's convictions can be affirmed on either the *Dirks* rule or on a misappropriation theory. The disclosure of information concerning the A&P acquisition among Ira Waldbaum's extended family was the result of ordinary familial interactions that can be expected in the case of family-controlled corporations. . . .

[Separate concurrence of MINER, Circuit Judge, and opinion by MAHONEY, Circuit Judge, concurring in part and dissenting in part, omitted.]

Notes and Questions

1. Is it realistic to expect that confidential business information will not be shared within families as in *Chestman*? Could Ira create a fiduciary relationship with members of his family? If so, how?

2. Would it make any difference if Chestman's source of information had been one of Ira's children? Why or why not?

NOTE ON RULE 10b5-2

In the fall of 2000, the SEC promulgated new regulations to address unsettled areas of securities fraud law. Rule 10b5-2 directly addresses the question, considered in *Chestman*, of when nonbusiness relationships may give rise to a duty of trust and confidence for purposes of the misappropriation theory of insider trading.

17 C.F.R. § 240.10b5-2
DUTIES OF TRUST OR CONFIDENCE
IN MISAPPROPRIATION INSIDER TRADING CASES

Preliminary Note to § 240.10b5-2: This section provides a non-exclusive definition of circumstances in which a person has a duty of trust or confidence for purposes of the "misappropriation" theory of insider trading under Section 10(b) of the Act and Rule 10b-5. The law of insider trading is otherwise defined by judicial opinions construing Rule 10b-5, and Rule 10b5-2 does not modify the scope of insider trading law in any other respect.

(a) Scope of Rule. This section shall apply to any violation of Section 10(b) of the Act (15 U.S.C. 78j(b)) and § 240.10b-5 thereunder that is based on the purchase or sale of securities on the basis of, or the communication of, material nonpublic information misappropriated in breach of a duty of trust or confidence.

(b) Enumerated "duties of trust or confidence." For purposes of this section, a "duty of trust or confidence" exists in the following circumstances, among others:

(1) Whenever a person agrees to maintain information in confidence;

(2) Whenever the person communicating the material nonpublic information and the person to whom it is communicated have a history, pattern, or practice of sharing confidences, such that the recipient of the information knows or reasonably should know that the person communicating the material nonpublic information expects that the recipient will maintain its confidentiality; or

(3) Whenever a person receives or obtains material nonpublic information from his or her spouse, parent, child, or sibling; provided, however, that the person receiving or obtaining the information may demonstrate that no duty of trust or confidence existed with respect to the information, by establishing that he or she neither knew nor reasonably should have known that the person who was the source of the information expected that the person would keep the information confidential, because of the parties' history, pattern, or practice of sharing and maintaining confidences, and because there was no agreement or understanding to maintain the confidentiality of the information.

Notes and Questions

1. To what extent did Rule 10b5-2 change existing law? Are the changes desirable? Do they bring greater clarity to this area of the law?

2. Did Rule 10b5-2 codify existing law in any respect? If so, is that desirable?

3. How would Rule 10b5-2 affect the analysis and outcome in *Chestman*?

4. Knowing Possession

UNITED STATES v. TEICHER
987 F.2d 112 (2d Cir. 1993)

ALTIMARI, Circuit Judge. . . .

BACKGROUND

The players in this case were involved in the business of arbitrage. Arbitrage entails trading in securities in companies that are the subject of changes in corporate control in order to take advantage of fluctuations in the price of these securities. Teicher, an arbitrageur, formed the Victor Teicher & Co., L.P. investment firm through which he managed investment pools for individual investors. Frankel was a research analyst in the arbitrage department of Drexel Burnham Lambert, Inc. ("Drexel").

Robert Salsbury, a key government witness, worked under Frankel performing financial analyses in the research unit at Drexel. During the same period, Michael David, another key government witness and a close personal friend of Salsbury, worked as an associate in the corporate department of the law firm of Paul, Weiss, Rifkind, Wharton & Garrison ("Paul Weiss"). Like Frankel and Teicher, David was interested in arbitrage.

The government's evidence at trial showed that from December 1985 until March 1986, David regularly provided Salsbury and Teicher with information that David had uncovered concerning possible acquisitions by Paul Weiss clients. David also provided Andrew Solomon, a trader at the brokerage firm of Marcus Schloss, Inc. ("Marcus Schloss") with the same Paul Weiss information he had disclosed to Teicher and Salsbury. Solomon, in turn, provided other confidential information to David who then passed it on to Teicher. The government's evidence also demonstrated that Salsbury had provided Teicher with the names of companies on Drexel's "phantom list" — a highly confidential list of companies that were the subject of mergers or takeovers by Drexel clients and in which trading by Drexel personnel was prohibited.

[While in possession of the tipped information, the defendants traded in the stocks of eight companies that were the subject of takeover bids. The indictment charged Teicher and Frankel, inter alia, with securities fraud, conspiracy, and mail fraud. The jury found them guilty on all counts.]

DISCUSSION

II. THE JURY CHARGE

Teicher and Frankel contend that the district court's jury charge erroneously instructed the jury that the defendants could be found guilty of securities fraud based upon the mere possession of fraudulently obtained material nonpublic information without regard to whether this information was the actual cause of the sale or purchase of securities. Specifically, Teicher and Frankel argue that the charge permitted the jury to find them guilty of securities fraud even if they had traded upon only publicly available information. We find this argument unpersuasive.

Under the misappropriation theory of securities fraud as adopted by this Circuit, "a person violates Rule 10b-5 when he misappropriates material nonpublic information in breach of a fiduciary duty or similar relationship of trust and confidence and uses that information in a securities transaction." United States v. Chestman, 947 F.2d 551, 566 (2d Cir. 1991) (in banc). In accordance with the misappropriation theory, the district court instructed the jury:

> The government charges that [the defendants,] knowing that information to have been misappropriated, received and exploited that information by using it for their own advantage.

In defining misappropriation, the district court charged:

> To misappropriate, in the context of this case, means to wrongfully take and use the information in violation of a fiduciary duty to hold the information in confidence.

Teicher and Frankel do not contest the propriety of these and similar portions of the charge. Rather, they focus on the part of the charge in which the court instructed:

> The government need not prove a causal relationship between the misappropriated material nonpublic information and the defendants' trading. That is, the government need not prove that the defendants purchased or sold securities because of the material nonpublic information that they knowingly possessed. It is sufficient if the government proves that the defendants purchased or sold securities while knowingly in possession of the material nonpublic information.

Placing great emphasis upon the term "use," they contend that the district court too broadly defined this word as the equivalent of mere possession. They posit the alternative theory that a defendant only "uses material nonpublic information where it can be proven that the trading was *causally connected* to the misappropriated information and hence, was proven not to have been conducted on an independent and proper basis." A causal connection standard would find no violation where a trader executes a previously and legitimately planned transaction after the trader wrongfully receives material nonpublic information which confirmed the transaction.

Although this argument is a novel one, the question of whether a violation of Rule 10b-5 requires an actual causal connection between the misappropriated information and the trading has been raised by commentators. See, e.g., 3 A. Bromberg & L. Lowenfels, *Securities Fraud & Commodities Fraud*, § 7.4 (622), p. 7:160.15 (1992). In support of their position that a causal connection is an element of the violation, Teicher and Frankel rely largely on cases which describe securities charges with phrases such as "trading on the basis of" but which did not address the possibility that the trading was *not* causally connected to the inside information. See, e.g., Dirks v. SEC, 463 U.S. 646, 648 (1983); SEC v. Materia, 745 F.2d at 199-200 (2d Cir. 1984).

In contrast, the government advances the view, which has been consistently endorsed by the SEC, that a violation of § 10(b) and Rule 10b-5 occurs when a trade is conducted in "knowing possession" of material nonpublic information obtained in breach of a fiduciary or similar duty. See, e.g., Sterling Drug Inc. Investigation, [1978 Transfer Binder] Fed. Sec. L. Rep. (CCH), ¶81,570, p. 80,298. . . .

A number of factors weigh in favor of a "knowing possession" standard. First, as the government points out, both § 10(b) and Rule 10b-5 require only that a deceptive practice be conducted "in connection with the purchase or sale of a security." We have previously stated that the "in connection with" clause must be "construed . . . flexibly to include deceptive practices 'touching' the sale of securities, a relationship which has been described as 'very tenuous indeed.'" United States v. Newman, 664 F.2d 12, 18 (2d Cir. 1981). Thus, for example, "the predicate act of fraud may be perpetrated on the source of the nonpublic information, even though the source may be unaffiliated with the buyer or seller of securities." *Chestman*, 947 F.2d at 566.

In addition, a "knowing possession" standard comports with the oft-quoted maxim that one with a fiduciary or similar duty to hold material nonpublic information in confidence must either "disclose or abstain" with regard to trading. See Chiarella v. United States, 445 U.S. 222, 227 (1979). When the fiduciary is an insider who is not in a position to make a public announcement, the fiduciary must abstain. It would be consistent with the "disclose or abstain" rule that a tippee acquire the same duty as his fiduciary tipper.

Finally, a "knowing possession" standard has the attribute of simplicity. It recognizes that one who trades while knowingly possessing material inside information has an informational advantage over other traders. Because the advantage is in the form of information, it exists in the mind of the trader. Unlike a loaded weapon which may stand ready but unused, material information can not lay idle in the human brain. The individual with such information may decide to trade upon that information, to alter a previously decided-upon transaction, to continue with a previously planned transaction even though publicly available information would now suggest otherwise, or simply to do nothing. In our increasingly sophisticated securities markets, where subtle shifts in strategy can produce dramatic results, it would be a mistake to think of such decisions as merely binary choices — to buy or to sell.

As a matter of policy then, a requirement of a causal connection between the information and the trade could frustrate attempts to distinguish between legitimate trades and those conducted in connection with inside information.

In any event, we need only rule with respect to the case before us. Viewing the jury charge in its entirety and based upon the record, we find that it is unnecessary to determine whether proof of securities fraud requires a causal connection, because any alleged defect in the instruction was harmless beyond doubt.

This case involves the fast-paced and perilous world of arbitrage. Arbitrageurs are in the business of gathering information. As described by Teicher, arbitrageurs "combin[e] publicly available information with rumors and other tidbits of immaterial nonpublic information in formulating investment strategies." By their own admission, Teicher and Frankel actively sought and received such "tidbits" in order to weave them into a material whole upon which they traded. It does not follow, that when one such piece of information is revealed to be material, in and of itself, and the trader knows it to be material, the trader might somehow consider the information irrelevant to the whole. . . .

It strains reason to argue that an arbitrageur who traded while possessing information he knew to be fraudulently obtained, knew to be material, knew to be nonpublic — and who did not act in good faith in so doing — did not also trade on the basis of that information. We find that on the facts of this case, no reasonable jury could have made such a distinction.

CONCLUSION

Based on the foregoing, the judgment of the district court is affirmed.[34]

Notes and Questions

1. The court expressed concern that under a causal connection test, a trader who executed a previously planned legitimate trade after receiving inside information would not violate Rule 10b-5. Why should execution of a legitimate trade ever be considered a violation? Cf. United States v. Smith, 155 F.3d 1051, 1069 (9th Cir. 1998) (proof of "use" is required in a criminal case).

2. The government's aggressive use of a theory whose contours remain indefinite has led to many calls for a legislative definition of what does and does not constitute illegal insider trading. Among the proposals that have been discussed are a statute drafted by the ABA Task Force on Regulation of Insider Trading and a modification of

---

34. Following their convictions, the SEC issued an administrative order barring Teicher, Frankel, and Victor Teicher & Co. from participating in various branches of the securities industry and from associating with registered and unregistered investment advisors. Teicher and Frankel unsuccessfully challenged the debarment as beyond the SEC's enforcement authority. See Teicher v. SEC, 177 F.3d 1016 (D.C. Cir. 1999). — ED.

that proposal by the Association of the Bar of the City of New York, see N.Y.L.J., Jan. 22, 1987, at 1, and legislation proposed by the SEC, see N.Y.L.J., Aug. 13, 1987, at 5.

Is a statutory or regulatory definition of insider trading needed? Why would Congress and the SEC be reluctant to undertake the task of defining it?

NOTE ON RULE 10b5-1

Although Congress and the SEC have yet to define insider trading, recently adopted regulations bring us closer in several respects. A companion provision to Rule 10b5-2, also adopted in the fall of 2000, specifically addresses the issue considered in *Teicher*. Rule 10b5-1 attempts to define when a person in possession of material nonpublic information trades "on the basis of" the information.

17 C.F.R. § 240.10b5-1
TRADING "ON THE BASIS OF" MATERIAL NONPUBLIC INFORMATION IN INSIDER TRADING CASES

Preliminary Note to § 240.10b5-1: This provision defines when a purchase or sale constitutes trading "on the basis of" material nonpublic information in insider trading cases brought under Section 10(b) of the Act and Rule 10b-5 thereunder. The law of insider trading is otherwise defined by judicial opinions construing Rule 10b-5, and Rule 10b5-1 does not modify the scope of insider trading law in any other respect.

(a) General. The "manipulative and deceptive devices" prohibited by Section 10(b) of the Act (15 U.S.C. 78j) and § 240.10b-5 thereunder include, among other things, the purchase or sale of a security of any issuer, on the basis of material nonpublic information about that security or issuer, in breach of a duty of trust or confidence that is owed directly, indirectly, or derivatively, to the issuer of that security or the shareholders of that issuer, or to any other person who is the source of the material nonpublic information.

(b) Definition of "on the basis of." Subject to the affirmative defenses in paragraph (c) of this section, a purchase or sale of a security of an issuer is "on the basis of" material nonpublic information about that security or issuer if the person making the purchase or sale was aware of the material nonpublic information when the person made the purchase or sale.

(c) Affirmative defenses.

(1)(i) Subject to paragraph (c)(1)(ii) of this section, a person's purchase or sale is not "on the basis of" material nonpublic information if the person making the purchase or sale demonstrates that:

(A) Before becoming aware of the information, the person had:

(1) Entered into a binding contract to purchase or sell the security,

(2) Instructed another person to purchase or sell the security for the instructing person's account, or

(3) Adopted a written plan for trading securities;

(B) The contract, instruction, or plan described in paragraph (c)(1)(i)(A) of this Section:

(1) Specified the amount of securities to be purchased or sold and the price at which and the date on which the securities were to be purchased or sold;

(2) Included a written formula or algorithm, or computer program, for determining the amount of securities to be purchased or sold and the price at which and the date on which the securities were to be purchased or sold; or

(3) Did not permit the person to exercise any subsequent influence over how, when, or whether to effect purchases or sales; provided, in addition, that any other person who, pursuant to the contract, instruction, or plan, did exercise such influence must not have been aware of the material nonpublic information when doing so; and

(C) The purchase or sale that occurred was pursuant to the contract, instruction, or plan. A purchase or sale is not "pursuant to a contract, instruction, or plan" if, among other things, the person who entered into the contract, instruction, or plan altered or deviated from the contract, instruction, or plan to purchase or sell securities (whether by changing the amount, price, or timing of the purchase or sale), or entered into or altered a corresponding or hedging transaction or position with respect to those securities.

(ii) Paragraph (c)(1)(i) of this section is applicable only when the contract, instruction, or plan to purchase or sell securities was given or entered into in good faith and not as part of a plan or scheme to evade the prohibitions of this section. . . .

(2) A person other than a natural person also may demonstrate that a purchase or sale of securities is not "on the basis of" material nonpublic information if the person demonstrates that:

(i) The individual making the investment decision on behalf of the person to purchase or sell the securities was not aware of the information; and

(ii) The person had implemented reasonable policies and procedures, taking into consideration the nature of the person's business, to ensure that individuals making investment decisions would not violate the laws prohibiting trading on the basis of material nonpublic information. These policies and procedures may include those that restrict any purchase, sale, and causing any purchase or sale of any security as to which the person has material nonpublic information, or those that prevent such individuals from becoming aware of such information.

Notes and Questions

1. How does the substantive rule adopted in Rule 10b5-1 compare with the ruling in *Teicher*?

2. Rule 10b5-1 contains enumerated affirmative defenses. Is it clear that these defenses should be recognized? If so, why?

3. Does Rule 10b5-1 apply to both buyers and sellers? Who is most likely to adopt a 10b5-1 plan and why?

PROBLEM 5-3

The CEO of a publicly traded company adopts a 10b5-1 trading plan to allow him to continue regularly buying the company's stock regardless of any unforeseen confidential good news he may receive in the future. Pursuant to the plan, his broker automatically purchases an additional 500 shares on the first Friday of every month at the prevailing market price when the market opens that day. After the plan has been in place for a year, the company's independent auditor and its chief financial officer inform the CEO that there are substantial accounting irregularities in the company's books. They tell him the irregularities have resulted in overstatement of corporate earnings for the past three years and that the company's stock is overvalued by at least 100 percent. As soon as they leave his office, the CEO calls his broker and instructs him to immediately cancel the plan.

Has the CEO violated Rule 10b5-1? Has he violated Rule 10b-5? Would it make any difference if the plan did not say anything about price?

5. Materiality

Insider trading is illegal only if the purchase or sale is made on the basis of "material" nonpublic information. The Supreme Court articulated the standard for materiality in securities cases in TSC Industries v. Northway, Inc.[35]

The question of materiality, it is universally agreed, is an objective one, involving the significance of an omitted or misrepresented fact to a reasonable investor. Variations in the formulation of a general test of materiality occur in the articulation of just how significant a fact must be or, put another way, how certain it must be that the fact would affect a reasonable investor's judgment. . . .

. . . An omitted fact is material if there is a substantial likelihood that a reasonable shareholder would consider it important in deciding how to vote.[36] This standard is fully consistent with *Mills'* general description of materiality as a requirement that "the defect have a significant *propensity* to affect the voting process." It does not require proof of a substantial likelihood that disclosure of the omitted fact would have caused the reasonable investor to change his vote. What the standard does contemplate is a showing of a substantial likelihood that, under all the circumstances, the omitted fact would have assumed actual significance in the deliberations of the reasonable shareholder. Put another way, there must be a substantial likelihood that the disclosure of the omitted fact would have been viewed by the reasonable investor as having significantly altered the "total mix" of information made available.[37]

---

35. 426 U.S. 438 (1976).

36. Or whether to purchase or sell. *TSC Industries* was decided in the context of proxy solicitation rules under the Securities Exchange Act of 1934. See 15 U.S.C. § 78n(a); 17 C.F.R. § 240.14a-9. — ED.

37. *TSC Industries*, 426 at 445, 449.

Notes and Questions

1. What was the nonpublic information at issue in *Chiarella, O'Hagan, Dirks*, and *Teicher*? What made it material?

2. Recall the facts in *Tarallo*, a case in which wildly exaggerated claims — e.g., that the defendants had developed an FDA approved detoxification system that would cleanse the user's body of all alcohol and drugs within 15 minutes — were the basis for the fraud claim. Are exaggerated claims like this material? Would a reasonable investor believe such claims? If not, would that undermine a finding of materiality?

B. THE HUMAN DIMENSION OF THE WALL STREET INSIDER TRADING SCANDAL

The discovery and criminal prosecution of widespread insider trading on Wall Street has left in its wake an enormous human toll. The following material should give you a sense of how and why so many professionals became caught up in illegal activity, how so many were actually caught engaging in it, and what it meant to be caught.

1. Wall Street's Army of Insiders

It should come as no surprise that lawyers and investment bankers are privy to inside information and thus may become participants in illegal schemes to trade on the basis of such information. But the litany of criminal defendants is far more extensive than that. It includes a veritable army of insiders. Corporate mergers and acquisitions provide an illustrative context for considering how so many people gain access to confidential information about corporate plans.

Beginning with the corporation itself, the executives, general counsel, and the board of directors all play critical roles in planning mergers and acquisitions. During the planning stage, counsel and corporate officers will consult with investment banks staffed with financial experts, research analysts, and merger and acquisition teams. The pool of insiders grows as law firms, public relations firms, financiers (including banks, bond dealers, and other lenders), proxy solicitors, and financial printers are called upon to play their respective roles in implementing the plan.

But this is only the tip of the iceberg. All of these professionals rely on associates, secretaries, and other support staff to move the process along. And beyond those who have a formal role to play in a merger or acquisition, there are inevitably family members and friends who will learn about the deal. They, in turn, may share what they know with their friends.[38]

But that is still not the end of the story. In addition to traditional insiders, temporary insiders, and others who had legitimate roles in the planning or execution of business deals involving inside information, the 98 defendants who were prosecuted for insider trading and related violations in the Southern District of New York during the 1980s included a dentist, a cab driver, a police officer, a broadcaster, a psychiatrist, and

---

38. Wall Street's Army of Insiders, N.Y. Times, May 18, 1986, at 1F.

several engineers. And so it goes on down the line. How do so many people who are so far removed personally and professionally from a merger or acquisition become privy to inside information? And what is the basis for prosecuting them? Is there a practicable way to keep the genie in the bottle?

IV. MISREPRESENTATION AND CONCEALMENT

Although the primary focus of this chapter is insider trading, Rule 10b-5 reaches other fraudulent conduct, including misrepresentation and concealment. In particular, Rule 10b-5(b) prohibits making "any untrue statement of a material fact" or failure to state "a material fact necessary in order to make the statements made, in the light of the circumstances under which they were made, not misleading." Consider this broad prohibition in the context of the following case study.

CASE STUDY: UNITED STATES v. STEWART[39]

Facts: The underlying facts of Martha Stewart's prosecution are widely known. ImClone, a pharmaceutical company founded by Stewart's longtime friend Sam Waksal, had applied for FDA approval of a promising cancer drug. Stewart, an ImClone stockholder, sold her ImClone stock the day before the FDA denied the application. The indictment alleged that immediately after receiving a tip that Waksal was selling his ImClone stock, Stewart instructed her broker to sell her stock as well. The tip had come from the broker, who said he expected ImClone's price to fall. Stewart was charged in a nine-count indictment with conspiracy, obstruction of justice, lying to the SEC and other government officials about the reason for the sale, obstruction of justice, and securities fraud.

Background: Martha Stewart, the founder of Martha Stewart Living Omnimedia (MSLO), served as the company's CEO and Chairman of the Board prior to her indictment. MSLO engages in book and magazine publishing, television production, merchandising, and Internet and catalog sales — all bearing the "Martha Stewart" brand. MSLO's 1999 prospectus stated:

> Martha Stewart as well as her name, her image and the trademarks and other intellectual property rights relating to these, are integral to our marketing efforts and form the core of our brand name. Our continued success and the value of our brand name therefore depends, to a large degree, on the reputation of Martha Stewart.[40]

MSLO is listed on the New York Stock exchange. When she sold the ImClone stock, Stewart held nearly 31 million shares — 62.6 percent — of MSLO's Class A common stock, and all of its Class B common stock — roughly another 31 million

---

39. Unless otherwise noted, factual details and specifics of the allegations in the indictment are derived from United States v. Stewart, S1-03-Cr-717 (MGC) (Superseding Indictment) (on file with the author).

40. United States v. Stewart, 305 F. Supp. 2d 368, 372 (S.D.N.Y. 2004).

shares. The market reacted negatively after it became publicly known that Stewart had sold her ImClone stock on the same day that the Waksal shares were sold, and MSLO's market price began to fall. The following week, when it was reported that Waksal had been arrested and charged with insider trading, the price of MSLO stock fell 5.6 percent.

Count 9 of the Indictment: Count 9 of the indictment charged Stewart with securities fraud. She was not charged with insider trading, however. Instead, the securities fraud count was based on the theory that Stewart had made false and misleading public statements about the reason she sold her ImClone stock. The charges were based on three series of statements about the sale.

Statements Stewart's Lawyer Made to the Wall Street Journal: Stewart's lawyer told the Wall Street Journal that Stewart's sale of ImClone stock was executed pursuant to an agreement to sell the stock if the price went below $60. The lawyer claimed that the agreement predated the sale by several weeks.

Stewart's June 12 Press Release: A press release that was attributed to Stewart explained that she had a preexisting agreement with her broker to sell if the price of the stock went below $60; that on the day of the sale, her broker had advised her that ImClone had fallen below $60; and that at the time of the sale, she did not have any nonpublic information about ImClone.

Stewart's June 18 Statement and Speech: In conjunction with a conference for securities analysts and investors at which she was scheduled to speak, Stewart issued another statement about the sale. This statement reiterated much of what she had said in the June 12 Press Release — in essence, that she sold her stock at a predetermined price based on a preexisting agreement with her broker. Stewart also broached the subject of the ImClone sale in her conference speech, stating: "I would like to address an issue in which all of you are probably interested."[41] She then repeated that the sale was pursuant to a standing arrangement with her stockbroker; that she had no insider information relating to ImClone when she sold the stock; that the sale "was based on information that was available to the public that day";[42] that she had cooperated fully with the SEC and the U.S. Attorney's Office; and that she was cooperating with an ongoing congressional investigation.

Notes and Questions

1. Since Stewart was not charged with insider trading, what was the government's theory of the case? Were her denials of wrongdoing related to securities transactions? Were they made in connection with the purchase or sale of securities? What mental state would the government have to prove to sustain the securities fraud charge?

2. Assuming arguendo that Stewart's statements were sufficiently securities-related, were they material under the *TSC Industries* test?

3. At the end of the trial, the judge granted Stewart's motion for a judgment of acquittal on the securities fraud charge. Should the charge have gone to the jury?

---

41. Id. at 374.
42. Id.

4. Assuming the factual allegations contained in the indictment are true, could the government have charged Stewart with insider trading? If so, what would the theory of the case be?

V. SECURITIES FRAUD PROSECUTIONS UNDER THE SARBANES-OXLEY ACT

Most of the criminal statutes considered in this course are found in the federal criminal code, which is codified in Title 18 of the United States Code. The securities fraud laws, which are codified in Title 15 of the Code, are among the few exceptions.[43] Most securities fraud prosecutions have historically proceeded under the Securities Exchange Act of 1934 (15 U.S.C. § 78ff) and/or fraud statutes of more general applicability (e.g., mail and wire fraud), because Title 18 did not have a provision that specifically addressed securities fraud. The Sarbanes-Oxley Act adds a new securities fraud offense that is modeled on the mail fraud statute,[44] which is considered in Chapter 4.

The new securities fraud provision, 18 U.S.C. § 1348, protects shareholders of publicly traded companies through two distinct prohibitions. Section 1348 makes it a crime to:

(1) knowingly execute or attempt to execute a scheme or artifice to defraud *in connection with any security* of a designated issuer; or
(2) obtain money or property through false or fraudulent pretenses, representations, or promises *in connection with the purchase or sale of any security* of a designated issuer.

There are obvious parallels between § 1348 and the mail fraud statute. Both statutes prohibit executing a "scheme or artifice" whose objective is "to defraud" or "to obtain money or property." And while both statutes prohibit fraudulent schemes, neither defines what constitutes fraud. It should be noted, however, that as used in the mail fraud statute, "fraud" is a nontechnical and highly elastic concept that differs from "fraud" as it is embodied in the securities laws. It is likely that courts construing § 1348 will rely on case law interpreting the mail fraud statute — rather than the securities laws — to flesh out these terms. It is also notable that because § 1348 is codified in the same part of the criminal code as the mail fraud statute, the term "scheme or artifice to defraud" includes a scheme to deprive another (including an individual, a corporate employer, or corporate shareholders) of the intangible right to honest services.[45]

There are two obvious differences between § 1348 and the mail fraud statute. First, unlike the mail fraud statute, § 1348 does not require proof of use of the mails or other jurisdictional facilities. Second, § 1348 is more limited in that it requires the scheme to defraud or to obtain money or property to be in connection with a publicly traded security. But while the phrase "in connection with the purchase or sale" of a security is

---

43. Other exceptions include tax crimes, which are codified in Title 26, and environmental crimes, which are scattered throughout major environmental regulatory statutes such as the Clean Air Act, the Clean Water Act, and the Resource Conservation and Recovery Act.

44. 18 U.S.C. § 1341. See Chapter 4.

45. 18 U.S.C. § 1346.

borrowed from the securities laws and has an established meaning, what the phrase "in connection with any security" is intended to connote is far less certain.

In keeping with generally more stringent criminal penalties authorized by Sarbanes-Oxley, violations of § 1348, the Securities Exchange Act, and the mail fraud statute are punishable by potentially severe sentences. A comparison of the penalties appears in Table 5-2.

TABLE 5-2
COMPARISON OF CRIMINAL FRAUD PENALTIES

FRAUD OFFENSE	MAXIMUM TERM	MAXIMUM FINE
Securities Fraud (15 U.S.C. § 78ff)	20 years	$5 million/ $25 million (org.)
Securities Fraud (18 U.S.C. § 1348)	25 years	$250,000/ $500,000 (org.)
Mail and Wire Fraud (18 U.S.C. §§ 1341, 1343)	20 years	$250,000/ $500,000 (org.)

Notes and Questions

1. What kinds of securities fraud cases will likely be more amenable to prosecution under § 1348 than under the Securities Exchange Act?

2. Would any of the cases in this chapter be easier to prosecute under § 1348?

3. Does § 1348 have the potential to significantly broaden the basis for prosecuting securities-related frauds in contexts not contemplated by the securities laws?

4. Does § 1348 encompass frauds that cannot be prosecuted under the mail fraud statute? If so, how significant is that? If not, was there an important reason to enact § 1348?

5. The mail fraud statute prohibits the *use of the mails* "for the purpose of executing" a scheme or artifice to defraud. Section 1348 prohibits *executing* or *attempting to execute* a scheme to defraud. Is that a meaningful difference? What would constitute executing a scheme to defraud under § 1348?

6

False Statements

I. INTRODUCTION

This chapter considers one species of "cover-up" crime — making false statements to deceive the government. The next two chapters take up the kindred offenses of perjury and obstruction of justice. These related theories of liability are frequently invoked to reach conduct that occurs during the course of a government investigation into other possible misconduct. Once it becomes clear that a suspect has resorted to questionable tactics to avoid detection, the government may seize the opportunity to prosecute a cover-up crime instead of the misconduct that was originally under investigation. One explanation for this phenomenon is that these crimes are often easy to prove and relatively simple for juries to grasp. Neither the prosecutor nor the jury needs to sift through truckloads of documents to determine whether the defendant lied, intimidated a witness, or ordered the destruction of a key piece of evidence.

The primary focus of this chapter is the federal false statements statute, 18 U.S.C. § 1001, which punishes making or using a false statement in any matter within the jurisdiction of any department or agency of the United States. Notably, section 1001 does not contain an oath requirement. Instead, it punishes *unsworn* falsifications relating to any matter within the jurisdiction of a federal department or agency.

The purpose of this statute is to prevent the use of fraud or trickery to subvert governmental processes. As a general matter, prosecutions under § 1001 typically involve using false information: (1) to obtain a monetary or proprietary benefit; (2) to obtain a privilege from the government; (3) to resist monetary claims by the government; and (4) to frustrate a lawful regulation.[1]

II. JURISDICTION

UNITED STATES v. RODGERS
466 U.S. 475 (1984)

Justice REHNQUIST delivered the opinion of the Court.

Respondent Larry Rodgers was charged in a two-count indictment with making "false, fictitious or fraudulent statements" to the Federal Bureau of Investigation (FBI)

---

1. See Friedman v. United States, 374 F.2d 363, 368 (8th Cir. 1967), for citations to illustrative cases.

Facts

and the United States Secret Service, in violation of 18 U.S.C. § 1001. Rodgers allegedly lied in telling the FBI that his wife had been kidnapped and in telling the Secret Service that his wife was involved in a plot to kill the President. Rodgers moved to dismiss the indictment for failure to state an offense on the grounds that the investigation of kidnappings and the protection of the President are not matters "within the jurisdiction" of the respective agencies, as that phrase is used in § 1001. The District Court for the Western District of Missouri granted the motion, and the United States Court of Appeals for the Eighth Circuit affirmed. We now reverse. The statutory language clearly encompasses criminal investigations conducted by the FBI and the Secret Service, and nothing in the legislative history indicates that Congress intended a more restricted reach for the statute.

On June 2, 1982, Larry Rodgers telephoned the Kansas City, Missouri, office of the FBI and reported that his wife had been kidnapped. The FBI spent over 100 agent hours investigating the alleged kidnapping only to determine that Rodgers' wife had left him voluntarily. Two weeks later, Rodgers contacted the Kansas City office of the Secret Service and reported that his "estranged girlfriend" (actually his wife) was involved in a plot to assassinate the President. The Secret Service spent over 150 hours of agent and clerical time investigating this threat and eventually located Rodgers' wife in Arizona. She stated that she left Kansas City to get away from her husband. Rodgers later confessed that he made the false reports to induce the federal agencies to locate his wife.

In granting Rodgers' motion to dismiss the indictment, the District Court considered itself bound by a prior decision of the Eighth Circuit in Friedman v. United States, 374 F.2d 363 (1967). *Friedman* also involved false statements made to the FBI to initiate a criminal investigation. In that case, the Court of Appeals reversed the defendant's conviction under § 1001, holding that the phrase "within the jurisdiction," as used in that provision, referred only to "the power to make final or binding determinations." Id., at 367.

The *Friedman* court noted that the current statutory language was first passed in 1934 at the urging of some of the newly created regulatory agencies. A predecessor provision punished false statements only when made "for the purpose and within the intent of cheating and swindling or defrauding the Government of the United States." In 1934, Congress deleted the requirement of a specific purpose and enlarged the class of punishable false statements to include false statements made "in any matter within the jurisdiction of any department or agency of the United States." The "immediate and primary purpose" of this amendment, the Eighth Circuit surmised, was to curtail the flow of false information to the new agencies, which was interfering with their administrative and regulatory functions.

> Though the statute was drafted in broad inclusive terms, presumably due to the numerous agencies and the wide variety of information needed, there is nothing to indicate that Congress intended this statute to have application beyond the purposes for which it was created. 374 F.2d, at 366.

Reading the term "jurisdiction" in this restrictive light, the Court of Appeals included within its scope the "power to make monetary awards, grant governmental privileges, or promulgate binding administrative and regulative determinations," while excluding "the mere authority to conduct an investigation in a given area without the power to dispose of the problems or compel action." Id., at 367. The court concluded that false statements made to the FBI were not covered by § 1001 because the FBI "had no power to adjudicate rights, establish binding regulations, compel the action or finally dispose of the problem giving rise to the inquiry." Id., at 368.

In the present case, the Court of Appeals adhered to its decision in *Friedman* and affirmed the dismissal of the indictment. The court acknowledged that two other Courts of Appeals had expressly rejected the reasoning of *Friedman*. See United States v. Adler, 380 F.2d 917, 922 (CA2 1967); United States v. Lambert, 501 F.2d 943, 946 (CA5 1974) (en banc). But the Eighth Circuit found its own analysis more persuasive. We granted certiorari to resolve this conflict.

It seems to us that the interpretation of § 1001 adopted by the Court of Appeals for the Eighth Circuit is unduly strained. Section 1001 expressly embraces false statements made in *any* matter within the jurisdiction of *any* department or agency of the United States. A criminal investigation surely falls within the meaning of "any matter," and the FBI and the Secret Service equally surely qualify as "department[s] or agenc[ies] of the United States." The only possible verbal vehicle for narrowing the sweeping language Congress enacted is the word "jurisdiction." But we do not think that term, as used in this statute, admits of the constricted construction given it by the Court of Appeals.

"Jurisdiction" is not defined in the statute. We therefore "start with the assumption that the legislative purpose is expressed by the ordinary meaning of the words used." Richards v. United States, 369 U.S. 1, 9 (1962). The most natural, nontechnical reading of the statutory language is that it covers all matters confided to the authority of an agency or department. Thus, Webster's Third New International Dictionary 1227 (1976) broadly defines "jurisdiction" as, among other things, "the limits or territory within which any particular power may be exercised: sphere of authority." A department or agency has jurisdiction, in this sense, when it has the power to exercise authority in a particular situation. See United States v. Adler, supra, at 922 ("the word 'jurisdiction' as used in the statute must mean simply the power to act upon information when it is received"). Understood in this way, the phrase "within the jurisdiction" merely differentiates the official, authorized functions of an agency or department from matters peripheral to the business of that body. . . .

There is no doubt that there exists a "statutory basis" for the authority of the FBI and the Secret Service over the investigations sparked by respondent Rodgers' false reports. The FBI is authorized "to detect and prosecute crimes against the United States," including kidnapping. 28 U.S.C. § 533(1). And the Secret Service is authorized "to protect the person of the President." 18 U.S.C. § 3056. It is a perversion of these authorized functions to turn either agency into a Missing Person's Bureau for domestic squabbles. The knowing filing of a false crime report, leading to an investigation and possible prosecution, can also have grave consequences for the individuals accused of crime. There is, therefore, a "valid legislative interest in protecting the integrity of [such] official inquiries," an interest clearly embraced in, and furthered by, the broad language of § 1001.

Limiting the term "jurisdiction" as used in this statute to "the power to make final or binding determinations," as the Court of Appeals thought it should be limited, would exclude from the coverage of the statute most, if not all, of the authorized activities of many "departments" and "agencies" of the Federal Government, and thereby defeat the purpose of Congress in using the broad inclusive language which it did. If the statute referred only to courts, a narrower construction of the word "jurisdiction" might well be indicated; but referring as it does to "any department or agency" we think that such a narrow construction is simply inconsistent with the rest of the statutory language.

The Court of Appeals supports its failure to give the statute a "literal interpretation" by offering several policy arguments in favor of a more limited construction. For example, the court noted that § 1001 carries a penalty exceeding the penalty for perjury and argued that Congress could not have "considered it more serious for one to informally volunteer an untrue statement to an F.B.I. agent than to relate the same story under oath before a court of law." Friedman v. United States, supra, at 366. A similar argument was made and rejected in United States v. Gilliland, 312 U.S., at 95. The fact that the maximum possible penalty under § 1001 marginally exceeds that for perjury provides no indication of the particular penalties, within the permitted range, that Congress thought appropriate for each of the myriad violations covered by the statute. Section 1001 covers "a variety of offenses and the penalties prescribed were maximum penalties which have a range for judicial sentences according to the circumstances and gravity of particular violations." Ibid.

Perhaps most influential in the reasoning of the court below was its perception that "the spectre of criminal prosecution" would make citizens hesitant to report suspected crimes and thereby thwart "the important social policy that is served by an open line of communication between the general public and law enforcement agencies." Friedman v. United States, supra, at 369. But the justification for this concern is debatable. Section 1001 only applies to those who "knowingly and willfully" lie to the Government. It seems likely that "individuals acting innocently and in good faith will not be deterred from voluntarily giving information or making complaints to the F.B.I." United States v. Adler, supra, at 922.

Even if we were more persuaded than we are by these policy arguments, the result in this case would be unchanged. Resolution of the pros and cons of whether a statute should sweep broadly or narrowly is for Congress. Its decision that the perversion of agency resources and the potential harm to those implicated by false reports of crime justifies punishing those who "knowingly and willfully" make such reports is not so "absurd or glaringly unjust," Sorrells v. United States, 287 U.S. 435, 450 (1932), as to lead us to question whether Congress actually intended what the plain language of § 1001 so clearly imports. . . .

The judgment of the Court of Appeals is reversed, and the case is remanded for further proceedings consistent with this opinion.

It is so ordered.

UNITED STATES v. WRIGHT
988 F.2d 1036 (10th Cir. 1993)

ANDERSON, Circuit Judge. . . .

BACKGROUND

During the period 1987-1989, Mr. Wright was the superintendent and manager of a water treatment plant and distribution system at Lake Tenkiller, near Vian, Oklahoma.

As part of his managerial duties he prepared and filed with the Sequoyah County (Oklahoma) Health Department monthly operating reports containing data on the suspended particulate matter (turbidity) in the water at his plant. These reports were false in that they purported to show information on turbidity from water samples when, in fact, no samples were analyzed or taken.

The reports, sampling, analytical, and record keeping requirements resulting in the type of data in question are required by federal regulations promulgated by the EPA pursuant to its authority and responsibility under the Act. The regulations require, among other things, daily monitoring of turbidity and submission to the state of monthly reports of the daily values within 10 days of the end of the month.

The Act permits a state to apply to the Administrator of the EPA for primary enforcement responsibility over drinking water standards. On March 30, 1977, the Administrator approved Oklahoma's application for primary enforcement responsibility and Oklahoma had that authority during the period in question. Within the State of Oklahoma, responsibility for enforcing drinking water standards has been given to the Department of Health, which provided the forms which Mr. Wright filled out and filed with the County Health Department. The County Health Department forwards filed forms to the State Health Department.

A federal grand jury indicted Mr. Wright on January 9, 1992, charging him with seven counts of violating 18 U.S.C. § 1001 by making false written statements in a matter within the jurisdiction of the EPA. After the district court denied his motion to dismiss the indictment on jurisdictional grounds, Mr. Wright entered into a plea agreement with the government pursuant to which he pled guilty to three counts of violating 18 U.S.C. § 1001, reserving his right to appeal the denial of his motion.

As part of the plea agreement, the parties stipulated that . . . all of the monthly reports he prepared concerning water turbidity were submitted by him to the Sequoyah County Health Department, and not to the EPA or any other federal agency or department.

The parties also stipulated that if a named responsible official of the EPA testified he would state that the EPA: (1) conducts annual evaluations of the Oklahoma public water system program under the Act; (2) makes semiannual visits to the Oklahoma State Department of Health to review the state public water system; (3) conducts biannual audits of the state program, during which operational reports are randomly selected for review; and (4) makes annual grants to the Oklahoma Department of Health which have ranged from approximately $500,000 to $700,000 since 1987. In addition, it was stipulated that such annual financial grants are dependent, in part, on the outcome of EPA's evaluation of the state public water program. The district court and the parties have treated these recitations as established facts, as do we.

DISCUSSION. . . .

The parties agree that "jurisdiction," as it is used in section 1001, is to be defined broadly. "The most natural, nontechnical reading of the statutory language is that it covers all matters confided to the authority of an agency or department." United States v. Rogers, 466 U.S. 475, 479 (1984). . . .

The false statement need not be made directly to the federal agency to be within its jurisdiction. . . .

Mr. Wright asserts that a writing does not fall within the jurisdiction of an agency unless there is a "direct relationship" between the writing and an authorized function of the agency. He then contends that there was no direct relationship between the reports he submitted and a function of the EPA "[b]ecause the EPA had surrendered primary authority for enforcement of Safe Drinking Water Act standards to the State of Oklahoma," and because he filed the report with the state, not the EPA. We disagree.

Regardless of the standard employed, the false turbidity data filed by Mr. Wright fell within the jurisdiction of the EPA. A grant of primary authority is not a grant of exclusive authority. Congress passed the Act "'to assure that water supply systems serving the public meet minimum national standards for the protection of public health.'" Montgomery County v. Environmental Protection Agency, 662 F.2d 1040, 1041 (4th Cir. 1981). The Act requires the Administrator to promulgate maximum contaminant level goals and national primary drinking water regulations. The regulations relating to the collection and reporting of turbidity data, described above, were promulgated pursuant to that charge and authority. The EPA retains the authority, in the discharge of its duties under the Act, to enforce its regulations; and, turbidity data clearly concern an authorized function of the EPA.

Furthermore, in this situation, the EPA is actively involved in assuring state compliance with national safe water standards. It audits, reviews, and evaluates the state of Oklahoma's program, including an inspection of the monthly reports of the type involved in this case. Such reports, therefore, directly implicate the ongoing function and mission of the agency. In addition, the Act *expressly* authorizes the EPA to take enforcement actions in states having primary enforcement authority.

Finally, EPA's funding of the Oklahoma public water program is conditioned, in part, on the results of its annual evaluations of that program. This court is in accord with other circuits which have found that a state agency's use of federal funds, standing alone, is generally sufficient to establish jurisdiction under section 1001.

CONCLUSION

For the reasons stated, we agree with the district court's denial of Wright's motion to dismiss the indictment, and we affirm the judgment of conviction.

Notes and Questions

1. How important is it that the EPA performed periodic evaluations of the Oklahoma program? Would it make a difference if the EPA had discretionary authority to evaluate the program, but did not exercise its power to do so?

2. What if the forms that Wright filled out were kept on file at the water treatment plant where he worked instead of being filed with the Sequoyah County Health Department? Would that affect the outcome?

3. The court in *Wright* said it agreed with other circuits that have found that a state agency's use of federal funds is ordinarily enough to establish jurisdiction under § 1001. What are the implications of that reading of the statute?

UNITED STATES v. STEINER PLASTICS MANUFACTURING CO.
231 F.2d 149 (2d Cir. 1956)

LUMBARD, Circuit Judge.

The defendant corporation is here appealing from its conviction and fines imposed totalling $45,500 for conspiracy and six counts in violation of 18 U.S.C. § 1001, which reads as follows:

> Whoever, in any matter within the jurisdiction of any department or agency of the United States knowingly and willfully falsifies, conceals or covers up by any trick, scheme, or device a material fact, or makes any false, fictitious or fraudulent statements or representations, or makes or uses any false writing or document knowing the same to contain any false, fictitious or fraudulent statement or entry, shall be fined not more than $10,000 or imprisoned not more than five years, or both.

In 1953 Steiner Plastics Mfg. Co., Inc., was engaged in the manufacture of plexiglass cockpit canopies pursuant to a subcontract from the Grumman Aircraft Engineering corporation, which was producing jet planes for the United States Navy. Malcolm Steiner was the President of Steiner Plastics and he and his wife were the sole stockholders. The contract with Grumman provided that all canopies produced by Steiner Plastics would be subject to inspection by Grumman and by the Navy. During the period in question these inspections took place at the Steiner plant in Glen Cove, New York. During 1953 difficulties developed in the production of the canopies and some 250 defective or incomplete canopies accumulated at the Steiner plant. Many of these were successfully reworked, but in June of 1953 approximately 100 canopies remained which could not successfully be reworked to pass inspection. A scheme was thereafter devised whereby some of these canopies were to be shipped without proper inspection by switching approval stamps and serial numbers from canopies which had previously been approved by Grumman and the Navy to other canopies which had not been so approved.

[The evidence clearly established that the switching had occurred, and the jury found Steiner Plastics guilty of conspiracy and violating § 1001.]

1. The defendant corporation first complains that there was no violation of § 1001 because the switching of approval stamps was not a matter "within the jurisdiction of any department or agency of the United States." The subcontract from Grumman, however, provided that the canopies produced by the defendant would be subject to inspection by representatives of the Navy. Moreover, the canopies involved in the counts on which the defendant was convicted were all shipped directly to the Navy by the defendant on government bills of lading. The scheme used by the corporation's employees was manifestly intended to deceive both the Navy and Grumman and thus it was clearly within the jurisdiction of an agency of the United States within the meaning of § 1001.

2. The defendant contends that since the trial court refused to admit evidence to show that the canopies in question were defective or had been rejected, there was a failure to establish that the defendant or its employees had falsified or concealed "a material fact" as required by the statute. The trial judge was correct, however, in ruling that no such evidence was necessary. The transfer of the approval stamps concealed at least the fact that the canopies to which they were transferred had not been approved. This was a material fact within the meaning of the statute. Nor does it make any difference that the indictment alleged that the canopies were in fact defective or had in fact been rejected. This was surplusage and was properly so treated by the trial judge. The government need not prove everything in the indictment, but only what is necessary to make out a violation of the statute. . . .

The conviction is affirmed.

 *Material fact*

Notes and Questions

1. In what sense was Steiner's switching of the cockpit canopies a matter within the jurisdiction of the federal government?

2. How did Steiner Plastics violate the statute? Is the company's liability premised on nondisclosure? Making a false representation? Concealment? Can mere nondisclosure support a conviction under § 1001?

3. Suppose that Steiner Plastics had been required to fill out a form requiring the company to verify that "the information supplied herein is true and correct." Steiner leaves a blank next to the question: "Have any of these canopies previously been rejected? If so, explain." The corporate agent who fills out the form knows that some of the canopies have been rejected. Does leaving the blank violate § 1001?[2]

4. During the course of its deliberations, the jury in *Steiner Plastics* sent the following question to the judge:

> Under United States laws can we hold the corporation responsible for the alleged criminal acts not only of the officers of the corporation but also of the alleged overt and criminal acts of its employees?

How should the judge answer the question?

III. DEPARTMENT OR AGENCY

For years courts have grappled with the definitional question of what constitutes a "department or agency" under the false statements statute. While there is little question that executive branch organs like the FBI and the Secret Service (*Rodgers*), the EPA (*Wright*), and the Navy (*Steiner Plastics*) qualify as agencies and departments under § 1001, what about Congress and the courts? In United States v. Bramblett,[3] the

Supreme Court rejected the defendant's argument that the statute is limited to false statements made to the executive branch of government. The Court found that the history and purpose of the statute demonstrate that the term "department" "was meant to describe the executive, legislative and judicial branches of the Government."[4]

But in 1995, the Supreme Court overruled *Bramblett* in Hubbard v. United States,[5] holding that the terms "department" and "agency" encompass only the executive branch of government. In response to the high Court's ruling, Congress amended § 1001 to restore the statute's breadth. As amended, § 1001 expressly applies to false statements within the jurisdiction of the executive, legislative, or judicial branch of the federal government, but with several notable exceptions.

UNITED STATES v. McNEIL
362 F.3d 570 (9th Cir. 2004)

HUG, Circuit Judge: . . .

I. BACKGROUND

On April 6, 2000, Christopher McNeil was indicted on one count of possessing false documents. He requested that the court appoint counsel to represent him and submitted a CJA-23 Financial Affidavit to support his request. The form requires the defendant to list his assets to determine if he qualifies financially for a court-appointed attorney. McNeil completed the form with the aid of Federal Defender Anthony Gallagher. McNeil admits that he omitted reference to real estate and several financial accounts that he owned at the time. Most of the accounts were in fictitious names, and McNeil argues that he did not list them on Gallagher's advice because of the possibility that such a disclosure would incriminate him. His T. Rowe Price account with a positive balance, however, was in his own name. McNeil admits that he did not tell Gallagher about this account.

Gallagher does not remember McNeil's case, but he testified that it was his custom to advise clients not to list assets that could be incriminating. Instead, Gallagher would make a notation on the form and tell the judge when the form was submitted that it was incomplete because of self-incrimination concerns. McNeil's form has no such notations, and Gallagher did not make a declaration to Magistrate Judge Cebull to that effect when the form was submitted.

On June 25, 2001, and on August 17, 2001, two federal grand juries indicted McNeil for making false statements on his CJA-23 Financial Affidavit in violation of 18 U.S.C. § 1001. McNeil pleaded not guilty to both counts. At the subsequent trial, the district judge refused to give a "good faith" instruction to the jury because he found that McNeil's failure to disclose the T. Rowe Price account to his attorney made him ineligible for that instruction. The jury convicted McNeil on both counts. On January 23, 2002, he was sentenced to a term of 18 months followed by 3 years of supervised release.

---

4. Id. at 509.
5. 514 U.S. 695 (1995).

McNeil now appeals, arguing that his statements were made in a judicial proceeding and are therefore not subject to prosecution under § 1001. He also argues that the district court erred by refusing to give the "good faith" jury instruction.

II. DISCUSSION

. . . This case presents a question of statutory interpretation of first impression in this circuit. Congress amended 18 U.S.C. § 1001 in 1996 to clarify the reach of the statute. This is the first opportunity we have had to address the newly constructed statute. As amended, the first section of the statute imposes criminal liability for, *inter alia*, knowingly and willfully making false statements "in any matter within the jurisdiction of the executive, legislative, or judicial branch of the Government." 18 U.S.C. § 1001(a). Subsection (b) creates an exception for judicial proceedings:

Subsection (a) does not apply to a party to a judicial proceeding, or that party's counsel, for statements, representations, writings, or documents submitted by such party or counsel to a judge or magistrate in that proceeding.

18 U.S.C. § 1001(b). Thus, to qualify for this exception from liability, McNeil must show that (1) he was a party to a judicial proceeding, (2) his statements were submitted to a judge or magistrate, and (3) his statements were made "in that proceeding."

McNeil was a party to a judicial proceeding when he made the statements because a judicial proceeding had been initiated against him. He had already been indicted on one count of possessing false identification documents when he made his false statements to Magistrate Judge Cebull.

Because McNeil's CJA-23 Financial Affidavit was presented to Magistrate Judge Cebull for use in determining whether McNeil qualified for court-appointed counsel, McNeil's statements satisfy the second requirement of submission to a judge or magistrate.

The final requirement to qualify for exemption from liability is that the statement must be made "in [a judicial] proceeding." This brings us to the pivotal issue in this case. We must determine whether the range of judicial activities implied by that phrase includes the inquiry into a defendant's financial status for purposes of appointing counsel. To do so, we start with the language of the statute itself. The Oxford English Dictionary defines "proceeding" as "the fact or manner of taking legal action; a legal action; an act done by authority of the court, assembly or society." (5th ed. 2002). Thus the term "proceeding" refers generally to legal actions and does not distinguish among different phases of an action.

Moreover, the Supreme Court has established the indictment as a definitional starting point for judicial "proceedings" in Sixth Amendment jurisprudence. Logically, every point between the indictment and the disposition would then be considered part of the "judicial proceeding."

Given this background of common understanding, the statute is clear on its face that "in that proceeding" refers to statements that are made as a part of a judicial proceeding, after it has officially begun. Once McNeil was indicted, the criminal proceeding against him had begun. His statement to Magistrate Judge Cebull was made as a part of that proceeding and therefore is exempted from liability under § 1001.

Prior to the amendment of § 1001 in 1996, this circuit had drawn a distinction between documents submitted for "housekeeping" and "adjudicative" functions, imposing liability for false statements submitted for the former, but making an exception for statements submitted for the latter. We did so because the statute, at that time, did not itself provide an exception for statements made in the context of advocacy in a judicial proceeding. . . .

As drafted, that statute created very broad liability, covering statements "in any matter within the jurisdiction of any department or agency of the United States." Id. We concluded that "neither Congress nor the Supreme Court intended the statute to include traditional trial tactics within the statutory terms 'conceals or covers up.'" *Plascencia-Orozco*, 768 F.2d at 1076 (quoting United States v. Morgan, 309 F.2d 234, 237 (D.C. Cir. 1962)). Thus, we construed the statute in such a way as to contain a limitation, by holding that it did not apply to statements made in connection with a court's "adjudicative" function.

In crafting the new version of § 1001, however, Congress has obviated the concern that led us to create the judicial function exception, and the distinction we drew between "housekeeping" and "adjudicative" functions is no longer necessary. The plain language of § 1001(b) carves out an exception to the conduct defined in § 1001(a), and that exception applies broadly to *all* submissions to a judge or magistrate in a proceeding. The statute covers "statements, representations, writings, or documents," without regard to the purpose or nature of the submission. Thus, there is no longer any reason or need to recognize a distinction between "housekeeping" and "adjudicative" functions. In the plain, literal sense, McNeil's submission of the CJA-23 Financial Affidavit was a "document[] submitted by [him] to a judge or magistrate in that proceeding." 18 U.S.C. § 1001(b). Section 1001(b) therefore exempts McNeil from liability under § 1001(a).[6]

Because we hold that McNeil's statements were protected by § 1001(b), we do not reach his second argument that the jury should have been given a "good faith" instruction.

III. CONCLUSION

The amended version of 18 U.S.C. § 1001 is unambiguous on its face. Statements made in judicial proceedings are excluded from liability under the statute by subsection (b). Because McNeil's statements were made in a judicial proceeding, they are not subject to prosecution under this statute. His conviction is therefore reversed.

---

6. Submitting a false CJA-23 form may subject a defendant to criminal liability under other statutes, for example, under 18 U.S.C. § 1621, the general statute on perjury, or 18 U.S.C. § 1623, which punishes the making of a false material declaration in any proceeding before, or ancillary to, any court. However, the indictment against McNeil did not charge him with having violated any statute other than 18 U.S.C. § 1001.

Notes and Questions

1. As a matter of policy, does it make sense to exclude the kinds of misstatements McNeil made from the coverage of § 1001? Would extending § 1001 liability to lying about one's eligibility for court-appointed counsel implicate concerns about criminalizing trial tactics?

2. Suppose McNeil was convicted on the original charge of possessing false documents. Two days before his sentencing hearing, his lawyer knowingly submits a forged letter to the court. The letter purports to be written by McNeil's doctor and urges the judge not to send McNeil to prison because he has a life-threatening medical condition. Would submission of the phony letter violate § 1001 as amended?

3. What was the purpose of the "housekeeping" and "adjudicative" distinction the *McNeil* court had recognized before § 1001 was amended? Why does the court conclude that § 1001 no longer preserves that distinction?

4. Would truthful disclosure of McNeil's assets have been incriminating? If so, is excluding his lies the best way to preserve his Fifth Amendment privilege?

5. Are there alternative theories of liability that might be sustained? If so, why did the government focus exclusively on § 1001?

6. Did McNeil's appointed lawyer provide sound advice when he told his client not to disclose all of his assets?

UNITED STATES v. PICKETT
353 F.3d 62 (D.C. Cir. 2004)

SENTELLE, Circuit Judge: . . .

I. BACKGROUND

On October 15, 2001, an anonymous letter delivered to Senator Thomas Daschle at his Senate office on Capitol Hill contained a white powder that tested positive for Anthrax — a dangerous, often deadly, disease-causing agent. Other similar Anthrax incidents occurred around the same time and geographic area. On November 7, 2001, while the Anthrax investigation was not only ongoing but much on the minds of law enforcement, members of Congress, and the public, Pickett committed what he now admits was a "bad joke." The facts of the incident are not in dispute. Appellant, then a Capitol Police officer, was on duty at a security post at the entrance to the Cannon Office Building tunnel, which connects the House Office Buildings to the Capitol Building. Because of the level of security measures occasioned by the Anthrax incident, which followed close on the heels of the tragic attacks on the United States on September 11, 2001, the tunnel was closed to members of the public, but open to authorized personnel including Members of the House of Representatives. The security post was accessible by members of the public and consisted largely of a podium, a desk, a magnetometer, and an x-ray machine. At approximately 5 P.M. on November 7, Officer Kari Morgansen left her seat at the podium and moved to the desk seat vacated by appellant, who was going on break. At the desk Officer Morgansen discovered a handwritten note and a small pile of white powder. The note read, "PLEASE INHALE YES THIS COULD BE? CALL YOUR DOCTOR FOR FLU—SYMPTOMS. THIS IS A CAPITOL POLICE TRAINING EXERCIZE [sic]! I HOPE YOU PASS!"

Officer Morgansen inquired of Officer John Caldwell, who was also on duty at the post, if he knew anything about the note or the powder. He did not. Neither of the officers believed that the powder was actually Anthrax. Nonetheless, because of the state of alert and the earlier incidents, they called a superior and blocked the powder and note from public view lest anyone become alarmed. The superior, Sergeant Turner, asked who else had been at the desk. Upon learning appellant had been sitting there, he contacted him by phone and asked him what was on the desk. After some delay, appellant advised that "it was a joke" and that the powder "was Equal." Although the powder was never tested, the government has never contended that it was actually Anthrax or anything other than the dietary sugar substitute appellant suggested. Sergeant Turner conducted some further investigation and reported the incident to the Criminal Investigation Division of the Capitol Police.

[Pickett was charged with making false statements in violation of § 1001 and obstructing the Capitol Police in violation of 40 U.S.C. § 212a-2(d). After a weeklong trial, the jury found him guilty of the false statements charge but not guilty of the obstruction charge. Pickett appealed.]

III. ANALYSIS

The count of conviction in the indictment charged that:

On or about November 7, 2001, in the District of Columbia, the defendant, JAMES JOSEPH PICKETT, in a matter within the jurisdiction of the legislative branch of the Government of the United States, that is, the United States Capitol Police, did knowingly and willfully make materially false, fictitious, and fraudulent statements and representations; that is, the defendant wrote a note and placed that writing at a United States Capitol Police security station with arrows directed to a nearby quantity of white powder, which writing stated — "PLEASE INHALE YES THIS COULD BE? CALL YOUR DOCTOR FOR FLU—SYMPTOMS. THIS IS A CAPITOL POLICE TRAINING EXERCIZE! [SIC] I HOPE YOU PASS!" — when the defendant knew the powder was not anthrax and his placement of the powder and the writing were not part of a United States Capitol Police training exercise.

Pickett contends that the District Court erred in denying his motion to dismiss this indictment for its failure to allege an essential element of the offense. More specifically, he argues that an indictment charging a violation of § 1001 by the making of a false statement "in a matter within the jurisdiction of the *legislative* branch of the Government" must further allege that the charged conduct fell within the specifications of 18 U.S.C. § 1001(c)(1) or (2). In this appeal, the Government has at no time claimed that whatever matter may have encompassed Pickett's alleged false statement was an administrative matter covered by subsection (1), and therefore, Pickett argues, the indictment was not valid without allegations that the "statement" was made in an investigation or review. . . .

... The Government's primary argument on appeal is that the requirement of § 1001 for an investigation is satisfied by the investigation which the false statement occasioned. This theory just does not square with the words of § 1001. That section requires first that the false statement be made "in any matter within the jurisdiction of the . . . legislative . . . branch." 18 U.S.C. § 1001(a). That it be made *in* a matter within the jurisdiction of the legislative branch would seem to contemplate that the matter existed at the time of the making of the statement. The section further requires that, with specific reference to the legislative branch, it will apply only to an "investigation or review, conducted pursuant to the authority of any committee, subcommittee, commission or office of the Congress, consistent with applicable rules of the House or Senate." 18 U.S.C. § 1001(c)(2). Not only was the investigation of the false statement not in existence so that the statement could have been made in it, the Government has pointed us to no evidence supporting the proposition that such investigation was pursuant to the authorities set out in subsection (c)(2). The Government's construction of the statute is not only unnatural and illogical, it would render subsection (2) meaningless. Presumably any false statement made in any matter within the legislative branch which became the subject of a prosecution would have been the subject of an investigation triggered by the statement. . . .

This leaves the Government's second theory for satisfaction of the "investigation or review" element. That second theory is that Pickett made a false statement in the concurrent investigation surrounding the Anthrax letters sent to Senator Daschle and others. This theory also fails. Not only has the Government not offered overwhelming and uncontroverted evidence that the statement was made in that investigation, it has offered none at all. The most the evidence shows is that the investigation was ongoing at the time of the alleged making of the statement, and that agents connected to that investigation were sent to all calls involving suspicious packages. The statute does not apply to statements made concurrently with an investigation, even if those statements concerned the same or similar subject matter. The statute requires that the statements be made *in* such a matter. The Government has offered no evidence to meet that requirement. . . .

[Concurring opinion by ROGERS, J., omitted.]

Notes and Questions

1. As interpreted by the court in *Pickett*, the investigation would have to have been ongoing when the alleged violation occurred. Why doesn't the statute apply to investigations triggered by the false statements?

2. Why weren't the false statements in *Pickett* made in the course of the investigation relating to the anthrax letters sent to Senator Daschle?

3. Is there a potentially viable alternative theory of the case?

4. Is § 1001, as amended, too narrowly drawn?

IV. FALSE STATEMENTS

A. FALSE PROMISES

UNITED STATES v. SHAH
44 F.3d 285 (5th Cir. 1995)

Garwood, Circuit Judge. . . .

Facts and Proceedings Below . . .

On June 9, 1992, the General Services Administration (GSA) issued a solicitation for the purchase of irons, ironing boards, and ironing board pads. The solicitation called for a bid from each of a number of prospective suppliers. Because the bid was to be negotiated, not sealed, the offeror was allowed to alter the price after submission but before the award. Among the prospective bidders was Omega Electronics (Omega), a small California company that had held the previous contract for steam irons with GSA. Omega had also previously dealt with GSA and the GSA contract specialist, Linda Brainard (Brainard), on an undisclosed number of small purchase contracts. Brainard testified that these contracts occasioned numerous telephone contacts between her and Shah, Omega's president.

On July 1, 1992, GSA mailed the solicitation for iron products to Omega's address in San Carlos, California. The solicitation contained the following language under section 13, entitled "Certificate of Independent Price Determination":

(a) The offeror certifies that —
(1) The prices in this offer have been arrived at independently, without, for the purpose of restricting competition, any consultation, communication, or agreement with any other offeror or competitor relating to (i) those prices, (ii) the intention to submit an offer, or (iii) the methods or factors used to calculate the prices offered;
(2) The prices in this offer have not been and will not be knowingly disclosed by the offeror, directly or indirectly, to any other offeror or competitor before bid opening (in the case of a sealed bid solicitation) or before contract award (in the case of a negotiated solicitation) unless otherwise required by law; and
(3) No attempt has been made or will be made by the offeror to induce any other concern to submit or not to submit an offer for the purpose of restricting competition.
(b) Each signature on the offer is considered to be a certification . . . that the signatory —
(1) . . . has not participated and will not participate in any action contrary to subparagraphs (a)(1) through (a)(3) above. . . .

The same solicitation was also sent to Kipper & Company, a New York concern specializing in the supply of hand and power tools to commercial and governmental customers. Jerome Kipper (Kipper), president of Kipper & Company, testified that he and Shah had spoken a "few times" on the telephone.[7] Besides these conversations, which occurred sometime in November or December of 1991, Shah and Kipper communicated only occasionally and very briefly during the early part of 1992.

On July 7, 1992, shortly after Omega received the GSA solicitation but one day before Omega sent it out, Shah telephoned Kipper and suggested that they share their bids. Shah explained that, by fixing and exchanging price information, they could rig the bidding and thus split the award. According to his plan, Shah would acquire the delivery depots west of the Mississippi, while Kipper would take those to the east. In response to this proposal, Kipper told Shah that he "questioned . . . [Shah's] ethic but admired his ambition." Although he clearly did not agree to trade price information, Kipper testified that he was "non-committal" at the close of the conversation. Shah again left his phone number.

The next day, July 8, 1992, Shah signed and mailed the solicitation to GSA, in which he certified that the prices contained in the bid "have not been and will not be disclosed." In the solicitation, he identified himself as the Managing Partner of Omega and listed the San Carlos, California, address as well as the telephone number earlier given to Kipper. Shah also filled in blanks throughout the solicitation, including information above and below section 13, the certification of independent price determination.

Kipper reported his July 7 conversation with Shah to both GSA and his attorney. Under the supervision of a GSA investigator, Kipper made two telephone calls to Shah on July 15, 1992, several days after both Kipper and Shah had submitted their bids to GSA. . . . Kipper testified that, during [the second] conversation, they agreed to fax to each other their bids and, further, that Shah requested confidentiality. They then carried out this agreement.[8]

On January 6, 1993, a grand jury returned a one-count indictment against Shah charging him with "knowingly and willfully" having made a "false, fictitious and fraudulent" statement to GSA, a government agency, contrary to 18 U.S.C. § 1001, namely "the statement that the prices in this offer have not been and will not be knowingly disclosed by the offeror, directly or indirectly, to any other offeror or competitor before bid opening or contract award.". . . After entering a plea of not guilty, Shah was tried and convicted before a jury in July 1993. At the close of the government's case (Shah presented no evidence), Shah properly but unsuccessfully moved for acquittal. . . .

DISCUSSION

On appeal, Shah contends . . . that a promise of future performance cannot, as a matter of law, constitute a violation of 18 U.S.C. § 1001.

---

7. During those conversations, Shah sought a price quote on a large quantity of Black & Decker irons.

8. Shah faxed Kipper a copy of the bid pages from his solicitation, and Kipper sent fictitious price information in exchange. The actual fax was retrieved by Kipper & Company's vice president, Adam Mellon, who authenticated the document at trial.

Section 1001 . . . prohibits the knowing and willful making of "false, fictitious or fraudulent statements or representations" on a matter "within the jurisdiction of any department or agency of the United States." The purpose of this broadly worded statute is "to protect the authorized functions of governmental departments and agencies from the perversion which might result from . . . deceptive practices." United States v. Gilliland, 312 U.S. 86, 93 (1941). To establish a violation, the government must prove five elements: "(1) a statement, that is (2) false (3) and material, (4) made with the requisite specific intent, [and] (5) within the purview of government agency jurisdiction." United States v. Puente, 982 F.2d 156, 158 (5th Cir. 1993). With regard to the "requisite specific intent," we have observed, "A false representation is one . . . made with an intent to deceive or mislead." United States v. Guzman, 781 F.2d 428, 431 (5th Cir. 1986).[9] In words more relevant to this case, the district court correctly instructed the jury that the government must prove "that the defendant made the false statement for the purposes of misleading the General Services Administration."

The central issue in this case, however, focuses only on the second element, falsity. We are asked to decide whether what Shah stated or represented in the solicitation could violate section 1001, and, if so, whether the government proved that it did. The critical language in the solicitation reads, "The prices in this offer have not been and will not be knowingly disclosed by the offeror . . . to any other offeror or competitor before . . . contract award." The statement was made when Shah submitted the solicitation on July 8, 1992. As of that date, there is no evidence that Shah had disclosed any price information. He had only proposed doing so the day before. It was not until July 15 that Shah actually disclosed the information. Therefore, only the "will not disclose" portion of the statement is at issue.

By disclosing his bid to a competitor, Shah broke a promise made and certified in the solicitation. As the government concedes, however, a broken promise is not alone a basis for criminal liability under section 1001. Otherwise, as Shah correctly points out, every breach of a governmental contract would be converted into a section 1001 false statement, thus exposing the breaching party to criminal prosecution. To establish a violation, then, the government must prove, among other things, that the statement "I will not disclose price information before the contract award" was false *when made*. Shah contends that this statement can be neither true nor false when made because it is simply a *prediction* of future performance. As such, the statement is either true or false only after the promise is carried out or broken. The government, on the other hand, argues that this statement clearly implies and manifests an intent which itself may render a promise true or false when made and which may be proved by circumstantial evidence of Shah's state of mind. According to the government, if Shah all the while intended to disclose price information, but nevertheless promised not to, he made a false and fraudulent statement to GSA in violation of section 1001.

---

9. Section 1001, however, "does not require an intent to defraud — that is, the intent to deprive someone of something by means of deceit." Lichenstein, 610 F.2d at 1277. In this sense, the [statute] seeks to protect more than the simple proprietary interests of the federal government; it "has for its object the protection and welfare of the government," specifically protection against "deceit, craft or trickery" designed "to interfere with or obstruct one of [the United States's [sic]] lawful government functions." McNally v. United States, 483 U.S. 350, 358 n.8 (1987). Section 1001 is thus distinct from general fraud statutes, such as the mail fraud statute, wherein "any benefit which the Government derives from the statute must be limited to the Government's interests as property holder." Id.

[The court characterized the precise issue as "whether a promise to perform can ever violate section 1001," a question on which neither side cited authority directly on point. To resolve this question, then, it was necessary to inquire whether Shah's statement was "capable of being termed true or false" — i.e., whether "a promise can be construed as 'a factual assertion.'" While Shah pressed the concern that the government's interpretation of what constitutes a false statement "would criminalize every broken promise," the court found the government's position far less sweeping.]

. . . *It is not breaking a promise that exposes a defendant to criminal liability, but making a promise with the intent to break it.* Whereas breaking a promise cannot retroactively render the promise false when stated, generally the making of a promise will necessarily imply an intent to perform, the absence of which may itself make a promise false when stated.

This distinction is critical. In the present context, the statement "I will not disclose prices" is something more than a prediction; it clearly contains a necessary implication, signified by the phrase "I will," that the maker intends to do what he promises. See Restatement (Second) of Torts § 530(1) cmt. c ("Since a promise *necessarily* carries with it the implied assertion of an intention to perform it follows that a promise made without such an intention is fraudulent. . . .") (emphasis added). The implication is necessary because the statement's meaning depends on it. In the setting of this case, the statement "I will not disclose prices, but I intend to disclose prices" is nonsense because the second clause negates the communicated meaning of the first.

That a promise can inherently be false when made is supported by case law not cited by either party. In Elmore v. United States, 267 F.2d 595 (4th Cir. 1959), the defendant was convicted of making false statements and representations on an application to the Farmers Home Administration in violation of the Commodity Credit Corporation Act. The defendant purchased surplus wheat from the government on the condition that the wheat be used only to feed livestock or poultry. Although the defendant certified as much, the wheat was later used for other purposes. Following his conviction, the defendant argued that "false statements" should be confined to "false statements of existing fact." . . . The court rejected this argument and read the statute to cover "false and fraudulent promises which the maker does not intend to perform." Id. In terms of frustrating the purpose of the act, the court could see no practical difference between false statements and false promises:

> [I]t cannot be supposed that Congress intended to direct the criminal sanctions of the act only against those who make false statements of existing fact and to exculpate those who should obtain surplus commodities by making false promises which they do not intend to fulfill. In practical effect, *a false promise fraudulently given amounts to a false statement of an existing intent* and it can be as destructive as the false statement of a material fact. We think Congress intended to cover it by the statute. Id. (emphasis added).

For the foregoing reasons, we reject Shah's contention that a "promise to perform" cannot, as a matter of law, ever violate section 1001. We hold that, under section 1001, a promise may amount to a "false, fictitious or fraudulent" statement if it is made without any present intention of performance and under circumstances such that it plainly, albeit implicitly, represents the present existence of an intent to perform. . . .

C ONCLUSION

For the foregoing reasons, the judgment of the district court is affirmed.

Notes and Questions

1. Does the decision to equate false promises with false statements create the risk that garden variety breaches of contract will be criminally prosecuted?

2. What is the difference between promises and predictions? Why should one be considered a statement when the other is not?

3. Suppose that during the negotiations with GSA, Shah discusses his company's record for timely performance. At one point he says: "Though I can't make any promises, I think we'll be able to deliver the products well ahead of the contract deadline." Shah knows the company cannot deliver before the contract deadline. Has he made a false statement?

4. Shah signed and mailed the solicitation to GSA on July 8. He agreed to exchange bid information with Kipper on July 15. Has the government proved that the statement was false at the time it was made? What evidence sheds light on this issue?

5. To be liable under § 1001, Shah must have "knowingly" made a false statement. Under the facts of this case, his knowledge of the falsity would be contingent on a finding that he had read the certification he signed and mailed in. Shah presented no evidence and thus did not testify. Has the government proved that he acted knowingly?

B. THE "EXCULPATORY NO" DOCTRINE

BROGAN v. UNITED STATES
522 U.S. 398 (1998)

S CALIA , J. delivered the opinion of the Court.

This case presents the question whether there is an exception to criminal liability under 18 U.S.C. § 1001 for a false statement that consists of the mere denial of wrongdoing, the so-called "exculpatory no."

I

While acting as a union officer during 1987 and 1988, petitioner James Brogan accepted cash payments from JRD Management Corporation, a real estate company whose employees were represented by the union. On October 4, 1993, federal agents from the Department of Labor and the Internal Revenue Service visited petitioner at his home. The agents identified themselves and explained that they were seeking petitioner's cooperation in an investigation of JRD and various individuals. They told petitioner that if he wished to cooperate, he should have an attorney contact the U.S. Attorney's Office, and that if he could not afford an attorney, one could be appointed for him.

The agents then asked petitioner if he would answer some questions, and he agreed. One question was whether he had received any cash or gifts from JRD when he was a union officer. Petitioner's response was "no." At that point, the agents disclosed that a search of JRD headquarters had produced company records showing the contrary. They also told petitioner that lying to federal agents in the course of an investigation was a crime. Petitioner did not modify his answers, and the interview ended shortly thereafter.

Petitioner was indicted for accepting unlawful cash payments from an employer in violation of 29 U.S.C. § 186(b)(1), (a)(2), (d)(2), and making a false statement within the jurisdiction of a federal agency in violation of 18 U.S.C. § 1001. He was tried, along with several co-defendants, before a jury in the United States District Court for the Southern District of New York, and was found guilty. The United States Court of Appeals for the Second Circuit affirmed the convictions. We granted certiorari on the issue of the "exculpatory no."

II

At the time petitioner falsely replied "no" to the Government investigators' question, 18 U.S.C. § 1001 provided:

> Whoever, in any matter within the jurisdiction of any department or agency of the United States knowingly and willfully falsifies, conceals or covers up by any trick, scheme, or device a material fact, or makes any false, fictitious or fraudulent statements or representations, or makes or uses any false writing or document knowing the same to contain any false, fictitious or fraudulent statement or entry, shall be fined not more than $10,000 or imprisoned not more than five years, or both.

By its terms, 18 U.S.C. § 1001 covers "any" false statement — that is, a false statement "of whatever kind," United States v. Gonzales, 117 S. Ct. 1032, 1035 (1997). The word "no" in response to a question assuredly makes a "statement," see e.g., Webster's New International Dictionary 2461 (2d ed. 1950) (def. 2: "That which is stated; an embodiment in words of facts or opinions"), and petitioner does not contest that his utterance was false or that it was made "knowingly and willfully." In fact, petitioner concedes that under a "literal reading" of the statute he loses.

Petitioner asks us, however, to depart from the literal text that Congress has enacted, and to approve the doctrine adopted by many Circuits which excludes from the scope of § 1001 the "exculpatory no." The central feature of this doctrine is that a simple denial of guilt does not come within the statute. There is considerable variation among the Circuits concerning, among other things, what degree of elaborated tale-telling carries a statement beyond simple denial. In the present case, however, the Second Circuit agreed with petitioner that his statement would constitute a "true 'exculpatory no' as recognized in other circuits," 96 F.3d at 37, but aligned itself with the Fifth Circuit (one of whose panels had been the very first to embrace the "exculpatory no," see Paternostro v. United States, 311 F.2d 298 (CA5 1962)), in categorically rejecting the doctrine, see United States v. Rodriguez-Rios, 14 F.3d 1040 (CA5 1994) (en banc).

Petitioner's argument in support of the "exculpatory no" doctrine proceeds from the major premise that § 1001 criminalizes only those statements to Government investigators that "pervert governmental functions"; to the minor premise that simple denials of guilt to Government investigators do not pervert governmental functions, to the conclusion that § 1001 does not criminalize simple denials of guilt to Government investigators. Both premises seem to us mistaken. As to the minor: We cannot imagine how it could be true that falsely denying guilt in a Government investigation does not pervert a governmental function. Certainly the investigation of wrongdoing is a proper governmental function; and since it is the very purpose of an investigation to uncover the truth, any falsehood relating to the subject of the investigation perverts that function. It could be argued, perhaps, that a disbelieved falsehood does not pervert an investigation. But making the existence of this crime turn upon the credulousness of the federal investigator (or the persuasiveness of the liar) would be exceedingly strange; such a defense to the analogous crime of perjury is certainly unheard-of. . . .[10]

In any event, we find no basis for the major premise that only those falsehoods that pervert governmental functions are covered by § 1001. . . .

The second line of defense that petitioner invokes for the "exculpatory no" doctrine is inspired by the Fifth Amendment. He argues that a literal reading of § 1001 violates the "spirit" of the Fifth Amendment because it places a "cornered suspect" in the "cruel trilemma" of admitting guilt, remaining silent, or falsely denying guilt. This "trilemma" is wholly of the guilty suspect's own making, of course. An innocent person will not find himself in a similar quandary. . . . And even the honest and contrite guilty person will not regard the third prong of the "trilemma" (the blatant lie) as an available option. The *bon mot* "cruel trilemma" first appeared in Justice Goldberg's opinion for the Court in Murphy v. Waterfront Comm'n of N.Y. Harbor, 378 U.S. 52 (1964), where it was used to explain the importance of a suspect's Fifth Amendment right to remain silent when subpoenaed to testify in an official inquiry. Without that right, the opinion said, he would be exposed "to the cruel trilemma of self-accusation, perjury or contempt." Id., at 55. In order to validate the "exculpatory no," the elements of this "cruel trilemma" have now been altered — ratcheted up, as it were, so that the right to remain silent, which was the liberation from the original trilemma, is now itself a cruelty. We are not disposed to write into our law this species of compassion inflation.

Whether or not the predicament of the wrongdoer run to ground tugs at the heart strings, neither the text nor the spirit of the Fifth Amendment confers a privilege to lie. "Proper invocation of the Fifth Amendment privilege against compulsory self-incrimination allows a witness to remain silent, but not to swear falsely." United States v. Apfelbaum, 445 U.S. 115, 117 (1980). Petitioner contends that silence is an "illusory" option because a suspect may fear that his silence will be used against him later, or may not even know that silence is an available option. As to the former: It is well established that the fact that a person's silence can be used against him — either as substantive evidence of guilt or to impeach him if he takes the stand — does not exert a form of pressure that exonerates an otherwise unlawful lie. See United States v. Knox, 396 U.S. 77, 81-82 (1969). And as for the possibility that the person under investigation

---

10. "The government need not show that because of the perjured testimony, the grand jury threw in the towel. . . . Grand jurors . . . are free to disbelieve a witness and persevere in an investigation without immunizing a perjurer." United States v. Abrams, 568 F.2d 411, 421 (CA5 1978).

may be unaware of his right to remain silent: In the modern age of frequently dramatized "Miranda" warnings, that is implausible. Indeed, we found it implausible (or irrelevant) 30 years ago, unless the suspect was "in custody or otherwise deprived of his freedom of action in any significant way," Miranda v. Arizona, 384 U.S. 436, 445 (1966). Petitioner repeats the argument made by many supporters of the "exculpatory no," that the doctrine is necessary to eliminate the grave risk that § 1001 will become an instrument of prosecutorial abuse. The supposed danger is that overzealous prosecutors will use this provision as a means of "piling on" offenses — sometimes punishing the denial of wrongdoing more severely than the wrongdoing itself. The objectors' principal grievance on this score, however, lies not with the hypothetical prosecutors but with Congress itself, which has decreed the obstruction of a legitimate investigation to be a separate offense, and a serious one. It is not for us to revise that judgment. Petitioner has been unable to demonstrate, moreover, any history of prosecutorial excess, either before or after widespread judicial acceptance of the "exculpatory no." And finally, if there is a problem of supposed "overreaching" it is hard to see how the doctrine of the "exculpatory no" could solve it. It is easy enough for an interrogator to press the liar from the initial simple denial to a more detailed fabrication that would not qualify for the exemption.

III . . .

. . . Because the plain language of § 1001 admits of no exception for an "exculpatory no," we affirm the judgment of the Court of Appeals.

It is so ordered. . . .

Justice GINSBURG, with whom Justice SOUTER joins, concurring in the judgment.

Because a false denial fits the unqualified language of 18 U.S.C. § 1001, I concur in the affirmance of Brogan's conviction. I write separately, however, to call attention to the extraordinary authority Congress, perhaps unwittingly, has conferred on prosecutors to manufacture crimes. . . .

At the time of Brogan's offense, § 1001 made it a felony "knowingly and willfully" to make "any false, fictitious or fraudulent statements or representations" in "any matter within the jurisdiction of any department or agency of the United States." That encompassing formulation arms Government agents with authority not simply to apprehend lawbreakers, but to generate felonies, crimes of a kind that only a Government officer could prompt.

This case is illustrative. Two federal investigators paid an unannounced visit one evening to James Brogan's home. The investigators already possessed records indicating that Brogan, a union officer, had received cash from a company that employed members of the union Brogan served. (The agents gave no advance warning, one later testified, because they wanted to retain the element of surprise.) When the agents asked Brogan whether he had received any money or gifts from the company, Brogan responded "No." The agents asked no further questions. After Brogan just said "No," however, the agents told him: (1) the Government had in hand the records indicating that his answer was false; and (2) lying to federal agents in the course of an investigation is a crime. Had counsel appeared on the spot, Brogan likely would have received and followed advice to amend his answer, to say immediately: "Strike that; I plead not guilty." But no counsel attended the unannounced interview, and Brogan divulged nothing more. Thus, when the interview ended, a federal offense had been completed—even though, for all we can tell, Brogan's unadorned denial misled no one.

A further illustration. In United States v. Tabor, 788 F.2d 714 (CA11 1986), an Internal Revenue Service agent discovered that Tabor, a notary public, had violated Florida law by notarizing a deed even though two signatories had not personally appeared before her (one had died five weeks before the document was signed). With this knowledge in hand, and without "warning Tabor of the possible consequences of her statements," the agent went to her home with a deputy sheriff and questioned her about the transaction. When Tabor, regrettably but humanly, denied wrongdoing, the Government prosecuted her under § 1001. An IRS agent thus turned a violation of state law into a federal felony by eliciting a lie that misled no one. . . .

As these not altogether uncommon episodes show, § 1001 may apply to encounters between agents and their targets "under extremely informal circumstances which do not sufficiently alert the person interviewed to the danger that false statements may lead to a felony conviction." United States v. Ehrlichman, 379 F. Supp. 291, 292 (DC 1974). Because the questioning occurs in a noncustodial setting, the suspect is not informed of the right to remain silent. Unlike proceedings in which a false statement can be prosecuted as perjury, there may be no oath, no pause to concentrate the speaker's mind on the importance of his or her answers. As in Brogan's case, the target may not be informed that a false "No" is a criminal offense until after he speaks.

At oral argument, the Solicitor General forthrightly observed that § 1001 could even be used to "escalate completely innocent conduct into a felony." More likely to occur, "if an investigator finds it difficult to prove some elements of a crime, she can ask questions about other elements to which she already knows the answers. If the suspect lies, she can then use the crime she has prompted as leverage or can seek prosecution for the lie as a substitute for the crime she cannot prove." Note, False Statements to Federal Agents: Induced Lies and the Exculpatory No, 57 U. Chi. L. Rev. 1273, 1278 (1990). If the statute of limitations has run on an offense—as it had on four of the five payments Brogan was accused of accepting—the prosecutor can endeavor to revive the case by instructing an investigator to elicit a fresh denial of guilt.[11] Prosecution in these circumstances is not an instance of Government "punishing the denial of wrongdoing more severely than the wrongdoing itself"; it is, instead, Government generation of a crime when the underlying suspected wrongdoing is or has become nonpunishable.

It is doubtful Congress intended § 1001 to cast so large a net. . . .

[Dissenting opinion of Justice Stevens omitted.]

---

11. Cf. United States v. Bush, 503 F.2d 813, 815-819 (CA5 1974) (after statute of limitations ran on § 1001 charge for defendant Bush's first affidavit containing a false denial, IRS agents elicited a new affidavit, in which Bush made a new false denial; court held that "Bush cannot be prosecuted for making a statement to Internal Revenue Service agents when those agents aggressively sought such statement, when Bush's answer was essentially an exculpatory 'no' as to possible criminal activity, and when there is a high likelihood that Bush was under suspicion himself at the time the statement was taken and yet was in no way warned of this possibility").

Notes and Questions

1. Was Brogan's § 1001 violation a "manufactured" crime? If so, why wasn't the majority concerned about applying the statute to this kind of case? Does this application of the statute come uncomfortably close to violating Brogan's Fifth Amendment privilege against self-incrimination?

2. At one point or another over time, at least six circuits embraced the "exculpatory no" doctrine. Since false denials of guilt fall within the literal text of the statute, how could a judicially created exception to liability gain such widespread acceptance? Is there a sound rationale for recognizing an "exculpatory no" exception?

3. Since *Brogan* rules out continued recognition of a judicially created "exculpatory no" doctrine, should Congress try to tailor the text of § 1001 to prevent prosecutorial misuse of the statute? If so, should it follow the lead of the lower courts and fashion a statutory "exculpatory no" exception?

4. How could Brogan's responses be "material" if the agents already knew the truth? Did his conduct pervert a governmental function?

C. MATERIALITY

As the court in *Shah* observed, materiality is an element of a § 1001 violation.[12] The test for materiality is whether the statement has a natural tendency to influence or is capable of influencing any governmental action or decision.[13] In determining whether a statement is material, the focus of the inquiry relates to its intrinsic capacity to influence, not its actual effect. Thus, neither actual influence nor reliance need be shown.[14]

What is the purpose of the materiality requirement? Does "material" mean something different than "relevant"?

PROBLEM 6-1

Lloyd, a lobbyist for the harness racing industry, offers Grubb, a powerful state legislator, $5,000 to kill a provision in a pending bill that is harmful to harness racing. Grubb declines the offer. A few days later, Grubb calls Lloyd and suggests that he and his wife really needed some time off and were thinking about a weekend getaway in Florida. Lloyd replies that he knows of a great resort on the coast and offers to make the arrangements. Lloyd later calls Grubb back, telling him that he has reserved the Presidential Suite at a posh Florida resort for the coming weekend, has bought first-class airline tickets for Grubb and his wife, and will send Grubb $2,500 "to go to the races" while he is there.

---

12. In United States v. Gaudin, 515 U.S. 506 (1995), the Supreme Court held that the issue of materiality is a mixed question of law and fact to be decided by the jury.
13. Id.
14. United States v. White, 270 F.3d 356 (6th Cir. 2001).

After Grubb and his wife enjoy a lavish weekend at the resort, Grubb successfully maneuvers behind the scenes to get the harness racing provision out of the bill. The legislation then passes without the provision, and Lloyd calls Grubb and promises to give him another $2,500 as a "down payment" on a second weekend in Florida. At the end of the conversation, Grubb invites Lloyd to join him for a drink after work and asks him to "bring the envelope" with him.

Unbeknownst to both parties, the telephone calls in which these arrangements were made were recorded by the FBI, which was investigating Lloyd in connection with another matter. The calls prompted an investigation into whether the vacations and cash that Lloyd gave Grubb constituted bribes. During an interview with an FBI agent, Grubb was asked whether he had ever received any gifts or payments from Lloyd. Rather than simply denying that he had, Grubb said: "Well yes, of course, but let me explain."

Grubb went on to say that Lloyd was a casual friend who occasionally bought him dinner at a nice restaurant or took him for a round of golf at the local country club — "but that's it. There's never been anything more substantial than that." Grubb's explanation led to his indictment for making false statements.

Has Grubb violated § 1001? Are his statements to the FBI agent material?[15]

V. CULPABLE MENTAL STATE

UNITED STATES V. YERMIAN
468 U.S. 63 (1984)

Justice POWELL delivered the opinion of the Court.

It is a federal crime under 18 U.S.C. § 1001 to make any false or fraudulent statement in any matter within the jurisdiction of a federal agency. To establish a violation of § 1001, the Government must prove beyond a reasonable doubt that the statement was made with knowledge of its falsity. This case presents the question whether the Government also must prove that the false statement was made with actual knowledge of federal agency jurisdiction.

I

Respondent Esmail Yermian was convicted in the District Court of Central California on three counts of making false statements in a matter within the jurisdiction of a federal agency, in violation of § 1001. The convictions were based on false statements respondent supplied his employer in connection with a Department of Defense security questionnaire. Respondent was hired in 1979 by Gulton Industries, a defense contractor. Because respondent was to have access to classified material in the course

---

15. Cf. United States v. LeMaster, 54 F.3d 1224 (6th Cir. 1995).

of his employment, he was required to obtain a Department of Defense Security Clearance. To this end, Gulton's security officer asked respondent to fill out a "Worksheet For Preparation of Personnel Security Questionnaire."

In response to a question on the worksheet asking whether he had ever been charged with any violation of law, respondent failed to disclose that in 1978 he had been convicted of mail fraud, in violation of 18 U.S.C. § 1341. In describing his employment history, respondent falsely stated that he had been employed by two companies that had in fact never employed him. The Gulton security officer typed these false representations onto a form entitled "Department of Defense Personnel Security Questionnaire." Respondent reviewed the typed document for errors and signed a certification stating that his answers were "true, complete, and correct to the best of [his] knowledge" and that he understood "that any misrepresentation or false statement . . . may subject [him] to prosecution under section 1001 of the United States Criminal Code."

After witnessing respondent's signature, Gulton's security officer mailed the typed form to the Defense Industrial Security Clearance Office for processing. Government investigators subsequently discovered that respondent had submitted false statements on the security questionnaire. Confronted with this discovery, respondent acknowledged that he had responded falsely to questions regarding his criminal record and employment history. On the basis of these false statements, respondent was charged with three counts in violation of § 1001.

At trial, respondent admitted to having actual knowledge of the falsity of the statements he had submitted in response to the Department of Defense security questionnaire. He explained that he had made the false statements so that information on the security questionnaire would be consistent with similar fabrications he had submitted to Gulton in his employment application. Respondent's sole defense at trial was that he had no actual knowledge that his false statements would be transmitted to a federal agency.[16]

Consistent with this defense, respondent requested a jury instruction requiring the Government to prove not only that he had actual knowledge that his statements were false at the time they were made, but also that he had actual knowledge that those statements were made in a matter within the jurisdiction of a federal agency. The District Court rejected that request and instead instructed the jury that the Government must prove that respondent "knew or should have known that the information was to be submitted to a government agency." Respondent's objection to this instruction was overruled, and the jury returned convictions on all three counts charged in the indictment.

The Court of Appeals for the Ninth Circuit reversed, holding that the District Court had erred in failing to give respondent's requested instruction. The Court of Appeals read the statutory terms "knowingly and willfully" to modify both the conduct of

---

16. Respondent maintained this defense despite the fact that both the worksheet and the questionnaire made reference to the Department of Defense, and the security questionnaire signed by respondent was captioned "Defense Department." The latter document also contained a reference to the "Defense Industrial Security Clearance Office," stated that respondent's work would require access to "secret" material, and informed respondent that his signature would grant "permission to the Department of Defense to obtain and review copies of [his] medical and institutional records." Nevertheless, respondent testified that he had not read the form carefully before signing it and thus had not noticed either the words "Department of Defense" on the first page or the certification printed above the signature block.

making false statements and the circumstances that they be made "in any matter within the jurisdiction of [a federal agency]." The court therefore concluded that "as an essential element of a section 1001 violation, the government must prove beyond a reasonable doubt that the defendant knew at the time he made the false statement that it was made in a matter within the jurisdiction of a federal agency." [708 F.2d] at 371. The Court of Appeals rejected the Government's argument that the "reasonably foreseeable" standard provided by the District Court's jury instructions satisfied any element of intent possibly associated with the requirement that false statements be made within federal agency jurisdiction.

The decision of the Court of Appeals for the Ninth Circuit conflicts with decisions by the three other Courts of Appeals that have considered the issue. We granted certiorari to resolve the conflict, and now reverse.

II

The only issue presented in this case is whether Congress intended the terms "knowingly and willfully" in § 1001 to modify the statute's jurisdictional language, thereby requiring the Government to prove that false statements were made with actual knowledge of federal agency jurisdiction. The issue thus presented is one of statutory interpretation. Accordingly, we turn first to the language of the statute.

A

. . . The statutory language requiring that knowingly false statements be made "in any matter within the jurisdiction of any department or agency of the United States" is a jurisdictional requirement. Its primary purpose is to identify the factor that makes the false statement an appropriate subject for federal concern. Jurisdictional language need not contain the same culpability requirement as other elements of the offense. Indeed, we have held that "the existence of the fact that confers federal jurisdiction need not be one in the mind of the actor at the time he perpetrates the act made criminal by the federal statute." United States v. Feola, 420 U.S. 671, 676-677, n.9 (1975). Certainly in this case, the statutory language makes clear that Congress did not intend the terms "knowingly and willfully" to establish the standard of culpability for the jurisdictional element of § 1001. The jurisdictional language appears in a phrase separate from the prohibited conduct modified by the terms "knowingly and willfully." Any natural reading of § 1001, therefore, establishes that the terms "knowingly and willfully" modify only the making of "false, fictitious or fraudulent statements," and not the predicate circumstance that those statements be made in a matter within the jurisdiction of a federal agency. Once this is clear, there is no basis for requiring proof that the defendant had actual knowledge of federal agency jurisdiction. The statute contains no language suggesting any additional element of intent, such as a requirement that false statements be "knowingly made in a matter within federal agency jurisdiction," or "with the intent to deceive the Federal Government." On its face, therefore, § 1001 requires that the government prove that false statements were made knowingly and willfully, and it unambiguously dispenses with any requirement that the Government also prove that those statements were made with actual knowledge of federal agency jurisdiction.

Respondent's argument that the legislative history of the statute supports a contrary interpretation is unpersuasive. . . .

III

Respondent argues that absent proof of actual knowledge of federal agency jurisdiction, § 1001 becomes a "trap for the unwary," imposing criminal sanctions on "wholly innocent conduct." Whether or not respondent fairly may characterize the intentional and deliberate lies prohibited by the statute (and manifest in this case) as "wholly innocent conduct," this argument is not sufficient to overcome the express statutory language of § 1001. Respondent does not argue that Congress lacks the power to impose criminal sanctions for deliberately false statements submitted to a federal agency, regardless of whether the person who made such statements actually knew that they were being submitted to the Federal Government. That is precisely what Congress has done here. In the unlikely event that § 1001 could be the basis for imposing an unduly harsh result on those who intentionally make false statements to the Federal Government, it is for Congress and not this Court to amend the criminal statute.[17]

IV

Both the plain language and the legislative history establish that proof of actual knowledge of federal agency jurisdiction is not required under § 1001. Accordingly, we reverse the decision of the Court of Appeals to the contrary.

It is so ordered.

Justice REHNQUIST, with whom Justice BRENNAN, Justice STEVENS, and Justice O'CONNOR join, dissenting.

It is common ground that in a prosecution for the making of false statements the Government must prove that the defendant actually knew that the statements were false at the time he made them. The question presented here is whether the Government must also prove that the defendant actually knew that his statements were made in a matter within "the jurisdiction of any department or agency of the United States." The Court concludes that the plain language and the legislative history of 18 U.S.C. § 1001 conclusively establish that the statute is intended to reach false statements made without actual knowledge of federal involvement in the subject matter of the false statements. I cannot agree.

---

17. In the context of this case, respondent's argument that § 1001 is a "trap for the unwary" is particularly misplaced. It is worth noting that the jury was instructed, without objection from the prosecution, that the Government must prove that respondent "knew or should have known" that his false statements were made within the jurisdiction of a federal agency. As the Government did not object to the reasonable foreseeability instruction, it is unnecessary for us to decide whether that instruction erroneously read a culpability requirement into the jurisdictional phrase. Moreover, the only question presented in this case is whether the Government must prove that the false statement was made with *actual* knowledge of federal agency jurisdiction. The jury's finding that federal agency jurisdiction was reasonably foreseeable by the defendant, combined with the requirement that the defendant had actual knowledge of the falsity of those statements, precludes the possibility that criminal penalties were imposed on the basis of innocent conduct.

The Court nonetheless proceeds on the assumption that *some* lesser culpability standard is required in § 1001 prosecutions, but declines to decide what that lesser standard is. Even if I agreed with the Court that actual knowledge of federal involvement is not required here, I could not agree with the Court's disposition of this case because it reverses the Court of Appeals without determining for itself, or remanding for the lower court to determine, whether the jury instructions in respondent's case were proper. I think that our certiorari jurisdiction is best exercised to resolve conflicts in statutory construction, and not simply to decide whether a jury in a particular case was correctly charged as to the elements of the offense. But here the Court, in a remarkable display of left-footedness, accomplishes neither result: reading its opinion from beginning to end, one neither knows what the congressionally intended element of intent is, nor whether the jury was properly instructed in this case. . . .

I respectfully dissent.

UNITED STATES v. GREEN
745 F.2d 1205 (9th Cir. 1984)

SKOPIL, Circuit Judge.

Green appeals his conviction on one count of mail fraud under 18 U.S.C. § 1341 and one count of filing a false official statement in violation of 18 U.S.C. § 1001. We affirm.

FACTS AND PROCEEDINGS BELOW

Appellant John Green was the quality assurance director for Con-Chem, Inc. ("Con-Chem"), a Los Angeles manufacturer of chemical coatings. In 1978 Con-Chem attempted to secure a contract with Bechtel Power Corporation ("Bechtel") to supply coatings for use in the "Level I area" of a nuclear power plant at Hope Creek, New Jersey. The Level I area consists of a chamber housing the reactor and cooling system and is a critical area of the nuclear plant from a safety standpoint.

In order for Con-Chem coatings to qualify for use in Level I areas they were required by the Nuclear Regulatory Commission ("NRC") to pass safety-related tests. Con-Chem began a testing program to obtain approval for Level I use of its coatings in 1977; the program came under the direction of Green in 1978.

Con-Chem's coatings performed poorly. Because testing indicated that Con-Chem materials were not suitable for Level I use, Green falsified the test report and delivered it to Bechtel. Later, Green sent Bechtel photographs which purportedly depicted tested samples. The samples in the photographs were actually new samples which had not been tested.

Several months later, a Con-Chem employee informed the FBI of Green's falsifications. [After his indictment on four counts of mail fraud and one count of making a false statement, Green was convicted on one of the mail fraud counts and on the false statements charge.]

2. JURY INSTRUCTIONS . . .

B. Merits . . .

(3)   Jurisdictional Knowledge

Green argues that it was error for the district court not to have instructed on jurisdictional knowledge. He relies on our decision in United States v. Yermian, 708 F.2d 365 (9th Cir. 1983), rev'd, 104 S. Ct. 2936 (1984). In reversing this count, the Supreme Court specifically held that actual knowledge that a matter is within the jurisdiction of a federal agency is not required in order to establish a violation of section 1001. The Supreme Court found it unnecessary to decide, however, whether some other less culpable mental state must be proved with respect to federal agency jurisdiction.

We are now squarely presented with the question reserved in *Yermian.* In deciding this matter of first impression, we have carefully reviewed the Supreme Court's decision in *Yermian* as well as the language and legislative history of section 1001. We are persuaded that no mental state is required with respect to federal involvement in order to establish a violation of section 1001.

First, no mental state with respect to federal jurisdiction is evident from the language of section 1001. There are simply no adverbs or phrases modifying the jurisdictional requirement. As the Supreme Court observed in *Yermian*:

> [t]he statutory language requiring that knowingly false statements be made "in any matter within the jurisdiction of any department or agency of the United States" is a jurisdictional requirement. Its primary purpose is to identify the factor that makes the false statements an appropriate subject for federal concern.

Id. at 2940. . . .

Finally, appellant argues that absent some state of mind requirement, section 1001 becomes a "trap for the unwary." To the contrary, the Court in *Yermian,* in response to this argument noted that "[i]n the unlikely event that § 1001 could be the basis for imposing an unduly harsh result on those who intentionally make false statements to the Federal Government, it is for Congress and not this court to amend the criminal statute." 104 S. Ct. at 2943. The short response to appellant's concern that absent a culpability requirement section 1001 becomes a trap for the unwary therefore is simply that Congress intended to cut a broadcloth.

While we understand appellant's concerns, we observe that section 1001 explicitly incorporates certain limitations which guard against its being so highly penal as to be infirm. First, in order to be within the scope of section 1001, the false statement must involve a matter within federal agency jurisdiction at the time it was made. Second, a person is guilty of violating section 1001 only if he "knowingly and willfully" makes a false statement. A person who knowingly and willfully makes a false statement cannot be deemed to have engaged in entirely innocent conduct. Finally, section 1001 has been construed as being applicable only to material misstatements or falsehoods.

No culpable mental state must be proved with respect to federal agency jurisdiction in order to establish a violation of section 1001. The trial judge did not abuse his discretion in refusing to give an instruction on jurisdictional knowledge.

Affirmed.

Notes and Questions

1. Reconsider the situation in *Yermian*. Suppose the only document Yermian falsified was his employment application and that the position he applied for did not require a security check. On the strength of the application, Gulton Industries hired him. A few years later, his supervisor decided to promote him to a more responsible position. Without consulting him, the supervisor attached Yermian's employment application to a letter to the Defense Department, recommending that Yermian be given a security clearance. During a review of the documentation, Yermian's false assertion that he had never been arrested was discovered. Did Yermian violate § 1001 under this variation of the facts? Does *Green* leave us rudderless on the question of what relationship the jurisdictional element bears to the other elements of a § 1001 violation? Does *Yermian* provide any better guidance?

VI. MULTIPLE PUNISHMENT

The Double Jeopardy Clause extends three discrete protections to criminal defendants. It prohibits prosecution for the same offense following conviction, prosecution for the same offense following acquittal, and imposition of multiple punishments for the same offense.[18] Although the Supreme Court has struggled for years to construct a coherent theory of when offenses are the "same" in this context, its most enduring test is found in Blockburger v. United States.[19] Under *Blockburger*, offenses are not the same for double jeopardy purposes if each requires proof of an element that the other does not. If each offense requires proof of a fact that is not required by the other, *Blockburger* permits imposition of multiple punishments, even though the evidence required to establish each of the crimes may substantially overlap.

UNITED STATES v. RAMOS
725 F.2d 1322 (11th Cir. 1984)

RONEY, Circuit Judge.

Defendant Reynaldo de Jesus Ramos was indicted, convicted, and sentenced for giving a false name, place, and date of birth and using false papers in applying for a passport in violation of 18 U.S.C. § 1001, and for making a false statement with the intent to secure a passport in violation of 18 U.S.C. § 1542. The defendant appeals his conviction on three grounds: (1) the trial court erred in convicting and sentencing him under both statutes because the same act and the same evidence constituted both offenses; (2) insufficiency of the evidence; and (3) the erroneous admission of hearsay testimony. We affirm.

---

18. North Carolina v. Pearce, 395 U.S. 711 (1969).
19. 284 U.S. 299 (1932).

The Supreme Court has recently reaffirmed that "where the same act or transaction constitutes a violation of two distinct statutory provisions, the test to be applied to determine whether there are two offenses or only one, is whether each provision requires proof of a fact which the other does not," Albernaz v. United States, 450 U.S. 333 (1981).

Ramos was sentenced to two concurrent two-year sentences under 18 U.S.C. § 1001 (Counts I and II), and a consecutive three-year term of probation under 18 U.S.C. § 1542 (Count III).

Section 1001 provides for penalties for

[w]hoever, in any matter within the jurisdiction of any department or agency of the United States knowingly and willfully falsifies, conceals or covers up by any trick, scheme, or device a material fact, or makes any false, fictitious, or fraudulent statements or representations, or makes or uses any false writing or document knowing the same to contain any false, fictitious, or fraudulent statement or entry.

Section 1542 penalizes

[w]hoever willfully and knowingly makes any false statement in an application for passport with intent to induce or secure the issuance of a passport under the authority of the United States, either for his own use or the use of another, contrary to the laws regulating the issuance of passports or the rules prescribed pursuant to such laws.

Properly applied § 1001 requires proof that the false statement be of a material fact, an element not needed for § 1542 where "any false statement" is sufficient. On the other hand, § 1542 requires that the false statement be made "with the intent to induce or secure . . . a passport." Although intent to deceive is necessary in § 1001, intent to defraud, that is "to deprive someone of something by means of deceit" is not. Thus, the *Blockburger* test is met. There are two offenses involved. The district court did not err in convicting and sentencing the defendant under both §§ 1001 and 1542.

This holding is consistent with the outcome in other cases in which convictions and sentences under both § 1001 and a more specific section have been challenged for multiplicity. See e.g., United States v. Carter, 526 F.2d 1276, 1278 (5th Cir. 1976) (§ 645(a) does not supplant § 1001; "§ 1001 requires a showing of materiality . . . § 645(a) requires that false statement be made for the purpose of influencing the action of the [Small Business Administration (SBA)], and does not require the government to show that the particular statement would have, in fact, affected the action of the SBA"); United States v. Diogo, 320 F.2d 898, 902 (2d Cir. 1963) (false statements to immigration authorities in violation of §§ 1001 and 1546).

Defendant's challenge to the sufficiency of the evidence on the question of the materiality of the misrepresentations is without merit. A material misrepresentation is one which has "a natural tendency to influence, or be capable of affecting or influencing, a government function." United States v. McGough, 510 F.2d 598, 602 (5th Cir. 1975). Defendant's false statement as to his name and identity is indisputably material to the agency's decisions whether to grant his passport application. The evidence presented by the government was sufficient to establish materiality. . . .

Affirmed.

Notes and Questions

1. What brought Ramos's conduct within the reach of § 1001? What brought it under § 1542? In what sense are the two crimes the same? In what sense are they different for double jeopardy purposes?[20]

VII. RELATED THEORIES OF LIABILITY

A. PROCUREMENT FRAUD

The canopy switching scheme in *Steiner Plastics* was intended to trick the government into accepting and paying for goods that failed to meet contract specifications. This is one of countless examples of procurement fraud, the most costly form of fraud against the federal government. In fiscal years 1986 and 1987, procurement fraud caused the Department of Defense alone losses of more than $99 million.[21] As *Steiner Plastics* illustrates, the false statements statute is a useful enforcement tool in this context. But when Congress specifically addressed this issue in the late 1980s, it demanded more stringent sanctions in a major new procurement fraud statute.

Modeled in part on the mail fraud statute, the Major Fraud Act of 1988 prohibits knowingly executing or attempting to execute a scheme to defraud the government or to fraudulently obtain money or property by making false or fraudulent representations relating to government contracts worth more than $1 million. In recognition of the complexity of major fraud investigations, prosecutions instituted under this provision are governed by a seven-year statute of limitations. Maximum criminal penalties vary depending on the magnitude of the fraud and the risk of personal injury, and convictions involving Defense Department contracts are punishable by temporary or long-term debarment.

UNITED STATES v. BROOKS
111 F.3d 365 (4th Cir. 1997)

NIEMEYER, Circuit Judge.

This case requires us to interpret for the first time the $1 million jurisdictional amount requirement of 18 U.S.C. § 1031(a), criminalizing "major fraud" against the United States.

Defendants Edwin Brooks, his sons John and Stephen Brooks, and their company, B&D Electric Supply, Inc., were charged with several crimes in relation to two

---

20. For examples of other contexts in which prosecutions under overlapping statutes have been unsuccessfully challenged on double jeopardy grounds see United States v. Woodward, 469 U.S. 105 (1985) (upholding convictions under both § 1001 and the currency reporting statute for failing to disclose the amount of currency the defendant was carrying); United States v. Beacon Brass Co., 344 U.S. 43 (1952) (indictment charging willful attempt to evade taxes by making a false statement, in violation of the Internal Revenue Code, and with making a false statement within the jurisdiction of a government agency, in violation of § 1001, is not duplicitous).

21. S. Rep. No. 503, 100th Cong., 2d Sess. 2 (1988).

subcontracts to provide electrical components to prime contractors engaged in refitting ships for the United States Navy. All four defendants were convicted of trafficking in counterfeit goods, in violation of 18 U.S.C. § 220(a), and of conspiracy to defraud the United States and to traffic in counterfeit goods, in violation of 18 U.S.C. § 371. Edwin Brooks, John Brooks, and B&D Electric were also convicted of "major fraud" against the United States in violation of 18 U.S.C. § 1031(a). . . .

I

The three Brooks defendants were operators of B&D Electric Supply, Inc., a marine electrical supply business which sold electrical parts to both civilian and military customers. The majority of B&D Electric's business consisted of reselling new components produced by well-established manufacturers of electrical parts. But B&D Electric also sold some electrical components which it custom-assembled, often out of used parts.

The charges at issue in this case arose from supply contracts that B&D Electric had with two prime contractors engaged by the United States Navy to refit several ships. B&D Electric contracted with the Jonathan Corporation to supply fourteen shipboard motor controllers meeting military specifications for a total price of $51,544. B&D Electric itself assembled these controllers from components but affixed to the controllers trademarks of the Cutler-Hammer Company, an approved military supplier of controllers. B&D Electric also supplied Ingalls Shipbuilding, Inc., with six rotary switches for a total price of $1,470, representing the switches as new when B&D Electric actually had assembled or rebuilt them. The dollar amount of the prime contract between Jonathan Corporation and the Navy was greater than $9 million, and prime contract between Ingalls Shipbuilding and the Navy was greater than $5 million.

II

Edwin Brooks, John Brooks, and B&D Electric challenge their convictions for major fraud against the United States in violation of 18 U.S.C. § 1031(a), on the jurisdictional ground that their two subcontracts did not satisfy the $1 million value prescribed by the statute. While the government does not dispute that the defendants' subcontracts were for amounts less than $1 million, it argues that the statute's jurisdictional requirement is established so long as the prime contract with the United States or any part thereof is worth $1 million. The issue is one of first impression for us.

As with all questions of statutory interpretation, we begin with the language of the statute, which provides:

Whoever knowingly executes, or attempts to execute, any scheme or artifice with the intent —

(1) to defraud the United States; or
(2) to obtain money or property by means of false or fraudulent pretenses, representations, or promises,

in any procurement of property or services as a prime contractor with the United States or as a subcontractor or supplier on a contract in which there is a prime contract with the United States, *if the value of the contract, subcontract, or any constituent part thereof, for such property or services is $1,000,000 or more* shall, subject to the applicability of subsection (c) of this section, be fined not more than $1,000,000, or imprisoned not more than 10 years, or both.

18 U.S.C. § 1031(a) (emphasis added). From a straightforward reading of this statute, we conclude that regardless of its privity with the United States, any contractor or supplier involved with a prime contract with the United States who commits fraud with the requisite intent is guilty so long as the prime contract, a subcontract, a supply agreement, or any constituent part of such a contract is valued at $1 million or more.

This reading recognizes that the seriousness of this species of fraud is measured not merely by the out-of-pocket financial loss incurred on a particular subcontract, but also by the potential consequences of the fraud for persons and property. In military contracts in particular, fraud in the provision of small and inexpensive parts can have major effects, destroying or making inoperable multi-million dollar systems or equipment, injuring service people, and compromising military readiness. By extending the statute's coverage even to minor contractors and suppliers whose fraudulent actions could undermine major operations, Congress enabled prosecutors to combat effectively the severe procurement fraud problem that Congress identified.

We understand that our reading is contrary to that espoused in dictum by the Second Circuit in United States v. Nadi, 996 F.2d 548 (2d Cir. 1993), the only other court to have interpreted the jurisdictional amount requirement of the major fraud statute. That court stated that for purposes of ascertaining the jurisdictional amount requirement of 18 U.S.C. § 1031(a), "the value of the contract is determined by looking to the *specific* contract upon which the fraud is based." Id. at 551 (emphasis added). It explained that "[t]his reading avoids the potential anomaly of small subcontractors whose subcontracts are valued at far less than $1,000,000 being prosecuted under the Act simply because the prime contract is for $1,000,000 or more." Id. But the jurisdictional amount requirement of the major fraud statute, like any bright line rule, dictates that some cases will fall outside of the scope of the law. We believe that our reading of the statute is no more anomalous than one which allows small subcontractors to escape prosecution under the provision, regardless of the cost of the overall project which their fraud affects, simply by ensuring that their own subcontract stays below the $1 million jurisdictional amount. The *Nadi* court's interpretation could significantly undermine the purpose of the statute because pervasive fraud on a multi-million dollar defense project would be unreachable under the statute, despite Congress' intent, if it were perpetrated in multiple separate subcontracts, each involving less than the jurisdictional amount.

The legislative history also supports our interpretation that the statute reaches fraud where any part of the prime contract or subcontract is valued at $1 million or more. In discussing the steady increase in procurement fraud losses, the Senate described its broad range of concern:

Procurement fraud is the most costly kind of fraud, accounting for about 18 percent of total losses. The Department of Defense reports losses of $99.1 million due to procurement fraud for fiscal years 1986 and 1987.

Prosecutions of individual companies reveal other disturbing facts:

Two corporate officials of Spring Works, Inc., were convicted of deliberately providing defective springs for installation in critical assemblies of the CH-47 helicopters, the Cruise Missile and the F-18 and B-1 aircraft.

Two corporate officials of MKB Manufacturing were sentenced for their role in the deliberate provision of defective gas pistons for installation in the M60 machine gun. Installation of the defective part would cause the machine gun to jam.

Thus, the evidence shows that besides causing financial losses, procurement fraud could cause the loss of life of American soldiers and could threaten national security.

These facts compel a legislative response.

S. Rep. No. 100-503, at 2 (1988), reprinted in 1988 U.S.C.C.A.N. 5969, 5969-70. The parts at issue in the Spring Works case were 21-cent springs, and the total value of the subcontract was $160.25. Yet, it was fraud like that perpetrated by Spring Works to which Congress was responding in 1988 with enactment of the major fraud statute. Undoubtedly, Congress was concerned with more than the most direct and narrow financial effects of fraud committed against the United States.

The legislative history also illuminates the meaning of the phrase in § 1031(a) at issue here, "value of the contract." In the section-by-section analysis, the Senate report states:

Section 1031(a) applies to procurement fraud "if the value of the contract, subcontract, or any constituent part thereof . . . is $1,000,000 or more." The phrase "value of the contract" refers to the value of the contract award, or the amount the government has agreed to pay to the provider of services whether or not this sum represents a profit to the contracting company. Furthermore, a subcontractor awarded a subcontract valued at $1,000,000 or more is covered by this section, regardless of the amount of the contract award to the contractor or other subcontractors.

S. Rep. No. 100-503, at 12 (1988), reprinted in 1988 U.S.C.C.A.N. 5969, 5975-76. Thus, for example, if a prime contractor had entered into three separate contracts, agreeing under each to supply the United States with $750,000 worth of equipment, but entered into a single supply contract with a subcontractor for $1 million worth of parts, the subcontractor would be covered by the Act. This Senate report explanation supports the interpretation that the statute applies to the entire procurement effort where any contractual component has a value of $1 million or more, so that a court should not confine its inquiry with regard to the jurisdictional amount of § 1031(a) to the value of the subcontract under which the fraud was perpetrated. As § 1031(a) provides, the statute applies to a government contractor, subcontractor, or supplier if "any constituent part" of the contract is worth more than $1 million.

Accordingly, the district court in this case did not err in taking into account the contract values of the Navy's prime contracts with Jonathan Corporation and Ingalls Shipbuilding. . . .

Affirmed.

Notes and Questions

1. Is it clear that Congress intended to bring subcontractors whose contracts are worth less than $1 million within the reach of the statute? If the value of the subcontract controls when it meets the $1 million requirement, why shouldn't it also control when it fails to meet that threshold amount?

2. Consider a hypothetical supplier who contracts to supply bubble wrap and other packing insulation to an electronics manufacturer. The contract specifies a rate of payment based on the cost of producing the insulation, but provides that the total contract price shall not exceed $5,000. Under the contract formula, the supplier's cost of producing the insulation is $4,200. Instead of billing this amount, the supplier overstates production costs by a modest amount and bills the manufacturer $4,800.

The electronics manufacturer, a subcontractor in a major Defense Department project, will use the insulation for shipping electronic components to the prime contractor. The prime contractor will pay the manufacturer a contract price of $500,000 for the components. The value of the prime contract with the government is $5 million. Has the bubble wrap supplier violated the Major Fraud Act? Does it matter whether the supplier knew the value of the prime contract?

UNITED STATES v. SAIN
141 F.3d 463 (3d Cir. 1998)

ROSENN, Circuit Judge.

[Sain and his company, Advanced Environmental Consultants (AEC), entered into a contract with the Army to construct and operate an industrial waste-water treatment plant. After AEC began to perform the contract, the Army modified the contract to incorporate a higher water purity standard, which increased AEC's performance costs. AEC submitted a series of inflated claims for reimbursement of costs associated with the contract changes. Among other things, AEC falsified the level of pollutants found in the water and misrepresented the grade and quantity of carbon it used in the purification process. AEC substantiated its false claims with bogus checks and purchase orders. Sain and AEC were convicted of 46 counts of fraud in violation of the Major Fraud Act. Sain argued on appeal that he was improperly charged with committing a separate violation of the Act for each false claim he submitted.]

III . . .

C . . .

By its plain language, the statute criminalizes each knowing "*execution*" of the fraudulent scheme and not simply devising the fraudulent scheme itself. The statute's contemplation that defendants could be convicted of "multiple counts" supports this reading. See 18 U.S.C. § 1031(c) (providing for a maximum fine of $10 million for defendants convicted of "multiple counts"). Our reading of the statute is consistent with this and other circuits' interpretation of the bank fraud statute, 18 U.S.C. § 1344,[22] which contains language virtually identical to the Major Fraud Act. "The circuits that have addressed multiplicity in the context of bank fraud have consistently held that the . . . statute 'punishes each execution of a fraudulent scheme rather than each act in furtherance of such a scheme.'" United States v. Harris, 79 F.3d 223, 232 (2d Cir. 1996) (collecting cases from the Third, Fifth, Seventh, Ninth, and Tenth circuits).

Our determination that a defendant may be punished for each knowing execution of the fraudulent scheme does not end the inquiry, however. Not every act in furtherance of a fraudulent scheme is a separate "execution" of the scheme. In determining whether an action is a separate execution of a fraudulent scheme, courts look to whether the actions are substantively and chronologically independent from the overall scheme. See *Harris*, 79 F.3d at 232. In the instant case, each of the 46 false claims constituted a separate execution of the scheme. Each was substantively independent from the overall scheme because each sought to obtain a separate amount of money from the government and caused the government a distinct loss. There is no evidence that the defendants had determined a specific amount of money that they wanted to obtain and took several steps to get that single amount. Rather, the evidence established that the defendants intended to obtain as much money as possible. Further, the false claims were chronologically distinct from each other in that each was submitted weeks or months apart over an approximately three-and-one-half-year period. In sum, we hold that a defendant may be separately punished under the Major Fraud Act for each execution of the fraudulent scheme and that each of Sain's false claims constituted a chronologically and substantially separate execution of the fraudulent scheme. . . .

IV

Accordingly, the judgment and sentence of the district court will be affirmed.

Notes and Questions

1. Why would Congress choose to punish "each execution" of the scheme rather than the fraudulent scheme itself? In the context of the mail fraud statute, the answer seems relatively clear. By invoking the use of the mails as the jurisdictional base, the statute does indirectly what it cannot directly do. Since the underlying rationale is the need to protect the integrity of the United States mails, the mail fraud statute punishes each use of the mails in furtherance of the fraudulent scheme whether or not Congress could directly punish the fraud itself. Are the same considerations at work in the context of the Major Fraud Act?

---

22. The bank fraud statute provides:

Whoever knowingly executes, or attempts to execute, a scheme or artifice — (1) to defraud a financial institution; or (2) to obtain any of the moneys, funds, credits, assets, securities, or other property owned by, or under the custody or control of, a financial institution, by means of false or fraudulent pretenses, representations, or promises; shall be fined not more than $1,000,000 or imprisoned not more than 30 years or both.

2. Is the court's approach to determining what constitutes a separate execution sound?

3. Suppose AEC had submitted only one inflated claim for reimbursement. When would the execution be complete? When the bogus claim was filed? When it was paid? Why is this an important issue? Cf. United States v. Reitmeyer, 356 F.3d 1313 (10th Cir. 2004).

B. FALSE CLAIMS

The false claims statute, 18 U.S.C. § 287, punishes knowingly making false, fictitious, or fraudulent claims against the government for money or property. The false claims statute has been used extensively in procurement fraud cases, and its coverage frequently overlaps the false statements statute and the Major Fraud Act. But unlike those provisions, the false claims statute requires that a claim for money or property be physically presented to the government.

UNITED STATES v. MAHER

582 F.2d 842 (4th Cir. 1978)

K. K. HALL, Circuit Judge.

Defendant, Alvin Michael Maher, appeals his criminal conviction on eleven counts of filing false, fictitious, or fraudulent claims with the United States government in violation of the False Claims Act, 18 U.S.C. § 287. The primary issue presented in this appeal is whether the district court properly instructed the jury that under § 287 the criminal intent essential for conviction is not limited to a specific intent to defraud. At trial, the defendant conceded the basic facts of the government's case but maintained he was innocent because he acted without a specific intent to defraud the government. . . .

At trial, the government presented evidence showing that, during the year in which defendant was promoted from vice-president to president of his corporate employer, he caused false vouchers to be submitted to an agency of the federal government requesting payments totalling approximately $68,000 more than should have been paid to his employer under its contracts with that agency. The defendant contended that he did so with no intent to cheat the government or to gain unfair advantage for himself or his company.

During the time in question, defendant worked for General Environments Corporation ("GEC"), which tested equipment and conducted experiments for various commercial and government clients. GEC's contracts with these clients could be categorized as either "fixed-price" contracts or "time-and-materials" contracts, depending upon the manner in which GEC was to be paid for its work. Under its "fixed-price" contracts, GEC agreed to perform experiments for a certain amount and to bill periodically on the basis of percentage of completion. Under its "time-and-materials" contracts, GEC agreed to perform experiments for a price *not to exceed* a certain amount and to bill periodically on the basis of the amount of labor and materials actually employed in the experiments up to the date of billing. According to the defendant's theory of defense, it was GEC's practice, at least for its contracts with government clients, to stop work on an experiment and seek additional funding from the client any-time GEC's costs met or exceeded its contract price. This practice was followed for such "cost overruns" under both "fixed-price" contracts and "time-and-materials" contracts.

During 1972, one of GEC's government clients was the Mobility Equipment Research and Development Center ("MERDC") of the Department of the Army of Fort Belvoir, Virginia. GEC and MERDC entered into various "time-and-materials" contracts most of which required GEC to conduct several experiments, or "tasks," with separate maximum prices allocated to each task. The hourly rate to be billed by GEC included its overhead and profit and varied according to the classification of labor utilized for each task. GEC billed MERDC monthly for work on these "time-and-materials" contracts. Its monthly billings were prepared by the company bookkeeper based upon time sheets which were filled out and signed by the GEC employees who worked on the MERDC contracts.

In 1972 the defendant became president of GEC. During that year, before and after his promotion, whenever the bookkeeper submitted MERDC billings to the defendant for his approval, he instructed her to change them to reflect more hours than were shown on the employees' time sheets. She made the billing changes that he specified, prepared new time sheets to conform to those billing changes, traced over the employees' signatures on the new time sheets and destroyed the original ones. The defendant told her these changes were necessary because the employees did not know to which contract they should charge their hours and that their signatures had to be traced because there was not time to have the employees sign the revised time sheets. Three GEC project managers, whose time sheets had been altered, testified that, in fact, they knew on which contracts they were working and that they recorded hours on their time sheets according to time spent working on those contracts. They said they were never told that they made errors on their time sheets. The defendant testified that no one in the government knew GEC was billing for the fictitious hours and that he did not discuss his practice of having hours changed on company time sheets with anyone at GEC. Approximately 5,300 fictitious hours, representing $68,000 in false claims, were billed on these MERDC contracts as a result of the defendant's instructions to the bookkeeper. The bookkeeper testified that the practice of changing time sheets ended when defendant left GEC in November, 1973.

Defendant admitted giving these instructions but maintained he was innocent because he acted for a legitimate business purpose and without a motive to defraud the government. He testified that he knew the MERDC contracts were to be paid at an hourly rate for work actually performed, but nevertheless thought they should be billed on the same basis as "fixed-price" contracts, that is, if he considered work on a MERDC task to be one half complete, he should have the bookkeeper bill one half of the maximum price allocated to that task regardless of the amount of labor actually employed.

Defendant testified that this approach to billing for the MERDC tasks furthered a legitimate business purpose because these tasks were experiments which could not be performed efficiently if they were delayed pending receipt of additional funding each time a cost overrun occurred. When cost overruns did occur, GEC would not get additional contracts and the government would not get fair value for its money. Consistent with this defense, he claimed he knew employees were adjusting hours on their time sheets to prevent cost overruns and delays in their work. One GEC project manager testified that he charged hours on his own time sheets which were actually spent working on MERDC tasks to "fixed-price" contracts in order to prevent cost over-runs and delays in completion of those "fixed-price" contracts pending GEC's request for additional funding. Defendant testified that he was aware that some hours were shifted away from MERDC contracts and he wanted to shift them back "to make it come out even." Therefore, in all, he contended that he would have the MERDC tasks billed on the basis of his personal estimations of the percentage each task was completed rather than on the amount of labor employed as shown on the employees' time sheets.

The primary issue presented in this appeal is whether the intent essential for conviction under § 287 is limited to an intent to defraud. This statute reads as follows:

> Whoever makes or presents to any person or officer in the civil, military, or naval service of the United States, or to any department or agency thereof, any claim upon or against the United States, or any department or agency thereof, knowing such claim to be false, fictitious, or fraudulent, shall be fined not more than $10,000 or imprisoned not more than five years, or both.

18 U.S.C. § 287. . . .

The defendant contends that the court committed error in refusing to instruct the jury that the intent essential for conviction under § 287 is limited to a specific intent to defraud the government. The instructions proffered by defendant on his theory of defense, which the court refused to give, implied that unless the jury found that in submitting the false claims the defendant acted with a purpose to either cheat the government or to unjustly benefit himself or his company, he should be found innocent. We disagree. . . .

First, we do not find that the statute specifies an intent to defraud as an element to be proved under § 287. The language of the statute states the terms, "false, fictitious or fraudulent," in the disjunctive, and we interpret this to mean that three kinds of claims may be submitted in violation of § 287 and not merely claims which are fraudulent. The statute is silent on motive and criminal intent and only specifies that the claims be submitted with a knowledge that they are false, fictitious or fraudulent. . . .

[W]e think that § 287 does not require proof of a specific intent to defraud, as defendant defines that term, because the purpose of § 287 will not be furthered by limiting criminal prosecutions to instances where the defendant is motivated solely by an intent to cheat the government or to gain an unjust benefit. The plain purpose of § 287 is to assure the integrity of claims and vouchers submitted to the government. Federal criminal statutes written in language similar to § 287 which have specified intent to defraud as an element to be proved have been interpreted to require only proof that the defendant acted "for the purpose of impairing, obstructing, or defeating" a lawful function of the government. Pina v. United States, 165 F.2d 890, 893 (9th Cir. 1948). In *Pina*, it was held as well-settled, that "the contemplated infliction of a monetary loss upon the Government is not a necessary ingredient of an intent to defraud the United States." 165 F.2d at 893. Such an interpretation is consistent with common law, in that, a common law prosecution for forging or for uttering a false writing could not be defended by a showing that the defendant's purpose was only to use the false writing as a device to collect a bona fide debt. . . .

Therefore, judgment of conviction is affirmed.

Notes and Questions

1. The defense in *Maher* was that the billing manipulation served a legitimate business purpose and that the defendant tried to ensure that, in the end, the proper amounts were billed to each project. If that were literally true, should the conduct violate the False Claims Act? What evidence in *Maher* supports a finding of criminal intent?

2. In what respects are False Claims Act violations similar to violations of § 1001? In what sense are they dissimilar?

3. To what extent are violations of the False Claims Act similar to violations of the Major Fraud Act? In what sense are they dissimilar?

4. Although a false statement or a scheme to defraud may be preparatory to the submission of a false claim, the false statements and major fraud statutes allow the government to deal with the problem at a much earlier stage. In view of that difference, when would it be more advantageous for the prosecutor to charge a government contractor with violating the false claims statute instead of a § 1001 violation?

C. CERTIFICATION OF CORPORATE FINANCIAL REPORTS

In response to "growing doubt about whether audited financial statements are believable,"[23] the Sarbanes-Oxley Act makes corporate managers assume responsibility for financial representations their companies make. A new criminal statute, 18 U.S.C. § 1350, requires chief executives and chief financial officers to certify the accuracy of periodic financial reports filed with the SEC. Section 1350 requires CEOs and CFOs to certify in writing that the financial statements comply with SEC reporting requirements and that they fairly present the company's financial condition in all material respects.

An SEC rule implementing the certification requirements requires executives to certify that: (1) they have reviewed the report they are filing; (2) based on their knowledge, the report contains no untrue statement of a material fact and does not omit any material fact necessary to make the statements in the report not misleading; (3) the information included in the report fairly presents the company's financial condition, results or operations, and cash flows in all material respects; and (4) they have disclosed any significant deficiencies in the company's internal controls — and any fraud involving employees who have a significant role in the company's internal controls — to the company's auditors and to the audit committee of the board of directors.[24] Neither the statute nor the SEC rule requires that the certification be sworn.

Section 1350 creates a two-tier system of liability based on the certifying officer's level of culpability. Under § 1350(c)(1), it is a crime to certify a financial report *knowing* that it does not comply with the statutory and SEC regulatory requirements. Under § 1350(c)(2), it is a more serious crime to *willfully* certify a financial report while *knowing* that it does not comply with the statutory requirements.

---

23. S. Rep. No. 107-205, at 25 (2002) (quoting testimony of Richard Breeden, former Chairman of the SEC).

24. See 17 C.F.R. § 240.15d-14 (2002). The rule is promulgated principally to implement § 302 of Sarbanes-Oxley, which imposes more detailed certification requirements than does the criminal statute discussed above.

A comparison of penalties under § 1350 and the false statements statute appears in Table 6-1.

TABLE 6-1
COMPARISON OF FALSE STATEMENT PENALTIES

OFFENSE	MAXIMUM TERM	MAXIMUM FINE
False Statements (18 U.S.C. § 1001)	5 years	$250,000/$500,000 (org.)
False Certifications (18 U.S.C. § 1350)	10 years	$1,000,000
Willful Violation	20 years	$5,000,000

Notes and Questions

1. What is the difference between knowledge and willfulness in this context? When would a corporate officer knowingly certify a false financial report without also willfully certifying it?

2. Section 1350 is captioned "Failure of corporate officers to certify financial reports." Does the statute impose liability for omissions?

3. What is the relationship between § 1350 and § 1001? When would a certification that violated § 1350 not violate § 1001 as well? What does § 1350 accomplish that § 1001 does not? Would a prosecution resulting in a CEO's conviction for violating both § 1350 and § 1001 withstand scrutiny under the double jeopardy test followed by the court in *Ramos*?

4. In the wake of the corporate fraud scandals, several top executives who have been criminally charged have relied on an "I was out of the loop" defense. For example, WorldCom CEO Bernie Ebbers, who presided over the largest corporate fraud scandal in United States history, claimed that he was not detail oriented, was not involved in the company's finances, and didn't understand accounting.[25] What, if any, impact is § 1350 likely to have on the viability of such claims?

---

25. Despite his claim that he didn't know about the fraud, the jury convicted Ebbers of conspiracy, securities fraud, and making a false filing with the SEC.

7

Perjury and False Declarations

I. INTRODUCTION

Two important federal statutes — the perjury statute, 18 U.S.C. § 1621, and the false declarations statute, 18 U.S.C. § 1623 — punish making false statements under oath.[1] These statutes often cover the same territory, for each applies to sworn falsifications made before federal courts and grand juries. The statutes differ, however, in three important respects: (1) the perjury statute applies to a broader range of proceedings, (2) the perjury statute contains more rigorous proof requirements on the issue of falsity, and (3) the false declarations statute provides a limited defense of recantation. These distinctions are explored at greater length below.

II. MAKING MATERIAL FALSE STATEMENTS

The perjury and false declarations statutes punish the making of false statements with respect to a material matter. As is true in prosecutions under § 1001, the test for materiality is not whether the statement has any actual effect on the proceeding, but is, instead, whether the statement has the capacity or tendency to influence the outcome of the proceeding.[2]

BRONSTON v. UNITED STATES
409 U.S. 352 (1973)

Mr. Chief Justice BURGER delivered the opinion of the Court.

We granted the writ in this case to consider a narrow but important question in the application of the federal perjury statute, 18 U.S.C. § 1621: whether a witness may be

---

1. Although liability under each statute is premised on sworn false statements, no particular form of oath is required and no proof is needed to establish that the oath was administered by someone who had authority to do so. All the government must prove is that the falsehood was made after administration of an oath authorized by law. Subornation of perjury is an independent crime. See 18 U.S.C. § 1622.

2. Whether or not a statement is material is a mixed question of law and fact to be determined by the jury. United States v. Gaudin, 515 U.S. 506 (1995).

convicted of perjury for an answer, under oath, that is literally true but not responsive to the question asked and arguably misleading by negative implication.

Petitioner is the sole owner of Samuel Bronston Productions, Inc., a company that between 1958 and 1964, produced motion pictures in various European locations. For these enterprises, Bronston Productions opened bank accounts in a number of foreign countries; in 1962, for example, it had 37 accounts in five countries. As president of Bronston Productions, petitioner supervised transactions involving the foreign bank accounts.

In June of 1964, Bronston Productions petitioned for an arrangement with creditors under Chapter XI of the Bankruptcy Act, 11 U.S.C. §§ 701 et seq. On June 10, 1966, a referee in bankruptcy held a § 21(a) hearing to determine, for the benefit of creditors, the extent and location of the company's assets. Petitioner's perjury conviction was founded on the answers given by him as a witness at that bankruptcy hearing, and in particular on the following colloquy with a lawyer for a creditor of Bronston Productions:

Q: Do you have any bank accounts in Swiss banks, Mr. Bronston?
A: No, sir.
Q: Have you ever?
A: The company had an account there for about six months, in Zurich.
Q: Have you any nominees who have bank accounts in Swiss banks?
A: No, sir.
Q: Have you ever?
A: No, sir.

It is undisputed that for a period of nearly five years, between October 1959 and June 1964, petitioner had a personal bank account at the International Credit Bank in Geneva, Switzerland, into which he made deposits and upon which he drew checks totaling more than $180,000. It is likewise undisputed that petitioner's answers were literally truthful. (a) Petitioner did not at the time of questioning have a Swiss bank account. (b) Bronston Productions, Inc., did have the account in Zurich described by petitioner. (c) Neither at the time of questioning nor before did petitioner have nominees who had Swiss accounts. The Government's prosecution for perjury went forward on the theory that in order to mislead his questioner, petitioner answered the second question with literal truthfulness but unresponsively addressed his answer to the company's assets and not to his own — thereby implying that he had no personal Swiss bank account at the relevant time.

At petitioner's trial, the District Court instructed the jury that the "basic issue" was whether petitioner "spoke his true belief." Perjury, the court stated, "necessarily involves the state of mind of the accused" and "essentially consists of wilfully testifying to the truth of a fact which the defendant does not believe to be true"; petitioner's testimony could not be found "wilfully" false unless at the time his testimony was given petitioner "fully understood the questions put to him but nevertheless gave false answers knowing the same to be false." The court further instructed the jury that if petitioner did not understand the question put to him and for that reason gave an unresponsive answer, he could not be convicted of perjury. Petitioner could, however, be convicted if he gave an answer "not literally false but when considered in the context in which it was given, nevertheless [constituted] a false statement."[3] The jury began its deliberations at 11:30 A.M. Several times it requested exhibits or additional instructions from the court, and at one point, at the request of the jury, the District Court repeated its instructions in full. At 6:10 P.M., the jury returned its verdict, finding petitioner guilty on the count of perjury before us today and not guilty on another charge not here relevant.

In the Court of Appeals, petitioner contended, as he had in post-trial motions before the District Court, that the key question was imprecise and suggestive of various interpretations. In addition, petitioner contended that he could not be convicted of perjury on the basis of testimony that was concededly truthful, however unresponsive. A divided Court of Appeals held that the question was readily susceptible of a responsive reply and that it adequately tested the defendant's belief in the veracity of his answer. The Court of Appeals further held that, "[for] the purposes of 18 U.S.C. § 1621, an answer containing half of the truth which also constitutes a lie by negative implication, when the answer is intentionally given in place of the responsive answer called for by a proper question, is perjury." 453 F.2d 555, 559. In this Court, petitioner renews his attack on the specificity of the question asked him and the legal sufficiency of his answer to support a conviction for perjury. The problem of the ambiguity of the question is not free from doubt, but we need not reach that issue. Even assuming, as we do, that the question asked petitioner specifically focused on petitioner's personal bank accounts, we conclude that the federal perjury statute cannot be construed to sustain a conviction based on petitioner's answer.

The statute, 18 U.S.C. § 1621, substantially identical in its relevant language to its predecessors for nearly a century, is "a federal statute enacted in an effort to keep the course of justice free from the pollution of perjury." United States v. Williams, 341 U.S. 58, 68 (1951). We have held that the general federal perjury provision is applicable to federal bankruptcy proceedings. Hammer v. United States, 271 U.S. 620 (1926). The need for truthful testimony in a § 21(a) bankruptcy proceeding is great, since the proceeding is "a searching inquiry into the condition of the estate of the bankrupt, to assist in discovering and collecting the assets, and to develop facts and circumstances which bear upon the question of discharge." Travis v. United States, 123 F.2d 268, 271 (CA10 1941). Here, as elsewhere, the perpetration of perjury "well may affect the dearest concerns of the parties before a tribunal. . . ." United States v. Norris, 300 U.S. 564, 574 (1937).

---

3. The District Court gave the following example "as an illustration only":

[If] it is material to ascertain how many times a person has entered a store on a given day and that person responds to such a question by saying five times when in fact he knows that he entered the store 50 times that day, that person may be guilty of perjury even though it is technically true that he entered the store five times.

The illustration given by the District Court is hardly comparable to petitioner's answer; the answer "five times" is responsive to the hypothetical question and contains nothing to alert the questioner that he may be sidetracked. Moreover, it is very doubtful that an answer which, in response to a specific quantitative inquiry, baldly understates a numerical fact can be described as even "technically true." Whether an answer is true must be determined with reference to the question it purports to answer, not in isolation. An unresponsive answer is unique in this respect because its unresponsiveness by definition prevents its truthfulness from being tested in the context of the question — unless there is to be speculation as to what the unresponsive answer "implies."

There is, at the outset, a serious literal problem in applying § 1621 to petitioner's answer. The words of the statute confine the offense to the witness who "willfully . . . states . . . any material matter which he does not believe to be true." Beyond question, petitioner's answer to the crucial question was not responsive if we assume, as we do, that the first question was directed at personal bank accounts. There is indeed an implication in the answer to the second question that there was never a personal bank account; in casual conversation this interpretation might reasonably be drawn. But we are not dealing with casual conversation and the statute does not make it a criminal act for a witness to willfully state any material matter that implies any material matter that he does not believe to be true.[4]

The Government urges that the perjury statute be construed broadly to reach petitioner's answer and thereby fulfill its historic purpose of reinforcing our adversary fact-finding process. We might go beyond the precise words of the statute if we thought they did not adequately express the intention of Congress, but we perceive no reason why Congress would intend the drastic sanction of a perjury prosecution to cure a testimonial mishap that could readily have been reached with a single additional question by counsel alert — as every examiner ought to be — to the incongruity of petitioner's unresponsive answer. Under the pressures and tensions of interrogation, it is not uncommon for the most earnest witnesses to give answers that are not entirely responsive. Sometimes the witness does not understand the question, or may in an excess of caution or apprehension read too much or too little into it. It should come as no surprise that a participant in a bankruptcy proceeding may have something to conceal and consciously tries to do so, or that a debtor may be embarrassed at his plight and yield information reluctantly. It is the responsibility of the lawyer to probe; testimonial interrogation, and cross-examination in particular, is a probing, prying, pressing form of inquiry. If a witness evades, it is the lawyer's responsibility to recognize the evasion and to bring the witness back to the mark, to flush out the whole truth with the tools of adversary examination.

It is no answer to say that here the jury found that petitioner intended to mislead his examiner. A jury should not be permitted to engage in conjecture whether an unresponsive answer, true and complete on its face, was intended to mislead or divert the examiner; the state of mind of the witness is relevant only to the extent that it bears on whether "he does not believe [his answer] to be true." To hold otherwise would be to inject a new and confusing element into the adversary testimonial system we know. Witnesses would be unsure of the extent of their responsibility for the misunderstandings and inadequacies of examiners, and might well fear having that responsibility tested by a jury under the vague rubric of "intent to mislead" or "perjury by implication." The seminal modern treatment of the history of the offense concludes that one consideration of policy overshadowed all others during the years when perjury first emerged as a common-law offense: "that the measures taken against the offense must

---

4. Petitioner's answer is not to be measured by the same standards applicable to criminally fraudulent or extortionate statements. In that context, the law goes "rather far in punishing intentional creation of false impressions by a selection of literally true representations, because the actor himself generally selects and arranges the representations." In contrast, "under our system of adversary questioning and cross-examination the scope of disclosure is largely in the hands of counsel and presiding officer." A.L.I. Model Penal Code § 208.20, Comment (Tent. Draft No. 6, 1957, p. 124).

not be so severe as to discourage witnesses from appearing or testifying." New York Law Revision Commission, Study on Perjury 23 (1935). . . .

Thus we must read § 1621 in light of our own and the traditional Anglo-American judgment that a prosecution for perjury is not the sole, or even the primary, safeguard against errant testimony. While "the lower federal courts have not dealt with the question often," and while their expressions do not deal with unresponsive testimony and are not precisely in point, "it may be said that they preponderate against the respondent's contention." United States v. Norris, 300 U.S., at 576. The cases support petitioner's position that the perjury statute is not to be loosely construed, nor the statute invoked simply because a wily witness succeeds in derailing the questioner — so long as the witness speaks the literal truth. The burden is on the questioner to pin the witness down to the specific object of the questioner's inquiry. . . .

It may well be that petitioner's answers were not guileless but were shrewdly calculated to evade. Nevertheless, we are constrained to agree with Judge Lumbard, who dissented from the judgment of the Court of Appeals, that any special problems arising from the literally true but unresponsive answer are to be remedied through the "questioner's acuity" and not by a federal perjury prosecution.

Reversed.

Notes and Questions

1. Was the question "Do you have any bank accounts in Swiss banks, Mr. Bronston?" ambiguous? If so, what alternative interpretations come to mind, and how could the ambiguity be cured? If the prosecution asks an ambiguous question, will the ambiguity automatically preclude basing a perjury prosecution on the answer to the question?[5]

2. If a witness intends to mislead the questioner in order to conceal the facts, what more is needed to support a perjury conviction and why? Should the court so readily accept deception under oath as a fact of life? Is the term "adversarial system" intended to include chicanery? Can a defense lawyer ethically counsel a witness to give evasive answers like the one that became the basis of Bronston's perjury prosecution?

3. After *Bronston*, could a perjury prosecution legitimately be based on the answer to a question containing an inaccurate factual premise?[6]

PROBLEM 7-1

Bronston, a cigarette smoker, worked in a plant where he was exposed to hazardous chemical fumes. Upon learning that he had developed a debilitating lung disease, he filed a workers' compensation claim. The company, of course, blamed Bronston's noxious habit instead of the ambient air in the plant. Assume the following colloquy occurred between Bronston and the company's lawyer during Bronston's deposition.

---

5. Cf. United States v. Camper, 384 F.3d 1073, 1076 (9th Cir. 2004) (distinguishing statements that contain "some ambiguity" and those that are "fundamentally ambiguous").

6. Cf. United States v. DeZarn, 157 F.3d 1042 (6th Cir. 1998).

Q: Mr. Bronston, how many cigarettes do you smoke per day?

A: Well, that would be hard to say exactly. It varies from day to day, and I don't usually keep count.

Q: Well, let me see if we can make it a little easier to pin this down. How many cigarettes did you smoke yesterday? Do you remember that?

A: I guess so. Let's see, I smoked one at the breakfast table while I read the paper. Then I smoked another one while I was driving to work — no, make that two. The traffic was terrible. Then I smoked a couple at lunch and a couple more during the afternoon. And I smoked a few more after dinner.

Despite his apparently vague recollection, Bronston knew he had smoked more than a pack of cigarettes the previous day, but he wasn't sure about the precise number he had smoked. Has he committed perjury?

Suppose the colloquy had gone something like this:

Q: Mr. Bronston, did you smoke any cigarettes before noon yesterday?

A: Yes, I did.

Q: How many did you smoke before noon?

A: I smoked one at the breakfast table before I left for work.

Assume that Bronston had smoked only one cigarette at the breakfast table, but that he smoked two more while he was driving to work. Is his response literally true? Could it be made the basis of a perjury prosecution?

UNITED STATES v. WALSER
3 F.3d 380 (11th Cir. 1993)

DUBINA, Circuit Judge.

This appeal presents a novel question: can one who intentionally causes an innocent party to commit perjury unwittingly . . . be held liable as a principal under 18 U.S.C. § 2? This question arises from Virginia Nell Walser's ("Walser") appeal from her convictions for perjury and aiding and abetting, in violation of 18 U.S.C. §§ 1623 and 2(b), and making false and fraudulent statements to a government agency or department, in violation of 18 U.S.C. § 1001. For the reasons that follow, we affirm.

I. FACTS

Walser and her husband farmed in Marion, Alabama. In 1989 a federal grand jury indicted them for defrauding the Federal Crop Insurance Corporation ("FCIC") and the Southern Crop Insurance Corporation ("SCIC") by submitting fraudulent crop insurance claims.[7] The government had alleged that the Walsers failed to report all the soybeans they produced on acreage insured by the SCIC. Specifically, the government

---

7. The FCIC is an agency of the United States Department of Agriculture that provides crop insurance to farmers. Farmers pay premiums and, if a loss is suffered, collect from the premium pool. The SCIC is a private company that sells and services crop insurance for the FCIC.

claimed that Walser and her husband surreptitiously grew approximately 4,980 bushels of insured soybeans and sold them under another name. Thus, the government contended, the Walsers were overpaid on their subsequent crop loss claims because they grew and sold more soybeans than were reported to the SCIC.

At trial, the Walsers defended by claiming that those 4,980 bushels of soybeans were an uninsured crop derived from another farm. They contended that Walser notified the SCIC of these uninsured beans through a document known as an SCI-013 form, entitled Statement of Facts ("SCI-013"). The SCI-013 is a standard form used for all correspondence with the SCIC.

Walser called Richmond Morrow ("Morrow"), an FCIC claims specialist, as a defense witness. Pursuant to a subpoena, Morrow brought certain documents from his file to the trial. Two were admitted into evidence. The first was a letter dated July 14, 1986, from Walser to Morrow at the FCIC. It stated as follows:

Dear Mr. Morrow,
    I am sending you a copy of the SCI-013 Statement of Facts that I have attached to my 1986 acreage report.[8] My crop insurance is with reinsurance, but due to the confussion [sic] in 1985 soybean production I wanted a copy of this statement, that was attached to my acreage report, on record with you in your office.

Sincerely,
/s/Virginia N. Walser

The second document was the SCI-013 form referred to in Walser's letter. Entitled "Southern Crop Insurance Agency, Incorporated, Statement of Facts" and also dated July 14, 1986, it stated as follows:

I have broadcast approximately 300 acres of soybeans on the Bob Rees place, ASCS farm number 024. These soybeans will not be covered by crop insurance. So there will not be a confussion [sic] or mix up between the production of soybeans covered by crop insurance and the production on farm 024, I am attaching a copy of this statement to my acreage report.

The SCI-013 form sent to Morrow thus purported to show that the 4,980 bushels of soybeans at issue were not insured beans harvested from Walser's farm, but were uninsured beans planted on a farm owned by a man named Bob Rees.

A jury acquitted Walser and her husband of all charges.

After the trial, special agent William Doles ("Agent Doles") of the Office of the Inspector General ("OIG"), United States Department of Agriculture ("USDA"), examined the SCI-013 form. He noticed that the name of the printer, AAA Printing & Graphics ("AAA"), appeared at the bottom of the form. Agent Doles contacted AAA and learned that AAA did not print and deliver the SCI-013 form to the SCIC until July 22, 1986, one week after the July 14, 1986, date used by Walser on the form sent to Morrow. It thus appeared that Walser prepared and back-dated a false document.

A second federal grand jury returned a three-count indictment against Walser based on this and other evidence of alleged false statements. Count I charged Walser with

---

8. An acreage report is part of a farmer's crop insurance policy. Farmers are required to notify the crop insurance company by a certain date how many acres have been planted and whether those acres represent insured or uninsured crops.

perjury and aiding and abetting by knowingly and willfully causing Morrow to present false evidence under oath, in violation of 18 U.S.C. §§ 1623 and 2(b). Counts II and III charged Walser with willfully and knowingly making and causing to be made false, fictitious and fraudulent statements and representations of material fact to the Agriculture Stabilization Conservation Service ("ASCS"), an agency of the USDA, in violation of 18 U.S.C. § 1001. These counts stemmed from two 1989 disaster claims in which Walser provided false testimony and documentary evidence purporting to show that she purchased certain fruit and vegetable seeds, when in fact she had not.

[Walser was convicted on all three counts.]

A. EVIDENCE AS TO COUNT I

At the 1992 trial Agent Doles testified that he examined all official FCIC and SCIC files pertaining to Walser before her first trial and found no mention of the uninsured soybeans purportedly planted on Bob Rees' farm. He further examined Walser's 1986 soybean acreage reports and, contrary to Walser's statement in her letter to Morrow, found no copy of the SCI-013 attached to them. Those acreage reports were dated July 14, 1986, the same date used by Walser when she created the SCI-013 form and the accompanying letter. Each acreage report was marked on the reverse side: "Received July 28, 1986." The SCI-013 form retrieved from Morrow's files had no date stamp. Agent Doles testified that he did not examine Morrow's files because Morrow, as an FCIC official, was not authorized to maintain official SCIC files. In sum, Agent Doles testified that neither Walser's 1986 acreage reports nor any other document in the FCIC or SCIC official files indicated that Walser informed the SCIC of uninsured soybeans.

Morrow testified that Walser sent him the SCI-013 and the accompanying letter, although he could not recall when he received them. He noted that it was unusual for him to have SCIC documents because he worked for the federal government and the SCIC was a private organization. He kept the documents, however, because he routinely filed all correspondence. He further testified that after Walser subpoenaed the documents in his file she called Morrow to ensure he possessed the subpoenaed documents. Morrow told her that he did. Walser then explained that Morrow need not give the OIG a copy of the SCI-013 because it had one already. Morrow testified that he felt tricked by Walser because he now knew the SCI-013 Walser sent him to be false and back-dated.

Robert Hagan ("Hagan"), the owner of AAA, testified that the SCIC ordered 5,000 SCI-013 Statement of Fact forms on July 10, 1986. Prior to this order, another printing company printed the forms. The old forms did not identify the printer. AAA delivered the first 500 forms on July 22 and the remainder on July 28. No AAA forms were printed or delivered prior to July 14, 1986. . . .

II. ANALYSIS . . .

B. WALSER'S PERJURY AND AIDING AND ABETTING CONVICTION

Count I of the indictment charged that Walser

knowingly and willfully assisted and caused Richmond Morrow, a witness under oath . . . to use and present a written document, knowing the same to contain a false material declaration; that is, VIRGINIA NELL WALSER caused to be introduced into evidence, through the witness Morrow, a document which she knew to have been falsely made and back-dated, to-wit: Form SCI-013 entitled Southern Crop Insurance Agency, Inc., Statement of Facts, relating to 300 acres of soybeans, dated July 14, 1986; All in violation of Title 18, United States Code, Section 1623 and Section 2.

Section 1623 of Title 18 of the United States Code makes it a crime for any person under oath

in any proceeding before or ancillary to any court or grand jury of the United States [to] knowingly make[] any false material declaration or make[] or use[] any other information, including any book, paper, document, record, recording, or other material, knowing the same to contain any false material declaration. . . .

The government does not contend that Walser knowingly used false information under oath. Rather, it argues that Walser aided and abetted the commission of perjury, and thus, via operation of 18 U.S.C. § 2(b), is liable as a principal. Walser argues that her conviction under 18 U.S.C. § 1623 cannot be based upon application of the aiding and abetting provision of § 2(b) because she was never placed under oath in regard to the offenses alleged in Count I of the indictment. Thus, she claims, she had no legal capacity to commit the crime of perjury. . . . Section 2(b) of the aiding and abetting statute provides that

(b) Whoever willfully causes an act to be done which if directly performed by him or another would be an offense against the United States, is punishable as a principal.

18 U.S.C. § 2(b).

"The standard test for determining guilt by aiding and abetting is to determine whether a substantive offense was committed by someone, whether there was an act by the defendant which contributed to and furthered the offense, and whether the defendant intended to aid its commission." United States v. Jones, 913 F.2d 1552, 1558 (11th Cir. 1990). Title 18 U.S.C. § 2, however, does not establish a separate crime. Rather, it merely permits one who aids and abets the commission of a crime to be punished as a principal. An individual, therefore, may be indicted as a principal for the commission of a substantive crime and convicted upon evidence that he or she aided and abetted only.

Further, an individual is criminally culpable for causing an intermediary to commit a criminal act even though the intermediary has no criminal intent and is innocent of the substantive crime. . . .

We reject Walser's contention that § 2(b) may not be applied to perjury claims arising under § 1623. Section 2(b) applies generally to all federal criminal statutes and prohibits one from causing another to do any act that would be illegal if one did it personally. The purpose of § 2 is to permit a person operating from behind the scenes to be convicted even though that person is not expressly prohibited by the substantive statute from engaging in the acts made criminal by Congress. . . .

Walser knew the document she sent to Morrow was false and back-dated. Indeed, the SCI-013 form she used had not even been printed or delivered by the date she purportedly wrote it. By falsifying and back-dating the SCI-013, then introducing it at trial through the innocent testimony of Morrow, Walser knowingly caused a fraudulent document to be entered into evidence during a court proceeding. Morrow lacked the criminal intent to commit perjury. As a witness under oath, he merely had the capacity to commit perjury. Section 2, however, operates to unite Morrow's capacity to commit perjury with Walser's intent that perjury be committed. Walser, as the crime's instigator and malefactor, adopted Morrow's capacity to commit perjury, including his status as a witness under oath. She is thus liable as a principal. . . . For the foregoing reasons, we affirm Walser's perjury conviction. . . .

Affirmed.

Notes and Questions

1. The prohibitions in § 1623 extend to making or using any document or record knowing it contains a false material declaration. It is clear that Walser made the false documents at issue. Is her making the documents the basis for her conviction? Or is her liability based on her use? If so, in what sense did she use them?[9]

2. Suppose that the grand jury had subpoenaed the documents from Morrow, who dutifully turned them over. Would Walser be guilty of perjury before the grand jury?

3. What if the grand jury subpoenas Walser's copy of the documents? Walser knows they are false and wants to avoid committing perjury. As she sees it, there are five options: (1) disobey the subpoena and refuse to produce the documents, (2) tell the U.S. Attorney that the documents no longer exist, (3) destroy the documents, (4) comply with the subpoena but advise the U.S. Attorney that the documents are false, or (5) simply comply with the subpoena. What would you advise?

Is pleading the Fifth Amendment privilege against self-incrimination another available option? If so, would there be any downside risks to using this strategy?

III. THE TWO-WITNESS RULE

The "two-witness rule" is an evidentiary rule that prohibits basing a perjury conviction solely upon an oath against an oath. Two policies historically were asserted in support of the rule. First, "equally honest witnesses may well have differing recollections of the same event."[10] Thus, something more than one person's word against another's was historically required.[11] Second, the two-witness rule was designed to protect a truthful witness from unfounded charges raised by someone aggrieved by the witness's testimony.

---

9. Cf. *United States v. Gellene*, 182 F.3d 578 (7th Cir. 1999) (law firm partner's nondisclosure of potential conflict of interest during testimony at fee hearing constituted "use" of misleading written declaration submitted to the court at an earlier stage of the proceedings).

10. *Weiler v. United States*, 323 U.S. 606 (1945).

11. *United States v. Beach*, 296 F.2d 153 (4th Cir. 1961).

UNITED STATES v. DAVIS
548 F.2d 840 (9th Cir. 1977)

BRUCE R. THOMPSON, District Judge.

This is an appeal from the conviction of the defendant, Ricky Allen Davis, on seven counts of perjury pursuant to Section 1621 of Title 18, United States Code.

On October 18, 1975, a service station situated on the United States Naval Ammunition Depot at Lualualei, Oahu, Hawaii, was burglarized. As the crime occurred within the exclusive jurisdiction of the United States, the FBI commenced an investigation into the matter. Shortly thereafter, a marine, Curt Allen Gustafson, became the target of the FBI investigation, as a result of fingerprints matching his being found at the scene of the burglary. At that time, Gustafson was assigned to the marine barracks at the Waikele branch of the Naval Ammunition Depot in Hawaii.

Special Agent Hilton J. Lui of the FBI, was assigned to the Lualualei burglary investigation. During the course of his investigation Lui questioned several marines who were also stationed with Gustafson at Waikele, regarding any information they might possess concerning the burglary. As a result of information received during one such interview, Lui directed the attention to the defendant, Ricky Allen Davis, a fellow marine and an acquaintance of Gustafson.

On January 14, 1976, Lui interviewed the defendant. During the course of this interview, Davis admitted being a friend of Gustafson, but denied any knowledge as to whether Gustafson had played a role in the burglary. In early February, the federal grand jury convened in Hawaii for the purpose of investigating the burglary. Davis was subpoenaed to appear and to testify concerning his knowledge, if any, of Gustafson's involvement in the crime.

According to the testimony of Lui, Davis, upon receipt of the grand jury subpoena on February 3, 1976, desired to make a statement to the FBI. Lui testified that during the February 3rd interview, Davis indicated that he had been apprised of Gustafson's role in the Lualualei burglary by Gustafson himself during a conversation between the two.

During the course of this interview, Lui simultaneously took written notes of Davis' responses to various questions. Subsequent to this interview, but while still in the presence of Davis, Lui composed a written statement based on his notes and presented it to the defendant for his signature. Lui testified that before obtaining the defendant's signature, he read the statement out loud to Davis and instructed him to make any corrections or deletions he desired. With no corrections, additions, or deletions being made, Davis' statement as composed by Lui read as follows:

> About one and a half weeks before November 4, 1975, the approximate date Curt Gustafson left the Marine Corps, he mentioned to me and said that he went to Lualualei on the night of the burglary at the gas station and broke into this gas station which is located there between the road from NAVMAG Lualualei and Radio Transmitting Facility (RTF) Lualualei. About two or three days later while we were going to the beach, we were driving on a deserted road in Makaha and Gustafson mentioned to me and pointed out an area we were passing as the area where the safe which they took from the burglary was dumped. I recall that Gustafson told me that they didn't get into the safe. Gustafson did not mention to me the other name of the individuals that participated in the burglary. Also, Gustafson did not mention to me of the other items.
>
> Gustafson did not mention any details to me as far as robbing the gas station.

After Davis was read the statement, he incorporated the following verification in his own handwriting.

> I make this statement consisting of two pages without any coercion against me and attest the statement is true and correct.

Davis then signed the statement.

Three days later, Davis had a slightly different version as to what transpired during the February 3 interview with Lui. In his appearance before the federal grand jury on February 6th, Davis, while under oath, denied having any knowledge as to who had robbed the Lualualei service station. He further denied that Gustafson had ever indicated to him, in any fashion, that he had ever committed the burglary.

When asked during the trial to explain the noticeable discrepancies between his testimony and that of Lui's, Davis testified that he had never told Lui anything concerning Gustafson's involvement in the burglary. In refuting the contents of the FBI statement that he had personally verified and signed, Davis' testimony is somewhat incredible. He recalled being read a statement by Agent Lui before signing it, but denied that the statement in evidence and the statement that he was read were the same. When asked if he had read the statement before signing it, Davis contended that he had only glanced at certain portions of the statement, and had apparently overlooked the sentence implicating Gustafson.

The defendant was charged with seven counts of perjury emanating from his testimony before the federal grand jury, and was subsequently convicted by a jury on all seven counts.

Counts I, III, V and VI all directly concern whether Gustafson even mentioned anything to Davis concerning his (Gustafson's) participation in the Lualualei burglary or his conduct on the particular night of the burglary. Count II is a much more general charge concerning whether Davis had any idea who had committed the Lualualei burglary. Count IV is based on defendant's denial before the grand jury that Agent Lui had carefully gone over the whole statement with Davis and that Davis had read the statement before signing it. Count VII of the indictment charged that the defendant committed perjury during his appearance before the federal grand jury when he denied telling Agent Lui that he was told of Gustafson's participation in the burglary by Gustafson himself.

This Circuit follows the traditional "two witness rule" which requires that the falsity of the defendant's statements must be proved by the testimony of two witnesses or the testimony of one witness, plus corroborating evidence. The corroborative evidence required need not be independently sufficient to establish the defendant's guilt, and may be circumstantial in nature. This Circuit has held that the corroborating evidence is sufficient if it, together with the direct evidence, is inconsistent with the innocence of the defendant. In United States v. Weiner, 479 F.2d 923, 927-28 (2d Cir. 1973), the court construed the rule requiring that the corroborating evidence be inconsistent with the innocence of the defendant to mean no more than

> such evidence must tend to substantiate that part of the testimony of the principal prosecution witness which is material in showing that the statement made by the accused under oath was false. This is to say that the two-witness rule is satisfied by corroborative

evidence of sufficient content and quality to persuade the trier that what the principal prosecution witness testified to about the falsity of the accused's statement under oath was correct.

In the present situation, Lui testified at trial that during the February 3, 1976, interview with Davis, Davis admitted having a conversation with Gustafson, where he was told of Gustafson's involvement in the burglary. Lui's testimony was further corroborated by the introduction into evidence of the verified and signed statement of Davis. This statement amounted to a written admission by Davis and was entirely consistent with the testimony given by Lui. In Vetterli v. United States, 198 F.2d 291, 293 (9th Cir.), vac. on other grds., 344 U.S. 872 (1952), we emphasized:

> Admissions of a party charged with perjury, if made under such circumstances as render them clearly admissible, seem to us to have a sound corroborative value.

The defendant contends that the use of this signed statement to satisfy the corroborative evidence requirement of the two-witness rule amounts to bootstrapping in that the statement was written and composed by Lui. We disagree. Where one witness testifies to the fact of perjury, independent corroborative evidence suffices under the two-witness rule if it tends to confirm the truth of the witness's testimony in material respects and thereby induces belief in his testimony. Since the corroborative evidence need not be strong nor even independently sufficient in itself, it may be supplied by the defendant's own conduct. Once the two-witness rule is satisfied, it is for the jury to decide the trustworthiness of the evidence, what weight should be accorded it, and the credibility of the witnesses. In addition to the testimony of Lui and the signed admission of Davis, further corroboration was provided by the defendant's testimony at trial.

Defendant Davis' testimony at the trial was so confusing and contradictory as to prompt cross-examination by his own counsel. . . . The jurors would have been quite justified in concluding that defendant had in fact admitted perjury before the grand jury in his trial testimony and had himself supplied the corroboration to satisfy the requirements of the two-witness rule. . . .

Affirmed.

Notes and Questions

1. What was the false statement that provided the basis for the perjury prosecution in *Davis*? What was the corroborating evidence?

2. Suppose that Davis is questioned about the specifics of his conversation with Gustafson. The prosecutor asks: "Did Gustafson tell you whether he had any accomplices in the burglary?" Davis responds: "I don't remember." The prosecutor presses him further, asking, "Didn't Gustafson tell you that several individuals had assisted him in committing the burglary?" Again, Davis responds, "I really can't recall that he did." Davis actually remembers the conversation quite well and knows Gustafson had two accomplices.

If Davis is indicted for perjury on the basis of these answers, what hurdle does the two-witness rule pose for the prosecution? Is an exception to the rule warranted in a case like this?[12]

NOTE ON INCONSISTENT DECLARATIONS

The false declarations statute expressly abandons the two-witness rule. Section 1623(e) provides that "[p]roof beyond a reasonable doubt under this section is sufficient for conviction. It shall not be necessary that such proof be made by any particular number of witnesses or by documentary or other type of evidence." Thus, under § 1623, evidence provided by a single witness may establish the falsity of the defendant's sworn declaration.

Section 1623 liberalizes the evidentiary rules even more. If the government can prove that the defendant made two inconsistent declarations under oath, one of which was necessarily false, it need not prove which statement is false. If both statements are "material to the point in question" and are irreconcilably inconsistent, proof that the witness knowingly made the statements is sufficient. 18 U.S.C. § 1623(c)(1). In prosecutions instituted under this theory, however, the statute provides that it is a defense "that the defendant at the time he made each declaration believed the declaration was true." Was it necessary for the statute to spell out this defense?

PROBLEM 7-2

Owen Canby, a professor of obstetrics, is hired as an expert witness and consultant to A. H. Robins, maker of the Dalkon Shield birth control device. Canby is a key witness for Robins in several lawsuits brought by women who claim they have been seriously injured by the device.

At a federal trial held in Florida in early 1993, Professor Canby is asked by Robins' lawyer whether he has conducted experiments on the device. Canby responds that he is supervising studies being conducted by a microbiologist and a specialist in the labeling of bacteria. In the course of his testimony, he draws diagrams to explain the experiments. He further testifies that, based partly upon the experiments, he has concluded that the Dalkon Shield is not unreasonably dangerous.

Eight months later, in a deposition taken in San Francisco in an unrelated Dalkon Shield case filed in federal court, a lawyer asks him whether he has done any experimental work on the device. This time he responds "no." When asked another question as to whether some experiments have been done under his supervision, he again responds "no."

The government wants to prosecute him for perjury. Under what theory or theories might the grand jury indict? Cf. Professor Is Charged with Lying for Maker of Birth Control Device, N.Y. Times, Mar. 4, 1988, at 1.

The New York Times article states that after the inconsistent testimony came to light, the FBI undertook to determine whether the lawyers knew about it. Why would

---

12. Cf. Gebhard v. United States, 422 F.2d 281 (9th Cir. 1970).

the FBI be interested in what the lawyers knew? Does it matter whether Robins' attorneys were aware of the inconsistencies in the professor's testimony? Cf. ABA Model Rules of Professional Conduct, Rules 3.3, 3.4.

IV. THE RECANTATION DEFENSE

The crime of perjury is complete when a witness makes a false statement under oath. Thus, if the witness later corrects or retracts the lie, it is no defense to a perjury charge. The Supreme Court explained the rule against permitting witnesses to purge themselves by recanting their false testimony in United States v. Norris, 300 U.S. 564, 574, 576 (1939), as follows.

> . . . It is argued that to allow retraction of perjured testimony promotes the discovery of the truth and, if made before the proceeding is concluded, can do no harm to the parties. The argument overlooks the tendency of such a view to encourage false swearing in the belief that if the falsity be not discovered before the end of the hearing it will have its intended effect, but, if discovered, the witness may purge himself of crime by resuming his role as witness and substituting the truth for his previous falsehood. It ignores the fact that the oath administered to the witness calls on him freely to disclose the truth in the first instance and not put the court and the parties to the disadvantage, hindrance and delay of ultimately extracting the truth by cross examination, by extraneous investigation, or other collateral means. . . .
>
>   . . . The plain words of the statute and the public policy which called for its enactment alike demand we should hold that the telling of a deliberate lie by a witness completes the crime defined by the law. This is not to say that the correction of an innocent mistake, or the elaboration of an incomplete answer, may not demonstrate that there was no willful intent to swear falsely.

The false declarations statute departs from this traditional rule and recognizes a limited defense of recantation.

UNITED STATES v. SHERMAN
150 F.3d 306 (3d Cir. 1998)

McKEE, Circuit Judge. . . .

I. STATEMENT OF FACTS

On October 23, 1996, Robert J. Sherman was indicted on five counts of perjury under 18 U.S.C. § 1621. The indictment stemmed from Sherman's testimony in the medical malpractice trial of Samuel and Gail Gassert v. Latif Awad, M.D. and Geisinger Medical Center. Sherman—a longtime obstetrician/gynecologist—had testified as the plaintiffs' medical expert in that trial. When cross examined about his qualifications as an expert, Sherman had testified that he was licensed to practice medicine in the District of Columbia, Virginia and Massachusetts and that none of his licenses had ever been revoked, suspended or restricted. He further testified that he had never been subject to any disciplinary proceedings by any hospital or medical society. He did, however, acknowledge that he had once been named in a medical malpractice case fifteen years earlier, involving a problem with a "D & C," but he described it as "routine." When Sherman provided that testimony, he knew that all of his licenses had been revoked, and defense counsel ultimately elicited this admission from Sherman. Because that testimony is at the heart of this appeal, we will quote the relevant exchange at length:

Q: At the present time you are licensed to practice medicine in Virginia.
A: Yes.
Q: Over the course of your practice, which has been about how many years now?
A: Thirty years.
Q: Okay, over the course of your practice, how many states have you ever been licensed to practice in?
A: I was licensed in Massachusetts, Virginia, Maryland, and D.C.
Q: And you've continued to keep your license current in Virginia.
A: That's all.
Q: Do you remember at the time of your retirement in 1985, do you remember what states you had licenses in?
A: I don't have that handy at the moment.
Q: Well, were you licensed to practice medicine in Virginia in 1985?
A: Yes. Yes.
Q: How about Massachusetts?
A: I moved away from Massachusetts so I didn't bother with that. . . .
Q: Did you ever have your privileges at any of those hospitals either revoked, suspended or restricted?
A: No. . . .
Q: Did you ever have any of your hospital privileges in Boston or in the Boston area revoked, suspended or restricted?
A: No.
Q: Have you ever been subject to any disciplinary proceedings by any —

(Objection and objection overruled)

Q: Dr. Sherman, have you ever been subject to any disciplinary proceedings by a hospital or medical society?
A: No.
Q: Have you ever been named as a defendant in a medical malpractice suit?

(Objection and objection overruled)

A: I had a malpractice case about 15 years ago myself, yes.
Q: Could you tell us what that was about?
A: It was settled somehow or other, but there was a routine case.
Q: Was that an OB/GYN case?
A: Yes.

Q: And it was routine?

A: Well, there was a D & C problem.

Q: You mentioned that over the course of your practice you were licensed in four states that you told us about. Have any of those licenses ever been revoked, suspended or restricted in any fashion?

A: No, I let them — I let them go because I had no intention of going back to active OB.

Q: So you let your license in Massachusetts lapse?

A: Yes.

Q: And you let your license in Maryland lapse?

A: Yes.

Q: And you let your license in the District of Columbia lapse?

A: Yes. . . .

Q: Go back to your licensures, Doctor. Isn't it true that you had your license to practice medicine in the District of Columbia revoked in 1977?

A: Yes, it was. Yes, but —

Q: Isn't it true that you had your license to practice medicine in Massachusetts revoked in 1983?

(Objection and objection overruled)

A: Yes.

Q: Isn't it true that you had your license to practice medicine in Virginia revoked in 1979?

A: But it was reinstated.

Q: The question to you, Doctor, is isn't it true that your license to practice medicine in Virginia was revoked in 1979?

A: Yes.

Q: And it was not until . . . 1993 that your license was reinstated in Virginia.

A: Yes.

Q: And wasn't [your] license in Virginia reinstated on a probationary status?

A: Yes. . . .

Q: And according to the order of reinstatement you were not to engage in the practice of medicine until such time as you successfully passed the special purpose examination.

A: Yes.

Q: Did you pass that examination?

A: I have to take it on March 17th.

Q: Do you have plans to take it?

A: Yes.

Q: But you have not yet complied with that particular requirement.

A: Not yet.

Q: I see. If you have not complied with a particular term or condition of reinstatement, has your license in Virginia in fact been reinstated?

A: Has it been reinstated?

Q: Has it been actually reinstated?

A: It has been reinstated subject to that, yes.

Q: Could you go into the state of Virginia today and treat patients?

A: I don't treat any patients at the —

Q: If you wanted to, could you, with your restricted license, go into Virginia today and treat patients?

A: No.

Q: After your license was revoked in Massachusetts in March of 1983, you requested in 1992 reinstatement, did you not?

A: Yes.

Q: That was denied, wasn't it?

A: Yes.

Q: Didn't you have a license to practice in Maine?

A: Yes.

Q: And you made a license renewal to Maine in 1983 which was denied, didn't you?

A: At that time. It is under advisement for renewal at this time. . . .

Q: Doctor you told us that 15 years ago you were subject — you were a defendant in a routine medical malpractice suit, weren't you?

A: Yes.

Q: You know where I'm going, don't you, Doctor?

A: Yes.

Q: Do you remember a patient by the name of Rita McDowell?

A: Yes.

Q: Rita McDowell came into your clinic for an abortion, didn't she?

A: Yes.

Q: She was 16 years of age.

A: Yes.

Q: You performed an incomplete abortion on her.

A: I did not.

Q: Doctor, as a result of the procedure that you performed on Rita McDowell, she died didn't she?

A: Absolutely not.

Q: Rita McDowell did not die?

A: She died at D.C. General Hospital as a result of a CVP line which perforated the lungs, and she died of cardiac arrest on that score.

Q: Doctor, the reason that your license was revoked in D.C. in 1977 was because of the Rita McDowell case, wasn't it?

A: Yes.

Q: And the reason that your license was revoked in D.C. was because you, as a practice, were performing incomplete septic abortions on your patients.

A: That is your opinion but not mine.

Sherman was subsequently indicted for perjury under 18 U.S.C. § 1621. Count I of the indictment charged him with testifying that none of his licenses to practice medicine had ever been revoked, suspended or restricted. Count II charged him with testifying that he had allowed his license to practice medicine in Massachusetts to lapse, when in fact it had been revoked. Count III charged him with testifying that he had only allowed his license to practice medicine in the District of Columbia to lapse. It had also been revoked. Count IV charged him with testifying that he had never been subject to disciplinary proceedings by a medical society, when in fact he had been subjected to such proceedings in the District of Columbia, the Commonwealth of Massachusetts and the Commonwealth of Virginia. Count V charged him with testifying that 15 years prior he had been named in a routine medical malpractice case involving a D & C, which was ultimately settled, "when in fact . . . the Board of Medicine of the District of Columbia had found that the defendant performed an incomplete abortion on a 16-year old girl in order to increase his fees by making later surgical procedures necessary, resulting in the patient's death . . . [and] the revocation of defendant's license to practice medicine . . . and . . . criminal prosecution."

Sherman moved to dismiss the indictment, arguing that the government had denied him the due process of law by depriving him of the defense of recantation that is available under 18 U.S.C. § 1623, but not under 18 U.S.C. § 1621. See 18 U.S.C. § 1623(d). The district court agreed and dismissed the indictment. . . .

II. DISCUSSION

A. THE DISTINCTIONS BETWEEN THE TWO STATUTES

The sole issue before us is whether the district court erred in dismissing the five-count indictment against Sherman. The court held that the government lacked the discretion to charge Sherman under the general perjury statute, 18 U.S.C. § 1621, rather than the false swearing statute, 18 U.S.C. § 1623, as the latter statute more specifically applied to his conduct, and not prosecuting under that statute improperly deprived Sherman of the defense of recantation which is available under 18 U.S.C. § 1623(d), but which does not apply to 18 U.S.C. § 1621. . . .

We have previously noted the distinctions between the two statutes: (1) § 1623 does not require that the prosecution employ the "two-witness rule" for proving perjury; (2) § 1623 has a reduced mens rea requiring only that one "knowingly" commit perjury rather than "willfully," as is required under § 1621; and (3) § 1623 is restricted to testimony before grand juries and courts and is therefore more limited in reach than § 1621.

In United States v. Lardieri, 506 F.2d 319 (3d Cir. 1974), we examined the congressional intent behind these overlapping statutes. We stated:

It was the congressional judgment that the overall purpose of Section 1623, obtaining more truthful responses from witnesses before courts and grand juries, would be best accomplished by facilitating perjury convictions for those who had violated their oaths. In order to remove encumbrances from such convictions, Congress abandoned the two-witness rule, discontinued the requirement that the prosecutor prove the truth of one of two irreconcilable statements under oath, and required only a "knowing" rather than a "willful" state of mind. The Senate Judiciary Committee described the intent of the Section as follows:

A subpoena can compel the attendance of a witness. . . . But only the possibility of some sanction such as a perjury prosecution can provide any guarantee that his testimony will be truthful.

Today, however, the possibility of perjury prosecution is not likely, and if it materializes, the likelihood of a conviction is not high. . . .

(Section 1623) creates a new federal false declaration provision that will not be circumscribed by rigid common law rules of evidence.

506 F.2d at 322 (citing S. Rep. No. 91-617, at 57-59 (1969)).

Thus, Congress changed the law in order to facilitate perjury prosecutions. It also sought to enhance the truth-seeking process by allowing perjurers to recant perjured testimony and thereby escape conviction.

> The congressional effort to improve truth telling in judicial proceedings was thus twofold. Congress magnified the deterrent role of the criminal law by easing the Government's path to perjury convictions and the emphasis here was plainly on pressure calculated to induce the witness to speak the truth at all times. Congress also extended absolution to perjurers who recant under prescribed conditions, admittedly an endeavor to secure truth through correction of previously false testimony. Each of these techniques has its own virtue, and it was, of course, the prerogative of Congress to put them to use; but it is evident that in some degree they unavoidably must work at cross-purposes. Recantation, for all its value in ultimately unveiling the truth, may well prove to be a disincentive to veracity in the first instance; to the extent that a perjurer can sidestep prosecution simply by recanting, he is hardly the more prompted to tell the truth in the beginning. By the same token, the deterrent effect of any statute punishing perjury is weakened in the same measure that recantation holds out the promise of possible escape. And indisputably, maximum deterrence of perjury is necessarily inconsistent with maximum range for recantation.

United States v. Moore, 613 F.2d 1029, 1041 (D.C. Cir. 1979).

B. PROSECUTORIAL DISCRETION

When Sherman testified about his background, he violated 18 U.S.C. § 1621 as well as 18 U.S.C. § 1623. With certain exceptions, when conduct runs afoul of more than one prohibition of the criminal law, prosecutors have discretion to choose under which statute to prosecute. United States v. Batchelder, 442 U.S. 114, 125 (1979). . . .

. . . [Sections] 1621 and 1623 are separate statutes that operate independently of each other, and the government can normally elect upon which of those two statutes to base its prosecution. "[A] defendant has no constitutional right to elect which of two applicable federal statutes shall be the basis of his indictment and prosecution." Id.

However, notwithstanding the breadth of prosecutorial discretion, a prosecutor's charging decision cannot be "motivated solely by a desire to [achieve] a tactical advantage by impairing the ability of a defendant to mount an effective defense, [in such a case] a due process violation might be shown." Id. Here, Sherman argues that the prosecution did just that. The district court accepted Sherman's argument that he was denied due process of the law because the prosecutor deliberately secured a tactical advantage in denying him a defense that he was entitled to assert by indicting him under § 1621 rather than § 1623. . . .

1. Recantation Under 18 U.S.C. § 1623(d)

Under 18 U.S.C. § 1623(d) the defense of recantation is available: (1) "if, at the time the admission is made, the declaration has not substantially affected the proceeding"; or (2) "it has not become manifest that such falsity has been or will be exposed." Here, the district court concluded that Sherman could have asserted the defense as his perjury had not substantially affected the proceeding when he recanted. Understandably, the court concluded that it was irrelevant that the perjury had been exposed prior to the recantation because the statute was drafted in the disjunctive so Sherman needed only to satisfy one of the two conditions, not both of them. The court held that the government's reliance upon 18 U.S.C. § 1621 deprived Sherman of the defense Congress wrote into § 1623 and that Sherman's right to due process of the law had therefore been violated.

The government contends that the district court erred in reading § 1623(d) in the disjunctive rather than the conjunctive, because both prongs must be met before a recantation defense is available. Since Sherman's perjury was exposed prior to his attempted recantation, the government argues that his right to due process of the law could not have been denied because he was not entitled to the recantation defense. Thus, our inquiry is focused upon whether Sherman was entitled to the defense of recantation under 18 U.S.C. § 1623(d). . . .

18 U.S.C. § 1623(d) is deceptive in its apparent clarity. It says "or" and Sherman argues that Congress intended the statute to mean exactly that. However, reading the statute as Sherman argues we must results in a statute that is both inconsistent with, and frustrating to, Congress' twofold intent in enacting the legislation. If Sherman is correct, one could commit perjury with impunity. A witness could violate his or her oath in the comfort of knowing that no perjury prosecution was possible so long as he or she recanted as soon as it appeared the perjury would be disclosed. A recantation at that point, under Sherman's interpretation, would shield the conduct even if the judicial proceedings had been substantially [a]ffected by the false testimony. Similarly, a witness could escape prosecution even after the false nature of it had been disclosed and hope to successfully argue that the proceedings had not been substantially [a]ffected because there had been a recantation. . . .

[D]espite the disjunctive phrasing in § 1623(d), the New York statute it was based upon is drafted in the conjunctive. Section 210.25 of the New York Penal Law states:

> In any prosecution for perjury, it is an affirmative defense that the defendant retracted his false statement in the course of the proceeding in which it was made before such false statement substantially affected the proceeding *and* before it became manifest that its falsity was or would be exposed.

N.Y. Penal Code § 210.25 (McKinney 1965) (emphasis added). See also *Lardieri*, 506 F.2d at 323 n. 6. Moreover, the wording of the New York statute is consistent with the court decision upon which it is based. People v. Ezaugi, 141 N.E.2d 580 (N.Y. 1957). . . .

Only if both statutory conditions exist at the time of recantation will Congress' dual purpose of deterring perjury through more effective prosecutions and encouraging truthful testimony be furthered. Congress clearly did not intend to remove the twin impediments of the "two-witness" rule and the burden of proving which of two conflicting statements was actually false only to replace them with a "get out of jail free card." Accordingly, we conclude that Congress intended to limit the defense of recantation in 18 U.S.C. § 1623(d) only to those instances where the perjurer recants before the "declaration has not substantially affected the proceeding," and "it has not become manifest that such falsity has been or will be exposed."

Here, that did not happen. Sherman's revelation came too late to allow him to rely upon it to defend himself from prosecution under the general perjury statute. Accordingly, we must reject his argument that the prosecutor's decision to charge him under 18 U.S.C. § 1621 rather than 18 U.S.C. § 1623 deprived him of a defense in violation of his right to due process of the law. . . .

Here, Sherman answered "yes" when defense counsel began his impeachment of Sherman by asking: "[y]ou know where I am going with this don't you?" It is difficult to imagine a scenario that more clearly demonstrates why Congress could not have intended § 1623(d) to be read in the disjunctive. . . .

In interpreting 18 U.S.C. § 1623(d), it may appear that there is tension between the language of the statute and the canons of statutory construction. However, "[t]he strict-construction rule governing interpretation of criminal statute is not [] to be woodenly applied." Strict construction "cannot provide a substitute for common sense, precedent and legislative history. . . ." *Moore*, 613 F.2d at 1044. . . .

III. CONCLUSION

For the foregoing reasons, we will reverse the order of the district court dismissing the government's indictment against Sherman and remand for proceedings consistent with this opinion.

Notes and Questions

1. Approving the analysis in *Moore*, the *Sherman* court joined other circuits that have held that "or" means "and" in the recantation provision, and this is now the majority view. *Sherman* and *Moore* reached this conclusion partly on policy grounds, partly on the legislative history, and partly on their notions of common sense.

The Eighth and Second Circuits, in contrast, have concluded that "or" means "or" in § 1623. In United States v. Smith[13] and United States v. Kahn,[14] the courts found that, when accorded its ordinary meaning, the plain language of the statute is unambiguous and thus controls. Although the legislative history relied on by *Moore* and *Sherman* could create "some uncertainty about the language Congress intended to enact, it does not create an ambiguity in an otherwise plainly worded statute."[15] Thus, in these circuits a witness may recant perjured testimony *either* before it becomes manifest that the falsehood will be exposed *or* before the testimony substantially affects the proceeding.

Which is the better rule?

2. What is the proper relationship between § 1621 and § 1623? Sherman argued that he was denied due process because he was charged under § 1621 and was thus deprived of the recantation defense afforded under § 1623. The court in *Sherman* found

---

13. 35 F.3d 344 (8th Cir. 1994).
14. 472 F.2d 272 (2d Cir. 1973).
15. *Smith*, 35 F.3d at 347.

no due process violation. What constraints limit the prosecutor's discretion to choose which statute to invoke? Are they adequate?[16]

3. To whom must exposure of the falsehood be manifest? Was exposure of the lies manifest in *Sherman*? What is the purpose of the manifest exposure limitation on the recantation defense?

4. When will a falsehood have substantially affected the proceedings?[17] Had Sherman's lies had that effect? What is the purpose of this limitation?

5. What constitutes recantation? Sherman's belated admissions that his licenses had been revoked are tantamount to a repudiation of his earlier claims that he was licensed to practice in four states. Is outright repudiation of the falsehoods required, or will something less suffice?[18]

6. Is the defense of recantation a jury question? When should the defense be raised?[19]

7. Recall the facts in Problem 7-2. What if after lying in the Florida proceeding, Professor Canby unequivocally recants the perjury in the California proceeding. Does he have a valid defense under § 1623?

8. What about the lawyering in *Sherman*? Are there any obvious deficiencies? If so, how could they have been cured?

9. The ABA Model Rules of Professional Conduct impose a duty of candor toward the court. Rule 3.3,[20] Candor Toward the Tribunal, provides:

(a) lawyer shall not knowingly: . . .

   (3) offer evidence that the lawyer knows to be false. If a lawyer, the lawyer's client, or a witness called by the lawyer, has offered material evidence and the lawyer comes to know of its falsity, the lawyer shall take reasonable remedial measures, including, if necessary, disclosure to the tribunal. A lawyer may refuse to offer evidence, other than the testimony of a defendant in a criminal matter, that the lawyer reasonably believes is false.

COMMENT . . .

REMEDIAL MEASURES . . .

[10] Having offered material evidence in the belief that it was true, a lawyer may subsequently come to know that the evidence is false. Or, a lawyer may be surprised when the lawyer's client, or another witness called by the lawyer, offers testimony the lawyer knows to be false, either during the lawyer's direct examination or in response to cross-examination by the opposing lawyer. In such situations or if the lawyer knows of the falsity of testimony elicited from the client during a deposition, the lawyer must take reasonable remedial measures. In such situations, the advocate's proper course is to remonstrate with the client confidentially, advise the client of the lawyer's duty of candor to the tribunal and seek the client's cooperation with respect to the withdrawal or correction of the false statements or evidence. If that fails, the advocate must take further remedial action. If

---

16. Cf. *Kahn*, 472 F.2d at 283 ("We find not a little disturbing the prospect of the government employing § 1621 whenever a recantation exists, and § 1623 when one does not, simply to place perjury defendants in the most disadvantageous trial position").

17. Cf. United States v. Crandall, 363 F. Supp. 648 (W.D. Pa. 1973).

18. Cf. United States v. Scivola, 766 F.2d 37 (1st Cir. 1985).

19. Cf. United States v. Fornaro, 894 F.2d 508 (2d Cir. 1990).

20. As amended February 5, 2002.

withdrawal from the representation is not permitted or will not undo the effect of the false evidence, the advocate must make such disclosure to the tribunal as is reasonably necessary to remedy the situation, even if doing so requires the lawyer to reveal information that otherwise would be protected by Rule 1.6.[21] It is for the tribunal then to determine what should be done — making a statement about the matter to the trier of fact, ordering a mistrial or perhaps nothing.

[11] The disclosure of a client's false testimony can result in grave consequences to the client, including not only a sense of betrayal but also loss of the case and perhaps a prosecution for perjury. But the alternative is that the lawyer cooperate in deceiving the court, thereby subverting the truth-finding process which the adversary system is designed to implement. See Rule 1.2(d). Furthermore, unless it is clearly understood that the lawyer will act upon the duty to disclose the existence of false evidence, the client can simply reject the lawyer's advice to reveal the false evidence and insist that the lawyer keep silent. Thus the client could in effect coerce the lawyer into being a party to fraud on the court.

How can the ABA rule be reconciled with the witness's rights under § 1623(d)? Consider the following hypothetical situations.

a.   Sherman falsely testifies under oath that he is licensed to practice medicine in four states, that his medical privileges have never been revoked by any hospital, and that the only malpractice suit ever brought against him was "routine."

During a break in Sherman's testimony in chief, the plaintiff's lawyer who hired him as an expert discovers that Sherman's testimony about his credentials is false. What should the lawyer do?

b.   Sherman gives the same false testimony, but this time the lawyer who hired him as an expert is the lawyer for the defense. By the time the lawyer learns of the falsity, the judge has already granted his motion for a directed verdict on three counts of the complaint, based on the strength of Sherman's testimony. The remainder of the case has been sent to the jury. What should the lawyer do?

Would the lawyer's ethical obligations be different in either of the hypotheticals if the witness was the lawyer's client rather than someone he hired to testify as an expert on his client's behalf?

NOTE ON COMPETENT TRIBUNALS AND ANCILLARY PROCEEDINGS

The perjury statute punishes making a sworn false statement that is within the jurisdiction of any tribunal authorized by federal law to administer an oath. Thus, this offense may be committed by testifying falsely before a federal court or grand jury, a congressional committee, a governmental department or agency, or a notary public. In contrast, the false declarations statute is limited to sworn false statements "in a proceeding before or ancillary to" a federal court or grand jury. The statute does not define what ancillary proceedings are, but case law requires that "certain notions of formality and convention" be observed before a proceeding will fall within the reach of § 1623.[22]

---

21. Relating to the confidentiality of client information.
22. United States v. Tibbs, 600 F.2d 19, 21 (6th Cir. 1979).

In Dunn v. United States,[23] the Supreme Court construed the ancillary proceedings language to require a context at least as formal as a deposition. Thus, for example, giving a sworn statement in an interview in a private lawyer's office would lack the requisite degree of formality to constitute an ancillary proceeding.

V. IMMUNIZED TESTIMONY

UNITED STATES v. APFELBAUM
445 U.S. 115 (1980)

Mr. Justice REHNQUIST delivered the opinion of the Court. . . .

I

The grand jury had been investigating alleged criminal activities in connection with an automobile dealership located in the Chestnut Hill section of Philadelphia. The investigation focused on a robbery of $175,000 in cash that occurred at the dealership on April 16, 1975, and on allegations that two officers of the dealership staged the robbery in order to repay loan-shark debts. The grand jury also heard testimony that the officers were making extortionate extensions of credit through the Chestnut Hill Lincoln-Mercury dealership.

In 1976, respondent Apfelbaum, then an administrative assistant to the District Attorney in Philadelphia, was called to testify because it was thought likely that he was an aider or abettor or an accessory after the fact to the allegedly staged robbery. When the grand jury first sought to question him about his relationship with the two dealership officials suspected of the staged robbery, he claimed his Fifth Amendment privilege against compulsory self-incrimination and refused to testify. The District Judge entered an order pursuant to 18 U.S.C. § 6002 granting him immunity and compelling him to testify.[24] Respondent ultimately complied with this order to testify.[25]

---

23. 442 U.S. 100 (1979).

24. Title 18 U.S.C. § 6002 provides:

Whenever a witness refuses, on the basis of his privilege against self-incrimination, to testify or provide other information in a proceeding before or ancillary to —

    (1)   a court or grand jury of the United States,
    (2)   an agency of the United States, or
    (3)   either House of Congress, a joint committee of the two Houses, or a committee or a subcommittee of either House,

and the person presiding over the proceeding communicates to the witness an order issued under this part, the witness may not refuse to comply with the order on the basis of his privilege against self-incrimination; but no testimony or other information compelled under the order (or any information directly or indirectly derived from such testimony or other information) may be used against the witness in any criminal case, except a prosecution for perjury, giving a false statement, or otherwise failing to comply with the order.

25. After the issuance of the immunity order, respondent had still refused to testify before the grand jury. He agreed to testify after being held in civil contempt under 28 U.S.C. § 1826 and confined for six days.

[In his grand jury testimony, Apfelbaum made two series of allegedly false statements that resulted in his indictment.]

At trial, the Government introduced into evidence portions of respondent's grand jury testimony in order to put the charged statements in context and to show that respondent knew they were false. . . . Respondent objected to the use of all the immunized testimony except the portions charged in the indictment as false. The District Court overruled the objection and admitted the excerpts into evidence on the ground that they were relevant to prove that respondent had knowingly made the charged false statements. The jury found respondent guilty on both counts of the indictment.

The Court of Appeals for the Third Circuit reversed, holding that because the immunized testimony did not constitute "the corpus delicti or core of a defendant's false swearing indictment" it could not be introduced. 584 F.2d 1264, 1265 (1978). We granted certiorari because of the importance of the issue and because of a difference in approach to it among the Courts of Appeals. . . .

II

Did Congress intend the federal immunity statute, 18 U.S.C. § 6002, to limit the use of a witness' immunized grand jury testimony in a subsequent prosecution of the witness for false statements made at the grand jury proceeding? Respondent contends that while § 6002 permits the use of a witness' false statements in a prosecution for perjury or for making false declarations, it establishes an absolute prohibition against the use of truthful immunized testimony in such prosecutions. But this contention is wholly at odds with the explicit language of the statute, and finds no support even in its legislative history.

It is a well-established principle of statutory construction that absent clear evidence of a contrary legislative intention, a statute should be interpreted according to its plain language. Here 18 U.S.C. § 6002 provides that when a witness is compelled to testify over his claim of a Fifth Amendment privilege, "no testimony or other information compelled under the order (or any information directly or indirectly derived from such testimony or other information) may be used against the witness in any criminal case, *except a prosecution for perjury, giving a false statement, or otherwise failing to comply with the order*." (Emphasis added.) The statute thus makes no distinction between truthful and untruthful statements made during the course of the immunized testimony. Rather, it creates a blanket exemption from the bar against the use of immunized testimony in cases in which the witness is subsequently prosecuted for making false statements.

The legislative history of § 6002 shows that Congress intended the perjury and false-declarations exception to be interpreted as broadly as constitutionally permissible. The present statute was enacted as a part of the Organized Crime Control Act of 1970, after a re-examination of the broad transactional immunity statute enacted in response to this Court's decision in Counselman v. Hitchcock, 142 U.S. 547 (1892). See Kastigar v. United States, 406 U.S. 441, 452, and n.36 (1972). Its design was not only to bring about uniformity in the operation of immunity grants within the federal system, but also to restrict the grant of immunity to that required by the United States Constitution. Thus, the statute derives from a 1969 report of the National Commission on the Reform of the

Federal Criminal Laws, which proposed a general use immunity statute under which "the immunity conferred would be confined to the scope required by the Fifth Amendment." And as stated in both the Senate and House Reports on the proposed legislation:

> This statutory immunity is intended to be as broad as, but no broader than, the privilege against self-incrimination. . . . It is designed to reflect the use-restriction immunity concept of Murphy v. Waterfront Commission, 378 U.S. 52 (1964) rather [than] the transaction immunity concept of Counselman v. Hitchcock, 142 U.S. 547 (1892).

In light of the language and legislative history of § 6002, the conclusion is inescapable that Congress intended to permit the use of both truthful and false statements made during the course of immunized testimony if such use was not prohibited by the Fifth Amendment.

III

The limitation placed on the use of relevant evidence by the Court of Appeals may be justified, then, only if required by the Fifth Amendment. Respondent contends that his conviction was properly reversed because under the Fifth Amendment his truthful immunized statements were inadmissible at his perjury trial, and the Government never met its burden of showing that the immunized statements it introduced into evidence were not truthful. The Court of Appeals, as noted above, concluded that the Fifth Amendment prohibited the use of all immunized testimony except the "corpus delicti" or "core" of the false swearing indictment.

In reaching its conclusion, the Court of Appeals initially observed that a grant of immunity must be coextensive with the Fifth Amendment. It then reasoned that had respondent not been granted immunity, he would have been entitled under the Fifth Amendment to remain silent. And if he had remained silent, he would not have answered any questions, truthfully or falsely. There consequently would have been no testimony whatsoever to use against him. A prosecution for perjury committed at the immunized proceeding, the Court of Appeals continued, must be permitted because "as a practical matter, if immunity constituted a license to lie, the purpose of immunity would be defeated." Such a prosecution is but a "narrow exception" carved out to preserve the integrity of the truth-seeking process. But the subsequent use of statements made at the immunized proceeding, other than those alleged in the indictment to be false, is impermissible because the introduction of such statements cannot be reconciled with the privilege against self-incrimination.

A

There is more than one flaw in this reasoning. Initially, it presumes that in order for a grant of immunity to be "coextensive with the Fifth Amendment privilege," the witness must be treated as if he had remained silent. This presumption focuses on the effect of the assertion of the Fifth Amendment privilege, rather than on the protection the privilege is designed to confer. In so doing, it calls into question the constitutionality of all immunity statutes, including "transactional" immunity statutes as well as "use" immunity statutes such as § 6002. Such grants of immunity would not provide a full and complete substitute for a witness' silence because, for example, they do not bar the use of the witness' statements in civil proceedings. Indeed, they fail to prevent the use of such statements for any purpose that might cause detriment to the witness other than that resulting from subsequent criminal prosecution.

This Court has never held, however, that the Fifth Amendment requires immunity statutes to preclude all uses of immunized testimony. Such a requirement would be inconsistent with the principle that the privilege does not extend to consequences of a noncriminal nature, such as threats of liability in civil suits, disgrace in the community, or the loss of employment. . . .

The reasoning of the Court of Appeals is also internally inconsistent in that logically it would not permit a prosecution for perjury or false swearing committed during the course of the immunized testimony. If a witness must be treated as if he had remained silent, the mere requirement that he answer questions, thereby subjecting himself to the possibility of being subsequently prosecuted for perjury or false swearing, places him in a position that is substantially different from that he would have been in had he been permitted to remain silent.

All of the Courts of Appeals, however, have recognized that the provision in 18 U.S.C. § 6002 allowing prosecutions for perjury in answering questions following a grant of immunity does not violate the Fifth Amendment privilege against compulsory self-incrimination. And we ourselves have repeatedly held that perjury prosecutions are permissible for false answers to questions following the grant of immunity.

It is therefore analytically incorrect to equate the benefits of remaining silent as a result of invocation of the Fifth Amendment privilege with the protections conferred by the privilege — protections that may be invoked with respect to matters that pose substantial and real hazards of subjecting a witness to criminal liability at the time he asserts the privilege. For a grant of immunity to provide protection "coextensive" with that of the Fifth Amendment, it need not treat the witness as if he had remained silent. Such a conclusion, as noted above, is belied by the fact that immunity statutes and prosecutions for perjury committed during the course of immunized testimony are permissible at all.

B

[Although it is firmly established that "the Fifth Amendment 'does not endow the person who testifies with a license to commit perjury,'" the Court was unwilling to decide the case on that basis alone.]

Perjury prosecutions based on immunized testimony, even if they be but a "narrow exception" to the principle that a witness should be treated as if he had remained silent after invoking the Fifth Amendment privilege, are permitted by our cases. And so long as they are, there is no principle or decision that limits the admissibility of evidence in a manner peculiar only to them. To so hold would not be an exercise in the balancing of competing constitutional rights, but in a comparison of apples and oranges.[26] For even if

---

26. Thus, the Court of Appeals' position is basically a halfway house that does not withstand logical analysis. If the rule is that a witness who is granted immunity may be placed in no worse a position than if he had been permitted to remain silent, the principle that the Fifth Amendment does not protect false

both truthful and untruthful testimony from the immunized proceeding are admissible in a subsequent perjury prosecution, the exception surely would still be properly regarded as "narrow," once it is recognized that the testimony remains inadmissible in all prosecutions for offenses committed prior to the grant of immunity that would have permitted the witness to invoke his Fifth Amendment privilege absent the grant. . . .

. . . [T]he Fifth Amendment does not prevent the use of respondent's immunized testimony at his trial for false swearing because, at the time he was granted immunity, the privilege would not have protected him against false testimony that he later might decide to give. Respondent's assertion of his Fifth Amendment privilege arose from his claim that the questions relating to his connection with the Chestnut Hill auto dealership would tend to incriminate him. The Government consequently granted him "use" immunity under § 6002, which prevents the use and derivative use of his testimony with respect to any subsequent criminal case except prosecutions for perjury and false swearing offenses, in exchange for his compelled testimony. . . .

Reversed.

[Concurring opinions of BRENNAN, J., and BLACKMUN, J., omitted.]

Notes and Questions

1. Does the constitutional right to testify include the right to commit perjury? If a lawyer admonishes his client that unless she testifies truthfully, the lawyer will withdraw, does that deprive the client of her Sixth Amendment right to counsel?[27]

2. Recall the facts of Problem 7-2 again. Suppose that in the 1993 Florida trial, Professor Canby falsely testified that he conducted experiments on the Dalkon Shield and that the tests conclusively proved the product was safe. Later subpoenaed to appear before a grand jury that was investigating the testing and marketing of the Dalkon Shield, he invoked his Fifth Amendment privilege against self-incrimination. After being given a grant of immunity under § 6002, he admitted that his Florida testimony was false, but he falsely denied that Robins' attorneys knew that he had not conducted any safety experiments on the Dalkon Shield. May Canby's immunized testimony be used in a prosecution against him for perjury committed during the Florida trial?

3. In conjunction with its investigation of Whitewater defendant Webster Hubbell for obstruction of justice, the Independent Counsel subpoenaed thousands of documents in Hubbell's possession — including personal financial records, tax returns, and bank records. Hubbell refused to comply on Fifth Amendment grounds. After then being granted immunity, he produced more than 13,000 pages of documents relating to his financial affairs. The Independent Counsel later used these records to build a criminal tax fraud case against him.

Conceding that all of the evidence for the tax fraud charge was derived directly or indirectly from Hubbell's act of producing his financial records, the Independent Counsel made "no bones about the fact" that the subpoenaed documents were critical to

---

statements serves merely as a piece of a legal mosaic justified solely by stare decisis, rather than as part of a doctrinally consistent view of that Amendment.

27. Cf. Nix v. Whiteside, 475 U.S. 157 (1986).

his ability to develop the tax fraud case. The Supreme Court held this derivative use of documents that Hubbell had been compelled to produce was improper and ruled that the government must prove that it developed its case against the witness from wholly independent sources.[28]

Suppose the initial investigation had been for tax-related offenses. What were the Independent Counsel's alternatives for building a case against Hubbell? Could he have obtained Hubbell's records with a search warrant? Could he have acquired some of the same information by obtaining a Dun & Bradstreet report on Hubbell? Subpoenaed records in the possession of Hubbell's banks and credit card companies? Talked to Hubbell's accountant? Acquired Hubbell's tax records from the IRS? What kinds of obstacles do these modes of investigation implicate?

VI. PERJURY BY GOVERNMENT WITNESSES

In the preceding section we explored legal pitfalls that can arise when a witness who has been immunized from prosecution under § 6002 lies under oath. The Court in *Apfelbaum* focused on the witness's potential liability for perjury despite the grant of immunity. We now turn the tables and focus briefly on issues that may arise when someone is (or may have been) convicted on the basis of a witness's perjured testimony.

Post-trial allegations of prosecutorial misconduct — often the basis for a motion for a new trial — rarely succeed. Although one might assume that perjury committed by a government witness would automatically entitle the defendant to a new trial, quite the opposite is true. Even if the witness is shown to have lied under oath, the defendant faces additional significant evidentiary hurdles that are rarely overcome.

Issues that arose two months after Martha Stewart and her stockbroker, Peter Bacanovic, were convicted of deceiving regulators about the circumstances surrounding the sale of Stewart's ImClone stock brought this point into sharp focus in United States v. Stewart.[29] Several months after the jury convicted Stewart and Bacanovic, newly discovered evidence suggested that the government's expert witness had lied on the stand. That led to a defense motion for a new trial based on the claim that the convictions were obtained on the basis of the perjured testimony.

These claims are always difficult to win. As the court in *Stewart* put it, such motions should be granted "only with great caution and in the most extraordinary circumstances."[30]

Courts are reluctant to upset jury verdicts because of alleged witness perjury for several important reasons. First, the standard of review is quite high. If the prosecution was unaware that the witness perjured himself, the defendant has the burden of proving that the jury "probably would have acquitted" the defendant if the witness had testified truthfully.[31] Second, if the prosecution knew or should have known that the witness was lying, the defendant must prove that there was a "reasonable likelihood" that the perjured testimony could have influenced the jury.[32]

---

28. United States v. Hubbell, 530 U.S. 27 (2000).
29. United States v. Stewart, 433 F.3d 273 (2d Cir. 2006) (Stewart I).
30. Id. at 296 (quoting United States v. Sanchez, 969 F.2d 1409, 1414 (2d Cir. 1992)).
31. United States v. Wallach, 935 F.2d 445, 446 (2d Cir. 1991).
32. Stewart I, 433 F.3d 273 at 297; United States v. Damblu, 134 F.3d 490, 493 (2d Cir. 1998).

In most cases, these are virtually insurmountable burdens of proof, and in *Stewart*, the cards were clearly stacked against the defendants.

First, even if the government's witness had lied and the government had been aware of the perjury, the witness's conclusions were corroborated by substantial independent evidence, including the expert witness for the defense. Indeed, Bacanovic's lawyer told the jury that "our expert and their expert really agreed on almost everything about the main important points."[33]

Second, the expert witness — who testified about his analysis of ink on a crucial document in the case — was not accused of lying about the results of the test. He allegedly lied about his personal participation in performing the test and about his knowledge of a book project several of his colleagues had proposed. These issues had little or no bearing on the issue of whether Stewart and Bacanovic had lied about the sale of her stock, so the defense could not show there was a "reasonable likelihood" that the false testimony influenced the jury.[34]

But there were even more compelling reasons for upholding the jury's verdict: (1) since the allegedly false testimony was collateral to the main issues, it was not material under § 1621; (2) the jury verdict was supported by substantial independent evidence;[35] and (3) the jury's special verdicts made it abundantly clear that the allegedly false testimony had not influenced the outcome.[36]

Notes and Questions

1. Why isn't a conviction based on perjured testimony automatically void?

2. Assuming the government's expert witness in *Stewart* testified falsely, was his testimony prejudicial? Does it matter whether the substance of his perjured testimony would not have influenced the jury's verdict? Could his testimony nonetheless be deemed prejudicial because the jury did not have an opportunity to weigh the expert's overall credibility in light of the alleged perjury?

3. Assuming that the expert lied when he claimed that he personally participated in conducting the ink analysis and that he knew about his colleagues' book proposal, is that important in the grand scheme of things? Should these lies have had any bearing on the judge's ruling on Stewart's motion for a new trial?

4. The standard of review for a challenge to a conviction based on perjured testimony is high. The usual test inquires whether the prosecution knew or should have known the testimony was perjured and whether "there is any reasonable likelihood that the perjured testimony influenced the jury." In the event that the prosecution did not know of the alleged perjury, an even more stringent standard of review applies. The test is whether "but for the perjured testimony, the defendant would most likely not have been convicted." Is this standard too speculative?

---

33. United States v. Stewart, 323 F. Supp. 2d 606, 614 (S.D.N.Y. 2004) (citing trial transcript at 4657) (Stewart II).

34. Id. at 615 (quoting United States v. Damblu, 134 F.3d 490, 493 (2d Cir. 1998).

35. The testimony of at least four witnesses close to the events supported the jury's verdict. Id. at 612, 621.

36. 3 Kathleen F. Brickey, Corporate Criminal Liability § 13:10.10 (2d ed. 1991-1994 & 2010-2011 Cumulative Supplement). For a fuller account of the special jury verdicts in *Stewart*, see Kathleen F. Brickey, Mostly Martha, 44 Washburn L.J. 517, 527-535, 546-551 (Appendices A-C) (2005).

8

Obstruction of Justice

I. INTRODUCTION

The federal obstruction of justice statutes serve two distinct but related purposes: (1) they protect participants in judicial and administrative proceedings from the use of force, intimidation, or corrupt means to influence them in the discharge of their duties; and (2) they preserve the integrity of the judicial and administrative decision-making process.

The principal statutory tools have historically been 18 U.S.C. § 1503, which applies to participants in civil and criminal judicial proceedings; 18 U.S.C. § 1505, which applies to participants in administrative agency and congressional proceedings; and 18 U.S.C. § 1510, which applies to participants in federal criminal investigations. The Victim and Witness Protection Act of 1982 altered the traditional role of these statutes and created two new offenses — tampering with witnesses, victims, and informants (18 U.S.C. § 1512) and retaliating against witnesses, victims, and informants (18 U.S.C. § 1513).

The Sarbanes-Oxley Act added four new offenses to the existing panoply of obstruction of justice statutes. The new provisions focus primarily on evidence tampering — particularly destruction, alteration, and concealment of documents — and retaliating against witnesses or informants, including corporate whistleblowers. As might be expected, parts of the new laws overlap with existing statutes, while others dovetail with them to fill interstitial gaps.

II. PENDING JUDICIAL PROCEEDINGS

The basic obstruction of justice statute, 18 U.S.C. § 1503, prohibits specific acts such as threatening jurors and officers of the court. For purposes of most white collar prosecutions, however, the heart of the statute is its omnibus clause, which forbids corruptly endeavoring "to influence, obstruct, or impede, the due administration of justice." This language highlights the principal concern of the statute, which is not so much "doing 'justice' in the sense of 'fairness' and 'rightness'" as it is preserving the "judicial procedure" through which legal and factual issues are adjudicated.[1] Thus, it is "the process of arriving at an appropriate judgment in a pending case" that the statute safeguards.[2] Just as society has an interest in affording the accused a fair trial, it has a legitimate interest in the adjudication of guilt and the imposition of punishment where warranted.

UNITED STATES v. SIMMONS
591 F.2d 206 (3d Cir. 1979)

ADAMS, Circuit Judge.

This appeal presents inter alia the question whether a grand jury investigation is pending for purposes of the obstruction of justice statute, 18 U.S.C. § 1503, when a subpoena to produce records and to testify before a regularly sitting grand jury has been issued upon application of an Assistant United States Attorney but when at the time of the alleged obstruction of justice the grand jury itself has no knowledge of the subpoena or the matters under investigation.

Barry Simmons was a writ server for the Philadelphia Traffic Court. In mid-July, 1977, two deputy writ servers employed by Simmons reported to the FBI that Simmons was engaged in an illegal scheme of changing the dates on scofflaw notices for which the statute of limitations had run and then mailing such notices. On July 28, 1977, the FBI secured a subpoena ordering the telephone company to produce before a regularly sitting grand jury on August 5, 1977, records of the toll calls made from Simmons' business and private telephones. Also, on August 4, 1977, subpoenas were served on Simmons and several of his employees directing them to appear before the grand jury on August 12, 1977, and to bring records and documents relating to priority scofflaw notifications.

According to the evidence introduced at trial, upon being served with a subpoena, Simmons proceeded to destroy documents in his possession that were referred to in such subpoena and to instruct his employees as to what they were to say to the investigators. For such conduct, Simmons was indicted by the grand jury on August 12, 1978, on two counts of obstruction of justice — the first count charging him with destruction of documents and the second count charging him with instructing his employees to withhold information from the grand jury — and was convicted and sentenced after a jury trial.

The obstruction of justice statute imposes criminal sanctions upon anyone who "corruptly . . . influences, obstructs, or impedes, or endeavors to influence, obstruct, or impede, the due administration of justice." 18 U.S.C. § 1503. A prerequisite for conviction is the pendency at the time of the alleged obstruction of some sort of judicial proceeding that qualifies as an "administration of justice." Thus, for example, the obstruction of an investigation that is being conducted by the FBI, or by any similar governmental agency or instrumentality, does not constitute a § 1503 violation because such agencies or instrumentalities are not judicial arms of the government "administering justice." On the other hand, obstruction of a pending grand jury investigation is punishable under the statute.

---

1. United States v. Howard, 569 F.2d 1331, 1337 (5th Cir. 1978).
2. Haili v. United States, 260 F.2d 744, 746 (9th Cir. 1958).

issue

At issue here is at what point does an investigation by law enforcement officers cross the threshold to become a pending grand jury investigation for purposes of such statute. On this matter, the jury was instructed, over objections by defense counsel,

> that when an Assistant United States Attorney issues a subpoena or subpoenas in further-ance of a grand jury investigation for the purpose of presenting evidence to the grand jury, there is a grand jury investigation pending within the meaning of that statute.

jury instr

The only evidence submitted on the question of pendency was proof that a grand jury had been constituted and empaneled and that subpoenas were then issued to the telephone company, to Simmons, and to several of his employees, to appear before such grand jury.

Simmons asserts that the jury charge was erroneous and that the evidence was insufficient to establish the pendency of a grand jury investigation on the date he is alleged to have obstructed justice. In support of this assertion, Simmons points out that the evidence fails to establish that at that time the grand jury was investigating, or even had knowledge of, defendant's traffic court activities. Each of the subpoenas to testify before the grand jury set forth on its face that it was issued on application of an Assistant United States Attorney, and no evidence was produced at trial to indicate that such attorney was instructed by the grand jury to obtain those subpoenas or that he was acting as an agent for the grand jury when applying for them. Therefore, Simmons argues, the evidence at best supports the conclusion that there was an investigation by the FBI or the United States Attorney's office, but not that there was a pending grand jury inves-tigation, as required for a § 1503 conviction.

Much of the force behind Simmons' argument is undercut by our discussion of the "pendency" issue in United States v. Walasek, 527 F.2d 676, 678 (3d Cir. 1975). There, Judge Hunter disposed of a similar challenge to a conviction under § 1503 in the following manner:

> Appellant would have us adopt a rigid rule that a grand jury proceeding is not "pending" until a grand jury has actually heard testimony or has in some way taken a role in the decision to issue the subpoena. He offers no authority for such a rule, and we are not inclined to adopt it. Appellant is correct in his observation that a grand jury subpoena may become an instrumentality of an investigative agency, without meaningful judicial super-vision. Nevertheless, the remedy against potential abuses is not to establish a rule, easily circumvented, by which some formal act of the grand jury will be required to establish "pendency." The remedy is rather to continue to inquire, in each case, whether the subpoena is issued in furtherance of an actual grand jury investigation, i.e., to secure a presently contemplated presentation of evidence before the grand jury. See United States v. Ryan, 455 F.2d 728 (9th Cir. 1972).
>
> Without attempting to articulate any necessary minimum set of circumstances, we are persuaded that the present record is sufficient to establish the "pendency" of a judicial proceeding.

Simmons submits, however, that unlike *Walasek*, his case does not present the "necessary minimum set of circumstances" required to sustain a jury finding of "pendency." In particular, Simmons distinguishes *Walasek* on the ground that at the time of the alleged destruction of subpoenaed documents under Walasek's supervision a witness had been called — not merely subpoenaed — to testify before the grand jury, and upon his refusal to testify had been granted immunity. Under those circumstances, Simmons asserts, it is clear that the grand jury was already cognizant of, and involved in, the investigation. . . .

We disagree with Simmons' interpretation of *Ryan* as well as with the standard for "pendency" which he urges upon us. As already noted in *Walasek*, *Ryan* involved the unusual situation wherein the IRS, unable to secure records by administrative subpoenas, caused an Assistant United States Attorney to obtain the subpoenas and to furnish them to IRS agents for service. The subpoenaed documents were delivered directly to the IRS, and the grand jury to which the matter had been assigned was eventually dismissed without ever having been told about the subpoenas and without investigating any matters related to them. More than fourteen months elapsed before another grand jury indicted Ryan. "Thus, by means of grand jury subpoenas, the I.R.S. obtained the records which it was unable to secure by an administrative subpoena."[3] It was therefore transparent in *Ryan* that, in terms of the *Walasek* test, the subpoenas were not "issued in furtherance of an actual grand jury investigation, i.e., to secure a presently contemplated presentation of evidence before the grand jury."[4]

With respect to whether the grand jury must be aware of the subpoena or involved in the investigation in some other way at the time of the alleged obstruction of justice, it is our view that adding such a gloss to the test laid down in *Walasek* would frustrate the purpose of the obstruction of justice statute. Section 1503 is a contempt statute. It was enacted as the counterpart to 18 U.S.C. § 401, whose reach is limited to conduct occurring in the presence of the court. As such, § 1503 allows punishment of actions taken with the specific intent to impede the administration of justice. So long as a defendant has such specific intent, he may not circumvent the court's contempt power by pressing "empty technicalities." Thus, in *Walasek* we refused to identify "some formal act of the grand jury [that] will be required to establish 'pendency,'" nor adopt "a rigid rule that a grand jury proceeding is not 'pending' until a grand jury has actually heard testimony or has in some way taken a role in the decision to issue the subpoena."[5] The requirement urged by Simmons — that the grand jury be aware of the subpoena or otherwise involved in the investigation at the time of the alleged obstruction of justice — likewise appears not to serve a useful function.

First, such requirement ignores the reality of the manner in which a grand jury operates and the mechanism by which subpoenas are issued. In In re Grand Jury Proceedings, 486 F.2d 85, 90 (3d Cir. 1973), we observed, albeit somewhat critically, that

> although grand jury subpoenas are occasionally discussed as if they were the instrumentalities of the grand jury, they are in fact almost universally instrumentalities of the United States Attorney's office or of some other investigative or prosecutorial department of the executive branch.

Furthermore, the prosecutorial authorities could easily nullify the effect of such a rigid rule by adding to their procedures the formal act of advising the grand jury of the subpoena when it is issued.

---

3. *Ryan*, supra, 455 F.2d at 732.
4. 537 F.2d 678.
5. Id.

Consequently, rather than require that the grand jury be cognizant of the subpoena or otherwise involved in the investigation, we hold that an investigation by a law enforcement agency ripens into a pending grand jury investigation for purposes of § 1503 when officials of such agency apply for, and cause to be issued, subpoenas to testify before a sitting grand jury. To the extent that, as demonstrated by *Ryan*, "a grand jury subpoena may become an instrumentality of an investigative agency, without meaningful judicial supervision," we reiterate our conviction that the remedy against such abuse is not to establish a rigid rule, but "rather to continue to inquire, in each case, whether the subpoena is issued in furtherance of an actual grand jury investigation, i.e., to secure a presently contemplated presentation of evidence before the grand jury." *Walasek*, supra.

Besides challenging his conviction on the ground that no grand jury investigation was pending, Simmons raises other grounds for reversal. We have reviewed each of these contentions and find them to be without merit. Accordingly, the judgment of the district court will be affirmed.

Notes and Questions

1. If someone falsifies subpoenaed documents, why should it matter that the subpoena was issued to help the IRS obtain evidence it had otherwise been unable to acquire? If the IRS had a legitimate reason for wanting the records, doesn't the act of falsifying them impede the due administration of justice?

Would submitting false documents that had been subpoenaed by the IRS violate a companion provision, § 1505, which prohibits corrupt efforts "to influence, obstruct, or impede the due and proper administration of the law under which any pending proceeding is being had before any department or agency of the United States"? When is a proceeding pending before an administrative agency?[6]

2. When does a proceeding cease to be pending? In *Simmons*, did the proceeding terminate with the issuance of the indictment? When the grand jury's term expired? When the jury convicted Simmons? When he was sentenced? At some other point in time?[7]

3. While courts are in agreement that § 1503 requires a pending grand jury proceeding, there is a split of authority when the charge is conspiracy to obstruct justice. Although at least one circuit requires that a proceeding be pending when the conspiracy is formed,[8] several others recognize that a punishable conspiracy may be found even though no proceeding is pending when the agreement is formed.[9] In United States v. Vaghela,[10] the court qualified this principle. Drawing on analogous Supreme Court

---

6. Cf. Rice v. United States, 356 F.2d 709, 712 (8th Cir. 1966) (Congress has chosen "a comprehensive term meaning the *action* of a proceeding — a particular step or series of steps adopted for the accomplishment of something").

7. Cf. United States v. Fulbright, 105 F.3d 443 (9th Cir. 1997); United States v. Bashaw, 982 F.2d 168 (6th Cir. 1992); United States v. Johnson, 605 F.2d 729 (4th Cir. 1979).

8. See United States v. Cihack, 137 F.3d 252, 263 (5th Cir. 1998).

9. See United States v. Vaghela, 169 F.3d 729, 734-735 (11th Cir. 1999); United States v. Messerlian, 832 F.2d 778, 799 (3d Cir. 1987).

10. 169 F.3d 729 (11th Cir. 1999).

precedents,[11] the court required that the conspiratorial objective have "the natural and probable effect of interfering with the due administration of justice" in a way that is more than merely "speculative."[12]

> [T]he requirement that the actions defendants conspired to take have "the natural and probable effect of interfering with the due administration of justice" is not so narrow as to preclude a conspiracy to obstruct specific future judicial proceedings, for example, an agreement to bribe members of a grand jury should one be struck in the future. See United States v. Perlstein, 126 F.2d 789, 794 (3d Cir. 1942). This was the thrust of the Third Circuit's decision in United States v. Messerlian, 832 F.2d 778 (3d Cir. 1987). In that case, the court upheld the conviction for conspiracy to obstruct justice of several state troopers who took steps to prevent a future federal grand jury investigation into a trooper's fatal assault of an arrestee who was in custody following his arrest for drunk driving.[13] The Third Circuit held that the defendants were properly convicted of conspiracy to obstruct justice because "the federal proceeding need not be pending at the time the conspiracy is formed" and that the government merely had to prove that "the conspirators undertook to obstruct the due administration of justice in a federal proceeding that they anticipated would commence in the future." Because the direct object of the actions agreed to by the conspirators in *Messerlian* was to prevent or otherwise obstruct the commencement of a grand jury investigation into the circumstances surrounding the arrestee's death, we agree with the Third Circuit that sufficient evidence existed to convict the *Messerlian* defendants of conspiracy to obstruct justice. Accordingly, we disagree with the Fifth Circuit position to the extent that it holds that a conviction for conspiracy to obstruct justice will always require a pending judicial proceeding to be in existence at the time the defendants formed the conspiracy.
>
> Thus, in order to sustain a conviction for conspiracy to obstruct justice under 18 U.S.C. § 371 and 18 U.S.C. § 1503, the government need not always show that a judicial proceeding existed at the time the defendants formed the conspiracy, but must demonstrate that the actions the conspirators agreed to take were directly intended to prevent or otherwise obstruct the processes of a specific judicial proceeding in a way that is more than merely "speculative.". . .[14]

UNITED STATES v. LUNDWALL
1 F. Supp. 2d 249 (S.D.N.Y. 1998)

Parker, District Judge.

Richard A. Lundwall and Robert W. Ulrich, two former officials of Texaco, Inc., are charged in a two count Superceding Indictment with conspiring to obstruct justice in violation of 18 U.S.C. § 371 and with obstruction of justice in violation of 18 U.S.C. § 1503. They move to dismiss on the ground that § 1503 does not apply to civil discovery matters. Since we conclude that § 1503 reaches the willful destruction of documents during civil litigation, defendants' motion is denied.

---

11. See United States v. Aguilar, 515 U.S. 593, 601 (1995).

12. *Vaghela*, 169 F.3d at 734.

13. These steps included "agreeing not to report the fact that [state trooper] Messerlian had assaulted [the arrestee], . . . failing to provide routine information to the hospital concerning the circumstances of [the arrestee's] death, . . . knowingly omitting accounts of the alleged assault from statements prepared during interviews with [several witnesses], . . . fabricating a story [regarding how the arrestee came to be injured, and] . . . making false declarations before the grand jury." *Messerlian*, 832 F.2d at 784.

14. *Vaghela*, 169 F.3d at 734-735.

Indictment

The Indictment charges that defendants' conduct occurred during the pendency in this District of a civil class action employment discrimination law suit styled Roberts v. Texaco, Inc., 94 Civ. 2915 (CLB). The *Roberts* plaintiffs alleged that Texaco had racially discriminated against its African-American employees. During pretrial preparations for *Roberts*, Texaco's legal department had allegedly advised certain Texaco officials, including Ulrich, of the pendency of the lawsuit and of the need to retain documents relevant to the lawsuit. A few months later, Lundwall was deposed and was requested on the record to produce documents pertaining to Texaco's minority employees. As a result of the request made by plaintiffs' counsel in the *Roberts* suit, Lundwall and Ulrich, among others, were given responsibility for collecting responsive documents for production. Following the requests made during Lundwall's deposition and memorialized in a subsequent follow-up letter, Lundwall, Ulrich and others are alleged to have first withheld and then destroyed documents sought by plaintiffs' counsel and required to be produced in *Roberts*.

Roberts

The Indictment charges that defendants' conduct violated 18 U.S.C. § 1503, which provides, in part:

1503

> Whoever . . . *corruptly, or by threats or force or by threatening letter or communication, influences, obstructs, or impedes, or endeavors to influence, obstruct or impede, the due administration of justice*, shall [be guilty of a federal crime].

Arg

The defendants move to dismiss on the ground that § 1503 does not apply to their conduct. Their principal contention is that the statute has never been used to prosecute individuals charged with the destruction or concealment of documents during civil discovery. See Richmark Corp. v. Timber Falling Consultants, Inc., 730 F. Supp. 1525, 1532-33 (D. Or. 1990). . . .

Cases involving prosecutions for document destruction during civil pretrial discovery are notably absent from the extensive body of reported § 1503 case law. Defendants contend that this absence precludes the application of § 1503 to their alleged conduct. . . .

Defendants' conduct as alleged in the Indictment seems to us to fall comfortably within the reach of the text of § 1503. As we have seen, the Indictment alleges that defendants, knowing that relevant documents were to be produced in ongoing civil litigation, deliberately concealed and destroyed them. In doing so, defendants are charged with having acted "corruptly" as opposed to inadvertently or with some innocent motive. The alleged document destruction and concealment is claimed by the government to have "influenced or impeded" or, at the very least, "attempted to influence or impede" the development of facts and claims asserted in the *Roberts* litigation. And defendants' conduct is alleged to have impeded the "due administration of justice":

> [T]he words "due administration of justice" import a free and fair opportunity to every litigant in a pending cause in federal court to learn what he may learn (if not impeded or obstructed) concerning the material facts and to exercise his option as to introducing testimony or such facts. The violation of the law may consist in preventing a litigant from learning facts which he might otherwise learn, and in thus preventing him from deciding for himself whether or not to make use of such facts.

Wilder v. United States, 143 F. 433, 441 (4th Cir. 1906).

Cases analyzing § 1503 reinforce an understanding that § 1503 reaches an extensive range of misconduct. "The broad scope of the statute and the evils it sought to combat . . . was the 'outgrowth of Congressional recognition of the variety of corrupt methods by which the proper administration of justice may be impeded or thwarted . . . [which are] limited only by the imagination of the criminally inclined.'" United States v. Solow, 138 F. Supp. 812, 815 (S.D.N.Y. 1956). "[T]he omnibus clause [of § 1503] is broad enough to cover any act committed corruptly, in an endeavor to impede or obstruct justice." United States v. Brenson, 104 F.3d 1267, 1275 (11th Cir.). "The statute [§ 1503] reaches all corrupt conduct capable of producing an effect that prevents justice from being duly administered." Id. at 1275. . . .

[W]e find no basis [in the legislative history or case law] for concluding either that § 1503 has consistently been applied more narrowly than is required by its text or that failing to do so would lead to a wrong result. The case law demonstrates that § 1503 has been repeatedly applied in a wide variety of civil matters. See, e.g., United States v. Muhammad, 120 F.3d 688 (7th Cir. 1997) (upholding obstruction conviction where defendant, a juror in a civil case, solicited a bribe from a litigant in that case in exchange for a promise to sway the jury); United States v. London, 714 F.2d 1558 (11th Cir. 1983) (affirming conviction under § 1503 for lawyer's presentation of fraudulent civil judgment to his client after resolution of lawsuit); Roberts v. United States, 239 F.2d 467, 470 (9th Cir. 1956) ("obstruction of justice statute is broad enough to cover the attempted corruption of a prospective witness in a civil action in a Federal District Court"); Wilder v. United States, 143 F. at 440 (rejecting contention that obstruction of justice in civil litigation is not an offense against the United States).

At the same time, a long line of cases holds that the willful destruction or concealment of documents sought in grand jury proceedings violates § 1503.

Defendants argue that this extensive body of cases establishes that to the extent that § 1503 is applied to the concealment or destruction of documents, its reach is limited to acts occurring in the context of such proceedings as grand jury investigations. Yet, again, nothing in these cases or in the language of the statute requires such a result. The omnibus clause of § 1503 is broad and does not, on its face, refer to grand jury proceedings. While a grand jury proceeding certainly complies with the Supreme Court's requirement that there be some pending judicial proceeding for the "due administration of justice" element of the statute to be met, see Pettibone v. United States, 148 U.S. 197, 207 (1893), nothing in the statute or its legislative history limits the definition of a pending judicial proceeding. The frequency with which cases reported under § 1503 involve grand jury proceedings probably indicates only that this area is one that attracts the attention of prosecutors far more frequently than matters of civil litigation. The pendency of a civil action — such as Roberts — in federal district court also satisfies the "pending proceeding" requirement, and the holdings of the cases in the context of a grand jury proceeding — that willful concealment and destruction of documents amount to § 1503 obstruction — therefore apply with equal force to both civil and criminal cases.

Of course, there are a great many good reasons why federal prosecutors should be reluctant to bring criminal charges relating to conduct in ongoing civil litigation. Civil litigation typically involves parties protected by counsel who bring frequently exaggerated claims that, under the supervision of a judicial officer, are narrowed and ultimately compromised during pretrial proceedings. Prosecutorial resources would risk quick depletion if abuses in civil proceedings — even the most flagrant ones — were the subject of criminal prosecutions rather than civil remedies. Thus, for numerous prudential reasons, prosecutors might avoid entering this area. But that is quite different from concluding that § 1503 precludes their doing so.

Defendants contend that they were not subpoenaed or directed by a court to furnish the information sought by the *Roberts* plaintiffs in their discovery requests. They also submit that the Indictment is overbroad, charging them not only with concealing and destroying documents requested by the *Roberts* plaintiffs, but also with concealing and destroying documents likely to be requested by them. But the law is clear that neither a subpoena nor a court order directing the production of documents must be issued or served as a prerequisite to a § 1503 prosecution, and that the concealment and destruction of documents likely to be sought by subpoena is actionable under the statute. . . .

Finally, defendants claim that the facts underlying the charges present nothing more than a civil discovery dispute and that if they engaged in discovery abuses, the federal courts possess broad statutory and inherent powers under Fed. R. Civ. P. 37 and 28 U.S.C. § 1927 to impose civil sanctions, including the imposition of monetary penalties, the entering of a default, and the dismissal of defenses.

This case, however, goes beyond civil discovery abuse remediable through civil sanctions. Defendants here are not charged with concealing and destroying documents they incorrectly concluded were not sought, or erroneously thought to be irrelevant or burdensome. Rather, they are charged with seeking to impair a pending court proceeding through the intentional destruction of documents sought in, and highly relevant to, that proceeding. For a variety of reasons, the panoply of tools used to address civil discovery problems such as monetary sanctions, orders of preclusion, or dismissal of claims or defenses might at times be insufficient. Civil discovery rules are primarily directed to the parties and their counsel. Here, the Indictment does not involve the misconduct of Texaco (the defendant in the *Roberts* litigation) or its counsel but that of individuals who appear to have been acting independently of their employer and its attorneys. Thus, it seems that the parties and their counsel in *Roberts* were apparently acting consistently with the requirements of the discovery provisions of the Federal Rules of Civil Procedure. Under these unusual circumstances, the government's contention that civil remedies are inadequate seems to us to be correct. . . .

. . . Rule 37 sanctions are designed for a limited purpose — to further the ends of the Federal Rules of Civil Procedure. Their purpose is to police discovery, to curb both negligent and intentional discovery lapses, and to keep the parties from benefitting in the lawsuit as a result of their own misconduct — all with the goal of insuring "the just, speedy, and inexpensive determination" of the particular lawsuit. As such, civil sanctions — in contrast to criminal ones — are only marginally punitive. Unlike criminal sanctions, civil sanctions are inadequate to effect either general or specific deterrence, or to protect the integrity of the court and the due administration of justice, especially under egregious circumstances such as are alleged in the Indictment.

Finally, precisely because Rule 37 sanctions and criminal sanctions serve different purposes and are addressed to different ends, they are not mutually exclusive. Where conduct in the context of discovery is contumacious, it may very well warrant both types of sanctions, and it is well established that a court may impose both civil and criminal sanctions in connection with the same contumacious behavior.

CONCLUSION

For the foregoing reasons, defendants' motion to dismiss the Indictment on the ground that it does not state an offense is denied.

So ordered.

Notes and Questions

1. The court notes that obstruction-of-justice cases arising out of wrongs that occur during civil pretrial discovery are "notably absent." Why would prosecutors be reluctant to bring criminal charges stemming from obstructive conduct in civil cases, but be eager to prosecute when such conduct relates to criminal investigations? What makes *Lundwall* the exception rather than the rule?

2. Is it clear that civil sanctions are inadequate to redress the wrong in *Lundwall*? If so, why? What additional purposes does criminal prosecution serve in this context?

3. The court observed that civil and criminal sanctions are not mutually exclusive and may simultaneously be imposed for the same contumacious acts. When would it be appropriate to impose both civil and criminal sanctions? Who decides what sanctions to impose?

4. If the documents had not yet been subpoenaed when the defendants destroyed them, why would the act of concealment or destruction implicate § 1503?

5. Lundwall secretly tape-recorded a number of conversations in which Texaco executives discussed destroying documents requested by plaintiffs in the discrimination suit and made racially disparaging remarks. After the tapes were publicly disclosed, Texaco quickly settled the bias suit for $176 million.

At the criminal trial, defense lawyers argued that this was the first time the government had sought criminal convictions for destruction of documents that had not been subpoenaed and that Lundwall and Ulrich did not have sufficient legal guidance on how the unsubpoenaed documents should be handled. After three weeks of trial and four days of deliberations, the jury acquitted both Lundwall and Ulrich of obstruction of justice.[15]

III. ENDEAVORING TO INFLUENCE OR IMPEDE

Section 1503 punishes corrupt endeavors to influence the administration of justice. By using the term "endeavors," Congress avoided the technicalities of the law of attempt. The statute punishes *any* effort to do what the statute forbids, provided that the conduct has "at least a reasonable tendency" to corrupt a legal proceeding.[16] Thus, conduct that falls far short of an attempt may violate the statute.

---

15. Adam Bryant, 2 in Texaco Case Found Not Guilty, N.Y. Times, May 13, 1998, at A1; Tim Whitmire, Tapes Don't Stick in Court: Ex-Texaco Executives Walk, Chicago Sun-Times, May 13, 1998, at 3.

16. United States v. Harris, 558 F.2d 366, 369 (7th Cir. 1977).

UNITED STATES v. COLLIS
128 F.3d 313 (6th Cir. 1997)

Boggs, Circuit Judge. Ronald Collis was convicted of obstructing justice when he submitted a forged letter to a district court in support of leniency at a supervised release violation hearing. . . .

I

This appeal stems from a parole violation after an earlier conviction. In 1990, Collis pled guilty to embezzling over $200,000 from a pension fund. As a result of this guilty plea, Collis was sentenced in federal court to a term of 12 months in a half-way house and three years of supervised release. The stay at the half-way house, however, did not stem Collis's predilection for embezzlement. About six months after being released, Collis began embezzling funds from Perfection Industries, where he was working at the time as the in-house accountant. This resulted in state criminal proceedings beginning against him and ultimately resulted in his pleading guilty in Detroit Recorder's Court to the lesser charge of attempted embezzlement.

Collis's probation officer, Charlene Minor, learned of the Recorder's Court case and also learned that Collis had left the state without seeking permission. As a result, she prepared a supervised release violation petition alleging that Collis had committed a new offense while on release and that he had left the district without permission. A revocation hearing was held and United States District Court Judge Zatkoff found that Collis had committed both of the alleged violations. He then invited Collis's counsel, Noel Lippman, to address the court before imposing sentence. In response, Lippman handed the judge three letters, all of which had been given to Lippman by Collis.

One of the letters was forged.[17] The letter appeared to be signed by Thomas P. Schwanitz, the principal owner of the firm where Collis had been working, and was on the firm's letterhead. It is this letter that forms the basis for the obstruction of justice charge:

> I am writing to you on behalf of my employee, tax manager, Ronald Collis. He will be in your courtroom on May 12, 1994.
>
> Mr. Collis has been my employee since January 17, 1994, however, I have known Mr. Collis since 1974. As an employer, Mr. Collis has been an ideal employee. . . . One would never know the problems he faces, and the vast amount of tragedy he is [sic] and has faced over the last five years.
>
> On a personal level, our office was quite skeptical of employing him, however, the skepticism has been replaced. Mr. Collis is a man trying to rehabilitate himself through many facets. He has for the last year and a half been under the care of a psychologist. He meets on a weekly basis, and has also been under medication proscribed [sic] by the doctor, and takes the medication religiously.

---

17. The other two letters — one from his brother and one from his psychiatrist — were not forged and are not relevant to this appeal. The letter from Collis's brother attempted to take the blame for Collis's unpermitted trip out of Michigan, and the letter from the psychiatrist briefly recommended that Collis continue with psychiatric treatment.

In addition, Mr. Collis has been doing community service work without any recognition. He has devoted many evenings since January, 1994 to help the accounting students of Mount Clemens's High School for their national evaluations. . . .

Mr. Collis last month wrote and was published in the California Medical Journal an article on "How to Help Avoid Employee Embezzlement and Fraud." He would not accept any remuneration for the article, as he felt it was part of his recovery.

Currently, the Michigan Association of CPA's has asked our firm to represent them at career day for Farmington High School, and Ferndale High School. We are currently awaiting your decision on Mr. Collis since he would be the employee we would have represent the MACPA because of his motivational speaking.

. . . Financially, things have been very difficult for Mr. Collis, since he is the sole support of his wife and child, plus he is supporting a second family.

However, as you are aware, Mr. Collis agreed to make restitution to Perfection Industries, Inc. at the rate of $555.55 per month for the next 36 months. Mr. Collis has made all of his payments to date. Also, Chief Justice Robeson has delayed entering a guilty plea and may be placed [sic] Mr. Collis on probation in the future next to insure all restitution payments are being made.

I would very much like Mr. Collis to be given a second chance in this case. Judge Robeson too thought so in going along with the agreement made with the prosecutor.

If you find Mr. Collis is in violation of his supervised release, I would ask that you consider other alternatives than that of sending him to jail. . . .

I thank you for the time in reading this letter, and hope that you will take this into account at Mr. Collis' hearing.

After receiving the three letters, Judge Zatkoff sentenced Collis to eight months in prison. No additional supervised release or fine was imposed.

Sometime after the revocation sentence had become final, a member of Judge Zatkoff's staff learned that the Schwanitz letter was a fabrication. The matter was then referred to the United States Attorney's Office and resulted in a two-count indictment, including the obstruction of justice charge.

During trial, Lippman was called to testify. He testified that he received the Schwanitz letter from Collis before the hearing and that the letter had originally been furnished to him unsigned. After making some suggested changes to the letter, Lippman returned it to Collis. The signed version was subsequently presented to Lippman by Collis, along with a letter from Collis's brother and a letter from his psychiatrist.

Schwanitz also testified at trial. He testified that he did not draft, sign or even see the letter. He also testified that the letter contained several other falsehoods. For one, he testified that Collis was not going to represent the Michigan Association of CPAs at career day. He was also unaware that Collis's CPA license was inactive and he was unaware of the supervised release violation proceeding. In addition, it was shown at trial that Collis had never submitted the embezzlement article for publication.

Judge Zatkoff testified at trial as well. He indicated that the letters submitted by Collis are the type he normally receives and relies on and that he had read the forged letter submitted by Collis before he imposed sentence. Collis did not testify at trial and continues to maintain that he did not provide the Schwanitz letter to his attorney.

II

Collis argues first that the Schwanitz letter could not have formed the basis of an obstruction of justice charge because there was no evidence the letter affected the court's determination of guilt or the sentence imposed. While Collis's argument is styled as a challenge to the sufficiency of the indictment, it is more appropriately viewed as a challenge to the sufficiency of the evidence at trial. Under either analysis, however, Collis's argument lacks merit.

Statute

A. SUFFICIENCY OF THE INDICTMENT . . .

In order to satisfy § 1503, the government must prove that (1) there was a judicial proceeding; (2) the defendant had knowledge or notice of the pending proceeding; and (3) the defendant acted corruptly with the intent of influencing, obstructing, or impeding the proceeding in the due administration of justice. . . . It is this third element that Collis argues was not satisfied. He claims that Judge Zatkoff's testimony that he normally receives and relies on such letters fails to establish that the letter had any actual effect on his sentencing decision. This argument is misplaced. The government need not show that the false statements actually obstructed justice. Collis's letter need only have "the natural and probable effect of impeding justice" to constitute a violation of § 1503. The letter does so.

First, it paints the defendant in a very favorable light and indicates that despite his troubled past, his employer completely trusts him and holds him in high esteem. Second, the letter indicates that Collis will continue to be employed should he remain out of prison, enabling him to continue to pay restitution. Third, the letter indicates that Collis has taken responsibility for his past actions and has endeavored to stop others from following in his path.

This court's decision in United States v. Essex, 407 F.2d 214, 218 (6th Cir. 1969), does not alter the analysis.[18] Unlike Essex, Collis was charged not only with submitting the false letter but also with endeavoring to obstruct and influence the sentencing process by seeking leniency using the letter. Moreover, *Essex*'s holding has been severely limited by this court in subsequent cases.

Rather, we believe this case is more closely analogous to United States v. Barber, 881 F.2d 345 (7th Cir. 1989), where the Seventh Circuit upheld an obstruction of justice charge. In *Barber*, the defendant, a former attorney on probation at the time a former client was being sentenced, sent forged letters to the court urging a stiff sentence for his former client. The letters were written on the fraudulently acquired stationery of local businesses and bore forged signatures of the owners of those businesses. As a result, Barber's probation was revoked based on a violation of § 1503. In rejecting Barber's claim that he did not obstruct justice, the Seventh Circuit held that "[t]he false letters

---

18. In *Essex,* the defendant had signed a false affidavit, which was then used by James Hoffa in a motion for a new trial. In the affidavit, Essex had falsely stated that she had had sex with several jurors in Hoffa's criminal case while the jury was sequestered. This court agreed with the district court that the gravamen of Essex's offense was the "rendering of false testimony and nothing more," which was insufficient to state an obstruction of justice offense because "perjury alone lacks the element of obstruction." Id. at 218.

establish that the defendant, in mailing the letters to the sentencing judge, acted 'corruptly'"; that they constituted an endeavor to influence the former client's sentencing; and that they were the kind of letters that could properly be considered by the district court and that *could have* altered the sentence had Barber's conduct gone undiscovered. Id. at 351. . . .

V

For the foregoing reasons, Collis's conviction and sentence are affirmed.

Notes and Questions

1. What language in § 1503 brought Collis's conduct within the reach of the statute? Would it have made a difference if the forgery was so obvious that Judge Zatkoff immediately knew the letter was counterfeit?

2. What was the role of Collis's lawyer in this affair? Collis gave Lippman an unsigned copy of the letter before the hearing. Lippman made suggested changes. At the hearing, Lippman handed the letter to the judge. Does this implicate Lippman in any wrongdoing? Did Lippman have a duty to check the letter's authenticity or veracity?

UNITED STATES v. GRIFFIN
589 F.2d 200 (5th Cir. 1979)

WISDOM, Circuit Judge. . . .

I

In September 1975, an Argentinian aircraft bound for Panama crashed at Miami International Airport. A bank bag containing $15,046 was discovered in the wreckage. In October the Federal Bureau of Investigation began to investigate whether the flight was connected to loansharking activities, including the transportation of money out of the country. The investigation soon focused on Charles "Bob" Ebeling and John Cifarelli who were placed under electronic surveillance.

In January 1976, the FBI intercepted a number of conversations between the defendant Griffin and Ebeling. In these conversations, they discussed various ways to recover the money found in the crash. They also talked about a debt that Griffin owed Ebeling. Ebeling spoke of attempting to collect from a number of people indebted to him and said that he owed a substantial amount of money himself. The names of several individuals, including Jack, Dominick, and Angelo, figured prominently in the conversations. Although the FBI never identified these individuals, one name the defendant mentioned, Felix Herrero, was identified as a passenger who died in the Miami crash.

On March 9, 1976, Griffin was called to testify before a grand jury investigating the financing of loansharking operations and the possible movement of money from the

United States to South America. In response to questions concerning the crash, the debts, and the individuals mentioned in the conversations, Griffin either flatly denied knowledge or relied on an inability to recall the facts about which he was questioned. The following answers illustrate the nature of his testimony:

Q. What's your relationship with Bob, also known as Charles William Ebeling?

A. None, I just met him at the track and that's it. I don't even know his name.

Q. Do you know anything about a plane crash of a plane going to South America?

A. Know anything about? No, sir.

Q. Have you ever discussed with Mr. Ebeling, Bob, anything about a plane [crashing] on its way to South America?

A. Not that I can recall, with him. . . .

Q. Do you know Felix Herrer[]o?

A. No, I do not. I know a Felix, but it is not Herrer[]o.

Q. Do you know an individual named Jack?

A. Jack?

Q. Yes.

A. Jack, not that I can recall. In regards to what?

Q. In regards to anything.

A. No.

Q. Did Mr. Ebeling ever tell you that if you didn't pay him the money you owed him you'd put him in the middle between him and some other people, put him in a bad spot?

A. I would put him in a bad spot?

Q. Yes, if you didn't pay him the money you owed him?

A. No.

Q. Do you know an individual named Dominick?

A. No, sir.

Q. Do you know anyone named Angelo?

A. No, sir.

Q. Do you know brothers named Dominick, Angelo?

A. No. . . .

At his trial, Griffin testified that his grand jury testimony was true or innocently incorrect. He explained that he had fabricated the conversations about the money found in the airplane crash to avoid a joint financial venture proposed by Ebeling. Other conversations, Griffin said, were engineered by Ebeling to impress his wife. On December 6, 1977, the jury found Griffin guilty of obstructing justice. He was sentenced to 6 months imprisonment and 2 years probation. . . .

II

. . . The defendant urges us . . . to recognize a distinction between one who induces a witness to commit perjury, conduct which we expressly held forbidden by the concluding clause of § 1503 in U.S. v. Partin, 5 Cir. 1977, 552 F.2d 621, and one who perjures himself. . . .

The clear implication of our analysis in *Partin* and *Howard* is that perjury constitutes an offense against the effective administration of justice. Although we left that question unanswered in *Partin*, we held there that one who conspired to induce a witness to testify falsely could be prosecuted under the omnibus clause of § 1503, not because the means chosen to obstruct justice violated the specific wording of the first part of the statute but because the object of the conspiracy was to obstruct justice. In *Howard* we relied on *Partin* in holding that the omnibus clause aims at all conduct that results in an obstruction of justice. We explained further that using threats to prevent a grand jury witness from testifying has the result of destroying evidence. Although the accomplishment of this result by use of threats or bribes falls under the first clause, the destruction of evidence by the defendant alone comes under the omnibus clause. Similarly, using threats or bribes to prevent a grand jury witness from testifying truthfully has the result of concealing and altering the nature of evidence. If such conduct constitutes an obstruction of the administration of justice, as we held in *Partin*, then so does testifying falsely; the result in either case is the same.

The same conclusion was reached by the Court of Appeals for the Second Circuit in U.S. v. Cohn, 2 Cir. 1971, 452 F.2d 881. Relying on the plain language of the statute, the *Cohn* court held that an obstruction of justice results when attempts to gather relevant evidence by a judicial body, which is charged by law with the task of investigating and punishing crime, are frustrated by the use of corrupt or false means. "The blatantly evasive witness achieves this effect as surely by erecting a screen of feigned forgetfulness as one who burns files or induces a potential witness to absent himself." 452 F.2d at 1884.

The *Cohn* court, however, characterized the gist of the defendant's offense as the concealment of knowledge from the grand jury rather than the injection of falsehood into the proceedings. And the indictment charged Cohn with evasive as well as false testimony. Griffin reminds us that evasive testimony, which obstructs the system's administration of justice in a procedural way by blocking the grand jury investigation, must be distinguished from testimony which is false. Although perjury may distort the truth, the defendant contends that it does not impede the judicial process; the criminal system is in fact designed to deal with falsehood through cross-examination and other means. Because Griffin was charged with giving only false testimony, he insists that the indictment does not state an offense amounting to an obstruction of the administration of justice.

Our Court, however, has long recognized that the purpose of § 1503 is to protect not only the procedures of the criminal system but also the very goal of that system — to achieve justice. "The statute is one of the most important laws ever adopted. It is designed to protect witnesses in Federal courts and also to prevent a miscarriage of Justice." Samples v. United States, 5 Cir. 1941, 121 F.2d 263, 265. The perjurious witness can bring about a miscarriage of justice by imperiling the innocent or delaying the punishment of the guilty. Thus, had Griffin's testimony been merely false, it might well have come under the terms of the omnibus clause of § 1503, nonetheless. Such a case is not before us, however.

The defendant has ignored the actual nature of his testimony. We find it impossible to differentiate a flat refusal to testify from an evasive answer or a falsehood such as Griffin's: "No; I don't know; Not that I can recall." By falsely denying knowledge of events and individuals when questioned about them, Griffin hindered the grand jury's attempts to gather evidence of loansharking activities as effectively as if he refused to answer the questions at all. Whether Griffin's testimony is described in the indictment as "evasive" because he deliberately concealed knowledge or "false" because he blocked the flow of truthful information is immaterial. In either event, the government must, and in this case did, charge in the indictment and prove at trial that the testimony had the effect of impeding justice.

[Griffin argued that the legislative history required a different result because § 1503 is derived from the federal contempt statute and perjury is not summarily punishable as contempt.]

We disagree. In the first place, we find that the defendant's testimony in this case amounted to contemptuous conduct. Moreover, we doubt that the limitation on a federal judge's power to punish perjury summarily is also a limitation on the power to punish under § 1503.

Originally all false swearing was punishable summarily as criminal contempt in the federal courts. In a series of decisions, however, the Supreme Court cautioned against the indiscriminate use of the contempt power to punish the perjurious witness. In Ex parte Hudgings, 1919, 249 U.S. 378, a witness was held in contempt by the trial judge after he repeatedly asserted that he could not recall a certain event. The Court ordered relief, explaining that it hesitated to permit a court to impose summary punishment whenever it disbelieved a witness with the object of confining the witness until the court exacted from him a character of testimony which the court would deem to be truthful. In a later decision, In re Michael, 1945, 326 U.S. 224, the Supreme Court reviewed the propriety of a contempt citation imposed on a witness before the grand jury who answered willingly but whose testimony the trial judge disbelieved after hearing contradictory testimony by other witnesses. Justice Black wrote:

> All perjured relevant testimony is at war with justice, since it may produce a judgment not resting on truth. Therefore it cannot be denied that it tends to defeat the sole ultimate objective of a trial. It need not necessarily, however, obstruct or halt the judicial process. For the function of trial is to sift the truth from a mass of contradictory evidence, and to do so the fact finding tribunal must hear both truthful and false witnesses. 326 U.S. at 227-28.

Undeniably, the Supreme Court found that perjury alone does not have a necessarily inherent obstructive effect on the administration of justice. The Court made clear, however, that false testimony can amount to contemptuous conduct when added to the element of perjury there is the "'further element of obstruction to the Court in the performance of its duty.'" In re Michael, 326 U.S. at 228, quoting Ex parte Hudgings, 249 U.S. at 383. As an example, the Court cited with approval a case where the requisite element of obstruction was found in sham inability to remember and blocking of the court's inquiry. This additional element is present in the case before us. Griffin's testimony did not merely require the grand jury to ascertain the truth by resolving contradictory evidence; his denial of knowledge had the effect of closing off avenues of inquiry entirely. . . .

III

Turning finally to the record of the grand jury proceeding, we find that Griffin's false testimony was material because it had the natural effect of dissuading the grand jury from its investigation of alleged loansharking in Florida by Ebeling and others. The testimony need not be directed to the primary subject under investigation; it is material if it is relevant to any subsidiary issue or is capable of supplying a link to the main issue under consideration. The questions concerning the airplane crash, the debt owed to Ebeling, and the persons mentioned in the monitored calls were either concerned with the subsidiary issue of transportation of money out of the country or were aimed at eliciting a link to the alleged loansharker.

The judgment of the district court is affirmed.

Notes and Questions

1. Why is perjury alone insufficient to violate § 1503? What facts supply the additional element needed for obstruction? Which kinds of lies will, and which will not, violate § 1503?

PROBLEM 8-1

Recall the facts in *Bronston* (see Chapter 7), in which Bronston gave an evasive answer when asked whether he had any Swiss bank accounts. In reversing Bronston's conviction, the Court said that even if Bronston had intended to deceive by giving an unresponsive answer, that was irrelevant to liability under the perjury statute. Suppose that, preparatory to the bankruptcy hearing, Bronston and his lawyer had the following conversation:

Attorney: You've got to tell the truth. Do not under any circumstances lie. But the one thing you want to avoid, if you can, is admitting you had those Swiss accounts.

Bronston: How can I do that?

Attorney: Well, for one thing, listen carefully to what you are being asked, and answer the questions as narrowly as possible — but still tell the truth. Don't volunteer any information. Don't say anything that you're not specifically asked by the creditors' lawyers.

Bronston: Okay.

Attorney: And another thing. You can be evasive. You know, make the creditors' lawyers earn their keep. Make them probe and pry to get the information they want. That's their responsibility.

Bronston: Yeah. That's right.

Attorney: The toughest part will be if you're asked directly, "Did you have any Swiss accounts?"

Bronston: Can I say, "Well, that's kind of hard to recall?"

Attorney: No, no. Don't say that. That would be perjury. Let's think a minute. . . . Wait, I've got it. If you're asked whether you ever had any Swiss accounts, you can truthfully say, "The company had two accounts."

Bronston: Great! That's absolutely true.

Does this prehearing strategy implicate the obstruction of justice statute? Does it matter that evasive testimony will not support a conviction under the perjury statute? In what respects are obstruction of justice and perjury similar? In what respects are they dissimilar?

Putting aside, for the moment, the potential criminality of the conduct, could the lawyer ethically give that advice to the client?[19]

UNITED STATES v. AGUILAR
515 U.S. 593 (1995)

Chief Justice REHNQUIST delivered the opinion of the Court. . . .

Many facts remain disputed by the parties. Both parties appear to agree, however, that a motion for post-conviction relief filed by one Michael Rudy Tham represents the starting point from which events bearing on this case unfolded. Tham was an officer of the International Brotherhood of Teamsters, and was convicted of embezzling funds from the local affiliate of that organization. In July 1987, he filed a motion under 28 U.S.C. § 2255 to have his conviction set aside. The motion was assigned to Judge Stanley Weigel. Tham, seeking to enhance the odds that his petition would be granted, asked Edward Solomon and Abraham Chalupowitz, a.k.a. Abe Chapman, to assist him by capitalizing on their respective acquaintances with another judge in the Northern District of California, respondent Aguilar. Respondent knew Chapman as a distant relation by marriage and knew Solomon from law school. Solomon and Chapman met with respondent to discuss Tham's case, as a result of which respondent spoke with Judge Weigel about the matter.

Independent of the embezzlement conviction, the Federal Bureau of Investigation (FBI) identified Tham as a suspect in an investigation of labor racketeering. On April 20, 1987, the FBI applied for authorization to install a wiretap on Tham's business phones. Chapman appeared on the application as a potential interceptee. Chief District Judge Robert Peckham authorized the wiretap. The 30 day wiretap expired by law on May 20, 1987, but Chief Judge Peckham maintained the secrecy of the wiretap under 18 U.S.C. § 2518(8)(d) after a showing of good cause. During the course of the racketeering investigation, the FBI learned of the meetings between Chapman and respondent. The FBI informed Chief Judge Peckham, who, concerned with appearances of impropriety, advised respondent in August 1987 that Chapman might be connected with criminal elements because Chapman's name had appeared on a wiretap authorization.

---

19. Cf. ABA Model Rules of Professional Conduct, Rule 1.2(d), Comments [6] & [7] (lawyer may not counsel client to engage in fraudulent conduct or suggest how client's wrongdoing might be concealed); Rule 3.3(a)(2), Comment [2] (lawyer must disclose material fact when disclosure is necessary to avoid assisting fraud); ABA Model Code of Professional Responsibility DR 7-102 (lawyer may not participate in concealment or knowing nondisclosure of that which lawyer is required by law to reveal).

[Aguilar, who mistakenly believed that Chapman's telephones were wiretapped, later disclosed that information to his nephew, intending that the nephew would pass it along to Chapman.]

At this point, respondent's involvement in the two separate Tham matters converged. Two months after the disclosure to his nephew, a grand jury began to investigate an alleged conspiracy to influence the outcome of Tham's habeas case. Two FBI agents questioned respondent. During the interview, respondent lied about his participation in the Tham case and his knowledge of the wiretap.

[Aguilar was indicted and convicted for obstructing justice and disclosing a wiretap. The court of appeals reversed.]

I . . .

The first case from this Court construing the predecessor statute to § 1503 was Pettibone v. United States, 148 U.S. 197 (1893). There we held that "a person is not sufficiently charged with obstructing or impeding the due administration of justice in a court unless it appears that he knew or had notice that justice was being administered in such court." The Court reasoned that a person lacking knowledge of a pending proceeding necessarily lacked the evil intent to obstruct. Recent decisions of courts of appeals have likewise tended to place metes and bounds on the very broad language of the catchall provision. The action taken by the accused must be with an intent to influence judicial or grand jury proceedings; it is not enough that there be an intent to influence some ancillary proceeding, such as an investigation independent of the Court's or grand jury's authority. Some courts have phrased this showing as a "nexus" requirement — that the act must have a relationship in time, causation or logic with the judicial proceedings. In other words, the endeavor must have the "'natural and probable effect'" of interfering with the due administration of justice. This is not to say that the defendant's actions need be successful; an "endeavor" suffices. But as in *Pettibone*, if the defendant lacks knowledge that his actions are likely to affect the judicial proceeding, he lacks the requisite intent to obstruct.

Although respondent urges various broader grounds for affirmance, we find it unnecessary to address them because we think the "nexus" requirement developed in the decisions of the courts of appeals is a correct construction of § 1503. . . . We do not believe that uttering false statements to an investigating agent — and that seems to be all that was proven here — who might or might not testify before a grand jury is sufficient to make out a violation of the catchall provision of § 1503.

The Government did not show here that the agents acted as an arm of the grand jury, or indeed that the grand jury had even summoned the testimony of these particular agents. The Government argues that respondent "understood that his false statements would be provided to the grand jury" and that he made the statements with the intent to thwart the grand jury investigation and not just the FBI investigation. The Government supports its argument with a citation to the transcript of the recorded conversation between Aguilar and the FBI agent at the point where Aguilar asks whether he is a target of a grand jury investigation. The agent responded to the question by stating:

There is a Grand Jury meeting. Convening I guess that's the correct word. Um some evidence will be heard I'm . . . I'm sure on this issue.

Because respondent knew of the pending proceeding, the Government therefore contends that Aguilar's statements are analogous to those made directly to the grand jury itself, in the form of false testimony or false documents.

We think the transcript citation relied upon by the Government would not enable a rational trier of fact to conclude that respondent knew that his false statement would be provided to the grand jury, and that the evidence goes no further than showing that respondent testified falsely to an investigating agent. Such conduct, we believe, falls on the other side of the statutory line from that of one who delivers false documents or testimony to the grand jury itself. Conduct of the latter sort all but assures that the grand jury will consider the material in its deliberations. But what use will be made of false testimony given to an investigating agent who has not been subpoenaed or otherwise directed to appear before the grand jury is far more speculative. We think it cannot be said to have the "natural and probable effect" of interfering with the due administration of justice.

Justice Scalia's dissent criticizes our treatment of the statutory language for reading the word "endeavor" out of it, inasmuch as it excludes defendants who have an evil purpose but use means that would "only unnaturally and improbably be successful." This criticism is unwarranted. Our reading of the statute gives the term "endeavor" a useful function to fulfill: it makes conduct punishable where the defendant acts with an intent to obstruct justice, and in a manner that is likely to obstruct justice, but is foiled in some way. Were a defendant with the requisite intent to lie to a subpoenaed witness who is ultimately not called to testify, or who testifies but does not transmit the defendant's version of the story, the defendant has endeavored to, but has not actually, obstructed justice. Under our approach, a jury could find such defendant guilty.

Justice Scalia's dissent also apparently believes that *any* act, done with the intent to "obstruct . . . the due administration of justice," is sufficient to impose criminal liability. Under the dissent's theory, a man could be found guilty under § 1503 if he knew of a pending investigation and lied to his wife about his whereabouts at the time of the crime, thinking that an FBI agent might decide to interview her and that she might in turn be influenced in her statement to the agent by her husband's false account of his whereabouts. The intent to obstruct justice is indeed present, but the man's culpability is a good deal less clear from the statute than we usually require in order to impose criminal liability. . . .

. . . We remand for proceedings consistent with this decision.

So ordered.

Justice SCALIA, with whom Justice KENNEDY and Justice THOMAS join, concurring in part and dissenting in part.

I

[The Court has long recognized that the term "endeavor" reaches "'*any effort or essay*'" to impede the administration of justice. That broad construction of what constitutes an endeavor to impede justice did not, however, leave § 1503's prohibition without limits. Section 1503 reaches only *purposeful* efforts to obstruct justice. That is, the actor must have that specific object in mind.

Although the Court's "nexus" requirement is facially similar to *Pettibone*'s "natural and probable consequence" rubric, it is actually a very different standard.]

. . . Instead of reaffirming that "natural and probable consequence" is one way of establishing intent, [the Court] *substitutes* "natural and probable effect" *for* intent, requiring that factor even when intent to obstruct justice is otherwise clear. But while it is quite proper to derive an *intent* requirement from § 1503's use of the word "endeavor," it is quite impossible to derive a "*natural and probable consequence*" requirement. One would be "endeavoring" to obstruct justice if he intentionally set out to do it by means that would only unnaturally and improbably be successful. As we said in *Russell*, "any effort or essay" corruptly to influence, obstruct, or impede the due administration of justice constitutes a forbidden endeavor, as we held in *Osborn*, an effort that is *incapable* of having that effect. . . .

II

The Court apparently adds to its "natural and probable effect" requirement the requirement that the defendant *know* of that natural and probable effect. Separate proof of such knowledge is not, I think, required for the orthodox use of the "natural and probable effect" rule discussed in *Pettibone*: Where the defendant intentionally commits a wrongful act that *in fact* has the "natural and probable consequence" of obstructing justice, "the unintended wrong may derive its character from the wrong that was intended.". . .

While inquiry into the state of the defendant's knowledge seems quite superfluous to the Court's opinion (since the act performed did not have the requisite "natural and probable effect" anyway), it is necessary to my disposition of the case. As I have said, I think an act committed *with intent to obstruct* is all that matters; and what one can fairly be thought to have intended depends in part upon what one can fairly be thought to have known. The critical point of knowledge at issue, in my view, is not whether "respondent knew that his false statement *would be provided* to the grand jury" (a heightened burden imposed by the Court's knowledge-of-natural-and-probable-effect requirement), but rather whether respondent knew — or indeed, even erroneously *believed* — that his false statement *might* be provided to the grand jury (which is all the knowledge needed to support the conclusion that the purpose of his lie was to mislead the jury). Applying the familiar standard of Jackson v. Virginia, 443 U.S. 307 (1979), to the proper question, I find that a rational juror could readily have concluded beyond a reasonable doubt that respondent had corruptly endeavored to impede the due administration of justice, i.e., that he lied to the FBI agents intending to interfere with a grand jury investigation into his misdeeds.

Recorded conversations established that respondent knew a grand jury had been convened; that he had been told he was a target of its investigation; and that he feared he would be unable to explain his actions if he were subpoenaed to testify. Respondent himself testified that, at least at the conclusion of the interview, it was his "impression" that his statements to the FBI agents would be reported to the grand jury. The evidence further established that respondent made false statements to the FBI agents that minimized his involvement in the matters the grand jury was investigating. Viewing this evidence in the light most favorable to the Government, I am simply unable to conclude that no rational trier of fact could have found beyond a reasonable doubt that respondent lied specifically because he thought the agents *might* convey what he said to the grand jury — which suffices to constitute a corrupt endeavor to impede the due administration of justice. In fact, I think it would be hard for a juror to conclude otherwise. . . .

The "nexus" requirement that the Court today engrafts into § 1503 has no basis in the words Congress enacted. I would reverse that part of the Court of Appeals' judgment which set aside respondent's conviction under that statute.

[Opinion of Justice STEVENS, concurring in part and dissenting in part, omitted.]

Notes and Questions

1. Is Justice Scalia correct in asserting that the majority distorted *Pettibone*'s reference to the "natural and probable consequence" of the conduct in question? If so, does the Court's decision significantly rein in the scope of the statute?

2. Justice Scalia cites several items of evidence supporting the conclusion that Judge Aguilar's lies were intended to thwart the grand jury investigation. But the majority concluded that the evidence was insufficient. What more will the government have to prove, and what evidence is needed to prove it?

3. What if Judge Aguilar knew about the grand jury investigation and lied to the FBI agent for the purpose of getting the agent to pass false information on to the grand jury? Would *Aguilar* prohibit treating this as a violation of § 1503?[20]

UNITED STATES v. CINTOLO
818 F.2d 980 (1st Cir. 1987)

SELYA, Circuit Judge.

This case deals with the manner in which one member of the criminal defense bar chose, in his own sense, to read and to act upon the bitter letter of the law. In the bargain, the case presents important questions concerning the relation of an attorney to the fabric of federal law which Congress has woven to prevent obstruction of justice.

In December 1984, a grand jury sitting in the District of Massachusetts returned an indictment against William J. Cintolo, a practicing criminal defense attorney, charging him with one count of conspiracy to obstruct justice, 18 U.S.C. §§ 371, 1503, and two substantive counts of obstruction of justice, 18 U.S.C. § 1503. After a lengthy trial, the jury found the defendant guilty on the conspiracy count, but not guilty on the substantive obstruction counts. Cintolo was thereafter sentenced to a prison term, the execution of which was stayed pending appeal. We affirm. . . .

I

Cintolo's indictment and ultimate conviction grew out of the judicially sanctioned electronic surveillance of an apartment at 98 Prince Street in Boston's North End. These

---

20. Cf. United States v. Grubb, 11 F.3d 426 (4th Cir. 1993).

premises were used by Gennaro Angiulo and his associates as a headquarters and office for the operation of illegal gambling and loansharking businesses. "Loansharking" is a term of criminal art which may roughly be defined as the unlawful lending of money at usurious rates of interest, repayment being encouraged by the employment (or threatened employment) of unorthodox collection measures, involving, inter alia, the breaking of bones.

The Federal Bureau of Investigation (FBI) monitored the conversations which took place on the premises from January 19 to May 3, 1981. The surveillance was conducted primarily by means of hidden microphones clandestinely emplaced within the apartment. These devices recorded conversations between Angiulo and his confederates, including Cintolo. In addition, a concealed exterior camera surreptitiously photographed persons entering and leaving the headquarters.

What this intensive scrutiny revealed vis-a-vis the appellant can usefully be summarized by reference to the true bill which the grand jury returned. The indictment charged that Cintolo conspired with Angiulo and others to violate 18 U.S.C. § 1503. The gravamen of the accusation was that Cintolo did "corruptly endeavor to influence, obstruct and impede the due administration of justice" by befouling the proceedings of a federal grand jury investigating the criminal activities of the Angiulo gang. According to the indictment, Cintolo set out to accomplish this nefarious end through the use of his position as attorney of record for Walter LaFreniere, a witness before the grand jury, to acquire information about the ongoing investigation for Angiulo's benefit. The indictment further charged Cintolo with knowingly assisting Angiulo in his efforts to inhibit LaFreniere, after the latter had been granted immunity, from testifying truthfully before the grand jury, or from cooperation in any way with the investigation.

Tape recordings played for the jury at Cintolo's trial established that LaFreniere and his father-in-law, Louis Venios, possessed damaging information linking various members of Angiulo's organization to illegal gambling and loansharking activities. Among other things, the evidence disclosed that both Venios and LaFreniere had been extended substantial credit to cover unpaid gambling debts, and that each had been subjected to exacting pressure from various of Angiulo's minions to remit the overdue sums. When subpoenas issued to Venios and LaFreniere indicated that the grand jury was investigating possible violations of 18 U.S.C. §§ 892-94 (making, financing, and collecting extortionate extensions of credit), Angiulo recognized the legal peril which faced him and his confreres. Notwithstanding that on March 12, 1981, after first being interviewed by FBI agent Quinn, LaFreniere appeared before the grand jury and refused to testify on Fifth Amendment grounds. . . .

[Angiulo and Cintolo had numerous conversations about the grand jury investigation, and it was clear that Angiulo was very concerned about LaFreniere, who possessed highly incriminating information about Angiulo and his gang. At one point Angiulo's concern was so great that he ordered two of his henchmen to kill LaFreniere. Fortunately for LaFreniere, the FBI overheard the conversation via its electronic monitors and warned him of the plot.

The gist of Cintolo's discussions with Angiulo about LaFreniere was that LaFreniere should refuse to testify on Fifth Amendment grounds and, if granted immunity, to continue to invoke the Fifth Amendment and go to jail for contempt. Cintolo carefully explained this strategy to LaFreniere, telling him that the maximum time he could be jailed for contempt was eighteen months.

When LaFreniere appeared before the grand jury a second time, he again refused to testify on Fifth Amendment grounds. He was then granted immunity, which deprived him of any Fifth Amendment protections. At that time Angiulo and Cintolo continued their strategy discussions, and it was clear that the object was to have LaFreniere invoke the Fifth Amendment and thus commit contempt. LaFreniere read the grand jury a statement Cintolo had prepared for him and, invoking the Fifth Amendment, refused to testify. Several weeks later he was held in contempt and sentenced to serve eighteen months in jail. Although Cintolo represented LaFreniere throughout this period, the court disqualified him from continuing to represent Angiulo. Cintolo maintained that at all times he had been acting in LaFreniere's best interests.]

II . . .

. . . [A]ppellant and the amici beseech us to announce an unprecedented rule of law designed, they contend, to insulate lawyers from encroachments on the "zealous representation" of clients accused of crime. So long as an attorney tenders a facially legitimate explanation for conduct performed in the course of his defense of a client, they urge, a factfinder must evaluate the behavior *on that basis*. In constructing this sort of paradigm, the lawyer's word alone creates what amounts to an irrebuttable presumption which debars the jury — despite the existence of mounds of circumstantial evidence — from drawing contradictory inferences as to the attorney's motives or intent. Put another way, if defense counsel's actions of and by themselves do not amount to a crime, then a factfinder may not criminalize the conduct on the basis of conclusions reached, no matter how reasonably, about *why* the actions were performed. Hidden motivations, howsoever corrupt, remain forever hidden in a world where veniremen are not allowed to peer beneath the surface of things.

We find no support in precedent, principle, or policy for such an anti-lapsarian rule, and decline to cleave so deep a chasm in the criminal law for the exclusive benefit of attorneys who knowingly involve themselves in the corruption of their clients. As important a role as defense counsel serve — and we do not minimize its importance one whit — the acceptance of a retainer by a lawyer in a criminal case cannot become functionally equivalent to the lawyer's acceptance of a roving commission to flout the criminal law with impunity. A criminal lawyer has no license to act as a lawyer-criminal. . . .

In Cole v. United States, 329 F.2d 437 (9th Cir. 1964), the court affirmed the § 1503 conviction of an individual who had pressed a grand jury witness to stand mute by invocation of his Fifth Amendment prerogative. The defendant's motive, the prosecution contended, was to protect both himself and a close friend from the slings and arrows of a pending grand jury investigation. The Ninth Circuit noted that: "the constitutional privilege against self-incrimination is an integral part of the due administration of justice, designed to do and further justice, and to the exercise of which there is an absolute right in every witness." Id. at 443. Nevertheless, while "[a] witness violates no duty to claim it, . . . one who bribes, coerces, forces or threatens a witness to claim it, or advises with corrupt motive the witness to take it, can and does himself obstruct or influence the due administration of justice." Id.

Cole, to be sure, did not involve a lawyer-client relationship. Yet the case explicitly suggested that an attorney who *corruptly* advised a client to wind the toga of the Fifth Amendment about him could well be subject to obstruction of justice liability notwithstanding any "privilege" he might claim to have in rendering such advice. After all, the high[-]minded purposes which underlie the constitutional protection are disserved, not furthered, if a third party — lawyer or not — has carte blanche to manipulate an individual's use of the privilege corruptly to impede the due administration of justice.

To like effect is the decision in United States v. Cioffi, 493 F.2d 1111 (2d Cir. 1974). . . .

These cases are instructive for the purposes at hand. Notwithstanding that the means used by the appellant might be regarded as lawful, if viewed in a vacuum, clear proof of improper motive could surely serve to criminalize that conduct. And, Cintolo's corrupt intent seems especially evident when contrasted with the actions scrutinized in the foregoing cases. Viewing the facts and the inferences therefrom most favorably to the government, as we are required to do, there was an ample basis for the jury to find — in significant contradistinction to *Cole* and *Cioffi* — that the appellant was not counseling LaFreniere to invoke legitimate rights for his own benefit. On this unhappy record, a factfinder could well have believed beyond a reasonable doubt that Cintolo acted as part of a high pressure, no-holds-barred campaign to induce his nominal client, LaFreniere, to commit a criminal contempt. Though Cintolo's acts in fostering the intimidation of LaFreniere were not in themselves *overtly* unlawful, they seem to us, in this context, to have been fully actionable under 18 U.S.C. § 1503. . . .

[Cintolo relied on United States v. Herron, 28 F.2d 122 (N.D. Cal. 1928), a case that reached a result the court found highly dubious. But even assuming arguendo the correctness of the result, *Herron* was distinguishable because the lawyer advised a client who would in fact have been protected against self-incrimination by invoking the Fifth Amendment.]

The remaining cases hawked by the appellant offer no sturdier support for his position. In Maness v. Meyers, 419 U.S. 449 (1975), for instance, the Court reversed the conviction of an attorney who had counseled his client not to respond to a subpoena duces tecum in a civil case, citing Fifth Amendment grounds. The Court noted however, that the lawyer had acted "in the good-faith belief that if [his] client produced the materials he would run a substantial risk of self-incrimination." Id. at 455. See also id. at 465-66 ("The privilege against compelled self-incrimination would be drained of its meaning if counsel . . . could be penalized for advising his client in good faith to assert it."). The Court quoted an earlier decision, In re Watts, 190 U.S. 1, 29 (1903), to the effect that "if an attorney acts in good faith and in the honest belief that his advice is well founded and in the just interests of his client, he cannot be held liable for error in judgment." 419 U.S. at 467. The clear implication of these comments is that, in the absence of a facially legitimate and bona fide basis for interposition of the Fifth Amendment, i.e., in the absence of good faith on the lawyer's part, guilt may be predicated on the conduct. In our view, we are scrupulously faithful to *Maness* and to *Watts*, insofar as they have pertinence, when we lay stress on the evidence from which the jury could logically have inferred Cintolo's corrupt motive, want of good faith, and lack of any "honest belief" that LaFreniere had any residual right, after receiving immunity, to maintain his silence — or that doing so would benefit LaFreniere in any legally cognizable sense. . . .

. . . Acceptable notions of evenhanded justice require that statutes like § 1503 apply to all persons, without preferment or favor. As sworn officers of the court, lawyers should not seek to avail themselves of relaxed rules of conduct. To the exact contrary, they should be held to the very highest standards in promoting the cause of justice. See ABA Model Code of Professional Responsibility EC 1-5 ("A lawyer should maintain high standards of professional conduct and should encourage fellow lawyers to do likewise."); EC 9-6 ("Every lawyer owes a solemn duty to uphold the integrity and honor of this profession; to encourage respect for the law and for the courts and judges thereof; . . . to conduct himself so as to reflect credit on the legal profession and to inspire the confidence, respect, and trust of his clients and of the public."). . . .

In sum, the government presented plethoric evidence from which the jury could reasonably have found the appellant guilty of conspiring to obstruct the due administration of justice. His role as a defense attorney did not insulate him from the criminal consequences of his corruptly-motivated actions. Accordingly, the district court did not err in denying the defendant's motion for judgment of acquittal. . . .

Notes and Questions

1. Cintolo claimed that he was acting in LaFreniere's best interests in advising him to refuse to testify on Fifth Amendment grounds. What facts undercut the credibility of his claim? What other matters, if any, should Cintolo have discussed with LaFreniere before advising him to plead the Fifth Amendment at all costs? Is it ever proper for a lawyer to advise a client to commit contempt?

2. Does the result in *Cintolo* put criminal defense lawyers in an untenable position? How far does it intrude into the attorney-client relationship? Does this open the door, for example, for a grand jury to inquire into a lawyer's decision to seek a postponement of his client's trial?

3. Cintolo and the amici argued that a corrupt motive cannot be found unless the conduct is otherwise independently unlawful. Is that a sound argument? Can you think of other examples where a corrupt motive turns otherwise lawful conduct into unlawful conduct?

4. Cintolo and the amici also argued that lawyers should have a blanket exemption from grand jury scrutiny of traditional lawyering decisions. Is a blanket exemption warranted? Could a lawyer properly pay a client $100,000 to invoke the Fifth Amendment?

5. Suppose that LaFreniere's wife had sincerely urged him to refuse to testify on Fifth Amendment grounds because she believed he would incriminate himself. Is she privileged to do this, or would this be obstruction of justice?

6. Suppose that Cintolo sincerely believes that LaFreniere's testimony will be self-incriminating. But when he advises LaFreniere to invoke the Fifth Amendment, his motive is to protect another client. Is Cintolo privileged to do this?[21]

7. Suppose that four grand jury witnesses, each of whom individually could validly assert the Fifth Amendment, agree to "stonewall" when they are called to testify by invoking the privilege against self-incrimination. Would that constitute conspiracy to

---

21. Cf. ABA Model Rules of Professional Conduct, Rule 1.9; ABA Model Code of Professional Responsibility, Canon 5 & EC 5-21 through 5-24.

obstruct justice? To turn the question around, what does it mean that each of the witnesses could "validly" assert the privilege? When, if ever, is a witness not entitled to assert it?

PROBLEM 8-2

Eve Tarlow, an employee of a metal processing company, knows that toxic waste from the plant is being illegally disposed of by unlicensed midnight dumpers. Tarlow is convinced that the waste haulers are connected with organized crime, but she is uncertain about whether anyone in the company is involved or is even aware of the suspected mob connection.

The illegal waste disposal eventually comes to light, and the company and several waste haulers are indicted for illegal dumping. During the course of the investigation, an Assistant United States Attorney interviewed Tarlow, and she provided solid evidence of the illegal dumping practices.

When the case came to trial, Tarlow was subpoenaed to testify, but she refused to do so on the ground that she feared for her life and the well-being of her family because of the haulers' reputed involvement with organized crime. Within the past year, she said, a material witness in a murder prosecution of a local organized crime figure was killed by a car bomb.

The judge told her that if she was in danger, she would be provided protection by the FBI and, if necessary, sequestered in a safe location during the trial. If that would not satisfy her, she could enter the witness protection program, have her identity changed, and be relocated to another part of the country. Tarlow replied that she did not want "to become someone else" or, for that matter, to uproot her family. But she went on to say that she still would not be safe under the witness protection program because organized crime is "everywhere." After several rounds of fruitless negotiations, the judge held her in contempt and ordered her to jail.

After it became clear that she was not going to cooperate, Tarlow was indicted for obstruction of justice. Has she violated § 1503? What competing policy considerations are implicated?[22]

NOTE ON LAWYER LIABILITY

As the decision in *Cintolo* illustrates, giving corrupt legal advice to a witness may constitute obstruction of justice. Predictably, this result does not sit well with some members of the bar, who — like Cintolo — believe that a lawyer's prerogative to provide legal advice is sacrosanct. The tension is palpable. On the one hand, lawyers — as officers of the court — are obliged to counsel their clients to obey the law. On the other hand, defense lawyers fear that vigorous and zealous representation of their clients could lead to criminal prosecution. Congress tried to resolve this tension in 1986 by providing a "safe harbor" for lawyers faced with this dilemma. The provision,

---

22. Compare United States v. Banks, 942 F.2d 1576 (11th Cir. 1991), with People v. Carradine, 287 N.E.2d 670 (Ill. 1972).

18 U.S.C. § 1515(c), states that nothing in the obstruction of justice statutes prohibits or punishes "the providing of lawful, bona fide, legal representation services in connection with or anticipation of an official proceeding."

The first reported case to construe the safe harbor provision was United States v. Kloess.[23] The issue in *Kloess* was whether § 1515(c) provides an affirmative defense to an obstruction of justice charge or whether it defines an element of the crime. This question has obvious practical implications. If § 1515 provides an affirmative defense, the lawyer would have the burden of producing evidence that he was providing bona fide legal representation rather than committing a crime. If § 1515 defines an element of the crime, the government would have to prove a negative — i.e., that the lawyer was not providing bona fide legal representation. The court in *Kloess* concluded that § 1515 provides an affirmative defense that allocates the burden of proof as follows:

> There has been a twentieth-century trend toward requiring the government to bear the burden of persuasion on certain affirmative defenses. An examination of the cases reveals, however, "a quite divided jurisprudence, without any clear default rule as to how affirmative defenses generally should be treated." United States v. Dodd, 225 F.3d 340, 348 (3d Cir. 2000).
>
> There is agreement, however, on one sort of affirmative defense. Any defense which tends to negate an *element* of the crime charged, sufficiently raised by the defendant, must be *disproved* by the government. "The Due Process Clause requires that the prosecutor bear the burden of persuasion beyond a reasonable doubt only if the [defense] makes a substantial difference in punishment and stigma. The requirement of course applies *a fortiori* if the [defense] makes the difference between guilt and innocence." Patterson v. New York, 432 U.S. 197, 226 (1977) (Powell, J., dissenting). Therefore, if the defendant introduces evidence that has the effect of negating any element of the offense, the government must disprove that defense beyond a reasonable doubt. *Patterson,* 432 U.S. at 210.
>
> Section 1515(c) provides such an affirmative defense. To violate Section 1512(b)(3), the defendant must knowingly act with the *specific* intent to hinder or delay the communication to the court of the commission of a federal offense or probation violation. In order to convict a defendant under Section 1512(b)(3), the government must prove that the defendant acted with an improper purpose. Section 1515(c) provides a complete defense to the statute because one who is performing bona fide legal representation does not have an improper purpose. His purpose — to zealously represent his client — is fully protected by the law. Section 1515(c), therefore, constitutes an affirmative defense which negates an element of the offense stated in Section 1512(b)(3).
>
> The Due Process Clause "protects the accused against conviction except upon proof beyond a reasonable doubt of *every fact* necessary to constitute the crime with which he is charged." In re Winship, 397 U.S. 358, 364 (1970). No defendant can be convicted under Section 1512(b)(3) unless the government proves *every* element of the offense beyond a reasonable doubt. Since the proper invocation of Section 1515(c) raises an inference of lawful purpose which negates the *mens rea* element of Section 1512(b)(3), the defendant is entitled to an acquittal if the government does not overcome the inference.
>
> A defendant-lawyer seeking the safe harbor of Section 1515(c) must affirmatively show that he is entitled to its protection. This is a minimal burden. Evidence tending to show that the defendant is a licensed attorney who was validly retained to perform the legal representation which constitutes the charged conduct is sufficient to raise an

---

23. 97 F. Supp. 2d 1084 (M.D. Ala. 2000).

inference of innocent purpose. Any requirement to do more would unconstitutionally shift the burden to the defendant to prove his innocence by negating an element of the statute — the required *mens rea.* This the Constitution forbids.

Once the Section 1515(c) defense has been fairly raised, the government must undertake to prove its case, including the requisite improper purpose, by adducing evidence that the charged conduct did not constitute lawful, bona fide representation. . . .

Having fairly raised the Section 1515(c) defense to culpability under Section 1512(b)(3), the defendant is entitled to an acquittal unless the jury finds that the government proved beyond a reasonable doubt that the defendant's conduct did not constitute lawful, bona fide legal representation.[24]

Notes and Questions

1. To what extent does § 1515(c) provide lawyers protection they otherwise would not have? Is this protection needed? Is it significant that § 1515(c) was on the books for 14 years before the first reported decision that applied it was handed down?

2. What is the practical effect of the court's holding in *Kloess*? Will it have the same impact regardless of which obstruction of justice statute the defendant is charged under? Compare the facts and prosecutorial theories in *Cintolo* and *Kloess*.

   a. The defendant in *Cintolo* advised a putative client to refuse to testify. Cintolo was charged with corruptly endeavoring to impede the administration of justice, in violation of the omnibus clause in § 1503.

   b. The defendant in *Kloess* represented a client named Gene Easterling, a convicted felon. While Easterling was on probation, the police stopped him for a traffic violation and found a pistol in his car. Not surprisingly, his gun possession violated the terms of his probation. During the traffic stop, Easterling gave the police a driver's license that falsely identified him as Craig Wallace, and he was charged under this assumed name with possessing a firearm without a permit. Kloess wrote a letter to the judge stating that his client, "Craig Wallace," intended to plead guilty to the possession charge in absentia. He also prepared an affidavit notifying the court that Wallace would enter a guilty plea through his lawyer, Kloess. When the deception was discovered, Kloess was charged under § 1512(b)(3) with engaging in misleading conduct toward another with intent to hinder, delay, or prevent the communication of information concerning a violation of conditions of probation to a federal judge.

Does the ruling in *Kloess* have the same or different effects under these two scenarios?

3. Regardless of § 1515(c)'s effect, is the lawyer's conduct in *Kloess* ethical? Is it legal?

---

24. United States v. Kloess, 251 F.3d 941 (11th Cir. 2001). Accord United States v. Mintmire, 507 F.3d 1273 (11th Cir. 2007).

IV. THE VICTIM AND WITNESS PROTECTION ACT

In 1982, Congress enacted the Victim and Witness Protection Act to expand the scope of the obstruction of justice statutes, including §§ 1503 and 1505. The Act deleted the statutory references to "witnesses" in both of these provisions and incorporated a variety of specific protections in a new obstruction statute, § 1512, which prohibits tampering with a witness, victim, or informant.

A. NONCOERCIVE WITNESS TAMPERING

1. Section 1503: The Omnibus Clause

UNITED STATES v. LESTER
749 F.2d 1288 (9th Cir. 1984)

SNEED, Circuit Judge. . . .

I. BACKGROUND

This case involves a conspiracy to prevent Leslie Brigham from testifying in a federal prosecution of Felix Mitchell, the alleged leader of an Oakland narcotics gang. In April 1983, the Oakland police department arrested Brigham for murder. While in custody, Brigham began cooperating with federal authorities as they prepared to prosecute Mitchell. Mitchell had been arrested in February 1983.

On April 17, 1983, while still in custody, Brigham was approached by Mitchell's attorney. The attorney urged Brigham not to cooperate with the federal authorities. In addition, she showed Brigham a note, authored by Mitchell, which directed him to refrain from testifying against Mitchell or speaking to the Justice Department Strike Force Attorney.

On or about April 15, 1983, Lester met with McGill and others to arrange Brigham's release from jail. This meeting apparently followed up a prior meeting in February 1983, attended by Lester and Mitchell, where Mitchell expressed concern that his own arrest was imminent and that Brigham might cooperate with the authorities. At the April 15 meeting, Lester said that the gang should get Brigham out of jail "because he [Brigham] was going to talk against Felix Mitchell." Accordingly, Lester approved the use of the gang's money for the purpose of securing Brigham's release; he instructed McGill to take $1000 to post as the cash part of Brigham's bail.

Before Lester or McGill could arrange Brigham's release, however, the Oakland police released Brigham into the temporary protection of the FBI. On April 18, 1983, the FBI checked Brigham and his wife into a San Francisco motel. Two days later, the couple left the motel and went to Brigham's sister's home in Oakland. There, Brigham called Tony Mitchell, Felix Mitchell's brother, and left a message that he was at his sister's home. A short time later, Lester called Brigham's sister and found to his surprise that Brigham was there. Apparently frightened, Brigham immediately called the Justice Department Attorney. While he was on the phone, however, Lester, Lester's brother

Tony, and Tony Mitchell walked in. Brigham pretended he was talking to someone other than the Justice Department Attorney, and he abruptly cut off the conversation. After some discussion and a telephone conversation with Mitchell, the parties agreed that Brigham should leave town for a time.

Brigham, accompanied by Lester's brother, then went to a motel in Alameda. Lester's brother paid for the room and left Brigham $300 in cash. He told Brigham to wait there until McGill came by in the morning.

McGill met Brigham the next day. The two stayed with their wives at another Alameda motel for three days. Needing money, Brigham and McGill drove to the house of Annie MacDonald, who gave McGill $500.

Brigham, McGill, and their wives then departed for San Diego, where they stayed for roughly three weeks. One of Mitchell's girlfriends paid for the accommodations in cash. While in San Diego, McGill periodically received money from Oakland, which he divided with Brigham. Evidence suggested that Lester's brother sent the money. On returning to Oakland, Brigham was arrested by the FBI.

Lester and McGill were charged by indictment with conspiracy, obstructing justice, and obstructing a criminal investigation. The government's case rested primarily on the testimony of two witnesses: Brigham and Norbert Bluitt, another alleged member of the gang. The jury returned guilty verdicts against both defendants on all counts. The district judge granted Lester's Rule 29 motion for acquittal on the two substantive counts, but he affirmed the conspiracy conviction; the judge acquitted McGill of the conspiracy count, but he affirmed the conviction as to the two substantive counts. . . .

III. APPLICABILITY OF SECTION 1503

A. STATUTORY COVERAGE

Both Lester's appeal of his conspiracy conviction and the government's appeal of Lester's substantive count acquittal and of McGill's conspiracy acquittal center on the applicability of 18 U.S.C. § 1503 to witness-related offenses. Lester and McGill contend that by enacting the Victim and Witness Protection Act of 1982 (Act), Congress intended to remove witness tampering from section 1503 and to consolidate all such offenses in a new provision, 18 U.S.C. § 1512. The government argues that the omnibus clause in section 1503 — which prohibits "endeavors to influence, obstruct, or impede, the due administration of justice" — reaches witness tampering of the type presented in this case.

Prior to the enactment of 18 U.S.C. § 1512, section 1503 prohibited influencing or intimidating "any witness . . . any grand or petit juror, or officer in or of any court of the United States" or injuring any of them for discharging their duties in court. The Act removed from section 1503 all references to witnesses and enacted section 1512 to protect witnesses, victims, and informants. The Act, however, left the omnibus provision of section 1503 intact. Lester and McGill argue that the Act evinces a congressional intent to redress all forms of witness tampering under section 1512, leaving section 1503 to remedy only tampering with court officers and jurors. We disagree.

As originally enacted, section 1503 had two objectives: "'It [was] designed to protect witnesses in Federal courts and also to prevent a miscarriage of Justice by corrupt methods.'" Catrino v. United States, 176 F.2d 884, 887 (9th Cir. 1949). Undeniably,

Congress passed the Act "to strengthen existing legal protections for victims and witnesses of Federal crimes." S. Rep. No. 532, 97th Cong., 2d Sess. 9 (1982), reprinted in 1982 U.S. Code Cong. & Ad. News 2515, 2515. And Congress may well have intended to remove the protection of witnesses from section 1503. It by no means follows, however, that Congress intended to reduce the effectiveness of section 1503 in combatting "miscarriage[s] of Justice by corrupt methods." See United States v. Beatty, 587 F. Supp. 1325, 1333 (E.D.N.Y. 1984). Yet this is precisely the result to which the defendant's urged construction would lead. If witness tampering should fall exclusively under section 1512, and if the accused used a method other than one prescribed in section 1512 (intimidation, physical force, threats, harassment, or misleading conduct), that conduct would no longer be prohibited. Neither section 1503 nor section 1512 would cover it.

An examination of the scope of section 1512 and the scope of section 1503 prior to the enactment of section 1512 makes this clear. The witness tampering reached by section 1512 involves the use of force or coercion. Section 1512(a) proscribes knowing use of intimidation, physical force, threats, or misleading conduct to "cause or induce any person to . . . be absent from an official proceeding to which such person has been summoned by legal process. . . ." 18 U.S.C. § 1512(a)(2)(D).[25] With the exception of misleading conduct, which is not alleged in the present case, all of the activities proscribed by the provision involve some element of coercion. Similarly, section 1512(b) prohibits intentional harassment that "hinders, delays, prevents, or dissuades any person from . . . attending or testifying in an official proceeding . . ." 18 U.S.C. § 1512(b)(1).[26] Although section 1512(b) apparently requires less force or intimidation than does section 1512(a), the gist of the offense is coercive conduct. As the Senate report notes, section 1512(b) "covers any conduct that maliciously hinders, delays, prevents, or dissuades a witness or victim from . . . attending or testifying in an official proceeding . . . *if the conduct is done with intent to intimidate, harass, harm, or injure another person.*" S. Rep. No. 532, 97th Cong., 2d Sess. 17 (1982), reprinted in 1982 U.S. Code Cong. & Ad. News 2515, 2523 (discussing section 1512(a)(2), the precursor of section 1512(b)). . . .

. . . [S]ection 1503 embraces the conduct of Lester and McGill who are charged, inter alia, with conspiracy to obstruct justice by hiding the witness Brigham to prevent his appearance at the trial of Felix Mitchell. Their efforts to secrete Brigham, manifestly done with the purpose of preventing his testimony, constitute a corrupt endeavor to obstruct justice in violation of section 1503, at least as that provision stood prior to the Act. We do not believe Congress intended to change this result. Yet under the construction of the Act urged by Lester and McGill, noncoercive witness tampering — including hiding a witness — would fall outside both section 1512 and section 1503. Neither the legislative history nor the Second Circuit's decision in United States v. Hernandez, 730 F.2d 895 (2d Cir. 1984) (exploring interplay between sections 1503 and 1512), supports such a result.

---

25. This provision is now codified as § 1512(b)(2)(D). — Ed.
26. This provision is now codified as § 1512(d)(1). — Ed.

First, we cannot assume that when the Act was passed Congress was unaware of the wide assortment of cases extending the reach of section 1503 to noncoercive conduct, including noncoercive witness tampering. On that assumption, it would be improper to hold that Congress silently decriminalized noncoercive, but nevertheless corrupt, efforts to interfere with witnesses. Rather, we believe that Congress enacted section 1512 to prohibit specific conduct comprising various forms of coercion of witnesses, leaving the omnibus provision of section 1503 to handle more imaginative forms of criminal behavior, including forms of witness tampering, that defy enumeration.

The legislative history supports this view. The Senate version of section 1512 contained an omnibus provision which was very similar to that of section 1503. In explaining its inclusion of the omnibus provision, the Senate Judiciary Committee noted that it intended the clause to reach interference with witnesses, victims, or informants that did not employ the means (coercion and deception) specified in other provisions of section 1512:

> There must also be protection against the rare type of conduct that is the product of the inventive criminal mind and which also thwarts justice. . . .
> . . . The Committee does not intend that the doctrine of ejusdem generis be applied to limit the coverage of this subsection. Instead, the analysis should be functional in nature to cover conduct the function of which is to tamper with a witness, victim, or informant in order to frustrate the ends of justice . . . irrespective of whether [there was] employed deception, intimidation, threat, or force. . . .

S. Rep. No. 532, 97th Cong., 2d Sess. 18 (1982), reprinted in 1982 U.S. Code Cong. & Ad. News 2515, 2524. Congress deleted the omnibus provision, however, and did not adopt it. In explaining this decision, Senator Heinz said:

> Subsection (3) of section 1512(a) of the Senate passed bill, general obstruction of justice residual clause of the intimidation section, was taken out of the bill as beyond the legitimate scope of this witness protection measure. It also is probably duplicative of abstrusion [sic] of justice statutes already in the books.

128 Cong. Rec. S13063 (daily ed. Oct. 1, 1982).

Congress' decision to forgo adoption of the section 1512 omnibus clause reflects, we believe, its intent to limit section 1512 to instances of witness tampering involving coercion or deception, leaving inventive tampering by other means to section 1503. Such a construction leaves no gap in federal criminal law coverage of witness interference. This is what Congress intended. . . .

In the present case, Lester and McGill hid a witness from the authorities to prevent his testimony at the Mitchell trial. Both Lester and McGill strenuously assert that no one coerced Brigham to go to San Diego. Taking that assertion at face value, their conduct lies outside "intimidation and harassment of witnesses"; however, it falls precisely within the residual omnibus clause of section 1503. Here it is not the witness but the "administration of justice" that stands in need of protection. Extending that protection is the province of section 1503, not section 1512. . . .

We affirm Lester's conviction for conspiracy and set aside the judgments of acquittal on Lester's substantive counts and McGill's conspiracy count and restore the jury verdicts.

Notes and Questions

1. In 1988, § 1512(b) was amended to read:

Whoever knowingly uses intimidation or physical force, threatens, *or corruptly persuades* another person, or attempts to do so, or engages in misleading conduct toward another person, with intent to —

(1) Influence, delay, or prevent the testimony of any person in an official proceeding [violates this provision].

Does this amendment completely fill the gap that the *Lester* court was concerned about? If so, should § 1512 be treated as the exclusive provision under which witness tampering can be prosecuted?[27] Does it matter whether other gaps remain?

2. The court in *Lester* also upheld McGill's conviction for conspiracy to violate 18 U.S.C. § 1510. That statute prohibits endeavoring to obstruct, delay, or prevent the communication of information about a federal crime to a criminal investigator through bribery. McGill argued that this provision becomes inapplicable once official proceedings have been instituted. The court disagreed, noting that the danger that a witness is exposed to arises from the fact of communication of the information to the government, not from the timing of the communication.

2. Section 1512: Corrupt Persuasion

ARTHUR ANDERSEN LLP v. UNITED STATES
544 U.S. 696 (2005)

Chief Justice REHNQUIST delivered the opinion of the Court. . . .

Enron Corporation, during the 1990's, switched its business from operation of natural gas pipelines to an energy conglomerate, a move that was accompanied by aggressive accounting practices and rapid growth. Petitioner audited Enron's publicly filed financial statements and provided internal audit and consulting services to it. Petitioner's "engagement team" for Enron was headed by David Duncan. Beginning in 2000, Enron's financial performance began to suffer, and, as 2001 wore on, worsened.[28] On August 14, 2001, Jeffrey Skilling, Enron's Chief Executive Officer (CEO),

---

27. Cf. United States v. Masterpol, 940 F.2d 760 (2d Cir. 1991).

28. During this time, petitioner faced problems of its own. In June 2001, petitioner entered into a settlement agreement with the Securities and Exchange Commission (SEC) related to its audit work of Waste Management, Inc. As part of the settlement, petitioner paid a massive fine. It also was censured and enjoined from committing further violations of the securities laws. In July 2001, the SEC filed an amended complaint alleging improprieties by Sunbeam Corporation, and petitioner's lead partner on the Sunbeam audit was named.

unexpectedly resigned. Within days, Sherron Watkins, a senior accountant at Enron, warned Kenneth Lay, Enron's newly reappointed CEO, that Enron could "implode in a wave of accounting scandals." She likewise informed Duncan and Michael Odom, one of petitioner's partners who had supervisory responsibility over Duncan, of the looming problems.

On August 28, an article in the Wall Street Journal suggested improprieties at Enron, and the SEC opened an informal investigation. By early September, petitioner had formed an Enron "crisis-response" team, which included Nancy Temple, an in-house counsel. On October 8, petitioner retained outside counsel to represent it in any litigation that might arise from the Enron matter. The next day, Temple discussed Enron with other in-house counsel. Her notes from that meeting reflect that "some SEC investigation" is "highly probable."

On October 10, Odom spoke at a general training meeting attended by 89 employees, including 10 from the Enron engagement team. Odom urged everyone to comply with the firm's document retention policy.[29] He added: "'[I]f it's destroyed in the course of [the] normal policy and litigation is filed the next day, that's great. . . . [W]e've followed our own policy, and whatever there was that might have been of interest to somebody is gone and irretrievable.'" On October 12, Temple entered the Enron matter into her computer, designating the "Type of Potential Claim" as "Professional Practice — Government/Regulatory Inv[estigation]." Temple also e-mailed Odom, suggesting that he "'remin[d] the engagement team of our documentation and retention policy.'"

On October 16, Enron announced its third quarter results. That release disclosed a $1.01 billion charge to earnings. The following day, the SEC notified Enron by letter that it had opened an investigation in August and requested certain information and documents. On October 19, Enron forwarded a copy of that letter to petitioner.

On the same day, Temple also sent an e-mail to a member of petitioner's internal team of accounting experts and attached a copy of the document policy. On October 20, the Enron crisis-response team held a conference call, during which Temple instructed everyone to "[m]ake sure to follow the [document] policy." On October 23, Enron CEO Lay declined to answer questions during a call with analysts because of "potential lawsuits, as well as the SEC inquiry." After the call, Duncan met with other Andersen partners on the Enron engagement team and told them that they should ensure team members were complying with the document policy. Another meeting for all team members followed, during which Duncan distributed the policy and told everyone to comply. These, and other smaller meetings, were followed by substantial destruction of paper and electronic documents.

On October 26, one of petitioner's senior partners circulated a New York Times article discussing the SEC's response to Enron. His e-mail commented that "the

---

29. The firm's policy called for a single central engagement file, which "should contain only that information which is relevant to supporting our work." The policy stated that, "in cases of threatened litigation, . . . no related information will be destroyed." It also separately provided that, if petitioner is "advised of litigation or subpoenas regarding a particular engagement, the related information should not be destroyed." Policy Statement No. 780 set forth "notification" procedures for whenever "professional practice litigation against [petitioner] or any of its personnel has been commenced, has been threatened or is judged likely to occur, or when governmental or professional investigations that may involve [petitioner] or any of its personnel have been commenced or are judged likely."

problems are just beginning and we will be in the cross hairs. The marketplace is going to keep the pressure on this and is going to force the SEC to be tough." On October 30, the SEC opened a formal investigation and sent Enron a letter that requested accounting documents.

Throughout this time period, the document destruction continued, despite reservations by some of petitioner's managers.[30] On November 8, Enron announced that it would issue a comprehensive restatement of its earnings and assets. Also on November 8, the SEC served Enron and petitioner with subpoenas for records. On November 9, Duncan's secretary sent an e-mail that stated: "Per Dave — No more shredding. . . . We have been officially served for our documents." Enron filed for bankruptcy less than a month later. Duncan was fired and later pleaded guilty to witness tampering.

In March 2002, petitioner was indicted in the Southern District of Texas on one count of violating § 1512(b)(2)(A) and (B). The indictment alleged that, between October 10 and November 9, 2001, petitioner "did knowingly, intentionally and corruptly persuade . . . other persons, to wit: [petitioner's] employees, with intent to cause" them to withhold documents from, and alter documents for use in, "official proceedings, namely: regulatory and criminal proceedings and investigations." A jury trial followed. When the case went to the jury, that body deliberated for seven days and then declared that it was deadlocked. The District Court delivered an "*Allen* charge," Allen v. United States, 164 U.S. 492 (1896), and, after three more days of deliberation, the jury returned a guilty verdict. The District Court denied petitioner's motion for a judgment of acquittal.

The Court of Appeals for the Fifth Circuit affirmed. It held that the jury instructions properly conveyed the meaning of "corruptly persuades" and "official proceeding"; that the jury need not find any consciousness of wrongdoing; and that there was no reversible error. Because of a split of authority regarding the meaning of § 1512(b), we granted certiorari.

[18 U.S.C. § 1512(b)(2)(A) & (B)] provide in relevant part:

> Whoever knowingly uses intimidation or physical force, threatens, or corruptly persuades another person, or attempts to do so, or engages in misleading conduct toward another person, with intent to . . . cause or induce any person to . . . withhold testimony, or withhold a record, document, or other object, from an official proceeding [or] alter, destroy, mutilate, or conceal an object with intent to impair the object's integrity or availability for use in an official proceeding . . . shall be fined under this title or imprisoned not more than ten years, or both.

In this case, our attention is focused on what it means to "knowingly . . . corruptly persuad[e]" another person "with intent to . . . cause" that person to "withhold" documents from, or "alter" documents for use in, an "official proceeding."

---

30. For example, on October 26, John Riley, another partner with petitioner, saw Duncan shredding documents and told him "this wouldn't be the best time in the world for you guys to be shredding a bunch of stuff." On October 31, David Stulb, a forensics investigator for petitioner, met with Duncan. During the meeting, Duncan picked up a document with the words "smoking gun" written on it and began to destroy it, adding "we don't need this." Stulb cautioned Duncan on the need to maintain documents and later informed Temple that Duncan needed advice on the document retention policy.

"We have traditionally exercised restraint in assessing the reach of a federal criminal statute, both out of deference to the prerogatives of Congress and out of concern that 'a fair warning should be given to the world in language that the common world will understand, of what the law intends to do if a certain line is passed,' McBoyle v. United States, 283 U.S. 25, 27 (1931)." United States v. Aguilar, 515 U.S. 593, 600 (1995).

Such restraint is particularly appropriate here, where the act underlying the conviction — "persua[sion]" — is by itself innocuous. Indeed, "persuad[ing]" a person "with intent to . . . cause" that person to "withhold" testimony or documents from a Government proceeding or Government official is not inherently malign. Consider, for instance, a mother who suggests to her son that he invoke his right against compelled self-incrimination or a wife who persuades her husband not to disclose marital confidences.

Nor is it necessarily corrupt for an attorney to "persuad[e]" a client "with intent to . . . cause" that client to "withhold" documents from the Government. In Upjohn Co. v. United States, 449 U.S. 383 (1981), for example, we held that Upjohn was justified in withholding documents that were covered by the attorney-client privilege from the Internal Revenue Service (IRS). No one would suggest that an attorney who "persuade[d]" Upjohn to take that step acted wrongfully, even though he surely intended that his client keep those documents out of the IRS' hands.

"Document retention policies," which are created in part to keep certain information from getting into the hands of others, including the Government, are common in business. It is, of course, not wrongful for a manager to instruct his employees to comply with a valid document retention policy under ordinary circumstances.

Acknowledging this point, the parties have largely focused their attention on the word "corruptly" as the key to what may or may not lawfully be done in the situation presented here. Section 1512(b) punishes not just "corruptly persuad[ing]" another, but "*knowingly* . . . corruptly persuad[ing]" another. The Government suggests that "knowingly" does not modify "corruptly persuades," but that is not how the statute most naturally reads. It provides the mens rea — "knowingly" — and then a list of acts — "uses intimidation or physical force, threatens, or corruptly persuades." We have recognized with regard to similar statutory language that the mens rea at least applies to the acts that immediately follow, if not to other elements down the statutory chain. The Government suggests that it is "questionable whether Congress would employ such an inelegant formulation as 'knowingly . . . corruptly persuades.'" Long experience has not taught us to share the Government's doubts on this score, and we must simply interpret the statute as written.

The parties have not pointed us to another interpretation of "knowingly . . . corruptly" to guide us here.[31] In any event, the natural meaning of these terms provides a clear answer. "[K]nowledge" and "knowingly" are normally associated with awareness, understanding, or consciousness. See Black's Law Dictionary 888 (8th ed. 2004) (hereinafter Black's); Webster's Third New International Dictionary 1252-1253 (1993) (hereinafter Webster's 3d); American Heritage Dictionary of the English Language 725 (1981) (hereinafter Am. Hert.). "Corrupt" and "corruptly" are normally associated with

---

31. The parties have pointed us to two other obstruction provisions, 18 U.S.C. §§ 1503 and 1505, which contain the word "corruptly." But these provisions lack the modifier "knowingly," making any analogy inexact.

wrongful, immoral, depraved, or evil. See Black's 371; Webster's 3d 512; Am. Hert. 299-300. Joining these meanings together here makes sense both linguistically and in the statutory scheme. Only persons conscious of wrongdoing can be said to "knowingly . . . corruptly persuad[e]." And limiting criminality to persuaders conscious of their wrongdoing sensibly allows § 1512(b) to reach only those with the level of "culpability . . . we usually require in order to impose criminal liability." United States v. Aguilar, 515 U.S., at 602.

The outer limits of this element need not be explored here because the jury instructions at issue simply failed to convey the requisite consciousness of wrongdoing. Indeed, it is striking how little culpability the instructions required. For example, the jury was told that, "even if [petitioner] honestly and sincerely believed that its conduct was lawful, you may find [petitioner] guilty." The instructions also diluted the meaning of "corruptly" so that it covered innocent conduct.

The parties vigorously disputed how the jury would be instructed on "corruptly." The District Court based its instruction on the definition of that term found in the Fifth Circuit Pattern Jury Instruction for § 1503. This pattern instruction defined "corruptly" as "'knowingly and dishonestly, with the specific intent to subvert or undermine the integrity'" of a proceeding. The Government, however, insisted on excluding "dishonestly" and adding the term "impede" to the phrase "subvert or undermine." The District Court agreed over petitioner's objections, and the jury was told to convict if it found petitioner intended to "subvert, undermine, or impede" governmental factfinding by suggesting to its employees that they enforce the document retention policy.

These changes were significant. No longer was any type of "dishonest[y]" necessary to a finding of guilt, and it was enough for petitioner to have simply "impede[d]" the Government's factfinding ability. As the Government conceded at oral argument, "'impede'" has broader connotations than "'subvert'" or even "'undermine,'" and many of these connotations do not incorporate any "corrupt[ness]" at all. The dictionary defines "impede" as "to interfere with or get in the way of the progress of" or "hold up" or "detract from." Webster's 3d 1132. By definition, anyone who innocently persuades another to withhold information from the Government "get[s] in the way of the progress of" the Government. With regard to such innocent conduct, the "corruptly" instructions did no limiting work whatsoever.

The instructions also were infirm for another reason. They led the jury to believe that it did not have to find *any* nexus between the "persua[sion]" to destroy documents and any particular proceeding. In resisting any type of nexus element, the Government relies heavily on § 1512(e)(1), which states that an official proceeding "need not be pending or about to be instituted at the time of the offense." It is, however, one thing to say that a proceeding "need not be pending or about to be instituted at the time of the offense," and quite another to say a proceeding need not even be foreseen. A "knowingly . . . corrup[t] persaude[r]" cannot be someone who persuades others to shred documents under a document retention policy when he does not have in contemplation any particular official proceeding in which those documents might be material.

We faced a similar situation in *Aguilar*. Respondent Aguilar lied to a Federal Bureau of Investigation agent in the course of an investigation and was convicted of "'corruptly endeavor[ing] to influence, obstruct, and impede [a] . . . grand jury investigation'" under § 1503. All the Government had shown was that Aguilar had uttered false statements to an investigating agent "who might or might not testify before a grand jury." We held that § 1503 required something more — specifically, a "nexus" between the obstructive act and the proceeding. "[I]f the defendant lacks knowledge that his actions are likely to affect the judicial proceeding," we explained, "he lacks the requisite intent to obstruct." 515 U.S. at 599.

For these reasons, the jury instructions here were flawed in important respects. The judgment of the Court of Appeals is reversed, and the case is remanded for further proceedings consistent with this opinion.

It is so ordered.

Notes and Questions

1. The Court concluded that § 1512(b) requires consciousness of wrongdoing and that the jury instructions did not adequately convey that requirement. Is it possible to "corruptly" perform an act without knowing it is wrongful?

2. In deciding that "knowingly" modifies "corruptly persuades," the Court said that a restrained interpretation of § 1512(b) was particularly appropriate because "'persuasion' — is itself innocuous." It gave as illustrative examples a mother who advises her son to withhold evidence by invoking his privilege against self-incrimination and a wife who asks her husband to keep marital confidences secret. Are these examples analogous to what Andersen employees allegedly did? Suppose the mother had told her son to bury a gun that they both knew his friend had used to kill someone. Assuming that their purpose was to keep the police from finding the gun, would the son be acting "corruptly" even if he did not know his conduct was illegal?

What about the lawyer in *Cintolo*? Where does his conduct fit on the *Andersen* Court's spectrum of culpability?

3. One of the Court's chief concerns seems to be the potential for criminalizing good-faith compliance with corporate document retention policies — e.g., that it is "not wrongful for a manager to instruct his employees to comply with a *valid* document retention policy under *ordinary* circumstances."[32] What do "valid" and "ordinary" mean in this context? Does Andersen's document destruction satisfy this standard?

4. The Andersen indictment alleged that Andersen partners engaged in "wholesale destruction" of Enron-related documents following "urgent and mandatory meetings" at which they were told to work overtime if necessary to shred the documents and delete computer files. According to the allegations, tons of Enron documents were shredded and — because the shredder at Andersen's office at Enron was in constant use — dozens of trunks of Enron documents were transported across town to Andersen's main Houston office to handle the overload.[33]

In January 2002, Andersen issued a press release acknowledging that David Duncan had called an urgent meeting to expedite the shredding of Enron documents and that Andersen had deleted "thousands of e-mails" and "rushed" the disposal of many documents. The press release continued: "These activities were on such a scale

---

32. 125 S. Ct. at 2135.
33. Indictment, United States v. Arthur Andersen LLP, CRH-02-121, at 5-6 (S.D. Tex. Mar. 3, 2002).

and of such a nature as to remove any doubt that Andersen's policies and reasonable good judgment were violated."[34]

Contrast the Court's recitation of the facts and its description of § 1512(b)(2)(A) and (B). Do they adequately capture the essence of the allegations and of Andersen's own admissions? Is it important whether they do?

5. Some critics of the Andersen prosecution have cited the Supreme Court's decision as proof of government overreaching in prosecuting the firm. Does the Court's opinion address the merits of the case against Andersen?

6. Andersen claimed that the prosecution was a gross abuse of power that caused irreparable reputational harm and left the firm in ruins. But to put Andersen's claim in context, consider other recent investigations of Andersen clients for various forms of financial and accounting fraud, shown in Table 8-1. Is it clear that the Enron-related obstruction-of-justice prosecution was the source of Andersen's demise? Assuming arguendo that it was, should prosecutors have refrained from criminally charging the firm?

TABLE 8-1
Financial and Accounting Fraud Investigations of Arthur Andersen Clients[35]

CLIENT	INVESTIGATION	AGENCY
Baptist Foundation of Arizona*	Ponzi Scheme/Concealing Losses	State Regulators, State Attorney General, State Prosecutor
CMS Energy	Overstated Revenue by $4.4 Billion in 2000 and 2001	SEC, CFTC,[36] U.S. Attorney
Dynegy*	Sham Trades to Inflate Revenue	SEC, CFTC, DOJ,[37] State Regulators
Enron*	Inflated Earnings and Off-Book Special-Purpose Entities	SEC, DOJ
Freddie Mac	Smoothing Earnings	SEC, DOJ
Global Crossing*	Accounting Practices and Network Swaps to Inflate Revenue	SEC, DOJ
Halliburton	Method of Recording Revenue	SEC
McKesson*	Inflated Revenue and Earnings	SEC, DOJ, U.S. Attorney
Peregrine Systems*	Inflated Revenue by $100 Million in 3 years	SEC, DOJ
Qwest Communications*	Inflated Revenue in 2000 and 2001	SEC, DOJ, U.S. Attorney, State District Attorney
Sunbeam	Accounting Fraud	SEC, DOJ
Waste Management	Inflated Revenue by $1 Billion during 1992-1996	SEC
WorldCom*	Concealed Losses and Inflated Revenue by $1.38 Billion in 2001	SEC, DOJ, U.S. Attorney

---

34. Press Release, Arthur Andersen, LLP, Andersen Announces Preliminary Enron-Related Disciplinary and Administrative Actions (Jan. 15, 2002).

35. Adapted from Kathleen F. Brickey, Andersen's Fall from Grace, 81 Wash. U. L.Q. 917, 952-954 (2003). An asterisk indicates that one or more individuals were indicted in connection with the fraud.

36. Commodities Future Trading Commission.

37. Department of Justice.

As the facts in *Andersen* suggest, lawyers in the corporate law world may encounter a host of thorny ethical questions, including what to do when it becomes clear that the client or the client's agent intends to commit a crime. Consider the following case in point.

MICHIGAN STATE BAR COMMITTEE ON PROFESSIONAL AND JUDICIAL ETHICS, INFORMAL OPINION RI-345
(October 24, 2008)

A corporation is engaged in litigation. The chief executive officer (CEO) of the corporation has informed the corporation's litigation attorney that he intends to destroy documents relevant to the dispute that are subject to a court discovery order. The corporation is closely held but has a board of directors to which the CEO is accountable; and the CEO is not the sole shareholder. The CEO has directed the lawyer not to produce the documents in response to the order and has threatened to terminate her if she does. The lawyer possesses copies of the documents, and the CEO has requested that she return them to the corporation. The lawyer asks what steps should be taken under the ethical rules to address the CEO's threatened misconduct.

The lawyer's obligations are to the corporation. Although in most instances, the Rules of Professional Conduct defer to other law in determining who is the client, Michigan Rule of Professional Conduct ("MRPC") 1.13(a) provides that the client is the corporation, not the CEO:

> A lawyer employed or retained to represent an organization represents the organization as distinct from its directors, officers, employees, members, shareholders, or other constituents.

In representing the corporation, the lawyer is to communicate with the client so as to permit informed decisions regarding the representation under MRPC 1.4(b), and is to take steps to prevent reasonably foreseeable harm to the client, as set forth in MRPC 1.13(b):

> If a lawyer for an organization knows that an officer, employee, or other person associated with the organization is engaged in action, intends to act, or refuses to act in a matter related to the representation that is a violation of a legal obligation to the organization, or a violation of law which reasonably might be imputed to the organization, and that is likely to result in substantial injury to the organization, the lawyer shall proceed as is reasonably necessary in the best interest of the organization. In determining how to proceed, the lawyer shall give due consideration to the seriousness of the violation and its consequences, the scope and nature of the lawyer's representation, the responsibility in the organization, and the apparent motivation of the person involved, the policies of the organization concerning such matters, and any other relevant considerations. Any measures taken shall be designed to minimize disruption of the organization and the risk of revealing information relating to the representation to persons outside the organization. Such measures may include among others:
>
> (1)   asking reconsideration of the matter;
>
> (2)   advising that a separate legal opinion on the matter be sought for presentation to appropriate authority in the organization; and

(3) referring the matter to higher authority in the organization, including, if warranted by the seriousness of the matter, referral to the highest authority that can act in behalf of the organization as determined by applicable law.

The Committee assumes that the CEO's threat to destroy documents that are subject to a discovery order, if carried out, would be "a violation of law which reasonably could be imputed to the organization, and that is likely to result in substantial injury to the organization. . . ."[38] Accordingly, the lawyer is required to proceed as reasonably necessary to protect the best interest of the corporation, taking into account MRPC 1.13(b) and other relevant considerations. The particular steps required of the lawyer will depend on such factors as the governance structure of the organization, the degree of independence of the board, and the CEO's relationship with higher authority.

The lawyer should first attempt to dissuade the CEO from the threatened course of conduct. In asking the CEO to reconsider, the lawyer may discuss such matters as the corporation's duty to comply with court orders and applicable law, any relevant corporate policies such as those involving ethical obligations and document retention, the lawyer's recommendation that a second opinion be obtained regarding the implications of the threatened conduct, and the lawyer's intent to refer the matter to higher authority in the corporation if the CEO does not recant.

If the CEO cannot be dissuaded, the lawyer should consult with higher authority, here presumably the corporation's board of directors. If the CEO is a member of the board, the lawyer should exercise care to assure that any independent directors are duly informed.[39] In referring the matter to higher authority, the lawyer may, as necessary, advise the board that the lawyer's ethical obligations would likely require withdrawal from representing the corporation, and appropriate disclosure to the tribunal, if the CEO carries out the threat and the misconduct is not otherwise rectified.

The objectives of MRPC 1.13 are met if the lawyer's referral to higher authority redresses the CEO's threatened misconduct. However, if the lawyer reasonably believes after counseling and remonstrating with the client that the CEO has not retracted his threat, the lawyer should preserve any pertinent documents, or copies thereof, in her possession until the matter of discovery compliance is resolved. Otherwise, the lawyer risks violating MRPC 3.4(a), which provides that a lawyer shall not "unlawfully obstruct another party's access to evidence; unlawfully . . . destroy or conceal a document . . . or assist another person to do any such act." The Comment to the Rule emphasizes that:

> [d]ocuments and other items of evidence are often essential to establish a claim or defense . . . [T]he right of an opposing party . . . to obtain evidence through discovery or subpoena is an important procedural right. The exercise of that right can be frustrated if relevant material is . . . concealed or destroyed. Other law makes it an offense to destroy material for purpose of impairing its availability in a pending proceeding or one whose commencement can be foreseen.

---

38. Determining when destruction of evidence is a violation of law and analyzing applicable legal authorities are outside of the Committee's jurisdiction. For purposes of this Opinion, we assume that the CEO's threatened misconduct, if carried out, would be a violation of law regarding preservation of evidence subject to a court order.

39. The lawyer's duty to maintain the confidentiality of client secrets does not, of course, prohibit the lawyer from disclosing communications with the CEO to higher authority within the client corporation. This is true even if the disclosure is against the interests of the CEO or other constituents of the corporation. See generally Restatement of the Law Governing Lawyers, 3d § 96.

The lawyer should decline to return the documents to the CEO or the corporation. Doing so with the knowledge of the CEO's intentions could be considered assisting the client in destroying or concealing a document having potential evidentiary value in violation of MRPC 3.4(a). Returning the documents may serve also to assist the client in conduct the lawyer knows to be illegal or fraudulent, addressed in MRPC 1.2(c).

The lawyer may continue the representation of the corporation notwithstanding the CEO's threat to destroy documents. The Comment to MRPC 1.16 counsels that "[t]he lawyer is not obliged to . . . withdraw simply because a client suggests such a course of conduct [that is illegal or violates the Rules of Professional Conduct or other law]." MRPC 1.16(a)(1) provides that a lawyer shall withdraw if "the representation will result in violation of the Rules of Professional Conduct or other law." Faced with the CEO's threatened misconduct, however, continued representation of the corporation is consistent with the lawyer's previously discussed obligations under MRPC 1.13(b). Such representation will not result in violation of the Rules or other law, but fulfills the lawyer's ethical duties and may forestall a violation of law by the client.

Notes and Questions

1. The lawyer has an ethical obligation to avoid harm to the client. Who is the client in this case? How might the client be harmed if the lawyer were to comply with the CEO's request?

2. Does the CEO's threatened misconduct violate any of the obstruction of justice statutes we have considered thus far? If so, which statute or statutes?

3. Assuming arguendo that the threatened misconduct constitutes some form of obstruction of justice, at what point will the lawyer risk becoming a party to the crime? Under what theory would the risk be incurred?

NOTE ON EVIDENCE TAMPERING AND DOCUMENT DESTRUCTION

In a direct response to the *Andersen* decision, the Sarbanes-Oxley Act provided prosecutors with two new statutory theories for pursuing obstruction of justice charges based on document destruction, alteration, and falsification, in addition to the amendments expanding the scope of § 1512. The Senate Report specifically refers to Andersen's document destruction and retention policy in its discussion of why new obstruction of justice laws were needed.[40]

The first concern relates to the destruction or alteration of records in federal investigations. The Court in *Andersen* was receptive to Andersen's arguments against criminalizing requests or orders to destroy documents relating to matters that may not be the subject of active investigations or that may be covered by legitimate corporate document retention policies. But Congress was not. When it enacted the Sarbanes-Oxley Act, Congress pointedly addressed these matters by making clear its intention to broadly prohibit evidence tampering in anticipation of government investigations.

---

40. The Corporate and Criminal Fraud Accountancy Act of 2002, S. Rep. No. 107-146, at 15-16 (May 6, 2002).

Consider § 1519, which reaches virtually all forms of tampering with tangible evidence. Section 1519 makes it a crime to *knowingly* alter, destroy, mutilate, conceal, or falsify any record, document, or tangible object with *intent to impede*, obstruct, or influence the *investigation* or *administration* of *any matter* within the *jurisdiction* of any department or agency of the United States, or any bankruptcy case; or *in relation to* or *contemplation of* any such matter or case.

The jurisdictional language in § 1519 tracks the jurisdictional language found — until recently — in the false statements statute, 18 U.S.C. § 1001, considered in Chapter 6. A department or agency has "jurisdiction" in a matter when it has statutory authority to act.[41] That is true whether or not the agency has actually exercised its power and authority over the matter and regardless of whether its jurisdiction is exclusive.[42]

A related question under this statute is what constitutes a "department or agency" of the United States. In decisions construing the same jurisdictional language formerly found in the false statements statute, courts ultimately concluded that while the executive and legislative branches are governmental departments and agencies, the judicial branch is not.[43]

Congress also addressed the Supreme Court's collateral concern about destruction of corporate audit records that may be regulated by a legitimate document retention program. The Sarbanes-Oxley Act specifically addresses the question of when it is permissible to alter or destroy corporate audit papers.

The new provision, 18 U.S.C. § 1520, imposes record retention requirements on accountants who audit corporations that are subject to the reporting requirements of the Securities Exchange Act of 1934. Section 1520 requires auditors to retain all audit or review workpapers for five years. Although § 1520 does not specify what documents should be deemed exempt from the retention requirements, it directs the SEC to promulgate appropriate rules and regulations concerning the retention of workpapers and other, similar documents — including electronic records — that contain conclusions, opinions, analyses, or financial data relating to the audit.[44] It is a crime to knowingly and willfully violate the record retention requirements.

3. Section 1512: Misleading Conduct

Section 1512 also punishes misleading conduct that is intended to affect another's participation in an official proceeding, impair the availability of evidence in an official proceeding, or impede the reporting of information relating to the commission of a federal crime to law enforcement authorities or a judge. Section 1515 defines "misleading conduct" to include making false or misleading statements or inviting reliance on false or misleading evidence.

---

41. United States v. Rodgers, 466 U.S. 475 (1984).

42. Thus, for example, while the SEC has jurisdiction to investigate securities fraud, to initiate civil or administrative proceedings against securities law violators, and to promulgate rules and regulations implementing the securities laws, the Justice Department also has jurisdiction to investigate and prosecute securities fraud.

43. See Hubbard v. United States, 514 U.S. 695 (1995) (overruling United States v. Bramblett, 348 U.S. 503 (1955)). As noted in Chapter 6, Congress has since amended § 1001 to expressly include the judicial branch of government in its jurisdictional language, albeit for relatively limited purposes.

44. 17 C.F.R. § 210.2-06 (2005).

W tampering (handwritten)

UNITED STATES v. GABRIEL
125 F.3d 89 (2d Cir. 1997)

MESKILL, Circuit Judge. . . .

BACKGROUND

indictment (handwritten)

Defendants-appellants James M. Gabriel and Gerard E. Vitti were both executive vice presidents at Chromalloy Research and Technology Division (CRT), a division of Chromalloy Gas Turbine Corporation. CRT is one of the nation's largest jet engine repair stations serving most of the world's airlines.

In 1992, the government learned that CRT was misrepresenting the nature of some of its jet engine repairs. After an extensive investigation Gabriel and Vitti were indicted on multiple counts of mail fraud, wire fraud and making false statements to the Federal Aviation Administration (FAA). Gabriel was indicted separately for witness tampering. After a six-week trial, a jury convicted Gabriel on two counts of mail fraud, two counts of wire fraud, two counts of making false statements to the FAA, and one count of witness tampering. Vitti was convicted on one count of wire fraud. . . .

[The indictment alleged two different fraudulent schemes relating to jet engine repairs that CRT had agreed to perform. The first, which was unrelated to the obstruction of justice charge, involved faulty repairs CRT made on jet engines used on wide-bodied passenger jets. CRT falsely certified that it had made the repairs in accordance with the manufacturer's specifications. This scheme led to Gabriel's convictions of mail and wire fraud and of making false statements, and to Vitti's conviction of wire fraud. The second, which was the subject of the witness tampering charge, related to repairs on a low pressure turbine case.]

B. THE LPT CASE SCHEME

In 1990, Qantas Airline contracted with CRT to repair a low pressure turbine (LPT) case. Gabriel repeatedly misled Qantas into believing that CRT would perform the repair when Gabriel knew that the work was to be performed at a related facility in Florida with which Qantas earlier had experienced problems.

After the Florida facility repaired the LPT case, the LPT case was shipped to CRT for transhipment to Qantas. A CRT quality control inspector inspected the part and determined that it had been damaged and was "irreparable scrap." Nevertheless, Gabriel ordered the LPT case shipped to Qantas after some purely cosmetic work was done. The packing slip that accompanied the LPT case falsely stated that the LPT case was suitable to be returned to service. Moreover, Gabriel sent a fax to Qantas falsely stating that the LPT case was "100% serviceable."

Qantas put the LPT case into service, and the LPT case flew approximately 1,200 hours until the FAA discovered the improper repair and directed Qantas to remove the LPT case from use. Subsequent inspection revealed that the LPT case was unserviceable and that as a result of the improper repair, it had started to come apart. . . .

C. WITNESS TAMPERING

When a grand jury began to investigate Gabriel's involvement in the LPT case scheme, CRT hired outside counsel to determine what had happened. When CRT's counsel asked Gabriel about the repair, Gabriel falsely stated that he had previously disclosed to Qantas that the LPT case was only partially serviceable. Further, in an attempt to support that story, Gabriel sent a fax to Donald Mealing, the Qantas representative with whom Gabriel had dealt. The fax was headed "ONGOING GOVT INVESTIGATION AT CRT," and stated, in pertinent part:

> I am going to call you with our attorneys within the next several days. . . . The questions they will ask you are relative to your memory of our meeting in [Sydney] at [Qantas] covering acceptance criteria and the very nature of this case that it was difficult to salvage. It is important that you think this through before they talk on the issue. Note *I've cited the case* had [numerous problems]. . . . All of these points supported the case was a "dog" but *we shipped it as partially serviceable.*

For sending that fax, Gabriel was charged with witness tampering. The government's theory was that Gabriel was attempting to mislead Mealing into believing that Gabriel had previously disclosed to Qantas that the case was "partially serviceable," and that Gabriel intended Mealing to believe that lie and to repeat it to the grand jury.

DISCUSSION . . .

E. WITNESS TAMPERING

As discussed above, even though a CRT inspector concluded that the LPT case was unserviceable scrap after it had been repaired, Gabriel falsely represented to Qantas that the part was "100% serviceable." Eventually, the grand jury and CRT's investigators began to suspect that the repair work had been fraudulently performed. When CRT's investigators asked Gabriel about the repair, Gabriel falsely stated that he had previously disclosed the faults in the LPT case to Qantas. Further, in an attempt to support that story, Gabriel sent the fax to Donald Mealing, the Qantas representative with whom Gabriel had dealt, quoted earlier in this opinion.

Gabriel was convicted of violating 18 U.S.C. § 1512(b)(1), which makes it a crime to "corruptly persuade[] another person, or attempt[] to do so, or engage[] in misleading conduct toward another person, with intent to — influence . . . the testimony of any person in an official proceeding." The government's theory was that Gabriel was attempting to mislead Mealing into believing that Gabriel had previously disclosed that the LPT case was only partially serviceable, and that Gabriel intended to have Mealing believe that lie and repeat it to the grand jury. See United States v. Rodolitz, 786 F.2d 77, 82 (2d Cir. 1986) (section 1512(b) applies to "the situation where a defendant tells a potential witness a false story as if the story were true, intending that the witness believe the story and testify to it before the grand jury").[45]

---

45. Mealing eventually testified before the grand jury, and although the record is not clear on this point, it appears that Mealing was not fooled by Gabriel's misrepresentations.

On appeal, Gabriel contends, as he did unsuccessfully below, that the government was required to prove that his actions were likely to affect Mealing's grand jury testimony. Gabriel further contends that because Mealing was in Australia and beyond the grand jury's subpoena power, there was insufficient evidence to prove that Mealing was likely to testify, and therefore, there was insufficient evidence to prove that Gabriel's actions were likely to affect Mealing's testimony. However, our decision in United States v. Romero, 54 F.3d 56 (2d Cir. 1995), undercuts that argument.

In *Romero*, the defendant was convicted of violating 18 U.S.C. § 1512(a)(1)(C), which makes it a crime to kill a person "with intent to — prevent the communication by any person to a law enforcement officer . . . of information relating to the commission or possible commission of a Federal offense." On appeal, we rejected the argument that the government had to prove that the victim "was willing to cooperate or that an investigation was underway." Id. at 62. Rather, we held that:

> The government need prove only an intent to kill for the purpose of interfering with communication with federal law enforcement officials. The victim need not have agreed to cooperate with any federal authority or even to have evinced an intention or desire to so cooperate. There need not be an ongoing investigation or even any intent to investigate. Rather, the killing of an individual with the intent to frustrate the individual's *possible cooperation* with federal authorities is implicated by the statute.

Id.

The elements of subsection (b)(1), which Gabriel was convicted of violating, are similar to the elements of subsection (a)(1)(C) that we construed in *Romero*. Both sections make it illegal to engage in certain conduct (corruptly persuading/misleading or killing) with an intent to achieve a specified result (influencing testimony in an official proceeding or preventing the communication of crimes to federal authorities). Further, both sections serve the same basic purpose — the prevention of "tampering with a witness . . . or an informant." Accordingly, we base our interpretation of section 1512(b)(1) on our decision in *Romero*, and conclude that the government was not required to prove that Mealing was likely to testify or that Gabriel's actions were likely to affect Mealing's testimony. Rather, the government was required to prove only that Gabriel endeavored corruptly to persuade or mislead Mealing with the intent of influencing Mealing's *potential* testimony before a grand jury.

Gabriel contends, nevertheless, that the Supreme Court's decision in United States v. Aguilar, 515 U.S. 593 (1995), which was decided after we decided *Romero*, requires that a "likely to affect" requirement be incorporated into section 1512. . . . As in this case, the government's theory in *Aguilar* was that the defendant lied to the FBI agents with the intent that the FBI agents would believe the lie and repeat it to the grand jury. . . .

Although the facts in this case and in *Aguilar* are similar — each defendant was convicted for telling a lie to a potential witness with the intent that the witness would believe the lie and repeat it to a grand jury — that is where the similarity between these two cases ends. A comparison of the statutes that underlie the convictions demonstrates that the "likely to affect" requirement that the *Aguilar* Court incorporated into section 1503 should not be incorporated into section 1512.

As mentioned above, the omnibus clause of section 1503 makes it a crime to "corruptly . . . endeavor[] to influence, obstruct, or impede, the due administration of justice." The *Aguilar* Court plainly was concerned about the "very broad language" of this clause. Further, the Court indicated that without a "likely to affect" requirement, the provision would not provide "fair warning . . . to the world . . . of what the law intends to do if a certain line is passed." Id. at 599-600. Accordingly, the *Aguilar* Court incorporated a "likely to affect" requirement into section 1503.

Here, unlike the omnibus clause of section 1503, section 1512(b) uses language that provides fair notice to the world of what line cannot be crossed. Section 1512(b) has two elements that are germane to the offenses charged: (1) that the defendant engaged in misleading conduct or corruptly persuaded a person, and (2) that the defendant acted with an intent to influence the person's testimony at an official proceeding. Both of the alternative possibilities in the first element provide fair notice — "misleading conduct" is defined with particularity in a later section, § 1515(a)(3), and we previously have held that "corruptly persuade" is not unduly vague, see United States v. Thompson, 76 F.3d 442, 452 (2d Cir. 1996).[46] Further, the second element, intent to influence a person's testimony at an official proceeding, is also reasonably specific. Accordingly, there is no reason to narrow section 1512(b) by incorporating a "likely to affect" requirement as the *Aguilar* Court did to section 1503.

Moreover, the *Aguilar* Court held that the "likely to affect" requirement was not satisfied by making a false statement to a potential witness who *might* testify before a grand jury that was *already* impaneled and investigating Aguilar. It stands to reason, therefore, that uttering a false statement to a person who *might* testify before a grand jury that *might* be impaneled would not satisfy the "likely to affect" requirement either. Therefore, if a "likely to affect" requirement were incorporated into section 1512(b), an official proceeding would have to be pending at the time of the defendant's conduct to warrant a conviction. However, section 1512(e)(1) specifically provides that "an official proceeding need not be pending or about to be instituted at the time of the offense." Therefore, if a "likely to affect" requirement were incorporated into section 1512(b), it would create a direct conflict with section 1512(e)(1) — indicating that a "likely to affect" requirement should not be incorporated into section 1512(b). . . .

Accordingly, despite the factual similarity between this case and *Aguilar*, we conclude that the government was not required to prove that Gabriel's actions were "likely to affect" Mealing's testimony before the grand jury. Rather, the government was required to prove only that Gabriel misled or corruptly persuaded Mealing with the intent to interfere with Mealing's *potential* testimony before the grand jury.

Here, the jury reasonably could conclude that Gabriel acted with the requisite intent. Gabriel concedes that he sent the fax to Mealing with the intent to interfere with CRT's internal investigation, but Gabriel argues that the fax would not support an inference that he intended to interfere with the grand jury investigation. From the body of the fax, the jury reasonably could have concluded that Gabriel's sole intention was to interfere with CRT's investigators. If the jury had so concluded, it would have been compelled to find Gabriel innocent because section 1512(b)(1) prohibits interference only with official proceedings. However, the jury also reasonably could have concluded

---

46. But see *Aguilar*, 515 U.S. at 600 & n.1 (declining to decide whether section 1503's use of the term "corruptly" renders the section vague or overbroad).

that Gabriel intended to interfere with the grand jury investigation. Gabriel knew that there was an ongoing grand jury investigation at the time he sent the fax and Gabriel knew that Mealing could be a damaging witness. Further, although the body of the fax discussed only the CRT investigation, the fax was headed "ONGOING GOVT INVESTIGATION AT CRT." From these facts, the jury reasonably could have concluded that Gabriel sent the fax with the intent, at least in part, of interfering with Mealing's potential testimony before the grand jury.[47] . . .

CONCLUSION

We affirm Gabriel's and Vitti's convictions. . . .

Notes and Questions

1. Is the distinction the court drew between the omnibus clause of § 1503 and the witness tampering statute persuasive? Do the two statutes serve the same or different purposes?

2. Suppose Gabriel and Mealing both knew that CRT had misrepresented that the LPT case was 100 percent serviceable and that CRT had never acknowledged any problems with the repairs. If Gabriel had asked Mealing to tell the investigators that CRT shipped the case as partially serviceable in the hope that this would derail the investigation, would that have constituted misleading conduct under § 1512(b)? Why or why not? If not, would Gabriel's conduct constitute witness tampering under a different theory?

4. Section 1512: Harassment

UNITED STATES v. WILSON
796 F.2d 55 (4th Cir. 1986)

ERVIN, Circuit Judge. . . .

I

On April 3, 1985, Wilson was being escorted by U.S. Marshals from a district courtroom, where he had been brought in on a writ to testify on behalf of the government in the trial of United States v. Joseph James McDermott. Three other government

---

47. We note that although not argued by Gabriel, the jury also reasonably could have concluded that Gabriel's sole intent was to interfere with the FBI investigation, and if the jury had so concluded, it would have been compelled to find Gabriel innocent. See 18 U.S.C. § 1512(b)(1) (prohibiting only interference with "official proceedings"); id. § 1515(a)(1) (defining "official proceeding" and not including government investigations). However, the jury reasonably could have concluded that Gabriel was more concerned about the grand jury investigation, and that therefore, Gabriel acted, at least in part, to interfere with that investigation.

witnesses in the same trial, Pauline Virginia Sawyer, Kimberly Renee Lindsey, and Patrick Charles Malone, were sitting in the hallway outside of the courtroom. As Wilson walked past the three, he pointed at each witness and with a sneer said in a low tone of voice: "Your asses belong to Joe" and "you are a bunch of jokes and should be in jail too."

Sawyer, Lindsey and Malone stated that they understood these comments to be threats regarding their testimony in the *McDermott* trial. Sawyer, who had not testified yet, became so upset that she attempted to leave the courthouse and temporarily decided not to testify against McDermott. Lindsey, who had testified for the government, but had not been excused yet by the court, was upset and frightened by the comments. Malone, who had testified and had been excused by the court, felt the statements were idle threats toward him.

The government brought a three count indictment against Wilson, charging that he did

> intentionally harass [Sawyer — Count One; Lindsey — Count Two; Malone — Count Three], thereby attempting to hinder, delay, prevent and dissuade [each one] from testifying in an official proceeding, in violation of Title 18, United States Code, Section 1512(b)(1).[48]

After the jury returned a guilty verdict on all three counts, the district court acquitted Wilson on the charges relating to Lindsey and Malone, finding that the facts as to those two counts fell outside the purview of § 1512(b)(1). The court reasoned that neither Malone nor Lindsey were actually harassed and dissuaded from giving testimony against McDermott, since both had already testified. The court further reasoned that Malone was no longer a witness, having been excused by the court before Wilson made the statements, and thus he could not be protected by a "witness protection statute."

We cannot accept the lower court's judgment. First, the evidence was substantial enough to sustain the jury's verdict that the witnesses were harassed; each justifiably reacted adversely to Wilson's statements. Cf. 128 Cong. Rec. H8469 (daily ed. Oct. 1, 1982) (purpose of § 1512(b) is to "reach thinly-veiled threats that create justifiable apprehension" in a witness).

Second, the court erroneously assumed that § 1512(b)(1) applies only to conduct that actually dissuades testimony. The statute, and the indictment upon which Wilson was tried, both state that "attempts to" dissuade testimony are sufficient for conviction. The success of an attempt or possibility thereof is irrelevant; the statute makes the endeavor a crime.

Finally, Malone retained his witness status, despite his previous excusal by the court. Section 1512(b)'s protection of a person who has been called to testify at a trial continues throughout the duration of that trial. The *McDermott* trial was ongoing at the time Wilson made the comments. Accordingly, threats to the excused witness Malone violated § 1512(b).

---

48. This provision is now codified as § 1512(d)(1). — ED.

II

Next, we must address Wilson's contention that he should be acquitted on all three counts because he lacked the intent to harass the witnesses. We reject this argument because, viewing the evidence in the light most favorable to the government, there is substantial evidence of Wilson's intent. Wilson knew that the three witnesses were in the hallway for the purpose of testifying against McDermott. Wilson did not know that Lindsey and Malone had already testified. Wilson spoke in a low tone of voice, so that the U.S. Marshals could not hear him. He made the comments with a sneer on his face while pointing at the witnesses. The statements, "your asses belong to Joe" and "you are a bunch of jokes and should be in jail too" could reasonably be interpreted as harassing remarks. Furthermore, Wilson's intent can be inferred from the adverse reactions the witnesses suffered upon hearing the threats. . . .

Wilson also argues on appeal that the court erred in instructing the jury that "harass" is defined as

> conduct that was designed and intended to badger, disturb or pester for the unlawful purpose or purposes as alleged in the indictment counts.

Wilson requested that harass be defined as "repeated attacks." We can find no error in either the jury instructions or the lower court's refusal to adopt Wilson's request.

The term "harass," as it is used in § 1512(b), is not defined by statute. Section 1515 in 18 U.S.C. contains definitions for § 1512 terms, but harass is omitted. This implies that Congress intended that "harass" take its ordinary meaning in § 1512.

The ordinary meaning for harass includes both a single act and a series of acts. See Black's Law Dictionary 645 (5th ed. 1979); The American Heritage Dictionary 600 (5th ed. 1970). Thus, the court did not err by refusing to limit the definition of harass to "repeated attacks." In addition, defining harass as conduct that would "badger, disturb or pester," was in accordance with the common meaning of the word, and was sufficiently broad to allow the jury to find that "harass" requires more than one act. Accordingly, the instruction contained no reversible error. . . .

Affirmed in part, reversed in part, and remanded.

Notes and Questions

1. Section 1512 does not define what harassment is. What did Congress mean? Does the statute sweep too broadly? Might it be subject to attack on due process grounds?

5. Tampering with Records or Otherwise Impeding an Official Proceeding

The Sarbanes-Oxley Act amended the witness tampering statute to provide a new liability provision that fills a gap left by § 1512(b) (corruptly persuading another to destroy or alter evidence) and § 1503 (corruptly endeavoring to impede the administration of justice). The new provision, § 1512(c), makes it a crime to *corruptly*

- Alter, destroy, mutilate, or conceal a record, document, or other object, or attempt to do so;
- Act with *intent* to impair the object's integrity or availability for use in an *official proceeding*; or
- Otherwise obstruct, influence, or impede an *official proceeding* or attempt to do so.[49]

The maximum prison term for violating § 1512(c) is twice as long as the maximum term for violating § 1512(b).

Notes and Questions

1. Like several other new laws created by the Sarbanes-Oxley Act, § 1512(c) overlaps with preexisting law. The conduct prohibited by the first prong of § 1512(c) is explicitly included in § 1512(b)'s conduct elements. Does § 1512(c) differ significantly in its focus?

2. The conduct prohibited by the first prong of § 1512(c) is also implicitly included in § 1503's omnibus clause, which prohibits corruptly endeavoring to obstruct or impede the due administration of justice. Why would Congress find it advantageous (or even desirable) to include the same prohibition in § 1512(c)?

3. The second prong of § 1512(c) broadly prohibits conduct that *otherwise* obstructs, influences, or impedes an official proceeding. What kinds of conduct would fall within this broad prohibition?

4. Under both prongs of § 1512(c), the defendant must act "corruptly." What does that mean in this context? Are courts likely to import Andersen's "consciousness of wrongdoing" and "nexus" requirements into this provision?

5. What is the difference between an "official" proceeding under § 1512 and a "pending" proceeding under § 1503?

6. Section 1512(c) authorizes a maximum prison term of 20 years, while its companion provision, § 1512(b), authorizes a maximum term of 10 years. Is it clear that these penalties are proportionate to the relative severity of the offenses?

B. THREATS AND INTIMIDATION

UNITED STATES v. WILLARD
230 F.3d 1093 (9th Cir. 2000)

GRABER, Circuit Judge. . . .

FACTUAL AND PROCEDURAL BACKGROUND

In June 1999, a federal jury convicted Defendant's husband, Clifford Willard, of taking their daughter from one state to another for the purpose of sexually abusing her.

---

49. The addition of this provision, which is designated as § 1512(c), necessitated the renumbering of all of the succeeding subsections. Thus, sections that were previously designated as subsections (c)-(h) are now designated as subsections (d)-(i).

It was Mr. Willard's second criminal conviction arising from his ongoing sexual moles-
tation of his and Defendant's daughter. Their daughter testified against her father at the
second trial.

In October 1998, before Mr. Willard's trial, Defendant attempted to convince the
daughter not to testify against her father. While driving home from dinner with her
then 18-year-old daughter and the daughter's husband, Defendant told the daughter
that she did not want her to testify and that God would not like it if she testified.
Defendant also told the daughter that Defendant would have her prosecuted for perjury
if she testified against her father. The daughter reported her mother's conduct to an FBI
agent.

Defendant's efforts to discourage her daughter from testifying against Mr. Willard
resulted in her indictment in the present case for attempting to intimidate a witness.
At trial, the daughter and her husband testified that Defendant had instructed the
daughter not to testify against her father. A jury convicted Defendant of the charged
offense. . . .

SUFFICIENCY OF THE EVIDENCE

Defendant first claims that insufficient evidence supported her conviction under 18
U.S.C. § 1512. We disagree.

To establish a violation of that statute, the government must prove that the defendant "knowingly used intimidation or physical force, threatened, or corruptly persuaded
another person, or attempted to do so, or engaged in misleading conduct toward another
person, with intent to influence, delay, or prevent the testimony of any other person in
an official proceeding." 18 U.S.C. § 1512(b)(1). It is not necessary to show that the
defendant actually obstructed justice or prevented a witness from testifying. The statutory focus is on the defendant's endeavor.

The evidence in the record is sufficient to sustain Defendant's conviction. Both
Defendant's daughter and her daughter's husband testified that Defendant tried to persuade the daughter not to testify at Mr. Willard's federal trial. Moreover, their testimony
established that Defendant threatened her daughter with criminal prosecution and dire
spiritual consequences if she testified. That evidence was enough to allow a rational trier
of fact to find the essential elements of the witness-intimidation statute. We therefore
affirm Defendant's conviction. . . .

Judgment of conviction affirmed. . . .

Notes and Questions

1. In *Wilson*, a government witness was charged with *harassment* for pointing at
three other witnesses, sneering, and making what two of them thought were verbal
threats. In *Willard*, a mother was charged with *intimidation* for telling her daughter that
she should not testify against her father and that if she testified, "God would not like it"
and the daughter would be prosecuted for perjury. Is it clear why *Willard* was a case of

intimidation but *Wilson* was not? What is the distinction between "corrupt persuasion," "harassment," and "intimidation"?

UNITED STATES v. MILLER
531 F.3d 340 (6th Cir. 2008)

GRIFFIN, Circuit Judge.

Following a jury trial, defendant Shawn Joseph Miller was found guilty on two counts of committing wire fraud, two counts of money laundering, and one count of witness tampering, in violation of 18 U.S.C. § 1512(b)(3). Thereafter, the district court sentenced Miller to an above-Guidelines term of 125 months of imprisonment. . . .

I.

Miller operated two Ohio corporations, McClure, Becker & Associates, Inc. and McClure, Becker & Ramono Financial, Inc. (collectively "McClure Becker"), that purported to be engaged in the business of purchasing and selling credit card debt portfolios to brokers and collection agencies. In conducting this business, McClure Becker maintained a checking account with First Merit Bank in Sheffield, Ohio. Miller was a signatory on the account.

Between September 2002 and December 2003, Miller used McClure Becker to defraud others by selling non-existent and fraudulent debt portfolios. . . .

After receiving wire transfer payments in exchange for the sale of the fraudulent portfolios, Miller converted the funds into cash and cashier's checks through the First Merit account. Miller then mostly used these funds for personal use, including gambling vacations to Las Vegas and Windsor, Ontario. However, when confronted with the fraudulent nature of his portfolios by clients, Miller occasionally used the proceeds in a manner consistent with a "ponzi scheme," applying funds received from subsequent brokers to pay off previous clients.

The FBI began investigating Miller in April 2004. Miller apparently learned of the investigation and, in July 2005, met with Sherry Lynn Rains, an employee of First Merit Bank who opened McClure Becker's account with the bank. Miller warned Rains that if she talked to anyone about the investigation, "including the FBI," he would sue her for defamation of character. Miller also stated to Rains that the FBI was not looking into his business. Rains informed Miller that she had spoken with the FBI in December 2003 and that she had no other information to provide investigators. . . .

IV.

. . . Miller challenges the sufficiency of the evidence offered against him at trial to support his conviction for witness tampering. He argues that the threat of exercising his right to sue for defamation is not a threat for purposes of criminal liability under 18 U.S.C. § 1512(b)(3). We disagree. . . .

Miller argues that his statement to witness Sherry Lynn Rains that he would sue her for defamation if she spoke with the FBI regarding its investigation of defendant cannot be considered a "threat" within the meaning of § 1512 because he has the legal right to initiate legal proceedings. His argument, however, is seriously flawed because it rests upon an inaccurate assumption. Although Miller claims that he has the right to file a defamation claim against Rains, "there is no constitutional right to file frivolous litigation." Wolfe v. George, 486 F.3d 1120, 1125 (9th Cir. 2007). The problem with his argument is that Miller threatened to sue Rains for defamation solely on the basis of her cooperation with the FBI, regardless of the veracity of Rains's statements to investigators. Miller has no right to institute baseless legal proceedings for the purpose of harassment, and cannot hide behind the First Amendment to shield him from prosecution under § 1512.

Although we have not had many opportunities to discuss § 1512, we find United States v. Bryant, 966 F.2d 1454 (Table) (6th Cir. June 12, 1992), instructive. In *Bryant,* the defendant William Ackison, the Ironton (OH) chief of police, was convicted on two counts of tampering with a witness, in violation of § 1512(b)(1) and § 1512(c)(2). The underlying incidents occurred during an FBI investigation into the conduct of a fellow Ironton police officer, in the course of which the FBI informed Ackison that it would be interviewing all of the Ironton officers. Ackison responded by sending a memorandum to the entire police department, which informed officers of the investigation and stated that "[n]o personnel of this department has to talk to [the FBI investigator] if they do not wish to." Several members of the police department testified that they interpreted the memorandum to mean that Ackison did not want Ironton officers to speak to the FBI, and two officers testified that Ackison either stated explicitly, or implied suggestively, that they would be fired if they cooperated with the FBI investigation. On review of the sufficiency of the evidence, this court held that "there was abundant evidence to support all of the convictions of both defendants," including Ackison.

Like Ackison, Miller ordered Rains not to cooperate with an ongoing investigation and stated that negative pecuniary effects would occur if she disobeyed his direction. On cross-examination, Rains testified that she considered Miller's order to be a threat, explaining that Miller "threatened to take me to court and sue me for defamation of character. If that's a threat, then yes, that's a threat."

We hold that, viewing the evidence in the light most favorable to the government, the jury could have reasonably accepted Rains's testimony that Miller's statement was a threat and could have reasonably inferred that it was made for the purpose of preventing communication to the FBI in connection with its investigation of Miller. Miller's conviction is affirmed. . . .

Notes and Questions

1. Is the conduct in *Miller* an example of witness tampering by the use of threats or intimidation? Or is this a case of harassment, or even, perhaps, corrupt persuasion? How much does (or should) it matter?

NOTE ON RETALIATION AGAINST WITNESSES AND INFORMANTS

The Victim and Witness Protection Act prohibits the use of violence or threats of violence to retaliate against a witness for participating in an official proceeding or providing information about a federal crime to a law enforcement officer. The Sarbanes-Oxley Act expanded the scope of the statute to protect parties who provide information about a federal crime to law enforcement officers from *nonviolent* forms of retaliation.

The new provision, § 1513(e), prohibits knowingly, with *intent to retaliate*, taking any action that is harmful to *any person* — including *interference* with the lawful employment or livelihood of *any person* — for providing truthful information about the commission or possible commission of a federal crime to a law enforcement officer. The term "law enforcement officer" includes federal officers and employees who are legally authorized to investigate or prosecute an offense.[50]

Notes and Questions

What kinds of harmful acts does § 1513(e) reach? As you consider the following questions, try to catalog the full range of conduct this provision prohibits.

1. Section 1513(e) specifically prohibits interference with another person's lawful employment or livelihood. What kinds of conduct are included in this prohibition?

2. Does § 1513(e) reach infliction of economic harm that is not related to one's employment or livelihood?

3. Does § 1513(e) contemplate infliction of noneconomic harm? If so, what kinds of harm would be included?

4. Does § 1513(e) require that the retaliatory action be directed against the person who provided information to law enforcement authorities? Or may the retaliatory acts be directed against a third person? What policy considerations are in play?

V. THE FIFTH AMENDMENT PRIVILEGE

A. THE ACT OF PRODUCTION DOCTRINE

The defendant in *Griffin* was convicted of obstruction of justice by lying under oath. While he was under investigation for possible loan sharking and money laundering activities, Griffin falsely denied knowledge of the plane crash, the debts, and specific individuals that he and Ebeling discussed in conversations recorded by the FBI, and he falsely claimed he could not recall other important facts as well. His motivation for lying was undoubtedly to avoid implicating himself in criminal conduct. But instead of digging himself out of a hole, this series of lies only compounded his legal problems.

In situations like this, a witness can lawfully avoid giving damaging testimony against himself by invoking the Fifth Amendment privilege against self-incrimination

---

50. 18 U.S.C. § 1515(a)(4).

and refusing to answer questions that call for incriminating responses. If the government considers the testimony crucial, it can obtain a grant of immunity — as in *Cintolo* — that requires the witness to testify but forbids the government from using the compelled testimony or any evidence derived from it against the witness in a criminal prosecution.[51] The same would be true if the witness is subpoenaed to produce self-incriminating documents. As long as his Fifth Amendment claim is well founded, he may decline to produce the records on Fifth Amendment grounds.

While the Fifth Amendment route to avoiding self-incrimination seems relatively straightforward, in the corporate world it is fraught with tortuous twists and turns. It is well settled that corporations have no Fifth Amendment privilege against self-incrimination.[52] Thus, a corporation cannot refuse to comply with a subpoena on Fifth Amendment grounds. But what about a custodian of corporate records who would (or arguably would) incriminate himself by producing the subpoenaed records? Can the custodian resist the subpoena on the ground that he would be personally incriminated by the records? At one point the answer seemed clear. In Wilson v. United States, the Supreme Court held that the custodian could not assert a Fifth Amendment privilege under those circumstances.[53] If his testimony would be self-incriminating, however, he could not be compelled to testify regarding the whereabouts of missing records he failed to produce. Thus, for example, although the custodian would be required to produce incriminating corporate books and records, he could not be compelled to testify that 15 boxes of subpoenaed documents remained hidden in his garage.

But could the custodian be compelled to give testimony identifying the records he did produce? In Curcio v. United States, the Court observed that "[t]he custodian's act of producing books or records in response to a subpoena duces tecum is itself a representation that the documents produced are those demanded by the subpoena."[54] Thus, to require the custodian to identify the records would merely make explicit that which was "implicit in the production itself."[55]

It is through this "act of production" doctrine that ambiguity crept into the law. First, what are the testimonial aspects of producing subpoenaed documents? And second, to what extent is the act of production equivalent to compelled self-incrimination?

The Court considered the testimonial aspects of record production in Fisher v. United States.[56] In *Fisher*, the Court observed that "[t]he act of producing evidence in response to a subpoena . . . has communicative aspects of its own, wholly aside from the contents of the papers produced. Compliance with the subpoena tacitly concedes the existence of the papers demanded and their possession and control by the [custodian]."[57]

Neither *Curcio* nor *Fisher* found the act of production to be self-incriminating. In United States v. Doe, however, the Court held that a sole proprietor could refuse to produce the proprietorship's records on Fifth Amendment grounds because the act of

---

51. 18 U.S.C. § 6002. See supra Chapter 7.
52. Hale v. Henkel, 201 U.S. 43 (1906).
53. 221 U.S. 361 (1911).
54. 354 U.S. 118, 125 (1957).
55. Id.
56. 425 U.S. 391 (1976).
57. Id. at 410.

complying with the subpoena — that is, producing the records — establishes their authenticity and the proprietor's possession of them.[58]

Doe was the first case in which the Court held that the communicative aspects of producing subpoenaed business records were sufficiently incriminating to justify non-compliance with a subpoena on Fifth Amendment grounds. Not surprisingly, the Court's reliance on the testimonial character of the act of production led the lower courts on a merry chase to determine whether corporate officers might similarly resist subpoenas to produce corporate records on Fifth Amendment grounds.

Until the last week of the Supreme Court's October 1987 term, case law on this point was, in a word, in shambles. The Second and Third Circuits had applied *Doe*'s holding to corporate agents, for example, but required the corporation to appoint another agent to produce the subpoenaed records.[59] The Fourth, Fifth, Sixth, Eighth, and Eleventh Circuits, in contrast, had viewed *Doe*'s holding as applicable only to sole proprietorships and nothing beyond. Thus, those courts denied corporate officers any personal Fifth Amendment right to resist a subpoena to produce the entity's records.[60] Suffice it to say that the underlying theories in these cases varied considerably from jurisdiction to jurisdiction.

It was at this point that the Supreme Court stepped in to resolve the conflict among the circuits. In Braswell v. United States,[61] the president of a corporation was subpoenaed to produce corporate books and records. Braswell moved to quash the subpoena on the ground that the act of producing the records would violate his Fifth Amendment privilege against self-incrimination. So far, the case sounds like *Wilson* — where we began — in which the Court held that corporate custodians may not assert a Fifth Amendment privilege to refuse to produce corporate documents. But *Braswell* added a new twist. Mr. Braswell had operated his business for 15 years as a sole proprietorship. When he decided to incorporate, he complied with the state corporation law by naming three directors — himself, his wife, and his mother. His wife and mother served, respectively, as corporate secretary-treasurer and vice president, although neither had any operative authority over corporate affairs. Thus, although Braswell was doing business in the corporate form, his small corporate operation looked very much like a sole proprietorship.

The Court held that because Braswell had been summoned in his capacity as corporate custodian, he could not resist the subpoena on Fifth Amendment grounds. To recognize a personal privilege in this context, the Court posited, "would have a detrimental impact on the Government's efforts to prosecute 'white-collar crime,' one of the most serious problems confronting law enforcement authorities."[62] That would be true, in the Court's view, because the most telling evidence of wrongdoing within an organization is likely to be found in the company's official books and records, which would be shielded from outside scrutiny if courts were to recognize the custodian's claim of

---

58. 465 U.S. 605 (1984). The Eleventh Circuit refused to extend the rule in *Doe* to a sole *shareholder*, as opposed to a sole proprietor. See In re Grand Jury, 816 F.2d 569 (11th Cir. 1987).

59. See, e.g., In re Two Grand Jury Subpoenae Duces Tecum, 769 F.2d 52 (2d Cir. 1985); In re Grand Jury Matter (Brown), 768 F.2d 525 (3d Cir. 1985) (en banc).

60. See, e.g., In re Grand Jury Subpoena (85-W-71-5), 784 F.2d 857 (8th Cir. 1986); In re Grand Jury Subpoena Duces Tecum, 795 F.2d 904 (11th Cir. 1986); United States v. Lang, 792 F.2d 1235 (4th Cir. 1986); In re Grand Jury Proceedings, 771 F.2d 143 (6th Cir. 1986).

61. 487 U.S. 99 (1988).

62. Id. at 115.

a personal privilege. Thus, to let a corporate custodian resist a subpoena on Fifth Amendment grounds would impede enforcement efforts against both the individual custodian and the corporation whose documents he keeps.

But what about the obvious alternatives embraced by some circuit courts of appeal? Why not, for example, permit the subpoenaed custodian to assert a Fifth Amendment privilege and let the court direct the corporation to appoint another agent to comply with the subpoena? Because, the Court said, the custodian is best able to comply with the subpoena and may be the only person with knowledge of the records in question.[63]

The other obvious solution would be to grant the custodian immunity for any testimonial aspects of his producing the subpoenaed records. But that solution was no more satisfactory to the Court. For even though the immunized acts could be used against the corporation, a grant of immunity could seriously impede the government's effort to prosecute the custodian.

But then, in a "peculiar attempt to mitigate the force of its . . . holding,"[64] the Court stated that when the custodian produces subpoenaed records, he acts in a purely representative capacity. It therefore follows, the majority thought, that the government may not use the *individual's* act of production in a prosecution against him, but could use the *corporation's* act of production against the individual. This means that the government cannot tell the jury who produced the records, but it can provide evidence that the subpoena was served on a corporate custodian and that records were received in response to the subpoena. The jury would then be permitted to infer that the records were authentic and were those to which the subpoena referred. In some instances, the jury would also be permitted to infer the identity of the custodian. But the government cannot introduce evidence that directly reveals who the custodian was. The Court did not disclose the source of this protection, but the dissent posits that if it derives from the Fifth Amendment, then "the necessary support for the majority's case has collapsed."[65]

Notes and Questions

1. Did the majority in *Braswell* reach a logical compromise? What if the Court had held that the Fifth Amendment requires the appointment of another agent to produce and authenticate the subpoenaed documents? Would an agent who was unfamiliar with the documents be able to fully comply?

2. Can a corporate custodian who does not have possession of subpoenaed corporate records be required to testify as to their whereabouts? If the custodian testifies that she does not have the records, has she waived the Fifth Amendment privilege?[66]

---

63. Since Braswell was the only active officer in the business, this is undoubtedly true in his case. But is that not also true with respect to true sole proprietorships?

64. 487 U.S. at 128 (Kennedy, J., dissenting).

65. Id.

66. Cf. In re Grand Jury Subpoena Dated April 9, 1996, 87 F.3d 1198 (11th Cir. 1996).

B. THE ENRON INVESTIGATION

CASE STUDY: SEC v. LAY

The Enron investigation is emblematic of the utility of adopting a building block approach to developing criminal cases, beginning with mid-level managers and working the way up to the top. The massive fraud at Enron was extraordinarily complex and required sifting through thousands of pages of documents. But in addition to the need to enlist the cooperation of knowledgeable insiders to assist in this essential task, the government first has to obtain access to the documents. The SEC's investigation of Enron CEO Ken Lay illustrates how tortuous the route can sometimes be.

It all began on January 2, 2002, when the SEC issued a subpoena to Lay ordering him to produce Enron documents on January 9 and to testify before the SEC on January 23. But that was just the opening scene in a two-year legal struggle over Lay's refusal to comply with the subpoena. Despite his protestations to the contrary, Lay was — quite simply — highly uncooperative for a variety of reasons, including a claim that the subpoenaed documents were shielded by the Fifth Amendment. After a year and a half of delays in producing the documents, the SEC formally asked the court to enforce the subpoena. The SEC's memorandum in support of its enforcement action explains the Fifth Amendment issues.

On January 2, 2002, pursuant to the Formal Order and the SEC's Rules of Practice and Investigations, the SEC served Lay with a subpoena requiring that he produce documents by January 9, 2002 and appear for testimony on January 23, 2002. Service was proper. At the time of service, Lay was the Chairman and CEO of Enron. Under Lay's employment agreement, all documents relating to Enron's business generated during his employment (during business hours or otherwise and whether on company premises or otherwise) are the "sole and exclusive property" of Enron.

The SEC subpoena requested documents concerning Enron, appointment books, calendars, and similar documents reflecting meetings and conversations concerning Enron and related entities, and documents regarding entities that Lay had an interest in and that had a relationship with Enron. The SEC asked Lay to identify any documents withheld for any reason, including assertion of a privilege, and to represent that all documents required to be produced pursuant to the subpoena had been produced. On or before January 9, 2002, the SEC gave Lay permission to produce documents on a rolling basis.

On January 16 and 22, 2002, Lay produced thousands of pages of documents in response to the subpoena. Lay produced, among other things, documents containing his handwriting relating to meetings and other activities while he was Chairman and/or CEO of Enron. The documents also include Lay's handwriting on calendars and daytimers reflecting personal matters, such as social engagements, golf outings, and family events. In the production of January 22, 2002, Lay withheld three documents on the basis of the attorney client privilege or work product doctrine. However, in these January 2002 productions, Lay did not assert the Fifth Amendment as a basis for withholding any documents.

On January 23, 2002, Lay resigned as Chairman and CEO of Enron. Upon his resignation, Lay was required to return to Enron all documents relating to Enron's business. On February 13, 2002, Lay appeared for testimony before the SEC in Washington, D.C. pursuant to the subpoena. Lay declined to answer questions, asserting his Fifth Amendment right against self-incrimination. On February 21, 2002, Lay produced additional documents in response to the subpoena. In connection with this production, and for the first time, Lay asserted the Fifth Amendment as a basis for withholding "certain responsive documents." Lay claimed he was entitled to withhold the documents under the Fifth Amendment and the act of production doctrine set forth in United States v. Hubbell, 530 U.S. 27 (2000). Lay made the same Fifth Amendment claim in subsequent letters to the SEC.

During the course of several telephone calls in January 2003, Lay's attorneys informed the SEC that the documents being withheld by Lay on Fifth Amendment grounds were comprised of approximately two files of papers, and included copies of Enron memoranda and other documents bearing Lay's handwriting and annotations, as well as copies of letters, position papers, and speeches in draft form. Lay's attorneys also stated that in determining, at least in part, whether such materials should be withheld, an assessment was made to determine whether the documents reflected Lay's "thought processes." The SEC informed Lay's attorneys that it disagreed with Lay's claim of Fifth Amendment protection. Lay continues to withhold documents responsive to the SEC's subpoena. . . .

The documents subpoenaed from Lay relate to Enron. Lay's description of documents he has withheld strongly suggests these are corporate records. According to Lay's counsel, he is withholding copies of Enron memoranda and other documents bearing Lay's handwriting and annotations, as well as copies of letters, position papers, and speeches in draft form. The documents were generated during Lay's tenure at Enron, and subpoenaed before he left Enron. These type of documents, to the extent they reflect the activities of Lay during his tenure as Chairman and CEO of Enron, are corporate records.

As the Supreme Court has repeatedly held, an individual may not invoke his personal Fifth Amendment privilege to avoid producing the documents of a collective entity that are in his custody, even if his production of those documents would prove personally incriminating. This principle of law is well settled and based on sound reasoning. Collective entities are not protected by the Fifth Amendment. These artificial entities may act only through their agents, and when such agents hold corporate records they do so in a representative rather than a personal capacity. When corporate records are subpoenaed, the custodian's act of production is not deemed a personal act, but rather the act of the corporation. To permit an individual holding corporate records to withhold them based on his Fifth Amendment privilege would be tantamount to a claim of privilege by the corporation, which it does not have. *Braswell*, 487 U.S. at 109-110. . . .

The same principles apply to corporate records in the possession of a person who is no longer employed by the corporation. Bellis v. United States, 417 U.S. at 88 and 96 n.3. . . .

. . . Indeed, Lay's employment agreement dictates that documents relating to Enron are company property and should have been returned to the company upon Lay's resignation. Lay holds corporate records of Enron in a representative capacity and cannot assert the Fifth Amendment with respect to such records.[67]

In its reply to Lay's memorandum opposing the Commission's application to enforce the subpoena, the SEC revealed its increasing frustration at Lay's apparent lack of candor and disingenuousness.

Despite Lay's concession that he has no Fifth Amendment right to withhold corporate records from the SEC and the fact that he has produced the *same* documents at issue to

---

67. Memorandum of the Securities and Exchange Commission in Support of Its Application for Orders to Show Cause, for an In Camera Review, and Requiring Obedience to Subpoena, SEC v. Lay, Misc. No. 03-1962 (D.D.C. Sept. 29, 2003).

parties in other proceedings, including production to the bankruptcy examiner apparently *after* the SEC filed this action, Lay continues to withhold corporate records from the SEC. In light of the foregoing, Lay's continued refusal to designate and produce corporate records to the SEC, unless the SEC "agrees" to his terms, is an outrage and belies his self-serving and disingenuous claim that he has been fully cooperative with the SEC. This Court should not permit Lay to continue this charade.

Lay has demonstrated a frankly whimsical approach to asserting his Fifth Amendment rights. Lay initially produced documents to the SEC without invoking the Fifth Amendment. Lay later asserted the Fifth Amendment in refusing to testify to the SEC, and selectively invoked the Fifth Amendment with respect to documents, withholding some documents and producing others. Yet Lay has already produced the same records he has withheld from the SEC to at least two parties. Further, just days ago, Lay submitted to questioning by the bankruptcy examiner, apparently without invoking his Fifth Amendment rights. Thus, when conditions suit his purposes Lay talks and provides documents, but when called to answer to law enforcement authorities, he invokes the Constitution, remaining silent and withholding documents. By what logic can Lay claim that he continues to hold a Fifth Amendment right to refuse compliance with the SEC's subpoena when he has produced the same documents to others? . . .

Given Lay's concession that he has no Fifth Amendment right to withhold corporate records, the only issue is whether Lay has any right to withhold personal records. Here, Lay's prior production of the same records to other parties, including a production to a party apparently just days ago, is fatal to his claim of privilege regarding personal records. Thus, while the SEC had expressed no desire to obtain Lay's personal records if he had a legitimate Fifth Amendment act of production privilege under *Hubbell*, the SEC is entitled to personal records given Lay's waiver of this privilege. . . .

. . . Lay has already communicated information about the existence, custody, and authenticity of any personal records called for in the subpoena by producing the same records to others. In fact, apparently after the SEC filed this action, Lay took the extraordinary step of producing the same records to the bankruptcy examiner. Lay has informed the SEC of these prior productions, so the act of production of the same records to the SEC would not disclose any new custodial information to the SEC. As to the second point, Lay's act of production to yet another party, the SEC, can hardly be considered potentially incriminating. Unlike *Hubbell*, Lay's production to the SEC would not be the first disclosure by Lay that the documents exist. Lay certainly cannot have any bona fide legal concerns attaching to his physical act of producing the subpoenaed records given the fact that he has now produced them to third parties — the plaintiffs in the class action lawsuit and the bankruptcy examiner — contemporaneous to his being, in his words, "pulverized" by Congress and the media. It is too little too late for Lay to now claim protection for the act of producing personal records. In light of Lay's prior productions, he cannot claim a Fifth Amendment act of production privilege to withhold personal records under Hubbell. . . .

. . . Curiously, Lay recently entered into a confidentiality agreement with counsel for the bankruptcy examiner and produced the same documents sought by the SEC in the instant action. This production apparently occurred while this very same subpoena enforcement action was pending with the Court. Lay refused to answer questions posed by the SEC based on the Fifth Amendment, yet days ago submitted to questioning by the bankruptcy examiner. . . .[68]

---

68. Reply of the Securities and Exchange Commission in Support of Its Application for Order Requiring Obedience to Subpeona, SEC v. Lay, Misc. No. 03-1962 (D.D.C. October 2003).

A few weeks after the SEC filed this reply, Lay entered into an agreement to comply with the Commission's subpoena and to waive any claim of privilege relating to documents that he produced as corporate records. The agreement also provided that the SEC could use all of the documents in future proceedings against him free of any assertion of privilege.

> The SEC may use all documents produced by Lay and any leads derived therefrom, directly or indirectly, for any law-enforcement purpose, including in any future action or proceeding it may bring against Lay. Lay shall not assert the Fifth Amendment as a basis to exclude the admission into evidence of all documents or the use of all documents in pre-trial proceedings or for any other law-enforcement purpose of the SEC. Further, Lay shall not assert at any time for any purpose that the SEC's use of the documents, directly or indirectly, violated any Fifth Amendment rights Lay may possess, and Lay shall not make such an assertion as a basis to dismiss any future SEC action or proceeding or any other action or proceeding against Lay.[69]

---

69. Stipulation and Order Requiring Production of Records, SEC v. Lay, Misc. No. 03-1962 (D.D.C. Nov. 7, 2003).

9

Bribery of Public Officials

I. INTRODUCTION

Our system of government is premised on the assumption that those who occupy positions of public trust will act for the common good and that issues affecting the national interest will be resolved on the merits. Thus, because society has a vested interest in the objective and unbiased judgment of its public officials, myriad forms of public corruption are treated as serious criminal matters.[1]

That citizens will try to influence official action, on the other hand, is also a given in our system of government. Public interest groups, paid lobbyists, large-scale media campaigns, and individual letters to elected representatives demonstrate this principle at work every day. The power to persuade, moreover, is not limited to reasoned argument, spirited debate, or emotional appeal. Money talks, and it would be naive to assume that campaign contributions, speaking honoraria, and other, similar payments from the business community are necessarily motivated by a spirit of detached generosity. Nor should we forget that the Constitution immunizes elected officials from external inquiry into speech or debate occurring in either house of Congress. Thus, the principle that official acts and decisions should be based on the merits may be more difficult to implement than we might first have assumed.

The materials in this chapter focus primarily on two traditional crimes — bribery and gratuity — to explore the tension between legitimate and illegitimate efforts to influence or reward public officials.[2] They also explore how statutes that punish federal program bribery and extortion under color of official right fit into the complex network of laws designed to curb official corruption.

---

1. See, e.g., 18 U.S.C. §§ 203, 204, 205, 207, 208, and 209; 26 U.S.C. § 7214.
2. Beyond the many federal statutes aimed specifically at public corruption, the mail and wire fraud statutes are ancillary enforcement tools that are widely used in public corruption prosecutions. See Chapter 4. In addition, bribery, mail fraud, and wire fraud are predicate crimes under the Racketeer Influenced and Corrupt Organizations Act (RICO), a versatile statute that has proven to be useful in the context of ongoing patterns of public corruption. See Chapter 10.

II. BRIBERY OF PUBLIC OFFICIALS

The principal federal bribery statute, 18 U.S.C. § 201, defines two distinct offenses — bribery and gratuity. Although both crimes revolve around the giving or receipt of something of value in connection with an official act, each is directed at a separate evil. Bribery is corruptly attempting to influence a public official in the performance of official acts by giving the official valuable consideration. Simply put, a bribe is a quid pro quo for an official act or decision. In contrast, gratuity consists of rewarding a public official on account of an official act, even if the payor's intent is benign. A gratuity is the payment of additional, off-the-book compensation for the performance of an official act. Because § 201 condemns the use of public office for private gain, it punishes both the giving and the receipt of bribes and gratuities.

A. OFFICIAL ACTS

The bribery statute makes it unlawful for a public official to solicit or accept anything of value "for or because of an official act performed or to be performed by him." Section 201(a) defines "official act" as

> any decision or action on any question, matter, cause, suit, proceeding or controversy, which may at any time be pending, or which may by law be brought before any public official, in his official capacity, or in his place of trust or honor.

UNITED STATES v. PARKER
133 F.3d 322 (5th Cir. 1998)

Emilio M. Garza, Circuit Judge.

Joann A. Parker ("Mrs. Parker") appeals her conviction and sentence for conspiracy to commit public bribery and five counts of public bribery in violation of 18 U.S.C. §§ 201(b)(2)(C) and 371. Ralph Parker ("Mr. Parker") appeals his conviction for conspiracy to commit public bribery and three counts of public bribery under the same statutes. We affirm.

I

The Social Security Administration ("SSA") Office of Hearings and Appeals employed Mrs. Parker as a clerk to Administrative Law Judge ("ALJ") John Aronson. She led a group that helped certain individuals to fraudulently obtain Supplemental Security Income ("SSI") benefits in return for money. The scheme began when Mrs. Parker met Niknitta Simmons ("Simmons") at a hearing where Simmons was appealing the denial of SSI benefits for her son, Kevin Simmons. ALJ Aronson advised Simmons that additional documentation would be necessary for a favorable ruling on Kevin's claim. Mrs. Parker approached Simmons after the hearing and offered to help. A few days later, Mrs. Parker gave Simmons a letter approving Kevin's benefits.

Mrs. Parker thereafter called Simmons and demanded money for her help. Simmons refused to pay, and Kevin's benefits were terminated. Mrs. Parker advised Simmons that Kevin's benefits would be reinstated if Simmons paid her.

Simmons went to several SSA offices and reported Mrs. Parker's demands. Investigators from the SSA and FBI contacted Simmons, and she agreed to assist them by permitting FBI Agent Karen Jenkins to record her telephone conversations with Mrs. Parker. In multiple recorded conversations, Mrs. Parker demanded payment for having Kevin's benefits approved initially and for having those benefits reinstated. At a meeting at Simmons' home, Mrs. and Mr. Parker took $500, as captured on videotape by the FBI. Mrs. Parker thereafter demanded more money, which Simmons paid, and Mrs. Parker gave Simmons a letter purportedly bearing ALJ Aronson's signature reinstating Kevin's benefits.

Agent Jenkins and a SSA agent interviewed Mrs. Parker about her contacts with Simmons. The agents advised Mrs. Parker of her rights and she signed a written waiver before confessing to fraudulently approving benefits for Kevin Simmons, Raymond Henry, Georgette Lemon, Yvette Scott, and Karen Johnson. Mrs. Parker stated that two other SSA employees had assisted her and implicated Mr. Parker. Mrs. Parker admitted that she had approved benefits by taking letters addressed to different persons, changing the names and dates of those letters to match those of the applicants who had paid her money, and forging the signature of ALJ Aronson.

II

A

Mrs. Parker first argues that the indictment charging her with conspiracy to commit public bribery and public bribery under 18 U.S.C. § 201(b)(2)(C) was deficient because she lacked the authority to grant or deny benefits. Mrs. Parker's duties included assisting ALJ Aronson before and during the hearings, recording and taking notes at those hearings, and typing and mailing ALJ Aronson's decisions. Mrs. Parker had access to the office's computer system, but was not authorized to approve benefits or sign ALJ Aronson's name. Thus, Mrs. Parker essentially argues that the only acts which we should examine in determining whether she violated section 201(b)(2)(C) are those within the scope of her authority, such as typing and mailing opinions.

Section 201(b)(2)(C) prohibits public officials from being induced to do or omit any act in violation of their official duty. Acts that violate an official's duty are extremely broad in scope. Section 201(a) broadly defines an "official act" as "any decision or action on any question, matter, cause, suit, proceeding or controversy, which may at any time be pending, or which may by law be brought before any public official, in such official's official capacity, or in such official's place of trust or profit." 18 U.S.C. § 201(a)(3). This broad definition of "official act" reflects Congress' intent to "include any decision or action taken by a public official in his capacity as such." S. Rep. No. 87-2213 (1962), reprinted in 1962 U.S.C.C.A.N. 3852, 3856. Official acts that violate an official's official duty are not limited to those proscribed by statutes and written rules and regulations, but may also be found in "established usage," because "duties not completely defined by written rules are established by settled practice, and action taken in the course of their performance must be regarded as within the provisions of the above-mentioned statutes against bribery." United States v. Birdsall, 233 U.S. 223, 231 (1914). Official acts that violate an official's official duty are also not limited to those within the official's specific authority. See e.g., United States v. Gjieli, 717 F.2d 968, 972 (6th Cir. 1983).

Mrs. Parker does not dispute that the individuals for whom she fraudulently approved benefits had appeals pending in her office. Because the appeals were pending in her "place of trust or profit," her actions fall within the statutory definition of "official act." See United States v. Dobson, 609 F.2d 840, 842 (5th Cir. 1980) (holding that the actions of a government employee in preparing a memorandum fell within the definition of an "official act" because the decision in question was pending in his "place of trust or profit"). Her abuse of the SSA facilities and equipment and the responsibility that ALJ Aronson gave her enabled her to alter and forge the decisions. Mrs. Parker could create fictitious letters approving benefits because she had access to the official networked computer system. She was able to "cut and paste" segments of one document onto another and make them appear real. As access to government computer systems becomes more prevalent, opportunities for this kind of nefarious behavior will become more common. We therefore hold that the term "official act" encompasses use of governmental computer systems to fraudulently create documents for the benefit of the employee or a third party for compensation, even when the employee's scope of authority does not formally encompass the act. See e.g., United States v. Carson, 464 F.2d 424, 433 (2d Cir. 1972) (interpreting the bribery statute broadly to cover a congressional aide's attempts to intercede with Executive Branch officials on behalf of bribers even though the scope of his job authority did not extend to such intercession). Mrs. Parker's actions were thus covered by section 201(b)(2)(C) and the indictment was not deficient. . . .

Affirmed.

Notes and Questions

1. Did Mrs. Parker have any authority to decide whether applicants would receive benefits? In what sense did her demands for money to approve benefits constitute an official act?

2. Mrs. Parker was a clerical worker. What made her a public official?

3. Should the bribery statute be construed to encompass conduct that is outside the public official's scope of authority?

UNITED STATES v. ARROYO
581 F.2d 649 (7th Cir. 1978)

MARKEY, Chief Judge.

[Anthony Arroyo was a Small Business Administration (SBA) loan officer who reviewed loan applications for their creditworthiness. On August 19, 1975, Arroyo received a $35,000 loan application from Orlando Fernandez. Arroyo reviewed the file and recommended that the loan be made. Although Arroyo's supervisor approved the loan on August 26, 1975, Fernandez was not informed of the approval. A few days later, Fernandez went to see Sanchez, a business counselor at the economic development corporation through which the loan was processed, and asked about the loan. Sanchez told him that there would be no money until SBA authorization was received and that Arroyo was the only person who could help him.

Over the next seven months, through a series of contacts with Sanchez and Arroyo, Fernandez was told that the loan would cost him $800. Although SBA records reflected disbursements of $20,000 in January and $10,000 in February pursuant to the loan application, Arroyo told Fernandez in March that to obtain a loan, he would have to pay Arroyo $800.

Arroyo and Sanchez were convicted of conspiracy to solicit a bribe, and Arroyo was convicted of soliciting and receiving a bribe, in violation of § 201.]

THE DISTRICT COURT'S JURY INSTRUCTION

The material portions of the jury charge are:

[T]he term "official act" means any decision or act or any question, matter, cause, suit, proceeding or controversy which may at any time be pending or which may, by law, be brought before any public official in his official capacity or in his place of trust or profit. . . . In order for the crime of bribery to be committed, it is not necessary that the public official actually have the power to perform the act that he promises in return for the money. What is necessary is that the public official solicit or receive the money on the representation that the money is for the purpose of influencing his performance of some official act. . . .

[The] government must prove beyond a reasonable doubt each of the following elements: One, that the defendant Anthony Arroyo was during the time charged in the indictment a public official as defined in the law; namely, a loan officer of the United States Small Business Administration.

Two, that the defendant Anthony Arroyo did corruptly ask, demand, exact, solicit, seek, accept, receive and agree to receive money from Orlando Fernandez. And that three, that the defendant Anthony Arroyo represented or caused to be represented to Orlando Fernandez that this money was in return for Anthony Arroyo's being influenced in his performance of an official act, as that term has previously been defined.

THE DEFENDANTS' REQUESTED JURY INSTRUCTION

The district court refused this requested instruction, which paraphrases the language of the court in Woelfel v. United States, 237 F.2d 484, 488 (4th Cir. 1956):

If you believe that the defendants' requests for or solicitations of the gratuity were not made until after the employee had exhausted his power of decision or action in connection with the loan and were not made under any prior promise or understanding that a gratuity would be forthcoming, then the defendants' actions did not constitute a transgression and you must find them not guilty.

APPELLANTS' CONTENTIONS

Arroyo and Sanchez contend that it is not a violation of 18 U.S.C. § 201(c)(1) . . . to solicit or accept money when the solicitation activity commenced after the public official had completely performed his official action. . . .

Further, Arroyo and Sanchez assert that Arroyo may have solicited a gratuity, . . . but not a bribe. . . .

OPINION . . .

Arroyo's and Sanchez' contentions, if accepted, would encourage the very conduct Congress condemned. Under the proffered interpretation, a public official could hurriedly and surreptitiously perform his official act, and then corruptly solicit and encourage the bribe, by creating the impression in the potential briber's mind that his official act had not yet been taken.

That is what Arroyo did here. Dealing with a loan program for the economically disadvantaged, Arroyo approved Fernandez' credit worthiness without ever talking with him about the loan and within a few days of receiving the loan application. The loan was authorized on August 26, 1975. Yet on August 28, 1975, when Fernandez asked about the delay of the loan, Arroyo expressly and falsely represented that "he had it," creating the false impression that the application was still pending before him. Fernandez, an unsophisticated immigrant to our shores, and seeking to enter the economic mainstream as a small business entrepreneur, could have gained no other impression. Indeed, the most sophisticated native-born could have gained no other. Then, when Fernandez asked if it would "cost" him, Arroyo did not say, "No, of course not. You are dealing with the United States Government and we don't do things that way," or words to that effect. Arroyo said, "See Sanchez." The return-for-being-influenced element of the offense was correctly stated by the district court in its jury charge: "that the defendant Anthony Arroyo represented or caused to be represented to Orlando Fernandez that this money was in return for Anthony Arroyo's being influenced in his performance of an official act, as that term has previously been defined."

The operative language of § 201(c)(1) is "[whoever], being a public official . . . corruptly . . . solicits . . . anything of value for himself . . . in return for . . . being influenced in his performance of any official act."[3] "Official act" is defined in § 201(a) as "any . . . action . . . which may *at any time* be pending . . . before any public official, in his official capacity. . . ." (Emphasis added.) Congress having used broad language in these provisions, we find no intent to limit their coverage to future acts. Congress did not intend for a public official, who had solicited and encouraged a bribe with a false representation that the official act was in futuro, to escape liability for bribe-solicitation by proving that he had successfully hidden the truth of past performance from the bribe-payer.

Arroyo and Sanchez seize upon the words "being influenced" as indicating that § 201(c)(1) requires that the bribe be paid to influence a future act, arguing that one cannot be influenced to do what has already been done. The argument is without merit in this case, for it disregards the lead-in phrase "in return for." That phrase brings into play the purpose of the bribe and thus the mind of the bribe-payer. Though more careful draftsmanship might have added "or apparently being" after "being," the section prohibits solicitation of payment "in return for being influenced." As illustrated

---

3. This provision is now codified as § 201(b)(2)(A). — ED.

by § 201(c), the gravamen of the offense lies in the corrupt solicitation, which would fail if the solicitee were told the truth. Bribes are paid, and solicited, in exchange for what the payer believes he is paying for. The bribe solicitor will always create the impression that the action sought is yet to come and is contingent on the bribe. The solicitation, against which the section is directed, is the same, whether the yet-to-come impression be objectively true or false. Further, § 201(c)(1), in listing one of the "in return for" elements, speaks of "*being* influenced in his performance of any official act" (emphasis added). It does not speak of "being influenced *to* perform any official act."

The broad language of the statute, and the purpose it was designed to accomplish, preclude the narrow construction sought by Arroyo and Sanchez. . . .

Affirmed.

Notes and Questions

1. The crime of bribery is committed when a public official seeks or receives something of value in return for "being influenced in the performance of any official act." In *Arroyo*, the loan had been recommended and approved before the official solicited the $800 payment. Did the payment come too late to influence Arroyo's decision to recommend the loan? If so, how can his solicitation be considered bribery?

2. Would it make a difference if Arroyo had solicited the bribe before he recommended the loan to his supervisor but had fully intended to recommend approval of the loan in any event?[4]

3. Did Fernandez violate § 201 by paying Arroyo the $800? If so, should it be a defense that he was economically coerced?

4. The crime of gratuity is committed when a public official seeks or receives something of value "for or because of" an official act. Does the conduct in *Arroyo* fit more neatly under this language?

B. MOTIVE AND INTENT

UNITED STATES v. SUN-DIAMOND GROWERS OF CALIFORNIA
526 U.S. 398 (1999)

Justice SCALIA delivered the opinion of the Court. . . .

I

Respondent is a trade association that engaged in marketing and lobbying activities on behalf of its member cooperatives, which were owned by approximately 5,000 individual growers of raisins, figs, walnuts, prunes, and hazelnuts. Petitioner United States is represented by Independent Counsel Donald Smaltz, who, as a consequence of

---

4. Cf. United States v. Alfisi, 308 F.3d 144 (2d Cir. 2002).

his investigation of former Secretary of Agriculture Michael Espy, charged respondent with, inter alia, making illegal gifts to Espy in violation of § 201(c)(1)(A). . . .

Count One of the indictment charged Sun-Diamond with giving Espy approximately $5,900 in illegal gratuities: tickets to the 1993 U.S. Open Tennis Tournament (worth $2,295), luggage ($2,427), meals ($665), and a framed print and crystal bowl ($524). The indictment alluded to two matters in which respondent had an interest in favorable treatment from the Secretary at the time it bestowed the gratuities. [First, member cooperatives that received grants to defray foreign marketing expenses stood to lose from proposed changes in the grant program, which was administered by the Department of Agriculture. Second, Sun-Diamond sought the Department's assistance in trying to persuade the EPA either not to phase out a low-cost pesticide many growers used or at least to mitigate the impact of the proposed change.]

Although describing these two matters before the Secretary in which respondent had an interest, the indictment did not allege a specific connection between either of them — or between any other action of the Secretary — and the gratuities conferred.

[Sun-Diamond moved to dismiss Count One of the indictment because it failed to allege a nexus between the gratuities and an official act. The district court denied the motion, finding that if Sun-Diamond provided the gratuities to Espy because of his official position, that would violate the statute. Sun-Diamond was convicted on Count One.]

The Court of Appeals reversed the conviction on Count One and remanded for a new trial, stating:

> Given that the "for or because of any official act" language in § 201(c)(1)(A) means what it says, the jury instructions invited the jury to convict on materially less evidence than the statute demands — evidence of gifts driven simply by Espy's official position. 138 F.3d 961, 968 (D.C. Cir. 1998).

In rejecting respondent's attack on the indictment, however, the court stated that the Government need not show that a gratuity was given "for or because of" any particular act or acts: "That an official has an abundance of relevant matters on his plate should not insulate him or his benefactors from the gratuity statute — as long as the jury is required to find the requisite intent to reward past favorable acts or to make future ones more likely." Id. at 969. . . .

II

Initially, it will be helpful to place § 201(c)(1)(A) within the context of the statutory scheme. Subsection (a) of § 201 sets forth definitions applicable to the section — including a definition of "official act," § 201(a)(3). Subsections (b) and (c) then set forth, respectively, two separate crimes — or two pairs of crimes, if one counts the giving and receiving of unlawful gifts as separate crimes — with two different sets of elements and authorized punishments. The first crime, described in § 201(b)(1) as to the giver, and § 201(b)(2) as to the recipient, is bribery, which requires a showing that something of value was corruptly given, offered, or promised to a public official (as to the giver) or corruptly demanded, sought, received, accepted, or agreed to be received or accepted by a public official (as to the recipient) with intent, inter alia, "to influence any official act" (giver) or in return for "being influenced in the performance of any official act" (recipient). The second crime, defined in § 201(c)(1)(A) as to the giver, and § 201(c)(1)(B) as to the recipient, is illegal gratuity, which requires a showing that something of value was given, offered, or promised to a public official (as to the giver), or demanded, sought, received, accepted, or agreed to be received or accepted by a public official (as to the recipient), "for or because of any official act performed or to be performed by such public official."

The distinguishing feature of each crime is its intent element. Bribery requires intent "to influence" an official act or "to be influenced" in an official act, while illegal gratuity requires only that the gratuity be given or accepted "for or because of" an official act. In other words, for bribery there must be a *quid pro quo* — a specific intent to give or receive something of value in exchange for an official act. An illegal gratuity, on the other hand, may constitute merely a reward for some future act that the public official will take (and may already have determined to take), or for a past act that he has already taken. The punishments prescribed for the two offenses reflect their relative seriousness: Bribery may be punished by up to 15 years' imprisonment, a fine of $250,000 ($500,000 for organizations) or triple the value of the bribe, whichever is greater, and disqualification from holding government office. See 18 U.S.C. §§ 201(b) and 3571. Violation of the illegal gratuity statute, on the other hand, may be punished by up to two years' imprisonment and a fine of $250,000 ($500,000 for organizations). See §§ 201(c) and 3571.

The District Court's instructions in this case, in differentiating between a bribe and an illegal gratuity, correctly noted that only a bribe requires proof of a quid pro quo. The point in controversy here is that the instructions went on to suggest that § 201(c)(1)(A), unlike the bribery statute, did not require any connection between respondent's intent and a specific official act. It would be satisfied, according to the instructions, merely by a showing that respondent gave Secretary Espy a gratuity because of his official position — perhaps, for example, to build a reservoir of goodwill that might ultimately affect one or more of a multitude of unspecified acts, now and in the future. The United States, represented by the Independent Counsel, and the Solicitor General as amicus curiae, contend that this instruction was correct. The Independent Counsel asserts that "section 201(c)(1)(A) reaches any effort to buy favor or generalized goodwill from an official who either has been, is, or may at some unknown, unspecified later time, be *in a position to act* favorably to the giver's interests." The Solicitor General contends that § 201(c)(1)(A) requires only a showing that a "gift was motivated, at least in part, by the recipient's *capacity to exercise governmental power or influence* in the donor's favor" without necessarily showing that it was connected to a particular official act.

In our view, this interpretation does not fit comfortably with the statutory text, which prohibits only gratuities given or received "for or because of *any official act performed or to be performed*.". . .

Besides thinking that this is the more natural meaning of § 201(c)(1)(A), we are inclined to believe it correct because of the peculiar results that the Government's alternative reading would produce. It would criminalize, for example, token gifts to the President based on his official position and not linked to any identifiable act — such as the replica jerseys given by championship sports teams each year during ceremonial White House visits. Similarly, it would criminalize a high school principal's gift of a school baseball cap to the Secretary of Education, by reason of his office, on the occasion of the latter's visit to the school. That these examples are not fanciful is demonstrated by the fact that counsel for the United States maintained at oral argument that a group of farmers would violate § 201(c)(1)(A) by providing a complimentary lunch for the Secretary of Agriculture in conjunction with his speech to the farmers concerning various matters of USDA policy — so long as the Secretary had before him, or had in prospect, matters affecting the farmers. Of course the Secretary of Agriculture *always* has before him or in prospect matters that affect farmers, just as the President always has before him or in prospect matters that affect college and professional sports, and the Secretary of Education matters that affect high schools.

It might be said in reply to this that the more narrow interpretation of the statute can also produce some peculiar results. In fact, in the above-given examples, the gifts could easily be regarded as having been conferred, not only because of the official's position as President or Secretary, but also (and perhaps principally) "for or because of" the official acts of receiving the sports teams at the White House, visiting the high school, and speaking to the farmers about USDA policy, respectively. The answer to this objection is that those actions — while they are assuredly "official acts" in some sense — are not "official acts" within the meaning of the statute, which, as we have noted, defines "official act" to mean "any decision or action on any question, matter, cause, suit, proceeding or controversy, which may at any time be pending, or which may by law be brought before any public official, in such official's official capacity, or in such official's place of trust or profit." 18 U.S.C. § 201(a)(3). Thus, when the violation is linked to a particular "official act," it is possible to eliminate the absurdities *through the definition of that term.* When, however, no particular "official act" need be identified, and the giving of gifts by reason of the recipient's mere tenure in office constitutes a violation, nothing but the Government's discretion prevents the foregoing examples from being prosecuted. . . .

Our refusal to read § 201(c)(1)(A) as a prohibition of gifts given by reason of the donee's office is supported by the fact that when Congress has wanted to adopt such a broadly prophylactic criminal prohibition upon gift giving, it has done so in a more precise and more administrable fashion. For example, another provision of Chapter 11 of Title 18, the chapter entitled "Bribery, Graft, and Conflicts of Interest," criminalizes the giving or receiving of any "supplementation" of an Executive official's salary, without regard to the purpose of the payment. See 18 U.S.C. § 209(a). Other provisions of the same chapter make it a crime for a bank employee to give a bank examiner, and for a bank examiner to receive from a bank employee, "any loan or gratuity," again without regard to the purpose for which it is given. See §§ 212-213. A provision of the Labor Management Relations Act makes it a felony for an employer to give to a union representative, and for a union representative to receive from an employer, anything of value. 29 U.S.C. § 186. With clearly framed and easily administrable provisions such as these on the books imposing gift-giving and gift-receiving prohibitions specifically based upon the holding of office, it seems to us most implausible that Congress intended the language of the gratuity statute — "for or because of any official act performed or to be performed" — to pertain to the office rather than (as the language more naturally suggests) to *particular* official acts.

Finally, a narrow, rather than a sweeping, prohibition is more compatible with the fact that § 201(c)(1)(A) is merely one strand of an intricate web of regulations, both administrative and criminal, governing the acceptance of gifts and other self-enriching actions by public officials.

[The Court described various other criminal and civil statutes and administrative regulations that restrict the giving and receipt of salary supplements or other things of value to past or present government officials.]

More important for present purposes, however, this regulation, and the numerous other regulations and statutes littering this field, demonstrate that this is an area where precisely targeted prohibitions are commonplace, and where more general prohibitions have been qualified by numerous exceptions. Given that reality, a statute in this field that can linguistically be interpreted to be either a meat axe or a scalpel should reasonably be taken to be the latter. Absent a text that clearly requires it, we ought not expand this one piece of the regulatory puzzle so dramatically as to make many other pieces misfits. As discussed earlier, not only does the text here not require that result; its more natural reading forbids it.

III . . .

We hold that, in order to establish a violation of 18 U.S.C. § 201(c)(1)(A), the Government must prove a link between a thing of value conferred upon a public official and a specific "official act" for or because of which it was given. We affirm the judgment of the Court of Appeals, which remanded the case to the District Court for a new trial on Count One. Our decision today casts doubt upon the lower courts' resolution of respondent's challenge to the sufficiency of the indictment on Count One — an issue on which certiorari was neither sought nor granted. We leave it to the District Court to determine whether that issue should be reopened on remand.

It is so ordered.

Notes and Questions

1. After *Sun-Diamond Growers*, do both the bribery and gratuity provisions effectively require the government to allege and prove specific intent? What is the difference, if any, between giving a thing of value to an official with intent to influence an official act and giving the same official a thing of value for or because of a "particular official act"?

2. After *Sun-Diamond Growers*, how would the government go about proving whether the lobbyist gave gifts to Secretary Espy to influence his official acts (bribery) or gave them for or because of a particular official act (gratuity)? What kinds of evidence would the government need to develop?

3. Since no specific quid pro quo is required to commit the crime of gratuity, what is the harm? What makes the payment of gratuities corrupt?

4. What about payments made to a public official that are motivated by "a desire to create a better working atmosphere" or by a desire to express "appreciation for [the official's] speedy and favorable [action]"?[5] Are they within the scope of § 201 after *Sun-Diamond Growers*? If a taxpayer takes an IRS auditor to lunch to thank her for a favorable audit, should this be deemed a crime? Does it matter whether the meal was lavish or simple? Whether the taxpayer's gesture was spontaneous or carefully planned?

UNITED STATES v. ANDERSON
509 F.2d 312 (D.C. Cir. 1974)

SPOTTSWOOD W. ROBINSON, III, Circuit Judge. . . .

I. THE FACTUAL BACKGROUND

Anderson was a registered congressional lobbyist for Spiegel, Inc.,[6] a Chicago-based merchandiser. Since Spiegel conducted its sales primarily through the mails, its financial well-being was directly related to the level of third-class mail rates. Daniel B. Brewster was a United States Senator, and a member of the Senate Committee on Post Office and Civil Service. It was the alleged bribery of Brewster by Anderson, as the alter ego of Spiegel, that gave birth to this litigation.

The theory of the prosecution was that Anderson on several occasions delivered monies to Brewster with corrupt intent to influence his action on postal-rate legislation coming before him in his official capacity. An indictment so charged, and the jury, at Anderson's trial jointly with Spiegel and Brewster, found Anderson guilty as charged.

The Government's case against Anderson, and by the same token the jury's verdict, rested notably upon the testimony of John Francis Sullivan, formerly an aide to Brewster, and Betsey Shipley Norton, a close friend of Anderson. . . .

In January, 1967, . . . Anderson conferred with Brewster and Sullivan in their Senate offices. Anderson revealed his connection with Spiegel and voiced Spiegel's opposition to higher postal rates. As the meeting drew to a close, Anderson gave Brewster an envelope containing $5,000 in cash, and Brewster told Anderson that he "would do all he possibly could to be of assistance to Spiegel. . . ." The $5,000 was placed in a safe in Sullivan's office, and was subsequently used for cash expenditures.

On April 5, 1967, a bill seeking postal-rate raises was introduced in Congress. Shortly thereafter, Anderson obtained from Spiegel a check for $13,500 payable to

---

5. United States v. Barash, 412 F.2d 26, 29 (2d Cir. 1969).

6. Hereinafter we refer to Spiegel, Inc., as "Spiegel." Two individuals having the surname "Spiegel" are later mentioned. We co[n]join their first names to distinguish them.

DCCME[7] and, with help from Betsey Norton, converted it into cash. Later that month Anderson, accompanied by a man introduced as Morris Spiegel, again called on Brewster and Sullivan. There was discussion of the pending bill, during which Morris Spiegel handed an envelope to Brewster. Inside the envelope was $4,500 in cash, which also found its way into the DCCME bank account.

A third payment was made in July, 1967. . . .

IV. THE TRIAL EVENTS . . .

B. THE REQUESTED INSTRUCTIONS

At trial, Anderson's counsel requested, and the judge refused, two instructions which assertedly were essential to the jury's understanding of the theory of his defense. One would have told the jury that

> [i]t is not corrupt in itself to influence or to attempt to influence a Senator or other legislator, nor is it corrupt in itself for a Senator to be influenced in respect to his actions, vote or decision on legislation. It is a part of the duty of every Senator to pay heed to and consider the views of all responsible parties on any matter of legislation before him.

The other request would have said that

> [a] lobbyist is a person who is paid for the purpose of attempting to influence the passage or defeat of legislation by the Congress of the United States. This is neither illegal nor improper. The only legal restriction on a lobbyist is that he or she must be properly registered with the Clerk of the House of Representatives or the Secretary of the Senate. In this case Mr. Anderson was so registered.

We think the judge properly rejected both.

We have no problem with the portion of the first request which spoke to the obligation of legislators to consider responsible views on pending legislation. But we cannot subscribe to an instruction indicating that influencing or attempting to influence a legislator in the performance of an official act cannot amount to bribery. A gift or promise of something of value with intent to exert such an influence *is* bribery; the influencing is legally innocent only if unaccompanied by that factor. If Anderson's first request incorporated that qualification, it did so all too subtly, and unless the qualification was clear the instruction asked for was misleading. The second instruction Anderson sought suffers from a similar infirmity. While we do not quarrel with the accuracy as distinguished from the relevance of Anderson's general definition of a lobbyist, we encounter difficulty with the statement that "[the] only legal restriction on a lobbyist is" proper registration. It may be that registration is the only precondition to lobbying, but a lobbyist is nonetheless under the same legal restrictions imposed by the bribery laws upon everybody else; in a word, that one who violates those laws is a lobbyist is no defense. Anderson's second request, like the first, could have misled the jury, and the trial judge rightly declined to give it. Certainly the profession of lobbying is honorable; just as surely, influence devoid of unlawful means is innocuous, but Anderson's instructions implied much more.

---

7. DCCME was the acronym for a fictitious political committee. — ED.

We are advertent to the consideration that, as Anderson argues, an accused is entitled to instructions addressed to his theory of the case when properly requested and framed. But here the function of the lobbyist was thoroughly ventilated before the jury by Anderson's testimony, and the instructions the trial judge gave the jury adequately explained the requirement of corrupt intent — the element toward which Anderson directed his main defense — even to the extent of exonerating campaign contributions inspired by the recipient's general position of support on particular legislation. In this fashion the jury was informed of Anderson's occupational and operational background, and the judge's instructions furnished the jury with sufficient guidance to enable the distinction of lawful contributions from bribes. These circumstances considered, Anderson is not in [a] position to urge that the judge should have done more. . . .

V. THE POST-VERDICT EVENTS . . .

A. THE BREWSTER VERDICT

While the jury found Anderson guilty of bribery, it acquitted Brewster of that offense and fixed his guilt instead at unlawful receipt of gratuities. Anderson claims that these verdicts are fatally inconsistent, and that reversal of his conviction is accordingly required. He argues that the Government's evidence details such a course of conduct between Brewster and himself that no distinction between their acts or intent could rationally be drawn. He reasons that in the presence of such factual similarity the jury erred in finding that he corruptly intended to give money to Brewster to influence his official action, but that Brewster lacked a corresponding intent in the receipt of such monies.

We note initially that inconsistent verdicts are not self-vitiating. Beyond that, the verdicts as to Anderson and Brewster, respectively, are not per se inconsistent. The payment and the receipt of a bribe are not interdependent offenses, for obviously the donor's intent may differ completely from the donee's. Thus the donor may be convicted of giving a bribe despite the fact that the recipient had no intention of altering his official activities, or even lacked the power to do so.

As ever so recently we recognized, these mental elements are the factors differentiating the offense of bribery from the lesser offense of unlawfully receiving gratuities. Here, on the evidence, the jury could reasonably conclude that Anderson gave Brewster monies with corrupt intent to influence his vote on the proposed rate-increase legislation, and that Brewster, though insensitive to any influence, accepted the monies with knowledge that Anderson's purpose was to reward him for his stance on such legislation. . . .

. . . Upon careful consideration of Anderson's contentions in light of the record, we have found no error. For the reasons stated herein, the judgment of his conviction has been affirmed.

Notes and Questions

1. The statute requires that a bribe be "corruptly" given or received. What does "corruptly" mean in this context? Would substituting "knowingly" be an improvement?[8]

2. What differentiates lobbying — an "honorable" pursuit — from criminal influence peddling?

3. Anderson's backup argument was that the payments were gratuities rather than bribes. What is the significance of this argument? Why would Anderson prefer that the payments be classified as gratuities?

4. The court tells us that, with one exception, all of the payments to Senator Brewster came from Spiegel's corporate coffers. That fact, when combined with the argument that the payments were actually campaign contributions, raises the specter of yet another possible offense. The Federal Election Campaign Act prohibits direct corporate campaign contributions and authorizes criminal penalties for knowing and willful violations.[9]

C. THING OF VALUE

Although bribes and gratuities are commonly payments of money, § 201 provides that the exchange or payment of "anything of value" will suffice.

UNITED STATES v. WILLIAMS
705 F. 2d 603 (2d Cir. 1983)

NEWMAN, Circuit Judge.

Harrison A. Williams, Jr., formerly United States Senator from New Jersey, and Alexander Feinberg, an attorney and close friend of Williams, appeal from judgments of conviction entered in the District Court for the Eastern District of New York (George C. Pratt, Judge) after a jury trial on bribery and related charges arising out of the Abscam undercover "sting" operation. . . .

I

. . . The indictment alleged a conspiracy and eight substantive violations, arising out of Williams' conduct, aided and abetted by Feinberg, in promising to use his position as a United States Senator to help obtain government contracts for the purchase of titanium from a mining venture in which the defendants held an interest. The promises were alleged to have been made in connection with two transactions, the first, a proposed loan of $100 million ostensibly to have been financed by a fictitious entity known as Abdul Enterprises, Ltd. This entity, purporting to be an enterprise of two wealthy Arab sheiks, was the cover of an elaborate "sting" operation conducted by

---

8. Cf. Working Papers of the National Commission on Reform of Federal Criminal Laws 686 (1970).
9. See generally 2 Kathleen F. Brickey, Corporate Criminal Liability §§ 10:01-10:62 (2d ed. 1993).

agents of the Federal Bureau of Investigation. The second transaction, also proposed by the Abscam operatives, involved a second Arab group's offer to purchase the mining venture for a sum that would have yielded all the owners of the venture an estimated $70 million profit.

[In exchange for his promise to help the sheiks obtain government contracts, Senator Williams received stock in three corporations related to the mining venture. The stock turned out to be worthless. Williams was convicted of bribery, gratuity, conflict of interest, and interstate travel to facilitate the bribery.]

. . . [A]ppellants contend that the phrase "anything of value," receipt of which is proscribed by the statutes punishing bribery, 18 U.S.C. § 201(c),[10] and unlawful gratuity, 18 U.S.C. § 201(g),[11] means something that objectively has actual value. Their point in this regard is that the stock received by the Senator had no commercial value, and that Judge Pratt erred when he told the jury that stock could be a thing of value "if, regardless of its actual worth in the commercial world, you find that the defendant believed that the stock had value for himself." We think Judge Pratt correctly construed the statutes to focus on the value that the defendants subjectively attached to the items received. The phrase "anything of value" in bribery and related statutes has consistently been given a broader meaning to carry out the congressional purpose of punishing misuse of public office. Corruption of office occurs when the officeholder agrees to misuse his office in the expectation of gain, whether or not he has correctly assessed the worth of the bribe. When the Senator received shares of stock in the three corporations organized to hold the properties of the mining venture, he expected these shares to have considerable value, representing not only the potential value of the properties but also the benefit of the contemplated loan of $100 million. . . .

The judgments appealed from are affirmed.

Notes and Questions

1. The court in *Williams* adopts a purely subjective test for what constitutes a thing of value. If it had been readily apparent to all but Senator Williams that the proffered stock was worthless, would there have been a solid justification for upholding his conviction for agreeing to accept a "thing of value"?

2. Even though the stock the undercover agents offered Senator Williams as a quid pro quo for his assistance in obtaining government contracts was worthless, it was nonetheless an offer of what appeared to be a tangible benefit. But what if the quid pro quo had been something intangible, such as an offer to provide the Senator sexual favors from a prominent socialite in exchange for his help in obtaining the contracts? Would that constitute a "thing of value" under the reasoning in *Williams*?

---

10. Now codified as § 201(b). — ED.
11. Now codified as § 201(c). — ED.

D. PUBLIC OFFICIALS

Section 201 defines the term "public official" to include members of Congress; government officers and employees, or anyone "acting for or on behalf of" the federal government "in any official function, under or by authority of" a federal governmental department or agency; and jurors.[12]

1. Appointed Officials

DIXSON v. UNITED STATES
465 U.S. 482 (1984)

Justice MARSHALL delivered the opinion of the Court.

These consolidated cases present the question whether officers of a private, nonprofit corporation administering and expending federal community development block grants are "public officials" for purposes of the federal bribery statute. 18 U.S.C. § 201(a).

I

In 1979, the city of Peoria received two federal block grants from the Department of Housing and Urban Development (HUD). The first was a $400,000 Community Development Block Grant; the second a $638,000 Metro Reallocation Grant. Both grants were funded through the Housing and Community Development Act of 1974 (HCDA). Under that Act, the Secretary of HUD is authorized to dispense federal block grants to state and local governments and nonprofit community organizations for urban renewal programs such as the rehabilitation of residential structures, code enforcement in deteriorating areas, and the construction of public works projects.

The city of Peoria subsequently designated United Neighborhoods, Inc. (UNI), a community-based, social-service organization, to be the city's subgrantee in charge of the administration of the federal block grant funds. UNI in turn hired petitioner Dixson to serve as the corporation's Executive Director and petitioner Hinton as its Housing Rehabilitation Coordinator. Petitioner Dixson was responsible for the general supervision of UNI's programs, including fiscal control and execution of contracts. Petitioner Hinton's duties included contracting with persons applying for housing rehabilitation assistance, and contracting with demolition firms.

A federal grand jury named petitioners in an 11-count indictment filed on March 12, 1981. The indictment charged that petitioners, as "public officials" under 18 U.S.C. § 201(a), had sought a series of bribes in return for "being influenced in their performance of an official act in respect to the awarding of housing rehabilitation contracts" in violation of 18 U.S.C. § 201(c)(1), (2). According to the Government's evidence at trial, petitioners used their positions to extract $42,694 in kickbacks from contractors

---

12. The statute also extends its protection to witnesses in federal judicial, congressional, and administrative proceedings.

seeking to work on UNI's housing rehabilitation projects. One contractor testified how he was approached by petitioner Hinton and persuaded to pay petitioners 10 percent of each housing rehabilitation contract that petitioners awarded him. The contractor explained that on 10 occasions, he received first draw checks from UNI for 20 percent of the contract price, deposited the check at his bank, and paid half the amount of the check in cash to petitioners. A second contractor testified as to substantially the same arrangement.

Before trial, petitioners moved to dismiss the indictment on the grounds that they were not "public officials" within the meaning of the federal statute. Their motions were denied, and following a jury trial in the United States District Court for the Central District of Illinois, petitioners were convicted as charged. The District Court sentenced each to 7-1/2 years' imprisonment, to be followed by 3 years' probation.

II

[Under the Housing and Community Development Act, HCDA grantees must assure HUD that they will comply with financial accountability and other regulatory requirements. In addition, nonprofit organizations that administer HCDA funds are subject to non-HUD requirements (such as a uniform audit procedure) imposed on all recipients of federal grants. Although the first contracts between UNI and the city of Peoria did not expressly mention HCDA or characterize UNI as a subgrantee, UNI was aware of both the federal government's role in the grant agreements and its own involvement in a federal program.]

III

[The petitioners claimed that as executives of a nonprofit corporation that was not affiliated with the federal government, they were not public officials. The government contended that they were because they acted "for or on behalf of" the United States "in an official function" under HUD authority. But the executives countered that they did not act "for or on behalf of" the government because neither they nor UNI had entered into an agreement with the federal government or any subdivision thereof. The government read the "for or on behalf of" language more expansively to mean that all private parties who administer federally funded and supervised programs should be deemed public officials.]

A

[Federal bribery statutes have always contained broad jurisdictional language, and courts have historically construed the jurisdictional element expansively.]

Of particular relevance to the instant case is the House Judiciary Committee's citation of the Second Circuit's decision in United States v. Levine, 129 F.2d 745 (CA2 1942), as an example of how the judiciary had in the past properly construed the federal bribery laws. The *Levine* decision involved the application of the 1909 bribery statute to a low-level official in a decentralized federal assistance program. The defendant in

Levine worked for a locally administered price stabilization program, the Market Administrator of the New York Metropolitan Milk Marketing Area, and was responsible for receiving milk handlers' market surplus claims, and checking them for accuracy. Levine solicited a bribe from one of the handlers within his jurisdiction in return for his promise to prevent investigations of the claims.

Although hired by a Market Administrator who, in turn, had been appointed by the Secretary of Agriculture, Levine himself was neither employed by the United States nor paid with federal funds. Nevertheless, Levine's duties were critical to the proper administration of the federally assisted New York Milk Marketing Area. Because claims for payment were not rechecked by anyone else, his duties resulted in expenditures from the Federal Treasury. After reviewing these facts, the Second Circuit concluded that, notwithstanding the absence of a direct contractual bond between the defendant and the United States, Levine's responsible position made him a "public official" for purposes of the federal bribery laws. By explicitly endorsing the Second Circuit's analysis in *Levine*, the House Judiciary Committee strongly intimated that the phrase "acting for or on behalf of the United States" covers something more than a direct contractual bond. . . .

. . . We agree with the Government that § 201(a) has been accurately characterized as a "comprehensive statute applicable to all persons performing activities for or on behalf of the United States," whatever the form of delegation of authority. To determine whether any particular individual falls within this category, the proper inquiry is not simply whether the person had signed a contract with the United States or agreed to serve as the Government's agent, but rather whether the person occupies a position of public trust with official federal responsibilities. Persons who hold such positions are public officials within the meaning of § 201 and liable for prosecution under the federal bribery statute.

B

Given the structure of the HCDA program and petitioners' responsible positions as administrators of the subgrant, we have little difficulty concluding that these persons served as public officials for purposes of § 201(a). As executives of UNI, petitioners had operational responsibility for the administration of the HCDA grant program within the city of Peoria. In allocating the federal resources made available to the city through the HCDA grant program, petitioners were charged with abiding by federal guidelines, which dictated both where and how the federal funds could be distributed. By accepting the responsibility for distributing these federal fiscal resources, petitioners assumed the quintessentially official role of administering a social service program established by the United States Congress.

Lest there be any doubt that Congress intended § 201(a) to cover local officials like petitioners, one need only compare petitioners to the defendant in *Levine*, whose conviction the House Judiciary Committee explicitly endorsed. Both Levine and petitioners worked in decentralized federal assistance programs. Both Levine and petitioners effectively determined who would be the beneficiary of federal dollars, and both solicited bribes to influence their official decisions. Levine held a position of public trust with official federal responsibilities: to collect and investigate the accuracy of data submitted by milk producers in support of their claims for federal subsidies. Petitioners held a position of public trust with official federal responsibilities: allocating federal resources, pursuant to complex statutory and regulatory guidelines, in the form of residential rehabilitation contracts. Indeed, in certain respects, petitioners performed duties that were more clearly "official" and more obviously undertaken "for or on behalf of the United States" than the responsibilities of the defendant in *Levine*. Where Levine was paid through a levy imposed on local businesses participating in the marketing order, petitioners' salaries were completely funded by the HCDA grant. Where Levine simply compiled data that were submitted to the Department of Agriculture for eventual disbursement, petitioners personally bestowed the benefits of the HCDA program to residents of Peoria. . . .

IV . . .

B.

By finding petitioners to be public officials within the meaning of § 201(a), we do not mean to suggest that the mere presence of some federal assistance brings a local organization and its employees within the jurisdiction of the federal bribery statute or even that all employees of local organizations responsible for administering federal grant programs are public officials within the meaning of § 201(a). To be a public official under § 201(a), an individual must possess some degree of official responsibility for carrying out a federal program or policy. Our opinion today is, therefore, fully consistent with Krichman v. United States, 256 U.S. 363 (1921), in which this Court ruled that a baggage porter, although employed by a federally controlled railroad, could not be said to have "acted for or on behalf of the United States" because the porter lacked any duties of an official character. Similarly, individuals who work for block grant recipients and business people who provide recipients with goods and services cannot be said to be public officials under § 201(a) unless they assume some duties of an official nature.

We recognize that the manner in which the HCDA block grant program combines local administration with federal funding initially creates some confusion as to whether local authorities administering HCDA grants should be considered public officials under the federal bribery statute. However, when one examines the structure of the program and sees that the HCDA vests in local administrators like petitioners Hinton and Dixson the power to allocate federal fiscal resources for the purpose of achieving congressionally established goals, the confusion evaporates and it becomes clear that these local officials hold precisely the sort of positions of national public trust that Congress intended to cover with the "acting for or on behalf of" language in the bribery statute. The Federal Government has a strong and legitimate interest in prosecuting petitioners for their misuse of Government funds. As this Court has said in another, closely related context, grant funds to state and local governments "are as much in need of protection from [fraud] as any other federal money, and the statute does not make the extent of [grant moneys'] safeguard dependent upon the bookkeeping devices used for their distribution." United States ex rel. Marcus v. Hess, 317 U.S. 537, 544 (1943) (holding that one who contracts with a local governmental unit to work on federally funded projects can "cheat the United States" through the state intermediary).

Because we agree with the Seventh Circuit that petitioners were public officials under § 201(a), the judgment of the Court of Appeals is affirmed.

It is so ordered.

Justice O'CONNOR, with whom Justice BRENNAN, Justice REHNQUIST, and Justice STEVENS join, dissenting. . . .

I

The language of § 201 and of its predecessors, as the Court's opinion points out, is intentionally broad. But that fact merely creates the interpretive problem — it does not resolve it. . . .

The legislative history of § 201 from the 87th Congress, which enacted the current version of the statute, contains two items that bear on the meaning of the statute's "acting for . . ." language. The Court relies heavily on these two items. One, however, offers no support for the Court's reading, and the other offers support of, at best, weak and uncertain significance.

First, the Court notes that the House Judiciary Committee cited United States v. Levine as an example of judicial construction of the statute. The Court concludes that this citation establishes congressional intent to include within the coverage of the bribery statute persons other than those with direct contractual bonds to the United States. That conclusion is surely correct. But saying that the class covered by the statute includes more than direct contractors does not begin to define the class actually covered and, in particular, does not imply that the class includes individuals employed by federal grant recipients or by their subgrantees.

Moreover, the *Levine* case itself does not suggest inclusion of such individuals. The individual involved in *Levine* was an employee of a person appointed by the Federal Government to carry out a federally defined regulatory task. As an employee of an agent of the United States, he was obviously acting for the United States. An employee of a grantee or subgrantee of the United States is in a quite different position. It is by no means obvious that such a person is acting for the United States, since a grantee does not necessarily have an agency relationship with the United States. Indeed, as the Court concedes, not all recipients of federal grant funds are acting for the United States: for example, recipients of science research funds are surely not acting for the United States, even when they use some of those funds to purchase assistance in accordance with the federally approved grant proposal. That Congress approved the *Levine* case simply cannot support an inference that Congress intended the bribery statute to cover persons in petitioners' position. . . .

I respectfully dissent.

Notes and Questions

1. Justice O'Connor's dissent emphasizes that not all recipients of federal grants are public officials. Is the majority suggesting that all or most grant recipients are? Why would the dissenters exclude recipients of science research funds? Would the majority likewise exclude them?

2. Do all or most individuals who have contracts with the federal government (excluding suppliers, of course) qualify as public officials? Can a corporation ever be considered a public official?

3. The majority's litmus test is "whether the person occupies a position of public trust with official federal responsibilities." What does that mean? Does Justice O'Connor hit or miss the mark when she says this standard provides no more guidance than the statutory language?

2. Elected Officials

UNITED STATES v. BREWSTER
408 U.S. 501 (1972)

Mr. Chief Justice BURGER delivered the opinion of the Court.

This direct appeal from the District Court presents the question whether a Member of Congress may be prosecuted under 18 U.S.C. §§ 201(c)(1), 201(g), for accepting a bribe in exchange for a promise relating to an official act. Appellee, a former United States Senator, was charged in five counts of a 10-count indictment.[13] Counts one, three, five, and seven alleged that on four separate occasions, appellee, while he was a Senator and a member of the Senate Committee on Post Office and Civil Service,

> directly and indirectly, corruptly asked, solicited, sought, accepted, received and agreed to receive [sums] . . . in return for being influenced in his performance of official acts in respect to his action, vote, and decision on postage rate legislation which might at any time be pending before him in his official capacity . . . in violation of Sections 201(c)(1) and 2, Title 18, United States Code.

Count nine charged that appellee

> directly and indirectly, asked, demanded, exacted, solicited, sought, accepted, received and agreed to receive [a sum] . . . for and because of official acts performed by him in respect to his action, vote and decision on postage rate legislation which had been pending before him in his official capacity . . . in violation of Sections 201(g) and 2, Title 18, United States Code.

Before a trial date was set, the appellee moved to dismiss the indictment on the ground of immunity under the Speech or Debate Clause, Art. I, § 6, of the Constitution, which provides:

> [F]or any Speech or Debate in either House, they [Senators or Representatives] shall not be questioned in any other Place.

---

13. The remaining five counts charged the alleged bribers with offering and giving bribes in violation of 18 U.S.C. § 201(b).

After hearing argument, the District Court ruled from the bench:

> Gentlemen, based on the facts of this case, it is admitted by the Government that the five counts of the indictment which charge Senator Brewster relate to the acceptance of bribes in connection with the performance of a legislative function by a Senator of the United States.
>
> It is the opinion of this Court that the immunity under the Speech and [sic] Debate Clause of the Constitution, particularly in view of the interpretation given that Clause by the Supreme Court in *Johnson*, shields Senator Brewster, constitutionally shields him from any prosecution for alleged bribery to perform a legislative act.
>
> I will, therefore, dismiss the odd counts of the indictment, 1, 3, 5, 7 and 9, as they apply to Senator Brewster. . . .

II

The immunities of the Speech or Debate Clause were not written into the Constitution simply for the personal or private benefit of Members of Congress, but to protect the integrity of the legislative process by insuring the independence of individual legislators. The genesis of the Clause at common law is well known. In his opinion for the Court in United States v. Johnson, 383 U.S. 169 (1966), Mr. Justice Harlan canvassed the history of the Clause and concluded that it

> was the culmination of a long struggle for parliamentary supremacy. Behind these simple phrases lies a history of conflict between the Commons and the Tudor and Stuart monarchs during which successive monarchs utilized the criminal and civil law to suppress and intimidate critical legislators. Since the Glorious Revolution in Britain, and throughout United States history, the privilege has been recognized as an important protection of the independence and integrity of the legislature. Id., at 178.

Although the Speech or Debate Clause's historic roots are in English history, it must be interpreted in light of the American experience, and in the context of the American constitutional scheme of government rather than the English parliamentary system. We should bear in mind that the English system differs from ours in that their Parliament is the supreme authority, not a coordinate branch. Our speech or debate privilege was designed to preserve legislative independence, not supremacy.[14] Our task, therefore, is to apply the Clause in such a way as to insure the independence of the legislature without altering the historic balance of the three co-equal branches of Government. . . .

In United States v. Johnson the Court reviewed the conviction of a former Representative on seven counts of violating the federal conflict-of-interest statute, 18 U.S.C. § 281 (1964), and on one count of conspiracy to defraud the United States, 18 U.S.C. § 371 (1964). The Court of Appeals had set aside the conviction on the count for conspiracy to defraud as violating the Speech or Debate Clause. Mr. Justice Harlan, speaking for the Court, cited the oft-quoted passage of Mr. Justice Lush in Ex parte Wason, L.R. 4 Q.B. 573 (1869):

---

14. Cella, The Doctrine of Legislative Privilege of Freedom of Speech and Debate: Its Past, Present and Future as a Bar to Criminal Prosecutions in the Courts, 2 Suffolk L. Rev. 1, 15 (1968); Note, The Bribed Congressman's Immunity from Prosecution, 75 Yale L.J. 335, 337-338 (1965).

> I am clearly of opinion that we ought not to allow it to be doubted for a moment that the motives or intentions of members of either House cannot be inquired into by criminal proceedings *with respect to anything they may do or say in the House*. Id., at 577 (emphasis added).

In Kilbourn v. Thompson, 103 U.S. 168 (1881), the first case in which this Court interpreted the Speech or Debate Clause, the Court expressed a similar view of the ambit of the American privilege. There the Court said the Clause is to be read broadly to include anything "generally done in a session of the House by one of its members in relation to the business before it." Id., at 204. This statement, too, was cited with approval in *Johnson*. Our conclusion in *Johnson* was that the privilege protected Members from inquiry into legislative acts or the motivation for actual performance of legislative acts.

In applying the Speech or Debate Clause, the Court focused on the specific facts of the *Johnson* prosecution. The conspiracy-to-defraud count alleged an agreement among Representative Johnson and three codefendants to obtain the dismissal of pending indictments against officials of savings and loan institutions. For these services, which included a speech made by Johnson on the House floor, the Government claimed Johnson was paid a bribe. At trial, the Government questioned Johnson extensively, relative to the conspiracy-to-defraud count, concerning the authorship of the speech, the factual basis for certain statements made in the speech, and his motives for giving the speech. The Court held that the use of evidence of a speech to support a count under a broad conspiracy statute was prohibited by the Speech or Debate Clause. The Government was, therefore, precluded from prosecuting the conspiracy count on retrial, insofar as it depended on inquiries into speeches made in the House.

It is important to note the very narrow scope of the Court's holding in *Johnson*:

> We hold that a prosecution under a general criminal statute dependent on such inquiries [into the speech or its preparation] necessarily contravenes the Speech or Debate Clause. We emphasize that our holding is limited to prosecutions involving circumstances such as those presented in the case before us. 383 U.S., at 184-185.

The opinion specifically left open the question of a prosecution which, though possibly entailing some reference to legislative acts, is founded upon a "narrowly drawn" statute passed by Congress in the exercise of its power to regulate its Members' conduct. Of more relevance to this case, the Court in *Johnson* emphasized that its decision did not affect a prosecution that, though founded on a criminal statute of general application, "does not draw in question the legislative acts of the defendant member of Congress or his motives for performing them." Id., at 185. The Court did not question the power of the United States to try Johnson on the conflict-of-interest counts, and it authorized a new trial on the conspiracy count, provided that all references to the making of the speech were eliminated.[15]. . .

Johnson thus stands as a unanimous holding that a Member of Congress may be prosecuted under a criminal statute provided that the Government's case does not rely

---

15. On remand, the District Court dismissed the conspiracy count without objection from the Government. Johnson was then found guilty on the remaining counts, and his conviction was affirmed. United States v. Johnson, 419 F.2d 56 (CA4 1969).

on legislative acts or the motivation for legislative acts. A legislative act has consistently been defined as an act generally done in Congress in relation to the business before it. In sum, the Speech or Debate Clause prohibits inquiry only into those things generally said or done in the House or the Senate in the performance of official duties and into the motivation for those acts.

It is well known, of course, that Members of the Congress engage in many activities other than the purely legislative activities protected by the Speech or Debate Clause. These include a wide range of legitimate "errands" performed for constituents, the making of appointments with Government agencies, assistance in securing Government contracts, preparing so-called "news letters" to constituents, news releases, and speeches delivered outside the Congress. The range of these related activities has grown over the years. They are performed in part because they have come to be expected by constituents, and because they are a means of developing continuing support for future elections. Although these are entirely legitimate activities, they are political in nature rather than legislative, in the sense that term has been used by the Court in prior cases. But it has never been seriously contended that these political matters, however appropriate, have the protection afforded by the Speech or Debate Clause. Careful examination of the decided cases reveals that the Court has regarded the protection as reaching only those things "generally done in a session of the House by one of its members in relation to the business before it," Kilbourn v. Thompson, supra, at 204, or things "said or done by him, as a representative, in the exercise of the functions of that office," Coffin v. Coffin, 4 Mass. 1, 27 (1808).

[Brewster argued that a broader reading of the Speech or Debate Clause would not allow wrongdoers to escape punishment because each house of Congress has the power to punish its own members. But the Court was unpersuaded. Not only was the Court concerned that a Member of Congress could be compelled to defend what in essence was a criminal charge before a political tribunal and without the procedural safeguards afforded in a criminal trial; the Court was also concerned that the scope of congressional jurisdiction is unclear — as, for example, in the instant case where the wrongdoing occurred during Brewster's term of office but remained undiscovered until after he left office. To accept Brewster's argument would, in the Court's view, confer immunity for a wide range of criminal conduct "simply because the acts in question were peripherally related to [a congressman's] holding office."]

III

An examination of the indictment brought against appellee and the statutes on which it is founded reveals that no inquiry into legislative acts or motivation for legislative acts is necessary for the Government to make out a prima facie case. Four of the five counts charge that appellee "corruptly asked, solicited, sought, accepted, received and agreed to receive" money "in return for being influenced . . . in respect to his action, vote, and decision on postage rate legislation which might at any time be pending before him in his official capacity." This is said to be a violation of 18 U.S.C. § 201(c), which provides that a Member who "corruptly asks, demands, exacts, solicits, seeks, accepts, receives, or agrees to receive anything of value . . . in return for . . . (1) being influenced in his performance of any official act" is guilty of an offense.

The question is whether it is necessary to inquire into how appellee spoke, how he debated, how he voted, or anything he did in the chamber or in committee in order to make out a violation of this statute. The illegal conduct is taking or agreeing to take money for a promise to act in a certain way. There is no need for the Government to show that appellee fulfilled the alleged illegal bargain; acceptance of the bribe is the violation of the statute, not performance of the illegal promise.

Taking a bribe is, obviously, no part of the legislative process or function; it is not a legislative act. It is not, by any conceivable interpretation, an act performed as a part of or even incidental to the role of a legislator. It is not an "act resulting from the nature, and in the execution, of the office." Nor is it a "thing said or done by him, as a representative, in the exercise of the functions of that office," 4 Mass., at 27. Nor is inquiry into a legislative act or the motivation for a legislative act necessary to a prosecution under this statute or this indictment. When a bribe is taken, it does not matter whether the promise for which the bribe was given was for the performance of a legislative act as here or, as in *Johnson*, for use of a Congressman's influence with the Executive Branch. And an inquiry into the purpose of a bribe "does not draw in question the legislative acts of the defendant member of Congress or his motives for performing them." 383 U.S., at 185.

Nor does it matter if the Member defaults on his illegal bargain. To make a prima facie case under this indictment, the Government need not show any act of appellee subsequent to the corrupt promise for payment, for it is *taking* the bribe, not performance of the illicit compact, that is a criminal act. If, for example, there were undisputed evidence that a Member took a bribe in exchange for an agreement to vote for a given bill and if there were also undisputed evidence that he, in fact, voted against the bill, can it be thought that this alters the nature of the bribery or removes it from the area of wrongdoing the Congress sought to make a crime?

Another count of the indictment against appellee alleges that he "asked, demanded, exacted, solicited, sought, accepted, received and agreed to receive" money "for and because of official acts performed by him in respect to his action, vote and decision on postage rate legislation which had been pending before him in his official capacity. . . ." This count is founded on 18 U.S.C. § 201(g), which provides that a Member of Congress who "asks, demands, exacts, solicits, seeks, accepts, receives, or agrees to receive anything of value for himself for or because of any official act performed or to be performed by him" is guilty of an offense. Although the indictment alleges that the bribe was given for an act that was actually performed, it is, once again, unnecessary to inquire into the act or its motivation. To sustain a conviction it is necessary to show that appellee solicited, received, or agreed to receive, money with knowledge that the donor was paying him compensation for an official act. Inquiry into the legislative performance itself is not necessary; evidence of the Member's knowledge of the alleged briber's illicit reasons for paying the money is sufficient to carry the case to the jury.

Mr. Justice White rests heavily on the fact that the indictment charges the offense as being in part linked to Brewster's "action, vote and decision on postage rate legislation." This is true, of course, but our holding in *Johnson* precludes any showing of how he acted, voted, or decided. The dissenting position stands on the fragile proposition that it "would take the Government at its word" with respect to wanting to prove what we all agree are protected acts that cannot be shown in evidence. Perhaps the

Government would make a more appealing case if it could do so, but here, as in that case, evidence of acts protected by the Clause is inadmissible. The Government, as we have noted, need not prove any specific act, speech, debate, or decision to establish a violation of the statute under which appellee was indicted. To accept the arguments of the dissent would be to retreat from the Court's position in *Johnson* that a Member may be convicted if no showing of legislative act is required.

Mr. Justice Brennan suggests that inquiry into the alleged bribe is inquiry into the motivation for a legislative act, and it is urged that this very inquiry was condemned as impermissible in *Johnson*. That argument misconstrues the concept of motivation for legislative acts. The Speech or Debate Clause does not prohibit inquiry into illegal conduct simply because it has some nexus to legislative functions. In *Johnson*, the Court held that on remand, Johnson could be retried on the conspiracy-to-defraud count, so long as evidence concerning his speech on the House floor was not admitted. The Court's opinion plainly implies that had the Government chosen to retry Johnson on that count, he could not have obtained immunity from prosecution by asserting that the matter being inquired into was related to the motivation for his House speech.

The only reasonable reading of the Clause, consistent with its history and purpose, is that it does not prohibit inquiry into activities that are casually or incidentally related to legislative affairs but not a part of the legislative process itself. Under this indictment and these statutes no such proof is needed.

We hold that under this statute and this indictment, prosecution of appellee is not prohibited by the Speech or Debate Clause. Accordingly the judgment of the District Court is reversed and the case is remanded for further proceedings consistent with this opinion.

Reversed and remanded.

[Dissenting opinions by Justice WHITE and Justice BRENNAN omitted.]

Notes and Questions

1. Is proof that Brewster accepted cash to influence his vote on the postal legislation tantamount to an inquiry into why he voted the way he did? If so, why isn't that inquiry foreclosed by the Speech or Debate Clause?

2. Is the distinction between a legislative act (which is protected under the Speech or Debate Clause) and an act relating to legislation (which is not protected) entirely clear? Does the Court in *Brewster* give sufficient guidance on how to distinguish one from the other?

3. Does the Speech or Debate Clause protect legislative status as well as legislative acts? Would it have been permissible to introduce evidence that Senator Brewster was a member of the Senate Committee on Post Office and Civil Service?[16]

4. What if Brewster's top aide had prepared a statistical report on the economics of the mail order industry for Brewster's use during committee deliberations. Is the aide's conduct immunized by the Speech or Debate Clause?[17]

---

16. Cf. United States v. Rostenkowski, 59 F.3d 1291 (D.C. Cir. 1995); United States v. Swindall, 971 F.2d 1531 (11th Cir. 1992).

17. Cf. Gravel v. United States, 408 U.S. 606 (1972).

5. For an interesting sidelight on a highly publicized dispute over whether a congressional committee could be compelled to give a tobacco company access to documents the company claimed had been stolen from it, see Brown & Williamson Tobacco Corp. v. Williams, 62 F.3d 408 (D.C. Cir. 1995).

E.   COOPERATING WITNESSES

Although the primary focus of § 201 is on preventing corruption of public officials, the statute also prohibits bribing witnesses before federal tribunals to influence their testimony, or paying gratuities "for or because of" a federal witness's sworn testimony.

UNITED STATES v. WARE
161 F.3d 414 (6th Cir. 1998)

I. BACKGROUND

[Robert Ware and four others were charged with conspiracy to distribute cocaine and cocaine base. Two of Ware's codefendants testified against him at trial pursuant to plea agreements under which they were allowed to plead guilty to fewer counts than they had been charged with. Ware was convicted on three counts and sentenced to 30 years in prison. On appeal, Ware argued that, by offering leniency to codefendants and cooperating witnesses in exchange for their testimony against him, the government violated 18 U.S.C. § 201(c)'s prohibition against offering anything of value to a witness for or because of the witness's testimony. In making this argument, Ware relied on the Tenth Circuit's decision in United States v. Singleton, 144 F.3d 1343 (10th Cir. 1998) (*Singleton I*).]

II. DISCUSSION . . .

B.

On July 1, 1998, a panel of the 10th Circuit held that it was a violation of § 201(c)(2) for a federal prosecutor to enter into an agreement with an accomplice to the defendant on trial whereby the accomplice agreed to testify truthfully in return for leniency, including a possible § 5K1.1 motion from the government for downward departure [of his sentence under the Sentencing Guidelines] (*Singleton I*). . . . The decision was vacated on July 10, 1998, by the 10th Circuit and set for en banc hearing in November 1998.

A number of district courts have addressed this issue in the wake of *Singleton* and rejected the rationale of the *Singleton* decision.

Section 201(c)(2) of Title 18 of the United States Code provides

(c) Whoever — ...

   (2) directly or indirectly, gives, offers or promises anything of value to any person, for or because of the testimony under oath or affirmation given or to be given by such person as a witness upon a trial, hearing, or other proceeding, before any court, any committee of either House or both Houses of Congress, or any agency, commission, or officer authorized by the laws of the United States to hear evidence or take testimony, or for or because of such person's absence therefrom; ...

shall be fined under this title or imprisoned for not more than two years, or both.

   The *Singleton* court broadly interpreted the term "whoever" to include the United States government. We disagree. During the more than three decades that this provision has been around, no court until the *Singleton* panel has read this section to apply to the government. We think there are a variety of valid reasons for that, as we shall explain.

   To begin with, we conclude that the reach of § 201(c)(2) is limited by the canon of statutory interpretation that says that the general words of a statute do not include the government or affect its rights unless the text of the statute expressly includes the government. Nardone v. United States, 302 U.S. 379, 383 (1937). The *Nardone* Court made the cursory statement that "the cases in which [the canon] has been applied fall into two classes." Id. The first is where application of the statute to the government "would deprive the sovereign of a recognized or established prerogative[,] title or interest." Id. The second is where application of a statute to public officers would create an obvious absurdity. Id. at 384. This case fits into both of those classes.

   The prosecutorial prerogative to recommend leniency in exchange for testimony dates back to the common law in England and has been recognized and approved by Congress, the courts, and the Sentencing Commission of the United States. In the Whiskey Cases, 99 U.S. 594 (1878), the Supreme Court acknowledged:

   Prosecutors in such a case should explain to the accomplice that he is not obliged to criminate himself, and inform him just what he may reasonably expect in case he acts in good faith, and testifies fully and fairly as to his own acts in the case, and those of his associates. When he fulfills those conditions he is equitably entitled to a pardon, and the prosecutor, and the court if need be, when fully informed of the facts, will join in such a recommendation.

Id. at 604.

   The Supreme Court has repeatedly upheld the plea bargaining practices historically utilized in the United States' criminal justice system. In Brady v. United States, 397 U.S. 742, 751-53 (1970), for example, the Court said,

   The issue we deal with [the validity of a guilty plea entered after the defendant learned that his codefendant had pled guilty and was available to testify against him] is inherent in the criminal law and its administration because guilty pleas are not constitutionally forbidden, because the criminal law characteristically extends to judge or jury a range of choice in setting the sentence in individual cases, and because both the State and the defendant often find it advantageous to preclude the possibility of the maximum penalty authorized by law. . . .

. . . [W]e cannot hold that it is unconstitutional for the State to extend a benefit to a defendant who in turn extends a substantial benefit to the State. . . .

A contrary holding would require the States and Federal Government to forbid guilty pleas altogether. . . .

Brady, 397 U.S. at 751-53. . . .

In carrying out his legitimate business it has always been properly within the prosecutor's prerogatives to offer these kinds of promises in return for a benefit to the government, often in the form of the defendant's cooperation. Plea agreements which make the government's promise to the defendant contingent upon the defendant's testifying in the trials of other offenders are certainly contemplated by the Federal Rules of Criminal Procedure. Rule 11(e), which sets out the procedure governing plea agreements, does not detail the kinds of commitments that the government may require of a criminal defendant in exchange for the government's promise to dismiss certain charges, or to permit a guilty plea to a lesser offense or to seek or recommend leniency in the sentence to be imposed; nonetheless, it is clear from the context of the rule and the Committee Notes detailing its history, not to mention decades of case law, that more may be required of the defendant than his simply giving up his right to trial. . . . The [Advisory Committee] notes to the 1975 amendments to Rule 11 are explicit:

> Proposed Rule 11(e) contemplates 4 different types of plea agreements. . . . [It is apparent, though not explicitly stated, that Rule 11(e) contemplates that the plea agreement may bind the defendant to do more than just plead guilty or nolo contendere. *For example, the plea agreement may bind the defendant to cooperate with the prosecution in a different investigation. The Committee intends by its approval of Rule 11(e) to permit the parties to agree on such terms in a plea agreement.*]

Fed. R. Crim. P. 11 advisory committee's notes (brackets in original) (emphasis added).

In Giglio v. United States, 405 U.S. 150 (1972), an assistant United States Attorney neglected to disclose the government's promise to a government witness that he would not be prosecuted if he cooperated. The Supreme Court held that the failure to disclose the promise to the defense effectively resulted in a due process violation, and, accordingly, the government must disclose a promise of leniency to a witness provided in exchange for testimony by that witness. Similarly, the Supreme Court held in Delaware v. Van Arsdall, 475 U.S. 673, 679-80 (1986), that the fact that a witness had had a pending charge against him dismissed was evidence "that a jury might reasonably have found [that it] furnished the witness a motive for favoring the prosecution in his testimony"; calling it a "prototypical form of bias on the part of the witness," the Court held that a refusal to permit a defendant to question the witness about the dismissal of the charge was a violation of the Sixth Amendment right to confrontation. Although the Supreme Court did not squarely address the legitimacy of such promises in these cases, the Court's holdings implicitly sanction promises of leniency. . . .

Circuit courts have followed suit, recognizing plea agreements conditioned upon testimony by co-defendants or co-conspirators. As stated by the Fifth Circuit, "no practice is more ingrained in our criminal justice system than the practice of the government calling a witness who is an accessory to the crime for which the defendant is charged and having that witness testify under a plea bargain that promises him a reduced sentence." United States v. Cervantes-Pacheco, 826 F.2d 310, 315 (5th Cir. 1987).

If 18 U.S.C. § 201(c)(2), which nowhere mentions the government, is nonetheless read to include the government, then a federal prosecutor's use of testimony obtained by means of plea agreements — one of the principal benefits to the government from plea agreements — is a criminal act. We think it is obvious that such a reading of the statute would deprive the sovereign of an established and recognized prerogative.

[The court also rejected the notion that the *Singleton* rule only limits agents of the sovereign rather than the sovereign itself. When the AUSA enters into a plea agreement, introduces immunized trial testimony, or moves for a downward departure under § 5K1.1, these are acts of the government itself.]

Even if we were to consider the AUSA as simply an agent or servant of the government, however, we conclude that this case falls within the second class of cases mentioned in *Nardone*. Those are the cases where the application of the statute to public officers would work an obvious absurdity. *Nardone*, 302 U.S. at 384.

The most obvious absurdity such a reading works is that AUSAs who entered into any plea agreements pursuant to Rule 11(e) would be subject to fines and imprisonment. This result cannot be avoided by attempting to argue that the language of the statute forbids only the use of the testimony from a witness who has entered into the plea agreement, not the plea agreement itself. Because a defendant who enters into a plea agreement pursuant to Rule 11 must appear before the court and enter his plea, the defendant's entry of that plea is testimony. "Central to the plea and the foundation for entering judgment against the defendant is the defendant's admission in open court that he committed the acts charged in the indictment. He thus stands as a witness against himself." Brady v. United States, 397 U.S. at 748. If § 201(c)(2) applies to AUSAs at all, it applies to those who obtain the guilty plea itself by bargaining.

To apply § 201(c)(2) to the government in the person of the AUSA works the further absurdity of making criminal that which is explicitly permitted pursuant to other sections of the United States Code as well as the Sentencing Guidelines. The Sentencing Reform Act, enacted by Congress in 1984, among other things, established the United States Sentencing Commission, charged with the duty of promulgating and distributing to the federal courts guidelines to be used in sentencing. See 28 U.S.C. § 994(a). The Act explicitly requires the Commission to

assure that the guidelines reflect the general appropriateness of imposing a lower sentence than would otherwise be imposed, including a sentence that is lower than that established by statute as a minimum sentence, to take into account a defendant's substantial assistance in the investigation or prosecution of another person who has committed an offense.

28 U.S.C. § 994(n). . . .

Equally, although perhaps somewhat less obviously, absurd is the effect on the statutory scheme providing for immunity of witnesses that would result from applying § 201(c)(2) to public officers. Sections 6001 through 6005 of Title 18, enacted in 1970 as part of the Organized Crime Control Act, expressly provide that immunity from prosecution may be given to witnesses under certain conditions. Section 6003 specifically authorizes a United States Attorney, with the approval of the Attorney General or various underlings of that office, to request from a United States district court an order granting immunity to a witness whose testimony the United States Attorney considers necessary in the public interest. Certainly there is no purpose for a grant of immunity to a witness except to obtain his testimony. And certainly immunity from prosecution is "something of value" given "for or because of the testimony under oath or affirmation." 18 U.S.C. § 201(c)(2). Do we then assume that the Congress enacted these immunity provisions with the intention that they be utilized by the United States Attorneys under pain of criminal sanction?

Legislative History

[The court's review of the legislative history to § 201 revealed no evidence of congressional intent to affect the government's long-standing prerogative to negotiate plea agreements with cooperating witnesses.]

The *Singleton* court, and the district courts who have chosen to follow the rationale of *Singleton*, United States v. Mays, No. 97-CR-127 (E.D. Tenn. Sept. 18, 1998); United States v. Fraguela, 1998 WL 560352 (E.D. La. Aug. 27, 1998); United States v. Lowery, 15 F. Supp. 2d 1348 (S.D. Fla. 1998), focus on the unreliability of testimony induced by plea agreements and the tainting of the judicial process. The *Lowery* decision, adopted in its entirety by the courts in *Fraguela* and *Mays*, reasoned that including the government and plea agreements "within the reaches of Section 201(c)(2) ensures that the judicial process will remain untainted by the admission of purchased testimony." 15 F. Supp. 2d at 1355. As one district court correctly pointed out, however, "the disclosure of the plea agreements to defense before trial, cross-examination of cooperating witnesses, and jury instructions all provide opportunity to ferret out false testimony that an interested witness might give because of a government promise." United States v. Reid, 19 F. Supp. 2d 534, 537 (E.D. Va. 1998). . . .

III. Conclusion

For the foregoing reasons, the conviction of Robert Ware, Jr., is affirmed.

[Concurring opinion of Wellford, Circuit Judge, omitted.]

Notes and Questions

1. What are the full implications of the rationale in *Singleton I*? Would prosecutors violate § 201 by hiring expert witnesses to testify? By paying the expenses of witnesses who lived outside the jurisdiction? Could a court appoint and compensate an expert witness with impunity?

2. Sitting en banc, the Tenth Circuit rejected the panel opinion's rationale in *Singleton I* and ruled that § 201 does not apply to federal prosecutors who offer leniency in exchange for a cooperating witness's testimony. United States v. Singleton, 165 F.3d 1297 (10th Cir. 1999) (*Singleton II*).

3. To what extent do *Ware* and *Singleton II* immunize a prosecutor's conduct from the reach of § 201? Suppose two of the government's key witnesses were reluctant to testify. Neither was suspected of criminal wrongdoing, so a plea bargain was not an available inducement to testify. Could the prosecutor offer each of them $500 to appear as witnesses? Is the $500 inducement qualitatively different from a five-year reduction in sentence?

4. Now suppose a key witness is a prime suspect in a criminal investigation. What if the prosecutor promises not to prosecute if the witness will embellish his testimony to make the government's case look stronger? If the witness agrees to testify to facts beyond his knowledge, is the prosecutor's conduct within the reach of § 201?

5. Most of the discussion in *Ware* and *Singleton II* centers on the proper scope of the term "whoever." Thus, the assumption in both opinions is that an offer of leniency is "anything of value" within the contemplation of the statute. Can an argument be made that a decision to forgo prosecution or to secure a reduced sentence is not a thing of value under § 201? Cf. United States v. Condon, 170 F.3d 687 (7th Cir. 1999).

UNITED STATES v. IHNATENKO
482 F.3d 1097 (9th Cir. 2007)

TALLMAN, Circuit Judge.

Mykola Ihnatenko and Mykhailo Yurchenko appeal their convictions for conspiracy to possess cocaine aboard a vessel subject to the jurisdiction of the United States and possession of cocaine with intent to distribute aboard a vessel subject to the jurisdiction of the United States. . . .

II

Appellants contend that the government violated 18 U.S.C. § 201(c)(2) in providing compensation in exchange for the cooperation of a witness, Rene Franco-Zapata (Franco). The district court rejected this argument. We affirm.

Franco received three types of benefits in exchange for his agreement to testify on behalf of the government. These benefits include: (1) cash payments to housing providers and to him and his family in excess of $200,000 over a fifteen-month period; (2) promises not to prosecute him or his daughter for any drug crimes; and (3) provision of resident alien cards allowing Franco and his family to live and work in this country. We have previously held that § 201(c)(2) does not prohibit the government from providing immigration benefits or immunity from prosecution to a cooperating witness. See United States v. Feng, 277 F.3d 1151, 1154 (9th Cir. 2002) (immigration benefits); United States v. Smith, 196 F.3d 1034, 1038-40 (9th Cir. 1999) (immunity); see also United States v. Mattarolo, 209 F.3d 1153, 1160 (9th Cir. 2000) (leniency).

Thus, the only issue we must decide is whether the government's provision of cash benefits or government-paid housing to a cooperating witness violates § 201(c)(2) and warrants a new trial. . . .

Paid informants play a vital role in the government's infiltration and prosecution of major organized crime and drug syndicates like this one. We have recognized that

> our criminal justice system could not adequately function without information provided by informants and without their sworn testimony in certain cases. . . . [I]t is a well-known phenomen[on] that the higher-ups in criminal enterprises attempt to insulate themselves from detection and exposure by having their unlawful schemes carried out by others. Without informants, law enforcement authorities would be unable to penetrate and destroy organized crime syndicates, drug trafficking cartels, bank frauds, telephone solicitation scams, public corruption, terrorist gangs, money launderers, espionage rings, and the likes. . . .

United States v. Bernal-Obeso, 989 F.2d 331, 334-35 (9th Cir. 1993). Recognizing the important contribution of cooperating witnesses and informants in our criminal justice system — and the substantial danger that such persons face from retaliation — Congress authorized in the Witness Security Reform Act multiple forms of government assistance, including relocation, housing, and payment to meet basic living expenses. See 18 U.S.C. § 3521(b)(1). Such compensation is necessary to assure the safety of those who turn against their former compatriots in the underworld.

We today join our sister circuits and hold that 18 U.S.C. § 201(c)(2) does not prohibit the government from paying fees, housing, expenses, and cash rewards to any cooperating witness, so long as the payment does not recompense any corruption of the truth of testimony. See *Smith,* 196 F.3d at 1039 n.5 (noting that "18 U.S.C. § 201(c)(2) might apply to a wayward prosecutor who bribes a witness to lie on the stand"). In reaching this conclusion we stress, as did the Third and Fourth Circuits, that "'a defendant's right to be apprised of the government's compensation arrangement with the witness, and to inquire about it on cross-examination, must be vigorously protected.'" United States v. Harris, 210 F.3d 165, 167 (3d Cir. 2000). The district court did so here, and Franco was exhaustively cross-examined on these benefits by eight defense lawyers in their efforts to discredit him.

In addition, we note that, even if appellants had proven a violation of § 201(c)(2), they would not be entitled to a new trial under that statute. *Smith,* 196 F.3d at 1040 (recognizing that the only remedy authorized by § 201(c)(2) is criminal prosecution of the prosecutor, leading to imprisonment or fine). It is not a rule of exclusion that may be invoked by defendants to thwart their criminal prosecutions.

Affirmed.

Notes and Questions

1. The cooperating witness in *Ihnatenko* received cash benefits exceeding $200,000, immunity from prosecution, and immigration assistance. Does this go beyond what the court in *Ware* said was permissible under § 201(c)(2)?

2. Is it troubling that in addition to approving substantial housing assistance and living expenses, the court in *Ihnatenko* condoned giving cooperating witnesses cash rewards? At what point does a "reward" become indistinguishable from a bribe?

3. Suppose a key witness refuses to testify at a major drug trial unless the prosecutor gives her $100,000 in cash. If the prosecutor meets her demand, has he violated § 201(c)(2)?

4. Suppose that after the key witness receives the $100,000, she testifies at trial and the Drug Kingpin is convicted largely on the basis of her testimony. Suppose further that the payment is later determined to have been a bribe. What is the remedy?

III. FEDERAL PROGRAM BRIBERY

In 1984 Congress enacted the federal program bribery statute, 18 U.S.C. § 666, which prohibits payoffs to state and local officials who are agents of an organization or government entity that receives more than $10,000 in federal funds in any one-year period. In enacting this provision, Congress intended "to create new offenses to supplement the ability of the United States to vindicate significant acts of theft, fraud, and bribery involving Federal monies that are disbursed to private organizations or State and local governments pursuant to a Federal program."[18] Violations of § 666 are punishable by a maximum term of ten years' imprisonment and/or a fine of up to $250,000.

SALINAS v. UNITED STATES
522 U.S. 52 (1997)

Justice KENNEDY delivered the opinion of the Court. . . .

I

This federal prosecution arose from a bribery scheme operated by Brigido Marmolejo, the Sheriff of Hidalgo County, Texas, and petitioner Mario Salinas, one of his principal deputies. In 1984, the United States Marshals Service and Hidalgo County entered into agreements under which the county would take custody of federal prisoners. In exchange, the Federal Government agreed to make a grant to the county for improving its jail and also agreed to pay the county a specific amount per day for each federal prisoner housed. Based on the estimated number of federal prisoners to be maintained, payments to the county were projected to be $915,785 per year. The record before us does not disclose the precise amounts paid. It is uncontested, however, that in each of the two periods relevant in this case the program resulted in federal payments to the county well in excess of the $10,000 amount necessary for coverage under

---

18. S. Rep. No. 98-225, at 369 (1984), reprinted in 1984 U.S.C.C.A.N. 3182, 3510. Although § 666(a)(1)(A) reaches various forms of theft, embezzlement, and fraud, the material included in this section of Chapter 9 focuses exclusively on the bribery provision, § 666(a)(1)(B), (a)(2).

18 U.S.C. § 666. (We denied certiorari on the question whether the monies paid to the county were "benefits" under a "Federal program" under § 666(b), and we assume for purposes of this opinion that the payments fit those definitions.)

Homero Beltran-Aguirre was one of the federal prisoners housed in the jail under the arrangement negotiated between the Marshals Service and the county. He was incarcerated there for two intervals, first for 10 months and then for 5 months. During both custody periods, Beltran paid Marmolejo a series of bribes in exchange for so-called "contact visits" in which he remained alone with his wife or, on other occasions, his girlfriend. Beltran paid Marmolejo a fixed rate of six thousand dollars per month and one thousand dollars for each contact visit, which occurred twice a week. Petitioner Salinas was the chief deputy responsible for managing the jail and supervising custody of the prisoners. When Marmolejo was not available, Salinas arranged for the contact visits and on occasion stood watch outside the room where the visits took place. In return for his assistance with the scheme, Salinas received from Beltran a pair of designer watches and a pickup truck.

Salinas and Marmolejo were indicted and tried together, but only Salinas' convictions are before us. Salinas was charged with one count of violating RICO, 18 U.S.C. § 1962(c), one count of conspiracy to violate RICO, § 1962(d), and two counts of bribery in violation of § 666(a)(1)(B). The jury acquitted Salinas on the substantive RICO count but convicted him on the RICO conspiracy count and the bribery counts. A divided panel of the Court of Appeals for the Fifth Circuit affirmed. . . .

II

Salinas contends the Government must prove the bribe in some way affected federal funds, for instance by diverting or misappropriating them, before the bribe violates § 666(a)(1)(B). The relevant statutory provisions are as follows:

> (a) Whoever, if the circumstance described in subsection (b) of this section exists —
>
> (1) being an agent of an organization, or of a State, local, or Indian tribal government, or any agency thereof — . . .
>
>> (B) corruptly . . . accepts or agrees to accept, anything of value from any person, intending to be influenced or rewarded in connection with any business, transaction, or series of transactions of such organization, government, or agency involving any thing of value of $5,000 or more . . .
>
> shall be fined under this title, imprisoned not more than 10 years, or both.
>
> (b) The circumstance referred to in subsection (a) of this section is that the organization, government, or agency receives, in any one year period, benefits in excess of $10,000 under a Federal program involving a grant, contract, subsidy, loan, guarantee, insurance, or other form of Federal assistance. . . .
>
> (d) As used in this section — . . .
>
>> (5) the term "in any one-year period" means a continuous period that commences no earlier than twelve months before the commission of the offense or that ends no later than twelve months after the commission of the offense. Such period may include time both before and after the commission of the offense.

The enactment's expansive, unqualified language, both as to the bribes forbidden and the entities covered, does not support the interpretation that federal funds must be affected to violate § 666(a)(1)(B). Subject to the five-thousand-dollar threshold for the business or transaction in question, the statute forbids acceptance of a bribe by a covered official who intends "to be influenced or rewarded in connection with any business, transaction, or series of transactions of [the defined] organization, government or agency." § 666(a)(1)(B). The prohibition is not confined to a business or transaction which affects federal funds. The word "any," which prefaces the business or transaction clause, undercuts the attempt to impose this narrowing construction.

Furthermore, the broad definition of the "circumstances" to which the statute applies provides no textual basis for limiting the reach of the bribery prohibition. The statute applies to all cases in which an "organization, government, or agency" receives the statutory amount of benefits under a federal program. The language reaches the scheme alleged, and proved, here.

Neither does the statute limit the type of bribe offered. It prohibits accepting or agreeing to accept "anything of value." The phrase encompasses all transfers of personal property or other valuable consideration in exchange for the influence or reward. It includes, then, the personal property given to Salinas in exchange for the favorable treatment Beltran secured for himself. The statute's plain language fails to provide any basis for the limiting § 666(a)(1)(B) to bribes affecting federal funds. . . .

The construction Salinas seeks cannot stand when viewed in light of the statutory framework in existence before § 666 was enacted and the expanded coverage prescribed by the new statute. Before § 666 was enacted, the federal criminal code contained a single, general bribery provision codified at 18 U.S.C. § 201. Section 201 by its terms applied only to "public official[s]," which the statute defined as "officer[s] or employee[s] or person[s] acting for or on behalf of the United States, or any department, agency or branch of Government thereof, including the District of Columbia, in any official function, under or by authority of any such department, agency, or branch." The Courts of Appeals divided over whether state and local employees could be considered "public officials" under § 201(a). Compare United States v. Del Toro, 513 F.2d 656, 661-662 (CA2 1975), with United States v. Mosley, 659 F.2d 812, 814-816 (CA7 1981), and United States v. Hinton, 683 F.2d 195, 197-200 (CA7 1982), aff'd sub nom. Dixson v. United States, 465 U.S. 482 (1984). Without awaiting this Court's resolution of the issue in *Dixson*, Congress enacted § 666 and made it clear that federal law applies to bribes of the kind offered to the state and local officials in *Del Toro*, as well as those at issue in *Mosley* and *Hinton*.

As this chronology and the statutory language demonstrate, § 666(a)(1)(B) was designed to extend federal bribery prohibitions to bribes offered to state and local officials employed by agencies receiving federal funds. It would be incongruous to restrict § 666 in the manner Salinas suggests. The facts and reasoning of *Del Toro* give particular instruction in this respect. In that case, the Second Circuit held that a city employee was not a "public official" under § 201(a) even though federal funds would eventually cover 100% of the costs and 80% of the salaries of the program he administered. *Del Toro*, 513 F.2d at 662. Because the program had not yet entered a formal request for federal funding, the Second Circuit reasoned, "[t]here were no existing committed federal funds for the purpose." Ibid. The enactment of § 666 forecloses this type of limitation. Acceptance of Salinas' suggestion that a bribe must affect federal

funds before it falls within § 666(a)(1)(B) would run contrary to the statutory expansion that redressed the negative effects of the Second Circuit's narrow construction of
§ 201 in *Del Toro*. We need not consider whether the statute requires some other kind
of connection between a bribe and the expenditure of federal funds, for in this case the
bribe was related to the housing of a prisoner in facilities paid for in significant part by
federal funds themselves. And that relationship is close enough to satisfy whatever
connection the statute might require. . . .

The judgment of the Court of Appeals is affirmed.

Notes and Questions

1. What is the federal government's interest in criminalizing the conduct in
Salinas? Is it strong enough to justify a statute that reaches virtually every state and
local government employee in the country? Does § 666 put prosecutors in the business
of enforcing federal standards of "good government" at the state and local levels?

2. What is the purpose of the requirement that the bribery involve an agent of an
organization or governmental agency that receives more than $10,000 in federal assis-
tance? Is the Court's holding that the bribery need not affect federal funds consistent
with it?

3. To what extent do § 201 and § 666 overlap? If § 666 had been on the books at
the time, could the prosecutor have charged the defendants in *Dixson* with federal
program bribery?

4. Could the government have prosecuted Salinas and the sheriff under § 201
using *Dixson*'s "federal official" test?

5. From a prosecutor's perspective, when would it be advantageous to charge a
violation of § 666 rather than § 201? To charge a violation of § 201 rather than § 666?

6. Should § 666 be construed to reach the payment or acceptance of gratuities as
well as bribes?[19]

UNITED STATES v. DeLAURENTIS
230 F.3d 659 (3d Cir. 2000)

FULLAM, District Judge.

The government appeals from the district court's pretrial dismissal of two counts
of an indictment. . . .

The two dismissed counts charged the defendant James V. DeLaurentis, the
Supervisor of Detectives for the Hammonton Police Department, in Hammonton, New
Jersey, with violations of 18 U.S.C. § 666 (theft or bribery involving programs
receiving federal funds). The dismissal was based upon the district court's conclusion
that the government's evidence did not suffice to show a nexus between the alleged
bribes and any federal interest or program, under the standards set forth in this court's
recent decision in United States v. Zwick, 199 F.3d 672 (3d Cir. 1999). We conclude
that the order appealed from must be reversed. . . .

---

19. Cf. United States v. Jennings, 160 F.3d 1006 (4th Cir. 1998); United States v. Bonito, 57 F.3d
167 (2d Cir. 1995).

[I]t is our view that the district judge misapplied the substantive law, as clarified in the *Zwick* case. On this issue, we labor under the same handicap as the district court, namely, the fact that there has not yet been a trial, hence no actual assessment of the government's evidence can be made. In the interest of providing guidance to the district court for the future conduct of the trial, however, we consider it appropriate to register our firm conclusion that, if the government's evidence is to the same effect as the parties and the district court have thus far assumed it will be, it would suffice to permit a jury to convict the defendant of violating 18 U.S.C. § 666.

The statute criminalizes bribery committed by "an agent . . . of a State, local, or Indian tribal government, or any agency thereof . . . in connection with any business, transaction, or series of transactions of such . . . government[,] or agency involving anything of value of $5,000 or more . . . ," but only if

> the organization, government, or agency receives, in any one year period, benefits in excess of $10,000 under a Federal program involving a grant, contract, subsidy, loan, guarantee, insurance, or other form of Federal assistance.

It is undisputed that the defendant was, at all relevant times, the Supervisor of Detectives in the Hammonton, New Jersey, Police Department, and was thus an agent of a local government or agency. It is also undisputed that the town of Hammonton was the recipient of federal funds, amounting to at least $25,000 per year for a three-year period. A literal reading of the statute would suggest that, if the defendant solicited or accepted bribes to influence or reward him in the performance of his police duties, he would be subject to punishment under the statute. But, as this court decided in United States v. Zwick, and as other courts have also determined, the literal language of the statute must be considered in conjunction with the concepts of federalism embodied in our Constitution. For a conviction under § 666, therefore, the evidence must show some connection between the defendant's bribery activities and the funds supplied by the federal government, or the programs supported by those federal funds.

In United States v. Zwick, this court undertook an exhaustive review of the judicial decisions which have addressed the somewhat elusive definition of the required nexus. That discussion need not be repeated here. We concluded that, although it is not necessary to show that the bribery activities of the defendant actually impacted the federal funds themselves, or had a direct bearing on the expenditure of those funds, it must appear that there is some connection between the bribery activities and a federal interest. In the *Zwick* case itself, the federal funds consisted of a small disaster relief fund which was used for snow-removal and flood-control. The bribery occurred in connection with developers being granted sewer access permits and landscaping contracts which, so far as the evidence disclosed, were totally unrelated to the federal grant or the activities funded by the federal grant. The court set aside the conviction, but remanded for a new trial to afford the government an opportunity to attempt to show such a connection. (The trial judge had ruled that no such connection need be shown.)

In the present case, the defendant was the Supervisor of Detectives, and among his other duties he was assigned to assist the New Jersey Division of Alcoholic Beverage Control in the enforcement of the state alcoholic beverage laws, under the supervision of the chief of police, who was the defendant's father. The federal funds were received from the Department of Justice under the Community Oriented Policing Services Program ("COPS Fast"), and were used by the Hammonton Police Department to pay the salary of an additional police officer (who happened to be the defendant's brother) for street patrol duties.

The indictment charges that the defendant accepted bribes for interceding with the town council to permit renewal of the license of a particular bar which had been the focus of much police activity because of fighting, drug sales, disorderly conduct, underage drinking, public drunkenness, public urination, public lewdness, etc.

The evidence outlined by the government would permit a rational jury to conclude that the defendant's successful intercession enabled this problem establishment to remain open, necessitating a disproportionate allocation of police manpower, to the detriment of street patrol activities elsewhere in the town. Indeed, the official records submitted by the government purport to show that, on several occasions, the very same officer whose salary is being paid with federal funds was dispatched to this problem bar to quell disturbances or make arrests.

Thus, this case differs markedly from the *Zwick* situation. It more nearly resembles Salinas v. United States, 522 U.S. 52 (1997). In that case, the federal government provided funds for physical improvements to a state prison, and paid a per diem fee for each federal prisoner housed there. A corrections officer accepted bribes to permit a federal prisoner to have conjugal visits. The Supreme Court had no difficulty in concluding that the defendant was properly convicted under § 666.

When it supplied the town of Hammonton with $75,000 to strengthen its police patrols, the federal government had a legitimate interest in discouraging police corruption affecting the patrol activities it was financing. There is no Constitutional impediment to applying § 666 in this case.

The district court's order dismissing Counts Two and Six of the indictment is vacated, and this case is remanded for trial on all counts of the indictment.

Notes and Questions

1. A post-*Salinas* split of authority developed on the question of what relationship, if any, must exist between the illegal conduct and the federal funding. What federalism concerns led the courts in *DeLaurentis* and *Zwick* to require a nexus between the bribe and the federal program? Is the holding in *DeLaurentis* consistent with *Salinas*?

2. What factual distinctions led the court to conclude that the required nexus between the bribery and the federal funds was satisfied in *DeLaurentis* but was lacking in *Zwick*? Is the Third Circuit's standard likely to promote consistency in future judicial decisions?

SABRI v. UNITED STATES
541 U.S. 600 (2004)

Justice SOUTER delivered the opinion of the Court. . . .

I

Petitioner Basim Omar Sabri is a real estate developer who proposed to build a hotel and retail structure in the city of Minneapolis. Sabri lacked confidence, however, in his ability to adapt to the lawful administration of licensing and zoning laws, and offered three separate bribes to a city councilman, Brian Herron, according to the grand jury indictment that gave rise to this case. At the time the bribes were allegedly offered (between July 2, 2001, and July 17, 2001), Herron served as a member of the Board of Commissioners of the Minneapolis Community Development Agency (MCDA), a public body created by the city council to fund housing and economic development within the city.

Count 1 of the indictment charged Sabri with offering a $5,000 kickback for obtaining various regulatory approvals, and according to Count 2, Sabri offered Herron a $10,000 bribe to set up and attend a meeting with owners of land near the site Sabri had in mind, at which Herron would threaten to use the city's eminent domain authority to seize their property if they were troublesome to Sabri. Count 3 alleged that Sabri offered Herron a commission of 10% on some $800,000 in community economic development grants that Sabri sought from the city, the MCDA, and other sources.

The charges were brought under 18 U.S.C. § 666(a)(2), which imposes federal criminal penalties on anyone who

> corruptly gives, offers, or agrees to give anything of value to any person, with intent to influence or reward an agent of an organization or of a State, local or Indian tribal government, or any agency thereof, in connection with any business, transaction, or series of transactions of such organization, government, or agency involving anything of value of $5,000 or more.

For criminal liability to lie, the statute requires that

> the organization, government, or agency receiv[e], in any one year period, benefits in excess of $10,000 under a Federal program involving a grant, contract, subsidy, loan, guarantee, insurance, or other form of Federal assistance. § 666(b).

In 2001, the City Council of Minneapolis administered about $29 million in federal funds paid to the city, and in the same period, the MCDA received some $23 million of federal money.

Before trial, Sabri moved to dismiss the indictment on the ground that § 666(a)(2) is unconstitutional on its face for failure to require proof of a connection between the federal funds and the alleged bribe, as an element of liability. [T]he District Court agreed with him that the law was facially invalid. A divided panel of the Eighth Circuit reversed, holding that there was nothing fatal in the absence of an express requirement to prove some connection between a given bribe and federally pedigreed dollars, and that the statute was constitutional under the Necessary and Proper Clause in serving the objects of the congressional spending power. Judge Bye dissented out of concern about the implications of the law for dual sovereignty.

We granted certiorari to resolve a split among the Courts of Appeals over the need to require connection between forbidden conduct and federal funds. We now affirm.

II

Sabri raises what he calls a facial challenge to § 666(a)(2): the law can never be applied constitutionally because it fails to require proof of any connection between a bribe or kickback and some federal money. It is fatal, as he sees it, that the statute does not make the link an element of the crime, to be charged in the indictment and demonstrated beyond a reasonable doubt. Thus, Sabri claims his attack meets the demanding standard set out in United States v. Salerno, 481 U.S. 739, 745 (1987), since he says no prosecution can satisfy the Constitution under this statute, owing to its failure to require proof that its particular application falls within Congress's jurisdiction to legislate.

We can readily dispose of this position that, to qualify as a valid exercise of Article I power, the statute must require proof of connection with federal money as an element of the offense. We simply do not presume the unconstitutionality of federal criminal statutes lacking explicit provision of a jurisdictional hook, and there is no occasion even to consider the need for such a requirement where there is no reason to suspect that enforcement of a criminal statute would extend beyond a legitimate interest cognizable under Article I, § 8.

Congress has authority under the Spending Clause to appropriate federal monies to promote the general welfare, Art. I, § 8, cl. 1, and it has corresponding authority under the Necessary and Proper Clause, Art. I, § 8, cl. 18, to see to it that taxpayer dollars appropriated under that power are in fact spent for the general welfare, and not frittered away in graft or on projects undermined when funds are siphoned off or corrupt public officers are derelict about demanding value for dollars. Congress does not have to sit by and accept the risk of operations thwarted by local and state improbity. Section 666(a)(2) addresses the problem at the sources of bribes, by rational means, to safeguard the integrity of the state, local, and tribal recipients of federal dollars.

It is true, just as Sabri says, that not every bribe or kickback offered or paid to agents of governments covered by § 666(b) will be traceably skimmed from specific federal payments, or show up in the guise of a quid pro quo for some dereliction in spending a federal grant. Cf. Salinas v. United States, 522 U.S. 52, 56-57 (1997) (The "expansive, unqualified" language of the statute "does not support the interpretation that federal funds must be affected to violate § 666(a)(1)(B)"). But this possibility portends no enforcement beyond the scope of federal interest, for the reason that corruption does not have to be that limited to affect the federal interest. Money is fungible, bribed officials are untrustworthy stewards of federal funds, and corrupt contractors do not deliver dollar-for-dollar value. Liquidity is not a financial term for nothing; money can be drained off here because a federal grant is pouring in there. And officials are not any the less threatening to the objects behind federal spending just because they may accept general retainers. It is certainly enough that the statutes condition the offense on a threshold amount of federal dollars defining the federal interest, such as that provided here, and on a bribe that goes well beyond liquor and cigars.

For those of us who accept help from legislative history, it is worth noting that the legislative record confirms that § 666(a)(2) is an instance of necessary and proper legislation. The design was generally to "protect the integrity of the vast sums of money distributed through Federal programs from theft, fraud, and undue influence by bribery," see S. Rep. No. 98-225, p. 370 (1983), in contrast to prior federal law affording only two limited opportunities to prosecute such threats to the federal interest: 18 U.S.C. § 641, the federal theft statute, and § 201, the federal bribery law. Those laws had proven inadequate to the task. The former went only to outright theft of unadulterated federal funds, and prior to this Court's opinion in Dixson v. United States, 465 U.S. 482 (1984), which came after passage of § 666, the bribery statute had been interpreted by lower courts to bar prosecution of bribes directed at state and local officials. Thus we said that § 666 "was designed to extend federal bribery prohibitions to bribes offered to state and local officials employed by agencies receiving federal funds," thereby filling the regulatory gaps. Congress's decision to enact § 666 only after other legislation had failed to protect federal interests is further indication that it was acting within the ambit of the Necessary and Proper Clause.

Petitioner presses two more particular arguments against the constitutionality of § 666(a)(2), neither of which helps him. First, he says that § 666 is all of a piece with the legislation that a majority of this Court held to exceed Congress's authority under the Commerce Clause in United States v. Lopez, 514 U.S. 549 (1995), and United States v. Morrison, 529 U.S. 598 (2000). But these precedents do not control here. In *Lopez* and *Morrison*, the Court struck down federal statutes regulating gun possession near schools and gender-motivated violence, respectively, because it found the effects of those activities on interstate commerce insufficiently robust. The Court emphasized the noneconomic nature of the regulated conduct, commenting on the law at issue in *Lopez*, for example, "that by its terms [it] has nothing to do with 'commerce' or any sort of economic enterprise, however broadly one might define those terms." 514 U.S., at 561. The Court rejected the Government's contentions that the gun law was valid Commerce Clause legislation because guns near schools ultimately bore on social prosperity and productivity, reasoning that on that logic, Commerce Clause authority would effectively know no limit. In order to uphold the legislation, the Court concluded, it would be necessary "to pile inference upon inference in a manner that would bid fair to convert congressional authority under the Commerce Clause to a general police power of the sort retained by the States." *Lopez,* 514 U.S., at 567.

No piling is needed here to show that Congress was within its prerogative to protect spending objects from the menace of local administrators on the take. The power to keep a watchful eye on expenditures and on the reliability of those who use public money is bound up with congressional authority to spend in the first place, and Sabri would be hard pressed to claim, in the words of the *Lopez* Court, that § 666(a)(2) "has nothing to do with" the congressional spending power. Id., at 561.

Sabri next argues that § 666(a)(2) amounts to an unduly coercive, and impermissibly sweeping, condition on the grant of federal funds as judged under the criterion applied in South Dakota v. Dole, 483 U.S. 203 (1987). This is not so. Section 666(a)(2) is authority to bring federal power to bear directly on individuals who convert public spending into unearned private gain, not a means for bringing federal economic might to bear on a State's own choices of public policy.[20] . . .

. . . The judgment of the Court of Appeals for the Eighth Circuit is affirmed.

[Concurring opinions by KENNEDY, J., and THOMAS, J., omitted.]

---

20. In enacting § 666, Congress addressed a legitimate federal concern by licensing federal prosecution in an area historically of state concern. In upholding the constitutionality of the law, we mean to express no view as to its soundness as a policy matter.

Notes and Questions

1. What federal interests justify the conclusion that § 666 is a legitimate exercise of congressional power? Could Congress have addressed those concerns differently by requiring states that receive federal funding to prosecute the types of corruption that § 666 prohibits? If so, why would Congress choose to federalize this species of bribery?

2. The Court discounts the defendant's argument that § 666 exceeds congressional authority under *Lopez* and *Morrison*. How does *Sabri* differ from those cases?

3. How does the Supreme Court's approach in *Sabri* differ from the Third Circuit's approach in *DeLaurentis*?

4. Does the holding in *Sabri* mean that there are no constitutional limits on the scope of § 666? Could a court properly hold that there must be a nexus between the bribe and the agency that receives federal funds? That the agency must directly receive federal funding?[21]

5. The Court in *Sabri* said that "[m]oney is fungible" and "can be drained off here because a federal grant is pouring in there." What does the Court mean? Can § 666 now be read to extend to the corruption of an agent of Local Agency A, which does not receive federal funds, because Local Agency B receives federal assistance? Stated differently, does *Sabri* answer the question whether § 666 would apply in the following contexts?

   a. D bribes a city meat inspector who works for an agency that does not receive federal funds. The city parks department receives more than $10,000 in federal funds a year.[22]

   b. D, an auto mechanic, offers a public high school principal unlimited free car repairs if the principal will hire him to teach shop.[23]

   c. D bribes a city official to eliminate taxes on real estate that D owns. The city receives substantial federal funds.[24]

6. After *Sabri*, could Congress make it a crime to rob welfare recipients?

UNITED STATES v. COPELAND
143 F.3d 1439 (11th Cir. 1998)

BLACK, Circuit Judge.

Appellants Virgil M. Copeland and John J. Winders appeal their convictions for accepting and making illegal kickbacks and bribes and for filing false tax returns. We vacate their convictions for bribery under 18 U.S.C. § 666 and § 2, but affirm their convictions on all other counts.

---

21. Cf. United States v. Shelton, 99 Fed. Appx. 136, 141 (9th Cir. 2004) (unpublished); United States v. Jackson, 313 F.3d 231 (5th Cir. 2002); United States v. Moeller, 987 F.2d 1134, 1137 (5th Cir. 1993).
22. Cf. United States v. Santopietro, 166 F.3d 88, 98 (2d Cir. 1999).
23. Cf. United States v. Sabri, 326 F.3d 937, 956 (8th Cir. 2003) (Bye, J., dissenting).
24. Cf. United States v. Brunshtein, 344 F.3d 91, 97-98 (2d Cir. 2003).

I. BACKGROUND

From the early 1980s until 1992, Appellant Virgil M. Copeland served as a manager in the Facilities Operations Division of the Marietta, Georgia, plant of Lockheed Aeronautical Systems Company (Lockheed). Copeland's responsibilities at Lockheed included finding off-site space for Lockheed to lease, arranging for the relocation of transferred Lockheed executives, and choosing contractors to perform building, maintenance, and repair projects.

Appellant John J. Winders was a licensed real estate appraiser and broker who assisted Lockheed in acquiring real estate and off-site lease premises. Winders and Copeland have been friends for over 20 years, and between 1991 and 1994, Winders earned approximately $100,000 in commissions from Lockheed-related business that Copeland referred to him.

Appellants' convictions stem from their involvement in a series of transactions in which Copeland improperly referred work to Winders and agreed on behalf of Lockheed to pay abnormally high commissions to Winders. In return, Winders paid Copeland approximately $15,000. In addition to his dealings with Winders, Copeland accepted payments from Robert Sherwood, a self-employed contractor to whom Copeland awarded several Lockheed construction projects, and William Mann, the owner of several contracting and construction companies that performed work for Lockheed.

Following a jury trial, Copeland was convicted of five counts of accepting kickbacks, in violation of 41 U.S.C. §§ 52-54, five counts of bribery, in violation of 18 U.S.C. § 666 and § 2, and three counts of filing false tax returns, in violation of 26 U.S.C. § 7206(1). Winders was convicted under the same statutory provisions of three counts of providing kickbacks, three counts of bribery, and one count of filing a false tax return.

On appeal, Appellants assert, among other claims, that the Government failed to prove the statutory prerequisites of 18 U.S.C. § 666. We agree, and therefore vacate the Defendants' bribery convictions and remand to the district court for resentencing consistent with this opinion.

II. DISCUSSION

The Anti-Bribery Act, 18 U.S.C. § 666, prohibits the unlawful acceptance or offering of anything of value of $5,000 or more, if the person taking the bribe is an agent of an organization subject to the statute. Whether an organization falls within the scope of the statute is determined pursuant to § 666(b), which provides:

> The circumstance referred to in subsection (a) of this section is that the organization, government, or agency receives, in any one year period, benefits in excess of $10,000 under a Federal program involving a grant, contract, subsidy, loan, guarantee, insurance, or other form of Federal assistance.

In the present case, the Government alleges that Lockheed is an organization within the scope of the statute because it is a prime contractor for the United States

Department of Defense. In response, Appellants argue that a quid pro quo contractual relationship does not satisfy the requirements of § 666(b). . . .

Section 666(b) provides that the benefits an organization receives under a federal program can be in the form of a grant, *contract*, subsidy, loan, guarantee, insurance, or other form of Federal *assistance*." A straightforward reading of this text indicates that § 666(b) encompasses many situations in which the government receives consideration in return for federal assistance. See United States v. Marmolejo, 89 F.3d 1185, 1189-91 (5th Cir. 1996) (applying § 666 to a county jail that received federal assistance in exchange for housing federal inmates), affirmed in part sub nom. Salinas v. United States, 118 S. Ct. 469 (1997); *Rooney*, 986 F.2d at 33-35 (holding that a government sponsored loan qualified as a benefit under a federal program, even though the recipient was required to repay the entire loan plus interest).

The scope of § 666, however, is not limitless; the statute clearly indicates that only those contractual relationships constituting some form of "Federal assistance" fall within the scope of the statute. Thus, organizations engaged in purely commercial transactions with the federal government are not subject to § 666.

Having reached this conclusion based on a plain reading of § 666(b), we normally would not engage in any additional analysis. However, since some circuits have found § 666(b) to be ambiguous on its face, it is worth noting that our conclusion is consistent with the statute's legislative history, which provides in part:

> [T]he term "Federal program involving a grant, a contract, a subsidy, a loan, a guarantee, insurance, or another form of Federal assistance" [is to] be construed broadly, consistent with the purpose of this section to protect the integrity of the vast sums of money distributed through Federal programs from theft, fraud, and undue influence by bribery. However, the concept is not unlimited. The term "Federal program" means that there must exist a specific statutory scheme authorizing the Federal assistance in order to promote or achieve certain policy objectives. Thus, not every Federal contract or disbursement of funds would be covered. For example, if a government agency lawfully purchases more than $10,000 in equipment from a supplier, it is not the intent of this section to make a theft of $5,000 or more from the supplier a Federal crime.

S. Rep. 98-225 at 370 (1984), reprinted in 1984 U.S.C.C.A.N. 3182, 3511. This passage shows that Congress did not intend the statute to apply to the federal government's ordinary commercial transactions.

Based on a plain reading of the statute, we conclude that the Government failed to prove that Lockheed is an organization that receives benefits pursuant to a federal program as required by § 666(b). Nothing in the record indicates that Lockheed receives any form of federal assistance or is in any way engaged in something other than purely commercial transactions with the government. The Government attempts to distinguish defense contracts from other commercial transactions by noting that the government provides Lockheed with detailed specifications for aircraft and that Congress annually appropriates specific sums for aircraft procurement, testing, and research and development. Although these factors make defense contracts unique, they do not show that Lockheed received benefits under a federal program through a contract or any other form of federal assistance. Punishing the Appellants' conduct might further the statute's goal of protecting the integrity of federal funds, but it is not the role of this Court to expand the scope of § 666 to encompass such behavior.

III. CONCLUSION

The Government failed to prove that Lockheed is an organization that received, in any one year period, benefits in excess of $10,000 under a federal program involving a grant, contract, subsidy, loan, guarantee, insurance, or other form of federal assistance. Accordingly, we vacate the Defendants' convictions for bribery under 18 U.S.C. § 666 and § 2, affirm their convictions in all other respects, and remand for resentencing consistent with this opinion. . . .

Notes and Questions

1. As a government contractor, Lockheed received millions of dollars from the federal government. Why isn't this enough to bring it within the reach of the statute? When, if ever, would a corporation constitute an organization covered by § 666? Is it clear what transactions should be deemed "purely commercial"?

2. Apart from commercial enterprises, what kinds of "organizations" that receive federal funding are within the reach of the statute?

3. What kinds of contractual relationships are within the scope of § 666? Suppose there had been no federal grant for jail improvement in *Salinas*, but the jail had a contract with the Federal Bureau of Prisons to house federal prisoners for a per diem fee. Would Salinas and the sheriff have violated § 666? If the Bureau of Prisons entered into a per diem contract with the jail, would it make any difference whether the jail was operated by the county at taxpayer expense or was privately operated by a for-profit corporation?

4. In Fischer v. United States, 529 U.S. 667 (2000), the Court considered what qualifies as a "benefit" under § 666. The Court held that hospitals and other health care providers that participate in the Medicare program receive "benefits," notwithstanding that the elderly and disabled are the primary program beneficiaries.

> . . . To determine whether an organization participating in a federal assistance program receives "benefits," an examination must be undertaken of the program's structure, operation, and purpose. The inquiry should examine the conditions under which the organization receives the federal payments. The answer could depend, as it does here, on whether the recipient's own operations are one of the reasons for maintaining the program. Health care organizations participating in the Medicare program satisfy this standard.
>
> The Government has a legitimate and significant interest in prohibiting financial fraud or acts of bribery being perpetrated upon Medicare providers. Fraudulent acts threaten the program's integrity. They raise the risk participating organizations will lack the resources requisite to provide the level and quality of care envisioned by the program.

Id. at 681-682.

IV. EXTORTION UNDER COLOR OF OFFICIAL RIGHT

Another statute that intersects with § 201 is the Hobbs Act, 18 U.S.C. § 1951. The Hobbs Act prohibits interfering with commerce by robbery or extortion, and it defines extortion to include obtaining the property of another, with his consent, "under color of official right." This prong of the definition clearly contemplates wrongful use of public office, including influence peddling.

EVANS v. UNITED STATES
504 U.S. 255 (1992)

Justice STEVENS delivered the opinion of the Court. . . .

I

Petitioner was an elected member of the Board of Commissioners of DeKalb County, Georgia. During the period between March 1985 and October 1986, as part of an effort by the Federal Bureau of Investigation (FBI) to investigate allegations of public corruption in the Atlanta area, particularly in the area of rezonings of property, an FBI agent posing as a real estate developer talked on the telephone and met with petitioner on a number of occasions. Virtually all, if not all, of those conversations were initiated by the agent and most were recorded on tape or video. In those conversations, the agent sought petitioner's assistance in an effort to rezone a 25-acre tract of land for high-density residential use. On July 25, 1986, the agent handed petitioner cash totaling $7,000 and a check, payable to petitioner's campaign, for $1,000. Petitioner reported the check, but not the cash, on his state campaign-financing disclosure form; he also did not report the $7,000 on his 1986 federal income tax return. Viewing the evidence in the light most favorable to the Government, . . . we assume that the jury found that petitioner accepted the cash knowing that it was intended to ensure that he would vote in favor of the rezoning application and that he would try to persuade his fellow commissioners to do likewise. Thus, although petitioner did not initiate the transaction, his acceptance of the bribe constituted an implicit promise to use his official position to serve the interests of the bribegiver.

In a two-count indictment, petitioner was charged with extortion in violation of 18 U.S.C. § 1951 and with failure to report income in violation of 26 U.S.C. § 7206(1). He was convicted by a jury on both counts. With respect to the extortion count, the trial judge gave the following instruction:

> The defendant contends that the $8,000 he received from agent Cormany was a campaign contribution. The solicitation of campaign contributions from any person is a necessary and permissible form of political activity on the part of persons who seek political office and persons who have been elected to political office. Thus, the acceptance by an elected official of a campaign contribution does not, in itself, constitute a violation of the Hobbs Act even though the donor has business pending before the official.

However, if a public official demands or accepts money in exchange for [a] specific requested exercise of his or her official power, such a demand or acceptance does constitute a violation of the Hobbs Act regardless of whether the payment is made in the form of a campaign contribution.

In affirming petitioner's conviction, the Court of Appeals noted that the instruction did not require the jury to find that petitioner had demanded or requested the money, or that he had conditioned the performance of any official act upon its receipt. The Court of Appeals held, however, that "passive acceptance of a benefit by a public official *is* sufficient to form the basis of a Hobbs Act violation if the official knows that he is being offered the payment in exchange for a specific requested exercise of his official power. The official need not take any specific action to induce the offering of the benefit." 910 F.2d 790, 796 (CA11 1990) (emphasis in original).

This statement of the law by the Court of Appeals for the Eleventh Circuit is consistent with holdings in eight other Circuits. Two Circuits, however, have held that an affirmative act of inducement by the public official is required to support a conviction of extortion under color of official right. Because the majority view is consistent with the common-law definition of extortion, which we believe Congress intended to adopt, we endorse that position.

II

It is a familiar "maxim that a statutory term is generally presumed to have its common-law meaning." Taylor v. United States, 495 U.S. 575, 592 (1990). As we have explained: "[W]here Congress borrows terms of art in which are accumulated the legal tradition and meaning of centuries of practice, it presumably knows and adopts the cluster of ideas that were attached to each borrowed word in the body of learning from which it was taken and the meaning its use will convey to the judicial mind unless otherwise instructed. In such case, absence of contrary direction may be taken as satisfaction with widely accepted definitions, not as a departure from them." Morissette v. United States, 342 U.S. 246, 263 (1952).

At common law, extortion was an offense committed by a public official who took "by colour of his office" money that was not due to him for the performance of his official duties. A demand, or request, by the public official was not an element of the offense. Extortion by the public official was the rough equivalent of what we would now describe as "taking a bribe." It is clear that petitioner committed that offense. The question is whether the federal statute, insofar as it applies to official extortion, has narrowed the common-law definition.

Congress has unquestionably *expanded* the common-law definition of extortion to include acts by private individuals pursuant to which property is obtained by means of force, fear, or threats. [The statute provides:]

(2) The term "extortion" means the obtaining of property from another, with his consent, induced by wrongful use of actual or threatened force, violence, or fear, or under color of official right.

18 U.S.C. § 1951. . . .

Although the present statutory text is much broader than the common-law definition of extortion because it encompasses conduct by a private individual as well as conduct by a public official, the portion of the statute that refers to official misconduct continues to mirror the common-law definition. There is nothing in either the statutory text or the legislative history that could fairly be described as a "contrary direction," Morissette v. United States, 342 U.S., at 263, from Congress to narrow the scope of the offense. . . .

The two courts that have disagreed with the decision to apply the common-law definition have interpreted the word "induced" as requiring a wrongful use of official power that "begins with the public official, not with the gratuitous actions of another." United States v. O'Grady, 742 F.2d, at 691; see United States v. Aguon, 851 F.2d at 1166 ("'inducement' can be in the overt form of a 'demand,' or in a more subtle form such as 'custom' or 'expectation'"). If we had no common-law history to guide our interpretation of the statutory text, that reading would be plausible. For two reasons, however, we are convinced that it is incorrect.

First, we think the word "induced" is a part of the definition of the offense by the private individual, but not the offense by the public official. In the case of the private individual, the victim's consent must be "induced by wrongful use of actual or threatened force, violence or fear." In the case of the public official, however, there is no such requirement. The statute merely requires of the public official that he obtain "property from another, with his consent, . . . [or] under color of official right." The use of the word "or" before "under color of official right" supports this reading.

Second, even if the statute were parsed so that the word "induced" applied to the public officeholder, we do not believe the word "induced" necessarily indicates that the transaction must be *initiated* by the recipient of the bribe. Many of the cases applying the majority rule have concluded that the wrongful acceptance of a bribe establishes all the inducement that the statute requires. They conclude that the coercive element is provided by the public office itself. And even the two courts that have adopted an inducement requirement for extortion under color of official right do not require proof that the inducement took the form of a threat or demand.

Petitioner argues that the jury charge with respect to extortion allowed the jury to convict him on the basis of the "passive acceptance of a contribution."[25] He contends that the instruction did not require the jury to find "an element of duress such as a demand," and it did not properly describe the quid pro quo requirement for conviction if the jury found that the payment was a campaign contribution.

We reject petitioner's criticism of the instruction, and conclude that it satisfies the quid pro quo requirement of McCormick v. United States, 500 U.S. 257 (1991), because the offense is completed at the time when the public official receives a payment in return for his agreement to perform specific official acts; fulfillment of the quid pro quo is not an element of the offense. We also reject petitioner's contention that an affirmative step

---

25. Petitioner also makes the point that "[t]he evidence at trial against [petitioner] is more conducive to a charge of bribery than one of extortion." Although the evidence in this case may have supported a charge of bribery, it is not a defense to a charge of extortion under color of official right that the defendant could also have been convicted of bribery. . . .

We agree with the Seventh Circuit in United States v. Braasch, 505 F.2d 139, 151, n.7 (1974), that "'the modern trend of the federal courts is to hold that bribery and extortion as used in the Hobbs Ac[t] are not mutually exclusive. United States v. Kahn, 472 F.2d 272, 278 (2d Cir. 1973).'"

is an element of the offense of extortion "under color of official right" and need be included in the instruction. As we explained above, our construction of the statute is informed by the common-law tradition from which the term of art was drawn and understood. We hold today that the Government need only show that a public official has obtained a payment to which he was not entitled, knowing that the payment was made in return for official acts.[26]

Our conclusion is buttressed by the fact that so many other courts that have considered the issue over the last 20 years have interpreted the statute in the same way. Moreover, given the number of appellate court decisions, together with the fact that many of them have involved prosecutions of important officials well known in the political community, it is obvious that Congress is aware of the prevailing view that common-law extortion is proscribed by the Hobbs Act. The silence of the body that is empowered to give us a "contrary direction" if it does not want the common-law rule to survive is consistent with an application of the normal presumption identified in *Taylor* and *Morissette*. . . .

The judgment is affirmed. . . .

Justice KENNEDY, concurring in part and concurring in the judgment.

The Court gives a summary of its decision in these words: "We hold today that the Government need only show that a public official has obtained a payment to which he was not entitled, knowing that the payment was made in return for official acts." In my view the dissent is correct to conclude that this language requires a quid pro quo as an element of the Government's case in a prosecution under 18 U.S.C. § 1951, and the Court's opinion can be interpreted in a way that is consistent with this rule. Although the Court appears to accept the requirement of a quid pro quo as an alternative rationale, in my view this element of the offense is essential to a determination of those acts which are criminal and those which are not in a case in which the official does not pretend that he is entitled by law to the property in question. Here the prosecution did establish a quid pro quo that embodied the necessary elements of a statutory violation. . . .

With regard to the question whether the word "induced" in the statutory definition of extortion applies to the phrase "under color of official right," I find myself in substantial agreement with the dissent. Scrutiny of the placement of commas will not, in the final analysis, yield a convincing answer, and we are left with two quite plausible interpretations. Under these circumstances, I agree with the dissent that the rule of lenity requires that we avoid the harsher one. We must take as our starting point the assumption that the portion of the statute at issue here defines extortion as "the obtaining of property from another, with his consent, induced . . . under color of official right."

I agree with the Court, on the other hand, that the word "induced" does not "necessarily indicat[e] that the transaction must be *initiated* by the" public official. Something beyond the mere acceptance of property from another is required, however, or else the word "induced" would be superfluous. That something, I submit, is the quid pro quo. The ability of the official to use or refrain from using authority is the "color of

---

26. The dissent states that we have "simply made up" the requirement that the payment must be given in return for official acts. On the contrary, that requirement is derived from the statutory language "under color of official right," which has a well-recognized common-law heritage that distinguished between payments for private services and payments for public services. See, e.g., Collier v. State, 55 Ala. 125 (1877), which the dissent describes as a "typical case."

official right" which can be invoked in a corrupt way to induce payment of money or to otherwise obtain property. The inducement generates a quid pro quo, under color of official right, that the statute prohibits. The term "under color of" is used, as I think both the Court and the dissent agree, to sweep within the statute those corrupt exercises of authority that the law forbids but that nevertheless cause damage because the exercise is by a governmental official.

The requirement of a quid pro quo means that without pretense of any entitlement to the payment, a public official violates § 1951 if he intends the payor to believe that absent payment the official is likely to abuse his office and his trust to the detriment and injury of the prospective payor or to give the prospective payor less favorable treatment if the quid pro quo is not satisfied. The official and the payor need not state the quid pro quo in express terms, for otherwise the law's effect could be frustrated by knowing winks and nods. The inducement from the official is criminal if it is express or if it is implied from his words and actions, so long as he intends it to be so and the payor so interprets it. . . .

The requirement of a quid pro quo in a § 1951 prosecution such as the one before us, in which it is alleged that money was given to the public official in the form of a campaign contribution, was established by our decision last Term in McCormick v. United States, 500 U.S. 257 (1991). Readers of today's opinion should have little difficulty in understanding that the rationale underlying the Court's holding applies not only in campaign contribution cases, but in all § 1951 prosecutions. That is as it should be, for, given a corrupt motive, the quid pro quo, as I have said, is the essence of the offense.

Because I agree that the jury instruction in this case complied with the quid pro quo requirement, I concur in the judgment of the Court.

[Concurrence of Justice O'CONNOR and dissent of Justice THOMAS omitted.]

Notes and Questions

1. Is it clear after *Evans* what the element of inducement requires?

2. What must the government prove to establish extortion under color of official right?

3. The Court in *Evans* noted that McCormick v. United States, 500 U.S. 257 (1991), held that a quid pro quo is required in the context of campaign contributions. Is the quid pro quo requirement limited to cases involving campaign contributions, or does it apply in other contexts as well? Are there sound reasons why campaign contributions might be treated differently from other payments to public officials?[27]

4. Could the government have prosecuted the defendants in *Sun-Diamond Growers* under the Hobbs Act? What is the difference between bribery and extortion?

5. In Scheidler v. National Organization for Women, Inc.,[28] the Court revisited the question of what constitutes "extortion" under the Hobbs Act. *Scheidler* was a civil

---

27. Cf. United States v. Blandford, 33 F.3d 685 (6th Cir. 1994).
28. 537 U.S. 393 (2003).

RICO suit[29] brought by the National Organization for Women against a network of abortion protest organizations and individuals. The protestors' goal was to shut down clinics that provide women's reproductive health services, including abortions. The suit alleged that the protestors violated the Hobbs Act by obstructing access to clinics, trespassing on and damaging clinic property, and using violence or threats of violence against clinic employees and patients. At issue in this appeal was whether the protestors "obtained" property from the clinics by causing losses such as inability to operate their businesses and property damage. Stated differently, did the protestors obtain property by using threats of violence to induce the clinics to "give up" intangible property rights? The Court held they did not.

> There is no dispute in these cases that petitioners interfered with, disrupted, and in some instances completely deprived respondents of their ability to exercise their property rights. Likewise, petitioners' counsel readily acknowledged at oral argument that aspects of his clients' conduct were criminal.[30] But even when their acts of interference and disruption achieved their ultimate goal of "shutting down" a clinic that performed abortions, such acts did not constitute extortion because petitioners did not "obtain" respondents' property. Petitioners may have deprived or sought to deprive respondents of their alleged property right of exclusive control of their business assets, but they did not acquire any such property. Petitioners neither pursued nor received "something of value from" respondents that they could exercise, transfer, or sell. United States v. Nardello, 393 U.S. 286, 290 (1969). To conclude that such actions constituted extortion would effectively discard the statutory requirement that property must be obtained from another, replacing it instead with the notion that merely interfering with or depriving someone of property is sufficient to constitute extortion.[31]

---

29. The RICO issues in the case are considered in Chapter 10.

30. "Question: But are we talking about actions that constitute the commission of some kind of criminal offense in the process? . . ."

"Mr. Englert: Oh yes. Trespass."

"Question: Yes, and other things, destruction of property and so forth, I suppose."

"Mr. Englert: Oh, yes. . . ."

"Question: I mean, we're not talking about conduct that is lawful here."

"Mr. Englert: We are not talking about extortion, but we are talking about some things that could be punished much less severely. It has never been disputed in this case . . . that there were trespasses." Tr. of Oral Arg. 8-9.

31. *Scheidler*, 537 U.S. at 404.

10

RICO

I. INTRODUCTION

RICO — the Racketeer Influenced and Corrupt Organizations Act — was enacted as Title IX of the Omnibus Crime Control Act of 1970. This innovative statute was designed to strike at the economic base of organized crime by imposing severe criminal penalties (including forfeiture of crime-related assets), providing the government with bold civil enforcement powers, and creating a private civil cause of action allowing injured parties to recover treble damages and the cost of suit, including attorneys' fees. Notwithstanding that RICO targets activities traditionally associated with organized crime, Congress defined "racketeering activity" broadly to include white collar crimes such as mail fraud, securities fraud, and bribery. Thus, despite RICO's usefulness as a tool to combat organized crime, prosecutors have come to view the statute as "a significant weapon against white collar . . . criminals" as well.[1]

II. THE ENTERPRISE

RICO's scheme of liability is premised on three discrete types of conduct: (1) investing in an enterprise; (2) acquiring an interest in or maintaining control over an enterprise; and (3) conducting the affairs of an enterprise — through a pattern of racketeering activity. The enterprise element thus is central to every RICO prosecution.

Congress defined the term "enterprise" to include "any individual, partnership, corporation, association, or other legal entity, and any union or group of individuals associated in fact although not a legal entity." 18 U.S.C. § 1961(4). That definition did little, however, to stem the tide of litigation challenging the breadth of the enterprise concept.

---

1. U.S. Dept. of Justice, An Explanation of the Racketeer Influenced and Corrupt Organizations Statute 2 (4th ed.).

UNITED STATES v. TURKETTE
452 U.S. 576 (1981)

Justice WHITE delivered the opinion of the Court. . . .

I

Count Nine of a nine-count indictment charged respondent and 12 others with conspiracy to conduct and participate in the affairs of an enterprise engaged in interstate commerce through a pattern of racketeering activities, in violation of 18 U.S.C. § 1962(d). The indictment described the enterprise as "a group of individuals associated in fact for the purpose of illegally trafficking in narcotics and other dangerous drugs, committing arsons, utilizing the United States mails to defraud insurance companies, bribing and attempting to bribe local police officers, and corruptly influencing and attempting to corruptly influence the outcome of state court proceedings. . . ." The other eight counts of the indictment charged the commission of various substantive criminal acts by those engaged in and associated with the criminal enterprise, including possession with intent to distribute and distribution of controlled substances, and several counts of insurance fraud by arson and other means. The common thread to all counts was respondent's alleged leadership of this criminal organization through which he orchestrated and participated in the commission of the various crimes delineated in the RICO count or charged in the eight preceding counts.

After a 6-week jury trial, in which the evidence focused upon both the professional nature of this organization and the execution of a number of distinct criminal acts, respondent was convicted on all nine counts. He was sentenced to a term of 20 years on the substantive counts, as well as a 2-year special parole term on the drug count. On the RICO conspiracy count he was sentenced to a 20-year concurrent term and fined $20,000.

On appeal, respondent argued that RICO was intended solely to protect legitimate business enterprises from infiltration by racketeers and that RICO does not make criminal the participation in an association which performs only illegal acts and which has not infiltrated or attempted to infiltrate a legitimate enterprise. The Court of Appeals agreed. We reverse.

II

In determining the scope of a statute, we look first to its language. If the statutory language is unambiguous, in the absence of "a clearly expressed legislative intent to the contrary, that language must ordinarily be regarded as conclusive." . . .

Section 1962(c) makes it unlawful "for any person employed by or associated with any enterprise engaged in, or the activities of which affect, interstate or foreign commerce, to conduct or participate, directly or indirectly, in the conduct of such enterprise's affairs through a pattern of racketeering activity or collection of unlawful debt." The term "enterprise" is defined as including "any individual, partnership, corporation, association, or other legal entity, and any union or group of individuals associated in fact although not a legal entity." § 1961(4). There is no restriction upon the associations embraced by the definition: an enterprise includes any union or group of individuals associated in fact. On its face, the definition appears to include both legitimate and illegitimate enterprises within its scope; it no more excludes criminal enterprises than it does legitimate ones. Had Congress not intended to reach criminal associations, it could easily have narrowed the sweep of the definition by inserting a single word, "legitimate." But it did nothing to indicate that an enterprise consisting of a group of individuals was not covered by RICO if the purpose of the enterprise was exclusively criminal. . . .

Section 1961(4) describes two categories of associations that come within the purview of the "enterprise" definition. The first encompasses organizations such as corporations and partnerships, and other "legal entities." The second covers "any union or group of individuals associated in fact although not a legal entity." The Court of Appeals assumed that the second category was merely a more general description of the first. Having made that assumption, the court concluded that the more generalized description in the second category should be limited by the specific examples enumerated in the first. But that assumption is untenable. Each category describes a separate type of enterprise to be covered by the statute — those that are recognized as legal entities and those that are not. The latter is not a more general description of the former. . . .

A . . . reason offered by the Court of Appeals in support of its judgment was that giving the definition of "enterprise" its ordinary meaning would create several internal inconsistencies in the Act. With respect to § 1962(c), it was said:

> If "a pattern of racketeering" can itself be an "enterprise" for purposes of section 1962(c), then the two phrases "employed by or associated with any enterprise" and "the conduct of such enterprise's affairs through [a pattern of racketeering activity]" add nothing to the meaning of the section. The words of the statute are coherent and logical only if they are read as applying to legitimate enterprises. 632 F.2d, at 899.

This conclusion is based on a faulty premise. That a wholly criminal enterprise comes within the ambit of the statute does not mean that a "pattern of racketeering activity" is an "enterprise." In order to secure a conviction under RICO, the Government must prove both the existence of an "enterprise" and the connected "pattern of racketeering activity." The enterprise is an entity, for present purposes a group of persons associated together for a common purpose of engaging in a course of conduct. The pattern of racketeering activity is, on the other hand, a series of criminal acts as defined by the statute. The former is proved by evidence of an ongoing organization, formal or informal, and by evidence that the various associates function as a continuing unit. The latter is proved by evidence of the requisite number of acts of racketeering committed by the participants in the enterprise. While the proof used to establish these separate elements may in particular cases coalesce, proof of one does not necessarily establish the other. The "enterprise" is not the "pattern of racketeering activity"; it is an entity separate and apart from the pattern of activity in which it engages. The existence of an enterprise at all times remains a separate element which must be proved by the Government. . . .

Finally, it is urged that the interpretation of RICO to include both legitimate and illegitimate enterprises will substantially alter the balance between federal and state enforcement of criminal law. This is particularly true, so the argument goes, since included within the definition of racketeering activity are a significant number of acts made criminal under state law. But even assuming that the more inclusive definition of enterprise will have the effect suggested,[2] the language of the statute and its legislative history indicate that Congress was well aware that it was entering a new domain of federal involvement through the enactment of this measure. Indeed, the very purpose of the Organized Crime Control Act of 1970 was to enable the Federal Government to address a large and seemingly neglected problem. The view was that existing law, state and federal, was not adequate to address the problem, which was of national dimensions. That Congress included within the definition of racketeering activities a number of state crimes strongly indicates that RICO criminalized conduct that was also criminal under state law, at least when the requisite elements of a RICO offense are present. As the hearings and legislative debates reveal, Congress was well aware of the fear that RICO would "[move] large substantive areas formerly totally within the police power of the State into the Federal realm." 116 Cong. Rec. 35217 (1970) (remarks of Rep. Eckhardt). In the face of these objections, Congress nonetheless proceeded to enact the measure, knowing that it would alter somewhat the role of the Federal Government in the war against organized crime and that the alteration would entail prosecutions involving acts of racketeering that are also crimes under state law. There is no argument that Congress acted beyond its power in so doing. That being the case, the courts are without authority to restrict the application of the statute.

Contrary to the judgment below, neither the language nor structure of RICO limits its application to legitimate "enterprises." Applying it also to criminal organizations does not render any portion of the statute superfluous nor does it create any structural incongruities within the framework of the Act. The result is neither absurd nor surprising. On the contrary, insulating the wholly criminal enterprise from prosecution under RICO is the more incongruous position.

Section 904(a) of RICO, 84 Stat. 947, directs that "[t]he provisions of this Title shall be liberally construed to effectuate its remedial purposes." With or without this admonition, we could not agree with the Court of Appeals that illegitimate enterprises should be excluded from coverage. We are also quite sure that nothing in the legislative history of RICO requires a contrary conclusion. . . .

The judgment of the Court of Appeals is accordingly reversed.

Justice STEWART agrees with the reasoning and conclusion of the Court of Appeals as to the meaning of the term "enterprise" in this statute. Accordingly, he respectfully dissents.

Notes and Questions

1. The defendants were charged with conspiracy to conduct the affairs of an enterprise through a pattern of racketeering activity. In what sense did the 13 conspirators constitute an enterprise?

---

2. RICO imposes no restrictions upon the criminal justice systems of the States. See 84 Stat. 947 ("Nothing in this title shall supersede any provision of Federal, State, or other law imposing criminal penalties or affording civil remedies in addition to those provided for in this title."). Thus, under RICO, the States remain free to exercise their police powers to the fullest constitutional extent in defining and prosecuting crimes within their respective jurisdictions. That some of those crimes may also constitute predicate acts of racketeering under RICO, is no restriction on the separate administration of criminal justice by the States.

2. The Court said that evidence introduced to establish the enterprise element may coalesce with evidence used to prove a pattern of racketeering. That being true, what distinguishes the enterprise from the pattern of racketeering activity?

3. The court of appeals was concerned about issues of federalism because the term "racketeering activity" includes nine categories of state crimes, thus creating federal jurisdiction over matters that are ordinarily entrusted to state law enforcement authorities. Why would Congress extend federal jurisdiction this far? What are the implications of its decision to do so?

4. In addition to the types of enterprises specifically enumerated in the statute, courts have held that an association of corporations or an association of individuals and corporations may constitute a RICO enterprise. See, e.g., United States v. Aimone, 715 F.2d 822 (3d Cir. 1983) (a group of private citizens and public officials associated with a construction company constituted an enterprise); United States v. Thevis, 665 F.2d 616 (5th Cir. 1982) (a group of individuals associated with various corporations to conduct a pornography business constituted an enterprise); United States v. Huber, 603 F.2d 387 (2d Cir. 1979) (an association of six hospital supply corporations the defendant controlled constituted a single enterprise). Similarly, associations of various types of business ventures may also constitute an enterprise. See, e.g., United States v. Navarro-Ordas, 770 F.2d 959 (11th Cir. 1985) (association of banks, family business ventures, and corporations); United States v. Hewes, 729 F.2d 1302 (11th Cir. 1984) (network of companies formed for fraudulent purposes).

BOYLE v. UNITED STATES
129 S. Ct. 2237 (2009)

Justice ALITO delivered the opinion of the Court. . . .

I

A

The evidence at petitioner's trial was sufficient to prove the following: Petitioner and others participated in a series of bank thefts in New York, New Jersey, Ohio, and Wisconsin during the 1990's. The participants in these crimes included a core group, along with others who were recruited from time to time. Although the participants sometimes attempted bank-vault burglaries and bank robberies, the group usually targeted cash-laden night-deposit boxes, which are often found in banks in retail areas.

Each theft was typically carried out by a group of participants who met beforehand to plan the crime, gather tools (such as crowbars, fishing gaffs, and walkie-talkies), and assign the roles that each participant would play (such as lookout and driver). The participants generally split the proceeds from the thefts. The group was loosely and informally organized. It does not appear to have had a leader or hierarchy; nor does it appear that the participants ever formulated any long-term master plan or agreement.

From 1991 to 1994, the core group was responsible for more than 30 night-deposit-box thefts. By 1994, petitioner had joined the group, and over the next five years, he participated in numerous attempted night-deposit-box thefts and at least two attempted bank-vault burglaries.

In 2003, petitioner was indicted for participation in the conduct of the affairs of an enterprise through a pattern of racketeering activity, in violation of 18 U.S.C. § 1962(d). . . .

B

In instructing the jury on the meaning of a RICO "enterprise," the District Court relied largely on language in United States v. Turkette, 452 U.S. 576 (1981). The court told the jurors that, in order to establish the existence of such an enterprise, the Government had to prove that: "(1) [t]here [was] an ongoing organization with some sort of framework, formal or informal, for carrying out its objectives; and (2) the various members and associates of the association function[ed] as a continuing unit to achieve a common purpose." Over petitioner's objection, the court also told the jury that it could "find an enterprise where an association of individuals, without structural hierarchy, form[ed] solely for the purpose of carrying out a pattern of racketeering acts" and that "[c]ommon sense suggests that the existence of an association-in-fact is oftentimes more readily proven by what it does, rather than by abstract analysis of its structure."

Petitioner requested an instruction that the Government was required to prove that the enterprise "had an ongoing organization, a core membership that functioned as a continuing unit, and an ascertainable structural hierarchy distinct from the charged predicate acts." The District Court refused to give that instruction.

[Boyle was convicted, inter alia, of participating and conspiring to participate in the affairs of an enterprise through a pattern of racketeering activity, in violation of 18 U.S.C. §§ 1962(c) and (d).]

II

A

RICO makes it "unlawful for any person employed by or *associated with any enterprise* engaged in, or the activities of which affect, interstate or foreign commerce, to conduct or participate, directly or indirectly, in the conduct of such enterprise's affairs through a pattern of racketeering activity or collection of unlawful debt." 18 U.S.C. § 1962(c) (emphasis added).

The statute does not specifically define the outer boundaries of the "enterprise" concept but states that the term "includes any individual, partnership, corporation, association, or other legal entity, and any union or group of individuals associated in fact although not a legal entity." § 1961(4). This enumeration of included enterprises is obviously broad, encompassing "*any* . . . group of individuals associated in fact." The term "any" ensures that the definition has a wide reach, and the very concept of an association in fact is expansive. In addition, the RICO statute provides that its terms are to be "liberally construed to effectuate its remedial purposes."

In light of these statutory features, we explained in *Turkette* that "an enterprise includes any union or group of individuals associated in fact" and that RICO reaches "a group of persons associated together for a common purpose of engaging in a course of conduct." 452 U.S., at 580, 583. Such an enterprise, we said, is proved by evidence of an ongoing organization, formal or informal, and by evidence that the various associates function as a continuing unit." Id., at 583. . . .

[T]he specific question on which we granted certiorari is whether an association-in-fact enterprise must have "an ascertainable structure beyond that inherent in the pattern of racketeering activity in which it engages." We will break this question into three parts. First, must an association-in-fact enterprise have a "structure"? Second, must the structure be "ascertainable"? Third, must the "structure" go "beyond that inherent in the pattern of racketeering activity" in which its members engage?

"Structure." We agree with petitioner that an association-in-fact enterprise must have a structure. In the sense relevant here, the term "structure" means "[t]he way in which parts are arranged or put together to form a whole" and "[t]he interrelation or arrangement of parts in a complex entity." American Heritage Dictionary 1718 (4th ed. 2000); see also Random House Dictionary of the English Language 1410 (1967) (defining structure to mean, among other things, "the pattern of relationships, as of status or friendship, existing among the members of a group or society").

From the terms of RICO, it is apparent that an association-in-fact enterprise must have at least three structural features: a purpose, relationships among those associated with the enterprise, and longevity sufficient to permit these associates to pursue the enterprise's purpose. As we succinctly put it in *Turkette,* an association-in-fact enterprise is "a group of persons associated together for a common purpose of engaging in a course of conduct." 452 U.S., at 583.

That an "enterprise" must have a purpose is apparent from meaning of the term in ordinary usage, *i.e.,* a "venture," "undertaking," or "project." Webster's Third New International Dictionary 757 (1976). The concept of "associat[ion]" requires both interpersonal relationships and a common interest. Section 1962(c) reinforces this conclusion and also shows that an "enterprise" must have some longevity, since the offense proscribed by that provision demands proof that the enterprise had "affairs" of sufficient duration to permit an associate to "participate" in those affairs through "a pattern of racketeering activity." . . .

"Ascertainable." Whenever a jury is told that it must find the existence of an element beyond a reasonable doubt, that element must be ascertainable or else the jury could not find that it was proved. Therefore, telling the members of the jury that they had to ascertain the existence of an ascertainable structure would have been redundant and potentially misleading.

"Beyond that inherent in the pattern of racketeering activity." This phrase may be interpreted in least two different ways, and its correctness depends on the particular sense in which the phrase is used. If the phrase is interpreted to mean that the existence of an enterprise is a separate element that must be proved, it is of course correct. As we explained in *Turkette*, the existence of an enterprise is an element distinct from the pattern of racketeering activity and "proof of one does not necessarily establish the other." 452 U.S., at 583.

On the other hand, if the phrase is used to mean that the existence of an enterprise may never be inferred from the evidence showing that persons associated with the enterprise engaged in a pattern of racketeering activity, it is incorrect. We recognized in *Turkette* that the evidence used to prove the pattern of racketeering activity and the evidence establishing an enterprise "may in particular cases coalesce." Ibid.

C

The crux of petitioner's argument is that a RICO enterprise must have structural features in addition to those that we think can be fairly inferred from the language of the statute. Although petitioner concedes that an association-in-fact enterprise may be an "'informal'" group and that "not 'much'" structure is needed, he contends that such an enterprise must have at least some additional structural attributes, such as a structural "hierarchy," "role differentiation," a "unique *modus operandi*," a "chain of command," "professionalism and sophistication of organization," "diversity and complexity of crimes," "membership dues, rules and regulations," "uncharged or additional crimes aside from predicate acts," an "internal discipline mechanism," "regular meetings regarding enterprise affairs," an "enterprise 'name,'" and "induction or initiation ceremonies and rituals."

We see no basis in the language of RICO for the structural requirements that petitioner asks us to recognize. As we said in *Turkette*, an association-in-fact enterprise is simply a continuing unit that functions with a common purpose. Such a group need not have a hierarchical structure or a "chain of command"; decisions may be made on an ad hoc basis and by any number of methods—by majority vote, consensus, a show of strength, etc. Members of the group need not have fixed roles; different members may perform different roles at different times. The group need not have a name, regular meetings, dues, established rules and regulations, disciplinary procedures, or induction or initiation ceremonies. While the group must function as a continuing unit and remain in existence long enough to pursue a course of conduct, nothing in RICO exempts an enterprise whose associates engage in spurts of activity punctuated by periods of quiescence. Nor is the statute limited to groups whose crimes are sophisticated, diverse, complex, or unique; for example, a group that does nothing but engage in extortion through old-fashioned, unsophisticated, and brutal means may fall squarely within the statute's reach.

The breadth of the "enterprise" concept in RICO is highlighted by comparing the statute with other federal statutes that target organized criminal groups. For example, 18 U.S.C. § 1955(b), which was enacted together with RICO as part of the Organized Crime Control Act of 1970, defines an "illegal gambling business" as one that "involves five or more persons who conduct, finance, manage, supervise, direct, or own all or part of such business." A "continuing criminal enterprise," as defined in 21 U.S.C. § 848(c), must involve more than five persons who act in concert and must have an "organizer," supervisor, or other manager. Congress included no such requirements in RICO. . . .

IV

The instructions the District Court judge gave to the jury in this case were correct and adequate. These instructions explicitly told the jurors that they could not convict on the RICO charges unless they found that the Government had proved the existence of an enterprise. The instructions made clear that this was a separate element from the pattern of racketeering activity.

The instructions also adequately told the jury that the enterprise needed to have the structural attributes that may be inferred from the statutory language. As noted, the trial judge told the jury that the Government was required to prove that there was "an ongoing organization with some sort of framework, formal or informal, for carrying out its objectives" and that "the various members and associates of the association func-tion[ed] as a continuing unit to achieve a common purpose."

Finally, the trial judge did not err in instructing the jury that "the existence of an association-in-fact is oftentimes more readily proven by what it does, rather than by abstract analysis of its structure." This instruction properly conveyed the point we made in *Turkette* that proof of a pattern of racketeering activity may be sufficient in a par-ticular case to permit a jury to infer the existence of an association-in-fact enterprise.

We therefore affirm the judgment of the Court of Appeals.

Justice STEVENS, with whom Justice BREYER joins, dissenting.

In my view, Congress intended the term "enterprise," as it is used in the Racketeer Influenced and Corrupt Organizations Act (RICO), to refer only to business-like enti-ties that have an existence apart from the predicate acts committed by their employees or associates. The trial judge in this case committed two significant errors relating to the meaning of that term. First, he instructed the jury that "an association of individu-als, without structural hierarchy, form[ed] solely for the purpose of carrying out a pat-tern of racketeering acts" can constitute an enterprise. And he allowed the jury to find that element satisfied by evidence showing a group of criminals with no existence beyond its intermittent commission of racketeering acts and related offenses. Because the Court's decision affirming petitioner's conviction is inconsistent with the statutory meaning of the term enterprise and serves to expand RICO liability far beyond the bounds Congress intended, I respectfully dissent. . . .

Notes and Questions

1. Is the result in *Boyle* consistent with the holding in *Turkette*? If so, can the posi-tion that Justice Stevens stakes out in his dissent in *Boyle* be reconciled with the fact that he joined the majority opinion in *Turkette*?

2. Does the majority's opinion in *Boyle* collapse the distinction between the terms "enterprise" and "pattern of racketeering activity"? Is it plausible that a jury would dis-tinguish the two concepts when the same evidence is used to prove both of these ele-ments where the enterprise is alleged to be a group of individuals who are associated in fact?

3. Justice Stevens' dissent in *Boyle* posits that Congress intended the term "enter-prise" to encompass only business-like entities. Does the statute's definition of the term "enterprise" as including "any individual, partnership, corporation, association, or other legal entity" in the first clause of § 1961(4) support that view? Are entities that are not "business-like" included in this part of the definition?

4. Justice Stevens' dissent suggests that the second part of the definition of "enter-prise" implies that other informal entities — i.e., those that consist of "any union or group of individuals associated in fact although not a legal entity" — should have the "business-like" characteristics of more formal entities like partnerships and corpora-tions. Is this the most plausible reading of the statute?

PROBLEM 10-1

Governor Arlen Aubrey and three of his top aides engage in a scheme to grant executive clemency to convicted felons and immunity from extradition to fugitive felons in exchange for bribes. Their conduct violates the state's bribery statute and has continued over a substantial period of time. Bribery is a state predicate crime included in RICO's definition of racketeering activity.

The Assistant United States Attorney handling the grand jury investigation is seeking a RICO indictment alleging that the four defendants have conducted the affairs of an enterprise (the Governor's office) through a pattern of racketeering activity. Is the Governor's office a RICO enterprise? Would naming the Governor's office as the enterprise raise additional federalism issues? Is there a better way to frame the indictment?[3]

NATIONAL ORGANIZATION FOR WOMEN v. SCHEIDLER
510 U.S. 249 (1994)

Chief Justice REHNQUIST delivered the opinion of the Court.

We are required once again to interpret the provisions of the Racketeer Influenced and Corrupt Organizations (RICO) chapter of the Organized Crime Control Act of 1970 (OCCA), 18 U.S.C. §§ 1961-1968. Section 1962(c) prohibits any person associated with an enterprise from conducting its affairs through a pattern of racketeering activity. We granted certiorari to determine whether RICO requires proof that either the racketeering enterprise or the predicate acts of racketeering were motivated by an economic purpose. We hold that RICO requires no such economic motive.

I

Petitioner National Organization for Women, Inc. (NOW) is a national nonprofit organization that supports the legal availability of abortion; petitioners Delaware Women's Health Organization, Inc. (DWHO) and Summit Women's Health Organization, Inc. (SWHO) are health care centers that perform abortions and other medical procedures. Respondents are a coalition of antiabortion groups called the Pro-Life Action Network (PLAN), Joseph Scheidler and other individuals and organizations that oppose legal abortion, and a medical laboratory that formerly provided services to the two petitioner health care centers.

Petitioners sued respondents in the United States District Court for the Northern District of Illinois, alleging violations of the Sherman Act, 15 U.S.C. §§ 1 et seq., and RICO's § 1962(a), (c), and (d), as well as several pendent state-law claims stemming from the activities of antiabortion protesters at the clinics. According to respondent Scheidler's congressional testimony, these protesters aim to shut down the clinics and persuade women not to have abortions. See, e.g., Abortion Clinic Violence, Oversight Hearings before the Subcommittee on Civil and Constitutional Rights of the House Committee on the Judiciary, 99th Cong., 1st and 2d Sess., 55 (1987) (statement of

---

3. Cf. United States v. Thompson, 685 F.2d 993 (6th Cir. 1982).

Joseph M. Scheidler, Executive Director, Pro-Life Action League). Petitioners sought injunctive relief, along with treble damages, costs, and attorneys' fees. They later amended their complaint, and pursuant to local rules, filed a "RICO Case Statement" that further detailed the enterprise, the pattern of racketeering, the victims of the racketeering activity, and the participants involved.

The amended complaint alleged that respondents were members of a nationwide conspiracy to shut down abortion clinics through a pattern of racketeering activity including extortion in violation of the Hobbs Act, 18 U.S.C. § 1951. Section 1951(b)(2) defines extortion as "the obtaining of property from another, with his consent, induced by wrongful use of actual or threatened force, violence, or fear, or under color of official right." Petitioners alleged that respondents conspired to use threatened or actual force, violence, or fear to induce clinic employees, doctors, and patients to give up their jobs, give up their economic right to practice medicine, and give up their right to obtain medical services at the clinics. Petitioners claimed that this conspiracy "has injured the business and/or property interests of the [petitioners]." According to the amended complaint, PLAN constitutes the alleged racketeering "enterprise" for purposes of § 1962(c).

[The district court dismissed both claims on the ground that NOW had failed to allege the enterprise had some profit-seeking purpose. The court of appeals affirmed, finding that "non-economic crimes committed in furtherance of non-economic motives are not within the ambit of RICO."]

III

We turn to the question of whether the racketeering enterprise or the racketeering predicate acts must be accompanied by an underlying economic motive. Section 1962(c) makes it unlawful "for any person employed by or associated with any enterprise engaged in, or the activities of which affect, interstate or foreign commerce, to conduct or participate, directly or indirectly, in the conduct of such enterprise's affairs through a pattern of racketeering activity or collection of unlawful debt." Section 1961(1) defines "pattern of racketeering activity" to include conduct that is "chargeable" or "indictable" under a host of state and federal laws. RICO broadly defines "enterprise" in § 1961(4) to "includ[e] any individual, partnership, corporation, association, or other legal entity, and any union or group of individuals associated in fact although not a legal entity." Nowhere in either § 1962(c), or in the RICO definitions in § 1961, is there any indication that an economic motive is required.

The phrase "any enterprise engaged in, or the activities of which affect, interstate or foreign commerce" comes the closest of any language in subsection (c) to suggesting a need for an economic motive. Arguably an enterprise engaged in interstate or foreign commerce would have a profit-seeking motive, but the language in § 1962(c) does not stop there; it includes enterprises whose activities "affect" interstate or foreign commerce. Webster's Third New International Dictionary 35 (1969) defines "affect" as "to have a detrimental influence on — used especially in the phrase *affecting commerce*." An enterprise surely can have a detrimental influence on interstate or foreign commerce without having its own profit-seeking motives.

The Court of Appeals thought that the use of the term "enterprise" in § 1962(a) and (b), where it is arguably more tied in with economic motivation, should be applied to restrict the breadth of use of that term in § 1962(c). . . .

We do not believe that the usage of the term "enterprise" in subsections (a) and (b) leads to the inference that an economic motive is required in subsection (c). The term "enterprise" in subsections (a) and (b) plays a different role in the structure of those subsections than it does in subsection (c). Section 1962(a) provides that it "shall be unlawful for any person who has received any income derived, directly or indirectly, from a pattern of racketeering activity . . . to use or invest, directly or indirectly, any part of such income, or the proceeds of such income, in acquisition of any interest in, or the establishment or operation of, any enterprise which is engaged in, or the activities of which affect, interstate or foreign commerce." Correspondingly, § 1962(b) states that it "shall be unlawful for any person through a pattern of racketeering activity or through collection of an unlawful debt to acquire or maintain, directly or indirectly, any interest in or control of any enterprise which is engaged in, or the activities of which affect, interstate or foreign commerce." The "enterprise" referred to in subsections (a) and (b) is thus something acquired through the use of illegal activities or by money obtained from illegal activities. The enterprise in these subsections is the victim of unlawful activity and may very well be a "profit-seeking" entity that represents a property interest and may be acquired. But the statutory language in subsections (a) and (b) does not mandate that the enterprise be a "profit-seeking" entity; it simply requires that the enterprise be an entity that was acquired through illegal activity or the money generated from illegal activity.

By contrast, the "enterprise" in subsection (c) connotes generally the vehicle through which the unlawful pattern of racketeering activity is committed, rather than the victim of that activity. Subsection (c) makes it unlawful for "any person employed by or associated with any enterprise . . . to conduct or participate . . . in the conduct of such enterprise's affairs through a pattern of racketeering activity. . . ." Consequently, since the enterprise in subsection (c) is not being acquired, it need not have a property interest that can be acquired nor an economic motive for engaging in illegal activity; it need only be an association in fact that engages in a pattern of racketeering activity.[4] Nothing in subsections (a) and (b) directs us to a contrary conclusion.

The Court of Appeals also relied on the reasoning of United States v. Bagaric, 706 F.2d 42 (2d Cir. 1983), to support its conclusion that subsection (c) requires an economic motive. In upholding the dismissal of a RICO claim against a political terrorist group, the *Bagaric* court relied in part on the congressional statement of findings which prefaces RICO and refers to the activities of groups that "'drain[] billions of dollars from America's economy by unlawful conduct and the illegal use of force, fraud, and corruption.'" 706 F.2d, at 57, n. 13 (quoting OCCA, 84 Stat. 922). The Court of Appeals for the Second Circuit decided that the sort of activity thus condemned required an economic motive.

We do not think this is so. Respondents and the two courts of appeals, we think, overlook the fact that predicate acts, such as the alleged extortion, may not benefit the

---

4. One commentator uses the terms "prize," "instrument," "victim," and "perpetrator" to describe the four separate roles the enterprise may play in section 1962. See Blakey, The RICO Civil Fraud Action in Context: Reflections on Bennett v. Berg, 58 Notre Dame L. Rev. 237, 307-325 (1982).

protestors financially but still may drain money from the economy by harming businesses such as the clinics which are petitioners in this case. . . .

In United States v. Turkette, 452 U.S. 576 (1981), we faced the analogous question of whether "enterprise" as used in § 1961(4) should be confined to "legitimate" enterprises. Looking to the statutory language, we found that "[t]here is no restriction upon the associations embraced by the definition: an enterprise includes any union or group of individuals associated in fact." Id., at 580. Accordingly, we resolved that § 1961(4)'s definition of enterprise "appears to include both legitimate and illegitimate enterprises within its scope; it no more excludes criminal enterprises than it does legitimate ones." Id., at 580-581. We noted that Congress could easily have narrowed the sweep of the term "enterprise" by inserting a single word, "legitimate." Instead, Congress did nothing to indicate that "enterprise" should exclude those entities whose sole purpose was criminal.

The parallel to the present case is apparent. Congress has not, either in the definitional section or in the operative language, required that an "enterprise" in § 1962(c) have an economic motive. . . .

We therefore hold that petitioners may maintain this action if respondents conducted the enterprise through a pattern of racketeering activity. The questions of whether the respondents committed the requisite predicate acts, and whether the commission of these acts fell into a pattern, are not before us. We hold only that RICO contains no economic motive requirement.

The judgment of the Court of Appeals is accordingly reversed.

[Concurring opinion by Justice SOUTER omitted.]

Notes and Questions

1. The Court notes that the role of the enterprise in subsections (a) and (b) differs from its role in subsection (c), because (a) and (b) contemplate an economic transaction — i.e., investment in an enterprise or acquisition of an enterprise. Does that leave open the possibility of requiring those enterprises to have an economic motive?

2. When the *NOW* case went to trial in 1998, the jury found in favor of the plaintiffs and awarded monetary damages that, when trebled as the civil RICO statute requires, totaled about $260,000. Although the civil RICO statute authorizes courts to grant a variety of equitable remedies, it neither expressly authorizes nor prohibits granting injunctions to private civil litigants. The trial judge in *NOW* nonetheless issued a permanent injunction against continued RICO violations.[5]

The case made its way to the Supreme Court for a second time in 2003, when the Court ruled that the plaintiffs had failed to prove a RICO violation based on extortion under the Hobbs Act because the defendants did not attempt to obtain property from them.[6] The Court vacated the injunction without addressing the question whether the civil RICO provision authorizes private litigants to seek injunctive relief, and that issue has yet to be resolved.

---

5. See National Organization for Women v. Scheidler, 1999 U.S. Dist. LEXIS 11980 (N.D. Ill. July 16, 1999).

6. Scheidler v. National Organization for Women, Inc., 537 U.S. 393 (2003).

NOTE ON INTERSTATE COMMERCE REQUIREMENT

As the Court observed in *NOW*, a RICO enterprise must be engaged in — or its activities must affect — interstate or foreign commerce. As is true in virtually every other context, however, this jurisdictional requirement may be satisfied by the presence of minimal contact with interstate commerce. Because RICO does not require proof that any of the racketeering activity had an interstate dimension, the prosecution need only show that the enterprise itself has some involvement with commerce. Thus, for example, using the mails or interstate telephone systems, purchasing goods from out-of-state vendors, and purchasing real estate in another state have been held to satisfy the interstate commerce element.

The Supreme Court unexpectedly reconsidered the breadth of Congress's power to exercise commerce-based criminal jurisdiction in two cases decided during its 1994 term. In United States v. Lopez, 514 U.S. 549 (1995), the Court struck down an exercise of Commerce Clause jurisdiction for the first time in more than 50 years when it declared the Gun-Free School Zones Act unconstitutional. The Court in *Lopez* recognized that Congress has the power to regulate commerce in three distinct ways. It can (1) regulate the use of the channels of interstate commerce; (2) regulate instrumentalities of commerce, or people or things in commerce; or (3) regulate activities that affect commerce. Since the Gun-Free School Zones Act did not purport to regulate the use of the channels of interstate commerce or to protect persons or things in commerce, the Court found that the Act could be upheld only if it regulated activities that "substantially affect" interstate commerce. The Court ruled that the Act did not pass muster under this test because gun possession in school zones is unrelated to commerce, because the Act contained no express jurisdictional element (e.g., that the gun or its possessor must have traveled in interstate commerce), and because there were no congressional findings supporting a nexus between the regulated conduct and commercial intercourse.

In a second Commerce Clause case — decided just a week later — the Court put to rest speculation about whether the "substantially affects" test applies to all statutes that rely on commerce-based jurisdiction. United States v. Robertson, 514 U.S. 669 (1995), made clear that it does not. In *Robertson*, a unanimous Court held that to pass constitutional muster, a substantial effect on commerce need be shown only when the regulated activity is wholly intrastate. Thus, if the person or entity in question is *engaged in* commerce — e.g., Robertson operated a gold mine that purchased equipment from out-of-state suppliers and hired out-of-state workers — no showing that the mining activity *affected* commerce is required.

Five years later, the Court reconsidered the constitutional boundaries of commerce-based jurisdiction in United States v. Morrison, 529 U.S. 598 (2000). In *Morrison*, the Court struck down a provision of the Violence Against Women Act that authorized victims of gender-motivated violence to bring private civil suits in federal court. Although the challenged provision contained no express jurisdictional element, Congress indicated that it relied on its Commerce Clause power as a basis for enacting the statute. In addition, Congress accumulated a "mountain of data" detailing harmful effects that domestic violence has on interstate commerce, and — in contrast with the Gun-Free School Zones Act — included specific findings to that effect. The Court in *Morrison* nonetheless invalidated the statute, holding that Congress lacks power under the Commerce Clause to regulate "noneconomic, violent criminal conduct based solely on that conduct's aggregate effect on interstate commerce." Id. at 617. Although the Court stopped short of ruling that Commerce Clause jurisdiction can never be based on the aggregate effects of noneconomic activity on commerce, it emphasized that all of the prior cases that upheld aggregate effects jurisdiction were construing statutes that regulated economic activity.

Morrison's "economic/noneconomic" distinction is amorphous at best. Is a gang of street muggers who regularly prey on elderly victims and steal their valuables engaged in economic activity for purposes of Commerce Clause jurisdiction? Would the answer be clearer if the gang targeted only victims who were withdrawing money at automated teller machines? Would it be clearer still if the gang's principal activity was robbing commercial banks? It is likely that *Morrison*'s "economic/noneconomic" distinction will be difficult to apply and will require courts to indulge in ad hoc line-drawing exercises with little concrete guidance.[7]

In the meantime, despite *Lopez*'s insistence that intrastate conduct must have a "substantial" effect on interstate commerce before federal jurisdiction kicks in, the lower courts have continued to construe the "substantially affects" test to require only a minimal effect on interstate commerce. Thus, for example, causing someone to cancel an $8,800 contract with an out-of-state company[8] or causing the seasonal use of a truck to transport, intrastate, a pecan harvest a short distance to an out-of-state broker[9] have been found to substantially affect interstate commerce.

III. PATTERN OF RACKETEERING ACTIVITY

RICO forbids participating in the affairs of an enterprise through a pattern of racketeering activity. Thus, like the enterprise requirement, the "pattern" and "racketeering activity" elements are key components of a RICO violation.

The term "racketeering activity" is defined to include more than 70 federal crimes, often referred to as predicate crimes or predicate acts. Although the defendant need not be formally charged with or tried for committing the predicate crimes, a RICO indictment must allege — and the prosecutor must prove to the jury's satisfaction — that the defendant was involved in the commission of at least two predicate crimes and that the underlying criminal conduct was "indictable" under one or more of the enumerated federal statutes.

A. THE PATTERN REQUIREMENT

RICO is not concerned with isolated criminal acts. Instead, it targets multiple criminal offenses that form a "pattern" of racketeering activity. The definition of this

---

7. Cf. Solid Waste Agency v. Army Corps of Engineers, 531 U.S. 159 (2001) (holding, on statutory construction grounds, that the Army Corps of Engineers exceeded its authority under the Clean Water Act by promulgating regulations that broadly asserted jurisdiction over all intrastate waters that provide habitat for migratory birds, but noting the government's argument that the Corps could regulate such waters stretched Commerce Clause jurisdiction to its outer bounds).

8. DeFalco v. Bernas, 244 F.3d 286 (2d Cir. 2001).

9. United States v. Grassie, 237 F.3d 1199 (10th Cir. 2001).

term has proven troublesome because rather than telling us what a pattern of racketeering activity *is*, the statute tells us what a pattern of racketeering *requires*. A pattern of racketeering activity "requires at least two acts of racketeering activity, one of which occurred after the effective date of this [Act] and the last of which occurred within ten years (excluding any period of imprisonment) after the commission of a prior act of racketeering activity." 18 U.S.C. § 1961(5). Why should this definition be problematic?

H.J., INC. v. NORTHWESTERN BELL TELEPHONE
492 U.S. 229 (1989)

Justice BRENNAN delivered the opinion of the Court. . . .

Petitioners, customers of respondent Northwestern Bell Telephone Co., filed this putative class action in 1986 in the District Court for the District of Minnesota. Petitioners alleged violations of § 1962(a), (b), (c), and (d) by Northwestern Bell and the other respondents — some of the telephone company's officers and employees, various members of the Minnesota Public Utilities Commission (MPUC), and other unnamed individuals and corporations — and sought an injunction and treble damages under RICO's civil liability provisions, § 1964(a) and (c).

The MPUC is the state body responsible for determining the rates that Northwestern Bell may charge. Petitioners' five-count complaint alleged that between 1980 and 1986 Northwestern Bell sought to influence members of the MPUC in the performance of their duties — and in fact caused them to approve rates for the company in excess of a fair and reasonable amount — by making cash payments to commissioners, negotiating with them regarding future employment, and paying for parties and meals, for tickets to sporting events and the like, and for airline tickets. Based upon these factual allegations, petitioners alleged in their first count a pendent state-law claim, asserting that Northwestern Bell violated the Minnesota bribery statute as well as state common law prohibiting bribery. They also raised four separate claims under § 1962 of RICO. Count II alleged that, in violation of § 1962(a), Northwestern Bell derived income from a pattern of racketeering activity involving predicate acts of bribery and used this income to engage in its business as an interstate "enterprise." Count III claimed a violation of § 1962(b), in that, through this same pattern of racketeering activity, respondents acquired an interest in or control of the MPUC, which was also an interstate "enterprise." In Count IV, petitioners asserted that respondents participated in the conduct and affairs of the MPUC through this pattern of racketeering activity, contrary to § 1962(c). Finally, Count V alleged that respondents conspired together to violate § 1962(a), (b), and (c), thereby contravening § 1962(d).

[Because it was bound by Eighth Circuit precedent that required proof of multiple illegal schemes to establish a "pattern" of racketeering activity, the district court dismissed the complaint, and the court of appeals affirmed.]

II

In Sedima, S.P.R.L. v. Imrex Co., 473 U.S. 479 (1985), . . . we suggested that RICO's expansive uses "appear to be primarily the result of the breadth of the predicate offenses, in particular the inclusion of wire, mail, and securities fraud, and the failure of Congress and the courts to develop a meaningful concept of 'pattern'" — both factors that apply to criminal as well as civil applications of the Act. Congress has done nothing in the interim further to illuminate RICO's key requirement of a pattern of racketeering; and as the plethora of different views expressed by the Court of Appeals since *Sedima* demonstrates, developing a meaningful concept of "pattern" within the existing statutory framework has proved to be no easy task.

It is, nevertheless, a task we must undertake in order to decide this case. Our guides in the endeavor must be the text of the statute and its legislative history. We find no support in those sources for the proposition, espoused by the Court of Appeals for the Eighth Circuit in this case, that predicate acts of racketeering may form a pattern only when they are part of separate illegal schemes. Nor can we agree with those courts that have suggested that a pattern is established merely by proving two predicate acts, or with amici in this case who argue that the word "pattern" refers only to predicates that are indicative of a perpetrator involved in organized crime or its functional equivalent. In our view, Congress had a more natural and commonsense approach to RICO's pattern element in mind, intending a more stringent requirement than proof simply of two predicates, but also envisioning a concept of sufficient breadth that it might encompass multiple predicates within a single scheme that were related and that amounted to, or threatened the likelihood of, continued criminal activity.

A

We begin, of course, with RICO's text, in which Congress followed a "pattern [of] utilizing terms and concepts of breadth." Russello v. United States, 464 U.S. 16, 21 (1983). As we remarked in *Sedima*, the section of the statute headed "definitions" does not so much define a pattern of racketeering activity as state a minimum necessary condition for the existence of such a pattern. Unlike other provisions in § 1961 that tell us what various concepts used in the Act "mean," § 1961(5) says of the phrase "pattern of racketeering activity" only that it "requires at least two acts of racketeering activity, one of which occurred after [October 15, 1970] and the last of which occurred within ten years (excluding any period of imprisonment) after the commission of a prior act of racketeering activity." It thus places an outer limit on the concept of a pattern of racketeering activity that is broad indeed.

Section 1961(5) does indicate that Congress envisioned circumstances in which no more than two predicates would be necessary to establish a pattern of racketeering — otherwise it would have drawn a narrower boundary to RICO liability, requiring proof of a greater number of predicates. But, at the same time, the statement that a pattern "requires at least" two predicates implies "that while two acts are necessary, they may not be sufficient." *Sedima*, supra, at 496, n.14; id., at 527 (Powell, J., dissenting). Section 1961(5) concerns only the minimum number of predicates necessary to establish a pattern; and it assumes that there is something to a RICO pattern beyond simply the number of predicate acts involved. The legislative history bears out this interpretation, for the principal sponsor of the Senate bill expressly indicated that "proof of two acts of racketeering activity, without more, does not establish a pattern." 116 Cong. Rec. 18940 (1970) (statement of Sen. McClellan). Section 1961(5) does not identify, though, these additional prerequisites for establishing the existence of a RICO pattern.

In addition to § 1961(5), there is the key phrase "pattern of racketeering activity" itself, from § 1962, and we must "start with the assumption that the legislative purpose is expressed by the ordinary meaning of the words used." Richards v. United States, 369 U.S. 1, 9 (1962). In normal usage, the word "pattern" here would be taken to require more than just a multiplicity of racketeering predicates. A "pattern" is an "arrangement or order of things or activity," 11 Oxford English Dictionary 357 (2d ed. 1989), and the mere fact that there are a number of predicates is no guarantee that they fall into any arrangement or order. It is not the number of predicates but the relationship that they bear to each other or to some external organizing principle that renders them "ordered" or "arranged." The text of RICO conspicuously fails anywhere to identify, however, forms of relationship or external principles to be used in determining whether racketeering activity falls into a pattern for purposes of the Act.

It is reasonable to infer, from this absence of any textual identification of sorts of pattern that would satisfy § 1962's requirement, in combination with the very relaxed limits to the pattern concept fixed in § 1961(5), that Congress intended to take a flexible approach, and envisaged that a pattern might be demonstrated by reference to a range of different ordering principles or relationships between predicates, within the expansive bounds set. For any more specific guidance as to the meaning of "pattern," we must look past the text to RICO's legislative history, as we have done in prior cases construing the Act.

The legislative history, which we discussed in *Sedima*, shows that Congress indeed had a fairly flexible concept of a pattern in mind. A pattern is not formed by "sporadic activity," S. Rep. No. 91-617, p. 158 (1969), and a person cannot "be subjected to the sanctions of title IX simply for committing two widely separated and isolated criminal offenses," 116 Cong. Rec. 18940 (1970) (Sen. McClellan). Instead, "[t]he term 'pattern' itself requires the showing of a relationship" between the predicates, and of "'the threat of continuing activity,'" ibid., quoting S. Rep. No. 91-617, at 158. "It is this factor of *continuity plus relationship* which combines to produce a pattern." Ibid. (emphasis added). RICO's legislative history reveals Congress' intent that to prove a pattern of racketeering activity a plaintiff or prosecutor must show that the racketeering predicates are related, and that they amount to or pose a threat of continued criminal activity.

B

For analytic purposes these two constituents of RICO's pattern requirement must be stated separately, though in practice their proof will often overlap. The element of relatedness is the easier to define, for we may take guidance from a provision elsewhere in the Organized Crime Control Act of 1970 (OCCA), of which RICO formed Title IX. OCCA included as Title X the Dangerous Special Offender Sentencing Act, 18 U.S.C. §§ 3575 et seq. (now partially repealed). Title X provided for enhanced sentences where, among other things, the defendant had committed a prior felony as part of a pattern of criminal conduct or in furtherance of a conspiracy to engage in a pattern of criminal conduct. As we noted in *Sedima*, Congress defined Title X's pattern requirement solely in terms of the *relationship* of the defendant's criminal acts one to another: "criminal conduct forms a pattern if it embraces criminal acts that have the same or similar purposes, results, participants, victims, or methods of commission, or otherwise are interrelated by distinguishing characteristics and are not isolated events." 18 U.S.C.

§ 3575(e). We have no reason to suppose that Congress had in mind for RICO's pattern of racketeering component any more constrained a notion of the relationships between predicates that would suffice.

RICO's legislative history tells us, however, that the relatedness of racketeering activities is not alone enough to satisfy § 1962's pattern element. To establish a RICO pattern it must also be shown that the predicates themselves amount to, or that they otherwise constitute a threat of, continuing racketeering activity. As to this continuity requirement, § 3575(e) is of no assistance. It is this aspect of RICO's pattern element that has spawned the "multiple scheme" test adopted by some lower courts, including the Court of Appeals in this case. But although proof that a RICO defendant has been involved in multiple criminal schemes would certainly be highly relevant to the inquiry into the continuity of the defendant's racketeering activity, it is implausible to suppose that Congress thought continuity might be shown only by proof of multiple schemes. The Eighth Circuit's test brings a rigidity to the available methods of proving a pattern that simply is not present in the idea of "continuity" itself; and it does so, moreover, by introducing a concept — the "scheme" — that appears nowhere in the language or legislative history of the Act. We adopt a less inflexible approach that seems to us to derive from a common-sense, everyday understanding of RICO's language and Congress' gloss on it. What a plaintiff or prosecutor must prove is continuity of racketeering activity, or its threat, *simpliciter*. This may be done in a variety of ways, thus making it difficult to formulate in the abstract any general test for continuity. We can, however, begin to delineate the requirement.

"Continuity" is both a closed- and open-ended concept, referring either to a closed period of repeated conduct, or to past conduct that by its nature projects into the future with a threat of repetition. It is, in either case, centrally a temporal concept — and particularly so in the RICO context, where what must be continuous, RICO's predicate acts or offenses, and the relationship these predicates must bear one to another, are distinct requirements. A party alleging a RICO violation may demonstrate continuity over a closed period by proving a series of related predicates extending over a substantial period of time. Predicate acts extending over a few weeks or months and threatening no future criminal conduct do not satisfy this requirement: Congress was concerned in RICO with long-term criminal conduct. Often a RICO action will be brought before continuity can be established in this way. In such cases, liability depends on whether the threat of continuity is demonstrated.

Whether the predicates proved establish a threat of continued racketeering activity depends on the specific facts of each case. Without making any claim to cover the field of possibilities — preferring to deal with this issue in the context of concrete factual situations presented for decision — we offer some examples of how this element might be satisfied. A RICO pattern may surely be established if the related predicates themselves involve a distinct threat of long-term racketeering activity, either implicit or explicit. Suppose a hoodlum were to sell "insurance" to a neighborhood's storekeepers to cover them against breakage of their windows, telling his victims he would be reappearing each month to collect the "premium" that would continue their "coverage." Though the number of related predicates involved may be small and they may occur close together in time, the racketeering acts themselves include a specific threat of repetition extending indefinitely into the future, and thus supply the requisite threat of continuity. In other cases, the threat of continuity may be established by showing that the predicate acts or offenses are part of an ongoing entity's regular way of doing business. Thus, the threat of continuity is sufficiently established where the predicates can be attributed to a defendant operating as part of a long-term association that exists for criminal purposes. Such associations include, but extend well beyond, those traditionally grouped under the phrase "organized crime." The continuity requirement is likewise satisfied where it is shown that the predicates are a regular way of conducting defendant's ongoing legitimate business (in the sense that it is not a business that exists for criminal purposes), or of conducting or participating in an ongoing and legitimate RICO "enterprise."

The limits of the relationship and continuity concepts that combine to define a RICO pattern, and the precise methods by which relatedness and continuity or its threat may be proved, cannot be fixed in advance with such clarity that it will always be apparent whether in a particular case a "pattern of racketeering activity" exists. The development of these concepts must await future cases, absent a decision by Congress to revisit RICO to provide clearer guidance as to the Act's intended scope.

III

Various amici urge that RICO's pattern element should be interpreted more narrowly than as requiring relationship and continuity in the senses outlined above, so that a defendant's racketeering activities form a pattern only if they are characteristic either of organized crime in the traditional sense, or of an organized-crime-type perpetrator, that is, of an association dedicated to the repeated commission of criminal offenses. Like the Court of Appeals' multiple scheme rule, however, the argument for reading an organized crime limitation into RICO's pattern concept, whatever the merits and demerits of such a limitation as an initial legislative matter, finds no support in the Act's text, and is at odds with the tenor of its legislative history. . . .

IV

Petitioners' complaint alleges that at different times over the course of at least a 6-year period the noncommissioner respondents gave five members of the MPUC numerous bribes, in several different forms, with the objective — in which they were allegedly successful — of causing these Commissioners to approve unfair and unreasonable rates for Northwestern Bell. RICO defines bribery as a "racketeering activity" so petitioners have alleged multiple predicate acts.

Under the analysis we have set forth above, and consistent with the allegations in their complaint, petitioners may be able to prove that the multiple predicates alleged constitute "a pattern of racketeering activity," in that they satisfy the requirements of relationship and continuity. The acts of bribery alleged are said to be related by a common purpose, to influence Commissioners in carrying out their duties in order to win approval of unfairly and unreasonably high rates for Northwestern Bell. Furthermore, petitioners claim that the racketeering predicates occurred with some frequency over at least a 6-year period, which may be sufficient to satisfy the continuity requirement. Alternatively, a threat of continuity of racketeering activity might be established at trial by showing that the alleged bribes were a regular way of conducting Northwestern Bell's ongoing business, or a regular way of conducting or participating in the conduct of the alleged and ongoing RICO enterprise, the MPUC.

The Court of Appeals thus erred in affirming the District Court's dismissal of petitioners' complaint for failure to plead "a pattern of racketeering activity." The judgment is reversed and the case is remanded for further proceedings consistent with this opinion.

It is so ordered.

Justice SCALIA, with whom THE CHIEF JUSTICE, Justice O'CONNOR, and Justice KENNEDY join, concurring in the judgment. . . .

Elevating to the level of statutory text a phrase taken from the legislative history, the Court counsels the lower courts: "continuity plus relationship." This seems to me about as helpful to the conduct of their affairs as "life is a fountain." Of the two parts of this talismanic phrase, the relatedness requirement is said to be the "easier to define," yet here is the Court's definition, in toto: "[C]riminal conduct forms a pattern if it embraces criminal acts that have the same or similar purposes, results, participants, victims, or methods of commission, or otherwise are interrelated by distinguishing characteristics and are not isolated events." This definition has the feel of being solidly rooted in law, since it is a direct quotation of 18 U.S.C. § 3575(e). Unfortunately, if normal (and sensible) rules of statutory construction were followed, the existence of § 3575(e) — which is the definition contained in another Title of the Act that was explicitly not rendered applicable to RICO — suggests that whatever "pattern" might mean in RICO, it assuredly does not mean that. "[W]here Congress includes particular language in one section of a statute but omits it in another section of the same Act, it is generally presumed that Congress acts intentionally and purposely in the disparate inclusion or exclusion." Russello v. United States, 464 U.S. 16, 23 (1983). But that does not really matter, since § 3575(e) is utterly uninformative anyway. It hardly closes in on the target to know that "relatedness" refers to acts that are related by purposes, results, participants, victims, . . . methods of commission, *or* [just in case that is not vague enough] *otherwise*." Is the fact that the victims of both predicate acts were women enough? Or that both acts had the purpose of enriching the defendant? Or that the different coparticipants of the defendant in both acts were his co[-]employees? I doubt that the lower courts will find the Court's instructions much more helpful than telling them to look for a "pattern" — which is what the statute already says.

The Court finds "continuity" more difficult to define precisely. "Continuity," it says, "is both a closed- and open-ended concept, referring either to a closed period of repeated conduct, or to past conduct that by its nature projects into the future with a threat of repetition." I have no idea what this concept of a "closed period of repeated conduct" means. Virtually all allegations of racketeering activity, in both civil and criminal suits, will relate to past periods that are "closed" (unless one expects plaintiff or the prosecutor to establish that the defendant not only committed the crimes he did, but is still committing them), and all of them must relate to conduct that is "repeated," because of RICO's multiple-act requirement. . . . [T]he Court tells us that predicate acts extending, not over a "substantial period of time," but only over a "few weeks or months and threatening no future criminal conduct" do not satisfy the continuity requirement. Since the Court has rejected the concept of separate criminal "schemes" or "episodes" as a criterion of "threatening future criminal conduct," I think it must be saying that at least a few months of racketeering activity (and who knows how much more?) is generally for free, as far as RICO is concerned. The "closed period" concept is a sort of safe harbor for racketeering activity that does not last too long, no matter how many different crimes and different schemes are involved, so long as it does not otherwise "establish a threat of continued racketeering activity." A gang of hoodlums that commits one act of extortion on Monday in New York, a second in Chicago on Tuesday, a third in San Francisco on Wednesday, and so on through an entire week, and then finally and completely disbands, cannot be reached under RICO. I am sure that is not what the statute intends, but I cannot imagine what else the Court's murky discussion can possibly mean. . . .

It is, however, unfair to be so critical of the Court's effort, because I would be unable to provide an interpretation of RICO that gives significantly more guidance concerning its application. . . .

That situation is bad enough with respect to any statute, but it is intolerable with respect to RICO. For it is not only true, as Justice Marshall commented in Sedima, S.P.R.L. v. Imrex Co., 473 U.S. 479 (1985), that our interpretation of RICO has "quite simply revolutionize[d] private litigation" and "validate[d] the federalization of broad areas of state common law of frauds," id., at 501 (dissenting opinion), so that clarity and predictability in RICO's civil applications are particularly important; but it is also true that RICO, since it has criminal applications as well, must, even in its civil applications, possess the degree of certainty required for criminal laws. No constitutional challenge to this law has been raised in the present case, and so that issue is not before us. That the highest Court in the land has been unable to derive from this statute anything more than today's meager guidance bodes ill for the day when that challenge is presented. . . .

Notes and Questions

1. Does the Court's opinion clarify what a "pattern" is? Or should Congress revisit the pattern requirement? If so, what would be a more satisfactory definition?

2. How long must criminal activity continue before it will constitute a closed-ended period? In some circuits, it must last at least a year or more.[10] Is this approach consistent with *H.J. Inc.*'s statement that in combining continuity and relationship, Congress "had a fairly flexible concept of a pattern in mind"?

3. Justice Scalia's concurring opinion invites a vagueness challenge. Is it likely that the Court would seriously entertain an argument that RICO is unconstitutionally vague?

4. Justice Scalia complained that "if normal (and sensible) rules of statutory construction were followed, the existence of § 3575(e) — which is the definition contained in another Title of the Act that was explicitly not rendered applicable to RICO — suggests that whatever 'pattern' might mean in RICO, it assuredly does not mean that." Why does he believe that?

---

10. Cf. Tabas v. Tabas, 47 F.3d 1280 (3d Cir. 1995).

In the same calendar year that it decided *H.J., Inc.*, the Court considered an analogous issue in United States v. Monsanto, 491 U.S. 600 (1989). In *Monsanto*, the challenged statute was a provision of the Comprehensive Forfeiture Act, which requires forfeiture of all property derived from specified criminal activity. The defendant argued that since the forfeiture statute did not expressly include assets earmarked to pay attorneys' fees, the Court should interpret the law to exempt them. Rejecting that position, the Court observed that the Comprehensive Forfeiture Act was enacted as part of an omnibus law that also contained the Victims of Crime Act (VCA), which contains its own forfeiture provision. The VCA forfeiture statute requires forfeiture of collateral profits — e.g., profits from books and movies — the defendant derived from his crime. But it expressly exempts from forfeiture payments made "for legal representation . . . in matters arising from the offense."

> Thus, Congress adopted expressly — in a statute enacted simultaneously with the one under review in this case — the precise exemption from forfeiture which respondent asks us to imply into [the Comprehensive Forfeiture Act]. The express exemption from forfeiture of assets that could be used to pay attorney's fees in [the Victims of Crime Act] indicates to us that Congress understood what it was doing in omitting such an exemption from [the Comprehensive Forfeiture Act in the same omnibus law].

Monsanto, 491 U.S. at 610-611.

Can the reasoning and results in *H.J., Inc.* and *Monsanto* be reconciled?

5. Although the vast majority of RICO prosecutions are premised on a pattern of racketeering activity theory, it is also possible to violate RICO through collection of an unlawful debt. Unlawful debt includes (1) a gambling debt incurred in connection with an illegal gambling business; and (2) a usurious loan made in the course of conducting a loansharking business, if the rate of interest is at least twice the enforceable rate under state or federal law. Because the term "unlawful debt" requires that the debt be incurred in connection with an illegal gambling or lending business, this theory of liability obviously contemplates cases in which the government proves multiple acts of unlawful debt collection. But in contrast with the definition of "pattern of racketeering activity," which requires proof of at least two predicate acts, unlawful debt collection includes collection of "a" debt in violation of designated gambling or usury laws. Thus, proof of a single act of unlawful debt collection that is related to the operation of an illegal gambling or lending business can be sufficient to establish a RICO violation.

B. STATE PREDICATE CRIMES

Although most crimes defined as racketeering activity are federal offenses, a limited number of state crimes may also serve as RICO predicate crimes. The definition of racketeering activity includes "any act or threat involving murder, kidnapping, gambling, arson, robbery, bribery, extortion, dealing in obscene matter, or dealing in narcotic or dangerous drugs, which is chargeable under State law and punishable by imprisonment for more than one year." 18 U.S.C. § 1961(1)(A).

UNITED STATES v. GARNER
837 F.2d 1404 (7th Cir. 1987)

RIPPLE, Circuit Judge. . . .

I. GENERAL BACKGROUND

This case involves the payment of bribes by private sewer contractors to sewer inspectors of the City of Chicago. Sewer work on private property in Chicago is performed by contractors regulated by the city. All contractors must be licensed by the city, and a permit and inspection must be obtained for most sewer work.

Sewer contractors pay a fee to the city to obtain work permits. The amount of this fee varies depending on the job that will be done. Before a contractor begins a job, he is required to contact the Department of Sewers and report the type, location, and price of the work. This information is then transmitted to a central desk for assignment to an inspector. The inspector travels to the jobsite to check the contractor's work, handle citizen complaints, and accept the check or money order for the permit fee. Inspections are performed after the work is completed but before the excavation is filled in. Inspectors are not entitled to any payment other than the permit fee. After inspecting the job and accepting the permit fee, the inspectors return the fee to the permit desk by interoffice mail.

The government does not contend that the defendants ever failed to remit the permit fee. Rather, this case involves the payment of additional amounts to inspectors by contractors. At trial, the government presented evidence demonstrating that sewer contractors, as a matter of course, gave inspectors from $10 to $20 per inspection. The government contended that this system was the product of a conspiracy among the sewer inspectors, and that the receipt of these additional payments constituted acts of bribery and extortion. The defendants contended that there was no conspiracy among the inspectors, and that the additional payments to inspectors were mere gratuities and were not intended as bribes nor induced by extortion.

On July 17, 1985, a grand jury returned an 84-count indictment against 14 defendants, all of whom were inspectors for the Department of Sewers of the City of Chicago. In Count 1 of the indictment, all 14 defendants were charged with conspiracy in violation of the RICO statute, 18 U.S.C. § 1962(d). This count of the indictment alleged that the defendants had agreed to conduct the affairs of the Department of Sewers through a pattern of racketeering activity, and it incorporated by reference the predicate acts alleged in the later individual RICO counts. In counts 2-15, each of the 14 defendants was charged with one count of violating the RICO statute, 18 U.S.C. § 1962(c). The indictment alleged numerous acts of racketeering activity by each defendant in violation of the Illinois bribery statute and the Illinois official misconduct statute. In Counts 16-84, each defendant was charged in five counts with extortion under color of official right in violation of the Hobbs Act.

. . . The government's case centered on the testimony of more than 50 witnesses. Most of the witnesses were contractors or their agents who had paid money to inspectors. Many of these witnesses testified under a grant of immunity. Four witnesses were not contractors or their agents, including one of the most important witnesses, Aubrey Blunt, a sewer inspector, who testified under a plea bargain agreement.

The government also introduced a substantial amount of documentary evidence. Many of the sewer contractors retained records of various jobs, and some even kept records of payments to inspectors. Records of the Department of Sewers also were introduced that identified which inspectors had been assigned to particular jobs. Most of the evidence of bribery and extortion was provided by the direct testimony of contractors. As to each defendant, several contractors testified that they made payments to the inspector and that these payments were accepted. At least five contractors testified against each inspector.

The government did not provide as much evidence about the purpose of the payments. A number of contractors characterized the payments as "the system" or the "cost of doing business" in Chicago. Most witnesses testified that they had been trained to pay inspectors by a friend, relative, or co-worker in the business. In a few cases, the inspector explicitly requested payments. In other cases, the contractor paid the inspector for the purpose of encouraging the inspector to look the other way when there was an improper permit or when improper materials were used. Most common, however, was the statement that the payments were made to avoid generalized fears of harassment or delays.

Most of the defendants used the ambiguity regarding the purpose of the payments as their primary defense. These defendants contended that the payments were a long-standing tradition in the industry, that they represented nothing more than mere gratuities, and that there was no expectation by either contractors or inspectors of a quid pro quo. Defendants Harold Knies and Hensley Garner, however, did not use this defense.

[The jury found the defendants not guilty of conspiracy but convicted them on the individual RICO count and found seven of them guilty of extortion.]

III. RICO ISSUES

A. THE ILLINOIS OFFICIAL MISCONDUCT STATUTE

1. Holding of the District Court

The defendants filed a motion to strike any references in the indictment to the Illinois official misconduct statute. That statute proscribes the unlawful acceptance of a payment knowing that it was given to reward past or future favors. The defendants contended that violations of that statute do not constitute predicate acts under the RICO statute. The court denied the defendants' motion. . . .

2. Analysis

The RICO statute defines "racketeering activity" as "any act . . . involving . . . bribery . . . which is chargeable under state law and punishable by imprisonment for more than one year." 18 U.S.C. § 1961(1)(A). The defendants argue that the court committed reversible error when it ruled that a violation of the Illinois official misconduct statute was an "act involving bribery." The defendants argue that the plain meaning of the word "bribery" only includes acts done with a corrupt intent or when there is an agreement that the recipient of the bribe will provide a quid pro quo. Because the Illinois official misconduct statute prohibits the receipt of illegal gratuities, and the statute has no requirement of corrupt intent or a quid pro quo, the defendants submit that a violation of the statute cannot be a RICO predicate act. This conclusion is reinforced, they note, by the fact that Illinois has a separate statute that explicitly prohibits "bribery." . . .

The labels placed on a state statute do not determine whether that statute proscribes bribery for purposes of the RICO statute. Congress intended for "bribery" to be defined generically when it included bribery as a predicate act. Thus, any statute that proscribes conduct which could be generically defined as bribery can be the basis for a predicate act. As the Third Circuit pointed out in United States v. Forsythe, 560 F.2d 1127, 1137 (3d Cir. 1977), the congressional statement in the legislative history of RICO that "state offenses are included by generic designation" manifests a legislative intent to incorporate the Supreme Court's holding in United States v. Nardello, 393 U.S. 286 (1969), into the RICO statute. The *Forsythe* court said:

> *Nardello* stands for the proposition that alleging a state violation which falls within the generic category of the predicate offense is adequate to charge a violation of the Travel Act. The test for determining whether the charged acts fit into the generic category of the predicate offense is whether the indictment charges a type of activity generally known or characterized in the proscribed category, namely, any act or threat involving bribery.

560 F.2d at 1137.

The parties disagree as to whether the Illinois official misconduct statute proscribes bribery in the generic sense. As the defendants point out, the statute does not require corrupt intent or an agreement to perform a quid pro quo. But we cannot agree with the defendants that the statute does not proscribe bribery as Congress intended to define that word. As the district court demonstrated, the RICO statute also defines "racketeering activity" as "any act which is indictable under . . . title 18, United States Code: Section 201 (relating to bribery). . . ." 18 U.S.C. § 1961(1)(B). Section 201(c)(1)(B) of title 18 makes it a felony for a public official to unlawfully "receive . . . anything of value personally for or because of any official act performed or to be performed by such official. . . ." Thus, the receipt of an illegal gratuity by a federal public official constitutes a RICO predicate act. We see no reason why Congress would have defined bribery more broadly for federal officials than for state officials, particularly when it is remembered that Congress intended for RICO to "be liberally construed to effectuate its remedial purpose." Pub. L. 91-452, Title IX, Section 904(a), reprinted in 1970 U.S. Code Cong. & Admin. News 4007, 4036.

The defendants contend that the parenthetical clause "relating to bribery" in 18 U.S.C. § 1961(1)(B) means that Congress only intended to incorporate as predicate acts those violations of section 201 that relate to the common definition of bribery. To the contrary, when read in context, the parenthetical "relating to bribery" does not limit the incorporation of section 201, but describes it. Congress incorporated many federal criminal statutes as RICO predicate acts, and each incorporation was followed by a descriptive parenthetical. As another court has said, the "parentheticals are only 'visual aids,' designed to guide the reader through what would otherwise be a litany of numbers." United States v. Perkins, 596 F. Supp. 528, 531 (E.D. Pa. 1984).

Our conclusion is further supported by precedent from the Third Circuit. In *Forsythe*, the Third Circuit pointed out that the RICO statute incorporates state offenses according to their generic designation. The court then said that, under Pennsylvania law, there were several offenses fitting within the generic category of bribery, and that bribery is defined generically as "conduct which is intended, at least by the alleged briber, as an assault on the integrity of a public office or an official action." 560 F.2d at 1137 n.23. In *Perkins*, the court interpreted *Forsythe* to mean that the receipt of an unlawful gratuity was within the generic designation of bribery. We agree with the *Forsythe* court that "the test for determining whether the charged acts fit into the generic category of the predicate offense is whether the indictment charges a type of activity generally known or characterized in the proscribed category, namely, any act or threat involving bribery." 560 F.2d at 1137. We also agree with the court in *Perkins* that an unlawful gratuity is an attack on the integrity of public officials and falls comfortably within the generic classification of bribery. . . .

[W]e affirm the judgment of the district court. . . .

Notes and Questions

1. The court said that the statute's references to state crimes are generic. What does that mean? Why would Congress use generic designations for state predicate crimes?

2. Why would Congress choose to "federalize" state crimes in the first instance? Doesn't this pose a threat to federal-state relations by intruding on a domain in which the states have a very real concern? Does RICO in effect punish defendants for violating state laws?

PROBLEM 10-2

Adams, a Chicago sewer inspector who routinely accepts bribes from sewer contractors, is charged with violating the Illinois official misconduct statute. His trial in state court results in an acquittal. Baker, another sewer inspector who also accepts bribes, is later charged with official misconduct under the same statute, but the trial court dismisses the case because the prosecution is barred by the Illinois statute of limitations. A year later, a federal grand jury indicts Adams and Baker for violating RICO, citing only violations of the Illinois official misconduct statute as predicate crimes. Does the RICO indictment properly allege offenses that are "chargeable" and "punishable" under Illinois law?[11]

To change the focus, assume the indictment does not name any state predicate crimes. Instead, it alleges that the predicate crime is bribery of public officials, in violation of 18 U.S.C. § 201. The indictment charges Adams and Baker with five counts of § 201 bribery and one RICO count. The jury acquits them of bribery but convicts them on the RICO charge. Should the RICO convictions stand?[12] Does the jury's verdict of acquittal on the counts charging bribery — the predicate crime — necessarily indicate insufficient evidence to convict on the RICO count?

NOTE ON THE DUAL SOVEREIGNTY DOCTRINE

Problem 10-2 posited successive state and federal prosecutions based upon the same conduct. Once the specific statutory construction and evidentiary questions in 10-2 are

---

11. Compare United States v. Davis, 576 F.2d 1065 (3d Cir. 1978), and United States v. Frumento, 563 F.2d 1083 (3d Cir. 1977), and Von Bulow v. Von Bulow, 634 F. Supp. 1284 (S.D.N.Y. 1986), with United States v. Louie, 625 F. Supp. 1327 (S.D.N.Y. 1985).

12. Cf. United States v. Powell, 469 U.S. 57 (1984).

resolved, the next logical inquiry is whether the federal RICO prosecution can go forward in light of the failed state prosecutions based on the same conduct. Have we now reached the point at which double jeopardy considerations bring the process to a halt?

Although this may look for all the world like a double jeopardy problem, it is not. The dual sovereignty doctrine permits successive state and federal prosecutions based upon the same conduct.[13] This doctrine is shaped by the concern that federal law enforcement efforts could be seriously frustrated by allowing a state to preempt a federal prosecution simply because the state prosecution was prior in time. Similarly, if a prior federal prosecution preempted a state prosecution for the same conduct, that would work a marked change in the traditional allocation of law enforcement responsibilities. States, not the federal government, have historically had primary responsibility for defining and prosecuting crimes.[14]

In what respects could a contrary rule frustrate the vindication of federal interests? Of state interests? Why do states have primary law enforcement responsibility? Do statutes like RICO cause erosion of that responsibility? Do other developments at the federal level?

Notwithstanding that successive state and federal prosecutions are constitutionally permissible, the federal government generally defers to a state that has already prosecuted for the same conduct.[15] That deference reflects the understanding that the state prosecution will usually serve the same interests the federal government seeks to vindicate. Is that more or less likely to be true in the context of a federal RICO prosecution?

And even without constitutional prohibition against successive state and federal prosecutions or a federal policy that favors deferring to the states, if the underlying conduct in both prosecutions is the same, why wouldn't the second prosecution be barred by the principle of collateral estoppels?

IV. RELATIONSHIP BETWEEN PERSON AND ENTERPRISE

REVES v. ERNST & YOUNG
507 U.S. 170 (1993)

Justice BLACKMUN delivered the opinion of the Court.[16]

[Reves, a trustee in bankruptcy, sued accounting firm Arthur Young (later known as Ernst & Young) on behalf of a farmer's co-op (the "Co-Op") and some of its creditors in connection with the firm's role in performing the Co-Op's annual financial audits during a two-year period. Arthur Young used unorthodox accounting methods to fix the value of the Co-Op's assets and, on the basis of its own questionable accounting techniques, certified the adequacy of the Co-Op's financial statements. Arthur Young took these actions without consulting or informing the Co-Op's board. Although the firm

---

13. Abbatte v. United States, 359 U.S. 187 (1959). The Supreme Court has also held that the dual sovereignty doctrine applies with equal force to successive state prosecutions by different sovereigns. Heath v. Alabama, 474 U.S. 82 (1985).

14. Abbatte v. United States, 359 U.S. 187, 195 (1959).

15. This policy, which is generally known as the Petite policy, was first announced in Petite v. United States, 361 U.S. 529 (1960).

16. Justice Scalia and Justice Thomas do not join Part IV-A of this opinion.

opined that the Co-Op was solvent, it did so without disclosing what was in truth the Co-Op's dire financial condition. Two years later, the Co-Op filed for bankruptcy.

The Trustee's lawsuit charged, inter alia, that — as the Co-Op's outside auditor — Arthur Young had violated RICO by participating in the affairs of an enterprise (the Co-Op) through a pattern of racketeering activity. Applying an "operation or management" test, the trial court granted Arthur Young's motion for summary judgment on the RICO claim, ruling that the firm and its auditors did not "conduct" or "participate in the conduct" of the Co-Op's affairs as required by § 1962(c). The court of appeals agreed.]

III . . .

The narrow question in this case is the meaning of the phrase "to conduct or participate, directly or indirectly, in the conduct of such enterprise's affairs." The word "conduct" is used twice, and it seems reasonable to give each use a similar construction. As a verb, "conduct" means to lead, run, manage, or direct. Webster's Third New International Dictionary 474 (1976). Petitioners urge us to read "conduct" as "carry on," so that almost any involvement in the affairs of an enterprise would satisfy the "conduct or participate" requirement. But context is important, and in the context of the phrase "to conduct . . . [an] enterprise's affairs," the word indicates some degree of direction.

The dissent agrees that, when "conduct" is used as a verb, "it is plausible to find in it a suggestion of control." The dissent prefers to focus on "conduct" as a noun, as in the phrase "participate, directly or indirectly, in the conduct of [an] enterprise's affairs." But unless one reads "conduct" to include an element of direction when used as a noun in this phrase, the word becomes superfluous. Congress could easily have written "participate, directly or indirectly, in [an] enterprise's affairs," but it chose to repeat the word "conduct." We conclude, therefore, that as both a noun and a verb in this subsection "conduct" requires an element of direction.

The more difficult question is what to make of the word "participate." This Court previously has characterized this word as a "term . . . of breadth." Petitioners argue that Congress used "participate" as a synonym for "aid and abet." That would be a term of breadth indeed, for "aid and abet" "comprehends all assistance rendered by words, acts, encouragement, support, or presence." Black's Law Dictionary 68 (6th ed. 1990). But within the context of § 1962(c), "participate" appears to have a narrower meaning. We may mark the limits of what the term might mean by looking again at what Congress did not say. On the one hand, "to participate . . . in the conduct of . . . affairs" must be broader than "to conduct affairs" or the "participate" phrase would be superfluous. On the other hand, as we already have noted, "to participate . . . in the conduct of . . . affairs" must be narrower than "to participate in affairs" or Congress' repetition of the word "conduct" would serve no purpose. It seems that Congress chose a middle ground, consistent with a common understanding of the word "participate" — "to take part in." Webster's Third New International Dictionary 1646 (1976).

Once we understand the word "conduct" to require some degree of direction and the word "participate" to require some part in that direction, the meaning of § 1962(c) comes into focus. In order to "participate, directly or indirectly, in the conduct of such enterprise's affairs," one must have some part in directing those affairs. Of course, the word "participate" makes clear that RICO liability is not limited to those with primary responsibility for the enterprise's affairs, just as the phrase "directly or indirectly" makes clear that RICO liability is not limited to those with a formal position in the enterprise,[17] but *some* part in directing the enterprise's affairs is required. The "operation or management" test expresses this requirement in a formulation that is easy to apply. . . .

V

Petitioners argue that the "operation or management" test is flawed because liability under § 1962(c) is not limited to upper management but may extend to "any person employed by or associated with [the] enterprise." We agree that liability under § 1962(c) is not limited to upper management, but we disagree that the "operation or management" test is inconsistent with this proposition. An enterprise is "operated" not just by upper management but also by lower-rung participants in the enterprise who are under the direction of upper management.[18] An enterprise also might be "operated" or "managed" by others "associated with" the enterprise who exert control over it as, for example, by bribery.

The United States also argues that the "operation or management" test is not consistent with § 1962(c) because it limits the liability of "outsiders" who have no official position within the enterprise. The United States correctly points out that RICO's major purpose was to attack the "infiltration of organized crime and racketeering into legitimate organizations," S. Rep. No. 91-617, at 76, but its argument fails on several counts. First, it ignores the fact that § 1962 has four subsections. Infiltration of legitimate organizations by "outsiders" is clearly addressed in subsections (a) and (b), and the "operation or management" test that applies under subsection (c) in no way limits the application of subsections (a) and (b) to "outsiders." Second, § 1962(c) is limited to persons "employed by or associated with" an enterprise, suggesting a more limited reach than subsections (a) and (b), which do not contain such a restriction. Third, § 1962(c) cannot be interpreted to reach complete "outsiders" because liability depends on showing that the defendants conducted or participated in the conduct of the "*enterprise's* affairs," not just their *own* affairs. Of course, "outsiders" may be liable under § 1962(c) if they are "associated with" an enterprise and participate in the conduct of *its* affairs — that is, participate in the operation or management of the enterprise itself — but it would be consistent with neither the language nor the legislative history of § 1962(c) to interpret it as broadly as petitioners and the United States urge.

---

17. For these reasons, we disagree with the suggestion of the Court of Appeals for the District of Columbia Circuit that § 1962(c) requires "significant control over or within an enterprise." Yellow Bus Lines, Inc. v. Drivers, Chauffeurs & Helpers Local Union 639, 913 F.2d 948, 954 (1990) (en banc) (emphasis added).

18. At oral argument, there was some discussion about whether low-level employees could be considered to have participated in the conduct of an enterprise's affairs. We need not decide in this case how far § 1962(c) extends down the ladder of operation because it is clear that Arthur Young was not acting under the direction of the Co-Op's officers or board.

In sum, we hold that "to conduct or participate, directly or indirectly, in the conduct of such enterprise's affairs," one must participate in the operation or management of the enterprise itself. . . .

The judgment of the Court of Appeals is affirmed.

It is so ordered.

Justice SOUTER, with whom Justice WHITE joins, dissenting. . . .

The word "conduct" occurs twice in § 1962(c), first as a verb, then as a noun. . . . [T]he majority goes astray in quoting only the verb form of "conduct" in its statement of the context for divining a meaning that must fit the noun usage as well. Thus, the majority reaches its pivotal conclusion that "in the context of the phrase 'to conduct . . . [an] enterprise's affairs,' the word indicates some degree of direction." To be sure, if the statutory setting is so abbreviated as to limit consideration to the word as a verb, it is plausible to find in it a suggestion of control, as in the phrase "to conduct an orchestra." (Even so, the suggestion is less than emphatic, since even when "conduct" is used as a verb, "the notion of direction or leadership is often obscured or lost; e.g. an investigation is *conducted* by all those who take part in it." 3 Oxford English Dictionary 691 (2d ed. 1989).)

In any event, the context is not so limited. . . . The term, when used as a noun, is defined by the majority's chosen dictionary as, for example, "carrying forward" or "carrying out," Webster's Third New International Dictionary 473 (1976), phrases without any implication of direction or control. The suggestion of control is diminished further by the fact that § 1962(c) covers not just those "employed by" an enterprise, but those merely "associated with" it, as well. And associates (like employees) are prohibited not merely from conducting the affairs of an enterprise through a pattern of racketeering, not merely from participating directly in such unlawful conduct, but even from indirect participation in the conduct of an enterprise's affairs in such a manner. The very breadth of this prohibition renders the majority's reading of "conduct" rather awkward, for it is hard to imagine how the "operation or management" test would leave the statute with the capacity to reach the indirect participation of someone merely associated with an enterprise. I think, then, that this contextual examination shows "conduct" to have a long arm, unlimited by any requirement to prove that the activity includes an element of direction. But at the very least, the full context is enough to defeat the majority's conviction that the more restrictive interpretation of the word "conduct" is clearly the one intended.

What, then, if we call it a tie on the contextual analysis? The answer is that Congress has given courts faced with uncertain meaning a clear tie-breaker in RICO's "liberal construction" clause, which directs that the "provisions of this title shall be liberally construed to effectuate its remedial purposes." . . . [I]n this instance, the "liberal construction" clause plays its intended part, directing us to recognize the more inclusive definition of the word "conduct," free of any restricting element of direction or control. . . .

Even if I were to adopt the majority's view of § 1962(c), however, I still could not join the judgment, which seems to me unsupportable under the very "operation or management" test the Court announces. If Arthur Young had confined itself in this case to the role traditionally performed by an outside auditor, I could agree with the majority that Arthur Young took no part in the management or operation of the Co-op. But the record on summary judgment, viewed most favorably to Reves, shows that Arthur Young created the very financial statements it was hired, and purported, to audit. Most

importantly, Reves adduced evidence that Arthur Young took on management responsibilities by deciding, in the first instance, what value to assign to the Co-op's most
important fixed asset . . . and Arthur Young itself conceded below that the alleged activity went beyond traditional auditing. . . .

For our purposes, the line between managing and auditing is fairly clear. In
describing the "respective responsibilities of management and auditor," Arthur Young
points to the Code of Professional Conduct developed by the American Institute of Certified Public Accountants (AICPA). This auditors' code points up management's ultimate responsibility for the content of financial statements:

> The financial statements are management's responsibility. The auditor's responsibility is
> to express an opinion on the financial statements. Management is responsible for adopting
> sound accounting policies and for establishing and maintaining an internal control struc-
> ture that will, among other things, record, process, summarize, and report financial data that
> is consistent with management's assertions embodied in the financial statements. . . . The
> independent auditor may make suggestions about the form or content of the financial state-
> ments or draft them, in whole or in part, based on information from management's account-
> ing system. 1 CCH AICPA Professional Standards, SAS No. 1, § 110.02 (1982).

In short, management chooses the assertions to appear in financial statements; the
auditor "simply expresses an opinion on the client's financial statements." These standards leave no doubt that an accountant can in no sense independently audit financial
records when he has selected their substance himself.

The evidence . . . indicates that Arthur Young did indeed step out of its auditing
shoes and into those of management, in creating the financial record on which the
Co-op's solvency was erroneously predicated. . . .

Notes and Questions

1. Is the statute as clear as the majority in *Reves* evidently thought it was? Does
the "operation and management" test help to clarify § 1962(c)? Or does it further
muddy the waters?

2. How high up in the corporate hierarchy must an actor be to participate in the
operation or management of the company?

3. To what extent does *Reves* shield outsiders from RICO liability? Do the Court's
limitations on § 1962(c) liability reflect sound policy?

PROBLEM 10-3

Recall the facts in United States v. Parker, supra in Chapter 9. Mrs. Parker was a
clerk to an administrative law judge in the Social Security Administration whose duties
consisted of typing and mailing the judge's opinions. Using the Administration's computer system — and acting outside the scope of her authority — she helped a number of
applicants obtain Supplemental Social Security Income benefits in return for bribes.
After *Reves*, if Mrs. Parker had been charged with violating § 1962(c), could the
government prove that she conducted or participated in the conduct of the Social Security Administration's affairs?

PROBLEM 10-4

Harry Hustler, a criminal defense lawyer, represents many clients who are prosecuted by the State's Attorney's Office. He and J. D. Thomas, an Assistant State's Attorney, have an informal arrangement through which Thomas, whenever possible, will give Hustler's clients favorable treatment in charging decisions and plea negotiations in exchange for cash.

After the FBI uncovers this cozy arrangement, a federal grand jury indicts Hustler and Thomas for violating § 1962(c). Is Hustler associated with the State's Attorney's Office? If so, has he conducted or participated in the conduct of its affairs?[19]

McCULLOUGH v. SUTER
757 F.2d 142 (7th Cir. 1985)

POSNER, Circuit Judge.

The question for decision — one of first impression so far as we are able to determine — is whether a sole proprietor can be an "enterprise" with which its proprietor can be "associated" within the meaning of a provision of the Racketeer Influenced and Corrupt Organizations Act, 18 U.S.C. § 1962(c), which makes it "unlawful for any person employed by or associated with any enterprise engaged in, or the activities of which affect, interstate or foreign commerce, to conduct or participate, directly or indirectly, in the conduct of such enterprise's affairs through a pattern of racketeering activity or collection of unlawful debt." There are no cases on the question and no pertinent legislative history.

Richard Suter, who under the name of the National Investment Publishing Company advises people about investments and buys coins for investment on their behalf, received $23,000 from the Utica National Bank to buy coins for R. D. McCullough's self-employed retirement account, which the bank manages. Suter represented that he used the money to buy coins, but he sent only three coins, together worth less than $10,000, to the bank, and the bank and McCullough brought this suit. Later Suter pleaded guilty to two counts of having used the mails to defraud coin investors such as the bank and McCullough, in violation of the federal mail-fraud statute. After a bench trial, the district court in this case found that Suter had defrauded the plaintiffs of $14,000, and awarded them treble their damages, plus attorney's fees, under the civil damages provision of the RICO statute, 18 U.S.C. § 1964(c).

There is no question that Suter's fraudulent activity constituted a pattern of racketeering activity as that term is defined in the statute, or that Suter conducted the affairs of the National Investment Publishing Company through this pattern, or that this conduct caused the injury to the plaintiffs of which they complain. Hence they are entitled to recover damages under the RICO statute provided that a sole proprietorship can be an "enterprise" with which the proprietor can be "associated." We think it can be. The statute provides that "'enterprise' includes any individual, partnership, corporation, association, or other legal entity, and any union or group of individuals associated in fact although not a legal entity." 18 U.S.C. § 1961(4). A sole proprietorship is a

---

19. Cf. United States v. Yonan, 800 F.2d 164 (7th Cir. 1986).

recognized legal entity, and, provided it has any employees, is in any event a "group of individuals associated in fact." . . .

There would be a problem if the sole proprietorship were strictly a one-man show. If Suter had no employees or other associates and simply did business under the name of the National Investment Publishing Company, it could hardly be said that he was associating with an enterprise called the National Investment Publishing Company; you cannot associate with yourself, any more than you can conspire with yourself, just by giving yourself a *nom de guerre*. We therefore held in Haroco, Inc. v. American National Bank & Trust Co., 747 F.2d 384, 399-402 (7th Cir. 1984), that an enterprise (a national banking association in that case) could not associate with itself for purposes of section 1962(c). But Suter had several people working for him; this made his company an enterprise, and not just a one-man band; and all section 1962(c) requires, as we said in *Haroco*, is "some separate and distinct existence for the person [Suter] and the enterprise [National Investment Publishing Company]," 747 F.2d at 402.

It is true that if Suter were all by himself, and yet adopted the corporate form for his activity, he might well fall under section 1962(c), for the corporation would be an enterprise within the meaning of section 1961(4). And from this it could be argued that since subsection (4) defines enterprise so broadly, even a sole proprietorship is an enterprise and Suter is therefore caught by section 1962(c) — thus showing the absurdity of ever treating a sole proprietorship as an enterprise. But these cases are different. If the one-man band incorporates, it gets some legal protections from the corporate form, such as limited liability; and it is just this sort of legal shield for illegal activity that RICO tries to pierce. A one-man band that does not incorporate, that merely operates as a proprietorship, gains no legal protections from the form in which it has chosen to do business; the man and the proprietorship really are the same entity in law and fact. But if the man has employees or associates, the enterprise is distinct from him, and it then makes no difference, so far as we can see, what legal form the enterprise takes. The only important thing is that it be either formally (as when there is incorporation) or practically (as when there are other people besides the proprietor working in the organization) separable from the individual.

The other issues raised by Suter on this appeal have no possible merit. The judgment for the plaintiff is affirmed.

NOTE ON RELATIONAL ELEMENTS

Section 1962(c) contemplates a relationship between a person and an enterprise. It requires that a "person" be employed by or associated with an "enterprise." Section 1962(c) also contemplates interaction between the person and the enterprise. The person must "conduct" or "participate" in the conduct of the affairs of the enterprise. Thus, because the "person" is the wrongdoer — i.e., he or she conducts the affairs of the enterprise through a pattern of racketeering activity — the person is the proper defendant. The enterprise is not.

Because it would be conceptually difficult to find the requisite relationship and interaction if there were only a single individual or entity, the majority of circuits that have ruled on this point have held — as the *McCullough* court did — that the person and the enterprise must be separate and distinct.[20]

Until recently, there was a split of authority on the question whether one who is formally affiliated with a corporate enterprise could be deemed a person who is separate from it. Late in its 2000 term, the Supreme Court clarified the law on this point. In Cedric Kushner Promotions, Ltd. v. King,[21] the trial court had dismissed a civil RICO suit against boxing promoter Don King on the ground that King, while acting in his capacity as president and sole shareholder of Don King Productions, was not a "person" distinct from the "enterprise."[22]

Although it did not quarrel with the premise that § 1962(c) requires the person and enterprise to be separate and distinct, the Supreme Court reversed. Noting that the fundamental reason for incorporating is to create a distinct legal entity whose rights, obligations, powers, and privileges differ from those of its owners and employees, the Court found that King was a natural person with a distinct identity apart from the corporate legal entity, notwithstanding his status as a corporate owner/employee.

In contrast with § 1962(c), § 1962(a) and (b) do not contemplate a relationship between the person and the enterprise as an essential predicate for liability. Subsection (a) is directed at the use or investment of the proceeds of racketeering activity to acquire, establish, or operate an enterprise. In this context, it is possible for the person and the enterprise to be the same.[23] A corporation that sells worthless securities, for example, may invest the proceeds of the sales in its own stock or may use them for operating capital.

Similarly, § 1962(b) contains no relational requirement. It targets acquiring or maintaining an interest in or control of an enterprise through a pattern of racketeering activity. Thus, for example, a single corporation could engage in a fraudulent stock manipulation scheme to squeeze out minority shareholders in violation of subsection (b)'s requirements.[24]

Because neither § 1962(a) nor (b) contains a relational element, an enterprise that is a wrongdoer can be named as the defendant.

V. RICO CONSPIRACIES

SALINAS v. UNITED STATES
522 U.S. 52 (1997)

Justice KENNEDY delivered the opinion of the Court. . . .

[Salinas was a deputy sheriff who worked in a local jail that received federal funds to house federal prisoners. He accepted bribes from a federal prisoner in exchange for allowing the prisoner private contact visits with women twice a week.[25]]

---

20. See, e.g., Kehr Packages v. Fidelcor, Inc., 926 F.2d 1406 (3d Cir. 1991).
21. 533 U.S. 158 (2001).
22. The Second Circuit affirmed the suit's dismissal.
23. See, e.g., Busby v. Crown Supply, 896 F.2d 833 (4th Cir. 1990) (en banc).
24. See, e.g., Landry v. Air Line Pilots Ass'n, 901 F.2d 404 (5th Cir. 1990).
25. A fuller statement of facts appears in Chapter 9. — ED.

. . . Salinas was charged with one count of violating RICO, 18 U.S.C. § 1962(c), one count of conspiracy to violate RICO, § 1962(d), and two counts of bribery in violation of § 666(a)(1)(B). The jury acquitted Salinas on the substantive RICO count but convicted him on the RICO conspiracy count and the bribery counts. A divided panel of the Court of Appeals for the Fifth Circuit affirmed.

III

Salinas directs his . . . challenge to his conviction for conspiracy to violate RICO. There could be no conspiracy offense, he says, unless he himself committed or agreed to commit the two predicate acts requisite for a substantive RICO offense under § 1962(c). Salinas identifies a conflict among the Courts of Appeals on the point. Decisions of the First, Second, and Tenth Circuits require that, under the RICO conspiracy provision, the defendant must himself commit or agree to commit two or more predicate acts. Eight other Courts of Appeals, including the Fifth Circuit in this case, take a contrary view. . . .

. . . The Government's theory was that Salinas himself committed a substantive § 1962(c) RICO violation by conducting the enterprise's affairs through a pattern of racketeering activity that included acceptance of two or more bribes, felonies punishable in Texas by more than one year in prison. The jury acquitted on the substantive count. Salinas was convicted of conspiracy, however, and he challenges the conviction because the jury was not instructed that he must have committed or agreed to commit two predicate acts himself. His interpretation of the conspiracy statute is wrong.

The RICO conspiracy statute, simple in formulation, provides:

> It shall be unlawful for any person to conspire to violate any of the provisions of subsection (a), (b), or (c) of this section. 18 U.S.C. § 1962(d).

There is no requirement of some overt act or specific act in the statute before us, unlike the general conspiracy provision applicable to federal crimes, which requires that at least one of the conspirators have committed an "act to effect the object of the conspiracy." § 371. The RICO conspiracy provision, then, is even more comprehensive than the general conspiracy offense in § 371.

In interpreting the provisions of § 1962(d), we adhere to a general rule: When Congress uses well-settled terminology of criminal law, its words are presumed to have their ordinary meaning and definition. See Morissette v. United States, 342 U.S. 246, 263 (1952). The relevant statutory phrase in § 1962(d) is "to conspire." We presume Congress intended to use the term in its conventional sense, and certain well-established principles follow.

A conspiracy may exist even if a conspirator does not agree to commit or facilitate each and every part of the substantive offense. The partners in the criminal plan must agree to pursue the same criminal objective and may divide up the work, yet each is responsible for the acts of each other. See Pinkerton v. United States, 328 U.S. 640, 646 (1946) ("And so long as the partnership in crime continues, the partners act for each other in carrying it forward."). If conspirators have a plan which calls for some conspirators to perpetrate the crime and others to provide support, the supporters are as guilty as the perpetrators. As Justice Holmes observed: "[P]lainly a person may conspire for the commission of a crime by a third person." United States v. Holte, 236 U.S. 140, 144 (1915). A person, moreover, may be liable for conspiracy even though he was incapable of committing the substantive offense.

The point Salinas tries to make is in opposition to these principles, and is refuted by Bannon v. United States, 156 U.S. 464 (1895). There the defendants were charged with conspiring to violate the general conspiracy statute, which requires proof of an overt act. One defendant objected to the indictment because it did not allege he had committed an overt act. We rejected the argument because it would erode the common-law principle that, so long as they share a common purpose, conspirators are liable for the acts of their co-conspirators. . . . The RICO conspiracy statute, § 1962(d), broadened conspiracy coverage by omitting the requirement of an overt act; it did not, at the same time, work the radical change of requiring the Government to prove each conspirator agreed that he would be the one to commit two predicate acts.

Our recitation of conspiracy law comports with contemporary understanding. When Congress passed RICO in 1970, the American Law Institute's Model Penal Code permitted a person to be convicted of conspiracy so long as he "agrees with such other person or persons that they or one or more of them will engage in conduct that constitutes such crime." American Law Institute, Model Penal Code § 5.03(1)(a) (1962). As the drafters emphasized, "so long as the purpose of the agreement is to facilitate commission of a crime, the actor need not agree 'to commit' the crime." American Law Institute, Model Penal Code, Tent. Draft No. 10, p. 117 (1960). . . .

A conspirator must intend to further an endeavor which, if completed, would satisfy all of the elements of a substantive criminal offense, but it suffices that he adopt the goal of furthering or facilitating the criminal endeavor. He may do so in any number of ways short of agreeing to undertake all of the acts necessary for the crime's completion. One can be a conspirator by agreeing to facilitate only some of the acts leading to the substantive offense. It is elementary that a conspiracy may exist and be punished whether or not the substantive crime ensues, for the conspiracy is a distinct evil, dangerous to the public, and so punishable in itself.

It makes no difference that the substantive offense under subsection (c) requires two or more predicate acts. The interplay between subsections (c) and (d) does not permit us to excuse from the reach of the conspiracy provision an actor who does not himself commit or agree to commit the two or more predicate acts requisite to the underlying offense. True, though an "enterprise" under § 1962(c) can exist with only one actor to conduct it, in most instances it will be conducted by more than one person or entity; and this in turn may make it somewhat difficult to determine just where the enterprise ends and the conspiracy begins, or, on the other hand, whether the two crimes are coincident in their factual circumstances. In some cases the connection the defendant had to the alleged enterprise or to the conspiracy to further it may be tenuous enough so that his own commission of two predicate acts may become an important part of the Government's case. Perhaps these were the considerations leading some of the Circuits to require in conspiracy cases that each conspirator himself commit or agree to commit two or more predicate acts. Nevertheless, that proposition cannot be sustained as a definition of the conspiracy offense, for it is contrary to the principles we have discussed.

In the case before us, even if Salinas did not accept or agree to accept two bribes, there was ample evidence that he conspired to violate subsection (c). The evidence showed that Marmolejo [the Hidalgo County Sheriff] committed at least two acts of racketeering activity when he accepted numerous bribes and that Salinas [one of Marmolejo's principal deputies] knew about and agreed to facilitate the scheme. This is sufficient to support a conviction under § 1962(d). . . .

The judgment of the Court of Appeals is affirmed.

Notes and Questions

1. Reves v. Ernst & Young held that to establish liability under § 1962(c), the government must prove that the defendant participated in the operation or management of the enterprise. In response to *Reves*, some courts held that the operation and management test applies to a conspiracy to violate § 1962(c) — i.e., the conspirators must have agreed to participate in the operation or management of the enterprise.[26] Other courts reached the opposite conclusion, holding that under § 1962(d), the conspirators need only agree to the overall objective of the RICO conspiracy.

The Court in *Salinas* did not expressly address this issue. What, if any, impact should *Salinas* have on the resolution of this question?

VI. CIVIL LIABILITY

Wisely or not, Congress created a private civil RICO action for damages. 18 U.S.C. § 1964(c). Although civil litigants were slow to warm to the provision, once its potential was fully understood, a virtual flood of civil RICO suits inundated the federal court system. Lured by the prospect of recovering treble damages and attorneys' fees, plaintiffs increasingly have sought to resolve ordinary commercial disputes between reputable business firms through civil RICO suits. Needless to say, this has rankled the business community and has made the scope of civil RICO liability a perpetual subject of controversy, both in the business community and in Congress.

To establish a cause of action, the civil RICO plaintiff must allege and prove all of the elements of a criminal violation. That is, the plaintiff must show the existence of an enterprise; an interstate commerce connection; a person who committed the RICO violation; a pattern of racketeering activity; and one of the relationships between the racketeering activity and the enterprise designated in §§ 1962(a), (b), or (c), or a conspiracy to violate § 1962(a), (b), or (c). In addition, the plaintiff must prove injury to his or her business or property by reason of the RICO violation.

---

26. See, e.g., Neibel v. Trans World Assurance Co., 108 F.3d 1123 (9th Cir. 1997); United States v. Antar, 53 F.3d 568 (3d Cir. 1995).

A. INJURY TO BUSINESS OR PROPERTY

SEDIMA, S.P.R.L. v. IMREX CO.
473 U.S. 479 (1985)

Justice WHITE delivered the opinion of the Court.

The Racketeer Influenced and Corrupt Organizations Act (RICO), provides a private civil action to recover treble damages for injury "by reason of a violation of" its substantive provisions. 18 U.S.C. § 1964(c). The initial dormancy of this provision and its recent greatly increased utilization[27] are now familiar history. In response to what it perceived to be misuse of civil RICO by private plaintiffs, the court below construed § 1964(c) to permit private actions only against defendants who had been convicted on criminal charges, and only where there had occurred a "racketeering injury." While we understand the court's concern over the consequences of an unbridled reading of the statute, we reject both of its holdings. . . .

In 1979, petitioner Sedima, a Belgian corporation, entered into a joint venture with respondent Imrex Co. to provide electronic components to a Belgian firm. The buyer was to order parts through Sedima; Imrex was to obtain the parts in this country and ship them to Europe. The agreement called for Sedima and Imrex to split the net proceeds. Imrex filled roughly $8 million in orders placed with it through Sedima. Sedima became convinced, however, that Imrex was presenting inflated bills, cheating Sedima out of a portion of its proceeds by collecting for nonexistent expenses.

In 1982, Sedima filed this action in the Federal District Court for the Eastern District of New York. The complaint set out common-law claims of unjust enrichment, conversion, and breach of contract, fiduciary duty, and a constructive trust. In addition, it asserted RICO claims under § 1964(c) against Imrex and two of its officers. Two counts alleged violations of § 1962(c), based on predicate acts of mail and wire fraud. A third count alleged a conspiracy to violate § 1962(c). Claiming injury of at least $175,000, the amount of the alleged over-billing, Sedima sought treble damages and attorney's fees.

[The District Court dismissed the RICO counts of the complaint because they failed to allege any "RICO-type injury." Although the court did not specify precisely what that might mean, it indicated that there must be "some sort of distinct 'racketeering injury'" or "'competitive injury'" that differed from the injury that would result directly from the commission of the predicate acts of mail and wire fraud. The court of appeals agreed. The court also ruled that the RICO counts were defective because they did not allege that the defendants had previously been convicted of the RICO violation or any of the underlying predicate crimes.]

The decision below was one episode in a recent proliferation of civil RICO litigation within the Second Circuit and in other Courts of Appeals. In light of the variety of approaches taken by the lower courts and the importance of the issues, we granted certiorari. We now reverse. . . .

---

27. Of 270 District Court RICO decisions prior to this year, only 3% (nine cases) were decided throughout the 1970's, 2% were decided in 1980, 7% in 1981, 13% in 1982, 33% in 1983, and 43% in 1984. Report of the Ad Hoc Civil RICO Task Force of the ABA Section of Corporation, Banking and Business Law 55 (1985) (hereinafter ABA Report); see also id., at 53a (table).

III

The language of RICO gives no obvious indication that a civil action can proceed only after a criminal conviction. The word "conviction" does not appear in any relevant portion of the statute. To the contrary, the predicate acts involve conduct that is "chargeable" or "indictable," and "offense[s]" that are "punishable," under various criminal statutes. As defined in the statute, racketeering activity consists not of acts for which the defendant has been convicted, but of acts for which he could be. Thus, a prior-conviction requirement cannot be found in the definition of "racketeering activity." Nor can it be found in § 1962, which sets out the statute's substantive provisions. Indeed, if either § 1961 or § 1962 did contain such a requirement, a prior conviction would also be a prerequisite, nonsensically, for a criminal prosecution, or for a civil action by the Government to enjoin violations that had not yet occurred.

The Court of Appeals purported to discover its prior-conviction requirement in the term "violation" in § 1964(c). However, even if that term were read to refer to a criminal conviction, it would require a conviction under RICO, not of the predicate offenses. That aside, the term "violation" does not imply a criminal conviction. It refers only to a failure to adhere to legal requirements. This is its indisputable meaning elsewhere in the statute. Section 1962 renders certain conduct "unlawful"; § 1963 and § 1964 impose consequences, criminal and civil, for "violations" of § 1962. We should not lightly infer that Congress intended the term to have wholly different meanings in neighboring subsections. . . .

The Court of Appeals was of the view that its narrow construction of the statute was essential to avoid intolerable practical consequences. First, without a prior conviction to rely on, the plaintiff would have to prove commission of the predicate acts beyond a reasonable doubt. This would require instructing the jury as to different standards of proof for different aspects of the case. To avoid this awkwardness, the court inferred that the criminality must already be established, so that the civil action could proceed smoothly under the usual preponderance standard.

We are not at all convinced that the predicate acts must be established beyond a reasonable doubt in a proceeding under § 1964(c). In a number of settings, conduct that can be punished as criminal only upon proof beyond a reasonable doubt will support civil sanctions under a preponderance standard. There is no indication that Congress sought to depart from this general principle here. . . .

The court below also feared that any other construction would raise severe constitutional questions, as it "would provide civil remedies for offenses criminal in nature, stigmatize defendants with the appellation 'racketeer,' authorize the award of damages which are clearly punitive, including attorney's fees, and constitute a civil remedy aimed in part to avoid the constitutional protections of the criminal law." 741 F.2d at 500, n.49. We do not view the statute as being so close to the constitutional edge. As noted above, the fact that conduct can result in both criminal liability and treble damages does not mean that there is not a bona fide civil action. The familiar provisions for both criminal liability and treble damages under the antitrust laws indicate as much. Nor are attorney's fees "clearly punitive." As for stigma, a civil RICO proceeding leaves no greater stain than do a number of other civil proceedings. Furthermore, requiring conviction of the predicate acts would not protect against an unfair imposition of the "racketeer" label. If there is a problem with thus stigmatizing a garden variety defrauder by means of a civil action, it is not reduced by making certain that the defendant is guilty of fraud beyond a reasonable doubt. . . .

Finally, we note that a prior-conviction requirement would be inconsistent with Congress' underlying policy concerns. Such a rule would severely handicap potential plaintiffs. A guilty party may escape conviction for any number of reasons — not least among them the possibility that the Government itself may choose to pursue only civil remedies. Private attorney general provisions such as § 1964(c) are in part designed to fill prosecutorial gaps. This purpose would be largely defeated, and the need for treble damages as an incentive to litigate unjustified, if private suits could be maintained only against those already brought to justice. . . .

IV

In considering the Court of Appeals' second prerequisite for a private civil RICO action — "injury . . . caused by an activity which RICO was designed to deter" — we are somewhat hampered by the vagueness of that concept. Apart from reliance on the general purposes of RICO and a reference to "mobsters," the court provided scant indication of what the requirement of racketeering injury means. It emphasized Congress' undeniable desire to strike at organized crime, but acknowledged and did not purport to overrule Second Circuit precedent rejecting a requirement of an organized crime nexus. The court also stopped short of adopting a "competitive injury" requirement; while insisting that the plaintiff show "the kind of economic injury which has an effect on competition," it did not require "actual anticompetitive effect." 741 F.2d at 496.

[The Court found no language in the statute or the legislative history to support a distinct "racketeering injury" requirement. The statute merely confers standing on one who has suffered injury to business or property as a result of conduct constituting the violation.]

Underlying the Court of Appeals' holding was its distress at the "extraordinary, if not outrageous," uses to which civil RICO has been put. 741 F.2d at 487. Instead of being used against mobsters and organized criminals, it has become a tool for everyday fraud cases brought against "respected and legitimate 'enterprises.' " Ibid. Yet Congress wanted to reach both "legitimate" and "illegitimate" enterprises. The former enjoy neither an inherent incapacity for criminal activity nor immunity from its consequences. The fact that § 1964(c) is used against respected businesses allegedly engaged in a pattern of specifically identified criminal conduct is hardly a sufficient reason for assuming that the provision is being misconstrued. Nor does it reveal the "ambiguity" discovered by the court below. "[T]he fact that RICO has been applied in situations not expressly anticipated by Congress does not demonstrate ambiguity. It demonstrates breadth." Haroco, Inc. v. American National Bank & Trust Co. of Chicago, 747 F.2d at 398.

It is true that private civil actions under the statute are being brought almost solely against such defendants, rather than against the archetypal, intimidating mobster.[28] Yet

---

28. The ABA Task Force found that of the 270 known civil RICO cases at the trial court level, 40% involved securities fraud, 37% common-law fraud in a commercial or business setting, and only 9% "allegations of criminal activity of a type generally associated with professional criminals." ABA Report, at 55-56. Another survey of 132 published decisions found that 57 involved securities transactions and 38 commercial and contract disputes, while no other category made it into double figures. American Institute

this defect — if defect it is — is inherent in the statute as written, and its correction must lie with Congress. It is not for the judiciary to eliminate the private action in situations where Congress has provided it simply because plaintiffs are not taking advantage of it in its more difficult applications.

We nonetheless recognize that, in its private civil version, RICO is evolving into something quite different from the original conception of its enactors. Though sharing the doubts of the Court of Appeals about this increasing divergence, we cannot agree with either its diagnosis or its remedy. The "extraordinary" uses to which civil RICO has been put appear to be primarily the result of the breadth of the predicate offenses, in particular the inclusion of wire, mail, and securities fraud, and the failure of Congress and the courts to develop a meaningful concept of "pattern." We do not believe that the amorphous standing requirement imposed by the Second Circuit effectively responds to these problems, or that it is a form of statutory amendment appropriately undertaken by the courts. . . .

The judgment below is accordingly reversed, and the case is remanded for further proceedings consistent with this opinion.

It is so ordered.

Justice MARSHALL, with whom Justice BRENNAN, Justice BLACKMUN, and Justice POWELL join, dissenting. . . .

I

The Court's interpretation of the civil RICO statute quite simply revolutionizes private litigation; it validates the federalization of broad areas of state common law of frauds, and it approves the displacement of well-established federal remedial provisions. We do not lightly infer a congressional intent to effect such fundamental changes. To infer such intent here would be untenable, for there is no indication that Congress even considered, much less approved, the scheme that the Court today defines.

The single most significant reason for the expansive use of civil RICO has been the presence in the statute, as predicate acts, of mail and wire fraud violations. Prior to RICO, no federal statute had expressly provided a private damages remedy based upon a violation of the mail or wire fraud statutes, which make it a federal crime to use the mail or wires in furtherance of a scheme to defraud. Moreover, the Courts of Appeals consistently had held that no implied federal private causes of action accrue to victims of these federal violations. The victims normally were restricted to bringing actions in state court under common-law fraud theories. . . .

The only restraining influence on the "inexorable expansion of the mail and wire fraud statutes" has been the prudent use of prosecutorial discretion. Prosecutors simply do not invoke the mail and wire fraud provisions in every case in which a violation of the relevant statute can be proved.

The responsible use of prosecutorial discretion is particularly important with respect to criminal RICO prosecutions — which often rely on mail and wire fraud as

---

of Certified Public Accountants, The Authority to Bring Private Treble-Damage Suits Under "RICO" Should Be Removed 13 (Oct. 10, 1984).

predicate acts — given the extremely severe penalties authorized by RICO's criminal provisions. . . .

In the context of civil RICO, however, the restraining influence of prosecutors is completely absent. Unlike the Government, private litigants have no reason to avoid displacing state common-law remedies. Quite to the contrary, such litigants, lured by the prospect of treble damages and attorney's fees, have a strong incentive to invoke RICO's provisions whenever they can allege in good faith two instances of mail or wire fraud. Then the defendant, facing a tremendous financial exposure in addition to the threat of being labeled a "racketeer," will have a strong interest in settling the dispute. The civil RICO provision consequently stretches the mail and wire fraud statutes to their absolute limits and federalizes important areas of civil litigation that until now were solely within the domain of the States. . . .

In summary, in both theory and practice, civil RICO has brought profound changes to our legal landscape. Undoubtedly, Congress has the power to federalize a great deal of state common law, and there certainly are no relevant constraints on its ability to displace federal law. Those, however, are not the questions that we face in this case. What we have to decide here, instead, is whether Congress in fact intended to produce these far-reaching results. . . .

[Dissent of Justice POWELL omitted.]

Notes and Questions

1. If the Court had endorsed the prior-conviction theory, what impact would that have had on civil RICO litigation? If Congress wanted to narrow the scope of civil RICO liability, would the addition of a prior-conviction requirement make sense?

2. Why did the Court reject the special "racketeering injury" requirement adopted by the court of appeals? If the high Court had endorsed it, what impact would that have had on civil RICO litigation? Should Congress consider defining more specifically (or narrowly) what qualifies as an injury to business or property?

3. The court of appeals described the uses to which the civil RICO statute has been put as "extraordinary and outrageous." What prompted the court to demonize civil RICO actions so vehemently? Do the majority and/or Justice Marshall view this as a fair characterization? If the statute is being used in ways that Congress did not envision, why wouldn't the Court adopt a more limiting construction?

4. Is it clear which is easier to prove — a criminal RICO violation or a civil RICO case? Are the elements precisely the same? How, if at all, does the "burden of proof" issue complicate matters?

5. Justice Marshall attached importance to the competing considerations that drive case selection by criminal prosecutors and civil plaintiffs. Does his point hit the mark? Should these considerations have had any bearing on the outcome in *Sedima*?

6. Mail, wire, and securities fraud are often identified as the underlying predicate crimes in criminal prosecutions. Yet few decisions involving criminal RICO convictions lash out at the use of these white collar fraud statutes as predicate crimes. Why might courts be more hostile to civil suits than to criminal prosecutions in this context?

7. Is there a legitimate argument that, as currently construed, the civil RICO statute creates serious federalism concerns? If so, what are they and why didn't they influence the outcome in *Sedima*?

NOTE ON RICO REFORM

As the opinions in *Sedima* suggest, the inclusion of mail, wire, and securities fraud in the litany of federal predicate crimes has made it possible to use the civil RICO statute in business disputes involving garden variety commercial fraud. In response to the business community's vociferous criticism of such "abusive" uses of civil RICO actions, Congress has considered various proposals to "reform" § 1964(c). Over the years, the concept of civil RICO reform has remained constant — "reform" is synonymous with limiting the scope of liability. Some reform efforts focused on a proposal containing a "gatekeeper" provision that would have required the court to dismiss a suit if the underlying criminal conduct was not "egregious" or if the defendant was not a major participant in the alleged violation.[29]

Others have targeted specific theories of liability. Two studies conducted in the mid-1980s led to a different approach. They revealed that 40 percent of the known civil RICO cases at the trial level involved securities fraud[30] and nearly half of the published civil RICO decisions involved securities transactions.[31] Responding to a wide range of perceived abuses in securities litigation — including, but not limited to, civil RICO litigation — Congress enacted the Private Securities Litigation Reform Act of 1995. In addition to "reforming" other aspects of securities litigation, the Act amended the civil RICO statute to severely limit civil RICO actions based on securities fraud.

SEC. 107. AMENDMENT TO RACKETEER INFLUENCED AND CORRUPT ORGANIZATIONS ACT

Section 1964(c) of title 18, United States Code, is amended by inserting before the period, "except that no person may rely upon any conduct that would have been actionable as fraud in the purchase or sale of securities to establish a violation of section 1962. The exception contained in the preceding sentence does not apply to an action against any person that is criminally convicted in connection with the fraud, in which case the statute of limitations shall start to run on the date on which the conviction becomes final."

The Conference Committee report explained what it intended to accomplish through this amendment.

The Conference Committee amends section 1964(c) of title 18 of the U.S. Code to remove any conduct that would have been actionable as fraud in the purchase or sale of securities as racketeering activity under civil RICO. The Committee intends this amendment to eliminate securities fraud as a predicate offense in a civil RICO action. In addition, the

---

29. This proposal, H.R. 1717, was approved by the House Judiciary Committee in 1991 but later died on the vine.

30. Report of the Ad Hoc Civil RICO Task Force of the ABA Section of Corporation, Banking and Business Law 55-56 (1985).

31. American Institute of Certified Public Accountants, The Authority to Bring Private Treble-Damage Suits Under "RICO" Should Be Removed, Oct. 10, 1984, at 13.

Conference Committee intends that a plaintiff may not plead other specified offenses, such as mail or wire fraud, as predicate acts under civil RICO if such offenses are based on conduct that would have been actionable as securities fraud.[32]

Notes and Questions

1. The amendment prohibits basing a civil RICO action on securities fraud unless the defendant has been "convicted in connection with the fraud." Does that language require that the defendant be convicted of violating the securities laws? Or would conviction of mail or wire fraud in a securities-related case suffice?

2. In view of the 1995 amendment, what are the potential ramifications for plea bargains in securities fraud prosecutions and in RICO prosecutions that allege securities fraud as a predicate crime?

3. Is there a principled basis for eliminating securities fraud as a predicate crime for civil RICO actions but retaining it as a predicate crime for criminal RICO cases?

4. In view of the harsh criticisms that have been leveled against RICO, the picture would not be complete without noting that while at the same time Congress has publicly sought to reform the civil RICO provision by narrowing its scope, it has quietly been broadening both civil and criminal liability by inserting more than 20 additional federal predicate crimes into the definition of racketeering activity. How can this be rationally explained?

LIBERTAD v. WELCH
53 F.3d 428 (1st Cir. 1995)

TORRUELLA, Chief Judge.

A group of individuals and organizations representing women who have sought or will seek family planning services in Puerto Rico ("Appellants") brought this action against certain individuals and organizations ("Appellees") who oppose abortion and coordinate anti-abortion demonstrations at women's health clinics in Puerto Rico. The Appellants appeal from the district court's grant of summary judgment disposing of their claims brought under §§ 1962(c) and (d) of the Racketeer Influenced and Corrupt Organizations Act ("RICO").

I. BACKGROUND

A. THE PARTIES

Appellants initiated this action on behalf of women seeking reproductive health services and their health care providers. Among the named plaintiffs are two women using the pseudonyms "Lydia Libertad" and "Emilia Emancipacion." Both Libertad and Emancipacion are Puerto Rico residents and have sought reproductive health services on the island. [Other plaintiffs included three reproductive health services clinics and

---

32. Private Securities Litigation Reform Act of 1995, S. Rep. No. 104-98, at 19 (1995).

their directors or administrators, and Grupo Pro Derechos Reproductivos, an abortion rights organization.]

Defendant Father Patrick Welch is the head of the anti–abortion rights organization Pro-Life Rescue Team ("PLRT"), also a named defendant. [Other named defendants were also leaders or members of various anti–abortion rights groups.]

B. EVENTS LEADING TO THIS ACTION

. . . Some or all of the Appellees staged protest demonstrations, which they refer to as "rescues," at the plaintiff clinics on five occasions: September 26, 1992, September 28, 1992, December 17, 1992, December 24, 1992, and January 8, 1993. During each of the five protests, Appellees blockaded the clinics so that clinic personnel and patients could not enter. Each blockade was carried out in a similar manner. Typically, the protests began before the clinics opened, with Appellees blocking access to the clinics and parking lots by physically obstructing the entrances, linking their arms tightly together and refusing to allow anyone to pass through. Outside, the protesters shouted slogans through megaphones to clinic personnel and patients, told patients that they were "murderers," screamed insults at clinic personnel, and videotaped or photographed people as they attempted to enter and leave the clinics. The protesters also defaced the clinic property by affixing difficult-to-remove stickers depicting fetuses on the walls and entrances, and by scrawling graffiti on the clinic walls. During these blockades, litter was strewn around clinic property and on the properties of surrounding businesses. In addition to effectively shutting down the clinics for all or part of a day, these protests caused extensive and costly property damage to the clinics.

[When the police tried to arrest them, the protestors used a variety of tactics to make apprehending them a difficult and time-consuming task.]

The blockades demand that local law enforcement officials expend a significant amount of time and resources; between forty-five and sixty officers are usually deployed for each protest. Law enforcement officials testified that they are overwhelmed by the protesters' tactics, that they are unable to either deter the blockades or keep the clinics open during the blockades. . . .

II. PRELIMINARY DISCUSSION . . .

B. STANDING . . .

There are three irreducible, minimum constitutional elements of standing. First, a plaintiff must have suffered an "injury in fact" — an invasion of a legally-protected interest which is (a) concrete and particularized, and (b) actual or imminent, not conjectural or hypothetical. Second, there must be a causal connection between the injury and the conduct complained of, such that the injury is fairly traceable to the challenged action of the defendant and not the result of the independent action of some third party not before the court. Finally, it must be likely, and not merely speculative, that the injury will be redressed by a favorable decision. . . .

In addition to these constitutionally required elements, the doctrine of standing also involves prudential considerations. Specifically, a court must determine 1) whether a plaintiff's complaint falls within the zone of interests protected by the law invoked; 2) whether the plaintiff is asserting its own rights and interests, and not those of third parties; and 3) that the plaintiff is not asking the court to adjudicate abstract questions of wide public significance which amount to generalized grievances more appropriately addressed by the legislature.

1. Appellants' Standing to Bring a RICO Claim

Appellees first contend that Appellants lack standing to assert claims under § 1962(c) and (d) of RICO. Specifically, they argue that Libertad, Emancipacion, and Grupo Pro Derechos Reproductivos ("Grupo Pro Derechos") lack standing to bring a RICO claim because they suffered no injury to business or property. Second, Appellees argue that the three clinics and [their directors or administrators] lack standing under RICO because they have failed to show that Appellees' actions proximately caused them any injury.

a. Do Libertad and Emancipacion Have Standing?

Libertad and Emancipacion are women who have sought reproductive health services at the blockaded clinics. Libertad submitted a sworn statement in support of Appellants' opposition to summary judgment, in which she described her experience at the WMC. She stated that the anti-abortion protesters intimidated her and made her angry; however, the protesters did not prevent her from attending her appointment at the clinic and obtaining an abortion.

Emancipacion testified at the summary judgment hearing about her experience at the blockaded clinic. Unlike Libertad, Emancipacion was intimidated enough by the Appellees' blockade and protest tactics that she was deterred from entering the clinic for her appointment. Emancipacion eventually returned to the clinic on a different day, however, and there is no indication that the delay caused her any physical harm.

Although we acknowledge that both women reasonably felt intimidated and harassed, neither woman suffered any injury to business or property, as is required for standing to sue under RICO. We therefore hold that Libertad and Emancipacion do not have standing to maintain this RICO claim.

b. Does the Grupo Pro Derechos Have Standing?

Appellant Grupo Pro Derechos is an association of feminist and human rights organizations and individuals. The group's mission is to defend women's reproductive rights, and to work for quality women's health services, sex education, and family planning. It allocates some of its resources to providing protection for women who patronize a blockaded clinic, and sues on its own behalf and on behalf of its members.

We have combed through the voluminous record and have been unable to find any evidence, or even any specific allegation, that the Grupo Pro Derechos has sustained any injury to business or property as a result of Appellees' conduct. One of the organization's members, Ms. Nancy Herzig Shannon, testified that while at one of the blockaded clinics, she received a death threat from a protester. She is not herself a named plaintiff, however, and she did not testify about any injury sustained by the group, such as expended resources, property damage, forgone business activities, or extortionate threats to its general membership. While the conduct of the protesters, lawful and unlawful, certainly conflicts with the group's mission and renders their objectives more difficult to achieve, this by itself does not give rise to an injury to the group's business or property interests. We therefore hold that the Grupo Pro Derechos does not have standing to maintain this RICO cause of action.[33]

c. Do the Remaining Appellants Have Standing?

Appellees claim that the remaining Appellants, the three clinics and their directors or administrators, lack standing to bring the RICO claim because they have failed to show that Appellees' acts proximately caused them injury. Even a cursory review of the record, particularly of the testimony adduced at the summary judgment hearing, belies this argument. The record is replete with evidence of the extensive property damage caused by Appellees' blockades at the clinics: broken locks, damaged gates, vandalism, strewn litter on the grounds, to list examples. Appellee Welch and his followers also did damage inside the clinics, ripping out electrical sockets and jamming door locks. The blockades also delayed or prevented the clinics from conducting business on those days. We therefore find that Appellants have sufficiently shown injury to business or property, and that this injury was proximately caused by Appellees.

As to the third, "redressibility" element of standing, Appellants seek, among other things, declaratory and injunctive relief from the Appellees' blockade activities — the same activities that caused their injury. This satisfies the "necessary causal connection between the injury alleged and the relief requested," Vote Choice, Inc. v. DiStefano, 4 F.3d 26, 37 (1st Cir. 1993), and we therefore find that the remaining Appellants have established the constitutional requirements necessary to confer standing.

Over and above these constitutional requisites, an analysis under the standing doctrine also embraces prudential concerns regarding the proper exercise of the court's jurisdiction. The remaining Appellants satisfy these concerns. They are asserting their own rights and interests in conducting their lawful business; their grievances are particularized and concrete; and the Appellants fall within the zone of interests contemplated by the explicit terms of the RICO statute — namely, "persons injured in [their] business or property" by an alleged pattern of racketeering activity. § 1964(c).

Accordingly, we hold that the remaining Appellants — the clinics, Caceres, Oficinas, Rivera, Gonzalez, and Castro — all have standing to maintain this RICO claim.

Notes and Questions

1. In *Libertad*, three sets of plaintiffs all claimed to have suffered injury from the same course of conduct. Why did some of them have standing while others did not?

2. Under what circumstances would plaintiffs who are clients of the clinics have standing to sue? Would they have standing if they had sustained physical injuries? If they suffered emotional distress?

3. When, if ever, would an association like the Grupo Pro Derechos have standing?

---

33. Plaintiffs like Libertad and Emancipacion could have standing to sue under RICO, if they were to submit sufficient evidence of injury to business or property such as lost wages or travel expenses, actual physical harm, or specific property damage sustained as a result of a RICO defendant's actions. The record before us, however, does not sufficiently establish this required element. . . .

B. CAUSATION

COMMERCIAL CLEANING SERVICES, L.L.C. v. COLIN
SERVICE SYSTEMS, INC.
271 F.3d 374 (2d Cir. 2001)

LEVAL, Circuit Judge: . . .

BACKGROUND . . .

A. The Complaint . . .

1. The Parties

[Commercial Cleaning Services (Commercial) and Colin Service Systems (Colin)] each provide janitorial services for commercial buildings. According to the complaint, Commercial is a small company that has bid against Colin for competitively awarded janitorial service contracts in the Hartford area. Colin operates throughout the Eastern seaboard and is described in the complaint as one of the nation's largest corporations engaged in the business of cleaning commercial facilities. The complaint was filed as a national class action on behalf of Colin's competitors.

2. The "Illegal Immigrant Hiring Scheme"

The complaint alleges that Commercial and the members of the plaintiff class are victims of Colin's pattern of racketeering activity in violation of 18 U.S.C. § 1962(c), referred to as "the illegal immigrant hiring scheme." The theory of the case, succinctly stated, is that Colin obtained a significant business advantage over other firms in the "highly competitive" and price-sensitive cleaning services industry by knowingly hiring "hundreds of illegal immigrants at low wages." Colin's illegal immigrant hiring scheme allows it to employ large numbers of workers at lower costs than its competitors must bear when operating lawfully. Colin allegedly pays undocumented workers less than the prevailing wage, and does not withhold or pay their federal and state payroll taxes, or workers' compensation insurance fees. The complaint refers to Colin's prosecution in 1996 by the United States Department of Justice for, among other things, hiring at least 150 undocumented workers, continuing to employ aliens after their work authorizations had expired, and failing to prepare, complete, and update employment documents.

The allegations assert that Colin is part of an enterprise composed of entities associated-in-fact that includes employment placement services, labor contractors, newspapers in which Colin advertises for laborers, and "various immigrant networks that assist fellow illegal immigrants in obtaining employment, housing and illegal work permits." The complaint neither describes how the undocumented workers allegedly hired by Colin entered the country, nor claims that Colin had knowledge of how those workers came to the United States. It alleges that Colin's participation in the affairs of the enterprise through the illegal immigrant hiring scheme violates 8 U.S.C. § 1324(a), which prohibits hiring certain undocumented aliens, and which is a RICO predicate offense if committed for financial gain. See 18 U.S.C. § 1961(1)(F).

3. The Pratt & Whitney Contracts

What apparently led to this lawsuit was Commercial's loss of lucrative cleaning contracts to Colin. In 1994, Commercial obtained a contract to clean Pratt & Whitney's facility at Southington, Connecticut. After successfully performing on that contract for approximately one year, however, Commercial was underbid by Colin for cleaning contracts at other Pratt & Whitney facilities in the area. The complaint alleges that, through the illegal immigrant hiring scheme, Colin could offer Pratt & Whitney and other potential customers access to "a virtually limitless pool of workers on short notice" at significantly lower prices than other firms could offer by operating lawfully. As a result, Pratt & Whitney and other large contractors for cleaning services accepted Colin's lower bids over Commercial's.

[The trial court granted Colin's motion to dismiss, ruling that Commercial lacked standing to sue because the complaint failed to allege a direct injury that was proximately caused by the illegal immigrant hiring scheme.]

DISCUSSION

I. CIVIL RICO STANDING . . .

B. *Proximate Cause*

RICO grants standing to pursue a civil damages remedy to "any person injured in his business or property by reason of a violation of [18 U.S.C. § 1962]." In order to bring suit under § 1964(c), a plaintiff must plead (1) the defendant's violation of § 1962, (2) an injury to the plaintiff's business or property, and (3) causation of the injury by the defendant's violation. Commercial's appeal turns in part on whether its complaint satisfies the causation requirement.

RICO's use of the clause "by reason of" has been held to limit standing to those plaintiffs who allege that the asserted RICO violation was the legal, or proximate, cause of their injury, as well as a logical, or "but for," cause. See Holmes v. Securities Investor Protection Corp., 503 U.S. 258, 268 (1992). The requirement that a defendant's actions be the proximate cause of a plaintiff's harm represents a policy choice premised on recognition of the impracticality of asserting liability based on the almost infinite expanse of actions that are in some sense causally related to an injury. In marking that boundary, the Supreme Court has emphasized that a plaintiff cannot complain of harm so remotely caused by a defendant's actions that imposing legal liability would transgress our "ideas of what justice demands, or of what is administratively possible and convenient." Id.

C. *"Direct Relation" Test*

Colin contends that the chain of causation between its alleged hiring of undocumented workers and Pratt & Whitney's decision to award cleaning contracts to Colin instead of Commercial is too long and tenuous to meet the proximate cause test of *Holmes*. The defendants in *Holmes* were alleged to have participated in a conspiracy to manipulate the value of the stock of several companies. Two broker-dealers who dealt in large amounts of the manipulated stock were put into liquidation when they experienced financial difficulties after the fraud was disclosed and the value of the manipulated stock precipitously declined. The Securities Investor Protection Corporation (SIPC) alleged that the defendants' securities and wire-fraud offenses amounted to a pattern of racketeering activity within the meaning of the RICO statute. It brought suit, based on a subrogation theory, on behalf of certain of the injured broker-dealer firms' customers who became unsecured creditors of the firms when the firms became insolvent.

The *Holmes* Court applied a proximate cause test requiring a "direct relation between the injury asserted and the injurious conduct alleged." Id. at 268. The "direct relation" requirement generally precludes recovery by a "plaintiff who complains of harm flowing merely from the misfortunes visited upon a third person by the defendant's acts." Id. The Court found that the link between the customers' losses SIPC sought to recover and the defendants' stock manipulation was too remote to satisfy the direct relation test. It explained that "the broker-dealers simply cannot pay their bills, and only that intervening insolvency connects the conspirators' acts to the losses suffered by the . . . customers." Id. at 271. The Court noted in contrast that the liquidating trustees suing directly on behalf of the defunct broker-dealers would have been the proper plaintiffs. . . .

D. Evaluation of Plaintiff's Claim in Relation to the Proximate Cause Test

We conclude that Commercial's complaint, when evaluated in light of these considerations, adequately states a direct proximate relationship between its injury and Colin's pattern of racketeering activity. The *Holmes* Court gave three policy reasons for limiting RICO's civil damages action only to those plaintiffs who could allege a direct injury. First, the less direct an injury is, the more difficult it becomes to determine what portion of the damages are attributable to the RICO violation as distinct from other, independent, factors. Second, if recovery by indirectly injured plaintiffs were not barred, courts would be forced, in order to prevent multiple recovery, to develop complicated rules apportioning damages among groups of plaintiffs depending on how far each group was removed from the defendant's underlying RICO violation. Third, there was no need to permit indirectly injured plaintiffs to sue, as directly injured victims could be counted on to vindicate the aims of the RICO statute, and their recovery would fix the injury to those harmed as the result of the injury they suffered.

1. Difficulty of Determining Damages Attributable to the RICO Violation

The district court found plaintiff's claim deficient on the first *Holmes* factor, because a fact finder would be required to determine whether Commercial's lost business to Colin was the result of the illegal immigrant hiring scheme as opposed to independent business reasons, such as the comparative quality of the companies' services, their comparative business reputations, the fluctuations in demand for their services, or other reasons customers might have for selecting one cleaning company over another. The district court concluded that, even if a fact finder could make such a determination, the calculation of damages attributable to the illegal immigrant hiring scheme would be "daunting, if not impossible."

The difficulty of proof identified in *Holmes*, however, was quite different from the circumstances of this case. Here, the plaintiffs bid against the defendant as direct competitors. The complaint asserts that Pratt & Whitney chose Colin because Colin submitted "significantly lower" bids in a "highly competitive" price-sensitive market. According to the complaint, Colin was able to underbid its competitors because its scheme to hire illegal immigrant workers permitted it to pay well below the prevailing wage for legal workers. Although we do not deny that there may be disputes as to whether the plaintiff class lost business because of defendant's violation of § 1324(a) or for other reasons, the plaintiff class was no less directly injured than the insolvent broker-dealers in *Holmes*, whose trustees, the Court indicated, would be proper plaintiffs. If plaintiffs can substantiate their claims, the plaintiffs may well show that they lost contracts directly because of the cost savings defendant realized through its scheme to employ illegal workers. . . .

Colin objects that any reduced labor costs were due to its alleged underpayment of workers and failure to pay other employment-related costs of doing business, not its participation in the illegal immigrant hiring scheme. In other words, Colin claims that Commercial complains of an injury caused by the low wages paid to Colin's workers — and not by their immigration status. Of course, paying workers less than the prevailing wage and failing to withhold payroll taxes are not RICO predicate acts. Nonetheless, the purpose of the alleged violation of 8 U.S.C. § 1324(a), the hiring of illegal alien workers, was to take advantage of their diminished bargaining position, so as to employ a cheaper labor force and compete unfairly on the basis of lower costs. By illegally hiring undocumented alien labor, Colin was able to hire cheaper labor and compete unfairly. The violation of § 1324(a) alleged by the complaint was a proximate cause of Colin's ability to underbid the plaintiffs and take business from them.

2.   Difficulty of Apportioning Damages Among Injured Parties

The *Holmes* Court warned that if courts did not limit recovery to injuries directly related to the RICO violation, they would be forced to devise complicated rules apportioning damages among plaintiffs at different degrees of separation from the violative acts alleged. . . .

Unlike the situation in *Holmes*, Commercial and its fellow class members are not alleging an injury that was derivative of injury to others. Commercial does not seek to recover based on "the misfortunes visited upon a third person by the defendant's acts." *Holmes*, 503 U.S. at 268. It claims to have lost profits directly as the result of Colin's underbidding, which it achieved through its violation of § 1324(a). We have stated a plaintiff has standing where the plaintiff is the direct target of the RICO violation. As discussed above, the theory of Commercial's claim is that Colin undertook the illegal immigrant hiring scheme in order to undercut its business rivals, thus qualifying them as direct targets of the RICO violation. . . .

3.   Ability of Other Parties to Vindicate Aims of the Statute

In relation to the third *Holmes* policy factor, the Supreme Court has observed that "the existence of an identifiable class of persons whose self-interest would normally motivate them to vindicate the public interest in [RICO] enforcement diminishes the justification for allowing a more remote party . . . to perform the office of a private attorney general." Associated Gen. Contractors of California, Inc. v. California State Council of Carpenters, 459 U.S. 519. Colin argues that this factor weighs against Commercial's standing, because other parties, such as state and federal authorities charged with collecting unpaid taxes and workers' compensation fees, may sue to vindicate the statute. Moreover, the INS, which enforces § 1324(a), has already obtained Colin's agreement to pay $1 million for violations of the immigration laws.

Once again, Colin misses the point. If the existence of a public authority that could prosecute a claim against putative RICO defendants meant that the plaintiff is too remote under *Holmes*, then no private cause of action could ever be maintained, for every RICO predicate offense, as well as the RICO enterprise itself, is separately prosecutable by the government. In *Holmes*, those directly injured could be expected to sue, and their recovery would redound to the benefit of the plaintiffs suing for indirect injury. Here, in contrast, suits by governmental authorities to recover lost taxes and fees would do nothing to alleviate the plaintiffs' loss of profits. There is no class of potential plaintiffs who have been more directly injured by the alleged RICO conspiracy than the defendant's business competitors, who have a greater incentive to ensure that a RICO violation does not go undetected or unremedied, and whose recovery would indirectly cure the loss suffered by these plaintiffs. . . .

CONCLUSION

The judgment of the district court is vacated, and the case is remanded for further proceedings consistent with this opinion.

Notes and Questions

1. The Supreme Court in *Holmes* required that there be a direct causal connection between the racketeering activity and the injury the plaintiff asserts. Why isn't the injury in *Commercial Cleaning* too remote? What is the racketeering activity?

2. What if the parties in *Commercial Cleaning* had not been head-to-head competitors? Suppose that Commercial Cleaning Services specialized in providing cleaning services to public schools in the state of Bliss. Commercial Cleaning had controlled 90 percent of the public school business in the state for more than ten years. Pratt & Whitney, which had a major facility in the state of Bliss, contracted with Colin Service Systems. Colin underbid all of its competitors for the Pratt & Whitney contract by $2 an hour because its work force consisted primarily of illegal immigrants. Commercial Cleaning did not bid on the contract. After the Pratt & Whitney contract was announced, the state of Bliss public school system decided to renegotiate all of its contracts in an understandable effort to cut its own costs. It refused to renew its contract with Commercial Cleaning unless Commercial reduced its labor costs by $2 an hour. Assuming that Colin's hiring of illegal aliens violated 8 U.S.C. § 1324(a), a RICO predicate crime, would Commercial Cleaning have a viable civil RICO claim?

3. The direct versus indirect injury distinction embraced in *Holmes* has confounded the lower courts. To test your understanding of the distinction *Holmes* meant to draw, consider the following hypotheticals.

a. Bernie Ebbers depletes the assets of WorldCom by borrowing hundreds of millions of dollars from the corporation in nonrepayable loans. Have the stockholders been directly injured by his conduct?

b. A labor union's health and benefit fund has incurred millions of dollars of expenses associated with its members' smoking-related illnesses. The fund contends that tobacco companies have concealed the health hazards associated with smoking for more than 40 years. Has the fund suffered an injury to business or property by reason of the tobacco companies' wrongdoing?

c. Barton, Inc., is a subcontractor that provides concrete for major construction projects. Coulter, a prime contractor, loses the bid for redeveloping a public housing project. Coulter has proof that Donaldson, the successful prime contractor, bribed housing authority officials to get the contract. If the contract had been awarded on the merits, Coulter would have received it and Barton would have received the concrete supply contract. Donaldson won't do business with Barton. Has Barton suffered an injury to business or property under the civil RICO provision?

d. Sherry Wilson, an Enron accountant, discovers massive accounting fraud in the company's books. She tells her superiors about the fraud and says that Enron's stock is virtually worthless. In the time-honored tradition of retaliating against the bearer of bad tidings, Enron fires her. Is her loss of employment a direct injury under the civil RICO statute?

ANZA v. IDEAL STEEL SUPPLY CORP.
547 U.S. 451 (2006)

Justice KENNEDY delivered the opinion of the Court. . . .

I . . .

Respondent Ideal Steel Supply Corporation (Ideal) sells steel mill products along with related supplies and services. It operates two store locations in New York, one in Queens and the other in the Bronx. Petitioner National Steel Supply, Inc. (National), owned by petitioners Joseph and Vincent Anza, is Ideal's principal competitor. National offers a similar array of products and services, and it, too, operates one store in Queens and one in the Bronx.

Ideal sued petitioners in the United States District Court for the Southern District of New York. It claimed petitioners were engaged in an unlawful racketeering scheme aimed at "gain[ing] sales and market share at Ideal's expense." According to Ideal, National adopted a practice of failing to charge the requisite New York sales tax to cash-paying customers, even when conducting transactions that were not exempt from sales tax under state law. This practice allowed National to reduce its prices without affecting its profit margin. Petitioners allegedly submitted fraudulent tax returns to the New York State Department of Taxation and Finance in an effort to conceal their conduct.

Ideal's amended complaint contains, as relevant here, two RICO claims. The claims assert that petitioners, by submitting the fraudulent tax returns, committed various acts of mail fraud (when they sent the returns by mail) and wire fraud (when they sent them electronically). Mail fraud and wire fraud are forms of "racketeering activity" for purposes of RICO. Petitioners' conduct allegedly constituted a "pattern of racketeering activity," because the fraudulent returns were submitted on an ongoing and regular basis.

Ideal asserts in its first cause of action that Joseph and Vincent Anza violated § 1962(c). . . .

[The district court dismissed the complaint, but the Second Circuit vacated the judgment, ruling that Anza had standing to sue because the complaint alleged that National's failure to collect and pay sales taxes on cash transactions gave (and was intended to give) National an unfair competitive advantage over Anza.]

II . . .

Applying the principles of *Holmes* to the present case, we conclude Ideal cannot maintain its claim based on § 1962(c). Section 1962(c), as noted above, forbids conducting or participating in the conduct of an enterprise's affairs through a pattern of racketeering activity. The Court has indicated the compensable injury flowing from a violation of that provision "necessarily is the harm caused by predicate acts sufficiently related to constitute a pattern, for the essence of the violation is the commission of those acts in connection with the conduct of an enterprise." Sedima, S.P.R.L. v. Imrex Co., 473 U.S. 479, 497 (1985).

Ideal's theory is that Joseph and Vincent Anza harmed it by defrauding the New York tax authority and using the proceeds from the fraud to offer lower prices designed to attract more customers. The RICO violation alleged by Ideal is that the Anzas conducted National's affairs through a pattern of mail fraud and wire fraud. The direct victim of this conduct was the State of New York, not Ideal. It was the State that was being defrauded and the State that lost tax revenue as a result.

The proper referent of the proximate-cause analysis is an alleged practice of conducting National's business through a pattern of defrauding the State. To be sure, Ideal asserts it suffered its own harms when the Anzas failed to charge customers for the applicable sales tax. The cause of Ideal's asserted harms, however, is a set of actions (offering lower prices) entirely distinct from the alleged RICO violation (defrauding the State). The attenuation between the plaintiff's harms and the claimed RICO violation arises from a different source in this case than in *Holmes*, where the alleged violations were linked to the asserted harms only through the broker-dealers' inability to meet their financial obligations. Nevertheless, the absence of proximate causation is equally clear in both cases.

This conclusion is confirmed by considering the directness requirement's underlying premises. One motivating principle is the difficulty that can arise when a court attempts to ascertain the damages caused by some remote action. The instant case is illustrative. The injury Ideal alleges is its own loss of sales resulting from National's decreased prices for cash-paying customers. National, however, could have lowered its prices for any number of reasons unconnected to the asserted pattern of fraud. It may have received a cash inflow from some other source or concluded that the additional sales would justify a smaller profit margin. Its lowering of prices in no sense required it to defraud the state tax authority. Likewise, the fact that a company commits tax fraud does not mean the company will lower its prices; the additional cash could go anywhere from asset acquisition to research and development to dividend payouts.

There is, in addition, a second discontinuity between the RICO violation and the asserted injury. Ideal's lost sales could have resulted from factors other than petitioners' alleged acts of fraud. Businesses lose and gain customers for many reasons, and it would require a complex assessment to establish what portion of Ideal's lost sales were the product of National's decreased prices.

The attenuated connection between Ideal's injury and the Anzas' injurious conduct thus implicates fundamental concerns expressed in *Holmes*. Notwithstanding the lack of any appreciable risk of duplicative recoveries, which is another consideration relevant to the proximate-cause inquiry, these concerns help to illustrate why Ideal's alleged injury was not the direct result of a RICO violation. Further illustrating this point is the speculative nature of the proceedings that would follow if Ideal were permitted to maintain its claim. A court considering the claim would need to begin by calculating the portion of National's price drop attributable to the alleged pattern of racketeering activity. It next would have to calculate the portion of Ideal's lost sales attributable to the relevant part of the price drop. The element of proximate causation recognized in *Holmes* is meant to prevent these types of intricate, uncertain inquiries from overrunning RICO litigation. It has particular resonance when applied to claims brought by economic competitors, which, if left unchecked, could blur the line between RICO and the antitrust laws.

The requirement of a direct causal connection is especially warranted where the immediate victims of an alleged RICO violation can be expected to vindicate the laws by pursuing their own claims. Again, the instant case is instructive. Ideal accuses the Anzas of defrauding the State of New York out of a substantial amount of money. If the allegations are true, the State can be expected to pursue appropriate remedies. The adjudication of the State's claims, moreover, would be relatively straightforward; while it may be difficult to determine facts such as the number of sales Ideal lost due to National's tax practices, it is considerably easier to make the initial calculation of how much tax revenue the Anzas withheld from the State. There is no need to broaden the universe of actionable harms to permit RICO suits by parties who have been injured only indirectly.

The Court of Appeals reached a contrary conclusion, apparently reasoning that because the Anzas allegedly sought to gain a competitive advantage over Ideal, it is immaterial whether they took an indirect route to accomplish their goal. This rationale does not accord with *Holmes*. A RICO plaintiff cannot circumvent the proximate-cause requirement simply by claiming that the defendant's aim was to increase market share at a competitor's expense. When a court evaluates a RICO claim for proximate causation, the central question it must ask is whether the alleged violation led directly to the plaintiff's injuries. In the instant case, the answer is no. We hold that Ideal's § 1962(c) claim does not satisfy the requirement of proximate causation. . . .

Justice THOMAS, concurring in part and dissenting in part.

The Court today limits the lawsuits that may be brought under the civil enforcement provision of the Racketeer Influenced and Corrupt Organizations Act (RICO or Act) by adopting a theory of proximate causation that is supported neither by the Act nor by our decision in Holmes v. Securities Investor Protection Corporation, on which the Court principally relies. The Court's stringent proximate-causation requirement succeeds in precluding recovery in cases alleging a violation of § 1962(c) that, like the present one, have nothing to do with organized crime, the target of the RICO statute. However, the Court's approach also eliminates recovery for plaintiffs whose injuries are precisely those that Congress aimed to remedy through the authorization of civil RICO suits. Because this frustration of congressional intent is directly contrary to the broad language Congress employed to confer a RICO cause of action, I respectfully dissent from Part II of the Court's opinion.

I

The language of the civil RICO provision, which broadly permits recovery by "[a]ny person injured in his business or property by reason of a violation" of the Act's substantive restrictions plainly covers the lawsuit brought by respondent. . . .

In *Holmes*, the Court explained that "a plaintiff who complained of harm flowing merely from the misfortunes visited upon a third person by the defendant's acts was generally said to stand at too remote a distance to recover." The plaintiff in *Holmes* was indirect in precisely this sense. . . .

Here, in contrast, it was not *New York's injury* that caused respondent's damages; rather, it was petitioners' own conduct — namely, their underpayment of tax — that permitted them to undercut respondent's prices and thereby take away its business. Indeed, the Court's acknowledgment that there is no appreciable risk of duplicative recovery here, in contrast to *Holmes,* is effectively a concession that petitioners' damages are not indirect, as that term is used in *Holmes*. The mere fact that New York is a direct victim of petitioners' RICO violation does not preclude Ideal's claim that it too is a direct victim. Because the petitioners' tax underpayment directly caused respondent's injury, *Holmes* does not bar respondent's recovery.

The Court nonetheless contends that respondent has failed to demonstrate proximate cause. It does so by relying on our observation in *Holmes* that the directness requirement is appropriate because "'[t]he less direct an injury is, the more difficult it becomes to ascertain the amount of a plaintiff's damages attributable to the violation, as distinct from other, independent, factors.'" . . .

The Court's reliance on the difficulty of ascertaining the amount of Ideal's damages caused by petitioners' unlawful acts to label those damages indirect is misguided. *Holmes* . . . simply held that one reason that *indirect* injuries should not be compensable is that such injuries are difficult to ascertain. We did not adopt the converse proposition that any injuries that are difficult to ascertain must be classified as indirect for purposes of determining proximate causation. . . .

It is nonetheless worth noting that the Court overstates the difficulties of proof faced by respondent in this case. Certainly the plaintiff in this case, as in all tort cases involving damage to business, must demonstrate that he suffered a harm caused by the tort, and not merely by external market conditions. But under the facts as alleged by Ideal, National did not generally lower its prices, so the Court need not inquire into "any number of reasons" that it might have done so. Instead, it simply *ceased charging tax* on cash sales, allegedly, and logically, because it had ceased reporting those sales and accordingly was not itself paying sales tax on them. Nor is it fatal to Ideal's proof of damages that National could have continued to charge taxes to its customers and invested the additional money elsewhere. Had National actually done so, it might be difficult to ascertain the damages suffered by Ideal as a result of that investment. But the mere fact that National *could have* committed tax fraud without readily ascertainable injury to Ideal does not mean that its tax fraud *necessarily* caused no readily ascertainable injury in this case. Likewise, the Court is undoubtedly correct that "Ideal's lost sales could have resulted from factors other than petitioners' alleged tax frauds." However, the means through which the fraudulent scheme was carried out — with sales tax charged on noncash sales, but no tax charged on cash sales — renders the damages more ascertainable than in the typical case of lost business. In any event, it is well within the expertise of a district court to evaluate testimony and evidence and determine what portion of Ideal's lost sales are attributable to National's lower prices and what portion to other factors. . . .

[Opinion of Justice BREYER, concurring in part and dissenting in part, omitted.]

Notes and Questions

1. If Ideal could prove that National purposely stopped collecting sales taxes on cash transactions to gain a competitive edge, why wouldn't Ideal be directly harmed by National's conduct? Does the Court's decision allow National to get away with intentional harm to its direct competitor? Is it fair to require Ideal to prove causation at the motion-to-dismiss stage?

2. Suppose the New York sales tax on the cash transactions had been 6 percent. That would translate into a savings of $300 on a $5,000 purchase for the buyer. Suppose that Ideal could prove the following: (a) National's cash sales increased when it stopped collecting the sales tax on them; (b) the number of cash transactions with Ideal's own customers dwindled after National stopped collecting the sales tax; and (c) Ideal's transactions with customers who bought on credit remained fairly constant. Would that adequately address the majority's concerns? How difficult would it be to compute Ideal's damages?

3. The majority thought that, as in *Holmes*, the direct victim — here the State of New York — could vindicate its own interests by suing National. Does *Holmes* (and, by extension, *Anza*) preclude the possibility that there may be multiple victims with compensable RICO injuries?

4. The Court in *Anza* said that the cause of Ideal's alleged harm was "a set of actions (offering lower prices) entirely distinct from the alleged RICO violation (defrauding the State)." Compare the court's statement in *Commercial Cleaning* to the effect that Commercial's asserted injury was proximately caused by Colin's hiring illegal immigrant workers, in violation of 8 U.S.C. § 1324, for the purpose of taking "advantage of their diminished bargaining position, so as to employ a cheaper labor force and compete unfairly on the basis of lower costs." Was the asserted harm in *Commercial Cleaning* caused by the predicate act of illegal hiring, which gave Colin the ability to underbid Commercial Cleaning? Or was it caused by Colin's decision to pay them below-market wages? After *Anza*, does it matter?

5. Putting aside for the moment your answer to Note 4, how, if at all, would the decision in *Anza* affect the result in the hypotheticals posed in Note 3 of the *Commercial Cleaning* Notes and Questions?

WILLIAMS v. MOHAWK INDUSTRIES, INC.
465 F.3d 1277 (11th Cir. 2006)

PER CURIAM. . . .

I. BACKGROUND

Mohawk is the second largest carpet and rug manufacturer in the United States and has over 30,000 employees. According to the plaintiffs, Mohawk has conspired with recruiting agencies to hire and harbor illegal workers in an effort to keep labor costs as low as possible. For example, according to the plaintiffs' complaint,

> Mohawk employees have traveled to the United States Border, including areas near Brownsville, Texas, to recruit undocumented aliens that recently have entered the United States in violation of federal law. These employees and other persons have transported undocumented aliens from these border towns to North Georgia so that those aliens may procure employment at Mohawk. Mohawk has made various incentive payments to employees and other recruiters for locating workers that Mohawk eventually employs and harbors.

Furthermore, "[v]arious recruiters, including Mohawk employees, have provided housing to these illegal workers upon their arrival in North Georgia and have helped them find illegal employment with Mohawk." Additionally, Mohawk knowingly or recklessly accepts fraudulent documentation from the illegal aliens.

The plaintiffs further allege that Mohawk has concealed its efforts to hire and harbor illegal aliens by destroying documents and assisting illegal workers in evading detection by law enforcement. According to plaintiffs' complaint, Mohawk takes steps to shield those illegal aliens from detection by, among other things, helping them evade detection during law enforcement searches and inspections at Mohawk's facilities.

According to the complaint, Mohawk's widespread and knowing employment and harboring of illegal workers has permitted Mohawk to reduce labor costs. Mohawk has done so by reducing the number of legal workers it must hire and, thereby, increasing the labor pool of legal workers from which Mohawk hires. This practice permits Mohawk to depress the wages it pays its legal hourly workers.

Finally, the plaintiffs allege that Mohawk is "able to save substantial sums of money" by paying its workers reduced wages. Furthermore, Mohawk knows that illegal workers are less likely to file worker's compensation claims, and, therefore, Mohawk is able to save additional monies. . . .

II. FEDERAL RICO CLAIMS . . .

A. PATTERN OF RACKETEERING ACTIVITY . . .

According to 18 U.S.C. § 1961(1)(F), "'racketeering activity' means any act which is indictable under the Immigration and Nationality Act, section 274 (relating to bringing in and harboring certain aliens), . . . if the act indictable under such section of such Act was committed for the purpose of financial gain." In this case, the plaintiffs have alleged that the defendant has engaged in an open and ongoing pattern of violations of section 274 of the Immigration and Nationality Act. . . . According to the plaintiffs' complaint, Mohawk has committed hundreds, even thousands, of violations of federal immigration laws. Consequently, we conclude that the plaintiffs have properly alleged a "pattern of racketeering activity." . . .

C. INJURY TO BUSINESS OR PROPERTY INTEREST UNDER RICO . . .

[T]his case is similar to the Ninth Circuit's *Mendoza* decision, where legally documented agricultural workers sued fruit growers under RICO alleging that the growers depressed wages by hiring illegal workers. . . . [T]he Ninth Circuit concluded that "what is required is precisely what the employees allege here: a legal entitlement to business relations unhampered by schemes prohibited by the RICO predicate statutes." Given that a relationship clearly exists between plaintiff workers and their employer, Mohawk, we conclude that a similar business interest exists in this case, and that the employees' alleged injury to their business interests satisfies the business-interest requirement. Consequently, the plaintiffs have alleged a sufficient injury to a business interest to pursue their RICO claims.

D. "BY REASON OF" THE SUBSTANTIVE RICO VIOLATIONS

We now turn to the "by reason of" requirement contained in § 1964(c). The "by reason of" requirement implicates two concepts: (1) a sufficiently direct injury so that a plaintiff has standing to sue; and (2) proximate cause. . . .

(i) Proximate Cause

It is well-established that RICO plaintiffs must prove proximate causation in order to recover. *Anza* makes clear that courts should scrutinize proximate causation at the pleading stage and carefully evaluate whether the injury pled was proximately caused by the claimed RICO violations.

More importantly, in *Anza*, the United States Supreme Court instructed that "[w]hen a court evaluates a RICO claim for proximate causation, the central question it must ask is whether the alleged violation led directly to the plaintiff's injuries." This central question stems from the Supreme Court's earlier decision in *Holmes,* which examined "the common-law foundations of the proximate-cause requirement" and specifically the "demand for some direct relation between the injury asserted and the injurious conduct alleged." Although *Anza* does not require plaintiffs to show that the injurious conduct is the sole cause of the injury asserted, *Anza* does emphasize that in RICO cases there must be "some direct relation" between the injury alleged and the injurious conduct in order to show proximate cause. . . .

Turning back to this case, we conclude that the plaintiffs have alleged sufficient proximate cause to withstand defendant Mohawk's motion to dismiss. According to their complaint, Mohawk has hired illegal workers "[i]n an effort to keep labor costs as low as possible." Furthermore, "Mohawk's employment and harboring of large numbers of illegal workers has enabled Mohawk to depress wages and thereby pay all of its hourly employees, including legally employed workers who are members of the class, wages that are lower than they would be if Mohawk did not engage in this illegal conduct." Again, the complaint alleges that "Mohawk's widespread employment and harboring of illegal workers has substantially and unlawfully increased the supply of workers from which Mohawk makes up its hourly workforce. This unlawful expansion of the labor pool has permitted Mohawk to depress the wages that it pays all its hourly employees. . . ." The plaintiffs also allege that "[o]ne purpose and intended effect of Mohawk's widespread employment and harboring of illegal workers is to deprive Mohawk's hourly workforce of any individual or collective bargaining power" and that they "were injured by direct and proximate reason of Mohawk's illegal conduct."

Given these allegations, which we must assume are true at this Rule 12(b)(6) stage of the litigation, it is clear that the plaintiffs have alleged a sufficiently direct relation between their claimed injury and the alleged RICO violations. In short, according to the complaint, Mohawk's widespread scheme of knowingly hiring and harboring illegal workers has the purpose and direct result of depressing the wages paid to the plaintiffs. Simply put, wholesale illegal hiring depresses wages for the legal workers in north Georgia where Mohawk is located. According to plaintiffs, Mohawk's illegal conduct had a substantial and direct effect on wages that Mohawk pays to legal workers.

In response, Mohawk asserts that other economic factors contribute to the plaintiffs' wages, that illegal hiring is just one of myriad factors affecting wages, and that therefore plaintiffs have not satisfied *Anza*'s proximate-cause requirements. However, plaintiffs persuasively reply that Mohawk's argument ignores that Mohawk's conduct has grossly distorted those normal market forces by employing literally *thousands* of illegal, undocumented aliens at its manufacturing facilities in north Georgia, thus depriving plaintiffs of "business relations unhampered by schemes prohibited by the RICO predicate statutes." Plaintiffs submit that their complaint focuses on only what is happening in the particular narrow labor market that Mohawk dominates in north Georgia. We agree with plaintiffs that their complaint alleges a sufficiently direct injury to satisfy *Anza* and *Holmes,* especially given the recognition of a direct correlation between illegal hiring and lower wages.

More importantly, as plaintiffs point out, in both *Holmes* and *Anza,* the Supreme Court emphasized that dismissal was appropriate because a more direct victim could bring suit. . . .

The concerns expressed in *Anza* and *Holmes* are not present in this case. There is no more direct[ly] injured party who could bring suit. Mohawk posits the United States as the only other victim because of its interest in enforcing immigration laws. But as plaintiffs aptly point out, the United States is responsible for all federal criminal laws which includes RICO's other predicate acts. Under Mohawk's theory, the United States would arguably be the most direct victim of all RICO predicate, criminal acts. Congress, however, criminalized the employment of illegal workers in part to protect legal workers. It is consistent with civil RICO's purposes — to expand enforcement beyond federal prosecutors with limited public resources — to turn victims (here, Mohawk's legal workers) into prosecutors as private attorneys general seeking to eliminate illegal hiring activity by their *own* employer.

Anza's concern about speculative damages, "intricate, uncertain injuries," and unwieldy apportionment are not implicated in this case because plaintiffs allege an injury fundamentally different from that in *Anza*. The plaintiff in *Anza* was a competitor suing for damages for lost opportunity or lost sales. In contrast, plaintiffs are Mohawk's own employees who seek to recover the diminution in wages they receive directly from Mohawk. Further, *Anza*'s concern about blurring the line between RICO and antitrust laws is wholly missing here.

We also recognize that Mohawk asserts that the cause of plaintiffs' alleged harms is a set of actions (paying lower wages) "entirely distinct" from the alleged RICO violation (hiring illegal workers). We disagree. As noted earlier, it has long been recognized that hiring illegal workers on substandard wage terms depresses the wage scales of legal workers. Moreover, plaintiffs are not suing about the hiring of illegal workers on the west coast depressing the wages of legal workers on the east coast. Rather, plaintiffs' complaint is a narrow one about a single employer's — Mohawk's — hiring of thousands of illegal workers at its manufacturing facilities in north Georgia depressing the wages of legal workers of the same employer, Mohawk, at the same manufacturing facilities in the same limited geographical area. Accordingly, under the particular factual circumstances of this case, we conclude that plaintiffs' complaint satisfies the direct relationship requirement imposed by *Holmes* and *Anza*'s interpretation of the "by reason of" language in the federal RICO statute. . . .

Although the plaintiffs' evidence in this case may not ultimately prove the proximate-cause requirement, we conclude that the plaintiffs' complaint states a sufficiently direct relation between their alleged injury and Mohawk's alleged unlawful predicate acts to withstand Mohawk's motion to dismiss. Consequently, we join the Sixth and Ninth Circuits in concluding that employees such as the ones in this case have alleged sufficient proximate cause to proceed with their RICO claims. . . .

Notes and Questions

1. *Commercial Cleaning*, *Anza*, and *Williams* all dealt with allegedly predatory business practices, but in different factual contexts. *Commercial Cleaning* and *Williams* both dealt with illegal immigrant hiring schemes, but the litigants in *Commercial Cleaning* were direct competitors, while the litigants in *Williams* were an employer and its legal workers. In *Anza*, in contrast, the litigants were direct competitors, but the focus was on the defendant's efforts to gain an undeserved market advantage rather than on the defendant's hiring practices per se. How important are these factual distinctions to the outcomes in these cases?

2. Is it clear that the documented workers were the most directly injured parties? Why weren't the undocumented workers who were exploited by Mohawk the proper plaintiffs?

3. What kinds of evidence would the plaintiffs in *Williams* need to present in order to establish a cognizable RICO injury?

HEMI GROUP, LLC v. CITY OF NEW YORK, NY
130 S. Ct. 983 (2010)

Chief Justice ROBERTS delivered the opinion of the Court in part.

The City of New York taxes the possession of cigarettes. Hemi Group, based in New Mexico, sells cigarettes online to residents of the City. Neither state nor city law requires Hemi to charge, collect, or remit the tax, and the purchasers seldom pay it on their own. Federal law, however, requires out-of-state vendors such as Hemi to submit customer information to the States into which they ship the cigarettes.

Against that backdrop, the City filed this lawsuit under the Racketeer Influenced and Corrupt Organizations Act (RICO), alleging that Hemi failed to file the required customer information with the State. That failure, the City argues, constitutes mail and wire fraud, which caused it to lose tens of millions of dollars in unrecovered cigarette taxes. Because the City cannot show that it lost the tax revenue "by reason of" the alleged RICO violation we hold that the City cannot state a claim under RICO. We therefore reverse the Court of Appeals' decision to the contrary.

I . . .

    B . . .

The City alleges that Hemi's "interstate sale of cigarettes and the failure to file Jenkins Act reports identifying those sales" constitute the RICO predicate offenses of mail and wire fraud in violation of § 1962(c), for which § 1964(c) provides a private cause of action. Invoking that private cause of action, the City asserts that it has suffered injury in the form of lost tax revenue — its "business or property" in RICO terms — "by reason of" Hemi's fraud. . . .

II . . .

    A . . .

Our decision in *Anza* confirms that the City's theory of causation is far too indirect. . . .

The City's claim suffers from the same defect as the claim in *Anza*. Here, the conduct directly responsible for the City's harm was the customers' failure to pay their taxes. And the conduct constituting the alleged fraud was Hemi's failure to file Jenkins Act reports. Thus, as in *Anza*, the conduct directly causing the harm was distinct from the conduct giving rise to the fraud.

Indeed, the disconnect between the asserted injury and the alleged fraud in this case is even sharper than in *Anza*. There, we viewed the point as important because the same party — National Steel — had both engaged in the harmful conduct and committed the fraudulent act. We nevertheless found the distinction between the relevant acts sufficient to defeat Ideal's RICO claim. Here, the City's theory of liability rests not just on separate *actions*, but separate actions carried out by separate *parties*.

The City's theory thus requires that we extend RICO liability to situations where the defendant's fraud on the third party (the State) has made it easier for a *fourth* party (the taxpayer) to cause harm to the plaintiff (the City). Indeed, the fourth-party taxpayers here only caused harm to the City in the first place if they decided not to pay taxes they were legally obligated to pay. Put simply, Hemi's obligation was to file the Jenkins Act reports with the State, not the City, and the City's harm was directly caused by the customers, not Hemi. We have never before stretched the causal chain of a RICO violation so far, and we decline to do so today.

One consideration we have highlighted as relevant to the RICO "direct relationship" requirement is whether better situated plaintiffs would have an incentive to sue. The State certainly is better situated than the City to seek recovery from Hemi. And the State has an incentive to sue — the State imposes its own $2.75 per pack tax on cigarettes possessed within the State, nearly double what the City charges. We do not opine on whether the State could bring a RICO action for any lost tax revenue. Suffice it to say that the State would have concrete incentives to try. . . .

B

The City offers a number of responses. It first challenges our characterization of the violation at issue. In the City's view, the violation is not merely Hemi's failure to file Jenkins Act information with the State, but a more general "systematic scheme to defraud the City of tax revenue." Having broadly defined the violation, the City contends that it has been directly harmed by reason of that systematic scheme.

But the City cannot escape the proximate cause requirement merely by alleging that the fraudulent scheme embraced all those indirectly harmed by the alleged conduct. Otherwise our RICO proximate cause precedent would become a mere pleading rule. In *Anza*, for example, Ideal alleged that National's scheme "was to give National a competitive advantage over Ideal." But that allegation did not prevent the Court from concluding that National's fraud directly harmed only the State, not Ideal. As the Court explained, Ideal could not "circumvent the proximate-cause requirement simply by claiming that the defendant's aim was to increase market share at a competitor's expense." Id., at 460.[34]

Our precedent makes clear, moreover, that "the compensable injury flowing from a [RICO] violation . . . 'necessarily is the harm caused by [the] predicate acts.'" Id., at 457. In its RICO statement, the City alleged that Hemi's failure to file Jenkins Act reports constituted the predicate act of mail and wire fraud. The City went on to allege that this predicate act "directly caused" its harm, but that assertion is a legal conclusion about proximate cause — indeed, the very legal conclusion before us. The only fraudulent *conduct* alleged here is a violation of the Jenkins Act. Thus, the City must show that Hemi's failure to file the Jenkins Act reports with the State led directly to its injuries. This it cannot do. . . .

---

34. Even if we were willing to look to Hemi's intent, as the dissent suggests we should, the City would fare no better. Hemi's aim was not to defraud the City (or the State, for that matter) of tax revenue, but to sell more cigarettes. Hemi itself neither owed taxes nor was obliged to collect and remit them. This all suggests that Hemi's alleged fraud was aimed at Hemi's competitors, not the City. But *Anza* teaches that the competitors' injuries in such a case are too attenuated to state a RICO claim.

The City at various points during the proceedings below described its injury as the lost "opportunity to tax" rather than "lost tax revenue." It is not clear that there is a substantive distinction between the two descriptions. In any event, before this Court, the City's argument turned on lost revenue, not a lost opportunity to collect it. Indeed, in its entire brief on the merits, the City never uses the word "opportunity" (or anything similar) to describe its injury.

Perhaps the City articulated its argument in terms of the lost revenue itself to meet Hemi's contention that an injury to the mere "opportunity to collect" taxes fell short of RICO's injury to "property" requirement.

That is not to say, however, that the City would fare any better on the causation question had it framed its argument in terms of a lost opportunity. Hemi's filing obligation would still be to the State, and any harm to the City would still be caused directly by the customers' failure to pay their taxes. Whatever the City's reasons for framing its merits arguments as it has, we will not reformulate them for it now. . . .

The judgment of the Court of Appeals for the Second Circuit is reversed, and the case is remanded for further proceedings consistent with this opinion.

It is so ordered.

Notes and Questions

1. Did the Court in *Hemi* decide the question whether lost tax revenue constitutes an injury to business or property?

2. Assuming arguendo that lost tax revenue constitutes an injury to business or property, would the City's lost opportunity to collect tax revenue constitute an injury to its business or property?

3. Was the City's injury directly attributable to the unpaid taxes? If so, why did its civil RICO claim fail? What was the predicate crime?

VII. ASSET FORFEITURE

One of the most potent sanctions RICO imposes on criminal defendants is forfeiture. Upon conviction, the statute requires forfeiture of any interest the defendant has acquired or maintained through the RICO violation (including profits, proceeds, and income), any interest the defendant has in an enterprise that was used in the RICO violation, and any contractual right that afforded the defendant a source of influence over an enterprise used in the RICO violation. 18 U.S.C. § 1963. The purpose of the RICO forfeiture provision is to separate the convicted racketeer from the economic power base that enabled him to use or acquire an enterprise to further long-term criminal activity. Since the forfeiture statute enables prosecutors to pursue all assets that have been tainted by the defendant's crimes, that occasionally means that this criminal punishment may be visited upon innocent third parties who have unwittingly come into possession of such assets.

A. FORFEITABLE INTERESTS

The forfeiture statute is broadly applicable to virtually any property that is connected with a RICO violation. Section 1963(a) provides that upon conviction, the defendant shall forfeit:

(1) any interest . . . acquired or maintained in violation of section 1962;
(2) any —
    (A) interest in;
    (B) security of;
    (C) claim against; or
    (D) property or contractual right of any kind affording a source of influence over:
        any enterprise which the person has established, operated, controlled, conducted,
    or participated in the conduct of, in violation of section 1962; and
(3) any property constituting, or derived from, any proceeds which the person obtained,
directly or indirectly, from racketeering activity . . . in violation of section 1962.

The categories of property that are subject to forfeiture are comprehensive. They include real property as well as "tangible and intangible personal property, including rights, privileges, interests, claims, and securities."[35] These rights, privileges, and interests include such things as union offices, pensions, and voting rights in corporate stock that provide a source of influence over the enterprise. There is a split of authority on the question whether the term "proceeds" should be construed to include the gross receipts the defendants derived from their racketeering activity or whether it should be limited to profits they received from their crimes.

It is generally accepted that for purposes of the forfeiture statute, RICO defendants are jointly and severally liable. As a practical matter, this means that the government is not required to prove the specific amount of proceeds attributable to each defendant. Thus, for example, where four RICO defendants received a total of $1 million from their racketeering activity, any one of them may be ordered to forfeit the entire amount, regardless of how they may have allocated the division of the proceeds among themselves.

Notes and Questions

1. How should courts construe the term "proceeds" under § 1963(a)(3)? What are the pros and cons of making "gross receipts" rather than "profits" subject to forfeiture? Would it be unreasonable to require the government to prove that the defendants profited from their criminal activity? Would such a requirement defeat the purpose of the forfeiture statute?

2. In United States v. Rubin,[36] the court upheld a forfeiture order that required the defendant to forfeit all of his union management offices after he was convicted of violating RICO by embezzling union funds and failing to keep union records. What

---

35. 18 U.S.C. § 1963(b).
36. 559 F.2d 975 (5th Cir. 1977).

language in § 1963 would support this result? As a practical and policy matter, why would Rubin's managerial positions in various unions be subject to forfeiture?

3. What is the basis for construing the forfeiture statute as imposing joint and several liability on RICO defendants? What is the theoretical and practical significance of that rule?

B. THIRD PARTY INTERESTS

Criminal forfeiture proceedings can (and sometimes do) implicate the rights of innocent third parties. Because RICO forfeitures are mandatory criminal penalties that are imposed as part of the sentence at the end of the criminal trial, forfeiture orders are entered without prior adjudication of third-party interests. Not all cases will pose the problem of third parties who claim superior rights to the forfeited assets. But in some instances, there may be co-owners, purchasers, or creditors who have a legitimate interest in the assets or who claim to own them outright. Although the RICO forfeiture statute provides third-party claimants an opportunity to be heard and to establish their interest in the forfeited property, the point in time when the third party acquired the interest is crucial.

The forfeiture statute specifically addresses two categories of third-party interests. First, if the third party had a vested right, title, or interest in the assets at the time when the conduct giving rise to the forfeiture occurred, the forfeiture is invalid to the extent of the claimant's proven interest.[37] This boils down to the question of who owned what interests in the property when the RICO violation occurred. Second, claimants who acquire an interest in the assets after the conduct giving rise to forfeiture occurs may prevail by proving that they are bona fide purchasers for value of a legal right, title, or interest in the property and that they were "reasonably without cause to believe that the property was subject to forfeiture" at the time of purchase.[38] To prevail under this theory, the claimant must prove that he: (1) entered into a bona fide transaction with the defendant; (2) gave valuable consideration for the asset; and (3) was, at the time he acquired his interest in the forfeitable asset, reasonably without cause to believe the property was tainted by criminal conduct.

C. ATTORNEYS' FEES

RICO's forfeiture statute is, in most pertinent respects, identical to the forfeiture provisions in the Continuing Criminal Enterprise statute (CCE), a drug kingpin law. RICO and CCE both authorize the pretrial restraint of assets to preserve their availability for forfeiture after trial. By the mid-1980s, the use of pretrial restraining orders to freeze a defendant's assets and the potential adverse impact of forfeitures on innocent third parties emerged as serious concerns. Three key questions came to the fore: (1) whether the statutes authorize pretrial restraint of assets the defendant intends to use to pay a criminal defense lawyer; (2) whether assets the defendant has already

---

37. 18 U.S.C. § 1963(*l*)(6)(A).
38. 18 U.S.C. § 1963(*l*)(6)(B).

transferred to his lawyer may be declared forfeited; and (3) whether the Sixth Amendment right to counsel prohibits pretrial restraints and/or forfeiture orders that effectively deprive a criminal defendant of money needed to hire a lawyer.

In United States v. Monsanto,[39] the Supreme Court addressed the statutory construction issue: whether assets that are set aside, or have already been paid, for a criminal defense lawyer's services are subject to forfeiture. Concluding that they are, the Court looked to what the statute categorized as forfeitable assets: "real property . . . tangible and intangible personal property, including rights, privileges, interest, claims, and securities."[40] Because the statute does not expressly exclude them, the Court found no basis for exempting assets earmarked to pay a lawyer's fees.

In Caplin & Drysdale v. United States,[41] the high Court addressed the question that flows from *Monsanto* — whether forfeiture of attorneys' fees impermissibly infringes on the Sixth Amendment right to counsel.

CAPLIN & DRYSDALE v. UNITED STATES
491 U.S. 617 (1989)

Justice WHITE delivered the opinion of the Court. . . .

I

In January 1985, Christopher Reckmeyer was charged in a multicount indictment with running a massive drug importation and distribution scheme. The scheme was alleged to be a continuing criminal enterprise (CCE), in violation of 21 U.S.C. § 848. Relying on a portion of the CCE statute that authorizes forfeiture to the Government of "property constituting, or derived from . . . proceeds . . . obtained" from drug-law violations, § 853(a), the indictment sought forfeiture of specified assets in Reckmeyer's possession. At this time, the District Court, acting pursuant to § 853(e)(1)(A), entered a restraining order forbidding Reckmeyer to transfer any of the listed assets that were potentially forfeitable.

Sometime earlier, Reckmeyer had retained petitioner, a law firm, to represent him in the ongoing grand jury investigation which resulted in the January 1985 indictments. Notwithstanding the restraining order, Reckmeyer paid the firm $25,000 for preindictment legal services a few days after the indictment was handed down; this sum was placed by petitioner in an escrow account. Petitioner continued to represent Reckmeyer following the indictment.

On March 7, 1985, Reckmeyer moved to modify the District Court's earlier restraining order to permit him to use some of the restrained assets to pay petitioner's fees; Reckmeyer also sought to exempt from any postconviction forfeiture order the assets that he intended to use to pay petitioner. However, one week later, before the District Court could conduct a hearing on this motion, Reckmeyer entered a plea agreement with the

---

39. 491 U.S. 600 (1989).
40. Id. at 607 (citing 21 U.S.C. § 853(b)).
41. 491 U.S. 617 (1989).

Government. Under the agreement, Reckmeyer pleaded guilty to the drug-related CCE charge, and agreed to forfeit all of the specified assets listed in the indictment. The day after Reckmeyer's plea was entered, the District Court denied his earlier motion to modify the restraining order, concluding that the plea and forfeiture agreement rendered irrelevant any further consideration of the propriety of the court's pretrial restraints. Subsequently, an order forfeiting virtually all of the assets in Reckmeyer's possession was entered by the District Court in conjunction with his sentencing.

[Caplin & Drysdale filed a petition claiming that the firm was a bona fide purchaser for value and that it was therefore entitled to a share of Reckmeyer's forfeitable assets for fees it claimed it was owed for representing him. The firm also argued that as a matter of statutory construction, attorney's fees were exempt from forfeiture and that if they were not, the statute was unconstitutional. The trial court rejected the statutory construction and unconstitutionality arguments, but granted the firm's claim for a share of Reckmeyer's assets. The Fourth Circuit affirmed.

Caplin & Drysdale argued that this application of the forfeiture statute impermissibly burdened the defendant's right to counsel of choice, but the Court noted that although the Sixth Amendment guarantees criminal defendants the right to counsel, that right is limited to adequate representation by lawyers the defendant can afford or, if he cannot afford to hire a lawyer, to be represented by competent appointed counsel.]

. . . The forfeiture statute does not prevent a defendant who has nonforfeitable assets from retaining any attorney of his choosing. Nor is it necessarily the case that a defendant who possesses nothing but assets the Government seeks to have forfeited will be prevented from retaining counsel of choice. Defendants like Reckmeyer may be able to find lawyers willing to represent them, hoping that their fees will be paid in the event of acquittal, or via some other means that a defendant might come by in the future. The burden placed on defendants by the forfeiture law is therefore a limited one.

Nonetheless, there will be cases where a defendant will be unable to retain the attorney of his choice, when that defendant would have been able to hire that lawyer if he had access to forfeitable assets, and if there was no risk that fees paid by the defendant to his counsel would later be recouped under § 853(c). It is in these cases, petitioner argues, that the Sixth Amendment puts limits on the forfeiture statute.

This submission is untenable. Whatever the full extent of the Sixth Amendment's protection of one's right to retain counsel of his choosing, that protection does not go beyond "the individual's right to spend his own money to obtain the advice and assistance of . . . counsel." Cf. Walters v. National Assn. of Radiation Survivors, 473 U.S. 305, 370 (1985) (Stevens, J., dissenting). A defendant has no Sixth Amendment right to spend another person's money for services rendered by an attorney, even if those funds are the only way that that defendant will be able to retain the attorney of his choice. A robbery suspect, for example, has no Sixth Amendment right to use funds he has stolen from a bank to retain an attorney to defend him if he is apprehended. The money, though in his possession, is not rightfully his; the government does not violate the Sixth Amendment if it seizes the robbery proceeds, and refuses to permit the defendant to use them to pay for his defense. "[N]o lawyer, in any case, . . . has the right to accept stolen property, or . . . ransom money, in payment of a fee. . . . The privilege to practice law is not a license to steal." Laska v. United States, 82 F.2d 672, 677 (CA10 1936). . . .

. . . [T]he property rights given the Government by virtue of the forfeiture statute are more substantial than petitioner acknowledges. In § 853(c), the so-called "relation-back" provision, Congress dictated that "[a]ll right, title and interest in property" obtained by criminals via the illicit means described in the statute "vests in the United States upon the commission of the act giving rise to forfeiture." 21 U.S.C. § 853(c). As Congress observed when the provision was adopted, this approach, known as the "taint theory," is one that "has long been recognized in forfeiture cases," including the decision in United States v. Stowell, 133 U.S. 1 (1890). . . .

In sum, § 853(c) reflects the application of the long-recognized and lawful practice of vesting title to any forfeitable assets, in the United States, at the time of the criminal act giving rise to forfeiture. Concluding that Reckmeyer cannot give good title to such property to petitioner because he did not hold good title is neither extraordinary [n]or novel. Nor does petitioner claim, as a general proposition that the relation-back provision is unconstitutional, or that Congress cannot, as a general matter, vest title to assets derived from the crime in the Government, as of the date of the criminal act in question. Petitioner's claim is that whatever part of the assets that is necessary to pay attorney's fees cannot be subjected to forfeiture. But given the Government's title to Reckmeyer's assets upon conviction, to hold that the Sixth Amendment creates some right in Reckmeyer to alienate such assets, or creates a right on petitioner's part to receive these assets, would be peculiar.

There is no constitutional principle that gives one person the right to give another's property to a third party, even where the person seeking to complete the exchange wishes to do so in order to exercise a constitutionally protected right. . . .

We therefore reject petitioner's claim of a Sixth Amendment right of criminal defendants to use assets that are the Government's — assets adjudged forfeitable, as Reckmeyer's were — to pay attorney's fees, merely because those assets are in their possession. . . .

IV

For the reasons given above, we find that petitioner's statutory and constitutional challenges to the forfeiture imposed here are without merit. The judgment of the Court of Appeals is therefore affirmed.

Justice BLACKMUN, with whom Justice BRENNAN, Justice MARSHALL, and Justice STEVENS join, dissenting.

Those jurists who have held forth against the result the majority reaches in these cases have been guided by one core insight; that it is unseemly and unjust for the Government to beggar those it prosecutes in order to disable their defense at trial. The majority trivializes "the burden the forfeiture law imposes on a criminal defendant." Instead, it should heed the warnings of our district court judges, whose day-to-day exposure to the criminal-trial process enables them to understand, perhaps far better than we, the devastating consequences of attorney's fee forfeiture for the integrity of our adversarial system of justice.

The criminal forfeiture statute we consider today could have been interpreted to avoid depriving defendants of the ability to retain private counsel — and should have been so interpreted, given the grave "constitutional and ethical problems" raised by the forfeiture of funds used to pay legitimate counsel fees. But even if Congress in fact required this substantial incursion on the defendant's choice of counsel, the Court should have recognized that the Framers stripped Congress of the power to do so when they added the Sixth Amendment to our Constitution. . . .

Notes and Questions

1. If Reckmeyer had had no other assets to pay his legal fees, would the outcome in *Caplin & Drysdale* have been different?

2. Is a pretrial order that restrains potentially forfeitable assets tantamount to determining guilt before trial? Why are pretrial restraining orders permitted?

3. The opinion in *Caplin & Drysdale* makes it reasonably clear that the result would be the same whether or not the assets in question were earmarked for or had already been paid to the lawyers when the restraining orders were issued. Why couldn't the lawyers claim a superior interest in the assets as payment for their services?

4. Why does the majority so easily dismiss the Sixth Amendment claims?

UNITED STATES v. MOFFITT, ZWERLING & KEMLER, P.C.
83 F.3d 660 (4th Cir. 1996)

WILKINSON, Chief Judge: . . .

I

In late August, 1991, William Paul Covington retained the law firm of Moffitt, Zwerling & Kemler to defend him against charges of drug trafficking and money laundering. Covington was then the subject of a grand jury investigation and many of his personal and business assets had already been seized. To secure the firm's representation, Covington was required to pay $100,000 up front. On August 23, 1991, Covington partially paid the fee with a wad of bills fished from his pocket that amounted to $17,000; the next day he delivered another $86,800 in cash, stored in a cracker box or a shoe box. Much of the $103,800 payment was in the form of $100 bills.

Neither William Moffitt nor John Zwerling asked Covington the source of the $103,800, though Moffitt apparently told Covington that, though they could accept cash, they could not accept "funny money." Covington refused a receipt for both payments because, he said, the F.B.I. might find it. The law firm thereafter filed the required Internal Revenue Service Form 8300 reflecting the cash payments from Covington, but failed to identify Covington as the source of the cash transfer.

Once retained, the firm notified prosecutors that they represented Covington. In a series of meetings with law firm members, the prosecutors outlined the nature of their case against Covington and provided a list of assets seized from Covington. These seizures included his home, four cars, a boat, hundreds of thousands of dollars in cash, a motorcycle, and assets of his auto service and towing businesses, namely, two tow trucks and two bank accounts. Prosecutors also disclosed a 50-page affidavit, prepared by an IRS investigator, that supported search and seizure warrants executed against Covington. Among other things, the affidavit reported that Covington had accumulated or spent a vast amount of money in the previous few years, money which the investigator concluded could only have come from drug trafficking activity. Moreover, the investigator revealed that Covington used his businesses to facilitate drug sales and to launder drug profits.

On October 30, 1991, the grand jury indicted Covington on a variety of drug trafficking, firearm, and money laundering offenses. A superseding indictment was returned on January 9, 1992. Both the original and the superseding indictment contained counts providing for the forfeiture of "any and all properties constituting, or derived from, proceeds" obtained as a result of the illegal activity and any properties used to facilitate that activity. Such assets "included, but [were] not limited to" cash of up to $168,000 that the government had not yet located.

On May 12, 1992, after obtaining the approval of the Department of Justice, the government filed a bill of particulars identifying the $103,800 paid to the law firm as subject to forfeiture. It also sought and obtained a restraining order to prevent dissipation of the fee.

In August, 1992, the district court disqualified the law firm from continuing to represent Covington. The judge observed that the most important reason for the disqualification was Covington's statement that while he wanted to plead guilty, he could not because one of his lawyers informed him that such a plea would place the law firm's acceptance of the fee in an unfavorable light. Another important reason for the disqualification related to the government's intention to use evidence concerning Covington's legal fee at trial. New counsel was then appointed.

On September 25, 1992, Covington entered a guilty plea. He was sentenced in February, 1993 to 262 months in prison. At sentencing, pursuant to 21 U.S.C. § 853, and with Covington's consent, the $103,800 fee paid to the law firm was ordered forfeited. Subsequently, the law firm sought to vacate the forfeiture order. It filed a petition asserting that it was "reasonably without cause to believe" that the fee was subject to forfeiture. The district court rejected the petition. In re Moffitt, Zwerling & Kemler, P.C., 846 F. Supp. 463 (E.D. Va. 1994) ("Moffitt I").

Thereafter, the government sought a final decree of forfeiture to collect the $103,800 from Moffitt, Zwerling. The firm maintained, however, that recovery was limited to the $3,695 that remained unspent at the time the district court entered the May, 1992 restraining order. Nearly all of the $103,800 fee was spent, in fact, as early as January, 1992. In response, the government pursued a number of remedies to retrieve some or all of the fee. . . .

[The law firm did not dispute the trial court's finding that Covington's fee was paid with proceeds of his criminal activity.]

III

Moffitt, Zwerling . . . argues that its fee was not subject to forfeiture because it qualified as an innocent transferee whose assets could not be forfeited. It was, it claims, "reasonably without cause to believe that the property was subject to forfeiture." After an extensive evidentiary hearing, however, the district court disagreed, concluding that: "[T]he record, taken as a whole, compels the conclusion that the Law Firm's belief that the cash fee came from legitimate sources was not reasonable in the circumstances." Moffitt I, 846 F. Supp. at 472.

We can find no fault with the district court's conclusion. Covington approached Moffitt, Zwerling as a known target of a far-reaching drug trafficking investigation. As the law firm knew, the government suspected that Covington was the leader of a major cocaine ring, and the government had seized nearly all of his personal and business assets. The extensive seizures were, as the law firm also knew, based on a judicial officer's determination that there was probable cause to believe the assets were subject to forfeiture. Covington himself told the firm's partners that he used his businesses to facilitate drug dealing, and the firm was aware of the government's conclusion that the considerable amount of money Covington had accumulated and spent could have only resulted from his drug trafficking activities. Despite this, the firm accepted from Covington two immense cash payments, totalling $103,800 and largely comprised of $100 bills, over a two-day period. At Covington's request, the firm did not give him a receipt for the $103,800 because Covington feared the receipt might fall into the hands of the F.B.I. Such circumstances were, to put it mildly, highly suspicious.

The firm contends that its partners believed, based on their extensive interviews with him, that Covington had "squirreled" away substantial assets from legitimate business activity. And the firm asserts that Covington was informed that he could not pay in "funny money." The district court found, however, that Covington advised the firm's partners that he was broke, and for that reason continued to engage in illegal activity. In addition, during the supposedly extensive interviews with Covington, the firm's partners tiptoed around the most pertinent questions. They did not even ask Covington what legitimate sources of income he had. And, conspicuously, they avoided asking Covington exactly where he had obtained the $103,800 in cash to pay his legal fee. In their meetings with Covington the lawyers did not seek to obviate doubts that any person would have had about the source of Covington's substantial cash payment. The meetings, in fact, create the impression that the participants were engaging in some sort of wink and nod ritual whereby they agreed not to ask — or tell — too much.

Based on this record, the district court observed, there was nothing less than a "mass of evidence available to the Law Firm partners in August 1991 that pointed convincingly to the conclusion that the cash fee constituted, or was derived from, drug trafficking proceeds." Id. at 475. We agree. Both what the law firm knew in August, 1991, and what it declined to inquire about, convinces us that it reasonably had cause to know that the $103,800 was subject to forfeiture. . . .

IV

The government thereafter sought a final decree of forfeiture for the $103,800. According to the law firm, the government's recovery was limited to $3,695, the amount of the fee that remained when the restraining order was entered in May, 1992. Seeking to recover the full amount of the fee, however, the government argued that under 21 U.S.C. § 853 the law firm was obligated to remit to the government the entire $103,800. The district court rejected this argument, but observed that the government might have other remedies available to it, such as a state law conversion action, to recover the fee. Consequently, the government brought common law actions of conversion and detinue under Virginia law to recover the full $103,800. . . .

V . . .

We affirm the district court's judgment that the government has stated the elements of a conversion action. Conversion is the "wrongful exercise or assumption of authority . . . over another's goods. . . ." United Leasing Corp. v. Thrift Ins. Corp., 440 S.E.2d 902, 905 (Va. 1994). To make out a conversion action in Virginia the government must have had an immediate right to possess the $103,800 at the time it was allegedly wrongfully converted by the law firm. The key dispute is whether the government had such a right to possession.

Under the relation back doctrine codified in § 853(c), the government had the right to possess the $103,800 at the time the law firm received it in August, 1991. No provision of the [Comprehensive Forfeiture Act of 1984] suggests that § 853(c) cannot be relied upon to establish one element of a conversion action. Moffitt, Zwerling emphasizes, however, that the government did not actually gain title to the $103,800 until the entry of the forfeiture order. But once the forfeiture order was entered, the government's title dated back in time to the criminal activity giving rise to the forfeiture, a date which necessarily was prior to August, 1991. The government therefore had a right to possess the $103,800 in August, 1991. . . .

For the foregoing reasons, the district court's judgment is affirmed in part, and reversed in part. . . .

Notes and Questions

1. What are the pivotal facts that precluded the law firm from establishing that it was a bona fide purchaser for value?

2. What is the significance of Covington's mode of payment? Is it unlawful to pay legal fees in cash?

3. Does the forfeiture statute put lawyers in a more disadvantageous position than it does other creditors? Suppose that Covington had paid his stockbroker or his country club dues in cash derived from drug dealing. Could the government have seized the payments from the broker or the country club under the forfeiture statute?

4. As *Moffitt* and *Caplin & Drysdale* illustrate, the forfeiture statute can be used to reach tainted assets in a third party's hands. But if, as in *Moffitt*, the third party has

already dissipated all or almost all of the assets, the government is in a difficult spot. Although the forfeiture statute provides for forfeiture of substitute assets in the defendant's hands,[42] the substitute assets provision does not apply to assets that have been transferred to third parties.

Does this loophole encourage third parties who knowingly receive tainted money to get rid of it quickly? If so, does it defeat the purpose of allowing forfeiture of assets in third parties' hands?

5. The court in *Moffitt* ruled that the forfeiture statute does not override state common law remedies and that the government had stated the elements of an action for conversion. How does the government's ability to sue in conversion improve its position?

6. Another option available to the government in a case like *Moffitt* is to try to locate property derived from criminal proceeds. Suppose that William Moffitt's share of Covington's legal fee is $50,000. He takes the cash to a jewelry store and buys himself a Rolex watch. If the government can trace it to the legal fee, the watch is subject to forfeiture. Is this an equitable rule?

7. What other options are available to the government? Celebrity defense lawyer F. Lee Bailey became entangled in a dispute over the receipt of proceeds from his clients' telemarketing scam. Bailey — who had control over the assets — violated a court order to turn them over to the court. The dispute ultimately resulted in Bailey's citation for contempt of court, service of six weeks of a six-month jail sentence, and disbarment from the Florida and Massachusetts bars.[43]

UNITED STATES v. STEIN
435 F. Supp. 2d 330 (S.D.N.Y. 2006)

KAPLAN, District Judge. . . .

Most of the defendants in this case worked for KPMG, one of the world's largest accounting firms. KPMG long has paid for the legal defense of its personnel, regardless of the cost and regardless of whether its personnel were charged with crimes. The defendants who formerly worked for KPMG say that it is obligated to do so here. KPMG, however, has refused.

If that were all there were to the dispute, it would be a private matter between KPMG and its former personnel. But it is not all there is. These defendants (the "KPMG Defendants") claim that KPMG has refused to advance defense costs to which the defendants are entitled because the government pressured KPMG to cut them off. The government, they say, thus violated their rights and threatens their right to a fair trial.

---

42. Thus, for example, if Covington's drug dealing had generated only $100,000 and he had paid all of it to the law firm, the government could seize other assets that he owns, including cars, boats, jewelry, securities, bank accounts, and, in most states, the defendant's home.

43. See United States v. McCorkle (Bailey), 321 F.3d 1292 (11th Cir. 2003) (considering forfeiture and contempt proceedings relating to Bailey's alleged mishandling of a drug client's funds); The Florida Bar v. Bailey, 803 So. 2d 683 (Fla. 2001) (disbarring Bailey in Florida for a minimum of five years); In the Matter of F. Lee Bailey, 786 N.E.2d 337 (Mass. 2003) (affirming judgment of disbarment in Massachusetts based on Florida disciplinary proceedings); Region in Brief: F. Lee Bailey Bids to Get Law License Back, Boston Herald, Mar. 10, 2005, at 031 (reporting a federal court hearing contesting Bailey's Massachusetts disbarment); Florida Disbars F. Lee Bailey over Stock Funds, N.Y. Times, Nov. 22, 2001, at A24; F. Lee Bailey Freed from Jail in Dispute over Drug Money, N.Y. Times, Apr. 20, 1996, § 1, at 12.

Having heard testimony from KPMG's general counsel, some of its outside lawyers, and government prosecutors, the Court concludes that the KPMG Defendants are
right. KPMG refused to pay because the government held the proverbial gun to its head.
Had that pressure not been brought to bear, KPMG would have paid these defendants'
legal expenses. . . .

KPMG's POLICY ON PAYMENT OF LEGAL FEES

KPMG's policy prior to this matter concerning the payment of legal fees of its
partners and employees is clear. While KPMG's partnership agreement and by-laws are
silent on the subject, the parties have stipulated as follows:

"1. Prior to February 2004, . . . it had been the longstanding voluntary practice of
KPMG to advance and pay legal fees, without a preset cap or condition of cooperation
with the government, for counsel for partners, principals, and employees of the firm in
those situations where separate counsel was appropriate to represent the individual in any
civil, criminal or regulatory proceeding involving activities arising within the scope of the
individual's duties and responsibilities as a KPMG partner, principal, or employee.
"2. This practice was followed without regard to economic costs or considerations
with respect to individuals or the firm.
"3. With the exception of the instant matter, KPMG is not aware of any current or
former partner, principal, or employee who has been indicted for conduct arising within
the scope of the individual's duties and responsibilities as a KPMG partner, principal, or
employee since [two partners] were indicted and convicted of violation of federal criminal
law in 1974. Although KPMG has located no documents regarding payment of legal fees
in that case, KPMG believes that it did pay pre- and post-indictment legal fees for the individuals in that case."

The Court infers and finds that KPMG in fact paid the pre- and post-indictment
legal fees for the individuals in the 1974 criminal case. Moreover, the extent to which
KPMG has gone is quite remarkable. In one recent situation involving KPMG's relationship with Xerox Corporation, it paid over $20 million to defend four partners in a
criminal investigation and related civil litigation brought by the Securities and
Exchange Commission. . . .

B. THE SIXTH AMENDMENT RIGHT TO COUNSEL

1. The Nature and Scope of the Right to Counsel . . .

The Sixth Amendment provides that "[i]n all criminal prosecutions, the accused
shall enjoy the right to . . . have the Assistance of Counsel for his defence." As already
has been demonstrated, however, this guarantees more than the mere presence of a lawyer at a criminal trial. It protects, among other things, an individual's right to choose
the lawyer or lawyers he or she desires and to use one's own funds to mount the defense
that one wishes to present. . . . The government nevertheless argues that the KPMG
Defendants have no Sixth Amendment rights at stake here for two principal reasons.

a.   Attachment of Sixth Amendment Rights

[The government first argued that because "the Sixth Amendment right to counsel attaches only upon the formal initiation of a criminal proceeding" such as arraignment, indictment, or preliminary hearing, the defendants' Sixth Amendment claims could not stand. But the court disagreed, observing that because the government's purpose was to minimize the defendants' access to resources they needed to mount their defenses, it was "not unfair" to hold the government accountable.]

The government first argues that the Sixth Amendment right to counsel attaches only upon the initiation of a criminal proceeding. As the Thompson Memorandum was adopted and the USAO did its handiwork before the KPMG Defendants were indicted, it contends, there was no Sixth Amendment violation.

It is true, of course, that the Sixth Amendment right to counsel typically attaches at the initiation of adversarial proceedings — at an arraignment, indictment, preliminary hearing, and so on. But the analysis can not end there. The Thompson Memorandum on its face and the USAO's actions were parts of an effort to limit defendants' access to funds for their defense. Even if this was not among the conscious motives, the Memorandum was adopted and the USAO acted in circumstances in which that result was known to be exceptionally likely. The fact that events were set in motion prior to indictment with the object of having, or with knowledge that they were likely to have, an unconstitutional effect upon indictment cannot save the government. This conduct, unless justified, violated the Sixth Amendment.

The government argues that this conclusion will open the door for future defendants to argue that all sorts of pre-indictment actions violate the Sixth Amendment and thus hamstring every investigation and prosecution. This is singularly unpersuasive. The government here acted with the purpose of minimizing these defendants' access to resources necessary to mount their defenses or, at least, in reckless disregard that this would be the likely result of its actions. In these circumstances, it is not unfair to hold it accountable.

b.   "Other People's Money"

The government next argues that the KPMG Defendants have no right, under the Sixth Amendment or otherwise, to spend "other people's money" on expensive defense counsel. The rhetoric is appealing, but the characterization of the issue — and therefore the conclusion — are wrong.

The argument is based on Caplin & Drysdale, Chartered v. United States and United States v. Monsanto, which held that the Sixth Amendment does not create[] a right for those in possession of property forfeitable to the United States to spend that money on their legal defense. That is hardly surprising — the money belongs to the government. But that is not the issue here.

Caplin & Drysdale recognized that the Sixth Amendment does protect a defendant's right to spend his own money on a defense. Here, the KPMG Defendants had at least an expectation that their expenses in defending any claims or charges brought against them by reason of their employment by KPMG would be paid by the firm. The law protects such interests against unjustified and improper interference. Thus, both the expectation and any benefits that would have flowed from that expectation — the legal fees at issue now — were, in every material sense, their property, not that of a third party. The government's contention that the defendants seek to spend "other people's money" is thus incorrect. . . .

Notes and Questions

1. The court indicates that if KPMG had departed from its practice of indemnifying legal expenses without prompting from the government, there would be no Sixth Amendment violation. Stated differently, KPMG's employees have no Sixth Amendment right to have their employer pay their legal fees. How does the employees' expectation of indemnification ripen into a constitutional right to payment of legal fees if — but only if — the government influenced KPMG's decision not to indemnify?

2. If the government influences KPMG not to indemnify the cost of its employees' legal defense, has it effectively denied them the right to counsel? Of the right to counsel of choice?

3. At what point in time did the government's pressure on KPMG encroach on the employees' Sixth Amendment rights? When does the right to counsel attach?

4. *Monsanto* and *Caplin & Drysdale* found that criminal defendants do not have the right to pay their legal fees with "other people's money." The court in *Stein* distinguishes those cases on the ground that the money the defendants sought to use to pay their lawyers was subject to forfeiture and thus belonged to the government. Did the money the Stein defendants sought via indemnification belong to them? Or did it belong to KPMG?

5. Although KPMG agreed to pay its employees' legal fees, it capped the amount that it would indemnify them at $400,000 apiece. Are there practical reasons — apart from government coercion — that might explain its decision?

6. HealthSouth CEO Richard Scrushy reportedly spent $32 million defending charges that he orchestrated a $2.7 billion fraud at the company.[44] Should the huge amounts that high-profile white collar defendants spend on legal fees influence the court's view of KPMG's obligation (or the extent of its obligation) to indemnify?

7. Assuming the court is correct in concluding that exertion of government influence over KPMG's decision whether it will indemnify its employees is improper, what is the proper remedy? Should the court dismiss the indictment? Order the government to reimburse the employees? Order KPMG to indemnify them?

8. On appeal, the Second Circuit considered this issue, ruling that Judge Kaplan lacked ancillary jurisdiction to resolve the fee dispute between KPMG and its employees. The court suggested, however, that dismissal of the indictment might serve as an alternative remedy to vindicate the defendants' rights.[45]

On remand, Judge Kaplan dismissed the charges against 13 former partners and employees who had been denied indemnification they would have received but for the government's pressure on KPMG to cooperate.[46] On appeal, the Second Circuit upheld the dismissal and affirmed Judge Kaplan's ruling that the defendants had been denied

---

44. An arbitrator ruled that HealthSouth was obligated to pay $17 million of the fees.
45. Stein v. KPMG, LLP, 486 F.3d 753 (2d Cir. 2007) (*Stein II*).
46. United States v. Stein, 495 F. Supp. 2d 390 (S.D.N.Y. 2007) (*Stein III*).

their Sixth Amendment right to counsel when the government caused KPMG to condition the payment of their legal fees, to place a cap on the fee amounts it would pay, and ultimately to discontinue fee payments altogether. Since the government had not cured the Sixth Amendment violation and no other remedy would restore the defendants to their original position, the Court of Appeals affirmed the dismissal of the indictment against the 13 defendants.[47]

The court seems to acknowledge that there may be circumstances under which the government would be justified in interfering with the defendant's right to be represented by counsel of choice. When would such interference be warranted?

D. CONSTITUTIONAL LIMITS

Although RICO requires forfeiture of *any* interest acquired or maintained in violation of § 1962, as well as *any* interest, claim against, or right affording a source of influence over a RICO enterprise and *any* property constituting or derived from proceeds of racketeering activity, the Supreme Court has held that criminal forfeitures are subject to scrutiny under the Eighth Amendment's Excessive Fines Clause. Under established Eighth Amendment principles, the initial burden of proof is on the defendant to establish that a fine or forfeiture is excessive for Eighth Amendment purposes. If the defendant makes a prima facie showing of disproportionality, the government bears the burden of rebutting that showing by establishing that the fine or forfeiture is justly proportional.

1. *Alexander I*

In Alexander v. United States,[48] the Court considered a constitutional challenge to a forfeiture order that required the defendant — who owned a large-scale pornography operation — to forfeit his interest in 31 businesses that were used to conduct his adult entertainment business plus nearly $9 million acquired through racketeering activity. In addition, he was sentenced to serve a 6 year prison term and to pay a $100,000 fine.

Rejecting Alexander's Eighth Amendment challenge to the forfeiture as grossly disproportionate to the seriousness of his crime, the Court acknowledged that the Excessive Fines Clause limits governmental power to exact payments as punishment for an offense. And because in personam criminal forfeitures — like those imposed under RICO — are a form of monetary punishment that is equivalent to traditional fines, they are subject to Eighth Amendment scrutiny.

Invoking these Eighth Amendment principles, Alexander argued that forfeiture of his entire business as punishment for selling a few obscene items was an excessive penalty, but the Court disagreed with his characterization of the offense.

> Petitioner . . . argues that the forfeiture order in this case — considered atop his 6-year prison term and $100,000 fine — is disproportionate to the gravity of his offenses and therefore violates the Eighth Amendment, either as a "cruel and unusual punishment" or

---

47. United States v. Stein, 541 F.3d 130 (2d Cir. 2008) (*Stein IV*).
48. 509 U.S. 544 (1993).

as an "excessive fine." The Court of Appeals, though, failed to distinguish between these two components of petitioner's Eighth Amendment challenge. Instead, the court lumped the two together, disposing of them both with the general statement that the Eighth Amendment does not require any proportionality review of a sentence less than life imprisonment without the possibility of parole. But that statement has relevance only to the Eighth Amendment's prohibition against cruel and unusual punishments. Unlike the Cruel and Unusual Punishments Clause, which is concerned with matters such as the duration or conditions of confinement, "[t]he Excessive Fines Clause limits the Government's power to extract payments, whether in cash or in kind, as punishment for some offense." Austin v. United States, 113 S. Ct. 2801 (1993). The *in personam* criminal forfeiture at issue here is clearly a form of monetary punishment no different, for Eighth Amendment purposes, from a traditional "fine." Accordingly, the forfeiture in this case should be analyzed under the Excessive Fines Clause.

Petitioner contends that forfeiture of his entire business was an "excessive" penalty for the Government to exact "on the basis of a few materials the jury ultimately decided were obscene." It is somewhat misleading, we think, to characterize the racketeering crimes for which petitioner was convicted as involving just a few materials ultimately found to be obscene. Petitioner was convicted of creating and managing what the District Court described as "an enormous racketeering enterprise." It is in the light of the extensive criminal activities which petitioner apparently conducted through this racketeering enterprise over a substantial period of time that the question of whether or not the forfeiture was "excessive" must be considered. We think it preferable that this question be addressed by the Court of Appeals in the first instance. . . . [49]

Although the Court's ruling in *Alexander I* made it clear that in personam forfeitures are like criminal fines and thus are subject to scrutiny under the Excessive Fines Clause of the Eighth Amendment, the Court notably provided no guidance to the lower courts on what factors should be considered and what relative weight each should be given.

2. *Alexander II*

On remand, the Eighth Circuit ruled that although the trial court had made extensive findings and stated detailed reasons for its forfeiture order, the court had not conducted the proportionality analysis the Supreme Court now required.[50] Thus, in *Alexander II* the Eighth Circuit directed the trial court to analyze the proportionality issue in light of the voluminous record from Alexander's four-month trial and the related forfeiture proceedings, and to make additional findings of fact and conclusions of law on the excessiveness issue. *Alexander II* also gave the trial court some guidance on how to proceed.

The Eighth Circuit first reaffirmed the commonly accepted principle that the initial burden of proof is on the defendant to show gross disproportionality. If the defendant succeeds in making a prima facie showing that the amount ordered to be forfeited is excessive, the trial court must then consider the government's evidence of just proportionality. In balancing the two, the court of appeals suggested that the trial court should

---

49. Alexander v. United States, 509 U.S. 544 (1993) (*Alexander I*).
50. United States v. Alexander, 32 F.3d 1231 (8th Cir. 1994) (*Alexander II*).

consider the extent and duration of the defendant's criminal conduct, the gravity of his crimes, the amount of property forfeited, and, perhaps, personal gain and motive. The court, however, said this list of factors is neither "complete" nor exhaustive."

Notes and Questions

1. Do the factors the court articulated in *Alexander II* provide adequate guidance to the trial court?

2. As noted earlier, profits and proceeds of RICO violations are made forfeitable under § 1963(a). If the court orders the defendant to forfeit proceeds he obtained from his criminal activity, is the forfeiture equivalent to punishment? Should forfeitures of criminal profits and proceeds be subject to scrutiny for disproportionality under the Excessive Fines Clause of the Eighth Amendment?

3. *Alexander III*

The forfeiture order under review required Alexander to forfeit 10 pieces of real estate; interests in 18 noncorporate businesses (including inventory, accounts receivable, vehicles, equipment, office furniture, computers, safes, televisions, and videocassette recorders); 15 bank accounts; inventory and equipment in 13 other noncorporate businesses; personal property including 8-millimeter projectors and videocassette recorders; 3 vehicles; and nearly $9 million in proceeds of racketeering activity that occurred between 1985 and 1988.

On remand, the trial court affirmed the forfeiture order, holding that Alexander had failed to make a prima facie showing of disproportionality. Alexander appealed again, challenging the district court's findings and conclusions regarding which assets were subject to forfeiture. The Eighth Circuit found all of his challenges to be without merit and affirmed. The legal arguments are not particularly worthy of note, but the following excerpt from the Eighth Circuit's opinion in *Alexander III* provides an instructive glimpse at the trial court's proportionality hearing.

GIBSON, Circuit Judge. . . . [51]

The district court recognized that Alexander must make a prima facie showing of gross disproportionality before the court will consider the government's counter-evidence of just proportionality. . . . The court concluded that Alexander "entirely failed to come forward with any cognizable evidence establishing the dollar value of his holdings." The court specifically referred to the several amounts Alexander claimed to have held, varying from "$25 million," to "many millions" to "$2 million." The court pointed out that Alexander failed to submit any evidence of the value of his business, such as a certified appraisal, audited financial statements, or any value based on a capitalization of income

---

51. In his brief, Alexander identifies and values the items forfeited: ten parcels of real property valued at $1,040,334.06; fifteen bank accounts totalling $5,017.47; fourteen bookstores valued at least at $2,000,000; personal property and equipment liquidated at auction and private sale for $47,297.47; 113.8 tons of "presumptively protected" magazines, videos, and novelties; 1,033 boxes of magazines, videos, and novelty items from a California warehouse; three motor vehicles valued at $12,000; and monies acquired from the RICO enterprise from the years 1985 through 1988, totalling $8,910,548.10.

stream, an offer of a comparable sale, or a specific asset listing and valuation. Because the court could not calculate "base holdings," the court concluded it was impossible to determine the proportion of fines and, ultimately, determine if the forfeiture was disproportionate.

The court also commented on Alexander's lack of credibility based on discrepancies in Alexander's trial testimony and his declarations. Alexander had stated to the Supreme Court that his business was worth $25 million, but on his Chapter 7 bankruptcy schedule, he stated, under penalty of perjury, that his business was worth approximately $2 million. The court found "unworthy of belief," Alexander's valuation of his assets. The court referred to evidence that Alexander failed to keep records of receipts and that there were "vast unreported sums of money." As one example, the court recounted evidence that Alexander maintained only a personal monthly declaration of quarters he collected and counted from unmetered "peep show" vending machines, and that these records did not square with testimony from a bank employee who stated that Alexander deposited substantial amounts of quarters into different bank accounts, often retaining large amounts of cash in $50 and $100 denominations. The court stated that between the time of Alexander's conviction and the seizure of his assets, Alexander requested and received control of his business and assets and, during that time, he "secreted assets, attempted bulk sales, and engaged in . . . a series of shenanigans designed to obstruct the Court's orderly processes and enrich himself before the marshal seized his inventory and equipment." Under these circumstances, the court concluded that the United States had no duty to inventory Alexander's holdings and rejected Alexander's argument that he should be relieved of his burden to show gross disproportionality.

The district court then considered the extent and duration of Alexander's criminal activities. The court compared Alexander's maximum consecutive sentences (171 years and statutory fines of $6,400,000) with his imposed sentence (72 months and $100,000 fine, special assessments, and costs), specifically noting that the court did not order a higher fine because of the forfeiture. The court concluded that the imposed sentence was appropriate and Alexander failed to make any showing that the forfeiture was grossly disproportionate to his criminal activity. . . . [52]

Notes and Questions

1. Why does the initial burden of proof fall on the defendant? What are the practical ramifications of requiring the defendant to make a prima facie showing of disproportionality? Why did Alexander fare so poorly?

2. Is the punishment imposed on Alexander proportionate to his crimes?

---

52. United States v. Alexander, 108 F.3d 853 (8th Cir. 1997) (*Alexander III*).

11

Tax Fraud

I. INTRODUCTION

The Internal Revenue Code largely relies on a system of voluntary compliance. Individual taxpayers who receive a threshold amount of gross income during any tax year must file a tax return that reports the income and assesses the amount of tax due.[1] Corporations, in contrast, must file annual returns regardless of the amount of earnings and profits received during the tax year.[2] Because this system depends on corporate and individual taxpayers to perform this annual rite on their own initiative, the criminal and civil penalty provisions in the Code play the crucial role of stimulating maximum compliance. Simply put, the penalty provisions are designed to deter those who might otherwise choose to opt out of the system.

This chapter focuses on key Code sections that are the heart of the criminal tax enforcement scheme. These provisions are directed at attempts to evade or defeat a tax; failure to perform required acts such as collecting or paying over a tax, filing a return, or supplying required information; and submitting fraudulent and false statements to the government.

II. WILLFULNESS

The unifying theme that draws the criminal tax provisions together is the requisite culpable mental state. Notwithstanding that some tax crimes are misdemeanors and others are felonies, all require proof of the element of willfulness. Although early Supreme Court decisions strongly suggested that, in the tax context, willfulness connotes "bad faith and evil intent,"[3] the Court later explained that the reference to "evil motive" meant nothing more than intent to violate the law. Thus, in the criminal tax context, willfulness means "a voluntary, intentional violation of a known legal duty."[4] United States v. Bishop, 412 U.S. 346, 360 (1973).

---

1. See 26 U.S.C. § 6012(a)(1).
2. See 26 U.S.C. § 6012(a)(2).
3. United States v. Murdock, 290 U.S. 389, 398 (1933).
4. United States v. Pomponio, 429 U.S. 10, 11 (1976).

A. PROOF OF CULPABILITY

UNITED STATES v. GUIDRY
199 F.3d 1150 (10th Cir. 1999)

BRORBY, Circuit Judge.

A jury found Appellant Anita L. Guidry guilty of three counts of knowingly and willfully filing a false tax return in violation of 26 U.S.C. § 7206(1). . . .

BACKGROUND

Anita L. Guidry was the architect of an embezzlement scheme that allowed her to line her pockets with approximately $3 million belonging to her employer, Wichita Sheet Metal.[5] While the embezzlement scheme itself is not directly in issue here, understanding the facts surrounding the scheme is a necessary predicate to resolving the issues before us. Accordingly, we begin with a cursory examination of Mrs. Guidry's background and her embezzlement.

Mrs. Guidry graduated from Wichita State University with a Bachelor's Degree in Business Administration. Her resume lists her major area of study as accounting, and she listed her occupation as accountant on several tax returns filed with the Internal Revenue Service. Wichita Sheet Metal hired Mrs. Guidry as an assistant to the controller of the company in 1986, and she subsequently became the controller in 1987, a position she held until she resigned in 1997. As controller, Mrs. Guidry not only supervised nearly every employee in the office, but she was an authorized signatory on the company checking account.

Mrs. Guidry's embezzlement scheme consisted of submitting checks, already signed by her and made payable to the company's bank, to Freda Moore or John Griffit, owners of Wichita Sheet Metal, for their signature. Mrs. Guidry wrote the checks in $10,000 or $9,000 increments, and she told Mrs. Moore and Mr. Griffit the checks were for federal tax payments. After collecting the proper signature, Mrs. Guidry cashed the checks at the company bank and pocketed the cash. Finally, to prevent discovery of her scheme, Mrs. Guidry altered the company's books to make it appear the money she had taken for personal pleasures was actually used to purchase inventory for the company. This created a discrepancy between the actual inventory and the inventory reflected on the company's books. The company's owners eventually asked for a detailed audit of the discrepancy, which ultimately led to the discovery of Mrs. Guidry's embezzlement.

Mrs. Guidry had financial responsibilities at home in addition to those at work. As the accountant in the family, Mrs. Guidry prepared the joint federal tax returns she filed on behalf of herself and her husband for 1993, 1994, and 1995. According to

---

5. Mrs. Guidry used her stolen money to make sure she had plenty of pockets to line. During the years of her embezzlement, Mrs. Guidry spent over $1.2 million on clothing from one retailer alone — GM Clotheshorse. Her employer, Wichita Sheet Metal, eventually took possession of 1,300 dresses, 182 pairs of shoes, 164 hats, 40 belts, 27 purses, two fur coats, and boxes of jewelry that included over 400 pairs of earrings, all of which Mrs. Guidry had kept in several rented storage units. Mrs. Guidry's former employers certainly have the inventory, if not the experience, to open their own boutique should the sheet metal business turn sour.

Mrs. Guidry's husband, these returns were prepared elaborately, which fact is buttressed by the returns themselves. The Guidrys painstakingly itemized their deductions, taking charitable deductions of $7,513 in 1993, $11,692 in 1994, and $13,102 in 1995. Not surprisingly, however, none of the returns reported the embezzled income. In 1993, Mrs. Guidry cashed forty checks through her embezzlement scheme for a total amount of $400,000. The Guidrys declared a total income, combined husband and wife, of $82,817 on their federal income tax return in 1993. In 1994, fifty-nine checks were cashed for a total of $563,000, and the Guidrys declared a total income of $88,547. In 1995, it was sixty-four checks cashed for $576,000, compared to a total declared income of $90,883.

While investigating Mrs. Guidry's embezzlement, Special Agent Martin McCormick of the Internal Revenue Service participated in the execution of a search warrant at the Guidry home. While searching for bank records, Special Agent McCormick opened a drawer in a file cabinet marked "taxes" and observed "tax booklets identical to those that are mailed to everyone by the Internal Revenue Service every year at the first of the year." The 1993 tax booklet the Internal Revenue Service provided with the Individual Income Tax Return listed embezzled income as taxable income that must be reported. The 1994 and 1995 tax booklets did not specifically contain this language, but instead referenced a publication the taxpayer could request which did specifically state embezzled income must be reported as taxable income.

DISCUSSION . . .

II. THE JURY INSTRUCTIONS

Mrs. Guidry . . . assigns error to the district court's jury instructions, claiming the instructions inadequately defined the term "willfully" as it pertains to the crime of filing a false tax return. . . .

The Supreme Court addressed the statutory definition of "willful" as it is applied in the tax code in Cheek v. United States, 498 U.S. 192 (1991). The Court held its cases "conclusively establish that the standard for the statutory willfulness requirement is the 'voluntary, intentional violation of a known legal duty.'" Id. at 200-01 (quoting United States v. Bishop, 412 U.S. 346, 360 (1973)). The district court's instructions in the current case tracked the *Cheek* language almost verbatim: "For the purpose of this instruction, the term 'willfully' means to voluntarily and intentionally violate a known legal duty." . . .

III. SUFFICIENCY OF THE EVIDENCE

Mrs. Guidry . . . complains the evidence at trial was insufficient to sustain the jury's verdict. This argument presents a high hurdle, and one Mrs. Guidry fails to surmount. . . .

Mrs. Guidry contends the "only" evidence supporting willfulness consists of her background and experience in accounting, the testimony to the effect Internal Revenue Service documents listed embezzled income as taxable income, and Agent McCormick's testimony he observed some Internal Revenue Service tax booklets in Mrs. Guidry's files at her home. Seeing a lack of evidence, Mrs. Guidry then goes on to cite our decision in

McCarty v. United States, 409 F.2d 793 (10th Cir. 1969), for the proposition that "willful-ness cannot be inferred from a mere understatement of income." Id. at 795 (citing Spies v. United States, 317 U.S. 492 (1943)). This analysis suffers from two fatal flaws: it fails to view all the evidence in the light most favorable to the Government, and it provides an incomplete view of the Supreme Court's guidance in *Spies*.

While it is well established willfulness cannot be inferred solely from an under-statement of income, willfulness can be inferred from

> making false entries of alterations, or false invoices or documents, destruction of books or records, concealment of assets or covering up sources of income, handling of one's affairs to avoid making the records usual in transactions of the kind, and any conduct, the likely effect of which would be to mislead or to conceal.

Spies, 317 U.S. at 499. This conduct can be used to prove willfulness "even though the conduct may also serve other purposes such as concealment of other crime." *Spies*, 317 U.S. at 499. The jury heard sufficient evidence to support its finding of willfulness in this case.

First, the jury heard evidence of Mrs. Guidry's expertise in accounting via her degree in business and her work experience as the controller of a company. The evidence showed Mrs. Guidry prepared the family taxes, and did so "elaborately" according to her husband. An investigator observed tax booklets from unknown years in Mrs. Guidry's files, and the jury learned the tax booklets specific to the years in question in this case either stated embezzled income should be reported, or referenced a second Internal Revenue Service document where taxpayers might receive that information. The evidence also showed: an ever-burgeoning disparity between the Guidrys' reported income and their actual income as complemented by the embezzlement scheme; the embezzled cash was used to purchase goods, making the money more difficult to detect; the Guidrys took significant charitable deductions on their taxes while not reporting the embezzled income; and the money was embezzled in increments of $9,000 or $10,000. Mrs. Guidry argues the jury should not have been allowed to take evidence of the embezzlement scheme itself into account, but such an argument defies logic.

Concealment of income can have more than one purpose. Such activity can show a desire to conceal the theft from the employer, and it can tend to show a purposeful attempt to conceal such income from the Internal Revenue Service. In addition, an infer-ence of willfulness can be supported by a "consistent pattern of underreporting large amounts of income." Holland v. United States, 348 U.S. 121, 139 (1954). "Criminal willfulness can be inferred when a defendant does not supply her tax preparer with evi-dence of substantial items of income." United States v. Stokes, 998 F.2d 279, 281 (5th Cir. 1993). In *Stokes*, the Ninth Circuit upheld a conviction under § 7206(1) when the defendant did not disclose illegal income to her tax preparer. It makes little sense to apply one standard to a person who withholds information from a tax preparer, and another standard to a self-preparer who withholds similar information from the Internal Revenue Service directly. The jury was free to conclude Mrs. Guidry had accounting expertise, that information stating embezzled income was to be reported as income on the tax return was available to her, and that she would have availed herself of the infor-mation. The jury was also free to examine the way the embezzlement scheme was designed to conceal assets, and infer Mrs. Guidry's intent was to avoid paying a known tax liability. As in *Spies*, Mrs. Guidry "claims other motives animated [her] in these matters. We intimate no opinion. Such inferences are for the jury." *Spies*, 317 U.S. at 500. Our holding is limited to the unique facts of this case. Given the combination of Mrs. Guidry's background and training, the details of her embezzlement scheme and attempts to conceal her income, and the testimony concerning the presence and contents of federal tax booklets, the evidence was sufficient to support the jury's verdict in this case. . . .

Accordingly, we affirm. . . .

[Opinion of Lucero, J., concurring in part and dissenting in part, omitted.]

Notes and Questions

1. Unlike most other contexts, "willfulness" under the tax laws requires intentional violation of a "known" legal duty. What if Mrs. Guidry claimed she did not know that embezzled money was taxable as income? Would the government still be able to prove her violation was willful?

2. Since there was no proof that Mrs. Guidry ever read the tax booklets found during the search of her home, why were the booklets relevant to her culpability?

3. Mrs. Guidry bought more than $1 million of clothing from a single retailer. Is the court suggesting that spending embezzled money is an act of concealment that supports an inference of willfulness? If she concealed the money, isn't that equally consistent with a purpose of avoiding detection of the embezzlement by her employer?

4. Did the court hold Mrs. Guidry to a higher standard because she had bookkeeping experience? If so, does that impermissibly shift the inquiry from what she knew to what she should have known?

5. The court said that willfulness can't be inferred solely from an understatement of income, but then went on to say that a consistent pattern of underreporting can support an inference of willfulness. Do these propositions contradict one another?

UNITED STATES v. OLBRES
61 F.3d 967 (1st Cir. 1995)

Selya, Circuit Judge.

In 1989, an employee of the Internal Revenue Service (IRS) noticed a Rolls Royce belonging to the defendants, Anthony and Shirley Olbres, parked outside a restaurant in Exeter, New Hampshire. The presence of so opulent a vehicle in so bucolic a setting piqued the taxman's interest. He initiated an investigation that led, in succession, to an audit, an indictment, a trial, and a conviction for income tax evasion pursuant to a jury verdict.[6] . . .

---

6. The statute of conviction provides in relevant part:

Any person who willfully attempts in any manner to evade or defeat any tax imposed by [the Internal Revenue Code] or the payment thereof shall, in addition to other penalties provided by law, be guilty of a felony. . . .

26 U.S.C. § 7201 (1988).

I. BACKGROUND

We start by relating certain (essentially uncontradicted) facts that serve to put the appeal into initial perspective. In 1974, the Olbreses — he an industrial designer, she a schoolteacher destined to become a self-taught bookkeeper — launched a proprietorship, Design Consultants (DC), to conceive, construct, and erect exhibit booths for trade shows. At first, the proprietors comprised the entire work force. The business grew steadily, and by 1987 DC employed 23 persons and had revenues in excess of $1,900,000. Despite the phenomenal growth of the business, Shirley Olbres continued to handle the books, toiling part-time, mostly at home. Her working materials consisted of an invoice log (in which she recorded bills sent and payments received), and three journals reflecting, respectively, cash receipts, cash disbursements, and petty cash.

Beginning in 1976, the defendants retained the services of an accountant, Wilson Dennett. Dennett compiled income tax returns and financial statements, but did not perform bookkeeping or kindred services. He prepared the tax returns in reliance on information supplied by the defendants. For the tax year at issue on this appeal — 1987 — Shirley Olbres drafted a summary of the defendants' books and records for Dennett's use. She and her husband then met with Dennett to answer questions. When Dennett completed the return, the defendants came to his office and signed it.

The defendants maintained various bank accounts during 1987. These included business checking and savings accounts at Indian Head Bank (IHB). Defendants deposited most of their business receipts into the business checking account, but occasionally deposited business receipts into the business savings account. While Shirley Olbres recorded all sums deposited into the business checking account in the cash receipts journal, she did not make comparable entries showing deposits made to the business savings account. During the same time frame, the defendants also maintained payroll and petty cash accounts at a second bank, and a rent-receipts account in the name of Seabrook Properties at yet a third financial institution.

The IRS started its investigation into the defendants' tax returns in 1989. Revenue Agent Leonard Kaply . . . determined, inter alia, that the defendants had substantially underreported their income on their joint federal income tax returns for the years 1986 through 1988. For 1987, Kaply's audit indicated that the defendants had failed to report nearly $750,000 in income from three sources: (1) business receipts deposited directly into the business savings account and not recorded in the cash receipts journal; (2) rebates from a transportation company that had contracted with DC to move trade show booths from place to place; and (3) certain income from rental property. In the course of the audit, the defendants gave Agent Kaply the cash receipts journal, but claimed to have misplaced the invoice log and the passbook for the business savings account (either of which would have revealed much of the unreported income). It was only when the IRS issued a summons to IHB that it discovered the business savings account, with its trove of unreported funds.

The IRS concluded that the defendants willfully failed to report substantial amounts of income on their 1986, 1987, and 1988 federal tax returns ($150,954 in 1986, $748,991 in 1987, and $175,432 in 1988). The defendants conceded the underreporting, but denied criminal responsibility, saying that they lacked any intent to defraud. A federal grand jury returned a three-count indictment charging the defendants with willfully attempting to evade income tax for those three years. . . .

II. ANALYSIS . . .

B. SUFFICIENCY OF THE EVIDENCE

In this instance, our assignment is simplified. Because the defendants do not dispute that they signed the 1987 tax return and that they substantially understated their income in the process, the question of guilt reduces to whether the underreporting occurred willfully, that is, whether it constituted "a voluntary, intentional violation of a known legal duty," United States v. Pomponio, 429 U.S. 10, 12 (1976). The trial focused on this narrow issue. The government contended that the defendants deliberately understated their 1987 income, while the defendants — who claimed to have signed the return without reading it — contended that they were guilty only of inadvertence, aggravated by the hiring of a maladroit accountant.

In a tax evasion case in which the defendants assert that blind reliance on their accountant, not criminal intent, caused an underreporting, the critical datum is not whether the defendants ordered the accountant to falsify the return, but, rather, whether the defendants knew when they signed the return that it understated their income. So here: if the evidence introduced at trial, taken in a pro-government light, permitted the jury to infer that the defendants (a) were aware of the contents of their return, and (b) knew that their reportable income significantly exceeded the income reflected therein, then the jury lawfully could find that the defendants acted willfully, and, hence, violated 26 U.S.C. § 7201. We turn to this two-part inquiry, and then buttress the results with additional evidence of willfulness.

1. Knowledge of the Return's Contents

This facet of the inquiry need not occupy us for long. A jury may permissibly infer that a taxpayer read his return and knew its contents from the bare fact that he signed it.

Here, moreover, the jury had before it other circumstantial evidence indicating that the defendants knew the contents of their return. Dennett's wife, who worked with him, testified that when Dennett prepared a tax return for signature, the return was bundled into a packet with a cover sheet that summarized its contents. The bottom portion of the cover sheet contained the bill for the tax preparation services. The defendants testified that it was their habit to go to Dennett's office, sign the completed return, and pay the bill. The jury could reasonably infer that, in order to have paid the accountant's bill, the defendants must have read the portion of the cover sheet that detailed the return's contents.

2. Knowledge of the Understatement

The most compelling proof that the defendants knew that the figure reported on their 1987 return substantially understated their true income is the product of simple arithmetic. Tama Mitchell, a government witness, analyzed the defendants' 1987 return and found that the disposable funds available to them in that year, based on the information contained in the return, totalled $24,695. Mitchell further testified that the defendants made expenditures of more than $620,656 during the year.[7] In the same period, their overall savings increased by $334,003. After subtracting net deposits of loan proceeds, Mitchell's analysis demonstrated that the defendants' combined expenditures and accretions to savings in 1987 exceeded the cash available to them, according to their tax return, by $580,989.

To be sure, the evidence pertaining to the defendants' lavish spending is circumstantial and suggestive, not direct and irrefutable. Yet, the arithmetic furnishes a sturdy infrastructure capable of supporting a reasonable inference that the defendants must have been aware that their 1987 return substantially underreported their income. Even if one were to accept the defendants' self-serving hypothesis that the accountant's incompetence sparked the myriad misstatements embedded in the return, the jury could still reasonably infer that, when the defendants signed the return, they must have gained an awareness that the numbers could not possibly be accurate.

The proposition that the defendants knew their return understated their income derives support from other evidence as well. For example, during 1986, Anthony Olbres (who had unrestricted access to DC's books and records) provided fiscal and marketing information to Dennett so that the latter could prepare a financial statement in connection with a prospective sale of the business. When completed, the financial statement projected 1987 revenues in the amount of $1,976,000. The projection proved to be prophetic — DC's actual 1987 gross receipts totalled $2,014,059 — but the defendants reported gross receipts on the 1987 tax return in a far smaller amount ($1,265,069). Based on this progression of events, a rational jury could plausibly infer that Anthony Olbres had sufficient knowledge of DC's financial matters to recognize the huge discrepancy between projected revenues and reported revenues, and to appreciate the significance of the gap. Likewise, the jury could infer from Shirley Olbres' position as DC's bookkeeper that she, too, must have recognized the massive understatement of income.

3. Other Evidence of Willfulness

In this case, the jury heard other evidence capable of supporting a permissible inference that the defendants acted willfully in underreporting their income. For one thing, the defendants themselves from time to time bypassed their business checking account and deposited substantial amounts of money (including approximately $145,000 in payments from a single customer, Digital Equipment Corp.) directly into their business savings account. They knew that these payments constituted income, yet they neither recorded them in the cash receipts journal nor reported them on their 1987 tax return. To make matters worse, the two source materials that most easily could have identified the unreported income — the invoice log and the passbook for the business savings account — were withheld from the defendants' accountant; and, coincidentally, the same source materials conveniently disappeared during the IRS audit. While the defendants maintained other books and records from which the existence of these funds

---

7. Mitchell's computations did not include all the defendants' annual expenditures, but established a baseline by concentrating on major cash purchases during the year, e.g., an outlay of $158,000 in June to purchase a Rolls Royce Corniche convertible; an outlay of $32,450 in August to purchase a Range Rover; and an infusion of roughly $140,000 to a brokerage account.

could perhaps be gleaned, it is readily evident that a jury plausibly could infer from these facts that the defendants clumsily attempted to conceal income from both their tax preparer and their government.

Of course, the defendants' counter-argument — that the evidence indicates nothing more than that they were remarkably slipshod in their business practices — is also plausible. Withal, the option to choose between these inferences belonged to the jury, not the judge, and the jury had a perfect right to reject the defendants' counter-argument and draw the inference urged by the government. . . .

4. Recapitulation

To sum up, the record, read favorably to the verdict, supports the following findings: (1) the defendants signed the 1987 tax return; (2) they knew the contents of the return at the time they signed it, and they knew that it significantly understated their taxable income; (3) they knew their business had made substantially more money than the return reflected; (4) they had received revenues during the tax year which they knew were taxable, such as business receipts and transportation rebates, yet they neither deposited those revenues in the business checking account nor recorded their receipt in the usual manner, but, instead, diverted the revenues to other bank accounts; (5) they deliberately understated the amounts of rental income received when transmitting data to their accountant preliminary to the accountant's preparation of their tax return; and (6) they withheld materials from the accountant (and, later, from the IRS auditor) that would have pointed to the existence and extent of the undeclared income. Notwithstanding the defendants' denials and regardless of the exculpatory evidence that lurked in the record, these findings enabled a rational jury to conclude, beyond a reasonable doubt, that the defendants were guilty of income tax evasion. . . .

Notes and Questions

1. What if the only evidence of intent in *Olbres* had been that the defendants signed the return? Would their signing of the return, standing alone, support a finding of willfulness?

2. Is the court in *Olbres* suggesting that willfulness can be inferred from sloppy business practices?

3. The court in *Guidry* seemed to think that Mrs. Guidry's spending more than $1 million on clothing was an act of concealment. Could the same be said of the Olbres' lavish spending?

B. IGNORANCE OR MISTAKE

Taxpayers sometimes claim that their violation was not willful because they mistakenly believed the conduct in question was lawful. This issue arises most frequently in prosecutions against tax protesters.

CHEEK v. UNITED STATES
498 U.S. 192 (1991)

Justice WHITE delivered the opinion of the Court.

Title 26, § 7201 of the United States Code provides that any person "who willfully attempts in any manner to evade or defeat any tax imposed by this title or the payment thereof" shall be guilty of a felony. Under 26 U.S.C. § 7203, "any person required under this title . . . or by regulations made under authority thereof to make a return . . . who willfully fails to . . . make such return" shall be guilty of a misdemeanor. This case turns on the meaning of the word "willfully" as used in §§ 7201 and 7203.

I

Petitioner John L. Cheek has been a pilot for American Airlines since 1973. He filed federal income tax returns through 1979 but thereafter ceased to file returns.[8] He also claimed an increasing number of withholding allowances — eventually claiming 60 allowances by mid-1980 — and for the years 1981 to 1984 indicated on his W-4 forms that he was exempt from federal income taxes. In 1983, petitioner unsuccessfully sought a refund of all tax withheld by his employer in 1982. Petitioner's income during this period at all times far exceeded the minimum necessary to trigger the statutory filing requirement.

As a result of his activities, petitioner was indicted for 10 violations of federal law. He was charged with six counts of willfully failing to file a federal income tax return for the years 1980, 1981, and 1983 through 1986, in violation of 26 U.S.C. § 7203. He was further charged with three counts of willfully attempting to evade his income taxes for the years 1980, 1981, and 1983 in violation of 26 U.S.C. § 7201. In those years, American Airlines withheld substantially less than the amount of tax petitioner owed because of the numerous allowances and exempt status he claimed on his W-4 forms. The tax offenses with which petitioner was charged are specific intent crimes that require the defendant to have acted willfully.

At trial, the evidence established that between 1982 and 1986, petitioner was involved in at least four civil cases that challenged various aspects of the federal income tax system.[9] In all four of those cases, the plaintiffs were informed by the courts that many of their arguments, including that they were not taxpayers within the meaning of

---

8. Cheek did file what the Court of Appeals described as a frivolous return in 1982.

9. In March 1982, Cheek and another employee of the company sued American Airlines to challenge the withholding of federal income taxes. In April 1982, Cheek sued the IRS in the United States Tax Court, asserting that he was not a taxpayer or a person for purposes of the Internal Revenue Code, that his wages were not income, and making several other related claims. Cheek and four others also filed an action against the United States and the [Commissioner of Internal Revenue] in Federal District Court, claiming that withholding taxes from their wages violated the Sixteenth Amendment. Finally, in 1985 Cheek filed claims with the IRS seeking to have refunded the taxes withheld from his wages in 1983 and 1984. When these claims were not allowed, he brought suit in the District Court claiming that the withholding was an unconstitutional taking of his property and that his wages were not income. In dismissing this action as frivolous, the District Court imposed costs and attorneys' fees of $1,500 and a sanction under Rule 11 in the amount of $10,000. The Court of Appeals agreed that Cheek's claims were frivolous, reduced the District Court sanction to $5,000 and imposed an additional sanction of $1,500 for bringing a frivolous appeal.

the tax laws, that wages are not income, that the Sixteenth Amendment does not authorize the imposition of an income tax on individuals, and that the Sixteenth Amendment is unenforceable, were frivolous or had been repeatedly rejected by the courts. During this time period, petitioner also attended at least two criminal trials of persons charged with tax offenses. In addition, there was evidence that in 1980 or 1981 an attorney had advised Cheek that the courts had rejected as frivolous the claim that wages are not income.[10]

Cheek represented himself at trial and testified in his defense. He admitted that he had not filed personal income tax returns during the years in question. He testified that as early as 1978, he had begun attending seminars sponsored by, and following the advice of, a group that believes, among other things, that the federal tax system is unconstitutional. Some of the speakers at these meetings were lawyers who purported to give professional opinions about the invalidity of the federal income tax laws. Cheek produced a letter from an attorney stating that the Sixteenth Amendment did not authorize a tax on wages and salaries but only on gain or profit. Petitioner's defense was that, based on the indoctrination he received from this group and from his own study, he sincerely believed that the tax laws were being unconstitutionally enforced and that his actions during the 1980-1986 period were lawful. He therefore argued that he had acted without the willfulness required for conviction of the various offenses with which he was charged.

In the course of its instructions, the trial court advised the jury that to prove "willfulness" the Government must prove the voluntary and intentional violation of a known legal duty, a burden that could not be proved by showing mistake, ignorance, or negligence. The court further advised the jury that an objectively reasonable good-faith misunderstanding of the law would negate willfulness but mere disagreement with the law would not. The court described Cheek's beliefs about the income tax system and instructed the jury that if it found that Cheek "honestly and reasonably believed that he was not required to pay income taxes or to file tax returns," a not guilty verdict should be returned.

After several hours of deliberation, the jury sent a note to the judge that stated in part:

> We have a basic disagreement between some of us as to if Mr. Cheek honestly & reasonably believed that he was not required to pay income taxes. . . .
>
> Page 32 [the relevant jury instruction] discusses good faith misunderstanding & disagreement. Is there any additional clarification you can give us on this point?

The District Judge responded with a supplemental instruction containing the following statements:

> [A] person's opinion that the tax laws violate his constitutional rights does not constitute a good faith misunderstanding of the law. Furthermore, a person's disagreement with the government's tax collection systems and policies does not constitute a good faith misunderstanding of the law.

---

10. The attorney also advised that despite the Fifth Amendment, the filing of a tax return was required and that a person could challenge the constitutionality of the system by suing for a refund after the taxes had been withheld, or by putting himself "at risk of criminal prosecution."

At the end of the first day of deliberation, the jury sent out another note saying that it still could not reach a verdict because "we are divided on the issue as to if Mr. Cheek honestly & reasonably believed that he was not required to pay income tax." When the jury resumed its deliberations, the District Judge gave the jury an additional instruction. This instruction stated in part that "an honest but unreasonable belief is not a defense and does not negate willfulness," and that "advice or research resulting in the conclusion that wages of a privately employed person are not income or that the tax laws are unconstitutional is not objectively reasonable and cannot serve as the basis for a good faith misunderstanding of the law defense." The court also instructed the jury that "persistent refusal to acknowledge the law does not constitute a good faith misunderstanding of the law." Approximately two hours later, the jury returned a verdict finding petitioner guilty on all counts.[11]

Petitioner appealed his convictions, arguing that the District Court erred by instructing the jury that only an objectively reasonable misunderstanding of the law negates the statutory willfulness requirement. The United States Court of Appeals for the Seventh Circuit rejected that contention and affirmed the convictions. . . . Because the Seventh Circuit's interpretation of "willfully" as used in these statutes conflicts with the decisions of several other Courts of Appeals, we granted certiorari. . . .

II

The general rule that ignorance of the law or a mistake of law is no defense to criminal prosecution is deeply rooted in the American legal system. Based on the notion that the law is definite and knowable, the common law presumed that every person knew the law. This common-law rule has been applied by the Court in numerous cases construing criminal statutes.

The proliferation of statutes and regulations has sometimes made it difficult for the average citizen to know and comprehend the extent of the duties and obligations imposed by the tax laws. Congress has accordingly softened the impact of the common-law presumption by making specific intent to violate the law an element of certain federal criminal tax offenses. Thus, the Court almost 60 years ago interpreted the statutory term "willfully" as used in the federal criminal tax statutes as carving out an exception to the traditional rule. This special treatment of criminal tax offenses is largely due to the complexity of the tax laws. In United States v. Murdock, 290 U.S. 389 (1933), the Court recognized that:

> Congress did not intend that a person, by reason of a bona fide misunderstanding as to his liability for the tax, as to his duty to make a return, or as to the adequacy of the records he maintained, should become a criminal by his mere failure to measure up to the prescribed standard of conduct. Id., at 396. . . .

---

11. A note signed by all 12 jurors also informed the judge that although the jury found petitioner guilty, several jurors wanted to express their personal opinions of the case and that notes from these individual jurors to the court were "a complaint against the narrow & hard expression under the constraints of the law." At least two notes from individual jurors expressed the opinion that petitioner sincerely believed in his cause even though his beliefs might have been unreasonable.

III

A

Willfulness, as construed by our prior decisions in criminal tax cases, requires the Government to prove that the law imposed a duty on the defendant, that the defendant knew of this duty, and that he voluntarily and intentionally violated that duty. We deal first with the case where the issue is whether the defendant knew of the duty purportedly imposed by the provision of the statute or regulation he is accused of violating, a case in which there is no claim that the provision at issue is invalid. In such a case, if the Government proves actual knowledge of the pertinent legal duty, the prosecution, without more, has satisfied the knowledge component of the willfulness requirement. But carrying this burden requires negating a defendant's claim of ignorance of the law or a claim that because of a misunderstanding of the law, he had a good-faith belief that he was not violating any of the provisions of the tax laws. This is so because one cannot be aware that the law imposes a duty upon him and yet be ignorant of it, misunderstand the law, or believe that the duty does not exist. In the end, the issue is whether, based on all the evidence, the Government has proved that the defendant was aware of the duty at issue, which cannot be true if the jury credits a good-faith misunderstanding and belief submission, whether or not the claimed belief or misunderstanding is objectively reasonable.

In this case, if Cheek asserted that he truly believed that the Internal Revenue Code did not purport to treat wages as income, and the jury believed him, the Government would not have carried its burden to prove willfulness, however unreasonable a court might deem such a belief. Of course, in deciding whether to credit Cheek's good-faith belief claim, the jury would be free to consider any admissible evidence from any source showing that Cheek was aware of his duty to file a return and to treat wages as income, including evidence showing his awareness of the relevant provisions of the Code or regulations, of court decisions rejecting his interpretation of the tax law, of authoritative rulings of the Internal Revenue Service, or of any contents of the personal income tax return forms and accompanying instructions that made it plain that wages should be [reported] as income.

We thus disagree with the Court of Appeals' requirement that a claimed good-faith belief must be objectively reasonable if it is to be considered as possibly negating the Government's evidence purporting to show a defendant's awareness of the legal duty at issue. Knowledge and belief are characteristically questions for the factfinder, in this case the jury. Characterizing a particular belief as not objectively reasonable transforms the inquiry into a legal one and would prevent the jury from considering it. It would of course be proper to exclude evidence having no relevance or probative value with respect to willfulness; but it is not contrary to common sense, let alone impossible, for a defendant to be ignorant of his duty based on an irrational belief that he has no duty. . . .

It was therefore error to instruct the jury to disregard evidence of Cheek's understanding that, within the meaning of the tax laws, he was not a person required to file a return or to pay income taxes and that wages are not taxable income, as incredible as such misunderstandings of and beliefs about the law might be. Of course, the more unreasonable the asserted beliefs or misunderstandings are, the more likely the jury will consider them to be nothing more than simple disagreement with known legal duties imposed by the tax laws and will find that the Government has carried its burden of proving knowledge.

B

Cheek asserted in the trial court that he should be acquitted because he believed in good faith that the income tax law is unconstitutional as applied to him and thus could not legally impose any duty upon him of which he should have been aware. Such a submission is unsound, not because Cheek's constitutional arguments are not objectively reasonable or frivolous, which they surely are, but because the *Murdock-Pomponio* line of cases does not support such a position. Those cases construed the willfulness requirement in the criminal provisions of the Internal Revenue Code to require proof of knowledge of the law. This was because in "our complex tax system, uncertainty often arises even among taxpayers who earnestly wish to follow the law," and "it is not the purpose of the law to penalize frank difference of opinion or innocent errors made despite the exercise of reasonable care." United States v. Bishop, 412 U.S. 346, 360-361 (1973).

Claims that some of the provisions of the tax code are unconstitutional are submissions of a different order. They do not arise from innocent mistakes caused by the complexity of the Internal Revenue Code. Rather, they reveal full knowledge of the provisions at issue and a studied conclusion, however wrong, that those provisions are invalid and unenforceable. Thus in this case, Cheek paid his taxes for years, but after attending various seminars and based on his own study, he concluded that the income tax laws could not constitutionally require him to pay a tax.

We do not believe that Congress contemplated that such a taxpayer, without risking criminal prosecution, could ignore the duties imposed upon him by the Internal Revenue Code and refuse to utilize the mechanisms provided by Congress to present his claims of invalidity to the courts and to abide by their decisions. There is no doubt that Cheek, from year to year, was free to pay the tax that the law purported to require, file for a refund and, if denied, present his claims of invalidity, constitutional or otherwise, to the courts. Also, without paying the tax, he could have challenged claims of tax deficiencies in the Tax Court, with the right to appeal to a higher court if unsuccessful. Cheek took neither course in some years, and when he did was unwilling to accept the outcome. As we see it, he is in no position to claim that his good-faith belief about the validity of the Internal Revenue Code negates willfulness or provides a defense to criminal prosecution under §§ 7201 and 7203. Of course, Cheek was free in this very case to present his claims of invalidity and have them adjudicated, but like defendants in criminal cases in other contexts, who "willfully" refuse to comply with the duties placed upon them by the law, he must take the risk of being wrong.

We thus hold that in a case like this, a defendant's views about the validity of the tax statutes are irrelevant to the issue of willfulness, need not be heard by the jury, and if they are, an instruction to disregard them would be proper. For this purpose, it makes no difference whether the claims of invalidity are frivolous or have substance. It was therefore not error in this case for the District Judge to instruct the jury not to consider Cheek's claims that the tax laws were unconstitutional. However, it was error for the court to instruct the jury that petitioner's asserted beliefs that wages are not income and that he was not a taxpayer within the meaning of the Internal Revenue Code should not be considered by the jury in determining whether Cheek had acted willfully.

IV

For the reasons set forth in the opinion above, the judgment of the Court of Appeals is vacated, and the case is remanded for further proceedings consistent with this opinion.

It is so ordered. . . .

Justice SCALIA, concurring in the judgment.

I concur in the judgment of Court because our cases have consistently held that the failure to pay a tax in the good-faith belief that it is not legally owing is not "willful." I do not join the Court's opinion because I do not agree with the test for willfulness that it directs the Court of Appeals to apply on remand.

As the Court acknowledges, our opinions from the 1930s to the 1970s have interpreted the word "willfully" in the criminal tax statutes as requiring the "bad purpose" or "evil motive" of "intentionally violating a known legal duty." It seems to me that today's opinion squarely reverses that long-established statutory construction when it says that a good-faith erroneous belief in the unconstitutionality of a tax law is no defense. It is quite impossible to say that a statute which one believes unconstitutional represents a "known legal duty." . . .

Justice BLACKMUN, with whom Justice MARSHALL joins, dissenting.

It seems to me that we are concerned in this case not with "the complexity of the tax laws," but with the income tax law in its most elementary and basic aspect: Is a wage earner a taxpayer and are wages income?

The Court acknowledges that the conclusively established standard for willfulness under the applicable statutes is the "voluntary, intentional violation of a known legal duty." That being so, it is incomprehensible to me how, in this day, more than 70 years after the institution of our present federal income tax system with the passage of the Revenue Act of 1913, any taxpayer of competent mentality can assert as his defense to charges of statutory willfulness the proposition that the wage he receives for his labor is not income, irrespective of a cult that says otherwise and advises the gullible to resist income tax collections. One might note in passing that this particular taxpayer, after all, was a licensed pilot for one of our major commercial airlines; he presumably was a person of at least minimum intellectual competence.

The District Court's instruction that an objectively reasonable and good faith misunderstanding of the law negates willfulness lends further, rather than less, protection to this defendant, for it added an additional hurdle for the prosecution to overcome. Petitioner should be grateful for this further protection, rather than be opposed to it.

This Court's opinion today, I fear, will encourage taxpayers to cling to frivolous views of the law in the hope of convincing a jury of their sincerity. If that ensues, I suspect we have gone beyond the limits of common sense.

While I may not agree with every word the Court of Appeals has enunciated in its opinion, I would affirm its judgment in this case. I therefore dissent.

Notes and Questions

1. What facts militate against Cheek's claim that he sincerely believed that his wages were not subject to taxation? Given those facts, how could a jury find in his favor?

2. Is it important that, after he challenged claims of tax deficiencies, Cheek was "unwilling to accept the outcome"?

Suppose that, on remand, the court correctly instructs the jury that Cheek's wages were subject to taxation but that if he held a good-faith belief that they were not, he did not act willfully. Finding his belief was sincere, the jury acquits him. Before discharging him, the court sternly lectures Cheek that his position is frivolous and that he must pay taxes on his income. Cheek fails to mend his ways, and two years after the acquittal, he is indicted again for failure to file during the two-year period. Can he still claim he has a good faith belief that he is not obligated to file a tax return? If not, have we taken away the fact finding function that the Court found so important? If so, is the Court equating "good faith belief" with obstinacy?

This question is not as far-fetched as it may seem. Irwin Schiff, one of the best-known spokesmen for the tax protest movement and the author of a book that advises fellow travelers how to avoid paying taxes, was convicted twice of tax evasion in the 1980s and served four years in prison.[12]

In 2004, he was indicted again — for tax evasion, conspiracy, preparing thousands of bogus returns that cost the government $56 million in unpaid taxes, failing to report nearly $4 million from sales at his bookstore over a five-year period, and hiding income and assets by using offshore accounts and an illegal Oregon bank, whose owners had also been convicted of tax crimes in 2002. Schiff continued to maintain that the income tax laws are illegal and that he was not required to comply with them. In the latest twist, he claimed he was delusional and believed, among other things, that only he was capable of correctly interpreting the tax laws.[13]

Suffice it to say, his theories did not sit well with the jury. Upon conviction, the 77-year-old Schiff was jailed without bond pending sentencing and was later sentenced to serve more than 13 years in prison and pay more than $4.2 million in restitution.[14]

3. Is Justice Scalia on target when he argues that one cannot intentionally violate a known legal duty if one believes the law is unconstitutional?

4. What kinds of evidence may the defendant introduce to establish his belief that wages are not taxable income? Should Cheek be permitted to testify regarding what the law is, or ought to be? To introduce tax protest literature into evidence?[15]

5. Suppose the trial court had instructed the jury that in deciding whether Cheek acted in good faith, it could consider whether his claimed belief was reasonable, and

---

12. David Cay Johnston, The Anti-Tax Man Cometh, N.Y. Times, July 5, 1995, at D1.

13. Tax-Resistance Promoter Is Convicted in Scam, Wall St. J., Oct. 25, 2005, at A4. His sentencing hearing was scheduled for January 2006; David Cay Johnston, Federal Grand Jury Indicts Protester for Tax Evasion, N.Y. Times, Mar. 25, 2004, at C8; David Cay Johnston, Tax Protester Tells Federal Court That He Is Delusional, N.Y. Times, Feb. 7, 2004, at C3.

14. Anti-Tax Advocate Receives 13 Years, N.Y. Times, Feb. 25, 2006, at B2; Tax-Resistance Promoter Is Convicted in Scam, Wall St. J., Oct. 25, 2005, at A4.

15. Cf. United States v. Sassak, 881 F.2d 276 (6th Cir. 1989); United States v. Hairston, 819 F.2d 971 (10th Cir. 1987).

that a farfetched belief is much less likely to be honestly held. Would that instruction be proper?[16]

6. On retrial, a properly instructed jury convicted Cheek on all counts. He was sentenced to jail for a year and a day and was fined $62,000.

7. According to Justice Department officials, the "sincere belief" claim has emerged as the defense of choice in tax protest cases after *Cheek*.[17] Although prosecutions in which the defense is raised often result in acquittals, misdemeanor convictions, or hung juries,[18] renewed efforts to crack down on tax deniers have netted some significant convictions and punishments.[19]

UNITED STATES V. COHEN
510 F.3d 1114 (9th Cir. 2007)

TALLMAN, Circuit Judge.

These consolidated appeals follow the convictions and sentences of a well-known recidivist tax protestor, Irwin Schiff, and two of his acolytes, Cynthia Neun and Lawrence Cohen. After Schiff's last release from prison in 1991 for income tax evasion, he opened a store in Las Vegas, Nevada, where he sold books, audio tapes, videos and instructional packages, many created by him, explaining how to "legally stop paying income taxes."[20] Cohen and Neun worked at the store, and, together with Schiff, they provided "consultation services" to clients who wished to avoid paying federal income taxes. They encouraged their clients to file "zero returns," federal individual income tax returns containing a zero on every line related to income and expenses, and, in most cases, seeking an improper refund of all federal income taxes withheld during the tax year for which it was filed.

Following a twenty-three day joint trial in which Schiff represented himself, the jury returned guilty verdicts with respect to many of the counts in the indictment. In particular, Cohen was convicted of one count of aiding and assisting in the filing of a false federal income tax return in violation of 26 U.S.C. § 7206(2), for which he received a thirty-three month sentence. At trial, the district court summarily convicted Schiff of fifteen counts of criminal contempt pursuant to 18 U.S.C. § 401 based on his

---

16. Cf. United States v. Pensyl, 387 F.3d 456, 458-459 (6th Cir. 2004).

17. David Cay Johnston, Another Income Tax Denier Will Have His Day in Court: Case Highlights a Change in U.S. Tactics, N.Y. Times, Jan. 19, 2005, at C3; David Cay Johnston, U.S. Discloses That Use of Tax Evasion Plans Is Extensive, N.Y. Times, May 22, 2002, at C4; David Cay Johnston, Couple in New Hampshire Convicted of Tax Evasion, N.Y. Times, Apr. 15, 1995, at A34 [hereinafter Couple Convicted]. See also David Cay Johnston, Tax Protester Pleads Guilty to Filing False Claims, N.Y. Times, June 29, 2005, at C2.

18. See, e.g., David Cay Johnston & Carolyn Marshall, Tax Evaders Win a Case over I.R.S.: Jury Frees Preparer of False Returns, N.Y. Times, June 24, 2005, at C1; David Cay Johnston, Mistrial Is Declared in Tax Withholding Case, N.Y. Times, Nov. 27, 2003, at C4; Couple Convicted, supra note 17.

19. See, e.g., David Cay Johnston, Tax Cheat Sentenced to 6 Years for Defying I.R.S., N.Y. Times, Apr. 14, 2005, at C3; 7-Year Sentence in U.S. Tax Case, N.Y. Times, May 1, 2004, at B2; David Cay Johnston, Tax Evader Pleads Guilty in Fraud Case, N.Y. Times, Feb. 14, 2004, at B4; David Cay Johnston, Two Plotters Are Sentenced in Big Tax Evasion Scheme, N.Y. Times, Nov. 16, 2002, at B3.

20. In United States v. Schiff, 379 F.3d 621, 630 (9th Cir. 2004), we upheld a preliminary injunction on the sale of a book authored by Schiff, The Federal Mafia: How the Government Illegally Imposes and Unlawfully Collects Income Taxes, finding that it constituted fraudulent commercial speech.

unruly courtroom behavior. Schiff's total sentence for those convictions was twelve months in prison to be served consecutively to his tax evasion and conspiracy sentence.

Cohen argues that his conviction must be overturned because the district court wrongfully excluded the expert testimony of his psychiatrist who would have offered evidence of Cohen's mental state. We agree, and we reverse Cohen's conviction, vacate his sentence, and remand for a new trial. . . .

II

A

. . . On June 14, 2005, Cohen's lawyer filed a notice, pursuant to Federal Rule of Criminal Procedure 12.2, that he intended to offer expert testimony by psychiatrist Dr. Norton A. Roitman relating to Cohen's "mental disease . . . bearing on . . . the issue of guilt." Attached to that notice was a report prepared by Dr. Roitman, who had met with Cohen on two occasions at the request of Cohen's attorney.

In the report, Dr. Roitman diagnoses Cohen as suffering from a narcissistic personality disorder, and concludes that Cohen "did not intend to violate the law, as would be the case with a criminal who acted out of a desire for personal gain" but rather "[h]is behavior is driven by a mental disorder as opposed to criminal motivation. . . . Although it is true Mr. Cohen was not delusional or psychotic and was in possession of basic mental faculties, his will was in the service of irrational beliefs as a result of narcissistic personality disorder." The report also notes that

> Because [Cohen's] beliefs are fixed and have led him to significant adverse consequences, he is irrational to the point of dysfunction, demonstrated by his stubborn adherence in the face of overwhelming contradictions and knowledge of substantial penalty. . . . Despite evidence to the contrary, his psychological needs dominated his mentation. . . . This is the nature of the narcissistic personality in which the sufferer could essentially pass a lie detector test when asked commonsensical questions while giving improbable answers.

The government moved to bar Dr. Roitman from testifying and the district court agreed, reasoning that Dr. Roitman failed to explain "how the alleged mental disorders negate mens rea. Rather, [his] opinion[] merely explain[s] or justif[ies] [Cohen's] conduct." . . .

C

Federal Rules of Evidence 702 and 704(b) govern the admissibility of Dr. Roitman's testimony, and we examine the exclusion of his testimony under both of these rules.[21] . . .

---

21. Rule 702 provides, "If scientific . . . knowledge will assist the trier of fact to understand the evidence or to determine a fact in issue, a witness qualified as an expert . . . may testify thereto in the form of an opinion or otherwise." Rule 704(b) prohibits the expert from offering "an opinion or inference as to whether the defendant did or did not have the mental state or condition constituting an element of the crime charged or of a defense thereto."

1

The threshold issue is whether Dr. Roitman's testimony would have assisted the trier of fact within the meaning of Rule 702. According to Cohen, Dr. Roitman's testimony would have bolstered the contention that Cohen had a good faith belief that he was acting in accordance with the law, thereby negating the mens rea element of 26 U.S.C. § 7206(2), which requires that a defendant "[w]illfully" assist in the filing of a false return. *See* Cheek v. United States, 498 U.S. 192, 201 (1991) (holding that a defendant cannot be convicted of violating a federal tax law if he harbors a good faith belief that he was not violating any of the provisions of the tax laws). The government counters that Dr. Roitman's report was irrelevant because nothing in it suggested

> that defendant was not capable of forming the requisite mens rea for the charged offenses. On the contrary, as the District Court found, Dr. Roitman's report did no more than explain why defendant intentionally violated his known legal duties. The report does not remotely suggest that defendant lacked the mental aptitude to understand his legal duties or the ability to act volitionally.

Cohen argues that United States v. Finley, 301 F.3d 1000, 1007 (9th Cir. 2002), controls and we agree. There, Finley was seeking funding to open a chain of bookstores when he met Leroy Schweitzer, a supposed investment guru who claimed to have recorded liens against various banks which could be drawn upon by the issuance of certain negotiable instruments. Schweitzer gave Finley several of these bogus instruments, claiming that they were worth nearly seven million dollars. Every institution presented with one of these instruments refused to honor it, including the IRS. Finley persisted in attempting to pay off his tax debt with these instruments, and he was eventually prosecuted for, inter alia, making a false claim against the United States in violation of 18 U.S.C. § 287. At trial, the district court excluded under Rule 702 testimony from Finley's psychologist that Finley lacked the intent to defraud due to his delusional disorder "in which . . . information from the real world . . . is so grossly distorted that the person ends up with" bizarre, irrational and fixed beliefs.

We reversed, reasoning that the excluded testimony

> would have offered an explanation as to how an otherwise normal man could believe that these financial instruments were valid and reject all evidence to the contrary. While Finley could and did testify about how and why he believed the instruments were valid, only a trained mental health expert could provide a counterweight to the government's allegations against Finley.

The facts in *Finley* are strikingly similar to those in the present case. Schweitzer convinced Finley that certain financial instruments were genuine; Schiff convinced Cohen that one could legally submit a zero return. Expert testimony proffered by Finley and Cohen suggested they had a tendency to cling doggedly to their beliefs even in the face of overwhelming contradictions. The *Finley* court determined that the expert testimony could have helped the defendant counter the government's argument that he knew the financial instruments were false; similarly, Dr. Roitman's testimony would have helped Cohen counter the government's suggestion that Cohen knew the zero returns were false.

We disagree with the government that Dr. Roitman's report can only be read to mean that Cohen knew what he was doing was wrong but did it anyway. In fact, the opposite is true: a fair reading of Dr. Roitman's report suggests that once Cohen adopted Schiff's views, Cohen would not change his mind. The report specifically states that Cohen "did not intend to violate the law." If Dr. Roitman had been allowed to testify to that effect, his testimony would have assisted the trier of fact within the meaning of Rule 702.

The government's reliance on United States v. Scholl, 166 F.3d 964, 970 (9th Cir. 1999), is misplaced. There, a defendant charged with filing false tax returns argued that the district court had erred in excluding under Rule 702 the testimony of an expert on compulsive gambling who would have testified that pathological gamblers, like the defendant, "have distortions in thinking and 'denial,' which impact their ability and emotional wherewithal to keep records." We affirmed, noting that there was no evidence presented at the *Daubert* hearing that addicted gamblers were incapable of truthfully reporting their gambling income. "[E]vidence that compulsive gamblers are in denial. . . . would not tend to show that Scholl did not believe his tax return to be correct. . . ."

Scholl is easily distinguishable from the present case. According to his expert's report, a narcissistic personality disorder like Cohen's can cause a person to continue to believe something to be true despite overwhelming evidence of its patent absurdity. By contrast, there was no evidence in *Scholl* that an addiction to gambling could cause a person to believe that a false tax return omitting winnings was true.

. . . The only question, which we discuss below, is how far Dr. Roitman should have been permitted to go in explaining his expert conclusions as they related to Cohen's ability to form the intent to evade the tax laws.

2

Rule 704(b) is a limitation on Rule 702. Even if expert testimony would "assist the trier of fact" within the meaning of Rule 702, such testimony may be excluded under Rule 704(b) if the testimony "state[s] an opinion or inference as to whether the defendant did or did not have the mental state or condition constituting an element of the crime charged. . . ." Fed. R. Evid. 704(b). With respect to the type of inference precluded under Rule 704(b), the court has stated that the expert may not "draw[] an inference which would necessarily compel the conclusion" that the defendant lacked the requisite mens rea. . . . United States v. Morales, 108 F.3d 1031, 1037 (9th Cir. 1997).

We have little doubt that if Dr. Roitman had been permitted to testify as to all of the conclusions contained in his report, some of that proffered testimony as contained in his report would have invaded the province of the jury and violated Rule 704(b). However, the best way for the district court to have insured the exclusion of the potentially inadmissible aspects of Dr. Roitman's testimony was not to bar him from testifying altogether, but to sustain the government's objections to particular questions likely to elicit inadmissible evidence under the rule. The district court also could have discussed with the parties before he testified the limits that would be imposed on the scope of Dr. Roitman's testimony.

If the district court had followed that course of action, then Dr. Roitman's testimony, like the expert testimony at issue in *Morales* and *Finley,* would have gone to a predicate matter — whether Cohen suffered from a Narcissistic Personality Disorder. Even if the jury had accepted this diagnosis, the jury would still have been required to determine what impact, if any, that condition might have on Cohen's ability to form the requisite *mens rea* — the intent to evade the tax laws. As in *Finley,* the jury could have accepted the Roitman diagnosis but determined nonetheless that Cohen knew the zero returns were false. . . .

3

The government argues that even if Dr. Roitman's testimony was admissible under Rules 702 and 704(b), it should have been excluded under Rule 403.[22] We disagree. Dr. Roitman's testimony would have been highly probative on the issue of whether Cohen could have formed the requisite mens rea, and was unlikely to cause significant confusion with the jury if properly constrained by compliance with the rules of evidence. . . .

4

[T]he exclusion of Dr. Roitman's testimony left Cohen without any way to explain the effect that his mental disorder may have had on his ability to form the requisite mens rea. We therefore reverse Cohen's conviction, vacate his sentence, and remand for a new trial. . . .

Notes and Questions

1. Is the outcome in *Cohen* a logical extension of the analysis in *Cheek*? Does *Cohen* affect your thinking about the approach the Court adopted in *Cheek*?

2. The court in *Cohen* stated that "once Cohen adopted Schiff's views, Cohen would not change his mind." Does it make any difference whether Cohen "would" not or "could" not change his mind? Does Dr. Roitman's report shed meaningful light on this question?

3. Narcissistic Personality Disorder is defined by the Diagnostic and Statistical Manual of Mental Disorders as "a pervasive pattern of grandiosity, need for admiration, and a lack of empathy."[23] How is this definition relevant to the question whether Cohen willfully violated the tax laws?

4. Recall the facts in *Guidry*. Do Mrs. Guidry's shopping habits suggest arguments that might be raised in her defense?

5. Are any aspects of the proffered expert opinion described in Dr. Roitman's report inadmissible under Rule 704(b)?

6. When all was said and done, Cohen pleaded guilty to one count of aiding and assisting in the preparation of a false tax return and agreed to pay restitution for the taxes he owed.

---

22. Federal Rule of Evidence 403 provides that relevant evidence may be excluded "if its probative value is substantially outweighed by the danger of unfair prejudice, confusion of the issues, or misleading the jury. . . ."

23. American Psychiatric Association, Diagnostic and Statistical Manual of Mental Disorders 714 (4th ed. 2000).

For reasons you can probably surmise, curious mental oddities seem to flourish in the defense of criminal tax prosecutions. In Spies v. United States, for example, the defendant claimed that his noncompliance with the tax laws was not willful because he had a psychological disturbance "amounting to something more than worry but something less than insanity."[24] Taxpayers in other cases have claimed that neurological disorders,[25] obsessive compulsive personality disorder,[26] tax phobia,[27] diminished intellectual capacity,[28] mental distress brought on by stressful family situations,[29] and other emotional difficulties prevented them from fulfilling their obligations under the tax laws.

One theory is that some taxpayers suffer from a clinically demonstrable "failure to file syndrome."[30] Typically, taxpayers who claim they are afflicted by this malady have an obsessive-compulsive personality and a history of procrastination. Although the "syndrome" has yet to be successfully invoked as a defense in a criminal tax prosecution, one lawyer claims to have influenced the IRS to drop a criminal investigation of his client, a throat surgeon, who produced a stack of claim forms representing several hundred thousand dollars in insurance reimbursements he had never submitted.[31] Given that 25 percent of the population in the United States (excluding those who suffer mere personality disorders) suffer from some type of at least mild psychological disorder, recognition of a failure to file syndrome as a defense in criminal tax cases "would suggest some exciting possibilities for reinventing tax administration."[32]

But consider the tale of Irwin Schiff, a notorious and colorful tax protester whom we encountered briefly in *Cohen*. While he was on the witness stand at trial, Schiff boasted that he had helped thousands of people avoid paying billions of dollars in taxes over the years. On appeal from his ensuing fraud conviction, his lawyer sought leniency at sentencing on the ground that Schiff was mentally ill. But the argument that Schiff's mental condition warranted lenient treatment was to no avail. Citing the government's

---

24. Spies v. United States, 317 U.S. 492, 493 (1943).

25. See, e.g., United States v. McCaffrey, 181 F.3d 854 (7th Cir. 1999) (claiming that depression and a neurological disorder that required defendant to sleep for all but four hours each day prevented him from filing timely returns).

26. United States v. Sinigaglio, 925 F.2d 339 (9th Cir. 1991) (trial court did not abuse discretion by refusing to allow expert testimony that defendant's obsessive compulsive personality disorder prevented him from forming willful state of mind); Tax Report: Court Notes, Wall St. J., May 10, 2000, at 1, col. 5 (reporting district court's rejection of argument that taxpayer was disabled by obsessive compulsive disorder that caused her to hoard paper and objects).

27. See, e.g., Kemmerer v. Commissioner, T.C. Memo 1993-394, 66 T.C.M. (CCH) 550 (1993) (claiming that "simple phobia of tax documents and preparing tax returns" constituted a mental infirmity that prevented taxpayer from preparing and filing returns).

28. See, e.g., United States v. Edwards, 90 F.R.D. 391 (E.D. Va. 1981) (excluding expert testimony on taxpayer's claim of diminished intellectual capacity (or "stupidity," as the court characterized it) for failure to give proper notice, under Federal Rule of Criminal Procedure 12.2(b), of intent to claim a mental disease, defect, or other condition affecting defendant's capacity to possess the requisite mental state).

29. See, e.g., Carlson v. United States, 126 F.3d 915 (7th Cir. 1997) (claiming mental distress caused by child's illness justified failure to pay income taxes and quarterly estimates).

30. Eliott Silverman & Stephen J. Coleman, "Failure to File" Syndrome: Legal and Medical Perspectives, N.Y.L.J., Feb. 4, 1994, at 1.

31. Milo Geyelin, Late Tax Filers Offer New Plea: Mental Malady, Wall St. J., Apr. 18, 1994, at B1.

32. James W. Wetzler & Scott Wetzler, Enforcement, Not Prozac, for Nonfilers, N.Y.L.J., Mar. 7, 1994, at 1.

substantial loss of tax revenue and the widespread lawlessness that Schiff's tax avoidance scheme had blatantly encouraged, the judge sentenced the 78-year-old Schiff to serve more than 13 years in prison and to pay more than $4 million in restitution.

C. RELIANCE ON PROFESSIONAL ADVICE

BURSTEN V. UNITED STATES
395 F.2d 976 (5th Cir. 1968)

BEN C. DAWKINS, JR., District Judge.

[Bursten, a lawyer, was indicted for evading federal income taxes. The indictment alleged that Bursten reported no taxable income in 1957, a year when he knew that his income exceeded $152,000. Although Bursten filed what he called an "amended" 1957 return, which the IRS received in mid-1960, the Service had no record of receiving any earlier return for the year in question. The amended return reported a capital gain of $156,000, against which Bursten offset a carryover capital loss of $140,000 and other losses of $14,000. The return thus reported no taxable income for the year.

The government produced testimony to the effect that the carryover loss could not be substantiated and that the capital gain should have been treated as ordinary income. Bursten testified, inter alia, that his tax counsel, William Goldworn, specifically advised him to claim the carryover loss on his 1957 return. Goldworn also testified that he thought the loss was properly reported. Bursten was found guilty as charged.]

II

Appellant . . . contends that the trial judge committed reversible error in refusing to give to the jury the following specially requested instruction:

> If you find that the defendant had discussed this matter with competent tax counsel and that the tax return herein was prepared pursuant to that advice, then you must find that the defendant did not willfully file a false return or make a false statement, and you should bring in a verdict of not guilty.

We agree that there is substantial merit in this contention for the following reasons:
In Perez v. United States, 297 F.2d 12 (5th Cir. 1961), we held:

> It is elementary law that the defendant in a criminal case is entitled to have presented instructions relating to a theory of defense for which there is any foundation in the evidence. . . . A charge is erroneous which ignores a claimed defense with such a foundation. . . . The charge to which he is entitled, upon proper request, in such circumstances is one which precisely and specifically, rather than merely generally or abstractly, points to his theory of defense, . . . and one which does not unduly emphasize the theory of the prosecution, thereby de-emphasizing proportionally the defendant's theory. . . .

Review of the record here leaves little or no doubt as to why appellant requested the quoted instruction. One of the essential elements to be proved by the Government here was that he, appellant, *willfully* evaded the federal income tax laws. To have been successful, the Government must have proved, beyond a reasonable doubt, that appellant willfully filed a false income tax return with intent to defraud the Government. Thus, if the jury believed that appellant honestly relied on the advice of his tax counsel, Goldworn, it might have found that the element of willfulness was lacking and have acquitted. Moreover, there is no doubt that there was adequate basis in the record for this requested instruction.

Careful review of this quite lengthy record reveals why this instruction was refused by the District Judge:

Mr. Booth: Which one are you refusing?

The Court: Well, that "advice"; that's no excuse at all for a lawyer, particularly. It's no excuse at all. (Emphasis added.)
[We must note here, as a matter of judicial knowledge, that most lawyers have only scant knowledge of the tax laws.]

Mr. Osman: I give this to the Court and ask him if he is going to have a charge on that?

The Court: If this were the law, then I could get advice from anybody.

Mr. Soltz: Well, it says, "competent."

The Court: Well, that's silly. You can always find a crook that will give you any advice that you don't owe any tax.

Moreover, we note from the Charge Conference, this:

Mr. Booth: Your Honor, it certainly goes on the question of what the intent was from what he was advised and what he believed.

The Court: Well, I'm not saying intent —

Mr. Booth: Whether it's the law or not.

The Court: That's a matter of argument. I agree with you that he may have been foolish enough to believe that so-called professor we had here —

Mr. Booth: He teaches at the graduate school.

The Court: I don't care what school he teaches in, *he is not a good tax man.* (Emphasis added.)

Mr. Booth: Well, on the question of intent, that really doesn't make much difference.

The Court: No, he may have given that advice. I don't say he didn't; and if he did, I don't say that this man is guilty in this case if he believed him.

Mr. Booth: That's what the testimony shows.

The Court: That's up to the jury. I'm not going to decide that.

This clearly establishes that this instruction was refused because the trial judge thought "he [Goldworn] [was] not a good tax man." In the very same colloquy with defense counsel, the trial judge also noted that whether appellant relied upon advice given by Goldworn was up to the jury. As was stated in Strauss v. United States: . . .

. . . We agree that the substance (though not necessarily the wording) of these charges should have been given. Defendant's dissatisfaction here is not pettifoggery over nuances of words. His objections go to the refusal to submit substantive defenses. (376 F.2d 416, 418-419)

While the record reveals that the trial judge gave a *general* instruction to the jury on the element of intent, the authorities cited and quoted from conclusively hold that appellant was entitled to a more specific charge in light of his contention that he relied on advice of his tax counsel. This failure to give such a specific charge, even though it should have been reworded, so as to indicate that, to rely on this defense, appellant should have been found to have given *all* the facts to his advisor, was reversible error. . . .

Reversed and remanded.

Notes and Questions

1. Under almost universally recognized general principles of criminal law, reliance on the advice of private counsel is not a defense. What rationale supports that rule? Should the rule be retained? What, if anything, justifies a departure from the rule in a case like *Bursten*? Is the justification unique to the tax laws?

2. On retrial, Cheek was convicted of willfully failing to file and willfully attempting to evade his income taxes. Like Bursten, Cheek claimed he relied on the advice of counsel. He testified that his post-1982 actions were attributable to "bum legal advice." He stated that three different lawyers had advised him that the federal tax system was based on voluntary compliance and that his various lawsuits had been dismissed purely on procedural grounds. He did not seek advice until after he had ceased filing returns, and it was unclear whether he asked for or received advice about the legality of possible future conduct. He argued on appeal that the trial court erred in refusing to instruct the jury on an advice of counsel defense. Why would he seek the advice of three different lawyers? Does it matter whether he followed their advice? Are these questions relevant to the determination of whether he was entitled to an advice of counsel instruction?[33]

3. If, as the court in *Bursten* believed, the advice Bursten received from his lawyer is relevant to the issue of liability, what limitations should be imposed? Consider the following problem.

PROBLEM 11-1

Blake, a high school graduate, owned Blake Snacks & Chips, a successful snack food distributorship. When he originally formed the company, which he operated as a sole proprietorship, Blake kept the company's books himself. In 1998, however, the State Worker's Compensation Board found his recordkeeping woefully inadequate and told him to hire a bookkeeper. Blake accordingly hired Hunter Accounting LLP to maintain the company's books and prepare his tax returns.

---

33. Cf. United States v. Cheek, 3 F.3d 1057 (7th Cir. 1993).

After studying Blake's operation, Hunter set up an accounting system for the company. Hunter told Blake to report his sales and costs to Hunter's office. The sales figures were to be determined by the figures that appeared on Blake's "load-out" sheets, which identified what products had been loaded onto trucks at Blake's warehouse for delivery to retail stores. The costs were to be determined by invoices reflecting the price of goods delivered to Blake's warehouse. In reporting sales and costs, Blake provided Hunter summaries instead of the original invoices and load-out sheets.

Beginning in 1984, Blake's supplier began giving him rebates on the cost of products as well as bonuses and promotional funds. Blake processed the rebates, bonuses, and promotional payments through a "clearing account" separate from the company's "business account." Blake pocketed the money that was processed through the clearing account, so it never made its way into the company's accounting system.

In 1988 Blake was indicted for willfully filing false and fraudulent tax returns for the years 1984-1988. Blake did not dispute that the returns for those years understated his income. His defense was, instead, that his understatement of income and tax liability was not willful because: (1) he relied on the accounting system set up by Hunter; and (2) his ignorance of accounting principles left him unaware that Hunter's system would not result in the reporting of his true income. Will this defense fly?[34]

III. TAX EVASION

One of the Revenue Code's principal criminal enforcement tools is § 7201, which defines the felony of attempting to evade or defeat a tax or the payment of a tax. When the government proceeds under this section, it establishes a prima facie case by showing: (1) that an additional tax was due and owing; (2) an attempt to evade the liability; and (3) willfulness.

A. ATTEMPT TO EVADE OR DEFEAT

Tax evasion is a multifaceted concept. In its simplest manifestation, it is a crime of omission. The taxpayer willfully fails to file a return or to pay a tax due and owing. This crime of omission is a misdemeanor under § 7203. In its more serious form, tax evasion consists of a willful attempt to evade or defeat a tax or to defeat the payment of a tax. 26 U.S.C. § 7201. The element that distinguishes these two crimes is § 7201's requirement of an "attempt." The Supreme Court has concluded that the attempt element requires proof of an affirmative act undertaken with the purpose of evading or defeating a tax — as opposed to passive neglect, which would suffice under § 7203.[35]

---

34. Cf. United States v. Daniels, 617 F.2d 146 (5th Cir. 1980).
35. Spies v. United States, 317 U.S. 492 (1943).

UNITED STATES v. EAKEN
17 F.3d 203 (7th Cir. 1994)

WILL, District Judge. . . .

I. BACKGROUND

Until 1988, when he requested that his name be removed from the list of attorneys licensed to practice in Illinois, defendant Eaken practiced law in Illinois. In 1984, Eaken was requested by clients to act as the administrator of the estate of Ms. Mary Oma Lane, which was being probated in Cook County, Illinois. As administrator, he received approximately $190,754.55 and opened an estate account at the Municipal Trust and Savings Bank in Bourbonnais, Illinois, where he conducted his personal and business banking. In addition to the estate account, he held at the bank a personal checking account, a checking account for his law practice, an account for Briar Center Partners, and a corporate account for Briar Center Partners, Ltd. In 1985, Eaken began withdrawing funds from the estate account and transferring these funds into his personal and business accounts.

Between January and October 1985, Eaken used withdrawal forms to make 34 withdrawals from the estate account, leaving a balance of only $501.89. During the same time period, Eaken made 25 deposits totalling approximately $100,000.00 into his "William E. Eaken, Attorney" account. He made five deposits totalling approximately $14,000.00 into the "Briar Center Partners, Ltd." account. Finally, he made one deposit of approximately $57,000.00 into the "Briar Capital Corporation" account. Thus, over $26,000.00 of the estate withdrawals remains unaccounted for. Eaken apparently used the embezzled estate funds for immediate expenditures such as the purchase of land for Briar Capital Corporation, to pay for the construction of a building, and for his various personal and professional expenses.

In 1984, Eaken employed an attorney to represent him with respect to the administration of the estate; this attorney subsequently withdrew because he was having problems communicating with the defendant. At the defendant's trial, another attorney testified that Eaken in December 1986 retained him to oppose in probate court the appointment of a special administrator of the estate to replace Eaken as administrator. At Eaken's request, this attorney informed the probate court that Eaken and his former attorney were having problems and further represented to the probate court that the estate would be closed shortly. However, Eaken failed to close the estate. As a result, a rule to show cause was issued against him in 1987. Finally, Eaken informed the probate court that he had depleted the assets of the estate. At trial, Eaken admitted that he was not forthcoming to the probate court and claimed that his motive was to conceal the embezzlement until he could replenish the estate funds. Throughout his testimony, Eaken insisted that he at no time had any intention to evade his tax obligations to the IRS.

It is undisputed that Eaken failed to file a tax return for 1985. On April 17, 1986, however, he did file a request for an extension of time in which to file for 1985, along with a payment of $1700.00. At the trial, an Internal Revenue Service agent testified that Eaken had admitted to him his failure to file his tax return for 1985, and his embezzlement of funds from the estate. Another IRS agent conducted an analysis of the flow of funds from the estate account to the defendant's personal accounts during 1985; this agent testified that $197,842.93 was withdrawn from the estate account and that all but $26,423.27 was deposited into the defendant's accounts. Based on these withdrawals, the agent estimated that Eaken's tax liability for 1985 was approximately $82,774.76.

Eaken was indicted for willfully attempting to evade or defeat the payment of taxes, in violation of 26 U.S.C. § 7201, and for failure to file a tax return, in violation of 26 U.S.C. § 7203. Following the trial, the jury found Eaken guilty on both counts. . . .

II. DISCUSSION . . .

B. SUFFICIENCY OF THE EVIDENCE

Section 7201 provides that "any person who willfully attempts in any manner to evade or defeat any tax" has committed the crime of tax evasion. 26 U.S.C. § 7201. In order to prove tax evasion under this section, the government must demonstrate the existence of a tax deficiency, that the defendant acted willfully, and that the defendant took an affirmative act to elude or defeat the obligatory payment of tax. . . .

Eaken contends that no overt act evincing an intent to avoid the payment of income taxes was proved by the government. The indictment alleged that he evaded his tax obligations under § 7201 through the following actions: (1) failing to make an income tax return on or before April 15, 1986; (2) acquiring in excess of $197,800.00 through a series of illegal withdrawals from the estate account; (3) refusing to appear before the probate court for estate proceedings; (4) refusing to file an accounting or to deliver the assets of the estate; (5) securing the services of an attorney to represent that another attorney was being obtained to represent the defendant and that the estate would soon be closed; and (6) attempting to conceal by diverting the funds into multiple bank accounts, including accounts of business partnership entities other than Eaken's own business account.

It is well established that the affirmative act required under 26 U.S.C. § 7201 must demonstrate something more than a mere passive failure to pay the income tax. This court has previously held that "reprehensible actions, designed to hinder detection of the strictly local crime of embezzlement, do not constitute such affirmative conduct as clearly and reasonably infers a motive to evade or defeat the tax." United States v. Mesheski, 286 F.2d 345, 347 (7th Cir. 1961). In *Mesheski*, we reversed a defendant's conviction for tax evasion where a tax preparer converted the tax payments of his clients to his own use and subsequently failed to pay taxes on the amounts embezzled from his clients.

In *Mesheski*, the defendant prepared the returns and received payment from the taxpayers in cash or in checks payable to his order. He then prepared his own checks payable to the district director of the IRS, as well as envelopes addressed to that official, which he exhibited to the taxpayers, who were also given receipts and informed that their tax obligations had been discharged. Thus, Mesheski's actions forestalled investigation by the taxpayers who would not thereafter expect to receive either cancelled checks or receipts from the IRS. The concealment in *Mesheski* was only from the taxpayers themselves; there was no independent proof of concealment from the IRS. Although Mesheski had committed affirmative acts with regard to his clients, we found that the evidence regarding his own tax obligations disclosed nothing other than mere passive failure to pay. We there held that there "must be something more, some affirmative positive act to attempt to defeat or evade the tax." Id. at 346.

Eaken argues that his case is identical to Mesheski's and that the evidence presented at trial fails to establish any affirmative positive act to attempt to defeat or evade the tax. He claims that, like Mesheski, he merely failed to file a tax return and thus cannot be convicted under § 7201. He further argues that even if we find that he took affirmative steps to conceal the fact of his embezzlement, none of these actions reflect any intent to evade his income tax obligations. Based on the evidence presented at trial, we disagree. In *Mesheski*, while the defendant attempted to conceal his embezzlement from the clients, he took no affirmative steps which could be interpreted to constitute an attempt to evade or defeat his own tax obligations. *Mesheski* presented for our review a case of embezzlement coupled with the mere passive failure to pay income tax on funds embezzled from other taxpayers.

Unlike *Mesheski*, it is undisputed that Eaken took additional affirmative steps to conceal his own receipt of the embezzled funds from the estate account. First, Eaken made 34 individual withdrawals from the estate account; to make these withdrawals, he used withdrawal forms rather than checks. Second, the majority of the withdrawn funds was deposited into three separate accounts, two of which were not in Eaken's name. Significantly, over $26,000.00 of the embezzled funds remains unaccounted for. Despite the fact that Eaken's name was among the names on the signature card for each account, the parcelling of the embezzled funds among three different accounts at the same bank constitutes an affirmative act which may reasonably be interpreted as an attempt to conceal Eaken's receipt of the embezzled funds as his income. In fact, such manipulation of funds is common among tax evasion and money laundering schemes.

Eaken insists that his actions evidence only an intent to conceal his crime of embezzlement, and that they do not rise to the level of willful affirmative action required by the Supreme Court in *Spies*. Again, we disagree. These actions can clearly constitute willful affirmative acts under *Spies*; that Court stated, "if the tax-evasion motive plays *any part* in such conduct the offense [under § 7201] may be made out *even though the conduct may also serve other purposes such as the concealment of other crime*." 317 U.S. at 499 (emphasis added). No doubt these actions assisted Eaken's execution of the embezzlement scheme. However, a rational trier of fact could also find that by these actions he intended to conceal his receipt of the embezzled funds as income from the IRS.

Whether the affirmative positive acts of depositing the embezzled funds into multiple bank accounts evidence an attempt to evade tax obligations obviously depends upon Eaken's intent with regard to these acts. For example, by these acts Eaken could have intended merely to conceal the money from the estate beneficiaries. Similarly, by these acts Eaken could have intended to conceal the embezzlement from the probate court. Indeed, Eaken insisted at trial that this was his only intent with regard to his actions. However, it is also reasonable to conclude from the evidence presented at trial that by these acts Eaken intended to conceal from the IRS his receipt of the embezzled funds as income during the year 1985.

The defendant further argues on appeal that the absence of a tax evasion motive is revealed by the fact that he sought an extension in time for the filing of his 1985 return and paid $1700.00 to the IRS. However, as the government correctly points out, this fact supports an alternative interpretation: Eaken's actions reveal his awareness of tax obligations, yet he paid as an estimate of his 1985 tax obligation only $1700.00 to the IRS when his actual tax obligation to the IRS was over $80,000.00. It is quite plausible to believe that he was actually trying to mislead the IRS by proposing that his income for 1985 was relatively modest as compared to what it actually was. . . .

Having been properly instructed regarding the requirement that an affirmative positive act and willfulness be proved, the jury concluded that by his actions Eaken willfully attempted to evade or defeat his tax obligations for the year 1985. Based on the evidence presented at trial, we believe that a rational jury could have found the elements of willfulness and an affirmative act of tax evasion as articulated by the Supreme Court in *Spies*. Accordingly, the defendant's conviction on Count 1 is affirmed. . . .

Notes and Questions

1. How important is it that Eaken deposited embezzled funds into three different bank accounts? If the accounts had all been under his name or the name of his firm, would the deposits constitute an affirmative act to evade or defeat? Would depositing all of the funds into a single account under Eaken's name have been an affirmative act?

2. Why is it significant that more than $26,000 in embezzled funds remained unaccounted for?

3. As was true in *Guidry*, Eaken claimed that he intended to conceal the embezzlement from the estate. Unlike Mrs. Guidry, however, Eaken maintained that his concealment was a temporary step that would last only until he could restore the funds to the estate. Is this difference relevant?

4. What were the affirmative acts in *Guidry* and *Olbres*?

B. METHODS OF PROOF

Some, but not all, of the federal tax crimes require proof of unreported income. Because concealment is the essence of so many tax evasion cases, direct proof of the exact amount of unreported income may not be possible. Tax evaders are notorious for keeping poor records or destroying what records they have. Thus, the government may use indirect (i.e., circumstantial) methods of proof to establish guilt. To require otherwise "would be tantamount to holding that skil[l]ful concealment is an invincible barrier to proof."[36]

---

36. United States v. Johnson, 319 U.S. 503, 518 (1943). "[I]ndeed, the inherent secrecy of [a] cash hoard makes it impossible for any but the keeper to know even of its existence, let alone the amount. . . . The government [is] not obliged to prove a proposition inherently impossible to establish." United States v. Normile, 587 F.2d 784, 786-87 (5th Cir. 1979).

1. Net Worth Method

UNITED STATES v. BENCS
28 F.3d 555 (6th Cir. 1994)

Joiner, Senior District Judge.

Ronald Bencs was charged with conspiring to defraud the United States, evading income tax, money laundering, and structuring financial transactions to avoid cash reporting requirements applicable to transactions in excess of $10,000. The government claimed generally that Bencs was involved in a large marijuana selling business, and attempted to shelter his drug profits from taxes and hide them from detection. The jury convicted on all counts. . . .

I

A

In 1988, the IRS criminal investigation unit investigated Bencs' accountant, Robert Gross, for allegedly helping a drug dealer launder drug proceeds and evade income tax on those proceeds. Agents searched Gross' office in April 1988, and, among other documents, seized the financial records of Ronald Bencs and his company, Diversified Financial Enterprises.

In reviewing those records, IRS agents Cappara and Kacarab noted that Bencs' net worth was approximately $1.2 million, but that his reported income did not justify this accumulation of wealth. The agents researched public records, bank records and tax returns, and interviewed a number of people, including Bencs, to account for the discrepancy. Bencs told the agents that Diversified's business was, in fact, diversified, and that the company had sources of income from striping parking lots; selling jewelry, art work and Christmas trees; and renovating houses. Bencs also claimed nontaxable sources of income in the form of loans from various individuals and banks. Bencs denied receiving income from illegal activities.

Contrary to Bencs' denial, the investigation indicated that Bencs was involved in a large marijuana distribution operation. Raymond Russell testified that he started selling marijuana to Bencs in 1972, and sold 300 to 500 pounds per month to him in 1973 and 1974. Russell testified that he sold 9000 pounds of marijuana for Bencs between 1980 and approximately 1985. Bencs occasionally bought cocaine from Russell during this period in amounts of one-half to one kilogram at a time. Russell's activity for the years 1985-89 abated somewhat. He testified that during this four-year period, he sold marijuana to Bencs on two occasions, one involving 40 pounds and one involving 60 pounds. Russell also borrowed $16,000 from Bencs to buy cocaine and repaid Bencs in 1986 or 1987 with 500 pounds of marijuana.

Michael McCarthy testified that from 1974 to 1976 he transported Russell's marijuana from Arizona, delivering it to Bencs in Cleveland. McCarthy testified that his dealings with Bencs resumed in 1983 and continued to 1985, when he again transported marijuana to Bencs, delivering 200-300 pounds on each trip. He and Bencs each made a profit of $100 per pound. Finally, George Abraham testified that between 1974 and 1983 he sold marijuana to Bencs in 200-300 pound amounts. These transactions took place at varying intervals, as seldom as once [every] six months and as frequently as two times per week.

Bencs formed Diversified in 1978, naming himself president. Bencs was the sole shareholder, and Gross maintained the financial records. Kacarab analyzed the deposits to and checks written against Diversified's account for the years 1983-88, demonstrating at trial that a total of $376,460.28 in cash was deposited, and only $41,680 in checks. Most of these checks were from individuals, or were government checks endorsed by the individuals to Diversified. A total of $318,374 was disbursed from the account in payroll checks to Bencs. Kacarab testified that a payroll check was usually negotiated shortly after a cash deposit was made. Diversified's bank records and tax returns did not reflect expenses customarily incurred by businesses engaged in sales and contracting work, such as cost of goods sold, rent, utilities, and labor. Diversified's tax returns reflected losses for all years but one, when it reported a $241 gain.

Cappara and Kacarab undertook a net worth analysis of Bencs and his company, necessitated because Bencs transacted business almost exclusively in cash and had records inadequate to determine his tax liability. The agents calculated Bencs' net worth at the end of 1983, and then for each of the years that followed through 1988. Included in the net worth computation were known income; personal, nondeductible expenditures for which documentation existed; bank account balances; real property; vehicles; securities; and other assets, such as loan receivables and an interest in a partnership. After subtracting liabilities, the agents then calculated Bencs' net worth for each tax year in question. The agents concluded that Bencs' net worth for the years 1984-88 exceeded his reported income in amounts ranging between $68,000 and $99,000, and that he had underpaid income tax for those years in amounts ranging between $21,000 and $40,000. Bencs presented an expert witness at trial who concurred in Kacarab's methodology and used most of his calculations. The expert's totals differed principally because he included Bencs' alleged ownership of coins, Krugerrands and jewelry in calculating Bencs' net worth as of the end of 1983, valuing them at $200,000. . . .

II . . .

D. SUFFICIENCY OF THE EVIDENCE . . .

2. *Tax Evasion*

Section 7201 provides that "any person who willfully attempts in any manner to evade or defeat any tax imposed by this title or the payment thereof shall . . . be guilty of a felony[.]" 26 U.S.C. § 7201. The government may prove tax evasion through the net worth method, pursuant to which a taxpayer's net worth is calculated at the beginning of the relevant period and then at the end. The difference between these two amounts may be attributed to taxable income if the government proves that the taxpayer had one or more sources of taxable income. Holland v. United States, 348 U.S. 121 (1954).

In approving the net worth method in *Holland*, the Court cautioned that the method is "so fraught with danger for the innocent that the courts must closely scrutinize its use." Id. at 125. Thus, "an essential condition . . . is the establishment, with reasonable certainty, of an opening net worth, to serve as a starting point from which to calculate future increases in the taxpayer's assets." Id. at 132. A defense often asserted in net worth cases is that the government's opening net worth is not accurate because of substantial cash or assets on hand at the starting point. This "favorite defense," as characterized by the Supreme Court, is one which the government has great difficulty refuting. Id. at 127. Nonetheless, the government's failure to investigate leads furnished by the taxpayer can result in serious injustice. "When the Government fails to show an investigation into the validity of such leads, the trial judge may consider them as true and the Government's case insufficient to go to the jury." Id. at 136.

Net worth increases must be attributable to taxable income. However, where the government proves a source of taxable income, it need not negate all the possible nontaxable sources of the alleged net worth increases, such as gifts, loans, and inheritances. Proof of a source of taxable income carries with it the negation of untaxable income.

Bencs attacks the legitimacy of the government's net worth analysis by claiming that the government's starting figure for the end of 1983 was too low, because it did not take into account an alleged coin, Krugerrand and jewelry collection. Bencs also claims that the agents did not pursue leads furnished by him and did not fully investigate his financial status as of the end of 1983. The agents testified, however, that they researched Bencs' financial statements and tax returns. None substantiated Bencs' ownership or acquisition in 1983 of a coin collection, and none reflected a sale of such items after that date. Although a number of Bencs' witnesses claimed to have seen his coin collection, none verified that the collection existed as of the beginning of the net worth period. The agents also interviewed Bencs' alleged jewelry source, and learned that Bencs had purchased a total of 25 pieces over a ten-year period, at a cost of only $5000 per year.

The jury properly was left to decide whether Bencs owned those assets at the end of 1983. Based on this record, a rational trier of fact could conclude that Bencs' opening net worth was that which the government proved, and not Bencs' inflated figure.

Bencs also contends that the evidence in support of his tax evasion convictions is insufficient because the testimony at trial did not reflect the same volume of drug sales for 1987 and 1988 as had existed in prior years. The government's financial proof reflected that Bencs had underreported his income by $69,000 and $68,000 for the years 1987 and 1988. The government also proved that Bencs had a source of taxable income during this period—drug dealing. Bencs himself claims to have had other sources of taxable income. It was not necessary, as Bencs concedes, for the government to prove that all of the unreported income was illegally derived. Having proved a likely source of taxable income, the government was not required to negate all possible sources of untaxable income. Even now, Bencs does not contend that nontaxable income explains the entire amount of unreported income.

The evidence, when viewed in the light most favorable to the government, was sufficient to support the jury's guilty verdicts on all of the tax evasion charges, including those for 1987 and 1988. We therefore affirm his convictions. . . .

Notes and Questions

1. As the court in *Bencs* observed, *Holland* requires the government to follow leads furnished by the taxpayer in net worth cases. Is it necessary for the government to follow *all* leads? Does the rationale supporting the leads rule apply when the government can prove specific items of unreported income?[37]

2. The court in *Bencs* said that where the government proves a source of taxable income, it need not disprove all possible nontaxable sources of increased net worth. Must the government prove the exact source and amount of taxable income? Or will a likely source suffice?[38] What are some examples of nontaxable sources of income? Why shouldn't the government bear the burden of negating all of them?

2. Bank Deposits and Cash Expenditures Method

The net worth method works reasonably well when the taxpayer has used his increased wealth to purchase durable property or other tangible investments. But if the taxpayer consumes the increased wealth (e.g., spends it all on lavish vacations instead of buying a yacht) or hides it in an offshore account, the net worth method is useless because the taxpayer is (or seems) no wealthier at the end of the tax year than before. In that event, variants of the net worth method may be used.

UNITED STATES v. ABODEELY
801 F.2d 1020 (8th Cir. 1986)

HENLEY, Senior Circuit Judge.

Defendant Joseph Abodeely was indicted by the grand jury for two counts of criminal tax evasion in violation of 26 U.S.C. § 7201 for the tax years of 1978 and 1979. Following a jury trial in the United States District Court for the Northern District of Iowa, the defendant was convicted on both counts. . . .

Joseph Abodeely derived his income from several business ventures. These included the Unique Motel, the Food Factory (a fast food restaurant), and the Meeting Place (a bar featuring exotic dancers and located near the Unique Motel). Abodeely filed an income tax return, along with his wife, for the 1978 tax year in which he stated their net taxable income was a negative $627.00. They declared a net taxable income for 1979 of $25,443.00. The government set out to prove that Abodeely's taxable income was substantially greater than the amount he stated in his tax returns for those two years. The government utilized the "bank deposits and cash expenditures" method to demonstrate that Abodeely received more income than he reported on his tax returns.

Evidence was introduced regarding various potential sources of the unreported income.[39] Among these potential sources were Abodeely's six trips to Las Vegas during

---

37. Cf. Swallow v. United States, 307 F.2d 81 (10th Cir. 1962).

38. See Holland v. United States, 348 U.S. 121 (1954).

39. The government argued that Abodeely had ten separate sources of unreported income: (1) money from room rentals at the Unique Motel that were not recorded; (2) prostitution income; (3) automobile sales; (4) Meeting Place — bar tabs, over the counter sales, and cover charges which were not rung up on

1978 and 1979. Abodeely had established credit with the MGM Grand Hotel and could receive markers from the cashier. A marker is an advance or loan which may be exchanged at the hotel's casino for chips in order to gamble. During each trip Abodeely received markers for between $12,000.00 and $16,000.00. Abodeely would then pay back these markers, in cash, on his subsequent trips. Abodeely's gambling activity was also rated by MGM. On his March, 1978 trip Abodeely was graded a B-30. The "B" indicated that Abodeely placed bets of $50.00 to $75.00 per bet. The "30" is time played in increments of fifteen minutes. Thus, "30" indicated he played seven and one-half hours. Mr. Abodeely's rating never fell below "B" for any of the six trips. This rating is used by the MGM to determine whether a player is to receive complimentary benefits. Room, food and beverage will be given if the player places a minimum of $7,500.00 in bets. Airfare will also be given if the amount of the bets exceeds $10,000.00. Abodeely received complimentary room, food, beverage and airfare on each occasion during 1978 and 1979. The records from the MGM do not disclose whether Abodeely won, lost, or broke even while gambling.

In addition to the gambling evidence, the trial court also permitted the government to introduce evidence of Abodeely's involvement in promoting prostitution. Kim Golston testified that she worked for Abodeely for between four and six weeks in 1979. Golston would use a room at the Unique Motel and Abodeely would send men to her room. Golston would split the money that she received from the prostitution sixty/forty with Abodeely, Abodeely receiving sixty per cent. Another witness testified that she overheard Abodeely tell one of the dancers who worked for him that "if she couldn't hook for him she could move out of her apartment" at the Unique Motel.

Abodeely argues that the trial court erred in admitting this testimony because it was not relevant, or, if relevant, its probative value was outweighed by the danger of unfair prejudice. . . .

In order to obtain a conviction for income tax evasion under 26 U.S.C. § 7201, the government must prove, beyond a reasonable doubt, the following elements:

(1) That there is a tax deficiency for the relevant year that is due and owing;
(2) That the defendant knowingly and wilfully failed to pay; and
(3) That the failure to pay was in an attempt to evade or defeat the tax due.

Abodeely's claims of error do not challenge the government's proof of the second and third elements. Defendant challenges the introduction of evidence as it relates to the first element — proof of a tax deficiency.

In order to prove a tax deficiency, "the government must show first that the taxpayer had unreported income, and second, that the income was taxable." United States v. Fogg, 652 F.2d 551, 555 (5th Cir. Unit B 1981); see United States v. Vannelli, 595 F.2d 402, 405-06 (8th Cir. 1979) ("In a tax evasion prosecution it is necessary to show that an individual received more income than he reported. In order to do this, the government must establish potential sources from which this unreported income was derived."). Proof of unreported taxable income by direct means is extremely difficult and often impossible. By the very fact that a taxpayer has failed to report the income,

---

the cash register; (5) rental of exotic dancers to V.F.W. post; (6) United Airline coupons; (7) assistance fees from Rapid Chevrolet for help in selling cars; (8) back door sales of televisions, radios and stereos; (9) Las Vegas gambling; and (10) rental income from other property.

it behooves him to obscure any trace of its existence. Therefore, direct methods of proof, which depend on the taxpayer's voluntary retention of records of the income, fail. Accordingly, the government has armed itself with an arsenal of indirect methods of proof which rely on circumstantial evidence to disclose unreported taxable income. These methods include:

(1) "Net worth," Holland v. United States, 348 U.S. 121 (1954);
(2) "Cash expenditures," Taglianetti v. United States, 398 F.2d 558 (1st Cir. 1968), aff'd per curiam, 394 U.S. 316 (1969); and
(3) "Bank deposits," United States v. Esser, 520 F.2d 213 (7th Cir. 1975).

The government may choose to proceed under any single theory of proof or a combination method, including a combination of circumstantial and direct proofs. The government denominates the method it used at trial in this case as the "bank deposits and cash expenditures" method. The "bank deposits" or "bank deposits and cash expenditures" method has been variously defined. The foundation of the method requires that the government "initially introduce evidence to show (1) that, during the tax years in question, the taxpayer was engaged in an income producing business or calling; (2) that he made regular deposits of funds into bank accounts; and (3) that an adequate and full investigation of those accounts was conducted in order to distinguish between income and non-income deposits." United States v. Morse, 491 F.2d 149, 152 (1st Cir. 1974). All non-taxable deposits are then excluded from the gross deposits and amounts on deposit from prior years are not included. *Morse*, 491 F.2d at 152. The figure arrived at after this "purification" is the net taxable bank deposits. Under a "pure" bank deposits approach, no further proof is necessary and "the jury is entitled to infer that the difference between the balance of deposited items and reported income constitutes unreported income." *Esser*, 520 F.2d at 217. The bank deposit method requires that the taxpayer's income be circulated through his bank accounts. If the income is simply received or converted into cash exclusive of his bank accounts and subsequently spent, its existence is not reflected in the bank deposits analysis. Likewise, unless the unreported income is converted into durable or investment property (automobiles, real estate, etc.), it will not be discovered in a net worth analysis. Therefore, the bank deposits and cash expenditures method, an augmentation of the bank deposits method, is sometimes used by the government to prove the existence of unreported income.

Under this augmented approach the underlying bank deposits foundation must be laid to establish the initial taxable income. To this figure the government then adds any other income which the taxpayer received but did not deposit in any bank account. . . . Under any method the government must demonstrate, beyond a reasonable doubt, that the unreported income came from a taxable source. There are two different ways that the government can show the taxable nature of the income.

First, the government may choose to negative all possible sources of non-taxable income. If this is done, there is no necessity of proving a likely source of the income. United States v. Massei, 355 U.S. 595 (1958) (per curiam). Under the bank deposits approach this would require the government to "do everything that is reasonable and fair [in] the circumstance to identify any non-income transactions and deduct them from total deposits." *Esser*, 520 F.2d at 217. The same is true in a bank deposits and cash expenditures case. The second approach is to prove a likely source from which the jury could reasonably find that the income sprung. *Holland*, 348 U.S. at 138. Proof of a likely source of the income necessarily negatives possible non-taxable sources. Appellant argues that *Holland* is a net worth case and has no bearing on a bank deposits and cash expenditures case.

This court does not completely agree. Under any § 7201 tax evasion case the government must show unreported taxable income as an element of its proof. Further, the net worth and bank deposits and cash expenditures methods both rely on circumstantial evidence, and the various safeguards expressed in *Holland* regarding the use of circumstantial evidence apply equally. Therefore, under any circumstantial method of proof, it is incumbent on the government to prove that the excess income is taxable.

Gains from unlawful activity are taxable. Here, gambling and prostitution evidence is relevant because it has the tendency to make it more probable that Abodeely had unreported income from a taxable source. "All relevant evidence is admissible" unless otherwise excluded. Fed. R. Evid. 402. The prostitution evidence was plainly relevant because the testimony of Golston clearly reveals that Abodeely was receiving taxable income. The testimony concerning a requirement that a dancer "hook" or "move" tended to show that appellant was in the prostitution business for profit.

This court is somewhat troubled by the gambling evidence, but does conclude that it was marginally relevant. The evidence reveals that Abodeely made six trips to Las Vegas during the tax years in question and made wagers in excess of $10,000.00 on each trip. From this evidence three conclusions may be drawn. First, the conclusion urged by the government, that Abodeely won at gambling and received income. Second, Abodeely may have lost. Losing, however, would also indicate unreported income because the losses would have to be covered. Abodeely always repaid his markers in cash on the subsequent trip. If he was losing money, this indicates a substantial unreported income source necessary to satisfy the losses. The third possibility is that Abodeely broke even; this would indicate no income from gambling and also might not evidence any other income source. Abodeely argues that he simply took the markers to use the cash as an interest free loan for cash flow at his various businesses. This explanation is plainly at odds with MGM's rating of Abodeely and the complimentary airfare which he was extended. The various inferences that may be drawn, but which a jury was not required to draw, from this evidence weigh in favor of evidencing an income source.

Apart from relevance Abodeely urges that the probative value of the questioned evidence is outweighed by the danger of unfair prejudice.

Evidence of this nature is undoubtedly prejudicial to the defendant. The rule requires, however, that the probative value be substantially outweighed by the danger of unfair prejudice. . . .

The court has no conceptual difficulty with the evidence concerning prostitution. While it is certainly prejudicial, it is highly probative of unreported taxable income. The gambling evidence, while having less direct probative value, is much less prejudicial, and indeed if its admission was error (which this court does not conclude), the error was harmless beyond a reasonable doubt. After all, having been shown that Abodeely ran a bar and a brothel, even the most straitlaced Iowa jury could hardly have been adversely affected by a showing of his participation in the legal, though perhaps sinful and worldly in the eyes of a midwestern jury, activity of gambling in Nevada. . . .

Abodeely's conviction is affirmed.

Notes and Questions

1. How does the bank deposits method differ from the net worth method of proof? What does the cash expenditures method add to the mix?

2. Why would the government avoid using the net worth method in a case like *Abodeely*?

3. What methods of proof would be appropriate to prove the tax deficiencies in *Guidry*, *Olbres*, and *Eaken*?

IV. FALSE DECLARATIONS

In contrast with punishable attempts to evade or defeat a tax, liability under the false declarations provision (a.k.a. "tax perjury" statute) is not premised on a finding of an unsatisfied tax liability. Instead, § 7206(1) is directed at willfully making and sub-scribing "any return, statement, or other document, which contains or is verified by a written declaration that is made under the penalties of perjury, and which [the declarant] does not believe to be true and correct as to every material matter." Thus, the false dec-laration need not have any actual tax consequences.

A. MATERIAL MATTERS

UNITED STATES v. DiVARCO
484 F.2d 670 (7th Cir. 1973)

PELL, Circuit Judge.

The defendants Joseph DiVarco and Joseph Arnold were charged in separate counts of an indictment with willfully and knowingly making and subscribing to a false statement on their respective 1965 federal income tax returns, which returns were veri-fied by written declarations that they were made under the penalties of perjury, in vio-lation of 26 U.S.C. § 7206(1). The two defendants were also indicted for conspiracy in violation of 18 U.S.C. § 371 in that they conspired with Irwin Davis, an unindicted co-conspirator, in violation of 26 U.S.C. § 7206(1) to report a false source of income from Chemical Mortgage & Investment Corporation, of which Davis was a stockholder and agent, "so as to conceal from the Internal Revenue Service of the United States the true source of the income reported and to prevent examination by the said Internal Rev-enue Service as to the truth or falsity of the income reported."

A jury found the defendants guilty as charged. . . .

Appellants contend that since there was no showing by the Government that they had in fact understated their income, 26 U.S.C. § 7206(1) was not applicable and only the general federal false statement statute, 18 U.S.C. § 1001, related to their alleged misconduct. Prosecution under that section was allegedly barred by the statute of limitations. The district court in a memorandum opinion, United States v. DiVarco, 343

F. Supp. 101 (N.D. Ill. 1972), concluded that the source of income was a "material matter" and that the willful and knowing misstatement of the source of income was covered by the prohibition in § 7206(1).

It is true, as contended by the defendants and observed by Judge Will in his opinion, that most, if not all, of the cases involving misstatement of source of income also involved an understatement of taxable income. However, "[one] of the more basic tenets running through all the cases is that the purpose behind the statute is to prosecute those who intentionally falsify their tax returns regardless of the precise ultimate effect that such falsification may have." 343 F. Supp. at 103.

We agree with and adopt Judge Will's opinion as to materiality. The plain language of the statute does not exclude the matter of the source of income from the definition of "material matter." In light of the need for accurate information concerning the source of income so that the Internal Revenue Service can police and verify the reporting of individuals and corporations, a misstatement as to the source of income is a material matter. . . .

Appellants also contend that, as in Spies v. United States, 317 U.S. 492 (1943), it was incumbent on the Government to prove specific intent and evil motive and purpose. Since the Government never proved that appellants had other sources of income which they were seeking not to disclose, it is argued that the proof of evil purpose was insufficient. While *Spies* involved a violation of the predecessor to 26 U.S.C. § 7201, which proscribed attempts to "evade or defeat any tax" and not false swearing on a return, nevertheless, it is clear that willfulness under § 7206(1) also requires proof of bad purpose or evil motive. United States v. Bishop, 412 U.S. at 359. This is not to say, however, that the evil motive must have been to evade the payment of taxes, which was what was involved in *Spies*. Here there was evidence from which the jury could have found, and apparently did, that the defendants reported income but falsely reported the source. Evil motive, of course, was not admitted. It seldom is. Of necessity, it is ordinarily proven by other evidence from which the inference may fairly be drawn that the evil motive existed at the pertinent time. . . .

The evidence was more than sufficient to sustain the charge of violation of § 7206(1). . . .

Affirmed.

UNITED STATES v. GREENBERG
735 F.2d 29 (2d Cir. 1984)

Kearse, Circuit Judge.

Defendant Jack Greenberg appeals from a judgment entered in the United States District Court for the Eastern District of New York after a jury trial before Jacob Mishler, Judge, convicting him on one count of filing a materially false corporate income tax return, in violation of 26 U.S.C. § 7206(1); two counts of filing materially false personal income tax returns, in violation of § 7206(1); and one count of willfully failing to file a federal income tax return, in violation of 26 U.S.C. § 7203. . . .

BACKGROUND

The sufficiency of the government's evidence to prove that Greenberg filed, and assisted in filing, false income tax returns is not disputed. Greenberg was an accountant who was also a participant in a joint venture called P.R.P. Industries, Inc. ("PRP"). With respect to the charge that Greenberg aided and abetted the filing of a false corporate income tax return for PRP's 1978 fiscal year, in violation of § 7206(1), government witnesses testified that Greenberg had instructed them, *inter alia*, to classify as PRP business expenses expenditures that were solely for the personal benefit of Greenberg's co-venturer, and to classify as loans payments that in fact were investments in other businesses or were compensation to the co-venturers. Notwithstanding these misallocations, PRP reported more income than it should have for that fiscal year, and its net taxable income was stated in the proper amount.

With respect to the charges that Greenberg filed, jointly with his wife, false personal income tax returns for the years 1976 and 1977, in violation of § 7206(1), the evidence was that for each of those years, Greenberg overreported his wife's income and underreported his own. For 1976, Mrs. Greenberg was reported to have had a gross income of some $32,000, when in fact she had none; Greenberg was reported to have had earnings of some $4400, when in fact his earnings were approximately $25,000. For 1977, Mrs. Greenberg was reported to have had gross income of some $35,000, when in fact she had none; Greenberg was reported to have had gross receipts of some $66,000, when in fact his gross receipts were more than $100,000. Greenberg testified that the purpose of these false allocations was to present a picture that would enable Mrs. Greenberg to obtain credit in her own name despite having no occupation. Notwithstanding these misallocations, the variance between the taxes paid by the Greenbergs and the taxes actually owing under a proper allocation was $48.

In its charge with respect to the counts alleging violations of § 7206(1), the court instructed the jury that there could be no violation unless the false statements were material. . . .

DISCUSSION . . .

Where a false statement is made to a public body or its representative, materiality refers to the impact that the statement may reasonably have on the ability of that agency to perform the functions assigned to it by law. The question is not what effect the statement actually had; its actual effect would plainly present an issue of fact. The question is rather whether the statement had the potential for an obstructive or inhibitive effect. . . .

[W]e are not persuaded that the court erred in concluding that the misstatements in the PRP return and in Greenberg's personal income tax returns were material. The purpose of § 7206(1) is not simply to ensure that the taxpayer pay the proper amount of taxes — though that is surely one of its goals. Rather, that section is intended to ensure also that the taxpayer not make misstatements that could hinder the Internal Revenue Service ("IRS") in carrying out such functions as the verification of the accuracy of that return or a related tax return.

Greenberg's argument that the misstatements were not material because they resulted in, at most, minimal underpayments of taxes ignores the potential of the misstatements for impeding the IRS's performance of its responsibilities. The fraudulent description of PRP's payment of its owners' personal expenses as business expenses, for example, presented a distorted picture of both PRP's expenses and of the owners' income. The fraudulent allocation of income to Mrs. Greenberg on the joint personal returns, with the corresponding underreporting of Greenberg's own income, gave a similar distorted view. All of these distortions had the potential for hindering the IRS's efforts to monitor and verify the tax liability of PRP and the Greenbergs.

In short, the district court correctly determined that the false statements made and assisted by Greenberg were material.

CONCLUSION . . .

The judgment of conviction is affirmed.

Notes and Questions

1. If the false statements in *DiVarco* and *Greenberg* did not relate to a tax deficiency, why were they material?

B. TRUE AND CORRECT

SIRAVO v. UNITED STATES
377 F.2d 469 (1st Cir. 1967)

COFFIN, Circuit Judge.

Defendant appeals from judgments of conviction on three counts for wilfully making and subscribing false tax returns in 1958, 1959, and 1960, in violation of 26 U.S.C. § 7206(1), and on one count for wilfully failing to file a tax return in 1961 in violation of 26 U.S.C. § 7203.

Defendant's returns during 1958-1960 showed as income only wages (not exceeding $7,500 in any of the tax years in question) paid by Siravo Motor Sales. In each year the tax due was less than tax withheld and refund was applied for. Evidence at trial showed that during these years defendant operated TransLux Jewelry Co., which assembled jewelry components as a subcontractor for various manufacturers, receiving for this work the following amounts: 1958 — $22,242.83; 1959 — $28,976.22; 1960 — $54,319.47; 1961 — $71,362.73.

Defendant made no entry on his form 1040 opposite the heading "profit (or loss) from business from separate Schedule C," nor did he file a separate Schedule C ("Profit (or Loss) From Business or Profession"). He signed the customary declaration.[40]

---

40. "I declare under the penalties of perjury that this return (including any accompanying schedules and statements) has been examined by me and to the best of my knowledge and belief is a true, correct, and complete return."

While the evidence indicated that the defendant's jewelry assembly work must have required a number of people, there was no evidence as to the amount of any costs or expenses, whether of materials, labor, or overhead.

The first three counts charged that defendant "did wilfully . . . make and subscribe . . . a . . . tax return . . . which was verified by a written declaration that it was made under the penalties of perjury, and which . . . he did not believe to be true and correct as to every material matter in that . . . he failed and omitted to disclose . . . substantial gross receipts from a business activity. . . ."

Defendant's principal contention is that 26 U.S.C. § 7206(1) describes a form of perjury, that a basic requirement of perjury is a false statement of fact, and that failure to attach a separate Schedule C reporting "gross receipts" is neither a constructive misrepresentation of taxable income nor a false statement. He therefore attacks the sufficiency of both the indictment and the evidence. The government denies that section 7206(1) is a perjury statute and that a false statement of facts is an essential element of this crime. It argues that a violation of the section can consist of the knowing and wil[l]ful omission of facts.

In our view it is unnecessary to resolve this dispute in semantics, for we hold that a return that omits material items necessary to the computation of income is not "true and correct" within the meaning of section 7206. If an affirmative false statement be required, it is supplied by the taxpayer's declaration that the return is true and correct, when he knows it is not. Therefore, the government has made out a violation of the section, whether it be labelled "a perjury statute," Kolaski v. United States, 5 Cir., 1966, 362 F.2d 847, or "similar in nature," Hoover v. United States, 5 Cir., 1966, 358 F.2d 87.

Our decision is grounded first on the language of the statute. If "true" and "correct" are not to be construed as precisely synonymous, therefore redundant, they must mean something more than that no false figures have been used and that the arithmetic is accurate. In fact, the two terms together are commonly construed as meaning that the document described is both accurate and complete.

Moreover, we think this construction is necessary to effect the statutory "self-assessing" approach to income taxation. As the Supreme Court said in United States v. Carroll, 1953, 345 U.S. 457, 460 (dictum), "The code and regulations must be construed in light of the purpose to locate and check upon recipients of income and the amounts they receive." In the context of this case, defendant's contrary construction comes down to this: The return of an employee who earned $10,000 a year and reported only $8,000 would not be "true and correct," while that of a corporation director who reported fees of $5,000 but omitted an accounting for the receipt of $1,000,000 in rents would be "true and correct." Or, to reverse the pattern in this case, defendant would have to say that a return showing an accounting for a taxpayer's business resulting in a net profit of $7,500 and omitting wage payments of $50,000 would also be "true and correct." We cannot conclude that Congress, in devising "a variety of sanctions for the protection of the system and the revenues," Spies v. United States, 1943, 317 U.S. 492, 495, intended to place such a premium on the telling of half truths. . . .

The fourth count charged that defendant, having a gross income of $73,209.24 in 1961, wilfully and knowingly failed to file a return. The trial court correctly instructed the jury that total receipts must be reduced by the cost of goods sold and other costs representing a return of capital to arrive at gross income for a manufacturing business, and that, even if the government did not prove the exact amount of income stated in the indictment, it was sufficient if the evidence showed that receipts exceeded cost of goods sold by at least $600. But there was no evidence as to the amount of costs, except the testimony that substantially all materials were supplied by defendant's customers. Defendant argues that since labor costs are part of the cost of goods sold and since there was testimony that the volume of business was impossible for one man to handle, the government has not carried its burden of showing that he did not have labor costs off-setting the proved gross receipts.

We do not agree that the government has any such burden. The applicable rule here is that uniformly applied in tax evasion cases — that evidence of unexplained receipts shifts to the taxpayer the burden of coming forward with evidence as to the amount of offsetting expenses, if any.[41] Indeed, this case is necessarily included in that rule. For in a tax evasion case the government's ultimate burden is to show that the taxpayer received not only gross income but also taxable income, after deduction of capital *and* non-capital expenses. If that is satisfied by proof of sales receipts, absent explanation, so must be the lesser burden here. . . .

Affirmed.

Notes and Questions

1. Must a return contain literally untrue or incorrect information to violate the tax perjury statute?

2. Suppose that Siravo had filed Form 1040A instead of Form 1040. Form 1040A seeks information about total wages, salaries, tips, interest income, and other types of income not relevant to this hypothetical. All of the information Siravo provided on Form 1040A was literally true. But assume Siravo knew that he had received substantial unreported gross receipts from manufacturing and selling seasonal wreaths. Although Form 1040A did not inquire about income from manufacturing and sales, the proper form — Form 1040 — required disclosure of the gross receipts. Has Siravo violated § 7206(1)? By filing the wrong form — Form 1040A — has he implicitly represented that he has reported all of his income?[42] If not, how should the government proceed?

3. The federal false statements statute, 18 U.S.C. § 1001, punishes the making of a false statement with respect to any matter within the jurisdiction of a United States department or agency. Do false statements covered by § 7206(1) also fall within the ambit of § 1001? If so, are there double jeopardy implications?[43]

---

41. Of course, when the defendant does offer evidence of offsetting costs, the burden is on the government to persuade the jury that the costs are not allowable.

42. Cf. United States v. Borman, 992 F.2d 124 (7th Cir. 1993).

43. Cf. Blockburger v. United States, 284 U.S. 299 (1932).

12

Currency Reporting Crimes and Money Laundering

I. INTRODUCTION

Money laundering is a mechanism for concealing income or its illegal source or use to make the transaction appear to be legitimate.[1] Although it is commonly associated with drug trafficking, as a practical matter money laundering is used to conceal and/or legitimize proceeds of a broad array of criminal activity, including bribery, mail fraud, and securities fraud. In addition to enabling those who possess proceeds of crime to introduce illicit funds into legitimate channels of commerce, money laundering often facilitates the commission of ancillary crimes like tax evasion as well.

The federal government's initiatives to combat money laundering began with the enactment of currency reporting statutes in the 1970s. These laws require that transactions involving large amounts of cash be reported to the Treasury Department regardless of whether the transaction is tainted by criminal activity or is wholly legitimate. More recently, Congress augmented this regulatory framework by expanding the categories of transactions subject to the reporting requirements and by enacting the Money Laundering Control Act of 1986, which criminalizes moving illegally derived funds into or out of legitimate banking channels as well as moving legally derived funds through the banking system to avoid tax or reporting requirements.

II. CURRENCY REPORTING CRIMES

Of the many ancillary enforcement tools available to the Internal Revenue Service (IRS), two statutes are of particular importance. They are the Bank Secrecy Act[2] and Internal Revenue Code § 6050I.[3] These statutes require the reporting of transactions

---

1. See President's Commission on Organized Crime, Interim Report to the President and Attorney General, The Cash Connection: Organized Crime, Financial Institutions, and Money Laundering 7 (1984).

2. See generally 3 Kathleen F. Brickey, Corporate Criminal Liability §§ 11:38-11:55 (2d ed. 1994).

3. See generally id. §§ 11:56-11:64.

involving large amounts of currency, regardless of whether the transactions are related to criminal conduct. Failure to file required reports is an independent crime.

A. THE BANK SECRECY ACT

Congress enacted the Bank Secrecy Act to give the government access to information that has "a high degree of usefulness in criminal, tax, or regulatory investigations or proceedings."[4] Of the three titles contained in the Act, Title II — the Currency and Foreign Transactions Reporting Act (CFTRA) — is most important for present purposes. CFTRA's regulatory scheme enables the government to monitor large monetary transactions (including exports and imports of currency) and the use of foreign financial accounts.[5] Congress found this legislation was needed because secret currency transactions — particularly the concealment of assets in secret foreign bank accounts — had led to the loss of hundreds of millions of dollars in tax revenues and jeopardized the financial soundness of some corporations.

1. Transporting Monetary Instruments

The provisions relating to importing or exporting monetary instruments are directed at those who knowingly transport or cause the transportation of monetary instruments into or out of the United States and those who receive monetary instruments that have been physically transported into the United States.[6] Reports of the movement of currency into and out of the country must be filed with the Customs Service. The threshold jurisdictional amount that triggers the reporting requirement is $10,000.

To establish a criminal violation of this statute, the government must prove two culpable mental states. First, it must show that the person "knowingly" transported or

---

4. 12 U.S.C. §§ 1829b(a)(1), 1951 & 1953(a); 31 U.S.C. § 5311 (formerly codified at 31 U.S.C. § 1051).

5. Many federal regulatory schemes, including some that contain criminal penalties, are not self-executing. Instead, they rely heavily on administrative agencies with special technical expertise to flesh out the substantive rules. That is especially true in the case of CFTRA, a barebones statute that authorizes the Secretary of the Treasury to promulgate rules governing the reporting of information that has a high degree of usefulness to government regulators.

It has long been settled that when a criminal penalty is set by statute, Congress may constitutionally delegate to an administrative agency the power to write substantive rules and regulations, the violation of which will be a crime subject to the statutory penalty. United States v. Grimaud, 220 U.S. 506 (1911). This principle "has not wavered a millimeter" since *Grimaud*. Gellhorn, Administrative Prescription and Imposition of Penalties, 1970 Wash. U. L.Q. 265, 266.

6. 31 U.S.C. §§ 5316-5317, 5321(a)(2), (c) (formerly codified at 31 U.S.C. §§ 1101-1105). Statutory and regulatory exemptions exist for many businesses, including banks, common carriers that are unaware they are transporting monetary instruments, and securities brokers and dealers that mail or ship monetary instruments by mail or common carrier. 31 U.S.C. § 5316(c) (formerly codified at 31 U.S.C. § 1101(c)); 31 C.F.R. § 103.23(c).

The term "monetary instrument" is not limited to domestic coins and currency. It includes foreign coins and currency, traveler's checks, negotiable instruments, investment securities, and securities in bearer form as well. 31 U.S.C. § 5312(a)(3) (formerly codified at 31 U.S.C. § 1052); 31 C.F.R. § 103.11.

received monetary instruments that exceed the jurisdictional amount of $10,000.[7] Once that is established, the government must then show that the failure to report was "willful."[8] As is true in criminal tax prosecutions, the element of willfulness in this context connotes an intentional violation of a known legal duty.[9]

Monetary instruments transported in violation of the reporting requirements are subject to seizure and forfeiture while they are in the process of being transported.[10]

UNITED STATES v. FORTY-SEVEN THOUSAND NINE HUNDRED EIGHTY DOLLARS ($47,980) IN CANADIAN CURRENCY
804 F.2d 1085 (9th Cir. 1986)

WALLACE, Circuit Judge.

BSP Investment and Development, Ltd. (BSP) appeals from a judgment of civil forfeiture in favor of the United States. . . .

I

BSP is a Canadian corporation whose principal officers and shareholders are Stark and Pascoe. On February 22, 1979, Stark and Pascoe entered the United States by automobile, carrying with them $47,980 in Canadian currency, which belonged to BSP. Stark and Pascoe were routinely stopped at the United States Customs Port of Entry at Eastport, Idaho, and questioned regarding the purpose of their visit to the United States and what property they carried with them.

Inspection of their car produced a briefcase containing a large quantity of currency, packaged in envelopes. When the customs inspector asked Stark and Pascoe if they were carrying over $5,000,[11] they lied to him, stating that they had only $4,000. When the customs inspector told Pascoe and Stark that he wished to count their currency, Stark and Pascoe produced three envelopes, containing a total of approximately $12,000. When the customs agent drew their attention to the reporting requirement for transportation of more than $5,000, Pascoe stated that he had not wished to be bothered with the disclosure forms, which he referred to as "I.R.S." forms. In view of the circumstances, however, Pascoe had a change of heart, and stated that he and Stark wished to declare the $12,000 they had produced. With further search, the customs inspector found additional envelopes of money, and was told that it amounted to approximately $20,000. Ultimately, $47,980 in Canadian currency was found in the briefcase by customs officers.

Customs authorities seized the currency because Stark and Pascoe had failed to declare it upon entry, as required by 31 U.S.C. § 1101, recodified as 31 U.S.C. § 5316. One day later, on February 23, 1979, the Customs Service sent Stark a "Notice of Seizure and Information for Claimants" offering three alternatives with respect to the

---

7. 31 U.S.C. § 5316(a) (formerly codified at 31 U.S.C. § 1101(a)).
8. 31 U.S.C. § 5322 (formerly codified at 31 U.S.C. §§ 1058, 1059).
9. See, e.g., United States v. Dichne, 612 F.2d 632 (2d Cir. 1979).
10. 31 U.S.C. § 5317(a) (formerly codified at 31 U.S.C. § 1105).
11. The original jurisdictional amount was $5,000. It is now $10,000. — ED.

seized currency. Stark was informed that if he did nothing the matter would be referred to the United States Attorney within 60 days for institution of judicial forfeiture proceedings. Stark could instead expressly request that the matter be immediately referred. Alternatively, he could file a petition for administrative relief. He was informed that by filing for administrative relief he would be requesting the Customs Service not to refer the matter to the United States Attorney for the institution of judicial forfeiture proceedings while the administrative petition was pending. On April 20, 1979, BSP filed a petition for administrative relief. Ten days later the Customs Service advised BSP that administrative relief would not be considered until the United States [A]ttorney decided whether to file criminal charges, because the currency might be used as evidence in a criminal trial. The criminal investigation ended when the Customs Service advised BSP on August 13, 1979, that no criminal prosecution would be pursued. Nearly four months later, on December 11, 1979, the Customs Service decided to deny remission of forfeiture and, on December 17, referred the matter to the United States Attorney for prosecution of a civil forfeiture action. Four months thereafter, on April 1, 1980, the United States Attorney filed this in rem forfeiture action.

[The district court found that the 14-month delay between the seizure and the institution of the forfeiture proceeding violated due process and granted summary judgment for BSP. The Ninth Circuit affirmed, but granted rehearing after the Supreme Court decided United States v. Eight Thousand Eight Hundred and Fifty Dollars in United States Currency, 461 U.S. 555 (1983) (*$8,850*). In *$8,850*, the Court applied the four-factor balancing test of Barker v. Wingo, 407 U.S. 514 (1972) (*Barker*), and found an 18-month delay in the initiation of forfeiture proceedings did not violate due process. On remand, the district court found no due process violation.]

II . . .

Under *Barker*, four factors must be weighed to determine whether due process was denied. These are the length of delay, the reason for the delay, the defendant's assertion of its right to speedy determination, and prejudice. This test is flexible, "balancing the interests of the claimant and the Government to assess whether the basic due process requirement of fairness has been satisfied in a particular case," and none of the four factors represents "a necessary or sufficient condition for finding unreasonable delay." *$8,850*, 461 U.S. at 565. . . .

B

As pointed out in *$8,850*, the possibility of a criminal proceeding justifies delay in instituting a civil forfeiture suit. A criminal conviction may result in forfeiture, rendering civil proceedings unnecessary. Moreover, a prior civil suit "might serve to estop later criminal proceedings and may provide improper opportunities for the claimant to discover the details of a contemplated or pending criminal prosecution." A thorough criminal investigation may be very time consuming. We have no indication that the criminal investigation in this case, which terminated six months after the currency was seized, was unreasonably lengthy. BSP, Stark, and Pascoe can hardly complain that it terminated in a decision *not* to seek criminal indictments. If the government were forced to initiate criminal proceedings without adequate investigation it might have made a premature decision to prosecute, at considerable cost to Stark, Pascoe, and BSP.

[The court found that a similar interest in avoiding unnecessary judicial proceedings counseled against precipitous decisions regarding the granting of administrative relief; that BSP had requested administrative relief and hence did not request immediate judicial proceedings; and that the 14-month delay had not prejudiced BSP.]

D . . .

Considering the balance of factors in this case, we agree with the district court that the delay encountered here was reasonable and did not abridge the fundamental fairness guaranteed by due process of law.

III

BSP argues that the district court misconstrued the governing statute [and] contends that forfeiture requires a willful refusal to declare currency, undertaken with knowledge of the legal reporting requirements.

A

Section 1101 requires any person who "knowingly transports . . . monetary instruments of more than $5,000 at one time . . . to a place in the United States from or through a place outside the United States" to file a report regarding the amount and kind of instruments so transported, ownership, and other information. See 31 U.S.C. § 5316. The statutory language thus suggests that a person is subject to the reporting requirements if he knows he is transporting more than $5,000, regardless of knowledge of the reporting statute.

Congress imposed criminal penalties for violations of section 1101, providing that any person "willfully violating" its reporting provisions shall be subject to a fine and possible imprisonment. 31 U.S.C. § 1058, recodified as 31 U.S.C. § 5322. By imposing criminal penalties on "willful" violations alone, Congress's choice of words suggests that it recognized violations of section 1101 may be either willful or nonwillful — that is, with or without knowledge that the failure to report is illegal. . . .

In the civil forfeiture provision, by contrast, Congress did not include any scienter requirement. The statute provides simply that: "A monetary instrument being transported may be seized and forfeited to the United States Government when a report on the instrument under section 5316 of this title has not been filed or contains a material omission or misstatement." 31 U.S.C. § 5317(b). This language does not suggest that failure to file a report must be done with the knowledge that the report is required by law. Moreover, it is consistent with the general rule that under forfeiture enactments "the innocence of the owner of the property subject to forfeiture has almost uniformly been rejected as a defense." Calero-Toledo v. Pearson Yacht Leasing Co., 416 U.S. 663, 683 (1974). As we held before in this case, "the statute and regulations clearly impose a duty to report at least by the time of inspection, and *a failure to report at that time completes the violation.*" *Canadian Currency II*, 726 F.2d at 534 (emphasis added).

Consistent with this position, several courts have held that knowledge of reporting requirements is not required for civil forfeiture. . . .

The Eleventh Circuit, in United States v. One (1) Lot of Twenty-four Thousand Nine Hundred Dollars ($24,900.00) in U.S. Currency, 770 F.2d 1530 (11th Cir. 1985), however, has interpreted the "knowingly transports" language of section 1101 to mean that for purposes of civil forfeiture the failure to report must be committed with knowledge of the reporting requirement and an intent to break the law. We have already rejected the Eleventh Circuit's interpretation. In United States v. One Hundred Twenty-Two Thousand Forty-Three Dollars ($122,043.00) in United States Currency, 792 F.2d 1470 (9th Cir. 1986), we held that the government need not prove knowledge of the reporting requirement as an element of its civil forfeiture case. Id. at 1473-74. That case controls our disposition of this appeal. As we stated:

> The plain language of the statutory provisions, 31 U.S.C. §§ 5316-5317, does not include knowledge of the reporting requirement as an element for forfeiture. The only knowledge requirement is that the person know that he or she is transporting more than $5,000 out of the country.

Id. at 1474. . . .
   Affirmed.

STEPHENS, District Judge, dissenting.

As the forfeiture statute, 31 U.S.C. Section 1101 (recodified as 31 U.S.C. Section 5316) has evolved through judicial interpretation, one bite at a time, it has lost almost all semblance of fairness, as fairness is viewed by the ordinary citizen. I invite attention to Judge Beezer's dissent and especially footnote 9 in United States v. One Hundred Twenty-Two Thousand Forty-Three Dollars ($122,043.00) in United States Currency, 792 F.2d 1470 (9th Cir. 1986). Judge Beezer's concern arises out of a requirement to report currency when leaving the United States while our *Canadian Currency* case involves entry into the United States, but both cases involve situations where the person transporting the currency may not be aware of the requirement to report the currency. The Secretary could avoid one major element of unfairness by requiring that all persons entering or leaving the United States be given a written explanation of the reporting requirements before any questions are asked concerning transportation of currency. . . .

Notes and Questions

1. The violation in *$47,980* that led to the forfeiture was a civil violation of the reporting requirements. As a practical matter, does the statute impose strict liability? What differentiates civil and criminal violations?

2. What mental state did Pascoe and Stark possess? What evidence is relevant to that determination?

3. Why wasn't a delay of 14 months too long to satisfy due process requirements?

4. CFTRA authorizes both criminal and civil forfeitures. The forfeiture in *$47,980* arose out of a civil proceeding. Most civil forfeiture proceedings are "in rem." That is, the action is brought against the property sought to be forfeited—here, nearly $50,000

in currency — on the legal fiction that the property is the guilty party.[12] Although civil forfeiture proceedings are usually triggered by illicit (often criminal) use of the property, civil forfeitures are independent from criminal proceedings and may be brought even if the wrongdoer (who may or may not be the owner) is never prosecuted. Thus, the guilt or innocence of the owner is normally irrelevant.[13]

Historically, the government has had the burden of establishing probable cause that the property was used in the commission of a crime and was thus subject to forfeiture. Once the government established probable cause, the burden shifted to the owner to prove by a preponderance of the evidence that the property was not subject to forfeiture. After a decade of reform efforts initiated by members of the legal community and other interested groups, Congress enacted the Civil Asset Forfeiture Reform Act of 2000,[14] which made important substantive and procedural changes in the rules. Significantly, the Act shifts the burden of proof to the government, recognizes an innocent owner defense, and allows successful claimants to recover reasonable costs and attorneys' fees from the government.

NOTE ON FORFEITURES AS "EXCESSIVE FINES"

Many forfeiture statutes are drafted broadly to reach virtually any property that is related to or involved in the underlying criminal conduct. The criminal forfeiture provision in the Bank Secrecy Act, for example, requires the court to "order the defendant to forfeit *all* property, real or personal, involved in the offense and any property traceable thereto."[15] Several applications of such broadly worded provisions have prompted constitutional challenges based on Eighth Amendment grounds. The crux of these arguments is that the specific forfeiture in issue is excessive and therefore violates the Eighth Amendment prohibition against excessive fines. That, of course, assumes that a criminal forfeiture is the equivalent of a fine for Eighth Amendment purposes.

The seminal case on this point is United States v. Bajakajian.[16] In *Bajakajian*, the defendant attempted to leave the United States without reporting $357,144 in cash, in violation of the Bank Secrecy Act. The District Court found that the reporting violation was unrelated to any other illegal activities and that the defendant, who was reluctant to report the currency because of "cultural differences," intended to use proceeds of lawful activity to pay a lawful debt. Thus, the court concluded that forfeiture of the entire amount would be excessively harsh. Instead, the court ordered a $15,000 forfeiture and sentenced Bajakajian to three years' probation and a $5,000 fine. The Supreme Court affirmed, holding that forfeiture of the entire amount of the unreported currency would violate the Excessive Fines Clause of the Eighth Amendment because it would be grossly disproportionate to the gravity of the offense.

The Eighth Amendment provides: "Excessive bail shall not be required, nor excessive fines imposed, nor cruel and unusual punishments inflicted." This Court has had little

---

12. Goldsmith-Grant Co. v. United States, 254 U.S. 505, 518 (1921).
13. Cf. id. at 509 ("The jury found the car guilty. . . .").
14. Pub. L. No. 106-185, 114 Stat. 202 (2000), codified at 18 U.S.C. § 983.
15. 31 U.S.C. § 5317(c)(1)(A).
16. 542 U.S. 321 (1997).

occasion to interpret, and has never actually applied, the Excessive Fines Clause. We have, however, explained that at the time the Constitution was adopted, "the word 'fine' was understood to mean a payment to a sovereign as punishment for some offense." Browning-Ferris Industries of Vt., Inc. v. Kelco Disposal, Inc., 492 U.S. 257, 265 (1989). The Excessive Fines Clause thus "limits the government's power to extract payments, whether in cash or in kind, 'as punishment for some offense.'" Austin v. United States, 509 U.S. 602, 609-610 (1993). Forfeitures — payments in kind — are thus "fines" if they constitute punishment for an offense.

We have little trouble concluding that the forfeiture of currency ordered by § 982(a)(1) constitutes punishment. The statute directs a court to order forfeiture as an additional sanction when "imposing sentence on a person convicted of" a willful violation of § 5316's reporting requirement. The forfeiture is thus imposed at the culmination of a criminal proceeding and requires conviction of an underlying felony, and it cannot be imposed upon an innocent owner of unreported currency, but only upon a person who has himself been convicted of a § 5316 reporting violation. . . .

The Government specifically contends that the forfeiture of respondent's currency is constitutional because it involves an "instrumentality" of respondent's crime. According to the Government, the unreported cash is an instrumentality because it "does not merely facilitate a violation of law," but is "the very sine qua non of the crime." The Government reasons that "there would be no violation at all without the exportation (or attempted exportation) of the cash."

Acceptance of the Government's argument would require us to expand the traditional understanding of instrumentality forfeitures. This we decline to do. Instrumentalities historically have been treated as a form of "guilty property" that can be forfeited in civil in rem proceedings. In this case, however, the Government has sought to punish respondent by proceeding against him criminally, in personam, rather than proceeding in rem against the currency. It is therefore irrelevant whether respondent's currency is an instrumentality; the forfeiture is punitive, and the test for the excessiveness of a punitive forfeiture involves solely a proportionality determination.

Because the forfeiture of respondent's currency constitutes punishment and is thus a "fine" within the meaning of the Excessive Fines Clause, we now turn to the question of whether it is "excessive."

The touchstone of the constitutional inquiry under the Excessive Fines Clause is the principle of proportionality: The amount of the forfeiture must bear some relationship to the gravity of the offense that it is designed to punish. Until today, however, we have not articulated a standard for determining whether a punitive forfeiture is constitutionally excessive. We now hold that a punitive forfeiture violates the Excessive Fines Clause if it is grossly disproportional to the gravity of a defendant's offense.

The text and history of the Excessive Fines Clause demonstrate the centrality of proportionality to the excessiveness inquiry; nonetheless, they provide little guidance as to how disproportional a punitive forfeiture must be to the gravity of an offense in order to be "excessive." Excessive means surpassing the usual, the proper, or a normal measure of proportion. The constitutional question that we address, however, is just how proportional to a criminal offense a fine must be, and the text of the Excessive Fines Clause does not answer it.

Nor does its history. . . .

We must therefore rely on other considerations in deriving a constitutional excessiveness standard, and there are two that we find particularly relevant. The first, which we have emphasized in our cases interpreting the Cruel and Unusual Punishments Clause, is that judgments about the appropriate punishment for an offense belong in the first instance to the legislature. The second is that any judicial determination regarding the gravity of a particular criminal offense will be inherently imprecise. Both of these principles counsel against requiring strict proportionality between the amount of a punitive forfeiture and the gravity of a criminal offense, and we therefore adopt the standard of gross disproportionality articulated in our Cruel and Unusual Punishments Clause precedents. . . .

Under this standard, the forfeiture of respondent's entire $357,144 would violate the Excessive Fines Clause. Respondent's crime was solely a reporting offense. It was permissible to transport the currency out of the country so long as he reported it. Section 982(a)(1) orders currency to be forfeited for a "willful" violation of the reporting requirement. Thus, the essence of respondent's crime is a willful failure to report the removal of currency from the United States. Furthermore, as the District Court found, respondent's violation was unrelated to any other illegal activities. The money was the proceeds of legal activity and was to be used to repay a lawful debt. Whatever his other vices, respondent does not fit into the class of persons for whom the statute was principally designed: He is not a money launderer, a drug trafficker, or a tax evader.[17] And under the Sentencing Guidelines, the maximum sentence that could have been imposed on respondent was six months, while the maximum fine was $5,000. Such penalties confirm a minimal level of culpability.

The harm that respondent caused was also minimal. Failure to report his currency affected only one party, the Government, and in a relatively minor way. There was no fraud on the United States, and respondent caused no loss to the public fisc. Had his crime gone undetected, the Government would have been deprived only of the information that $357,144 had left the country. The Government and the dissent contend that there is a correlation between the amount forfeited and the harm that the Government would have suffered had the crime gone undetected. We disagree. There is no inherent proportionality in such a forfeiture. It is impossible to conclude, for example, that the harm respondent caused is anywhere near 30 times greater than that caused by a hypothetical drug dealer who willfully fails to report taking $12,000 out of the country in order to purchase drugs.

Comparing the gravity of respondent's crime with the $357,144 forfeiture the Government seeks, we conclude that such a forfeiture would be grossly disproportional to the gravity of his offense. It is larger than the $5,000 fine imposed by the District Court by many orders of magnitude, and it bears no articulable correlation to any injury suffered by the Government. . . .

For the foregoing reasons, the full forfeiture of respondent's currency would violate the Excessive Fines Clause. . . .

Justice KENNEDY, with whom THE CHIEF JUSTICE, Justice O'CONNOR, and Justice SCALIA join, dissenting.

For the first time in its history, the Court strikes down a fine as excessive under the Eighth Amendment. The decision is disturbing both for its specific holding and for the broader upheaval it foreshadows. At issue is a fine Congress fixed in the amount of the currency respondent sought to smuggle or to transport without reporting. If a fine calibrated with this accuracy fails the Court's test, its decision portends serious disruption of a vast range of statutory fines. The Court all but says the offense is not serious anyway. This disdain for the statute is wrong as an empirical matter and disrespectful of the separation of powers. . . .

---

17. Nor, contrary to the dissent's repeated assertion, is respondent a "smuggler." Respondent owed no customs duties to the Government, and it was perfectly legal for him to possess the $357,144 in cash and to remove it from the United States. His crime was simply failing to report the wholly legal act of transporting his currency.

. . . The majority suggests in rem forfeitures of the instrumentalities of crimes are not fines at all. The point of the instrumentality theory is to distinguish goods having a "close enough relationship to the offense" from those incidentally related to it. Austin v. United States, 509 U.S. 602, 628 (Scalia, J., concurring in part and concurring in judgment). From this, the Court concludes the money in a cash smuggling or non-reporting offense cannot be an instrumentality, unlike, say, a car used to transport goods concealed from taxes. There is little logic in this rationale. The car plays an important role in the offense but is not essential; one could also transport goods by jet or by foot. The link between the cash and the cash-smuggling offense is closer, as the offender must fail to report while smuggling more than $10,000. The cash is not just incidentally related to the offense of cash smuggling. It is essential, whereas the car is not. Yet the car plays an important enough role to justify forfeiture, as the majority concedes. A fortiori, the cash does as well. Even if there were a clear distinction between instrumentalities and incidental objects, when the Court invokes the distinction it gets the results backwards. . . .

The majority does not explain why respondent's knowing, willful, serious crime deserves no higher penalty than $15,000. It gives only a cursory explanation of why forfeiture of all of the money would have suffered from a gross disproportion. The majority justifies its evisceration of the fine because the money was legal to have and came from a legal source. This fact, however, shows only that the forfeiture was a fine, not that it was excessive. As the majority puts it, respondent's money was lawful to possess, was acquired in a lawful manner, and was lawful to export. It was not, however, lawful to possess the money while concealing and smuggling it. Even if one overlooks this problem, the apparent lawfulness of the money adds nothing to the argument. If the items possessed had been dangerous or unlawful to own, for instance narcotics, the forfeiture would have been remedial and would not have been a fine at all. See *Austin*, 509 U.S. at 621. If respondent had acquired the money in an unlawful manner, it would have been forfeitable as proceeds of the crime. As a rule, forfeitures of criminal proceeds serve the nonpunitive ends of making restitution to the rightful owners and of compelling the surrender of property held without right or ownership. Most forfeitures of proceeds, as a consequence, are not fines at all, let alone excessive fines. Hence, the lawfulness of the money shows at most that the forfeiture was a fine; it cannot at the same time prove that the fine was excessive.

In assessing whether there is a gross disproportion, the majority concedes, we must grant "'substantial deference'" to Congress' choice of penalties. Yet, ignoring its own command, the Court sweeps aside Congress' reasoned judgment and substitutes arguments that are little more than speculation. . . .

The crime of smuggling or failing to report cash is more serious than the Court is willing to acknowledge. The drug trade, money laundering, and tax evasion all depend in part on smuggled and unreported cash. Congress enacted the reporting requirement because secret exports of money were being used in organized crime, drug trafficking, money laundering, and other crimes. Likewise, tax evaders were using cash exports to dodge hundreds of millions of dollars in taxes owed to the Government.

The Court does not deny the importance of these interests but claims they are not implicated here because respondent managed to disprove any link to other crimes. Here, to be sure, the Government had no affirmative proof that the money was from an illegal source or for an illegal purpose. This will often be the case, however. By its very nature, money laundering is difficult to prove; for if the money launderers have done their job, the money appears to be clean. The point of the statute, which provides for even heavier penalties if a second crime can be proved, is to mandate forfeiture regardless. . . .

In my view, forfeiture of all the unreported currency is sustainable whenever a willful violation is proven. The facts of this case exemplify how hard it can be to prove ownership and other crimes, and they also show respondent is far from an innocent victim. For one thing, he was guilty of repeated lies to Government agents and suborning lies by others. Customs inspectors told respondent of his duty to report cash. He and his wife claimed they had only $15,000 with them, not the $357,144 they in fact had concealed. He then told customs inspectors a friend named Abe Ajemian had lent him about $200,000. Ajemian denied this. A month later, respondent said Saeed Faroutan had lent him $170,000. Faroutan, however, said he had not made the loan and respondent had asked him to lie. Six months later, respondent resurrected the fable of the alleged loan from Ajemian, though Ajemian had already contradicted the story. As the District Court found, respondent "has lied, and has had his friends lie." He had proffered a "suspicious and confused story, documented in the poorest way, and replete with past misrepresentation."

Respondent told these lies, moreover, in most suspicious circumstances. His luggage was stuffed with more than a third of a million dollars. All of it was in cash, and much of it was hidden in a case with a false bottom. . . .

In short, respondent was unable to give a single truthful explanation of the source of the cash. The multitude of lies and suspicious circumstances points to some form of crime. Yet, though the Government rebutted each and every fable respondent proffered, it was unable to adduce affirmative proof of another crime in this particular case.

Because of the problems of individual proof, Congress found it necessary to enact a blanket punishment. One of the few reliable warning signs of some serious crimes is the use of large sums of cash. So Congress punished all cash smuggling or non-reporting, authorizing single penalties for the offense alone and double penalties for the offense coupled with proof of other crimes. The requirement of willfulness, it judged, would be enough to protect the innocent. The majority second-guesses this judgment without explaining why Congress' blanket approach was unreasonable. . . .

Given the severity of respondent's crime, the Constitution does not forbid forfeiture of all of the smuggled or unreported cash. Congress made a considered judgment in setting the penalty, and the Court is in serious error to set it aside. . . .

Notes and Questions

1. The majority took the dissenters to task for calling Bajakajian a smuggler. The dissenters, in turn, took the majority to task for failing to appreciate the seriousness of Bajakajian's crime. Is there merit to either or both of these views? What bearing do they have on the question whether forfeiture of the entire amount is constitutionally permissible?

2. While the majority found that forfeiture of the entire amount would be grossly disproportional to the gravity of the crime, the dissenters believed that it would be precisely proportional. What might account for such disparate views? Does the majority in *Bajakajian* say what threshold amount would be proportional?

3. *Bajakajian* is the first case in which the Supreme Court struck down a fine under the Excessive Fines Clause. The dissent worried that the decision "portends serious disruption of a vast range of statutory fines." Why? What are the implications of the majority's approach?

4. The majority concluded that punitive forfeitures are subject to scrutiny as excessive fines, but that remedial forfeitures are not. When is a forfeiture remedial? Aren't all forfeitures punitive to some extent?

The majority also noted that its Eighth Amendment analysis applies in the context of civil forfeitures. When is a civil forfeiture punitive? Was the civil forfeiture in *$47,980* remedial or punitive? If it was punitive, was it excessive in light of *Bajakajian*?

5. The forfeiture in *Bajakajian* was an in personam criminal forfeiture. Criminal and civil forfeitures differ in several important respects. First, criminal forfeiture proceedings are directed toward the defendant (in personam) rather than the property (in rem). Second, criminal forfeitures are intended as punishment for the underlying crime. Third, criminal forfeitures are premised on a finding that the defendant is guilty of the crime(s) giving rise to forfeiture. Thus, unlike civil forfeitures, which are independent of criminal proceedings, criminal forfeiture determinations are part of a criminal trial.

2. Domestic Currency Transactions

CFTRA also monitors domestic currency transactions involving more than $10,000. The currency reporting requirements apply to financial institutions at which a deposit, withdrawal, currency exchange, or other physical transfer of more than $10,000 in currency occurs. "Financial institution" is a term of broad import that includes not only banks and similar institutions, but extends to registered securities brokers and dealers; currency dealers and exchangers; issuers of checks, money orders, and similar instruments; licensed carriers with annual revenues exceeding $1 million; and other similar businesses.[18]

RATZLAF v. UNITED STATES
510 U.S. 135 (1994)

Justice GINSBURG delivered the opinion of the Court. . . .

I

On the evening of October 20, 1988, defendant-petitioner Waldemar Ratzlaf ran up a debt of $160,000 playing blackjack at the High Sierra Casino in Reno, Nevada. The casino gave him one week to pay. On the due date, Ratzlaf returned to the casino with cash of $100,000 in hand. A casino official informed Ratzlaf that all transactions involving more than $10,000 in cash had to be reported to state and federal authorities. The official added that the casino could accept a cashier's check for the full amount due without triggering any reporting requirement. The casino helpfully

---

18. 31 U.S.C. § 5312(a)(2) (formerly codified at 31 U.S.C. § 1052(e)); 31 C.F.R. § 103.11.

placed a limousine at Ratzlaf's disposal, and assigned an employee to accompany him to banks in the vicinity. Informed that banks, too, are required to report cash transactions in excess of $10,000, Ratzlaf purchased cashier's checks, each for less than $10,000 and each from a different bank. He delivered these checks to the High Sierra Casino.

Based on this endeavor, Ratzlaf was charged with "structuring transactions" to evade the banks' obligation to report cash transactions exceeding $10,000; this conduct, the indictment alleged, violated 31 U.S.C. §§ 5322(a) and 5324(3). The trial judge instructed the jury that the Government had to prove defendant's knowledge of the banks' reporting obligation and his attempt to evade that obligation, but did not have to prove defendant knew the structuring was unlawful. Ratzlaf was convicted, fined, and sentenced to prison.[19] Ratzlaf maintained on appeal that he could not be convicted of "willfully violating" the antistructuring law solely on the basis of his knowledge that a financial institution must report currency transactions in excess of $10,000 and his intention to avoid such reporting. To gain a conviction for "willful" conduct, he asserted, the Government must prove he was aware of the illegality of the "structuring" in which he engaged. The Ninth Circuit upheld the trial court's construction of the legislation and affirmed Ratzlaf's conviction. We granted certiorari, and now conclude that, to give effect to the statutory "willfulness" specification, the Government had to prove Ratzlaf knew the structuring he undertook was unlawful. We therefore reverse the judgment of the Court of Appeals.

II

A

Congress enacted the Currency and Foreign Transactions Reporting Act in response to increasing use of banks and other institutions as financial intermediaries by persons engaged in criminal activity. The Act imposes a variety of reporting requirements on individuals and institutions regarding foreign and domestic financial transactions. The reporting requirement relevant here, 31 U.S.C. § 5313(a), applies to domestic financial transactions. Section 5313(a) reads:

> When a domestic financial institution is involved in a transaction for the payment, receipt, or transfer of United States coins or currency (or other monetary instruments the Secretary of the Treasury prescribes), in an amount, denomination, or amount and denomination, or under circumstances the Secretary prescribes by regulation, the institution and any other participant in the transaction the Secretary may prescribe shall file a report on the transaction at the time and in the way the Secretary prescribes. . . .[20]

---

19. Ratzlaf's wife and the casino employee who escorted Ratzlaf to area banks were codefendants. For convenience, we refer only to Waldemar Ratzlaf in this opinion.

20. By regulation, the Secretary ordered reporting of "transactions in currency of more than $10,000." 31 C.F.R. § 103.22(a) (1993). Although the Secretary could have imposed a report-filing requirement on "any . . . participant in the transaction," 31 U.S.C. § 5313(a), the Secretary chose to require reporting by the financial institution but not by the customer. 31 C.F.R. § 103.22(a) (1993).

To deter circumvention of this reporting requirement, Congress enacted an anti-structuring provision, 31 U.S.C. § 5324, as part of the Money Laundering Control Act of 1986. Section 5324,[21] which Ratzlaf is charged with "willfully violating," reads:

> No person shall for the purpose of evading the reporting requirements of section 5313(a) with respect to such transaction — . . .
>   (3) structure or assist in structuring, or attempt to structure or assist in structuring, any transaction with one or more domestic financial institutions.

The criminal enforcement provision at issue, 31 U.S.C. § 5322(a), sets out penalties for "[a] person willfully violating," inter alia, the antistructuring provision. Section 5322(a) reads:

> A person willfully violating this subchapter or a regulation prescribed under this subchapter (except section 5315 of this title or a regulation prescribed under section 5315) shall be fined not more than $250,000, or imprisoned for not more than five years, or both.

B

Section 5324 forbids structuring transactions with a "purpose of evading the reporting requirements of section 5313(a)." Ratzlaf admits that he structured cash transactions, and that he did so with knowledge of, and a purpose to avoid, the banks' duty to report currency transactions in excess of $10,000. The statutory formulation under which Ratzlaf was prosecuted, however, calls for proof of "willfulness" on the actor's part. The trial judge in Ratzlaf's case, with the Ninth Circuit's approbation, treated § 5322(a)'s "willfulness" requirement essentially as surplusage — as words of no consequence. Judges should hesitate so to treat statutory terms in any setting, and resistance should be heightened when the words describe an element of a criminal offense.

"Willful," this Court has recognized, is a "word of many meanings," and "its construction [is] often . . . influenced by its context." Spies v. United States, 317 U.S. 492, 497 (1943). Accordingly, we view §§ 5322(a) and 5324(3) mindful of the complex of provisions in which they are embedded. In this light, we count it significant that § 5322(a)'s omnibus "willfulness" requirement, when applied to other provisions in the same sub-chapter, consistently has been read by the Courts of Appeals to require both "knowledge of the reporting requirement" and a "specific intent to commit the crime," i.e., "a purpose to disobey the law." See United States v. Bank of New England, N.A., 821 F.2d 844, 854-859 (CA1 1987); United States v. Eisenstein, 731 F.2d 1540, 1543 (CA11 1984).

Notable in this regard are 31 U.S.C. § 5314, concerning records and reports on monetary transactions with foreign financial agencies, and § 5316, concerning declaration of the transportation of more than $10,000 into, or out of, the United States. Decisions involving these provisions describe a "willful" actor as one who violates "a known legal duty." See, e.g., United States v. Sturman, 951 F.2d 1466, 1476-1477 (CA6 1991);

---

21. Subsequent to Ratzlaf's conviction, Congress recodified § 5324(1)-(3) as § 5324(a)(1)-(3), without substantive change. In addition, Congress added subsection (b) to replicate the prohibitions of subsection (a) in the context of international currency transactions. For simplicity, we refer to the codification in effect at the time the Court of Appeals decided this case.

United States v. Warren, 612 F.2d 887, 890 (CA5 1980); United States v. Dichne, 612 F.2d 632, 636 (CA2 1979); United States v. Granda, 565 F.2d 922, 924-926 (CA5 1978).

A term appearing in several places in a statutory text is generally read the same way each time it appears. We have even stronger cause to construe a single formulation, here § 5322(a), the same way each time it is called into play.

The United States urges, however, that § 5324 violators, by their very conduct, exhibit a purpose to do wrong, which suffices to show "willfulness":

> On occasion, criminal statutes — including some requiring proof of "willfulness" — have been understood to require proof of an intentional violation of a known legal duty, i.e., specific knowledge by the defendant that his conduct is unlawful. But where that construction has been adopted, it has been invoked only to ensure that the defendant acted with a wrongful purpose. See Liparota v. United States, 471 U.S. 419, 426 (1985).
>
> The anti-structuring statute, 31 U.S.C. § 5324, satisfies the "bad purpose" component of willfulness by explicitly defining the wrongful purpose necessary to violate the law: it requires proof that the defendant acted with the purpose to evade the reporting requirement of Section 5313(a). Brief for United States 23-25.

"'[S]tructuring is not the kind of activity that an ordinary person would engage in innocently,'" the United States asserts. It is therefore "reasonable," the Government concludes, "to hold a structurer responsible for evading the reporting requirements without the need to prove specific knowledge that such evasion is unlawful."

Undoubtedly there are bad men who attempt to elude official reporting requirements in order to hide from Government inspectors such criminal activity as laundering drug money or tax evasion. But currency structuring is not inevitably nefarious. Consider, for example, the small business operator who knows that reports filed under 31 U.S.C. § 5313(a) are available to the Internal Revenue Service. To reduce the risk of an IRS audit, she brings $9,500 in cash to the bank twice each week, in lieu of transporting over $10,000 once each week. That person, if the United States is right, has committed a criminal offense, because she structured cash transactions "for the specific purpose of depriving the Government of the information that Section 5313(a) is designed to obtain." Nor is a person who structures a currency transaction invariably motivated by a desire to keep the Government in the dark. But under the Government's construction an individual would commit a felony against the United States by making cash deposits in small doses, fearful that the bank's reports would increase the likelihood of burglary,[22] or in an endeavor to keep a former spouse unaware of his wealth.[23]

Courts have noted "many occasions" on which persons, without violating any law, may structure transactions "in order to avoid the impact of some regulation or tax."

---

22. See United States v. Dollar Bank Money Market Account No. 1591768456, 980 F.2d 233, 241 (CA3 1992) (forfeiture action under 18 U.S.C. § 981(a)(1)(A) [involving a cash gift deposited by the donee in several steps to avoid bank's reporting requirement]; court overturned grant of summary judgment in Government's favor, noting that jury could believe donee's "legitimate explanations for organizing his deposits in amounts under $10,000," including respect for donor's privacy and fear that information regarding the donor — an "eccentric old woman [who] hid hundreds of thousands of dollars in her house" — might lead to burglary attempts).

23. See Aversa, 984 F.2d, at 495 (real estate partners feared that "paper trail" from currency transaction reports would obviate efforts to hide existence of cash from spouse of one of the partners).

United States v. Aversa, 762 F. Supp. 441, 446 (NH 1991), aff'd in part, 984 F.2d 493 (CA1 1993). . . .

In current days, as an amicus noted, countless taxpayers each year give a gift of $10,000 on December 31 and an identical gift the next day, thereby legitimately avoiding the taxable gifts reporting required by 26 U.S.C. § 2503(b).

In light of these examples, we are unpersuaded by the argument that structuring is so obviously "evil" or inherently "bad" that the "willfulness" requirement is satisfied irrespective of the defendant's knowledge of the illegality of structuring. Had Congress wished to dispense with the requirement, it could have furnished the appropriate instruction.

C

In § 5322, Congress subjected to criminal penalties only those "willfully violating" § 5324, signaling its intent to require for conviction proof that the defendant knew not only of the bank's duty to report cash transactions in excess of $10,000, but also of his duty not to avoid triggering such a report. There are, we recognize, contrary indications in the statute's legislative history. But we do not resort to legislative history to cloud a statutory text that is clear. . . .

We do not dishonor the venerable principle that ignorance of the law generally is no defense to a criminal charge. In particular contexts, however, Congress may decree otherwise. That, we hold, is what Congress has done with respect to 31 U.S.C. § 5322(a) and the provisions it controls. To convict Ratzlaf of the crime with which he was charged, the jury had to find he knew the structuring in which he engaged was unlawful.[24] Because the jury was not properly instructed in this regard, we reverse the judgment of the Ninth Circuit and remand this case for further proceedings consistent with this opinion.

It is so ordered.

Justice BLACKMUN, with whom THE CHIEF JUSTICE, Justice O'CONNOR, and Justice THOMAS join, dissenting. . . .

I

"The general rule that ignorance of the law or a mistake of law is no defense to criminal prosecution is deeply rooted in the American legal system." Cheek v. United States, 498 U.S. 192, 199 (1991). The Court has applied this common-law rule "in numerous cases construing criminal statutes." Ibid.

Thus, the term "willfully" in criminal law generally "refers to consciousness of the act but not to consciousness that the act is unlawful." *Cheek*, 498 U.S., at 209 (Scalia, J., concurring in judgment). . . .

---

24. The dissent asserts that our holding "largely nullifies the effect" of § 5324 by "making prosecution for structuring difficult or impossible in most cases." Even under the dissent's reading of the statute, proof that the defendant knew of the bank's duty to report is required for conviction; we fail to see why proof that the defendant knew of his duty to refrain from structuring is so qualitatively different that it renders prosecution "impossible." . . .

Unlike other provisions of the subchapter, the antistructuring provision identifies the purpose that is required for a § 5324 violation: "evading the reporting requirements." The offense of structuring, therefore, requires (1) knowledge of a financial institution's reporting requirements, and (2) the structuring of a transaction for the purpose of evading those requirements. These elements define a violation that is "willful" as that term is commonly interpreted. The majority's additional requirement that an actor have actual knowledge that structuring is prohibited strays from the statutory text, as well as from our precedents interpreting criminal statutes generally and "willfulness" in particular. . . .

The majority . . . contends that § 5322(a)'s willfulness element, when applied to the subchapter's other provisions, has been read by the courts of appeals to require knowledge of and a purpose to disobey the law. In fact, the cases to which the majority refers stand for the more subtle proposition that a willful violation requires knowledge of the pertinent reporting requirements and a purpose to avoid compliance with them. Consistent with and in light of that construction, Congress' 1986 enactment prohibited structuring "for the purpose of evading the reporting requirements." The level of knowledge imposed by the term "willfully" as it applies to all the underlying offenses in the subchapter on reporting requirements is "knowledge of the reporting requirements."

The Court next concludes that its interpretation of "willfully" is warranted because structuring is not inherently "nefarious." It is true that the Court, on occasion, has imposed a knowledge-of-illegality requirement upon criminal statutes to ensure that the defendant acted with a wrongful purpose. See, e.g., Liparota v. United States, 471 U.S. 419, 426 (1985). I cannot agree, however, that the imposition of such a requirement is necessary here. First, the conduct at issue — splitting up transactions involving tens of thousands of dollars in cash for the specific purpose of circumventing a bank's reporting duty — is hardly the sort of innocuous activity involved in cases such as Liparota, in which the defendant had been convicted of fraud for purchasing food stamps for less than their face value. Further, an individual convicted of structuring is, by definition, aware that cash transactions are regulated, and he cannot seriously argue that he lacked notice of the law's intrusion into the particular sphere of activity. By requiring knowledge of a bank's reporting requirements as well as a "purpose of evading" those requirements, the antistructuring provision targets those who knowingly act to deprive the Government of information to which it is entitled. In my view, that is not so plainly innocent a purpose as to justify reading into the statute the additional element of knowledge of illegality.[25] In any event, Congress has determined that purposefully structuring transactions is not innocent conduct.

---

25. The question is not whether structuring is "so obviously 'evil' or inherently 'bad' that the 'willfulness' requirement is satisfied irrespective of the defendant's knowledge of the illegality of structuring." The general rule is that "willfulness" does not require knowledge of illegality; the inquiry under exceptional cases such as Liparota is whether the statute criminalizes "a broad range of apparently innocent conduct," 471 U.S., at 426, such that it requires no element of wrongfulness.

The majority expresses concern about the potential application of the antistructuring law to a business operator who deposits cash twice each week to reduce the risk of an IRS audit. First, it is not at all clear that the statute would apply in this situation. If a person has legitimate business reasons for conducting frequent cash transactions, or if the transactions genuinely can be characterized as separate, rather than artificially structured, then the person is not engaged in "structuring" for the purpose of "evasion." See United States v. Brown, 954 F.2d, at 1571; S. Rep. No. 99-433, p. 22 (1986). Even if application of § 5324 were theoretically possible in this extreme situation, the example would not establish prohibition of a

In interpreting federal criminal tax statutes, this Court has defined the term "willfully" as requiring the "voluntary, intentional violation of a known legal duty." *Cheek* v. *United States*, 498 U.S., at 200. Our rule in the tax area, however, is an "exception to the traditional rule," applied "largely due to the complexity of the tax laws." *Cheek*, 498 U.S., at 200. The rule is inapplicable here, where, far from being complex, the provisions involved are perhaps among the simplest in the United States Code.

II . . .

The majority's interpretation of the antistructuring provision is at odds with the statutory text, the intent of Congress, and the fundamental principle that knowledge of illegality is not required for a criminal act. Now Congress must try again to fill a hole it rightly felt it had filled before. I dissent.

Notes and Questions

1. Would a properly instructed jury be likely to find Ratzlaf guilty under these facts? What evidence is relevant to knowledge of illegality?

2. Is the majority equating "specific intent" with "knowledge of illegality"? Is it possible to intend to evade reporting requirements without knowing that the means used to do so are illegal? What is the difference between evasion and avoidance in this context?

3. The Court in *Ratzlaf* cited *Cheek* for the premise that as a general matter, ignorance of the law is no excuse. *Cheek*, of course, went on to hold that a good-faith misunderstanding of the law, no matter how unreasonable, negates a finding of willfulness in a criminal tax prosecution. Is the *Ratzlaf* Court suggesting this rule should also apply in the context of currency reporting violations? If so, would such a rule be justified?[26]

4. Recall that willfulness has a special meaning in the context of tax crimes — a voluntary, intentional violation of a known legal duty — because of the complexity of the tax laws. Is it important that the majority opinion in *Ratzlaf* states that in deciding what willfulness means in the context of criminal CFTRA violations, the complexity of the CFTRA's provisions must be kept in mind? The *Ratzlaf* dissent categorically states that "far from being complex, the provisions involved here are perhaps among the simplest in the United States Code."

5. Does the *Ratzlaf* majority make a persuasive case for the premise that currency structuring is not inherently nefarious?

6. Less than a year after the Court decided *Ratzlaff*, Congress amended the antistructuring statute to include its own penalty provision and to make it clear that the only culpable mental state required is the purpose to avoid the reporting requirements.[27]

7. Courts in some cases cite the defendant's status as a stockbroker, lawyer, or bank employee as a factor that may support an inference of knowledge that it is illegal to

---

"broad range of apparently innocent conduct" as in *Liparota*, and it would not justify reading into the statute a knowledge-of-illegality requirement.

26. Cf. *United States v. Aversa*, 984 F.2d 493 (1st Cir. 1993).

27. See 31 U.S.C. § 5324(c).

structure or assist others in structuring currency transactions. Does that lead to liability based on what the defendant should have known as opposed to what he actually knew?

3. Enhanced Penalties

Willful violations of the currency reporting requirements are punishable as felonies.[28] The authorized maximum penalties are doubled for willful violations that occur while the actor is "violating another law of the United States" and for violations that are "a part of a pattern of any illegal activity involving more than $100,000 in a 12-month period."[29]

UNITED STATES v. ST. MICHAEL'S CREDIT UNION
880 F.2d 579 (1st Cir. 1989)

BOWNES, Circuit Judge.

This case arises out of the alleged illegal activities of St. Michael's Credit Union and one of its employees, Janice Sacharczyk. St. Michael's was convicted of failing to file Currency Transaction Reports with the Internal Revenue Service on thirty-nine occasions during the period from September, 1983 to September, 1984 in violation of the Currency Transactions Reporting Act. Sacharczyk was convicted of knowingly and willfully aiding and abetting St. Michael's failure to file. These omissions formed the basis for additional convictions of both defendants for concealing, by trick, scheme and device, material facts from the IRS under 18 U.S.C. § 1001. Defendants appeal their convictions. . . .

II. FACTS

St. Michael's was a small financial institution that catered to the people who lived in and around Lynn, Massachusetts. A great deal of its operation was devoted to serving the needs of the ethnic Polish community in Lynn. The organization and management of St. Michael's was, by all accounts, unprofessional and deficient. Due in part to this mismanagement, it was taken over by Massachusetts Share Insurance Corporation in September, 1984.

Janice Sacharczyk was employed at the credit union and served as its bookkeeper, computer operator, clerk, and treasurer. On December 13, 1983, she resigned her position as treasurer but continued to work at the credit union until September 6, 1984, despite bearing a child in the spring of 1984. Her main responsibility at the credit union was "to prove" its books to ensure that all of the money that went in or out was accounted for in the records. She also ran the computers and accessed information contained therein for others. Occasionally, she approved checks and obtained more money for tellers who had used up their initial allotment of cash.

---

28. 31 U.S.C. § 5322(a) (authorizing a maximum fine of $250,000 and/or term of imprisonment of up to 5 years). The statute originally classified willful violations as misdemeanors.

29. 31 U.S.C. § 5322(b) (authorizing a maximum fine of $500,000 and/or term of imprisonment of up to 10 years).

For eight weeks between September and November 1983, St. Michael's was audited by John DiPerna, the Banking Examiner for the Credit Union Division of the Banking Commission of Massachusetts. DiPerna testified at trial that the audit was to "evaluate the assets and ascertain that all the liabilities in the institution[] are shown on the balance sheet" and to ensure the institution's compliance with state and federal laws and regulations.

During the audit, a member of DiPerna's staff discovered that on two occasions, St. Michael's had failed to file CTRs with the IRS. Although the law requiring the filing of CTRs had been passed in the 1970's, it was only in 1982 or 1983 that DiPerna was instructed by the federal government to enforce the law's provisions against state institutions. DiPerna met with Sacharczyk to discuss the CTRs. He told her that CTRs must be filled out and filed with the IRS whenever there are withdrawals or deposits of currency exceeding $10,000. DiPerna testified that "it was evident that they [defendants] were unaware of the law. . . ." As was his custom at the time, DiPerna told Sacharczyk that if St. Michael's filed the CTRs for the two transactions, he would not report the omissions as violations. He also gave Sacharczyk an outdated and incomplete copy of the regulations that govern CTRs. Omitted from the regulations were the sections that dealt with civil and criminal penalties for the failure to file. DiPerna left the credit union telling "them to start keeping track of currency transactions over $10,000."

In February, 1984, DiPerna returned to St. Michael's for a "bring-up exam." At that time, Sacharczyk showed him xerox copies (showing only the fronts) of the CTRs he had told her to file with the IRS (the French and Perry CTRs). She stated that they had been sent to the IRS and, therefore, DiPerna did not mention them in his audit report. These CTR forms detailed both the reasons for requiring CTRs and the civil and criminal penalties for failing to file.

Contrary to the averment of Sacharczyk that the CTRs were sent to the IRS, Yvonne Covington, the IRS official in charge of keeping records on CTR filings, testified that no CTRs were filed by St. Michael's between September 1983 and October 1984. . . .

In September, 1984, agents of the IRs' Financial Task Force began an investigation of St. Michael's. Special Agent DeAngelis questioned Sacharczyk concerning her knowledge of CTRs. She stated that DiPerna had discussed them with her and that she had filed CTRs for the two currency transactions that DiPerna had brought to her attention. She then searched the basement and produced xeroxed copies of the CTRs she claimed to have sent to the IRS. Sacharczyk told the agents that St. Michael's had no official policy regarding CTRs. When the agents asked her whether there was a CTR compliance officer at St. Michael's, she responded "no." When asked whose responsibility it would be to file CTRs, she stated that either the Manager, Barbara Szczawinski, or herself would be responsible.

The Task Force investigation of St. Michael's uncovered a number of $10,000 transactions for which no CTRs had been filed. These formed the basis for the indictment in this case. . . . Sacharczyk and St. Michael's were convicted on thirty-nine counts of felonious failure to file CTRs and on one count of concealing material facts from the IRS. . . .

III. The Currency Transactions Reporting Act Convictions...

B. A "Pattern of Illegal Activity"

The Currency Transactions Reporting Act defines both felony and misdemeanor offenses for knowing and willful failures to file CTRs. The felony provisions are implicated when:

> A person willfully violat[es] this subchapter or a regulation prescribed under this subchapter (except section 5315 of this title or a regulation prescribed under section 5315), while violating another law of the United States or as part of a pattern of illegal activity involving transactions of more than $100,000 in a 12-month period. . . .

31 U.S.C. § 5322(b). In the case at bar, the government charged the defendants with felonious violations, alleging that the acts named in the indictment constituted a "pattern of illegal activity involving transactions of more than $100,000 in a 12-month period." The trial judge instructed the jury that it could find there was a pattern of illegal activity if it determined "beyond a reasonable doubt that there were repeated and related violations" of the Act. The defendants argue that the government has failed to produce any evidence that could support a finding that the transactions named in the indictment formed a "pattern of illegal activity." We cannot agree.

In United States v. Bank of New England, N.A., 821 F.2d 844 (1st Cir. 1987), we dealt with the issue of what constitutes a "pattern of illegal activity" under 31 U.S.C. § 5322(b). We affirmed the felony convictions of the Bank for failing to file CTRs for thirty-one currency transactions, each involving the same individual customer and the same form of currency transfer. In interpreting the meaning of the phrase "pattern of illegal activity," we examined the limited case law on point. We concluded that to form a pattern under the Act, the transactions must be "repeated *and* related." *Bank of New England*, 821 F.2d at 853. Although the trial judge in that case had charged the jury that a pattern could be established by proving repeated violations, she did not instruct that the transactions also must be related. We found that did not constitute plain error because:

> Under the evidence adduced, it was clear that the repeated failures by the Bank to report were directly related to the withdrawals by McDonough [the individual customer]. These failures were not isolated events; they entailed repeated failures to file CTRs on similar transactions by the same customer. The similarity of the transactions, coupled with the frequency and regularity of their repetition, establish a related scheme.

Id.

Sacharczyk and St. Michael's argue mightily that here, unlike in *Bank of New England*, there is absolutely no evidence that would link the currency transfers named in the indictment to one another. They stress that the indictment charged fifty different violations of the Act involving twenty-five different customers. They point out that the transactions named in the indictment consisted of differing forms of currency transfers: cash withdrawals, cash deposits, purchases of Treasurer's checks, loan proceeds, and the cashing of third-party checks. Absent evidence of some relation among these transactions, Sacharczyk and St. Michael's contend that they are simply repeated, "isolated events," which are prosecutable only under the misdemeanor provision of the Act.[30] Although this is a plausible reading of the "repeated and related" standard set forth in *Bank of New England*, we believe it proves too much and refuse to read that standard so narrowly.

At the outset, we reaffirm that to establish a pattern of illegal activity under the Act, the government must prove that the transactions involved were both repeated and related to one another. In the normal prosecution under 31 U.S.C. § 5322(b), a financial institution is indicted for failing to file CTRs for a limited number of transactions; the institution has filed CTRs for certain transfers while failing to file them for others. To prove a pattern of illegal activity in such a case, the government must establish an underlying relationship or linkage among the unreported transactions. To do this it might prove, inter alia, a common feature among the customers involved, the forms of transfers of currency, and/or the purposes for which the funds were used.

In a case like the one at bar, however, where a financial institution has systematically failed to file any CTRs, the above approach is inapt. While a relationship must still be established, it may be proven without linking the underlying transactions. The necessary connection can be shown by proving that the financial institution chronically and consistently failed to file any CTRs. By showing a consistent failure to report, the government has proven an overall relationship among the transactions. There is a pattern of not reporting.

The language of the statute and its legislative history support this interpretation. 31 U.S.C. § 5311 declares that the purpose of the statute is "to require certain reports or records where they have a high degree of usefulness in criminal, tax, or regulatory investigations or proceedings." We agree with the Second Circuit that, in passing this legislation

> Congress was largely concerned with the fact that the relative freedom accorded domestic and foreign currency transactions by American law in combination with the secrecy accorded currency transactions by certain foreign nations facilitated major criminal schemes, such as the laundering of money earned in criminal enterprises, the evasion of income taxes by gambling establishments, and the perpetuation of multinational securities frauds. In selecting among remedies, Congress rejected substantive restrictions on monetary or currency transactions but instead provided for a system of compulsory record-keeping and reporting designed to diminish the advantages accorded such illegal activities by existing domestic and foreign law.

Dickinson, 706 F.2d at 91-92. "Congress evidently believed that to effectively fight petty criminals, members of the underworld, white collar criminals, and income tax evaders it was necessary for financial institutions to maintain adequate records." United States v. Kattan-Kassin, 696 F.2d 893, 896 (11th Cir. 1983).

When the government proves that a financial institution has willfully failed to file CTRs for any of its reportable transactions or that it has filed for only a few out of a vast number of its reportable transactions, a sufficient relationship has been established between those acts to constitute a pattern of illegal activity and thereby trigger the Act's

---

30. The court's reference to "the misdemeanor provision of the Act" is to the basic penalty provision, § 5322(a), which imposes criminal punishment for willful violations. Although willful violations were originally classified as misdemeanors, the statute has since been amended to make them felonies. — ED.

felony provision. Congress placed the responsibility for filing CTRs on the financial institutions. It is incongruous to believe that Congress intended that a financial institution could insulate itself from felony prosecution by showing that it had not filed CTRs for any of its reportable transactions. Such a systemic disregard of the Act's reporting requirements is an open invitation to money launderers and other criminals to use the financial institution for hiding their ill-gotten gains. . . .

We hold that under the standards outlined above, there was sufficient evidence for the jury to have found that St. Michael's failure to file any CTRs comprised "a pattern of illegal activity." . . .

Notes and Questions

1. In *St. Michael's Credit Union*, the pattern of illegal activity consisted of a series of currency reporting violations. Should the statute be construed to require a pattern of independent illegal activity?

2. The defendants were found guilty of violating the currency reporting requirements as part of a "pattern" of illegal activity. In contrast with the transactions in *Bank of New England*, which all involved cash withdrawals by the same customer using the same modus operandi, the transactions in *St. Michael's Credit Union* included five different forms of currency transactions conducted with 25 different customers. What is required to establish a pattern under the Bank Secrecy Act? How do the transactions in this case satisfy the pattern element? Is the pattern element in the Bank Secrecy Act comparable to the pattern element found in RICO?

3. The defendants were convicted of 39 counts of failure to file currency reports. Did Congress intend to subject them to enhanced penalties for each individual failure to file? Or is the statute intended to punish the pattern of illegal activity itself? What rationale would support subjecting each failure to report to enhanced punishment?

4. Suppose the only transaction in question was a single customer's deposit of $15,000 cash and that Sacharczyk embezzled it for her personal use. If she failed to file a CTR reporting the customer's deposit, what penalties should she be subject to and why?

B. SECTION 6050I

Section 6050I of the Internal Revenue Code contains a currency reporting requirement similar to CFTRA's. Section 6050I requires any person who is engaged in a trade or business to report the receipt of more than $10,000 in cash in one or more related transactions in the course of the trade or business.[31] The term "transaction" (i.e., the underlying event that generates the cash) includes sales, rentals, cash exchanges, custodial arrangements, payments of loans and debts (including attorneys' fees), and conversion of cash into negotiable instruments.[32] A transaction is reportable if any part of

---

31. Some financial institutions are exempt from the reporting requirement. See 31 U.S.C. § 5312(a)(2)(A)-(G),(J),(R), and (S).

32. The regulations are codified at 26 C.F.R. § 1.6050I-1.

it occurs in the United States. Like CFTRA, § 6050I forbids structuring transactions for the purpose of avoiding the reporting requirements.

A businessperson who receives more than $10,000 in cash in a reportable transaction must file an IRS Form 8300, which requires the name, address, occupation, and Social Security number of the payor, the date and nature of the transaction, and the amount involved.

Willful violation of § 6050I is a felony.[33]

1. Attorney-Client Privilege

UNITED STATES v. GOLDBERGER & DUBIN, P.C.
935 F.2d 501 (2d Cir. 1991)

VAN GRAAFEILAND, Circuit Judge.

Attorneys Ronald P. Fischetti, Mark F. Pomerantz, Paul A. Goldberger, Lawrence A. Dubin, the law firms of Fischetti, Pomerantz & Russo and Goldberger & Dubin, P.C., and intervenors John Doe No. 1 and John Doe No. 2 appeal from orders of the United States District Court for the Southern District of New York (Broderick, J.) requiring the attorneys and their firms to provide the Internal Revenue Service, pursuant to 26 U.S.C. § 6050-I,[34] with the names of clients who paid them cash fees in excess of $10,000. We affirm.

Internal Revenue Code section 6050-I requires "[a]ny person . . . engaged in a trade or business, and who, in the course of such trade or business, receives more than $10,000 in cash in 1 transaction (or 2 or more related transactions)" to file a return specified as Form 8300. When completed, a Form 8300 contains the cash payor's name and other identifying information. During 1986 and 1987, Fischetti, Pomerantz & Russo received cash fees in excess of $10,000 from two individuals identified in this proceeding as John Doe No. 1 and John Doe No. 2. Both payors retained the Fischetti firm to represent them in connection with criminal indictments; both were advised of section 6050-I's reporting requirements, and both requested their attorneys not to disclose their identities as payors. Goldberger and Dubin, P.C. similarly received cash fees in excess of $10,000 from, or on behalf of, each of three individuals, but none of these three has intervened.

Respondents filed a Form 8300 disclosing the cash fee payment in each case but did not identify the payor. Following an unproductive exchange of correspondence with respondents, the IRS issued summonses directing them to appear and produce information identifying the payors. Upon respondents' refusal to comply, the government petitioned the district court for enforcement of the summonses. John Doe No. 1 and John Doe No. 2 were granted leave to intervene in the summons enforcement proceedings. In a bench ruling after oral argument, the district court held that respondents must comply with the IRS summonses and provide the payor information.

---

33. 26 U.S.C. § 7203.

34. The official section number is 6050I. However, because this has the appearance of a 5-digit number, we have inserted a hyphen to avoid confusing those readers who are otherwise unfamiliar with the section.

Financial-reporting legislation plays an important role in the economic life of our country. Prominent among statutes of this nature are those that require reports of substantial currency transactions. See, e.g., the Bank Secrecy or Currency and Foreign Transactions Reporting Act of 1970 (the Bank Secrecy Act) and the Trading with the Enemy Act, both of which have survived constitutional challenges.

The record-keeping and reporting provisions of the Bank Secrecy Act were based upon congressional findings that they "have a high degree of usefulness in criminal, tax, and regulatory investigations or proceedings."

Congress incorporated section 6050-I(a) in the Tax Reform Act of 1984 in an additional effort to unearth the "underground economy." In section 6050-I(a)(1), Congress expanded the reporting requirements for cash transactions in excess of $10,000 to apply to "[a]ny person who is engaged in a trade or business." Extensive lobbying efforts to exempt attorneys from the reach of this amendment were unsuccessful. Appellants now seek to secure from the judiciary what their lobbyists were unable to get from Congress.

Appellants' allegations of unconstitutionality merit only brief discussion. Their contentions relative to the Fourth and Fifth Amendments have been rejected consistently in cases under the Bank Secrecy Act by both the Supreme Court and this court. The reporting requirements of the 1984 Tax Reform Act, like those of the Bank Secrecy Act, target transactions without regard to the purposes underlying them and do not require reporting of information that necessarily would be criminal.

Respondents' principal constitutional argument, that section 6050-I deprives them of their Sixth Amendment right to counsel, is equally without merit. . . .

Section 6050-I stops far short of the forfeiture statutes that were at issue in Caplin & Drysdale, Chartered v. United States, 491 U.S. 617 (1989) and United States v. Monsanto, 491 U.S. 600 (1989), in which the preclusion of the defendants from using seized assets to pay their attorneys was held not to violate the Sixth Amendment. Section 6050-I does not preclude would-be clients from using their own funds to hire whomever they choose. To avoid disclosure under section 6050-I, they need only pay counsel in some other manner than with cash. The choice is theirs. None of the appellants has advanced a legitimate reason why payment other than in cash cannot be made. Statements such as "[s]ome clients may not have non-cash assets" are somewhat less than persuasive. Equally unpersuasive is the argument that a would-be client might elect to take his business to an unscrupulous lawyer who would ignore the reporting requirements of section 6050-I.

Although the unscrupulous lawyer might not be the client's first choice, the Sixth Amendment does not guarantee the client the right to his first choice. In Morris v. Slappy, 461 U.S. 1, 13-14 (1983), the Court rejected the claim that the Sixth Amendment guarantees a "meaningful relationship between an accused and his counsel."

In sum, we hold that section 6050-I passes constitutional muster. Appellants' contention that section 6050-I conflicts with the traditional doctrine of attorney-client privilege also is without merit. . . . The doctrine protects only those disclosures that are necessary to obtain informed legal advice and that would not be made without the privilege. The privilege cannot stand in the face of countervailing law or strong public policy and should be strictly confined within the narrowest possible limits underlying its purpose. Advice given in connection with an ongoing or proposed illegality or fraud does not qualify for the privilege. The privilege against disclosure belongs to the client, not to the attorney.

Application of the foregoing principles in the instant case makes it clear that, absent special circumstances, concerning which there is no evidence whatever herein, the identification in Form 8300 of respondents' clients who make substantial cash fee payments is not a disclosure of privileged information. In both In re John Doe, 781 F.2d at 248 and In re Shargel, 742 F.2d at 63 & 64 n.6, we held that the disclosure of fee information and client identity is not privileged even though it might incriminate the client. That asserted possibility does not constitute a "special circumstance" warranting a claim of privilege. This case readily is distinguishable from cases such as Marchetti v. United States, 390 U.S. 39, 48-49 (1968) (the gambler's registration case), in which the "direct and unmistakable consequence" of the disclosure requirements was the incrimination of the person making the disclosure. No such "direct linkage" is apparent in section 6050-I.

When members of the Fischetti firm returned the incomplete 8300 Forms to the IRS, they included notes indicating that disclosure of the client information "would violate NYCPLR § 4503" which codifies the attorney-client privilege law of New York. They erred twice in so doing. In the first place, in actions such as the instant one, which involve violations of federal law, it is the federal common law of privilege that applies. Secondly, even if New York State law were to be applied, a communication to an attorney would not be considered confidential unless it was made in the process of obtaining legal advice; and fee arrangements between attorney and client do not satisfy this requirement in the usual case. Matter of Priest v. Hennessy, 409 N.E.2d 983 (N.Y. 1980). Moreover, said the *Priest* court, "even where the technical requirements of the privilege are satisfied, it may, nonetheless, yield in a proper case, where strong public policy requires disclosure." That surely should be the case where, as here, the attorney-client privilege doctrine collides head on with a federal statute that implicitly precludes its application.

The importance of client identification as a means of uncovering tax evasion is apparent from the briefs of appellants' amici, which state that "the wholesale enforcement of attorney 8300 Forms would require thousands of attorneys each year to provide client-information to the government" (Association of the Bar of the City of New York Committee on Criminal Advocacy at 7) and "threatens profoundly to affect the adversarial system of justice in the United States" (American Bar Association at 6). In its "General Explanation of the Revenue Provisions of the Deficit Reduction Act of 1984," the Staff of the Joint Committee on Taxation, 98th Cong., 2d Sess., stated:

> Congress was concerned that approximately 80 percent of the revenue lost through non-compliance is attributable to the underreporting of income. For 1981, the Internal Revenue Service estimated that taxpayers filing returns failed to report $134 billion of income and nonfilers failed to report $115 billion. The $250 billion of underreporting reduced tax receipts by an estimated $55 billion. Unreported income connected with illegal activities was estimated to result in an additional $9 billion of lost revenue. Congress believed that reporting on the spending of large amounts of cash would enable the Internal Revenue Service to identify taxpayers with large cash incomes.

The words of a statute should be given their normal meaning and effect in the absence of a showing that some other meaning was intended. The practice of law is treated as a "trade or business" under both the income tax laws and the Sherman

Act. There is no indication that Congress intended those words to be interpreted any differently in section 6050-I. Indeed, Congress's rejection of the lobbying efforts to secure a specific exclusion of the legal profession from this customary definition is strong evidence that Congress did not wish to do so.[35] The clear and unmistakable intent of Congress in enacting the currency reporting statutes was to enable the IRS to identify taxpayers with large cash incomes. To the extent that the congressional intent, as expressed in section 6050-I, conflicts with the attorney-client privilege, the latter must give way to the former.

Because attorneys are not excepted by the Constitution from complying with section 6050-I, they are subject to the civil and criminal penalties designed to induce such compliance. Although sections 6721-6724 of the Internal Revenue Code provide specific penalties for failure to comply with information-reporting requirements of the code, such penalties are not necessarily exclusive. Section 1001 of Title 18 of the United States Code, the purpose of which is to protect the government from fraud and deceit regardless of whether it results in monetary loss, makes it unlawful for anyone to knowingly and willfully conceal or cover up a material fact in any matter within the jurisdiction of any department or agency of the United States. It has been applied, together with 18 U.S.C. § 371 (conspiracy to defraud the United States) and 18 U.S.C. § 2(b) (aiding and abetting), to both bank officers and depositors who cause the bank to violate the reporting requirements of the Bank Secrecy Act.

The frauds against the government prohibited by these sections are not restricted to fraud, as that term has been used in the common law. Assuming that the necessary elements of knowledge and willfulness are found to exist, there is no reason why sections 371, 2(b), and 1001 should not be applied to attorneys and their clients. In short, "in the absence of allegations as to special circumstances — we see no reason why an attorney should be any less subject to questioning about fees received from a taxpayer than should any other person who has dealt with the taxpayer." Colton v. United States, 306 F.2d 633, 637-38 (2d Cir. 1962).

In the instant case, as in most cases, the moving force behind nondisclosure is the client, not the lawyer. Indeed, it is the lawyer's duty to counsel against such wrongful nondisclosure, not to encourage it. A client, for whose benefit the attorney-client privilege exists, should not be permitted to claim the privilege, either directly or through his attorney, for the purpose of concealing his own ongoing or contemplated fraud. . . .

Affirmed.

Notes and Questions

1. Are there limits to what the government can (or should be willing to) do to eradicate the underground economy? If so, does the enforcement action in *Goldberger* exceed them?

2. Section 6050I imposes reporting requirements on "[a]ny person who is engaged in a trade or business." While recognizing that § 6050I may justify a lawyer's disclosure of client confidences despite local disciplinary rules to the contrary, a District of

---

35. The ABA and other lawyers' organizations also unsuccessfully urged the IRS to exempt attorneys' fees from regulations issued under § 6050I. 51 Fed. Reg. 31610 (Sept. 4, 1986). — ED.

Columbia Bar Ethics panel ruled that § 6050I cannot *require* disclosure because "substantial good faith arguments exist as to whether law firms are a 'trade or business' within the meaning of section 6050I."[36] Section 162 of the Internal Revenue Code allows deduction of ordinary and necessary expenses incurred in carrying on a trade or business. Lawyers and law firms routinely deduct as business expenses, under § 162, the cost of office rent, furniture, computers, photocopy and fax machines, law books, salaries, travel, paper, paper clips, and countless other items that are essential to running a law office.

Is it likely that the District of Columbia Bar Association would seriously contend that lawyers are not engaged in a trade or business for purposes of § 162? Are there really "substantial good faith arguments" about whether law firms are a trade or business for purposes of § 6050I as the Ethics Committee Opinion asserts?

3.In United States v. Ritchie,[37] a criminal defense lawyer challenged an IRS summons requiring him to divulge the identities of clients who paid him in cash. The district court found the IRS had three legitimate grounds for seeking this information: (1) the clients were obtaining advice from a "well-known criminal defense attorney"; (2) they wanted their identities kept secret; and (3) they paid the lawyer with large amounts of cash.[38]

The court of appeals rejected the first two grounds, stating for the reason that "[o]ur legal system requires that the innocent and the guilty alike be permitted to consult counsel on legal matters without attaching [a] penalty to the exercise of that right."[39] To permit the government to rely on consultation with counsel as a reason for seeking information about the client would impose an undue burden on the right to consult a lawyer.

But the court found the third reason was legitimate. The suspect act is not consulting a lawyer. Instead, it is "paying over $10,000 in cash *for anything* — in this case legal services."[40] The IRS investigation was related not to the fact of representation. It was, instead, a function of how the client paid the fee.

> We must conclude that there is no reason to grant law firms a potential monopoly on money laundering simply because their services are personal and confidential; other businesses must divulge the identity of their cash-paying clients in keeping with lawful revenue regulations and law firms should not be an exception to this rule. We therefore hold that the simple fact that these clients paid for legal services with large amounts of cash is a sufficient "reasonable basis" upon which to issue [a] John Doe summons.[41]

In what respect would adoption of the lawyer's position be tantamount to giving law firms a monopoly on money laundering?

---

36. District of Columbia Bar Ethics Committee, Opinion No. 214.
37. 15 F.3d 592 (6th Cir. 1994).
38. Id. at 600.
39. Id.
40. Id. at 601.
41. Id.

Other circuits considering the point have similarly rejected claims that the attorney-client privilege shields disclosure of client information required by Form 8300.[42]

The court in *Goldberger* observed that lawyers are subject to an array of civil and criminal penalties for failure to comply with the reporting requirements. In an effort to improve compliance by lawyers who do not file Form 8300 or who file incomplete forms, the IRS announced that it would begin assessing intentional disregard penalties against them. This could make noncompliance a costly proposition, for the penalty is the greater of $25,000 or the amount of cash received in the unreported transaction, up to a maximum of $100,000.[43]

LEFCOURT v. UNITED STATES
125 F.3d 79 (2d Cir. 1997)

WALKER, Circuit Judge.

Plaintiff-appellant Gerald B. Lefcourt, P.C. ("Lefcourt" or "the law firm") appeals from the May 16, 1996 judgment entered in the United States District Court for the Southern District of New York (Robert P. Patterson, Jr., District Judge), granting the United States' motion for summary judgment and denying plaintiff's cross-motion for summary judgment in plaintiff's tax refund action. In so doing, the district court affirmed the imposition of a $25,000 penalty by the Internal Revenue Service ("IRS") on the ground that Lefcourt had intentionally failed to comply with certain reporting requirements set forth in 26 U.S.C. § 6050I and that the law firm had not established "reasonable cause" for doing so.

Lefcourt has advanced a number of reasons for failing to file the information required by § 6050I, all of which are animated by a concern for the sensitive relationship that exists between attorney and client. We recognize the importance of this privilege and the impulse of attorneys to defend it vigorously, as Lefcourt has done here. However, for the following reasons, we affirm the judgment of the district court.

BACKGROUND . . .

During the summer of 1993, Lefcourt, a law firm specializing in criminal defense work, undertook the representation of a client facing federal drug and money laundering charges. The client paid Lefcourt over $10,000 in cash for legal services. On July 9, 1993, the law firm submitted a Form 8300 to the IRS, stating that it had received in excess of $10,000, and particularizing the date of the payment. The firm, however,

---

42. United States v. Sindel, 53 F.3d 874 (8th Cir. 1995); United States v. Under Seal (In re Grand Jury Proceedings No. 92-4), 42 F.3d 876 (4th Cir. 1994); In re Subpoena to Testify Before the Grand Jury, 39 F.3d 973 (9th Cir. 1994); United States v. Leventhal, 961 F.2d 936 (11th Cir. 1992) (per curiam). Cf. In re Grand Jury Proceedings, 33 F.3d 1060 (8th Cir. 1994) (attorney-client privilege does not protect identity of client who gave lawyer a $100 counterfeit bill).

43. IRS News Release, IRS Seeks Greater Compliance with Form 8300 Requirements (Dec. 7, 1993).

deliberately omitted the payor's name. In doing so, Gerald Lefcourt, the law firm's name partner, attached to the Form 8300 an affidavit asserting that revealing the client-identifying information called for by § 6050I would prejudice the interests of a client whom the law firm was actively representing and that the confidentiality of the information was protected by the Fifth and Sixth Amendments of the Constitution and by the Lawyers' Code of Professional Responsibility.

On December 14, 1993, the IRS served the law firm with a Notice of Proposed Penalties under 26 U.S.C. § 6721(e), which allows for the imposition of a penalty where "intentional disregard" of § 6050I's reporting requirements is established. Over the following four months, Lefcourt initiated numerous correspondences with the IRS to request a conference with the IRs's Office of Appeals concerning the proposed penalty, and to explain the basis for its failure to provide the name of its client on the Form 8300. The overtures resulted in an apparently unsuccessful pre-settlement conference between Lefcourt and the IRS on April 12, 1994: on August 8, 1994 the IRS assessed the law firm a $25,000 penalty pursuant to § 6721.

In September of 1994, the law firm paid the full amount of the assessed penalty and, on that date, claimed a refund for the same amount. The following day, the IRS notified Lefcourt that no refund would be granted. On December 6, 1994, Lefcourt brought this refund action in the district court pursuant to 28 U.S.C. § 1346(a)(1).

In May 1995, while the case was pending before the district court, the law firm filed an amended Form 8300 that provided the name of the client that had previously been omitted from the form that was filed on July 9, 1993.

Both parties moved for summary judgment before the district court. In an opinion and order dated May 13, 1996, the district court granted the government's motion and denied Lefcourt's, reasoning principally that Lefcourt intentionally disregarded § 6050I's filing requirements, thereby triggering the penalty for willful noncompliance set forth in 26 U.S.C. § 6721, and that the law firm failed to establish that it acted with the reasonable cause required to qualify for the mandatory waiver of penalties set forth in 26 U.S.C. § 6724. This appeal followed.

DISCUSSION . . .

I. INTENTIONAL DISREGARD

We first turn to the question of whether, by declining to provide its client's name as called for by Form 8300, the law firm acted with "intentional disregard" of § 6050I's filing requirements.

As noted earlier, 26 U.S.C. § 6050I requires "any person . . . engaged in a trade or business" who "in the course of such trade or business, receives more than $10,000 in cash . . ." to file a report with the IRS that specifies the person from whom the cash was received, the amount of cash received, the date and nature of the transaction, and "such other information as the Secretary may prescribe." 26 U.S.C. § 6050I(a), (b). When a party is deemed to have failed to file the information required by § 6050I because of "intentional disregard of the filing requirement," the Internal Revenue Code provides that the party shall be fined the greater of $25,000 or the amount of cash received in the transaction. Title 26, section 301.6721-1(f)(2)(ii), of the Code of Federal

Regulations indicates that "a failure is due to intentional disregard if it is a knowing or willful . . . failure to include correct information."

The district court found that the $25,000 penalty was properly assessed against Lefcourt because the government satisfied its burden of demonstrating that the law firm acted with intentional disregard of its legal obligations — that is, that "[p]laintiff knew what § 6050I required and voluntarily, consciously, and intentionally failed to comply."

On appeal, Lefcourt argues that the district court applied the incorrect *mens rea* standard to § 6721's enhanced penalty provision. Lefcourt takes the position that under § 6721, a good faith belief in the legality of one's conduct — even where that belief later proves to be mistaken or unreasonable — precludes a finding of intentional disregard. Put another way, Lefcourt argues that one must be aware of the law's requirements in order to disregard them, and thus, a subjective good faith belief that one's conduct is lawful precludes the imposition of the penalty. Lefcourt suggests that Congress chose to adopt this heightened "bad faith" requirement because the penalties provided for by the statute are severe.

The principal case Lefcourt points to is Cheek v. United States, 498 U.S. 192 (1991). . . .

Lefcourt's reliance on *Cheek*'s willfulness standard is unavailing. *Cheek* was a criminal case, and we are persuaded that its rationale does not apply in the context of the civil tax penalties at issue here. Describing the genesis of the "special treatment of criminal tax offenses," id. at 200, the Court in *Cheek* explained that Congress did not intend that a taxpayer "should become a criminal" based on a "bona fide misunderstanding as to his liability," id. . . .

Cases construing analogous civil penalty provisions in the tax code and, in particular, provisions requiring a showing of willfulness also persuade us that no heightened *mens rea* is required in this context. Courts considering such provisions define willfulness in terms of "voluntary, conscious, and intentional" conduct. Indeed, as this circuit has explained before *Cheek* in the slightly different context of 26 U.S.C. § 6672 (which provides for penalties upon willful failure to collect withholding tax), an "individual's bad purpose or evil motive in failing to collect and pay the taxes 'properly play[s] no part in the civil definition of willfulness.'" Hochstein v. United States, 900 F.2d 543, 548 (2d Cir. 1990).

Section 6721 does not use the term "willful"; it uses the term "intentional disregard." But 26 C.F.R. § 301.6721-1(f)(2)(ii) defines "intentional disregard" as synonymous with "willfulness." Thus, in our view, the "intentional disregard" set forth in § 6721's penalty provision means conduct that is willful, a term which in this context requires only that a party act voluntarily in withholding requested information, rather than accidentally or unconsciously. Once it is determined, as it was here, that the failure to disclose client-identifying information was done purposefully, rather than inadvertently, it is irrelevant that the filer may have believed he was legally justified in withholding such information. The only question that remains is whether the law required its disclosure.

As it is uncontested that Lefcourt was aware that Form 8300 asked for its client's identity and nonetheless chose to refuse to provide the name, there is no dispute that Lefcourt acted voluntarily. We thus agree with the district court that, as a matter of law,

Lefcourt's failure to disclose the client-identifying information was willful and in "intentional disregard" of the law firm's obligation. . . .

. . . We therefore affirm the judgment of the district court.

Notes and Questions

1. The argument that this was not a case of intentional disregard was premised on the assertion that Lefcourt held a good faith belief that he could lawfully withhold the information to protect client confidentiality. Consider some additional facts that the court of appeals did not recite. Lefcourt assisted the American Bar Association and the National Association of Criminal Defense Lawyers in unsuccessful efforts to persuade the Justice Department to exempt lawyers from the reporting requirements or to adopt guidelines that would spell out when lawyers could refuse to supply information by asserting the attorney-client privilege. He was also a signatory on an amicus brief filed in United States v. Goldberger & Dubin, supra, where the court ruled that client identity and fee information are not exempt from disclosure under § 6050I.[44]

How, if at all, do these facts affect Lefcourt's claim that he did not intentionally disregard the reporting requirements and that he had reasonable cause to believe he could withhold the information? Was Lefcourt's failure to supply the required information objectively reasonable under the circumstances?

2. The IRS announced its intention to assess civil penalties against lawyers who intentionally disregard the cash reporting requirements in December 1993. Although there have undoubtedly been other cases in which penalties were imposed, *Lefcourt* is the first reported case in which a lawyer or law firm challenged a penalty imposed under § 6721(e) in this context. Is it problematic that lawyers may incur substantial penalties for protecting client confidences in accordance with state ethical rules?

2. Designated Reporting Transactions

The scope of the § 6050I reporting requirements was considerably broadened in 1992 to reach "designated reporting transactions." The term "designated reporting transaction" is defined to mean retail sales that fit within one of three specifically defined categories of goods or services: (1) consumer durables — i.e., tangible personal property that, under ordinary usage, is suitable for personal consumption or use and has an expected useful life of at least one year; (2) collectibles — i.e., artwork, gems, coins, and the like; and (3) travel or entertainment activity — i.e., transportation and accommodations sold in the same transaction or a series of related transactions. If the retailer receives more than $10,000 in cash in connection with any of these types of sales, the transaction must be reported.

Notably, in this context, cashier's checks, bank drafts, traveler's checks, and money orders having a face amount of *not more than* $10,000 are deemed to be cash. Thus, if the aggregate value of such monetary instruments and/or currency exceeds $10,000, the transaction is reportable.

---

44. See Lefcourt v. United States, 1996 WL 252363 (S.D.N.Y. May 14, 1996).

What are the implications of this extension of § 6050I? Why would Congress and the IRS be interested in these kinds of transactions?

PROBLEM 12-1

Greta Glamor purchases a $15,000 diamond necklace from a retail jeweler. She gives the jeweler $8,000 in traveler's checks and a $7,000 personal check in payment for the necklace. Is the jeweler required to report the transaction?

PROBLEM 12-2

Greta's next stop is at the local Toyota dealer. She buys a $25,000 Camry using a $4,000 cashier's check, a $2,000 money order, $6,000 in cash, and a $13,000 traveler's check. Must the dealer report the transaction?

PROBLEM 12-3

Greta's shopping spree ends at her travel agent's office. She asks the travel agent to arrange a month-long trip to Spain to see the bullfights. The total amount of the accommodations, airline tickets, and admission fees adds up to $13,500. She pays for the trip with a cashier's check in the amount of $11,000 and $2,500 in cash. Is this a reportable transaction?

III. MONEY LAUNDERING

The federal government's efforts to combat money laundering include a variety of approaches contained in an interrelated network of statutes and regulations. The first line of attack was to require the creation of a paper trail documenting large cash transactions conducted with financial institutions. As we have seen, the currency reporting requirements — first imposed under the Bank Secrecy Act — have been periodically refined and augmented to reflect changing regulatory needs. One drawback to this approach is that it generates an overwhelming load of paperwork. In 1998, financial institutions alone filed some 12.5 million currency transaction reports with the Treasury Department. Needless to say, this burdensome volume of filings creates an enforcement nightmare.

The Money Laundering Control Act of 1986 (18 U.S.C. §§ 1956 & 1957) broadens the reach of anti-money laundering laws in several notable respects. First, § 1956 prohibits conducting a financial transaction when the actor knows the transaction involves the proceeds of unlawful activity.

In addition to requiring knowledge that the transaction involves proceeds from some form of unlawful activity, § 1956 requires proof of collateral criminal intent. The actor must *intend*: (1) to promote "the carrying on of specified unlawful activity"; or

(2) to commit tax evasion or fraud. Alternatively, the actor must *know* that the financial transaction is designed: (1) to "conceal or disguise the nature, location, source, ownership, or control of the proceeds of specified unlawful activity"; or (2) to avoid federal or state currency reporting requirements, including those imposed by the Bank Secrecy Act.[45] "Specified unlawful activity" is a term of broad import. It encompasses most RICO predicate crimes in addition to a lengthy list of other federal offenses, including financial institution crimes, customs violations, and various forms of fraud.[46] Thus, although § 1956 reaches money laundering transactions designed to conceal proceeds generated by drug trafficking, gambling, and organized crime activities, liability under § 1956 is often triggered by financial transactions related to white collar crime.[47]

UNITED STATES v. TENCER
107 F.3d 1120 (5th Cir. 1997)

DAVIS, Circuit Judge. . . .

I

Appellants Tencer and Lazar, both licensed chiropractors, worked at the Allied Chiropractic Clinic ("Allied") in Kenner, Louisiana. Tencer, who owned the clinic, turned over the bulk of his practice to Lazar, his employee, in 1989; thereafter, Tencer generally supervised the clinic's financial affairs while Lazar treated patients on a day-to-day basis. From sometime in 1988 to early 1992, Allied submitted false insurance claims to three insurance companies, Blue Cross/Blue Shield of Louisiana ("Blue Cross"), Mail Handlers Benefit Plan ("Mail Handlers"), and National Association of Letter Carriers ("NALC"), and collected proceeds for patients who were not treated at all or who received only minimal treatment.

To execute the fraud, the appellants paid insurance premiums for some patients who, in return, signed multiple sign-in sheets indicating their presence in the office awaiting treatment. Those sheets were then used to generate false insurance claims. Appellants followed a similar pattern with patients recruited from local and federal government agencies; patients with good insurance benefits for chiropractic services were paid to sign their names and the names of family members on the clinic's sign-in sheets. They were also compensated for referring coworkers to Allied.

While Allied apparently provided some legitimate services, many patients testified that they and their family members received either no treatment or only cursory treatment consisting of brief massages or the application of heat pads. Yet, the claim forms Allied submitted for these same patients reported complicated diagnoses and elaborate treatment regimens. As a result of the scheme, Allied submitted hundreds of fraudulent claims and collected more than $450,000 in insurance proceeds related to these patients.

---

45. 18 U.S.C. § 1956(a)(1).
46. Id. § 1956(c)(7).
47. Approximately 18,500 defendants were prosecuted for money laundering from 1994-2001. DOJ Issues Report on Money Laundering Prosecutions from 1994 Through 2001, Crim. L. Rep. (BNA), July 23, 2003, at 456.

[Tencer was convicted of conspiracy, mail fraud, and money laundering in violation of 18 U.S.C. § 1956.]

II . . .

B

Tencer . . . challenges the sufficiency of the evidence supporting his conviction for money laundering. . . . To support a conviction under 18 U.S.C. § 1956, the money laundering statute, the government must prove that the defendant 1) conducted or attempted to conduct a financial transaction, 2) which the defendant knew involved the proceeds of a specified unlawful activity, 3) with the intent to conceal or disguise the nature, location, source, ownership, or control of the proceeds of unlawful activity.

1

Tencer contends first that the government failed to produce sufficient evidence to establish the concealment element of six of the money laundering counts. Those counts stemmed from six transfers of funds by wire and check from various money market accounts throughout the country into one account in Tencer's name at California Federal Bank in Las Vegas, Nevada. A brief description of the facts is necessary to understand Tencer's argument.

Between May 1989 and April 1992, Tencer opened bank accounts in various banks across the country and deposited checks drawn on his personal account at Fidelity Homestead and on the Allied Clinic account at Whitney National Bank. On July 9, 1992, a little more than a week after federal agents had executed a search warrant at Allied Clinic, Tencer faxed instructions to several of the regional banks where he had accounts. He directed those banks to transmit his funds on deposit by mailing cashier[']s checks by Federal Express to an Algiers, Louisiana, address at which Tencer neither worked nor resided. On July 13, 1992, Tencer opened an account at California Federal Bank in Las Vegas, Nevada, using some of the cashier[']s checks; his initial deposit totaled $662,637.06. He told employees at the Las Vegas bank that he was moving into the area and needed cash to buy a business. He also directed banks that had not yet mailed cashier[']s checks to the Algiers address to wire funds totaling $312,297.89 to the account at California Federal Bank. The next day, Tencer deposited an $89,832.10 cashier[']s check into the account and withdrew $9,900.[48] Later that day, Tencer arranged to have the entire balance in the account — roughly $1,055,000 — delivered to him in cash at a local airport. Before the funds could be picked up by a security company and delivered to Tencer, a seizure warrant was executed on the California Federal account.

Tencer argues that the government has presented no evidence that he sought to conceal the nature, source, ownership, or control of the funds. He contends that when he opened the regional accounts initially and later transferred those balances to the California Federal account, he used his own name and handled his own transactions. No third parties were used, and a paper trail clearly connected Tencer to both the regional and California Federal accounts.

---

48. Withdrawals of more than $10,000 in cash require the completion of a Currency Transaction Report; according to a bank official, withdrawals slightly below the regulated amount are not unusual.

The government counters that the use of a false identity is not essential to a money laundering conviction. It contends that Tencer's request that funds be sent to an address at which he neither worked nor resided, his use of a Las Vegas bank hundreds of miles away from his home and business to consolidate funds, and his false statements to bank employees about his plans to move to the area demonstrated his intent to conceal.

We reject as overly narrow Tencer's view that § 1956's concealment element is satisfied only by an attempt to disguise the defendant's identity. Several circuits, including this one, have recognized that the government need not "prove with regard to any single transaction that the defendant removed all trace of his involvement with the money or that the particular transaction charged is itself highly unusual." United States v. Willey, 57 F.3d 1374, 1386 (5th Cir. 1995). Thus, the fact that Tencer did not seek to conceal his identity while depositing funds in the California Federal account does not require us to reverse his conviction on these counts.

Tencer argues that this Court's decision in United States v. Dobbs, 63 F.3d 391 (5th Cir. 1995), supports reversal. In *Dobbs*, the defendant deposited proceeds of bank fraud into his wife's bank account, converted other proceeds into cashier[']s checks, and then used the account and checks for family and business expenses. This Court found insufficient evidence to sustain the defendant's money laundering convictions because the transactions were "open and notorious" and no third parties were used to make purchases or hide his activity.

In *Dobbs*, unlike today's case, the government produced no evidence that the transactions were conducted to disguise the relationship between the defendant and the fraudulent proceeds. Whereas Dobbs openly used fraudulently obtained funds to pay for business and family expenses, Tencer endeavored to consolidate illicit funds in a city that was hundreds of miles from his home and where large cash transactions are commonplace. He asked regional banks to wire funds to an address to which he had no connection. His false statements to bank officials showed an intent to minimize attention to the transactions. Based on the evidence in the record, a jury could infer that Tencer was attempting to conceal the nature of the funds and facilitate laundering of the proceeds of his fraudulent activities. . . .

VII . . .

[T]he judgment of the district court is affirmed. . . .

Notes and Questions

1. If Tencer used his own identity while doing business with his own banks, why weren't the transactions deemed "open and notorious" as in *Dobbs*? How important are the timing of the transfers and the locations of the various banks?

2. What is the purpose of the provision at issue in *Tencer* and *Dobbs*? Why should it make any difference whether the transactions were conducted openly or under cover?

UNITED STATES v. CAMPBELL
977 F.2d 854 (4th Cir. 1992)

Ervin, Chief Judge.

The United States appeals from the district court's grant of Ellen Campbell's motion for judgment of acquittal on charges of money laundering, 18 U.S.C. § 1956(a)(1)(B)(i), and engaging in a transaction in criminally derived property, 18 U.S.C. § 1957(a). . . .

I

. . . In the summer of 1989, Ellen Campbell was a licensed real estate agent working at Lake Norman Realty in Mooresville, North Carolina. During the same period, Mark Lawing was a drug dealer in Kannapolis, North Carolina. Lawing decided to buy a house on Lake Norman. He obtained Campbell's business card from Lake Norman Realty's Mooresville office, called Campbell, and scheduled an appointment to look at houses.

Over the course of about five weeks, Lawing met with Campbell approximately once a week and looked at a total of ten to twelve houses. Lawing and Campbell also had numerous phone conversations. Lawing represented himself to Campbell as the owner of a legitimate business, L & N Autocraft, which purportedly performed automobile customizing services. When meeting with Campbell, Lawing would travel in either a red Porsche he owned or a gold Porsche owned by a fellow drug dealer, Randy Sweatt, who would usually accompany Lawing. During the trips to look at houses, which occurred during normal business hours, Lawing would bring his cellular phone and would often consume food and beer with Sweatt. At one point, Lawing brought a briefcase containing $20,000 in cash, showing the money to Campbell to demonstrate his ability to purchase a house.

Lawing eventually settled upon a house listed for $191,000 and owned by Edward and Nancy Guy Fortier. The listing with the Fortiers had been secured by Sara Fox, another real estate agent with Lake Norman Realty. After negotiations, Lawing and the Fortiers agreed on a price of $182,500, and entered into a written contract. Lawing was unable to secure a loan and decided to ask the Fortiers to accept $60,000 under the table in cash and to lower the contract price to $122,500.[49] Lawing contacted Campbell and informed her of this proposal. Campbell relayed the proposal to Fox, who forwarded the offer to the Fortiers. The Fortiers agreed, and Fox had the Fortiers execute a new listing agreement which lowered the sales price and increased the commission percentage (in order to protect the realtors' profits on the sale).

Thereafter Lawing met the Fortiers, Fox and Campbell in the Mooresville sales office with $60,000 in cash. The money was wrapped in small bundles and carried in a brown paper grocery bag. The money was counted, and a new contract was executed

---

49. Lawing's explanation to Campbell of this unorthodox arrangement was that the lower purchase price would allow Lawing's parents to qualify for a mortgage. Lawing would then make the mortgage payments on his parents' behalf. Lawing justified the secrecy of the arrangement by explaining that his parents had to remain unaware of the $60,000 payment because the only way he could induce their involvement was to convince them he was getting an excellent bargain on the real estate.

reflecting a sales price of $122,500. Lawing tipped both Fox and Campbell with "a couple of hundred dollars."

William Austin, the closing attorney, prepared closing documents, including HUD-1 and 1099-S forms, reflecting a sales price of $122,500, based on the information provided by Campbell. Campbell, Fox, Austin, Lawing, Lawing's parents and the Fortiers were all present at the closing. The closing documents were signed, all reflecting a sales price of $122,500.

Campbell was indicted on a three count indictment alleging: 1) money laundering, in violation of 18 U.S.C. § 1956(a)(1)(B)(i); 2) engaging in a transaction in criminally derived property, in violation of 18 U.S.C. § 1957(a); and 3) causing a false statement (the HUD-1 form) to be filed with a government agency, in violation of 18 U.S.C. § 1001. She was tried and convicted by a jury on all three counts. After the verdict, the district court granted Campbell's motion for judgment of acquittal with respect to the money laundering and transaction in criminally derived property counts. . . .

II . . .

The money laundering statute under which Campbell was charged applies to any person who:

> knowing that the property involved in a financial transaction represents the proceeds of some form of unlawful activity, conducts or attempts to conduct such a financial transaction which in fact involves the proceeds of specified unlawful activity . . . knowing that the transaction is designed in whole or in part . . . to conceal or disguise the nature, the location, the source, the ownership, or the control of the proceeds of specified unlawful activity. . . .

18 U.S.C. § 1956(a)(1). The district court found, and Campbell does not dispute, that there was adequate evidence for the jury to find that Campbell conducted a financial transaction which in fact involved the proceeds of Lawing's illegal drug activities. The central issue in contention is whether there was sufficient evidence for the jury to find that Campbell possessed the knowledge that: (1) Lawing's funds were the proceeds of illegal activity, and (2) the transaction was designed to disguise the nature of those proceeds.

In assessing Campbell's culpability, it must be noted that the statute requires actual subjective knowledge. Campbell cannot be convicted on what she objectively should have known. However, this requirement is softened somewhat by the doctrine of willful blindness. In this case, the jury was instructed that:

> The element of knowledge may be satisfied by inferences drawn from proof that a defendant deliberately closed her eyes to what would otherwise have been obvious to her. A finding beyond a reasonable doubt of a conscious purpose to avoid enlightenment would permit an inference of knowledge. Stated another way, a defendant's knowledge of a fact may be inferred upon willful blindness to the existence of a fact.
>
> It is entirely up to you as to whether you find any deliberate closing of the eyes and inferences to be drawn from any evidence. A showing of negligence is not sufficient to support a finding of willfulness or knowledge.

> I caution you that the willful blindness charge does not authorize you to find that the defendant acted knowingly because she should have known what was occurring when the property at 763 Sundown Road was being sold, or that in the exercise of hindsight she should have known what was occurring or because she was negligent in failing to recognize what was occurring or even because she was reckless or foolish in failing to recognize what was occurring. Instead, the Government must prove beyond a reasonable doubt that the defendant purposely and deliberately contrived to avoid learning all of the facts.

Neither party disputes the adequacy of these instructions on willful blindness or their applicability to this case.

As outlined above, a money laundering conviction under section 1956(a)(1)(B)(i) requires proof of the defendant's knowledge of two separate facts: (1) that the funds involved in the transaction were the proceeds of illegal activity; and (2) that the transaction was designed to conceal the nature of the proceeds. In its opinion supporting the entry of the judgment of acquittal, the district court erred in interpreting the elements of the offense. After correctly reciting the elements of the statute, the court stated, "in a prosecution against a party other than the drug dealer," the Government must show "*a purpose of concealment*" and "knowledge of the drug dealer's activities." This assertion misstates the Government's burden. The Government need not prove that the defendant had the *purpose* of concealing the proceeds of illegal activity. Instead, as the plain language of the statute suggests, the Government must only show that the defendant possessed the *knowledge* that the transaction was designed to conceal illegal proceeds.[50]

This distinction is critical in cases such as the present one, in which the defendant is a person other than the individual who is the source of the tainted money. It is clear from the record that Campbell herself did not act with the purpose of concealing drug proceeds. Her motive, without question, was to close the real estate deal and collect the resulting commission, without regard to the source of the money or the effect of the transaction in concealing a portion of the purchase price. However, Campbell's motivations are irrelevant. Under the terms of the statute, the relevant question is not Campbell's purpose, but rather her knowledge of Lawing's purpose.[51]

The sufficiency of evidence regarding Campbell's knowledge of Lawing's purpose depends on whether Campbell was aware of Lawing's status as a drug dealer. Assuming for the moment that Campbell knew that Lawing's funds were derived from illegal activity, then the under the table transfer of $60,000 in cash would have been sufficient, by itself, to allow the jury to find that Campbell knew, or was willfully blind to the fact,

---

50. The other portion of the district court's statement, that the Government must show Campbell possessed "knowledge of the drug dealer's activities," is also incorrect. The statute requires only a showing that the defendant had knowledge that "the property involved in a financial transaction represents the proceeds of *some form of illegal activity*." 18 U.S.C. § 1956(a)(1). . . .

51. We have no difficulty in finding that Lawing's purpose satisfied the statutory requirement that the transaction be "designed in whole or in part . . . to conceal or disguise the nature, the location, the source, the ownership, or the control of the proceeds of specified unlawful activity. . . ." 18 U.S.C. § 1956(a)(1)(B). The omission of $60,000 from all documentation regarding the sales price of the property clearly satisfies this standard — concealing both the nature and the location of Lawing's illegally derived funds. See United States v. Lovett, 964 F.2d 1029, 1034 (10th Cir. 1992) (money laundering transaction need not necessarily conceal the identity of the participants in the transaction; concealment of the funds themselves is sufficient). Accordingly, we need not address the Government's alternative argument that Lawing concealed ownership of the funds by placing title to the Lake Norman property in the name of his parents.

that the transaction was designed for an illicit purpose. Only if Campbell was oblivious to the illicit nature of Lawing's funds could she credibly argue that she believed Lawing's explanation of the under the table transfer of cash and was unaware of the money laundering potential of the transaction. In short, the fraudulent nature of the transaction itself provides a sufficient basis from which a jury could infer Campbell's knowledge of the transaction's purpose, if, as assumed above, Campbell also knew of the illegal source of Lawing's money.[52] As a result, we find that, in this case, the knowledge components of the money laundering statute collapse into a single inquiry: Did Campbell know that Lawing's funds were derived from an illegal source?

The Government emphasizes that the district court misstated the Government's burden on this point as well, by holding that the Government must show Campbell's "knowledge of the drug dealer's activities." As the text of the statute indicates, the Government need only show knowledge that the funds represented "the proceeds of some form of unlawful activity." 18 U.S.C. § 1956(a)(1); see also 18 U.S.C. § 1956(c)(1) (money laundering provision requires "that the person knew the property involved in the transaction represented proceeds from some form, though not necessarily which form, of [specified unlawful] activity"). Practically, this distinction makes little difference. All of the Government's evidence was designed to show that Campbell knew that Lawing was a drug dealer. There is no indication that the jury could have believed that Lawing was involved in some form of criminal activity other than drug dealing. As a result, the district court's misstatement on this point is of little consequence.

The evidence pointing to Campbell's knowledge of Lawing's illegal activities is not overwhelming. First, we find that the district court correctly excluded from consideration testimony by Sweatt that Lawing was a "known" drug dealer. Kannapolis, where Lawing's operations were located, is approximately fifteen miles from Mooresville, where Campbell lived and worked, and, as the district court pointed out, there was no indication that Lawing's reputation extended over such an extensive "community."

However, the district court also downplayed evidence that we find to be highly relevant. Sara Fox, the listing broker, testified at trial that Campbell had stated prior to the sale that the funds "may have been drug money." The trial court discounted this testimony because it conflicted with Fox's grand jury testimony that she did not recall Campbell ever indicating that Lawing was involved with drugs. In evaluating the testimony in this manner, the trial court made an impermissible judgment on witness credibility — a judgment that was clearly within the exclusive province of the jury. When ruling on a motion for judgment of acquittal the district court is obligated to weigh the evidence in the light most favorable to the Government. Under that standard, Fox's testimony regarding Campbell's statement that the funds "may have been drug money" should have been accepted as completely true.

---

52. In this respect the present case is completely distinguishable from the principal case relied upon by the district court, United States v. Sanders, 929 F.2d 1466 (10th Cir. 1991). In that case, the court overturned two money laundering convictions of a defendant who, with funds admittedly derived from an illegal source, had purchased two automobiles. Unlike the present case, there was nothing irregular about the transactions themselves. The court found the transactions to be devoid of any attempt "to conceal or disguise the source or nature of the proceeds" and found that application of the money laundering statute to "ordinary commercial transactions" would "turn the money laundering statute into a 'money spending statute,'" a result clearly not intended by Congress. Id. at 1471-72. The present case, by contrast, presents a highly irregular financial transaction which, by its very structure, was designed to mislead onlookers as to the amount of money involved in the transaction.

In addition, the Government presented extensive evidence regarding Lawing's lifestyle. This evidence showed that Lawing and his companion both drove new Porsches, and that Lawing carried a cellular phone, flashed vast amounts of cash, and was able to be away from his purportedly legitimate business for long stretches of time during normal working hours. The district court conceded that this evidence "is not wholly [sic] irrelevant" to Campbell's knowledge of Lawing's true occupation, but noted that Lawing's lifestyle was not inconsistent with that of many of the other inhabitants of the affluent Lake Norman area who were not drug dealers. Again, we find that the district court has drawn inferences from the evidence which, while possibly well-founded, are not the only inferences that can be drawn. It should have been left to the jury to decide whether or not the Government's evidence of Lawing's lifestyle was sufficient to negate the credibility of Campbell's assertion that she believed Lawing to be a legitimate businessman.

We find that the evidence of Lawing's lifestyle, the testimony concerning Campbell's statement that the money "might have been drug money," and the fraudulent nature of the transaction in which Campbell was asked to participate were sufficient to create a question for the jury concerning whether Campbell "deliberately closed her eyes to what would otherwise have been obvious to her." As a result, we find that a reasonable jury could have found that Campbell was willfully blind to the fact that Lawing was a drug dealer and the fact that the purchase of the Lake Norman property was intended, at least in part, to conceal the proceeds of Lawing's drug selling operation. Accordingly, we reverse the judgment of acquittal on the money laundering charge. . . .

Notes and Questions

1. Why is Campbell's purpose irrelevant under the statute? What differentiates knowledge from purpose?

2. Campbell's statement that the funds Lawing used to buy the property "may have been drug money" suggests *suspicion* that Lawing was involved in drugs, but suspicion falls short of knowledge. At what point along the continuum does suspicion ripen into knowledge? What facts did Campbell "know" that are relevant to the issue of culpability?

3. To what extent is Lawing's lifestyle relevant to Campbell's culpability? Does it matter whether he is a relative stranger dealing with her in an arm's-length real estate transaction? Is the fact that he drove expensive cars and spent a significant amount of time during the work week looking at real estate enough to charge her with knowledge that he was a drug dealer? Are those facts equally consistent with a wholly innocent explanation?

4. To what extent does the statute impose a duty on the Campbells of the world to "know your customer"? Does it make sense to require Campbell to police how Lawing acquires and spends his money?

Violations of § 1956 are often charged in tandem with violations of § 1957, which dovetails with the currency reporting requirements imposed by the Bank Secrecy Act and § 6050I. The currency reporting statutes do not make it unlawful to deposit or withdraw large amounts of currency or to acquire expensive goods and services with cash. They merely require the creation of a paper record of such transactions for government inspection. Section 1957 goes a step further by making it illegal to knowingly engage "in a monetary transaction in criminally derived property that is of a value greater than $10,000 and is derived from specified unlawful activity."[53] Since the term "monetary transaction" includes bank deposits and withdrawals, the thrust of § 1957 is to freeze criminals who have large amounts of tainted money out of legitimate banking channels.[54] As in § 1956, "specified unlawful activity" includes most RICO predicate crimes in addition to customs violations and a variety of frauds.

UNITED STATES v. JOHNSON
971 F.2d 562 (10th Cir. 1992)

Brown, Senior District Judge.

The defendant-appellant Robert Johnson was charged in a sixty-three count indictment with various violations of the Money Laundering Control Act of 1986 (18 U.S.C. §§ 1956 & 1957). A jury found him guilty on all but one count. Appellant was sentenced by the district court to 405 months imprisonment. On appeal, Johnson raises several challenges to the propriety of the convictions and the sentence.

The government alleged that the defendant masterminded a "peso scheme" which defrauded investors out of millions of dollars. According to the government, the defendant convinced investors that he was buying Mexican pesos at a discount rate and then reselling the pesos for their market value in American dollars. Johnson told potential investors that he had served in the war in Vietnam with a man from Mexico whose father was highly placed in the Mexican government. Johnson said that through this contact he had access to Mexican citizens and businesses that wanted to exchange pesos for dollars. The Mexicans wanted to convert their money to dollars, Johnson explained, because the peso was rapidly losing its value and the Mexicans preferred to hold a more stable currency. The defendant told investors that, depending on the number of trades he could make in a day, an investor could realize anywhere from fifteen to twenty-five per cent profit per week.[55]

Several individuals who sent money to the defendant for investment in the peso scheme testified at the defendant's trial. They each testified that they began by giving relatively small amounts of money to the defendant for investment in the peso deal. At the defendant's request, they transferred money they wanted to invest in the deal by means of a wire transfer from their own bank to the defendant's account at the Sooner Federal Savings & Loan in Broken Arrow, Oklahoma. Shortly thereafter, the defendant

---

53. 18 U.S.C. § 1957(a).

54. Note the symbiotic relationship between § 1957 and the currency reporting requirements. Section 1957 applies only to monetary transactions involving more than $10,000, which is the threshold reporting amount under the Bank Secrecy Act. If the actor structures deposits in smaller amounts to avoid running afoul of § 1957, he runs the risk of violating the antistructuring rule in the Bank Secrecy Act if the structuring is also animated by the desire to avoid filing a currency transaction report.

55. A black market in the exchange of pesos apparently sprang up in reaction to attempts by the Mexican government in 1982 to regulate transfers of that currency. See United States v. Nivica, 887 F.2d 1110, 1113 (1st Cir. 1989).

would wire back the amount of "profit" supposedly made by the investor from the purchase and sale of pesos. The amount wired back by the defendant was often fifteen to twenty per cent of the initial investment. The huge "profits" being made by investors apparently convinced them to invest heavily in the scheme and numerous individuals wired a steady stream of money to the defendant. Several of the investors who testified at trial sent upwards of half a million dollars to the defendant. The defendant managed to gain their complete confidence.

An Internal Revenue Service agent who had examined the defendant's bank records determined that about five and a half million dollars were deposited into the defendant's account in shortly over a year's time. The agent further determined that approximately $1.8 million of that amount was withdrawn out of the account and was used by the defendant to purchase various items, including a house, a car, and assorted cashier's checks. Approximately $1.3 million worth of liquid assets was seized from the defendant when he was arrested. The remainder of the money had been intermittently wired back to investors in the form of "profits."

Agent

We find it unnecessary for purposes of this opinion to fully recount the evidence presented by the government relating to the defendant's involvement in the peso scheme; we simply observe that the evidence overwhelmingly supported a conclusion that the scheme was fraudulent and that the defendant was not using the investors' money to purchase and resell pesos.

Counts two and three of the indictment charged the defendant with violations of 18 U.S.C. § 1956(a)(1)(A)(i). That section provides:

> § 1956. Laundering of monetary instruments
>
> (a)(1) Whoever, knowing that the property involved in a financial transaction represents the proceeds of some form of unlawful activity, conducts or attempts to conduct such a financial transaction which in fact involves the proceeds of specified unlawful activity —
> (A)(i) with the intent to promote the carrying on of specified unlawful activity . . .
> shall be sentenced to, . . . imprisonment for not more than twenty years. . . .

The "specified unlawful activity" alleged in the indictment was wire fraud in violation of 18 U.S.C. § 1343. Count two of the indictment alleged that Johnson used the proceeds of a wire fraud to pay off the mortgage on his house in Tulsa in the amount of $122,796. Count three alleged that Johnson used wire fraud proceeds to purchase a 1989 Mercedes automobile. . . .

Arg

Appellant contends that the evidence did not show that the payment of the mortgage on his home was done "with the intent to promote the carrying on" of the wire fraud.[56] He argues that there was no evidence to support a conclusion that he paid off the mortgage in order to further the wire fraud activity. In response, the government points out that the defendant maintained an office in the home which he used to carry out much of the fraudulent activity.

---

56. Appellant does not assert that the evidence was insufficient to show that he violated the wire fraud statute. Also, appellant does not challenge the jury's determination that he conducted the financial transactions specified in counts two and three of the indictment knowing that the property involved therein represented the proceeds of the wire fraud activity.

Direct evidence of a defendant's intent is seldom available. Intent can be proven, however, from surrounding circumstances. We find that the evidence, when viewed in the light most favorable to the government, is sufficient to support the conviction on count two. The evidence clearly showed that the defendant used the office in his home to carry out the fraudulent scheme. In addition, the defendant's aura of legitimacy was bolstered in the minds of investors who saw the defendant's house. The circumstances give rise to an inference that the defendant paid the mortgage on the house so that he could continue using the office in furtherance of the fraudulent scheme. Although, as appellant points out, he could have retained the use of the office simply by continuing to make monthly mortgage payments, the fact is that he did not do so. Instead, he used wire fraud proceeds to retire the outstanding balance on the loan secured by the mortgage. Paying off the loan gave him the right to continue using the office and the home. The jury could legitimately infer that paying off the mortgage with wire fraud proceeds was done with the intent to promote the carrying on of the unlawful activity.

The evidence similarly supports the conviction on count three of the indictment. The evidence suggests that the defendant used the Mercedes described in count three to impress investors. The jury could conclude from the evidence that appellant purchased the car to promote the carrying on of his fraudulent scheme. Appellant argues that he had two Mercedes automobiles and that evidence was lacking to show that the one described in count three was used by him in furthering the peso scheme. He contends that the Mercedes described in count three was purchased for his wife. The defendant in fact told one of the investors that he had purchased this car for his wife. But the record contains some evidence that contradicts this assertion. Testimony indicated that the defendant used this particular car both before and after he was separated from his wife. Also, after the defendant talked about the car with the same investor mentioned above, the investor went and talked to the auto dealer who sold the car to the defendant. The dealer spoke very highly of the defendant, who had put a down payment of approximately $66,000 on the car. After speaking with the auto dealer and others about the defendant, the investor was persuaded that the defendant was a legitimate businessman. This evidence suggests that the defendant used the car to persuade investors to invest in his scheme. His use of the car in this manner further tends to show that he purchased the car with that purpose in mind. Taken as a whole, the evidence supports the jury's finding that the defendant engaged in the financial transaction of purchasing the car with the intent to promote the carrying on of the wire fraud activity.

Appellant's next argument is that the evidence was insufficient to support the convictions on counts four through sixty-three of the indictment. These counts were brought under 18 U.S.C. § 1957, which provides in part:

> § 1957. Engaging in monetary transactions in property derived
> from specified unlawful activity

> (a) Whoever, . . . knowingly engages or attempts to engage in a monetary transaction in criminally derived property that is of a value greater than $10,000 and is derived from specified unlawful activity, shall be punished as provided in subsection (b). . . .
> (f) As used in this section —
> (1) the term "monetary transaction" means the deposit, withdrawal, transfer, or exchange, in or affecting interstate or foreign commerce, of funds or a monetary instrument . . . by, through, or to a financial institution. . . .

> (2) the term "criminally derived property" means any property constituting, or derived from, proceeds obtained from a criminal offense; . . .

Counts four through thirty-one of the indictment against the defendant alleged violations of § 1957 based on twenty-eight separate wire transfers of funds from investors to the defendant's account in Tulsa, Oklahoma. Counts thirty-two through fifty-seven were based upon wire transfers of funds from the defendant's account to individual investors. The final charges in the indictment, counts fifty-eight through sixty-three, were based upon withdrawals by the defendant from his account in the form of cashier's checks. The funds involved in all of the transactions were alleged to be the proceeds of wire fraud.

Appellant's primary argument pertains to counts four through thirty-one. He argues that the transfer of funds from the investors to his account did not violate § 1957 because those transfers were not monetary transactions in "criminally derived property."[57] . . . He points to the definition of criminally derived property, which is "any property constituting . . . proceeds obtained from a criminal offense." § 1957(f)(2). He argues that he did not obtain the proceeds of the wire fraud until they were credited to his account. Thus, he maintains, the transaction in which those funds were wired to him did not involve "criminally derived property." . . .

Under § 1957, "criminally derived property" means any property constituting, or derived from, proceeds obtained from a criminal offense. Because there is no other "property" at issue here, we are only concerned with the funds transferred by the investors to the defendant. We agree with appellant that under the facts presented here, the transfer of funds from the investors to the defendant's account did not constitute violations of § 1957.

Both the ordinary meaning of the word "obtained" and the legislative history behind § 1957 suggest that this section was not intended to apply to transactions of the type alleged in counts four through thirty-one. We turn first to the language of the statute. The statute itself defines criminally derived property in terms of proceeds "obtained" from a criminal offense. . . . "Obtain" most commonly means "to gain or attain possession or disposal of usually by some planned action or method." Webster's Third New International Dictionary, 1559 (1961). This suggests that Congress viewed a violation of § 1957 as occurring only after the individual involved in the specified criminal activity gained possession or disposal of the proceeds generated by the criminal activity. . . .

The underlying criminal activity in this case was wire fraud, which the defendant accomplished by causing the investors to wire funds to his account. Whether or not the funds that were wired to the defendant were "criminally derived property" depends upon whether they were proceeds obtained from a criminal offense at the time the defendant engaged in the monetary transaction. We find they were not. Section 1957 appears to be drafted to proscribe certain transactions in proceeds that have already been obtained by an individual from an underlying criminal offense. The defendant did not have possession of the funds nor were they at his disposal until the investors transferred

---

57. The essential elements of a § 1957 violation are that (1) the defendant engage or attempt to engage (2) in a monetary transaction (3) in criminally derived property that is of a value greater than $10,000 (4) knowing that the property is derived from unlawful activity, and (5) the property is, in fact, derived from "specified unlawful activity." United States v. Lovett, 964 F.2d 1029 (10th Cir. 1992). . . .

them to him. The defendant therefore cannot be said to have obtained the proceeds of the wire fraud until the funds were credited to his account. Thus, the transfers alleged in counts four through thirty-one of the indictment were not transactions in criminally derived property and the defendant's convictions on those counts are reversed.

Appellant's next argument is that the evidence was insufficient as to counts thirty-two through sixty-three of the indictment. These counts alleged violations of § 1957 based on transfers of funds from the defendant's account to the investors in the peso scheme. Appellant argues that the government did not show that the funds that he wired out of his account were the proceeds of wire fraud, stating "It is entirely possible that the funds paid out . . . came from sources other than the investors."

We find that the evidence here was sufficient for the jury to conclude that these funds were in fact derived from specified unlawful activity. The evidence showed that over five and a half million dollars were deposited into the defendant's account at the Sooner Federal Savings & Loan. The government presented evidence that at least $2.4 million of this amount was from specific instances of wire fraud. The testimony and the defendant's bank records indicated that most of the remainder, about $3 million, came from other investors in the peso scheme. The source of approximately 1.2% of the funds deposited in the defendant's account could not be determined. The amount of funds withdrawn from the defendant's account in the transactions set forth in counts thirty-two through sixty-three was approximately $1.8 million. An examination of the defendant's bank records gave no indication that the funds in the defendant's account came from any source other than investors in the alleged peso trades. Under the circumstances, the evidence was sufficient for the jury to find that the funds withdrawn were derived from the specified unlawful activity.

The government had the burden of showing that the criminally derived property used in the monetary transactions was in fact derived from specified unlawful activity. This does not mean, however, that the government had to show that funds withdrawn from the defendant's account could not possibly have come from any source other than the unlawful activity. Once proceeds of unlawful activity have been deposited in a financial institution and have been credited to an account, those funds cannot be traced to any particular transaction and cannot be distinguished from any other funds deposited in the account. The "tainted" funds may be commingled with "untainted" funds, with the result being simply a net credit balance in favor of the depositor. The credit balance gives the depositor a claim against the bank and allows him to withdraw funds to the extent of the credit. In the context of a withdrawal, the portion of § 1957 requiring a showing that the proceeds were in fact "derived from specified unlawful activity" could not have been intended as a requirement that the government prove that no "untainted" funds were deposited along with the unlawful proceeds. Such an interpretation would allow individuals to avoid prosecution simply by commingling legitimate funds with proceeds of crime. This would defeat the very purpose of the money-laundering statutes. . . .

CONCLUSION

The convictions on counts two, three, and thirty-two through sixty-three are affirmed. The convictions on counts four through thirty-one are reversed. . . .

Notes and Questions

1. Counts 2 and 3 charged that Johnson violated § 1956 by paying off the mortgage on his house (where his office was located) and by buying a Mercedes. Johnson did not challenge the jury's finding that he knew the money he used to buy the house and the car was derived from the fraud. What facts support the jury's finding of knowledge?

2. In addition to proof of knowledge that the money constituted proceeds of wire fraud, § 1956 requires proof that Johnson intended to promote the carrying on of wire fraud. Why were paying the mortgage and buying the car deemed evidence of intent to promote fraud?

3. Johnson made a $66,000 down payment on the Mercedes. Would the car dealer be in trouble if Johnson had made the payment in cash?

4. Counts 4 through 31 alleged violations of § 1957 based on wire transfers from the investors' own bank accounts to Johnson's account at an Oklahoma bank. Since Johnson never used the money to purchase and sell pesos as promised, these transfers constituted wire fraud. That being true, why wasn't the money the investors transferred into his account criminally derived property?[58]

If the investors had mailed Johnson checks, which he deposited himself, would we then have a monetary transaction in criminally derived property?

5. Counts 32 through 63 alleged violations of § 1957 based on wire transfers Johnson made from his account to the accounts of various investors. The source of some of the money in Johnson's account could not be determined. Johnson stated: "It is entirely possible that the funds paid out . . . came from sources other than the investors." If the source of some funds is unaccounted for, how did the government satisfy its burden of proving that the money Johnson wired to the investors was criminally derived property and that Johnson knew it was criminally derived?

Contrast the approach in *Johnson* with the Ninth Circuit's reasoning in United States v. Rutgard.[59] In *Rutgard*, the defendant was a wealthy ophthalmologist accused of Medicare fraud. Although the government proceeded on the theory that his entire medical practice was a fraud, the evidence established that the proceeds of the fraud amounted to only $46,000 of nearly $16 million in Medicare payments he received. Rutgard deposited $3.7 million from his practice and $1.9 million in municipal bonds into a family trust account during the time when the fraud occurred. After the government searched his office, he made two wire transfers out of the trust account — $5.6 million on May 5, and $1.9 million on May 6 — to an offshore bank. Shortly before the transfers occurred, the trust account held $8.5 million. After the transfers were made, more than $46,000 remained in the account. Thus, the question before the court was whether at least $10,000 of each transfer was criminally derived property (i.e., proceeds of the fraud).

> Section 1957 . . . does not speak to the attempt to cleanse dirty money by putting it in a clean form and so disguising it. This statute applies to the most open, above-board transaction. See 18 U.S.C. § 1957(f)(1) (broadly defining "monetary transaction"). The intent to commit a crime or the design of concealing criminal fruits is eliminated. . . .

---

58. Cf. United States v. Conley, 37 F.3d 970, 980 (3d Cir. 1994) (defining "proceeds" to include money derived from a completed offense or "a completed phase of an ongoing offense").

59. 116 F.3d 1270, 1291-1293 (9th Cir. 1997).

Section 1957 was enacted as a tool in the war against drugs. It is a powerful tool because it makes any dealing with a bank potentially a trap for the drug dealer or any other defendant who has a hoard of criminal cash derived from the specified crimes. If he makes a "deposit, withdrawal, transfer or exchange" with this cash, he commits the crime; he's forced to commit another felony if he wants to use a bank. This draconian law, so powerful by its elimination of criminal intent, freezes the proceeds of specific crimes out of the banking system. As long as the underlying crime has been completed and the defendant "possesses" the funds at the time of deposit, the proceeds cannot enter the banking system without a new crime being committed. . . .

The monetary transaction statute cannot be made wholly ineffective by commingling. To prevail, the government need show only a single $10,000 deposit of criminally-derived proceeds. Any innocent money already in the account, or later deposited, cannot wipe out the crime committed by the deposit of criminally-derived proceeds. Commingling with innocent funds can defeat application of the statute to a withdrawal of less than the total funds in the account, but ordinarily that fact presents no problem to the government which, if it has proof of a deposit of $10,000 of criminally-derived funds, can succeed by charging the deposit as the crime; or the government may prevail by showing that all the funds in the account are the proceeds of crime. Commingling will frustrate the statute if criminal deposits have been kept under $10,000. But that is the way the statute is written, to catch only large transfers. Moreover, if the criminal intent was to hide criminal proceeds, as would presumably be the case any time criminally derived cash was deposited with innocently derived funds to hide its identity, § 1956 can kick in and the depositor of amounts under $10,000 will be guilty of a § 1956 crime. . . .

Rutgard's convictions may be upheld if he transferred out of the account all the funds that were in it or if there was a rule or presumption that, once criminally-derived funds were deposited, any transfer from the account would be presumed to involve them for the purpose of applying § 1956. Rutgard did not transfer all the funds in the family trust account, however. The government showed that the account held $8.5 million on April 2, 1992 and $13,901 on July 2, 1992, the dates of the quarterly bank statements. But so far as evidence at trial goes, more than $46,000 remained in the account after the May 6 and 7 transfers. These transfers therefore did not necessarily transfer the $46,000 of fraudulent proceeds.

The alternative way of sustaining the convictions depends on a presumption, which the Fourth Circuit created in *Moore*, 27 F.3d at 976-77, but which we decline to create. The statute does not create a presumption that any transfer of cash in an account tainted by the presence of a small amount of fraudulent proceeds must be a transfer of these proceeds. . . . As the government did not prove that any fraudulently-derived proceeds left the account on May 5 or May 6, 1992, the monetary transfer counts were not proved beyond a reasonable doubt. . . .

Which approach is most faithful to the text of the statute? Is it possible that factual distinctions between *Johnson* and *Rutgard* make the result in each case right? What are the implications of the Fourth Circuit's creation of a presumption that any transfer of cash from an account in which legitimate and illegitimate assets are combined is a transfer of criminally derived proceeds?

UNITED STATES v. KENNEDY
64 F.3d 1465 (10th Cir. 1995)

EBEL, Circuit Judge.

Defendant-Appellant William R. Kennedy, Jr. ("Kennedy") was charged in a 109-count indictment for a massive scheme to defraud precious metals investors. A jury convicted Kennedy of one count of racketeering, 18 U.S.C. §§ 1962(c) & 1963, nine counts of mail fraud, 18 U.S.C. §§ 1341 & 2 (aiding and abetting), and seven counts of money laundering, 18 U.S.C. §§ 1956(a)(1)(A)(i) & 2 (aiding and abetting). . . .

BACKGROUND

In 1979, Kennedy helped found Western Monetary Consultants, Inc. ("WMC"). He served as WMC's president from the corporation's inception through his indictment in this case. WMC marketed itself as a large-scale seller of precious metals and coins. Through various literature mailings and a series of seminars, referred to as "war colleges," WMC advocated the purchase of tangible precious metals as a hedge against inflation caused by certain world events. Investors could purchase the metals from WMC either through cash transactions or through cash down-payments coupled with bank-financed loans.

When an investor agreed to purchase a certain quantity of metal from WMC, a WMC consultant would quote the investor an approximate price. The consultant would then contact the WMC trading department, which would locate the best price for the metal from one of its dealers. The consultant would then inform the investor of the exact price, which was to be "locked-in" at that point in time, and the investor would then transfer funds to WMC via check, often supplemented with funds from a bank loan. If WMC did not in turn provide the dealer with the purchase price within 48 hours of ordering, the dealer typically nullified the contract with WMC, requiring WMC to reorder at a new price.

Between 1984 and 1987, WMC increased its sales rapidly and began to experience serious cash shortages. Kennedy nevertheless continued to promote sales to new investors, without informing them that WMC was between ten to thirteen million dollars behind in filling backlogged orders. By March of 1988, WMC's cash shortages were so great that WMC filed for Chapter 11 bankruptcy protection, listing over 600 creditors from whom WMC had received over $18,000,000 towards orders that remained unfilled. WMC continued to operate thereafter under a confirmed reorganization plan.

In July of 1992, after a five year investigation of WMC's practices, the government indicted Kennedy and numerous other WMC participants. The 109-count indictment against Kennedy alleged a massive Ponzi scheme to defraud numerous precious metals investors. The government alleged that when WMC "locked-in" a price for an investor, it did so under the false pretenses that it would purchase the investor's metal immediately. However, rather than purchasing immediately, the government alleged that WMC frequently delayed purchases or failed to fill orders altogether. Specifically, the government alleged that WMC diverted many investors' funds to other uses, including speculating in futures markets, operating the *Conservative Digest* magazine, and financing personal endeavors. . . .

The government indicted Kennedy for the specific money laundering violations set forth in 18 U.S.C. § 1956, which provides in relevant part:

> (a)(1) Whoever, knowing that the property involved in a financial transaction represents the proceeds of some form of unlawful activity, conducts or attempts to conduct such a financial transaction which in fact *involves the proceeds of specified unlawful activity* —
>
>   (A)(i) with the intent to promote the carrying on of specified unlawful activity-
> . . . shall be sentenced to a fine . . . or imprisonment. . . .

18 U.S.C. § 1956(a)(1)(A)(i). The government alleged that Kennedy violated this statute by depositing checks or foreign currency from various investors into a WMC account. Each separate count represented a particular deposit involving a different named investor's funds. The government claimed that each of these deposits constituted financial transactions "involving the proceeds of specified unlawful activity" — namely, the proceeds of the mail fraud scheme described above.

Kennedy argues that these deposits cannot violate § 1956 because § 1956 only covers transactions that occur *after* a defendant has taken complete control of the funds from the predicate crime. Relying on United States v. Johnson, 971 F.2d 562 (10th Cir. 1992), Kennedy suggests that to state a § 1956 money laundering violation, the indictment would have had to allege another transaction, subsequent to his taking possession of the funds by depositing them into a WMC account. We disagree. All that is required to violate § 1956 is a transaction meeting the statutory criteria that takes place after the underlying crime has been completed. Thus, the central inquiry in a money laundering charge is determining when the predicate crime became a "completed" offense — and it is that inquiry that distinguishes this case from *Johnson*.

In *Johnson*, the defendant was charged with money laundering under a companion statute, 18 U.S.C. § 1957. Section 1957 prohibits "knowingly engaging or attempting to engage in a monetary transaction in criminally derived property," which is defined as "any property constituting, or derived from, proceeds obtained from a criminal offense." 18 U.S.C. § 1957(a), (f)(2). Each count against the defendant in *Johnson* was based on a wire transfer of funds from an investor's account directly into the defendant's account. Thus, the predicate crimes were the use of the wires in violation of 18 U.S.C. § 1343. Significantly, however, the only wirings that were alleged to support the predicate wire fraud crimes in *Johnson* were the very transfers of funds identified in the money laundering transactions. Based on that fact, we held that the wirings could not also be used to support convictions for § 1957 money laundering crimes.

Kennedy's case is thus distinguishable in one important and dispositive respect. As noted, the only use of the wires alleged in *Johnson* to prove the predicate wire fraud crimes were the very wire transfers that allegedly involved "criminally derived property" under the money laundering statute. In Kennedy's case, in contrast, the government alleged many prior mailings to prove the predicate mail fraud crimes, which occurred before the monetary transactions that formed the basis of his money laundering counts. Thus, unlike in *Johnson*, the illegal mailings in this case involved discrete, earlier mailings by Kennedy, rather than the receipt of funds by Kennedy from his victims. It was the subsequent and distinct transfers of funds that were alleged as the separate transactions involving "proceeds of specified unlawful activity" which constituted the alleged money laundering under § 1956.

This factual difference is important because Congress clearly intended the money laundering statutes to punish new conduct that occurs after the completion of certain criminal activity, rather than simply to create an additional punishment for that criminal activity. The "completion" of both wire and mail fraud occurs when any wiring or mailing is used in execution of a scheme; there is no requirement that the scheme actually defraud a victim into investing money for the crime to be complete. Thus, because the money deposits in Kennedy's case occurred after other mailings had already completed the predicate mail fraud crime, those transfers properly could be construed as new transactions involving the proceeds of mail fraud. In contrast, because the specific wire fraud violations alleged in *Johnson* were not complete until the wires were used to transfer the funds, those transfers could not be construed as new transactions to support a money laundering offense. Accordingly, we reject Kennedy's contention that his money laundering convictions must be set aside for failure to allege the "proceeds" element of those crimes. . . .

III. CONCLUSION

For the reasons stated above, we affirm.

Notes and Questions

1. Are the results in *Johnson* and *Kennedy* attributable to differences in the statutes, differences in the facts, or differences in the government's theory? Could the government have successfully framed its § 1957 case under a different theory in *Johnson*?

NOTE ON THE MEANING OF "PROCEEDS"

The money laundering statutes require, as an element of proof, that the offense involve proceeds of specified unlawful activity. But neither § 1956 nor § 1957 defines the term "proceeds," and there is no legislative history to shed light on the question of what Congress meant when it made this a key concept in the statutory scheme. Left with a blank slate to write on, the lower courts adopted differing views on the question whether "proceeds" means gross receipts or it means net profits.[60] The Supreme Court granted certiorari in United States v. Santos[61] to resolve the circuit split, but the case ended with a sharply divided Court that produced somewhat inconclusive results.

Writing for a four-Justice plurality, Justice Scalia announced the judgment of the Court, affirming the Seventh Circuit's ruling that under these money laundering statutes, "proceeds" means "profits." Scalia's opinion reasoned that the ordinary meaning of "proceeds" could reasonably be read to encompass either receipts or profits without doing violence to the coherence of the statutory scheme. But absent legislative history

---

60. Compare United States v. Grasso, 381 F.3d 160, 167 (3d Cir. 2004) ("proceeds" means gross receipts), with United States v. Scialabba, 282 F.3d 475, 476 (7th Cir. 2002) ("proceeds" means profits).

61. United States v. Santos, 553 U.S. 507 (2008).

to illuminate congressional intent, the plurality was persuaded that the rule of lenity required the Court to adopt the definition most favorable to the defendant. And since "profits" is a narrower concept than "receipts" and thus will always be more defendant friendly, the plurality's ruling would be that under §§ 1956 and 1957, "proceeds" always means "profits."

But that's not quite the end of the story. Justice Stevens, who cast the deciding vote, concurred in the judgment but on far more limited grounds. In Justice Stevens' view, the meaning of "proceeds" should be context specific. And because the statutes define the specified unlawful activity that must generate or be related to the proceeds to include myriad predicate crimes that run the gamut from drug and gambling offenses to white collar fraud, Justice Stevens would hold that under §§ 1956 and 1957, "proceeds" sometimes means net profits but at other times means gross receipts.

Thus, the Court in effect ruled out the interpretation that "proceeds" always means profits, but Justice Scalia's coalition could not command the necessary fifth vote to support the view that "proceeds" never means receipts.

13

Environmental Crimes

I. INTRODUCTION

One need not be an avid environmentalist to be conversant with terms like acid rain, ozone layer, greenhouse effect, and Love Canal. These terms telegraph shorthand messages about serious environmental concerns — air and water pollution, hazardous waste, and toxic substances, to name but a few.[1] Although surveys conducted in the 1970s and 1980s showed strong public support for sending polluters to jail, both Congress and the executive branch were slow to develop effective criminal enforcement tools to address these concerns. It was not until the 1970s that Congress recognized the need to address them with comprehensive environmental legislation, and it was only in 1980 that Congress authorized, for the first time, felony penalties for environmental crimes.[2]

Congress marked the beginning of modern environmental law with the enactment of the Clean Air Act and the Clean Water Act in the early 1970s. These landmark legislative achievements were soon followed by the enactment of the Resource Conservation and Recovery Act (RCRA), which provides "cradle to grave" regulation of hazardous waste, and the Comprehensive Environmental Response, Conservation and Liability Act (CERCLA) — also known as the Superfund law — which provides a mechanism for financing the cleanup of the worst hazardous waste sites in the country.

II. WATER POLLUTION: THE CLEAN WATER ACT

The Clean Water Act (CWA) outlaws discharging pollutants from a point source into navigable waters. Its first priority is to set water quality standards and regulate discharges of pollutants into public waterways. To attain those goals, the Act establishes

---

1. A 1984 survey by the Department of Justice Bureau of Justice Statistics revealed that the public ranked the knowing pollution of a city's water supply as more serious than heroin smuggling if the pollution caused 20 people to become ill but not sick enough to require medical treatment. Knowingly polluting the water supply with no reported ill effects was ranked as more serious than arson or supplying a robber with the floor plan of a bank. U.S. Dept. of Justice Bureau of Justice Statistics, The National Survey of Crime Severity, vii-viii (1985).

2. Kathleen F. Brickey, Environmental Crime at the Crossroads: The Intersection of Environmental and Criminal Law Theory, 71 Tul. L. Rev. 487, 495-496 (1996).

a system of national effluent standards on an industry-by-industry basis. The CWA permits controlled discharges of pollutants to the extent that they are consistent with the protection of public water supplies, agricultural and industrial uses, marine and wildlife, and recreational uses of the waterways.[3] Through the National Pollutant Discharge Elimination System (NPDES), a permit to discharge pollutants may be obtained from the Environmental Protection Agency (EPA) or a corresponding state agency.[4]

Knowing violations of the CWA are punished more severely than negligent violations, and violations that occur after a first conviction are punished twice as severely as first offenses. Both the civil and criminal penalty provisions authorize a separate fine for each day the violation continues.

A. DISCHARGE FROM A POINT SOURCE

1. Point Source

The CWA regulates discharges — i.e., releases — of pollutants into navigable waters. To violate the Act, the discharge must be from a "point source," a term of broad import that is defined to include:

> any discernible, confined and discrete conveyance, including but not limited to any pipe, ditch, channel, tunnel, conduit, well, discrete fissure, container, rolling stock, concentrated animal feeding operation or vessel or other floating craft, from which pollutants are or may be discharged.[5]

UNITED STATES v. PLAZA HEALTH LABORATORIES, INC.
3 F.3d 643 (2d Cir. 1993)

GEORGE C. PRATT, Circuit Judge. . . .

FACTS AND BACKGROUND

Villegas was co-owner and vice president of Plaza Health Laboratories, Inc., a blood-testing laboratory in Brooklyn, New York. On at least two occasions between April and September 1988, Villegas loaded containers of numerous vials of human blood generated from his business into his personal car, and drove to his residence at the Admirals Walk Condominium in Edgewater, New Jersey. Once at his condominium complex, Villegas removed the containers from his car and carried them to the edge of the Hudson River. On one occasion he carried two containers of the vials to the bulkhead that separates his condominium complex from the river, and placed them at low tide within a crevice in the bulkhead that was below the high-water line.

---

3. 33 U.S.C. § 1312(a).
4. 33 U.S.C. § 1342.
5. 33 U.S.C. § 1362(14).

On May 26, 1988, a group of eighth graders on a field trip at the Alice Austin House in Staten Island, New York, discovered numerous glass vials containing human blood along the shore. Some of the vials had washed up on the shore; many were still in the water. Some were cracked, although most remained sealed with stoppers in solid-plastic containers or ziplock bags. Fortunately, no one was injured. That afternoon, New York City workers recovered approximately 70 vials from the area.

On September 25, 1988, a maintenance worker employed by the Admirals Walk Condominium discovered a plastic container holding blood vials wedged between rocks in the bulkhead. New Jersey authorities retrieved numerous blood vials from the bulkhead later that day.

Ten of the retrieved vials contained blood infected with the hepatitis-B virus. All of the vials recovered were eventually traced to Plaza Health Laboratories.

Based upon the May 1988 discovery of vials, Plaza Health Laboratories and Villegas were indicted on May 16, 1989, on two counts each of violating § 1319(c)(2) and (3) of the Clean Water Act. A superseding indictment charged both defendants with two additional CWA counts based upon the vials found in September 1988.

[Two of the counts in the indictment charged the defendants with knowingly discharging pollutants from a "point source" without a permit. They were convicted on both counts. On appeal, Villegas argued that his conviction could not stand because the definition of point source did not contemplate individual human beings.]

DISCUSSION . . .

A. NAVIGATING THE CLEAN WATER ACT

The basic prohibition on discharge of pollutants is in 33 U.S.C. § 1311(a), which states:

> Except as in compliance with this section and sections 1312, 1316, 1317, 1328, *1342*, and 1344 of this title, the *discharge* of any *pollutant* by any person shall be unlawful.

Id. (emphasis added).

The largest exception to this seemingly absolute rule is found in 33 U.S.C. § 1342, which establishes the CWA's national pollutant discharge elimination system, or NPDES:

> (a) Permits for discharge of pollutants
>   (1) Except as provided in sections 1328 [aquaculture] and 1344 of this title [dredge and fill permits], the Administrator may, after opportunity for public hearing, issue a permit for the discharge of any pollutant . . . *notwithstanding section 1311(a) of this title*, upon condition that such discharge will meet . . . all applicable requirements under sections 1311, 1312, 1316, 1317, 1318, and 1343 of this title. . . .

33 U.S.C. § 1342(a) (emphasis added).

Reading § 1311(a), the basic prohibition, and § 1342(a)(1), the permit section, together, we can identify the basic rule, our rhumb line to clean waters, that, absent a permit, "the discharge of any pollutant by any person" is unlawful.

We must then adjust our rhumb line by reference to two key definitions —
"pollutant" and "discharge." "Pollutant" is defined, in part, as "biological materials . . .
discharged into water." 33 U.S.C. § 1362(6) (emphasis added).[6] "Discharge," in turn, is
"any addition of any pollutant to navigable waters *from any point source . . .*" (emphasis added). 33 U.S.C. § 1362(12).

As applied to the facts of this case, then, the defendant "added" a "pollutant"
(human blood in glass vials) to "navigable waters" (the Hudson River), and he did so
without a permit. The issue, therefore, is whether his conduct constituted a "discharge,"
and that in turn depends on whether the addition of the blood to the Hudson River
waters was "from any point source."

For this final course adjustment in our navigation, we look again to the statute.

> (14) The term "point source" means any discernible, confined and discrete convey-
> ance, including but not limited to any pipe, ditch, channel, tunnel, conduit, well, discrete
> fissure, container, rolling stock, concentrated animal feeding operation, or vessel or other
> floating craft, from which pollutants are or may be discharged. This term does not include
> agricultural stormwater discharges and return flows from irrigated agriculture.

33 U.S.C. § 1362(14).

During and after Villegas's trial, Judge Korman labored over how to define "point
source" in this case. At one point he observed that the image of a human being is not
"conjured up" by [C]ongress's definition of "point source." Ultimately, he never defined
the "point source" element but he did charge the jury:

> Removing pollutants from a container, and a vehicle is a container, parked next to a navi-
> gable body of water and physically throwing the pollutant into the water constitutes a dis-
> charge from a point source.

. . . Judge Korman held that the element "point source" may reasonably be read

> to include any discrete and identifiable conduit — *including a human being* — designated
> to collect or discharge pollutants produced in the course of a waste-generating activity
> (emphasis added).

As the parties have presented the issue to us in their briefs and at oral argument,
the question is "whether a human being can be a point source." Both sides focus on the
district court's conclusion . . . that, among other things, the requisite "point source"
here could be Villegas himself. . . .

1. Language and Structure of Act

Human beings are not among the enumerated items that may be a "point source."
Although by its terms the definition of "point source" is nonexclusive, the words used
to define the term and the examples given ("pipe, ditch, channel, tunnel, conduit, well,
discrete fissure," etc.) evoke images of physical structures and instrumentalities that

---

6. The term "pollutant" is defined to mean "dredged spoil, solid waste, incinerator residue, sewage,
garbage, sewage sludge, munitions, chemical wastes, biological materials, radioactive materials, heat,
wrecked or discarded equipment, rock, sand, cellar dirt and industrial, municipal and agricultural waste
discharged into water." 33 U.S.C. § 1362(6). — ED.

systematically act as a means of conveying pollutants from an industrial source to navigable waterways.

In addition, if every discharge involving humans were to be considered a "discharge from a point source," the statute's lengthy definition of "point source" would have been unnecessary. It is elemental that Congress does not add unnecessary words to statutes. Had Congress intended to punish any human being who polluted navigational waters, it could readily have said: "any person who places pollutants in navigable waters without a permit is guilty of a crime."

The Clean Water Act generally targets industrial and municipal sources of pollutants, as is evident from a perusal of its many sections. Consistent with this focus, the term "point source" is used throughout the statute, but invariably in sentences referencing industrial or municipal discharges. See, e.g., 33 U.S.C. § 1311 (referring to "owner or operator" of point source); § 1311(e) (requiring that effluent limitations established under the Act "be applied to all point sources of discharge"); § 1311(g)(2) (allows an "owner or operator of a point source" to apply to EPA for modification of its limitations requirements); § 1342(f) (referring to classes, categories, types, and sizes of point sources); § 1314(b)(4)(B) (denoting "best conventional pollutant control technology measures and practices" applicable to any point source within particular category or class); § 1316 ("any point source . . . which is constructed as to meet all applicable standards of performance"); § 1318(a) (administrator shall require owner or operator of any point source to install, use and maintain monitoring equipment or methods); and § 1318(c) (states may develop procedures for inspection, monitoring, and entry with respect to point sources located in state).

This emphasis was sensible, as "[i]ndustrial and municipal point sources were the worst and most obvious offenders of surface water quality. They were also the easiest to address because their loadings emerge from a discrete point such as the end of a pipe." David Letson, Point/Nonpoint Source Pollution Reduction Trading: An Interpretive Survey, 32 Nat. Resources J. 219, 221 (1992).

Finally on this point, we assume that Congress did not intend the awkward meaning that would result if we were to read "human being" into the definition of "point source." Section 1362(12)(A) defines "discharge of a pollutant" as "any addition of any pollutant to navigable waters from any point source." Enhanced by this definition, § 1311(a) reads in effect "the addition of any pollutant to navigable waters *from any point source by any person* shall be unlawful" (emphasis added). But were a human being to be included within the definition of "point source," the prohibition would then read: "the addition of any pollutant to navigable waters *from any person by any person* shall be unlawful," and this simply makes no sense. As the statute stands today, the term "point source" is comprehensible only if it is held to the context of industrial and municipal discharges. . . .

Convictions reversed; cross-appeal affirmed.

OAKES, Circuit Judge, dissenting:

I agree that this is not the typical Clean Water Act prosecution — though, as criminal prosecutions under the Act are infrequent, or at least result in few published judicial opinions, what is "typical" is as yet ill-defined. I also agree that the prosecutors in this case may not have defined the theory of their case before proceeding to trial as well as they might have, thereby complicating the task of determining whether the jury was asked to resolve the proper factual questions. However, because I do not agree that a person can never be a point source, and because I believe that Mr. Villegas' actions, as the jury found them, fell well within the bounds of activity proscribed by the Clean Water Act's bar on discharge of pollutants into navigable waters, I am required to dissent.

A. POINT SOURCE . . .

I begin with the obvious, in hopes that it will illuminate the less obvious: the classic point source is something like a pipe. This is, at least in part, because pipes and similar conduits are needed to carry large quantities of waste water, which represents a large proportion of the point source pollution problem. Thus, devices designed to convey large quantities of waste water from a factory or municipal sewage treatment facility are readily classified as point sources. Because not all pollutants are liquids, however, the statute and the cases make clear that means of conveying solid wastes to be dumped in navigable waters are also point sources. See, e.g., 33 U.S.C. § 1362(14) ("rolling stock," or railroad cars, listed as an example of a point source); Avoyelles Sportsmen's League, Inc. v. Marsh, 715 F.2d 897, 922 (5th Cir. 1983) (backhoes and bulldozers used to gather fill and deposit it on wetlands are point sources).

What I take from this look at classic point sources is that, at the least, an organized means of channeling and conveying industrial waste in quantity to navigable waters is a "discernible, confined and discrete conveyance." . . .

In short, the term "point source" has been broadly construed to apply to a wide range of polluting techniques, so long as the pollutants involved are not just human-made, but reach the navigable waters by human effort or by leaking from a clear point at which waste water was collected by human effort. . . .

. . . [T]o further refine the definition of "point source," I consider what it is that the Act does not cover: nonpoint source discharges.

Nonpoint source pollution is, generally, runoff: salt from roads, agricultural chemicals from farmlands, oil from parking lots, and other substances washed by rain, in diffuse patterns, over the land and into navigable waters.[7] The sources are many, difficult to identify and difficult to control. Indeed, an effort to greatly reduce nonpoint source pollution could require radical changes in land use patterns which Congress evidently was unwilling to mandate without further study.[8] The structure of the statute — which regulates point source pollution closely, while leaving nonpoint source regulation to the states under the Section 208 program — indicates that the term "point source" was

---

7. According to the EPA, nonpoint source pollution

is caused by diffuse sources that are not regulated as point sources and normally is associated with agricultural, silvicultural and urban runoff, runoff from construction activities, etc. Such pollution results in the human-made or human-induced alteration of the chemical, physical, biological, and radiological integrity of water. In practical terms, nonpoint source pollution does not result from a discharge at a specific, single location (such as a single pipe) but generally results from land runoff, precipitation, atmospheric deposition, or percolation.

EPA Office of Water Regulations and Standards, Nonpoint Source Guidance 3 (1987).

8. As Professors Anderson, Mandelker, and Tarlock have observed,

Congress expressed great faith in the ability of engineers to limit what came out of pipes but less faith in the ability of engineers to fix non-point source pollution:

included in the definition of discharge so as to ensure that nonpoint source pollution would not be covered. Instead, Congress chose to regulate first that which could easily be regulated: direct discharges by identifiable parties, or point sources.

This rationale for regulating point and nonpoint sources differently — that point sources may readily be controlled and are easily attributable to a particular source, while nonpoint sources are more difficult to control without radical change, and less easily attributable, once they reach water, to any particular responsible party — helps define what fits within each category. Thus, Professor Rodgers has suggested, "the statutory 'discernible, confined and discrete conveyance' . . . can be understood as singling out those candidates suitable for control-at-the-source." 2 William H. Rodgers, Jr., Environmental Law: Air and Water § 4.10 at 150 (1986). . . .

While Villegas' activities were not prototypical point source discharges . . . they much more closely resembled a point source discharge than a nonpoint source discharge. First, Villegas and his lab were perfectly capable of avoiding discharging their waste into water: they were, in Professor Rodgers' terms, a "controllable" source.

Furthermore, the discharge was directly into water, and came from an identifiable point, Villegas. Villegas did not dispose of the materials on land, where they could be washed into water as nonpoint source pollution. Rather, he carried them, from his firm's laboratory, in his car, to his apartment complex, where he placed them in a bulkhead below the high tide line. I do not think it is necessary to determine whether it was Mr. Villegas himself who was the point source, or whether it was his car, the vials, or the bulkhead: in a sense, the entire stream of Mr. Villegas' activity functioned as a "discrete conveyance" or point source. The point is that the source of the pollution was clear, and would have been easy to control. Indeed, Villegas was well aware that there were methods of controlling the discharge (and that the materials were too dangerous for casual disposal): his laboratory had hired a professional medical waste handler. He simply chose not to use an appropriate waste disposal mechanism.

Villegas' method may have been an unusual one for a corporate officer, but it would undermine the statute — which, after all, sets as its goal the elimination of discharges — to regard as "ambiguous" a Congressional failure to list an unusual method of disposing of waste. I doubt that Congress would have regarded an army of men and women throwing industrial waste from trucks into a stream as exempt from the statute. . . .

Conclusion

Accordingly, I would affirm the rulings of the district court.

There is no effective way as yet, other than land use control, by which you can intercept that runoff and control it in the way that you do a point source. We have not yet developed technology to deal with that kind of a problem. [Senate Debate on S. 2770, Nov. 2, 1971, reported in 1972 Legislative History, at 1315.]

Frederick R. Anderson, Daniel R. Mandelker & A. Dan Tarlock, Environmental Protection: Law and Policy 377 (2d ed. 1990).

Notes and Questions

1. Which of the following would constitute a discharge from a point source under the majority's view?

    a. A dump truck parks beside a river and dumps its contents directly into the water.

    b. The truck dumps its contents onto the river bank. The next day, a heavy rain washes the matter from the bank into the water.

    c. The truck dumps its load onto the river bank. Three laborers then shovel it into the water.

    d. The truck parks on the river bank. The three laborers climb onto the truck bed and shovel the contents over the side into the water.

2. At one point in his dissent, Judge Oakes expressed disbelief that Congress would have meant to exempt an army of men and women who threw industrial waste into the river from liability under the CWA. In his view, this would encourage corporations that are perfectly capable of complying with the Act "to ask their employees to stand between the company trucks and the sea." What did he mean by that?

3. Could Judge Oakes' reading of the statute lead to imposition of felony penalties for throwing a candy wrapper into navigable waters? If so, would it be possible to avoid this extreme result while at the same time recognizing that — in appropriate circumstances — an individual could nonetheless be deemed a point source?

4. The Refuse Act is a turn of the century statute that prohibits discharging "any refuse matter of any kind or description" (excluding certain kinds of sewage) into navigable waters.[9] It applies to all foreign substances that threaten navigation or pollute the water.[10] The Refuse Act contains two distinct prohibitions: (1) the act of discharging refuse into navigable waters and (2) depositing refuse on the bank of navigable waters where the refuse is "liable" to be washed into the water. Do these prohibitions provide a useful backup to the liability scheme in the CWA? How would they apply to the hypothetical situations posed in Question 1 above?

5. Unlike the CWA, the Refuse Act does not require proof of a culpable mental state to establish a criminal violation. Instead, it imposes strict liability. And unlike criminal violations of the CWA, which are felonies, Refuse Act violations are misdemeanors. How would these differences influence a prosecutor's decision about which statute to invoke?

2. Navigable Waters

The Clean Water Act applies only to discharges into navigable waters, but what makes a waterway "navigable" is a question that has dogged courts over the years. Clearly rivers, oceans, and other bodies of water that are navigable in fact fall within the coverage of the statute. But the dicier question is the extent to which waters that are

---

9. 33 U.S.C. § 407.
10. United States v. Standard Oil Co., 384 U.S. 224, 230 (1966).

not navigable in fact — such as wetlands, arroyos, and intermittent streams — are within the regulatory reach of the Act.

NORTHERN CALIFORNIA RIVER WATCH v. CITY OF HEALDSBURG
457 F.3d 1023 (9th Cir. 2006)

SCHROEDER, Chief Judge.

Defendant/Appellant City of Healdsburg ("Healdsburg") appeals the district court's judgment in favor of Plaintiff/Appellee Northern California River Watch ("River Watch"), an environmental group, in this litigation under the Clean Water Act ("CWA"). Plaintiff alleges that Healdsburg, without first obtaining a National Pollutant Discharge Elimination System ("NPDES") permit, violated the CWA by discharging sewage from its waste treatment plant into waters covered by the Act. Healdsburg discharged the sewage into a body of water known as "Basalt Pond," a rock quarry pit that had filled with water from the surrounding aquifer, located next to the Russian River.

[The district court held that the discharges into the Pond were discharges into the Russian River, a waterway protected by the CWA.]

BACKGROUND . . .

Basalt Pond was created in approximately 1967 when the Basalt Rock Company began excavating gravel and sand from land near the Russian River. After the top soil was ripped away, large machines tore out rock and sand. The result was a pit. The pit filled with water up to the line of the water table of the surrounding aquifer. Today, Basalt Pond, measuring one half mile in length and a quarter mile in breadth, contains 58 acres of surface water. The Pond lies along the west side of the Russian River, separated from the River by a levee.

It is undisputed that the Russian River is a navigable water of the United States. Its headwaters originate in Mendocino County, California. Its main course runs about 110 miles, flowing into the Pacific Ocean west of Santa Rosa.

The horizontal distance between the edge of the River and the edge of the Pond varies between fifty and several hundred feet, depending on the exact location and the height of the river water. Usually, there is no surface connection, because the levee blocks it and prevents the Pond from being inundated by high river waters in the rainy season.

In 1971, Healdsburg built a secondary waste-treatment plant on a 35-acre site located on the north side of Basalt Pond about 800 feet from and west of the Russian River. Prior to 1978, Healdsburg discharged the plant's wastewater into another water-filled pit located to the north. In 1978, Healdsburg began discharging into Basalt Pond. Although Healdsburg did not obtain an NPDES permit, it received a state water emission permit as well as permission from Syar Industries, Inc., the current owner and manager of land and operations at Basalt Pond.

The wastewater discharged into Basalt Pond from the plant was about 420 to 455 million gallons per year between 1998 and 2000. The volume of the Pond itself is somewhat larger — 450 to 740 million gallons. The annual outflow from the sewage plant, therefore, is sufficient to fill the entire Pond every one to two years. Basalt Pond would, of course, soon overflow in these circumstances were it not for the fact that the Pond drains into the surrounding aquifer.

Pond water in the aquifer finds its way to the River over a period of a few months and seeps directly into the River along as much as 2200 feet of its banks. . . .

The district court found that the concentrations of chloride in the groundwater between the Pond and the Russian River are substantially higher than in the surrounding area. Chloride, which already exists in the Pond due to naturally occurring salts, reaches the River in higher concentrations as a direct result of Healdsburg's discharge of sewage into the Pond. . . .

DISCUSSION

A. WETLANDS CONSTITUTING WATERS OF THE UNITED STATES

Congress passed the Clean Water Act in 1972. The Act's stated objective is "to restore and maintain the chemical, physical, and biological integrity of the Nation's waters." 33 U.S.C. § 1251(a). To that end, the statute, among other things, prohibits "the discharge of any pollutant by any person" except as provided in the Act. § 1311(a).

After the CWA was passed, an issue arose concerning the extent to which wetlands adjacent to navigable waters constitute "waters of the United States." In 1978, the Army Corps of Engineers ("ACOE") issued a regulation defining "waters of the United States" to include "adjacent wetlands." The regulations specifically provide that "[t]he term 'waters of the United States' means," among other things, "[w]etlands adjacent to waters." The regulations further specify that "[w]etlands separated from other waters of the United States by man-made dikes or barriers, natural river berms, beach dunes and the like are 'adjacent wetlands.'" 33 C.F.R. § 328.3(c).

The first issue is therefore whether Basalt Pond and its surrounding[s] are "wetlands adjacent to waters" within the meaning of the regulations. If so, we must decide whether such adjacent wetlands constitute "waters of the United States" protected under the Act.

[T]he Pond itself and its surrounding area are wetlands under the regulatory definition. The applicable regulations define wetlands as "those areas that are inundated or saturated by surface or groundwater." See 33 C.F.R. § 328.3(b). The record here reflects that the Russian River and surrounding area rest on top of a vast gravel bed extending as much as sixty feet into the earth. The gravel bed is a porous medium, saturated with water. Through it flows an equally vast underground aquifer. This aquifer supplies the principal pathway for a continuous passage of water between Basalt Pond and the Russian River. Beneath the surface, water soaks in and out of the Pond via the underground aquifer. This action is continuous, 24 hours a day, seven days a week, 365 days a year. Indeed, the parties have stipulated that the Pond and the River overlie the same unconfined aquifer and that the land separating the two is saturated below the water table.

Because Basalt Pond and surrounding wetlands were created by quarrying, they are man-made. This fact is not determinative of whether they qualify as navigable waters. Since Basalt Pond contains wetlands, the only remaining question is whether the adjacent wetlands constitute waters of the United States subject to the CWA.

The Supreme Court has consistently held, when interpreting the meaning of "adjacent wetlands" in the regulations, that in order for the Act to apply there must be some relationship between wetlands and an identifiable navigable water. The leading case is *Riverside Bayview Homes*, 474 U.S. 121, decided in 1985. The Supreme Court there upheld CWA jurisdiction over wetlands that directly abutted a navigable creek. The Court held that "the relationship between waters and their adjacent wetlands provides an adequate basis for a legal judgment that adjacent wetlands may be defined as waters under the Act." The Court left open the question of whether the CWA also protected wetlands other than those adjacent to open waters. Id. at 131-32.

In Solid Waste Agency of Northern Cook County v. United States Army Corps of Engineers, 531 U.S. 159 (2001) (*SWANCC*), the Supreme Court again interpreted the CWA term "navigable waters" and held that isolated ponds and mudflats, unconnected to other waters covered by the Act, were not "waters of the United States." The case involved ponds that had been formed as a result of an abandoned sand and gravel pit mining operation and were not "adjacent wetlands." The ACOE regulations defined the ponds nevertheless to be "waters of the United States," because they were "used as habitat by other migratory birds which cross state lines." Under this "Migratory Bird Rule," ponds that are isolated from navigable waters may constitute "waters of the United States" if they are used as habitat by migratory birds. The Supreme Court rejected that theory and held that the CWA does not protect isolated ponds without a significant nexus. The Court explained that, "[i]t was the significant nexus between wetlands and 'navigable waters' that informed our reading of the [Act] in *Riverside Bayview Homes*." Id. at 167.

The Supreme Court in *SWANCC*, therefore, invalidated the Migratory Bird Rule but did not purport to reconsider its prior holding regarding adjacent wetlands in *Riverside Bayview Homes*. . . .

In the last term, however, the Supreme Court discussed the intersection between *Riverside Bayview Homes* and *SWANCC*. United States v. Rapanos, 126 S. Ct. 2208 (2006). The *Rapanos* decision involved two consolidated cases.

The first consolidated case, *Rapanos I*, involved three land parcels near Midland, Michigan. [All three parcels contained at least several dozen acres of wetlands.] The wetlands at issue in all three parcels were neither directly adjacent to or entirely isolated from a navigable water of the United States. . . .

In *Rapanos*, a 4-4-1 plurality opinion, the Supreme Court addressed how the term "navigable waters" should be construed under the Act. The plurality, written by Justice Scalia for four Justices, would have reversed on the grounds that only those wetlands with a continuous surface connection to bodies that are "waters of the United States" are protected under the CWA. Justice Stevens, writing the dissent for four Justices, would have affirmed on the grounds that wetlands not directly adjacent to navigable waters, but adjacent to tributaries of navigable waters, are protected under the CWA. Justice Stevens argued that *Riverside Bayview Homes* is still the controlling precedent and does not require a "significant nexus" test.

Justice Kennedy, constituting the fifth vote for reversal, concurred only in the judgment and, therefore, provides the controlling rule of law. See Marks v. United States, 430 U.S. 188, 193 (1977) (explaining that "[w]hen a fragmented Court decides a case and no single rationale explaining the result enjoys the assent of five Justices, the holding of the Court may be viewed as that position taken by those Members who concurred in the judgments on the narrowest grounds"). Justice Kennedy took the view that wetlands come within the statutory phrase "navigable waters," if the wetlands have a "significant nexus" to navigable-in-fact waterways. He explained that a significant nexus exists "if the wetlands, either alone or in combination with similarly situated lands in the region, significantly affect the chemical, physical, and biological integrity of other covered waters more readily understood as 'navigable.'" *Rapanos*, 126 S. Ct. at 2248. "When, in contrast, wetlands' effects on water quality are speculative or insubstantial, they fall outside the zone fairly encompassed by the statutory term 'navigable waters.'" Id.

In addressing whether a hydrological connection satisfies the "significant nexus" test, Justice Kennedy explained that a "mere hydrologic connection should not suffice in all cases; the connection may be too insubstantial for the hydrologic linkage to establish the required nexus with navigable waters as traditionally understood." Id. at 2251. Rather, the "required nexus must be assessed in terms of the statute's goals and purposes," which are to "restore and maintain the chemical, physical, and biological integrity of the Nation's waters." Id. at 2248.

Justice Kennedy made clear that *SWANCC*'s holding "is not an explicit or implicit overruling of *Riverside Bayview Homes*. Rather, *SWANCC* provides further clarification of *Riverside Bayview Homes'* construction of the term "navigable waters." Id. at 2244-45. As Justice Kennedy explained in *Rapanos*:

> . . . Taken together these cases establish that in some instances, as exemplified by *Riverside Bayview*, the connection between a nonnavigable water or wetland and a navigable water may be so close, or potentially so close, that the Corps may deem the water or wetland a "navigable water" under the Act. In other instances, as exemplified by *SWANCC*, there may be little or no connection. Absent a significant nexus, jurisdiction under the Act is lacking.

Id. at 2241.

Applying these principles in this case, it is apparent that the mere adjacency of Basalt Pond and its wetlands to the Russian River is not sufficient for CWA protection. The critical fact is that the Pond and navigable Russian River are separated only by a man-made levee so that water from the Pond seeps directly into the adjacent River. This is a significant nexus between the wetlands and the Russian River and justifies CWA protection. . . . The district court's findings of fact support the conclusion that Basalt Pond and its wetlands "significantly affect the chemical, physical, and biological integrity of other covered waters understood as navigable in the traditional sense." Id. at 2248.

Moreover, there is an actual surface connection between Basalt Pond and the Russian River when the River overflows the levee and the two bodies of water commingle. Thus, there are several hydrological connections between Basalt Pond's wetlands and the Russian River that affect the physical integrity of the River. Basalt Pond drains into the aquifer and at least 26 percent of the Pond's volume annually reaches the River itself. There is also an underground hydraulic connection between the two bodies, so a change in the water level in one immediately affects the water level in the other.

In addition to these physical connections between Basalt Pond and the Russian River, the district court found that there is also a significant ecological connection. The wetlands support substantial bird, mammal and fish populations, all as an integral part of and indistinguishable from the rest of the Russian River ecosystem. Many of the bird populations at the Pond are familiar along the River, including cormorants, great egrets, mallards, sparrows, and fish-eaters. Fish indigenous to the River also live in the Pond due to the recurring breaches of the levee. As the district court observed, these facts make Basalt Pond indistinguishable from any of the natural wetlands alongside the Russian River that have extensive biological effects on the River itself.

The district court also found that Basalt Pond significantly affects the chemical integrity of the Russian River by increasing its chloride levels. The chloride from Basalt Pond reaches the River in higher concentrations as a direct result of Healdsburg's discharge of sewage into the pond. Mr. John Lambie testified at trial that the average concentration of chloride appearing upstream in the river is only 5.9 parts per million. In contrast, the average concentration of chloride seeping from Basalt Pond into the River is 36 parts per million, and the chloride concentration on the west side of the River adjacent to the Pond is 18 parts per million.

In sum, the district court made substantial findings of fact to support the conclusion that the adjacent wetland of Basalt Pond has a significant nexus to the Russian River. The Pond's effects on the Russian River are not speculative or insubstantial. Rather, the Pond significantly affects the physical, biological and chemical integrity of the Russian River, and ultimately warrants protection as a "navigable water" under the CWA. Appellant's discharge of wastewater into Basalt Pond without a permit, therefore, violates the CWA. . . .

Notes and Questions

1. Is it important that the Pond is adjacent to the River? Why isn't adjacency, standing alone, sufficient to confer CWA jurisdiction? Would the dissenters in *Rapanos* have found that adjacency alone is enough?

2. Is the hydrological link between the Pond and the River enough to satisfy Justice Kennedy's significant nexus test?

3. How would the Justices who formed the plurality in *Rapanos* likely have decided *River Watch*?

4. Why was Justice Kennedy's concurrence the "controlling" opinion in *Rapanos*?

B. PERMIT REQUIREMENT

UNITED STATES v. FREZZO BROTHERS, INC.
602 F.2d 1123 (3d Cir. 1979)

ROSENN, Circuit Judge.

Since the enactment in 1948 of the Federal Water Pollution Control Act ("the Act"), the Government has, until recent years, generally enforced its provisions to control water pollution through the application of civil restraints. In this case, however, the Government in the first instance has sought enforcement of the Act as amended in 1972, against an alleged corporate offender and its officers by criminal sanctions. . . .

I

Frezzo Brothers, Inc., is a Pennsylvania corporation engaged in the mushroom farming business near Avondale, Pennsylvania. The business is family operated with Guido and James Frezzo serving as the principal corporate officers. As a part of the mushroom farming business, Frezzo Brothers, Inc., produces compost to provide a growing base for the mushrooms. The compost is comprised mainly of hay and horse manure mixed with water and allowed to ferment outside on wharves.

The Frezzo's farm had a 114,000 gallon concrete holding tank designed to contain water run-off from the compost wharves and to recycle water back to them. The farm had a separate storm water run-off system that carried rain water through a pipe to a channel box located on an adjoining property owned by another mushroom farm. The channel box was connected by a pipe with an unnamed tributary of the East Branch of the White Clay Creek. The waters of the tributary flowed directly into the Creek.

Counts One through Four of the indictment charged the defendants with discharging pollutants into the East Branch of the White Clay Creek on July 7, July 20, September 20, and September 26, 1977. On these dates Richard Casson, a Chester County Health Department investigator, observed pollution in the tributary flowing into the Creek and collected samples of wastes flowing into the channel box. The wastes had the distinctive characteristics of manure and quantitative analysis of the samples revealed a concentration of pollutants in the water. The Government introduced meteorological evidence at trial showing that no rain had been recorded in the area on these four dates. Based on this evidence, the Government contended that the Frezzos had willfully discharged manure into the storm water run-off system that flowed into the channel box and into the stream.[11]

Investigator Casson returned to the Frezzo farm on January 12, 1978, to inspect their existing water pollution abatement facilities. Guido and James Frezzo showed Casson both the holding tank designed to contain the waste water from the compost wharves, and the separate storm water run-off system. Casson returned to the farm on May 9, 1978 with a search warrant and several witnesses. This visit occurred after a morning rain had ended. The witnesses observed the holding tank overflowing into the storm water run-off system. The path of the wastes from the Frezzo holding tank to the channel box and into the stream was photographed. James Frezzo was present at the time and admitted to Casson that the holding tank could control the water only 95% of the time. Samples were again collected, subjected to quantitative analysis and a high concentration of pollutants was found to be present. This incident gave rise to Count Five of the indictment.

Additional samples were collected from the channel box on May 14, 1978, after a heavy rain. Again, a concentration of pollutants was found to be present. This evidence served as the basis for Count Six of the indictment. At trial, the Government introduced evidence of the rainfall on May 9 and May 14 along with expert hydrologic testimony regarding the holding capabilities of the Frezzos' tank. The Government theorized that the holding tank was too small to contain the compost wastes after a

---

11. At the time when the violations occurred, the statute punished "willful" violations as well as negligent ones. A subsequent amendment deleted willfulness as a culpable mental state and replaced it with knowledge. — ED.

rainstorm and that the Frezzos had negligently discharged pollutants into the stream on the two dates in May.

The jury returned guilty verdicts on all six counts against the corporate defendant, Frezzo Brothers, Inc., and individual defendants, Guido and James Frezzo. . . .

III

The Frezzos . . . contend that the indictment should have been dismissed because the EPA had not promulgated any effluent standards applicable to the compost manufacturing business. The Frezzos argue that before a violation of § 1311(a) can occur, the defendants must be shown to have not complied with existing effluent limitations under the Act. The district court disagreed, finding no such requirement. We agree with the district court.

The core provision of the Act is found in § 1311(a) which reads:

> Except as in compliance with this section and sections 1312, 1316, 1317, 1328, 1342, and 1344 of this title, the discharge of any pollutants by any person shall be unlawful.

Section 1311(b) then sets out a timetable for the promulgation of effluent limitations for point sources and section 1312 provides for the establishment of water quality related effluent limitations. The Frezzos contend that they cannot have violated the Act because the EPA has not yet promulgated effluent limitations which they can be held to have violated.

[The court observed that the statute flatly prohibits discharging pollutants and that the prohibition requires no effluent regulations to activate it.]

. . . The basic policy of the Act is to halt uncontrolled discharges of pollutants into the waters of the United States. In fact, the Act sets forth "the national goal that the discharge of [all] pollutants into the navigable waters be eliminated by 1985." 33 U.S.C. § 1251(a)(1). We see nothing impermissible with allowing the Government to enforce the Act by invoking § 1311(a), even if no effluent limitations have been promulgated for the particular business charged with polluting. Without this flexibility, numerous industries not yet considered as serious threats to the environment may escape administrative, civil, or criminal sanctions merely because the EPA has not established effluent limitations. Thus, dangerous pollutants could be continually injected into the water solely because the administrative process has not yet had the opportunity to fix specific effluent limitations. Such a result would be inconsistent with the policy of the Act.

We do not believe . . . that the permit procedure urged by the Government is unduly burdensome on business. If no effluent limitations have yet been applied to an industry, a potential transgressor should apply for a permit to discharge pollutants under section 1342(a). The Administrator may then set up operating conditions until permanent effluent limitations are promulgated by EPA. The pendency of a permit application, in appropriate cases, should shield the applicant from liability for discharge in the absence of a permit. 33 U.S.C. § 1342(k). EPA cannot be expected to have anticipated every form of water pollution through the establishment of effluent limitations. The permit procedure, coupled with broad enforcement under § 1311(a) may, in fact, allow EPA to discover new sources of pollution for which permanent effluent standards are appropriate.

In the present case, it is undisputed that there was no pending permit to discharge pollutants; nor had Frezzo Brothers, Inc., ever applied for one. This case, therefore, appears to be particularly compelling for broad enforcement under sections 1311(a), 1319(c)(1). The Frezzos, under their interpretation of the statute, could conceivably have continued polluting until EPA promulgated effluent limitations for the compost operation. The Government's intervention by way of criminal indictments brought to a halt potentially serious damage to the stream in question, and has no doubt alerted EPA to pollution problems posed by compost production. We therefore hold that the promulgation of effluent limitation standards is not a prerequisite to the maintenance of a criminal proceeding based on violation of section 1311(a) of the Act. . . .

Accordingly, the judgment of the district court will be affirmed.

Notes and Questions

1. The national goal of the CWA is to eliminate the discharge of pollutants into navigable waters. Is the permit system consistent with that goal? Is a permit a license to pollute? What is the reason for including a permit system in the statutory scheme?

2. The defendants argued, unsuccessfully, that the EPA must provide written notice of the violation as a prerequisite to filing criminal charges. If the defendants were operating without the guidance of either an effluent standard for mushroom compost or a warning from the EPA, why would they be on notice that their conduct violated the law? How does "no effluent standard" + "no prior notification" = a willful or knowing violation? Does this result pose due process concerns?

3. What special problems of proof does the government face in a case like *Frezzo Brothers*?

C. KNOWING VIOLATIONS

UNITED STATES v. AHMAD
101 F.3d 386 (5th Cir. 1996)

SMITH, Circuit Judge.

Attique Ahmad appeals his conviction of, and sentence for, criminal violations of the Clean Water Act ("CWA"). Concluding that the district court erred in its instructions to the jury, we reverse and remand.

I

This case arises from the discharge of a large quantity of gasoline into the sewers of Conroe, Texas, in January 1994. In 1992, Ahmad purchased the "Spin-N-Market No. 12," a combination convenience store and gas station located at the intersection of Second and Lewis Streets in Conroe. The Spin-N-Market has two gasoline pumps, each of which is fed by an 8,000-gallon underground gasoline tank. Some time after Ahmad bought the station, he discovered that one of the tanks, which held high-octane gasoline, was leaking. This did not pose an immediate hazard, because the leak was at the top of the tank; gasoline could not seep out. The leak did, however, allow water to enter into the tank and contaminate the gas. Because water is heavier than gas, the water sank to the bottom of the tank, and because the tank was pumped from the bottom, Ahmad was unable to sell from it.

In October 1993, Ahmad hired CTT Environmental Services ("CTT"), a tank testing company, to examine the tank. CTT determined that it contained approximately 800 gallons of water, and the rest mostly gasoline. Jewel McCoy, a CTT employee, testified that she told Ahmad that the leak could not be repaired until the tank was completely emptied, which CTT offered to do for 65 cents per gallon plus $65 per hour of labor. After McCoy gave Ahmad this estimate, he inquired whether he could empty the tank himself. She replied that it would be dangerous and illegal to do so. On her testimony, he responded, "Well, if I don't get caught, what then?"

On January 25, 1994, Ahmad rented a hand-held motorized water pump from a local hardware store, telling a hardware store employee that he was planning to use it to remove water from his backyard. Victor Fonseca, however, identified Ahmad and the pump and testified that he had seen Ahmad pumping gasoline into the street. Oscar Alvarez stated that he had seen Ahmad and another person discharging gasoline into a manhole. Tereso Uribe testified that he had confronted Ahmad and asked him what was going on, to which Ahmad responded that he was simply removing the water from the tank.

In all, 5,220 gallons of fluid were pumped from the leaky tank, of which approximately 4,690 gallons were gasoline. Some of the gas-water mixture ran down Lewis Street and some into the manhole in front of the store.

The gasoline discharged onto Lewis Street went a few hundred feet along the curb to Third Street, where it entered a storm drain and the storm sewer system and flowed through a pipe that eventually empties into Possum Creek. When city officials discovered the next day that there was gasoline in Possum Creek, several vacuum trucks were required to decontaminate it. Possum Creek feeds into the San Jacinto River, which eventually flows into Lake Houston.

The gasoline that Ahmad discharged into the manhole went a different route: It flowed through the sanitary sewer system and eventually entered the city sewage treatment plant.[12] On January 26, employees at the treatment plant discovered a 1,000-gallon pool of gasoline in one of the intake ponds. To avoid shutting down the plant altogether, they diverted the pool of gasoline and all incoming liquid into a 5,000,000-gallon emergency lagoon.

The plant supervisor ordered that non-essential personnel be evacuated from the plant and called firefighters and a hazardous materials crew to the scene. The Conroe fire department determined the gasoline was creating a risk of explosion and ordered that two nearby schools be evacuated. Although no one was injured as a result of the discharge, fire officials testified at trial that Ahmad had created a "tremendous explosion hazard" that could have led to "hundreds, if not thousands, of deaths and injuries" and millions of dollars of property damage.

---

12. Conroe's sanitary sewer system is completely independent of its storm sewer system; the two serve different purposes, empty into different locations, and share no common pipes.

By 9:00 A.M. on January 26, investigators had traced the source of the gasoline back to the manhole directly in front of the Spin-N-Market. Their suspicions were confirmed when they noticed a strong odor of gasoline and saw signs of corrosion on the asphalt surrounding the manhole. The investigators questioned Ahmad, who at first denied having operated a pump the previous night. Soon, however, his story changed: He admitted to having used a pump but denied having pumped anything from his tanks.

Ahmad was indicted for three violations of the CWA: knowingly discharging a pollutant from a point source into a navigable water of the United States without a permit, in violation of 33 U.S.C. §§ 1311(a) and 1319(c)(2)(A) (count one); knowingly operating a source in violation of a pretreatment standard, in violation of 33 U.S.C. §§ 1317(d) and 1319(c)(2)(A) (count two); and knowingly placing another person in imminent danger of death or serious bodily injury by discharging a pollutant, in violation of 33 U.S.C. § 1319(c)(3) (count three). At trial, Ahmad did not dispute that he had discharged gasoline from the tank or that eventually it had found its way to Possum Creek and the sewage treatment plant. Instead, he contended that his discharge of the gasoline was not "knowing," because he had believed he was discharging water.

. . . The jury found Ahmad guilty on counts one and two and deadlocked on count three.

II

Ahmad argues that the district court improperly instructed the jury on the mens rea required for counts one and two. The instruction on count one stated in relevant part:

For you to find Mr. Ahmad guilty of this crime, you must be convinced that the government has proved each of the following beyond a reasonable doubt:

(1) That on or about the date set forth in the indictment,
(2) the defendant knowingly discharged
(3) a pollutant
(4) from a point source
(5) into the navigable waters of the United States
(6) without a permit to do so.

On count two, the court instructed the jury:

In order to prove the defendant guilty of the offense charged in Count 2 of the indictment, the government must prove beyond a reasonable doubt each of the following elements:

(1) That on or about the date set forth in the indictment
(2) the defendant,
(3) who was the owner or operator of a source,
(4) knowingly operated that source by discharging into a public sewer system or publicly owned treatment works
(5) a pollutant that created a fire or explosion hazard in that public sewer system or publicly owned treatment works.

Ahmad contends that the jury should have been instructed that the statutory mens rea — knowledge — was required as to each element of the offenses, rather than only with regard to discharge or the operation of a source. . . .

The principal issue is to which elements of the offense the modifier "knowingly" applies. The matter is complicated somewhat by the fact that the phrase "knowingly violates" appears in a different section of the CWA from the language defining the elements of the offenses. Ahmad argues that within this context, "knowingly violates" should be read to require him knowingly to have acted with regard to each element of the offenses. The government, in contrast, contends that "knowingly violates" requires it to prove only that Ahmad knew the nature of his acts and that he performed them intentionally. Particularly at issue is whether "knowingly" applies to the element of the discharge's being a pollutant, for Ahmad's main theory at trial was that he thought he was discharging water, not gasoline.

The Supreme Court has spoken to this issue in broad terms. In United States v. X-Citement Video, Inc., 115 S. Ct. 464, 467 (1994), the Court read "knowingly" to apply to each element of a child pornography offense, notwithstanding its conclusion that under the "most natural grammatical reading" of the statute it should apply only to the element of having transported, shipped, received, distributed, or reproduced the material at issue. The Court also reaffirmed the long-held view that "the presumption in favor of a scienter requirement should apply to each of the statutory elements which criminalize otherwise innocent conduct." Id. at 469.

Although X-Citement Video is the Court's most recent pronouncement on this subject, it is not the first. In Staples v. United States, 511 U.S. 600, 619-20 (1994), the Court found that the statutes criminalizing knowing possession of a machinegun require that defendants know not only that they possess a firearm but that it actually is a machinegun. Thus, an awareness of the features of the gun — specifically, the features that make it an automatic weapon — is a necessary element of the offense. More generally, the Court also made plain that statutory crimes carrying severe penalties are presumed to require that a defendant know the facts that make his conduct illegal.

Our own precedents are in the same vein. In United States v. Baytank (Houston), Inc., 934 F.2d 599, 613 (5th Cir. 1991), we concluded that a conviction for knowing and improper storage of hazardous wastes under 42 U.S.C. § 6928(d)(2)(A) requires "that the defendant know[] factually what he is doing — storing, what is being stored, and that what is being stored factually has the potential for harm to others or the environment, and that he has no permit. . . ." This is directly analogous to the interpretation of the CWA that Ahmad urges upon us. Indeed, we find it eminently sensible that the phrase "knowingly violates" in § 1319(c)(2)(A), when referring to other provisions that define the elements of the offenses § 1319 creates, should uniformly require knowledge as to each of those elements rather than only one or two. To hold otherwise would require an explanation as to why some elements should be treated differently from others, which neither the parties nor the caselaw seems able to provide.

In support of its interpretation of the CWA, the government cites cases from other circuits. We find these decisions both inapposite and unpersuasive on the point for which they are cited. In United States v. Hopkins, 53 F.3d 533, 537-41 (2d Cir. 1995), the court held that the government need not demonstrate that a § 1319(c)(2)(A) defendant knew his acts were illegal. The illegality of the defendant's actions is not an element of the offense, however. In United States v. Weitzenhoff, 35 F.3d 1275 (9th Cir.

1994), the court similarly was concerned almost exclusively with whether the language of the CWA creates a mistake-of-law defense. Both cases are easily distinguishable, for neither directly addresses mistake of fact or the statutory construction issues raised by Ahmad. . . .

IV

. . . The convictions are reversed and the case remanded.

Notes and Questions

1. Does *Ahmad*'s holding that the scienter requirement applies to each element of the offense require proof that the defendant knew he needed a permit to pump the tank's contents into the sewer system? Would it make sense to require Ahmad to know that he did not have a permit without also requiring knowledge of the permit requirement?

2. Would a properly instructed jury be likely to convict or acquit Ahmad? What evidence is probative on the issue of his claimed mistake about whether he was pumping water or gasoline? If you were the prosecutor, what additional evidence would you try to develop? What inferences would you ask the jury to draw?

3. Ahmad wanted to call two witnesses at trial who would have testified that he left the Spin-N-Market between 7:30 and 8:00 P.M. on January 25, but the district court excluded their testimony as irrelevant. The court of appeals held that this evidentiary ruling was in error. What factual issues would the proffered testimony be relevant to?

4. The CWA imposes felony penalties for knowingly discharging pollutants into navigable waters without a permit and misdemeanor penalties for negligently doing so. On remand, should the trial court instruct on the lesser included offense of negligent discharge? If so, on what theory?

UNITED STATES v. SINSKEY
119 F.3d 712 (8th Cir. 1997)

ARNOLD, Circuit Judge.

The defendants appeal their convictions for criminal violations of the Clean Water Act. We affirm the judgments of the trial court.

I

In the early 1990s, Timothy Sinskey and Wayne Kumm were, respectively, the plant manager and plant engineer at John Morrell & Co. ("Morrell"), a large meat-packing plant in Sioux Falls, South Dakota. The meat-packing process created a large amount of wastewater, some of which Morrell piped to a municipal treatment plant and the rest of which it treated at its own wastewater treatment plant ("WWTP"). After treating wastewater at the WWTP, Morrell would discharge it into the Big Sioux River.

One of the WWTP's functions was to reduce the amount of ammonia nitrogen in the wastewater discharged into the river, and the Environmental Protection Agency ("EPA") required Morrell to limit that amount to levels specified in a permit issued under the Clean Water Act ("CWA"). As well as specifying the acceptable levels of ammonia nitrogen, the permit also required Morrell to perform weekly a series of tests to monitor the amounts of ammonia nitrogen in the discharged water and to file monthly with the EPA a set of reports concerning those results.

In the spring of 1991, Morrell doubled the number of hogs that it slaughtered and processed at the Sioux Falls plant. The resulting increase in wastewater caused the level of ammonia nitrate in the discharged water to be above that allowed by the CWA permit. Ron Greenwood and Barry Milbauer, the manager and assistant manager, respectively, of the WWTP, manipulated the testing process in two ways so that Morrell would appear not to violate its permit. In the first technique, which the parties frequently refer to as "flow manipulation" or the "flow game," Morrell would discharge extremely low levels of water (and thus low levels of ammonia nitrogen) early in the week, when Greenwood and Milbauer would perform the required tests. After the tests had been performed, Morrell would discharge an exceedingly high level of water (and high levels of ammonia nitrogen) later in the week. The tests would therefore not accurately reflect the overall levels of ammonia nitrogen in the discharged water. In addition to manipulating the flow, Greenwood and Milbauer also engaged in what the parties call "selective sampling," that is, they performed more than the number of tests required by the EPA but reported only the tests showing acceptable levels of ammonia nitrogen. When manipulating the flow and selective sampling failed to yield the required number of tests showing acceptable levels of ammonia nitrogen, the two simply falsified the test results and the monthly EPA reports, which Sinskey then signed and sent to the EPA. Morrell submitted false reports for every month but one from August, 1991, to December, 1992.

As a result of their participation in these activities, Sinskey and Kumm were charged with a variety of CWA violations. After a three-week trial, a jury found Sinskey guilty of eleven of the thirty counts with which he was charged, and Kumm guilty of one of the seventeen counts with which he was charged. In particular, the jury found both Sinskey and Kumm guilty of knowingly rendering inaccurate a monitoring method required to be maintained under the CWA and Sinskey guilty of knowingly discharging a pollutant into waters of the United States in amounts exceeding CWA permit limitations. Each appeals his conviction.

II

Sinskey first challenges the jury instructions that the trial court gave with respect to 33 U.S.C. § 1319(c)(2)(A), which, among other things, punishes anyone who "knowingly violates" § 1311 or a condition or limitation contained in a permit that implements § 1311. . . .

The trial court gave an instruction, which it incorporated into several substantive charges, that in order for the jury to find Sinskey guilty of acting "knowingly," the proof had to show that he was "aware of the nature of his acts, performed them intentionally, and [did] not act or fail to act through ignorance, mistake, or accident." The instructions also told the jury that the government was not required to prove that Sinskey knew that his acts violated the CWA or permits issued under that act. Sinskey contests these instructions as applied to 33 U.S.C. § 1319(c)(2)(A), arguing that because the adverb "knowingly" immediately precedes the verb "violates," the government must prove that he knew that his conduct violated either the CWA or the NPDES [National Pollutant Discharge Elimination System] permit. We disagree.

Although our court has not yet decided whether 33 U.S.C. § 1319(c)(2)(A) requires the government to prove that a defendant knew that he or she was violating either the CWA or the relevant NPDES permit when he or she acted, we are guided in answering this question by the generally accepted construction of the word "knowingly" in criminal statutes, by the CWA's legislative history, and by the decisions of the other courts of appeals that have addressed this issue. In construing other statutes with similar language and structure, that is, statutes in which one provision punishes the "knowing violation" of another provision that defines the illegal conduct, we have repeatedly held that the word "knowingly" modifies the acts constituting the underlying conduct. See United States v. Farrell, 69 F.3d 891, 893 (8th Cir. 1995), and United States v. Hern, 926 F.2d 764, 766-68 (8th Cir. 1991).

In *Farrell*, for example, we discussed 18 U.S.C. § 924(a)(2), which penalizes anyone who "knowingly violates" § 922(*o*)(1), which in turn prohibits the transfer or possession of a machine gun. In construing the word "knowingly," we held that it applied only to the conduct proscribed in § 922(*o*)(1), that is, the act of transferring or possessing a machine gun, and not to the illegal nature of those actions. A conviction under § 924(a)(2) therefore did not require proof that the defendant knew that his actions violated the law.

We see no reason to depart from that commonly accepted construction in this case, and we therefore believe that in 33 U.S.C. § 1319(c)(2)(A), the word "knowingly" applies to the underlying conduct prohibited by the statute. Untangling the statutory provisions discussed above in order to define precisely the relevant underlying conduct, however, is not a little difficult. At first glance, the conduct in question might appear to be violating a permit limitation, which would imply that § 1319(c)(2)(A) requires proof that the defendant knew of the permit limitation and knew that he or she was violating it. To violate a permit limitation, however, one must engage in the conduct prohibited by that limitation. The permit is, in essence, another layer of regulation in the nature of a law, in this case, a law that applies only to Morrell. We therefore believe that the underlying conduct of which Sinskey must have had knowledge is the conduct that is prohibited by the permit, for example, that Morrell's discharges of ammonia nitrates were higher than one part per million in the summer of 1992. Given this interpretation of the statute, the government was not required to prove that Sinskey knew that his acts violated either the CWA or the NPDES permit, but merely that he was aware of the conduct that resulted in the permit's violation.

This interpretation comports not only with our legal system's general recognition that ignorance of the law is no excuse, but also with Supreme Court interpretations of statutes containing similar language and structure. In United States v. International Minerals & Chemical Corp., 402 U.S. 558 (1971), for example, the Court analyzed a statute that punished anyone who "knowingly violated" certain regulations pertaining to the interstate shipment of hazardous materials. In holding that a conviction under the statute at issue did not require knowledge of the pertinent law, the Court reasoned that the statute's language was merely a shorthand designation for punishing anyone who knowingly committed the specific acts or omissions contemplated by the regulations at issue, and that the statute therefore required knowledge of the material facts but not the relevant law. The Court also focused on the nature of the regulatory scheme at issue, noting that where "dangerous or . . . obnoxious waste materials" are involved, anyone dealing with such materials "must be presumed" to be aware of the existence of the regulations. Id. at 565. Requiring knowledge only of the underlying actions, and not of the law, would therefore raise no substantial due process concerns. Such reasoning applies with equal force, we believe, to the CWA, which regulates the discharge into the public's water of such "obnoxious waste materials" as the byproducts of slaughtered animals. . . .

Our confidence in this interpretation is increased by decisions of the only other appellate courts to analyze the precise issue presented here. See United States v. Hopkins, 53 F.3d 533, 541 (2d Cir. 1995), and United States v. Weitzenhoff, 35 F.3d 1275, 1283-86 (9th Cir. 1993). Both cases held that 33 U.S.C. § 1319(c)(2)(A) does not require proof that the defendant knew that his or her acts violated the CWA or the NPDES permits at issue.

Contrary to the defendants' assertions, moreover, United States v. Ahmad, 101 F.3d 386 (5th Cir. 1996), is inapposite. In *Ahmad*, a convenience store owner pumped out an underground gasoline storage tank into which some water had leaked, discharging gasoline into city sewer systems and nearby creeks in violation of 33 U.S.C. § 1319(c)(2)(A). At trial, the defendant asserted that he thought that he was discharging water, and that the statute's requirement that he act knowingly required that the government prove not only that he knew that he was discharging something, but also that he knew that he was discharging gasoline. The Fifth Circuit agreed, holding that a defendant does not violate the statute unless he or she acts knowingly with regard to each element of an offense. *Ahmad*, however, involved a classic mistake-of-fact defense, and is not applicable to a mistake-of-law defense such as that asserted by Sinskey and Kumm. Indeed, the Fifth Circuit noted as much, distinguishing *Hopkins* and *Weitzenhoff* on the grounds that those decisions involved a mistake-of-law defense.

Sinskey, joined by Kumm, also challenges the trial court's instructions with respect to 33 U.S.C. § 1319(c)(4), arguing that the government should have been required to prove that they knew that their acts were illegal. This argument has even less force with respect to § 1319(c)(4) — which penalizes a person who "knowingly falsifies, tampers with, or renders inaccurate any monitoring device or method required to be maintained" by the CWA — than it does with respect to § 1319(c)(2)(A). In § 1319(c)(4), the adverb "knowingly" precedes and explicitly modifies the verbs that describe the activities that violate the act.

We have repeatedly held that, in other statutes with similar language, the word "knowingly" refers only to knowledge of the relevant activities (in this case, the defendants' knowledge that they were rendering the monitoring methods inaccurate by aiding and abetting in the flow games and selective sampling). Based on this well established constructional convention, and the equally well known principle that a term that appears in a statute more than once should ordinarily be construed the same way each time, Ratzlaf v. United States, 510 U.S. 135, 143 (1994), we see no reason to read a requirement that a defendant know of the illegal nature of his or her acts into 33 U.S.C. § 1319(c)(4). Contrary to the defendants' assertions, moreover, requiring the government to prove only that the defendant acted with awareness of his or her conduct does not render § 1319(c)(4) a strict liability offense. . . .

III

Kumm attacks his conviction for violating 33 U.S.C. v1319(c)(4) on a number of grounds, first among them the sufficiency of the government's evidence. Kumm claims that the government's evidence established only that he failed to stop others from rendering inaccurate Morrell's monitoring methods, not that he affirmatively participated in the deceit either directly or by aiding and abetting those who did. As Kumm correctly argues, to convict him of aiding and abetting the monitoring scheme, the government must prove more than his mere association with, and knowledge of the activities of, Greenwood, Milbauer, and Sinskey. Instead, the government must show that Kumm associated himself with the misleading monitoring scheme, participated in it "as something [he] wished to bring about," and acted in such a way as to ensure its success. Encouraging the perpetrators of a crime in their efforts to effect that crime is therefore aiding and abetting the commission of a crime. . . .

[W]e believe that the evidence supports a verdict that he aided and abetted the misleading monitoring scheme by encouraging Greenwood to render Morrell's monitoring methods inaccurate and by discouraging him from complaining about it to others at the WWTP.

Kumm once reassured a worried Greenwood, for example, "not to worry about [the violations] because if we did get caught, Morrell's had enough lawyers and lobbyists that it wouldn't be a problem." Although Kumm knew of Greenwood's illegal activities, moreover, he praised Greenwood on employee evaluations and even recommended that Greenwood receive a raise. When Greenwood began complaining about the violations and campaigning for physical improvements at the WWTP to decrease future violations, Kumm silenced him. At a meeting of the plant's mechanical department, for example, Kumm told Greenwood that "now is not the time or the place to discuss those matters" when Greenwood raised the subject of the violations. Lastly, although Greenwood would "rant and rave" to Kumm several times a week about the permit violations and about getting the WWTP fixed, Kumm responded only by submitting to Morrell headquarters routine requests for future improvements that were similar to previous requests that had already been denied. We believe that these affirmative acts constitute sufficient evidence to support Kumm's conviction. . . .

For the foregoing reasons, we affirm the convictions in all respects.

Notes and Questions

1. Is Sinskey's argument that the actor must know the offending conduct violates the NPDES permit tantamount to arguing that ignorance of the law is an excuse? In what sense was Morrell's NPDES permit "the law"?

2. Is the *Sinskey* court correct in asserting that *Ahmad* can be neatly distinguished as a classic mistake of fact problem?

3. Many critics of environmental criminal enforcement argue that decisions like *Sinskey* and *Weitzenhoff* read the mens rea requirements out of the statute. Does *Sinskey*'s interpretation of the mens rea requirements transform CWA violations into strict liability crimes?

4. In *Weitzenhoff*, the defendants operated a municipal sewage treatment plant that had a permit limiting the amount of organic and solid matter allowed in the effluent discharged from the plant. After converting to a new system, the plant experienced a buildup of excess waste that the system lacked the capacity to treat. Rather than hauling the excess waste to another treatment plant as they had done in the past, the defendants regularly bypassed the pretreatment system and discharged untreated sewage directly into the ocean. The majority of the en banc court in *Weitzenhoff* concluded that if the defendants knew the relevant facts — i.e., if they knew they were discharging untreated sewage from the plant — they knowingly violated the NPDES permit. Five judges dissented. Consider the following excerpt from Judge Kleinfeld's dissent:

> The harm our mistaken decision may do is not necessarily limited to Clean Water Act cases. Dilution of the traditional requirement of a criminal state of mind, and application of the criminal law to innocent conduct, reduces the moral authority of our system of criminal law. If we use prison to achieve social goals regardless of the moral innocence of those we incarcerate, then imprisonment loses its moral opprobrium and our criminal law becomes morally arbitrary.
>
> We have now made felons of a large number of innocent people doing socially valuable work. They are innocent, because the one thing which makes their conduct felonious is something they do not know. It is we, and not Congress, who have made them felons. The statute, read in an ordinary way, does not. . . .
>
> . . . In this case, the defendants, sewage plant operators, had a permit to discharge sewage into the ocean, but exceeded the permit limitations. The legal issue for the panel was what knowledge would turn innocently or negligently violating a permit into "knowingly" violating a permit. Were the plant operators felons if they knew they were discharging sewage, but did not know that they were violating their permit? Or did they also have to know they were violating their permit? Ordinary English grammar, common sense, and precedent, all compel the latter construction.
>
> As the panel opinion states the facts, these two defendants were literally "midnight dumpers." They managed a sewer plant and told their employees to dump 436,000 pounds of sewage into the ocean, mostly at night, fouling a nearby beach. Their conduct, as set out in the panel opinion, suggests that they must have known they were violating their National Pollution Discharge Elimination System (NPDES) permit. But we cannot decide the case on that basis, because the jury did not. The court instructed the jury that the government did not have to prove the defendants knew their conduct was unlawful, and refused to instruct the jury that a mistaken belief that the discharge was authorized by the permit would be a defense. Because of the way the jury was instructed, its verdict is consistent with the proposition that the defendants honestly and reasonably believed that their NPDES permit authorized the discharges.
>
> This proposition could be true. NPDES permits are often difficult to understand and obey. The EPA had licensed the defendants' plant to discharge 976 pounds of waste per day, or about 409,920 pounds over the fourteen months covered by the indictment, into the ocean. The wrongful conduct was not discharging waste into the ocean. That was socially desirable conduct by which the defendants protected the people of their city from sewage-borne disease and earned their pay. The wrongful conduct was violating the NPDES permit by discharging 26,000 more pounds of waste than the permit authorized

during the fourteen months. Whether these defendants were innocent or not, in the sense of knowing that they were exceeding their permit limitation, the panel's holding will make innocence irrelevant in other permit violation cases where the defendants had no idea that they were exceeding permit limits. The only thing they have to know to be guilty is that they were dumping sewage into the ocean, yet that was a lawful activity expressly authorized by their federal permit. . . .

Are the dissenters justified in claiming that *Weitzenhoff* turns morally innocent people who do socially valuable work into felons? What are the practical implications of the dissenters' views?

5. Many environmental law scholars are critical of criminal enforcement of environmental standards. Their sense of unease revolves around three principal themes: (1) that environmental law is so complex that criminal enforcement of environmental standards is unfair; (2) that prosecutors enjoy reduced evidentiary burdens in environmental prosecutions; and (3) that the culpability requirements for environmental crimes are far too low. [13]

Do the culpability requirements in the environmental statutes contribute to the perception of unfairness in environmental criminal enforcement? If so, should a different level of culpability be required? If the culpability requirements remain the same, should good faith be a defense?

6. In *Sinskey*, defendant Kumm was convicted of aiding and abetting the monitoring scheme. Was his conviction based on affirmative acts or failure to act? Is the distinction between acts and omissions important in this context?

7. What if Kumm had asked Morrell for immediate assistance in making physical improvements to the plant but Morrell had refused to allocate any resources for that purpose? Would that affect Kumm's liability?

D. RESPONSIBLE CORPORATE OFFICER DOCTRINE

UNITED STATES v. HONG
242 F.3d 528 (4th Cir. 2001)

WILKINS, Circuit Judge. . . .

I

In September 1993, Hong acquired a wastewater treatment facility at Second and Maury Streets in Richmond, Virginia from Environmental Restoration Company, Inc. Hong initially operated the facility under the name ERC-USA but subsequently made several changes to the company name, eventually calling it Avion Environmental Group (Avion). Hong also moved the company's operations to a new facility on Stockton

---

13. See Kathleen F. Brickey, The Rhetoric of Environmental Crime: Culpability, Discretion, and Structural Reform, 84 Iowa L. Rev. 115 (1998) (examining and providing a counterpoint to these enforcement concerns).

Street in Richmond. Hong avoided any formal association with Avion and was not identified as an officer of the company. Nevertheless, he controlled the company's finances and played a substantial role in company operations. For example, Hong negotiated the lease for the Stockton Street facility,[14] participated in the purchase of a wastewater treatment system (discussed further below), reviewed marketing reports, urged Avion employees to make the company successful through the use of various marketing strategies, and controlled the payment of Avion's various expenses. Hong maintained an office at Avion from which he conducted business.

In late 1995, Hong and Robert Kirk, Avion's general manager, began to investigate the possibility of obtaining a carbon-filter treatment system for the Stockton Street facility, which lacked a system to treat wastewater. Hong and Kirk were specifically advised that the treatment system they were considering was designed only as a final step in the process of treating wastewater; it was not intended for use with completely untreated wastewater. Nevertheless, after purchasing the system, Avion used it as the sole means of treating wastewater. The system quickly became clogged. Hong was advised of the problem by Avion employees and inspected the treatment system himself on at least one occasion. Additionally, Bruce Stakeman, who sold the filtration media necessary for the system, advised Hong that the treatment system would not function properly unless it was preceded by an additional filtration mechanism. No additional filtration media were purchased, nor was an additional filtration system installed.

In May 1996, Avion employees began discharging untreated wastewater directly into the Richmond sewer system in violation of Avion's discharge permit. Untreated wastewater was discharged numerous other times during the remainder of 1996. Based on these activities, Hong subsequently was charged by information with 13 counts of negligently violating pretreatment requirements under the CWA. More specifically, Hong was charged with one count of failing to properly maintain and operate a treatment system and with 12 counts of discharging untreated wastewater. Each count of the information alleged that Hong committed the violations "as a responsible corporate officer."

The case was tried before a magistrate judge, who found Hong guilty on all counts. The magistrate judge imposed a fine of $1.3 million — $100,000 for each count of conviction — and sentenced Hong to 36 months imprisonment. . . .

. . . Hong now appeals his convictions and term of imprisonment. . . .

II

The provision of the CWA under which Hong was convicted applies to "any person who" negligently violates pretreatment requirements. 33 U.S.C. § 1319(c)(1)(A). The CWA defines "person" generally as "an individual, corporation, partnership, association, State, municipality, commission, or political subdivision of a State, or any interstate body." 33 U.S.C. § 1362(5). For purposes of § 1319(c), "person" is further defined to include "any responsible corporate officer." 33 U.S.C. § 1319(c)(6). As noted previously, the information charged Hong with negligently violating pretreatment requirements "as a responsible corporate officer." Hong argues that the Government failed to

---

14. Hong signed the lease for the Stockton Street facility as Avion's president.

prove that he was a responsible corporate officer. Specifically, he maintains that the Government failed to prove that he was a formally designated corporate officer of Avion and that, even if such proof was not required, the Government failed to prove that he exerted sufficient control over the operations of Avion to be held responsible for the improper discharges. We disagree with both contentions.

The "responsible corporate officer" doctrine was first articulated by the Supreme Court in United States v. Dotterweich, 320 U.S. 277 (1943). In *Dotterweich*, the president and general manager of a drug company argued that he could not be held criminally liable for the company's violations of the Federal Food, Drug, and Cosmetic Act. The Supreme Court rejected this contention, holding that all who had "a responsible share" in the criminal conduct could be held accountable for corporate violations of the law. Id. at 284 (explaining that "a corporation may commit an offense and all persons who aid and abet its commission are equally guilty").

The Court revisited the responsible corporate officer doctrine in United States v. Park, 421 U.S. 658 (1975). In elaborating on the concept of a "responsible share" in a violation that the defendant did not personally commit, the Court stated that the Government may satisfy its burden of proof by introducing "evidence sufficient to warrant a finding by the trier of the facts that the defendant had, by reason of his position in the corporation, responsibility and authority either to prevent in the first instance, or promptly to correct, the violation complained of, and that he failed to do so." *Park*, 421 U.S. at 673-74. The Court explicitly rejected the argument that the defendant must have brought the violation about through some "wrongful action." Id. at 673.

It is evident from these principles that the Government was not required to prove that Hong was a formally designated corporate officer of Avion. The gravamen of liability as a responsible corporate officer is not one's corporate title or lack thereof; rather, the pertinent question is whether the defendant bore such a relationship to the corporation that it is appropriate to hold him criminally liable for failing to prevent the charged violations of the CWA.

Regarding that question, Hong contends that the Government failed to prove that his relationship to Avion was such that he possessed authority to prevent the illegal discharges. Ample evidence supports the magistrate judge's finding of guilt, however. The evidence indicated that although Hong went to great lengths to avoid being formally associated with Avion, in fact he substantially controlled corporate operations. Furthermore, Hong was involved in the purchase of the filtration system and was aware, in advance, that the filtration media would quickly be depleted if used as Hong intended. And, the evidence supported a finding that Hong was in control of Avion's finances and refused to authorize payment for additional filtration media. Finally, Hong was regularly present at the Avion site, and discharges occurred openly while Hong was present. Accordingly, we affirm Hong's convictions. . . .

Notes and Questions

1. Hong was prosecuted on the theory that he was "a responsible corporate officer." Why would the government choose to proceed on that theory rather than on the theory that he was liable as "an individual"?

2. In determining that Hong was a responsible corporate officer, the court relied heavily on the "responsible share" standard of liability articulated in *Dotterweich* and *Park*.[15] The defendants in those cases were prosecuted under the Food, Drug, and Cosmetic Act. Unlike the CWA, which specifically makes "any responsible corporate officer" liable for negligent violations, the Food, Drug, and Cosmetic Act provision at issue in *Dotterweich* and *Park* makes no reference to responsible corporate officers. Hence, the responsible share standard of liability developed in that context is a judicial gloss on a public welfare statute. In *Dotterweich* and *Park*, moreover, the defendants were the presidents of their respective companies, whereas Hong had no formal association with Avion. Do these differences cast doubt on the wisdom of the *Hong* court's reliance on *Dotterweich* and *Park*?

3. Hong was convicted of negligently violating a CWA provision that fails to specify the applicable standard of care. In the absence of statutory guidance, how should the court decide whether Hong was negligent for purposes of this statute?[16]

4. If there was no statutory or judicially approved standard for what constitutes negligence under the CWA, did Hong have fair warning that his conduct was criminal?

NOTE ON THE BP GULF SPILL

At 9:50 P.M. on April 20, 2010, an explosion rocked BP's offshore oil rig Deepwater Horizon, killing 11 workers, injuring 17, and unleashing what has become the largest accidental oil spill in world history. For nearly three months the well gushed as much as 60,000 barrels per day into the Gulf of Mexico. Federal estimates place the total near 4.9 million barrels (by comparison, the infamous *Exxon Valdez* oil spill released a total of 750,000 barrels into Prince William Sound off of the coast of Alaska). The Deepwater Horizon rig was owned by Transocean Ltd. and leased by BP to drill one of its deepwater wells off of the Louisiana coast. Described as a "nightmare well" in internal BP emails, frequent drilling problems put the project well over budget and significantly behind schedule.

During the last leg of drilling, BP made a number of decisions that seemed to put the goals of saving money and time above safety, despite several warnings and recommendations from outside contractors, in addition to troubling results from BP's own internal tests. These decisions included: choosing to use a well design with few barriers to gas flow in lieu of a multi-barriered design; using 6 centralizers meant to center the pipe while guiding it into the well instead of the recommended 21; turning away a team brought on board to test the integrity of the cement bond in the well, even though internal tests predicted cement failure; defying industry best practice by only partially circulating drilling mud in the well; and neglecting to use a lockdown sleeve as a last resort to keep the seal at the well head from blowing out. Damning e-mails later surfaced, revealing that BP engineers were aware of the danger but that at least some of them were indifferent to the risks. As one engineer wrote in a now notorious e-mail exchange, "who cares, it's done, end of story, will probably be fine."

---

15. See supra Chapter 2.
16. Cf. United States v. Hanousek, 176 F.3d 1116 (9th Cir. 1999) (rejecting defendant's argument that gross negligence is required and ruling that ordinary negligence will suffice).

In the months that followed the explosion, BP and Transocean, the House Committee on Energy and Commerce, and numerous regulatory agencies all launched investigations designed to discover the cause of the spill and identify the responsible party or parties. These, in turn, brought detailed scrutiny to the decisions made during the last leg of drilling, which other industry players condemned in testimony before the House Committee and referred to as "horribly negligent." The investigations also focused on the failed blowout preventer on board the Deepwater Horizon, which was designed to trigger a "deadman" switch to clamp the well shut in an emergency.

Officials also pointed to regulatory failures that allowed BP to drill without following standard procedures and to operate without an effective emergency containment plan in the event that a spill occurred. The federal Minerals Management Service (MMS), which oversaw BP's offshore operations, approved the flawed drill plan and permitted BP to delay required testing of the blowout preventer that eventually failed.

Former BP CEO Tony Hayward became a magnet for vociferous criticism. Though not personally involved with the Deepwater Horizon project, Hayward had removed several layers of safety assurance from the corporate structure to give more decision-making power to lower-level managers and engineers more intimately involved in the projects.[17] He criticized the prior policy as inefficient and redundant. This was despite a refinery explosion in Texas, a large oil leak in Alaska, and 760 "egregious, willful" OSHA safety violations during his tenure (Sunoco had the next largest number of violations during that time, with 8). In a hearing before the House Committee on Energy and Commerce, the congressional body responsible for investigating the spill, Hayward was accused of fostering an atmosphere that put cost above safety, encouraging BP employees to take risks in order to improve the bottom line. His only response was that he was not involved in the decision-making process and that those in the best position to make key decisions had the power to do so, though he did not identify who those people were. Hayward agreed to step down as CEO on October 1.

Notes and Questions

1. It is widely expected that the investigations will culminate in one or more criminal prosecutions. The most likely environmental charges against BP would be Clean Water Act violations. Do the facts support bringing criminal charges against the company? What would the government need to prove to obtain a conviction under the CWA? Could Tony Hayward be charged as a responsible corporate officer? Should the government consider charging lower level corporate operatives?

2. The MMS approved BP's drilling plan for the Deepwater Horizon. How would the agency's approval affect the government's case?

3. Allegations of corruption within MMS have since led to calls for regulatory reform. In an industry where regulations seem to be lagging behind technological advances, the agency seemed far too willing to allow the oil companies to dictate acceptable practices. It was reported that employees from the regulated oil companies were treating MMS agency employees to sporting events, meals, and lavish gifts. The

---

17. In fact, BP policy is that any employee on board an oil rig who feels the conditions are unsafe can immediately stop operations at any time.

result? Leniency. MMS approved BP drilling plans that most other companies regarded as unsafe, allowed for delayed testing of the blowout preventer, and approved an emergency response plan that cited a Japanese home-shopping website and provided for the protection of "seals, sea otters, and walruses," none of which inhabit the Gulf of Mexico. How, if at all, do these allegations affect your evaluation of the relevance of the agency's approval to BP's potential liability?

4. Recall the discussion in Chapter 1 concerning the prosecution of a corporation as an entity. What legal rules and policies are at play in the BP case? What factors and policies should a prosecutor consider when deciding whether or not to file criminal charges against BP as an entity? How do BP's 760 "egregious, willful" OSHA violations affect your analysis? Do the circumstances here warrant a prosecution of the corporation?

E. KNOWING ENDANGERMENT

UNITED STATES v. BOROWSKI
977 F.2d 27 (1st Cir. 1992)

HORNBY, District Judge.

Congress enacted the Clean Water Act "to restore and maintain the chemical, physical, and biological integrity of the Nation's waters." 33 U.S.C. § 1251 (1988). As one means of improving water quality, Congress ordered the Environmental Protection Agency (EPA) to design pretreatment standards for industrial waste discharges into publicly-owned treatment works. Under the Act, someone who knowingly violates these standards and knows that he or she thereby places another person in imminent danger of death or serious injury commits a felony. Does this criminal sanction apply when the imminent danger is not to people at the publicly-owned treatment works, municipal sewers or other downstream locations affected by the illegal discharge, but rather to employees handling the pollutants on the premises from which the illegal discharge originates? We hold that it does not.

FACTS

The defendant John Borowski was the President and owner of Borjohn Optical Technology, Inc. and Galaxie Laboratory, Inc. ("Borjohn"). Borjohn operated a manufacturing facility in Burlington, Massachusetts, producing optical mirrors for use in aerospace guidance and sighting systems.

Borjohn used various rinses, dips and nickel plating baths to plate nickel onto its mirrors. When a mirror was improperly plated, Borjohn used a nitric acid bath to strip the nickel off. From time to time the nickel plating solutions and nitric acid stripping baths had to be replaced.

Borjohn disposed of its spent nickel plating baths and nitric acid baths by crudely dumping them directly into plating room sinks, without any form of pretreatment. Those sinks drained immediately into Borjohn's underground pipes which, at the property border line, fed into the Burlington municipal sewer system and from there into the Massachusetts Water Resource Authority's treatment works. Because the pollutants were ultimately discharged into a publicly-owned treatment works, Borjohn was subject to the EPA's pretreatment regulations. The EPA regulations prohibited nickel discharges into the publicly-owned treatment works in amounts exceeding 3.98 milligrams per liter and also prohibited concentrations of nitric acid discharges into the publicly-owned treatment works if they had a pH balance of less than 5. The nickel and nitric acid baths Borjohn discharged greatly exceeded these pretreatment standards.

According to medical experts, enormous health concerns are associated with exposure to nitric acid and nickel in the amounts involved here. Contact with the chemicals causes severe allergic reactions, chemical burns, serious skin disorders such as rashes and dermatitis, and cancer. Inhalation of nickel vapors and nitric acid fumes can cause breathing problems, nasal bleeding and serious damage to a person's respiratory tract. Various Borjohn employees testified to symptoms consistent with these health problems. Employees testified to having had "daily nose bleeds," headaches, chest pains, breathing difficulties, dizziness, rashes and blisters.

Repeated employee exposure to the chemicals was unavoidable. In discharging the spent nickel plating baths and nitric acid baths, for instance, Borjohn employees were told to bail out the harmful solutions by hand using a plastic bucket or a portable pump. Once a tank was nearly empty it was tipped over the edge of the sink and a scoop or small cup was used to scoop out any remaining solution. The employees were required to scrape the sides and bottom of nickel baths to extricate a layer of nickel byproduct called "extraneous plate out." Sometimes employees were told to dump "hot" nitric acid solutions into the sinks. This created an "alka seltzer" like appearance on the surface of the sink. Employees testified that the nickel and nitric acid solutions sometimes splashed and spilled directly onto their skin[]. Indeed, one employee complained that he was always "wet" with the solution and at times was scalded by the chemicals.

[The protective gear made available to the employees was grossly inadequate, and it was clear that Borjohn and Borowski knew the employees were exposed to serious health risks. Borjohn and Borowski were indicted under the CWA's knowing endangerment provision for knowingly discharging the nickel and nitric acid baths into the city sewer system and the publicly owned treatment plant, thereby placing Borjohn employees in imminent danger of death or serious bodily injury. Both Borjohn and Borowski were convicted.]

DISCUSSION

Section 1317(b) of the Clean Water Act directs the EPA to promulgate pretreatment standards for pollutants going into publicly-owned treatment works.[18] Subsection

---

18. Specifically, the EPA is to promulgate:

regulations establishing pretreatment standards for introduction of pollutants into treatment works . . . which are publicly owned for those pollutants which are determined not to be susceptible to treatment by such treatment works or which would interfere with the operation of such treatment works. . . . Pretreatment standards under this subsection . . . shall be established to

(d) prohibits the owner or operator of any source (a term that includes Borjohn and Borowski) from violating these standards. Section 1319(c)(3)(A) provides that anyone who "knowingly violates section . . . 1317 . . . , and who knows at that time that he thereby places another person in imminent danger of death or serious bodily injury" is guilty of a felony.[19]

We assume for purposes of this appeal that both defendants knowingly violated § 1317 and knew of the dangers to the Borjohn employees. It is undisputed that Borjohn employees were placed in imminent danger of serious bodily injury during their employment and that some of this danger occurred at the time of dumping chemical solutions into sinks that ultimately led to a publicly-owned treatment works. The question is whether the defendants, in knowingly violating § 1317, knew that they "thereby" placed the employees in imminent danger.

There is no single correct answer to this semantic puzzle. In one sense, it can be said that the knowing violation "thereby" placed the employees in danger. After all, the defendants knew that the sinks were connected to the publicly-owned sewer and treatment works and that the wastes would therefore illegally proceed without interruption to the publicly-owned treatment works. They also knew that the employees' actions in performing the dumping as instructed placed them in imminent danger. Arguably, therefore, through the knowing violation the defendants "thereby" endangered the employees. On the other hand, there could be no violation unless the wastes ultimately ended up in a publicly-owned sewer and treatment works. But the risks and dangers to these employees would have been the same if the plugs had always remained in the sinks so that no discharge to the publicly-owned treatment works (and therefore no § 1317 violation) ever occurred. The danger to the employees was inherent in their handling of the various chemical solutions, solutions that were part of the defendant's manufacturing process. They would have been subject to the identical hazards had they been dumping the chemicals into drums or other containers for appropriate treatment under the Act. In that respect, therefore, although the defendants knew that their employees were placed in imminent danger, that danger was not caused by the knowing violation of § 1317.

Since semantic analysis alone is insufficient, how is this puzzle to be resolved? Several factors assist us. First, the purpose of the statute is clear. The Clean Water Act is not a statute designed to provide protection to industrial employees who work with hazardous substances. Instead, section 1251(a) states: "The objective of this Act is to restore and maintain the chemical, physical, and biological integrity of the Nation's waters." The EPA is directed to promulgate pretreatment standards only so as to "prevent the discharge of any pollutant" that will pass through publicly-owned treatment works, interfere with the works, be incompatible with the works, or otherwise violate

---

prevent the discharge of any pollutant through treatment works . . . which are publicly owned, which pollutant interferes with, passes through, or otherwise is incompatible with such works.

33 U.S.C. § 1317(b).

19.

Knowing endangerment. (A) General rule. Any person who knowingly violates section 1317, and who knows at that time that he thereby places another person in imminent danger of death or serious bodily injury, shall, upon conviction, be subject to a fine of not more than $250,000 or imprisonment of not more than 15 years, or both. A person which is an organization shall, upon conviction of violating this subparagraph, be subject to a fine of not more than $1,000,000.

33 U.S.C. § 1319(c)(3).

effluent standards for the works. The EPA regulations reflect this same focus of concern on publicly-owned treatment works. The regulations' goals are:

> (a) To prevent the introduction of pollutants into POTWs which will interfere with the operation of a POTW, including interference with its use or disposal of municipal sludge;
> (b) To prevent the introduction of pollutants into POTWs which will pass through the treatment works or otherwise be incompatible with such works; and
> (c) To improve opportunities to recycle and reclaim municipal and industrial wastewaters and sludges.

40 C.F.R. § 403.2. One can read the entire statute and regulations in vain for any protection mechanism for industrial employees who work with wastes at the point of discharge.[20] Instead, other laws deal with industrial employee health and safety. The Occupational Safety and Health Act (OSHA) is the best known. 29 U.S.C. §§ 651 et seq. . . .

Second, Congress has passed a separate law dealing with the general handling, treatment and storage of hazardous substances. Specifically, the Resource Conservation and Recovery Act (RCRA) is a cradle-to-grave statute providing a full range of remedies designed to protect both health and the environment. The Clean Water Act, on the other hand, is not directed at the *handling* of pollutants. Indeed, under the Clean Water Act, if the publicly-owned treatment works were itself capable of removing the nickel and acid from Borjohn's discharges (thereby satisfying Clean Water Act goals), the works could seek to avoid the prohibition placed on Borjohn's discharge — yet the health hazard to the employees would obviously remain the same.[21] Moreover, unlike the Clean Water Act, RCRA exhibits explicit concern for industrial health. It has a provision specifically requiring the EPA to provide information about employee hazards to

---

20. Any concern for employees reflected in the regulations deals with "downstream" employees, i.e., employees of the publicly-owned works. See 40 C.F.R. § 403.5(b)(7) (prohibiting "pollutants which result in the presence of toxic gases, vapors, or fumes *within the POTW* in a quantity that may cause acute worker health and safety problems") (emphasis supplied).

At only three other points do the regulations reflect concern with health. First, 40 C.F.R. § 403.8(f)(1)(vi)(B) provides:

> The POTW shall have authority and procedures (after informal notice to the discharger) immediately and effectively to halt or prevent any discharge of pollutants *to the POTW* which reasonably appears to present an imminent endangerment to the health or welfare of persons (emphasis supplied).

This provision apparently permits a municipal works to take steps to prevent a discharge from reaching it. The danger contemplated, therefore, is to persons who would be endangered once the discharge reaches the municipal sewers or works. Second, 40 C.F.R. § 403.8(f)(2)(vii)(C) lists as a "significant noncompliance" any discharge that causes "interference or pass through (including endangering the health of POTW personnel or the general public)." Conspicuously missing is any reference to source employees. Third, the very next sentence lists as a significant noncompliance "any discharge of a pollutant that has caused imminent endangerment to human health, welfare or to the environment. . . ." 40 C.F.R. § 403.8(f)(2)(vii)(D). "Discharge" is defined as "the introduction of pollutants into a POTW. . . ." 40 C.F.R. § 403.3(g). The concern again, therefore, is for "downstream" effects.

None of these regulations was referred to by either the United States Attorney's Office or the defendants.

21. Conversely, there may be remedial measures (proper respirators and ventilation, protective clothing and procedures) that could alleviate the health risks to the workers, yet have no value in addressing Clean Water Act concerns of cleaning up the discharges.

the Secretary of Labor and OSHA for OSHA enforcement purposes. The Clean Water Act exhibits no equivalent concern for workplace dangers.

Finally, the well-known rule of lenity in applying criminal statutes applies here. Where there is ambiguity in a criminal statute, the ambiguity is to be construed in favor of the defendant. Our initial semantic exercise reveals the ambiguity in this statute.

These three factors lead us to conclude that a knowing endangerment prosecution cannot be premised upon danger that occurs before the pollutant reaches a publicly-owned sewer or treatment works. Section 1319(c)(3)(A) therefore does not apply to the defendants' conduct as set forth in this indictment.

[The CWA provides a defense to a knowing endangerment charge if the endangerment "was consented to by the person endangered," and both the danger and the offending conduct were reasonably foreseeable hazards of a particular occupation. The government argued that the court's interpretation of the knowing endangerment provision made this language meaningless, because only employees at the source of the discharge could both be endangered by the discharge and consent to the endangerment.]

. . . We find the premise to be faulty. In the course of ordinary industrial activity, illegal discharges will undoubtedly occur from time to time (human or mechanical failure) that the industrial manufacturer or other entity physically cannot correct or halt immediately. Such an entity, if it is also a good citizen, will inform the publicly-owned treatment works of the discharge so that any corrective steps possible can be taken downstream. These publicly-owned treatment works may then hire professional consultants to advise the publicly-owned treatment works how to handle these fully disclosed but illegal discharges until they are corrected or halted. These "downstream" actors — consciously and freely dealing with illegal substances after they have reached the publicly-owned sewers or treatment works — are legitimate subjects for the affirmative defense and give it appropriate content. The section does not, therefore, require us to give section 1319 the reading the United States Attorney urges, a reading that is inconsistent with the overall thrust of the Clean Water Act.

CONCLUSION

The endangered persons on whom this prosecution is based had no connection to the publicly-owned treatment works or municipal sewers, but were endangered solely as a result of their employment activities at their private place of employment prior to any illegal discharge reaching the public sewer or works. The defendants' conduct here was utterly reprehensible and may have violated any number of other criminal laws; but it did not violate the knowing endangerment provision of the Clean Water Act.

Accordingly, the judgments of conviction are vacated; judgments of acquittal shall be entered for both defendants on both counts.

Notes and Questions

1. What is the point of having a knowing endangerment provision if it does not apply to the endangered Borjohn employees? Whom does the statute protect and why?

2. If the court had concluded that the endangerment provision protected the employees, would the defendants have been able to prevail on the defense of consent? Why does the statute recognize consent as a defense?

3. Under the reasoning in *Borowski*, could BP be held liable under the CWA's knowing endangerment provision for the deaths of its employees and contractors aboard the Deepwater Horizon? If the spill continues to pose a risk to the health, safety, and livelihoods of the Gulf coast's countless inhabitants on a long-term basis, could this subject BP to liability for knowing endangerment?

4. There are also allegations that BP's initial estimates of the extent of the spill delayed much needed company and governmental response efforts and resource allocation (BP initially reported that only 5,000 barrels of oil were being released per day, but the actual measurement turned out to be between 40,000 and 60,000 barrels per day), held back underwater camera footage of the spill, and failed to provide proper protective equipment to volunteers and contractors cleaning up the oil. Are there potential knowing endangerment violations here?

5. The CWA places a premium on truthfulness, as reflected in its recordkeeping, reporting, and monitoring requirements. It is a crime under the Act to knowingly make a false material statement in any application, record, or other document required to be filed or maintained under the Act, or to knowingly falsify, tamper with, or render inaccurate any monitoring device or method the Act requires to be maintained. Do the facts in the BP case support the filing of criminal charges for violating these requirements? What would the government have to prove to obtain a conviction?

6. Recall that in Chapter 6 we considered liability under the general false statements statute, 18 U.S.C. § 1001. How, if at all, does the CWA false statements provision differ from its more general Title 18 counterpart? Would the facts in the BP incident support charges under § 1001?

III. AIR POLLUTION: THE CLEAN AIR ACT

The Clean Air Act provides a regulatory framework for federal and state air pollution control. The key components of this framework are the establishment of national ambient air standards by the EPA and the adoption of state implementation plans (SIPs) that set pollution emission limits and create a system to monitor compliance and enforcement. The principal enforcement provision, 42 U.S.C. § 7413, contains a broad range of criminal prohibitions, including knowing violation of an implementation plan, permit, order, or other regulatory requirement; knowing endangerment; and making false statements.

Prosecutors make sparing use of the criminal provisions in the Clean Air Act. In the first ten years of the environmental criminal enforcement program, Clean Air Act prosecutions accounted for fewer than 10 percent of environmental prosecutions. More than two-thirds of the Clean Air Act prosecutions arose out of demolition or renovation projects in which contractors and commercial property owners failed to comply with asbestos removal rules.[22]

---

22. Most of the remaining cases were related to auto emissions standards.

To establish a violation of the asbestos removal standards, the government must prove that the defendant is an "owner or operator" of a demolition or renovation operation involving asbestos removal.

UNITED STATES v. DIPENTINO
242 F.3d 1090 (9th Cir. 2001)

THOMPSON, Circuit Judge. . . .

BACKGROUND

The Las Vegas Convention and Visitors Authority ("Visitors Authority") hired Ab-Haz Environmental, Inc. ("Ab-Haz"), an asbestos abatement consulting firm, to oversee the removal of asbestos-containing materials from the Landmark Hotel and Casino in Las Vegas, Nevada, prior to its demolition. Rafiq Ali was the president and sole proprietor of Ab-Haz; Rocco Dipentino was an industrial hygienist employed by Ab-Haz as the on-site inspector at the Landmark. Under the terms of its contract with the Visitors Authority, Ab-Haz was required to: (1) survey the Landmark and identify the asbestos-containing materials that needed to be removed prior to demolition; (2) prepare specifications for how the asbestos removal job was to be performed; (3) assist the Visitors Authority in selecting an asbestos-removal contractor to remove the asbestos-containing materials; (4) serve as the Visitors Authority's on-site representative, providing day-to-day monitoring and oversight of the work to ensure that it was being performed in accordance with the law; and (5) inspect and certify that the site was free from asbestos following the completion of the asbestos-removal work.

The Clean Air Act classifies asbestos as a hazardous air pollutant. Emissions of hazardous air pollutants in violation of work practice standards promulgated by the Environment Protection Agency are prohibited. Under the work practice standard relevant to this case, an owner or operator of a demolition activity is required to remove all asbestos prior to demolition and must "adequately wet the [asbestos-containing] material and ensure that it remains wet until collected and contained" in leak-tight containers for proper disposal. An owner or operator of a demolition activity who knowingly violates a work practice standard is subject to criminal penalties. An employee who is carrying out his or her normal activities and acting under orders from the employer is liable only for knowing and willful violations.

The grand jury for the District of Nevada returned a two-count indictment against Ab-Haz, Rafiq Ali, Rocco Dipentino, and a defendant who was later acquitted, Richard Lovelace, who was the on-site inspector of the asbestos-removal contractor hired by the Visitors Authority. Count 1 of the indictment charged the defendants with knowingly conspiring to violate the Clean Air Act by removing regulated asbestos-containing materials from surfaces in the Landmark without complying with the applicable work practice standards. Count 2, paragraph A ("Count 2 ¶A") charged each defendant with knowingly violating the Clean Air Act by leaving scraped asbestos-containing debris on floors and other surfaces, where it was allowed to dry out, instead of placing the debris, while wet, into leak-proof containers for removal from the site. Count 2, paragraph B ("Count 2 ¶B") charged each defendant with knowingly violating the Clean Air Act by causing asbestos-covered facility components to fall from the ceiling to the floor, rather than carefully lowering such components so as not to dislodge asbestos. One government inspector described the removal project as "the worst [asbestos] abatement job I've seen."

[The jury convicted Ali and Dipentino of knowingly violating the Clean Air Act by allowing asbestos-containing debris to dry out before placing it into leak-proof containers, as charged in Count 2 ¶A of the indictment. Ali and Dipentino appealed.]

B. SUFFICIENCY OF THE EVIDENCE . . .

The Clean Air Act imposes criminal liability on an owner or operator if he or she knowingly violates the Act. The term "owner or operator" is defined under the asbestos regulations as "any person who owns, leases, operates, controls, or supervises the facility being demolished or renovated or any person who owns, leases, operates, controls or supervises the demolition or renovation operation, or both." 40 C.F.R. § 61.141. In determining whether a person is an owner or operator within the meaning of the Clean Air Act, the question is whether the person "had significant or substantial or real control and supervision over [the] project." United States v. Walsh, 8 F.3d 659, 662 (9th Cir. 1993).

The evidence established that Dipentino "had significant or substantial or real control and supervision" over the asbestos-abatement project at the Landmark and that he knowingly violated the relevant work practice standards charged in the indictment. The government presented evidence that Dipentino was employed by Ab-Haz as the Landmark's "on-site representative during the term of work"; that he was present at the site on a daily basis; that he performed inspections of areas that the asbestos-removal contractor had allegedly abated; that he prepared and signed final inspection reports certifying that rooms in the Landmark were clear of asbestos-containing material; and that he had the power to stop the asbestos-removal contractor's work for improper performance.

The government also presented evidence that Dipentino was licensed by the State of Nevada as an asbestos-abatement supervisor and consultant; that in support of his applications for those licenses, Dipentino certified that he had completed courses and training in environmental law requirements; that Dipentino co-authored with Rafiq Ali the asbestos survey of the Landmark, which revealed that the Landmark contained 328,000 square feet of asbestos-containing acoustical ceiling spray, 1250 linear feet of asbestos-containing fireproofing material on structural components such as beams, as well as asbestos-containing pipe insulation and other materials found throughout the facility; and that piles of asbestos-containing debris were discovered by inspectors after the Landmark abatement job was certified as completed. Although Dipentino argues that the jury could not reasonably have concluded that he knew, simply by looking, that the debris left to dry on the floors of the Landmark contained asbestos, the district court properly rejected this argument in a post-judgment order stating: "Knowledge that a debris pile contains asbestos, however, can also result from knowing the source and nature of the material in the debris pile. Plainly it can be concluded that a person knows a debris pile contains asbestos if that person knew that the debris pile was created from material that the person knew to contain asbestos." In sum, there was sufficient evidence to convict Dipentino. . . .

Notes and Questions

1. Ali was the president and sole proprietor of Ab-Haz. Dipentino was an industrial hygienist employed by Ab-Haz as the on-site inspector at the Landmark. As a "hired gun," in what sense was Dipentino an owner or operator? What did he own or operate? Was Ali also an owner or operator? Was Ab-Haz? Was Landmark?

2. Dipentino was convicted of knowingly violating the Clean Air Act. What must he know to be guilty? What evidence supports a finding that he had the requisite knowledge?

3. Although prosecutions under the Clean Air Act are few in number, they may not provide an accurate barometer of the level of criminal enforcement for air pollution. When reportable quantities of hazardous pollutants are released into the environment — including the air — the Comprehensive Environmental Response, Compensation, and Liability Act (CERCLA) imposes a duty to notify regulators. Failure to comply with the notification requirements provides an independent basis for criminal prosecution.

IV. HAZARDOUS WASTE

A. THE RESOURCE CONSERVATION AND RECOVERY ACT

The Resource Conservation and Recovery Act of 1976 (RCRA) is a far-reaching regulatory statute. It establishes "cradle to grave" regulation of the more than half a million individuals and firms that generate hazardous waste as well as those that treat, store, dispose of, or transport hazardous waste. RCRA's regulatory scheme is called "cradle to grave" because it is designed to enable the EPA to monitor the management of hazardous waste from the moment of its creation up through the time it is stored or disposed of.

The critical link in the chain is the manifest system. Producers of hazardous waste ("generators") must prepare a manifest that enables the EPA to trace the transportation, treatment, and disposal of the waste. RCRA also imposes stringent standards for handling hazardous waste together with numerous recordkeeping and labeling requirements. As is true under many environmental statutes, obtaining and complying with a permit to handle hazardous waste are capstones of the regulatory scheme.

Like the Clean Water Act, RCRA authorizes cumulative fines for each day that a violation occurs and punishes violations that occur after a first conviction twice as severely as a first offense.

1. Treatment, Storage, or Disposal Violations

UNITED STATES v. JOHNSON & TOWERS, INC.
741 F.2d 662 (3d Cir. 1984)

SLOVITER, Circuit Judge. . . .

I

The criminal prosecution in this case arose from the disposal of chemicals at a plant owned by Johnson & Towers in Mount Laurel, New Jersey. In its operations the company, which repairs and overhauls large motor vehicles, uses degreasers and other industrial chemicals that contain chemicals such as methylene chloride and trichloro-ethylene, classified as "hazardous wastes" under the Resource Conservation and Recovery Act (RCRA) and "pollutants" under the Clean Water Act. During the period relevant here, the waste chemicals from cleaning operations were drained into a holding tank and, when the tank was full, pumped into a trench. The trench flowed from the plant property into Parker's Creek, a tributary of the Delaware River. Under RCRA, generators of such wastes must obtain a permit for disposal from the Environmental Protection Agency (EPA). The EPA had neither issued nor received an application for a permit for Johnson & Towers' operations.

The indictment names as defendants Johnson & Towers and two of its employees, Jack Hopkins, a foreman, and Peter Angel, the service manager in the trucking department. According to the indictment, over a three-day period federal agents saw workers pump waste from the tank into the trench, and on the third day observed toxic chemicals flowing into the creek. [The defendants were charged with RCRA and CWA violations and with conspiracy.]

The counts under RCRA charged that the defendants "did knowingly treat, store, and dispose of, and did cause to be treated, stored and disposed of hazardous wastes without having obtained a permit . . . in that the defendants discharged, deposited, injected, dumped, spilled, leaked and placed degreasers . . . into the trench. . . ." The indictment alleged that both Angel and Hopkins "managed, supervised and directed a substantial portion of Johnson & Towers' operations . . . including those related to the treatment, storage and disposal of the hazardous wastes and pollutants" and that the chemicals were discharged by "the defendants and others at their direction." The indictment did not otherwise detail Hopkins' and Angel's activities or responsibilities.

Johnson & Towers pled guilty to the RCRA counts. Hopkins and Angel pled not guilty, and then moved to dismiss [the RCRA counts]. The court concluded that the RCRA criminal provision applies only to "owners and operators," i.e., those obligated under the statute to obtain a permit. Since neither Hopkins nor Angel was an "owner" or "operator," the district court granted the motion as to the RCRA charges but held that the individuals could be liable on these . . . counts under 18 U.S.C. § 2 for aiding and abetting. The court denied the government's motion for reconsideration and the government appealed to this court.

We hold that section 6928(d)(2)(A) covers employees as well as owners and operators of the facility who knowingly treat, store, or dispose of any hazardous waste, but that the employees can be subject to criminal prosecution only if they knew or should have known that there had been no compliance with the permit requirement of section 6925.

II

The single issue in this appeal is whether the individual defendants are subject to prosecution under RCRA's criminal provision, which applies to:

[a]ny person who — [. . .]
    (2) knowingly treats, stores, or disposes of any hazardous waste identified or listed under this subchapter either —
        (A) without having obtained a permit under section 6925 of this title . . . or
        (B) in knowing violation of any material condition or requirement of such permit.
    [. . .]

42 U.S.C. § 6928(d) (emphasis added). The permit provision in section 6925, referred to in section 6928(d), requires "each person owning or operating a facility for the treatment, storage, or disposal of hazardous waste identified or listed under this subchapter to have a permit" from the EPA.

[While the defendants argued that the criminal provision applies only to those responsible for obtaining a permit — i.e., owners and operators — the government maintained that the provision applies to anyone who treats, stores, or disposes of hazardous waste.]

B . . .

The original statute made knowing disposal (but not treatment or storage) of such waste without a permit a misdemeanor. Amendments in 1978 and 1980 expanded the criminal provision to cover treatment and storage and made violation of section 6928 a felony. The fact that Congress amended the statute twice to broaden the scope of its substantive provisions and enhance the penalty is a strong indication of Congress' increasing concern about the seriousness of the prohibited conduct.

Although Congress' concern may have been directed primarily at owners and operators of generating facilities, since it imposed upon them in section 6925 the obligation to secure the necessary permit, Congress did not explicitly limit criminal liability for impermissible treatment, storage, or disposal to owners and operators. The House Committee's discussion of enforcement contains several references relevant only to owners and operators, but it says, in addition: "This section *also* provides for criminal penalties for the person who . . . disposes of any hazardous waste without a permit under this title. . . ." H.R. Rep. No. 1491, supra at 31, 1976 U.S. Code Cong. & Ad. News at 6269 (emphasis added). The "also" demonstrates that the reach of section 6928(d)(2) is broader than that of the rest of the statute, particularly the administrative enforcement remedies. The acts that were made the subject of the criminal provision were distinguished in the House Report from the other conduct subject to administrative regulation because they were viewed as more serious offenses. As the Report explained, "[the] justification for the penalties section is to permit a broad variety of mechanisms so as to stop the illegal disposal of hazardous wastes." Id.

We conclude that in RCRA, no less than in the Food and Drugs Act, Congress endeavored to control hazards that, "in the circumstances of modern industrialism, are largely beyond self-protection." United States v. Dotterweich, 320 U.S. at 280. It would undercut the purposes of the legislation to limit the class of potential defendants to owners and operators when others also bear responsibility for handling regulated materials. The phrase "without having obtained a permit *under section 6925*" (emphasis added) merely references the section under which the permit is required and exempts from prosecution under section 6928(d)(2)(A) anyone who has obtained a permit; we conclude that it has no other limiting effect. Therefore we reject the district court's construction limiting the substantive criminal provision by confining "any person" in section 6928(d)(2)(A) to owners and operators of facilities that store, treat or dispose of hazardous waste, as an unduly narrow view of both the statutory language and the congressional intent.

III

A

Since we must remand this case to the district court because the individual defendants are indeed covered by section 6928(d)(2)(A), it is incumbent on us to reach the question of the requisite proof as to individual defendants under that section. . . .

We focus again on the statutory language:

[a]ny person who — [. . .]
(2) *knowingly* treats, stores, or disposes of any hazardous waste identified or listed under this subchapter either —
(A) without having obtained a permit under section 6925 of this title . . . or
(B) *in knowing violation* of any material condition or requirement of such permit.

42 U.S.C. § 6928(d) (1982) (emphasis added).

If the word "knowingly" in section 6928(d)(2) referred exclusively to the acts of treating, storing or disposing, as the government contends, it would be an almost meaningless addition since it is not likely that one would treat, store or dispose of waste without knowledge of that action. At a minimum, the word "knowingly," which introduces subsection (A), must also encompass knowledge that the waste material is hazardous. Certainly, "[a] person thinking in good faith that he was [disposing of] distilled water when in fact he was [disposing of] some dangerous acid would not be covered." United States v. International Minerals & Chemical Corp., 402 U.S. 558, 563-64 (1971).

Whether "knowingly" also modifies subsection (A) presents a somewhat different question. The district court concluded that it is not necessary to show that individual defendants prosecuted under section 6928(d)(2)(A) knew that they were acting without a permit or in violation of the law. Since we have already concluded that this is a regulatory statute which can be classified as a "public welfare statute," there would be a reasonable basis for reading the statute without any mens rea requirement. However, whatever policy justification might warrant applying such a construction as a matter of general principle, such a reading would be arbitrary and nonsensical when applied to this statute.

Treatment, storage or disposal of hazardous waste in violation of any material condition or requirement of a permit must be "knowing," since the statute explicitly so states in subsection (B). It is unlikely that Congress could have intended to subject to criminal prosecution those persons who acted when no permit had been obtained irrespective of their knowledge (under subsection (A)), but not those persons who acted in violation of the terms of a permit unless that action was knowing (subsection (B)). Thus we are led to conclude either that the omission of the word "knowing" in (A) was inadvertent or that "knowingly" which introduces subsection (2) applies to subsection (A).

As a matter of syntax we find it no more awkward to read "knowingly" as applying to the entire sentence than to read it as modifying only "treats, stores or disposes." . . .

B

However, our conclusion that "knowingly" applies to all elements of the offense in section 6298(d)(2)(A) does not impose on the government as difficult a burden as it fears. On this issue, we are guided by the Court's holding in United States v. International Minerals & Chemical Corp., 402 U.S. at 563, that under certain regulatory statutes requiring "knowing" conduct the government need prove only knowledge of the actions taken and not of the statute forbidding them. . . .

The Court recognized that under certain statutes, such as the income tax law, the government must show a purpose by defendant to bring about the forbidden result. However, the Court in *International Minerals*, construing a statute and regulations which proscribed knowing failure to record shipment of chemicals, stated,

[W]here, as here and as in *Balint* and *Freed, dangerous or deleterious devices or products or obnoxious waste materials are involved*, the probability of regulation is so great that anyone who is aware that he is in possession of them or dealing with them must be presumed to be aware of the regulation.

402 U.S. at 565 (emphasis added).

Even the dissenting Justices, viewing the highly regulated shipping industry, agreed that the officers, agents, and employees

are under a species of absolute liability for violation of the regulations despite the "knowingly" requirement. This, no doubt, is as Congress intended it to be. Cf. United States v. Dotterweich, 320 U.S. 277; United States v. Balint, 258 U.S. 250. Likewise, prosecution of regular shippers for violations of the regulations could hardly be impeded by the "knowingly" requirement for triers of fact would have no difficulty whatever *in inferring knowledge on the part of those whose business it is to know, despite their protestations to the contrary.*

402 U.S. at 569.

The indictment in this case specified the crime in the language of the statute. Thus it did not include language spelling out the knowledge requirements of the statute discussed in text. Nevertheless, in light of our interpretation of section 6928(d)(2)(A), it is evident that the district court will be required to instruct the jury, inter alia, that in order to convict each defendant the jury must find that each knew that Johnson & Towers was required to have a permit, and knew that Johnson & Towers did not have a permit. Depending on the evidence, the district court may also instruct the jury that such knowledge may be inferred. . . .

IV

In summary, we conclude that the individual defendants are "persons" within section 6928(d)(2)(A), that all the elements of that offense must be shown to have been knowing, but that such knowledge, including that of the permit requirement, may be inferred by the jury as to those individuals who hold the requisite responsible positions with the corporate defendant.

For the foregoing reasons, we will reverse the district court's order dismissing portions of . . . the indictment, and we will remand for further proceedings consistent with this opinion.

UNITED STATES v. HOFLIN
880 F.2d 1033 (9th Cir. 1989)

THOMPSON, Circuit Judge.

Douglas Hoflin appeals his felony conviction for aiding and abetting the disposal of hazardous waste during his tenure as Director of Public Works for the City of Ocean Shores, Washington, in violation of 42 U.S.C. § 6928(d)(2)(A). Hoflin also appeals his misdemeanor conviction for aiding and abetting the burial of sludge at the Ocean Shores sewage treatment plant, contrary to the conditions of the plant's operating permit in violation of 33 U.S.C. § 1319(c)(1).

Hoflin contends his conviction under 42 U.S.C. § 6928(d)(2)(A) requires proof that he knew there was no permit for disposal of the waste, and that the jury instructions omitted this element of the offense. He also contends that the jury instructions were inadequate to define the misdemeanor offense created by 33 U.S.C. § 1319(c)(1). We affirm.

BACKGROUND

Hoflin was the Director of the Public Works Department for Ocean Shores, Washington ("City"), from 1975 to 1980, when he left for personal reasons. In 1982, he returned as Assistant Director until he again became Director in 1983. As Director, Hoflin's responsibilities included supervising maintenance of roads and operation of a sewage treatment plant. The criminal prosecution in this case arose from the disposal of two types of waste generated by the City: paint left over from road maintenance and sludge removed from the kitchen of the City's golf course. These wastes were buried at the City's sewage treatment plant.

Hoflin and his successor, John Hastig, bought 3,500 gallons of paint for road maintenance from 1975 through 1982. As painting jobs were finished, 55-gallon drums which had contained paint were returned to the Public Works Department's yard. Drums which were empty were used elsewhere or given away. Fourteen drums which still contained paint remained. In the fall of 1982, Hastig moved these drums inside a building located on the Public Works Department yard to keep the paint from freezing. The fire marshal, however, ordered Hastig to return the drums to the outdoors because of the risk of explosion. Hoflin was aware that the drums had to be moved because of the flammable nature of their contents.

When Hoflin again became Director in 1983, he told Fred Carey, director of the sewage treatment plant, that he planned to dispose of the drums by burying them at the plant. Carey replied that burying the drums might jeopardize the plant's NPDES certificate,[23] but Hoflin said he was going to do it anyway.

Hoflin instructed an employee to haul the paint drums to the sewage treatment plant and bury them. Hoflin claimed he told the employee to bury only drums in which the contents had solidified, but the employee testified that Hoflin gave no such instruction. Around August, 1983, employees of Hoflin's department took the drums to the treatment plant, dug a hole on the grounds of the plant, and dumped the drums in. Some of the drums were rusted and leaking, and at least one burst open in the process. The hole was not deep enough, so the employees crushed the drums with a front end loader to make them fit. The refuse was then covered with sand.

Almost two years later, in March 1985, Carey reported the incident to state authorities. After inspecting the plant, the state authorities referred the matter to the Environmental Protection Agency ("EPA"). EPA employees recovered the drums, but because several of the drums had no lids or had been crushed, paint had already leaked into the soil. Ten of the fourteen drums recovered contained liquid material. [EPA tests confirmed that the contents of the drums were hazardous and could not be legally disposed of without a permit.] No such permit had been obtained.

The City owns a golf course which houses a restaurant. Periodically, the grease trap in the kitchen septic system is pumped out and the sludge is taken to the sewage treatment plant. Because this sludge contains so much grease, it kills the bacteria necessary for the treatment process and has to be specially burned. In September 1984, three truck loads of this sludge were transported to the City's sewage treatment plant, but Carey refused to accept delivery. Carey told Hoflin that accepting the sludge could jeopardize the plant's NPDES certificate. Hoflin told him to take it anyway and to bury it rather than treat it.[24] The sludge was then dumped into a depression on the grounds

---

23. The National Pollutant Discharge Elimination System ("NPDES") certificate is an operating permit issued to the City pursuant to the Clean Water Act, 33 U.S.C. § 1342. Any person seeking to discharge a pollutant directly into the navigable waters of the United States must obtain an NPDES certificate either from the Administrator of the Environmental Protection Agency ("EPA") or from a state agency authorized by the EPA.

24. The City's sewage treatment plant, run by Carey, has an NPDES permit for treating and discharging sewage. The plant operators treat waste water with bacteria in clay-lined lagoons to break down

of the plant and covered with a backhoe. This burial violated the plant's NPDES permit.

C. THE INDICTMENT

[The indictment charged Hoflin with conspiracy, disposing of the paint without a permit in violation of RCRA (42 U.S.C. § 6928(d)(2)), and disposing of the kitchen sludge in violation of the CWA. The jury acquitted him of conspiracy but convicted him on the RCRA and CWA charges.]

DISCUSSION

A. SECTION 6928(D)(2)(A)

On appeal from his conviction on Count II, Hoflin contends he did not know the City did not have a permit to dispose of the paint. . . .
. . . Section 6928(d) provides in pertinent part:

(d) Criminal Penalties
Any person who —
     (2) *knowingly* treats, stores or disposes of any hazardous waste identified or listed under this subchapter either —
          (A) without having obtained a permit under section 6925 of this title . . . ; or
          (B) in *knowing* violation of any material condition or requirement of such permit;
     shall, upon conviction, be subject to [fines, imprisonment, or both] (emphasis added).

It is Hoflin's position that "knowingly" in subsection (2) modifies both subsections (A) and (B). Under this interpretation, knowledge becomes an essential element of the crime defined by section 6928(d)(2)(A), and Hoflin could not be convicted on Count II without proof that he knew no permit had been obtained. . . .
     . . . The absence of the word "knowing" in subsection (A) is in stark contrast to its presence in the immediately following subsection (B). The statute makes a clear distinction between non-permit holders and permit holders, requiring in subsection (B) that the latter knowingly violate a material condition or requirement of the permit. To read the word "knowingly" at the beginning of section (2) into subsection (A) would be to eviscerate this distinction. Thus, it is plain that knowledge of the absence of a permit is not an element of the offense defined by subsection (A). The statute is not ambiguous. On the contrary, "the language is plain and the meaning is clear. Our statutory construction inquiry, therefore, is at an end." United States v. Patterson, 820 F.2d 1524, 1526 (9th Cir. 1987).
     Hoflin relies on United States v. Johnson & Towers, Inc., 741 F.2d 662 (3d Cir. 1984), to argue that this interpretation of the statute is unreasonable and could not have

---

organic materials, and then discharge the waste into ground waters. Section 54 of the NPDES permit requires the permit holder to provide all known, available and reasonable methods of treatment to prevent leachate from its solid waste material from entering surface waters or adversely affecting state ground waters.

been intended by Congress. In *Johnson & Towers*, the Third Circuit held that employees could be subjected to criminal prosecution under section 6928(d)(2)(A) only if they knew or should have known their employer had failed to obtain the required permit. In remanding the case to the district court for trial, the Third Circuit in *Johnson & Towers* stated that the necessary knowledge element could be inferred from proof that the individuals charged with violating section 6928(d)(2)(A) had "responsible positions with the corporate defendant," presumably meaning that based on the positions they held in the company it could be inferred they either knew or should have known whether a permit had been obtained. . . .

We respectfully decline to follow the Third Circuit's analysis in *Johnson & Towers*. Had Congress intended knowledge of the lack of a permit to be an element under subsection (A) it easily could have said so. It specifically inserted a knowledge element in subsection (B), and it did so notwithstanding the "knowingly" modifier which introduces subsection (2). In the face of such obvious congressional action we will not write something into the statute which Congress so plainly left out. . . . To adopt the Third Circuit's interpretation of subsection (A) would render the word "knowing" in subsection (B) mere surplusage.

The result we reach is also consistent with the purpose of RCRA. The overriding concern of RCRA is the grave danger to people and the environment from hazardous wastes. Such wastes typically have no value, yet can only be safely disposed of at considerable cost. Millions of tons of hazardous substances are literally dumped on the ground each year; a good deal of these can blind, cripple or kill. Many of such substances are generated and buried without notice until the damage becomes evident. . . .

Finally, our conclusion is consistent with RCRA's goals and the treatment Congress gave "knowledge" in 42 U.S.C. § 6928(d)(2)(A) and (B) to achieve these goals. The statute requires knowledge of violation of the terms of a permit under subsection (B) but omits knowledge that a permit is lacking as an element of disposing of hazardous waste without a permit under subsection (A). There is nothing illogical about this. Knowledge of the location of hazardous waste, from its generation through its disposal, is a major concern of RCRA. Those who handle such waste are, therefore, affirmatively required to provide information to the EPA in order to secure permits. Placing this burden on those handling hazardous waste materials makes it possible for the EPA to know who is handling hazardous waste, monitor their activities and enforce compliance with the statute. On the other hand, persons who handle hazardous waste materials without telling the EPA what they are doing shield their activity from the eyes of the regulatory agency, and thus inhibit the agency from performing its assigned tasks. We hold that knowledge of the absence of a permit is not an element of the offense defined by 42 U.S.C. § 6928(d)(2)(A).

Hoflin next argues that even if knowledge of the absence of a permit is unnecessary to a prosecution under section 6928(d)(2)(A), the government nonetheless must prove, and the jury must be instructed, that the defendant knew the material being disposed of was hazardous. We agree.

Subsection (2) applies to anyone who "knowingly treats, stores or disposes of any hazardous waste. . . ." The term "knowingly" modifies "hazardous waste" as well as "treats, stores or disposes of," and thus, one who does not know the waste he is disposing of is hazardous cannot violate section 6928(d)(2)(A). But this does not help Hoflin. The district court's instructions to the jury embodied this interpretation of the statute. The district court instructed the jury that in order to find Hoflin guilty on Count II, the jury had to find:

> First: That [Hoflin] knowingly disposed of or commanded and caused others to dispose of chemical wastes on or about August 1, 1983;
> Second: Defendant knew that the chemical wastes had the potential to be harmful to others or to the environment, or in other words, it was not an innocuous substance like water;
> Third: The wastes were listed or identified by the United States Environmental Protection Agency ("EPA") as a hazardous waste pursuant to RCRA;
> Fourth: The defendant had not obtained a permit from either EPA or the State of Washington authorizing the disposal under RCRA.

While these instructions did not use the word "hazardous" in paragraph Second, they did require the jury to find that Hoflin disposed of chemical waste which he knew "had the potential to be harmful to others or to the environment." This instruction was sufficient. . . .

Affirmed.

Notes and Questions

1. The holdings in *Hoflin* and *Johnson & Towers* conflict with one another. Which decision is more analytically sound? Is § 6928(d)(2) free from ambiguity, as the *Hoflin* court maintained? Should Congress rewrite § 6928(d)(2)? If so, how should it be changed?

2. The indictment in *Johnson & Towers* alleged that both Angel and Hopkins managed and directed a substantial part of the company's operations — including hazardous waste management operations — and that the chemicals in question were discharged at their direction. How important is their status as managers? Would subordinate employees acting under their direction and supervision also be liable?

3. Courts routinely analogize RCRA to public welfare statutes, often citing *Dotterweich*, *Park*, and *International Minerals*. In what respects is RCRA analogous to public welfare statutes?

4. The RCRA provision under consideration imposes felony penalties. The violations at issue in *Dotterweich*, *Park*, and *International Minerals* were misdemeanors. How important is this difference?[25]

5. Hoflin argued that the statute requires knowledge that the waste is hazardous, and the court of appeals agreed. But precisely what does that mean? Courts consistently conclude that knowledge that the waste is regulated — i.e., that EPA regulations identify it as hazardous — is not required. Nor is it required that the defendant know exactly what the substance is. All that is needed is "knowledge of the general hazardous character" of the waste — i.e., that it has "the potential to be harmful to others or the environment." United States v. Goldsmith, 978 F.2d 643, 646 (11th Cir. 1992). The court in *Hoflin* held that an instruction to that effect is sufficient. Is that a meaningful standard?

---

25. Cf. Staples v. United States, 511 U.S. 600 (1994).

6. The permit application and review process serves a number of important functions. The filing of an application puts the EPA on notice that the applicant intends to engage in activity that is regulated by RCRA. The application must provide a detailed description of the applicant's business operations and its facility, as well as relevant technical information such as the chemical composition of the waste the facility will handle. The EPA's in-depth review of the application enables the Agency to determine whether the facility will be in compliance with RCRA requirements and, if so, to prescribe precise conditions under which the business will be allowed to manage hazardous waste. Once a permit is issued, RCRA's recordkeeping and recording requirements enable the EPA to closely monitor the facility's compliance with the terms of its permit.

The indictments in *Hoflin* and *Johnson & Towers* alleged violations of § 6928(d)(2)(A), which prohibits treatment, storage, or disposal of hazardous waste without a permit. These are typical RCRA charges. During the first ten years of the Justice Department's environmental criminal enforcement program, more than half of the indictments in RCRA prosecutions charged that the defendants managed hazardous waste without a permit. In contrast, only a handful of prosecutions alleged violations of § 6928(d)(2)(B), which prohibits treating, storing, or disposing of hazardous waste in violation of the terms and conditions of a permit. It thus appears that the government gives priority to prosecuting cases in which the defendants are "rogue" operators who engage in highly regulated business activities without subjecting themselves to the rules of the game.[26]

2. Transportation Violations

UNITED STATES v. HAYES INTERNATIONAL CORP.
786 F.2d 1499 (11th Cir. 1986)

Kravitch, Circuit Judge. . . .

I. Background

Hayes International Corp. (Hayes) operates an airplane refurbishing plant in Birmingham, Alabama. In the course of its business, Hayes generates certain waste products, two of which are relevant to this case. First, Hayes must drain fuel tanks of the planes on which it works. Second, Hayes paints the aircraft with spray guns and uses solvents to clean the paint guns and lines, thereby generating a mix of paint and solvents.

L.H. Beasley was the employee of Hayes responsible for disposal of hazardous wastes. In early 1981, Beasley orally agreed with Jack Hurt, an employee of Performance Advantage, Inc., to dispose of certain wastes. Under the agreement, Performance Advantage would obtain from Hayes the valuable jet fuel drained from the planes; Performance Advantage would pay twenty cents per gallon for the jet fuel, and, at no charge, would remove other wastes from the Hayes plant including the mixture of paint and solvents. Performance Advantage was a recycler, and used the jet fuel to make

---

26. See generally Kathleen F. Brickey, Charging Practices in Hazardous Waste Crime Prosecutions, 62 Ohio St. L.J. 1077 (2001).

marketable fuel. Wastes were transported from Hayes to Performance Advantage on eight occasions between January 1981 and March 1982.

Beginning in August 1982, government officials discovered drums of waste generated by Hayes and illegally disposed of by Performance Advantage. Approximately six hundred drums of waste were found, deposited among seven illegal disposal sites in Georgia and Alabama. The waste was the paint and solvent which Performance Advantage had removed from Hayes. Some of the drums were simply dumped in yards, while others were buried.

The prosecutions in this case were brought under the Resource Conservation and Recovery Act. The Act creates a cradle to grave regulatory scheme to ensure that hazardous wastes are properly disposed of. Generators of waste are required to identify hazardous wastes and use a manifest system to ensure that wastes are disposed of only in facilities possessing a permit.

The regulatory scheme sets forth two different methods of identifying a hazardous waste. A waste is hazardous if it appears on a list of wastes adopted by the Environmental Protection Agency. The list appears at 40 C.F.R., Subpart D. A waste is also hazardous if it possesses certain characteristics. These characteristics are set forth in 40 C.F.R., Subpart C. The mixture of paint waste and solvent involved in this case was a characteristic waste based on its ignitability.

Beasley and Hayes each were convicted of eight counts of violating 42 U.S.C. § 6928(d)(1), which provides criminal sanctions for

> Any person who (1) knowingly transports any hazardous waste identified or listed under this subchapter to a facility which does not have a permit under section 6925 of this title.[27]

Hayes' liability is based on the actions of Beasley. It is undisputed that Performance Advantage did not have a permit.

In their motion for judgment notwithstanding the verdict and on appeal, the appellees raise three basic theories of defense, and argue that the government's evidence was insufficient to refute any of them. First they contend that they did not commit any "knowing" violation because they misunderstood the regulations. Second, they contend that they did not "know" that Performance Advantage did not have a permit. Third, they contend that they did not commit a knowing violation because they believed that Performance Advantage was recycling the waste. Under the regulations in force at the time, characteristic hazardous waste was not regulated if it was "beneficially used or reused [sic] or legitimately recycled or reclaimed." 40 C.F.R. § 261.6(a)(1), superseded effective July 5, 1985, 50 Fed. Reg. 665. . . .

II. The Elements of a Section 6928(d) Offense . . .

Congress did not provide any guidance, either in the statute or the legislative history, concerning the meaning of "knowing" in section 6298(d).[28] Indeed, Congress

---

27. The current version of the statute applies to anyone who "transports or causes to be transported." 42 U.S.C.A. § 6928(d)(1) (Supp. 1985).

28. Congress also created the offense of knowing endangerment, for which it did set forth some standards. 42 U.S.C. § 6928(e).

stated that it had "not sought to define 'knowing' for offenses under subsection (d); that process has been left to the courts under general principles." S. Rep. No. 172, 96th Cong., 2d Sess. 39 (1980), U.S. Code Cong. & Admin. News 1980, pp. 5019, 5038. . . .

WHETHER KNOWLEDGE OF THE REGULATIONS IS REQUIRED

[The court concluded that § 6928(d) does not require knowledge of the illegality of the conduct.]

. . . First, section 6928(d)(1) is not drafted in a manner which makes knowledge of illegality an element of the offense. . . . In addition, section 6928(d)(1) is undeniably a public welfare statute, involving a heavily regulated area with great ramifications for the public health and safety. As the Supreme Court has explained, it is completely fair and reasonable to charge those who choose to operate in such areas with knowledge of the regulatory provisions. Indeed, the reasonableness is borne out in this case, for the evidence at trial belied the appellees' profession of ignorance. Accordingly, in a prosecution under 42 U.S.C. § 6928(d)(1) it would be no defense to claim no knowledge that the paint waste was a hazardous waste within the meaning of the regulations; nor would it be a defense to argue ignorance of the permit requirement.

WHETHER KNOWLEDGE OF THE PERMIT STATUS IS REQUIRED

The government argues that the statute does not require knowledge of the permit status of the facility to which the wastes are transported. The Supreme Court has noted that statutes similarly drafted in the manner of section 6928(d) are linguistically ambiguous: it is impossible to tell how far down the sentence "knowingly" travels. . . .

In this case, the congressional purpose indicates knowledge of the permit status is required. The precise wrong Congress intended to combat through section 6928(d) was transportation to an unlicensed facility. Removing the knowing requirement from this element would criminalize innocent conduct; for example, if the defendant reasonably believed that the site had a permit, but in fact had been misled by the people at the site. If Congress intended such a strict statute, it could have dropped the "knowingly" requirement. . . .

The government does not face an unacceptable burden of proof in proving that the defendant acted with knowledge of the permit status. Knowledge does not require certainty; a defendant acts knowingly if he is aware "that that result is practically certain to follow from his conduct, whatever his desire may be as to the result." United States v. United States Gypsum Co., 438 U.S. 422 (1978). Moreover, in this regulatory context a defendant acts knowingly if he willfully fails to determine the permit status of the facility.

Moreover, the government may prove guilty knowledge with circumstantial evidence. In the context of the hazardous waste statutes, proving knowledge should not be difficult. The statute at issue here sets forth certain procedures transporters must follow to ensure that wastes are sent only to permit facilities. Transporters of waste presumedly are aware of these procedures, and if a transporter does not follow the procedures, a juror may draw certain inferences. Where there is no evidence that those who took the waste asserted that they were properly licensed, the jurors may draw additional inferences. Jurors may also consider the circumstances and terms of the transaction. It is common knowledge that properly disposing of wastes is an expensive task, and if someone is willing to take away wastes at an unusual price or under unusual circumstances, then a juror can infer that the transporter knows the wastes are not being taken to a permit facility.

In sum, to convict under section 6928(d)(1), the jurors must find that the defendant knew what the waste was (here, a mixture of paint and solvent), and that the defendant knew the disposal site had no permit. Knowledge does not require certainty, and the jurors may draw inferences from all of the circumstances, including the existence of the regulatory scheme.

III. ANALYSIS

A

We now turn to the three defenses appellees rely upon. The first is simply a mistake of law defense. They contend that they held a good faith belief that any waste sent to a recycler was exempt from the regulations, regardless of whether the waste was actually recycled. The discussion set forth above indicates that ignorance of the regulatory status is no excuse. There is no dispute that the appellees knew that the waste was a combination of paint and solvents; nor is there any dispute that the mixture was a hazardous waste. Accordingly, the evidence was sufficient for the jury to find the appellees knowingly transported hazardous waste.

B

The appellees' second defense is that the evidence was insufficient to show they knew that Performance Advantage did not have a permit. . . . The evidence shows that Hayes was not following the regulatory procedure for manifesting waste sent to a permit site, from which the jury could have inferred that the appellees did not believe Performance Advantage had a permit. This inference is strengthened by Hayes' own documents, which set forth this requirement. Performance Advantage also was not charging to haul away the waste (although obviously they found the overall deal advantageous), and Beasley thought he had made a good deal; accordingly the terms were such as to raise suspicion.

The appellees rely on Hurt's testimony that he had had an EPA "number," and that he could not recall whether he had given it to Beasley. Drawing all reasonable inferences in favor of the government, the jury could have found that Hurt did not give the EPA "number" to Beasley. In addition, the "number" was not a permit, and the jury could have inferred that Beasley did not believe the number evidenced an actual permit.[29] Accordingly, the jury could have found that there was no evidence that Performance Advantage professed to be a permit facility. Based on all the above, the jury could have found beyond a reasonable doubt that appellees knew Performance Advantage did not have a permit.

---

29. Indeed no permit actually existed.

C

Appellees' third defense is that they believed that Performance Advantage was recycling the waste. At the outset, we accept the theory of this mistake of fact defense. As the Supreme Court stated in United States v. International Minerals, 402 U.S. 558, 563-64 (1971), a case involving "knowing" shipment of dangerous chemicals, a person who believed "in good faith that he was shipping distilled water when in fact he was shipping some dangerous acid would not be covered." In this case, had the wastes been recycled, then no violation of the statute would have occurred. Accordingly, a good faith belief that the materials were being recycled is analogous to the good faith belief in *International Minerals* that the acid was actually water.

We believe, however, that there is sufficient evidence for the jury to have rejected the defense of mistake of fact. . . . In this case, three areas of the evidence could have led the jury to reject the mistake of fact defense.

First, are the negotiations that led to the arrangement. Jack Hurt, who negotiated the deal for Performance Advantage, testified at trial. He contacted Beasley in late 1980 or early 1981 about purchasing jet fuel from Hayes. After Hurt asked "what it would take" to obtain the right to purchase the jet fuel, the parties agreed that Performance Advantage would take away a load of the paint wastes, at no charge, and attempt to run them through their system to make fuel. The proposed deal was that Performance Advantage would obtain the jet fuel for twenty cents per gallon if it would also haul away the paint waste. Thirty drums of the paint waste were then shipped to the Performance Advantage plant. Hurt was not responsible for the test run at the plant, but his supervisor, Lyn Bolton, instructed him to find out if Performance Advantage could obtain the jet fuel without the paint waste. Hurt then told Beasley that Bolton did not want the paint waste, but Beasley replied that "he liked the deal the way it was; to take it all." Bolton then decided to take the paint waste as well as the jet fuel.

The inferences that the jury could have drawn from the above testimony are clear. Beasley knew that Performance Advantage had tested the paint sludge in its recycling system, and that after this test Performance Advantage did not want the paint sludge, even for free. If Performance Advantage found it desirable to run the waste through its system, it would not have objected to a deal in which it obtained the waste at no cost. Accordingly, the jury could infer from this exchange that Beasley knew that Performance Advantage did not intend to recycle the paint waste.

The second type of evidence showing appellees' knowledge consisted of internal documents from Hayes. For example, one document, a compliance memorandum from Hayes official Charles Reymann to Beasley, stated:

Hazardous waste with no resale value, which must be disposed of, shall be hauled to an EPA-approved disposal site. The hauler and the disposal site must both have an EPA interim permit number. A manifest must be used to identify the materials hauled, the hauler, and the disposal site. A copy of the manifest must be returned to Hayes by the disposal site operator.

The evidence showed that Performance Advantage did not want the paint waste, even at no charge, and Beasley therefore knew it had no resale value. The memorandum directed that wastes with no resale value be sent to EPA approved sites, and that manifests must be used to confirm disposition of the wastes. The jury could infer from

Beasley's violation of company procedures that he knew the disposition of the waste was improper. The documentary evidence also showed that proper disposition of the waste was Beasley's responsibility; the jury could infer from the fact that it was Beasley's business to know what happened to the waste, that indeed he did know.

Third, subsequent conversations between Hurt and Beasley removed any doubt whether Beasley thought the wastes were being recycled. . . .

. . . Beasley was directly told that the waste was being disposed of rather than recycled, and he nevertheless continued to ship waste to Performance Advantage; this indicates that the agreement was never premised on recycling of the waste. Accordingly, we conclude that the inferences would support conviction for shipments both before and after the conversation.

The judgments of acquittal notwithstanding the verdict as to both defendants are vacated. The case is remanded to the district court to enter judgment in accordance with the jury verdicts of guilty.

Reversed and remanded.

Notes and Questions

1. Suppose a transporter of hazardous waste does not know that a permit is required but knows that the facility does not have one. Would that knowledge be sufficient under *Hayes*? What if the transporter is ignorant of the permit requirement and has not asked whether the facility has one?

2. What if the transporter knows that the disposal facility has a permit but that the permit does not cover the substance being delivered to the facility?[30]

3. Does proof of shipment of hazardous waste to a facility without a permit always (or almost always) justify an inference of knowledge of the facility's permit status? If not, what more is needed?

UNITED STATES v. FIORILLO
186 F.3d 1136 (9th Cir. 1999)

PER CURIAM . . .

FACTS AND PROCEDURAL HISTORY

Diversey Corp. ("Diversey") is a company engaged in the manufacture and sale of industrial cleaning products. In 1992, Diversey discovered that two of its products, Slurry and Eclipse, would leak out of their containers in warm or humid weather. The two products are industrial-strength cleansers used in institutional settings and both are highly caustic.[31] After determining that the products were unsaleable, Diversey

---

30. Cf. United States v. MacDonald & Watson Waste Oil Co., 933 F.2d 35 (1st Cir. 1991).

31. Materials with a pH level greater than 12.5 are classified as hazardous under federal regulations. One of the Government's expert witnesses testified that Slurry and Eclipse had pH levels of 13 to 14. Each one-point difference in pH represents a tenfold increase in the materials' corrosiveness.

authorized its corporate distribution manager, Adrian Farris, to dispose of 30,000 gallons of the products.

Frank Fiorillo was the president and CEO of West Coast Industries, Inc. ("West Coast"). The company's primary business was the storage of a number of products at a warehouse located in Sacramento, California. Fiorillo, who had provided warehouse services to Diversey in the past, submitted a proposal for the disposal of the products to Farris on behalf of West Coast and SafeWaste Corp. ("SafeWaste"), Art Krueger's company. Farris agreed to the proposal and the parties entered into a contract on February 24, 1993, for the disposal of 10,000 gallons of Slurry and Eclipse. Under the contract, Diversey agreed to pay 50% of the contract costs when the products were transported to Fiorillo's warehouse and the remaining 50% upon submission of compliance documentation.

Diversey periodically received compliance documentation from Fiorillo and Krueger in the form of certificates of disposal, which were signed by Krueger. Ultimately, Diversey paid Krueger and Fiorillo $254,000 for the disposal of 30,000 gallons of the hazardous products. In reality, Fiorillo and Krueger only properly disposed of two of the eleven truckloads of Slurry and Eclipse by sending it to a facility in Nevada, which met the requirements set out in RCRA. The rest of the Slurry and Eclipse was stored at Fiorillo's warehouse in Sacramento in a cold room that Krueger leased from Fiorillo.

In August 1993, Rick Knighton, a former West Coast employee, informed David DeMello, a Sacramento County Fire Department official, that West Coast was storing Class A explosives at its warehouse.[32] DeMello, who had conducted earlier fire inspections of the warehouse, and another fire inspector, Robert Billett, went to the warehouse where they informed the receptionist that they were there to conduct an inspection. DeMello's and Billett's testimony conflicts over what happened next.

According to DeMello, the receptionist phoned someone who authorized the inspectors to enter the warehouse. Billett did not recall the receptionist getting permission to let them in. Rather, he remembered that she simply allowed them to proceed with the inspection. Regardless, before the men discovered any explosives, they were met by Fiorillo. DeMello testified that Fiorillo was cordial and polite when he greeted the two men. Fiorillo agreed to accompany the inspectors during the inspection. DeMello and Billett then discovered the Class A explosives, consisting of approximately 17,000 artillery shells, taking up about one-third of the warehouse. DeMello also discovered hazardous material, which covered an additional one-third of the warehouse, leaking from its containers about six feet from the explosives.

Over the course of the next few days, members of the fire department returned to the warehouse to ensure that proper cleanup was occurring and that no further violations were happening. About eight days after DeMello's discovery, the fire captain, Ed Vasques, received an anonymous tip that additional hazardous materials were being stored in a room that the fire inspectors had not discovered. DeMello, Vasques, and other officials conducted a re-inspection of the warehouse and discovered an unmarked door that was hidden behind several pallets of food and beverages.

---

32. When Knighton was a West Coast employee, he had contacted DeMello to inquire whether West Coast met the requirements to store Class A explosives in the Sacramento warehouse. DeMello informed Knighton that West Coast would not be approved to store Class A explosives at its warehouse.

Peter Bishop, an independent contractor hired by West Coast to assist in the cleanup, entered Fiorillo's office to get keys to the room. An investigator from the Sacramento County environmental office overheard Fiorillo say that there was nothing in the room, that he had done everything they wanted and that he had had enough. Nevertheless, Bishop came back out with the keys. A door outside the warehouse led into the cold room as did a door inside the warehouse. The keys did not work on the outside door, and when Bishop went to unlock the inside door, it was apparently unlocked. At this point, the county officials discovered the Slurry and Eclipse, which Krueger and Fiorillo had told Diversey was destroyed.

Fiorillo was charged with twelve counts of wire fraud (four of the counts were dismissed by the Government prior to trial), two counts of violating provisions of RCRA, and two counts of receiving Class A explosives without a permit. Krueger was charged with all of the same counts except those relating to the explosives. A jury found both men guilty of all the counts against them. . . .

C. TITLE 42 U.S.C. § 6928(D)(1)

The indictment charged Fiorillo and Krueger with "knowingly storing corrosive hazardous waste" in violation of 42 U.S.C. § 6928(d)(2) and with "knowingly transporting and causing to be transported a corrosive hazardous waste" in violation of 42 U.S.C. § 6928(d)(1).[33] The jury found both defendants guilty on both counts. Fiorillo and Krueger challenge their convictions for violating subsection 6928(d)(1), asserting that its "causes to be transported" provision applies only to those who generate hazardous waste for transport by others. The Government argues that the "causes to be transported" prohibition is not limited to hazardous waste generators and that the defendants properly were convicted of both storing and causing transportation of hazardous waste. We agree with the defendants that a person who merely receives hazardous waste does not "cause[]" that waste "to be transported" under section 6928(d)(1). We nevertheless affirm the defendants' convictions because the record shows that Fiorillo and Krueger took responsibility for and carried out the transportation of the Eclipse and Slurry from Diversey's storage location to the West Coast warehouse. . . .

Fiorillo and Krueger assert that their actions of unlawfully receiving and storing hazardous waste did not "cause[]" the transportation of that waste under section 6928(d)(1); the Government refutes this contention. The word "cause" has a plethora of meanings. Among its common definitions are "to bring about," "to compel," see BLACK'S LAW DICTIONARY 200 (5th ed. 1979), and "to effect by command, authority, or force," see WEBSTER'S NEW COLLEGIATE DICTIONARY 175 (1979). Various legal standards draw fine lines between types of "causation" — ranging from an indirect, peripheral contribution to an immediate and necessary precedent of an event. Looking at the

---

33. This subsection of the statute provides:
Any person who —

(1) knowingly transports or causes to be transported any hazardous waste identified or listed under this subchapter to a facility which does not have a permit under this subchapter shall, upon conviction, be subject to [a fine or imprisonment, or both].

42 U.S.C. § 6928(d)(1).

word "cause" itself, therefore, does not allow us to discern the specific actions to which Congress intended to attach criminal liability under section 6928(d)(1). The statute's overall structure reveals, however, that as Congress used the phrase here, "causes to be transported" does not include a warehouse's receipt of hazardous waste pursuant to a contract. Section 6928(d) contains a comprehensive, seven-item list of acts related to hazardous waste management for which the Federal government imposes criminal penalties. Each of the seven subdivisions addresses a particular category of prohibited activity. For example, subsection (d)(3) pertains to making false representations in required documentation of hazardous waste; subsection (d)(4) pertains to the destruction of, alteration of, or failure to file any required documentation; and subsection (d)(6) pertains to the exportation of hazardous waste to other countries. More pertinent to the issue before us, subsections (d)(1) and (d)(2) penalize two distinct sets of acts involving the handling of hazardous waste without a permit. Subsection (d)(1) addresses transporting and causing to be transported hazardous waste to a facility lacking a permit, whereas subsection (d)(2) addresses treating, storing, and disposing of hazardous waste without or in violation of a permit. By dividing these activities into two categories, Congress demonstrated that, despite the similarities between the prohibitions in subsections (d)(1) and (d)(2), it intended to distinguish between these two groups of conduct in some way. The principal distinction is that subsection (d)(1) describes activities connected to the creation and shipping of hazardous waste, while subsection (d)(2) covers only the receipt and processing of the waste. Stated another way, subsection (d)(1) pertains to the direction of hazardous waste to a facility that lacks a permit, whereas subsection (d)(2) addresses activities occurring at the unpermitted facility.

We acknowledged this distinction between subsections (d)(1) and (d)(2) when discussing a different aspect of those provisions in United States v. Speach, 968 F.2d 795 (9th Cir. 1992). *Speach* presented the issue of whether the Government must prove that a section 6928(d)(1) defendant knew that the recipient facility of the hazardous waste lacked a permit. We answered this question in the affirmative, relying in part upon the following reasoning:

> The two provisions [(d)(1) and (d)(2)] target different groups of defendants. Section 6928(d)(2)(A) imposes criminal liability on the person who knowingly treats, stores, or disposes of waste, when he or his facility lacks a permit, whether or not he knew that the permit was lacking. . . .
>
> In contrast, section 6928(d)(1) deals not with the violator's lack of a permit, but with the lack of a permit on the part of the person to whom the violator delivers hazardous waste.

Id. at 797. In this passage, *Speach* implicitly recognized that the violator of subsection (d)(1) is the person responsible for making the delivery of hazardous waste, not the person who merely accepts the shipment.[34] . . .

---

34. Subsection (d)(1) logically holds liable transporters and those causing transportation only for sending or delivering hazardous waste to a facility lacking a permit, because what the recipient does with the waste after accepting it is beyond the transporter's control. In contrast, subsection (d)(2)'s proscription of treating, storing, or disposing of hazardous waste without a permit, as well as in violation of any material condition or requirement of a permit, demonstrates Congress's concern in this provision with regulating the activities of processors, who, unlike transporters, "are in a position to control" those activities. United States v. MacDonald & Watson Waste Oil Co., 933 F.2d 35, 49 (1st Cir. 1991); see generally

Another of the seven categories of criminal conduct listed in section 6928 — subsection (d)(5) — provides the final piece of structural evidence upon which we rely in concluding that subsection (d)(1) does not apply to a person who merely receives and stores hazardous waste without a permit. Subsection (d)(5) imposes criminal penalties on any person who "knowingly transports without a manifest, or causes to be transported without a manifest, any hazardous waste [required] to be accompanied by a manifest." A "manifest" is "the form used for identifying the quantity, composition, and the origin, routing, and destination of hazardous waste," 42 U.S.C. § 6903(12); various provisions of the federal hazardous waste management laws hold *generators* of hazardous waste responsible for providing this form to the transporter. Subsection (d)(5), therefore, proscribes the same two activities that subsection (d)(1) addresses — transporting and causing to be transported — and imposes conditions with which only a generator of hazardous waste reasonably can comply. This provision reinforces our understanding that subsection (d)(1) pertains to persons responsible for the delivery of hazardous waste, not merely the receipt of it, because only a generator (who supplies the manifest) or a transporter (who must obtain it before undertaking the transportation) reasonably could be expected to comply with these requirements.

. . . When Congress enacted section 6928 in 1976, subsection (d)(1) prohibited only "knowingly" "transporting . . . hazardous waste . . . to a facility which does not have a permit." In 1984, Congress amended the statute, adding the "causes to be transported" language. The House Report accompanying the 1984 amendments explains the reasoning behind this addition:

> This provision clarifies the criminal liability of generators of hazardous waste who knowingly cause the waste to be transported to an unpermitted facility. Because the generator is in the best position to know the nature of his waste material, the regulatory scheme established by RCRA places a duty on the generator in the first instance to make arrangements to transport and dispose of his waste properly. EPA's ability to obtain criminal penalties against generators who knowingly cause the transportation of hazardous waste to an unpermitted facility is essential to the regulatory scheme.

H.R. Rep. No. 98-198, pt. I (1984), reprinted in 1984 U.S.C.C.A.N. 5576, 5613. Far from indicating that Congress meant subsection (d)(1) to apply to anyone who merely accepts delivery of a shipment of hazardous waste, the House Report strengthens our understanding, based upon the statute's language and structure, that this provision applies only to those persons responsible for initiating, arranging for, or actually performing the transportation of the waste. . . .

We must clarify that our interpretation of this provision does not mean that a person must be in the business of generating or transporting hazardous waste in order to run afoul of section 6928(d)(1). In some circumstances, the intended recipient of hazardous waste may also violate subsection (d)(1) by personally undertaking the transportation of the hazardous waste or by making arrangements for a third party to perform that task. Recognizing this possibility, we decline to adopt the interpretation of the statute, advocated by the defendants, that subsection (d)(1) applies only to generators and transporters of hazardous waste. Instead, we hold that the language of section 6928(d),

---

Speach, 968 F.2d at 797 (discussing each provision's limitation of liability to person in best position to know law's requirements).

its structure, and its legislative history dictate that subsection (d)(1) does not apply to a person who does not participate in or direct the transportation of hazardous waste, but merely receives that waste.

Turning our attention to these defendants' conduct, we first note that, because the jury found both defendants guilty of violating subsection (d)(1), we must construe the record in the light most favorable to the Government. According to Farris, he solicited bids from three companies, including SafeWaste, when he learned Diversey needed to dispose of the Eclipse and Slurry. In response to this inquiry, Fiorillo submitted to Farris a written proposal, dated January 26, 1993. Farris accepted Fiorillo's bid because it was the lowest and because they previously had had a good working relationship. On February 24, 1993, Farris, Fiorillo, and Krueger signed another document printed on West Coast letterhead that was substantially identical to the January 26 letter and that also was styled as a proposal letter from Fiorillo to Farris. As Farris testified, however, and as the writing itself indicates, the February 24 document actually was a memorialization of a meeting among the three men, and it constituted the contract to which all three were parties. The contract states:

> Per our meeting today with yourself [Farris], Art Krueger (Safewaste Corp.) and myself [Fiorillo], regarding your warehoused hazardous material. The following is our proposal for handling, *transportation*, disposal and EPA compliance documentation for Diversey products Eclipse, Slurry, and PEP in one and six gallon containers.

Service	Cost
. . . Freight (from current warehouse location or any "in-line" multiple stop locations to disposal site).	$1,760.00 per load . . .

> *Terms*
>
> A. On a load by load basis, 50% of the billing amount is to be paid upon confirmed pickup of the product from your warehouse site or the last stop on a multiple site pickup. . . .
>
> *Assumptions* . . .
>
> 2. You will deliver to us an accurate location, address, contact name and phone number of all inventory as described on your product disposal form.
>
> 3. You will give us the authority to request an accurate inventory and product condition description for each location.

Below Fiorillo's signature is the heading "Sign Off An [sic] Approval." Signature lines for Fiorillo, Krueger, and Farris as representatives of their respective corporations appear under this heading; all three signed this document on February 24, 1993.

Other evidence exists that Krueger and Fiorillo actually arranged for and conducted the transportation of the Eclipse and Slurry from Diversey's storage facilities. Throughout his extensive testimony, Farris frequently asserted that Fiorillo undertook the transportation and that Krueger participated in this activity, as well. Farris also offered examples of contacts he had had with both defendants that supported his account of Fiorillo's and Krueger's responsibilities. Significantly, there is no evidence in the record contradicting Farris's account that defendants undertook and incurred the costs of transporting the Eclipse and Slurry. Based upon this evidence, the jury reasonably could have determined that Fiorillo and Krueger did much more than simply receive the hazardous waste and store it: they proposed (and Farris agreed) that Diversey would pay them to make arrangements for transporting the waste to the West Coast warehouse. . . .

CONCLUSION . . .

The judgment is affirmed in part and reversed and remanded in part. . . .

Notes and Questions

1. Why does § 6928(d)(1) require generators and transporters to assume responsibility for ensuring that the facility receiving the shipment has a permit for the type of waste being delivered? Doesn't the ultimate responsibility rest with the facility itself?

2. The court in *Fiorillo* ruled that mere receipt of hazardous waste is not equivalent to causing its transportation. What criteria determine whether the intended recipient violates § 6928(d)(1)? In what sense did Fiorillo cause transportation of the waste? Was his participation in facilitating the transportation more than minimal? Would something less suffice? What if he simply had said to Diversey, "You bring me the hazardous waste and I'll get rid of it for you"?

3. Which, if any, of the defendants in *Fiorillo* could have been charged with violating § 6928(d)(2)?

4. Which, if any, of the participants in the waste disposal operations in *Hoflin* could have been charged with violating § 6928(d)(1)?

3. Knowing Endangerment

Like the CWA, RCRA contains a felony provision that punishes knowing endangerment. The RCRA endangerment section provides:

> Any person who knowingly transports, treats, stores, disposes of, or exports any hazardous waste identified or listed under [RCRA] in violation of [RCRA's criminal provisions] who knows at that time that he thereby places another person in imminent danger of death or serious bodily injury [commits an offense against the United States].

42 U.S.C. § 6928(e).

"Serious bodily injury" means bodily injury that involves a substantial risk of death, unconsciousness, extreme physical pain, protracted and obvious disfigurement, or protracted loss or impairment of the function of a bodily member, organ, or mental faculty. 42 U.S.C. § 6928(f)(6).

In United States v. Protex Industries, Inc., 874 F.2d 740 (10th Cir. 1989), the court upheld the corporation's conviction of knowingly endangering its employees by exposing them to toxic chemicals. The evidence established that several employees suffered from a type of psychoorganic syndrome that could result in permanent impairment of mental faculties and that their prolonged exposure to toxic chemicals had irreversibly increased their risk of contracting cancer. In upholding the conviction, the court proceeded on the unarticulated assumption that RCRA's knowing endangerment provision protects employees who are exposed to hazardous chemicals in the workplace. In contrast, in construing the CWA's knowing endangerment provision, the court in *Borowski*, supra, held the CWA provision did not protect the defendant's employees from workplace hazards. What explains these disparate results?

B. THE COMPREHENSIVE ENVIRONMENTAL RESPONSE, COMPENSATION, AND LIABILITY ACT

The Comprehensive Environmental Response, Compensation, and Liability Act (CERCLA) was enacted to deal with the increasingly serious problem of hazardous waste sites. Also known as the Superfund Act, its principal focus is the cleanup of hazardous waste sites. The term "hazardous substance" includes hazardous wastes under RCRA, hazardous air pollutants under the Clean Air Act, and other substances designated by the EPA as hazardous pursuant to CERCLA or the Toxic Substances Control Act.

The major criminal provision penalizes failure to notify the appropriate governmental agency of a release of a reportable quantity of hazardous substances into the environment. The duty to notify is imposed on a person in charge of a vessel or an offshore or onshore facility as soon as he knows of a reportable release.[35]

UNITED STATES v. CARR
880 F.2d 1550 (2d Cir. 1989)

PIERCE, Circuit Judge. . . .

Appellant David James Carr appeals from a judgment . . . convicting him under section 103 of the Comprehensive Environmental Response, Compensation and Liability Act of 1980 (CERCLA), 42 U.S.C. § 9603. Under section 103, it is a crime for any person "in charge of a facility" from which a prohibited amount of hazardous substance is released to fail to report such a release to the appropriate federal agency. Appellant, a supervisor of maintenance at Fort Drum, New York, directed a work crew to dispose of waste cans of paint in an improper manner, and failed to report the release of the hazardous substances — the paint — to the appropriate federal agency. At appellant's trial, the district court instructed the jury that appellant could be found to have been "in charge" of the facility so long as he had any supervisory control over the facility.

Appellant contends on appeal that this instruction was erroneous because (1) it extended the statutory reporting requirement to a relatively low-level employee, and (2) it allowed the jury to find that appellant was "in charge" so long as he exercised *any* control over the dumping. . . .

---

35. The term "facility" is defined broadly to include "any site or area where a hazardous substance has been deposited, stored, disposed of, or placed, or otherwise come to be located." 42 U.S.C. § 9601(9).

BACKGROUND

Appellant was a civilian employee at Fort Drum, an Army camp located in Watertown, New York. As a civilian employee at a military installation, he was supervised by Army officers. His position was that of maintenance foreman on the Fort's firing range, and as part of his duties he assigned other civilian workers to various chores on the range. In May 1986, he directed several workers to dispose of old cans of waste paint in a small, man-made pit on the range; at that time, the pit had filled with water, creating a pond. On Carr's instructions, the workers filled a truck with a load of cans and drove to the pit. They backed the truck up to the water, and then began tossing cans of paint into the pond. After the workers had thrown in fifty or so cans, however, they saw that paint was leaking from the cans into the water, so they decided instead to stack the remaining cans of paint against a nearby target shed. At the end of the day, the workers told Carr of the cans leaking into the pond, and warned him that they thought that dumping the cans into the pond was illegal. Two truckloads of paint cans remained to be moved the next day, so Carr told the workers to place those cans alongside the target shed.

Approximately two weeks later, Carr directed one of the workers to cover up the paint cans in the pond by using a tractor to dump earth into the pit. Another worker, however, subsequently triggered an investigation by reporting the disposal of the cans to his brother-in-law, a special agent with the Department of Defense. A 43-count indictment was returned against appellant, charging him with various violations of federal environmental laws. The indictment included charges under the Resource Conservation and Recovery Act (Counts 1-4), the CERCLA charges here at issue (Counts 5-6), and multiple charges under the Clean Water Act (Counts 7-43). Appellant pleaded not guilty, and a 6-day trial before a jury began on October 3, 1988.

After the government had presented its evidence, it filed with the court various proposed jury instructions, including one regarding the definition of the term "in charge." Over appellant's objection, the district court gave the government's proposed instruction to the jury, essentially unchanged, as follows:

> There has been testimony that the waste paint was released from a truck assigned to the workers by the Defendant David Carr. The truck, individually, and the area of the disposal constitute facilities within the meaning of [CERCLA]. So long as the Defendant had supervisory control or was otherwise in charge of the truck or the area in question, he is responsible under this law. The Defendant is not, however, required to be the sole person in charge of the area or the vehicle. If you find that he had any authority over either the vehicle or the area, this is sufficient, regardless of whether others also exercised control.

The jury acquitted appellant of all charges except Counts 5 and 6, the CERCLA charges. The district court imposed a suspended sentence of one year's imprisonment, and sentenced appellant to one year of probation. This appeal followed.

Discussion

I. THE MEANING OF "IN CHARGE" UNDER SECTION 103

Appellant raises two claims on this appeal, both of which arise out of the district court's instruction quoted above. The first claim turns on the meaning of the statutory term "in charge." Under section 103, only those who are "in charge" of a facility must report a hazardous release. There is, however, no definition of the term "in charge" within CERCLA. Appellant argues that the district court's instruction was erroneous because Congress never intended to extend the statute's reporting requirement to those, like Carr, who are relatively low in an organization's chain of command.

Our analysis of appellant's claim requires a review of the statute and its legislative history. The language of the statute itself sheds little light on the meaning of the term "in charge." Section 103 of CERCLA states only that:

> Any person in charge of a vessel or an offshore or an onshore facility shall, as soon as he has knowledge of any release (other than a federally permitted release) of a hazardous substance from such vessel or facility in quantities equal to or greater than those determined pursuant to [42 U.S.C. 9602], immediately notify the National Response Center established under the Clean Water Act of such release. The National Response Center shall convey the notification expeditiously to all appropriate Government agencies, including the Governor of any affected State.

42 U.S.C. § 9603(a) (1982). The regulations implementing the statute fail to define the term "in charge." See 40 C.F.R. § 302 (1988) (EPA regulations). Since its meaning is unclear, we turn to the legislative history in an effort to determine the scope Congress intended the term "in charge" to have.

When CERCLA was enacted in late 1980, Congress sought to address the problem of hazardous pollution by creating a comprehensive and uniform system of notification, emergency governmental response, enforcement, and liability. The reporting requirements established by section 103 were an important part of that effort, for they ensure that the government, once timely notified, will be able to move quickly to check the spread of a hazardous release. [CERCLA's reporting requirements were modeled on § 311 of the CWA.]

The legislative history of section 311 bears out appellant's argument that CERCLA's reporting requirements should not be extended to *all* employees involved in a release. "The term 'person in charge' [was] deliberately designed to cover only supervisory personnel who have the responsibility for the particular vessel or facility and not to include other employees," H.R. Conf. Rep. No. 940, 91st Cong., 2d Sess. 34 (1970), reprinted in 1970 U.S. Code Cong. & Admin. News 2712, 2719. Indeed, as the Fifth Circuit has stated, "to the extent that legislative history does shed light on the meaning of 'persons in charge,' it suggests at the very most that Congress intended the provisions of [section 311] to extend, not to every person who might have knowledge of [a release] (mere employees, for example), but only to persons who occupy positions of responsibility and power." United States v. Mobil Oil Corp., 464 F.2d 1124, 1128 (5th Cir. 1972).

That is not to say, however, that section 311 of the Clean Water Act — and section 103 of CERCLA — do not reach lower-level supervisory employees. The reporting requirements of the two statutes do not apply only to owners and operators, see United

States v. Greer, 850 F.2d 1447, 1453 (11th Cir. 1988), but instead extend to any person who is "responsible for the operation" of a facility from which there is a release, Apex Oil Co. v. United States, 530 F.2d 1291, 1294 (8th Cir. 1976). As the Fifth Circuit noted in *Mobil Oil*, imposing liability on those "responsible" for a facility is fully consistent with Congress' purpose in enacting the reporting requirements. Those in charge of an offending facility can make timely discovery of a release, direct the activities that result in the pollution, and have the capacity to prevent and abate the environmental damage.

Appellant's claim that he does not come within the reporting requirements of section 103 fails because we believe Congress intended the reporting requirements of CER-CLA's section 103 to reach a person — even if of relatively low rank — who, because he was in charge of a facility, was in a position to detect, prevent, and abate a release of hazardous substances. Appellant's more restrictive interpretation of the statute would only "frustrate congressional purpose by exempting from the operation of the [statute] a large class of persons who are uniquely qualified to assume the burden imposed by it." *Mobil Oil*, 464 F.2d at 1127.

II. THE BREADTH OF THE INSTRUCTION GIVEN

Appellant's second claim focuses more closely on the specific instruction given by the district court. The district court instructed the jury that "[i]f you find that [Carr] had any authority over either the vehicle or the area, this is sufficient [to convict], regardless of whether others also exercised control." Appellant contends that the district court, by instructing the jury that it had only to find that appellant exercised "any authority" over the facility at issue, effectively broadened the statute to reach any employee working at the facility. . . .

A careful review of the challenged instruction indicates that the district court sought, through the charge, to explain two important principles to the jury: (1) that the appellant must have exercised supervisory control over the facility in order to be held criminally liable for his failure to report the release, but (2) that the appellant need not have exercised *sole* control over the facility. By taking the language of the instruction out of context — by focusing too narrowly on the district court's use of the word "any" — appellant ignores the broader point that the district court was attempting to make to the jury. The court had already explained that the appellant must have had "supervisory control" over the facility in order to be found guilty. The subsequent, challenged portion of the instruction was therefore not directed at the breadth of authority that appellant must have had, but instead was intended to make clear that the appellant need not have been the sole person in charge of the facility. . . . [W]e hold that the instruction, though not ideal, was not erroneous. . . .

The judgment of the district court is, therefore, affirmed.

Notes and Questions

1. The jury was instructed that the defendant did not have to be the sole person in charge to be liable. Can more than one person be in charge of a facility at the same time? If so, do they all share responsibility for a failure to notify?

2. The duty to notify arises as soon as the person in charge knows of the release. Knowledge that the substance is regulated or poses a danger to public health or the environment is not required. As long as the actor knows what he is working with (e.g., asbestos), that will suffice.[36]

3. CERCLA's notification requirement has obvious Fifth Amendment implications. The reportable release might violate RCRA, the Clean Air Act, or the Clean Water Act, for example. Thus, the statute confers use immunity — comparable to the immunity statute the Supreme Court considered in United States v. Apfelbaum[37]on the person who reports the release.[38]

---

36. United States v. Buckley, 934 F.2d 84 (6th Cir. 1991).

37. See United States v. Apfelbaum, 445 U.S. 115 (1980) (construing the federal use immunity statute, 18 U.S.C. § 6002). *Apfelbaum* is considered supra in Chapter 7.

38. 42 U.S.C. § 9603(b)(3).

14

Sanctions

I. INTRODUCTION

When crimes are committed in an organizational setting, the question of what sanctions are appropriate may take on special significance. What are the penological objectives of prosecuting and sentencing corporate and white collar criminals?[1] Should those who commit white collar crimes (many of which are not committed for personal gain) be imprisoned like common muggers and thieves? Or do we unfairly apply a double standard if we incarcerate mainly "street criminals" and reserve community service, restitution, and kindred remedies for white collar offenders? What organizational sanctions are most effective?

Despite the lack of definitive answers to these and other, related questions, federal, state, and local governments increasingly rely on criminal sanctions to regulate wrongdoing in the business community. And once the specter of criminal liability has been raised, administrative mechanisms may trigger collateral consequences that are more severe than the authorized criminal penalties. They may include administrative suspension and debarment,[2] ineligibility to obtain a license,[3] loss

---

1. See Brent Fisse & John Braithwaite, The Impact of Publicity on Corporate Offenders (1983); Stanton Wheeler, Kenneth Mann & Austin Sarat, Sitting in Judgment: The Sentencing of White-Collar Criminals (1988); John C. Coffee, Corporate Crime and Punishment: A Non-Chicago View of the Economics of Criminal Sanctions, 17 Am. Crim. L. Rev. 419 (1980); John C. Coffee, "No Soul to Damn: No Body to Kick": An Unscandalized Inquiry into the Problem of Corporate Punishment, 79 Mich. L. Rev. 386 (1981); Brent Fisse, Reconstructing Corporate Criminal Law: Deterrence, Retribution, Fault, and Sanctions, 56 S. Cal. L. Rev. 1141 (1983); John B. McAdams, The Appropriate Sanctions for Corporate Criminal Liability: An Eclectic Alternative, 46 U. Cin. L. Rev. 989 (1978); Ilene Nagel & John L. Hagan, The Sentencing of White-Collar Criminals in Federal Courts: A Socio-Legal Exploration of Disparity, 80 Mich. L. Rev. 1427 (1982); Richard Posner, Optimal Sentences for White-Collar Criminals, 17 Am. Crim. L. Rev. 409 (1980).

2. See, e.g., 12 U.S.C. § 1818(g)(1) (authorizing suspension of indicted bank officials whose continued service threatens the interests of depositors or impairs public confidence in the bank); 17 C.F.R. § 201.2(a)(1) (authorizing temporary or permanent denial of the privilege of appearing or practicing before the SEC to lawyers and accountants who have engaged in unprofessional conduct or violated federal securities laws).

3. See, e.g., 18 U.S.C. § 922(g), (h) (forbidding shipment or receipt of firearms or ammunition in interstate commerce by one who is under indictment for or has been convicted of any state or federal crime punishable by a prison term of more than one year).

of benefits,[4] and even revocation of a corporation's charter.[5]

The materials in this chapter illustrate the difficulty of making the punishment fit both the crime and the criminal in corporate and white collar cases.

II. IMPRISONMENT

A. PRE-GUIDELINES SENTENCING

UNITED STATES v. BERGMAN
416 F. Supp. 496 (S.D.N.Y. 1976)

FRANKEL, District Judge.

Defendant is being sentenced upon his plea of guilty to two counts of an 11-count indictment. . . . It seems fitting now to report in writing the reasons upon which the court concludes that defendant must be sentenced to a term of four months in prison.[6]

I. DEFENDANT AND HIS CRIMES

Defendant appeared until the last couple of years to be a man of unimpeachably high character, attainments, and distinction. A doctor of divinity and an ordained rabbi, he has been acclaimed by people around the world for his works of public philanthropy, private charity, and leadership in educational enterprises. Scores of letters have come to the court from across this and other countries reporting debts of personal gratitude to him for numerous acts of extraordinary generosity. . . . In addition to his good works, defendant has managed to amass considerable wealth in the ownership and operation of nursing homes, in real estate ventures, and in a course of substantial investments.

Beginning about two years ago, investigations of nursing homes in this area, including questions of fraudulent claims for Medicaid funds, drew to a focus upon this defendant among several others. The results that concern us were the present indictment and two state indictments. After extensive pretrial proceedings, defendant embarked upon elaborate plea negotiations with both state and federal prosecutors. A state guilty plea and the instant plea were entered in March of this year. . . . As part of the detailed plea arrangements, it is expected that the prison sentence imposed by this court will comprise the total covering the state as well as the federal convictions.

For purposes of the sentence now imposed, the precise details of the charges, and of defendant's carefully phrased admissions of guilt, are not matters of prime

---

4. See, e.g., 18 U.S.C. § 218 (granting administrative agencies power to rescind any contract, grant, license, or right held by one who has been convicted of bribery, graft, or conflicts of interest under federal law, and authorizing the government to recover amounts expended or things delivered pursuant to the rescinded privilege).

5. See, e.g., Del. C. § 284(a).

6. The court considered, and finally rejected, imposing a fine in addition to the prison term. Defendant seems destined to pay hundreds of thousands of dollars in restitution. The amount is being worked out in connection with a state criminal indictment. Apart from defendant's further liabilities for federal taxes, any additional money exaction is appropriately left for the state court.

importance. Suffice it to say that the plea on Count One (carrying a maximum of five years in prison and a $10,000 fine) confesses defendant's knowing and [willful] participation in a scheme to defraud the United States in various ways, including the presentation of wrongfully padded claims for payments under the Medicaid program to defendant's nursing homes. Count Three, for which the guilty plea carries a theoretical maximum of three more years in prison and another $5,000 fine, is a somewhat more "technical" charge. Here, defendant admits to having participated in the filing of a partnership return which was false and fraudulent in failing to list people who had bought partnership interests from him in one of his nursing homes, had paid for such interests, and had made certain capital withdrawals. . . .

II. THE GUIDING PRINCIPLES OF SENTENCING . . .

The court agrees that this defendant should not be sent to prison for "rehabilitation." Apart from the patent inappositeness of the concept to this individual, this court shares the growing understanding that no one should ever be sent to prison *for rehabilitation*. That is to say, nobody who would not otherwise be locked up should suffer that fate on the incongruous premise that it will be good for him or her. Imprisonment is punishment.

. . . If someone must be imprisoned — for other, valid reasons — we should seek to make rehabilitative resources available to him or her. But the goal of rehabilitation cannot fairly serve in itself as grounds for the sentence to confinement.[7]

Equally clearly, this defendant should not be confined to incapacitate him. He is not dangerous. It is most improbable that he will commit similar, or any, offenses in the future. There is no need for "specific deterrence."

Contrary to counsel's submissions, however, two sentencing considerations demand a prison sentence in this case:

> *First*, the aim of *general deterrence*, the effort to discourage similar wrongdoing by others through a reminder that the law's warnings are real and that the grim consequence of imprisonment is likely to follow from crimes of deception for gain like those defendant has admitted.

> *Second*, the related, but not identical, concern that any lesser penalty would, in the words of the Model Penal Code, § 7.01(1)(c), "depreciate the seriousness of the defendant's crime." . . .

IV. "MEASURING" THE SENTENCE

In cases like this one, the decision of greatest moment is whether to imprison or not. . . .

The criminal behavior, as has been noted, is blatant in character and unmitigated by any suggestion of necessitous circumstance or other pressures difficult to resist. . . . [C]ompetent people, possessed of their faculties, make choices and are accountable

---

7. This important point, correcting misconceptions still widely prevalent, is developed more fully by Dean Norval Morris in The Future of Imprisonment (1974).

for them. In this sometimes harsh light, the case of the present defendant is among the clearest and least relieved. Viewed against the maxima Congress ordained, and against the run of sentences in other federal criminal cases, it calls for more than a token sentence. On the other side . . . [d]efendant's illustrious public life and works are in his favor, though diminished, of course, by what this case discloses. This is a first, probably a last, conviction. Defendant is 64 years old and in imperfect health, though by no means so ill, from what the court is told, that he could be expected to suffer inordinately more than many others of advanced years who go to prison.

Defendant invokes an understandable, but somewhat unworkable, notion of "disparity." He says others involved in recent nursing home fraud cases have received relatively light sentences for behavior more culpable than his. . . .

Our sentencing system, deeply flawed, is characterized by disparity. We are to seek to "individualize" sentences, but no clear or clearly agreed standards govern the individualization. The lack of meaningful criteria does indeed leave sentencing judges far too much at large. But the result, with its nagging burdens on conscience, cannot be meaningfully alleviated by allowing any handful of sentences in a short series to fetter later judgments. . . .

How, then, the particular sentence adjudged in this case? As has been mentioned, the case calls for a sentence that is more than nominal. Given the other circumstances, however — including that this is a first offense, by a man no longer young and not perfectly well, where danger of recidivism is not a concern — it verges on cruelty to think of confinement for a term of years. We sit, to be sure, in a nation where prison sentences of extravagant length are more common than they are almost anywhere else. By that light, the term imposed today is not notably long. For this sentencing court, however, for a nonviolent first offense involving no direct assaults or invasions of others' security (as in bank robbery, narcotics, etc.), it is a stern sentence. For people like Dr. Bergman, who might be disposed to engage in similar wrongdoing, it should be sufficiently frightening to serve the major end of general deterrence. For all but the profoundly vengeful, it should not depreciate the seriousness of his offenses. . . .

Notes and Questions

1. The court called Bergman's four-month sentence "stern." In what sense is it stern? Is it arguable that it is not?

2. The 11-count indictment charged Bergman with fraud that ran into millions of dollars. He pled guilty only to counts 1 and 3, and the plea bargain failed to mention the astronomical sums of money involved in the fraud. Should the magnitude of the fraud and/or Bergman's unwillingness to admit the scope of his crime affect the sentence imposed? Should Bergman's anticipated payment of large sums of money in restitution affect the court's decision on whether and how much to fine him? Why aren't "the precise details of the charges" and Bergman's "carefully phrased admissions of guilt" matters of prime importance?

BROWDER v. UNITED STATES

398 F. Supp. 1042 (D. Or. 1975), *aff'd mem.*, 544 F.2d 525 (9th Cir. 1976)

SKOPIL, District Judge.

[Browder pled guilty to pledging stolen securities that he transported in interstate commerce. He was sentenced to serve four 10-year terms and one 5-year term, 25 years of which were to run consecutively. Browder sought habeas corpus relief on numerous grounds, including the ground that the sentence constituted cruel and unusual punishment.]

IV

Petitioner's final argument is that imposition of a twenty-five year sentence for his "white collar" property crimes constituted cruel and unusual punishment and violated equal protection of the law.

The basis for petitioner's claim is a study he conducted of 100 cases involving similar white collar crimes. If accurate, his study contains startling statistics. Of the 100 defendants studied, 20% received fines, probation, or suspended sentences only for acts involving $350,000,000 or more. The others studied received light sentences for a variety of swindles in which the public became victim to members of the Mafia, labor union officials, mayors, attorneys, stock brokers, business executives, bankers, a former state Attorney General, a governor, a federal judge, and others.

I can only speculate on the motivations for sentences rendered in the individual cases listed. As Mr. Browder observes, "wherein the greater the offense against capital, the lesser the punishment imposed by the sentencing court." If Mr. Browder's study is accurate, the pattern of sentencing revealed is deplorable.

If there is a logic to this paradox, it eludes me. I cannot reconcile a policy of sending poorly educated burglars from the ghetto to jail when men in the highest positions of public trust and authority receive judicial coddling when they are caught fleecing their constituencies. Penology's recent enchantment with rehabilitation as a wholesale justification for imprisonment has dissolved in the face of numerous studies proving that rehabilitation rarely occurs. A minority of the prison population are rightfully locked up because they are too dangerous to release. If we are to justify imprisonment for the rest, it must be on the grounds of punishment or deterrence. And if this is our premise, the white collar criminal must come to expect equal or greater treatment than the common, nonviolent thief. The consequences of a white collar property crime tend to reach a higher magnitude in direct proportion to the level of status and power held by the criminal involved. The men Browder studied abused their influence to defraud thousands of people throughout the country out of millions of dollars. Apparently this has been tolerated through light sentencing because of the staggering proportions of the crime.

The defect in Browder's reasoning is his conclusion that because other white collar criminals have been receiving disparate treatment, he should too. As a matter of law, I cannot review the propriety of the sentence he received. The sentence was within statutory limits. 18 U.S.C. § 2315. Therefore it was a constitutional product of the trial court's discretion. As a matter of jurisprudence, I will comment on his sentence in the context of his study. The sentencing judge may have shared my dismay, and Browder's, at the pattern of white collar crime sentences. White collar crime pays. It will continue to do so as long as judges endorse it through their sentencing policy.

Imprisonment is hardly a panacea. Well-crafted parole and probation programs and requirements of restitution are usually better solutions. I doubt that deterrence will be very effective until the "executive" becomes convinced that if he embarks on a criminal adventure, he will be severely — though proportionately — punished. Certainty is the key. Edward Browder was convicted of pledging over $500,000 worth of stolen securities. He concedes his guilt for those crimes. The fact that they were accomplished by means of wit and charm rather than a burglar's tool does not minimize the damage done to the public. The judge who sentenced Browder obviously shared that view. It is a tragedy, if Browder's study is accurate, that fewer judges — and not more of them — subscribe to it also. Petitioner's petition is denied.

Notes and Questions

1. Which offense is more serious — defrauding the government of several million dollars (as in *Bergman*) or pledging stolen securities worth half a million dollars (as in *Browder*)? Which of the sentences in *Bergman* and *Browder* (if either) seems relatively proportional to the crime?[8]

2. Is it really necessary to imprison white collar offenders like Bergman and Browder? Is it likely that they will repeat their crimes if they are sentenced only to pay a fine?

3. Should it matter whether Browder's sentence was disproportionately harsh compared with sentences meted out for similar white collar crimes? That it was disproportionately lenient compared with sentences imposed for nonviolent "street" crimes?

B. GUIDELINES SENTENCING

A common theme in *Bergman* and *Browder* is the "deplorable" disparities in sentences meted out to similarly situated defendants and the "coddling" of white collar defendants by sentencing judges who rely heavily on fines and probation. Congress sought to address these and other perceived shortcomings in federal sentencing practices in the Sentencing Reform Act of 1984. The Act raised the authorized fine levels for most offenses, created the United States Sentencing Commission, directed the Commission to promulgate guidelines that reduce unwarranted sentencing disparities, revised federal probation laws to give the sentencing judge a wider range of options, and — significantly — abolished parole.

---

8. For an empirical view of how federal judges justify their sentencing decisions in white collar cases, see Stanton Wheeler, Kenneth Mann & Austin Sarat, Sitting in Judgment: The Sentencing of White Collar Criminals (1988).

The Sentencing Guidelines take a tough stance against white collar criminals. The Guidelines' philosophy is that deterrence can best be achieved in this context by requiring short but sure prison terms.

> . . . Under pre-guidelines sentencing practice, courts sentenced to probation an inappropriately high percentage of offenders guilty of certain economic crimes, such as theft, tax evasion, antitrust offenses, insider trading, fraud, and embezzlement, that in the Commission's view are "serious."
>
> The Commission's solution to this problem has been to write guidelines that classify as serious many offenses for which probation previously was frequently given and provide for at least a short period of imprisonment in such cases. The Commission concluded that the definite prospect of prison, even though the term may be short, will serve as a significant deterrent, particularly when compared with pre-guidelines practice where probation, not prison, was the norm.[9]

In consequence, the Guidelines designate many white collar offenses as serious crimes that merit prison time.

To give a few examples, under prior sentencing practices, 54 percent of those convicted of fraud and 57 percent of those convicted of tax crimes received probation without incarceration. The Sentencing Commission projected that under the Guidelines, only about 24 percent of fraud convictions and 3 percent of tax convictions would result in probation without incarceration. Before the Guidelines became effective, only 39 percent of antitrust convictions resulted in any imprisonment, and those that did averaged a sentence of 45 days. Under the Guidelines, most antitrust offenses and all bid rigging violations carry a recommended sentence of at least four months in addition to large fines. The Guidelines provide a range of authorized sentences for "each category of offense involving each category of defendant."[10]

1. Sentencing Guidelines Roadmap

To facilitate your understanding of how the Guidelines work, the following discussion walks you through seven basic steps the sentencing court takes in determining the appropriate guideline sentence,[11] using the defendants in *Bergman* and *Browder* to illustrate.

Step One: Determining the Base Offense Level

The first step in the sentencing process is determining the base offense level. Rather than trying to create a separate guideline for each of the estimated 3,000 federal crimes on the books, the Sentencing Commission began with generic guidelines that group similar types of offenses into discrete categories — e.g., offenses involving theft,

---

9. United States Sentencing Commission, Guidelines Manual ch. 1, pt. A, at 8 (Nov. 2009) [hereinafter Sentencing Guidelines].

10. 28 U.S.C. § 994(b).

11. This discussion is adapted in part from United States Sentencing Commission, Special Report to Congress: Mandatory Minimum Penalties in the Federal Criminal Justice System 20-26 (1991).

fraud, or deceit.[12] The purpose of this step is to rank the categories by the severity of the offense on a scale of 1 to 43, with the least serious offenses being assigned the lowest numbers. Thus, for example, a defendant convicted of unlawfully transferring nuclear weapons would begin with a much higher offense level than one convicted of odometer tampering.

The base offense level for most fraud offenses is 6. Thus, in a typical case, the sentencing judge would begin by assigning Bergman and Browder an offense level of 6.

Step Two: Specific Offense Characteristics

The court next looks at specific offense characteristics. The guideline that sets the base offense level also lists characteristics that are common to that category of offenses and that reflect the relative gravity of the crime. For example, the fraud guideline directs the court to consider the magnitude of the defendant's fraud. If the estimated or probable loss from the fraud was $5,000 or less, the offense level remains unchanged at 6. If the loss is more than $5,000, the offense level will increase anywhere from 1 to 18 levels, depending on the magnitude of the loss. In Bergman's case, the Medicaid fraud was estimated to be between $2 and $3 million in addition to an unquantified loss caused by his tax fraud. That would require adding roughly 18 levels to his offense score (now up to 24). In Browder's case, the fraud was estimated at about $500,000, so the court would increase his offense level by 14 (now up to 20).

Step Three: Chapter 3 Adjustments

Chapter 3 of the Guidelines provides adjustments to the offense level based on victim-related factors (e.g., an unusually vulnerable victim), the defendant's role in the offense (e.g., an aggravating or mitigating role), and specified types of conduct that obstruct justice. For purposes of this discussion, assume that no adjustments apply to Bergman and Browder.

Step Four: Multiple Counts

The Guidelines recognize that in some cases multiple counts of conviction will reflect multiple harms, but that in other cases they may not. In an effort to provide a rational and uniform way to determine how much a sentence should be increased when defendants are convicted of multiple counts, the Guidelines specify procedures for grouping closely related counts, for determining the offense level applicable to each group of counts, and for determining the combined offense level. For present purposes, assume the sentences in *Bergman* and *Browder* would remain unchanged by step four.

---

12. Sentencing Guidelines § 2B1.1.

Step Five: Acceptance of Responsibility

The Guidelines provide a 2-level decrease in the offense level if the defendant affirmatively demonstrates acceptance of personal responsibility for his crime.[13] Thus, for example, a defendant who voluntarily resigns from the position he held when he committed the crime (e.g., a union treasurer who embezzled union funds voluntarily resigns from office) or who voluntarily makes restitution before he is found guilty (e.g., the treasurer voluntarily restores the embezzled funds) may qualify for this reduction.[14] In some cases the defendant may qualify for another 1-level reduction if, in addition to accepting responsibility, he assisted authorities in the investigation or prosecution of his crime by providing complete information about his involvement in it or by giving timely notice of his intent to plead guilty.[15]

Both Bergman and Browder pled guilty, but a sentencing court might treat them differently for purposes of step five. Entering a guilty plea does not automatically entitle the defendant to an adjustment for acceptance of responsibility. Bergman's guilty plea, which followed "extensive pretrial proceedings" and was the product of "elaborate plea negotiations" with federal and state prosecutors, contained "carefully phrased admissions of guilt" for crimes charged in two counts of an 11-count indictment. His strategy was to concede as little as possible. In contrast, Browder — following the advice of his lawyer (whose assistance, Browder later claimed, was ineffective) — agreed to the consolidation of federal prosecutions pending in California, Florida, Georgia, and Oregon for purposes of sentencing. Under counsel's advice to avoid going to trial and thus reduce his exposure to a long sentence, he pled guilty in Oregon to all counts of three indictments and an information.

A sentencing judge might well conclude that Browder's guilty plea was more consistent with acceptance of responsibility than Bergman's and that it conserved valuable prosecutorial and judicial resources. That being true, assume that the judge would make a downward adjustment for Browder (which would lower his offense level to 18) but not for Bergman.

Step Six: Prior Criminal History

As was true in pre-guidelines sentencing, the defendant's prior criminal record is relevant to the punishment imposed. Under the Guidelines, the court takes into account

---

13. See id. § 3E1.1.

14. Id., Application Note 1.

This adjustment is not intended to apply to a defendant who puts the government to its burden of proof at trial by denying the essential factual elements of guilt, is convicted, and only then admits guilt and expresses remorse. Conviction by trial, however, does not automatically preclude a defendant from consideration for such a reduction. In rare situations a defendant may clearly demonstrate an acceptance of responsibility for his criminal conduct even though he exercises his constitutional right to a trial.

Id. § 3E1.1 Commentary, Application Note 2.

Is there a sound basis for providing a downward adjustment for acceptance of responsibility? Is it troublesome that defendants who exercise their constitutional right to a jury trial will only rarely qualify for a downward adjustment? Under what circumstances could a defendant who is convicted at trial qualify?

15. Id. § 3E1.1(b).

the number and seriousness of the defendant's previous crimes, whether the defendant is a career criminal, and other similar factors. Since Bergman and Browder were first-time offenders,[16] their sentences would be unaffected by the criminal history categories.

Step Seven: Determining the Applicable Sentencing Range

The court is now ready to turn to the sentencing table, a grid containing a vertical column that ranks offenses by their severity (with 1 representing the least and 43 representing the most serious offense level) and a horizontal column in which the sentencing range increases in severity depending on which of the six criminal history categories the defendant falls within.[17] When we left Bergman and Browder, their offense levels were, respectively, 24 and 18. If you consult the sentencing grid in the Guidelines, you will find that the applicable sentencing range for Bergman would be 51 to 63 months — considerably more than Judge Frankel imposed. The applicable sentencing range for Browder would be 27 to 33 months — considerably less than the sentence Judge Skopil upheld. Having arrived at this point (see Table 14-1), the sentencing judge may choose a sentence from any point in the designated range for each defendant.

TABLE 14-1
GUIDELINES SENTENCE CALCULATIONS

	BERGMAN		BROWDER	
	OFFENSE LEVEL	SENTENCING RANGE	OFFENSE LEVEL	SENTENCING RANGE
Step 1	6	0-6 mos.	6	0-6 mos.
Step 2	+18	51-63 mos.	+14	33-41 mos.
Step 3	0	—	0	—
Step 4	0	—	0	—
Step 5	0	—	–2	27-33 mos.
Step 6	0	—	0	—
Step 7	24	51-63 mos.	18	27-33 mos.

2. Relevant Conduct

The Sentencing Guidelines inevitably reflect a series of compromises the Sentencing Commission reached. One of the most fundamental and controversial questions the Commission considered was whether to adopt a "charge offense" or "real offense" sentencing regime. Under a "charge offense" system, sentences would be based solely on the offense of conviction — i.e., the elements of the crime the defendant was convicted of committing — and the applicable Guideline would specify limited aggravating and mitigating circumstances relevant to the offense. Under a "real offense" system, the sentence would reflect the details of the charges — e.g., specific circumstances relating to

---

16. In Browder's case, this isn't entirely clear. The sentencing judge referred to Browder as "the worst crook that has ever come before this Court" and called Browder's record "one of the most abominable records" he had ever seen. These comments prompted Browder to claim that his sentence had been calculated on the basis of "erroneous information in [his] criminal record." *Browder*, 398 F. Supp. at 1046.

17. Sentencing Guidelines ch. 5, pt. A., at 402, Sentencing Table. The Sentencing Table is reproduced in Part II of the supplement to this book.

the defendant's method of committing the crime, the victim's special vulnerability, or the defendant's criminal history. A "real offense" system would allow a greater range of factors — including uncharged conduct and the defendant's character or propensity to commit future crimes — to increase the severity of the sentence.[18]

The Sentencing Commission's compromise was to incorporate some features of each. Under the Guidelines, the "charge offense" ordinarily determines the base offense level. Once that level is set, the court considers "real offense" circumstances — including "relevant conduct" — that aggravate or mitigate the severity of the crime. In some cases, however, relevant conduct — i.e., circumstances extraneous to the elements of the offense of conviction — will play a role in setting the base offense level. Among them are cases in which the defendant committed other acts "that were part of the same course of conduct or common scheme or plan as the offense of conviction."[19]

UNITED STATES v. PINNICK
47 F.3d 434 (D.C. Cir. 1995)

TATEL, Circuit Judge.

Appellant Shannon O. Pinnick pled guilty to one count of a four-count indictment for fraud and received a twenty-one month sentence. He now claims that the district court erred when it considered the conduct alleged in the other three counts as "relevant conduct" under section 1B1.3 of the United States Sentencing Guidelines. . . .

I

Mr. Pinnick was indicted on four counts of fraud in a single indictment. Count one alleged that on October 1, 1992, under the alias Scott Bishop, he presented a counterfeit check for approximately $19,000 to open an account at a brokerage firm. Count two alleged that on the day before, using the same alias, he used another counterfeit check drawn on the same fictitious account to purchase an $18,000 car. Both counts alleged violation of 18 U.S.C. § 513(a). Count three alleged that two months earlier — on August 6, 1992 — appellant violated 18 U.S.C. §§ 1029 & 2 by using the names James Douglas and Scott Bishop to file a fraudulent application for a credit card account over the Prodigy computer network and by making purchases of almost $5,000 using that account during the following month. Count four charged that on December 28 and 29, 1992, appellant, claiming to be a Mr. Agbebaku, cashed five counterfeit checks totalling $6,000 drawn on Mr. Agbebaku's account at Riggs National Bank in violation of 18 U.S.C. § 1344.

Pursuant to a plea agreement, appellant pled guilty to count four of the indictment and the government dismissed the first three counts. At his plea colloquy, appellant admitted all of the allegations in count four. He also admitted using the aliases "Agbebaku" and "Bishop," but made no other statements regarding the offenses alleged

---

18. Stephen Breyer, The Federal Sentencing Guidelines and the Key Compromises upon Which They Rest, 17 Hofstra L. Rev. 1, 8-12 (1988).

19. Sentencing Guidelines § 1B1.3(a)(2).

in the other three counts. The district court accepted his plea and ordered a presentence investigation.

The presentence report recommended that the court consider counts one, two, and three as relevant conduct under section 1B1.3(a)(2) of the Sentencing Guidelines because the counts involved the "same course of conduct" as the offense of conviction. This recommendation increased the value of the loss used to determine the appellant's guideline range from $6,000 to $48,000, increasing his base offense level from level 11 to level 13. In addition, because appellant was on probation for another offense at the time of the credit card fraud alleged in count three, treating that count as relevant conduct added two points to his criminal history score, placing him in criminal history category III rather than category II.

Both in a letter to the probation officer who prepared the report and at the sentencing hearing, defense counsel objected to the use of counts one, two and three as relevant conduct. The government submitted no additional evidence. Relying entirely on the presentence report, the government argued that all four counts involved fraud, were similar in nature, and were part of the same crime spree.

The district court found that the allegations in the three dismissed counts qualified as relevant conduct, and therefore ruled that appellant's base offense level was 13 and that his criminal history was category III. . . .

On appeal, Mr. Pinnick argues that the district court should not have treated the three dismissed counts as relevant conduct. He argues that the government failed to prove that he committed the acts in the three dismissed counts, and that the court erred in finding that the dismissed counts were "part of the same course of conduct" as the offense of conviction. . . .

III . . .

For most offenses, the Guidelines require the sentencing court to consider only conduct intrinsic to the offense of conviction in determining the defendant's guideline range. The court may consider conduct related to other offenses when selecting the specific sentence within that range. For fraud and certain other offenses, however, the Guidelines provide a limited exception to this approach. Under section 1B1.3(a)(2), conduct which is part of a "common scheme or plan" or part of the "same course of conduct" as the offense of conviction qualifies as "relevant conduct" and is considered when determining the indicated guideline range.

The presentence report in this case said nothing about a "common scheme or plan," but concluded that the dismissed counts were part of the "same course of conduct" as appellant's offense of conviction. . . . Extraneous offenses qualify as part of the same course of conduct if "they are sufficiently connected or related to each other as to warrant the conclusion that they are part of a single episode, spree, or ongoing series of offenses." U.S.S.G. § 1B1.3(a)(2), comment. (n.9(B)). The sentencing court must evaluate and balance several factors, including "the degree of similarity of the offenses and the time interval between the offenses." Id. Also relevant are the "nature of the offenses" and whether the offenses can "readily be broken into discrete, identifiable units that are meaningful for purposes of sentencing." Id. comment. (n.9(B)) & backg'd. No single factor in this fact-based inquiry is dispositive. The absence of one factor requires a stronger presence of at least one of the other factors. The inquiry focuses on whether the defendant "repeats the same type of criminal activity over time" and "engages in an identifiable behavior pattern of specified criminal activity." United States v. Perdomo, 927 F.2d 111, 115 (2d Cir. 1991).

Where the defendant's offense of conviction and the acts offered as relevant conduct could be "separately identified" and were of a different "nature," we have found that the conduct was not part of the same course of conduct. See United States v. Jones, 948 F.2d 732, 737-38 (D.C. Cir. 1991). In *Jones*, the defendant was convicted of stealing bank statements from the mail and using the information to access the accounts. We held that an alleged embezzlement from his employer that occurred over a year earlier was not part of the same course of conduct.

Applying these principles, we hold that the district court's relevant conduct finding regarding the first two counts is not clearly erroneous. In each of the acts associated with counts one, two, and four, appellant, using an alias, presented a counterfeit check to obtain either cash, or, in count two, an automobile. The offenses involved similar instruments — counterfeit checks — and a similar method — using an alias — albeit a different alias in count four (Agbebaku) than in counts one and two (Bishop). It is true that the conduct in counts one and two preceded that in count four by three months, and that the acts are separately identifiable. Counts one and two are, however, more similar in nature and closer in time to appellant's offense of conviction than the embezzlement count was to the mail fraud conviction in *Jones*. In this case, the district court could reasonably conclude that these acts demonstrate that appellant "repeated the same type of criminal activity over time" and "engaged in an identifiable behavior pattern of specified criminal activity." See *Perdomo*, 927 F.2d at 115.

We do not agree, however, that the credit card fraud alleged in count three constitutes part of the same course of conduct as count four, the offense of conviction. Unlike counts one, two, and four, count three did not involve counterfeit checks. Like the embezzlement count in *Jones*, count three is both separately identifiable from count four and of a different nature. That counts three and four both involved fraud to obtain money is not enough. While substantial similarities exist between count three and counts one and two — they all involved the same alias and occurred within two months — the government must demonstrate a connection between count three and the *offense of conviction*, not between count three and the other offenses offered as relevant conduct. The credit card fraud in count three is thus not part of the same course of conduct as the offense of conviction. The district court committed clear error in treating it as relevant conduct.

Removing count three from consideration as relevant conduct does not affect appellant's base offense level. It remains at level 13. But because appellant was on probation at the time of the credit card fraud, excluding count three removes two points from his criminal history score, placing him in criminal history category II instead of category III. Eliminating count three as relevant conduct thus reduces appellant's indicated guideline range from 18-24 months to 15-21 months. Accordingly, we vacate the sentence and remand for resentencing. . . .

So ordered.

Notes and Questions

1. Is it appropriate to allow uncharged conduct to affect the severity of the sentence for the offense of conviction? What are the relative pros and cons of "charge offense" and "real offense" sentencing? Did the Sentencing Commission reach a reasonable compromise?

2. The *Pinnick* court's sentence was based in part on allegations — contained in two dismissed counts in the indictment — that Pinnick had cashed two other counterfeit checks using an alias. The court's finding that this was part of the same course of conduct was based exclusively on conclusions contained in the presentence report. Objecting to the use of the two dismissed counts in determining the sentence, defense counsel claimed the presentence report contained factual inaccuracies.

Is it fair to require the defendant to refute untested assertions contained in the presentence report? What kinds of sources will the probation officer likely rely on in preparing the report? Are defendants likely to have access to all or most of the sources?

3. Sentencing hearings are not constrained by the formal evidentiary and procedural rules that apply at trial. Thus, for example, the presentence report may rely on evidence that would have been excluded at trial because it was acquired in violation of established constitutional rights.[20] Should the Sentencing Commission have required more safeguards to ensure that relevant conduct evidence is both reliable and fairly obtained?

NOTE ON DOUBLE JEOPARDY

What are the double jeopardy implications of the result in *Pinnick*? Charges that were dismissed in conjunction with his guilty plea were considered "relevant conduct" that increased his sentence. What if he had not pled guilty and had gone to trial? Suppose the jury convicted him on count 1 but acquitted him on counts 2-4. Could the court consider the allegations of fraud in counts 2-4 as relevant conduct in calculating the Guidelines sentence? While this may feel like a double jeopardy problem, two recent Supreme Court decisions suggest it is not.

In Witte v. United States, 515 U.S. 389 (1995), the defendants were charged with conspiracy to possess and attempted possession of marijuana with intent to distribute. Witte pled guilty to the attempted possession charge and agreed to cooperate. Because sentences for federal drug charges are based partly on the quantity of drugs involved, the trial court took into account the amount of marijuana charged in the possession offense in calculating Witte's sentence. But the total drug quantity the court used to calculate the sentence also included cocaine involved in an uncharged importation offense, which the court found was included in the marijuana conspiracy. And once the court determined that the uncharged drug cocaine violation was part of the marijuana conspiracy, the cocaine offense became "relevant conduct" under the Guidelines. Thus, the Guidelines directed the court to include the drugs involved in the uncharged cocaine offense in its computation of the total quantity of drugs involved in the marijuana conspiracy, a step that substantially increased the sentence Witte received for the marijuana crime to which he pled guilty.

---

20. See, e.g., United States v. McCrory, 930 F.2d 63, 67-69 (D.C. Cir. 1991) (upholding use, at sentencing phase, of evidence obtained during illegal warrantless search; evidence that is inadmissible at trial may be admissible at sentencing).

After being sentenced on the marijuana charge, Witte was indicted again. The second indictment charged him with conspiracy to import and attempted importation of cocaine — accusations based on the same uncharged conduct the court had earlier used to compute his sentence for attempted possession of marijuana. Witte challenged the second prosecution on double jeopardy grounds, arguing that he had already been punished for the cocaine-related activities because they had been used to increase the sentence for his marijuana offense.

The Supreme Court rejected the challenge, holding that when a court uses uncharged criminal conduct to enhance a sentence that is within the legislatively authorized range of punishment for the crime of conviction, the enhancement does not constitute punishment for the uncharged conduct under the Double Jeopardy Clause. The sentence punishes the defendant only for the offense of conviction.

Courts have historically had broad discretion to consider factors relevant to the defendant's crime and character at the sentencing stage of the proceedings.

> [R]oughly speaking, [relevant conduct under the Guidelines] corresponds to those actions and circumstances that courts typically took into account when sentencing prior to the Guidelines' enactment. . . . [C]onsideration of information about the defendant's character and conduct at sentencing does not result in "punishment" for any offense other than the one of which the defendant was convicted. . . . [Instead, the defendant is] punished only for the fact that the *present* offense was carried out in a manner that warrants increased punishment. . . .

Id. at 402-403.

Two years later, in United States v. Watts, 519 U.S. 148 (1997),[21] the Court reaffirmed this view of double jeopardy law in a case strikingly similar to the *Pinnick* hypothetical above. In *Watts* the defendant was charged with two related offenses. The jury convicted him of one offense and acquitted him of the other. At sentencing, the trial court found by a preponderance of the evidence that he had committed the offense for which he was acquitted and thus factored it in as relevant conduct in determining the sentence for the offense of conviction. The defendant objected on double jeopardy grounds.

The high Court again rejected the challenge. First, the Court reiterated that *Witte* made it clear that sentence enhancements within the statutorily prescribed Guidelines range are not separate punishments for double jeopardy purposes. Second, it found the argument misunderstands the preclusive effect of an acquittal. When a jury returns a general verdict of not guilty, it merely decides there is a reasonable doubt as to guilt. An acquittal does not prove the defendant is innocent and thus does not preclude the sentencing judge from finding, by a preponderance of evidence, that the defendant committed the crime.

3. Judicial Fact Finding

As originally conceived, the Sentencing Guidelines envisioned a sentencing regime that would reduce unwarranted disparities in sentences imposed for similar offenses by minimizing the role judicial discretion played in sentencing decisions. Thus,

---

21. *Watts* was a consolidation of two separate cases on appeal.

the Guidelines imposed mandatory restrictions on how trial judges calculated Guidelines sentences, but they also relied heavily on judicial fact finding. Judges were required to apply a number of Guideline factors such as the role the defendant played in the offense (e.g., was he an organizer or supervisor), aggravating factors relating to the nature of the offense or the manner in which it was committed (e.g., did the offense cause serious or widespread harm), and other similar factors relating to the severity of the offense or the dangerousness of the offender.

As in *Witte* — where cocaine involved in an uncharged importation offense was used to enhance the sentence for the attempted marijuana possession offense to which Witte pled guilty — the factual underpinnings for the sentence need not have been facts introduced or proved at trial. Instead, the Guidelines gave judges leeway to make these factual determinations on their own — by a preponderance of the evidence — during the sentencing phase of the proceeding.

Heavy reliance on judicial fact finding ultimately raised Sixth Amendment concerns that cast considerable doubt on the continuing viability of the Guidelines. The genesis of those concerns was Apprendi v. New Jersey,[22] a case the Supreme Court decided in 2002. *Apprendi* involved a New Jersey hate crime statute that increased the maximum penalty from a 10 year prison term to a maximum of 20 years if the judge found that the defendant committed the crime "with a purpose to intimidate . . . because of race, color, gender, handicap, religion, sexual orientation or ethnicity."[23] The Court found this repugnant to the Sixth Amendment right to a jury trial and ruled that "[o]ther than the fact of a prior conviction, any fact that increases the penalty for a crime beyond the prescribed statutory maximum must be submitted to a jury."[24]

Two years later, in Ring v. Arizona, the Court extended this ruling to an Arizona statute that gave judges discretionary authority to impose the death penalty if they found that one of ten aggravating factors was present.[25] Two years after that, in Blakely v. Washington, the high Court invalidated a state sentencing guidelines scheme that permitted the sentencing judge to depart from the standard sentencing range for some violent felonies and to impose an "exceptional sentence" if there were "substantial and compelling reasons" to do so.[26] Taken together, *Apprendi*, *Ring*, and *Blakely* clearly laid the foundation for striking down the federal Sentencing Guidelines, at least in part.

In United States v. Booker,[27] the defendants were convicted of drug crimes. Applying the applicable federal Guideline, the judge found there were aggravating circumstances that warranted more than doubling the normal sentence imposed for the crimes. Writing in part for a sharply divided Court (the "merits" opinion), Justice Stevens ruled that under the reasoning in *Apprendi* and *Blakely*, imposition of enhanced sentences based on judicial findings of fact that are not reflected in the jury verdict or admitted by the defendant violates the Sixth Amendment.

But rather than throwing the baby out with the bath water, Justice Breyer, writing for a different majority in part (the "remedies" opinion), found that while the provisions making the Sentencing Guidelines mandatory were unconstitutional, they could be

---

22. 530 U.S. 466 (2000).
23. Id. at 468-469.
24. Id. at 490.
25. Ring v. Arizona, 536 U.S. 584 (2002).
26. Blakely v. Washington, 542 U.S. 296, 298 (2004).
27. 543 U.S. 220 (2005).

severed from the rest of the Guidelines, leaving the remaining Guidelines in place as advisory rather than binding sentencing principles.[28] Thus, Justice Breyer's opinion saved the Guidelines sentencing system by excising two provisions — one that required judges to impose a sentence within a stated Guidelines range, and one that specified appellate standards of review, including de novo review of sentences that are not within the Guidelines range.

Although *Booker* made it clear that the standard of appellate review was the reasonableness of the sentence imposed, this novel interpretation of the Guidelines left sentencing judges in limbo. What does "reasonable" mean in the context of a sentencing regime that is advisory and thus has no enforceable rules? If the Guidelines were now no longer mandatory, what weight should a trial judge give them? Should they be given "substantial weight"? Should they be considered "persuasive" or even "presumptively reasonable"? *Booker* left trial judges with an infinite range of possibilities but gave little guidance on which of them to choose.

Notes and Questions

1. How, if at all, will *Booker* and its progeny affect the reasoning and/or results in cases like *Pinnick*?

2. *Booker* and its progeny confer broad discretion on the trial judge to fashion individualized sentences that deviate from the normal Guidelines range. Is this consistent with the underlying goal of eliminating disparity in sentences that are imposed for the same or similar crimes?

3. Does *Booker* eliminate judicial fact finding at the sentencing stage?

4. What weight should a trial judge now give the Guidelines in calculating a sentence?

5. After *Booker*, the standard of review is the reasonableness of the sentence. What does "reasonable" mean in the context of a sentencing regime that is merely advisory?

6. More than 93 percent of defendants in the federal system plead guilty. Is *Booker* likely to affect plea bargains or bargaining practices? Can defendants be required to waive their *Booker* rights as a condition of a plea agreement?[29]

Booker ushered in an era of uncertainty about sentencing under the Guidelines regime. Thus, for example, *Booker* prompted litigants to question what weight a sentence

---

28. Before he became a member of the Supreme Court, Justice Breyer was, variously, a member of the original Sentencing Commission, a judge on the First Circuit Court of Appeals, and chief counsel to the Senate Judiciary Committee. In all three roles, he advocated adoption of a system of advisory sentencing guidelines. See Susan R. Klein, The Return of Federal Judicial Discretion in Criminal Sentencing, 39 Val. U. L. Rev. 693, 717-718 (2005). Although his preference for advisory guidelines did not prevail, as a member of the Commission he nonetheless played a pivotal role in the policy decisions that shaped the guidelines system that was in place when *Booker* was decided. His background as a Commissioner undoubtedly helps to explain his ability to command the support of four other Justices in *Booker*.

29. Cf. Memorandum from James Comey, Deputy Attorney General, to All Federal Prosecutors, Departmental Legal Positions and Policies in Light of *Blakely v. Washington*, at 4 (July 2, 2004) (directing line prosecutors to seek plea agreements in which the defendant waives all rights under *Blakely* and "agrees to have his sentence determined under the Sentencing Guidelines"). The Comey Memorandum can be accessed through the Department of Justice website at *http://www.usdoj.gov/dag/readingroom/blakely.htm*.

that falls within the guidelines range should be given. Should a sentence that is within the recommended guidelines range be accorded a presumption of reasonableness? In Rita v. United States,[30] the Supreme Court held that a presumption of reasonableness on appeal is permissible. But while the Court ruled that it is permissible for appellate courts to adopt a presumption that a sentence within the guidelines range is reasonable, it also made clear that appellate courts may *not* presume that sentences that are outside the recommended guidelines range are *unreasonable*.

Rita set the stage for a pair of cases[31] that tested the extent to which courts are free to depart from recommended guidelines sentences.

GALL v. UNITED STATES
552 U.S. 38 (2007)

Justice STEVENS delivered the opinion of the Court.

In two cases argued on the same day last Term we considered the standard that courts of appeals should apply when reviewing the reasonableness of sentences imposed by district judges. The first, Rita v. United States, 551 U.S. 338 (2007), involved a sentence *within* the range recommended by the Federal Sentencing Guidelines; we held that when a district judge's discretionary decision in a particular case accords with the sentence the United States Sentencing Commission deems appropriate "in the mine run of cases," the court of appeals may presume that the sentence is reasonable.

The second case, Claiborne v. United States, involved a sentence *below* the range recommended by the Guidelines, and raised the converse question whether a court of appeals may apply a "proportionality test," and require that a sentence that constitutes a substantial variance from the Guidelines be justified by extraordinary circumstances. We did not have the opportunity to answer this question because the case was mooted by Claiborne's untimely death. We granted certiorari in the case before us today in order to reach that question, left unanswered last Term. . . .

I

[While he was a sophomore in college, Gall joined a conspiracy to distribute a popular drug known as "ecstasy." His participation in the conspiracy netted him $30,000 for delivering ecstasy pills to his co-conspirators, who then sold them to consumers. Although Gall himself used controlled substances at the time, he stopped using drugs within a few months of joining the ring. Several months later, he notified his fellow conspirators that he was withdrawing from the conspiracy. Having "self-rehabilitated," Gall subsequently graduated from college, became gainfully employed, and remained drug-free. Despite his clean record, Gall was indicted for his role in the conspiracy and later pled guilty.

The probation officer's pre-sentencing report recommended a Guidelines sentence of 30-37 months in prison. At the sentencing hearing, the government did not contest

---

30. Rita v. United States, 127 S. Ct. 2456 (2007).
31. Kimbrough v. United States, 552 U.S. 85 (2007); Gall v. United States, 552 U.S. 38 (2007).

Gall's claim that he had been law abiding during the intervening years between his voluntary withdrawal from the conspiracy and the indictment. The prosecutor argued, however, that the recommended Guidelines sentence was nonetheless "appropriate" and "should be followed," particularly in light of the 30-35 month terms two of his co-conspirators had been sentenced to serve. Unpersuaded, the judge declined to impose a prison term and sentenced Gall to serve 36 months on probation.]

. . . In addition to making a lengthy statement on the record, the judge filed a detailed sentencing memorandum explaining his decision, and provided the following statement of reasons in his written judgment:

> The Court determined that, considering all the factors under 18 U.S.C. 3553(a), the Defendant's explicit withdrawal from the conspiracy almost four years before the filing of the Indictment, the Defendant's post-offense conduct, especially obtaining a college degree and the start of his own successful business, the support of family and friends, lack of criminal history, and his age at the time of the offense conduct, all warrant the sentence imposed, which was sufficient, but not greater than necessary to serve the purposes of sentencing.

At the end of both the sentencing hearing and the sentencing memorandum, the District Judge reminded Gall that probation, rather than "an act of leniency," is a "substantial restriction of freedom." In the memorandum, he emphasized:

> [Gall] will have to comply with strict reporting conditions along with a three-year regime of alcohol and drug testing. He will not be able to change or make decisions about significant circumstances in his life, such as where to live or work, which are prized liberty interests, without first seeking authorization from his Probation Officer or, perhaps, even the Court. Of course, the Defendant always faces the harsh consequences that await if he violates the conditions of his probationary term.

Finally, the District Judge explained why he had concluded that the sentence of probation reflected the seriousness of Gall's offense and that no term of imprisonment was necessary:

> Any term of imprisonment in this case would be counter effective by depriving society of the contributions of the Defendant who, the Court has found, understands the consequences of his criminal conduct and is doing everything in his power to forge a new life. The Defendant's post-offense conduct indicates neither that he will return to criminal behavior nor that the Defendant is a danger to society. In fact, the Defendant's post-offense conduct was not motivated by a desire to please the Court or any other governmental agency, but was the pre-Indictment product of the Defendant's own desire to lead a better life.

II

The Court of Appeals reversed and remanded for resentencing. Relying on its earlier opinion in United States v. Claiborne, it held that a sentence outside of the Guidelines range must be supported by a justification that "is proportional to the extent of the difference between the advisory range and the sentence imposed." Characterizing the difference between a sentence of probation and the bottom of Gall's advisory Guidelines range of 30 months as "extraordinary" because it amounted to "a 100% downward variance," the Court of Appeals held that such a variance must be — and here was not — supported by extraordinary circumstances. . . .

III

In *Booker* we invalidated both the statutory provision, 18 U.S.C. § 3553(b)(1), which made the Sentencing Guidelines mandatory, and § 3742(e), which directed appellate courts to apply a *de novo* standard of review to departures from the Guidelines. As a result of our decision, the Guidelines are now advisory, and appellate review of sentencing decisions is limited to determining whether they are "reasonable." Our explanation of "reasonableness" review in the *Booker* opinion made it pellucidly clear that the familiar abuse-of-discretion standard of review now applies to appellate review of sentencing decisions.

It is also clear that a district judge must give serious consideration to the extent of any departure from the Guidelines and must explain his conclusion that an unusually lenient or an unusually harsh sentence is appropriate in a particular case with sufficient justifications. For even though the Guidelines are advisory rather than mandatory, they are, as we pointed out in *Rita,* the product of careful study based on extensive empirical evidence derived from the review of thousands of individual sentencing decisions.

In reviewing the reasonableness of a sentence outside the Guidelines range, appellate courts may therefore take the degree of variance into account and consider the extent of a deviation from the Guidelines. We reject, however, an appellate rule that requires "extraordinary" circumstances to justify a sentence outside the Guidelines range. We also reject the use of a rigid mathematical formula that uses the percentage of a departure as the standard for determining the strength of the justifications required for a specific sentence.

As an initial matter, the approaches we reject come too close to creating an impermissible presumption of unreasonableness for sentences outside the Guidelines range. Even the Government has acknowledged that such a presumption would not be consistent with *Booker.*

The mathematical approach also suffers from infirmities of application. On one side of the equation, deviations from the Guidelines range will always appear more extreme — in percentage terms — when the range itself is low, and a sentence of probation will always be a 100% departure regardless of whether the Guidelines range is 1 month or 100 years. Moreover, quantifying the variance as a certain percentage of the maximum, minimum, or median prison sentence recommended by the Guidelines gives no weight to the "substantial restriction of freedom" involved in a term of supervised release or probation.

We recognize that custodial sentences are qualitatively more severe than probationary sentences of equivalent terms. Offenders on probation are nonetheless subject to several standard conditions that substantially restrict their liberty. Probationers may not leave the judicial district, move, or change jobs without notifying, and in some cases receiving permission from, their probation officer or the court. They must report regularly to their probation officer, permit unannounced visits to their homes, refrain from associating with any person convicted of a felony, and refrain from excessive drinking.

Most probationers are also subject to individual "special conditions" imposed by the court. Gall, for instance, may not patronize any establishment that derives more than 50% of its revenue from the sale of alcohol, and must submit to random drug tests as directed by his probation officer.

On the other side of the equation, the mathematical approach assumes the existence of some ascertainable method of assigning percentages to various justifications. Does withdrawal from a conspiracy justify more or less than, say, a 30% reduction? Does it matter that the withdrawal occurred several years ago? Is it relevant that the withdrawal was motivated by a decision to discontinue the use of drugs and to lead a better life? What percentage, if any, should be assigned to evidence that a defendant poses no future threat to society, or to evidence that innocent third parties are dependent on him? The formula is a classic example of attempting to measure an inventory of apples by counting oranges.

Most importantly, both the exceptional circumstances requirement and the rigid mathematical formulation reflect a practice — common among courts that have adopted "proportional review" — of applying a heightened standard of review to sentences outside the Guidelines range. This is inconsistent with the rule that the abuse-of-discretion standard of review applies to appellate review of all sentencing decisions — whether inside or outside the Guidelines range.

As we explained in *Rita*, a district court should begin all sentencing proceedings by correctly calculating the applicable Guidelines range. As a matter of administration and to secure nationwide consistency, the Guidelines should be the starting point and the initial benchmark. The Guidelines are not the only consideration, however. Accordingly, after giving both parties an opportunity to argue for whatever sentence they deem appropriate, the district judge should then consider all of the § 3553(a) factors to determine whether they support the sentence requested by a party. In so doing, he may not presume that the Guidelines range is reasonable. He must make an individualized assessment based on the facts presented. If he decides that an outside-Guidelines sentence is warranted, he must consider the extent of the deviation and ensure that the justification is sufficiently compelling to support the degree of the variance. We find it uncontroversial that a major departure should be supported by a more significant justification than a minor one. After settling on the appropriate sentence, he must adequately explain the chosen sentence to allow for meaningful appellate review and to promote the perception of fair sentencing.

Regardless of whether the sentence imposed is inside or outside the Guidelines range, the appellate court must review the sentence under an abuse-of-discretion standard. It must first ensure that the district court committed no significant procedural error, such as failing to calculate (or improperly calculating) the Guidelines range, treating the Guidelines as mandatory, failing to consider the § 3553(a) factors, selecting a sentence based on clearly erroneous facts, or failing to adequately explain the chosen sentence — including an explanation for any deviation from the Guidelines range. Assuming that the district court's sentencing decision is procedurally sound, the appellate court should then consider the substantive reasonableness of the sentence imposed under an abuse-of-discretion standard. When conducting this review, the court will, of course, take into account the totality of the circumstances, including the extent of any variance from the Guidelines range. If the sentence is within the Guidelines range, the appellate court may, but is not required to, apply a presumption of reasonableness. But if the sentence is outside the Guidelines range, the court may not apply a presumption of unreasonableness. It may consider the extent of the deviation, but must give due deference to the district court's decision that the § 3553(a) factors, on a whole, justify the extent of the variance. The fact that the appellate court might reasonably have concluded that a different sentence was appropriate is insufficient to justify reversal of the district court.

Practical considerations also underlie this legal principle. . . . "The sentencing judge has access to, and greater familiarity with, the individual case and the individual defendant before him than the Commission or the appeals court." Moreover, "[d]istrict courts have an institutional advantage over appellate courts in making these sorts of determinations, especially as they see so many more Guidelines sentences than appellate courts do."[32]

. . . As we shall now explain, the opinion of the Court of Appeals in this case does not reflect the requisite deference and does not support the conclusion that the District Court abused its discretion.

IV

As an initial matter, we note that the District Judge committed no significant procedural error. He correctly calculated the applicable Guidelines range, allowed both parties to present arguments as to what they believed the appropriate sentence should be, considered all of the § 3553(a) factors, and thoroughly documented his reasoning. The Court of Appeals found that the District Judge erred in failing to give proper weight to the seriousness of the offense, as required by § 3553(a)(2)(A), and failing to consider whether a sentence of probation would create unwarranted disparities, as required by § 3553(a)(6). We disagree.

Section 3553(a)(2)(A) requires judges to consider "the need for the sentence imposed . . . to reflect the seriousness of the offense, to promote respect for the law, and to provide just punishment for the offense." [The Court rejected the contention that the sentence did not adequately reflect the seriousness of the offense because it "ignored the serious health risks ecstasy poses."]

The Government's legitimate concern that a lenient sentence for a serious offense threatens to promote disrespect for the law is at least to some extent offset by the fact that seven of the eight defendants in this case have been sentenced to significant prison terms. Moreover, the unique facts of Gall's situation provide support for the District Judge's conclusion that, in Gall's case, "a sentence of imprisonment may work to promote not respect, but derision, of the law if the law is viewed as merely a means to dispense harsh punishment without taking into account the real conduct and circumstances involved in sentencing."

Section 3553(a)(6) requires judges to consider "the need to avoid unwarranted sentence disparities among defendants with similar records who have been found guilty of similar conduct." The Court of Appeals stated that "the record does not show that the district court considered whether a sentence of probation would result in unwarranted

---

32. District judges sentence, on average, 117 defendants every year. The District Judge in this case, Judge Pratt, has sentenced over 990 offenders over the course of his career. Only a relatively small fraction of these defendants appeal their sentence on reasonableness grounds.

disparities." As with the seriousness of the offense conduct, avoidance of unwarranted disparities was clearly considered by the Sentencing Commission when setting the Guidelines ranges. Since the District Judge correctly calculated and carefully reviewed the Guidelines range, he necessarily gave significant weight and consideration to the need to avoid unwarranted disparities. . . .

From these facts, it is perfectly clear that the District Judge considered the need to avoid unwarranted disparities, but also considered the need to avoid unwarranted *similarities* among other co-conspirators who were not similarly situated. The District Judge regarded Gall's voluntary withdrawal as a reasonable basis for giving him a less severe sentence than the three codefendants discussed with the AUSA, who neither withdrew from the conspiracy nor rehabilitated themselves as Gall had done. We also note that neither the Court of Appeals nor the Government has called our attention to a comparable defendant who received a more severe sentence.

Since the District Court committed no procedural error, the only question for the Court of Appeals was whether the sentence was reasonable — *i.e.,* whether the District Judge abused his discretion in determining that the § 3553(a) factors supported a sentence of probation and justified a substantial deviation from the Guidelines range. As we shall now explain, the sentence was reasonable. The Court of Appeals' decision to the contrary was incorrect and failed to demonstrate the requisite deference to the District Judge's decision.

V

The Court of Appeals gave virtually no deference to the District Court's decision that the § 3553(a) factors justified a significant variance in this case. Although the Court of Appeals correctly stated that the appropriate standard of review was abuse of discretion, it engaged in an analysis that more closely resembled *de novo* review of the facts presented and determined that, in its view, the degree of variance was not warranted.

The Court of Appeals thought that the District Court "gave too much weight to Gall's withdrawal from the conspiracy. . . ." This criticism is flawed in that it ignores the critical relevance of Gall's voluntary withdrawal, a circumstance that distinguished his conduct not only from that of all his codefendants, but from the vast majority of defendants convicted of conspiracy in federal court. The District Court quite reasonably attached great weight to the fact that Gall voluntarily withdrew from the conspiracy after deciding, on his own initiative, to change his life. This lends strong support to the District Court's conclusion that Gall is not going to return to criminal behavior and is not a danger to society. Compared to a case where the offender's rehabilitation occurred after he was charged with a crime, the District Court here had greater justification for believing Gall's turnaround was genuine, as distinct from a transparent attempt to build a mitigation case. . . .

Finally, the Court of Appeals thought that, even if Gall's rehabilitation was dramatic and permanent, a sentence of probation for participation as a middleman in a conspiracy distributing 10,000 pills of ecstasy "lies outside the range of choice dictated by the facts of the case." If the Guidelines were still mandatory, and assuming the facts did not justify a Guidelines-based downward departure, this would provide a sufficient basis for setting aside Gall's sentence because the Guidelines state that probation alone is not an appropriate sentence for comparable offenses. But the Guidelines are not mandatory, and thus the "range of choice dictated by the facts of the case" is significantly broadened. Moreover, the Guidelines are only one of the factors to consider when imposing sentence, and § 3553(a)(3) directs the judge to consider sentences other than imprisonment. . . .

The District Court quite reasonably attached great weight to Gall's self-motivated rehabilitation, which was undertaken not at the direction of, or under supervision by, any court, but on his own initiative. This also lends strong support to the conclusion that imprisonment was not necessary to deter Gall from engaging in future criminal conduct or to protect the public from his future criminal acts.

The Court of Appeals clearly disagreed with the District Judge's conclusion that consideration of the § 3553(a) factors justified a sentence of probation; it believed that the circumstances presented here were insufficient to sustain such a marked deviation from the Guidelines range. But it is not for the Court of Appeals to decide *de novo* whether the justification for a variance is sufficient or the sentence reasonable. On abuse-of-discretion review, the Court of Appeals should have given due deference to the District Court's reasoned and reasonable decision that the § 3553(a) factors, on the whole, justified the sentence. Accordingly, the judgment of the Court of Appeals is reversed.

[Concurring opinions of Justices SCALIA and SOUTER and dissenting opinions of Justices THOMAS and ALITO omitted.]

Notes and Questions

1. One of the purposes underlying the Guidelines sentencing regime is to promote uniformity — i.e., to eliminate unwarranted disparities in sentences. Yet Gall appears to be the only defendant who did not receive a substantial prison term. Why doesn't his sentence of probation raise significant concerns for the Court? When are substantial sentence *disparities* justified? When are substantial *similarities* in sentences unjustified?

2. The Court reiterated that the appropriate standard of review is abuse of discretion. Apart from the Court of Appeals' express requirement that a sentence outside the normal Guidelines range be justified by "extraordinary" circumstances, what factors suggest that the appellate court did not accord sufficient deference to the sentencing judge?

3. Now that the Guidelines are merely advisory, at what point should a sentencing judge take them into account? Should they be treated as a "starting point," an "ending point," or something in between?

4. What procedural hoops must a judge jump through before imposing a non-Guidelines sentence? Did the trial judge in *Gall* satisfy the procedural requirements before sentencing Gall to a term of probation?

5. Post-*Booker* case law — including *Rita, Gall,* and a handful of other Supreme Court decisions — endeavored to provide more concrete guidance to trial and appellate courts on several fronts, including what weight they should accord sentences prescribed by the Guidelines and, for appellate courts, how to conduct a reasonableness review under the deferential abuse of discretion standard.[33] The upshot of these rulings is

---

33. See Nelson v. United States, 129 S. Ct. 890 (2009); Spears v. United States, 129 S. Ct. 840 (2009); Gall v. United States, 128 S. Ct. 586 (2007); Kimbrough v. United States, 128 S. Ct. 558 (2007); Rita v. United States, 127 S. Ct. 2456 (2007).

roughly as follows: (1) sentencing judges may not presume that a sentence prescribed by the Guidelines is reasonable; (2) on appeal, a reviewing court may (but need not) presume that the sentence the trial judge imposed is reasonable; (3) a sentence outside the Guidelines range is not per se unreasonable, even though it may be based on the judge's policy disagreement with the applicable guideline; (4) the reviewing court may not presume that a sentence that is outside the specified Guidelines range is unreasonable; and (5) appellate courts must review all sentences under a deferential abuse of discretion standard regardless of how much the sentence may deviate from the normal Guidelines range.

Does this set of principles provide sufficient guidance to the lower courts? Does *Gall* resolve the question of what "reasonableness" means on appellate review?

4. Post-*Booker* Adjustments

In the post-*Booker* era, sentencing courts will consider a number of adjustments to the base offense level. These adjustments will generally fall within at least one of the following categories: enhancements, departures, and non-Guidelines factors. To facilitate consideration of sentencing adjustments, the sentencing record in United States v. Ebbers provides a baseline study. The government's sentencing memorandum lays the factual groundwork.

UNITED STATES v. EBBERS
GOVERNMENT'S MEMORANDUM OF LAW IN OPPOSITION
TO DEFENDANT'S SENTENCING MOTIONS
(June 24, 2005)

. . . BACKGROUND

On March 15, 2005, after an eight-week trial, a jury convicted Ebbers of one count of conspiracy to commit securities fraud, in violation of 18 U.S.C. § 371, one count of securities fraud, in violation of 15 U.S.C. § 78j(b), and seven counts of making false filings with the United States Securities and Exchange Commission ("SEC"), in violation of 15 U.S.C. § 78ff. As the Indictment in this case alleged — and as the evidence at trial overwhelmingly demonstrated — from October 2000 through June 2002, the defendant, the Chief Executive Officer of WorldCom, Inc. ("WorldCom") conspired with several other individuals in a scheme to defraud purchasers and sellers of World-Com common stock. The following factual summary is taken from the proof adduced at trial. . . .

II. EBBERS'S CRIMINAL CONDUCT

From in or about September 2000 through in or about June 2002, Ebbers and his co-conspirators engaged in an illegal scheme to deceive members of the investing public, WorldCom shareholders, securities analysts, the SEC, and others concerning WorldCom's true operating performance and financial results. As Ebbers and his co-conspirators knew, by no later than September 2000, WorldCom's true operating performance and financial results were in decline and had fallen materially below analysts' expectations. Ebbers nevertheless insisted that WorldCom publicly report financial results that met analysts' expectations. As a result, rather than disclosing WorldCom's true condition and suffer the ensuing decline in the price of WorldCom's common stock, Sullivan, with Ebbers's knowledge and approval, directed co-conspirators to make false and fraudulent adjustments to WorldCom's books and records.

Thereafter, from September 2000 through June 2002, for the purpose of disguising WorldCom's true operating performance and financial results, Ebbers and his co-conspirators caused WorldCom's reported figures for revenue, SG&A[34] and line cost expenses, EBITDA,[35] depreciation expense, net income, and EPS[36] to be falsely and fraudulently manipulated. As Ebbers and his co-conspirators knew, the aggregate effect of these adjustments, which were made in round-dollar amounts and consistently totaled hundreds of millions of dollars per quarter, was to present a materially false and misleading picture of WorldCom's true operating performance and financial results.

In furtherance of the scheme, Ebbers and his co-conspirators made repeated public statements in which they (a) falsely described WorldCom's operating performance and financial results, (b) omitted to disclose material facts necessary to make the statements that they made about WorldCom's operating performance and financial results complete, accurate, and not misleading, and (c) caused WorldCom to file financial statements with the SEC that presented a materially false and misleading description of WorldCom's operating performance and financial results. Through this scheme, Ebbers and his co-conspirators inflated and maintained artificially the price of WorldCom common stock.

On or about June 25, 2002, WorldCom announced that, as a result of an internal investigation, it would have to issue restated financial statements. In the days following this announcement, the price of WorldCom's common stock plummeted more than 90%, resulting in an aggregate decline in shareholder value of more than $2 billion. . . .

As was noted in the roadmap to Guidelines sentencing and in *Pinnick*, the Sentencing Guidelines begin with a base offense level and then provide a series of factors that are specific to the category of the particular offense and often to the individual offender that, where applicable, must be taken into account when calculating the sentence. Depending on the criminal activity involved, some of these factors may considerably enhance the length of the sentence imposed.

The sentencing process begins with a presentence report (PSR), in which the federal Probation Office prepares a report in which it calculates the applicable Guidelines sentence. In the *Ebbers* case, the base offense level was six, which would amount to a prison term of 0-6 months. But by the time the relevant enhancements were added to the mix, the PSR calculated the total offense level as 44, which translated into a sentence of

---

34. Selling, general, and administrative expenses. — ED.
35. Earnings before interest, taxes, depreciation, and amortization. — ED.
36. Earnings per share. — ED.

life in prison. The enhancements that so dramatically increased the recommended sentence included the amount of loss caused by the fraud, the number of victims, the amount of gain received as a result of the fraud, Ebbers' leadership role in devising and orchestrating the scheme, and his abuse of the position of trust that corporate officers and directors hold.

The findings and calculations contained in Ebbers' PSR are summarized in Table 14-2.

TABLE 14-2
EBBERS PRESENTENCE REPORT CALCULATIONS
BASE OFFENSE LEVEL PLUS ENHANCEMENTS

BASE OFFENSE LEVEL	**6**	**0-6 Months**
Loss (exceeds $2.2 billion)[37]	+26	
Victims (more than 50)	+4	
Gain (exceeds $1 million)	+2	
Role (organizer or leader)	+4	
Abuse of Position of Trust	+2	
Total Offense Level[38]	**44**	**Life Imprisonment**

a. Enhancements

As shown in Table 14-2, the base offense level for Ebbers' fraud was 6. Standing alone, that offense level would authorize imposition of no more than six months' imprisonment. But when all was said and done, the addition of a series of Guidelines enhancements raised his offense level to 44, which could carry a sentence of up to life in prison.

Not surprisingly, Ebbers objected to the Guidelines calculation contained in the pre-sentencing report in almost every respect. He argued that: enhancements based on the amount of loss, the number of victims, his deriving more than $1 million in gross receipts, his being a leader of criminal activity, and obstruction of justice were all inapplicable. The following text provides a context for considering the sentencing recommendations and evaluating Ebbers' objections to them.

Loss. The Guidelines adopt a sliding scale of enhancements based on the amount of loss caused by the fraud, provided that the amount of the loss exceeded $5,000. In determining the amount of loss resulting from a fraud offense, the sentencing court is not required to compute the loss with precision. The court need only make a reasonable estimate of the loss. In the context of the WorldCom fraud, such factors might include diminution in the value of the stock, the estimated number of victims multiplied by the

---

37. Although the PSR's recommendation for a 26-level increase was based on the conclusion that the loss exceeded $2.2 billion, the Guidelines would have triggered the 26-point enhancement upon a finding that the loss exceeded $100 million. The $100 million figure was the highest threshold amount for triggering an enhancement based on loss, and a 26-level increase was the largest loss-based enhancement under the 2001 version of the Guidelines, which the court found was applicable to Ebbers' conduct.

38. The total offense level exceeded the highest offense level — 43 — incorporated in the 2001 version of the Guidelines Sentencing Table.

average loss each victim incurred, the scope and duration of the fraud, and — in the context of securities fraud — the change of market capitalization resulting from disclosure of the fraud.

In the WorldCom case, the government established loss exceeding $100 million. The investment manager of Oppenheimer Capital testified that Oppenheimer owned approximately 200 million WorldCom shares on behalf of its client, which had a value of roughly $1.5 billion at WorldCom's peak. After WorldCom announced that it was restating its financial statements, Oppenheimer attempted to sell all of its approximately 200 million WorldCom shares but was able to sell only a million shares, resulting in a loss of approximately $200 million for its clients. Based on a calculation of total shares, moreover, the government demonstrated that a loss of more than $2 billion had occurred. Although the amount of loss ordinarily is not easily quantifiable, the court of appeals found that the loss caused by the WorldCom fraud clearly exceeded the $100 million threshold for Ebbers' 26-level enhancement. Although Ebbers argued that the decline in WorldCom's stock price was the result of market forces, the argument failed to carry the day.

Number of Victims. The Guidelines posit that frauds involving more than 50 victims by definition cause widespread harm and should be punished more severely than more limited fraudulent schemes. The principal victims of the WorldCom fraud were shareholders who bought or held WorldCom stock while the fraud was occurring and relied on the accuracy of WorldCom's financial statements or on the "integrity" of the market price.

Leadership Role. The Sentencing Guidelines provide for a four-level increase in the offense level if the defendant was an organizer or leader of criminal activity that involved five or more participants or that was otherwise extensive. This enhancement is appropriate where the defendant played a crucial role in planning, coordinating, and implementing the criminal scheme. A defendant qualifies as a leader as long as he organized or led at least one of the other participants. Under this standard, Ebbers clearly qualified as an organizer, as he was the driving force behind the fraud.

Ebbers and CFO Scott Sullivan engineered the fraud by improperly adjusting publicly reported revenues to meet the quarterly earnings estimates. At Ebbers' insistence, Sullivan instructed subordinates to make accounting adjustments that ultimately resulted in booking $3.8 billion in ordinary expenses as capital expenditures. By November 2002, WorldCom acknowledged that its illusory profits could top $9 billion.

Breach of Trust. If, as in the WorldCom fraud, the scheme involved violations of securities laws, the offense level will be increased by 4 if the defendant was an officer or director of a publicly traded company. The defendant need not be convicted of violating the securities laws, however. As long as the fraudulent scheme "involved" securities law violations, the defendant's conviction may be premised on a more general fraud statute such as mail or wire fraud. No specific finding of breach of trust is required, moreover. Officers and directors of publicly traded companies have heightened fiduciary duties, and as long as Ebbers was WorldCom's CEO at the time he committed the fraud, the enhancement automatically applies.

b. Downward Departures

Ebbers made a number of downward departure motions that the prosecution argued were inappropriate under Second Circuit law. Departures are allowed only if the court finds that there exists an aggravating or mitigating circumstance of a kind or degree not adequately taken into consideration by the Sentencing Commission in formulating the Guidelines and that the circumstance would justify a sentence outside the normal Guidelines range. Where a factor is already taken into account by the Guidelines, the court should depart only if the factor is present to an exceptional degree or if it otherwise distinguishes the case from the run-of-the mill case in which that factor is present. Because Ebbers sought the departure, he had the burden of showing by a preponderance of the evidence that the departure he sought should be granted.

Loss Versus Seriousness of Offense. The Guidelines state that there may be circumstances under which the offense level specified by the loss guideline could substantially overstate the seriousness of the offense. Thus, for example, where there are multiple defendants who each played the same organizational role in the fraud, it may be difficult to apportion the loss among them.[39] Similarly, the amount of loss may overstate the seriousness of the offense if there are multiple contributing causes. Although Ebbers argued that cases recognizing these principles supported his motion for a downward departure, the court disagreed. First, Ebbers clearly played the lead role in the World-Com fraud. He was both CEO and the instigator of the fraud. And even if other factors contributed to the decline of WorldCom's stock price, the sheer size of the loss still dwarfed even the largest amount of fraud contemplated by the loss tables. Ebbers also argued that the loss overstated the seriousness of the fraud because he received little or no personal gain. The absence of gain, however, is not a ground for departure.

Medical Condition. Under the Guidelines, a defendant's physical condition is usually not a ground for departure. A downward departure may be granted only in cases where the defendant suffers from an "extraordinary physical impairment" that cannot be adequately monitored and treated by the Bureau of Prisons.

Charity, Community Service, and Prior Good Works. Ebbers also sought a downward departure based on his exceptional history of community service and good works, but the Guidelines counsel against such departures. Civic or charitable work, public service, employment-related contributions, and similar prior good works are not ordinarily relevant in determining whether a sentence should be outside the normal Guidelines range. Courts should depart only if the factor is present to an exceptional degree, and no departure based purely on charitable work has been upheld in the Second Circuit, where Ebbers was prosecuted.

White collar criminals enjoy sufficient income and community status that they not only have the opportunity to engage in civic activities but are expected to do so. The Guidelines are intended to achieve sentencing parity for white collar and blue collar criminals, but this goal would be defeated if downward departures were allowed for

---

39. See, e.g., United States v. MacCaull, 2002 WL 31426006 (S.D.N.Y. Oct. 28, 2002) (unreported) (prosecution of 21 brokers in a stock boiler room operation that employed somewhere between 150 and 250 brokers).

white-collar criminals whose status facilitates their involvement in community service and charitable endeavors. Good works are laudable but fall far short of being so extraordinary as to justify a downward departure. Nor do the Sentencing Guidelines allow a downward departure merely because a defendant has shown kindness or because he has had an otherwise successful career. In any event, Ebbers did not document the specific amount of charitable contributions he made, so the prosecution argued there was no reason to believe that his charitable giving was exceptional.

Notes and Questions

1. Does measuring the sentence by the amount of loss ensure that a CEO or CFO of a large corporation will inevitably receive a sentence at the high end of the scale? If calculating Ebbers' offense largely on the basis of loss results in the equivalent of a life sentence, does the loss calculus exaggerate the seriousness of the crime? Is it relevant that the CEO or CFO may not have personally gained from the fraud?

2. Calculating a sentence on the basis of loss can be dauntingly complex. Should loss be measured by the decrease in the value of the corporation's shares after the fraud is revealed? How should other extrinsic factors be taken into account? And how should a court go about deciding how much of the loss is attributable to any particular defendant? The Fifth Circuit addressed these questions in United States v. Olis, 429 F.3d 540 (5th Cir. 2005), a case in which a mid-level manager was originally sentenced to 24 years in prison based largely on the trial court's calculation of the loss caused by the fraud. The court of appeals ruled that the loss calculation was erroneous and vacated the sentence. On remand, Olis was sentenced to a 6 year term. Should his status as a mid-level manager — rather than a high-level executive — be factored into the sentencing equation?

3. Under the Guidelines, a departure from the normal guideline range is warranted only if there is "an aggravating or mitigating circumstance of a kind, or to a degree, not adequately taken into consideration by the Sentencing Commission."[40] Under this policy the defendant's age, physical or mental condition, good character, vocational skills, charitable and community service, socioeconomic status, and other personal circumstances are "not ordinarily relevant" in determining the sentence.[41] If the circumstances are extraordinary, however, they may be taken into account. But the line between "ordinary" and "extraordinary" circumstances is exceedingly imprecise.[42]

Why would the Guidelines ordinarily exclude consideration of such personal factors? Should the Guidelines be more specific on these issues rather than leave the line-drawing function up to judges on a case-by-case basis?

---

40. Sentencing Guidelines § 5K2.0 (Policy Statement).
41. See Sentencing Guidelines §§ 5H1.1-5H1.6 (Policy Statements).
42. Compare United States v. Gaskill, 991 F.2d 82 (3d Cir. 1993) (upholding downward departure for defendant who was sole provider for manic-depressive wife who was unable to leave house or care for herself), and United States v. Pena, 930 F.2d 1486 (10th Cir. 1991) (upholding downward departure for single mother who was steadily employed and was the source of support for two infants and a 16 year-old daughter), with United States v. Goff, 20 F.3d 918 (8th Cir. 1994) (denying departure for defendant who provided sole support for three young sons and whose wife was disabled by depression and panic attacks), and United States v. Dyce, 91 F.3d 1462 (D.C. Cir. 1996) (denying departure for single mother of three children under the age of 4).

4. It was not contested that Ebbers had a serious heart condition. Under what circumstances would his medical condition provide a basis for a downward departure?

And what about age? Adelphia's CEO John Rigas, who was then 80 years old, was sentenced to a 15-year prison term, and the judge made it clear that but for Rigas's advanced years, his sentence would have been longer. In view of the surrounding circumstances, is the sentence the judge imposed too harsh?

5. Charitable good works are not ordinarily relevant. What would make good deeds sufficiently "extraordinary" to provide a basis for a downward departure?

6. What other types of factors should be considered as possible bases for providing downward departures? What about potential business failures that could (or would be likely to) occur as a result of the defendant's incarceration? Should the foreseeable effect of incarceration on innocent employees be considered in sentencing?

7. The kinds of personal characteristics and circumstances enumerated in Question 3 are disfavored, but not categorically excluded, as considerations for downward departures. But the Guidelines categorically exclude other characteristics such as race and gender as grounds for a downward departure. Why would the Sentencing Commission draw this distinction? Would it have been better to eliminate categorical exclusions altogether? Or at least to treat all categories of personal circumstances on par with one another?

UNITED STATES v. MARTIN
455 F.3d 1227 (11th Cir. 2006)

HULL, Circuit Judge.

This is the second time the government has appealed the sentence of defendant-appellee Michael Martin, a former HealthSouth Corporation ("HealthSouth") executive, who pled guilty to conspiracy to commit securities fraud and mail fraud and falsify books and records, and falsifying books and records. In both appeals the parties have agreed that Martin's advisory guidelines range is 108 to 135 months' imprisonment, and that Martin's substantial assistance to the government warrants a downward departure pursuant to U.S.S.G. § 5K1.1. The hotly contested dispute both times has been over whether the extremely lenient sentence the district court gave is reasonable.

The district court originally sentenced Martin to 60 months' probation. In the first appeal, this Court vacated that sentence for lack of a record capable of meaningful appellate review and remanded for resentencing.

At the resentencing, the government recommended a § 5K1.1 downward departure to 42 months' imprisonment, which equates to a 9-level departure. Instead, the district court granted Martin a 23-level downward departure and imposed a sentence of 7 days' imprisonment. The government again appeals. After review, we again vacate Martin's sentence in its entirety.

I. FACTUAL BACKGROUND . . .

[HealthSouth was one of the nation's largest health care providers, and its common stock was publicly traded.]

From at least 1994 until March 2003, a group of HealthSouth officers conspired to artificially inflate HealthSouth's reported earnings and earnings per share, and to falsify reports about HealthSouth's overall financial condition. . . . As a result, HealthSouth's public financial records overstated its financial position cumulatively by billions of dollars from 1994 to 2002, and public investors purchased overvalued shares of Health-South's stock, which plummeted from $3.91 per share to $.11 per share when the massive fraud was revealed.

Defendant Martin was employed by HealthSouth from 1989 to 2000, and served as its Chief Financial Officer ("CFO") from October 1997 until he resigned in March 2000. As early as 1994, Martin became aware that HealthSouth was not meeting its earnings-per-share projections. After Martin became CFO in 1997, he began reviewing quarterly preliminary income statements showing HealthSouth's true and accurate financial results, which showed that HealthSouth was not meeting earnings-per-share projections made by its Chief Executive Officer ("CEO"), Richard Scrushy. By Martin's own admission, at the direction of Scrushy, Martin falsified numbers to inflate HealthSouth's stated earnings to meet Scrushy's projections and Wall Street's expectations. . . .

. . . The most direct victims of the fraud were the investing public, HealthSouth shareholders, and the company. HealthSouth had many shareholders, some of whom invested their life savings in HealthSouth stock and saw their investment plummet to pennies per share. A conservative estimate of the stock value loss attributable to Martin's fraud was $1,390,800,000 or approximately $1.4 billion.

There were also many other collateral victims of Scrushy and Martin's fraud, including (1) HealthSouth employees, particularly those who were terminated and those who had participated in the company's stock ownership plan or pension fund; (2) employees of contractors who were dependent on HealthSouth contracts for income; (3) banks and other lenders who loaned money to HealthSouth based on falsified financial information; and (4) competing health service providers who lost business or financing based on the false information. See United States v. McVay, 447 F.3d 1348, 1350 (11th Cir. 2006).

Although many victims suffered devastating losses, HealthSouth's officers benefitted by receiving huge salaries and bonuses. Martin's income was over $14 million from just 1997 to 2000: $3,339,237 in 1997; $5,820,910 in 1998; $1,632,776 in 1999, and $4,080,959 in 2000. As detailed later, Martin agreed to a $2.375 million forfeiture, and the district court also imposed a $50,000 fine, both of which Martin immediately paid by check. At the time of the PSI in 2004, Martin had a net worth of over $8.9 million. . . .

III. DISCUSSION

Even after the Supreme Court's decision in United States v. Booker, 543 U.S. 220 (2005), in fashioning an appropriate sentence, the district court still must correctly calculate first the appropriate advisory Guidelines range. The district court then may consider imposing a more severe or more lenient sentence, and this Court reviews the ultimate sentence for reasonableness. "Before we conduct a reasonableness review of the ultimate sentence imposed, 'we first determine whether the district court correctly interpreted and applied the Guidelines to calculate the appropriate advisory Guidelines range.'" United States v. McVay, 447 F.3d 1348, 1353 (11th Cir. 2006). . . .

C. MARTIN'S SENTENCE

[Although the government did not dispute that Martin had provided substantial assistance that warranted a downward departure, it argued that the trial courts' 21-level departure and imposition of a 7 day sentence were "patently unreasonable" in view of his role in HealthSouth's massive and prolonged fraud.]

The government . . . relies on *McVay*, wherein this Court addressed the government's challenge to the same district court's extraordinary downward departure in sentencing one of Martin's co-conspirators. In that case, defendant McVay's guidelines range was 87 to 108 months' imprisonment, and the district court downwardly departed 21 levels (from an offense level 29 to an offense level 8) to a range of 0 to 6 months' imprisonment, and then imposed a sentence of 60 months' probation. *McVay*, 447 F.3d at 1349. As we did in the government's prior appeal in Martin's case, this Court vacated McVay's sentence and remanded, inter alia, because the district court failed to provide reasons for the departure, and thus the sentence was incapable of meaningful appellate review. As a result, this Court did not have occasion to decide the permissible extent of the § 5K1.1 departure or whether McVay's probationary sentence was reasonable. However, the Court in *McVay* did provide the following guidance about the reasonableness of a probationary sentence under the circumstances of the "multi-billion dollar securities fraud" at HealthSouth:

> We pause to note that, in the absence of truly compelling reasons — in the face of a multi-billion dollar securities fraud at the expense of the investing public — a six-month probationary term given to the Chief Financial Officer, Senior Vice-President, and Treasurer of the company at the time of the fraud (who signed the Form 10-Q with full knowledge of its falsity), is not easily reconcilable with the basic factors enumerated by Congress in § 3553(a), including the need for a sentence to reflect the seriousness of the offense, to promote respect for the law, and to provide just punishment.

Id. at 1357.[43]

In Martin's case, we now are squarely presented with the question of whether a 23-level departure under § 5K1.1 for his assistance and an ultimate sentence of 7 days' imprisonment for this multi-billion-dollar securities fraud are reasonable. The answer is easy: they are not.

The extent of the § 5K1.1 departure alone is unreasonable in this case. We fully accept the district court's determination that Martin's cooperation was extraordinary and merits a correspondingly extraordinary departure. Indeed, the government recognized this fact by recommending only a 42-month sentence even though (1) Martin's guidelines range was 108-135 months (i.e., from 9 to approximately 11 years), and (2) his statutory maximum was 15 years (i.e., 5 years on Count One and 10 on Count Two). We also recognize that there is always a range of reasonable § 5K1.1 choices that district courts are in the best position to make. However, the choice of a 23-level

---

43. In addition to its successful challenge to the sentence imposed in *McVay* and ultimately in *Martin*, the government had also successfully challenged the sentences of two other HealthSouth defendants who pled guilty and received exceptional downward departures from the same judge who sentenced Martin and McVay. See United States v. Livesay, 146 F. App'x 403 (11th Cir. 2005) (reversing sentence based on 18-level departure); United States v. Botts, 135 F. App'x 416 (11th Cir. 2005) (reversing sentence based on 26-level departure). — ED.

guidelines departure under § 5K1.1 to a 0-6 months guidelines range was unreasonable where Martin's crimes yielded an advisory guidelines range of 9-11 years' imprisonment and a potential sentence of 15 years. Martin's cooperation, while commendable and extremely valuable, is not a get-out-of-jail-free card. Martin's cooperation does not wash the slate clean. Yet departing 23 levels to a 0-6 months range effectively accomplishes that by permitting a sentence of no jail time at all, or 7 days, which is close to none. . . .

Turning to the ultimate sentence, the district court's 7-day sentence is shockingly short and wholly fails to serve the purposes of sentencing set forth by Congress in § 3553(a). Martin's crimes and the district court's punishment are so wildly disproportionate that we readily conclude that the district court's 7-day sentence is also unreasonable and must be vacated. We explain the many reasons why the district court erred in its consideration of the § 3553(a) factors, and why we, for the second time, must vacate Martin's sentence.

First, the district court's 7-day sentence wholly fails to take into account the nature and circumstances of the offense and the need for the sentence to reflect the seriousness of the crime. Martin knowingly participated in a massive and prolonged fraud, served as a leader in that fraud, financially benefitted substantially from the fraud, and cooperated only after the fraud was revealed. While the district court emphasized Martin's lack of a criminal record and viewed his fraudulent conduct as an "aberration" in his otherwise outstanding life, Martin's criminal history category of I already takes into account his lack of a criminal record. Despite this lack of a criminal record, Martin's offense conduct spanned a period of years, during which Martin consistently abused the public trust and played a leadership role in a conspiracy that resulted in over a billion dollars of loss harming thousands of victims. Martin's crimes are major league economic crimes that harmed not only individual victims but also many institutions and companies. This type and scale of crime is peculiarly corrosive to the economic life of the community, as demonstrated by the deleterious effects the large-scale fraud in this case had on the healthcare industry and the securities markets. Martin not only participated in this fraud for over three years as HealthSouth's CFO before finally resigning, he also chose not to approach authorities about the conspiracy until they had learned independently about his criminal conduct. Put simply, the 7-day sentence imposed by the district court wholly fails to take into account the egregious years-long nature of Martin's crimes.

The 7-day sentence imposed by the district court also utterly fails to afford adequate deterrence to criminal conduct. Because economic and fraud-based crimes are "more rational, cool, and calculated than sudden crimes of passion or opportunity," these crimes are "prime candidate[s] for general deterrence." Stephanos Bibas, White-Collar Plea Bargaining and Sentencing After Booker, 47 Wm. & Mary L. Rev. 721, 724 (2005). Defendants in white collar crimes often calculate the financial gain and risk of loss, and white collar crime therefore can be affected and reduced with serious punishment. Yet the message of Martin's 7-day sentence is that would-be white-collar criminals stand to lose little more than a portion of their ill-gotten gains and practically none of their liberty.

Our assessment is consistent with the views of the drafters of § 3553. As the legislative history of the adoption of § 3553 demonstrates, Congress viewed deterrence as "particularly important in the area of white collar crime." Congress was especially concerned that prior to the Sentencing Guidelines, "[m]ajor white collar criminals often [were] sentenced to small fines and little or no imprisonment. Unfortunately, this creates the impression that certain offenses are punishable only by a small fine that can be written off as a cost of doing business." S. Rep. No. 98-225, at 76 (1983). . . .

While the district court stated summarily that "[Martin's] devastating experience will deter others similarly situated from engaging in similar criminality," the district court failed to explain how Martin's 7-day sentence contributes to general deterrence in any way. The district court's confidence that "this defendant has been effectively deterred from any further criminal conduct" speaks to the goal of preventing recidivism, but not to the general need "to afford adequate deterrence to criminal conduct." . . .

Rather than deter crime by others, Martin's 7-day sentence suggests that those similarly situated to Martin could profit from fraudulent conduct and, even if caught, escape severe consequences by cooperating with the government after the fact.

Finally, the district court erred by justifying Martin's lenient sentence in part on the basis that "from the point of view of the government, the man most singularly responsible for this criminal conduct [Richard Scrushy] has been found not guilty and will serve no time at all." Regardless of the government's original theory of the overall fraud scheme in this case, § 3553(a)(6) does not permit the district court to compare Martin's sentence with the "sentence" of a man whom a jury acquitted of criminal conduct, however groundless that acquittal may seem in light of the evidence in this record. While the need for consistent sentences among similarly situated defendants is a statutory sentencing factor, § 3553(a)(6) confines that consideration to "the need to avoid unwarranted sentenc[ing] disparities among defendants with similar records who have been found guilty of similar conduct." 18 U.S.C. § 3553(a)(6). Because Scrushy was found not guilty, he is not a valid comparator for § 3553(a)(6) purposes. As a result, the fact that Scrushy will not serve prison time is utterly irrelevant to Martin's sentence.

In sum, we agree with the government's position in its brief: "If any sentence is unreasonable, it is this one." A much less substantial departure than that awarded by the district court would properly reward Martin for his substantial and extraordinary cooperation, encourage others in his position to cooperate, and satisfy the goals embodied in § 3553(a). Martin's cooperation, even viewed as extraordinary and commendable, cannot erase the enormity of Martin's underlying criminal conduct in the billion-dollar fraud scheme he played a major role in perpetrating.

We do not express an opinion as to what would constitute a reasonable sentence. The district court on remand will exercise discretion in fashioning an appropriate sentence consistent with what we have stated in this opinion, and there is a range of reasonable sentences. A 7-day sentence is not nearly within that range. It is not remotely commensurate with the seriousness and extensive scale of the crimes and does not promote respect for the law, does not provide just punishment for the offense, as § 3553(a)(2)(A) requires, and does not afford adequate deterrence to the criminal conduct here, as § 3553(a)(2)(B) mandates. Accordingly, we vacate Martin's sentence and remand this case for resentencing in a manner consistent with this opinion and with the Supreme Court's decision in *Booker*.

V. REASSIGNMENT

Finally, based on our review of the record and the elements that this Court considers in determining whether to reassign a case to a different judge where there is no indication of actual bias, we have determined it wiser to remand this case with instructions to reassign it to a different judge. This is the second appeal in Martin's case and the second time we have had to reverse the sentence that the district court gave Martin. On remand, the district court changed its sentence from 60 months' probation to only 7 days' imprisonment and failed to properly take into account the § 3553(a) factors. In light of the two reversals in this case and three other appeals in which we have reversed the same judge for extraordinary downward departures that were without a valid basis in the record, we find it likely that "the original judge would have difficulty putting his previous views and findings aside."

Notes and Questions

1. Since the government agreed with the court that Martin's cooperation was extraordinary and merited a significant downward departure and further agreed that the court properly calculated the applicable guidelines range, why was the sentence "shockingly short" and "wildly disproportionate"? What factors serve as counterweights to the trial court's reliance on the value of Martin's cooperation in determining the length of the sentence?

2. Martin's sentence included a $50,000 fine and $2.375 million forfeiture. His net worth exceeded $8.9 million, and he immediately paid his $50,000 fine and $2.375 million forfeiture by check. Should his wealth and liquidity be factored in during the sentencing phase of the proceeding?

3. Although Martin provided extensive cooperation and testified against Scrushy at trial, the jury found Scrushy not guilty. The trial judge rationalized Martin's seven-day sentence as follows: "According to the government, the man most guilty has been found not guilty and will serve no time at all."[44] Should Scrushy's acquittal be taken into account in evaluating Martin's cooperation for sentencing purposes?

4. It is highly unusual for an appellate court to reassign a case to a different district judge on remand. What prompted this move in *Martin*? What does this case tell us about the trial judge's attitude toward the Sentencing Guidelines? Was his approach consistent with *Booker*?

5. Martin's third sentencing proceeding resulted in the imposition of a 36 month prison term. Absent a downward departure, the applicable guidelines range was 109-135 months, and the government had recommended a 42 month sentence. Is the 36 month sentence reasonable in light of the relevant facts and circumstances?

c. Non-Guidelines Considerations

Federal sentencing law directs courts to consider a variety of non-Guidelines factors to ensure that the sentence imposed is "sufficient, but not greater than necessary," to serve the ends of justice.[45] Now that the Supreme Court has ruled that the Guidelines themselves are only advisory, non-Guidelines factors have assumed even greater significance in the sentencing process.

---

44. Michael Tomberlin, Ex-CFO to Serve Week in Prison, Birmingham News, Sept. 21, 2005, at E1.
45. See 18 U.S.C. § 3553(a).

UNITED STATES v. EBBERS
GOVERNMENT'S MEMORANDUM OF LAW IN OPPOSITION
TO DEFENDANT'S SENTENCING MOTIONS

. . . IV. Application of Factors Under 18 U.S.C. § 3553(a)

In light of the Supreme Court's decision in *Booker*, the Court must now consider an array of other factors, in addition to the Sentencing Guidelines, when determining the appropriate sentence for a defendant. In that regard, Ebbers provided the court with a detailed discussion of various factors under Section 3553(a) of Title 18. In weighing these factors, the Court should consider certain counterbalancing facts, as set forth below.

A. The Nature and Circumstances of the Offense

An initial factor for the Court to consider is the nature and circumstances of the offense. 18 U.S.C. § 3553(a)(1).

Here, the enormity of the crimes that Ebbers committed cannot be overstated: the fraud at WorldCom was the largest securities fraud in history. Along with Enron, the name WorldCom has become synonymous with fraud. The revelation of the fraud at WorldCom caused a dramatic blow to investor confidence and spawned a revolution in the enforcement of the securities laws. In direct response to the fraud at WorldCom, new laws were passed that strengthened the ability to police corporate misconduct and a Presidential Task force was created to monitor corporate fraud across the country.

One person established the culture that allowed this fraud to occur and, more fundamentally, specifically directed WorldCom employees to commit fraud rather than reveal WorldCom's true financial condition to the public: Bernard Ebbers. And what's more, Ebbers caused this fraud to occur for one reason: to prop up WorldCom's stock price in order to avoid personal financial ruin. In directing this fraud, not only did Ebbers fail to save himself from financial ruin, but his conduct hastened this former Fortune 500 company's trip into bankruptcy and caused literally tens of thousands — or more — of innocent shareholders to suffer billions of dollars in losses. These factors merit consideration in deriving the appropriate sentence.

B. The Court Should Consider General Deterrence

One of the factors the Court must consider in imposing sentence is the need for the sentence to "afford adequate deterrence to criminal conduct." 18 U.S.C. § 3553(a)(2)(B). Ebbers claims that "the message to corporate America has already been sent" by means of his highly publicized trial and conviction. The Government disagrees. Corporate executives across the country, and the American public as a whole, will be measuring the seriousness of Ebbers' conduct in part by the seriousness of his sentence. More importantly, corporate executives will, in the future, consider the sentence imposed on Ebbers whenever those executives are tempted to mislead shareholders or manipulate the financial statements of their companies. General deterrence serves an important function and works, perhaps even more effectively than in the context of other types of criminal conduct, to prevent financial crimes of the sort committed by

Ebbers. Thus, to effect the goal of general deterrence, the Court should impose a sentence commensurate with the nature and seriousness of his crime and sufficient to cause others who may be tempted to engage in similar conduct to refrain from criminal activity for fear of the potential sanctions that might follow.

The defense argues that a substantial term of imprisonment is not necessary to achieve the goals of general deterrence in this case. The defense suggests that defendants such as Ebbers are peculiarly sensitive to the "ignominy" of conviction and, therefore, the fear of "ignominy" alone is sufficient to achieve general deterrence. This argument fails for two reasons. First, recent history has starkly demonstrated that the risk of a felony conviction alone has not been sufficient to deter corporate executives who are tempted to put their personal financial interests above their legal and fiduciary duties to make full and truthful disclosures to their shareholders and creditors. Second, the defense argument, at its core, relies on premises inimical to basic principles of equal application of the laws. The defense argument boils down to a claim that defendants who have all the advantages that education, business experience, reputation and wealth can provide, should be sentenced more lightly because, for them, the embarrassment of conviction and the stigma of prison are more devastating.

C. THE NEED TO AVOID UNWARRANTED SENTENCE DISPARITIES

The Sentencing Guidelines were promulgated, in part, to minimize disparities in federal sentences. Although those Guidelines are no longer mandatory, the importance of eliminating sentencing disparities remains an important factor which the Court must separately consider pursuant to 18 U.S.C. § 3553(a)(7).

Although securities fraud prosecutions are by no means rare in this District, there have been very few recent sentences in cases which involved truly similar criminal conduct. Measured in terms of the extent of the harm caused (both in terms of the financial losses and number of victims), the scope and complexity of the schemes, and duration of the schemes, Ebbers's conduct is rare. However, there are three fairly analogous cases within the past ten years: John Rigas, Patrick Bennett and Steven Hoffenberg.

John J. Rigas was the founder, Chairman of the Board of Directors and Chief Executive Officer of Adelphia, which in 2002 was the sixth largest cable television service provider in the United States. Rigas and his co-conspirators simply looted Adelphia for their personal benefit and the benefit of their family. Further, like Ebbers, Rigas lied to public investors about Adelphia's financial and operational performance by fraudulently: (a) understating Adelphia's debts to banks and concealing the size of Adelphia's liability for borrowings by the Rigas family under various co-borrowing agreements; (b) overstating Adelphia's EBITDA in nearly every quarterly and year-end financial report; (c) overstating the number of Adelphia's subscribers and the pace at which Adelphia was rebuilding its physical plant; and (d) representing that the Rigas family had invested cash of more than $1.6 billion to purchase newly-issued Adelphia securities, when in fact those securities had effectively been stolen from Adelphia.

Rigas's fraudulent schemes wreaked financial havoc on both Adelphia and the many thousands of investors who entrusted billions of dollars to him and his co-conspirators as officers and fiduciaries of Adelphia. Between August 1998 and January 2002, Adelphia sold to the public approximately $4.5 billion in bonds and convertible notes. During that same period, Adelphia raised an additional $4.8 billion in capital through the public sale of newly issued common and preferred stock. As of January 2, 2002, 228,600,000 shares of Adelphia's Class A common stock had been issued to the public and were valued at $31.85 per share, for a market capitalization of approximately $7 billion. The majority of those investments, including essentially all of Adelphia's multi-billion dollar equity market capitalization, were lost as a direct result of the crimes perpetrated by the defendants.

On June 20, 2005, the Honorable Leonard B. Sand sentenced John Rigas to 15 years' imprisonment. This sentence was a non-Guidelines sentence, as Judge Sand calculated Rigas's Sentencing Guidelines range to be life imprisonment, with a statutory maximum of 215 years' imprisonment. In imposing a non-Guidelines sentence, Judge Sand made clear that he was considering Rigas's age (80 years old) and poor health. Were these factors not present, Judge Sand indicated that he would have imposed a greater sentence.[46]

Patrick Bennett was the CFO of the Bennett Funding Group ("BFG"), a company which specialized in providing equipment leasing and financing for office equipment. BFG started as a small family-owned business. Patrick Bennett's father was the Chairman of the company and his brother was the Chief Operating Officer. Although, unlike WorldCom, BFG never went public, BFG raised capital by selling debt securities and interests in the equipment leases that BFG originated. Following two jury trials, Bennett was convicted of numerous counts of money laundering, securities fraud, and bank fraud. The evidence at trial demonstrated that, among other schemes, Patrick Bennett (1) engaged in accounting fraud by inflating BFG's revenue as reported to debt-holders in audited financial statements in two separate years; and (2) securitized and sold to investors leases that did not exist and/or leases that had been previously sold to other investors. See United States v. Bennett, 252 F.2d 559, 560-61 (2d Cir. 2001). As a result of selling leases that did not exist, BFG quickly turned into both a massive accounting fraud and one of the largest Ponzi schemes ever prosecuted. The losses from Bennett's conduct, as found by the Probation Department, exceeded $600 million. Id. at 565. And the number of victims reached well into the thousands.

Bennett was sentenced under an earlier version of the Sentencing Guidelines which prescribed a sentencing range of 188 to 235 months. Id. at 561. At sentencing, the Honorable John S. Martin upwardly departed from that range and imposed a term of imprisonment of 30 years based, in part, on efforts by Patrick Bennett and his wife to shield some of the proceeds of the fraud from recovery by the victims. Bennett appealed from his sentence and the Second Circuit, finding that the wife's refusal to voluntarily return assets was not a proper basis for an upward departure, remanded for reconsideration of the upward departure. Id. at 565. Bennett also challenged the 30 year sentence on Eighth Amendment grounds. Even though the Circuit's remand mooted the Eighth Amendment issue, the Court took pains to resolve the question. In language that would be equally applicable on the facts here, the Court stated: "[w]hether the final sentence is thirty years or twenty years (or something in between), we think there is no disproportion between sentence and conduct. Bennett's conduct wiped out the savings of thousands of people, and is not longer than the sentences meted out in other large fraud cases." Id. at 567.

---

46. Indeed, Judge Sand sentenced Timothy Rigas, Adelphia's former CFO, to 20 years' imprisonment.

On remand, Judge Martin again upwardly departed and imposed a sentence of twenty-two years on the basis of the extraordinary amount of the loss, the number of victims, and Bennett's efforts to shield his assets by placing them in his wife's name while the scheme was ongoing. See United States v. Bennett, No. 02-1379 (2d Cir. Sep. 18, 2003) (unpublished).

Similarly, the Honorabl[e] Robert Sweet imposed a sentence of twenty years' imprisonment on Steven Hoffenberg. See United States v. Hoffenberg, 1997 WL 96563 (S.D.N.Y. Mar. 5, 1997). Hoffenberg was the CEO and Chairman of Towers Financial Corporation (Towers). Through various subsidiaries, Towers was engaged in the insurance business as well as providing receivables financing. Id. at *3-4. Although Hoffenberg's relevant conduct included schemes to defraud various insurance regulators, the principal offense for which he was sentenced involved the fraudulent sales of notes to investors. As a result of Hoffenberg's fraudulent note sales, more than 3,000 victims suffered losses of approximately $475 million. Id. at *6. After considering the factors set forth in Section 3553(a), Judge Sweet stated:

> The greatest weight must be given to retribution and just punishment. Here, an unstable individual with manic tendencies and a sense of grandiosity violated the law in order to satisfy his own greed and sense of entitlement. His acts resulted in the loss of the savings and investments of thousands of people. Not only must he be punished, he must be effectively barred from causing further damage to the society.

Id. at *14.

By any objective measure of the harm caused, Ebbers's conduct was as detrimental to shareholders as that of John Rigas and was demonstrably worse than that of Patrick Bennett and Steven Hoffenberg. The Government respectfully submits that the sentences imposed on Ebbers should therefore be proportionate to the sentences imposed in those cases.

Notes and Questions

1. One non-Guidelines statutory factor to be considered is "the nature and circumstances of the offense." Does this provide any real guidance to sentencing judges? Is it so indeterminate that a judge who dislikes the Guidelines could, in reality, disregard them altogether? Under the facts of the WorldCom fraud, how should Ebbers' offense be characterized for purposes of this sentencing factor?

2. When will a sentence afford "adequate deterrence"? How is the sentencing judge supposed to know whether a sentence will over-deter, under-deter, or provide just about the right level of deterrence?

3. The government's memorandum ends where the Sentencing Commission began: searching for a sentencing regime that will avoid unwarranted disparities. The government cites sentences that were imposed in three other cases of high-end fraud — arguably comparable to the fraud at WorldCom — as benchmarks for the sentence that Ebbers should receive. Is this an appropriate measure of disparity given the government's concession that "there have been very few recent sentences in cases which involved truly similar criminal conduct"?

Assuming arguendo that it is, are the three cases the government relied on sufficiently similar to justify using the sentences imposed as a guide for sentencing Ebbers? Are there salient differences? What criteria should be used to gauge whether the fraud at WorldCom was comparable to, worse than, or less egregious than the fraud at Adelphia? Than the fraud in the Patrick Bennett and Steven Hoffenberg cases?

Since the statutory goal is to avoid *unwarranted* disparity, the clear implication is that not all disparity is undesirable. When is disparity warranted?

NOTE ON THE EBBERS SENTENCE

By and large, Judge Jones agreed with the government and rejected most of Ebbers' sentencing arguments. In particular, she agreed with the PSR that the loss exceeded the Guidelines' threshold of more than $100 million and thus justified a 26-level increase in the base offense level. She also agreed that enhancements were warranted on the grounds that there were more than 50 victims, that Ebbers was a leader of the criminal scheme, and that Ebbers abused a position of trust.[47] Similarly, she rejected all of Ebbers' downward departure arguments, but indicated that she would take some of the factors into account in deciding what an appropriate sentence would be.

When all was said and done, Judge Jones found that the proper Guidelines offense level was 42 and that the corresponding sentence range was 30 years to life. But that was not the end of the road. Instead, after weighing the available options, she decided to impose a non-Guidelines sentence.

Notes and Questions

1. Does the sentence the judge imposed serve the ends of justice? Why would a sentence of 30 years be "excessive" and "unnecessary" but a sentence of 25 years be necessary and appropriate?

2. All parties appear to have assumed that a sentence of imprisonment would be imposed. Was prison the most appropriate sentence in Ebbers's case? Is he a threat to society? Is he likely to repeat his crimes?

3. Was it proper for the judge to consider the settlement in the class action securities litigation as part of the criminal sentencing calculus?

III. FINES

A. AUTHORIZED LEVELS

Monetary fines are usually imposed in white collar prosecutions. It is a frequent complaint, however, that the authorized fines for white collar offenses are woefully inadequate to either deter or punish. That is particularly true with respect to corporate

---

47. She rejected enhancements based on claims that Ebbers received more than $1 million from a financial institution as a result of the fraud and that he obstructed justice by testifying falsely at his trial.

defendants. Mail and wire fraud, for example, long mainstays of white collar prosecutions, for decades were punishable by a maximum fine of $1,000.[48]

Congress began to take interest in the adequacy of penalties for corporate and white collar offenses in the aftermath of the Watergate scandal. In addition to dramatically increasing authorized fines for many crimes, Congress took the significant step of creating bifurcated penalty structures that designate larger maximum fines for organizations than for individuals. The Antitrust Procedures and Penalties Act of 1974, for example, raised the stakes for antitrust defendants by reclassifying antitrust violations from misdemeanors to felonies and authorizing a fine of up to $100,000 for individuals and a maximum fine of $1 million for organizations.[49] Congress has since utilized similar bifurcated fine structures in many other statutes.

Although piecemeal revision of the criminal penalty provisions in the United States Code increased the deterrent value of fines for some crimes, it was an incomplete answer to the problem. Thus, in 1984, Congress adopted a global approach to reforming criminal fines in the Criminal Fine Enforcement Act. The revised penalties are not limited to Title 18 (i.e., criminal code) offenses. Instead, they apply to all federal statutes containing criminal penalty provisions (e.g., securities, tax, and environmental laws) regardless of which title of the United States Code they are codified in. The alternative fines authorized by the Act in most instances greatly exceed the fines authorized by specific criminal statutes. The alternative fine levels are set forth in Table 14-3.

TABLE 14-3
MAXIMUM FINES UNDER 18 U.S.C. § 3571

OFFENSE	INDIVIDUALS	ORGANIZATIONS
Felony	$250,000	$500,000
Misdemeanor resulting in death	$250,000	$500,000
Class A misdemeanor not resulting in death	$100,000	$200,000
Class B or C misdemeanor not resulting in death	$5,000	$10,000
Infraction	$5,000	$10,000

The court may deviate from these fine limitations if the offense is one that results in pecuniary gain to *any person* or that results in pecuniary harm to someone other than the offender. In either event the court may impose a fine of as much as twice the gross gain or loss, unless using gain or loss as a benchmark for calculating the fine would "unduly complicate or prolong the sentencing process."[50] These outer limits on fines do

---

48. That may explain the government's strategy in requiring E. F. Hutton to plead guilty to 2,000 counts of mail fraud in connection with the firm's questionable cash management practices. By charging such a large number of counts, the government was able to obtain the then-highest-ever fine in a white collar prosecution — $2 million. Although the use of multiple counts is not unusual in mail fraud prosecutions, the government's decision to charge 2,000 counts against Hutton was highly unusual.

49. 15 U.S.C. § 3.

50. 18 U.S.C. § 3571.

not apply to statutes that specifically authorize higher fines — as is true of a number of statutes today.[51]

B. CORPORATE FINES

In addition to creating a bifurcated system of fines for individuals and organizations and greatly increasing the maximum authorized fine, the Sentencing Reform Act and Sentencing Guidelines significantly changed the way in which corporations are fined. The Act directs the sentencing judge to consider the size of the corporation, what measures the organization has taken to discipline responsible employees, and what steps it has taken to prevent recurrence of the wrongdoing.[52]

The guidelines for sentencing organizations make the calculation of corporate fines more complicated than in the past.[53] Subject to *Booker*'s holding that courts should treat the Guidelines as advisory, the sentencing court will (1) employ one of three alternative methods for calculating a base fine; (2) determine the organization's "culpability score" on the basis of specified aggravating and mitigating factors; (3) use the culpability score to determine minimum and maximum multipliers; (4) multiply the base fine by those multipliers to arrive at the range of fines that may be imposed; and (5) select a fine from within that range, using as guidance another set of factors relating to considerations such as the organization's role in the offense, collateral consequences of conviction, the vulnerability of the victim, and other similar factors.

The aggravating factors focus on whether high level or other responsible personnel participated in or tolerated the criminal activity; whether the organization has a history of prior similar misconduct; whether the commission of the offense violated a judicial order or injunction; and whether the organization obstructed justice during the course of the investigation, trial, or sentencing.

The mitigating factors focus on whether the organization had an effective program to prevent and detect violations, and whether the organization promptly reported the offense, cooperated fully in the investigation, and accepted responsibility.

Notes and Questions

1. What disincentives does a corporation have to report an offense to the authorities and cooperate in the investigation? Are they outweighed by the prospect of a reduced fine? By the prospect of entering into a deferred prosecution agreement with the government?[54]

---

51. Cf. 18 U.S.C. § 1350 (Sarbanes-Oxley false certification offense punishable by a fine of $1 million for knowing violations and $5 million for willful violations).

52. 18 U.S.C. § 3572.

53. The organizational guidelines were submitted to Congress in 1991. For data on prior sentencing practices, see Mark A. Cohen, Corporate Crime and Punishment: A Study of Social Harm and Sentencing Practice in the Federal Courts, 1984-1987, 26 Am. Crim. L. Rev. 605 (1989); Jeffrey S. Parker, Criminal Sentencing Policy for Organizations: The Unifying Approach of Optimal Penalties (Appendix: United States Sentencing Commission Staff Study), 26 Am. Crim. L. Rev. 513, 594 (1989).

54. See, e.g., Letter from David N. Kelley, United States Attorney, Southern District of New York, to Robert S. Bennett, Esq., Re: KPMG — Deferred Prosecution Agreement (Aug. 26, 2005); Deferred Pros-

2. For an example of another type of incentive to report corporate wrongdoing and the grief it can sometimes cause, see United States v. Rockwell International Corp., 924 F.2d 928 (9th Cir. 1991).

_____

As we have seen in earlier chapters, one significant feature of the Sarbanes-Oxley Act's criminal provisions is the Act's reliance on increased criminal penalties. That being true, it should come as no surprise that the task of implementing the new penalties fell on the Sentencing Commission.

KATHLEEN F. BRICKEY, ENRON'S LEGACY
8 Buff. Crim. L. Rev. 221, 232-234 (2004)

Sarbanes-Oxley directed the United States Sentencing Commission to review existing sentencing guidelines applicable to high-end fraud, obstruction of justice, and other white collar crimes, with the expectation that the Commission would require longer sentences than in the past. Although critics predicted that Sarbanes-Oxley's enhanced penalties were unlikely to increase the length of sentences actually imposed, the revised guidelines require substantially longer prison time in several categories of cases. The guidelines amendments increase the minimum sentence for large-scale frauds by about 25 percent and triple the sentence for Enron-like frauds that endanger the solvency or financial security of a substantial number of victims or a publicly traded company. The amendments also increase sentences imposed on corporate officers and directors who are convicted of securities fraud by about 50 percent solely because they are corporate executives, and increase by more than five years the minimum sentence for crimes that cause economic loss of more than $400 million.

Sarbanes-Oxley also directed the Commission to review the organizational sentencing guidelines to ensure that authorized sentences are adequate to deter and punish institutional wrongdoing. After conducting a two-year review, the Commission adopted the first amendments to the organizational sentencing guidelines since they became law in 1991. Reflecting norms embedded in Sarbanes-Oxley, the amendments are designed to foster a culture of compliance.

The organizational guidelines require the sentencing court to consider a series of aggravating and mitigating factors in determining the appropriate sentence. If the corporation has an effective compliance program to prevent and detect criminal conduct, that will mitigate the sentence imposed. The Sarbanes-Oxley amendments retain this basic approach but adopt more rigorous criteria for evaluating what constitutes an effective compliance program.

First, in addition to requiring the exercise of due diligence to prevent and detect criminal wrongdoing, the amended guidelines broaden the stated objectives of corporate compliance programs to include promoting an institutional culture that "encourages *ethical* conduct" as well as a commitment to legal compliance.[55] Toward that end, the amended guidelines set minimum standards and procedures for devising, implementing,

_____

ecution Agreement Between Christopher J. Christie, United States Attorney, District of New Jersey, and Bristol-Myers Squibb Co. (June 13, 2005).

55. 2004 Guidelines Amendments § 8B2.1(a)(2) (emphasis added).

and enforcing the organization's compliance program. Second, the amendments broaden the role of senior management and the board of directors in implementing and monitoring compliance programs and disqualify the corporation from receiving a mitigated sentence based on its compliance program if high-level executives either participated in, condoned, or were willfully ignorant of the wrongdoing. And third, the amendments provide that periodic risk assessment is crucial to an effective compliance program.

Notes and Questions

1. One of the stated goals of the revised organizational Sentencing Guidelines is to promote an ethical corporate culture. In what sense do corporations have cultures? Are sentencing guidelines an appropriate vehicle for addressing business ethics?

2. Why should senior management and the board of directors be required to play an increased role in implementing and monitoring compliance programs?

3. If a corporation has an otherwise effective compliance program, is it appropriate to deny the corporation a mitigated sentence if one or two high-level executives were willfully ignorant of the wrongdoing?

UNITED STATES v. EUREKA LABORATORIES, INC.
103 F.3d 908 (9th Cir. 1996)

THOMPSON, Circuit Judge.

Defendant Eureka Laboratories, Inc. (ELI) and two of its managers were charged in an eight-count superseding information with conspiracy to defraud the United States and other crimes arising from ELI's alleged fraudulent manipulations of analytical tests, in violation of 18 U.S.C. §§ 287, 371, and 1001. After the trial began, ELI pleaded guilty to all counts.

During sentencing, the district court imposed a $1.5 million fine on ELI. The district court also ordered ELI to pay both restitution in the amount of $322,442 and a special assessment of $1600. . . .

FACTS

ELI is an analytical testing laboratory engaged in analyzing soil, air, and water samples provided by governmental and private clients. Between February 1991, and August 1993, ELI was awarded contracts with the United States Environmental Protection Agency (EPA), the United States Department of the Army (Army), and the United States Department of the Air Force (Air Force), to analyze environmental samples in connection with the evaluation and remediation of Superfund hazardous waste sites. ELI fraudulently manipulated analytical tests during its performance of these government contracts.

ELI was charged in an eight-count superseding information with conspiracy to defraud the United States and other crimes arising from its fraudulent activities. ELI pleaded guilty to all eight counts.

During sentencing, based upon the invoices paid to ELI on its government contracts and the reasonably foreseeable reprocurement costs incurred by the government agencies as a result of ELI's fraudulent conduct, the district court determined the estimated total loss to the government from ELI's fraudulent activities to be approximately $4.6 million. Using this figure as a base, the court determined that the sentencing guideline range for ELI's fine was between $6,425,013 and $9,178,590.

The presentence report recommended a departure below the fine calculated by reference to the guideline range because of ELI's financial condition. The probation officer calculated ELI's assets, including cash, property, and other equipment, at approximately $2.5 million. Between the years 1990 and 1993, ELI generated from $3.5 to $4.8 million in annual revenues. However, after 1993, ELI's revenues steadily deteriorated because of the government's criminal investigation and the EPA's subsequent debarment of ELI from further federal contracts.[56] In 1994, ELI's work force fell from as many as 78 employees to 35 employees, although it was still able to generate $1 million in revenues. In 1995, ELI's work force fell to 19 employees. During the first four months of 1995, ELI generated $264,000 in revenue. After that, ELI's business significantly deteriorated.

In light of ELI's assets and diminishing revenues, the Probation Department recommended a fine of $4,266,852, a substantial downward departure from the minimum guideline fine of $6,425,013. The amount of the recommended fine was equal to the total loss to the government agencies involved ($4,589,295), less the recommended restitution to those agencies ($322,443). To enable ELI to pay that fine, the probation office recommended that the fine be payable in installments over ELI's five-year period of probation.

On November 6, 1995, the date set for ELI's sentencing, the district court questioned whether ELI could pay a fine of $4.2 million (rounded off). The district court directed the probation office to appoint an independent auditor to determine ELI's net revenues over the past several years and to predict ELI's future business prospects.

[The independent auditor portrayed ELI's financial prospects as bleak. ELI then had a current book value of about $1.5 million. The auditor predicted that while ELI would continue to lose money over the next three years, it could make a profit by the fourth year. It was his expectation, however, that the firm would likely cease doing business within the period of a year.]

After considering the auditor's report, the district court decided to impose a $1.5 million fine, payable in installments over ELI's five-year period of probation.

Pursuant to 18 U.S.C. § 3663(a)(1), the district court also ordered ELI to make restitution to the EPA, Army, and Air Force in the aggregate amount of $322,442. The district court arrived at this figure by adding up the amounts ELI had charged these three government agencies for their contracts.

The district court also ordered ELI to pay a special assessment of $200 per count, a total of $1600.

On appeal, ELI argues that the district court erred, both in its factual determination that ELI would be able to pay the $1.5 million fine, and as a matter of law when, contrary to Guideline Section 8C3.3, the court imposed a fine that would jeopardize ELI's continued viability.

---

56. Government contracts had accounted for 60 to 70 percent of ELI's business. — ED.

DISCUSSION...

A. GUIDELINE SECTION 8C3.3

Guideline Section 8C3.3(a) requires a court to reduce a fine to the extent needed to avoid interfering with a defendant organization's ability to pay restitution to victims. Guideline Section 8C3.3(b) permits, but does not require, a court to reduce a fine upon a finding that a defendant organization is not, and is not likely to become, able to pay it. This discretion is authorized only to the extent necessary to avoid substantially jeopardizing the continued viability of the organization.

Contrary to ELI's interpretation, Guideline Section 8C3.3 does not prohibit a court from imposing a fine that jeopardizes an organization's continued viability. It permits, but does not require, a court in such circumstances and in its discretion, to reduce the fine. The only time a reduction is mandated under section 8C3.3 is if the fine imposed, without reduction, would impair the defendant's ability to make restitution to victims. Thus, even if the district court's fine would completely bankrupt ELI, neither section 8C3.3(a) nor section 8C3.3(b) precluded the court from imposing such a fine so long as the fine did not impair ELI's ability to make restitution. It did not.

The district court ordered the $1.5 million fine to be paid by ELI in five annual installments. Thus, the first year, the amount payable would be one-fifth of $1.5 million, or $300,000. The independent auditor estimated ELI's total current net assets at $1,516,000. Thus, ELI could first pay $322,442 in restitution to the government, and then from the remaining $1.19 million (rounded off) it could pay the initial $300,000 installment of the fine.

Because ELI would be able to make restitution to the government, the plain language of Guideline Section 8C3.3 did not require the district court to further reduce ELI's fine. . . .

C. FACTORS FROM 18 U.S.C. § 3572

A sentencing court is required by 18 U.S.C. § 3572 to consider several factors when deciding whether to impose a fine and in what amount.[57] . . .

---

57. 18 U.S.C. § 3572 provides:

In determining whether to impose a fine, and the amount, time for payment, and method of payment of a fine, the court shall consider, in addition to the factors set forth in section 3553(a) —

(1) the defendant's income, earning capacity, and financial resources;
(2) the burden that the fine will impose upon the defendant, any person who is financially dependent on the defendant, or any other person (including a government) that would be responsible for the welfare of any person financially dependent on the defendant, relative to the burden that alternative punishments would impose;
(3) any pecuniary loss inflicted upon others as a result of the offense;
(4) whether restitution is ordered or made and the amount of such restitution;
(5) the need to deprive the defendant of illegally obtained gains from the offense;
(6) the expected costs to the government of any imprisonment, supervised release, or probation component of the sentence;
(7) whether the defendant can pass on to consumers or other persons the expense of the fine; and
(8) if the defendant is an organization, the size of the organization and any measure taken by the organization to discipline any officer, director, employee, or agent of the organization responsible for the offense and to prevent a recurrence of such an offense.

The trial court, on its own initiative, ordered the appointment of an independent auditor to evaluate ELI's present net worth and future earning capacity. Based on that report, the trial court chose to impose a fine, the amount of which was approximately equal to ELI's net worth. In explaining that symmetry, the trial court observed that one of two things would happen to ELI. First, ELI could go out of business. If it did go out of business, it could liquidate its assets, valued at over $1.5 million, pay the amount of restitution, and apply the rest of its assets to the fine. Alternatively, ELI could remain in business and try to make a profit. Under either scenario, ELI would be able to make restitution and have assets left over to apply toward the fine. It might not be able to pay the entire fine, but that doesn't matter so long as the court considers, to the extent applicable, the section 3572 factors. Here the district court did that. It was not precluded by 18 U.S.C. § 3572 or by Guideline Section 8C3.3 from imposing on ELI a fine that jeopardized ELI's continued viability.

ELI's contention that the court should have considered the impact of the fine on ELI's "dependent" employees pursuant to section 3572(a)(2) is without merit. As a preliminary matter, the language of section 3572(a)(2) seems to refer to dependent family members of an individual defendant, not the employees of a corporate defendant. However, we need not decide that question. Even if section 3572(a)(2) applies to corporate defendants, the mere existence of dependent corporate employees does not preclude a fine on a corporation. Corporations always have employees who could be affected by the imposition of a corporate fine. This fact alone cannot allow a corporation that has engaged in illegal activity to escape paying a fine.

CONCLUSION

We conclude the district court did not err in imposing the $1.5 million fine on ELI. No statute or Guideline precludes imposition of a fine on a corporate defendant that jeopardizes the corporate defendant's continued viability.

Affirmed.

Notes and Questions

1. Why would a court impose a fine that would jeopardize a company's continued viability?

2. To what extent, if any, should a court take into account the impact of a corporate fine on the corporation's employees or on the economic well being of the community in which the company is located?

NOTE ON CORPORATE DEATH PENALTY

The federal Sentencing Guidelines authorize a corporate death penalty for "criminal purpose organizations." These are organizations that are operated primarily for a criminal purpose or primarily by criminal means.[58] The commentary gives as examples of such entities an organization that fronts for a fraudulent scheme, an organization that is established to participate in illegal drug trafficking, and a hazardous waste organization that has no legitimate way to dispose of the waste. If the court finds that a corporation is a criminal purpose organization, the guideline directs it to set the fine in an amount that will divest the company of all of its assets.

This provision was invoked for the first time in a prosecution against a government defense contractor who supplied substandard screws, bolts, nuts, and O-rings for space projects, misrepresenting them as highly tested products. The company, American Precision Components, Inc., admitted the fraud.

The company had a prior history of similar problems. In 1988, it was convicted of supplying substandard hardware to the Navy for use in a shipyard that built nuclear submarines. Notwithstanding the seriousness of the wrongdoing, the company was sentenced to pay only $125,000 in fines and was debarred from government contracts for just 18 months.

Barring anyone from ever starting the business up again, the judge in the space projects case ordered American Precision to go out of business permanently and directed that all of the company's cash on hand be seized and all of its assets sold.

The owner of American Precision was sentenced to five years in prison and fined $75,000. As part of a plea agreement, he had earlier forfeited $2.2 million and two luxury cars.

Notes and Questions

1. The court in *Eureka Laboratories* approved a fine that jeopardized the company's ability to continue doing business. Is this a backdoor way of imposing a corporate death penalty without first determining that the company was a criminal purpose organization? Would ELI qualify as a criminal purpose organization?

2. Apart from its involvement in the catastrophic oil spill in the Gulf of Mexico, BP has a checkered safety history. In 2005 an explosion at BP's Texas City oil refinery claimed the lives of 15 workers and injured 170 others. In 2006 unchecked corrosion in a BP Alaskan pipeline caused the largest spill on Alaska's north slope to date. In 2007 BP signed a plea agreement with the Department of Justice, pleading guilty to felony charges under the Clean Air Act for the Texas refinery explosion and to misdemeanor charges under the Clean Water Act for negligent maintenance of the Alaskan pipeline. In addition to being sentenced to pay heavy fines, BP was placed on probation and was ordered to comply with OSHA safety standards. Since the 2007 plea agreement, BP has been cited for 760 "willful, egregious" OSHA safety violations — mostly for failure to comply with OSHA's directives at the Texas City refinery. Would BP qualify under the Sentencing Guidelines as a criminal purpose organization? Would imposition of the corporate death penalty be a fitting punishment for BP?

---

58. Sentencing Guidelines § 8C1.1.

IV. ADMINISTRATIVE SANCTIONS

A. REVOCATION OF CORPORATE CHARTER

In addition to the wide range of judicially imposed penalties and administrative sanctions outlined in this chapter, state governments have an equally powerful remedial tool — revocation of the corporate charter — that is roughly equivalent to the Sentencing Guidelines' corporate death penalty. United States corporations obtain their charters from the state in which they are incorporated and receive the statutory benefits and protections provided the laws of that state. In exchange, corporations are subject to regulation in their state of incorporation and are only permitted to conduct lawful activity that is within the scope of their charters.

Engaging in activities that exceed those authorized by the corporate charter — e.g., committing fraud in violation of state law — will give the state grounds for revoking it. Delaware, a popular state for incorporation thanks to its favorable corporate tax structure, permits revocation of a corporation's charter "for abuse, misuse or nonuse of its corporate powers, privileges or franchises."[59] The legislature may dissolve a corporation or the state's Attorney General may move to revoke the charter in the Court of Chancery, which has the power to appoint receivers to administer and wind up the corporation's affairs. The corporation is in effect "dead" because it can no longer conduct business operations, make contracts, or be sued or prosecuted.[60]

Such extreme measures are not taken lightly, however, and courts ordinarily proceed with extreme caution, looking for "a sustained course of fraud, immorality, or violations of statutory law before deciding that there has been an abuse of charter privileges."[61] Types of abuse resulting in revocation have included fraudulently organizing as a nonprofit organization,[62] operating an illegal casino under a hotel charter,[63] and violating state libel laws.[64] Although revocation was a frequently invoked sanction in the nineteenth century, it has largely fallen into disuse in modern times.

There are exceptions, however. In 1976 the attorney general of California moved to revoke the charter of a water company that had been delivering contaminated water to the state's residents, but the company settled and sold off all of its assets before the charter could be revoked. New York's attorney general more recently revoked the charter of the Council for Tobacco Research in 1998 for undermining legitimate health and safety research.

---

59. 8 Del. C. § 284(a).

60. But cf. Melrose Distillers, Inc. v. United States, 359 U.S. 271 (1959).

61. Young v. Nat'l Ass'n for Advancement of White People, 109 A.2d 29, 31 (Del. Ch. 1954) (corporation chartered to study and foster race relations but which actively opposed admission of African American students to Delaware schools, intimidated school boards, and encouraged white parents to keep their children out of school, in violation of Delaware school laws).

62. Southerland v. Decimo Club, Inc., 142 A. 786 (Del. Ch. 1928) (private club chartered to operate a non-profit fraternal and social site was operated for the pecuniary benefit of its organizer, who received a substantial portion of its members' initiation fees).

63. State v. French Lick Springs Hotel Co., 82 N.E. 801 (Ind. App. 1907) (corporation organized for the purpose of operating a hotel and health spa conducted a casino for gambling, in violation of Indiana law, and contributed to the delinquency of minors by giving them free access to the casino).

64. People v. White Circle League of America, 97 N.E.2d 811 (Ill. 1951) (corporation formed to provide "education as to customs, civic and social standards" of its members disseminated racially inflammatory, scandalous, and libelous materials in violation of Illinois law).

As was noted above, under common law a dissolved corporation was not amenable to civil suit or criminal prosecution. It would thus be possible for management to evade prosecution simply by dissolving the corporation and reincorporating in a different state. In order to prevent voluntary dissolution for the purpose of avoiding liability, states began to enact "winding up" statutes that prolonged a corporation's existence for a sufficient period of time to allow orderly resolution of its remaining affairs. Every state now has some form of "winding up" statute, so dissolution no longer abates actions relating to liabilities or obligations incurred during the course of corporate operations.

In 2010 public outrage against BP following the catastrophic Gulf oil spill spurred a large-scale campaign to have Delaware revoke BP America's corporate charter. Led by Green Change, a network organization advocating greater environmental awareness, the anti-BP campaign encouraged supporters to contact Delaware's attorney general and state legislators to urge them to act to punish the company. Within a few months the campaign had thousands of followers on the social networking site Facebook, and "Revoke BP's Charter!" effectively became a mantra echoed by politicians and media talking heads alike. As noted in Chapter 13, the oil giant has been under fire from the government for years for its high-profile mishaps, which have resulted dozens of deaths and hundreds of injuries caused by BP-related environmental disasters. It remains to be seen whether BP's spill in the Gulf of Mexico will prove to be the last straw.

Notes and Questions

1. Before the disastrous oil spill in the Gulf, BP already had numerous prior violations under the Clean Air Act, the Clean Water Act, and OSHA.[65] The devastating environmental and economic effects of both the Alaskan and Gulf spills will likely be felt for decades. Evidence of negligent and reckless behavior regarding safety is piling up in connection with the blowout aboard the Deepwater Horizon rig. Does the state of Delaware have the power to revoke BP America's corporate charter? Would revocation of BP's charter be equivalent to imposing the "corporate death penalty" authorized by the Sentencing Guidelines?

2. BP is currently the largest energy supplier to the U.S. military. It holds six contracts with the Pentagon worth a total of $2.1 billion and is a major employer in the United States. It employs some 29,000 Americans — 7,000 alone at its BP America headquarters in Houston, the site of immense economic turmoil following the Enron collapse. Assuming arguendo that BP's conduct puts the company at risk of forfeiting its corporate charter, would Delaware be well advised to revoke BP's charter? Before you answer this question, consider the enormous economic consequences of the Gulf oil spill. New civil suits are being filed against BP every day by those adversely affected by the spill, and to date BP has already spent billions on cleanup efforts on its own initiative. Equally important, BP promised to pay $20 billion to cover private losses resulting from the spill. Would it be wise for Delaware authorities to initiate proceedings to revoke BP's charter — effectively cutting off its revenue generating operations — when the stakes are so high?

---

65. See supra Problem 13-1.

3. If the government decides to criminally prosecute BP, it could be years before an indictment is issued. How would revocation of BP's charter before indictment affect the prosecution? What about pending and future civil suits? Would it be fair for Delaware to consider the Gulf oil spill as a basis for initiating revocation proceedings before liability for the spill has been formally established?

4. BP America is simply part of a larger global corporation, BP PLC, based in the UK. What practical impact would revocation of its Delaware charter really have? What can be done to stop BP America from simply reincorporating in another state? Are there other remedies that would be more effective ways to control BP's U.S. operations?

5. Courts have held that a corporation does not escape liability by merging with a different company and assuming a new corporate persona. The rationale is essentially the same as the rationale for enacting "winding up" statutes — i.e., preventing wrong-doers from manipulating the corporate form to evade accountability. The same is typically true for corporations that sell off all of their assets before civil or criminal proceedings have begun, leaving behind only a corporate shell. A successor corporation that continues the business activity of its predecessor implicitly agrees to assume liabilities previously incurred by its predecessor. With that in mind, how would a BP fire sale or merger affect future legal proceedings against the corporation?

B. LOSS OF LICENSE

When a business operates in a highly regulated industry, one potential consequence of a criminal conviction is the temporary or permanent loss of license to engage in some or all of the company's normal business activities. Because the case study in Section C scrutinizes the aftermath of the conviction of E.F. Hutton (a large brokerage house) on 2,000 counts of mail fraud, the examples of licensing complications discussed in this section focus on state and federal laws pertaining to the securities industry.

To begin with the federal level, brokers must be registered with the SEC before they are permitted to use the mails to conduct securities transactions.[66] Once registered, brokers are subject to continuous monitoring by the SEC. A broker's criminal conviction triggers SEC enforcement powers that can seriously interfere with the broker's business operations. If the SEC determines that the conviction fits the statutory criteria, the commission may censure the broker, place limitations on the broker's operations, revoke the broker's registration, or suspend the broker for as long as 12 months. Offenses that will trigger these broad enforcement powers include:

1. an offense relating to the purchase or sale of securities, making sworn or unsworn false statements, bribery, or burglary, or conspiracy to commit any of those crimes;
2. an offense arising out of the conduct of the broker's business;
3. theft, embezzlement, or other specified acquisitive offenses; or
4. commission of specified federal crimes, including mail and wire fraud.[67]

---

66. 15 U.S.C. § 78o(a)(1).
67. 15 U.S.C. §§ 78o(b)(4)(B)(i)-(iv).

Under the Investment Advisers Act, those who engage in the business of advising others on the value of securities or the advisability of particular securities transactions, and those who regularly issue analyses or reports on those matters, must also register with the SEC.[68] As is true in the case of brokers, the SEC may censure, suspend, limit, or revoke the registration of investment advisors who are convicted of a felony or misdemeanor. The SEC may exercise these enforcement powers to the same extent and under virtually the same circumstances as those specified for brokers.[69]

Similarly, the Investment Company Act requires registration of virtually all investment companies.[70] But the sanctions under this Act progress a step further. Any person who is convicted of a felony or misdemeanor arising out of the purchase or sale of securities or the person's conduct as an underwriter, broker, dealer, or investment advisor is barred from being employed by or serving as an officer, director, or investment advisor of a registered investment company within ten years of the conviction.[71] Additionally, the SEC may prohibit — conditionally or unconditionally, permanently or temporarily — anyone who has willfully violated the Securities Act of 1933, the Securities Exchange Act of 1934, or specified provisions of the Investment Company Act, and anyone who has willfully aided and abetted such violations, from serving as an employee, officer, director, investment advisor, or principal underwriter for any investment company, bank, or insurance company.[72]

While the above possibilities are playing out at the SEC, the New York Stock Exchange may choose to enter the scene. If the Exchange finds that a listed company fails to satisfy the criteria for continued listing, delisting procedures may be initiated. In addition to a number of more specific criteria that may lead to delisting, the Exchange may take such action upon a finding that the company or its management has engaged in operations that are contrary to the public interest, has failed to make timely and accurate disclosures to the shareholders and the public, or has failed to observe good accounting practices in reporting the company's earnings or financial position.[73]

The New York Stock Exchange disciplinary rules also contemplate disciplinary action against members and their employees for specified types of conduct, including violating the Securities Exchange Act, violating Exchange rules or agreements, stock parking, making misstatements to the Exchange, committing fraud, and engaging in acts detrimental to the Exchange. The authorized sanctions include expulsion, suspension, limitations on the wrongdoer's the activities, imposition of fines, and censure.[74]

In addition to maintaining licenses that enable them to operate nationwide, individuals and organizations in the securities industry must also jump through various state regulatory hoops. To give one example, the Uniform Securities Act requires broker-dealers and investment advisors to register with the state commissioner of banking. As is true under federal law, conviction of any felony or of a misdemeanor involving a security or any aspect of the securities business may lead to suspension, denial, or revocation of state registration.[75]

---

68. 15 U.S.C. §§ 80b-2(a)(11), 80b-3.
69. 15 U.S.C. § 80b-3(e).
70. 15 U.S.C. § 80a-7.
71. 15 U.S.C. § 80a-9(a).
72. 15 U.S.C. § 80a-9(b).
73. New York Stock Exchange Listed Company Manual § 8.
74. New York Stock Exchange Guide, Rules of Board, Rule 476.
75. See, e.g., Conn. Gen. Stat. Ann. § 36b-15 (1996 & Supp. 2000).

Companies convicted of environmental crimes face a similar threat. Federal pollution permits are an invaluable commodity for manufacturers. If the EPA were to deny a company's application for a permit, that would severely handicap the company's operations and, perhaps, shut them down altogether. Violators can also be barred from competing for government contracts. Department of Defense standards, for example, require responsible business practices and a "satisfactory record of integrity and business ethics,"[76] which a criminal conviction would surely jeopardize. If convicted, a company like BP — which holds $2.1 billion worth of contracts with the Pentagon — would be in danger of debarment. Are there countervailing factors the government is likely to consider before pursuing this route?

C. CASE STUDY ON THE AFTERMATH OF CORPORATE CONVICTION UNITED STATES v. E. F. HUTTON & CO.

In 1985 the Justice Department charged E. F. Hutton with 2,000 counts of mail fraud for engaging in cash management practices akin to check kiting. Pursuant to a carefully crafted plea agreement, Hutton pled guilty to all counts. According to Hutton's president, the company agreed to the plea "to get the situation behind us and to get out of the media." Little did he realize then that the guilty plea was only the painful beginning of Hutton's woes and that the case would become a true cause célèbre.[77]

1. The Federal Investigation

DEPARTMENT OF JUSTICE PRESS RELEASE

FOR IMMEDIATE RELEASE   CRM
THURSDAY, MAY 2, 1985   (202) 633–2010

The Department of Justice today filed a criminal information charging E. F. Hutton & Company Inc., one of the nation's largest securities dealers, with 2,000 counts of mail and wire fraud.

The essence of the charges was that Hutton obtained the interest-free use of millions of dollars by intentionally writing checks in excess of the funds it had on deposit in various banks.

Attorney General Edwin Meese III said the filing of the criminal information with the federal district court in Scranton, Pennsylvania, was followed immediately by the entry of a guilty plea to all 2,000 counts of wire and mail fraud by the firm.

In accordance with a plea agreement between Hutton and the government, Judge William Nealon Jr. imposed the maximum criminal fine, $2 million, and assessed costs of the investigation of $750,000. The agreement also calls for payment of restitution to the banks, the Attorney General said. More than 400 banks throughout the United States are believed to have been affected.

---

76. Federal Acquisition Regulations, 48 C.F.R. 9.104-1(d)
77. Biden, Metzenbaum Blast Justice Department, Ask Why Hutton Officials Weren't Charged in Scam, Corp. Couns. Wkly. (BNA), Apr. 23, 1986, at 8.

The information charged that during the course of the scheme, which it said began about July 1980 and continued through February 1982, Hutton's drawings against uncollected funds totaled more than $1 billion, with daily overdrafts sometimes exceeding $250 million.

The purpose of the scheme, according to the information, was to obtain the daily, interest-free use of millions of dollars in bank funds, thereby avoiding the necessity to borrow funds at interest rates which, during the course of the scheme, reached an annual rate of 20 percent.

The information said the scheme, which closely resembled a check kite, was accomplished by Hutton's withdrawing from its depository accounts arbitrary amounts — unrelated to and in excess of the volume of customer funds it had deposited — and thereafter covering such excessive withdrawals by depositing covering checks drawn on other Hutton accounts. In addition, the defendant caused funds to be successively transferred between various of its branch and regional depository banks and utilized a multiplier formula arbitrarily to increase the amount of customer funds actually deposited, and exploited the opportunities thus created for delayed clearing times of deposit items, the information charged.

Meese also announced that, in a companion civil proceeding, Hutton and its corporate parent, the E. F. Hutton Group Inc., consented to the entry of an order of permanent injunction, pursuant to 18 U.S.C. Section 1345, enjoining the defendants from violations of the mail and wire fraud statutes (18 U.S.C. Sections 1341 and 1343), as well as the bank fraud statute (18 U.S.C. Section 1344). The injunction specifically prohibits the practices in question and mandates certain disclosures by Hutton to the banks with which it does business.

The E. F. Hutton Group Inc. was not a defendant in the criminal action.

The case represents, the Attorney General said, the first use by the Department of the civil injunctive authority conferred by Section 1345 and the first charges under Section 1344, albeit in a civil context, since the enactment of these provisions on October 12, 1984.

The defendants also consented to the appointment of a special master to determine, according to an agreed-upon formula, the amount of restitution that the securities dealer must pay to the banks and financial institutions which were victimized by the fraudulent conduct.

In addition, the defendants agreed to institute revised corporate procedures and policies to prohibit future violations and to instruct approximately 1,200 of their corporate officers and employees as to compliance with the permanent injunction. The defendants also have undertaken to file with the court affidavits from each such officer and employee attesting that each has received and read a copy of the plea agreement and all pleadings in the criminal and civil proceedings.

Investigation of the case was conducted by a special United States Postal Service investigative team of 25 postal inspectors, accountants and computer specialists led by Postal Inspector John A. Holland of Harrisburg, Pennsylvania. In addition, assistance and information were provided by the Federal Reserve Board, the Federal Deposit Insurance Corporation, the Securities and Exchange Commission and the New York State Banking Commission.

Prosecution was handled by Assistant United States Attorney Albert R. Murray, Jr., of the Middle District of Pennsylvania, Robert W. Ogren, chief of the Fraud Section of the Justice Department's Criminal Division, and Fraud Section attorney Peter B. Clark. . . .

STATEMENT
OF
STEPHEN S. TROTT
ASSISTANT ATTORNEY GENERAL
CRIMINAL DIVISION
BEFORE
THE
SUBCOMMITTEE ON CRIME
COMMITTEE ON THE JUDICIARY
HOUSE OF REPRESENTATIVES

CONCERNING
E. F. HUTTON CASE
ON
DECEMBER 6 AND 11, 1985

. . . The Hutton prosecution is without precedent in the federal system. Some of the practices embraced by our enforcement action were probably legal until enactment of the bank fraud statute last October. Nevertheless, they constituted serious abuses that threatened to inflict significant losses on banks. The perpetrators did not believe they were committing a crime, although in fact their acts now are clearly illegal and many of them were at the time. The investigation covered 3 years and ultimately involved the analysis of 7,000,000 documents. On top of these difficulties, we recognized that many of Hutton's most serious cash management abuses could not be reached by a conventional criminal prosecution.

Our prosecutors had to choose. The first option: a conventional prosecution of Hutton and two mid level individuals, would have been costly, inefficient, had a questionable prospect of success and could not reach the most widespread abuses of Hutton and the rest of the money management community. The second option: a comprehensive settlement that we judged would address most directly the serious problem of widespread money management abuses.

For what amounted to deceiving banks into giving it interest-free unsecured short-term loans, Hutton was required to plead guilty—not nolo contendere but guilty—to an unprecedented 2,000 felony counts of intentional mail and wire fraud. It was fined $2,000,000, the maximum the law allows for this unparalleled number of counts, and a sum which makes it the steepest fine in the history of our white collar enforcement effort. Hutton was also required to pay the Government $750,000 to cover the costs of the investigation. Those costs are ordinarily not recoverable, even with a jury verdict of guilty. Additionally, the new injunctive provision of 18 U.S.C. §1345 was used for the first time since its enactment by Congress in October 1984 to enjoin all of Hutton's cash management abuses, not just those precisely identified in the criminal information, many of which were not criminal prior to enactment of the Comprehensive Crime [Control] Act.

The Department of Justice also required that Hutton immediately make full and complete restitution, with interest, to each and every one of the bank victims without regard to the federal district in which they reside. Rarely is there a criminal fraud case where this much immediate benefit flows to victims. Usually victims['] interests are handled as an afterthought. It is incorrect to assume or infer that restitution is limited to the $8,000,000 Hutton has reserved for this purpose. Hutton is obligated to pay back the total amount obtained fraudulently, plus interest, whatever that may be. In sum, this is the most comprehensive program of restitution ever developed in a federal criminal case.

Notes and Questions

1. Mr. Trott emphasized that the government not only was able to obtain a global settlement via the plea agreement but also obtained more than it was entitled to by law. Should the government use the plea bargaining process to gain such concessions from criminal defendants? Does the government's decision to prosecute only the corporation have any bearing on this question?

2. Mr. Trott defended the Justice Department's departure from its customary policy of holding individuals criminally responsible in corporate prosecutions on tactical grounds. Moreover, all but a few of the middle-level employees who were potential targets of the investigation were granted immunity from prosecution in exchange for their cooperation in the investigation. Absent evidence that would warrant pursuing upper-echelon executives, government lawyers feared that prosecuting only lower-level managers might smack of "scapegoating."[78] This proved to be an extremely controversial decision, and the controversy later assumed even greater proportions when evidence suggesting high-level knowledge of and participation in the cash management practices began to surface.[79]

SEC rules require issuers of registered securities to file annual reports, known as Form 10-K Reports, disclosing matters important to regulators and stockholders — including legal proceedings that could have a material adverse effect on the corporation's financial position. The following excerpt shows how extensive the regulatory and other legal consequences of a criminal conviction can be.

E. F. HUTTON
1985 10-K REPORT

. . .

ITEM 3. LEGAL PROCEEDINGS

The Company and its subsidiaries are defendants in various legal actions relating to their securities, commodities, investment banking, insurance, leasing and mortgage

---

78. Biden, Metzenbaum Blast Justice Department, Ask Why Hutton Officials Weren't Charged in Scam, Corp. Couns. Wkly. (BNA), Apr. 23, 1986, at 8.

79. Hutton Plea Called a Mistake, N.Y. Times, July 11, 1985, at 25.

activities. Certain of these actions are brought on behalf of various classes of claimants and seek damages of material or indeterminate amounts. Although no assurance can be given, in the opinion of management these actions will not result in any material adverse effect on the consolidated financial position of the Company. Included in such actions are the following: . . .

On May 2, 1985, EFH entered a plea of guilty to an Information filed in the United States District Court for the Middle District of Pennsylvania. . . .

EFH is subject to numerous state and Federal regulatory and licensing statutes and to the rules of several self-regulatory organizations, most of which provide, inter alia, that conviction of crimes such as mail and wire fraud is a basis for revocation or suspension of licensure. As a result of the plea, EFH has been and is the subject of formal investigations and informal inquiries under certain of these regulatory and licensing statutes relating to EFH's receipt, movement and disbursement of funds. EFH has also responded to informal inquiries by other regulators. So far as EFH is aware, none of the statutes or rules to which it is subject provides that revocation or suspension of licensure is mandatory upon conviction, and all of them permit imposition of lesser penalties or no penalty at all should the regulatory body involved determine (under various standards generally relating to the public interest) that such action is appropriate.

At present, EFH is aware of the following orders, investigations and inquiries from the following regulatory and self-regulatory organizations. There can be no assurance that other investigations will not be commenced.

1. SECURITIES AND EXCHANGE COMMISSION

(a) On May 2, 1985, the Securities and Exchange Commission (the "Commission") granted EFH and Hutton Group a 180-day temporary exemption from certain provisions of the Investment Company Act of 1940, as amended, which, if applied to EFH, might have rendered it ineligible to serve as an investment advisor. On October 29, 1985, the Commission granted EFH and Hutton Group a further conditional temporary exemption for a period of one year commencing October 29, 1985, or until such earlier time as the Commission may direct unless extended by the Commission pending consideration of EFH's concurrent application for a permanent exemption. . . . Neither EFH nor Hutton Group may act as a managing or co-managing underwriter, investment adviser or promoter for any new management investment company, including any new series of existing registered investment companies, served by EFH, for the duration of the temporary order. During this period, EFH may, however, sponsor new unit investment trusts and new series of its existing unit investment trusts. No assurance can be given that EFH's request for a permanent exemption will be granted.

(b) On October 28, 1985, Hutton Group agreed to the issuance of a permanent civil injunction by the United States District Court for the District of Columbia (the "SEC Injunction") against future violations of Sections 13(a) and 13(b)(2) of the Securities Exchange Act of 1934 and Rules 13a-1 and 12b-20 thereunder. The Commission's Complaint alleged that Hutton Group's 1981 and 1982 Annual Reports on Form 10-K failed adequately to disclose the impact on net interest income of the practices underlying the plea and further alleged that Hutton Group failed to maintain a system of internal controls adequate to prevent such practices. Hutton Group consented to entry of the SEC Injunction without admitting or denying the allegations of the Complaint.

(c) On October 29, 1985, the Commission instituted an administrative proceeding against EFH pursuant to Section 15(b)(4) of the Securities Exchange Act of 1934, based upon the plea, the DOJ Injunction and the SEC Injunction, to determine what, if any, remedial sanctions would be appropriate in the public interest. Without admitting or denying the allegations of the Commission's order for proceedings, except admitting the fact of the cited court actions, EFH settled that proceeding and agreed to an order: (1) censuring EFH; (2) requiring EFH to employ an independent consultant, acceptable to the Commission and knowledgeable in broker-dealer operations, to examine EFH's current and historical policies and practices regarding the handling of customers' securities and monies to determine whether EFH's policies and practices conform to the Federal securities laws and regulations, the rules of self-regulatory organizations, and a broker-dealer's fiduciary duty to its customers, and submit a public report of his findings and recommendations to EFH and the Commission within 120 days of the Commission's order, which time period has been extended to April 15, 1986; (3) requiring EFH to adopt the recommendations of the consultant, unless otherwise directed by the Commission, within 45 days of the submission of the consultant's report; and (4) requiring EFH not to open any new branch offices until the later of 120 days from the date of the Commission's order or the date when EFH adopts the recommendations of the independent consultant. In evaluating such operations, such consultant may compare and contrast EFH's policies with prevailing industry practices. Hutton Group cannot predict what findings or recommendations will be contained in the report of such consultant or what the consequences of such findings or recommendations will be. EFH has retained an independent consultant in accordance with the condition referred to in subdivision (c)(2) above. . . .

2. Since October 1985, EFH has consented to various orders and injunctions with agencies of the States of Connecticut, Georgia, Hawaii, Massachusetts, Missouri, Nebraska, New York, New Mexico, Ohio, Virginia and Wisconsin. In each case, EFH consented to an order after the state's inquiry into the conduct underlying the plea or the DOJ Injunction. Under the consent orders, EFH has variously been placed on probation, has agreed to modify its procedures for disbursing payments to customers and to supervise closely such procedures, has been made subject to certain other administrative supervision and reporting requirements, and/or has been disqualified for limited periods of time from using the state's Uniform Limited Offering Exemption. Additionally, EFH has agreed to make payments to various states totalling approximately $375,000 and has agreed to contribute $200,000 to one or more charities designated by the Banking Commissioner of the State of Connecticut. EFH's ability to act as a securities dealer, underwriter or issuer has not been affected.

EFH has had and continues to have discussions and/or has responded to and continues to respond to formal and informal inquiries from securities, insurance and/or other regulatory agencies in many of the other states in which it is licensed. . . .

4. The New York Stock Exchange is conducting an inquiry pursuant to Exchange Rule 476 into the plea, the DOJ Injunction and the underlying conduct.

5. The United States Department of Labor has informed EFH that it intends to conduct an inquiry to determine what, if any, action should be taken pursuant to the

debarment provisions of Section 411 of the Employee Retirement Income Security Act of 1974 to restrict EFH from acting as an administrator or investment adviser to employee benefit plans.

6. A number of Congressional subcommittees have instituted or indicated an interest in instituting inquiries and investigations into the conduct of EFH relating to the plea.

7. In addition to the foregoing actions by governmental and regulatory bodies, EFH and/or Hutton Group and/or certain of their officers and directors have been named as defendants in a number of purported state and Federal class actions, and in an individual suit, variously brought under the Federal securities laws, and various state statutes and common-law principles, and in a number of purported derivative suits allegedly brought on behalf of Hutton Group. These actions relate to the Information and the DOJ Injunction referred to above and the events underlying them. Some of the class actions seek damages from all defendants based upon, inter alia, alleged fraudulent failure to disclose those events to purchasers of Hutton Group's common stock, or, in one case, call options thereon. The individual suit makes similar assertions on behalf of a purchaser and seller of put options on Hutton Group's stock. Four of the class actions seek damages on behalf of EFH's customers based upon alleged fraud in disbursing funds from banks located outside of the state in which the customers reside or located a long distance from the EFH office where the customer transacts business. One of those class actions additionally seeks damages on behalf of all banks that were allegedly injured by the conduct underlying the plea. In general, the derivative suits seek damages from the individual defendants on behalf of Hutton Group based upon, inter alia, alleged waste, negligence, fraud and/or mismanagement, breach of fiduciary duty, and violations of Federal securities laws by individual defendants in connection with these events. Additionally, EFH is a defendant in a third-party action in which a bank seeks to recover damages allegedly sustained as a result of the activities described in the Information. Certain of the class and derivative suits, the individual action and the third-party action also purport to assert claims under the Racketeer Influenced [and] Corrupt Organizations Act and seek various forms of injunctive relief. . . .

On May 17, 1985, Hutton Group announced that it had requested the Honorable Griffin B. Bell, former Attorney General of the United States, to conduct a full and independent investigation of the conduct underlying the plea and Injunction referred to above and make such findings and recommendations as he determined to be appropriate. On September 4, 1985, Judge Bell issued his report which, among other things, made certain recommendations concerning personnel actions to be taken and restructuring of various operations of EFH and Hutton Group. The Company's Board of Directors, at a special meeting held on September 4, 1985, approved the implementation of Judge Bell's recommendations.

In addition, John M. Pearce, an EFH employee who was sanctioned pursuant to the recommendations in the report of Griffin B. Bell (the "Bell Report"), commenced an action in January 1986 entitled John M. Pearce v. The E.F. Hutton Group Inc. and Griffin B. Bell in the United States District Court for the District of Columbia. Plaintiff seeks $10 million in compensatory damages and the same amount in punitive damages, plus attorneys' fees and costs, for alleged defamation and invasion of privacy in connection with the publication of the Bell Report and the imposition of sanctions against plaintiff by EFH. . . .

Notes and Questions

1. In light of the number and nature of pending and threatened regulatory investigations, injunctions, and lawsuits when this annual report was released, how could Hutton's management possibly opine that the legal proceedings would not have a material adverse effect on the company's financial condition?

2. The State Investigations

Hutton's 10-K Report notes that Hutton had consented to a number of orders and injunctions issued by state regulatory agencies. A brief look at the actions that some of them contemplated brings home the potentially serious consequences of those investigations.

In Connecticut, the state banking commissioner scheduled a hearing to consider revoking or suspending Hutton's license to do business in the state as a securities broker and investment advisor.[80] Massachusetts and Kansas also considered such action.[81] The Missouri securities commissioner considered declaring Hutton ineligible to use the state's private placement procedure, known as Regulation D. Under a "bad boy" provision in Missouri law, a firm is ineligible to make a Regulation D offering if the firm or its officers or directors have been convicted of a felony within the past five years. The commissioner indicated that he had previously been lenient in some felony cases involving Hutton vice presidents in other states. "We sort of agreed with them that if you have some account executive in Montana that has a felony conviction, it shouldn't keep you from using Regulation D in Missouri," he said. "But this is different. This is a conviction of the firm itself."

Although denial of access to Regulation D would not have disqualified Hutton from acting as a broker-dealer, it would have required review by the commissioner's office of every tax shelter Hutton underwrote — a time-consuming and costly procedure. Some observers speculated that Hutton's Missouri tax shelter business would dry up if the commissioner prohibited the firm from using Regulation D.[82]

Georgia fashioned a settlement with Hutton that served as a rough model for other states. Hutton signed a consent decree with the state that put the firm on probation for a year but allowed it to continue business as usual. The terms of probation required Hutton to file quarterly reports on its compliance with the terms of the plea agreement with federal prosecutors and with the recommendations of former Attorney General Griffin Bell, who conducted the internal investigation the plea agreement had ordered. In addition, Hutton agreed to reimburse the state $15,000 for its legal costs.[83] Several other states quickly followed suit.

---

80. Connecticut's Hutton Plan, N.Y. Times, June 1, 1985, at 28.
81. State May Act Against Hutton, St. Louis Post-Dispatch, May 8, 1985, at 1C.
82. Id.
83. Hutton Put on Probation in Georgia Settlement, N.Y. Times, Sept. 27, 1985, at 43.

STILL MORE GRIEF

Even with the settlement of state investigations well under way, Hutton's problems continued to mount. Hutton's municipal finance division, one of its strongest units, began to lose important customers because of the plea. The chief financial officer for the Metropolitan Transportation Authority (MTA), a New York state agency, reported that Hutton had been removed from all of the MTA's future underwritings. New York City removed Hutton as an underwriter for the city's largest bond financing ever — $592 million. At the same time, the Massachusetts Housing Finance Agency was considering whether to keep Hutton on its list of a small number of investment banks eligible to serve as managing underwriter to the agency. And so it went. Predictably, all of this hurt where it counts. Hutton's ranking in the municipal finance industry fell from second to eleventh in terms of the volume of issues the firm underwrote.[84]

By 1987, the firm's legal bills had reached $100 million, largely because of the fallout from the guilty plea. In the meantime, months of negative publicity generated by the investigations had sullied Hutton's reputation and disrupted the conduct of its business.[85] During this time, Hutton's financial condition continued to weaken, and the once preeminent firm unsuccessfully sought a prospective buyer that would bid high to acquire the firm. Although Shearson Lehman Brothers expressed interest in a possible acquisition, the two companies were unable to come to terms after Shearson offered $50 a share. Hutton wanted $55.[86] When the stock market collapsed on October 19, 1987, word that Hutton had suffered serious losses sealed the firm's fate. Soon thereafter Shearson in fact acquired Hutton — for a mere $29 a share.[87]

But that is not the end of the story. In 1988 the New York Stock Exchange concluded a two-year investigation of the sordid cash management affair. The Exchange censured former Hutton president George Ball, then-chairman of Prudential-Bache Securities Inc., for failure to supervise and control firm officials after indications of irregularities in Hutton's cash management practices had surfaced. The Exchange also censured Thomas Lynch, Hutton's former chief financial officer. In addition, the Stock Exchange fined Hutton approximately $400,000 — a penalty that Shearson ultimately would bear.[88]

Following that blow, Hutton was criminally charged with money laundering for conduct that occurred in the firm's Providence, Rhode Island, office. Before the charges were formally filed, Hutton's new parent, Shearson Lehman Hutton, disclosed to the SEC that Hutton would plead guilty to the felony charges. When the plea was entered, the company immediately paid a fine of $1.01 million, which had been set aside for that purpose before Shearson acquired Hutton. A former broker for Hutton who participated in the money laundering pled guilty in a related case. Shearson expected to be permitted to continue all of its securities business despite the felony convictions.[89]

---

84. Some Issuers Remove Hutton as Underwriter, N.Y. Times, July 8, 1985, at D1.

85. How They Tore Hutton to Pieces, N.Y. Times, Jan. 17, 1988, § 3, at 1.

86. E. F. Hutton, Losing Two-Year Struggle, Looking for a Buyer, N.Y. Times, Nov. 24, 1987, at A1.

87. The Slow Death of E. F. Hutton, Fortune, Feb. 29, 1988, at 82.

88. Censures in Hutton Case Reported, N.Y. Times, Feb. 29, 1988, at D1.

89. Hutton Charged with Laundering Money, N.Y. Times, May 7, 1988, § 1, at 39; Guilty Plea in Hutton Case, N.Y. Times, June 10, 1988, at D10; United States v. E. F. Hutton & Co., Legal Times, May 30, 1988, at 3.

Table of Cases

Table of Statutes

Index